Crosslinguistic Approaches to the Psychology of Language

Research in the Tradition of Dan Isaac Slobin

Edited by
Jiansheng Guo
Elena Lieven
Nancy Budwig
Susan Ervin-Tripp
Keiko Nakamura
Şeyda Özçalışkan

Psychology Press
Taylor & Francis Group
New York London

Psychology Press
Taylor & Francis Group
270 Madison Avenue
New York, NY 10016

Psychology Press
Taylor & Francis Group
27 Church Road
Hove, East Sussex BN3 2FA

© 2009 by Taylor & Francis Group, LLC
Psychology Press is an imprint of Taylor & Francis Group, an Informa business

Printed in the United States of America on acid-free paper
10 9 8 7 6 5 4 3 2 1

International Standard Book Number-13: 978-0-8058-5999-7 (Softcover) 978-0-8058-5998-0 (Hardcover)

Except as permitted under U.S. Copyright Law, no part of this book may be reprinted, reproduced, transmitted, or utilized in any form by any electronic, mechanical, or other means, now known or hereafter invented, including photocopying, microfilming, and recording, or in any information storage or retrieval system, without written permission from the publishers.

Trademark Notice: Product or corporate names may be trademarks or registered trademarks, and are used only for identification and explanation without intent to infringe.

Visit the Taylor & Francis Web site at
http://www.taylorandfrancis.com

and the Psychology Press Web site at
http://www.psypress.com

Contents

Dedication	ix
Contributors	xi
The Editors	xiii
Authors	xv
A Poetic Portrait of Dan Isaac Slobin	xix

Introduction   1

   Jiansheng Guo and Elena Lieven

PART I   LANGUAGE LEARNING IN CROSSLINGUISTIC PERSPECTIVE

Introduction   11

   Nancy Budwig and Susan Ervin-Tripp

1   Alligators All Around: The Acquisition of Animal Terms in English and Russian   17

   Jean Berko Gleason, Brenda Caldwell Phillips, Richard Ely, and Elena Zaretsky

2   Making Language Around the Globe: A Crosslinguistic Study of Homesign in the United States, China, and Turkey   27

   Susan Goldin-Meadow, Aslı Özyürek, Burcu Sancar, and Carolyn Mylander

3   "He Take One of My Tools!" vs. "I'm Building": Transitivity and the Grammar of Accusing, Commanding, and Perspective-Sharing in Toddlers' Peer Disputes   41

   Amy Kyratzis

4   Direction and Perspective in German Child Language   55

   Heike Behrens

5   One-to-One Mapping of Temporal and Spatial Relations   69

   Richard M. Weist

6   Effects of Lexical Items and Construction Types in English and Turkish Character Introductions in Elicited Narrative   81

   Aylin C. Küntay and Dilara Koçbaş

| 7 | Revisiting the Acquisition of Sesotho Noun Class Prefixes | 93 |

Katherine Demuth and David Ellis

| 8 | Dialogic Priming and the Acquisition of Argument Marking in Korean | 105 |

Patricia M. Clancy

PART II NARRATIVES AND THEIR DEVELOPMENT LINGUISTIC, COGNITIVE, AND PRAGMATIC PERSPECTIVES

| | Introduction | 121 |

Ruth A. Berman

| 9 | Sequencing Events in Time or Sequencing Events in Storytelling?: From Cognition to Discourse—With Frogs Paving the Way | 127 |

Michael Bamberg

| 10 | Plot and Evaluation: Warlpiri Children's Frog Stories | 137 |

Edith L. Bavin

| 11 | Clause Packaging in Narratives: A Crosslinguistic Developmental Study | 149 |

Ruth A. Berman and Bracha Nir-Sagiv

| 12 | The Many Ways to Search for a Frog Story: On a Fieldworker's Troubles Collecting Spatial Language Data | 163 |

Raphael Berthele

| 13 | Between Frogs and Black-Winged Monkeys: Orality, Evidentials, and Authorship in Tzotzil (Mayan) Children's Narratives | 175 |

Lourdes de León

| 14 | Learning to Express Motion in Narratives by Mandarin-Speaking Children | 193 |

Jiansheng Guo and Liang Chen

| 15 | Typological Constraints on Motion in French and English Child Language | 209 |

Maya Hickmann, Henriëtte Hendriks, and Christian Champaud

| 16 | Language and Affect: Japanese Children's Use of Evaluative Expressions in Narratives | 225 |

Keiko Nakamura

| 17 | Rethinking Character Representation and Its Development in Children's Narratives | 241 |

Ageliki Nicolopoulou

| 18 | Motion Events in English and Korean Fictional Writings and Translations | 253 |

Kyung-ju Oh

| 19 | Learning to Talk About Spatial Motion in Language-Specific Ways | 263 |

Şeyda Özçalışkan

| 20 | Learning to Tell a Story of False Belief: A Study of French-Speaking Children | 277 |

Edy Veneziano, Laetitia Albert, and Stéphanie Martin

PART III THEORETICAL PERSPECTIVES ON LANGUAGE DEVELOPMENT, LANGUAGE CHANGE, AND TYPOLOGY

| | Introduction | 293 |

Elena Lieven

| 21 | Can Apes Learn Grammar?: A Short Detour Into Language Evolution | 299 |

T. Givón and Sue Savage Rumbaugh

| 22 | Some Remarks on Universal Grammar | 311 |

Robert D. Van Valin, Jr.

| 23 | The Canonical Form Constraint: Language Acquisition Via a General Theory of Learning | 321 |

Thomas G. Bever

| 24 | Finiteness, Universal Grammar, and the Language Faculty | 333 |

Wolfgang Klein

| 25 | Grammaticization: Implications for a Theory of Language | 345 |

Joan Bybee

| 26 | What Does It Mean to Compare Language and Gesture? Modalities and Contrasts | 357 |

Eve Sweetser

| 27 | On Paradigms, Principles, and Predictions | 367 |

Matthew Rispoli

| 28 | Child Language, Aphasia, and General Psycholinguistics | 375 |

Lise Menn

| 29 | Main Verb Properties and Equipollent Framing | 389 |

Leonard Talmy

30	Path Salience in Motion Events	403
	Iraide Ibarretxe-Antuñano	
31	Continuity and Change in the Representation of Motion Events in French	415
	Anetta Kopecka	
32	Mixing and Mapping: Motion, Path, and Manner in Amondawa	427
	Wany Sampaio, Chris Sinha, and Vera da Silva Sinha	

PART IV LANGUAGE AND COGNITION
UNIVERSALS AND TYPOLOGICAL COMPARISONS

	Introduction	443
	Melissa Bowerman	
33	Language as Mind Tools: Learning How to Think Through Speaking	451
	Penelope Brown and Stephen C. Levinson	
34	Why Some Spatial Semantic Categories Are Harder to Learn Than Others: The Typological Prevalence Hypothesis	465
	Dedre Gentner and Melissa Bowerman	
35	Cognitive Predictors of Children's First and Second Language Proficiency	481
	Ludo Verhoeven and Anne Vermeer	
36	Relativistic Application of Thinking for Speaking	493
	Stéphanie Pourcel	
37	Thinking for Speaking and Channeling of Attention: A Case for Eye-Tracking Research	505
	Sven Strömqvist, Kenneth Holmqvist, and Richard Andersson	
38	Imagery for Speaking	517
	David McNeill	
39	Evidentials: An Interface Between Linguistic and Conceptual Development	531
	Ayhan Aksu-Koç	
40	How Deep Are Differences in Referential Density?	543
	Sabine Stoll and Balthasar Bickel	

Appendix A Dan Slobin's Mentors, Models, Influences, and Connections: A Self-Portrait	557
Appendix B Bibliography of Dan Isaac Slobin's Publications, 1960–	565
Author Index	575
Subject Index	583

Dedication

We are honored to dedicate this collection of cutting-edge research in the field of the crosslinguistic study of the psychology of language to Dan I. Slobin, a beloved friend, an ever stimulating colleague, and an inspiring and committed mentor.

The Editors: Guo, Elena, Nancy, Sue, Kei, and Şeyda

Contributors

The contributors of this volume are but a small portion of the long list of several generations of language and psychology researchers whose research and careers have been strongly influenced and closely related to Dan Slobin's research and activities. Here, we will briefly tell the readers who the editors are in relationship to Dan, and list all the contributors. But out there across the world, there are many researchers who will join us in celebrating Dan's scholarly achievement by reading and using this Festschrift.

The Editors

Jiansheng Guo   When I first went from China to Berkeley in 1986 to do my graduate studies in language acquisition, I was overwhelmed by Dan's enthusiastic energy, charismatic warmth, expansive knowledge, and capacious heart and mind. His sharp insights and never-ending interest in a wide range of intellectual issues across many disciplines were contagious, and forever exciting and stimulating. Dan consistently shows his students his trade-mark intellectual style by examining the issue from multiple directions and dimensions. He always approaches the understanding of language dialectically from both static and dynamic perspectives, never separating language use and language structure. He believes that "One cannot separate a theory of language *change* from a theory of language *structure*." He begins with the research question about the universal character of language in language acquisition, but he addresses the issue ingeniously, by looking at the vast variations of languages and the dynamic nuances in language change and development. A philosophical and dialectical remark of his struck me in my first year at Berkeley, and has been engraved in my mind ever since: "In a remarkable way, language maintains a universal character across all of these continuing changes, so that the more it changes, the more sure we can be of what it is." This motto has since inspired me to examine the complex and dynamic nature of any ostensibly simple and static phenomenon.

Elena Lieven   I first 'met' Dan Slobin through his writing. In the early 1970s, I was a graduate student at Cambridge in England, struggling to locate children's language development within Piagetian and Brunerian theories of developmental psychology, in a context where Chomskian 'accounts' were sweeping the board. I still remember the feelings of intense wonder, excitement, and gratitude when I discovered Dan's work. Wonder, because it opened up new worlds of relevant ideas from linguistics: the enormous range of differences between languages and the amazingly rapid way in which they can change over time. Excitement, because it provided alternative ways of thinking about the problem which felt both linguistically *and* psychologically much more promising. And gratitude, because here was an author who was directly addressing my concerns and who wrote wonderfully clearly and with humanity. A few years later I was lucky enough to meet Dan, and to try to convince him that differences between children learning the same language could provide another 'window' on the processes involved. We have been good friends ever since, a friendship encompassing music, beautiful places, both natural and human-made, and a great deal of arguing about language development!

Nancy Budwig   My arrival in Berkeley could not have been more perfectly timed. In my first semester the famous conference that paved the way for the *Crosslinguistic study of language acquisition* book series took place so my first year at Berkeley was extraordinarily lively. A student could not have asked for anything more than the mentoring team I was afforded at UCB. Dan's mentoring style fostered a rigorous scholarly atmosphere uniquely placed within a warm and friendly setting conducive for developing fresh ideas. Typically this happened outside the traditional classroom setting in informal venues—often Dan's living room where he held regular meetings or in Sue's dining room. This provided a model for the passion and fun to be found in academic life. One particularly salient memory of Dan is from my semester long experience working as his teaching assistant. To be honest, what I liked most about this was the sustained opportunity to debate with Dan the content of the integrative chapter he was writing for his 1985 volume. I vividly remember the day Dan finished the first complete readable draft of that (long!) chapter. It was the week-end, and he dropped off exams for me to grade; he also brought along a draft of the chapter for my feedback. I stayed awake all night literally not able to put the manuscript down and had to quickly grade the exams at dawn. Not every graduate student has that opportunity to share the intellectual excitement of many years of thinking solidifying as they did then for Dan. His razor-sharp vision of the field combined with his warm and loving ongoing support of my development has had long lasting impact—not only influencing my scholarship but also the mentorship model I have developed. For all of this, I am grateful.

Susan Ervin-Tripp   I was teaching child language in the Speech Department, and analyzing data from a child grammar project, one of the three independently developed around 1960 by Braine, Brown, and Ervin. Berkeley at that time was a hotbed of new ideas about language including Sidney Lamb's stratificational grammar and Hymes' and Gumperz' ethnography of communication, all of which overlapped in regular colloquia. When Dan came he helped us all develop the weekly evening informal seminar discussing "language, society, and the child," and began teaching psycholinguistics. His enthusiasm for continuing the work on child grammar that he had begun with Brown, and for using his extensive knowledge of other languages to extend the model, led him to become very active in training students from both psychology and other departments for field work. In 1966, while I was in Europe on sabbatical leave, we did an *Annual Review* chapter on psycholinguistics, for which I cannot identify the separate author segments, so seamlessly did we work. In 1971, he put together a panel at AAAS on contrasting child language theories in which both of us took constructivist positions. The idea of strategies for acquisition must have played a large role in our discussions; my article on strategies appeared in 1972. When I saw his 1973 paper on Operating Principles, I realized his theoretical and presentational abilities were exceptional, and that no one would forget the detailed and mnemonically organized OPs. We taught graduate seminars on child language together for decades, and shared students. His knowledge, incisive intelligence, and eagerness to expand the field helped make Berkeley a major center for this work. One attribute is not often mentioned: his managerial abilities. Dan is a planner and manager, and has succeeded in coordinating work from all over the world, leading to his long list of edited books.

Keiko Nakamura   My first meeting with Dan was in the spring of 1988, when I was busy visiting graduate programs in psychology. Over the past two decades, he has been an invaluable mentor and I have been constantly amazed by his strong dedication to his teaching and research. In particular, Dan's firm commitment to the crosslinguistic approach and his introduction of the Frog Story to the field as a methodological tool have influenced my own research on Japanese language development, especially my work on narratives.

Şeyda Özçalışkan   My initial acquaintance with Dan was at the University of California, Berkeley, where I studied as a graduate student under his supervision. He introduced me to the field of spatial language and cognition, and we worked on several projects together, examining crosslinguistic variation in the expression of spatial motion. Dan has been a wonderful mentor and an insightful collaborator ever since. Looking back, I still miss all the stimulating conversations we had back at Berkeley, with the topics ranging from the (im)possibilities of encoding manner in verb-framed languages, to reminiscences about life in Istanbul, Turkish music and politics. Dan has been a key figure in my intellectual development, and I feel very fortunate to have had the chance to be one of his doctoral students.

Authors

Ayhan Aksu-Koç
Department of Psychology
Yeditepe University
Kayışdağı, Istanbul
Turkey
and
Department of Psychology
Boğaziçi University
Bebek, Istanbul
Turkey

Laetitia Albert
Laboratoire MoDyCo-CNRS
Paris, France

Richard Andersson
Humanities Lab
Lund University
Lund, Sweden

Michael Bamberg
Department of Psychology
Clark University
Worcester, Massachusetts

Edith L Bavin
School of Psychological Science
La Trobe University
Victoria, Australia

Heike Behrens
Department of English
University of Basel
Basel, Switzerland

Ruth A. Berman
Department of Linguistics
Tel Aviv University
Ramat Aviv, Israel

Raphael Berthele
Département des Sciences du plurilinguisme et
  des langues étrangères
Departement Mehrsprachigkeits-und
  Fremdsprachenforschung
Université de Fribourg
Fribourg, Switzerland

Thomas G. Bever
Departments of Linguistics, Psychology,
  Language Reading and Culture
Programs in Cognitive Science and
  Neuroscience
University of Arizona
Tucson, Arizona

Balthasar Bickel
Department of Linguistics
University of Leipzig
Leipzig, Germany

Melissa Bowerman
Max Planck Institute for Psycholinguistics
Nijmegen, the Netherlands

Penelope Brown
Language Acquisition Group
Max Planck Institute for Psycholinguistics
Nijmegen, the Netherlands

Nancy Budwig
Department of Psychology
Clark University
Worcester, Massachusetts

Joan L. Bybee
Department of Linguistics
University of New Mexico
Albuquerque, New Mexico

Christian Champaud
Laboratoire Structures Formelles du Langage
CNRS & Université Paris
Paris, France

Liang Chen
Department of Communication Sciences and
  Disorders
The University of Georgia
Athens, Georgia

Patricia M. Clancy
Department of Linguistics
University of California, Santa Barbara
Santa Barbara, California

Katherine Demuth
Cognitive and Linguistic Sciences
Brown University
Providence, Rhode Island

David Ellis
Cognitive and Linguistic Sciences
Brown University
Providence, Rhode Island

Richard Ely
Department of Psychology
Boston University
Boston, Massachusetts

Susan Ervin-Tripp
Department of Psychology
University of California, Berkeley
Berkeley, California

Dedre Gentner
Psychology Department
Northwestern University
Evanston, Illinois

T. Givon
Institute of Cognitive and Decision Sciences
University of Oregon
Eugene, Oregon

Jean Berko Gleason
Department of Psychology
Boston University
Boston, Massachusetts

Susan Goldin-Meadow
Department of Psychology
University of Chicago
Chicago, Illinois

Jiansheng Guo
Department of Human Development
California State University, East Bay
Hayward, California

Henriëtte Hendriks
Research Centre for English and Applied
  Linguistics
University of Cambridge
Cambridge, U.K.

Maya Hickmann
Laboratoire Structures Formelles du Langage
Université Paris
Paris, France

Kenneth Holmqvist
Humanities Lab
Lund University
Lund, Sweden

Iraide Ibarretxe-Antuñano
Departamento de Lingüística
General e Hispánica Universidad de Zaragoza
Zaragoza, Spain

Wolfgang Klein
Max Planck Institute for Psycholinguistics
Nijmegen, the Netherlands

B. Dilara Koçbaş
Koç University
Istanbul, Turkey
and
Department of Language & Literacy Education
University of British Columbia
Vancouver, British Columbia, Canada

Anetta Kopecka
Max Planck Institute for Psycholinguistics
Nijmegen, the Netherlands

Aylin C. Küntay
Department of Psychology
Koç University
Istanbul, Turkey

Amy Kyratzis
Department of Education
University of California,
Santa Barbara, California

Lourdes de Leon
Center for Research and Higher Studies in
  Social Anthropology
Tlalpan, Mexico

Stephen C. Levinson
Language and Cognition Group
Max Planck Institute for Psycholinguistics
Nijmegen, the Netherlands

Elena Lieven
Max Planck Institute for Evolutionary
  Anthropology
Leipzig, Germany
and
School of Psychological Sciences
University of Manchester
Manchester, United Kingdom

Stéphanie Martin
Laboratoire MoDyCo-CNRS
Paris, France

David McNeill
Departments of Psychology and Linguistics
University of Chicago
Chicago, Illinois

Lise Menn
Institute of Cognitive Science and
  Department of Linguistics
University of Colorado
Boulder, Colorado

Carolyn Mylander
Department of Psychology
University of Chicago
Chicago, Illinois

Keiko Nakamura
Faculty of Letters
Keio University
Tokyo, Japan

Ageliki Nicolopoulou
Department of Psychology
Lehigh University
Bethlehem, Pennsylvania

Bracha Nir-Sagiv
Department of Linguistics
Tel Aviv University
Ramat Aviv, Israel

Kyung-ju Oh
Cambridge, Massachusetts

Şeyda Özçalışkan
Department of Psychology
Georgia State University
Atlanta, Georgia

Aslı Özyürek
Department of Linguistics
Radboud University
and
Max Planck Institute for Psycholinguistics
Nijmegen, the Netherlands
and
Department of Psychology
Koc University
Istanbul, Turkey

Brenda Caldwell Phillips
Department of Psychology
Boston University
Boston, Massachusetts

Stéphanie Pourcel
School of Linguistics & English Language
Bangor University
Wales, United Kingdom

Matthew Rispoli
Department of Speech and Hearing Science
University of Illinois at Urbana-Champaign
Champaign, Illinois

Wany Bernadete de Araujo Sampaio
Departamento de Línguas Vernáculas
Universidade Federal de Rondônia
Porto Velho, Brazil

Burcu Sancar
Department of Psychology
University of Chicago
Chicago, Illinois

Sue Savage-Rumbaugh
Great Ape Trust of Iowa
Des Moines, Iowas

Chris Sinha
Department of Psychology
University of Portsmouth
Portsmouth, United Kingdom

Vera da Silva Sinha
Department of Psychology
University of Portsmouth
Portsmouth, United Kingdom

Sabine Stoll
Department of Linguistics
Max Planck Institute for Evolutionary
 Anthropology
Leipzig, Germany

Sven Strömqvist
Centre for Languages and Literature
Lund University
Lund, Sweden

Eve Sweetser
Department of Linguistics
University of California, Berkeley
Berkeley, California

Leonard Talmy
Department of Linguistics
Center for Cognitive Science
University at Buffalo
State University of New York
Buffalo, New York

Robert D. Van Valin, Jr.
Department of General Linguistics
Institute for Language and Information
Heinrich Heine University
Düsseldorf, Germany
and
Department of Linguistics
University at Buffalo
The State University of New York
Buffalo, New York

Edy Veneziano
Institut de Psychologie
Université Paris Descartes-CNRS
Paris, France

Ludo Verhoeven
Behavioral Science Institute
Radboud University Nijmegen
Nijmegen, the Netherlands

Anne Vermeer
Department of Communication and
 Information Sciences
Tilburg University
Tilburg, the Netherlands

Richard M. Weist
Department of Psychology
State University of New York at Fredonia
Fredonia, New York

Elena Zaretsky
Department of Communication Disorders
University of Massachusetts-Amherst
Amherst, Massachusetts

A Poetic Portrait of Dan Isaac Slobin

Presented
at
The Special Symposium
in Honor of Dan Isaac Slobin
at
IASCL-10, Berlin, July 26, 2005

Chinese Characters

学海书林万里程
信步闲庭学意浓
五湖四海勤耕种
叶绿花香硕果红

Pinyin (Romanization)

Xué hǎi shū lín wàn lǐ chéng
Xìn bù xián tíng xué yì nóng
Wǔ hú sì hǎi qín gēng zhòng
Yè lǜ huā xiāng shuò guǒ hóng.

(Originally composed by Jiansheng Guo in Mandarin Chinese)

English

Oceans of scholarship and forests of
    books expand ten thousand miles,
Stroll away on an excursion engrossed
    in contemplation and smiles,
Tirelessly disseminate and cultivate
    across the five lakes and four seas,
Leaves are lush, flowers intoxicating,
    and bountiful fruit dazzling with
    ruby peace.

(English translation from Chinese by Jiansheng Guo)

Japanese

万里の海と森林を超える學問、
靜思と笑顔で散策し、
五つの湖、四つの海を努め耕し、
綠は茂、花は香り、果実は実る。

Banri no umi to shinrin o koeru gakumon,
Seishi to egao de sansaku shi,
Itsutsu no mizuumi, yottsu no umi o tsutome tagayashi,
Midori wa shige, hana wa kaori, kajitsu wa minoru.

(Japanese translation from Chinese by Keiko Nakamura)

Turkish

Uzanır okyanuslarca bilgi ve ormanlarca kitap yerkürenin binlerce metrekaresine,
Dalar bir gezintinin düşünmeler ve gülümsemelerle dolu dünyasına,
Yayar ve yetiştirir hiç yorulmadan beş göl ve dört deniz ötesine,
Ve bulur kendini yetişen yaprakların bolluğunun, çiçeklerin başdöndürücü
    kokusunun ve binbir meyvenin yakut renkli ışıltısının dünyasında.

(Turkish Translation from English by Şeyda Özçalışkan)

Introduction

JIANSHENG GUO
California State University, East Bay

ELENA LIEVEN
Max Planck Institute for Evolutionary Anthropology and University of Manchester

DAN ISAAC SLOBIN AND HIS CONTRIBUTIONS

Dan Slobin is a household name among scholars and students in the fields of linguistics and psychology. He has been a major intellectual and creative force in the field of child language development, typological linguistics, and psycholinguistics for the past 40 years. A pioneer, creative theorist, and researcher, he has insisted on a rigorous, crosslinguistic approach in his attempt to identify universal developmental patterns in language learning, to explore the effects of particular types of languages on psycholinguistic processes, to determine the extent to which universals of language and language behavior are determined by modality (vocal/auditory vs. manual/visual), and, finally, to investigate the relation between linguistic and cognitive processes. His insights from languages with radically different structures to those of English have revolutionized the questions we ask about the cognitive bases of children's language development, universals of language learning, and the contribution of formal and functional typological differences to understanding the psychology of language.

The Beginning of Crosslinguistic Studies

The field of crosslinguistic studies of psychology of language has come a long way since the Sterns published the first edition of their diary study in 1907 (Stern & Stern, 1907) and since the heyday of behaviorist structural linguistics in the 1950s and nativist generative linguistics in the 1960s. The psychology of language was created, with the term psycholinguistic being coined by 1953, thanks to a group of psychologically minded language scholars and a linguistically educated psychologist, J.B. Carroll, who used the term as the name of an interdisciplinary summer institute in 1953, organized by Osgood, an experimental psychologist, and Sebeok, a linguist (Osgood & Sebeok, 1954). One outcome was the Southwest Project in Comparative Psycholinguistics, focusing primarily on the Whorf hypothesis through a crosslinguistic experimental study of speakers of at least four languages of the American Southwest. Susan Ervin, then a graduate student, was assistant on that project, and later joined the faculty of the University of California, Berkeley.

Slobin arrived to join the psychology faculty at Berkeley in 1964 with a fresh PhD from Harvard, having worked with Roger Brown in his classic child language study research group and having been immersed in the intellectual debates around the philosophy of language, linguistics, and anthropology that characterized the Harvard–MIT environment at that time. By comparison with the early beginnings of crosslinguistic research, the critical move that Slobin made was to focus on syntax and on the "marvelous set of 'natural experiments' in which children with similar endowments master languages of varying forms" (Slobin, 1985, p. 5). As soon as he started at Berkeley, Slobin began to teach a course on psycholinguistics into which he incorporated child language material. He also became deeply involved with a group of scholars whose ideas went beyond the study of language structure, and beyond the English language alone. Coming "fresh from the heady days of early transformational grammar" (Slobin, Gerhardt, Kyratzis, & Guo, 1996, p. ix), he became attracted by the interdisciplinary research on language that was actively conducted by a group of pioneering Berkeley scholars, including Susan Ervin-Tripp in the Department of Speech, and John Gumperz, Dell Hymes, and their graduate students in the Anthropology Department, who were planning to do field work on language socialization in four societies coordinated by a field manual. Slobin plunged into this collaborative project, writing up the chapter on the comparative syntax section of the manual, and eventually editing the whole manual, published as *A Field Manual for Cross-Cultural Study of the Acquisition of Communicative Competence* (Slobin, 1967). The first encounter of 'crosslinguistic' in Slobin's publications is in 1979, in his coauthored paper with Ammon, titled *A Cross-Linguistic Study of the Processing of Causative Sentences* in the journal *Cognition* (Ammon & Slobin, 1979). By searching the word crosslinguistic on Google, we find an astronomical 677,000 entries. We have come a long way in the past 40 years, and we owe this in large part to Slobin.

Although Slobin's crosslinguistic approach encompasses a broad range of languages, he started his research program with a much smaller set. Soon after his work on the Manual, he developed a new major crosslinguistic acquisition project, in which samples of adult–child speech were gathered and comparable elicitation experiments were performed in Serbo-Croatian, Turkish, English, and Italian, involving several international research teams. The languages were not randomly chosen, but rather, he deliberately selected languages in which the syntactic challenges to children differed. The teams met in Dubrovnik in the summer of 1972 to coordinate their plans, the same summer as the International Symposium on First Language Acquisition met in Florence, during which the International Association for the Study of Child Language (IASCL) was voted into existence; its first triennial Congress was in Tokyo, Japan, in 1978. Slobin's project developed into the large-scale research program culminating in the five-volume series that is described in more detail in the introduction to Part I (Budwig & Ervin-Tripp, this volume).

In the late 1980s, Slobin embarked on another major crosslinguistic project, in collaboration with Ruth Berman (Berman & Slobin, 1987), originally intended to compare children's development of the tense/aspect systems of five different languages: English, Hebrew, German, Spanish, and Turkish. They investigated this issue through the analysis of children's elicited narratives based on the picture story book *Frog, where are you?* (Mayer, 1969). This resulted in a volume by Berman and Slobin (1994) in collaboration with 10 other scholars all over the world, which was followed by its sequel with a similar focus but a much larger crosslinguistic database, involving many more scholars across the five continents, covering wider perspectives and approaches (Strömqvist & Verhoeven, 2004). According to an incomplete count by Berman and Slobin (1994), research using the Frog book elicitation method was being conducted in 48 different languages in first language acquisition, and 17 languages in second language acquisition or bilingualism (see the introduction to Part II, Berman, this volume).

A Dynamic Thinker

Slobin's research defines and illustrates vision, broad-mindedness, and thinking which is both systemic and dynamic. Over the past 40 years, his research has been primarily concerned with processes of language acquisition and their relation to cognition and thinking on the one hand, and to culture and communication on the other. In both his theorizing and empirical work, his mind dances artfully among structure, function, social relations, communicative utility, and cognitive constraints. He first proposed the Operating Principles (OPs) to account for the many strategies children utilize in their construction of grammar (Slobin, 1971, 1973, 1982, 1985). The value of his OPs is not just in their comprehensive inclusiveness of processing strategies, but even more in the prediction that each OP can make about children's behavior, and the competing forces exerted on the language-learning child to shape the production and comprehension of language. This dynamic way of thinking is illustrated in two hypotheses that he presented in his paper *Language change in childhood and in history* (Slobin, 1977; also see Slobin, 1979). First, he proposed that the way language is structured is the product of the four competing constraints (charges, in his terms): the need for clarity in communication, the need to be humanly processible in ongoing time, given the speaker and hearer's cognitive constraints, the need for speed and ease of use, and the need for expressiveness. As Slobin (1979, p. 194) states, "We cannot understand the nature of Language without attending to the complex and contradictory pressures of these four charges." Second, he had the vision to see the connections between change during child language development, historical development, in language contact, and in the evolution of pidgin and Creole languages. Although his ultimate interest and goal was universal patterns of language, he focused his attention and energy on variation and change. In fact, he welcomed and celebrated variation and change in language by saying that "the study of language during its unstable or changing phases is an excellent tool for discovering the essence of language itself" (Slobin, 1977, p. 185). This ability to balance the systemic nature of language with its historical and acquisitional dynamics is summed up in the same paper, "In a remarkable way, language maintains a universal character across all of these continuing changes, so that the more it changes, the more sure we can be of what it is" (Slobin, 1977, p. 186; see Part III Introduction, Lieven, this volume).

The dynamic nature of Slobin's thinking is also reflected in his open-mindedness and constant modification of his theories based on interactions with colleagues and students and in reaction to accounts based on ever increasing available data from the field (much of which was, in turn, inspired by developments in his theorizing). A diligent learner, Slobin absorbed intellectual wisdom from a wide range of mentors and models. His thinking was strongly influenced by Roger Brown, Jerome Bruner, Noam Chomsky, Roman Jakobson, Eric Lenneberg, George Miller, and Lev Vygotsky (see Appendix A in this volume). These mentors provided a solid theoretical foundation for Slobin's initial research focus on the relationship between language structures and cognition. A congenial and challenging colleague, Slobin never stopped learning from his fellow researchers. Colleagues such as Susan Ervin-Tripp and John Gumperz were an important influence in developing the knowledge that context and culture played a vital role in the development of language structures and functions. Leonard Talmy and Melissa Bowerman challenged and helped to develop Slobin's changing ideas on the relationship between linguistic structure and human cognition. A nurturing and encouraging mentor, Slobin has also never stopped learning from his students. The Frog story was a method originally used by his student Michael Bamberg for his dissertation (Bamberg, 1985, 1987). Slobin then developed it into a widely used tool of narrative elicitation among language researchers. Students such as Julie Gerhardt (Gerhardt, 1983; Gee [Gerhardt] & Savasir, 1985) and Nancy Budwig (Budwig, 1986, 1995) emphasized how pragmatic functions may penetrate into the processing of language structures in child language development, and shape child language structures. In his recent writings and theorizing, pragmatic functions and cultural practices are always a necessary and integral component of his paradigm and hypothesis (e.g., Slobin, 1997, 2004).

Concerning the issue of universality and language specificity in child language development, Slobin's initial proposal was for a universal 'child grammar' subsequently developing into the particular language that children were learning (Slobin, 1985). As a result of ongoing and intense debate, above all with Melissa Bowerman (Bowerman, 1985), and in the face of newly available data, Slobin modified his original position, and starting in the late 1980s, developed his current view, which he referred to as 'Thinking for Speaking' (Slobin, 1987, 1991, 1996; see the introduction to Part IV, Bowerman, this volume). This new approach has resulted in many research projects and publications on typological issues in the linguistic conceptualization of space in motion events. This is a relatively rare and highly commendable example of a scientist who can change his mind in the face of new data and theory and be prepared to say so!

Slobin has more recently developed another line of research related to the acquisition of sign language. Here he is attempting to expand crosslinguistic studies to include "cross-modality" (vocal/auditory vs. manual/visual) comparisons. This gives a completely new dimension of the meaning of "crosslinguistic." To quote Judy Reilly's (2005) speech at the 10th IASCL special symposium celebrating Slobin's achievements:

> In the U.S., the field of study of sign languages was greatly expanded by Slobin's Harvard colleagues, Ursula Bellugi and Ed Klima, and many different sign languages have been studied. To

this field, Slobin has made two important contributions in significantly advancing the flourishing field. First, he and his group made an important methodological contribution by developing the Berkeley Transcription System (BTS), a transcription system taking into account the multidimensionality of signed languages that is compatible with CHILDES. Second, he has initiated crosslinguistic studies of signed and spoken languages, bringing sign languages into the mainstream of crosslinguistic research. Together these have permitted us and encouraged us to address basic issues of language structure and acquisition across modalities: spoken and signed.

This international project has led to a reconceptualization of the grammar in sign language (through Hoiting and Slobin's analysis of "polycomponential verbs," Hoiting & Slobin, 2002), showing that sign languages are radically different in structure from the spoken/written languages of the surrounding communities. This contrast has implications both for linguistic theory and for educational practice.

A Mind of Humanity

Slobin's research is consistently characterized by his focus on humanity. Ultimately his concerns are with the universal patterns of language, language change, and language development, but he has always paid close attention to the individual language users and their specific linguistic, cultural, social, and communicative contexts. Thus his research is consistently based on real speech data collected from contextualized discourse, rather than hypothetical data based on the intuitions of linguists about expectations of language patterning. His paradigms and the components of his paradigms make human sense for real communication, conceptualization, language use, and human cognitive capacities. Hence, although he was a psychology student at Harvard during the period when Chomskyan models were developing, he stayed away from the start from the algorithmic structures and principles that he felt have little connection with psychology of language and language users. At the same time, he retains a belief in a level of symbolic mental representation of language and conceptual structures.

Slobin is not only a highly influential thinker and researcher, but he has had a major role in organizing research and in the integration of scholars around the world into the international research community. With his ambitious plans, willingness to encourage and help, and artful skills of organization, he has collaborated with countless researchers, veteran and novice, in many research projects across all the five continents (Asia, Australasia, Europe, South America, and North America). He meets people in classrooms, seminars, workshops, conferences, committee meetings, and online by email. Any casual discussion could result in an eventual serious research collaboration that bears abundant fruit in grants, conference presentations, and publications. He generously gives out his own data to other people, friends, colleagues, or even total strangers from distant countries contacting him by email. He has also helped many scholars or graduate students to start their own academic networks and establish their own research enterprises. He is truly the center of research in the field in the literal sense. His selfless dedication to working with and helping other researchers has played an indispensable role in creating research networks in each of the fields with which he is involved and this is demonstrated by the range and number of contributors to this volume.

A 'Renaissance Man'

Slobin is a true 'Renaissance man,' with diverse talents and interests, academic and otherwise. He is a prolific researcher and writer. His first publication was in 1961 (see Slobin's bibliography in this volume), when he was 22 years of age, on second language teaching in elementary schools in Israel. He published his first paper in a peer-reviewed journal in *Word* in 1963 on Yiddish address pronouns. And he has never stopped writing and publishing since. In addition to his trademark five volumes of *The crosslinguistic study of language acquisition*, he authored and edited over a dozen books and monographs, and published over a hundred peer-reviewed journal papers and book chapters. He speaks at least seven languages (English, Yiddish, German, Spanish, Turkish, Russian, and French), and his knowledge of the linguistic structures of these languages is always on the tip of his tongue for detailed explanation and discussion. His memory about other people's language-related research is photographic, as natural as any reflexive reaction. His cultural knowledge and interests go beyond academia. He loves poetry (see the several poems he published in *Poems by linguists*, as listed in his bibliography) and music (he is a pianist, harpsichordist, and passionate opera fan) and has deep interests in visual art and politics.

Accomplishment and Recognition

Slobin's important theoretical contribution to the field, his remarkable organizational skills, and his academic talents have been widely recognized in many ways by many different organizations. He has received invitations from nearly every continent. He has been regularly invited to give plenary or keynote addresses at major international child language and linguistic conferences, ever since the 1970s, and almost every year since the 1990s, sometimes several times within a year. He travels frequently to Europe for regular meetings of several international committees. He has been a member and twice Chair since 1990 of the Scientific Council (Fachbeirat) of the Max Planck Institute for Psycholinguistics. He has received research grants from a variety of funding organizations in the U.S. and abroad. He is on the editorial board of many journals and book series. In 2001, he was invited to present a Master Lecture at SRCD's (Society for Research in Child Development) biannual meeting. In 2005, a special symposium was held in his honor at the 10th International Congress for the Study of Child Language in Berlin. The conference hall with a capacity of 1,000 people was packed.

THE BOOK

This book is a collection of 40 chapters reporting current research findings by leading scholars in the field of psychology of language. The 40 chapters are organized in four parts: each identifies and highlights one major field of research that Slobin's theorizing and research has inspired. Part I consists of 8 chapters focusing on empirical studies of child language development in crosslinguistic perspective. Part II consists of 12 chapters reporting current research concerning cognitive, linguistic, and pragmatic issues in narratives with both developmental and crosslinguistic orientations. Part III includes 12 chapters laying out different theoretical perspectives on language development, language change, and language typology. Part IV includes 8 chapters that investigate the relationship between language and the various forms of the thinking process. Each of these 40 chapters either involves explicit comparisons of two or more languages with clear theoretical guidance, or investigates issues within one language with a clear crosslinguistic/crosscultural research issue as its final goal. The definition of crosslinguistic not only involves many different spoken languages from different language types, but also extends to languages of different modality (spoken vs. sign languages vs. paralinguistic gestures). Thus, this volume not only follows the paths that Slobin has opened up for us, but also develops several new paths that he has inspired.

Hence, this book can serve both as a state-of-the-art review of the field, and as an advanced textbook for upper-level undergraduate and graduate students in the field. To help the readers better organize and conceptualize this vast field of research as represented by the many chapters, and appreciate Slobin's contribution to the field and the historical background of the development of the field in the past 40 years, each part of the volume starts with an introductory chapter, laying out the historical background, Slobin's contribution and accomplishment, the relevance of the chapters in each part, and future research directions.

We dedicate this volume to Dan Slobin. His vision and execution of a research program has provided a platform for moving our understanding of the psychology of language forward significantly in the past 40 years. To celebrate Slobin's life accomplishment in research is also to celebrate the accomplishment and maturity of the field. We hope all veteran researchers will enjoy this volume as a reflection of their hard work, energy, and intellectual endeavor. We hope all new joiners of the field will be inspired by this volume to carry on the research tradition of Dan Slobin's crosslinguistic studies of the psychology of language, and to develop the field yet further.

The editors would like to gratefully acknowledge and thank Larry Erlbaum, publisher, and Cathleen Petree, editor, who were so central to the initial stages of this book.

REFERENCES

Ammon, M. S., & Slobin, D. I. (1979). A cross-linguistic study of the processing of causative sentences. *Cognition, 7*, 3–17.

Bamberg, M. (1985). *Form and function in the construction of narratives: Developmental perspectives.* Unpublished doctoral dissertation, University of California, Berkeley.

Bamberg, M. (1987). *The acquisition of narratives: Learning to use language.* Berlin: Mouton de Gruyter.

Berman, R. A., & Slobin, D. I. (1987). *Five ways of learning how to talk about events: A crosslinguistic study of children's narratives* (Technical Report No. 46). Institute of Cognitive Studies, University of California, Berkeley.

Berman, R. A., & Slobin, D. I. (1994). *Relating events in narrative: A crosslinguistic developmental study.* Hillsdale, NJ: Lawrence Erlbaum Associates.

Bowerman, M. (1985). What shapes children's grammars? In D. I. Slobin (Ed.), *The crosslinguistic study of language acquisition: Vol. 2. Theoretical issues* (pp. 1257–1319). Hillsdale, NJ: Lawrence Erlbaum Associates.

Budwig, N. (1986). *Agentivity and control in early child language.* Unpublished doctoral dissertation, University of California, Berkeley.

Budwig, N. (1995). *A developmental-functionalist approach to child language.* Mahwah, NJ: Lawrence Erlbaum Associates.

Gee, J., & Savasir, I. (1985). On the use of *will* and *gonna*: Towards a description of activity-types for child language. *Discourse Processes, 8*, 143–175.

Gerhardt, J. (1983). *Tout se tient: Towards an analysis of activity-types to explicate the interrelation between modality and future reference in child discourse.* Unpublished doctoral dissertation, University of California, Berkeley.

Hoiting, N., & Slobin, D. I. (2002). Transcription as a tool for understanding: The Berkeley Transcription System for sign language research (BTS). In G. Morgan & B. Woll (Eds.), *Directions in sign language acquisition* (pp. 55–75). Amsterdam/Philadelphia: John Benjamins.

Mayer, M. (1969). *Frog, where are you?* New York, Dial Press.

Osgood, C. E., & Sebeok, T. A. (Eds.). (1954). Psycholinguistics: A survey of theory and research problems. *Journal of Abnormal Social Psychology, 49*(4,2), 1–203 [also as Supplement to *International Journal of American Linguistics*, XX, iv].

Reilly, J. (2005, July). From speech to sign language: Cross-modality comparisons. Paper presented at the Special Symposium in Honor of Dan Slobin, at the 10th International Congress for the Study of Child Language, Berlin, Germany.

Slobin, D. I. (Ed.). (1967). *A field manual for cross-cultural study of the acquisition of communicative competence.* Berkeley, CA: Language-Behavior Research Laboratory.

Slobin, D. I. (1971). Developmental psycholinguistics. In W. O. Dingwall (Ed.), *A survey of linguistic science* (pp. 298–411). College Park, MD: University of Maryland Linguistics Program.

Slobin, D. I. (1973). Cognitive prerequisites for the development of grammar. In C. A. Ferguson & D. I. Slobin (Eds.), *Studies of child language development* (pp. 175–208). New York: Holt, Rinehart & Winston. [Translations: Germany, Iceland, Poland, Russia]

Slobin, D. I. (1977). Language change in childhood and in history. In J. Macnamara (Ed.), *Language learning and thought* (pp. 185–214). New York: Academic Press.

Slobin, D. I. (1979). *Psycholinguistics* (2nd ed.). Glenview, IL: Scott Foresman. [Translation: Brazil]

Slobin, D. I. (1982). Universal and particular in the acquisition of language. In E. Wanner & L. R. Gleitman (Eds.), *Language acquisition: The state of the art* (pp. 128–172). Cambridge, UK: Cambridge University Press.

Slobin, D. I. (1985). Crosslinguistic evidence for the language-making capacity. In D. Slobin (Ed.), *The crosslinguistic study of language acquisition: Vol. 2. Theoretical issues* (pp. 1157–1256). Hillsdale, NJ: Lawrence Erlbaum Associates.

Slobin, D. I. (1987). Thinking for speaking. *Proceedings of the Annual Meeting of the Berkeley Linguistics Society, 13*, 435–444.

Slobin, D. I. (1991). Learning to think for speaking: Native language, cognition, and rhetorical style. *Pragmatics, 1*, 7–26.

Slobin, D. I. (1996). From "thought and language" to "thinking for speaking." In J. Gumperz & S. Levinson (Eds.), *Rethinking linguistic relativity* (pp. 70–96). Cambridge, UK: Cambridge University Press.

Slobin, D. I. (Ed.). (1997). *The crosslinguistic study of language acquisition: Vol. 5. Expanding the contexts*. Mahwah, NJ: Lawrence Erlbaum Associates.

Slobin, D. I. (2004). The many ways to search for a frog: Linguistic typology and the expression of motion events. In S. Strömqvist & L. Verhoeven (Eds.), *Relating events in narrative: Vol. 2. Typological and contextual perspectives* (pp. 219–257). Mahwah, NJ: Lawrence Erlbaum Associates.

Slobin, D. I., Gerhardt, J., Kyratzis, A., & Guo, J. (Eds.). (1996). *Social interaction, social context, and language: Essays in honor of Susan Ervin-Tripp*. Mahwah, NJ: Lawrence Erlbaum Associates.

Stern, C., & Stern, W. (1907). *Die Kindersprache*. Leipzig: Barth.

Strömqvist, S., & Verhoeven, L. (Eds.). (2004). *Relating events in narrative — Typological and contextual perspectives*. Mahwah, NJ: Lawrence Erlbaum Associates.

Part I

Language Learning in Crosslinguistic Perspective

Introduction

NANCY BUDWIG
Clark University

SUSAN ERVIN-TRIPP
University of California, Berkeley

> The central claim is that LMC constructs similar early grammars from all input languages. The surface forms will, of course, vary, since the materials provided by the input languages vary. What is constant are the basic notions that first receive grammatical expression, along with early constraints on the positioning of grammatical elements and the ways in which they relate to syntactic expression.
>
> **Dan I. Slobin (1985, p. 1161)**

> I will propose, however, that such theorists-including myself-have erred in attributing the origins of structure to the mind of the child, rather than to the interpersonal communicative and cognitive processes that everywhere and always shape language in its peculiar expression of content and relation.
>
> **Dan I. Slobin (2001, p. 407)**

Slobin argues that crosslinguistic study provides a *method* that "can be used to reveal both developmental universals and language-specific developmental patterns in the interaction of form and content" (Slobin, 1985, p. 5). While the specific proposals Slobin has endorsed over time have changed, the general idea that crosslinguistic study provides a method for revealing how children construct language anew has remained constant. How did Slobin come to build a lifetime program of research around crosslinguistic study?

Dan Slobin's development of the field of comparative child syntax can be foreseen from his own history. He grew up in a multilingual family, spent a year with his family in Vienna at 14 and by the time he went to graduate school he could speak Yiddish, Russian, Hebrew, Spanish, and German, so typological contrasts were familiar to him. As a senior at the University of Michigan he completed an honors thesis on psycholinguistics and heard Roger Brown talk about Jean Berko's work on children's grammatical creativity. The move to Harvard in 1960 to pursue a Ph.D. with Brown and with George Miller seemed a natural. He participated in the analysis of child syntax first on the transcripts of Adam, Eve, and Sarah in Brown's seminar. His dissertation was on grammatical processing, completed quickly to come to the job offered him by the Berkeley Psychology Department.

Arriving in Berkeley in 1963, he soon took part in an interdisciplinary seminar that met regularly to discuss communicative competence, a concept Dell Hymes proposed, which extended the boundary between competence and performance to include cultural and situational knowledge (see Ervin-Tripp, in press; Gumperz & Hymes, 1964). Dell Hymes, John Gumperz, Susan Ervin-Tripp, and Dan Slobin worked with students on a project to study crosslinguistic and cross-cultural contexts of language socialization. This led to the development of a Field Manual to help coordinate such research. Dan Slobin entered into this enterprise with gusto, taking on writing the comparative syntax section of the manual, and eventually editing the whole manual, called the Cross-Cultural Study of the Acquisition of Communicative Competence. Slobin had been told by a mentor that he should find a challenging topic rich enough for a lifetime commitment of his research. He had found it. This project made it clear to him that the method of comparative crosslinguistic study could provide a natural experiment for the study of the acquisition of grammar in relation to a cognitive common ground. Since cognition, he believed at the time, was everywhere alike, developmental differences would be due to the syntactic means available.

Soon after this work on the Manual, which continued in his coordination of the field workers, he developed a new major crosslinguistic acquisition project, in which samples of adult-child speech would be gathered and comparable elicitation experiments would be performed in Serbo-Croatian, Turkish, English, and Italian. He had deliberately chosen languages where the syntactic challenges to children differed. It was these two projects in cross-cultural work that laid the groundwork for his major theoretical proposal of Operating Principles. The importance of this project has over the years attracted participation from scholars working in a wide range of languages. Slobin has edited a series of books refining and enriching his first theoretical description; the contributions to this section are testimony to the enduring importance of the project.

The eight chapters in this section suggest ways that ongoing research has been influenced by Slobin's thinking about language learning in crosslinguistic perspective. Our introductory chapter is divided into three parts. First, we begin with a brief overview of some of the key aspects of Slobin's views on crosslinguistic study, beginning with his discussion of the language-making capacity, operating principles and basic child grammar and tracing this forward to his later work on language typology. We conclude this first section by considering ways the eight chapters draw upon Slobin's ideas about universals and particulars of acquisition. Second, we turn to two ways the authors in this section push Slobin's thinking in new directions, first by focusing on issues of methodology and second, examining *typology in use*. Finally, we offer our own reflections for future lines of research examining language development within a crosslinguistic perspective.

THE LANGUAGE-MAKING CAPACITY, BASIC CHILD GRAMMAR, AND THE SHIFT TOWARD LANGUAGE TYPOLOGY

In one way or another, the eight chapters in this section draw upon Slobin's discussion of the relative role of universals and particulars in the acquisition process. Slobin's original theoretical perspective was built on the idea of the language-making capacity (LMC) and operating principles. Slobin originally argued that the LMC and Operating Principles provide the child with mechanisms to construct similar grammars regardless of input language. These early grammars were referred to as Basic Child Grammar: "What is constant are the basic notions that first receive grammatical expression, along with early constraints on the positioning of grammatical elements and the ways in which they relate to syntactic expression" (Slobin, 1985, p. 1161). Later the idea that children start with a core set of basic notions that they give grammatical treatment to regardless of input language was retracted. In 1997, in the final volume of the crosslinguistic series, Slobin argued that there is a collection of grammatically relevant notions but "there are too many different packagings of such semantic and pragmatic characteristics to build in all of the possible packages in advance or rank them in terms of "naturalness" or "accessibility" (Slobin, 1997, p. 301). From here Slobin went on to argue that typological aspects of the input language as used in practice played a far greater role in children's use and development of grammatical systems than his earlier work had suggested.

The eight chapters in this section collectively develop aspects of arguments Slobin has made previously. Gleason, Phillips, and Ely focus on the lexicon, examining the acquisition of animal terms in Russian and English. They highlight the importance of studying lexical development crosslinguistically in order to conclude something about the universality of the acquisition process. Gleason et al. argue that animal terms are acquired as part of broader interaction routines that bridge to decontextualized discourse, and that despite some differences in frequency and density of the lexicon, there is universal interest by two-year-olds in talk about the animal world.

The other chapters focus more squarely on the acquisition of grammar. Two of the papers explicitly examine Slobin's early claims about Basic Child Grammar. Goldin-Meadow, Özyürek, Sancar, and Mylander undertook a remarkable extension of the comparative method to the homesign of deaf children born to hearing parents in China, Turkey and the United States. The children have contextual and gestural input to language formation, but they were not exposed to conventional sign language or to speech training. When the developmental course of homesign was followed, there were striking similarities in the types of semantic elements expressed, types of gesture combinations, and the order at sentence level. Among these similarities were focusing on patient first (by pointing or iconic gesture), and on results. They suggest, consistent with Slobin's discussion of Basic Child Grammar, that the constructions they found show conceptual starting points for grammatical notions that are highly accessible to all children. In contrast, Kyratzis challenges Slobin's early focus on the Manipulative Activity Scene. Consistent with Slobin's later ideas about more flexible starting points for children, Kyratzis argues that the transitivity parameters that children come to use in a particular situation may be shaped by the pragmatic uses they themselves put their language to, which in turn may derive from the pragmatic functions of language with peers, the language that they hear spoken around them in that situation, and by the socialization influences and ideologies that they are exposed to in their language community.

Several other chapters that focus on grammar are concerned with Slobin's more recent interest in the role of typology. Behrens, for example, looks at the early use of particles that encode deixis in German-speaking children and finds evidence that children follow the lexicalization patterns of their input language. Yet though the semantic distinctions are marked linguistically, they are acquired late. Similarly, Weist reports on the contrasts in the acquisition of one-to-one mapping of temporal and spatial relations in Polish and Finnish, finding support for the overall claim that children's ability to process form-function relations of a language is related to the morphosyntactic structure of a particular language. Küntay and Kocbas, in their comparative work on lexical items and construction types in English and Turkish character introductions in elicited narratives, highlight ways in which the relative ease of accessibility of certain constructions in the two languages produces differences in patterns of use of nominal constructions by children acquiring the two languages.

Nuanced discussion of Slobin's early position on universal starting points and his later advocacy for more flexible origins dependent on typological features of the input can be found in the chapters by Demuth et al. and Clancy. Demuth's early work suggested a challenge for Slobin's Operating Principles involving simplicity and order. Despite the fact that there are up to 18 singular/plural prefixes, 2-year-old Bantu-speaking children acquired these forms early and error free. Demuth's recent work casts light on even more delicate constraints on realization and omission. Further research on the southern Bantu language Sesotho has also found that some phonologically underspecified noun class prefixes can be 'optionally' dropped when followed by a nominal modifier. The Bantu-speaking children were sensitive both to agreement constraints and phonological constraints on the dropping of noun class prefixes.

Clancy also points out nuanced ways to link discussion of operating principles with typological issues. In her analysis of the dialogic environment for Korean argument markers, which draws on the notion of priming, she makes quite clear that there is a high predictability in similar contexts between null and realized morphemes for the partner and the child, suggesting that the child tracks the partner's practices. Structural priming is interpreted as a form of implicit learning, thus as a potential acquisition mechanism.

CONTRIBUTIONS TO SLOBIN'S LEGACY

While the chapters in this section provide ample support for various aspects of Slobin's work, collectively they also elaborate on his thinking in at least two ways. First, the chapters when taken together push us to think more deeply about methodology and the claims a research community can make at any given time in the light of current advances in technology and theorizing about units of analysis, and second, the chapters encourage us to ground a view of origins of grammar in terms of a view of *typology in interaction*. We now turn to a discussion of each of these points.

Method

One of the innovative aspects of the crosslinguistic project undertaken by Slobin was the ambitious vision to develop a common framework from which to approach the study of children's language learning. The original child research used adult eliciting or observations of adult-child talk. Kyratzis suggests that the heavy use of adult–child talk rather than peer talk in early research altered the pragmatic and priming contexts available in the data, distorting the syntax.

Since the original Slobin project was developed, the field of child language has seen tremendous methodological advances based on increasing use of technological tools. The most obvious is the greater ease of video recording. The advent of computer-aided analyses has facilitated new findings as well. At the technical level, several of the studies in this section discuss ways that new technology has been central to the work that they have done and afforded new conclusions. Behrens comments on the advantages of both large corpora and computer-aided analyses especially for observing patterns in relatively rare grammatical markers. Demuth et al. similarly comment on the ways larger corpora and new language analysis tools have altered the interpretation of the children's acquisition of Sesotho.

Goldin-Meadow et al. push us to think anew about what counts as a "natural experiment" in their examination of deaf children acquiring homesign, raising questions such as: how do children who have no access to input other than gestures construct a language system; and what differences from hearing children's first language tell us about language universals and language-medium particulars? The advent of digital video recordings has been central to this work as it has to research on sign language.

Other advances from the early field studies come in terms of selecting the units of study. The original crosslinguistic research focused on morphological systems relatively independently of one another. Advances in how psycholinguists view language systems and theoretical frameworks such as Construction Grammar have encouraged researchers in this volume such as Küntay et al. and Clancy to examine the interface between such subsystems as noun phrase character introductions and verb constructions.

Interaction Patterns

A second theme that emerges since Slobin began the original discussion of the crosslinguistic study of language learning has to do with interaction patterns. In the preface to the fifth volume of his series, Slobin (1997) noted the importance of relating socio-cultural factors and, in particular, the existence of a gap arising from the relative failure to examine the role of human interaction patterns on grammatical learning in crosslinguistic context. Several of the chapters in this section fill this gap by outlining the needed shift from conceiving of typology in terms of what is known about languages in the abstract, to looking at interaction patterns actually available to children. Several of the authors' contributions flesh out this important point. For instance, Gleason and colleagues discuss the role of context and gender in examining the typological patterns of animal terms used by the English- and Russian-speaking families they studied. Similarly Kyratzis shows how conversational partner (caregiver versus peer) altered the transitivity expression of two-year-old children, and notes ways in which caregivers' socialization goals in the preschool might have led English-speaking children to de-emphasize the agentive nature of their claims when interacting with their peers. Demuth et al. highlight ways in which the examination of actual caregiver speech to children influenced the re-examination of Bantu noun class prefixes. Clancy's analysis of priming focused on an available specific morphological input that affected child speech across stretches of discursive interaction. Finally, Goldin-Meadow and colleagues employ a detailed analysis of the input available to the deaf children they studied through their (hearing) caregiver's adult gestures. All of these studies ground a discussion of typology in the actual moment-to-moment analysis of input children receive when interacting with actual communicative partners. While noted in the final crosslinguistic volume, these studies illustrate ways to move beyond recognition of the need to incorporate more socio-cultural levels of analysis. Among the levels that need to be considered as affecting interaction patterns are differences in structuring of speech events, participants, turn-taking, pragmatic actions, social meaning, and dialectal/stylistic variation.

FUTURE PROSPECTS

Dan Slobin has made significant contributions to the field of child language through his ambitious vision of crosslinguistic study as a method of understanding language learning, and it is evident that his work will continue to be the starting point for many future studies. One of Slobin's major accomplishments was to forge new paths while connecting with ongoing debates. He has done so by reading broadly and holding discussions with a vast array of colleagues in diverse intellectual fields. For the field to remain as vibrant as Slobin's work has made it, it is imperative that researchers not only replicate and look for support for his ideas, but also push the boundaries of crosslinguistic work to keep up with new trends and constructs in related fields. The breadth of Slobin's vision has clearly contributed to the legacy that he has left to the field. It is by continuing to foster this broad vision by an openness to integrating new ideas from a range of inter-disciplinary fields that we will come to better understand language learning in crosslinguistic perspective as an aspect of communicative competence.

REFERENCES

Ervin-Tripp, S. (in press). Hymes on speech socialization. *Text & Talk: An Interdisciplinary Journal of Language, Discourse, & Communication Studies.*

Gumperz, J. J., & Hymes, D. H. (1964). *The ethnography of communication.* Washington, DC: American Anthropological Association.

Slobin, D. I. (1985). Crosslinguistic evidence for the Language-Making Capacity. In D. I. Slobin (Ed.), *The crosslinguistic study of language acquisition: Vol. 2. Theoretical issues* (pp. 1157–1256). Hillsdale, NJ: Lawrence Erlbaum Associates.

Slobin, D. I. (1997). The origins of grammaticizable notions: Beyond the individual mind. In D. I. Slobin (Ed.), *The crosslinguistic study of language acquisition: Vol. 5. Expanding the contexts* (pp. 265–323). Mahwah, NJ: Lawrence Erlbaum Associates.

Slobin, D. I. (2001). Form function relations: how do children find out what they are? In M. Bowerman & S. C. Levinson (Eds.), *Language acquisition and conceptual development* (pp. 406–449). Cambridge, UK: Cambridge University Press.

1

Alligators All Around
The Acquisition of Animal Terms in English and Russian

JEAN BERKO GLEASON,
BRENDA CALDWELL PHILLIPS, and RICHARD ELY
Boston University

ELENA ZARETSKY
University of Massachusetts, Amherst

> It is only by detailed examination of patterns of children's verbal interaction with others that we can form a picture of the child's activity in constructing a language.
>
> **Dan I. Slobin (1985, p. 1158)**

We share Dan's belief that language acquisition is an interactive process, and that actual data from many languages are needed if we are ever to understand the basically universal phenomenon that every child creates anew. Like Dan, we are students and admirers of Roger Brown, who inspired us to record and analyze what children and parents say as a first step toward building the science of developmental psycholinguistics.

INTRODUCTION

In this chapter we discuss children's acquisition of one particular domain of the lexicon: words referring to animals. Animals appear to be very important and attractive to even very young children, as well as to the adults around them. Adults, for instance, frequently point out animals (and not, for instance, rocks) to children, and the children reciprocate by paying attention. Baby talk words for animals are common. Books for infants are also filled with a great variety of living creatures, and animal toys abound. Some of children's earliest words refer to animals. For example, in the MacArthur–Bates Communicative Development Inventory (Dale & Fenson, 1996; Fenson et al., 1993, 1994) words such as *bear, bird, bunny, cat, kitty, dog,* and *duck* are in the comprehension vocabularies of 50% of 14-month-olds. Most of the 14-month-old's animal words, including *bear, bird, dog,* and *horse,* are very common and are included in counts of the 2000 most frequent words in English; others, e.g., *cat, chicken, cow,* and *fish,* are among the 5000 most frequent words (Francis & Kucera, 1982). By the age of 30 months, however, children's animal vocabularies have become very sophisticated: Over 70% of English-speaking children at this age understand or produce the words *alligator* and *zebra*. By any count, these are not common words: They do not appear among the commonest 2000 words of English, or even among the 5000 most frequently used words.

Animal terms contrast with children's other typical vocabulary in other ways as well: Alligators are not usually in the here-and-now, and in this respect they contrast with other early words (e.g., body parts, clothing, family members) whose referents are part of the child's immediate world. In fact, many of children's earliest animal terms refer primarily to pictured referents (*alligator*) or to facsimiles such as stuffed toy animals. Thus, conversations about animals are likely to be qualitatively different from conversations about more concrete aspects of children's lives and may provide an early route to decontextualization. Discussions about animals may also contribute to the child's emerging conceptualizations of the biological world. Finally, this early talk about animals may reflect children's natural propensity to be emotionally and intellectually attracted to other living things (Kahn, 1999; Kahn & Kellert, 2002). Recent research reveals that the development of a bond with animals is an important part of children's affective and social world (Melson, 2001, 2003). Little is known, however, about the acquisition of the animal lexicon across a range of children, although there has been some very interesting work on individual children (e.g., Clark, 1993, 1995). Clark reported that her son Damon began with one animal term, *dog*, at the age of 1;1,15, and rapidly acquired a variety of names of domestic and wild animals during his second year, at the end of which he had 25 terms, including *alligator, ladybug,* and *zebra* (Clark, 1993).

In this study we describe the animal lexicon of parents and children in a variety of corpora in English and Russian, drawn from the CHILDES database. In looking beyond English, we make a modest step toward understanding the principles that may underlie the acquisition of this semantic domain crosslinguistically. Children's ages range from infancy to middle childhood; settings are naturalistic, primarily in children's homes.

METHOD

Data

Using CHILDES (MacWhinney, 2000), we examined six corpora of children whose language was described as developing typically. As can be seen in Table 1.1, two of these corpora were longitudinal observations of English-speaking children between the ages of 2;3 and 5;2 (Brown, 1973: Adam and Sarah). Two corpora were cross-sectional datasets: Gleason Dinners (Masur & Gleason, 1980) contained 22 English-speaking children, and Warren (Warren-Leubecker, 1982) included 20 children. Their ages ranged between 1;6 and 6;2. Finally, in order to gain a crosslinguistic perspective, we included two longitudinal observations that are the only Russian data in the CHILDES database, Varya (from the Protassova Corpus) and Tanja (Bar-Shalom & Snyder, 1997, 1998), whose ages ranged between 1;6 and 2;11. With the exception of Sarah, who was from a working-class family, all children were from middle-class families. In all corpora, parents, mostly mothers, were the primary conversational partners, and parents and children were observed engaging in activities like toy play, book reading, and eating that were typical of everyday, routine child–parent interactions in literate households.

TABLE 1.1 Description of Corpora

Corpus	N	Age of Child(ren)	Setting
Brown (Adam)	1	2;3–4;11	home
Brown (Sarah)	1	2;3–5;2	home
Gleason	22	2;5–5;2	home, dinner
Warren	20	1;6–6;2	home, play
Protassova (Varya)	1	1;6–2;10	home, play
Tanja	1	2;5–2;11	home, play

Data Analysis

Using CLAN we extracted a list of all possible animal terms from each corpus. Variations of a basic animal morpheme, such as *dog, dogs, doggy, doggies*, were all treated as one type. Words with similar meanings (*cat* and *kitty*) but different basic morphemes were counted as different types. We examined each possible term in context to determine whether it was truly an animal noun. In this manner, we excluded from our counts the use of verbs such as *fly* and *duck*, and words like *robin* when it was used to refer to an individual named *Robin*. We then computed the number of types and tokens of animal terms for each speaker. Because our primary focus was on the animal lexicon *per se*, we excluded from analyses all references to animals like family pets or famous figures like *Dumbo* and *Bambi* who were identified by proper name *only*. So if a speaker referred by proper name to a pet or to a favorite stuffed animal (e.g., *Tuba* in Sarah's data and *Jocko* in Adam's), that name was not included as an animal term even though it clearly referred to an animal. Given these restrictions, our study clearly underestimates the degree to which children and parents talk about animals (Tannen, 2004).

In addition to analyzing types and tokens, we developed a coding scheme designed to capture how animal terms were used.

The first category, Contextual, encompassed animal terms used to talk about animals in the immediate present, within the current context, including representations of animals by pictures or toys, so long as they were actually there. This category also included the recitation or singing of nursery rhymes that incorporated animal terms (like *Three Blind Mice*). In addition, this category included two subordinate groupings of animal terms:

(a) Animal Characters included animal terms used as part of characters' names, as in *Donald Duck* or *Spiderman*.
(b) Food encompassed animal terms like *chicken* and *tuna fish* used to refer to food. There are some interesting questions related to this category: It is not clear when or to what extent children, and for that matter adults, connect to the concept of animal in their use of animal food terms. There is clearly much in our culture that encourages us *not* to think of a bleating little lamb when we see supermarket packages of neatly trimmed chops. Many of us have heard anecdotal tales of children's first realization of what it is they are having for dinner, and these tend not to be pretty stories. This is a topic that bears further investigation. For now, we categorize the term as *food* without further comment or moralization.

The second major category, Decontextual captured all uses of animal terms that made reference to animals or representations of animals that were not in the immediate surroundings. This encompassed narratives about past experiences with particular animals, or more general talk about the world of animals.

The third category, Metaphoric, referred to the metaphoric use of an animal term as in *eat like a pig*.

Finally, the fourth category, called Constituent, included animal terms that are constituents of compound words like *hotdog* and *chickenpox*. These often had at best tangential connections to the animal world.

We applied this coding scheme to the four longitudinal datasets (Adam, Sarah, Varya, and Tanja), but for purposes of this coding only, we limited the age range of our analyses in Adam's and Sarah's data to the first 3 years (up to 3;0) so that their results would be comparable to those of Varya and Tanja, whose observations ended shortly before age 3;0. In addition, we applied the coding scheme to the two cross-sectional datasets (Gleason and Warren).

RESULTS

Across all corpora there was a remarkable range of animal terms, indicating a large animal lexicon for even very young children. For example, individual children of preschool age produced as many as 96 different animal types. The frequency of use of animal terms varied considerably, ranging from a low of approximately 1 to 2 animal terms per 100 utterances in middle-class American family dinner conversations to more than 14 per 100 utterances in the play session of one Russian child. Children and adults used a wide range of types, many of which included rare words like *alligator* and *pelican*. As will be evident, the context clearly affects both the amount and nature of talk about animals.

Brown Corpus: Adam and Sarah

We examined the transcripts of these two children who were observed longitudinally between the ages of 2 and 5 by Roger Brown and his students at Harvard in the 1960s. The observations covered a range of typical at-home activities with parents, mostly mothers, and occasionally other adults and children.

Frequencies of types and tokens of animal terms across both corpora were similar for children and adults (Table 1.2). Adam used a total of 96 animal types and produced tokens at a rate of 6.2 per 100 utterances through age 4;11. Adult speakers in Adam's data used 102 types and produced tokens at a rate of 5.4 per 100 utterances across the same age range. Across the more restricted age range up to 3;0, Adam produced 67 types at a rate of 7.6 tokens per 100 utterances.

Sarah produced 91 types and generated tokens of animal terms at a rate of 6.0 per 100 utterances up to age 5;2. In Sarah's corpus, adults used 78 types and their tokens were at the rate of 4.0 per 100 utterances through the same age range. Again, looking at Sarah's data up to 3;0, Sarah produced 46 types, at a rate of 10.6 tokens per 100 utterances. Not only did these children have extensive animal lexicons, they produced some quite rare words: Adam's transcripts include *llama, octopus,* and *rhinoceros,* and Sarah talked about *weasels* and *baboons*.

In terms of function, most animal terms in both corpora were used contextually (Table 1.3). In Adam's case, 61% of his tokens were contextual, 20% decontextual. His mother's contextual rate was 54% and her decontextual rate was 31%, the highest among the longitudinal datasets, and the second highest overall. Both Adam and his mother used a relatively large proportion of animal terms that were constituents of compounds, most commonly the term *cowboy*. For Sarah, 86% of her use of animal terms was Contextual and 13% was Decontextual. Like Adam's mother, Sarah's mother's Contextual rate was lower than that of Sarah, 74%, but her production of Decontextualized terms, at nearly 22%, was higher than that of her daughter.

TABLE 1.2 Types and Tokens by Speakers for the Longitudinal Data

Corpus	Speaker	Types	Tokens per 100 Utterances
Longitudinal			
Brown (Adam)	child	96	6.2
Brown (Adam)	adults	102	5.4
Brown (Sarah)	child	91	6.0
Brown (Sarah)	adults	78	4.0
Protassova (Varya)	child	25	4.0
Protassova (Varya)	adults	27	6.5
Tanja	child	44	14.5
Tanja	adults	43	13.0

TABLE 1.3 Coding Categories by Corpus

Corpus/Speaker	Contextual[a]	Decontextual	Metaphoric	Constituent
Brown				
Adam – child	60.9	20.4	0.4	18.3
Adam – mother	54.1	30.8	0.8	14.3
Sarah – child	85.9	13.2	0.0	0.9
Sarah – mother	77.4	21.7	0.0	0.9
Gleason				
Children	67.6	22.1	0.0	10.3
Mothers	61.7	23.5	2.5	12.3
Fathers	48.8	32.6	4.7	14.0
Warren				
Children	78.3	13.8	0.3	7.6
Mothers	67.6	25.4	0.0	7.0
Fathers	70.7	19.7	0.0	9.6
Russian				
Varya – child	94.6	4.7	0.0	0.8
Varya – adults	83.9	16.1	0.0	0.0
Tanja – child	84.8	15.2	0.0	0.0
Tanja – adults	78.8	21.2	0.0	0.0

[a] The category Contextual included 2 subordinate categories, Food and Animal Characters, that are subsumed under the supraordinate category Contextual.

Gleason Corpus: Families at Dinner

The Gleason Dinner Corpus encompasses the dinner conversations of 22 children and their parents. Children ranged in age between 2;5 and 5;2. Across all speakers, there were 33 animal terms used, with a high degree of overlap among the speakers.

Children and fathers used animal terms at a rate of 1.1 per 100 utterances, mothers slightly more, 1.5 per 100 utterances. Although there were no statistically significant gender differences, girls (1.4 per 100 utterances) did use animal terms more than boys (0.8 per 100 utterances), and fathers of girls directed twice as many animal terms to their daughters as did fathers of boys to their sons (1.4 and 0.7 per 100 utterances, respectively).

Using our coding scheme the contextual subcategory Food not surprisingly represented the most common use in mothers, representing more than half of their overall total. Fathers were more likely than any other speaker to use animal terms to refer beyond the here-and-now, with the category Decontextual comprising approximately one third of their overall output. For children, contextual was the most frequent category of use, representing 44% of their total.

Warren Corpus; Children at Play

In contrast to the overall low frequency in dinner table discourse, the use of animal terms represented a significant portion of the play session conversations. Parents had been instructed to engage their child in play and conversation as they normally would, using the child's own books and toys; however, parents and children were explicitly instructed not to read to one another.

For children, 1 out of every 10 utterances contained an animal term. Overall, parents used more types (71) than children (55), but children produced somewhat more tokens than parents (10.7 per 100 utterances, vs. 8.3 for mothers and 8.5 for fathers). As in the dinner data, fathers directed more animal tokens per 100 utterances to girls (12.0) than to boys (5.0) and this time the difference was statistically significant. Girls produced somewhat more types and tokens than boys, but not significantly so. Mothers and fathers were similar in their rates of types and tokens. Once again, Contextual was the most common use across all speakers. Mothers, more than fathers and children, were likely to use animal terms decontextually (Table 1.3). In fact, their rate (25.4 per 100 utterances) was nearly twice that of their children (13.8 per 100 utterances).

The Warren data included children of a wider age range than the Gleason Corpus. There were significant negative correlations with age in the frequency with which children used types and tokens of animal terms, $r(20) = -.55, p < .05$ and $-.61, p < .01$, respectively. In other words, younger children produced more animal types and tokens than did older children.

Russian Corpus: Tanja and Varya (Protassova Corpus)

The very young child Tanja produced 44 animal types, and a very high rate of tokens: 14.5 per 100 utterances (Table 1.2). Adults in Tanja's files produced 27 types and tokens at the rate of 13 per 100 utterances. Varya produced 25 types and she produced tokens at the rate of 4 per 100 utterances; adults in Varya's files produced 27 types and they produced tokens at the rate of 6.5 per 100 utterances.

In terms of coding categories, contextual uses of animal terms was the most frequent category in children and adults in both datasets, ranging from 79% in the adults in Tanja's corpus to 95% by Varya herself. Decontextual animal terms were rare in Varya's data, representing less than 5% of the total, but were more frequent in Tanja's dataset (Table 1.3).

The Russian data also contain a very rich collection of morphological forms, diminutives, double diminutives, and inflected forms that is beyond our focus here. In general, there was a high degree of overlap among the Russian speakers, with the children and the adults sharing reference to common animals such as cats, dogs, cows, bears, horses, and fish. We also found that they all made reference to crocodiles, as did at least one American family, as our examples indicate. Here, Varya and her mother are playing together with some animal toys:

Mother:	Gde tut krokodily?
	Where are crocodiles?
Child:	Vot krokodily... kushajut kosti.
	Here are the crocodiles, eating bones.
	Na tebe, na tebe kost', krokodil'chik.
	Here, here, take the bone, crocodile (diminutive).
	Malen'kie krokodil'chiki.
	Little crocodilies.
Mother:	Idi ko mne, krokodil'chik.
	Come to me, little crocodile.

Decontextualized Talk

As we noted earlier, animals figured in some sophisticated, decontextualized talk with these young children. Some decontextualized talk took the form of narratives, with parents prompting children to describe events from the past. For example, in one family, a father asked his son David (age 4;2) about his *swanboat* ride, itself a compound word using an animal term. (For those who are not residents of Boston, it must be noted that swanboat rides are a well-known local phenomenon found in a downtown park.) David's mother followed up by asking him what he ate and if he fed the ducks in the park.

Mother:	But what about the poor ducks?
	Did they get any [peanuts and raisins]?
David:	I gave some things to them, too.

Later in this same family, David's mother talked about a visit to a friend's house. The focus of her conversation was animals.

Mother: You know what I saw today, David?
David: What?
Mother: At Betty's house.
She has a great big dog.
And, a big cat.
David: A what ...
Mother: And they were fighting with each other.

Equally as common as narratives focusing on animals was generic talk about the animal world, some of which was initiated by the children themselves. Theresa (4;1) made a rather startling pronouncement.

Theresa: Daddy!
Father: What sweetheart?
Theresa: Um do you know that ... three million whales died?
Father: Three million whales died?
Theresa: Yep!
Father: Since when?
Father: How do you know?
Mother: Um…
Theresa: Um…
Mother: Theresa um.
Theresa: Since thirteen years ago.
Father: [indecipherable].
Mother: Theresa [indecipherable] isn't that terrific?
Father: That's wonderful Theresa [indecipherable]; where'd you hear that thing about the whales?

In contrast to Theresa's authoritative pronouncements about whales, Adam is more guarded about some of his claims about the animal world. He initiates a conversation about owls by asking whether they can crawl. His mother replies:

Mother: I don't think they crawl ... no.
They walk ... don't they?
And fly.

Adam's mother (as well as the research assistant who is now a famous professor) go on to challenge Adam's evolving knowledge of owls.

Mother: What animals wake up in the morning?
Adam: Owls sleeping in the night.
Ursula: I thought owls sleep in the daytime
Adam: Owls sleeps, sleeps in the night.
Ursula: Oh?
Adam: Does owls sleep in the night?
Mother: I don't think so.

Finally, in one English-speaking family there is an extended discussion about bees, flowers, honey, and skunks. The child is an active participant, asking, for example, "How can bees make honey in this kind of flower?" and learning from her mother that "Actually, the bees make the honey in their bodies." There is extensive talk about worker bees, queen bees, and a mention of how bees do not fly at night because they cannot see, and how they are thus more prone to nocturnal attacks from skunks.

Adults and children in the Russian data also engage in decontextualized talk about animals, as in the following instance about a past trip to the zoo from the files of Tanja, who was 2;7 at the time.

Mother: Ty rasskazhi Eve, ty bila v zooparke?
          Tell Eva, did you go to the zoo?
Tanja: Da, v zooparke strausy.
          Yes, ostriches are in the zoo.
Mother: Prihodili v mashinu.
          Came to the car.
Tanja: Zhirafy, mishki zakryty.
          Giraffes and bears are locked up.

DISCUSSION

Our study suggests that animal terms are an important part of the young child's lexicon. The relatively large proportion of parent–child conversation devoted to talk about the animal world appears to reflect an early emergent interest in biology as well as an affective outlook on this same world. Of course this focus on the animal world is both reflected and enhanced by the presence of cultural artifacts such as animal toys and picture books. Parents are able to take advantage of children's natural tendency to be interested in and attracted to the animal world and engage them in relatively sophisticated conversations, some of which move beyond the here-and-now. As the examples earlier have illustrated, this decontextualized discourse provides children with a rich source of information about the animal world as well as an opportunity to expand their cognitive abilities.

The descriptive data we have presented suggest that context plays an important role in determining how parents and children talk about the animal world. In dinner table conversations, talk about the animal world was infrequent and, not surprisingly, a relatively sizable portion of this discourse focuses on animals as food. By contrast, in book reading and play, the largely middle-class parents in our data are apt to focus on the animal world, aided by picture books about animals and facsimiles of animals (e.g., stuffed animals). The ensuing conversations are likely to have a pedagogical function, presenting both parents and children with opportunities to explore in depth the characteristics of this unique domain.

The extent of this interest is reflected in the size of the animal lexicon. Both Adam and Sarah produced nearly 100 animal terms in observations that run through age 5. In order to get a sense of the relative size of the animal lexicon, we examined the vehicle lexicon (e.g., cars, trucks, trains) in two of the longitudinal datasets (Adam and Sarah). Vehicles of all sorts are pervasive in contemporary cultures. Children are more likely to have had real world experience with a wide variety of vehicles than with many of the animals they talked about, having ridden in cars and buses, for example, and having seen numerous instances of fire trucks, bulldozers, and airplanes. Analysis of the overall corpora reveals that Adam produced 67 vehicle types, and 1784 tokens, at a rate of 3.8 tokens per 100 utterances (compared with 96 types, 2839 tokens, and a rate of 6.2 tokens per 100 utterances for animal terms). Sarah produced substantially fewer vehicle terms, only 17 types overall and 254 tokens for a rate well below 1 per 100 utterances.

The difference between Adam's and Sarah's use of vehicle terms may reflect a broader gender difference, and it is interesting to note that this difference may be much greater than the animal lexicon differences we documented earlier in the Warren Corpus. Interest in the domain of vehicles and the acquisition of a lexicon supporting such an interest may be more gender dimorphic than the comparable interest in the animal world: Boys may be much more interested in vehicles than girls, and girls may be only somewhat more interested in animals than boys. In this regard, it is interesting to note that the young boy studied by Clark (1995), produced a richer vehicle lexicon (83 terms) than animal lexicon (62) by age 3;0. However, this was not the pattern found in Adam's data; to the degree that frequency reflects attention, sparrows and snails were of more interest to Adam than were scooters and spaceships.

Our data also reveal that talk about the here-and-now is the dominant form of talk about animals. However, there were some notable exceptions. We have already cited a number of examples of decontextual talk about the animal world. Such talk was particularly prevalent in the Gleason Corpus of dinner table conversations, where fathers were especially active in engaging children in decontextualized conversations about animals. This tendency of fathers to push the limits of their children's linguistic competence has been seen as a bridge to the larger world (Gleason, 1975).

Like the fathers in the Gleason Corpus, Adam's mother displayed a strong propensity to move beyond the here-and-now in her conversations with her son. This pull to move outside the immediate context was also evident in the Russian data. It is worth noting that while Varya's talk about animals was overwhelmingly contextually bound, the same was not true of the adults with whom she was interacting. Though less frequent overall (16%) than seen in other corpora, they still used animal terms decontextually at more than three times the rate of Varya herself, reflecting, we would argue, a strong tendency to decontextualize the ongoing conversation.

Finally, our data reveal that the animal world is particularly salient to younger children. This was seen in the negative correlations with age for the use of animal types and tokens in the Warren data. A similar pattern was evident in the Brown Corpus, where the token rate was notably higher through age 3;0 than at a later age. In this regard, Tanja, one of the youngest children, had the highest rate of tokens, with 14.5 produced per 100 utterances. As children grow older, they may speak less about animals, but by the age of 3 they have developed a rich lexicon that reflects their evolving cognitive and affective connection to the animal world.

FUTURE DIRECTIONS

We have raised some questions along the way that bear consideration and investigation in future research into children's cognitive, social, and linguistic development as it pertains to the domain of animals:

Are there gender differences in children's interest in the animal world and do parents treat boys and girls differently with respect to animals (cf. Laws, 2004)? Our results seem to indicate that fathers talk more to girls about animals and that girls show a greater interest in the animal world. If there are gender differences, would we also find them in preferred animals? For instance, do girls talk more about cats and horses in our society, and do boys refer more frequently to dogs?

Some of the animal terms we report here, particularly at the dinner table, refer to the animal as food. When do children come to understand the animal origins of their food? This is not a kind of cognitive achievement that our society encourages. Children may make school trips to the potato chip factory but not to the slaughterhouse, and animal products are packaged in a way that does not emphasize that they are body parts. Children who grow up on a farm may, of course, have a better and earlier understanding of the situation, but they may also suffer cognitive dissonance since they can have the experience of discovering that they are eating an animal that they know.

How important is parent input in establishing 'biophilia,' or the love of living things? Children from an early age seem attracted to the animal world, but this interest may be enhanced or even engendered by parental emphasis on animals. More specifically, if we conducted a study of all the things that parents call their children's attention to with phrases like "look at the …" or "see the …" what proportion of the pointed-at things would be alive? Similarly, we might ask what words parents diminutize in various languages, since the diminutive typically includes a positive, hypocoristic, affective component.

How does the size of the animal lexicon compare with other domains in children's language? Are animal terms young children's largest category, or are there other domains where a preschooler might have nearly 100 types? As we noted earlier here, the category of vehicles is also extensive, but does not have as many members as the animal category. Other researchers may find lexical domains that are as yet unexplored.

Finally, we must ask if the biophilia and emphasis on animals we have seen in English and in Russian is characteristic of only a few societies, or if the extended animal lexicon we have documented reflects a universal human cognitive and social predisposition. This calls for crosslinguistic and cross-cultural work in the spirit that Dan Slobin has pioneered.

REFERENCES

Bar-Shalom, E., & Snyder, W. (1997). Optional infinitives in Russian and their implications for the pro-drop debate. In M. Lindseth & S. Franks (Eds.), *Formal approaches to Slavic linguistics: The Indiana Meeting 1996*, (pp. 38–47). Ann Arbor, MI: Michigan Slavic Publications.

Bar-Shalom, E., & Snyder, W. (1998). Root infinitives in child Russian: A comparison with Italian and Polish. In R. Shillcock, A. Sorace, & C. Heycock (Eds.), *Language acquisition: Knowledge representation and processing. Proceedings of GALA '97*. Edinburgh, UK: The University of Edinburgh.

Brown, R. (1973). *A first language: The early stages*. Cambridge, MA: Harvard University Press.

Clark, E. (1993). *The lexicon in acquisition*. Cambridge, UK: Cambridge University Press.

Clark, E. (1995). Language acquisition: The lexicon and syntax. In J. L. Miller & P. D. Eimas (Eds.), *Speech, language, and communication*. San Diego, CA: Academic Press.

Dale, P. S., & Fenson, L. (1996). Lexical development norms for young children. *Behavior Research Methods, Instruments, & Computers, 28*, 125–127.

Fenson, L., Dale, P. S., Reznick, J., Bates, E., Thal, D., Pethick, S., et al. (1994). Variability in early communicative development. *Monographs of the Society for Research in Child Development, 59*(5, Serial No. 173).

Fenson, L., Dale, P. S., Reznick, J. S., Thal, D., Bates, E., Hartung, J. P., Pethick, S., et al. (1993). *The MacArthur Communicative Development Inventories: User's guide and technical manual*. Baltimore: Paul H. Brookes Publishing Co.

Francis, W. N., and Kucera, H. (1982). *Frequency analysis of English usage*. Boston: Houghton Mifflin.

Gleason, J. Berko. (1975). Fathers and other strangers: Men's speech to young children. *Proceedings of the 26th Annual Georgetown University Roundtable*, 289–297.

Kahn, P. H. (1999). *The human relationship with nature: Development and culture*. Cambridge, UK: MIT Press.

Kahn, P. H., & Kellert, S. R. (2002). *Children and nature: Psychological, sociocultural, and evolutionary investigations*. Cambridge, MA: The MIT Press.

Laws, K. R. (2004). Sex differences in lexical size across semantic categories. *Personality and Individual Differences, 36*, 23–32.

MacWhinney, B. (2000). *The CHILDES Project: Tools for analyzing talk. 3rd Edition. Vol. 2. The database*. Mahwah, NJ: Lawrence Erlbaum Associates.

Masur, E., & Gleason, J. Berko. (1980). Parent-child interaction and the acquisition of lexical information during play. *Developmental Psychology, 16*, 404–409.

Melson, G. F. (2001). *Why the wild things are: Animals in the lives of children*. Cambridge, MA: Harvard University Press

Melson, G. F. (2003). Child development and the human-companion animal bond. *American Behavioral Scientist, 47*(1), 31–39.

Slobin, D. (1985). Crosslinguistic evidence for the language-making capacity. In D. Slobin (Ed.), *The crosslinguistic study of language acquisition: Vol. 2. Theoretical issues* (pp. 1157–1248). Hillsdale, NJ: Lawrence Erlbaum Associates.

Tannen, D. (2004). Talking the dog: Framing pets as interactional resources in family discourse. *Research on Language and Social Interaction, 37*(4), 399–420.

Warren-Leubecker, A. (1982). *Sex differences in speech to children*. Unpublished doctoral dissertation, Georgia Institute of Technology, Athens.

2

Making Language Around the Globe
A Crosslinguistic Study of Homesign in the United States, China, and Turkey

SUSAN GOLDIN-MEADOW
University of Chicago, Chicago

ASLI ÖZYÜREK
Max Planck Institute for Psycholinguistics, Nijmegen
Koç University, Istanbul

BURCU SANCAR
University of Chicago, Chicago
Koç University, Istanbul

CAROLYN MYLANDER
University of Chicago, Chicago

At the present state of our knowledge, it is premature to attribute a particular organization of grammaticizable notions to the child at the beginning of language acquisition (*pace* Slobin, 1985). It would seem more plausible to endow the child with sufficient flexibility to discern and master the particular organization of the exposure language.

Dan I. Slobin (1997b, p. 296)

But what happens when a child is not exposed to a conventional language?
In 1985, Dan Slobin encouraged the field of language acquisition to take advantage of the fact that the world's languages constitute a range of "experiments of nature." Different types of languages pose different types of acquisition problems for the language-learning child. By observing children who are exposed to languages that vary systematically along one or more dimensions, we can get some sense of which aspects of languages, if any, present stumbling blocks to the language-learner. Moreover, to the extent that we see children *change* the input they receive, we get insight into the role children themselves play in shaping the language they learn—as Dan so eloquently put it, the child as "language-maker" (Slobin, 1985a).

Dan encouraged the field by pointing out the kinds of questions that can only be addressed by crosslinguistic studies (Slobin, 1985b) and by publishing the first two volumes of *The crosslinguistic study of language acquisition*. The encouragement was wildly successful. Language acquisition researchers, who up until this point had been narrowly focused on English, began expanding their horizons and their languages. There are now five volumes in Dan's influential crosslinguistic series exploring acquisition in 28 different languages.

Our work takes Dan's call to extend the range of environments within which we observe language-learning one step farther. What would happen if a child were not exposed to any language model whatsoever? Would such a child develop a communication system and, if so, which properties of language would the system contain? Put more simply—would such a child be able to make her own language?

The children we study are deaf with hearing losses so extensive that they cannot naturally acquire oral language, and born to hearing parents who have not yet exposed them to a conventional manual language. Under such inopportune circumstances, these deaf children might be expected not to communicate. Yet they do. Despite their impoverished language-learning conditions, American deaf children of hearing parents develop gestural communication systems, called "homesigns," that contain many of the properties of language (Goldin-Meadow, 2003a). Moreover, Chinese deaf children of hearing parents develop gesture systems similar to their American counterparts, suggesting that the deaf children's gesture systems are resilient, not only to the absence of a conventional language model, but also to some aspects of cultural variation. The purpose of this chapter is to extend the range of environments within which we observe gesture creation one step further to include a deaf child developing a homesign system in Turkey.

THE DEVELOPMENT OF HOMESIGN SYSTEMS: WHY TURKEY?

The deaf children in our studies are inventing their homesign gesture systems without benefit of a conventional language model, but they do not create these systems in a vacuum. They are exposed to the gestures that their hearing parents produce as they talk to their children, and those gestures differ from culture to culture (McNeill, 1992). Does the crosslinguistic variation in gesture have an impact on the gesture systems the deaf children create?

In previous work, we chose a Chinese culture as a second culture in which to explore the homesign gesture systems of deaf children in large part because the patterns of parent–child interaction in Chinese cultures differ greatly from those in American cultures (e.g., Chen & Uttal, 1988; Wu, 1985). For example, Chinese parents favor practices that result in more control over their interactions with their children than American parents (Lin & Fu, 1990). In addition, Chinese parents produce many more gestures when they speak to their children (hearing or deaf) than do American parents (Goldin-Meadow & Saltzman, 2000). Despite these differences, the Chinese deaf children in our studies invented homesign systems that were similar to the American deaf children's homesign systems in sentence-level structure (Goldin-Meadow & Mylander, 1998), word-level morphological structure (Goldin-Meadow, Mylander, & Franklin, 2007), narrative structure (Phillips, Goldin-Meadow & Miller, 2001), generic expressions (Goldin-Meadow, Gelman, & Mylander, 2005), and descriptions of motion events (Zheng & Goldin-Meadow, 2002).

Although the gestures Mandarin-speakers produce differ in quantity from those produced by English-speakers, they do not differ—at least from the deaf child's point of view—in quality. McNeill and Duncan (2000; see also McNeill, this volume) note that a primary difference between the gestures that accompany Mandarin vs. English resides in the timing of gesture in relation to speech. For example, action gestures (a downward blow) typically co-occur with the predicate in an English sentence ("the old lady *hit* him with a big stick"), but tend to occur out of synchrony with the predicate in a comparable Mandarin sentence ("old lady hold *big stick* him hit-down"). McNeill and Duncan suggest that this difference reflects the fact that English is a subject-prominent language, whereas Mandarin is a topic-prominent language. Interestingly, while this difference is an important one in understanding the relation between gesture and speech in these two languages and may be crucial to children who can hear, it is a difference that is *invisible* to the deaf child. Chinese and American deaf children would both see the downward blow, but would know nothing about where the gesture fell with respect to speech. From the deaf child's vantage point, the gesture models provided by hearing individuals in Chinese and American worlds do not differ.

In contrast to the gestures that accompany Mandarin, the gestures that accompany Turkish can look very different from those that accompany English, at least with respect to the expression of intransitive motion events (Kita & Özyürek, 2003; Özyürek & Kita, 1999; Özyürek et al., 2005). Turkish is a verb-framed language whereas English and Mandarin are satellite-framed languages (Talmy, 1985). This distinction depends primarily on the way in which the path of a motion is packaged. In a satellite-framed language, both path and manner can be encoded within a verbal clause; manner is encoded in the verb itself (*flew*) and path is coded as an adjunct to the verb, a satellite (e.g., *down* in the sentence "the bird flew down"). In a verb-framed language, path is bundled into the verb while manner is introduced constructionally outside the verb, in a gerund, a separate phrase, or clause (e.g., if English were a verb-framed language, the comparable sentence would be "the bird exits flying"). One effect of this typological difference is that manner can, depending upon pragmatic context (Allen et al., 2007; Papafragou & Gleitman, 2006), be omitted from sentences in verb-framed languages (Slobin, 1996). Importantly, these crosslinguistic differences have been shown to influence how manner and path are expressed in gesture. For example, Turkish speakers produce more manner-*only* gestures (e.g., fingers wiggling in place to represent feet alternating while walking) and path-*only* gestures (e.g., index finger crossing space to represent the trajectory of the walk) than English speakers, who produce more gestures containing *both* manner and path (fingers wiggling as the hand crosses space; Kita & Özyürek, 2003; Özyürek & Kita, 1999; Özyürek et al., 2005). These gestural patterns can be traced to the typological difference between English and Turkish—manner and path are expressed in two clauses in Turkish but in one clause in English.

Our goal here is to explore whether the different gestures that hearing speakers produce make a difference to a deaf child generating a homesign gesture system. We therefore examined the gestures produced by a deaf child of hearing parents growing up in Istanbul, and compared them to the gestures produced by the American and Chinese deaf children in our previous studies. If deaf children in all three cultures develop homesign systems with the same structure despite differences in the gestures they see, we will have increasingly compelling evidence for biases that children themselves bring to the language-making task. If, however, the gestures developed by the Turkish deaf child differ from those developed by the American and Chinese deaf children, we can begin to deduce how children's construction of a language-like gesture system is influenced by the models they see.

DEAFNESS AND LANGUAGE LEARNING

Deaf children born to deaf parents and exposed from birth to a conventional sign language such as American Sign Language acquire that language naturally; that is, these children progress through stages in acquiring sign language similar to those of hearing children acquiring a spoken language (Newport & Meier, 1985). However, 90% of deaf children are not born to deaf parents who could provide early exposure to a conventional sign language. Rather, they are born to hearing parents who rarely know conventional sign language and, quite naturally, expose their children to speech (Hoffmeister & Wilbur, 1980).

Unfortunately, it is extremely uncommon for deaf children with severe to profound hearing losses to acquire the spoken language of their hearing parents naturally; that is, without intensive and specialized instruction. Even with instruction, deaf children's acquisition of speech is markedly delayed when compared either to the acquisition of speech by hearing children of hearing parents, or to the acquisition of sign by deaf children of deaf parents. By age 5 or 6, and despite intensive early training programs, the average profoundly deaf child has a very reduced oral linguistic capacity (Conrad, 1979; Mayberry, 1992; Meadow, 1968).

Moreover, although many hearing parents of deaf children send their children to schools in which a manually coded system of a spoken language (e.g., Signed English) is taught, other hearing parents send their deaf children to "oral" schools in which sign systems are neither taught nor encouraged; thus, these deaf children are not likely to receive input in a conventional sign system, either at home or at school.

We observed a Turkish deaf child twice, at ages 3;4 and 3;6 (years;months), and compared the gestures he produced to those produced by four deaf children in America (1 in Philadelphia, 3 in Chicago) and four in Taiwan, Republic of China (Taipei), each observed twice between ages 3;8 and 4;11 (Goldin-Meadow & Mylander, 1998). All of the children were videotaped at home for approximately two hours per session interacting with their hearing mothers (and any other family members present) with a standard set of toys. The children were congenitally deaf with no recognized cognitive deficits. Cause of deafness was unknown. Each child had at least a 70 to 90 dB hearing loss in both ears, and even with hearing aids, none was able to acquire speech naturally. At the time of videotaping, none of the children could do more than produce an occasional spoken word in a highly constrained context, and none had been exposed to a conventional sign system.

SENTENCE-LEVEL STRUCTURE IN THE HOMESIGN SYSTEMS

We used the coding system described in Goldin-Meadow and Mylander (1984) and found that, like his counterparts in the United States and China, the Turkish child used three types of gestural lexical items: (1) Deictics were typically pointing gestures that maintained a constant kinesic form in all contexts. These deictics were used to single out objects, people, places, and the like. (2) Characterizing gestures were stylized pantomimes whose iconic forms varied with the intended meaning of each gesture (e.g., a fist pounded in the air as though hammering). (3) Markers were typically conventional head or hand gestures (e.g., head-shake, nod, two-handed "flip") that were used as modulators (e.g., to negate, affirm, doubt).

The Turkish deaf child, like the American and Chinese deaf children, concatenated his gestural lexical items into strings expressing the propositions or semantic relations typically found in child language. In previous work, we have found that homesigners' gesture strings share structural properties with the sentences produced by young children learning language from conventional language models and, in this sense, warrant the linguistic term "sentence." We focus here on two structural properties of these sentences: (1) patterned production and deletion of semantic elements in the surface structure of a sentence; and (2) patterned ordering of those elements within the sentence.

Gesture Production and Deletion Regularities

Production probability patterns describe the likelihood that a particular argument or predicate will be produced in a gesture sentence (e.g., when describing a mouse eating cheese, a gesture for the actor, mouse, is less likely to be produced than a gesture for the patient, cheese). In previous work, we have found that both American and Chinese homesigners produce gestures for transitive actors, patients, and intransitive actors at different rates (Feldman, Goldin-Meadow & Gleitman, 1978; Goldin-Meadow & Mylander, 1998). Gestures were produced significantly more often for patients (the cheese when describing a mouse eating cheese) and for intransitive actors (the mouse when describing a mouse moving to its hole) than for transitive actors (the mouse in a sentence describing a mouse eating cheese).[1] As can be seen in Figure 2.1, the Turkish child displayed this same pattern in his homesigns.

---

[1] We used context and the form of act gestures to decide whether a gesture sentence was transitive or intransitive. If, for example, the child was gesturing about his mother pushing a truck across the floor, his gesture sentence would be considered transitive if he produced a push gesture (a C-hand representing the mother's hand on the truck moving it across space) and intransitive if he produced a go gesture (a flat palm representing the truck moving across space). Note that if the child produced a pointing gesture at the truck along with the push gesture, the point would be classified as a patient (i.e., truck push). In contrast, if he produced a pointing gesture at the truck with the go gesture, the point would be classified as an intransitive actor (i.e., truck go). These decisions were made without regard for the order in which the gestures were produced; that is, the pointing gesture would be classified as a patient whether the child produced it before (truck push) or after (push truck) the push gesture.

MAKING LANGUAGE AROUND THE GLOBE 31

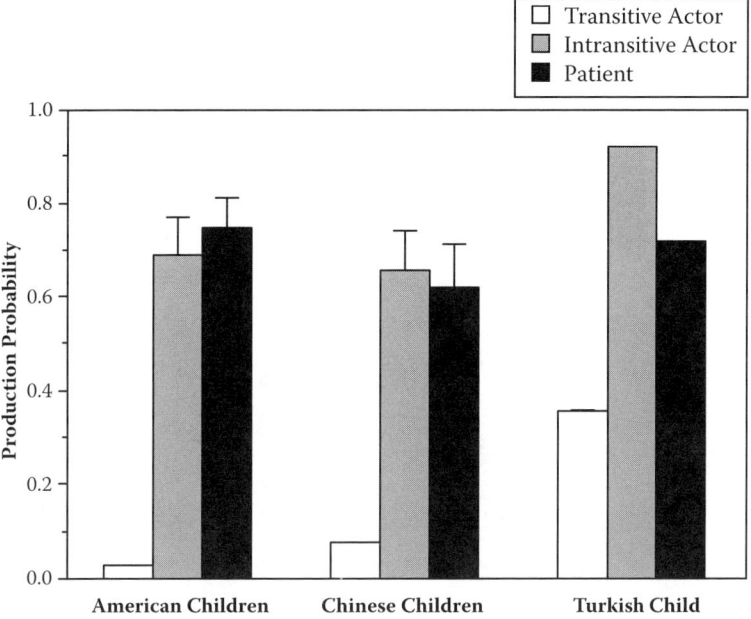

Figure 2.1 Production probability of transitive actors, intransitive actors, and patients in two-gesture sentences. The bars indicate standard errors for the American and Chinese children.

Interestingly, the particular structural pattern found in the deaf children's gesture sentences in all three cultures is an analog of a structural case-marking pattern found in natural human languages—*ergative* languages, in which patients and intransitive actors are marked in the same way and both different from transitive actors (cf. Dixon, 1979; Silverstein, 1976). In the deaf child's case, marking is by production/deletion. Gestures for the intransitive actor (the moving-mouse), tended be produced as often as gestures for the patient (the eaten-cheese), and more often than gestures for the transitive actor (the eating-mouse). The bars for the American and Chinese deaf children represent mean scores for four children. The bars for the Turkish deaf child represent only his data. Although the Turkish child produced gestures for actors (both transitive and intransitive) more often than the American and Chinese children, in all cultures, intransitive actors resembled patients more closely than they resembled transitive actors—the hallmark of the ergative pattern. It is also worth pointing out that none of the languages spoken in these deaf children's worlds (English, Mandarin, or Turkish) is ergative in structure.

Gesture Order Regularities

Gesture order patterns describe where a particular argument or predicate tends to appear in a gesture sentence. The American and Chinese deaf children produced gestures for intransitive actors before gestures for acts (*mouse*-go) and also produced gestures for patients before gestures for acts (*cheese*-eat). They thus placed intransitive actors in the same position as patients (the children did not produce enough transitive actors to determine a consistent order pattern for this semantic element). As can be seen in Figure 2.2, the Turkish deaf child also produced gestures for patients and intransitive actors before gestures for acts.

Deaf children who are exposed to conventional sign languages, not surprisingly, learn the ordering patterns of those languages—for example, SVO (subject–verb–object) in American Sign Language (Hoffmeister, 1978), SOV in the Sign Language of the Netherlands (Coerts, 2000). It is striking that the homesigners in our studies not only used consistent order in their gesture sentences,

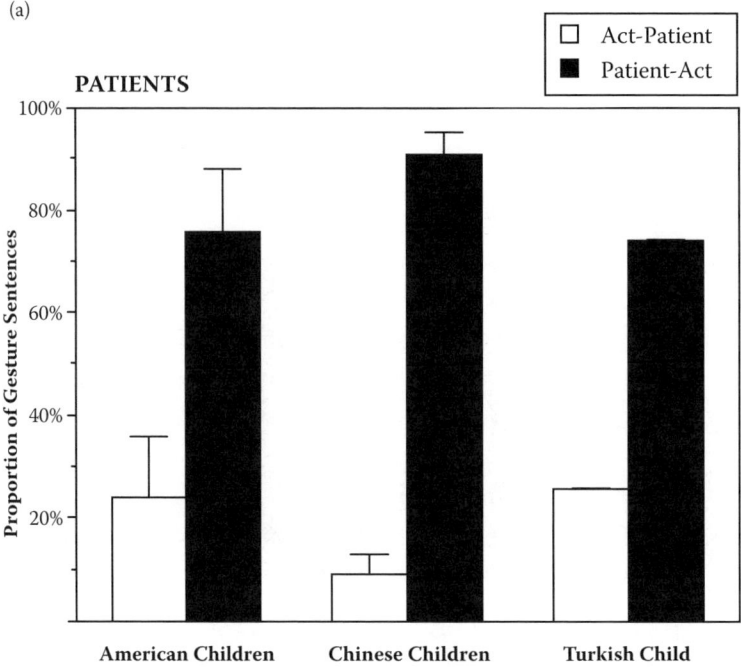

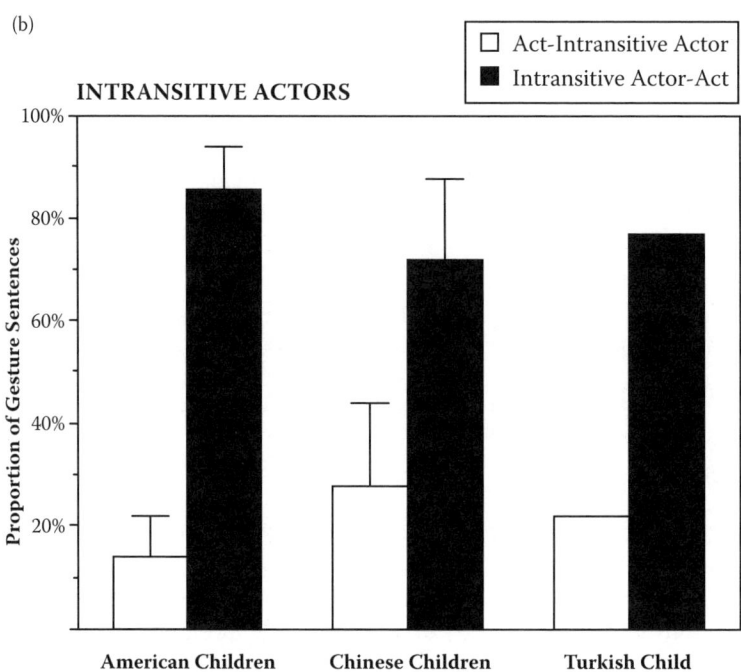

Figure 2.2 Position of patients (a) and intransitive actors (b) in two-gesture sentences containing acts. The bars indicate standard errors for the American and Chinese children.

but they all used an O-first (or patient-first) order—an order that is consistent with the patient-focus found in the children's production regularities.[2,3]

Thus, deaf children from three different cultures produce gesture sentences that are not haphazardly generated. Gestures are produced and positioned in sentences as a function of the semantic role they represent and, in this sense, display a simple syntax. Interestingly, the particular syntactic patterns found in the homesign systems in all three cultures were the same.

EXPRESSING PATH AND MANNER IN MOTION EVENTS

The differences manifested in the gestures that accompany speech in English- and Mandarin-speakers vs. Turkish-speakers have to do with the way manner and path are packaged in the verb, not how semantic elements are expressed and marked in a sentence. We therefore might expect our Turkish deaf child to differ from our American and Chinese deaf children, not in his sentence-level gesture structures, but in the gestures he produces to convey manner and path in motion events.

Following Zheng and Goldin-Meadow (2002), we isolated all of the gestures the Turkish child produced to convey crossing-space motions (motions in which a person or object moves or is moved to another location) and examined how many discourse units conveying a motion event contained gestures for the path and or manner of the motion. Contrary to our expectations that the homesigners' gestures would be influenced by the gestures produced by hearing speakers in their worlds, we found that the Turkish homesigner produced gestures for paths and motions at the same rate as the American and Chinese homesigners. Children from all three cultures produced path gestures in twice as many discourse units as manner gestures (Figure 2.3).

Although the production/deletion, ordering, and manner/path patterns we have found are suggestive, before reaching any firm conclusions we must first observe more deaf children in Turkey to determine how representative the child in our study is (there is, indeed, variation across individual homesigners within a culture, particularly in terms of morphological structure, Goldin-Meadow, Mylander, & Franklin, 2007). We also need to examine the gestures that the hearing parents of these particular deaf children produce. It is possible that these parents do not use gesture when they talk to their deaf children in the same ways as parents do when talking to their hearing children (although see Goldin-Meadow & Saltzman, 2000, for evidence that the gestural differences between hearing parents of deaf vs. hearing children are minimal, compared to the differences between hearing parents of Chinese vs. American children). Our future work will examine these possibilities.

LANGUAGE-MAKING SKILLS THAT DO NOT REQUIRE A LANGUAGE MODEL

Children who are exposed to conventional language models apply whatever language-learning skills they have to the linguistic inputs they receive, and the product is a linguistic system. There is no reason to believe that deaf children who are *not* exposed to a conventional language model have a

---

[2] Most of the gestures that the children used to convey patient arguments were pointing gestures (e.g., point at grape). However, the children did, on occasion, use a characterizing iconic gesture to refer to patients (e.g., an eat gesture used to refer to the grape) and when they did, they placed these iconic gestures in the same sentence-initial positions that their patient-points occupied (Goldin-Meadow, Butcher, Mylander, & Dodge, 1994).

[3] Importantly, the deaf children's ordering patterns are not reducible to the discourse status of the semantic elements—if we reanalyze the sentences in terms of whether an element is "new" or "old" to the discourse, we find that most of the children's gesture sentences are "old-old" or "new-new," and that the "old-new" sentences are approximately as frequent as "new-old" sentences. In other words, "new" elements do not consistently occupy the initial position in the deaf children's gesture sentences, nor do "old" elements (Goldin-Meadow & Mylander, 1984, p. 51).

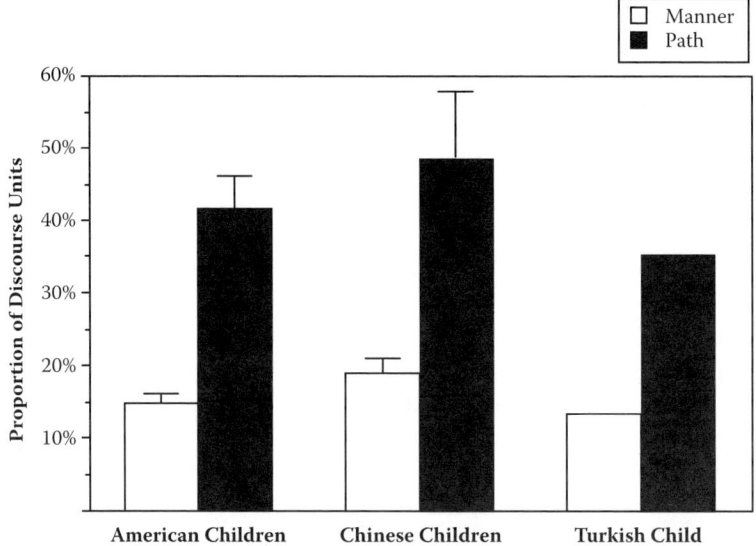

Figure 2.3 Proportion of discourse units expressing motion events that contain manner and path gestures. The bars indicate standard errors for the American, Chinese, and Turkish children.

different set of language-learning skills. However, they apply these skills to a very different input. Despite this radical difference in input, their product is also a set of linguistic properties. What kind of language-learning skills can create such a product in the absence of linguistically structured input? The deaf children's homesign systems offer hints as to what these skills might be, skills that might more aptly be called language-*making* than language-*learning*. The data we have described here suggest a number of such skills: the ability to segment ideas into word-like units, to combine those units into sentences, and to organize the sentences around an ergative pattern.

One of the most striking aspects of the deaf children's gestures is that it is not mime. The children could easily (and effectively) convey information by producing continuous and unsegmentable movements in mime-like fashion. For example, a child could elaborately pantomime a scene in which she is given a jar, twists off the lid, and blows a bubble in order to request the jar and comment on what she'll do when she gets it. But the deaf children don't behave like mimes. They produce discrete gestures concatenated into sentences—their gestures resemble beads on a string rather than one continuous strand. The basic process underlying the deaf children's gesture system appears to be *segmentation*.

Once segmented into smaller units, those newly segmented units need to be related to one another within a larger *combination*. At the sentence level, the children's solution to the combination problem is to construct sequences. But just stringing elements together is not enough. Imagine that a mime for the bubble-blowing scene is segmented into many discrete gestures. Although the gestures may adequately refer to the elements in the scene, they do not convey how those elements relate to one another. This relation, which is conveyed iconically in a mime, must be conveyed through other processes in sequences of discrete elements. One such process marks the elements in a sequence according to thematic role using deletion and order, devices that are found in all natural languages and in the deaf children's homesigns. These processes are necessary to tell who is doing what to whom.

We have also shown here that the homesign systems in three cultures can be described in terms of an *ergative* pattern. Unlike segmentation and combination, ergative constructions are not universal. In fact, ergative languages are not particularly frequent in the world's languages. Why then would children arrive at these constructions in the absence of linguistic input? Although it may be counterintuitive to speakers of English (which is not an ergative language), the ergative pattern may be a default organization for a language-learning child—in other words, it may require input to structure language in any other way. Indeed,

Zheng and Goldin-Meadow (2002) found that hearing children acquiring Mandarin, a language that allows deletion, not only delete a great deal but they delete according to an ergative pattern (and, as mentioned earlier, Mandarin is *not* an ergative language). Thus, the ergative structuring that we see in the deaf children crops up in hearing children when their language does not rule it out. Ergative structure is also found in very young English-learners who can only produce two words at a time (Goldin-Meadow & Mylander, 1984, pp. 62–64) and in children learning Korean, which is also not an ergative language (Choi, 1999; Clancy, 1993). Taken together, these data bear on what we might describe as the initial grammatical state – the state that children are in when they come to language-learning.

The way the deaf children instantiate an ergative pattern in their gesture systems is to omit gestures for transitive actors, which are typically subjects in conventional languages. Conventional languages vary according to whether they permit deletion of subjects (i.e., null subjects). Italian does (it's a null-subject language), English does not. Children need input to determine whether or not the language they are learning is a null-subject language.

The question we address here is whether children come to language-learning with a default bias to either omit or produce subjects. Hyams (1986) hypothesized that children start out with a grammar that licenses null subjects and need input from a conventional language to teach them whether subjects must be expressed in that language. Data from the deaf children's gesture systems—in particular, the fact that the children omit gestures for transitive actors, which tend to be subjects[4]—support Hyams' (1986) view that children come to language-learning with a default bias to omit subjects.

In some domains, however, children may come to the language-learning situation *without* a bias or default—and the deaf children can provide useful data here as well. For example, children exposed to conventional language models discover relatively early that they are learning either a right-branching (English) or a left-branching (Japanese) language (Lust & Wakayama, 1979). Discovering the branching direction of the language they are learning has ramifications throughout the children's linguistic system. Do children have a bias toward right- vs. left-branching systems before being exposed to linguistic input? No—at least according to the data on complex sentences in the deaf children's homesigns (Goldin-Meadow, 1987). The deaf children show no bias of any sort, suggesting that the initial grammatical state may be neutral on this dimension.

These constructions—obligatoriness of explicit subjects, and dominant branching organization (left vs. right)—are places where Slobin (1997a, p. 3) has hypothesized that children learn a general format or "solution" from the syntax of the language model to which they are exposed. Our findings suggest that a language model is indeed essential to obligatorily produce subjects and to have a branching direction, thus providing empirical support for Slobin's claim. However, our findings go one step further—they make it clear that these two cases are not identical. In one case (branching direction), the child does not appear to come to the language-learning situation with a bias. In the other case (obligatoriness of subjects), the child does—a bias to omit subjects (or at least agents).

PRIVILEGED FORMS AND MEANINGS

One of the original goals of Slobin's crosslinguistic enterprise was to identify commonalities in the early stages of language-learning that children across the globe display despite differences in the languages to which they are exposed—a set of privileged forms and meanings that crop up in children's language even if there is no explicit model for them in the language the children are learning. These privileged forms and meanings constitute a set of hypotheses as to how children might be expected to communicate in the absence of usable linguistic input, and the data we have described here provide support for those hypotheses.

---

[4] Note that, in the deaf children's gesture systems, transitive actors really are omitted, or more accurately not lexicalized, as opposed to never being there in the first place—otherwise we would not be able to explain the systematic actor production probability patterns we find in relation to underlying predicate frames (see Goldin-Meadow, 1985, 2003a).

Take, for example, consistent word order, which appears to be a privileged form in early child language (Goldin-Meadow, 2003a, pp. 26–27). Children look for ordering relations across words within a sentence, learning them easily if their language relies on word order to convey who-does-what-to-whom and imposing ordering regularities if their language does not display them. In line with these findings, we find that deaf children, exposed to no usable language whatsoever, impose ordering regularities on their homemade gesture systems. Word order does indeed seem to be a privileged form for language-learners.

In addition to privileged forms, we can also identify privileged meanings on the basis of the crosslinguistic literature. A focus on *results* seems to be a privileged meaning for language-learners (Goldin-Meadow, 2003a, pp. 25–26) and, here again, the deaf children's homesign gesture systems provide confirming evidence. Ergative patterns can be thought of as focusing on results, a tendency to see objects as affected by actions rather than as initiators of action. In the sentence "you go to the corner," the intransitive actor "you," has a double meaning. On the one hand, "you" refers to the goer, the actor, the initiator of the going action. On the other hand, "you" refers to the gone, the patient, the affectee of the going action. At the end of the action, "you" both "have gone" and "are gone," and the decision to emphasize one aspect of the actor's condition over the other is arbitrary. By treating intransitive actors like patients in terms of production probability (Figure 2.1) and order (Figure 2.2), the deaf children are highlighting the affectee properties of the intransitive actor over the initiator properties. Focusing on patients may be a default bias children bring to language-learning. When not exposed to a usable conventional language model, children display a patient bias in their self-generated communication systems. This bias is, of course, abandoned when a hearing child is exposed to a language model whose syntactic structures do not match the bias (e.g., Zheng & Goldin-Meadow, 2002).[5]

If a patient-focus is such a natural way of taking in a scene, why don't most of the world's languages design their structures to take advantage of what would appear to be an easily processed format. Slobin (1977) has outlined a number of pressures that language faces—pressures to be clear, processible, quick and easy, and expressive. Importantly, Slobin points out that these pressures do not necessarily all push language in the same direction. Thus, for example, the pressure to be semantically clear may come into conflict with pressures to be processed quickly or to be rhetorically expressive. The need to be clear may pressure languages to adopt structures that reinforce the patient-bias. However, at the same time, the need to be quick and expressive may pressure languages toward structures that do not have a patient focus. If the bias toward patients is as fundamental as our homesign data suggest, there may be a cognitive cost to overriding it—for example, there may be greater cognitive costs involved in processing sentences that do not organize around the patient than sentences that do. This would be an intriguing direction for future research (Goldin-Meadow, 2003b).

---

[5] It may be easier to guess actors than patients from context. If so, the bias to express patients found in the deaf children's gestures could stem from the child's tendency to express elements that are less predictable. However, we have found little support for the idea that predictability in context drives the deaf children's patterns of production and deletion. For example, in our analyses of underlying predicate frames, we examined production probability separately for first person actors (i.e., the child him or herself), second person actors (the communication partner), and third person actors. If predictability in context is the key, first and second person actors should tend to be omitted regardless of underlying predicate frame because their identity can be easily guessed in context (both persons are on the scene); and third person actors should be gestured quite often regardless of underlying predicate frame because they are less easily guessed from context. We found, however, that production probability patterns for first person, second person, and third person actors do not differ (Goldin-Meadow, 1985, p. 237). In other words, the structural patterns seen in the deaf children's gestures do not seem to reflect how likely a semantic element is to be inferred from context.

WHAT HOMESIGN CAN TELL US ABOUT HOW ALL CHILDREN LEARN LANGUAGE

The particular thoughts the deaf children convey in their gestures have not been influenced by a conventional language model. These thoughts come as close as we can currently envision to revealing the expressible and grammaticizable notions that children bring to the language-learning situation—thought before language. But data from the deaf children can address a second question about how children learn language, one that is central to the crosslinguistic study of language-learning that Slobin encouraged in 1985. Do young hearing children speak like native language users because they are exposed to different language models, or because they are growing up in different cultures? To the extent that the language model is, on its own, responsible for crosslinguistic differences at the earliest stages of language development, deaf children developing their gesture systems across different cultures *should not* reflect these differences—precisely because they do not have access to their culture's language model. On the other hand, to the extent that the culture within which the language model is embedded may also be responsible for the early crosslinguistic differences we see in language development, the deaf children *should* display the same differences as their hearing counterparts—since they too live in that culture (see, for example, Phillips et al., 2001). The deaf children's homesigns can, in this sense, serve as a baseline against which to evaluate the effects of a conventional language model (see Zheng & Goldin-Meadow, 2002, for an example of this line of work).

Slobin (1997b, p. 276) has suggested that certain grammatical forms and constructions may be more accessible than others to children.[6] However, it is not a simple matter to determine which notions are more, or less, accessible. Indeed, Slobin has made it clear that accessibility hierarchies cannot be discovered by surveying the array of languages that are spoken across the globe by adults. We need to look at children. If a child gives grammatical expression to a notion early in development, that notion is a good candidate for being high on the accessibility hierarchy. However, the age at which a construction appears in a child's language is affected by many factors, not the least of which is the language model to which the child is exposed.

We suggest that deaf children inventing their own gesture systems offer the most straightforward data on this question. If a deaf child is able to produce a grammatical construction without any guidance from a language model, that grammatical construction must be very high on the accessibility hierarchy—what we have called a resilient property of language. Thus, the constructions we have identified in the deaf children's homesign systems are likely to be highly accessible to all language-making children, serving as, what Slobin so aptly called the conceptual starting points for grammatical notions.

REFERENCES

Allen, S., Özyürek, A., Kita, S., Brown, A., Furman, R., & Ishizuka, T. (2007). Language-specific and universal influences in children's syntactic packaging of manner and path: A comparison of English, Japanese, and Turkish. *Cognition, 102,* 16–48.

Chen, C., & Uttal, D. H. (1988). Cultural values, parents' beliefs, and children's achievement in the United States and China. *Human Development, 31,* 351–358.

---

[6] Recently, Slobin (1996, 2003) has become convinced that language plays an important role in shaping how we think when we talk. Note, however, that the deaf children we study are creating their gesture systems without usable input from a conventional language model. Their homesign systems thus provide the best evidence that children can express language-like notions in language-like ways without a language model. But data from the deaf children could also provide evidence that language shapes thought. To the extent that the deaf children fail to express ideas that can be expressed in natural language, not only will we have evidence that a conventional language model is essential for expressing certain ideas, but we will also have pointers as to what those ideas might be (Goldin-Meadow, 2003b).

Choi, S. (1999). Early development of verb structures and caregiver input in Korean: Two case studies. *The International Journal of Bilingualism, 3*, 241–265.

Clancy, P. M. (1993). Preferred argument structure in Korean acquisition. In E. Clark (Ed.), *The proceedings of the twenty-fifth annual Child Language Research Forum* (pp. 307–314). Stanford, CA: Stanford University Center for the Study of Language and Information.

Coerts, J. A. (2000). Early sign combinations in the acquisition of Sign Language of the Netherlands: Evidence for language-specific features. In C. Chamberlain, J. P., Morford & R. Mayberry (Eds.), *Language acquisition by eye* (pp. 91–109). Mahwah, NJ: Lawrence Erlbaum Associates.

Conrad, R. (1979). *The deaf child*. London: Harper & Row.

Dixon, R. M. W. (1979). Ergativity. *Language, 55*, 59–138.

Feldman, H., Goldin-Meadow, S., & Gleitman, L. (1978). Beyond Herodotus: The creation of language by linguistically deprived deaf children. In A. Lock (Ed.), *Action, symbol, and gesture: The emergence of language* (pp. 361–414). New York: Academic Press.

Goldin-Meadow, S. (1985). Language development under atypical learning conditions: Replication and implications of a study of deaf children of hearing parents. In K. Nelson (Ed.), *Children's language* (Vol. 5, pp. 197–245). Hillsdale, NJ: Lawrence Erlbaum Associates.

Goldin-Meadow, S. (1987). Underlying redundancy and its reduction in a language developed without a language model: The importance of conventional linguistic input. In B. Lust (Ed.), *Studies in the acquisition of anaphora: Vol. II. Applying the constraints* (pp. 105–133). Boston, MA: D. Reidel Publishing Company.

Goldin-Meadow, S. (2003a). *The resilience of language: What gesture creation in deaf children can tell us about how all children learn language*. New York: Psychology Press.

Goldin-Meadow, S. (2003b). Thought before language: Do we think ergative? In D. Gentner & S. Goldin-Meadow (Eds.), *Language in mind: Advances in the study of language and thought* (pp. 493–522). Cambridge, MA: The MIT Press.

Goldin-Meadow, S., Butcher, C., Mylander, C., & Dodge, M. (1994). Nouns and verbs in a self-styled gesture system: What's in a name? *Cognitive Psychology, 27*, 259–319.

Goldin-Meadow, S., Gelman, S., & Mylander, C. (2005). Expressing generic concepts with and without a language model. *Cognition, 96*, 109–126.

Goldin-Meadow, S., & Mylander, C. (1984). Gestural communication in deaf children: The effects and noneffects of parental input on early language development. *Monographs of the Society for Research in Child Development, 49*, 1–121.

Goldin-Meadow, S. & Mylander, C. (1998). Spontaneous sign systems created by deaf children in two cultures. *Nature, 91*, 279–281.

Goldin-Meadow, S., Mylander, C., & Franklin, M. (2007). How children make language out of gesture: Morphological structure in gesture systems developed by American and Chinese deaf children. *Cognitive Psychology, 55*(2), 87–135.

Goldin-Meadow, S., & Saltzman, J. (2000). The cultural bounds of maternal accommodation: How Chinese and American mothers communicate with deaf and hearing children. *Psychological Science, 11*, 311–318.

Hoffmeister, R. (1978). *The development of demonstrative pronouns, locatives and personal pronouns in the acquisition of American Sign Language by deaf children of deaf parents*. Unpublished doctoral dissertation, University of Minnesota.

Hoffmeister, R., & Wilbur, R. (1980). Developmental: The acquisition of sign language. In H. Lane & F. Grosjean (Eds.), *Recent perspectives on American Sign Language* (pp. 61–78). Hillsdale, NJ: Lawrence Erlbaum Associates.

Hyams, N. (1986). *Language acquisition and the theory of parameters*. Boston: Reidel.

Kita, S., & Özyürek, A. (2003). What does cross-linguistic variation in semantic coordination of speech and gesture reveal? Evidence for an interface representation of spatial thinking and speaking. *Journal of Memory and Language, 48*, 16–32.

Lin, C.-Y. C., & Fu, V.R. (1990). A comparison of child-rearing practices among Chinese, immigrant Chinese, and Caucasian-American parents. *Child Development, 61*, 429–433.

Lust, B., & Wakayama, T. K. (1979). The structure of coordination in children's first language acquisition of Japanese. In F. R. Eckman & A. J. Hastings (Eds.), *Studies in first and second language acquisition* (pp. 134–152). Rowley, MA: Newbury House Publishers.

Mayberry, R. I. (1992). The cognitive development of deaf children: Recent insights. In F. Boller & J. Graffman (Series Eds.). S. Segalowitz & I. Rapin (Eds.), *Handbook of neuropsychology* (Vol. 7, pp. 51–68), Amsterdam: Elsevier.

McNeill, D. (1992). *Hand and mind*. Chicago: University of Chicago Press.

McNeill, D., & Duncan, S. (2000). Growth points in thinking-for-speaking. In D. McNeill (Ed.), *Speech and gesture: Window into thought and action* (pp. 141–161). New York: Cambridge University Press.

Meadow, K. (1968). Early manual communication in relation to the deaf child's intellectual, social, and communicative functioning. *American Annals of the Deaf, 113*, 29–41.

Newport, E. L., & Meier, R. P. (1985). The acquisition of American Sign Language. In D. I. Slobin (Ed.), *The crosslinguistic study of language acquisition: Vol. 1. The data* (pp. 881–938). Hillsdale, NJ: Lawrence Erlbaum Associates.

Özyürek, A., & Kita, S. (1999). Expressing manner and path in English and Turkish: Differences in speech, gesture, and conceptualization. *Proceedings of the Cognitive Science Society, 21*, 507–512.

Özyürek, A., Kita, S., Allen, S., Furman, R., & Brown, A. (2005). How does linguistic framing influence co-speech gestures? Insights from crosslinguistic differences and similarities. *Gesture, 5*, 216–241.

Papafragou, A., Massey, J., & Gleitman, L. (2006). When English proposes what Greek presupposes: The crosslinguistic encoding of motion events. *Cognition, 98*, B75–B87.

Phillips, S. B. V. D., Goldin-Meadow, S., & Miller, P. J. (2001). Enacting stories, seeing worlds: Similarities and differences in the cross-cultural narrative development of linguistically isolated deaf children. *Human Development, 44*, 311–336.

Silverstein, M. (1976). Hierarchy of features and ergativity. In R.M.W. Dixon (Ed.), *Grammatical categories in Australian languages* (pp. 112–171). Canberra: Australian Institute of Aboriginal Studies.

Slobin, D. I. (1977). Language change in childhood and history. In J. Macnamara (Ed.), *Language learning and thought* (pp. 185–214). New York: Academic Press.

Slobin, D. I. (1985a). Crosslinguistic evidence for the language-making capacity. In D. I. Slobin (Ed.), *A crosslinguistic study of language acquisition* (Vol. 2, pp. 1157–1256). Hillsdale, NJ: Lawrence Erlbaum Associates.

Slobin, D. I. (1985b). Introduction: Why study acquisition crosslinguistically? In D. I. Slobin (Ed.), *A cross-linguistic study of language acquisition* (Vol. 1, pp. 3–24). Hillsdale, NJ: Lawrence Erlbaum Associates.

Slobin, D. I. (1996). From "thought and language" to "thinking to speaking." In J. J. Gumperz & S. C. Levinson (Eds.), *Rethinking linguistic relativity* (pp. 70–96). Cambridge: Cambridge University Press.

Slobin, D. I. (1997a). The universal, the typological, and the particular in acquisition. In D. I. Slobin (Ed.), *A cross-linguistic study of language acquisition* (Vol. 5, pp. 1–39). Hillsdale, NJ: Lawrence Erlbaum Associates.

Slobin, D. I. (1997b). The origins of grammaticizable notions: Beyond the individual mind. In D. I. Slobin (Ed.), *A cross-linguistic study of language acquisition* (Vol. 5, pp. 265–323). Hillsdale, NJ: Lawrence Erlbaum Associates.

Slobin, D. I. (2003). Language and thought online: Cognitive consequences of linguistic relativity. In D. Gentner & S. Goldin-Meadow (Eds.), *Language in mind: Advances in the study of language and thought* (pp. 157–191). Cambridge, MA: The MIT Press.

Talmy, L. (1985). Lexicalization patterns: Semantic structure in lexical forms. In T. Shopen (Ed.), *Language typology and syntactic description: Vol. III. Grammatical categories and the lexicon* (pp. 57–149). Cambridge, UK: Cambridge University Press.

Wu, D. Y. H. (1985). Child training in Chinese culture. In W.-S. Tseng & D. Y. H. Wu (Eds.), *Chinese culture and mental health* (pp. 113–134). Orlando, FL: Academic Press.

Zheng, M., & Goldin-Meadow, S. (2002). Thought before language: How deaf and hearing children express motion events across cultures. *Cognition, 85*, 145–175.

3

"He Take One of My Tools!" vs. "I'm Building"
Transitivity and the Grammar of Accusing, Commanding, and Perspective-Sharing in Toddlers' Peer Disputes

AMY KYRATZIS
University of California, Santa Barbara

[W]e can define the prototypical transitive event as one in which an animate agent willfully brings about a physical and perceptible change of state or location in a patient by means of direct body contact. Such events are encoded in consistent grammatical fashion by about age two.

Dan I. Slobin (1981, p. 187)

I had the wonderful opportunity in the early 1990s to do a postdoctoral fellowship with Dan Slobin and Sue Ervin-Tripp, working on child language issues at the University of California, Berkeley's Psychology Department. I took courses from Dan and sat in on meetings of his research group, which was meeting at the time on the crosslinguistic study of language in narrative. I came to be influenced by Dan's dynamic approach of looking at how child speakers select forms to express particular discursive functions and semantic notions, and how language-specific, cognitive, communicative, and developmental factors enter into these choices. His view of children as active constructors of their own language, and his approach of looking at how language forms are selected by speakers in very specific contexts, is reflected in the work I did at Berkeley on children's causal constructions in narratives and arguments. This influence can also be seen in the analysis presented below, which examines the transitivity of very young children's verb constructions as used in their peer disputes. I feel very lucky to be among the many child language researchers today for whom Dan has been a teacher.

INTRODUCTION

In his early work, Slobin proposed that linguistic transitivity "appears among the first notions marked by grammatical morphemes" (Slobin, 1985) due to the fact that the Manipulative Activity Scene (MAS) that it reflected contained cognitive notions within the grasp of children in the sensorimotor period of development. Later, examining the different ways that languages have of describing motion (Slobin, 1996, 2003), he came to believe that language-specific, cultural, discursive, and social-interactive functions guide speakers' grammar use and acquisition. The current study examines very young children's use of verb constructions in the constrained discourse context of peer disputes. In defensive conflicts in which they are in dispute with a peer, would very young child speakers report the actions of these children using highly transitive forms consistent with the MAS? Or would they, in keeping with Thompson and Hopper's (2001) findings for conversations among adults, emphasize their own feelings, states, and reactions? The results suggest that parameters of transitivity vary with the speech act or pragmatic function the speaker elects to use. Results are discussed in light of Slobin's (e.g., 2003) recent position that cultural ways of speaking have an influence on the viewpoints that speakers take on events and the grammatical structures that they choose.

Slobin has dedicated his research to, among other things, accounting for the "cognitive and communicative bases of linguistic structures, and consequences for language acquisition and use" (Slobin, 2004, Research Overview). Over the years, he underwent a change in his thinking. In his earlier work, Slobin (1979) set forth several ways in which cognition imposes constraints on grammar. Although he also posited ways that discourse and information flow constrain grammar and determine its structure, in this early work, he believed that cognition was more important than ways of speaking and typological differences across languages in determining the order of acquisition of grammatical forms. For example, he interpreted researchers' findings that children acquiring Russian (Gvozdev, 1949), Hungarian (MacWhinney, 1973), Kaluli (Schieffelin, 1985), and other languages reserved the use of ergative and accusative markers to the subjects or "direct objects of verbs involving direct, physical action on things—such as 'give,' 'carry,' 'put,' and 'throw'" (Slobin, 1985, p. 1176), and omitted them in sentences with verbs such as "say" and "see" (Slobin, 1985, p. 1176), as follows. Slobin argued that the prototypical scene reflected in early-appearing ergative and accusative inflectional marking that was seen across these languages was the Manipulative Activity Scene (MAS), corresponding to Lakoff and Johnson's (1980) "prototypical direct manipulation." This scene was "the experiential gestalt of a basic causal event in which an agent carries out a physical and perceptible change of state in a patient by means of direct body contact or with an instrument under the agent's control" (Slobin, 1985, p. 1175). Although children could take different perspectives on this basic scene (Antinucci & Miller, 1976; Savasir, 1983), the MAS was early-emerging. Slobin argued that Manipulative Activity Scenes (MASs) are a part of Basic Child Grammar because they reflect cognitive notions within the grasp of children in the sensorimotor period of development. MAS's "regularly occur as part of frequent and salient activities and perceptions" (Slobin, 1985, p. 1175) and they correspond to "sensorimotor concepts of physical agency involving the hands and perceptual-cognitive concepts of change of state and change of location, along with some overarching notions of efficacy and causality, embedded in interactional formats of requesting, giving, and taking" (Slobin, 1985, p. 1175). For cognitive reasons, "both the Manipulative Activity Scene," and the perspectives that the child could take on it, "emerge early" (Slobin, 1985, p. 1183) in the course of language acquisition.

Several years later, during the 1990s, Slobin's views about the primacy of the role played by universal cognitive factors in determining the ease and order of acquisition of forms in first and second language learning changed. He came to believe that the relationship between language and thought went in the opposite direction. "We encounter the contents of the mind in a special way when they are being accessed for use. That is, the activity of thinking takes on a particular quality when it is employed in the activity of speaking … **I propose that, in acquiring a native language, the child learns particular ways of thinking for speaking**" (Slobin, 1996, p. 76). Examining the different ways that languages have of describing motion (Slobin, 1996, 2003) and examining the influence of these ways on corresponding typological features of languages as well as on the perceptions and cognitions of speakers of different languages, he came to believe, with other investigators of the time (Bowerman, 1996; Budwig, Stein, & O'Brien 2001; Duranti & Ochs, 1996; Ervin-Tripp, 1996; Hopper & Thompson, 1980; Ochs & Schieffelin, 1984; Thompson & Hopper,

2001), that language-specific, cultural, discursive, and social-interactive functions (Kuntay & Slobin, 2002) strongly guided speakers' grammatical choices and acquisition.

That cultural, linguistic, discursive, and social interactive functions may constrain how *transitivity* is used by very young children in early verb constructions was not an area that Slobin returned to in his research program, after his views on the relationship between thought and language changed in the 1990s. However, several investigators began to document discursive and cultural underpinnings of the transitivity and agency of adult speakers' verb constructions (Duranti & Ochs, 1996; Hopper & Thompson, 1980), and even of children's (Budwig, 1995; Budwig, Stein, & O'Brien, 2001). Slobin himself, in his work with Berman, noted that children, with age, "make increased use of a productive system of verb morphology to present a non-agentive perspective on events" (Berman & Slobin, 1994, p. 310) in narrative, as they increasingly take a global perspective on individual scenes within the story. A discursive factor, then, was viewed as influencing child speakers' marking of agency. Thompson and Hopper (2001) analyzed three face-to-face conversations among family members and friends from an archival dataset of adult conversations and found that these manifested a "low Transitivity of the clauses" (p. 53). They concluded that "the low Transitivity in our conversational data is to a considerable extent determined by the kinds of things we are doing when we talk with friends and acquaintances. We do not seem to talk much about events, let alone actions (as Hopper 1991, 1997 has also shown), but rather, our talk is mostly about 'how things are from our perspective'" (Thompson & Hopper, 2001, p. 53).

Thompson and Hopper (2001) attributed their finding that adults conversing with other adults used forms low in Transitivity to what the adults were doing with their language in those situations. Their conclusion is consistent with that of other research with both children and adults. The speech act or activity-type in which speakers are engaged, for example, whether they are describing the world or attempting to control the behavior of others (Budwig, 1996; Ervin-Tripp 1993, 1996; Gee & Savasir, 1985; Gordon & Ervin-Tripp, 1984; Savasir, 1983; Savasir & Gee, 1982), or whether they are taking a local perspective on individual scenes within a story, or a global one (Berman & Slobin, 1994), have been found to be key factors in determining how they talk about that event. Speakers may reserve more transitive constructions to situations in which they seek to express "a stance that assumes or assigns accountability to the participant role" (Duranti & Ochs, 1996, p. 183). For these reasons, the context in which the talk occurs is important to consider. Much of the data on which Slobin based his claims about the primacy of the MAS came from studies conducted in the early child language tradition, which usually involved periodic recording of spontaneous speech between the child and an adult (a parent or investigator) (e.g., Ervin & Miller, 1964) in the home. The verb constructions tended to occur in boasts by the child, or comments on just completed or ongoing events ("Dolly fall down"), or in requests (Ervin-Tripp, personal communication). The findings about the primacy of the MAS may have been due to the speech acts that young children tended to use at home when speaking with adults, but may not generalize to other contexts. It is important to expand the range of contexts examined when drawing conclusions about young children's language uses.

The present study extends Slobin's (and his colleagues') work on transitivity in children's early verb constructions by expanding the range of discourse contexts examined to include young children interacting with their peers in situations of dispute. The peer context may be expected to yield different results than the early child language studies, because, as found by Budwig in her own study of children's verb constructions, "there were differences in the kinds of talk about physical and social causation that took place when the children were interacting with a peer versus a caregiver" (Budwig, 1995, p. 42). On the basis of past research emphasizing the role of speech act and activity-type, the present study asks the following questions: what kinds of verb constructions do young children use when interacting with their peers, and to what extent are the constructions that they use influenced by the speech acts that they use in the event? In keeping with Slobin's (e.g., 2003) recent position that cultural ways of speaking have an influence on the grammatical structures that speakers choose, the present study also asks the following question: how are young children socialized to take viewpoints on events, in this case conflict events, by those in their language community? How do these viewpoints affect the transitivity of the forms they choose?

A STUDY OF VERB CONSTRUCTIONS

To address these questions, the verb constructions used by four target children in a specific category of peer disputes that were identified in a previously collected data set, a 500-hour videotape archive, were analyzed. The archive consists of video recordings of the naturally occurring interactions of children who were students in two toddler-infant day care centers. Video recordings of children's naturally occurring peer interactions were made at these day care sites twice weekly, for a period of 2 years. Children at the centers were aged 12 to 30 months. They came from middle-class families, and for most, English was the language spoken in the home. Each taping session lasted 2 hours. The focus of the original study, reflected in its title, was "Communicative Action in the Social Lives of Very Young Children," and the researchers focused their camera on peer social interactions of various sorts (e.g., disputes, pretend play, affect displays, etc.) that occurred during the video recording sessions.

The four target children, one girl (Kimmy), and three boys (Marcus, Devon, and Roger),[1] were selected on the basis of having fairly stable friendships or playmates. The subset of data from the archive used in this analysis consists of a specific category of peer conflicts identified for the four target children when they were in a given age range, that is, from the time they were 24 months until they were 30 months of age. These were conflicts in which the four target children were provoked by other children, and in which they made various defensive moves in response to the provocations. The age range focused on in this study, 24–30 months, is within the range of the studies on which the claims about the primacy of the MAS were based, although it may represent the upper part of the age range of some of those studies. Schieffelin (1985) and Savasir (1983) followed children from the time they were 24 months until they were 30 months or older. MacWhinney's (1973) subject Zoli was followed from the time he was 17 months to 26 months. Antinucci and Miller's (1976) participants were followed from 18 months of age to between 26 and 29 months.

These defensive conflicts were identified for a Master's thesis project conducted by Artemis Savarnejad (2003). Savarnejad's analysis examined the effectiveness of different conflict strategies used by the four target toddlers in defensive conflicts (in terms of terminating the provocation), while the present analysis focuses on linguistic aspects, specifically, transitivity parameters of the verb constructions in the defensive conflicts. A conflict of this (defensive) type was coded when a provoking move was committed by another child against one of the four target children (e.g., taking their toy hammer, knocking over the toy tower that they were building), and the target child opposed the provocation in some way, either through saying "no," issuing a command or prohibition, issuing a physical move (pushing), or giving a reason why the provocation should be terminated ("I'm building" said to a child who was knocking down the target child's toy tower). Usually, the provocation was sustained over several turns. Only when the opposition was resolved in some way (e.g., through one of the children procuring the disputed object) or ceased for a time (e.g., through the provocateur ceasing the provoking action, or through the two children resuming playing together without opposition, or separating for a time) was the conflict considered ended.

The present study analyzed the verb constructions used by the four target children in these disputes. The approach of looking at constructions within a constrained discourse such as peer disputes is modeled after Slobin's approach of studying forms in constrained discursive and semantic contexts (e.g., in narrative, as in Berman & Slobin, 1994, and in verbs of motion—Slobin 1996, 2003). This approach enables the analyst to identify specific effects of language functions and uses on forms. All the verb constructions used in defensive moves by these four children were identified and then analyzed for the speech act they encoded and for their transitivity. Transitivity of the verb construction was analyzed as follows. Hopper and Thompson (1980) identified ten components (number of participants, kinesis, aspect, punctuality, volitionality, affirmation, mode, agency, affectedness of object, and individuation of object, see p. 252). They argued that these are associated with transitivity through involving "a different facet of the effectiveness or intensity with which the action is

---

[1] All names of study children used in this report are pseudonyms.

transferred from one participant to the other" (Hopper & Thompson, 1980, p. 252). For example, a description that has telic aspect, that is viewed from its completion point rather than from inside the still-ongoing event, and that specifies an action that projects greater kinesis and agency—all of these features contribute to a description that projects greater "effectiveness or intensity with which the action is transferred from one participant to another (Hopper & Thompson, 1980, p. 252). To refer to Hopper and Thompson's (1980) multidimensional, composite view of the concept of transitivity, I will henceforth use the term "Transitivity" with a capital T as they did in that article (see also Thompson & Hopper, 2001, p. 28). Three of these components (1) the kinesis of the verb (whether the verb was high in action or kinesis e.g., "push," "hit," "take") or was a verb without much action or kinesis, such as "have," "be," or "say"); (2) whether there is mention of an object that is affected, and (3) aspect (whether a completion point was made explicit in the verb construction) were examined to assess the degree of Transitivity of the constructions produced by the children in their disputes.

There were three different speech acts in which the verb constructions occurred: Accusing Statements, Commands/Prohibitions, and Perspective Statements (see below). All verb constructions were coded exhaustively for these three types. Accusing Statements were reports in the second or third person describing the action of the child in the provoking role. In constructions 1 and 2 below, one target child complains to the nearby caregiver that the child in the provoking role took one of the tools that he was playing with, and another complains that the provoking child knocked his truck down.

(1) Marcus (29 mos.): She took ... he take one of my tools!
(2) Roger (30 mos.): They knock off my truck.

Similarly, in the construction below, Kimmy, one of the target children, complains to the child in the provoking role that he pushed her.

(3) Kimmy (26 mos.): You push me!

Commands/Prohibitions were directives spoken by the target children that asked the child in the provoking role to do something or to stop doing something, as in examples (4–8).

(4) Kimmy (26 mos.): No push me. (to peer who just pushed her)
(5) Kimmy (27 mos): No, stop! (to peer splashing her)
(6) Devon (30 mos.): Stop screaming me! (to peer screaming in his face)
(7) Devon (24 mos.): Go eat! (telling peer taking his food to return to his own spot at the table)
(8) Roger (30 mos.): You can't say 'hi.' (demanding that a child who keeps greeting him stop doing so)

Perspective Statements were the third kind of speech act that could occur in a defensive conflict. The term was used here to refer to a prevalent kind of statement identified by Thompson and Hopper (2001) in adult conversations, descriptions of how things appeared from the speaker's perspective. In this study Perspective Statements were defined as descriptions of how things appeared from the provoked child's perspective, more specifically, they were descriptions of states and actions used by that child as justifications. These statements seemed intended to persuade the addressee, the child in the provoking role, to produce some form of response (usually, cessation of the provoking action). For example, in one conflict, Example 8, a target child, Marcus, was provoked by another child who took his hammer while he was playing with several tools from a play tool box. In response, Marcus issued a directive, "put back in there!" with parameters of high Transitivity—a kinetic verb with a specified completion point. However, he also uttered several Perspective Statements with parameters of low Transitivity—stative verbs. These statements may be intended to persuade the child in the provoking role to see the defender's perspective and give his hammer back.

(9) Marcus (29 mos): (Put back in there!)
It's my tools.
That's for working.
That for working.
It's bang, bang.

Similarly, in another conflict in which a peer tried repeatedly to knock down the toy tower he was building, Marcus (Example 9) tried to use Commands ("let me do it") but also, in the same dispute, used a Perspective Statement, perhaps to make his directives seem more reasonable to his addressee.

(10) Marcus (28 mos.): I'm, I'm building.

Transitivity in Toddlers' Verb Constructions in Different Speech Acts Within Disputes

There were 83 defensive conflicts involving provocation of the four target children in the period from when these children were aged 24 to 30 months. In 58 of these 83 conflicts, verb constructions were produced by one of the four target children, in some cases at the rate of more than one per conflict, yielding a total of 125 verb constructions that were considered in the analysis. As described in the section on analysis, there were three different speech acts in which the verb constructions occurred: Accusing Statements, Commands/Prohibitions, and Perspective Statements. The speech act in which the verb construction was produced seemed to affect the Transitivity, so Transitivity features of the verb constructions are reported separately for different speech acts (see Table 3.1).

Table 3.1 reports the total number of verb constructions that were produced in Accusing Statements, Commands/Prohibitions, and Perspective Statements. Table 3.1 also reports the mean proportion of defensive verb constructions that had the following low Transitivity features: (1) kinesis = non-action; (2) no mention of an affected object; and (3) atelic (non-completed) aspect in each of these different speech acts. For example, the first proportion in the table was derived as follows. Of the 11 (total) verb constructions produced in Accusing Statements, 3 of these 11, or .3, had no kinesis. We focused on features of low Transitivity rather than high Transitivity, following some of the analyses in Thompson and Hopper (2001; see p. 37).

The first finding of note is that different frequencies of the speech act were encoded in the target children's verb constructions. The children were unlikely to use Accusing Statements in these defensive disputes. Only 11/125, or .1, of the verb constructions were produced in Accusing Statements. The most preferred category of speech act to be used with a verb construction in a dispute was Perspective Statements, yielding 61/125 verb constructions, that is, accounting for .5 of the constructions. How did these different speech acts support the use of parameters of Transitivity? As Thompson and Hopper (2001) noted, low Transitivity resides in features such as low kinesis of the verb, no affectedness of the object, and atelic aspect. Therefore, we examined children's constructions in disputes for these features.

TABLE 3.1 Proportion of Verb Constructions With Low Transitivity Parameters in Different Speech Acts

Low Transitivity Parameter	Accusing Statements	Speech Act Commands/ Prohibitions	Perspective Statements	Mean Across Different Speech Acts
No Kinesis	.3	.4	.8	.6
No Affected Obj	.3	.7	.9	.8
Atelic	.5	.8	.9	.8
Total Verb Constructions	11	53	61	125

As can be seen in Table 3.1, parameters of low Transitivity were the least likely to be produced in Accusing Statements. These constructions had the Transitivity parameter of no kinesis in only 3/11 or .3 of cases. No mention of an object, or mention of one that was not affected, occurred in 3/11 or .3 of cases. The feature of low Transitivity most likely to be produced in Accusing Statements was atelic aspect, which occurred in 6/11 or .5 of cases, but it was produced less frequently that in the other two speech acts, Commands and Perspective Statements. Accusing Statements tended to have parameters of high Transitivity, that is, verbs that were kinetic actions (e.g., "he take one of my tools! "you push me!," "they knock off my truck!"), verbs encoded with completed aspect, and verbs which were presented as having an object affected by the action. It appeared that when child speakers accused the provocateur, probably wishing to emphasize the actor's agency and the outcome of their action, they used features of high Transitivity, since these features convey "a different facet of the effectiveness or intensity with which the action is transferred from one participant to another" (Hopper & Thompson, 1980, p. 252).

As can be seen in Table 3.1, in contrast to Accusing Statements, low Transitivity features were produced more frequently in Commands. Although verbs denoting high kinesis could be produced ("no push me" "don't knock me down," "go away," "put back in there"), several of the verbs in Commands, rather than naming kinetic actions, instead specified the cessation of action ("stop," "stop it," "let me do it"). Or they specified verbs of saying ("you can't say 'hi'") or seeing ("watch out"). In total, kinesis = non-action occurred in 23/53, that is, in nearly half, or .4, of the Commands. A majority (39/53 or .7) of the verbs in Commands specified no object or one that was not affected. Although expressions such as "no you can't take it," "no push me," "get off me," "don't knock me down," and "stop screaming me," could occur, Command constructions were more likely to omit mention of an object that was affected by the action ("go eat," "get off," "put back in there"). Completion was also de-emphasized, in that the majority (42/53 or .8) of the verbs had either atelic aspect ("go eat," "you can't say 'hi'") or had indeterminable aspect (as in constructions such as "stop," or "let me go down," where no action was specified). In other words, in Commands, where the speaker might have mentioned an action ("move your body away so that I can go down the slide"), they said "stop" or "let me go down." By not specifying the actor's kinetic action, or by omitting mention of an object that was affected by the action ("go eat," "get off"), or by specifying no completion point for the action, the children may have been speaking from the "viewing arrangement" of one caught inside the event (see Langacker, 2001, for more about "viewing arrangement" as affecting use of the simple present).

As Table 3.1 indicates, of the three kinds of speech acts, Perspective Statements, which operated as complaints or statements of how things seemed from the speaker's perspective, were the highest of all three speech acts in features of low Transitivity. Non-action, stative verbs low in kinesis were named in 48/61 or .8 of these constructions (e.g., "it's my tools," "that's for working," "it's so loud"). The high rate of low-kinesis verbs in Perspective Statements was due to the fact that the majority of constructions were either "epistemic/evidential clauses" or "copular clauses" (Thompson & Hopper, 2001, pp. 38–39). They were verbs of saying, seeing, and feeling, such as "I say 'no,' I say 'stop'" and "I don't like it" and "I don't like that big horsie" (said to child who was putting a toy horse in the speaker's face). In other cases, they were copular clauses, including "That's for working," "it's my tools," "it's for bang, bang" (meaning, "it's for banging")—said to a child who was taking the speaker's toy hammer away, as well as "it's so loud" and "that's my bear," complaints intended to end a child's repeatedly calling the child speaker's name loudly or taking their toy bear. A high proportion (.9 or 55/61) of the Perspective Statements specified no object or one not affected by the action ("I'm building," "I can't cook," "I want go xxx" (meaning "I want to go to my backpack") said about a boy who was blocking the speaker's access to it). Perspective Statements usually (in 56/61 = .9 of cases) named non-completed, atelic actions ("I'm building," "I can't cook," "Now I'm using that"). In other words, kinesis was generally low, and even when it was not, the action was presented in its non-completed form and as having no affected object. Speakers may use these features of low Transitivity to emphasize how things seemed from their perspective. While speakers have a choice as to the perspective or "viewing arrangement" (Langacker, 2001, p. 16) to take on action, the child speakers here, in using atelic aspect, showed a preference for taking a "viewing arrangement" (Langacker,

2001, p. 16) on the action, that, rather than being from its endpoint, and viewing the action from a distal and uninvolved viewpoint, took the "viewing arrangement" of one who is still inside of and involved in the activity ("I can't cook," "I'm building") (Cook-Gumperz & Kyratzis, 2001; Langacker, 2001). Presenting no affected object, and using copular and stative verbs, may also go toward creating this effect.

A long example, Example 11, will help demonstrate how Perspective Statements emerged in sequences of interaction. Marcus and Devon, two of the target children of the study, are engaged in a conflict. (Marcus is the one who is in the defensive (provoked) role, so it is his verb constructions from this dispute that are counted in the analysis). As the example begins, Devon provokes Marcus by patting him on the head while Marcus builds a tower on the floor (lines 2–3.) Marcus himself uses a Perspective Statement in response to the provocation, in line 5. He describes his own words and feelings ("(I say) 'stop'"). The caregiver encourages Marcus to use his words ("you can tell him to stop," line 9, and "did you say 'okay' Marcus?"—line 16) and encourages the child in the provoking role to attend to the words and wishes of Marcus ("you might want to ask Marcus before you do it," line 11," and "I didn't hear him say anything," line 18). The child being provoked is responsive to the caregiver's encouragement to use his words, as he says "I say 'stop'" in line 5 and then more emphatically "I say 'no'" in line 22. These utterances would be coded as Perspective Statements, and they are characterized by parameters of low Transitivity (verbs with no kinesis, non-completed aspect, and no specification of an object that is affected). Marcus's use of Perspective Statements is not at first successful. When he says "I say 'stop'" (line 5), the child in the provoking role misrepresents him as saying "I say 'yeah'" (line 6) and also misrepresents Marcus's words to the caregiver, "he said 'okay'" (line 14). Only after several declarations of Marcus's words and feelings, and several appeals by Marcus to the caregiver, does the child in the provoking role give up his provocation (line 23). This example shows how children's use of Perspective Statements, speech acts carrying parameters of low Transitivity, arose in sequences of interaction at these daycare centers.

Example 11 (Marcus, 28 mos.)

[Marcus and Devon are building a tower together on the floor. Marcus climbs up on the couch, lies on his stomach. He disturbs the tower, which falls. Devon flings a tower piece at Marcus.]

1. Marcus: Oh no, oh no, oh no. [looking down at fallen tower]
2. [Devon begins to pat Marcus on the head with both hands]
3. [Devon moves onto the couch and continues patting Marcus's head]
4. Devon: Marcus likes.
5. Marcus: (I say) 'stop.' [continues building]
6. Devon: I say 'yeah,' I say 'no,' I say 'no.' [pretending to speak for Marcus]
7. C.G.: can't you do that, Marcus?
8. Marcus: No.
9. C.G.: Yeah, you can tell him to stop.
10. Devon: I say 'stop'! [yelling, pretends to speak for Marcus]
11. C.G.: You might want to ask Marcus before you do it.
12. Devon: I do it? [stops patting, looks at Marcus]
13. [Marcus pauses, stares off into space. Does not answer Devon]
14. Devon: He said 'okay.' [to C.G.]
15. Boy: No:o. [had been watching, to Devon]
16. C.G.: He said 'okay'? Did you say 'okay,' Marcus?
17. [Marcus does not answer]
18. C.G.: I didn't hear him say anything.
19. Marcus: No. [states firmly]
20. C.G.: He said 'no.' [to Devon]
21. Devon: I said 'don't'! [pats Marcus forcefully, pretends to speak for him]
22. Marcus: I say 'no.' [looking at C.G.]
23. [Devon goes over to C.G., speaks to her about something]

Summing across all three different speech acts with verb constructions in Table 3.1 (125 verb constructions in all), low Transitivity features were produced in a majority (.6–.8) of the verb constructions, depending on the Transitivity parameter examined. These findings are very much like Thompson and Hopper's (2001) results for adult conversational corpus data. "The clauses in English conversation are very low in Transitivity" (2001, p. 52). "Our talk is mostly about 'how things are from our perspective'" (Hopper, 1991, 1997) (Thompson & Hopper, 2001, p. 53). "Our data show that we describe states, reveal our attitudes, ascribe properties to people and situations, and give our assessments of situations and behavior" (Thompson & Hopper, 2001, p. 53). Through these means, "we display our identities" (Thompson & Hopper, 2001, p. 53). Like adults, the child speakers in the present dispute data avoided using parameters associated with high Transitivity, except when making accusations. They did not talk about actions in ways that emphasized the "effectiveness or intensity with which the action is transferred from one participant to another" (Hopper & Thompson, 1980, p. 252), preferring to focus on their own feelings and activities. Even when they mentioned the kinetic actions of the child provoking them, they presented these from the viewpoint of non-completed aspect and without an object that was affected. The children took a "viewing arrangement" (Langacker, 2001, p. 16) that was inside the action, focusing on how the action seemed from the perspective of one still involved within it, rather than on how the action seemed from a more distanced, telic perspective, or how it affected an object. Thus they did not focus on the other as an active agent producing effects on objects.

With young children aged 24–30 months, displaying identities was probably not an operative goal, as Thompson and Hopper (2001) argued was the case for the adult speakers in their conversational data. Why, then, do very young children talk about how things seem from their perspective? Our data suggested that this was related to the pragmatic functions toward which they used their language. They avoided using accusations, which, as Table 3.1 indicates, would have increased their use of parameters of high Transitivity. This is somewhat paradoxical. In situations of being provoked, it would seem that child speakers would wish to use Accusing Statements and parameters of high Transitivity, since these features convey "a different facet of the effectiveness or intensity with which the action is transferred from one participant to another" (Hopper & Thompson, 1980, p. 252), thereby allowing them to emphasize the addressee's effect on the environment, blame-worthiness, and "accountability" (Duranti & Ochs, 1996). Yet, they avoid doing so.

Since the results suggest that children prefer to use language in certain ways, for certain kinds of speech acts (for Perspective Statements and Commands, but not for Accusations), in disputes with other children, the next step in this inquiry would be to examine socialization influences on their preferred ways of using language in disputes. Is there something about the socialization practices at these child care centers that encourage children to use Perspective Statements carrying parameters of low Transitivity, and that discourage children from using Accusing Statements carrying parameters of high Transitivity? The preferred pragmatic functions toward which the children used their language in these disputes may have been a product of socialization. Caregivers at these child care centers were observed to encourage children to "use their words" to state their feelings and desires to other children, and to attend to the words of other children, during disputes. As seen in Example 11, the caregiver encouraged the child in the provoked role (Marcus) to use his words ("you can tell him to stop," line 9, and "did you say 'okay' Marcus?," line 16) and encouraged the child in the provoking role to attend to the words and wishes of Marcus ("you might want to ask Marcus before you do it," line 11, and "I didn't hear him say anything," line 18). When children were struggling or crying or looking plaintively to the caregivers, the caregivers were observed to encourage the children to express their feelings to one another ("you wanna go tell him that you want it?"). Accusations were discouraged. In one instance, we observed a child who was having her toys taken by another child use an Accusing Statement "he robbing this thing." The caregiver discouraged this by saying "you can't say that, you can tell him you don't like that."

To varying degrees, both of the child care centers utilized, and trained their child care professionals in, the RIE (Resources for Infant Educarers) Method, a curriculum which is based on ten principles (see Gonzalez-Mena & Eyer, 2001) and which is adapted and used in many infant and toddler centers in California. It should be noted that different centers vary greatly in how they implement the RIE Method. The ten principles are based on Magda Gerber's philosophy of child care. Gerber advises child care educators (see Gonzalez-Mena & Eyer, 2001) as well as parents (see Gerber & Johnson, 1998) to respect young infants and toddlers and encourage their "natural abilities" and self-confidence. With respect to conflict management, to the extent possible, young children are encouraged to work out their own conflicts. They are encouraged to "use their words" and express their likes and dislikes as a way of naturally avoiding frustration during conflict, and as a way of having their feelings respected. Gerber recommends "if your child is disturbed by another child's touching, before intervening, you may say 'Lani's touching you and it looks like you don't like it. You can tell Lani you don't like that.' This acknowledges your child's feelings while encouraging him to talk it out" (Gerber & Johnson, 1998, p. 191). As respect for infants and toddlers is encouraged, blaming children is discouraged. When a child acts aggressively, Gerber recommends to parents "allow him to express his feelings while making it clear that you will not allow him to hurt another child. This is better than making him feel guilty about his feelings" (Gerber & Johnson, 1998, p. 188). There seem to be operative ideologies at these centers, then, favoring the encouragement of children to work out their own conflicts, by describing their likes and feelings to other children (i.e., to use Perspective Statements), and disfavoring children blaming and accusing other children, hence possibly accounting for the results seen in Table 3.1. The qualitative analysis of one long example, as well as the researchers' impressions gained from observing hours of video recorded interactions between children and caregivers at these centers, illustrated that adults in the language community of these young children socialized particular ways for the children to take perspectives on events when they "think for speaking" (Slobin, 1996) in situations of peer dispute.

DISCUSSION

This analysis examined a grammatical feature, children's use of parameters of low and high Transitivity, in their early verb constructions. Slobin and his colleagues (1985) observed an early restrictedness of accusative and ergative marking to certain situations, and Slobin explained this restrictedness in terms of universal aspects of cognitive development, specifically, in terms of the prevalence of MASs in young children's descriptions of the world. In this study, we examined a very specific discourse context, one in which children were being provoked by other child peers in their daycare center. There were three main findings. First, the verb constructions that the children utilized in the context of peer disputes (low Transitivity) differed from the forms they were reported to notice and utilize in the early child language studies (high Transitivity). Second, the pragmatic functions toward which the children used their speech greatly influenced the parameters of Transitivity that they utilized, as Table 3.1 revealed. Third, although Accusing Statements would have increased children's use of parameters of high Transitivity, the children avoided the use of this pragmatic function. Instead, children favored the use of Perspective Statements that described how things seemed from their perspective and carried parameters of low Transitivity (non-kinetic verbs, no affected object, atelic aspect). Each of these findings is discussed in turn.

With regard to the first finding, it has been noted here that children utilized very different forms when interacting with a peer in this study than children have been noted use in other studies of early child language and the difference among studies bears discussion. Although it might be argued that the children in the present study were somewhat older than in some of the early studies (over 24 months, as opposed to under 24 months), as noted, some of the MAS studies were of children above the age of 24 months. Moreover, it is very difficult to obtain data of sustained peer interactions in which verbal constructions are used by children younger than 2 years. Also, it should be noted that the findings here are about children's preference for verb constructions and Transitivity parameters of particular types for use in interaction, rather than, as in the early studies, their use of verb constructions of particular sorts as a basis for extension of new morphemes. Nonetheless, across both the early studies and this one, children's active selection of linguistic marking is at issue.

Any methodological differences notwithstanding, the differences across studies in the saliency of the MAS for very young children are likely to reside in context differences across the studies, and underscore the importance of considering context when studying early child language. The role of context is consistent with prior research illustrating that the speech act or activity-type in which speakers are engaged influences the grammatical forms that they choose (Budwig, 1995; Clancy, 2004; Duranti & Ochs, 1996; Ervin-Tripp, 1993, 1996; Gee & Savasir, 1985; Gordon & Ervin-Tripp, 1984; Savasir, 1983; Savasir & Gee, 1982; Thompson & Hopper, 2001). Budwig (1995), for example, divided the coding of MAS into peer data and caregiver–child data, and found more agentive kinds of marking in the peer data. She found that the presence of caregivers diminished the children's marking of agentivity. The adult caregivers in the present data exerted a similar diminishing effect on children's agentive and accusative marking (i.e., high Transitivity), but their ideology influenced the way in which the peers interacted with one another (i.e., to avoid using accusations and forms with high Transitivty) rather than the way in which the children interacted with them. In the early child language studies, the context of adult–child interaction may have encouraged children to use forms with parameters of high Transitivity, because the children were commenting on interesting, just completed events for the purpose of gaining adults' attention, and may have wished to emphasize the "effectiveness or intensity with which the action is transferred from one participant to another" (Hopper & Thompson, 1980, p. 252). The same speaker's language forms may vary significantly across different contexts (Budwig, Stein, & O'Brien, 2001; Budwig, 1995; Ervin-Tripp, 1993, 1996), because the ways in which speakers use speech acts and take perspectives on events vary across different settings.

Now we turn the discussion to the second and third findings. As noted, the pragmatic functions toward which the children used their speech greatly influenced the parameters of Transitivity that they utilized, as Table 3.1 revealed. Although Accusing Statements would have increased children's use of parameters of high Transitivity, the children avoided the use of this pragmatic function. Instead, children favored the use of Perspective Statements that described how things seemed from their perspective and carried parameters of low Transitivity (non-kinetic verbs, no affected object, atelic aspect).

In attempting to account for this differential preference of children for Perspective Statements and Commands versus Accusing Statements as speech acts to use in disputes, and in attempting to account for the perspectives they chose to take on ongoing actions within disputes (as seen in the Transitivity parameters they selected), we suggested some possible influences of caregiver practices and child care ideologies utilized at the daycare centers at which these data were collected. To different degrees, these centers subscribed to a particular child care philosophy whereby educators encouraged children to express their likes and dislikes ("tell (other child) that you don't like that"). These practices may have accounted for young children's strong preference to use Perspective Statements and to use parameters of low Transitivity that was seen in Table 3.1. Future research should examine the influence of caregiver input and socialization directly, through detailed qualitative and quantitative analyses, as has been done in the work of Budwig (1996) and Lieven (e.g., Rowland, Pine, Lieven, & Theakston, 2003), for example, examining whether variation in caregiver input and encouragement of children to "use their words" and express their likes and dislikes across different centers impacts on the children's own use of Perspective Statements and statements carrying parameters of low Transitivity.

The finding that children's language choices were influenced by adult ideologies is consistent with the view that Slobin came to have in his later work when he argued that, rather than universals of cognition organizing the grammatical features of the languages that children come to acquire, "the contents of the mind" themselves are shaped "in a special way when they are being accessed for **use**" (Slobin, 1996, p. 76) through speaking. Slobin viewed these influences as being language-specific, with each language providing "a subjective orientation to the world of human experience" (Slobin, 1996, p. 91), and he viewed them as being situation-general; "once our minds have been trained in taking particular points of view for the purposes of speaking, it is exceptionally difficult for us to be retrained" (Slobin 1996, p. 91). Nonetheless, his views are not incompatible with more situation-specific and discursive influences on grammar and thinking. In his paper on "language and thought online," he quoted Gumperz and Levinson for their point that "world view" cannot be viewed as "detached from all the practices established for its use" (Gumperz & Levinson, 1996, p. 230; cited in Slobin, 2003, p. 18). In that paper, Slobin also wrote that "thinking-for-speaking effects" are "thus part of a much larger framework of online communication, negotiation, and action ... all of these ... are **processes**—that is, they unfold in time and are shaped in use" (Slobin, 2003, p. 18). Consistent with Slobin's ideas, the results of this analysis suggest that rather than being determined by a generalized "scene" like the Manipulative Activity Scene (see also Ninio's, 1999, findings on verbs expressing "object relations" as "pathbreaking verbs"), the Transitivity parameters that children come to use in a particular situation, and possibly the orientation that children take to an event at the moment of speaking, may be shaped by the pragmatic uses they themselves put their language toward, which in turn may derive from the language that they hear spoken around them in that situation, and by the socialization influences and ideologies that they are exposed to in their language community (Ochs & Schieffelin, 1984).

In conclusion, the results of this study suggest that there may be an ideologically preferred speech act (Gordon & Ervin-Tripp, 1984) to use, as well as an ideologically preferred "viewing arrangement" (see Langacker, 2001, p. 16) to take on events in a particular setting (e.g., in peer disputes) as viewed by those in the language community surrounding the child. The results also suggest that the adults use language in a way that encodes these favored speech acts and viewpoints (see also Duranti & Ochs, 1996), and that adults' language use determines how young children themselves encode events for the act of speaking and use speech acts and parameters of Transitivity in that setting. The children in this study were certainly familiar with more Accusing Statements that carried parameters of high Transitivity, that would have allowed them to emphasize their provocateur's completed action and its bad effect on an affected object, as they used such statements in a small proportion of the cases, but in general, they preferred using Perspective Statements and statements that carried parameters of low Transitivity, which allowed them to focus instead on their own internal feelings, desires, words, or ongoing activities. Even when they discussed others' kinetic actions, they took a perspective (non-completed, without emphasizing affectedness of an object) that emphasized how things seemed to them from inside the event. The idea that speakers take a preferred viewpoint on events within specific contexts and for specific purposes and acts of speaking is very much in alignment with Slobin's idea of "thinking for speaking." It is very important to keep in mind, however, that the viewpoint that is taken, both by the community of speakers, and by the children themselves, may be very different in another context. Although the current study extended the range of contexts in which young children's use of verb constructions and parameters of Transitivity have been studied to include the context of children interacting with their peers in disputes, more needs to be done. An important direction for future research is to study the same children's language development longitudinally, across a range of carefully defined discourse contexts.

REFERENCES

Antinucci, F., & Miller, R. (1976). How children talk about what happened. *Journal of Child Language, 3*, 167–189.

Berman, R., & Slobin, D. I. (1994). *Relating events in narrative.* Hillsdale, NJ: Lawrence Erlbaum Associates.

Bowerman, M. (1996). The origins of children's spatial semantic categories: cognitive vs. linguistic determinants. In J. J. Gumperz & S. C. Levinson (Eds.), *Rethinking linguistic relativity* (pp. 145–175). Cambridge, UK: Cambridge University Press.

Budwig, N. (1995). *A developmental-functionalist approach to child language.* Mahwah, NJ: Lawrence Erlbaum Associates.

Budwig, N. (1996). What influences children's patterning of forms and functions in early child language? In D. I. Slobin, J. Gerhardt, A. Kyratzis, & J. Guo (Eds.), *Social interaction, social context, and language: Essays in honor of Susan Ervin-Tripp* (pp. 143–156). Mahwah, NJ: Lawrence Erlbaum Associates.

Budwig, N., Stein, S., & O'Brien, C. (2001). Non-agent subjects in early child language: A crosslinguistic comparison. In K. Nelson, A. Aksu-Koc, & C. Johnson (Eds.), *Children's language: Vol. 11. Interactional contributions to language development* (pp. 49–67). Mahwah, NJ: Lawrence Erlbaum Associates.

Clancy, P. (2004). The discourse basis of constructions: Some evidence from Korean. In E. Clark (Ed.), *Proceedings of the 32nd Stanford Child Language Research Forum*. Stanford, CA: CSLI Publications.

Cook-Gumperz, J., & Kyratzis, A. (2001). Pretend play: Trial ground for the simple present. In M. Putz, S. Niemeier, & R. Dirven (Eds.), *Applied cognitive linguistics: I. Theory and language acquisition* (pp. 41–61). Berlin: Mouton de Gruyter.

Duranti, A., & Ochs, E. (1996). Use and acquisition of genitive constructions in Samoan. In D. I. Slobin, J. Gerhardt, A. Kyratzis, & J. Guo (Eds.), *Social interaction, social context, and language: Essays in honor of Susan Ervin-Tripp,* (pp. 175–189). Mahwah, NJ: Lawrence Erlbaum Associates.

Ervin, S. M., & Miller, W. (1964). The development of grammar in child language. *Monographs of the Society for Research in Child Development 29*, 9–34.

Ervin-Tripp, S. M. (1993). Constructing syntax from discourse. In E. V. Clark (Ed.), *Proceedings of the twenty-fifth annual Child Language Research Forum*. Stanford, CA: Center for the Study of Language and Information.

Ervin-Tripp, S. M. (1996). Context in language. In D. I. Slobin, J. Gerhardt, A. Kyratzis, & J. Guo (Eds.), *Social interaction, social context, and language: Essays in honor of Susan Ervin-Tripp* (pp. 21–36). Mahwah, NJ: Lawrence Erlbaum Associates.

Gee, J., & Savasir, I. (1985). On the use of *will* and *gonna*: Towards a description of activity-types for child language. *Discourse Processes, 8*, 143–175.

Gerber, M., & Johnson, A. (1998). *Your self-confident baby: How to encourage your child's natural abilities—from the very start*. New York: John Wiley & Sons.

Gonzalez-Mena, J., & Eyer, D. W. (2001). *Infants, toddlers, and caregivers: A curriculum of respectful, responsive care and education* (6th ed.) Boston: McGraw-Hill.

Gordon, D. P., & Ervin-Tripp, S. M. (1984). The structure of children's requests. In R. L. Schiefelbusch & J. Pickar (Eds.), *The acquisition of communicative competence* (pp. 295–322). Baltimore: University Park Press.

Gumperz, J. J., & Levinson, S. C. (1996). Introduction to part III. In J. J. Gumperz & S. C. Levinson, (Eds.), *Rethinking linguistic relativity* (pp. 225–231). Cambridge, UK: Cambridge University Press.

Gvozdev, A. N. (1949). *Formirovanie u rebenka grammatičeskogo stroja russkogo jazyka*. Moscow: Izd-vo Akademii Pedagogičeskix Nauk RSFSR. [Reprinted in A.N. Gvozdev (1961), *Voprosy izučenija detskoj reči* (pp. 149–467). Moscow: Izd-vo Akademii Pedagogičeskix Nauk RSFSR.]

Hopper, P. J. (1991). Dispersed verbal predicates in vernacular writing. *Berkeley Linguistics Society 17*, 402–413.

Hopper, P. J. (1997). Discourse and the category 'verb' in English. *Language and Communication, 17*(2), 93–102.

Hopper, P. J., & Thompson, S. A. (1980). Transitivity in grammar and discourse, *Language, 56*(2), 251–299.

Kuntay, A., & Slobin, D. I. (2002). Putting interaction back into child language: Examples from Turkish. *Psychology of Language and Communication, 6*, 5–14.

Langacker, R. W. (2001). Cognitive linguistics, language pedagogy, and the English present tense. In M. Putz, S. Niemeier, & R. Dirven (Eds.), *Applied cognitive linguistics: Theory and language acquisition* (I, pp. 3–39). Berlin: Mouton de Gruyter.

Lakoff, G., & Johnson, M. (1980). *Metaphors we live by*. Chicago: University of Chicago Press.

MacWhinney, B. J. (1973). *How Hungarian children learn to speak*. Unpublished doctoral dissertation. University of California, Berkeley.

Ninio, A. (1999). Pathbreaking verbs in syntactic development and the question of prototypical transitivity. *Journal of Child Language, 26*, 619–653.

Ochs, E., & Schieffelin, B. B. (1984). Language acquisition and socialization: Three developmental stories. In R. Shweder & R. LeVine (Eds.), *Culture theory: Essays in mind, self, and emotion* (pp. 276–320). Cambridge, UK: Cambridge University Press.

Rowland, C. F., Pine, J. M., Lieven, E. V., & Theakston, A. L. (2003). Determinants of acquisition order in wh-questions: Re-evaluating the role of caregiver speech. *Journal of Child Language, 30*, 609–635.

Savarnejad, A. (2003). *Conflict strategies in very young children*. Unpublished master's thesis, University of California, Santa Barbara.

Savasir, I. (1983). *How many futures?* Unpublished M.A. dissertation, University of California, Berkeley, Department of Psychology.

Savasir, I., & Gee, J. (1982). The functional equivalents of the middle voice in child language. *Proceedings of the Berkeley Linguistics Society, 8*, 607–616.

Schieffelin, B. B. (1985). The acquisition of Kaluli. In D. I. Slobin (Ed.), *The crosslinguistic study of language acquisition: Vol. 1. The data* (pp. 525–593). Hillsdale, NJ: Lawrence Erlbaum Associates.

Slobin, D. I. (1979). *Psycholinguistics* (2nd ed.). Glenview, IL: Scott Foresman, & Co.

Slobin, D. I. (1981). The origins of grammatical encoding of events. In W. Deutsch (Ed.), *The child's construction of language* (pp. 185–200). New York: Academic Press.

Slobin, D. I. (1985). Crosslinguistic evidence for the language-making capacity. In D. I. Slobin (Ed.), *The crosslinguistic study of language acquisition: Vol. 2. Theoretical issues* (pp. 1157–1256). Hillsdale, NJ: Lawrence Erlbaum Associates.

Slobin, D. I. (1996). From "thought and language" to "thinking for speaking." In J. J. Gumperz & S. C. Levinson (Eds.), *Rethinking linguistic relativity* (pp. 70–96). Cambridge, UK: Cambridge University Press.

Slobin, D. I. (2003). Language and thought online: Cognitive consequences of linguistic relativity. In D. Gentner & S. Goldin-Meadow (Eds.), *Language in mind: Advances in the investigation of language and thought* (pp. 157–192). Cambridge, MA: The MIT Press.

Slobin, D. I. (2004). Research overview. http://ihd.berkeley.edu/slobres.pdf.

Thompson, S. A., & Hopper, P. J. (2001). Transitivity, clause structure, and argument structure: Evidence from conversation. In J. Bybee & P. Hopper (Eds.), *Frequency and the emergence of linguistic structure* (pp. 27–60). Amsterdam: John Benjamins.

Direction and Perspective in German Child Language

HEIKE BEHRENS
University of Basel, Switzerland

The basic claim is that if a domain is elaborated in linguistic expression, users of that language will continually attend to and elaborate that domain cognitively.

Dan I. Slobin (2006, p. 99)

INTRODUCTION

The encoding of motion events has been one of Dan Slobin's most prominent topics over the past two decades. He and his collaborators analyzed cognitive and linguistic partitioning of motion events in a number of languages and took Len Talmy's (1985) distinction between verb-framed and satellite-framed languages as a point of departure. Verb-framed languages encode semantic information about the path of motion in the verb stem; satellite-framed languages use verb-related particles or affixes for the semantic encoding instead (e.g., *come out, drive in*). The effect of this typological divide on language processing and language acquisition was shown for children's narratives in the famous *Frog Stories* (Berman & Slobin, 1994), as well as for adults' rhetorical style, or literary translations (e.g., Slobin, 1996b, 2006). Moreover, these typological differences in dividing the conceptual space seem to account for differences in non-linguistic cognition like attention and memory, mental imagery, and gesture (Slobin, 1997, 2003, 2008). In short, we think for speaking (Slobin, 1996a): the language we speak guides our attention, and we need to arrange our mental representations such that we can easily activate them for linguistic encoding.

German is one of the languages investigated by Slobin and colleagues and is prominently satellite framed. About 20% of the verb tokens produced by children or adults are particle or prefix verbs (Behrens, 1998, 2003). Particles encode not only spatial, but also temporal information. In addition, many particle verbs have taken on abstract meanings. But apart from directional information like *up, down,* or *into*, German particles have another unique, but much less studied, feature: they can encode the perspective of the direction, whether it is toward the deictic center (*her* 'hither') or whether it is away from the deictic center (*hin* 'thither') (1a,b). *Hin* and *her* can form complex particles in combination with other directional particles (2a,b).

(1) a. Er geht zum Baum hin.
 'He goes to the tree thither.'
 b. Er kommt vom Baum her.

'He comes from the tree hither.'
(2) a. Er geht zur Tür hinaus.
'He goes to the door thither-out-of.'
b. Er kommt zur Tür herein.
'He comes to the door hither-into."

How and when do German children acquire this typologically rather rare distinction? Does the existence of these particles enhance a heightened sensitivity for deixis? The idea for this chapter originated in the mid-1990s in Nijmegen, when Dan Slobin, Melissa Bowerman, and I had a conversation on German particle verbs. Dan Slobin insisted that that German has a *hither–thither* distinction, which quite surprised me as a native speaker of German. Of course, I was aware of the lexical items, but I was unaware of the perspectival difference they encoded. Later, when I studied particle verbs more closely as a visiting scholar at Berkeley, I was relieved to find out that my lack of intuition is presumably due to the fact I am from Northern Germany, where this distinction is less common than in the more Southern parts.

THE SYSTEM OF GERMAN DIRECTIONAL AND PERSPECTIVAL PARTICLE VERBS

While inseparable prefix verbs like *belong* or *undo* are attested in all Germanic languages, separable particle verbs emerged in Old High German. Since the Early New High German period, German allows for double particles (Harnisch, 1982, p. 111; cf. also Leden, 1982, p. 184). Directional particles can be combined with either *hin* or *her* to mark source- or goal-oriented deixis (see 2 above), or with *dr-* (a short form of *da* 'there' to emphasize the endstate of the movement (3).

(3) *Er packt es auf den Tisch drauf.*
'He puts it onto the table there-onto.'

Not all combinations are possible with a locative reading. For example, *dr-aus* makes no sense because there is no endstate if one takes something out. The system with *hin* or *her* is less constrained, especially with verbs with a medium degree of specificity (Eichinger, 1989, p. 30ff.). Eichinger analyzed the combinations of complex particles with *hin/her* in the *Duden German Dictionary* and found that those motion verbs that have flexible orientation have the fewest constraints. While there seem to be few constraints regarding combination with double particles, there are preferences (Eichinger, 1989, p. 54; see Henzen, 1969, p. 282 ff. for lists of verbs that only take *hin* or *her*). *Hin* particles appear to be more frequent than *her* because speakers more frequently encode events that are oriented away from the deictic origo than verbs that are oriented towards the deictic origo (Eichinger, 1989, p. 75ff).

But the *hin/her* distinction is not always realized. In Northern Germany, speakers use a shortened *r*-form instead (*hin-auf* and *her-auf* become *r-auf* 'onto.' Shortening is attested in Southern Germany as well, but here speakers tend to use *n*-forms, e.g., *n-auf, n-ein*). In the shortened forms, the directional distinction is neutralized. Thus, these particles leave open whether the direction is hither or thither.

German thus has a fivefold system of directional and perspectival particle verbs:

Simple Particles

a) *auf* 'on,' *unter-* 'under,' *über-* 'over,' ...
b) *hin-* 'away from deictic center'/'thither,' *her-* 'toward deictic center'/ 'hither'

Double Particles

c) *hin-/her-* plus *auf/ab/an/unter/über*....
d) *r- / n-* plus *auf/ab/*....
e) *dr-* plus *auf/unter/*....

A look at the literature shows that although there is some systematicity, the domain of these combinatorial particles shows highly idiosyncratic or verb-specific semantics. Their syntax is complicated as well. Sometimes these elements fill argument positions of the simplex verb (4a), sometimes they are adjuncts (4b) which can be used in addition to the prepositional argument in a pleonastic construction (4c); Olsen 1999). Also, the placement of the particle can lead to meaning differences (cf. Zintl, 1982, p. 138).

(4) a. *Er packt es unter den Tisch*
'He puts it under the table.'
b. *Er packt es drunter.*
'He puts it there-under.'
c. *Er packt es unter den Tisch drunter.*
'He puts it under the table there-under.'

The *hin-/her-*, *r-/n-*, and *dr-*particles can replace the encoding of the target destination because their meaning entails goal or source information. Engelen (1995, p. 242) argues that these particle verbs are found in spoken rather than written language. If the source or goal is clear from the context, it is communicatively adequate to just use particle verbs without further specification by adverbs or prepositional phrases. Their dominance in spoken language may explain why these particles are hardly discussed at all in German grammars, although they pose a major problem for second language learners of German (Engelen, 1995, p. 242). Eisenberg (1998) discusses the directionality of *hin/her* in a footnote; the 1995 edition of the Duden-grammar devoted half a page to *hin* and *her* and the revised, and extended 2005 edition did not add information. Likewise, the three-volume grammar published by the "Institut für deutsche Sprache" (Zifonum, Hoffmann & Strecker, 1997) just provides a short list of such particles and mentions that they encode deixis. Helbig and Buscha (2002) in their grammar for second language learners do not give any information on the meaning of these particles.

Of course, there are several studies on directional particles in German. But due to the intricacies of this linguistic domain, they tend to focus on a particular semantic aspect and/or a restricted number of verbs or particles. A comprehensive survey of the possible combinations and their semantics is lacking. The present article does not attempt to fill this void, but investigates instead the frequency of this phenomenon in an extensive corpus of German child language. The aim is to find out how frequent and contrastive this system is in children's language.

THE DATA

Analyses are based on a 870,000 word corpus of the language development of six German children. They were recorded for various periods and with different sampling frequency (see Table 4.1). The Simone and Kerstin data (Miller, 1976) are available through the CHILDES network (MacWhinney, 2002). The data for Pauline, Sebastian, and Cosima where made available through Rosemarie Rigol; and the Leo corpus was collected at the MPI for Evolutionary Anthropology in Leipzig (Behrens, 2006).

The data were transcribed in a common format devised by the author. The morphosyntactic coding scheme paid particular attention to verb-particle constructions, and included identification of all particle verb constructions that were syntactically separated (Behrens, 2003). This coding allows for

TABLE 4.1 Data

Child	Source	Age Range	Word Tokens
Leo	Leipzig	1;11–4;11	495,667
Simone	Miller	1;9–4;0	85,786
Kerstin	Miller	1;3–3;9	54,938
Pauline	Rigol	0;0–7;11	84,786
Sebastian	Rigol	0;0–7;4	74,493
Cosima	Rigol	0;0–7;3	80,693
N=Words			**876,363**

the extraction of all verbs and their morphological properties, including particle verbs, even when they occur in discontinuous form. To increase legibility, all utterances are transcribed in standard orthography and markers of disfluencies, etc., were removed. The only symbols used here are round brackets to indicate segments that were not spoken, "#" to mark pauses or other types of hesitation, and "xxx" to mark segments that could not be transcribed.

In a first step, the relative frequency of directional particle verbs is established, and the rank order in the emergence of such verbs is compared across children. In a second step, qualitative analyses are carried out. Here, error analyses reveal semantic misanalyses of the German particle system. In addition, searches for complex paths and pleonastic constructions, i.e., constructions where children use particles and prepositions to encode the same path (e.g., *er geht durch den Wald hindurch* 'he goes through the woods thither-through') are carried out in order to investigate the degree of complexity children reach in their usage of these particles.

QUANTITATIVE ANALYSES

Proportion of Particle Verbs With hin- and her-

In a first analysis, I computed the proportion of verbs with *hin-* and *her-*particles as compared to the proportion of reduced *r*-forms (Table 4.2). Recall that it is possible for double particles to reduce the *hin-* and *her*-forms to *r-* when the second element starts with a vowel, e.g., *heraus* or *hinaus* become *raus* (*n*-forms were extracted as well but they play only a very marginal role and are not considered here). The reduction to *r-* or *n*-forms neutralizes the directional distinction. For the first analysis, the proportion of *r*-particle verbs and *hin-/her*-particle verbs was computed as a proportion of particle verbs in total (see Table 4.2). The ordering of the children reflects increases in both the age range covered and in sample size. For this analysis, the concrete utterances were not checked as to whether they encode motion events only. However, in this early phase of language development it is not likely that children use more abstract meanings with high frequency.

TABLE 4.2 Token Frequency of Directional Particles[1]

	Verb Tokens	Particle Verb Tokens	*r*-Tokens (% of particle verb tokens)	*hin-/her*-Tokens (% of particle verb tokens)
Kerstin	6,875	1,554	228 (15%)	186 (12%)
Simone	11,959	2,439	480 (20%)	142 (6%)
Pauline	10,131	1,958	394 (20%)	240 (12%)
Leo	54,684	13,657	2278 (17%)	734 (5%)

[1] The quantitative analyses could not be carried out for Cosima and Sebastian because their data are not fully coded yet.

TABLE 4.3 Number of Verb Stems (Types) With Particles

	Verb Stems (Types) With Particles	Verb Stems (Types) With r-Particles	Verb Stems (Types) With hin- or her-Particles	Verb Stems (Types) With hin- and her-Particles
Kerstin	75	23	14	2
Simone	135	65	20	4
Pauline	189	67	26	5
Leo	514	202	92	19

While the children differ in the relative proportion of *r-* versus *hin-/her-* particle verbs, their combined frequency falls within a rather narrow range of between 22% (Leo) and 32% (Pauline) of all particle verb tokens. That is, about a quarter to one third of all particle verbs show a morphological marker of directionality or perspective. But there are individual differences as well: Simone and Leo use relatively fewer *hin-* and *her-*forms (1% and 1.3% of all verb tokens) than Pauline (2.3%) and Kerstin (2.7%).

If we collapse the data from all four children, we find that *hin-*verbs are much more frequent than *her-*verbs (1013 tokens versus 291 tokens). However, the number of verb types does not differ much: Altogether, there are 110 different *hin-*verbs in the corpus as compared to 95 *her-*verbs. It can be concluded that *hin-*verbs have a lower type-token ratio, i.e., the individual verbs are used more frequently. In addition, more *hin-*verbs occur as unseparated morphological units, whereas *her-*verbs tend to be syntactically separated: In German syntax, separable particle verbs show the verb-second effect when they are finite (e.g., "wo kommst du her?" 'where come you hither?"). Only 40% of all *hin-*verbs, but 64% of the *her-*verbs occur in constructions where they are separated. These figures confirm findings in the literature that *hin-*verbs are more frequent and more lexicalized than *her-*verbs (Eichinger, 1989).

Table 4.3 lists the number of verb stems for each child that occur with particles (Column 1). To further differentiate particle use, the number of verb stems with a marker of directionality (*r-*particles, Column 2) and perspective (*hin-/her-*particles, Column 3) was computed. Again, sample size has a big effect here as smaller samples will yield less type variation (see below). But even in the smallest sample (Kerstin), more than a dozen verb stems occur with *hin-/her-*particles, and 23 with *r-*particles (note that many verbs can occur with both types of particles, hence the set of verb stems may be overlapping). In the largest sample of Leo there are 92 and 202 verb stems, respectively. In order to investigate how many verbs occur with a marker of either perspective, reverse concordances were extracted from the data. With this method, the lexicon is alphabetized from the end of the words such that all items with the same root but different prefixes occur together in the list (Column 4).

It is not surprising that the number of different verb stems varies greatly with sample size, since the likelihood of capturing low-frequency elements increases with sample size (see Tomasello & Stahl, 2004, for a general discussion of the relationship between sample size and chance of sampling relevant exemplars; and Malvern, Richards, Chipere, & Duran, 2004, for similar issues regarding the measurement of lexical development and diversity). However, we can conclude from these figures that at least one third, if not half, of all verb stems that occur with particles occur with a marker of directionality and/or perspective. For all children, the number of verbs that occur with *r-*particles is about 2 to 3 times higher than the number of verbs that occur with *hin-* or *her-*particles. But the mere occurrence of *hin-* and *her-*forms does not provide evidence for their productivity, as they could simply be lexically specific, i.e. tied to particular verb stems. Therefore, I examined how many verb stems were attested with *her-* as well as with *hin-* (Column 4). In (5) the verb stems that occur with both *hin-* and *her-*particles are listed together with the particles they occur with. For some verbs, the contrast may seem surprising because the verb stem itself denotes direction (e.g., *come, bring*). But recall that *hither* and *thither* denote direction to the *deictic* origo which can be different from the speaker. It is thus possible to bring something thither (= to me, the speaker) and hither (to the addressee, for example), or to come thither (to me, the speaker) or hither (to the addressee or another specified location). In terms of morphological complexity, all children use simple as well as double perspectival particles. The verb roots are verbs of motion (locomotion or putting), as well as verbs of looking and transfer.

(5) Verb stems that occur with both *hin-* and *her-*particles

Kerstin: (hinein-, her-)gucken 'look,' (hin-, herunter-)fallen 'fall'
Simone: (hin-, her-)bringen 'bring,' (hin-, her-, heraus-)kommen 'come,' (hin-, her-, herum-)fahren 'drive,' (hin-, her-)schauen 'look'
Pauline: (hin-, her-)kriegen 'get, receive," (hin-, hinein-, herein-)gehen 'go,' (hin-, her-) ziehen 'pull,' (hin-, hinein-, her-)kommen 'come,' (hin-, her-)fahren 'drive'
Leo:[†] (hinauf-, herum-, hinein-, herein-, hin-und-her-, hin-, hernunter²-) schieben 'push,' (herum-, hin-, hinunter-, hinein-)laufen 'run,' (hinein-, herein-, her-und-hin-, hin-, herum-, herunter-, hinaus-)fliegen 'fly,' (herab-, hin-)hängen 'hang,' (hin-, her-)bringen 'bring,' (herum-, hin-, hernunter-,² hernaus-,² heraus-)machen 'make,' (hinauf-, hinein-, hin-und-rein-, hin-, hinunter-, herunter-, hervor-, heraus-) gehen 'go,' (hinauf-, hinter-her-, hin-und-her-, heraus-)ziehen 'pull,' (hinein-, hin-, her-, hervor-, heraus-, herunter-) gucken 'look, watch,' (hinein-, hin-, hinunter-, herunter-, hinaus-, heraus-)fallen 'fall,' (hin-, her-, hinein-, hinunter-, hinaus-)stellen 'put standing,' (her-, hin-)rollen 'roll,' (herauf-, her-, hervor-, heraus-, herunter-, hinaus-)holen 'fetch,' (hinein-, herein-, hin-, hinterher-, her-, hervor-, heraus-, hinauf-, heran-, herunter-)kommen 'come,' (hinauf-, hindurch-, herum-, hinein-, hin-, hinterher-, her-, hinunter-, hernunter-,² hernein-,² herunter-, hinaus-, heraus-, hindurch-) fahren 'drive,' (hinunter-, hin-, heraus-)schmei-ßen 'throw,' (hin-, herum-) bauen 'build,' (hin-, her-, herunter-, hinaus-, hernaus-,² hervor-) schauen 'look,' (hin-, herunter-, hinauf-, herauf-, hinein-)klettern 'climb'

Emergence of Perspectival Particle Verbs

Since all children use verbs with *hin-* and *her-*, is it possible to find a "basic vocabulary" of such verbs that (a) are acquired early and (b) are shared between children? To this end the first ten verbs with *hin-* and *her-* were extracted. Table 4.4 shows the rank order and age of first mention.

Most children develop their inventory shortly after the second birthday. Only Kerstin and Sebastian show an increase about half a year later, between 2;7 and 2;11. This may be a trend (for Kerstin, seven new verbs are attested at 2;7), or it may be due to sampling. When Sebastian shows his peak after 2;7, the new forms are used in advanced syntactic constructions.

Two verbs are used early by all children (*hinsetzen* 'sit thither' 'sit down,' *hinlegen* 'lie/lay thither'), another one by four children (*hinstellen* 'put thither standing'). Again, that we do not find more overlap can be due to sampling. A look at the verb stems shows, however, that they are basic verbs of motion like *go, drive, fly,* verbs of putting, verbs of looking, and verbs of belonging (*fit*). There are currently no studies with frequency information on these verbs in adult corpora of spoken language, but it seems likely that many of these verbs are high-frequency verbs that are highly lexicalized (e.g., *hinsetzen, hinlegen, hinschmeissen*) with their counterpart being low frequency. In other words, it has yet to be investigated whether these verbs are part of productive pairs with varying perspectives, or just goal- or source-oriented lexicalized "singletons."

In sum, the quantitative analyses show that German children acquire verbs with perspectival particles (early) in their third year of life. In the naturalistic data many of these particles are attested earlier than in the narrative Frog Story data (Bamberg & Marchman, 1994, p. 221). For most

---

[2] Note that *hinkriegen* does not have a motion, but an abstract meaning ('to achieve something')
[3] Some of the particles Leo uses are marked with an asterisk because they are his own creations.

TABLE 4.4   Rank Order and Age of First Occurrence of Verbs With *hin-* and *her-*

Leo	Simone	Kerstin	Pauline	Cosima	Sebastian
hinstellen 'put thither standing' 2;0	*hingehen* 'go thither' 1;10	*hinsetzen* 'sit thither' 1;11	*hinlegen* 'lie/lay thither' 1;11	*hinsetzen* 'sit thither' 1;8	*hinhängen* 'hang thither' 2;6
hinsetzen 'sit thither' 2;0	*hinstellen* 'put thither' 1;10	*herkommen* 'come hither' 2;0	*hineinsetzen* 'place into thither' 1;11	*hineintun* 'put into thither' 2;1	*hinlegen* 'lie/lay thither' 2;7
hinfallen 'fall thither' 2;0	*hinsetzen* 'sit down' 1;11	*hingehen* 'go thither' 2;2	*hingehen* 'go thither' 1;11	*hinstellen* 'put thither standing' 2;3	*heraushüpfen* 'jump out of hither' 2;7
hergucken 'look hither' 2;1	*herkommen* 'come hither' 2;0	*hergucken* 'look hither' 2;7	*hinsetzen* 'sit thither' 2;0	*hinlegen* 'lie/lay thither' 2;4	*hineinfahren* 'drive into thither' 2;8
hingucken 'look thither' 2;1	*hinfahren* 'drive thither' 2;0	*hineingucken* 'look into thither' 2;7	*hineinkommen* 'come into thither' 2;2	*hinfallen* 'fall thither' 2;4	*hinwerfen* 'throw thither' 2;8
hinlegen 'lie/lay thither' 2;1	*hinstellen* 'put thither standing' 2;0	*hineintun* 'put into thither' 2;7	*hinlegen* 'lie/lay thither' 2;2	*hinschütten* 'heap up thither' 2;9	*hinsetzen* 'sit thither' 2;8
hinmachen 'make/place thither' 2;2	*hinlegen* 'lie/lay down' 2;0	*herunterfallen* 'fall down hither' 2;7	*hinschmeissen* 'throw thither' 2;2	*hingehen* 'go thither' 2;9	*hinfahren* 'drive thither' 2;9
herholen 'fetch hither' 2;2	*herauskommen* 'come out of thither' 2;0	*hinstellen* 'put thither standing' 2;7	*herziehen* 'pull hither' 2;3	*hinauskommen* 'come out of thither' 2;9	*hinbringen* 'bring thither' 2;9
hinkommen 'come/belong thither' 2;2	*hinfallen* 'fall thither' 2;1	*hinkommen* 'come hither' 2;7	*hinpassen* 'fit thither' 2;3	*hinwerfen* 'throw thither' 2;9	*hinhängen* 'hang thither' 2;11
hinfahren 'drive thither' 2;2	*hinfliegen* 'fly thither' 2;2	*hinlegen* 'lay down thither' 2;7	*hingehören* 'belong thither' 2;4	*hinkommen* 'come/belong thither' 2;10	*hingehen* 'go thither' 2;11

children, the quantitative data regarding type frequency and variation are inconclusive regarding the productivity of perspectival particles. Only the dense database of Leo provides a substantial number of verbs that are used with contrastive perspectival particles.

QUALITATIVE ANALYSES

Apart from frequency information, there are qualitative analyses to assess the degree of mastery with linguistic structures. In the following, I will present two analyses regarding the linguistic and conceptual path information. I extract from the data examples that show pleonastic encoding of the same path, and examples that encode complex paths within one clause. The reason for choosing the former is that the possibility for pleonastic encoding of paths by both a particle and a prepositional phrase is a particular feature of German (Olsen, 1996, 1999; cf. example 4c above): here, prepositional phrase and particle encode the same information. The reason for choosing the latter is to investigate whether young children are able to encode complex conceptual information in a condensed way by making use of the differential information in the preposition and the particle.

But first, the data will be screened for errors regarding the use of *hin* and *her*. Error analyses provide a window for productivity because we can assume that these constructions are not just rote learned.

Error Analysis

Real errors are hard to find because *hin* and *her* encode deictic perspective. In many contexts, both perspectives can be construed, even if they seem atypical. There is one such error from Cosima (6) and several from Leo (7).

(6) Cosima 2;10.14 *Wirf es mir mal hin.*
'Throw it me PT thither.
'Throw it towards me.'

Since Cosima specifies herself as the goal of the throwing, the correct particle would be *her*, not *hin*. This example can be interpreted as non-productive overgeneralization of the more frequent verb *hinwerfen* to the less common *herwerfen*. It is not clear whether she really understands the perspectival shift. Similar mismatches between the location of the subject of the clause and the direction of the deictic particle are attested for Leo (7).

(7) Directional mismatches for perspectival particles: Leo

Leo 2;5.22	*xxx Das Krokodil will eine Sandburg machen [?] heraufklettern.*
	'The crocodile wants a sand-castle make – climb- up-hither.'
Leo 2;6.08	*Die kommt vom Tunnel hinaus .*
	'It comes from tunnel thither-out.'
Leo 2;6.14	*Die kommt aus ‹m Tunnel hinaus.*
	'It comes out of the tunnel thither-out.'
Leo 2;10.08	*Und bald kam es aus den Tunnel hinaus.*
	'And soon it came from the tunnel thither-out.'
Leo 2;10.08	*Und bald kamen es aus den Tunnel hinaus.*
	'And soon came it from the tunnel thither-out.'
Leo 2;10.24	*Ich schiebe xxx die # Krabben wieder # herein.*
	'I push xxx the crabs again hither-into.'
Leo 2;11.13	*Ich habe ihn aus der Kiste hinausgeholt.*
	'I have it from the box thither-out-fetched.'
Leo 2;10.10	*Ha , also öffnete xxx Fenster xxx und blickte hinaus in das Fenster xxx.*
	'Ha! So opened xxx window xxx and looked thither-out into the window xxx.'

In addition, there are creative coinages of new forms. In (8), the perspective is correct, but the common way of phrasing is *auswählen* 'select out,' not *herauswählen*.

(8) Leo 2;8.7 *Wählt euch irgendeine Farbe heraus.*
Select REFL any color hither-out.
'Choose/pick any color.'

Most striking, though, are Leo's repeated blends of *hin* and *her* particles to a nonstandard *hern-* form (see the list of items above in (5)). Between 2;9 and 2;10 there are nine such examples. These blends encode both directions, *hither* (9) and *thither* (10).

(9) *hern*-blends to encode *hin* 'thither'

Leo 2;9.7	*Wieder herneingefahren in der Rakete.*
	'Again thither-into-drove in the rocket.'
Leo 2;9.19	*Ja, du schaust hernaus.*
	'Yes, you look out-thither.'

(10) *hern*-blends to encode *her* 'hither'

Leo 2;9.5	*Da kommt er dann hiernunter und da xx er wieder hoch.*
	'There he comes then here-down-hither and there he xx up again.'
Leo 2;9.5	*Und da wird er wieder hernuntergeschoben.*
	and there he is being pushed down-hither
Leo 2;9.7	*Wieder # hernausgefallen.*
	'Again fell-out-hither.'

These different types of errors and especially the creative new forms show that Leo is insecure about the *hin-/her*-system in the age range between 2;6 and 2;10. Such phases of insecurity and errors are usually taken to indicate that the system is restructuring. But the examples also show that it is quite hard to assess the underlying representation from naturalistic data. Even if examples look odd at first, it is often possible to construe a matching scenario, and the context information is usually not specific enough to rule out particular readings.

Pleonastic Constructions

In German, directional and perspectival particles can be used in addition to prepositions that specify the same direction. In this sense they are pleonastic because the same direction is encoded twice (Olsen, 1999). It is also possible that the prepositional phrase(s) or adverbials and the particles specify different directions in order to encode complex paths. In the following sections I will study the emergence of pleonastic constructions and complex paths.

First pleonastic constructions encoding the *into*-direction can be found as early as 2;4 (Examples 11a–c), but the examples also show that Leo has not mastered the construction. In Example (11a) Leo uses the wrong perspective (it should be *hin-*, not *her-*), and in Example (11c) the preposition is omitted.

(11) a. Leo 2;4.18   *Fliegt in Wasser herein.*
        'Flies in water hither-in.'
    b. Leo 2;4.19   *Die [Bahn]fährt in Tunnel hinein.* (2 times)
        'It [the train] drives in the tunnel into-thither.'
    c. Leo 2;4.23   *Der [Zug] fährt Tunnel hinein,*
        'It drives tunnel into-thither.'

The next example (12) occurs a month later, but remains an isolated example. Only at 2;7 do we find more pleonastic constructions (13) as well as first complex paths (see Example (16) below). The examples under (13) show that by age 2;8, the pleonastic construction is not limited to a single spatial dimension, but open to various directions (*out of, around, at/toward*).

(12) Leo 2;5.28   *… aus Düsenflugzeug kommt was heraus.*
    'Out-of steamjet comes something out-of-hither.'
(13) Leo 2;8.1   *Frederik kommt nich(t) aus 'M Mausefalle+Käfig heraus.*
    'Frederic comes not out of the mouse-trap out-of-hither.'
    Leo 2;8.1   *Du bist in den Wald hineingelaufen, um den Baum zu besteigen.*
    'You ran into the wood into-thither in order to climb the tree.'
    Leo 2;8.27   *Der Mond krei(st) um die Erde einmal herum.*
    'The moon circles around the earth one-time hither-around.'
    Leo 2;8.29   *Um an den Butterkeks heranzukommen*
    in-order-to at the cookie hither-at-get
    'In order to reach the cookie.'

Pleonastic paths with *hin* or *her* are not attested for Kerstin, Pauline, and Sebastian. Cosima produced an example at 4;11 (14), and Simone at 3;7 and 3;9 (15).

(14) Cosima 4;11.24   *Jetzt laufen wir um den Baum herum.*
'Now we run around the tree hither-around.'
(15) Simone 3;7.07   *Alle kommen jetzt mal aus (de)m Bett heraus.*
'And now all of you come out of the bed hither-out.'
Simone 3;9.18   *… der hat sein Fuß hineingesetzt in die Kuh.*
'He has thither-into-put his foot into the cow.'

All of these examples occur substantially later than those in the Leo-corpus. In order to check whether these children use pleonastic constructions at all, the search was extended to the more frequent *r-* particles. Here, the first examples where found between age 2;4 for Simone and 2;11 for Pauline. This is close to the age range in which we find pleonastic *hin-/her*-constructions for Leo. No example was found for Cosima. However, because her data are not fully coded the search could not be formulated as precisely as for the other children.

The examples for this construction type are few, and the isolated occurrences may not indicate the age of emergence. Nonetheless, the examples demonstrate that pleonastic constructions are a feature of German child language. We cannot draw conclusions, however, as to whether pleonastic constructions with *hin-/her*-particles are not produced by some children at all (perhaps because they are rare or unattested in the input), or whether they are simply missed due to low sampling density.

Complex Paths

Under the notion "complex path" I will discuss utterances that show "clause compacting" (Slobin, 1996b: 202), i.e., several segments of a path are encoded within a clause, rather than chained in different clauses. There are numerous examples for all children of complex syntactic constructions where prepositional phrases are used in addition to complex particles to encode the source or goal of the movement, or the means of transportation. And as shown in the previous section, prepositions are used to encode the same path that is already encoded by the particle. In the data we find several examples where the prepositional phrase encodes the path by a different preposition than the one that is part of the particle. However, the direction of movement stays the same, and the prepositional phrase does not single out particular segments of the path (16).

(16) Leo 2;7.12   *Der # kann nicht unter der Brücke hindurchfahren.*
'It cannot under the bridge thither-through-drive.'
Leo 3;7.21   *Das ist der Schuppenstrich, der über die Schwanzflosse hinweg führt.*
'That is the scale-line that leads-thither-away over the tail-fin.'

Thus, there is no evidence that German children in this age range make use of clause-compacting in constructions that include perspectival particles and prepositional phrases.

DISCUSSION

Does the existence of deictic or perspectival verbal particles enhance German children's awareness of deixis, as predicted by Slobin (2006)? Based on the analysis of a German corpus of six children up to age 7, the careful answer is: probably. All children acquire a repertoire of such particle verbs, which make up 1%–2.7% of the children's main verb tokens. While this percentage may seem low, we have to remember that verbs are a relatively frequent category in speech. Even in rather small samples we find more than a hundred examples. Second, all children under investigation encode a contrast between *hin* and *her* at least for a few verbs, which suggests that they understood the contrast between these particles.

However, it is not clear whether they see this contrast as a deictic one. There are only a few errors with mismatches between the subject or topic of a clause and the perspectival particle. A number of explanations can account for this. First, the low sampling rate of some corpora may have led to missing errors. Second, children could use these particle verbs in a non-productive fashion, simply replicating the most frequent lexicalized examples. If this were the case, Slobin's basic prediction that children follow the lexicalization patterns of the input language would be confirmed (Slobin, 2006, p. 99). But the naturalistic data do not allow us to conclude that the existence of particles that encode deixis really attunes children to this feature. Even Leo's errors and his coinage of a blend between *hin* and *her* only indicate that he is confused about the system, not that he has mastered it afterward. Rather, the children studied seem to use perspectival particles in order to encode the goal or source of a movement that is already intrinsic in or compatible with the verb semantics. For example, it is more natural to come hither than thither. In this case, the information encoded by the particles is semantically redundant (Krause, 1998), which also accounts for the fact that in spoken language, the *hin/her* distinction is frequently nullified by phonological reduction to *r*- or *n*-forms.

But production data provide only limited insight into the mental representation of the semantics of these particles. Clearly, controlled experimental or elicitation tasks are needed to work out the mental representation that child and adult speakers of German have for the *hin/her* system, and how they construe the situations in which they are used. Lexical frequency effects will most certainly play a role. For example, high frequency verbs like *hinsetzen* 'sit thither' to most people will simply mean 'sit down.' However, its less frequent counterpart *hersetzen* 'sit hither' evokes a more particular meaning, e.g., that somebody comes over to sit next to me. Given the dialectal variance, individual variation is to be expected as well. German perspectival particles may thus offer a chance to study the effect of language on conceptual representation even within a language.

REFERENCES

[Duden-Grammatik] (1995). *Duden Bd. 4: Grammatik der deutschen Gegenwartssprache* [Duden Volume 4: Grammar of contemporary German]. (5th ed.). Mannheim: Duden-Verlag.

[Duden-Grammatik] (2005). *Duden Bd. 4: Grammatik der deutschen Gegenwartssprache* [Duden Volume 4: Grammar of contemporary German]. (7th ed.). Mannheim: Duden-Verlag.

Bamberg, M., & Marchman, V. (1994). Foreshadowing and wrapping up in narrative. In R. A. Berman & D. I. Slobin (Eds.), *Relating events in narrative: A crosslinguistic developmental study* (pp. 555–590). Hillsdale, NJ: Lawrence Erlbaum Associates.

Behrens, H. (1998). How difficult are complex verbs: Evidence from German, English and Dutch. *Linguistics, 36*, 679–712.

Behrens, H. (2003). Verbal prefixation in German child and adult language. *Acta Linguistica Hungarica, 50*, 37–55.

Behrens, H. (2006). The input–output relationship in first language acquisition. *Language and Cognitive Processes, 21*, 2–24.

Berman, R. A., & Slobin, D. I. (Eds.) (1994). *Relating events in narrative: A crosslinguistic developmental study*. Hillsdale, NJ: Lawrence Erlbaum Associates.

Bybee, J., & Scheibman, J. (1999). The effects of usage of degrees of constituency: The reduction of "don't" in English. *Linguistics, 37*, 575–596.

Engelen, B. (1995). *Hinunter versus darunter. Beobachtungen und Überlegungen zu den Direktionaladverbien* ['Downwards' versus 'under': Observations and thoughts on directional adverbials]. In L. M. Eichinger & H. W. Eroms (Eds.), Dependenz und Valenz [*Dependency and valency*] (pp. 243–258). Hamburg: Buske.

Eichinger, L. M. (1989). *Raum und Zeit im Verbwortschatz des Deutschen: Eine valenzgrammatische Studie* [Space and time in the verb lexicon of German: A study from a valency grammar perspective]. Tübingen: Niemeyer.

Eisenberg, P. (1998). *Grundriß der deutschen Grammatik: Das Wort* [Layout of German grammar: The word]. Stuttgart: Metzler.

Harnisch, R. (1982): "*Doppelpartikelverben" als Gegenstand der Wortbildungslehre und Richtungsadverbien als Präpositionen. Ein syntaktischer Versuch* ["Double-particle verbs" as topic of word formation and directional adverbials as prepositions: A syntactic attempt]. In L. M. Eichinger (Ed.), *Tendenzen verbaler Wortbildung in der deutschen Gegenwartssprache* [Tendencies in verbal word formation in contemporary German] (pp. 107–133). Hamburg: Buske.

Helbig, G., & Buscha, J. (2002). *Deutsche Grammatik: Ein Handbuch für den Ausländerunterricht* [German grammar: A handbook for foreign language teaching]. (2nd ed.). Berlin: Langenscheidt.

Henzen, W. (1969): *Die Bezeichnung von Richtung und Gegenrichtung im Deutschen. Studien zu Umfang und Ausnutzung der mit Adverbien der Richtung zusammengesetzten Wortbildungsgruppen* [The encoding of direction and opposite direction in German. Studies on the range and use of word formation groups that are composed with directional adverbials]. Tübingen: Niemeyer.

Krause, M. (1998). Überlegungen zu hin-/her- +Präposition [Thoughts on prepositions with 'thither' and 'hither']. In T. Harden & E. Hentschel (Eds.), *Particulae particularum. Festschrift zum 60. Geburtstag von Harald Weydt* [The particularities of particles: Festschrift for Harald Weydt on his 60th birthday] (pp. 195–217). Tübingen: Stauffenburg.

Leden, A. (1982). Bedeutungen und Gebrauchsmöglichkeiten einiger Komposita: ausgehen, herausgehen, hinausgehen und eingehen, hereingehen, hineingehen [Meaning and applications of some compound verbs: go-out, go-hither-out, go-thither-out, and in-go, hither-go, thither-go]. In L. M. Eichinger (Ed.), *Tendenzen verbaler Wortbildung in der deutschen Gegenwartssprache* [Tendencies in verbal word formation in contemporary German] (pp. 193–195). Hamburg: Buske.

MacWhinney, B. (2000). *The CHILDES-Project: Tools for analyzing talk* (2 volumes) (3rd ed.). Mahwah, NJ: Lawrence Erlbaum Associates.

Malvern, D. D., Richards, B. J., Chipere, N., & Duran, P. (2004). *Lexical diversity and language development: quantification and assessment.* New York: Palgrave Macmillan.

Miller, M. (1976). *Zur Logik der frühkindlichen Sprachentwicklung: Empirische Untersuchungen und Theoriediskussion* [*The logic of language development in early childhood: empirical investigations and theoretical discussion*]. Stuttgart: Klett.

Olsen, S. (1996). Pleonastische Direktionale [Pleonastic directionals]. In G. Harras & M. Bierwisch (Eds.), *Wenn die Semantik arbeitet: Klaus Baumgärtner zum 65. Geburtstag* [When semantics works: Festschrift for Klaus Baumgärtner on his 65th birthday] (pp. 303–329). Tübingen: Niemeyer.

Olsen, S. (1999). Durch den Park durch, zum Bahnhof hin. Komplexe Präpositionalphrasen mit einfachem direktionalem Kopf [Through the park through, towards the station thither: Complex prepositional phrases with a simple directional head]. In H. Wegener (Ed.), *Deutsch kontrastiv. Typologisch vergleichende Untersuchungen zur deutschen Grammatik* [German contrastively: Comparative typological investigations on German grammar] (pp. 111–134). Tübingen: Stauffenburg.

Slobin, D. I. (1996a). From "thought and language" to "thinking for speaking." In J. J. Gumperz & S. C. Levinson (Eds.), *Rethinking linguistic relativity* (pp. 70–96). Cambridge, UK: Cambridge University Press.

Slobin, D. I. (1996b). Two ways to travel: Verbs of motion in English and Spanish. In M. Shibatani & S. A. Thompson (Eds.), *Grammatical constructions: Their form and meaning* (pp. 195–219). Oxford: Oxford University Press.

Slobin, D. I. (1997). Mind, code and text. In J. Bybee, J. Haiman, & S. A. Thompson (Eds.), *Essays on language function and language type* (pp. 437–467). Amsterdam: Benjamins.

Slobin, D. I. (2001). Form–function relations: How do children find out what they are? In M. Bowerman & S. Levinson (Eds.), *Language acquisition and conceptual development* (pp. 406–449). Cambridge, UK: Cambridge University Press.

Slobin, D. I. (2003). Language and thought online: Cognitive consequences of linguistic relativity. In D. Gentner & S. Goldin-Meadow (Eds.), *Language in mind: Advances in the study of language and cognition* (pp. 157–191). Cambridge, MA: MIT Press.

Slobin, D. I. (2006). What makes manner of motion salient? Explorations in linguistic typology, discourse, and cognition. In M. Hickman & S. Robert (Eds.), *Space in languages: Linguistic systems and cognitive categories* (pp. 83–101). Amsterdam: Benjamins.

Slobin, D. I. (2008). Relations between paths of motion and paths of vision: A crosslinguistic and developmental exploration. In Gathercole, V. M. (Ed.), *Routes to language: Studies in honour of Melissa Bowerman*. Mahwah, NJ: Lawrence Erlbaum Associates.

Talmy, L. (1985). Lexicalization patterns: Semantic structures in lexical forms. In T. E. Shopen (Ed.), *Language typology and syntactic description: Vol. 3. Grammatical categories and the lexicon* (pp. 57–149). Cambridge, UK: Cambridge University Press.

Tomasello, M., & Stahl, D. (2004). Sampling children's spontaneous speech: How much is enough. *Journal of Child Language, 31*, 101–121.

Zifonum, G., Hoffmann, L., & Strecker, B. (1997). *Grammatik der deutschen Sprache. Band 1–3 [Grammar of the German language]* Vol. 1–3. Berlin/New York: de Gruyter.

Zintl, J. (1982). Zur Syntax von hinaus/hinein, heraus/herein [On the syntax of thither-out/thither-in, hither-out/hither-in]. In L. M. Eichinger (Ed.), *Tendenzen verbaler Wortbildung in der deutschen Gegenwartssprache [Tendencies in verbal word formation in contemporary German]* (pp. 135–172). Hamburg: Buske.

5

One-to-One Mapping of Temporal and Spatial Relations

RICHARD M. WEIST
SUNY College at Fredonia

> Well before they were two years of age, two bilingual girls were productively and appropriately using a variety of Hungarian case endings on nouns indicating such locative relations as illative, elative, sublative, and superessive—that is, in plain English, the children were using inflections to express the directional notions of 'into', 'out of', and 'onto', and the positional notion of 'on top of'. At the same time they had barely begun to develop locative expressions on Serbo-Croatian, which requires a locative preposition before the noun along with some case inflection attached to the end of the noun.
>
> **Dan I. Slobin (1973, p. 182)**

*I*n 1980, when I returned from a 2-year Fulbright fellowship in Poznań, Poland, Dan invited me to spend some time at Berkeley in the summer. At that time, Dan was editing the first two volumes of the *Crosslinguistic Study of Language Acquisition*. After we became acquainted that summer at Berkeley, our paths crossed from time to time over a period of 25 years at IASCL conferences and at smaller meetings designed to brainstorm a functional theory of language acquisition. I was already immersed in crosslinguistic research at the time that we first met, and some of my work on Polish was aimed at an evaluation of operating principles, e.g., Weist (1983) on operating principle A. In this chapter, I discuss the way in which Slobin's (1973) *Cognitive Prerequisites* paper stimulated my research comparing Polish with Finnish in the acquisition of the spatial and temporal systems.

INTRODUCTION TO OPERATING PRINCIPLES

When Dan Slobin introduced the concept of Operating Principles in his 1973 chapter on cognitive prerequisites, he supported some of his arguments with observations of two Serbo-Croatian—Hungarian bilingual children. Slobin observed that there were some things about the spatial morphology of the Finno-Ugric language that facilitated acquisition as contrasted with the Slavic language. Applying the form of Slobin's argument to temporal morphology, we[1] hypothesized that there are

---

[1] While this chapter has a single author, the research behind the argument was accomplished by a cross-cultural team of scientists. That team included two trilinguals: Aleksandra Pawlak (Polish, English, Finnish) and Marja Atanassova (Finnish-Bulgarian, English) and two bilinguals: Hanna Wysocka (Polish, English) and Paula Lyytinen (Finnish, English).

properties of the temporal morphology of Slavic languages that should facilitate acquisition. These ideas motivated a series of crosslinguistic studies contrasting the acquisition of the temporal and spatial systems of Polish, Finnish, and English. In this chapter, I will review evidence supporting the hypothesis that the one-to-one mapping of salient semantic relations facilitates the acquisition of the morphology within a system within a language.

RESEARCH MOTIVATION

This chapter presents the argument that one-to-one morpheme-to-concept information processing facilitates the child's capacity to discover the essential components of spatial and temporal linguistic systems. This argument was at the core of a research project designed to investigate the relationship between language and thought, or more specifically between the acquisition of language and conceptual development (Weist, Lyytinen, Wysocka, & Atanassova, 1997; Weist, Atanassova, Wysocka, & Pawlak, 1999). The research was focused on space and time for three reasons: (1) it is adaptive for children to think about the arrangement of objects in space and events in time, (2) every language has systems for spatial location (e.g., Brown, 2001 on Tzeltal, with its environment-centered perspective) and temporal reference (e.g., Swift, 2004, on Inuktitut, having a future-non-future split and remote tenses), and (3) there has been considerable research on space and time in the linguistic domain (e.g., Bowerman & Choi, 2001, on space, and Behrens, 1993, 2001, on time) and in the conceptual domain (e.g., Newcombe & Huttenlocher, 2003, on space, and Bauer, 2006, on time). Therefore, the potential for language—thought interactions will exist in every culture, and this situation provides a rich environment for crosslinguistic investigations.

While there are many ways to think about space and time, three examples will provide adequate context for this analysis of morpheme-to-concept mapping: (1) psychological, (2) conventional, and (3) linguistic—functional. Languages express psychological and conventional space/time concepts within the lexicon. A person can express her/his perception of space/time with expressions like, *Space is confined/wide-open* or *Time flies/lingers on*, and a person can learn the conventions of his/her culture to specify distance (e.g., *inches/meters*) and direction (e.g., *east/west*) in space or extent (e.g., *days/years*) and point (e.g., *ten o'clock*) in time. However, a child can become a fluent speaker without expressing his/her feelings about space or time and without learning cultural conventions.

In contrast, languages have morpho-syntactic systems for locating objects in space and events in time (see Talmy, 1983, for space and Comrie, 1976 and 1985, for time). While second language learners in the un-tutored environment are typically slow to enter these systems, children acquire the essential components in a precocious manner (Weist, 2002). These systems express what Lucy (1992, p. 7) referred to as "habitual thought ... routine ways of attending to objects and events…," and therefore, the crosslinguistic differences in the structure of these morpho-syntactic systems have the potential to influence information processing and alter the course of conceptual development.

In order to access the spatial/temporal systems, the child must process the relevant functional morphology. In 1973, Slobin introduced the concept of Operating Principles (OPs) in his seminal chapter on the topic, "Cognitive Prerequisites for the Development of Grammar," and he expanded on this conceptual framework 12 years later (Slobin, 1985). Slobin made the basic assumption that, "Every normal human child constructs for himself the grammar of his native language," and in order for the child to do so, "(1) he must be able to cognize the physical and social events which are encoded in language, and (2) he must be able to process, organize and store linguistic information" (Slobin, 1973, pp. 175 and 176). In other words, there are two components to the construction of grammar; a conceptual development component and a linguistic information-processing component. Regarding the linguistic component, Slobin proposed a set of information-processing principles that represent the perceptual–conceptual procedures for the construction of grammar. According to his theory, "OPs [Operating Principles] function in the processing of linguistic input and in the organization and reorganization of stored linguistic material" (1985, p. 1159). In agreement with Slobin's contention that children are constructing grammatical systems, this chapter concerns the systems designed to locate objects in space and events in time. A network of operating principles ranging from detecting to organizing the elements of the system is needed to understand this process, and Slobin (1985) proposed such a network.[2]

Languages vary in the way in which they structure their space and time information. The manner in which a specific language structures that information can either facilitate or impede the application of operating principles (cf. "typological bootstrapping," Slobin, 2001, p. 441). When a single morpheme codes a single concept within a linguistic system, this one-to-one mapping should facilitate information processing in contrast to a many-to-one mapping. Considering data from Mikeš (1967, cited by Slobin), Slobin's (1973) initial example of this mapping prediction involved two bilingual children simultaneously learning the spatial locative systems of Hungarian (a Finno-Ugric language) and Serbo-Croatian (a Slavic language). Mapping in the Finno-Ugric spatial system approaches one-to-one, and mapping in the Slavic system is clearly many-to-one. At an early phase of acquisition, the children effectively used the inflectional morphology of Hungarian, but not of Serbo-Croatian. Slobin's observation and its relation to information processing provided the key to our crosslinguistic study of a Finno-Ugric language, Finnish and a Slavic language, Polish (see also Slobin, 1982, p. 164).

SPACE AND TIME SYSTEMS FOR POLISH AND FINNISH

There are two dimensions at the core of the most basic component of the spatial and temporal systems of these languages (see Table 5.1). In space, there are locative morphemes that specify direction relative to a referent object, i.e., toward, at, and away, and there is a dimension of spatial perspective which can be internal or external relative to language-specific properties of the referent object (see Bowerman, 1996, Figure 6.5). In English, the internal locative prepositions are *into*, *in*, and *out of*, and the external ones are *onto*, *on*, and *off of*. In time, the location of the temporal interval of the focal/primary event (i.e., event time (ET)) is established relative to the temporal interval of the speech act (i.e., speech time (ST)). ST is the unique referent event for "absolute" tense but not for relative or absolute-relative tenses, e.g., past prefect (see Comrie, 1985). In general, aspectual perspective may

TABLE 5.1 Two Core Dimensions of Spatial and Temporal Systems[a]

Direction/Tense	Spatial & Aspectual Perspective	
	Internal	External
Away/Past	*out of*/*was-were* verb-*ing*	*off of*/verb-*ed*
At/Present	*in*/*is-are* verb-*ing*	*on*/verb-*s*
Toward/Future	*into*/*will* be verb-*ing*	*onto*/*will* verb

[a] In space, direction refers to the trajectory of the figure relative to the referent object (or ground). The internal versus external distinction in perspective relates to the perceived containment versus support properties of the referent object. In time, given the moving ego metaphor, the self (and deictic center) is viewed as progressing through time creating the sense that ST moves away from ET for past tense and ST moves toward ET for future tense. The internal versus external distinction is related to the imperfective versus perfective aspectual distinction.

---

[2] There is an important difference between a hypothesis regarding how children process linguistic information (i.e., an operating principle) and a hypothesis regarding how children think about the information they are processing (i.e., the "Basic Child Grammar," Slobin, 1985). We accepted the former as an interesting testable hypothesis (Weist, 1983, p. 86 regarding OP-A), and we had a different analysis of the latter (Weist, Wysocka, Witkowska-Stadnik, Buczowska, & Konieczna, 1984, p. 370, on temporal perspectives; see also Bowerman's (1985, p. 1302–1303) comparison these two alternatives).

be viewed as internal versus external in "viewpoint" represented by imperfective versus perfective aspect (see Smith, 1991, p. 93). The direction by dimension matrix found in Table 5.1 contains six concepts for each system. Rather than a list of individual concepts, we argue that children acquire an interrelated set of concepts, i.e., a system (see Weist, Pawlak, & Carapella, 2004, regarding time). Furthermore, children integrate spatial and temporal systems into their general theory of grammar, and we have argued that Role and Reference Grammar represents the best estimate of the form of that grammar (see Van Valin, 2005). Van Valin's analysis of how children acquire such a grammatical system is beyond the scope of this chapter, but his most recent proposal is found in this volume (Van Valin, this volume).

In Finnish, the morpheme-to-concept mapping approaches one-to-one for the spatial concepts defined by the interaction of direction by perspective shown in Table 5.1. In addition to cases that code such relations as subject and direct object, Finnish has six cases primarily designed to code spatial concepts, e.g., away-internal is expressed with the elative case, noun-*stA*. In contrast to Finnish, Polish requires a many-to-one mapping to code the locative concepts outlined in Table 5.1. Polish always requires a preposition plus a noun suffix, and Polish can require a prefix on the verb as well. While Polish has a locative case, it utilizes the general case system to establish spatial location with each preposition having its unique case requirements, e.g., away-internal is expressed with *wy*-verb *z* noun-genitive. Adding to complexity, the exact form of the case ending depends on the gender and number of the noun.

The opposite situation is found in the temporal domain. Both languages have a past versus non-past split. Polish has a set of affixes designed to establish the distinction in aspectual perspective between imperfective and perfective, and in addition to the distinction between the past and non-past stem, Polish has a unique past tense morpheme, i.e., the suffix - *ł* [w]. Finnish has numerous mechanisms to establish values of aspectual perspective that sometimes involve a case contrast on the direct object and sometimes a locative case integrated into a complex verb form. Furthermore, Finnish has perfect tenses (i.e., absolute-relative tenses) as well as absolute tenses creating many ways to locate an event in the past and creating a many-to-one coding. The differences in the manner in which Polish and Finnish code spatial and temporal concepts are summarized in Table 5.2.

MONO-/BI-REFERENTIAL LOCATION IN SPACE/TIME

As Slobin (1973) argued some 30 years ago, we need to understand the role cognitive complexity, as well as linguistic complexity, plays in the construction of grammar. Spatial location and temporal reference vary in complexity (see Johnston & Slobin, 1979, on space and Weist, 1986, 1989, and 2002, on time). There are different ways to conceptualize relative complexity in space and in time. However, there is a common thread running through the analysis in the spatial and temporal domains. Conceptually simple spatial and temporal location requires a single referent object or event, and relatively complex location requires two or more referent objects or events. Applying the most transparent terminology, we made the distinction between mono-referential and bi-referential. For mono-referential location the place/time of the primary object/event is located relative to a single referent,

TABLE 5.2 Morpheme–Concept Mapping Within the Dimensions of Direction and Perspective: Prototypical Patterns for Finnish and Polish

Domain	Language	Morpheme X	Morpheme Y	Morpheme Z
Space	Finnish		Noun/Postposition-suffix	
	Polish	Verb-prefix	Preposition	Noun-suffix
Time	Finnish	Auxiliary-suffix	Verb-suffix	Noun-suffix
	Polish		Verb-affixes	

e.g., all of the entries in Table 5.1. The location of an object in space or an event in time is considered bi-referential when there are two or more referents. In the spatial domain, Kuczaj and Maratsos (1975) and Johnston and Slobin (1979) found that children were able to understand the *front/back* contrast when the referent object had distinctive features that identified a front versus a back side, e.g., visual apparatus and prototypical direction of motion. When a referent object is void of such features, the location of the primary object is more complex, requiring two referents, e.g., *The boy found the toy in front of the ball*. In the temporal domain, mono-referential location involves ET and ST (see Table 5.1). Temporal reference becomes more complex when reference time is included in the configuration, e.g., temporal adverbs and adverbial clauses, *The boy found the toy yesterday*. The analysis of caregiver–child interaction data reveals that children learning English produce mono-referential constructions approximately one year before bi-referential constructions (see Internicola & Weist, 2003, for space and Pawlak, Oehlrich & Weist, 2006, for time). The concepts of linguistic and cognitive complexity were integrated into our crosslinguistic research project.

SPACE/TIME RESEARCH HYPOTHESES

The research was guided by the following three-part hypothesis: (1) children who learn a language with one-to-one mapping of morphemes-to-concepts in the spatial and/or temporal domain gain an advantage in their opportunity to construct the related linguistic system, (2) information processing is facilitated by the structure of the Finnish spatial system and the Polish temporal system, and (3) the linguistic capacity to express the location of objects in space and/or events in time has the potential to accelerate cognitive development.

SPACE/TIME RESEARCH DESIGN

In this section of the chapter, I will outline the general research design that formed the foundation for two complex experiments, and then I will selectively discuss a few of the most salient findings as they pertain to the question of morpheme-to-concept mapping. In general, the research design was crosslinguistic with three languages, Polish, Finnish, and English, and the design was cross-sectional with 12 children at each of four levels (2-, 3-, 4, and 5-year-olds in one study and 3-, 4-, 5, and 6-year-olds in the second study). The children were evaluated in the conceptual and linguistic domains regarding their knowledge of spatial and temporal concepts. Within the linguistic domain, comprehension and production tests were administered by native speakers of the target language. The three research sites were Poznań, Poland, Jyväskylä, Finland, and Fredonia, New York. Regarding the relevance of one-to-one mapping to the acquisition process, the results of the comprehension tests for the Polish and Finnish children are the most relevant.

There were two kinds of comprehension tests. In the static test, the problems were presented in a book with two opposing illustrations, and in the dynamic test, the problems were presented on two video screens where a child actress acted out opposing scenarios. The test included both spatial and temporal problems having either mono-referential or bi-referential complexity. For example, Problems 1 and 2 were taken from the dynamic comprehension test of the Weist, et al., (1999) study.[3]

Problem 1. Space, mono-referential, & perspective (external/internal).

ENG The girl is taking the cover (off of/out of) the car.
POL Dziewczynka (z-dejmuje-Ø/wy-jmuje-Ø) pokrowiec-Ø z samochod-u.

---

[3] The following code was used to gloss the sentences: 3 third person, ABL ablative, ACC accusative, ELAT elative, FEM feminine, GEN genitive, IPFV imperfective, NPAST non-past, PART partitive, PAST past, PFV perfective, and SG singular.

girl (off-take_IPFV_NPAST-3_SG/out_of-take_IPFV_NPAST-3_SG) cover-ACC from car-GEN
FIN   Tyttö otta-a peittee-n (auto-n pää-ltä/auto-sta).
girl take_NPAST-3_SG cover-ACC (car-GEN top-ABL/car-ELAT)

Problem 2. Time, mono-referential, & aspect (internal/external).

ENG   The girl (was cutting/cut) a loaf of bread.
POL   Dziewczynka (kroi-ł-a-Ø/po-kroi-ł-a-Ø) chlebek-Ø.
girl (cut_IPFV-PAST-FEM-3_SG/PFV-cut-PAST-FEM-3_SG) bread-ACC
FIN   Tyttö leikkas-i-Ø (leipä-ä/leivä-n).
girl cut-PAST-3_SG (bread-PART/bread-ACC)

Problems 1 and 2 are both mono-referential, and they both present a contrast in perspective (see Table 5.1). In Problem 1, in Finnish, there is an ablative (–ltä) versus elative (–sta) contrast, while in Polish, a contrast in verb prefixes (z-/wy-) is combined with a preposition (z) and a genitive case suffix (-u) on a nominative singular noun. In Finnish the morphological contrast occurs in a single location on the referent noun (or postposition) utilizing two different locative cases, each with a single specific meaning. In Polish, the child is required to process an array of three morphemes where none of the individual elements is uniquely designed to code the specific locative meaning portrayed in the video. In Problem 2, we argue that in order to understand the difference in information processing, we need to consider how this particular contrast fits into the larger tense-aspect system that the children are constructing. In Problem 2, in Polish, imperfective versus perfective (Ø-/po-) aspect is contrasted with the absence versus presence of the prefix –po. In Polish, the perfective–imperfective distinction is always made within the verb morphology, i.e., prefix, suffix, or suppletion, and this is true for intransitive as well as transitive verbs. Finnish does not have aspect in the same sense as a Slavic language. Rather, Finnish has mechanisms that simulate aspectual meanings. In Problem 2, the distinction between an incomplete and a complete process is made with the partitive versus accusative case suffixes on the noun (-ä/-n). However, the partitive case has other functions, e.g., if the sentence was negated the direct object would be in the partitive case, and to make things more complicated, other mechanisms for creating aspectual meanings such as the progressive involve inflections on a form of the verb (Heinämäki, 1983). In general, we argue that children are constructing spatial and temporal systems, and a rich network of operating principles, such as those proposed by Slobin (1985), is needed to understand information processing at the system level as well as the level of the specific morphological contrast. In Problem 2, in Finnish, the partitive versus accusative contrast is simple by itself, but it is part of a complex tense-aspect system.

SPACE/TIME RESEARCH RESULTS

The Polish and Finnish children's capacity to comprehend mono- and bi-referential contrasts in spatial and temporal problems was evaluated in Experiment 2 in Weist et al. (1997). Children at age levels 2, 3, 4, and 5 years of age were presented with minimal morphological contrasts in a sentence–picture-matching task. The experimenter showed the children two illustrations (e.g., a girl in the process of drawing a flower and a girl having completed the flower drawing process), then she read two sentence alternatives (e.g., 'The girl (was drawing/drew) the flower'), and finally, she reread one of the sentence alternatives and asked the child to point to the matching picture. In general, the Polish and Finnish children were equally proficient at this task, and their performance improved significantly with age. Hence, the pictures were not somehow biased in favor of one or the other culture, and the samples of children were not more precocious in one culture than the other. In general, mono-referential problems were easier than bi-referential problems. This difference extended across languages and across the space and time domains indicating that conceptual development had a participating role. Finally, and most importantly, there was a significant interaction of language by space/time dimension. Finnish children were better on spatial problems than Polish children and Polish children were better on temporal problems than Finnish children. This finding supports the argument that one-to-one mapping facilitates access to the relevant grammatical system.

In the companion experiment, Weist et al. (1999) utilized a similar methodology to investigate the idea that the structure of the Finnish spatial system and the Polish temporal system promotes information processing and grammatical organization at the system level. In order to evaluate comprehension, the sentence–picture-matching procedure described above was utilized. However, in this experiment, the pictorial contrasts were presented with video performances as well as illustrations in a book. In general, the Polish children demonstrated a consistent relative advantage in the temporal dimension. While the Finnish children consistently performed at a high level on spatial problems, they only had a relative spatial advantage on the video comprehension test. When creating aspect problems for sentence–picture-matching tests, some combinations of lexical and grammatical aspect are difficult to implement. In an attempt to incorporate activity predicates into the mono-referential temporal problems, ambiguity was created (see Weist et al., 1999, for a full discussion and a control experiment). The defective problems were removed from the analysis, and the comprehension tests were balanced having three contrasts for each of the four distinctions (i.e., space versus time and mono- versus bi-referential). In this "truncated" design, we again found the interaction of language by space/time dimension, with the Finnish children showing a spatial advantage and the Polish children demonstrating a temporal advantage on both the still picture and the video picture comprehension tests. This finding again supports the argument that one-to-one mapping facilitates language acquisition, and the crosslinguistic experimental research design is required to prove this point.

COGNITIVE PRE-REQUISITES AND LINGUISTIC RELATIVITY

From my perspective, an invariant that runs through Slobin's work is captured by the following statement: "The role of linguistic input is to guide the child towards discovery and construction of the form-function relations inherent in the exposure language" (Slobin, 2001, p. 438). In his "cognitive pre-requisites" paper, Slobin proposed a set of information processing principles (i.e., operating principles) that guide this discovery process, and he presented a methodology to evaluate such operating principles, i.e., crosslinguistic investigation. The methodology was/is based on the fact that languages differ in the way in which they code form–function relations, e.g., 1-to-1 versus many-to-one mapping. By investigating how children acquire the same concepts, e.g., location in space and/or time, in typologically different languages, e.g., Polish and Finnish, it should be possible to determine how children process linguistic information. When the structure of the language matches the form of the operating principles, the acquisition process should be facilitated, i.e., "typological bootstrapping" (Slobin, 2001, p. 441). This crosslinguistic methodology assumes linguistic diversity, and linguistic diversity is a necessary condition for linguistic relativity. How does the discovery of form–function relations influence the child's thought processes, i.e., what are the implications of linguistic diversity for linguistic relativity? Slobin (1996, p. 76) proposed that linguistic relativity extended to the thought processes which function during communication, i.e., "…in acquiring a native language, the child learns particular ways of thinking for speaking," and together with Ruth Berman, other colleagues, and "The Frog Story," they demonstrated some of the differences in such thinking (see Berman & Slobin, 1994). Our space/time research project was designed to investigate the potential influence of linguistic relativity that extends beyond "thinking for speaking" to the Whorfian realm of habitual thinking about the location of objects in space and events in time. In other words, the research was designed to test the third of the three hypotheses listed above which I will repeat as follows: "The linguistic capacity to express the location of objects in space and/or events in time has the potential to accelerate cognitive development." This is a developmental variation on the Whorfian theme since it concerns the course of conceptual change and not necessarily the ultimate form.

In order to understand this hypothesis, we need to know the child's conceptual status when they begin to process functional morphology, and what kind of influence language might have on their thought processes. Infants can construct spatial and temporal (i.e., event sequence) representations prior to the acquisition of spatial and temporal functional morphology. After a penetrating review of the literature in the spatial domain, Newcombe and Huttenlocher (2003: 106) surmised that infants have the capacity to code location in terms of the following: (1) motor responses, (2) coincident cues, (3) data from their own movement, and (4) distance in continuous space. While infants can construct spatial representations, their capacity to think about those representations is limited, e.g., see Hazen, Lockman, and Pick (1978), and this leaves a considerable opportunity for language to influence the continued development of the child's thinking about space.

In the spatial domain, there has been considerable research on the relationship between language and thought. Contrasting data from Korean and English, Choi and Bowerman (1991) found that language can direct a child's attention to specific spatial distinctions and de-emphasize others. In a penetrating analysis of this process, Choi (2006) evaluated the changes in the relative sensitivity of children learning English and Korean to the distinction between the concepts of tight-fit versus loose-fit (or degree of fit). She found that children learning English became less sensitive to the distinction as their use of the English locative *in/on* contrast became more productive. There is a broader potential for the spatial system of a language to influence thought in languages that have an environment-centered (i.e., absolute) perspective and lack an observer-centered (i.e., relative) perspective, such as Tzeltal. Brown (2001) has shown that by approximately 3 years of age, children acquiring Tzeltal are able to utilize an environment-centered system of spatial perspective as contrasted with a viewer-centered system, and Levinson (2003) has shown that adult Tzeltal speakers are likely to employ an environment-centered solution to a 180 degree rotation problem in stark contrast to adult Dutch speakers. Hence, while the infant can code spatial location, the linguistic expression of spatial location influences thinking about space. My colleagues and I proposed that talking about space within the mono-referential system of the 2-year-old would facilitate thinking about higher-order spatial relations.

In the temporal domain, between the ages of 1 and 2 years, children can construct and retain multiple-component event representations (see Bauer's 1996 review). Factors that influence the adult's declarative memory also influence the child's memory, such as enablement relations between events in a sequence, multiple experiences with an event, and reminders related to the event. Bauer (1996, p. 39) conjectured that "verbal expression may be what determines whether a memory will survive the transition from infancy to early childhood." Along the same line of thinking, Fivush (e.g., Fivush, Haden, & Adam, 1995) has argued that the longevity of personal experience memories depends on the organization of cohesive narratives, i.e., "It is the canonical narrative form that gives personal memories their structure" (Fivush et al., 1995, p. 34). In fact, their major longitudinal study of children's memory for personal experiences confirmed their argument. Hence, even though the pre-linguistic infant has the capacity for declarative memory, the temporal structure of language can and does influence conceptual development.

In the temporal domain, we don't have research that compares with the work of Soonja Choi and her colleagues. For example, Mary Swift (2004) has conducted a longitudinal analysis of the emergence of the temporal system of Inuktitut, an Inuit language with a future–non-future split and an elaborate system of remote tenses. Children learning Inuktitut code future tense during a relatively early phase of acquisition as contrasted with children learning a language with a past–non-past split. However, this linguistic research was not accompanied by an evaluation of cognitive development in the temporal domain.[4]

---

[4] While the details of their research are beyond the scope of this chapter, an intriguing paradigm for the investigation of linguistic relativity in either the temporal or the spatial domain can be found in the research of Núñez and Sweetser (2006) concerning the relationship between language and gesture in Aymara where fluent speakers (with relatively limited Spanish) gesture forward when they talk about the past and behind when they talk about the future.

In our crosslinguistic research project, outlined in this chapter, we evaluated the child's higher-order capacity to conceptualize layouts in space and sequences of events in time, and the children demonstrated dramatic conceptual development during the period from 2 to 6 years of age. Furthermore, their conceptual development was correlated (i.e., co-varied) with their linguistic development in the spatial and temporal domains. While this shows that higher-order thinking advances with increased complexity in spatial and temporal language, it does not show that these changes in thought processes vary as a function of typological differences in the target languages, i.e., linguistic relativity. Support for linguistic relativity requires a crossover interaction, where Polish children excel on temporal conceptual tests and Finnish children excel on spatial conceptual tests. Such an interaction was not discovered, and the potential for relatively efficient linguistic information processing to accelerate conceptual development was not revealed. One-to-one form–function mapping extended to "thinking for speaking," but not to the Whorfian realm of "habitual thought," more specifically, not to the course of conceptual development (Weist et al., 1997, 1999).

In summary, the Polish–Finnish comparisons demonstrate that the morpho-syntactic structure of a language is related to the child's capacity to process the form–function relations of that language. A match between the child's operating principles and the form of the morpho-syntactic array creates the potential for efficient information processing. The difference between mono- and bi-referential location influences the timing of the acquisition of spatial and temporal contrasts. Locating objects in space and events in time within a mono-referential linguistic system contributes to children's capacity to think about the structure of their space–time experience and to the acquisition of a more complex bi-referential linguistic system. Therefore, conceptual and linguistic factors interact during the language acquisition process, confirming Slobin's (1973) original claim. Beyond information processing, children construct a grammar that integrates spatial and temporal systems.

REFERENCES

Bauer, P. J. (1996). What do infants recall of their lives? *American Psychologist, 51*, 29–41.
Bauer, P. J. (2006). *Remembering the times of our lives: Memory in infancy and beyond.* Mahwah, NJ: Lawrence Erlbaum Associates.
Behrens, H. (1993). *Temporal reference in German child language: Form and function of early verb use.* Zutphen: Koninklijke Wöhramann.
Behrens, H. (2001). Cognitive-conceptual development and the acquisition of grammatical morphemes: the development of time concepts and verb tense. In M. Bowerman & S. C. Levinson (Eds.), *Language acquisition and conceptual development* (pp. 450–474). Cambridge, UK: Cambridge University Press.
Berman, R. A., & Slobin, D. I. (1994). *Relating events in narrative: A crosslinguistic developmental study.* Hillsdale, NJ: Lawrence Erlbaum Associates.
Bowerman, M. (1985). What shapes children's grammars? In D. I. Slobin (Ed.), *The crosslinguistic study of language acquisition* (pp. 1257–1315). Hillsdale, NJ: Lawrence Lawrence Erlbaum Associates.
Bowerman, M. (1996). The origins of children's spatial semantic categories: cognitive versus linguistic determinants. In J. J. Gumperz & S. C. Levinson (Eds.), *Rethinking linguistic relativity* (pp. 145–176). Cambridge, UK: Cambridge University Press.
Bowerman, M., & Choi, S. (2001). Shaping meaning for language: Universal and language-specific in the acquisition of spatial semantic categories. In M. Bowerman & S. C. Levinson (Eds.), *Language acquisition and conceptual development* (pp. 475–511). Cambridge, UK: Cambridge University Press.
Brown, P. (2001). Learning to talk about motion UP and DOWN in Tzeltal: Is there a language specific bias for verb learning?. In M. Bowerman & S. C. Levinson (Eds.), *Language acquisition and conceptual development* (pp. 512–543). Cambridge, UK: Cambridge University Press.
Choi, S. (2006). Influence of language-specific input on spatial cognition: Categories of containment. *First Language, 26*, 207–232.
Choi, S., & Bowerman, M. (1991). Learning to express motion events in English and Korean: The influence of language-specific lexicalization patterns. *Cognition, 41*, 83–121.
Comrie, B. (1976). *Aspect.* London: Cambridge University Press.
Comrie, B. (1985). *Tense.* Cambridge, UK: Cambridge University Press.

Fivush, R., Haden, C., & Adam, S. (1995). Structure and coherence of preschoolers' personal narratives over time: Implications for childhood amnesia. *Journal of Experimental Child Psychology, 60,* 32–56.

Hazen, N. L., Lockman, J. J., & Pick, H. L. (1978). The development of children's representations of large-scale environments. *Child Development, 56,* 1195–1203.

Heinämäki, O. (1983). Aspect in Finnish. In C. de Groot & H. Tommola (Eds.), *Aspect bound* (pp. 153–178). Dordrecht, The Netherlands: Floris.

Internicola, R., & Weist, R. M. (2003). The acquisition of simple and complex spatial locatives in English: A longitudinal investigation. *First Language, 23,* 239–248.

Johnston, J. R., & Slobin, D. (1979). The development of locative expressions in English, Italian, Serbo-Croatian, and Turkish. *Journal of Child Language, 6,* 529–545.

Kuczaj, S., & Maratsos, M. (1975). On the acquisition of front, back, and side. *Child Development, 46,* 202–210.

Levinson, S. C. (2003). *Space in language and cognition.* Cambridge, UK: Cambridge University Press.

Lucy, J. A. (1992). *Language diversity and thought.* Cambridge, UK: Cambridge University Press.

Newcombe, N. S., & Huttenlocher, J. (2003). *Making space: The development of spatial representation and reasoning.* Cambridge, MA: The MIT Press.

Núñez, R. E., & Sweetser, E. (2006). With the future behind them: Convergent evidence from Aymara language and gesture in the crosslinguistic comparison of spatial construals of time. *Cognitive Science, 30,* 401–450.

Pawlak, A., Oehlrich, J. S., & Weist, R. M. (2006). Reference time in child English and Polish. *First Language, 26,* 281–297

Slobin, D. I. (1973). Cognitive pre-requisites for the acquisition of grammar. In C. A. Ferguson & D. I. Slobin (Eds.), *Studies of child language development* (pp. 175–208). New York: Holt.

Slobin, D. I. (1982). Universal and particular in the acquisition of language. In E. Wanner & L. Gleitman (Eds.), *Language acquisition: The state of the art* (pp. 128–170). Cambridge, UK: Cambridge University Press.

Slobin, D. I. (1985). Crosslinguistic evidence for the language-making capacity. In D. I. Slobin (Ed.), *The crosslinguistic study of language acquisition* (pp. 1157–1256). Hillsdale, NJ: Lawrence Erlbaum Associates.

Slobin, D. I. (1996). From "Thought and Language" to "Thinking for Speaking." In J. J. Gumperz & S. C. Levinson (Eds.), *Rethinking linguistic relativity* (pp. 70–96). Cambridge, UK: Cambridge University Press.

Slobin, D. I. (2001). Form-function relations: how do children find out what they are? In M. Bowerman & S. C. Levinson (Eds.), *Language acquisition and conceptual development* (pp. 406–449). Cambridge, UK: Cambridge University Press.

Smith, C. (1991). *The parameter of aspect.* Dordrecht, The Netherlands: Kluwer Academic Publishers.

Swift, M. D. (2004). *Time in child Inuktitut.* Berlin: Mouton de Gruyter.

Talmy, L. (1983). How language structures space. In H. Pick & L. Acredolo (Eds.), *Spatial orientation* (pp. 225–281). New York: Plenum Press.

Van Valin, R. D. (2005). *Exploring the syntactic–semantic interface.* Cambridge, UK: Cambridge University Press.

Van Valin, R. D. (in press). Some remarks on Universal Grammar. In J. Guo, E. Lieven, S. Ervin-Tripp, N. Budwig, S. Özçalişkan, & K. Nakamura (Eds.) *Crosslinguistic approaches to the psychology of language: Research in the tradition of Dan Isaac Slobin.* Hillsdale, NJ: Lawrence Erlbaum Associates.

Weist, R. M. (1983). Prefix versus suffix information processing in the comprehension of tense and aspect. *Journal of Child Language, 10,* 85–96.

Weist, R. M. (1986). Tense and aspect: Temporal systems in child language. In P. Fletcher & M. Garman (Eds.), *Language acquisition: studies in first language development* (pp. 356–374). Cambridge, UK: Cambridge University Press.

Weist, R. M. (1989). Time concepts in language and thought: Filling the Piagetian void from two to five years. In I. Levin & D. Zakay (Eds.), *Time and human cognition: A life span perspective* (pp. 63–118). Amsterdam: North-Holland.

Weist, R. M. (2002). Space and time in first and second language acquisition: A tribute to Henning Wode. In P. Burmeister, T. Piske, & A. Rohde (Eds.), *An integrated view of language development: Papers in honor of Henning Wode* (pp. 79–108). Trier, Germany: Wissenschaftlicher Verlag Trier (WVT).

Weist, R. M., Atanassova, M., Wysocka, H., & Pawlak, A. (1999). Spatial and temporal systems in child language and thought: A cross-linguistic study. *First Language, 19,* 267–312.

Weist, R. M., Lyytinen, P., Wysocka, J., & Atanassova M. (1997). The interaction of language and thought in children's language acquisition: A crosslinguistic study. *Journal of Child Language, 24,* 81–121.

Weist, R. M., Pawlak, A., & Carapella, J. (2004). Syntactic-semantic interface in the acquisition of verb morphology. *Journal of Child Language, 31*, 31–60.

Weist, R. M., Wysocka, H., Witkowska-Stadnik, K., Buczowska, E., & Konieczna, E. (1984). The defective tense hypothesis: On the emergence of tense and aspect in child Polish. *Journal of Child Language, 11*, 347–374.

6

Effects of Lexical Items and Construction Types in English and Turkish Character Introductions in Elicited Narrative

AYLIN C. KÜNTAY and DILARA KOÇBAŞ
Koç University

> I want to propose that rhetorical style is determined by the relative *accessibility* of various means of expression, such as lexical items and construction types. That is, *ease of processing* is a major factor in giving language-particular shape to narratives. At the same time, cultural practices and preferences reinforce habitual patterns of expression. The picture is complex … because various options compete or conspire to provide an overall shape to narrative production.
>
> D. I. Slobin (2004, p. 223)

The beginning of a story has serious implications for how it unfolds. This is why I seem to clearly remember my first three encounters with Dan Slobin. My first meeting with him was in the summer of 1988 in Üsküdar, Istanbul, as I was preparing to apply for graduate school in the United States. A friend of my family took me over to his home. Neither he nor I said much that day, except we did talk about me not having taken any linguistics and how hard it is for international students to financially survive in Berkeley. I am not so sure now whether he actually told me these things, but I left his place with such ideas in my mind.

The next time I interacted with Dan was when he called my family home in Teşvikiye, Istanbul, in the spring of 1989. He told me I was accepted to Berkeley. I did not talk much that day either, being exhilarated but really nervous. Dan felt I might have questions, and told me that I could send him an "email" with questions. When I went silent upon hearing this novel word, he rephrased it as "electronic mail." That exchange was momentous in making me realize that I was going to a world with new wonders and puzzles, having never left my own country, with its own wonders and puzzles. I was right. I was actually embarking on a journey of wonders and puzzles.

The third time was in August of 1989 in Tolman Hall, Berkeley, when the incoming students got together for an orientation meeting. Dan approached with a very friendly smile, and started elucidating some of these wonders and puzzles of the new world. I remember we talked about a various range of topics like how the fog clears up in the afternoons in the Bay Area, conflict in the Middle East, and Turkish morphology. I was struck, then and ever, by the breadth of Dan's interests and by his unpretentious mastery in approaching issues and problems, whether they are of intellectual or interpersonal nature.

For the next 18 years, Dan would become a beacon of wisdom for me, who would point to interesting directions of intellectual curiosity in a very non-imposing way. The work that we present in the following is an offshoot of many such directions.

INTRODUCTION

The ways speakers set up characters and their relations to one another right from the outset have implications for how their stories later unfold (Berman, 2001; Berman & Katzenberger, 2004). Pictured depiction of a frog in a jar in the bedroom of a little boy could plausibly lead to an interpretation of an enduring belongingness of the frog to the boy or a temporary investigative phase, where the captured frog is being admired by the boy to be soon released back to nature. In this chapter, we will examine the linguistic devices used to enact and interconnect the three main characters in the beginning of narratives produced by English and Turkish narrators of the Frog Story, a picturebook used by several researchers with participants of different ages learning a variety of languages (Bamberg, 1987; Berman & Slobin, 1994; Stromqvist & Verhoeven, 2004).

Several researchers thought that young children have difficulties with linguistic marking of referent identifiability with determiners, but there are some situations in which they use appropriate linguistic forms (e.g., Bamberg, 1987; Bennett-Kastor, 1983; Brown, 1973; Hickmann, Hendriks, Roland, & Liang, 1996; Kail & Hickmann, 1992; Karmiloff-Smith, 1981; Maratsos, 1976; Warden, 1981; Wigglesworth, 1990). These situations might have to do with the linguistic contexts, i.e., "lexical items and construction types," surrounding referential terms.

Many languages have specialized constructions such as presentational constructions (e.g., *Once upon a time there was an old man and a dog*) for presenting previously unidentified referents into discourse (Du Bois, 1980; Givón, 1995; Lambrecht, 1994; Schiffrin, 1994). Such constructions serve to decrease the informational load while this important function of introducing new referents gets achieved. There are developmental studies of narrative discourse that examine the association between 'local' markers such as determiners and 'global' or construction-level indications of newness such as word order (Hickman et al., 1996; Kail & Hickmann, 1992; Kail & Sanchez-Lopez, 1997). These studies found that most definite first mentions are in subject roles and most indefinite first mentions are in non-subject roles (Kail & Hickmann 1992; Kail & Sanchez-Lopez, 1997). This suggests that choice of a construction such as the presentative and the assignment of a referent into a non-subject role might predetermine usage of determiners at the level of the noun phrase. These studies, however, found crosslinguistic differences between how speakers mark main and secondary characters with indefinite determiners, suggesting the need for further research.

In this chapter, we investigate how the absence or presence of determiners in nominal constructions might be affected by verbal constructions such as transitive and presentational frames in different age groups speaking English and Turkish. The aim is to examine how speakers of Turkish, a language without a formal article system, compare to English speakers in presenting story characters into discourse. The emphasis will not be merely on the types of nouns used to introduce characters, but also on the types of constructions and argument roles in which these nouns are embedded. The specific questions listed below are all addressed with developmental and crosslinguistic comparisons in mind.

1. What is the order of mention of the three characters in the opening of the story?
2. What types of verbs are used to interrelate the boy and the frog?
3. What is the distribution of indefinite and definite first mentions for the main human character (i.e., the boy) and the secondary animal characters (i.e., the dog and the frog)?
4. In what types of constructions and what types of argument roles do indefinite first mentions prevail?

RELEVANT LINGUISTIC FEATURES: ENGLISH AND TURKISH

English has a formal article system that marks the identifiability of nouns by indefinite and definite articles, independent of the grammatical role that the noun plays in a construction. Turkish, on the other hand, has an indefinite numeral, *bi(r)*, which can be used optionally for indefinite noun phrases, but no definite determiners. However, when nouns fulfill non-subject grammatical roles, they receive casemarking, which implicates definiteness in the absence of the indefinite numeral.

With respect to verbal constructions, both languages have comparable multiple-argument constructions, intransitive constructions, and presentational constructions. Multiple-argument constructions include more than one constituent, such as in actor-patient (e.g., *the boy found a frog*) or comitative constructions (e.g., *kurbağa-sı-yla oynu-yor* 'frog-POSS-COM play-PROG'). Intransitive constructions have one constituent, such as in '*the boy is sitting in his room.*' Presentational constructions can be recognized by a frame as *X var* 'X exists' in Turkish, where X denotes the entity that is introduced into the discourse, generally in the focal preverbal slot (Sansa-Tura, 1986). English also has a presentational construction, involving intransitive verbs like *be* and *come*, the subjects of these verbs as presented elements, and the deictic adverbs *here* or *there* (Lambrecht, 1994).

FROG STORY DATABASES

The Turkish data come from the A. Aksu-Koç corpus (1994), and the A. Küntay corpus (1997). The English data are the T. Renner corpus (1988), and the G. Wigglesworth (1990) corpus, all downloaded from CHILDES. Table 6.1 presents the number of participants in each age and language group.

Mayer's picturebook, *Frog, where are you?* (1969) was used to elicit narratives ("frog stories") individually from each participant. Each participant examined the entire book, and then told the story from the beginning, while looking at the pictures. Except for the Küntay corpus, all the narratives were told to the adult experimenter. A procedure with naïve listeners was used in collecting the Küntay corpus.

A DEVELOPMENTAL AND CROSSLINGUISTIC ANALYSIS OF FIRST MENTIONS

In the following, we will first examine the order in which English and Turkish speakers of different ages initially mention the three main characters of the frog story, i.e., the boy, the dog, and the frog. Then we will show how they relate the boy to the frog, a theme of crucial importance for the remainder of the story. Finally, we will look at the relationship between indefinite nominal constructions and the types of verbal constructions embedding them.

Initial Ordering and Interrelating of Referents

An important initial task in telling the frog story is to interconnect story participants with one another in relation to the global narrative theme of loss and search. To use Berman's (2001) terms, the task

TABLE 6.1 Number of Participants in Each Age and Language Group

	Total	3 and 4 Years	5 and 6 Years	9 and 10 Years	Adults
English	140	38	36	34	32
Turkish	136	41	45	25	25

TABLE 6.2 Order of Mention of Characters in the Opening of the Story

	3 and 4 Years		5 and 6 Years		9 and 10 Years		Adults	
	Boy-First	Other-First	Boy-First	Other-First	Boy-First	Other-First	Boy-First	Other-First
English	10	22	22	11	32	2	32	0
Turkish	7	31	15	29	19	6	23	2

of initial interrelating of referents combines the *presentative* and *motivating* functions of story settings, that is, to introduce the characters in a way to motivate the remainder of the story.

All three characters are depicted in the first picture of the frog story. Although any one of the six orderings of these three characters is plausible, adult narrators of both languages tend to start their story with the human character, using a "boy-first" strategy. Once the human character is initialized (MacWhinney & Bates, 1978), then the other two characters are linguistically anchored to it through specialized constructions such as possessive or relative constructions, as shown in Example (1).

(1) *There's this little boy and he's enjoying his pet frog that he has in a bottle. He has a pet dog, too* (English 20L, T. Renner).

Table 6.2 presents the breakdown of the order of mention of story characters during the telling of the first page into "boy-first" and "other-first" strategies: 100% of English-speaking adults and 92% of Turkish-speaking adults introduce the boy to their story as the very first participant. Setting up the boy as the initial character is also a prevalent strategy for 9- and 10-year-olds in both language groups.

However, this tendency does not hold as strongly in preschool age children. In both language groups, 3- and 4-year-old children use one of the animal characters (either the dog or the frog) as their initial participant. 5- and 6-year-olds also tend to set up other characters as their first character, while the trend is stronger for Turkish-speaking participants (χ^2 (2, N = 77) = 6.76, $p < 0.01$). The other-first strategy in the younger age group, and the boy-first strategy in the two older age groups do not exhibit statistically significant crosslinguistic differences. In summary, English-speaking children predominantly start using the human character as their starting point from preschool ages on while Turkish-learning children do not adopt such a strategy before 9 years of age. In both age groups, however, there are significant differences in the extent of using a "boy-first" strategy between 5- and 6-year-olds and 9- and 10-year-olds (for Turkish, χ^2 (2, N = 69) = 9.59, $p < 0.005$; for English, (χ^2 (2, N = 67) = 6.41, $p < 0.01$). That is, there is a growing tendency to anchor the story around the boy right from the outset in both language groups, although the development is more protracted in the Turkish sample.

The first frame of the picturebook implies that the relationship of the boy and the two animals can be construed to be a pet-ownership one, because of the indoor surroundings and cultural frames associated with the entire setting. The construction of some such relationship between the three main characters has a bearing on the narrative action portrayed in subsequent frames, and therefore is usually explicitly stated by adult narrators of the frog story, through a possessive construction or a verb referring to the inferred means by which the frog was acquired. Below is an example featuring a possessive marking for the dog and a verb of acquisition (*bul* 'find') for the frog:

(2) *küçük bir çocukla bi köpeğ-i varmış bu*
'there was a little boy and a dog of this (boy)'
*ondan sonra bunlar bigün bi kurbaga **bul**-muşlar*
'and then they found a frog one day' (Adult G, A. Küntay)

TABLE 6.3 The Linguistic Encoding of the Relationship Between the Boy and the Frog in the First Frame, Adults vs. Preschool Children

	Relation	Turkish	English
Adult	Possessive marker	12 (48%)	17 (50%)
	Verbs of non-evident relation	10 (40%)	13 (38%)
	Verbs of looking	2 (8%)	4 (12%)
	No explicit relation	1 (4%)	—
Preschoolers	Verbs of looking	34 (40%)	10 (14%)
	No mention of frog, boy, or both	19 (22%)	27 (36%)
	No explicit relation	16 (19%)	15 (20%)
	Verbs of non-evident relation	7 (8%)	4 (5%)
	Descriptions of pictorially evident relation	6 (7%)	1 (1%)
	Possessive marker	4 (5%)	17 (23%)

Table 6.3 illustrates how adults and preschoolers offer an account of the relationship of the boy and the frog, which is crucial in establishing a motivational background for the search events to follow (Berman, 2001). The coding categories differentiated between picture-dependent and picture-inferrable ways of interrelating the frog and the boy. On one hand, the possessive marker and verbs of non-evident relations (such as *yakalamak* 'to catch,' *sevmek* 'to like/admire,' *bulmak* 'to find,' *avlamak* 'to hunt') encode relations that go beyond the immediately perceivable situation depicted in the first frame. On the other hand, verbs of looking (such as *bakmak* 'to look,' *seyretmek* 'to watch'), and descriptions of pictorially evident relations (such as *karşısında oturmak* 'to sit across,' *yanında* 'next to') remain within the boundaries of what is physically depicted in the first picture of the book. As can be seen in Table 6.3, many preschool children (22% in Turkish and 36% in English) fail to mention either the boy, the frog, or both ("No mention of frog, boy, or both"); around one-fifth in both languages do not set up any explicit relation between the two referents.

The adult narrators behave very similarly in the two languages. They either simply use a possessive construction, showing they assume a relationship of ownership between the boy and the frog (~ 50%) or use verbs of non-evident relation to encode their inferences about how the frog came to exist in a jar placed in what looks like the boy's bedroom (~ 40%). Only a few adults do not go beyond mentioning the frog as an object of the boy's gaze, leaving out all the inferrable connections between the two.

In contrast to adult narrators of English and Turkish, there are crosslinguistic differences in the way the relationship between the boy and the frog is set up for the preschool children. For Turkish children, the predominant way of relating the frog to the boy is through using verbs of looking (40%). English-speaking preschoolers, on the other hand, use more possessive markers. It is likely that young English-speaking children have more cultural access to a pet-ownership schema between a boy and a frog.

A comparison between preschoolers and adults suggests that (a) adults explicitly construct a relationship between the boy and the frog more often and (b) when this relationship is set up, preschoolers' expressions are more picture-bound. This does not mean that young children cannot draw inferences based on static pictorial representations. However, their lesser tendency to do so, compared to adults, shows that preschoolers undertake a differently constructed task when asked to tell a story by looking at the pictures of a book. It seems that they find it adequate to describe the objectively presented contents of the picture, including the identity and behavior of the participants. The nature of the interrelatedness between different characters does not get indicated beyond how they evidently interact within the boundaries of a particular scene. Such a self-enclosed scene description indicates that the preschoolers, as far as picturebook storytelling is concerned, do not "set the narrative scene" in relation to an understanding of the global story structure (Berman, 2001). As will be discussed in the next section, differences between younger and older narrators in the stance they take to the task of storytelling might lead to changes in the patterns of referential introductions.

Introductory Constructions

The analysis of first mention devices involves verbal constructions that encase the introductory referential forms and the types of nominal constructions that denote the referent.

The introductory verbal constructions were first classified into three categories: (1) multiple-argument constructions where more than one NP (Noun Phrase) is involved (e.g., *a boy got a new frog*), (2) intransitive constructions where the only NP is the introduced participant and the verb is not a presentative verb (e.g., *şimdi o otur-uyor* 'now he sit-PROG'), and (3) presentational constructions where the only NP is the introduced participant and the verb is a presentative verb (e.g., *there's a boy*).

The nominal constructions used to refer to the characters were categorized into (1) indefinite NPs prefaced by the indefinite determiner (i.e., *a/an* in English, *bi/bir* in Turkish), (2) definite NPs (proper nouns, pronouns, nouns prefaced by the definite determiner, *the*, in English), and (3) possessive NPs that are marked by possessive pronouns and/or possessive morphology.

Adult Patterns   First we present results from adult narrators displaying the patterns that the younger speakers are working toward. Tables 6.4 and 6.5 present the types of verbal and nominal constructions used for the three characters by adults in English and Turkish stories.

TABLE 6.4   Distribution of Different Nominal Marking in Different Constructions for the Boy in Adult Narratives in English and Turkish

	Multiple-Argument		Intransitive		Presentational	
	Indefinite	Definite	Indefinite	Definite	Indefinite	Definite
Turkish	1 / 4%	8 / 35%	3 / 13%	2 / 8%	8 / 35%	1 / 4%
English	2 / 6%	5 / 16%	5 / 16%	1 / 3%	16 / 52%	2 / 6%

TABLE 6.5   Distribution of Different Nominal Marking in Different Constructions for the Frog and the Dog in Adult Narratives in English and Turkish

		Multiple-Argument			Intransitive			Presentational		
		I	D	P	I	D	P	I	D	P
Frog	Turkish	10 / 43%	4 / 17%	1 / 4%	—	—	1 / 4%	5 / 22%	—	2 / 9%
	English	12 / 35%	2 / 6%	5 / 15%	—	—	1 / 3%	10 / 29%	1 / 3%	3 / 8%
Dog	Turkish	—	2 / 10%	5 / 25%	—	—	4 / 20%	7 / 35%	—	2 / 10%
	English	6 / 21%	1 / 3%	12 / 41%	1 / 3%	1 / 3%	2 / 7%	3 / 10%	1 / 3%	2 / 7%

Note: I = Indefinite; D = Definite; P = Possessive

The proportion of definiteness for the boy is higher in Turkish adult stories (47%) compared to English adult stories (25%). For both language groups, there appears to be a relation between the verbal construction type and (in)definiteness marking in the nominal construction. That is, one-argument presentational and intransitive constructions tend to include an indefinite first mention form for the boy more often than do multiple-argument constructions. The presentational construction, as a specialized device used for introduction of characters, appears more available to English speakers, whereas Turkish speakers more often opt for multiple-argument constructions. As discussed in Dasinger & Toupin (1994), English featutes postposed-postnominal subordinate clauses, allowing speakers to introduce a referent in a non-subject position through a presentational construction and immediately assert a proposition about it. English-speaking adults often use such constructions, merging the introductory function with provision of background or advancement of plot, as seen in Example 3. Since relative clauses are preposed-prenominal in Turkish, presentational clauses are not amenable to progression of narrative as in English, and therefore less frequently employed by Turkish adults.

(3) *There was once a little boy who had a pet dog and a pet frog who he used to keep in a glass jar in his bedroom* (Adult, Wigglesworth).

For the secondary characters, the dog and the frog, a third option of marking the status of the introductory noun phrase exists, that is, to relate it to a previously mentioned character, i.e., the boy. A common way to achieve this is to indicate a possession relation to the boy, either through nominal morphology (e.g., *his dog*, *köpeğ-i* 'dog-POSS') or a possession construction (e.g., *the boy has a dog*, *köpeğ-i var* 'dog-POSS exists'). The employability of possessive constructions for the dog and the frog, once the boy is introduced, decreases the proportion of inappropriate definite expressions for these characters in both languages. As Table 6.5 shows, only 17% of the Turkish adults use definite expressions for the frog, and 10% for the dog. These ratios are 9% and 6%, respectively, in the English-speaking adults' stories. Both groups of adults use more possessive constructions for the dog than the frog.

When we examine the number of indefinite nominal constructions for the frog and the dog across the two languages, the frequencies are the same (64% in English and 65% in Turkish for the frog, and 34% in English and 35% in Turkish for the dog), although the frog receives more indefinite modifiers than the dog. The frequency of indefinite marking for the frog (65%) is slightly higher than for the boy (52%) in the stories of Turkish adults while this relation is reversed for English adults (64% and 74%, respectively), who provide more indefinite marking for the boy. Although this crosslinguistic reversal might be due to different effects of perceived animacy and centrality of character on nominal constructions, it is plausibly an outcome of the preferred pattern of choice in verbal constructions. Turkish adults, when they use the initial referential expression for the frog in multiple argument constructions, mostly use it in nonsubject positions that require non-nominal casemarking. Since all casemarking implies definiteness in Turkish, adults appear to be counteracting this implication by providing an explicit indefinite numeral or using non-casemarked noun phrases for the frog.

In summary, when introduced in non-subject roles, adults of both languages predominantly use indefinite marking. The major difference between the adult Turkish and English stories is that Turkish speakers often use multiple-argument constructions for the boy, where the linguistic term for the boy in the subject grammatical role is not marked as an indefinite NP. The presentational construction is more available to English speakers than Turkish speakers, who often employ multiple-argument constructions where the boy is the definite subject. For the frog, on the other hand, since both groups use either the indefinite-presentational or indefinite object of multiple argument constructions, crosslinguistic differences are not observed.

As Lambrecht (1994) suggests, many languages have a grammatical constraint against indefinite NPs in subject position, since subjects are often the "given/topic" part of constructions. Although indefinite NPs are allowed as subjects in both English and Turkish, adults in both languages seem

TABLE 6.6 Distribution of Nominal Forms With Indefiniteness and Definiteness Marking in All Age Groups for Both Language Samples

	3 and 4 Years		5 and 6 Years		9 and 10 Years		Adults	
	Indefinite	Definite	Indefinite	Definite	Indefinite	Definite	Indefinite	Definite
English	10 43%	13 57%	13 45%	16 55%	16 52%	15 48%	23 74%	8 26%
Turkish	5 17%	25 83%	7 22%	35 78%	16 70%	7 30%	12 52%	11 48%

to entertain such a constraint. In other words, they tend not to employ an indefinite noun phrase for the boy in subject position in multiple-argument constructions.

Developmental Patterns In what follows, we will present how the frequency of (in)definiteness marking interacts with the type of verbal construction in the character introductions of English and Turkish speakers of different ages.

Table 6.6 shows the number and percentage of nouns marked for indefiniteness and definiteness used for first mention of the boy in all age groups. These data exclude cases where there were no mentions of the boy in the introductory page, but include verbless labelings such as 'a boy.'

The proportion of indefinite marking for the boy is higher in English-speaking narrators than Turkish-speaking narrators at preschool ages (χ^2 (2, N = 71) = 6.72, p < 0.01 for 5- to 6-year-olds; χ^2 (2, N = 53) = 4.61, p < 0.05 for 3- to 4-year-olds). From 9 to 10 years of age on, there are no crosslinguistic differences in the patterns of distribution of indefinite and definite nouns. In other words, the two older groups of narrators in the two languages preface the nominal for the boy with an indefinite determiner at comparable levels. The relative optionality of the indefinite determiner in Turkish as compared to English leads to less likelihood of its usage in preschool ages in Turkish. However, this difference diminishes for school-age children and adults, where more formulaic and conventional character introductions start to prevail.

Table 6.7 shows the number of different construction types that encase definite and indefinite noun phrases for the boy. These data, as opposed to Table 6.6, exclude verbless labelings where characters are introduced by nominal phrases. However, the data about verbless labelings are interesting in the sense that they are only used by the youngest age, 3- and 4-year-olds: In English, there were 7 such introductions for the boy, of which 5 had an indefinite pronoun. This age group also has 9 verbless labelings for the dog, and 8 for the frog, and most include an indefinite marker (6 out of 9 for the dog and 6 out of 8 for the frog). Considering the scarcity of indefinite constructions used in

TABLE 6.7 Number of Different Construction Frames for Indefinite and Definite First Mentions for the Boy by Different Age Groups in English and Turkish

		3 and 4 Years		5 and 6 Years		9 and 10 Years		Adults	
	Construction	I	D	I	D	I	D	I	D
English	Multiple-argument	—	8	—	15	3	12	2	5
	Intransitive	—	3	—	1	1	3	5	1
	Presentational	4		13	1	14	—	16	1
Turkish	Multiple-argument	—	15	2	19	5	5	1	8
	Intransitive	2	7	1	11	1	1	3	2
	Presentational	2	2	6	2	10	1	8	1

Note: I = Indefinite; D = Definite

TABLE 6.8 Distribution of Indefinite, Definite, and Possessive NPs Used for the Dog and the Frog by Different Age Groups in the Two Languages

		3 and 4 Years			5 and 6 Years			9 and 10 Years			Adults		
		I	D	P	I	D	P	I	D	P	I	D	P
Dog	English	4 29%	10 71%	—	12 40%	15 50%	3 10%	11 44%	7 28%	7 28%	10 36%	—	18 64%
	Turkish	5 14%	29 83%	1 3%	8 19%	31 74%	3 7%	7 39%	7 39%	4 22%	7 29%	2 8%	15 63%
Frog	English	9 50%	8 44%	1 6%	13 42%	12 39%	6 19%	25 74%	2 6%	7 21%	21 66%	3 9%	8 25%
	Turkish	9 29%	22 71%	—	13 32%	27 66%	1 2%	19 76%	5 20%	1 4%	14 61%	3 13%	6 26%

Note: I = Indefinite; D = Definite; P = Possessive

fuller constructions at this age, the fact that many are verbless constructions is revealing. In Turkish, verbless labelings are often definite.

The distribution of the indefinite forms into different types of constructions suggests that most indefinites for the boy occur in presentational constructions at all ages and for both languages. The connection between presentational constructions and the indefinite article appears especially strong in English. After 9 and 10 years, the strength of this connection weakens, leading to a few indefinite subjects of multiple-argument and intransitive frames. In Turkish, more than 50% of indefinites are attested in presentational constructions at all ages, although NPs in other kinds of constructions occasionally receive indefinite marking, at earlier ages than observed for English-speaking children. On the whole, however, definite nominal constructions used for the boy tend to be the subjects in intransitive or multiple-argument constructions, more often in the latter.

Turning our attention to the secondary characters, Table 6.8 presents the distribution of indefinite, definite, and possessive NPs used for the dog and the frog by different age groups in the two languages.

The crosslinguistic differences observed in the introductory devices of the younger groups for the boy are not observed for the secondary characters. In other words, at all ages studied, the distributions of different nominal constructions used for the dog and the frog are not statistically different across English and Turkish speakers.

In both languages, the amount of definite expressions used for both of the characters gradually disappears across ages. Although possessive constructions are few at preschool ages, they gain prevalence, especially for the dog, with age in both languages. The use of the possessive construction for the frog is less frequent overall in Turkish, and also employed less frequently by Turkish children than by English-speaking children.

Table 6.9 shows the number of different construction types that include the different types of nominal constructions for the dog and the frog. Preliminary analysis indicated that the grammatical role that the referent fulfills in a multiple-argument construction might play a role in the (in)definiteness marking it receives.

Although the dog tends to be introduced as subject, the frog mostly occupies a non-subject grammatical role in both languages. For the dog and the frog, there are some introductions in non-subject positions that are expressed in indefinite form by 5- to 6-year-olds and older narrators in English. The youngest narrators only use presentational constructions to embody the indefinite numeral. In Turkish, the dog mostly receives definite marking in subject positions, although the amount of indefiniteness for the frog gains prevalence from 5 to 6 years of age on.

Even though the number of definite nominals exceeds that of indefinite ones in the preschool ages, we see that the indefiniteness indicator is used more frequently for the frog than for the boy. There might be two partially related reasons for this: As previous research indicated (Bamberg, 1986,

TABLE 6.9 Distribution of Different Nominal Marking in Different Constructions for the Frog and the Dog Across Ages in English and Turkish

		Construction	3 and 4 Years			5 and 6 Years			9 and 10 Years			Adults		
			I	D	P	I	D	P	I	D	P	I	D	P
Dog	English	Multi-argument	—	8	—	9	14	3	7	6	4	7	—	12
		Intransitive	—	2	—	1	—	—	—	1	1	—	—	4
		Presentational	4	—	—	2	1	—	4	—	2	3	—	2
	Turkish	Multi-argument	3	26	1	1	26	3	2	7	3	—	2	7
		Intransitive	—	1	—	1	4	—	—	—	—	—	—	3
		Presentational	2	2	—	6	1	—	5	—	1	7	—	4
Frog	English	Multi-argument	2	3	1	9	8	5	21	2	5	19	2	6
		Intransitive	—	5	—	—	4	—	1	—	—	—	—	1
		Presentational	7	—	—	4	—	1	3	—	2	2	1	1
	Turkish	Multi-argument	3	13	—	5	16	1	10	3	—	9	3	3
		Intransitive	4	5	—	1	6	—	1	1	—	—	—	1
		Presentational	2	4	—	7	5	—	8	1	1	5	—	2

Note: I = Indefinite; D = Definite; P = Possessive

1987; Hickmann, 2003; Hickmann et al., 1996; Kail & Hickmann, 1992; Küntay, 2002; McGann & Schwartz, 1988; Wigglesworth, 1990), narrators use less indefinite and more presupposing forms for main characters than for secondary characters. Also, in both languages, there seems to be an association between usage of indefinite marker and non-subject grammatical roles, in which the frog gets introduced.

CONCLUSIONS

As Slobin points out, "… habitual patterns of language use are shaped by ease of accessibility of linguistic forms—to producer and receiver, as well as by the dynamics of cultural and aesthetic values and the perspectives and communicative aims of the speaker" (Slobin, 2004, p. 253). This study shows that patterns of usage of (in)definite nominal constructions depend on ease of accessibility of certain constructions in addition to the stance the participant assumes in relation to the task. Availability of a formal article system leads English speakers of younger ages to use more indefinite articles for the boy than their Turkish counterparts. However, from 9 years of age on, the effect disappears, probably because older speakers opt for more formulaic devices for opening stories than at younger ages. Another factor is the status of the character being introduced. No crosslinguistic differences are found in the (in)definiteness status of the introductory devices for the dog and the frog in any of the age groups. A decisive factor that might explain crosslinguistic differences for the boy at young ages and similarities for the other two characters is the type of construction or lexical form chosen to introduce characters. In both languages, a very high percentage of presentational constructions attract the indefinite marker. Hickmann et al. (1996) reports a similar association of predicate types with the usage of indefinite marking found in the four languages they studied (English, French, German, and Mandarin), with presentational constructions 'attracting' local markings of indefiniteness in all languages. We can confirm that the distribution of indefinite marking is related to the choice of construction.

The choice of construction, in turn, has to do with the stance narrators display in beginning their story. It is also interesting to note that one preschool-age child in the Turkish data who prefaced his introduction of the boy with an indefinite article started out by asking the following question to the experimenter:

(4) *burda ... yani böyle masalı mı anlatıcam yoksa burda neler var onu mu söyliycem?*
'here ... I wonder, shall I tell the story or talk about what there is here [= in this picture]?

Adult: *masalı anlatıcaksın evet*
'you're going to tell the story, right'

peki 'ok'
bir *çocuk ...* **bir** *çocuk yerde oturuyo*
'a child ... a child is sitting on the floor' (4-year-old, A. Küntay)

It might well be that the child opted to use an indefinite numeral to preface the first character introduced in a conventional way, because he actively constructed the task as a storytelling task as opposed to a picture-description. M. Gopnik (1989) has found that, in English-speaking young children's (4- to 6-year-olds) stories, most indefinite articles occur in stories with formal beginnings. She hypothesized that "the non-occurrence of a formal beginning is an indicator that the child has not adopted a story stance" (p. 236). The meta-textual question posed by the Turkish preschooler in Example 4 shows that there could be multiple stances to this task of picture-based storytelling.

A picture-description rather than a storytelling stance also leads to a random ordering of the mention of the three characters and interconnections of characters that encode merely visually available information. Such strategies can adequately describe the contents of the first picture, but might fall short of situating the rest of the narrative around a boy who has a dog and a frog. With age, narrators in both languages order the boy as the first character, anchoring the dog and the frog around it with possessive marking and/or verbs of non-evident relations.

Expressing the discourse function of introducing new characters in a story involves a choice between different constructions. The choice of an indefinite nominal construction appears to depend on the type of verbal construction used. That might be why, although preschoolers might use determiners appropriately in some contexts (Maratsos, 1976), their skills are fragile. Warden (1981) proposes that when preschool-age children are asked to produce full constructions, as in his experiments in comparison to Maratsos (1976), who prompted for simple noun phrases, they do not divert enough attention to producing appropriate indefinite articles. To explain the inconsistency in the adult-like usage of determiners, Warden proposes that "it is quite possible that the children were intermittently able to divert attention from syntax construction and the selection of content words to consider the rules of article use" (p. 93). This study shows that certain constructions are more amenable to provision of indefinite marking on the noun phrase than others, both for children and for older speakers, and in very different languages such as English and Turkish. Our findings are consistent with the suggestions of Pine and Lieven (1997) that the development of an adultlike determiner usage involves the progressive increase of the range of frames in which determiners appear.

REFERENCES

Aksu-Koç, A. (1994). Development of linguistic forms: Turkish. In R. Berman & D. I. Slobin (Eds.), *Relating events in narrative: A crosslinguistic development study.* Mahwah, NJ: Lawrence Erlbaum Associates.

Bamberg, M. (1986). A functional approach to the acquisition of anaphoric relationships. *Linguistics, 24,* 227–284.

Bamberg, M. (1987). *The acquisition of narratives: Learning to use language.* Berlin: Mouton de Gruyter.

Bennett-Kastor, T. (1983). Noun phrases and coherence in child narratives. *Journal of Child Language, 10,* 135–149.

Berman, R. A. (2001). Setting the narrative scene: How children begin to tell a story. In K.E. Nelson, A. Aksu-Koç, & C.E. Johnson (Eds.), *Children's language* (Vol. 10, pp. 1–30). Mahwah, NJ: Lawrence Erlbaum Associates.

Berman, R. A., & Katzenberger, I. (2004). Form and function in introducing narrative and expository texts: A developmental perspective. *Discourse Processes, 38,* 57–94.

Berman, R. A., & Slobin, D. I. (1994). Becoming a proficient speaker. In R. Berman & D. I. Slobin (Eds.), *Relating events in narrative: A crosslinguistic developmental study* (pp. 597–610). Hillsdale, NJ: Lawrence Erlbaum Associates.

Brown, R. A. (1973). *A first language*. Cambridge, MA: Harvard University Press.

Dasinger, L., & Toupin, C. (1994). The development of relative clause functions in narrative. In R. A. Berman & D. I. Slobin (Eds.), *Relating events in narrative: A crosslinguistic developmental study* (pp. 457–515). Hillsdale, NJ: Lawrence Erlbaum Associates.

Du Bois, J. W. (1980). Beyond definiteness: The trace of identity in discourse. In W. L. Chafe (Ed.), *The pear stories: Cognitive, cultural, and linguistics aspects of narrative production* (pp. 203–274). Norwood, NJ: Ablex Publishing Corporation.

Givón, T. (1995). Coherence in text vs. coherence in mind. In M. A. Gernsbacher & T. Givón (Eds.), *Coherence in spontaneous text* (pp. 59–115). Amsterdam/Philadelphia: John Benjamins.

Gopnik, M. (1989). The development of text competence. In M.-E. Conte, J. S. Petöfi, & E. Sözer (Eds.), *Text and discourse connectedness* (pp. 225–244). Amsterdam/Philadelphia: John Benjamins.

Hickmann, M. (2003). *Children's discourse: person, space and time across languages.* Cambridge, UK: Cambridge University Press.

Hickmann, M., Hendriks, H., Roland, F., & Liang, J. (1996). The marking of new information in children's narratives: A comparison of English, French, German, and Mandarin Chinese. *Journal of Child Language*, 3, 591–610.

Kail, M., & Hickmann, M. (1992). French children's ability to introduce referents in narratives as function of mutual knowledge. *First Language*, 12, 73–94.

Kail, M., & Sanchez-Lopez, I. (1997). Referent introductions in Spanish narratives as a function of contextual constraints: A crosslinguistic perspective. *First Language*, 17, 103–130.

Karmiloff-Smith, A. (1981). The grammatical marking of thematic structure in the development of language production. In W. Deutsch (Ed.), *The child's construction of language* (pp. 121–147). New York: Academic Press.

Küntay, A. C. (2002). Development of the expression of indefiniteness: Presenting new referents in Turkish picture-series stories. *Discourse Processes*, 33, 77–101.

Lambrecht, K. (1994). *Information structure and sentence form: Topic, focus, and the mental representation of discourse referents.* Cambridge, UK: Cambridge University Press.

MacWhinney, B., & Bates, E. (1978). Sentential devices for conveying givenness and newness: A cross-cultural developmental study. *Journal of Verbal Learning and Verbal Behavior*, 17, 539–558.

Maratsos, M. P. (1976). *The use of definite and indefinite reference in young children: An experimental study in semantic acquisition.* Cambridge, UK: Cambridge University Press.

Mayer, M. (1969). *Frog, where are you?* New York: Dial Press.

McGann, W., & Schwartz, A. (1988). Main character in children's narratives. *Linguistics*, 26, 215–233.

Pine, J. M., & Lieven, E.V. (1997). Slot and frame patterns and the development of the determiner category. *Applied Psycholinguistics*, 18, 123–138.

Sansa, Tura, S. (1986). Definiteness and referentiality in Turkish nonverbal sentences. In D. I. Slobin & K. Zimmer (Eds.), *Studies in Turkish linguistics* (pp. 165–194). Amsterdam/Philadelphia: John Benjamins.

Schiffrin, D. (1994). *Approaches to discourse.* Cambridge, MA: Blackwell.

Slobin, D. I. (2004). The many ways to search for a frog: Linguistic typology and the expression of motion events. In S. Strömqvist & L. Verhoeven (Eds.), *Relating events in narrative: Vol. 2. Typological and contextual perspectives* (pp. 219–257). Mahwah, NJ: Lawrence Erlbaum Associates.

Stromqvist, S., & Verhoeven, L. (Eds.). (2004). *Relating events in narrative: Vol. 2. Typological and contextual perspectives.* Mahwah, NJ: Lawrence Erlbaum Associates.

Warden, D. (1981). Learning to identify referents. *British Journal of Psychology*, 72, 93–99.

Wigglesworth, G. (1990). Children's narrative acquisition: A study of some aspects of reference and anaphora. *First Language*, 10, 105–125.

7

Revisiting the Acquisition of Sesotho Noun Class Prefixes[1]

KATHERINE DEMUTH and DAVID ELLIS

Brown University

Operating Principle A: Pay attention to the ends of words.

Dan I. Slobin (1973, p. 191)

The issue of how and when Sesotho noun class prefixes are acquired was the topic of a seminar Dan and I taught while I was a postdoctoral fellow at UC Berkeley from 1983–1985. Since Bantu languages have multiple singular and plural noun class prefixes, this was a topic of particular theoretical interest for Dan given his Operating Principles of paying attention to the beginnings and ends of words, and unique form–function mapping (Slobin 1973, 1985). The preliminary investigation of how Sesotho noun class prefixes are learned did not support these Operating Principles, with multiple singular and plural prefixes appearing gradually between the ages of 2 and 3 (Demuth, 1988). This chapter reports on recent research examining the noun class input Sesotho-speaking children actually hear. In so doing, it also provides insight into the grammatical structure of Sesotho, how it differs from other Bantu languages, and the learnability issues that arise. Equipped with this background it is now possible to better understand the apparent 'gradual' nature of the acquisition process, and to develop a more fine-grained model of how language learning takes place.

INTRODUCTION

The acquisition of the Bantu noun class prefix system has long been a topic of theoretical interest. Most of Africa's approximately 500 Bantu languages have between 13 and 18 noun class prefixes, though some have been lost, especially in languages serving as lingua francas. Compare, for example, the noun class system reconstructed for Proto-Bantu (Welmers, 1973) with those systems found today in closely related Setswana and Sesotho, and the more distant Cameroonian language Western Ejagam (Watters, 1980) (see also Guthrie, 1948; Meeussen, 1967). This is shown in Table 7.1.

---

[1] A previous version of this chapter was presented at the Bantu Acquisition Workshop at Smith College. We thank that audience, reviewers Nancy Budwig and Susan Ervin-Tripp, and members of the Brown Child Language Lab for helpful suggestions and discussion. We also thank Francina Moloi and 'Malillo Machobane for helping stimulate this research, and Thandie Hlabana for Sesotho consultation. Research for this chapter was supported in part by NIH grant R01MH60922 to the first author.

TABLE 7.1 Sample of Bantu Noun Class Systems

	Proto-Bantu	Setswana	Sesotho	W. Ejagam
1	mo-	mo-	mo-	N-
1a	ø	ø	ø	
2	va-	ba-	ba-	a-
2a	βo-	bo-	bo-	
3	mo-	mo-	mo-	N-
4	me-	me-	me-	
5	le-	le-	le-	e-
6	ma-	ma-	ma-	a-
7	ke-	se-	se-	
8-	βi-	di-	di-	bi-
9	ne-	N-	(N)-	N-
10	li-ne	diN-	di(N)-	
11	lo-	lo-		
12	ka-			
13	to-			
14	βo-	bo-	bo-	o-
15	ko-	γo-	ho-	
16	pa-	fa-		
17	ko-	γo-	ho-	
18	mo-	mo-		
19	pi-			i-
20	γo			
21	γI			
22	γa			
23	γe			

Many of these noun classes show singular–plural pairings, as shown (orthographically) in the Sesotho examples in (1).

(1) Sesotho singular/plural nouns and prefixes

	Singular		Plural	
1	mo-tho	2	ba-tho	'person'
1a	ø-mme	2a	bo-mme	'mother'
3	mo-se	4	me-se	'dress'
5	le-tsatsi	6	ma-tsatsi	'day'
7	se-tulo	8	di-tulo	'chair'
9	ø-tapole	10	di-tapole	'potato'
14	bo-hobe			'bread'

The complexity of this noun class system, and the fact that there are multiple morphological markers for the notion 'plural,' led Slobin (1973, 1985) to propose that there might be the tendency for children to use one plural noun class prefix, and overextend this to use with other plural nouns, showing unique form–function mapping. However, a review of the literature on the acquisition of Bantu noun class prefixes in Siswati, Sesotho, Setswana, and Zulu found little evidence for this position (cf. Demuth, 1988, 1992, 2003). Rather, children seem to acquire the Bantu noun class system with relative ease by the age of 3, typically showing errors of omission, but not errors of commission.

Demuth (1988) proposed that the lack of morphological overgeneralization was due in part to the agglutinative nature of most noun class prefixes, and to the phonologically transparent agreement system in which they participate. This is illustrated in the Sesotho examples in (2) below, where the numbers indicate the class to which the prefix belongs. A more phonetically transparent version of Lesotho orthography has been used (cf. Doke & Mofokeng, 1985). Numbers indicate noun class. Glosses are as follows: AGR = subject-verb agreement, COP = copula, FOC = focus, PRF = perfect.)

(2) a. Mo-sadi o-ngotse le-ngolo le-le-tle
   1-woman AGR1-wrote/PRF 5-letter 5-5-nice
   'The woman wrote a nice letter'
   b. Ba-sadi ba-ngotse ma-ngolo a-ma-tle
   2-women AGR2-wrote/PRF 6-letter 6-6-nice
   'The women wrote some nice letters'

Thus, although learning the gender and case marking system in German is difficult and protracted (Mills, 1986; Clahsen, Eisenbeiss, & Vainikka, 1994), learning the Bantu noun class and agreement system is comparably easy and error-free. The fact that Bantu noun class prefixes are morphologically easy to segment from the nominal stem and the fact that they participate in a relatively phonologically transparent agreement system provide mechanisms for early and error-free learning. At least this is the picture that has generally been offered to date.

Much of the original research on the acquisition of Bantu noun class prefixes was carried out in the 1970s and 1980s (Kunene, 1979; Suzman, 1980, 1991, 1996; Connelly, 1984; Tsonope, 1987; Demuth, 1988; Idiata, 1998). Most of this research examined data from longitudinal case studies of a few children for each language. The research by Kunene (1979) also included wug-tasks to nonce forms (Berko, 1958) for children learning Siswati, where occasional lack of segmentation and overgeneralization took place. Research on Sesotho, Setswana, and Sangu also suggested that 2-year-olds were more likely to show earlier use of noun class prefixes with monosyllabic noun stems (Tsonope, 1987; Demuth, 1992, 1994; Idiata, 1998). Demuth (1992, 1994) suggested that this was due to the fact that a second syllable was required to meet disyllabic (binary foot) word-minimality requirements (e.g., *mo-tho* > *motho* 'person,' but *le-phoqo* > *phoko* 'green corn stalk'). These studies also noted that between 2 and 2;6 there was a certain amount of variability in Sesotho prefix production, with alternation between null, filler syllable, and full-prefix forms, even for the same lexical item. However, none of these studies provided a quantitative perspective on the development of noun class prefixes (though see Ziesler & Demuth, 1995). Today, with computerized longitudinal developmental databases, such as the Demuth Sesotho Corpus, it is possible to examine more closely the course of noun class prefix development over time (see Demuth, 1992, and http://childes.psy.cmu.edu/ for further discussion of the children, data collection methods, and the data).

The existence of larger acquisition corpora, and the tools needed to exploit them, has also made it possible to examine more closely the input that children hear. This has been a critical methodological aspect of some of my early work on the acquisition of Sesotho passives (Demuth, 1989, 1990), and has recently become the focus of work by Tomasello and colleagues (e.g., Theakston, Lieven, & Tomasello, 2003). This process also often leads to a better understanding of the structure of the target language. Although many of the best-studied Bantu languages have excellent grammars and dictionaries, as well as a good body of theoretically sophisticated syntactic research, much is still not known about the structure of these languages. Yet, knowledge about the structure of the target language is critical for understanding the nature of the learning problem young language learners face.

In a study of children's acquisition of Sesotho noun class prefixes, Ziesler and Demuth (1995) observed that adults sometimes drop noun class prefixes in child-directed speech. They raised the possibility that this might have an effect on children's acquisition of noun class prefixes as well. However, it is only more recently that we have discovered that Sesotho-speaking adults selectively drop only certain noun class prefixes, and only under certain syntactic conditions (Machobane, 2003; Machobane, Moloi, & Demuth, 2004). If adults are dropping noun class prefixes, this raises questions about the actual nature of the input children hear, and the possible effects this might have on the acquisition of noun class prefixes. In the following section we present an analysis of the contexts in which null noun class prefixes are found in Sesotho and other closely related (Sotho) languages. In particular, we show that noun class prefixes that begin with a coronal consonant can be optionally dropped (realized as null) in the context of agreement. We then present new findings on the analysis of two Sesotho-speaking children between the ages of 2 and 3, showing how they learn the phonological and syntactic conditions under which noun class prefixes can be realized as null.

THE DISTRIBUTION OF NULL NOUN CLASS PREFIXES IN SESOTHO

Sesotho has 13 noun class prefixes. These are shown in (3) below. (Classes 1a and 2a take the same agreement forms as 1 and 2. Since they are also also restricted to humans, these are typically classified as a special sub-class of classes 1 and 2. Note also that classes 11, 12, and 13 have disappeared through internal processes of morpho-phonological change.)

(3) Sesotho noun class prefixes

	Singular		Plural
1	mo-	2	ba-
1a	ø-	2a	bo-
3	mo-	4	me-
5	<u>le-</u>	6	ma-
7	<u>se-</u>	8	<u>di-</u>
9	ø-	10	<u>di-</u>
14	bo-		

Those prefixes that contain a coronal consonant (underlined above) can be 'optionally' dropped, or realized as null, but only when followed by some form of agreement. Thus, the coronal classes 5, 7, 8, and 10 can be realized as null when the noun is followed by an agreeing morpheme (4a), but not when there is no agreeing morpheme (4b). In contrast, non-coronal noun class prefixes cannot be dropped, even when agreement is present (4c).

(4) a. Ba-tho ba-rata (di)-tapole tsa-ka
    2-people 2AGR-like 10-potatoes 10-my
    'The people like my potatoes'
  b. Ba-tho ba-rata *(di)-tapole
    2-people 2AGR-like 10-potatoes
    'The people like potatoes'

c. Neo o-rata °(ba)-na ba-ba-tle
Neo 1AGR-like 2-children 2-2-beautiful
'Neo likes beautiful children'

Any type of agreement appears to license null noun class prefixes. A sample of the types of agreement contexts is provided in (5).

(5) a. (Di)poleiti di-fihl-ile　　　　　Subject
　　　10-plate 10AGR-arrive-PRF
　　　'The plates arrived'
　b. Bea (se)eta se-na　　　　　　　Object
　　　put_down 7-shoe 7-this
　　　'Put this shoe down'
　c. (Le)sela le metsi　　　　　　　 Copula
　　　5-cloth 5COP 6water
　　　'The cloth is wet'
　d. Ke (se)kolo sa-ng?　　　　　　 Wh-word
　　　FOC 7-school 7-what
　　　'What kind of school is it?'

We suggest that the ability for the phonologically 'unmarked' noun class prefixes in Sesotho to optionally drop when the noun class prefix features are represented elsewhere in the phrase may be due to the different syntactic analyses of the noun class prefix across Bantu languages. If noun class prefixes actually mark number, as Carstens (1991, 1993) proposes, Sesotho appears to permit unmarked (coronal) prefix deletion if number (agreement) is marked elsewhere in the noun phrase (or determiner phrase). This suggests that noun class prefixes in Sesotho may be grammatical function items, whereas in other Bantu languages they may be bound morphemes that are listed in the lexicon. This contrast raises questions about the semantic content of noun class prefixes, the implications for syntactic structure, and the effects on how these morphemes are acquired. A fuller treatment of the syntax of these constructions goes beyond the scope of the present chapter (see Bresnan & Mchombo (1995), Myres (1987), Visser (2001), and Machobane (1993) for further discussion).

One of the questions that arises in any study of grammatical alternations is how frequently different forms of a construction actually appear. We therefore examined a sample of the adult input to two of the children in the Demuth Sesotho Corpus. This included an analysis of child-directed speech productions in the first and last sessions for Hlobohang (at 2;1 and 3 years) and Litlhare (at 2;1 and 3;2 years). In the first case we found that adults consistently dropped 20% of coronal noun class prefixes that contained agreement. No other noun class prefixes were dropped, except for a few cases of 'baby-talk' in the earlier session, where the adult imitated the child's attempt to produce *mo-roho* 'greens' as *ayo*, or *royo*. In the second case we found that adults consistently dropped 35% of coronal nouns with agreement in both sessions. Noun class prefixes were also dropped on a few locative nouns, which is also grammatical (e.g., *le-ifo > ifo* 'in the fire-place,' *le-saka > sak-eng* 'at the corral'). Under no other conditions did adults drop noun class prefixes in their speech to children. Thus, adults appear to drop 20–35% of coronal noun class prefixes that are followed by some sort of agreement, at least in their conversations with 2- to 3-year-olds. The extent of this dropping across discourse genres is not known, but it is grammatical, and is heard in adult-directed speech as well.

This distribution of null noun class prefixes should be clear to the Sesotho learner. That is, noun class prefixes are only dropped with those noun class prefixes that contain a coronal consonant, but then only when it occurs with agreement. However, given that the majority of the time (65–80%) these prefixes do not drop, this distribution presents a potential problem for the learner. Even when both phonological and syntactic licensing conditions are met, the realization of noun class prefixes as null is variable. This may make it more difficult for the learner to extract the phonological and syntactic generalizations under which this process is permitted. We might then expect learners to show a protracted course of acquisition, where the learning path is characterized by either phonological or syntactic overgeneralizations, or both. Alternatively, children might take a lexical approach, only dropping prefixes on those items they typically hear with a null prefix. In the following section we present results from these two children's acquisition of noun class prefixes over time, showing that overgeneralization does take place, but that there may be some lexical effects as well, at least for very high frequency lexical items.

The Acquisition of Sesotho Noun Class Prefixes

For this part of the study we examine all nouns produced by Hlobohang (boy, 2;1–3;0) and Litlhare (girl, 2;1–3;2). Prefixless nouns such as those in class 9, which accounted for much of the data, were excluded from the analysis. The total number of noun productions analyzed was therefore 1293 word tokens for Hlobohang and 1685 word tokens for Litlhare. All nouns containing a possible target prefix were then coded for the number of syllables in the noun stem (1, 2, 3 or more), the noun class (either coronal or non-coronal), the realization of the noun class prefix (null, filler (V or syllabic nasal), full), and the presence of any agreement. Subsequent analysis showed that fillers occurred in some of the children's prefix attempts, especially up to the age of 2;6 (17% for Hlobohang, 25% for Litlhare). From 2;7 onward, fillers dropped below 10% for both coronal and non-coronal target prefixes, indicating better overall mastery of CV prefix production.

Since previous reports had suggested that monosyllabic stems might be more likely to preserve noun class prefixes, we first examined prefix production as a function of the number of syllables per word. Hlobohang was significantly more likely to use noun class prefixes with monosyllabic nouns until 2;3 years. Litlhare also showed significantly more use of noun class prefixes with monosyllables until 2;4. Conversely, there was a greater likelihood of prefixes being truncated with words that were already a disyllabic foot. These findings confirm the proposals of Demuth (1992, 1994), showing that Sesotho-speaking children may be aware of the language's word-minimality effects, and that grammatical morphemes such as noun class prefixes are more likely to be produced in these prosodically licensed contexts. This contributes to a growing body of literature showing that prosodic factors may account for some of the reported early variable production of grammatical morphemes in many languages (cf. Gerken, 1996; Lleó & Demuth, 1999). However, this effect tends to disappear around 2;3, at least in the case of Sesotho noun class prefixes.

Thus, some of the early variability in the use of noun class prefixes in Sesotho may be due to the more consistent use of prefixes with monosyllabic noun stems, forming a disyllabic foot. Surprisingly, however, Litlhare occasionally dropped noun class prefixes on monosyllabic stems (e.g., *(le)jwe lena* 'this stone,' *(di)jo tsaka* 'my food'), and adults did the same! We suspect that the resulting monosyllabic noun prosodically cliticizes to the following modifier, resulting in a well-formed prosodic word. The prosodic structure of these forms, and the frequency with which they occur, is obviously an area for further research.

We then conducted three different analyses of the data to investigate the children's knowledge of the contexts in which Sesotho noun class prefixes can be optionally dropped. First, we examined the children's awareness that null prefixes are phonologically licensed by coronal consonants. Second, we explored their awareness of the syntactic agreement constraints. Finally, we investigated the possibility that the children's use of null prefixes was lexically determined.

Phonological Licensing of Null Noun Class Prefixes

We now address the issue of how and when children learn that only coronal prefixes can be realized as null. To do this we compared the production of coronal and non-coronal prefixes (including fillers), independent of agreement. As indicated in Figures 7.1 and 7.2, coronal prefixes were significantly less likely to be produced across all points in development for both children at $p < 0.05$.

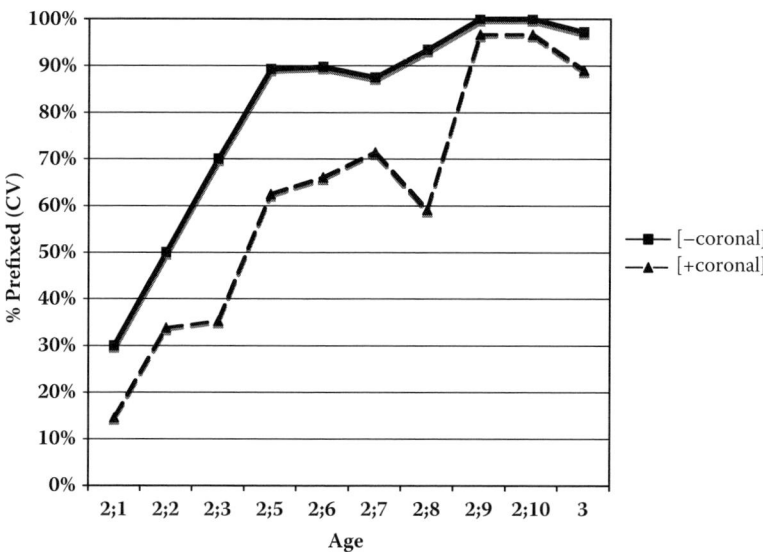

Figure 7.1 Hlobohang's production of coronal and non-coronal noun class prefixes.

Overall patterns of development for both children show that coronal prefixes are significantly less likely to be produced than non-coronal prefixes (Hlobohang: $\chi2 = 67.93$, $p < 0.001$; Litlhare: $\chi2 = 214.82$, $p < 0.001$).

Further analysis examined the children's production of coronal and non-coronal prefixes at each point in time. A significant difference in the production of the two phonologically distinct prefixes ($p < 0.05$) held for Hlobohang at all points except 2;7, and then again from 2;9–3 when he produced all prefixes at near or above 90%. The difference for Lithlare was also significant at all points ($p < 0.05$) except at 2;5.

Thus, both children produced coronal prefixes less often than non-coronal prefixes. This indicates some awareness of the phonological licensing of null noun class prefixes from early in acquisition. In the following section we examine their understanding that agreement is also required for licensing null prefixes.

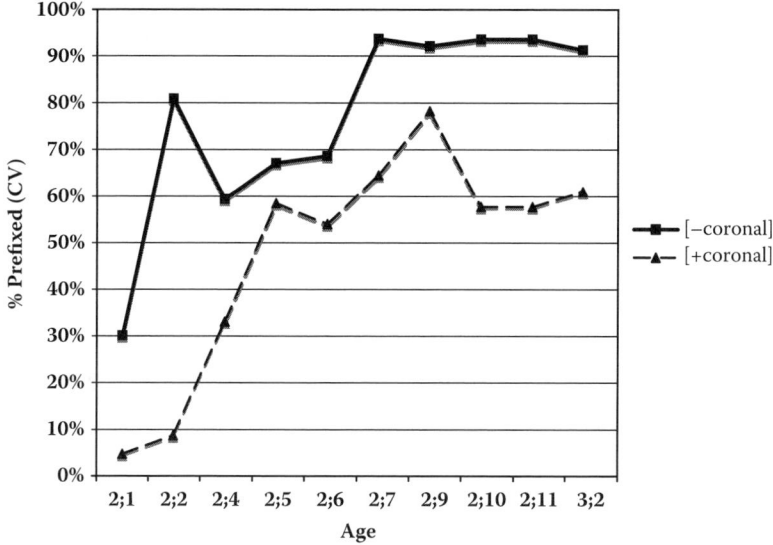

Figure 7.2 Litlhare's production of coronal and non-coronal noun class prefixes.

Syntactic Licensing of Null Noun Class Prefixes

Given both children's tendency to drop noun class prefixes more often when these contained coronal consonants, we then examined the data to determine if null prefixes were more likely to occur in the presence of agreement. In particular, we suspected that Litlhare's lowered prefix production with non-coronal prefixes at 2;4, 2;5, and 2;6 might have been due to the overgeneralization of agreement, thereby licensing the dropping of all prefixes that were coronal or had agreement. To investigate these possible overgeneralization effects, we combined the data for both children into two time periods: Time 1 (2;1-2;6) and Time 2 (2;7–3;0–3;2). The results are shown in (6).

(6) Percent production of noun class prefixes under different phonological and syntactic conditions

		Coronal		Non-Coronal	
		AGR	No AGR	AGR	No AGR
Hlobohang	Time 1	56%	62%	90%	80%
	Time 2	71%	90%	91%	96%
Litlhare	Time 1	37%	62%	69%	82%
	Time 2	59%	82%	99%	98%

At Time 1, Hlobohang showed evidence of phonological overgeneralization, dropping coronal prefixes regardless of the presence of agreement. By Time 2, however, he correctly used null coronal prefixes only when agreement was present, showing that he had learned the syntactic licensing conditions for null prefixes by this time. At both times, Hlobohang was extremely accurate at producing non-coronal prefixes. His poorer performance in the non-coronal no agreement cases was due to his unsuccessful attempts to produce the lexical item *moroho* 'greens' as *aya* or *royo*. Recall that this is the lexical item that adults also produced in baby-talk form.

In contrast, Litlhare exhibited syntactic overgeneralization at Time 1, dropping prefixes on both coronals and non-coronals that contained agreement. That is, she seemed to be aware of both the phonological and syntactic licensing conditions, but permitted null prefixes if either condition was met. Thus, Litlhare's initial analysis was that null prefixes were permitted at the union, rather than at the intersection, of the licensing conditions. By Time 2, however, she realized that null noun class prefixes were permitted only when both conditions were met. Thus, although she still dropped prefixes more often on coronals with no agreement than with non-coronals, she was much more likely to drop prefixes on coronals when agreement was present. Further examination of Litlhare's coronal nouns showed that prefixes were grammatically dropped on locative nouns (e.g., *(se)dibeng* 'at the well,' *(le)lwaleng* 'at the mill'), but also on nouns with three or four syllables not followed by agreement (e.g., *(le)sheleshele* 'porridge,' *(le)kotikoti* 'tin can,' *(di)namune* 'orange'), suggesting a prosodic complexity or word-length explanation for some of her coronal prefix deletions.

In sum, both children showed overgeneralization of null noun class prefixes, indicating that they are not simply matching the input they hear. Hlobohang overgeneralized to all coronals at Time 1, suggesting that he was aware of the phonological constraints on licensing null prefixes. Litlhare overgeneralized to both coronals and to all nouns with agreement at Time 1, showing that she was aware of both the phonological and syntactic licensing conditions. She continued to phonologically overgeneralize at Time 2. Further analysis would be needed to determine if this interacts with prosodic constraints on word-size.

These findings suggest that Sesotho-speaking 2-year-olds are making both phonological and syntactic generalizations about the conditions that license null prefixes. However, recall that adults employ null noun class prefixes on only 20–35% of those nouns that are licensed for null prefixes. We also noticed that some nouns are much more likely to be produced with null prefixes by adults when licensing conditions are met. In the next section we explored the possibility that children's use of null prefixes may also show evidence of lexical effects.

Lexical Effects

Recent research by Tomasello and colleagues (e.g., Pine, Lieven, & Rowland, 1998; Tomasello, 1992) has suggested that children's early grammars initially show evidence of lexical learning, and only later begin to exhibit evidence of syntactic generalization. This raises the possibility that the apparent grammatical licensing children exhibit with respect to null noun class prefixes may actually be reduced to lexical effects. That is, perhaps some lexical items are more likely to be produced with null prefixes in the input children hear such that the children themselves use null prefixes with only some lexical items.

One way to test for possible lexical effects is to measure the frequency with which certain items are used in the input children hear. We therefore calculated the frequency of coronal lexical items in the input children heard, and compared this with their prefix truncation rates. The analysis suggests there was no correlation between lexical frequency in the input and children's truncation rates on different lexical items. This is probably due to the fact that we have only coded a small proportion of the adult data (about 8 hours for each child). However, the lexical item most likely to exhibit a null prefix for both children and adults was the high-frequency lexical item *di-ntho* 'things.' Thus, children may have a tendency to produce null noun class prefixes on at least some high-frequency lexical items that have a relatively high instance of null prefixes in the input they hear. However, in the small sample of input we examined there was no overall evidence of lexical effects. It therefore appears that children are making early grammatical generalizations regarding the conditions under which null prefixes are licensed. That is, they are paying close attention to both the beginnings and ends of words very early in the acquisition process.

DISCUSSION

This study has shown that, despite some noise in the input, Sesotho-speaking 2-year-olds appear to have extracted both the phonological and syntactic generalizations that license null noun class prefixes. This is evidenced by their systematic forms of overgeneralization from 2;1 to 2;6. By 3, both children had begun to approach an adult-like grammar, dropping prefixes only in fully licensed contexts, and at about the same rate as that evidenced in the input they heard. This rapid learning is quite remarkable given the probabilistic nature of the input, where adults only variably produce null noun class prefixes, even when the phonological and syntactic context is met. Further research is needed to determine the possibility that discourse or other factors may also influence where and when adults produce null prefixes.

The findings presented here argue strongly against proposals that young language learners initially show only lexical learning, taking until the age of 3 or 4 to make grammatical generalizations (e.g., Tomasello, 1992). Rather, the present study shows that Sesotho-speaking children make both phonological and syntactic generalizations by the age of 2;6—overgeneralizing the use of null prefixes to words they have never heard produced in this way. This is consistent with recent findings on the acquisition of word order (e.g., Abbot-Smith, Lieven, & Tomasello, 2001; Narasimhan, Budwig, & Murty, 2005; Budwig, Narasimhan, & Srivastava, 2006), suggesting that, at least in some domains, 2-year-olds can make robust grammatical generalizations.

The Sesotho findings raise many questions regarding the acquisition of noun class prefixes in other Bantu languages. To date we have found that null noun class prefixes are only permitted in the closely related Sotho group of languages (Sesotho, Setswana, Sepedi). For other Bantu languages, then, the use of noun class prefixes is obligatory. We would predict that, modulo prosodic constraints, the learning of noun class prefixes in other Bantu languages should be earlier, at least for those languages with CV (consonant + vowel) noun class prefixes like Sesotho. On the other hand, Nguni languages like isiZulu, isiXhosa, and isiSwati have not only prefixes, but also pre-prefixes (note the initial copy vowel in isiZulu). These pre-prefixes are elided in the negative, and coalesce with conjunctions and other formatives (e.g., Xhosa: *na + isi-kolo > nesikolo*). Suzman (1991) reports that noun class prefixes in Zulu are only learned around 3;6, and Gxilishe (2005) reports the same for Xhosa. Kunene (1979) further shows some overgeneralization of singular/plural forms in wug-like overgeneralization tasks, suggesting that morphological segmentation of the noun class prefix may be more difficult in Nguni languages, with the more variable form of (pre)prefixes contributing to their later acquisition.

The availability of larger on-line child language corpora, from a number of different Bantu languages, now makes it possible to explore the acquisition of Bantu noun class prefixes in a more systematic, quantifiable manner. The flurry of activity on these issues in the 1970s and early 1980s, fueled in part by Slobin's (1973) proposals for unique form–function mapping, left the impression that Bantu noun class prefixes were acquired early and easily, with little morphological overgeneralization. Children learning a variety of Bantu languages were shown to make very few errors of commission, permitting multiple morphological forms for marking the concept of plural. However, the acquisition of Bantu noun class prefixes may be more complex than originally thought. In particular, the syntactic and semantic status of the noun class prefix is now open to question. It is not clear how this difference in syntactic structure or semantic interpretation might affect the language learning process. This is obviously an area for further research.

CONCLUSION

This study examined the phonological and syntactic licensing of null noun class prefixes by two Sesotho-speaking children between the ages of 2 and 3. First, it found that adults used null prefixes in up to 35% of licensed contexts. It then demonstrated that both children showed phonological overgeneralization at 2;6, and one showed syntactic overgeneralization at 2;6. Both had limited their overgeneralization by 3, closely approximating the adult system, with no apparent lexical effects. These findings indicate not only that the learning of Bantu noun class prefixes is more complex than originally thought, but also that 2-year-olds are making phonological and syntactic generalizations, even in the context of variable input. Thus, it appears that these children are paying attention to both the beginnings and ends of words, since information from the prefix and the presence of agreement following the noun are both critical for determining the context for null prefix use. This suggests that young language learners are capable of making sophisticated phonological and syntactic generalizations by the age of 2;6, simultaneously paying attention to multiple levels of linguistic structure. Given the availability of large longitudinal corpora today, it is now possible to consider Slobin's Operating Principles anew, providing a more quantitative context in which to evaluate the mechanisms underlying the learning of language. We offer this study as a step in that direction.

REFERENCES

Abbot-Smith, K., Lieven, E., & Tomasello, M. (2001). What pre-school children do and do not do with ungrammatical word orders. *Cognitive Development, 16*, 679–692.
Berko, J. (1958). The child's learning of English morphology. *Word, 14*, 150–177.
Bresnan, J., & Mchombo, S. (1995). The Lexical Integrity Principle: Evidence from Bantu. *NLLT, 13*, 181–252.
Budwig, N., Narasimhan, B., & Srivastava, S. (2006). Interim solutions: the acquisition of early verb constructions in Hindi. In E. Clark & B. Kelly (Eds.), *Constructions in acquisition*. Stanford, CA: CSLI.
Carstens, V. (1991). *The morphology and syntax of determiner phrases*. Unpublished Doctoral thesis, University of California, Los Angeles.

Carstens, V. (1993). On nominal morphology and DP structure. In S. Mchombo, (Ed.), *Theoretical aspects of Bantu grammar* (pp. 151–180). Stanford, CA: CSLI.

Clahsen, H., Eisenbeiss, S., & Vainikka, A. (1994). The seeds of structure. A syntactic analysis of the acquisition of case marking. In: T. Hoekstra & B. Schwartz (Eds.), *Language acquisition studies in generative grammar* (pp. 85–118). Amsterdam: John Benjamins.

Connelly. M. (1984). *Basotho children's acquisition of noun morphology*. Unpublished Doctoral thesis, University of Essex.

Demuth, K. (1988). Noun class agreement in Sesotho acquisition. In M. Barlow, & C. A. Ferguson (Eds.), *Agreement in natural language: Approaches, theories and descriptions* (pp. 305–321). CSLI: University of Chicago Press.

Demuth, K. (1989). Maturation and the acquisition of Sesotho passive. *Language, 65,* 56–80.

Demuth, K. (1990). Subject topic and the Sesotho passive. *Journal of Child Language, 17,* 67–84.

Demuth, K. (1992). Accessing functional categories in Sesotho: Interactions at the morpho-syntax interface. In J. Meisel (Ed.), *The acquisition of verb placement: Functional categories and V2 phenomena in language development* (pp. 83–107). Dordrecht: Kluwer Academic Publishers.

Demuth, K. (1994). On the 'underspecification' of functional categories in early grammars. In B. Lust, M. Suñer, & J. Whitman (Eds.), *Syntactic theory and first language acquisition: Cross-linguistic perspectives* (pp. 119–134). Hillsdale, NJ: Lawrence Erlbaum Associates.

Demuth, K. (2003). The acquisition of Bantu languages. In D. Nurse & G. Phillipson (Eds.), *The Bantu languages* (pp. 209–222). Richmond, Surrey, UK: Curzon Press.

Doke, C. M., & Mofokeng, S. M. (1985). *Textbook of Southern Sotho grammar*. Cape Town: Longman.

Gerken, L. A. (1996). Prosodic structure in young children's language production. *Language, 72,* 683–712.

Guthrie, M. (1948). Gender, number and person in Bantu languages. *Bulletin of the School of Oriental and African Studies, 18,* 545–555.

Gxilishe, D. S. (2005, November). The acquisition of noun class markers and subject agreement in Xhosa. Paper presented at the Bantu Acquisition Workshop, Smith College.

Idiata, D. F. (1998). *Some aspects of the children's acquisition of the Sangu language*. Unpublished Doctoral dissertation, University of Lyon II.

Kunene. E.C.L. (1979). The acquisition of Siswati as a first language: Morphological study with special reference to noun classes and some agreement markers. Unpublished Doctoral dissertation, University of California, Los Angeles.

Lleó, C., & Demuth, K. (1999). Prosodic constraints on the emergence of grammatical morphemes: Crosslinguistic evidence from Germanic and Romance languages. In A. Greenhill, H. Littlefield, & C. Tano (Eds.), *Proceedings of the 23rd annual Boston University Conference on Language Development* (pp. 407–418). Somerville, MA: Cascadilla Press.

Machobane, 'M. (1993). The ordering restriction between the Sesotho applicative and causative suffixes. *South African Journal of African Languages, 13,* 129–137.

Machobane, 'M. (2003). Variation in Bantu DP structure: Evidence from Sesotho. *Malawian Journal of Linguistics, 3,* 85–104.

Machobane, 'M., Moloi, F., & Demuth, K. (2004). *Some restrictions on Sesotho null noun class prefixes*. Master's thesis, & Brown University.

Meeussen, A. E. (1967). Bantu grammatical reconstructions. *Africana Linguistica III:* 79–121. Tervuren Musee Royal de l'Afrique Centrale, Annales no. 61.

Mills, A. E. (1986). *The acquisition of gender: A study of English and German*. Heidelberg: Springer.

Myres, S. (1987). *Tone and the structure of words in Shona*. Doctoral dissertation, University of Massachusetts, Amherst.

Narasimhan, B., Budwig, N., & Marty, L. (2005). Argument realization in Hindi caregiver-child discourse. *Journal of Pragmatics, 37,* 461–475.

Pine, J. M., Lieven, E. V. M., & Rowland, C. F. (1998). Comparing different models of the development of the English verb category. *Linguistics, 36,* 807–830.

Slobin, D. I. (1973). Cognitive prerequisites for the development of grammar. In C. A. Ferguson & D. I. Slobin (Eds.), *Studies of child language development* (pp. 175–209). New York: Holt Rinehart & Winston.

Slobin, D. I. (1985). Crosslinguistic evidence for the language-making capacity. In D. I. Slobin (Ed.), *The crosslinguistic study of language acquisition: Vol. 2. Theoretical Issues* (pp. 1157–1256). Hillsdale, NJ: Lawrence Erlbaum Associates.

Suzman, S. M. (1980). Acquisition of the noun class system in Zulu. *Papers and Reports on Child Language Development*. Stanford University, *19,* 45–52.

Suzman, S.M. (1991). *Language acquisition in Zulu.* Ph.D. dissertation. University of the Witwatersrand, Johannesburg.

Suzman, S.M. (1996). Acquisition of noun class systems in related Bantu languages. In C. Johnson & J. Gilbert (Eds.), *Children's language* (Vol. 9, pp. 87–104). Mahwah, NJ: Lawrence Erlbaum Associates.

Theakston, A., Lieven, E. V. M., & Tomasello, M. (2003). The role of the input in the acquisition of third person singular verbs in English. *Journal of Speech, Language, and Hearing Research, 24*, 863–877.

Tomasello, M. (1992). *First verbs: A case study of early grammatical development.* Cambridge, UK: Cambridge University Press.

Tsonope, J. (1987). *The acquisition of Setswana noun class and agreement morphology, with reference to demonstratives and possessives.* Unpublished Doctoral dissertation, State University of New York, Buffalo.

Visser, M. (2001). The category DP in Shosa and northern Sotho: A comparative syntax. In H. Thipa (Ed.), *Ahead of time: Studies in African languages presented in honour of Nompumelelo Jafta.* (pp. 108–127). Howick: Brevitaqs.

Watters, J. (1980). The Ejagam noun class system: Ekoid Bantu revisited. In L. Hyman (Ed.), *Noun classes in the Grassfields Bantu Borderland* (pp. 99–137). SCOPIL vol. 8. University of Southern California.

Welmers, W. E. (1973). *African language structures.* Berkeley: University of California Press.

Ziesler, Y., & Demuth, K. (1995). Noun class prefixes in Sesotho child-directed speech. In E. Clark (Ed.), *Proceedings of the 26th Child Language Research Forum, 13,* 26, 137–146. Stanford University: CSLI.

8

Dialogic Priming and the Acquisition of Argument Marking in Korean[1]

PATRICIA M. CLANCY

University of California, Santa Barbara

The task, then, is to propose a set of procedures for the construction of language. I have used the term "Operating Principle" (OP) to denote the "procedures" or "strategies" employed by LMC. … OPs, whatever their ultimate origin, are necessary prerequisites for the perception, analysis, and use of language in ways that will lead to the mastery of any particular input language.

Dan I. Slobin (1986, p. 1159)

When "Cognitive prerequisites for the development of grammar" (Slobin, 1973) was published, I was a new graduate student at Berkeley, fascinated by Dan's vision of the acquisition process as building on a universal set of cognitively based Operating Principles. Years later, when Dan launched his vast crosslinguistic project, I was thrilled to participate in the quest to understand the child's "Language-Making Capacity" (LMC), and the Operating Principles that comprise it. My final years at Berkeley were spent analyzing my Japanese acquisition data for contributions I could make to this quest. My graduate years thus began and ended with the challenge that Dan had set: to specify the nature of the human capacity for constructing grammar.

INTRODUCTION

The acquisition of morphology, which will be the topic of this chapter, is an important focus of the Operating Principles, many of which address the child's ability to extract potential morphemes from the stream of speech, map them to meanings/functions, and organize them into systems. For example, OP (ATTENTION) END OF UNIT specifies that children will attend to the last syllable of extracted speech units (Slobin, 1986, p. 1166). Children acquiring Japanese and Korean will find nominative, topic, and accusative morphemes at the ends of overt arguments, where they are prime candidates for extraction (Peters, 1986, p. 1034), especially when the marked argument is produced as a single intonation unit. Prior to their acquisition, argument-marking morphemes constitute "leftover segments in storage" as the child processes speech; not identified as content words, such

---

[1] I am grateful to Pamela Downing, Stefan Gries, Nancy Budwig, and Sue Ervin-Tripp for their many helpful comments on drafts of this chapter. Special thanks are due to Stefan Gries for his generous help with the statistics in this chapter. The data for this study were collected with funding from the Social Science Research Council, Korea Program.

105

segments serve as "the opening wedge for the discovery of grammatical morphemes" (Slobin, 1986, p. 1171). The child's task is to map these stored syllables to their meanings/functions.[2]

Where and when do Operating Principles function? If we assume that the everyday conversation that language-learning children participate in and observe is the primary site for operation of the cognitive processes underlying language acquisition, the question arises: Are there particular types of conversational sequences in caregiver–child speech that are especially conducive to acquisition, e.g., to the operation of cognitive processes involving the extraction and interpretation of morphemes and to their organization into morphological systems? In pursuing this question, the fundamental repetitiveness of everyday talk is a useful starting point (Peters, 1986, p. 1051–53). Two independent but convergent lines of research that shed light on the relevance of repetition in discourse to acquisition are Du Bois' work on dialogic syntax in linguistics and the research of Bock and others on structural priming in psychology.

Du Bois' (2001, p. 1) research on dialogic syntax focuses on "the speaker's active engagement with the words of those who have spoken before." When one speaker reuses lexical, syntactic, and other linguistic resources from the prior speaker's utterance, Du Bois proposes, "patterns match at varying levels of abstraction, from *identity of overt morphology* to abstract features to syntactic structures" (2001, p. 1, emphasis added). These patterns create "resonance," defined as "the activation of intrinsic potential affinity" between the two utterances (2001, p. 8). This resonance has consequences for the meaning of an utterance—semantically, pragmatically, and interactively. "Engaged forms produce engaged meanings," Du Bois claims (2001, p. 1). For example, structural parallelism may highlight a stance of alignment or non-alignment with the prior speaker (Du Bois, 2007), as M. Goodwin (1990, pp. 177–185) has noted in her analysis of "format tying" in children's arguments.

In this chapter I will be concerned with Korean children's reuse of argument-marking morphemes in caregiver–child dialogue, as in Example (1). The overt, marked argument is highlighted and the nominative marker is underlined.

(1) Adult is asking child (2;2 years of age) about scribbles on the wall.

Adult: ku-ke **nwu-ka** pyek-eyta kuly-ess-ni?
that-thing who-NOM wall-LOC draw-ANT-INTERR
'Who drew that on the wall?'
Child: **hyenswu-ka**.
Hyenswu-NOM
'Hyenswu (= I) (did).'

In question–answer sequences such as (1), reusing the nominative -*ka* highlights the dialogic relation between answer and question. According to Du Bois (2001), dialogicality is part of what speakers know about grammar: how to create resonance by using syntactic structures and morphological paradigms to relate one's current utterance to prior utterances.

Is resonance created deliberately or is it an involuntary by-product of language processing? While Du Bois' work on dialogic syntax emphasizes the discourse-functional motivations for resonance, psycholinguistic research focuses on priming as a processing mechanism. Bock and Griffin (2000, p. 1), for example, define priming as the "unintentional, pragmatically unmotivated tendency to repeat the general syntactic pattern of an utterance." It is important to recognize, however, that even if reuse of a form is functionally motivated and serves semantic, pragmatic, or interactional functions in the discourse context, involuntary priming can also have a facilitating effect on production.

---

[2] Revising his original view that there is a privileged set of grammaticizable notions to which morphemes are mapped (Slobin, 1986, pp. 1172–1174), Slobin (2001) has proposed that the meanings of grammatical morphemes are constrained only by the communicative exigencies of adult discourse. This directs the child's task outward, to the discourse in which the relevant meanings are to be found.

Thus priming and discourse-functional motivation can be seen as complementary forces that work together to create resonance.

In her initial study of structural priming, Bock (1986) demonstrated that speakers are more likely to use a particular syntactic structure, e.g., a double-object dative, if they have just heard and produced that structure. For example, subjects who heard and repeated a double-object dative sentence, such as *The governess made the princess a pot of tea*, were more likely to then describe a picture using a double-object dative, i.e., *The woman is showing the man a dress*, rather than a prepositional dative, i.e., *The woman is showing a dress to the man*. Subsequent research has verified that syntactic priming is a very robust effect; it is impervious to thematic roles (Bock & Loebell, 1990), and is found even in non-native speakers (Gries & Wulff, 2005) and when the priming language differs from the language that the speaker is producing (Loebell & Bock, 2003).

Interestingly, experiments in which natural dialogue is simulated have found priming effects of especially large magnitude (Branigan, Pickering, & Cleland, 2000). When two participants, one of whom is a confederate in the experiment, are engaged in a task, hearing the confederate's syntactic primes strongly elicits production of the primed structures by the other participant. Apparently, when structural priming occurs from comprehension to production in a context of joint engagement, as in everyday talk, it is very effective. This suggests that structural priming, arising as an automatic consequence of having processed a particular form or structure, is one reason why everyday conversation is so repetitive. One speaker's use of a particular morphological form or syntactic construction makes it cognitively easier for the same form or construction to be used again, facilitating the creation of resonance in dialogue. The prevalence of syntactic repetition in ordinary conversation and the existence of structural priming are obviously relevant to the acquisition of grammar. From the perspective of Slobin's theory, structural priming seems an ideal cognitive mechanism for children acquiring grammar to have in their Language-Making Capacity.

Although research on structural priming has focused primarily on syntactic constructions, there is also a large body of evidence that priming operates at the level of morphology as well. Most of these studies have investigated the processing of roots and affixes in morphologically complex words, but a number of experimental and corpus-based studies have addressed the priming of one grammatical morpheme by another. For example, experimental research has established priming of gender morphology in Serbo-Croatian (Gurjanov, Lukatela, Savic, & Turvey, 1985) and in Greek (Plemmenou, Bard, & Branigan, 2002), and of person and number inflections in German (Clahsen, Sonnenstuhl, Hadler, & Eisenbeiss, 2001), while sociolinguistic research on Spanish has found priming in interview discourse for the use of optional plural markers within a noun phrase (Poplack, 1980) and for the use of the first person pronoun *yo* (Cameron, 1994; Flores-Ferrán, 2002). In her analysis of the "*yo-yo* effect" in Colombian Spanish—the tendency for one use of the optional first person pronoun *yo* to be followed by another—Travis (2005) discovered that speakers are significantly more likely to use *yo* if another speaker has recently used *yo*, especially at a distance of no more than two clauses. In light of the extensive findings on morphological priming, I will assume for purposes of this study that the grammatical morphemes in an utterance, such as those indicating important syntactic functions and grammatical relations, can also act as structural primes for subsequent use of the same morpheme.

In this chapter I will address the role of priming in the acquisition of Korean argument-marking morphology. The three morphemes to be analyzed here—nominative, topic, and accusative markers—are not obligatory; they are used with varying frequency to mark overt arguments. In Korean grammar, S (the sole argument of an intransitive verb) and A (the more agent-like argument of a transitive verb) both take nominative marking with *-ka/-i*. The O argument (more patient-like argument of a transitive verb) takes accusative marking with *-(l)ul*. S, A, and O arguments may be marked as topics with *-(n)un*; the topic marker suppresses nominative and accusative morphemes but co-occurs with oblique argument markers. These three morphemes pose interesting challenges for the language-learning child, since they lack lexical content, are not used consistently in adult speech, and can have different functions depending on the discourse context.

To assess the potential role of morphological priming in Korean acquisition, I will address the following questions:

1. Is the child's production of nominative, topic, and accusative markers primed by prior occurrence of these morphemes?
2. Are there developmental changes with respect to priming?
3. What kinds of dialogic sequences in Korean caregiver–child conversation afford the opportunity for primed use of argument markers?

METHODOLOGY

Participants and Data

The participants in this study are two Korean girls, Hyenswu and Wenceng, who were audio recorded twice monthly for a year in their homes in Providence, Rhode Island. During the 90-minute recording sessions, the children interacted with their mothers and one or two research assistants. The children and their caregivers engaged in a variety of everyday activities during the sessions, such as playing with toys, making Lego constructions, eating snacks, and reading storybooks.

The data for this study consist of overt S, A, and O arguments produced by the children and their mothers in 13 recordings at 1-month intervals. In order to analyze developmental changes, each child's data are divided into early (the first 4 months of the study), mid (the middle 5 months), and late (the final 4 months) stages. The mothers' data come from three samples of 350 clauses each, taken from early, mid, and late months of the study, respectively. Table 8.1 presents the participants and data for this study, giving the number and percentage of unmarked arguments and arguments with nominative, topic, and accusative morphemes (arguments with other markers are not included).

Hyenswu is the less advanced child with respect to argument marking, having significantly more unmarked arguments and fewer marked arguments than Wenceng ($\chi^2 = 153.7636$, $df = 1$, $p < .001$). The two mothers differ along the same lines, with Hyenswu's mother having significantly more unmarked arguments and fewer marked arguments than Wenceng's mother ($\chi^2 = 10.5672$, $df = 1$, $p < .01$).

Data Coding

For purposes of this study, a primed argument is defined as an overt argument that is preceded by a main clause or utterance having an overt argument in the same role (S, A, or O). A primed morpheme is defined as an argument marker on an overt argument that is preceded by a main clause

TABLE 8.1 Participants and Data

Participant	Stage	Age	Unmarked Arguments	Marked Arguments	Total
Hyenswu (H)	1	1;10–2;1	239 (92.6%)	19 (7.4%)	258
	2	2;2–2;6	464 (83.8%)	90 (16.2%)	554
	3	2;7–2;10	586 (73.5%)	211 (26.5%)	797
H's mother (HM)		Adult	356 (64.5%)	196 (35.5%)	552
Wenceng (W)	1	1;8–1;11	241 (83.4%)	48 (16.6%)	289
	2	2;0–2;4	423 (59.3%)	290 (40.7%)	713
	3	2;5–2;8	455 (53.9%)	389 (46.1%)	844
W's mother (WM)		Adult	302 (54.7%)	250 (45.3%)	552

TABLE 8.2 Priming Contexts for Children's Production of Argument Markers

Dialogic Sequence	No Prime	Unmarked Prime	Marked Prime Same	Marked Prime Different
Priming Argument	—	NP	NP+Marker$_1$	NP+Marker$_1$
Child Argument	NP or NP+Marker	NP or NP+Marker	NP+Marker$_1$ or NP	NP+Marker$_2$ or NP

or utterance having an overt, marked argument in the same role. The priming utterance can be produced either by the child or the child's conversational partner.

Since Korean argument markers only occur on overt arguments, the children's production of overt arguments and of markers must be considered separately; either or both may be primed. Furthermore, it is possible that prior use of one argument marker may prime the child's use of a different marker; Bock (1989),[3] for example, has found that a Prepositional Phrase (PP) with one preposition can prime a PP with a different preposition. Priming will therefore be analyzed in terms of the dialogic sequences presented in Table 8.2, each of which affords different possibilities.

In "No prime" sequences, the prior utterance/clause has no overt argument in the same role as the child's argument (which may be unmarked or marked), and therefore lacks the necessary structural parallel with the child's utterance for priming. In "Unmarked prime" sequences, the prior utterance has an overt NP in the same argument role that could prime the child's production of an overt argument, but no marker to prime the child's use of an argument marker. If the child's argument is unmarked, it matches the prime's lack of marking; if the child's argument is marked, the marking is considered unprimed. In "Marked prime" sequences, there is an overt, marked NP in the prior clause/utterance having the same argument role as the child's NP; if the child's argument is marked, the marker can either be the same (Marker$_1$) or different (Marker$_2$) from the marker on the priming argument. If, on the other hand, the child's argument is unmarked, then the potential prime has failed to influence the child's production.

The definition of priming employed in this study is conservative in that only the immediately preceding utterance or main clause is treated as a potential environment for a priming argument. In addition, priming arguments are defined as requiring the same argument role—S, A, or O—as the primed argument, although S and A arguments may prime each other since both can take nominative marking. The distinction between S and A is maintained here since in these data S and A arguments differ in their frequencies of surface forms, semantic roles, and topic vs. nominative markers (Clancy, 2003, in press); other studies have also found early differentiation between S and A arguments (e.g., Choi, 1999; Rispoli, 1987; Schieffelin, 1986).

In coding the argument roles S, A, and O, the transitivity of verbs was coded on the basis of the discourse context, with native speaker assistance for questionable cases, e.g., uses of *hata* 'do' with no overt O argument. Reported speech and other object complements do not take the accusative marker in Korean and are not counted as O arguments. Utterances with an overt NP but no verb are coded as arguments of an elided token of the prior verb when this interpretation is warranted by the discourse context, e.g., in question–answer sequences such as Example (1).

RESULTS

First, let us consider the priming contexts in which the children use marked rather than unmarked arguments. Figure 8.1 presents the percentage of children's overt (marked and unmarked) arguments found in the following dialogic sequences: (1) the prior utterance/clause lacks an overt, potentially

---

[3] Bock (1989) concludes that grammatical morphemes are not "immanent" in structural frames, but the prepositions she considered, *for* vs. *to* in English datives, mark oblique arguments and are not comparable in frequency or function to nominative, topic, and accusative markers on Korean core arguments.

110 CROSSLINGUISTIC APPROACHES TO THE PSYCHOLOGY OF LANGUAGE

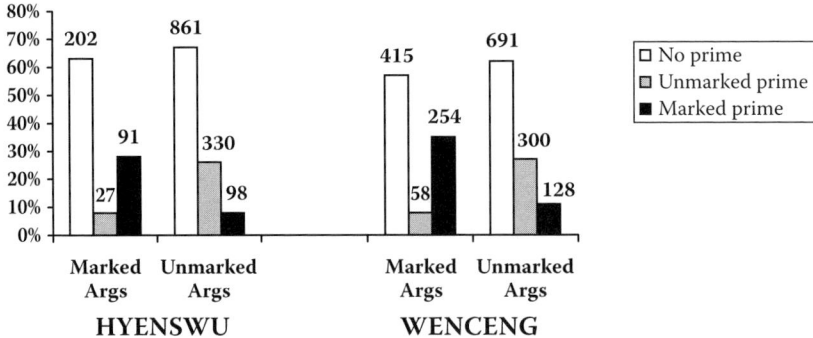

Figure 8.1   Distribution of marked and unmarked arguments by priming context.

priming argument in the same role as the child's argument ("No prime"), (2) the prior utterance/clause has an overt but unmarked argument in the same role ("Unmarked prime"), and (3) the prior utterance/clause has an overt marked argument in the same role ("Marked prime").

As Figure 8.1 shows, for both children the priming contexts of marked arguments are quite different from those of unmarked arguments. These differences are significant for both children (Hyenswu: $\chi^2 = 129.2967$, $df = 2$, $p < .001$; Wenceng: $\chi^2 = 199.7895$, $df = 2$, $p < .001$). Marked arguments are preferred following marked primes and unmarked arguments following unmarked primes, although the latter effect is significant only for Wenceng. Conversely, for both children marked arguments are dispreferred following unmarked primes, and unmarked arguments following marked primes. When there is no priming argument, marked and unmarked arguments occur in the frequencies expected by chance.

Does the preference for marked–marked and unmarked–unmarked sequences change during the course of the year? Figure 8.2 presents the frequencies of marked and unmarked arguments with respect to marked and unmarked primes in the early, mid, and late months of the year for Hyenswu; Figure 8.3 gives the same information for Wenceng. The percentage of overt arguments with no prime is not displayed, since the distribution of marked and unmarked arguments that lack a prime does not differ from chance for either child in early, mid, or late months of the year.

For both children, marked and unmarked arguments differ significantly in priming at each stage (Hyenswu: Early: $\chi^2 = 19.5913$, $df = 2$, $p < .001$; Mid: $\chi^2 = 50.4576$, $df = 2$, $p < .001$; Late: $\chi^2 = 60.3832$, $df = 2$, $p < .001$; Wenceng: Early: $\chi^2 = 28.1216$, $df = 2$, $p < .001$; Mid: $\chi^2 = 131.1519$, $df = 2$, $p < .001$; Late: $\chi^2 = 54.2463$, $df = 2, p < .001$). As we see in Figure 8.2, Hyenswu uses marked arguments much more frequently following marked primes throughout the year. In the early months of the year, 8 out of her total of 9 marked arguments are found after marked primes. This pattern is the strongest

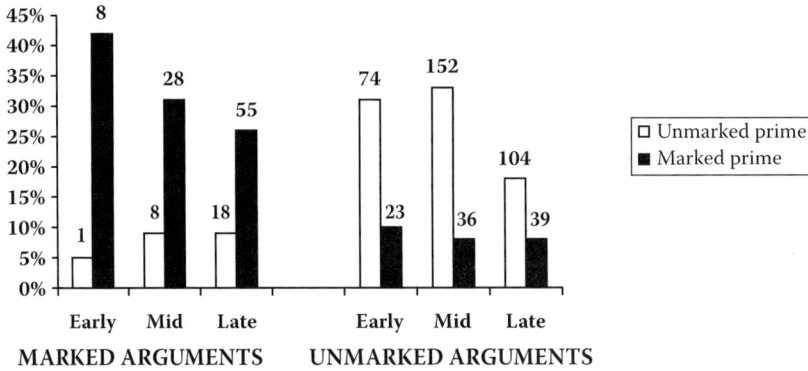

Figure 8.2   Hyenswu's marked vs. unmarked arguments with marked vs. unmarked primes.

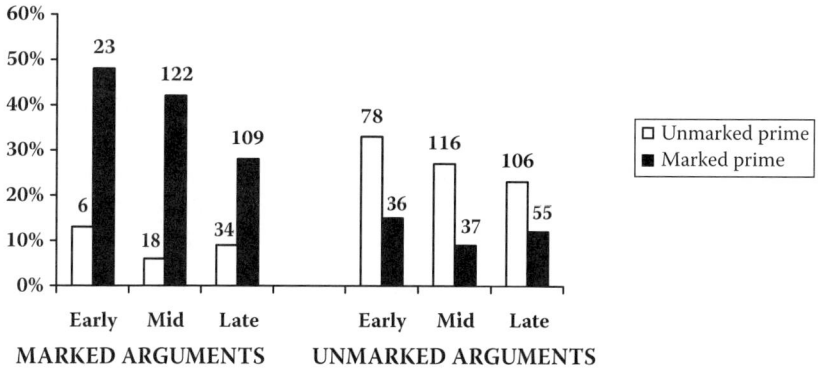

Figure 8.3 Wenceng's marked vs. unmarked arguments with marked vs. unmarked primes.

priming effect throughout the year. By mid-year, marked arguments are dispreferred following an unmarked prime; late in the year unmarked arguments are dispreferred following a marked prime. Cramer's V, which provides a measure of effect size, shows that these effects, which are significant only in combination, are not very strong, and peak mid-year (Early: 0.076, Mid: 0.091, Late: 0.076).

Figure 8.3 shows Wenceng's course of development, which is more compressed. In the early months of the year, Wenceng already uses a higher rate of marked arguments following marked primes, like Hyenswu. By mid-year this effect has become significant, and three other effects are also apparent, though not individually significant: Unmarked arguments are preferred following unmarked primes and dispreferred following marked primes, while marked arguments are dispreferred following unmarked primes. In the final months of the year these effects level out, with none reaching significance, and the strength of the association between marked arguments and marked primes weakens, becoming more similar to that of the other associations. As with Hyenswu, these effects, although significant at each stage in combination, are not large, and are strongest mid-year (Cramer's V: Early: 0.097, Mid: 0.184, Late: 0.064).

When a child produces a marked argument following a marked prime, both arguments usually have the same marker. For purposes of this analysis, "same" marker will be defined in terms of types, i.e., nominative, topic, and accusative; phonological differences between the allomorphs of each type of marker will be ignored. Overall, 86.8% of Hyenswu's primed markers and 84.3% of Wenceng's have "same marker" primes; there are no significant differences between the two children in their proportions of same/different argument markers ($\chi^2 = 0.4515$, $df = 1$, $p > .05$).

What kinds of dialogic sequences afford sites for primed production of argument markers? Question–answer exchanges provide a frequent source of primed argument markers in the data for both children. Example (2) illustrates contrastive use of the topic marker in a question–answer sequence.

(2) Wenceng (2;2) and the Research Assistant are playing with toy bottles, putting them into holders. Two are missing.

Res. Asst: **twu kay-nun** eti-lo ka pely-ess-e?
two CL-TOP where-LOC go:CONN finish-ANT-IE
'(Lit.) Where did two go?' (= 'Where are these two'?)
Wenceng: **hana-nun** salacy-e pely-ess-e.
one-TOP disappear-CONN finish-ANT-IE
'One has disappeared.'

According to Lee (1999), a contrastive topic marker is used to make an explicit contrast between the marked element and a specific set of contrasting elements from the discourse context that the speaker has in mind. In (2), the Research Assistant's contrast is between the bottles that are present and the two missing bottles; Wenceng's contrast is between the one missing bottle that has disappeared and the other missing bottle, which she apparently does not regard as gone for good. Reusing the topic marker from the prior utterance is both contextually appropriate and, due to priming, easy to accomplish.

When referents are repeated, contrasted, or otherwise related across utterances, the opportunity often arises for repetition of particular argument roles and markers. In Example (3), Hyenswu, who does not yet attend kindergarten, is being contrasted with her sister, who does.

(3) Hyenswu (2;6) has been listening to her five-year-old sister, who has just mentioned to their mother that she now goes to kindergarten.

Hyenswu: na-**nun**?
1p-TOP
'What about me?'
H's sister: hyenswu-**nun** hakkyo an ka-canh-a.
Hyenswu-TOP school NEG go:CONN-TAG-IE
'Hyenswu (= you) don't go to school.'
hyenswu-**nun** khu-myen ka-ya-ci. ku-ci?
Hyenswu-TOP big-COND go-NEC-COMM be.like.that-COMM
'Hyenswu (=you) will go when you're older. Right?'
Hyenswu: na-**nun** kwukmin hakkyo ka-ss-ta
1p-TOP elementary school go-ANT-INTRP
o-l ke-ya.[4]
come-ATTR(IRRL) thing-COP.IE
'I'll go to elementary school.'

In (3), repeated use of the topic marker to encode the ongoing contrast is appropriate, with each use potentially priming others.

Sequences with wh-questions and answers provide an important site for primed use of the nominative to mark focused constituents, as in Example (1). Hyenswu's earliest production of a primed nominative marker is given in Example (4).

(4) The session is just beginning and the adults are trying to engage Hyenswu (2;0) in conversation.

Res. Asst: hyenswu-ya meli **nwu-ka** call-a cw-ess-ni?
Hyenswu-VOC hair who-NOM cut-CONN give-ANT-INTERR
'Hyenswu, who cut your hair for you?'
Hyenswu: **emma-ka**.
mommy-NOM
'Mommy (did).'

This focal interpretation of the nominative, which Kuno (1973) calls "exhaustive listing" in his analysis of the Japanese nominative, has the approximate reading, 'It was mommy who cut my hair.' According to Lee (1999, p. 27), focal nominatives highlight a particular element from an evoked set of potential alternatives that are "shadowed, ignored or excluded" rather than explicitly contrasted with the marked element. The distinction between contrastive topics and focal nominatives may be subtle, but the child can come up with the appropriate marker by reusing the marker on the priming argument in each case, as well as by having acquired the constraints on appropriate usage.

---

[4] Here Hyenswu's use of *kassta olkeya* 'I will go and come back,' typically said when leaving for a quick errand, is inappropriate.

An activity that gives rise to many question–answer exchanges involving the nominative is storybook reading. Question prompts during storybook reading are an important source of primes for Wenceng's argument markers, as illustrated in Example (5).

(5) Wenceng (1;11) is being prompted by her mother to tell a story.

W's mother:	yeysnal-ey **mwe-ka** iss-ess-e?
	old.times-in what-NOM exist-ANT-IE?
	'Once upon a time there was what?'
Wenceng:	**mwulkoki-ka** sal-ko iss-ess-e.
	fish-NOM live-PROG-ANT-IE
	'A fish was living.' (=There lived a fish).

In this case her mother's question models nominative marking on a newly introduced story character in a presentative construction. Focusing the queried constituent with the nominative marker in the response is appropriate here, and can be facilitated by priming.

In Wenceng's data, question–answer sequences, including story prompts, are also a common context for primed use of the accusative morpheme, as illustrated in (6).

(6) Her mother is eliciting a Winnie-the-Pooh story from a picture book, with Wenceng (2;1) answering her questions.

W's mother:	kulemyen Roo-nun mwe ha-ko iss-nun-kes kath-uni?
	then Roo-TOP what do-PROG-ATTR-thing be.like-INTERR
	'Then what do you think Roo is doing?'
Wenceng:	pes-ko iss-e.
	remove-PROG-IE
	'(He)'s taking (it) off.'
W's mother:	mwe-**lul**?
	what-ACC
	'What?'
Wenceng:	sikyey-**lul**.
	watch-ACC.
	'(His) watch.'[5]

It is important to note that the most common discourse contexts for priming often overlap, e.g., Example (3) features contrastive repetition in a question–answer sequence.

In sum, quantitative analysis has shown that: (1) both children can produce argument markers without priming from early on; (2) the children's marked arguments are generally preceded by marked primes, and unmarked arguments by unmarked primes; (3) primed production of argument markers is present at the outset, while the preference for unmarked arguments following unmarked primes and the negative associations between marked primes–unmarked arguments and unmarked primes–marked arguments appear somewhat later; and (4) when primed, the children's production

---

[5] Abbreviations, taken mostly from Lee (1991), are as follows:

1P	first person	COND	conditional	NEC	necessitative
ACC	accusative	CONN	connective	NEG	negative
ANT	anterior	IE	informal ending	NOM	nominative
ATTR	attributive	IRRL	irrealis	PROG	progressive
CL	classifier	INTERR	interrogative	TAG	tag
COMM	committal	INTRP	interruptive	TOP	topic
		LOC	locative	VOC	vocative

of argument markers usually involves "same marker" priming. Qualitative analysis has revealed that there are certain (overlapping) types of dialogic sequences that afford sites for the priming of argument markers: question–answer sequences, sequences that maintain the same overtly mentioned referent across two or more utterances/clauses, and sequences in which paired forms, e.g., deictic pronouns or numbers, are used in successive utterances/clauses to pick out the same referent or to highlight different referents.

DISCUSSION

Research on structural priming, to my knowledge, has yet to focus on the type of morphological priming investigated here: reuse of argument markers. The results of this study suggest that morphological priming plays a role in Korean children's production of nominative, topic, and accusative argument markers. Both children use argument markers more frequently after having just heard and/or used the same marker in the prior utterance or clause. This finding supports Du Bois' (2001, p. 4) proposal that dialogic syntax creates "an ideal site for the on-going learning of all levels of linguistic structure," with language learners relying on "dialogic bootstrapping" to produce their own utterance by reusing the forms and functions of the prior utterance. The fact that the priming effects found in this study, although significant, are not very strong is consistent with a situation in which there are a number of factors responsible for children's usage of argument markers, of which priming is one.

What does priming contribute to the acquisition process? Priming does not seem to be necessary for production, since both children in this study produce argument markers without priming from early on. Nevertheless, priming can reduce the child's processing burden by facilitating production. Smith and Wheeldon (2001) have demonstrated that primed structures are produced more quickly, and have concluded that priming reduces the cognitive "cost" of processes underlying language production. As Wray (2002) notes with respect to formulaic language, when the child's cognitive load is reduced during production, more attention becomes available for other activities, such as the analysis of form and meaning. By making it easier to produce forms that are in the process of being acquired or have already been acquired, priming can facilitate further acquisition.

An obvious contribution of priming to language acquisition is that it provides children with practice in the dialogic construction of syntax, i.e., in coordinating their strategies for comprehension and production in such a way that they can create structural resonance with the utterances of their conversational partners. At first, the tendency to borrow forms and structures from previous utterances probably reflects very young children's need to reduce the cognitive cost of language production. By facilitating the reuse of structural features from prior talk, priming supports the dialogic engagement that is an important part of everyday conversation and paves the way for later, strategic uses of resonance, such as those documented by Du Bois (2001), Goodwin (1999), and others (e.g., Tannen, 1989).

Where does priming come from? Structural priming, Bock and Griffin (2000, p. 189) propose, "arises within a system that is organized for learning how to produce sequences of words, as a consequence of the learning processes themselves." While some researchers have interpreted structural priming as a matter of temporary, short-term activation (e.g., Wheeldon & Smith, 2003), Bock and Griffin (2000) have found that structural priming can persist over as many as ten intervening utterances. They therefore conclude that priming is actually a form of implicit, procedural learning; the act of processing a particular syntactic structure leaves behind changes in speakers' procedures for formulating and producing utterances. In fact, Bock and Griffin (2000, p. 189) suggest that the procedures underlying language production "may undergo fine-tuning in every episode of adult language production." Structural priming, they conclude, is "a dynamic vestige of the process of learning to perform language."

This leads us directly to the child's Language-Making Capacity. Let us assume that, as Bock and Griffin (2000) have proposed, structural priming is a universal cognitive mechanism that alters the procedures for producing sentences, increasing the accessibility of a particular form or structure each time that it is processed and/or produced. Couched as an operating principle, we have:

> OP (PRODUCTION): REUSE. If you have just heard or produced a particular grammatical form or structure, use it in your next utterance.

Of course, there are a number of forces that can counteract or limit the operation of this principle, the most important of which must be whether reuse would fit the child's communicative goals. As language acquisition progresses, the child will develop an understanding of the discourse contexts in which it is semantically and pragmatically appropriate to avoid repetition, e.g., when it is appropriate to use ellipsis or pronouns. When and how such forces interact with OP: REUSE is an important arena for future research. The relevant point here is that something like OP: REUSE surely has an important role to play in acquisition theory. Du Bois (2001, p. 9) has proposed that adult speakers usually follow the principle: "Maximize resonance." If adults are maximizing resonance, then OP: REUSE is not merely a developmental heuristic, it is a feature of adult grammar-in-use to be acquired by children.

How can OP: REUSE be integrated with other Operating Principles for the acquisition of grammatical morphemes? Korean argument markers must first be extracted from the stream of speech and distinguished from the content words that they follow. Operating principles such as OP: END OF UNIT focus attention on these NP-final markers; OP: UNITS and OP: UNIT FORMATION guide appropriate segmentation of heads and markers; and OP: FUNCTORS stores markers in relation to the argument that they mark (Slobin, 1986, p. 166–69, 1172, 1187). At an early stage, when the child has not sorted out the functions of these argument markers, OP: REUSE helps account for the interim production strategy OP: UNINTERPRETED FORMS, which specifies that the child uses frequent, perceptually salient elements in their usual position before discovering their functions (Slobin, 1986, p. 1200–1202). Even after forms have been appropriately segmented, stored, and interpreted, OP: REUSE specifies that priming will increase the accessibility of recently processed forms for use in production.

Can priming help the child figure out the meanings/functions of morphemes? By enabling the child to participate actively in the construction of dialogic contexts for the use of grammatical forms, OP: REUSE potentially increases the set of appropriate form-function pairs available to the language-learning child for the task of mapping forms to functions. When, for example, Korean children reuse the marker on a priming argument, they actually experience two contexts providing information about its function: the usage in the priming argument and their own subsequent, primed usage. Further research is necessary to ascertain the extent to which repeating argument markers in dialogic sequences results in correct usage.

What can OP: REUSE tell us about the nature of grammar and its acquisition? The findings of this study, like Du Bois' research, call attention to the fact that the form/function relationship in grammar is constructed and acquired dialogically. Bock's discovery of structural priming helps explain why this is so, and suggests that grammar does not just happen to be dialogic, it is designed to be dialogic. In this view our capacity and propensity to produce language dialogically reflect a fundamental principle of the way our minds operate. Formulated here as OP: REUSE, structural (including morphological) priming can be seen as one among the principles that Slobin has identified in his foundational research on cognitive universals underlying the process of language acquisition.

CONCLUSIONS

The results of this study suggest that morphological priming facilitates children's production, and potentially their acquisition, of grammatical morphemes. Morphological priming provides one type of evidence for the fundamentally dialogic nature of grammar and the process by which it is acquired. Further research is necessary to establish whether the same morphological priming effects documented here are also found among adults, to establish the duration of such effects at different stages in the child's development, including longer distances between morphemes than the one-clause duration considered in this study, and to clarify the role of priming in the acquisition process.

As this chapter suggests, in the years since the publication of *Crosslinguistic studies of language acquisition*, I have been struck by the ways in which linguistic and psycholinguistic research, such as Du Bois' work on dialogic syntax and Bock's studies of structural priming, bring me back to Slobin's Operating Principles. This reflects not only the extent of my nostalgia for the Berkeley years, but also the depth and continuing significance of Slobin's quest to uncover the fundamental principles of human cognition and their relevance for language acquisition. I offer this study and OP: REUSE as another small piece in the endlessly complex and fascinating picture of language acquisition that Dan Slobin has put together. His intellectual courage and vision in tackling the ultimate questions, such as the nature of the human Language-Making Capacity, are as inspiring to me now as in those early years in Berkeley, when he led the way for his many students. I am grateful for the privilege of being one of them.

REFERENCES

Bock, J. K. (1986). Syntactic persistence in language production. *Cognitive Psychology, 18*, 355–387.
Bock, J. K. (1989). Closed-class immanence in sentence production. *Cognition, 31*, 163–186.
Bock, J. K., & Griffin, Z. M. (2000). The persistence of structural priming: Transient activation or implicit learning? *Journal of Experimental Psychology: General, 129*, 177–192.
Bock, J. K., & Loebell, H. (1990). Framing sentences. *Cognition, 35*, 1–39.
Branigan, H., Pickering, M., & Cleland, A. (2000). Syntactic coordination in dialogue. *Cognition, 75*, B13–B25.
Cameron, R. (1994). Switch reference, verb class and priming in a variable syntax. *Proceedings of the thirtieth annual meeting of the Chicago Linguistic Society*, pp. 27–45.
Choi, S. (1999). Early development of verb structures and caregiver input in Korean: Two case studies. *International Journal of Bilingualism, 3*, 241–265.
Clahsen, H., Sonnenstuhl, I., Hadler, M., & Eisenbeiss, S. (2001). Morphological paradigms in language processing and language disorders. *Transactions of the Philological Society, 99*, 247–277.
Clancy, P. M. (2003). The lexicon in interaction: Developmental origins of Preferred Argument Structure. In J. W. Du Bois, L. E. Kumpf, & W. J. Ashby (Eds.), *Preferred Argument Structure: Grammar as architecture for function* (pp. 81–108). Amsterdam/Philadelphia: John Benjamins.
Clancy, P. M. (In press). The acquisition of argument structure and transitivity in Korean: A discourse-functional approach. In C. Lee, Y. Kim, & G. Simpson (Eds.), *Korean psycholinguistics: Part III. Handbook of East Asian psycholinguistics*. Cambridge, UK: Cambridge University Press.
Du Bois, J. W. (2001). Towards a dialogic syntax. Unpublished manuscript. University of California, Santa Barbara.
Du Bois, J. W. (2007). The stance triangle. In R. Englebretson (Ed.), *Stance in discourse: Subjectivity in interaction* (pp. 139–182). Amsterdam/Philadelphia: John Benjamins.
Flores-Ferrán, N. (2002). *Subject personal pronouns in Spanish narratives of Puerto Ricans in New York City: A sociolinguistic perspective*. Munich: Lincom Europa.
Goodwin, M. H. (1990). *He-said-she-said: Talk as social organization among black children*. Bloomington/Indianapolis: Indiana University Press.
Gries, S., & Wulff, S. (2005). Do foreign language learners also have constructions? Evidence from priming, sorting, and corpora. *Annual Review of Cognitive Linguistics, 3*, 182–200.
Gurjanov, M., Lukatela, G., Lukatela, K., Savic, M., & Turvey, M. T. (1985). Grammatical priming of inflected nouns by the gender of possessive adjectives. *Haskins Laboratories Status Report on Speech Research, 82–83*, 205–219.
Kuno, S. (1973). *The structure of the Japanese language*. Cambridge, MA: The MIT Press.
Lee, C. (1999). Contrastive topic: A locus of the interface, evidence from Korean and English. In K. Turner (Ed.), *The semantics/pragmatics interface from different points of view* (pp. 317–342). New York: Elsevier.
Loebell, H., & Bock, J. K. (2003). Structural priming across languages. *Linguistics, 41*, 791–834.

Peters, A. (1986). Language segmentation: Operating principles for the perception and analysis of language. In D. I. Slobin (Ed.), *The crosslinguistic study of language acquisition: Vol. 2. Theoretical issues* (pp. 1029–1067). Hillsdale, NJ: Lawrence Erlbaum Associates.

Plemmenou, E., Bard, E. G., & Branigan, H. P. (2002). Grammatical gender in the production of single words: Some evidence from Greek. *Brain and Language, 81,* 236–241.

Poplack, S. (1980). The notion of the plural in Puerto Rican Spanish: Competing constraints on (s) deletion. In W. Labov (Ed.), *Locating language in time and space* (pp. 55–67). New York: Academic Press.

Rispoli, M. (1987). The acquisition of transitive and intransitive action verb categories in Japanese. *First Language, 7,* 183–200.

Scheiffelin, B. B. (1985). The acquisition of Kaluli. In D. I. Slobin (Ed.), *The crosslinguistic study of language acquisition: Vol. 1. The data* (pp. 525–93). Hillsdale, NJ: Lawrence Erlbaum Associates.

Slobin, D. I. (1973). Cognitive prerequisites for the development of grammar. In C. A. Ferguson & D. I. Slobin (Eds.), *Studies of child language development* (pp. 175–208). New York: Holt, Rinehart & Winston.

Slobin, D. I. (1986). Crosslinguistic evidence for the Language-Making Capacity. In D. Slobin (Ed.), *The crosslinguistic study of language acquisition: Vol. 2. Theoretical issues* (pp. 1029–1067). Hillsdale, NJ: Lawrence Erlbaum Associates.

Slobin, D. I. (2001). Form-function relations: How do children find out what they are? In M. Bowerman & S. C. Levinson (Eds.), *Language acquisition and conceptual development* (pp. 406–449). Cambridge, UK: Cambridge University Press.

Smith, M., & Wheeldon, L. (2001). Syntactic priming in spoken sentence production: An online study. *Cognition, 78,* 123–164.

Tannen, D. (1989). *Talking voices: Repetition, dialogue and imagery in conversational discourse.* New York: Cambridge University Press.

Travis, C. E. (2005). The *yo-yo* effect: Priming in subject expression in Colombian Spanish. In R. Gess & E. J. Rubin (Eds.), *Selected papers from the thirty-fourth Linguistic Symposium on Romance Languages (LSRL), Salt Lake City, 2004* (pp. 329–349). Amsterdam/Philadelphia: John Benjamins.

Wheeldon, L. R., & Smith, M. C. (2003). Phrase structure priming: A short-lived effect. *Language and Cognitive Processes, 18,* 431–442.

Wray, A. (2002). *Formulaic language and the lexicon.* Cambridge, UK: Cambridge University Press.

Part II

Narratives and Their Development

Linguistic, Cognitive, and Pragmatic Perspectives

Introduction

RUTH A. BERMAN
Tel Aviv University

*I*t is fitting that a book dedicated to "research in the tradition of Dan Isaac Slobin" include a section on narratives. Constructing a narrative provides people with a compelling means for deploying their linguistic, cognitive, and pragmatic knowledge—three strands of inquiry that Slobin has consistently argued should not be treated as autonomous. And children's narrative development constitutes "a particularly privileged vantage point" for studying the complex relations between language and cognition (Venezeniano, Albert, & Martin, this volume). No coincidence, then, that Slobin's idea of *thinking for speaking* emerged out of his contemplation of narratives across languages and across the life-span, as did his view of language use as determined not only by the typological properties of a given language or group of languages but also by the *rhetorical preferences* of members of a given speech community and the expressive options selected by individual speaker-writers. As the chapters in this section indicate, narratives also afford a richly textured framework for the text-embedded study of *developing form/function relations*, a notion that Slobin early in his career transformed from its broadly developmental formulation by Werner and Kaplan (1963) into a focus on the relationship between linguistic forms and their discourse functions.

Psycholinguistically motivated research on narrative development took root in the early 1980s, pioneered by Hickmann (1980, 1982) and Karmiloff-Smith (1980, 1981). At the time, these scholars focused on reference to characters in the story, as a domain that sheds particular light on cognitive and pragmatic features of language acquisition. It was Slobin who moved the field from a focus on nominals to predicates, from reference to entities to *encoding of events*. When Slobin and I embarked on a project in the early 1980s (Berman & Slobin, 1987) to compare tense/aspect in English and Hebrew child language, Slobin suggested that we depart from the then prevailing paradigm, with its focus on the categorial and referential content of individual words or morphemes, by shifting to a text-embedded investigation of tense/aspect acquisition. This sent us to narratives, as a discourse genre anchored in dynamic events that proceed through time, affording a communicative context particularly suited to studying the development of temporality.

In method, we decided to deploy a picture-book story (Mercer Mayer's *"Frog, where are you?"*) that involved a longer, more complex set of episodes than the picture-series stimuli used by Hickmann and Karmiloff-Smith. Our choice of Mayer's remarkable little booklet was motivated by work of Slobin's then student, Michael Bamberg, whose 1987 monograph was the first published piece of "Frog Story" research (on German child language).[1] Since the Berman and Slobin (1994) crosslinguistic developmental study, the scale of Frog Story research has burgeoned considerably—as demonstrated by the collection edited by Strömqvist and Verhoeven (2004) and the studies listed in its appendices; and, as Slobin wrote in the preface, "a lot of little tadpoles have grown into frogs." This enterprise is brilliantly anchored in the pragmatics of storytelling as an activity by Clark's (2004) chapter "Variations on a ranarian theme" (pp. 457–476), and it is superbly summed up in typological perspective by Slobin's chapter on "The many ways to search for a frog" (Slobin, 2004a).[2]

By selecting to focus on temporality and hence on events, Slobin set the foundations for a rich flowering of usage-based typological and developmental research on *motion events*. Slobin's crosslinguistic probing of this domain in narrative has been fruitful in several directions. Most notably, it has

---

[1] The second was an article on Hebrew-language Frog Stories (Berman, 1988).
[2] Although not prepared to take official credit, Slobin was tirelessly involved in all facets of the book's production, from eliciting chapters to evaluating them for content and style, often writing detailed commentary to the authors.

helped recast the path-breaking verb-framed vs. satellite-framed typology of Talmy (1991, 2000)—Slobin's former student, then colleague, always friend—in a less dichotomous framework. Insights from Frog Story research underlie Slobin's (1997) conceptualization of "grammatically specified notions" as lying along a *cline* between grammar and lexicon and his (2004) narrative-embedded study of motion events as involving a third, *more mixed type* of language, termed 'equipollent.'

The twelve chapters in this section echo several of these themes, while reflecting other major features of Slobin's life and work as well. The first is *his impact on people* from around the world. Thus, half the chapters—like several of those in Berman and Slobin (1994)—are written by Slobin's former doctoral students—Bamberg, Guo, Nakamura, Nicolopolou, Oh, and Özçalişkan—and the other authors have all benefited from being associated with Slobin during their stays at Berkeley and his in Europe. The second is a *crosslinguistic approach* to language acquisition, heralded by Slobin's departure from the Anglo-centrism of the field, through the Berkeley field manual he edited (Slobin, 1967). In like spirit, the twelve chapters in this section analyze narratives in a range of languages—French (Veneziano et al), Swiss German (Berthele), Japanese (Nakamura), Mandarin Chinese (Guo & Chen), Tzotzil Mayan (de León), and Walpiri (Bavin)—as well as in crosslinguistic comparisons—English-French (Hickmann et al), English-Korean (Oh), English-Turkish (Özçalişkan), and English-Hebrew-Spanish (Berman & Nir-Sagiv). Having originally motivated rich research into the impact of target language typology on early acquisition (Section I of this volume), Slobin's subsequent work has played a major role in the study of how children and adults from different language backgrounds construe and construct the stories that they tell.

Since the 1970s, cognitivist perspectives have largely dominated research on narrative development—in story grammar analyses, mainly of text comprehension and retelling, on the one hand, and subsequently in "functional psycholinguistics" approaches to narrative text construction, on the other (Nicolopolou, 1997). In contrast, the chapters in this section reflect the broadness of Slobin's interests and his non-monolithic approach to language, to language development, and to narrative analysis. Thus, in largely *pragmatic perspective*, Bamberg uses "the frog-book project to show how an originally cognitive orientation to the language acquisition task that was mainly interested in children's grammatical marking of sequencing events in time could turn subversively into something much larger." Against this background, Bamberg calls for a refocusing on subjectively projective aspects of narrative acquisition and the role of narratives in the development of self-identity. In similar vein, Nicolopolou's penetrating analysis of different trends in narratology and narrative development leads her to conclude that "character representation and its development remain a surprisingly unexplored area in developmental research on narrative." To motivate more attention to this issue, Nicolopolou points to a "puzzling discrepancy" between the widely attested lack of reference to the inner life of characters in children's narratives until as late as age 8 to 9 years, contrasting with current narrative research showing that even 4-year-olds demonstrate social understanding and an ability to attribute mental states to others in order to explain the behavior of participants in a story. Relatedly, Nakamura's analysis of narrative evaluation in Frog Stories of Japanese-speaking children and adults demonstrates that even young preschoolers are capable of using culturally appropriate linguistic means for expressing affect in order to achieve "emotive communication."

The chapters in this section illustrate *varied procedures* for eliciting narratives. These include picture-series and animated cartoons (Hickmann et al.), retellings with and without intervention of a specially designed picture series (Veneziano et al), semi-structured personal-experience narratives that tap into "thinking for writing" (Berman & Nir-Sagiv), spontaneous conversation-embedded stories (de León, Nicolopoulou), and bi-directional translations of novels and short stories (Oh). The remaining six chapters devolve around "frogbook" studies in different population and from various perspectives, including comparisons of child and adult narrations in Bavin's analysis of plot structure in Warlpiri, in Nakamura's study of evaluative affect in Japanese, and de León's comparison of evidentials in Frog Stories as against spontaneous narratives in a Mayan language. The enterprise is enriched by Berthele's account of his travails in attempting to apply Frog Story procedures to a conservatively traditional Alpine community speaking the Muotathal dialect of Swiss German.

Several of the chapters in this section directly address the *verb-framed vs. satellite-framed opposition*, re-analyzing this typology through narrative-anchored motion events across varied age groups, languages, and language families. Together, they provide evidence for Slobin's demonstration that narratives highlight the need to go beyond a strictly dichotomous division into *verb-framed vs. satellite-framed* languages and an unequivocal favoring of either path or manner. Berthele's chapter lays new groundwork by extending such comparisons to the domain of dialectology, characterizing this typological distinction as lying along a *cline* from standard French to Swiss German and Romansh. Guo and Chen's analysis of Frog Story narratives of adults and children in Mandarin Chinese provides evidence for what Slobin termed "equipollently-framed languages" as a third language type, where path and manner are expressed by two linguistic forms that have roughly equal morpho-syntactic status. And Oh's analysis of the expression of manner of motion in Korean and English translation confirms the fact that "clusters of features" rather than all-or-nothing alternatives combine in these domains.

Related questions are raised in *developmental perspective* by Hickmann et al. They use a richly varied database to demonstrate what Slobin has termed "distributive" means of expressing the semantics of motion events, to show that while children may rely largely on the prototypical means for encoding motion in their language, they also use alternative, more marked linguistic structures for this purpose. Their English–French analyses support Slobin's (1996) proposal that the language used by children from a young age is closer to that of adult speakers of the language than to that of their peers from typologically different linguistic backgrounds. Özçalişkan, too, comments on what Berman (1986; 1993) has called "the typological imperative," noting that crosslinguistic variation is learned early on by children exposed to English and Turkish, two typologically very different languages.

Another developmental theme to emerge from these analyses of children's narratives, one that Slobin has considered deeply over the years, is the relation between *language and thought*. Fresh insight on this topic is provided by the conclusions drawn by Veneziano et al, to the effect that 6- to 7-year-olds "do not take on a mind-oriented approach to storytelling." In more linguistic perspective, Guo and Chen propose that a language with serial-verb constructions, like Mandarin Chinese, would be a good place to test for "a cognitivist bias" determining early acquisition over and above the impact of target language typology, but this might require younger children than the participants in their studies. Özçalişkan's English-Turkish comparisons demonstrate the role of grammaticalization in acquisition, providing fresh evidence for Slobin's (1996, 1997) insight that notions realized by grammaticized means of making a particular categorial distinction are acquired early on and are highly accessible to children as well as adult speakers of a given language. Thus, from early childhood, grammaticalization brings certain semantic and functional categories to the cognitive and hence to the expressive forefront of "thinking for speaking."

Yet another idea that Slobin was among the first to articulate concerns the interplay between a language's structural options and the *rhetorical preferences* of its speaker-writers as determining their expressive choices in constructing a narrative. This is echoed in the chapter by Guo and Chen on how children aged 3 to 9 compared with adults relate the contents of the Frog Story in Mandarin Chinese, and in Berman and Nir-Sagiv's comparison of the means favored for achieving narrative connectivity in personal-experience narratives produced by schoolchildren and adolescents in English and Hebrew compared with Spanish.

Cross-cultural comparisons of narrative construction in traditional cultures are provided by Berthele's investigation of a conservative community in the Swiss Alps in what he suggests may be a "non-narrative culture"; by Bavin's consideration of evaluative elements in the Warlpiri Frog Stories of children and adolescents raised in an aboriginal community in the central Australian desert; and by Nakamura's analysis of the expression of affect in stories told by Japanese-speaking children compared with adults. These studies extend Slobin's insights concerning the early impact of linguistic typology by demonstrating that even young children are sensitive to culturally appropriate forms of linguistic expression of narrative evaluation. These ideas are enriched by de León's ethnographic comparison of the use of evidentials for achieving narrative cohesion in Frog Story–based compared with free narratives told by child and adult speakers of Tzotzil Mayan, an indigenous language of Mexico, where "narratives typically unfold in dialogic or multiparty interaction in culturally grounded encounters." Her study demonstrates that the idea of what constitutes a "true story" needs to be evaluated in relation to the cultural context in which it is situated. These themes echo the concern voiced by Slobin in our original Frog Story study, where Mercer Mayer's book is described as "clearly a product of Western culture" (Berman & Slobin, 1994, p. 21), a concern that he was at pains to counter in the later, 2004 collection.

The chapters in this volume, then, provide richly varied insights into key themes in (narrative) "research in the tradition of Dan Isaac Slobin." They also point to directions for further research. One would be to test the generality of findings reported here by applying varied procedures for eliciting narratives across a single topic and/or population. This might help resolve apparently conflicting results for children's reference to mental states documented in the chapters by Nicolopolou compared with Veneziano et al.—as earlier suggested by Hickmann's (1995, 2003) interpretation of different findings in the domain of reference and see, too, Berman's (2004) comparison of Frog Stories with other types of Hebrew narratives. One way to do so is by eliciting different types of narratives from *the same children*, as de León does in comparing Frog Stories and free narratives produced by children raised in an oral culture. In this connection, too, Slobin has paved the way, by extending his analyses to different narrative sub-genres, "from children's oral narratives to the rhetorical style of novels, newspaper reports, and conversations (1996, 2000) and the 'discourse effects of linguistic typology' in novels in different languages and in multilingual translations (2003, 2004b)" (Berman & Nir-Sagiv, this volume).

A second, likewise integrative direction, would be to consider Rimmon-Kenan's (1983) claim that "we should consider character and plot as interdependent and analyze the forms of this interdependence" (cited by Nicolopolou, this volume). Psycholinguistically, this view is closely consistent with Slobin's appeal for a "distributed semantics," in the sense that diverse linguistic devices conspire together for expressing a particular conceptual category or discourse stance (Berman, 2005). Clearly, narratives are an excellent site for analyzing, along lines indicated in the chapter by Hickmann et al, the interaction between different cognitive and linguistic sub-domains—space and time, people and events.

Another theme that warrants further consideration for narrative research is the issue of individual rhetorical choice. Expressive preferences for realizing form-function relations in narrative will apply not only across a language, a speech community, or an age-group. Rather, rhetorical expressiveness may depend in part on *individual* abilities and propensities (Berman & Nir-Sagiv, 2007). In both these areas, there is a lot to learn from Slobin—first, because of the breadth of the contexts that he has considered, and second because he himself is a superb raconteur, with a rare gift for storytelling and for thinking for speaking and writing. One of many instances: On an afternoon in the summer of 1991, sitting in his study on Rose Street, wondering how to start writing up the Frog Story project, Slobin framed the issue in terms as succinct as they were illuminating. He asked: "What story should we tell about the frog story"? This was the jumping-off point for our deciding that the book would start with narrative functions, move on to linguistic forms, and then try the hardest job of all, relating the two in the texts we analyzed. The effort culminated (but did not end) in the coda that Slobin wrote about "Telling the Frog Story in Academia" (Berman & Slobin, 2004, p. 643). Those eighteen lines represent narrative competence and storytelling performance at their very best.

REFERENCES

Bamberg, M. (1987). *The acquisition of narratives: Learning to use language*. Berlin: Mouton de Gruyter.
Berman, R. A. (1986). The acquisition of morphology/syntax: A crosslinguistic perspective. In P. Fletcher & M. Garman (Eds.), *Language acquisition, 2nd ed.* (pp. 429–447). Cambridge, UK: Cambridge University Press.
Berman, R. A. (1988). On the ability to relate events in narratives. *Discourse Processes, 11*, 469–97.

Berman, R. A. (1993). Crosslinguistic perspectives on native language acquisition. In K. Hyltenstam & A. Viberg, (Eds.), *Progression and regression in language: Sociocultural, neuro-psychological, and linguistic perspectives* (pp. 245–266). Cambridge, UK: Cambridge University Press.

Berman, R. A. (2004). The role of context in developing narrative abilities. In S. Strömqvist & L. Verhoeven (Eds.) *Relating events in narrative: Typological and contextual perspectives* (pp. 261–280). Mahwah, NJ: Lawrence Erlbaum Associates.

Berman, R. A. (Ed.) (2005). Developing discourse stance across adolescence [Special issue]. *Journal of Pragmatics, 37*, 2.

Berman, R. A., & Nir-Sagiv, B. (2007). Comparing narrative and expository text construction across adolescence: A developmental paradox. *Discourse Processes, 43*, 79–120.

Berman, R. A., & Slobin, D. I. (1987). *Five ways of learning how to talk about events: A crosslinguistic study of children's narratives (Berkeley Cognitive Science Report No. 46)*. Berkeley, CA: Institute of Cognitive Science, University of California, Berkeley.

Berman, R. A., & Slobin, D. I. (1994). *Relating events in narrative: A crosslinguistic developmental study*. Hillsdale, NJ: Lawrence Erlbaum Associates.

Clark, H. H. (2004). Variations on a ranarian theme. In S. Strömqvist & L.Verhoeven (Eds.), *Relating events in narrative: Typological and contextual perspectives* (pp. 457–476). Mahwah, NJ: Lawrence Erlbaum Associates.

Hickmann, M. (1980). Creating referents in discourse: A developmental analysis of linguistic cohesion. In J. Kreiman & E. Ojeda (Eds.), *Papers from the Parasession on Pronouns and Anaphora* (pp. 192–203). Chicago: Chicago Linguistic Society.

Hickmann, M. (1982). The development of narrative skills: Pragmatic and metapragmatic aspects of discourse cohesion. Unpublished doctoral dissertation, University of Chicago.

Hickmann, M. (1987). The pragmatics of reference in child language: Some issues in developmental theory. In M. Hickmann (Ed.), *Social and functional approaches to language and thought* (pp. 165–184). Orlando: Academic Press.

Hickmann, M. (1995). Discourse organization and the development of reference to person, place, and time. In P. Fletcher & B. MacWhinney (Eds.), *The handbook of child language* (pp. 194–218). Oxford: Blackwell.

Hickmann, M. (2003). *Children's discourse: Person, space, and time across languages*. Cambridge, UK: Cambridge University Press

Karmiloff-Smith, A. (1980). Psychological processes underlying pronominalization and non-pronominalization in children's connected discourse. In J. Kreiman & E. Ojeda (Eds.), *Papers from the Parasession on Pronouns and Anaphora* (pp. 231–250). Chicago: Chicago Linguistic Society.

Karmiloff-Smith, A. (1981). The grammatical marking of thematic structure in the development of language production. In W. Deutsch (Ed.), *The child's construction of language* (pp. 121–147). New York: Academic Press.

Nicolopolou, A. (1997). Children and narratives: Toward an interpretive and sociocultural approach. In M. Bamberg (Ed.), *Narrative development: Six approaches* (pp. 179–216). Mahwah, NJ: Lawrence Erlbaum Associates.

Slobin, D. I. (Ed.), (1967). *A field manual for cross-cultural study of the acquisition of communicative competence*. University of California, Berkeley.

Slobin, D. I. (1996). From "thought and language" to "thinking to speaking." In J. J. Gumperz & S. C. Levinson (Eds.), *Rethinking linguistic relativity* (pp. 70–96). Cambridge, UK: Cambridge University Press.

Slobin, D. I. (1997). The origins of grammaticizable notions: Beyond the individual mind. In D. I. Slobin (Ed.), *The crosslinguistic study of language acquisition* (Vol. 5, pp. 267–323). Hillsdale, NJ: Lawrence Erlbaum Associates.

Slobin, D. I. (2000). Verbalized events: A dynamic approach to linguistic relativity and determinism. In S. Niemeir & R. Dirven (Eds.), *Evidence for linguistic relativity* (pp. 107–138). Amsterdam: John Benjamins.

Slobin, D. I. (2001). Form-function relations: How do children find out what they are? In M. Bowerman & S. C. Levinson (Eds.), *Language acquisition and conceptual development* (pp. 406–449). Cambridge, UK: Cambridge University Press.

Slobin, D. I. (2003). How people move. In C. L Moder & A. Martinovic-Zic (Eds.), *Discourse across languages and cultures* (pp. 195–210). Amsterdam: John Benjamins.

Slobin, D. I. (2004a). The many ways to search for a frog: Linguistic typology and the expression of motion events. In S. Strömqvist & L. Verhoeven (Eds.), *Relating events in narrative: Typological and contextual perspectives* (pp. 219–257). Mahwah, NJ: Lawrence Erlbaum Associates.

Slobin, D. I. (2004b). Relating events in translation. In D. Ravid & H. B. Shyldkrot (Eds.), *Perspectives on language and language development: Essays in honor of Ruth A. Berman* (pp. 115–130). Dordrecht, The Netherlands: Kluwer.

Strömqvist, S., & Verhoeven, L. (Eds.) (2004). *Relating events in narrative: Typological and contextual perspectives.* Mahwah, NJ: Lawrence Erlbaum Associates.

Talmy, L. (1991). Path to realization: A typology of event conflation. In L. Sutton, C. Johnson, & R. Shields (Eds.) *Proceedings of Berkeley Linguistics Society, 17* (pp. 480–519). Berkeley Linguistics Society.

Talmy, L. 2000. *Toward a cognitive semantics* (Vols. 1 and 2). Cambridge, MA: The MIT Press.

Werner, H., & Kaplan, B. (1963). *Symbol formation: An organismic-developmental approach to language and the expression of thought.* New York: Wiley.

9

Sequencing Events in Time or Sequencing Events in Storytelling?
From Cognition to Discourse— With Frogs Paving the Way

MICHAEL BAMBERG
Clark University

Culture and language co-construct each other in ongoing processes of speaking and engaging in cultural practices.

Dan I. Slobin (2003, p. 187)

This chapter is a short contribution to a volume that gives credit to Dan Slobin's accomplishments in the broad landscapes of child language and psycholinguistics, and it opens up the opportunity to look back and take stock of the impact of his work and current theorizing in these same fields. It is my goal to focus on what I will call a turning point—and Dan Slobin's influential role in it—from what broadly can be conceived of as a predominantly 'cognitive orientation' to what is now known as a more 'discursive' or 'pragmatic orientation' within the field of child language research. Although much child language research still is strongly anchored in cognitivism (and its bedfellow: nativism), and although these orientations are not necessarily mutually exclusive, it may be fruitful to show how the turn to discursive approaches to language acquisition came about and what it has to offer to students of child language in the present day. In examining this orientation shift, I will show that the issue of event sequencing was originally conceived of as a 'mindful' activity of the individual speaker in the service of constructing the plot. Yet, on closer examination, it grew into a discursive or dialogical activity between speakers in the service of 'self-presentation' and 'identity work.'

Let me start with a brief historical introduction of how the language acquisition task was conceived of at the height of the cognitive revolution.[1] In the early sixties (1960–1964), Dan Slobin was a student at the Harvard Center for Cognitive Studies and took classes with Roger Brown, Eric Lenneberg, George Miller, and Jerry Bruner. He also ventured down to the MIT campus to audit a Chomsky seminar. So it comes as no surprise that his early notions of the language acquisition task were framed in terms of innate concepts and the child's cognitive advances jointly impinging on meaningful concepts that became mapped onto linguistic forms in the child's linguistic development. While on the one hand, Slobin's assumptions were in agreement with Chomsky's position that all languages have

---

[1] Of course, any compilation of historical facts is not only retrospective but also from an ideological vantage point. My own is that of a discursive psychologist.

the same basic underlying structure and that humans operate with the same basic cognitive principles, his 1973 proposal of Operating Principles constituted a considerable departure from a strong deterministic nativist position. He posited that the child is equipped with cognitive predispositions or preferences to figure out how meanings can be mapped onto linguistic units. In order to do so, Dan needed to attend to the language specificity of the language with which the child grew up.

More specifically, Slobin defined the language acquisition task as learning to connect two aspects of language: the content aspect and the relational aspect. The content aspect was said to consist of the ability to refer to objects and events of experience, while the relational aspect highlighted the connection of these objects and events with one another. The first was said to take place typically in the form of lexical items or content words, while the second was accomplished by grammatical functors. Both interacted differently in different languages, particularly in typologically different languages, and Slobin claimed it was the child's task to figure out the ways his/her mother tongue split up the divide. More specifically, the child needed to attend to the kinds of systematic form–function relationships particular to his/her language. Later on (1997, 2001), Slobin more strongly emphasized a third component to be equally relevant for the language acquisition task. It consisted of another relational orientation, namely, to view the objects and events of experience from the speaker's discourse perspective.

In my contribution to this volume I will take off from this formulation of the relationship between content and how content items are related to each other and how the two orient in concert toward the discourse perspective of the speaker. I will use the frog-book project to show how an originally cognitive orientation to the language acquisition task that was mainly interested in children's grammatical marking of sequencing events in time could turn subversively into something much larger. However, before I head this way, let me briefly summarize the view of the child that was running parallel to this type of theorizing.

It was very clear, from early on, that the child was somewhat of an agent in the process of conducting the learning task. The child had to figure out the language specific intricacies all by him/herself—albeit with the kind of cognitive equipment s/he was developing, which in turn was assumed to be nested within the processes of a universal cognitive development. Thus, the course of the child's general development proceeds from mental development to linguistic development, placing the language learning task squarely within the domain of the child's cognitive development. Again, it comes as no surprise that, within this general framework of setting up the task of 'cracking the linguistic code,' the child's social development was consistently reduced to the *right* exposure to the *right* input that the well-equipped mind subsequently could process 'actively' into the *right* linguistic *knowledge*. In sum, it appeared as though Jerry Bruner's influence on Dan Slobin's early stages of developing 'Basic Child Grammars' in solving the puzzle of how meanings become mapped onto linguistic forms was minimal. Still, fast forwarding to Slobin's more recent formulations of the language acquisition task, which frame the child as 'learning to think for speaking and to listen for understanding in terms of the exposure language(s)' (2001, p. 441), these formulations equally give little space to the child's active explorations in his/her everyday language practices. Rather, the language itself comes to organize the child's language practices along the underlying typology of the target language (Slobin, 1997, 2001). Thus, what still sounds like a very cognitive solution of the language acquisition task, one that pays little attention to children's active role in the making of grammatical structures, nevertheless attempts to give language a major role in children's cognitive socialization. I will return later to potential implications of this perspective.

The Frog-Book Project: From 'Relating Events in Time' to 'Relating Events in Narrative'

The frog-book project[2] and the way it emerged and changed focus are an interesting example or mirror for how initial outlooks and perspectives within a domain of inquiry can change. When the

---

[2] The frog-book project resulted in the Berman and Slobin volume (1994) which was based on children's (and adults') tellings of the booklet *Frog, where are you?* This wordless picture booklet contains 24 pictures in which a boy and his dog try to find their pet frog, who had run away from home. Their search results in a happy ending depicted in the last picture where the boy and dog return home with a/the frog.

crosslinguistic team,[3] under the guidance of Dan Slobin and Ruth Berman, originally ventured out to gain crosslinguistic data with the frog-book as our elicitation tool, the task looked pretty straightforward. The beauty of using the wordless picture-book *Frog, where are you?* (Mayer, 1969) seemed to consist of exposing all our participants of different ages and in different languages to the same stimuli. Because we assumed that the interpretation of these stimuli is pretty much the same across different languages and cultures, naming the events depicted in these pictures would open up insights into how the language-specific means (e.g., tense and aspect markers) cut up the flow of time to solve the task. More specifically, having children of different age groups perform this task could have potentially delivered insights into the children's minds in terms of the cognitive underpinnings for the necessary but supposedly limited form–meaning mappings.

Of course, it was also very clear from the outset of the project that the participants in our study were doing more than simply naming the events depicted in the individual pictures. Ever since Labov and Waletzky's (1967/1997) seminal work on using narratives for sociolinguistic inquiry, it became obvious that speakers also seriate events and combine them into something like a plot, that is, a narrative structure that signals the point of its telling. Simultaneously, plots are kinds of content structures that are 'borrowed' from available repertoires of socioculturally shared plots with the purpose to lend social meaning to the telling of the particular narrative under consideration. Regarding this type of general task, the frog story is particularly rich, since it sets up opportunities for the narrator to encode a variety of temporal distinctions, such as sequence, simultaneity, prospection, retrospection, ongoing and completed events, and the like. Thus, for the frog-story project, the developmental task for children can be defined more concretely as learning to filter and package the information (cf. Berman & Slobin, 1994, pp. 9–16) so that the narrative plot of the search theme can come to existence. As Berman and Slobin put it in their introduction to the volume:

> The Leitmotif of our study is that form and function interact in development. Under 'form' we include a broad range of linguistic devices … along with lexical items encoding notions of temporality, manner, and causation. By 'function' we understand the purposes served by these forms in narrative discourse—purposes of constructing a text that is cohesive and coherent at all levels: within the clause, between adjacent clauses, and hierarchically relating larger text segments to one another. (Berman & Slobin, 1994, p. 4)

More concretely, Berman and Slobin (1994, pp. 517ff.) suggest that events are constructed linguistically by following a sequence of preverbal, cognitive decisions: The speaker selects (i) a topic, (ii) the locus of control and effect, (iii) an event view, and (iv) a degree of agency. Let me consider

picture 11   picture 12

Figure 9.1   Pictures 11 and 12 of *Frog, Where Are You?*

---

[3] Here are the other players on this team: Ayhan A. Aksu-Koç (Turkish), Virginia Marchman and Tanya Renner (English), Eugenia Sebastián (Spanish), and myself (German).

the presentation of two particular pictures of the frog-book, pictures 11 and 12, in which the dog apparently has caused a beehive to fall off a tree (in picture 11) and now (in picture 12) is being followed by a swarm of bees. First, the dog can be construed as *running away* from the bees and as being *pursued* or *chased* by them. In other words, a speaker can relate these characters in some form of character constellation that attributes motives for their movements through time and space. According to Berman and Slobin, speakers first can be assumed to select a topic, having a choice between *the bees* and *the dog*. Topic here refers to who is mentioned in subject position: the bees as active pursuers, the dog either as *running* or, by use of the passive voice, as *being followed, pursued* or *chased*. Regarding the speaker's selection of a locus of control, the choice of passive voice with the dog as topic is more likely to be recognized as construing the event from the dog's point of view—with the dog as the undergoer (locus of effect) and the bees as controller. Accordingly, making a decision as to how to view the event, speakers can choose between a cause-view (presenting an actor who causes a change of state in an undergoer—as in *the dog is being chased by the bees*), a become-view (orienting to a change of state, usually by way of an activity verb—as in *now the dog is running*), or a state-view (state description—as in *there is a dog*). Last, in selecting a degree of agency, the speaker also has a number of options. For instance, s/he can opt for a relatively high degree of agency (*the dog raced away because the bees were chasing him*), a mid degree (*the dog was being chased by the bees*), or a low degree (*the dog was running away from the bees*). Thus, selection of degree of agency in English can involve lexical choices of verbs and associated adverbs as well as placement of the controller in a peripheral phrase.

Concerning this particular constellation of pictorially presented information and the seemingly overwhelming number of choices, the question emerges: How can we find out what motivates speakers to select one particular perspective over all the other possible ones? It is obvious that the world does not 'come' with clear-cut event boundaries. It is speakers who use conventional (linguistic) means in order to construe events by 'stopping,' so to speak, time on the right and on the left of the unit, which is under construction and which we subsequently can call 'events.' Neither does the world 'come' in event sequences nor in terms of distinctions of what is figure and what is ground, telling us how to choose our linguistic devices to 'impose' perspective and degree of agency. Rather, decisions with regard to events, event sequences, and perspective fall within the domain of speakers' subjectivities. However, what factors are motivating these choices? In particular, how do young children learn to organize their perspectives? Within a predominantly cognitive framework, the answers to these questions have been pushed over to the domain of speakers' subjectivities and are not of concern for the language acquisition task.

Before I turn to the potential of a more discursive answer to these questions, let me briefly discuss an interchange between a mother and a daughter who recorded their interaction as a nightly routine that formed part of my dissertation data (Bamberg, 1985, 1987). Both mother and daughter had just turned on the recorder and were looking at the cover page of the booklet as in Figure 9.2.

Example 1:

1	mother	*schau mal da rufen die*
		'look there they are calling'
2	mother	*weisst du auch wen die da rufen*
		'do you know who they are calling for'
3	daughter	*ja den Frosch*
		'yes the frog'
4	mother	*ja und wo ist der*
		'right and where is he'
5	daughter	*der sitzt da unter dem Baum*
		'he's sitting there under the tree'
6	mother	*ja der hat sich da versteckt*
		'right he is hiding there'

cover page **picture 1**

Figure 9.2   Cover page and picture 1 of *Frog, Where Are You?*

<blockquote>

7 mother → *so jetzt geht die Geschichte los*
'so now the story begins'

8 mother   *da <u>war</u> also mal <u>ein</u> Junge*
'once there was a boy'

9 mother   *und der <u>hatte</u> zwei Freunde <u>einen</u> Hund und <u>einen</u> Frosch*
'and he <u>had</u> two friends a dog and a frog'

10 mother   *und eines Nachts dann*
'and then one night'

11 mother   *als die beiden <u>schliefen</u>*
'when both of them <u>were asleep</u>'

12 mother   *<u>schlich</u> sich der Frosch vom Trapez*
'the frog <u>snuck</u> away'

</blockquote>

It is important to realize that throughout the interaction both conversational partners make use of the present tense as long as they are engaging in a question-and-answer sequence over the characters depicted on the cover (lines 1–6). In addition, the characters are referred to by the use of definite marking (*die* 'they' in line 1; *den Frosch* 'the frog' in line 3), as if these characters either have been established as part of the ongoing discourse beforehand (anaphoric), or they are marked definite because they *are there* within the deictic reach of the interlocutors and therefore do not require an introduction into the discourse by the use of less definite marking. In line 7 the mother opens up the picture book and turns to the first picture of the story sequence. It is here that she announces that the story will begin (*die Geschichte geht los* 'the story starts'), marked by a tense change in the next proposition to the simple past (*war* 'was' in line 8) and reintroducing the character by use of an indefinite marker (*ein Junge* 'a boy'). From line 8 on, the story continues in the past tense.

What these changes in grammatical choices apparently signal is a perspective change. The activity or language game of finding characters on the cover page and descriptively labeling them is signaled as completed and a new activity has started. And the new language game is overtly referred to as 'storytelling.' Using the indefinite forms both for the boy ('a boy' in line 8) and for the dog and the frog ('a dog and a frog' in line 9) construes the characters as 'new,' or at least as though they require a new introduction because the discourse genre is new. This suggests that all previous references as well as the established talk about the story characters are eradicated. Similarly, switching tense from the present to the past signals a perspective change that has nothing to do with the temporal dimension that links what is told (as potentially conceptualized in the past) to the telling (in the here and now). Instead, what is called into the context of the here and now (*contextualized*) is the *new* 'perceived time' of the *new* language game between the two interlocutors. What we have on tape and represented in the transcript is that the use of linguistic forms as marking a change in language games is transformed nicely into a socialization practice for the child. In other words, the mother 'knows' what she is doing when she engages the child in question-and-answer routines that require correct linguistic labeling practices. Similarly, she 'knows' that she is engaging in storytelling a few seconds later. She even comments overtly on this change. By marking off these two language games and separating them from one another, the speaker signals for the interlocutor that such changes in contextualizing the goings-on are part of language practices. Such practices have their origins in interpersonal negotiations rather than in depictions of the world or of the ways we believe we have experienced the world.

While there is nothing particularly astonishing in the realization that picture-reading activities can be framed very differently, and that different frames are marked off linguistically and practiced with children in early book-reading activities, there is even more that we can take away from the example offered. First, tense distinctions (as all kinds of other temporality distinctions) do more than mark off events in the there-and-then and connect them into plot structures. They simultaneously organize the here and now; that is, they coordinate the time flow of the present in terms of the activities and practices that emerge between the interlocutors. Or, as Hanks (1996) puts it, these markers 'orient discourse genres to the reception that the practice is likely to get on the part of other agents in the field(s) to which it is addressed' (p. 245). Hanks also points out that it is through this kind of 'routine use, [that] genres become natural themselves, that is, they become so familiar as to be taken for granted. Their special features are invisible to actors who experience the world through them' (p. 246).

Second, if it is correct to assume that the form–function relationships regulate the communal and relational aspects between interlocutors in the here-and-now as much as they regulate the coordination between the events in the there-and-then,[4] then the learning task for the child needs to be reformulated. Rather than acquiring the necessary knowledge to map meaning onto linguistic forms to establish events and to relate these events appropriately 'in time,' we may want to entertain an alternative proposal: If it is not possible to simply read off the systematicity between form and function without already knowing what functions are in play, this kind of 'knowledge' may better be established through and *as* active participation in such practices. The example above may serve as a case in point.

Third, and most relevant, what the exercise in book-reading activities brings to our awareness is that the notion of the child as a cognizer of form-function relationships may require a similar kind of revision: If it is not possible to read the systematicities of form–function mappings off the language in use, then it may be more productive to reconceptualize the child as learning to *make* language systematic. 'Making language systematic' is not something the child doesn't know early on and learns about later, but rather it is something that is *done*—in daily routines and practices. It is an ongoing endeavor that does not result in a conclusive 'knowledge state,' as though once the child has acquired the 'correct knowledge,' his/her practices became 'right.' According to a practice orientation, the act of speaking 'involves a dialectic between the expressive projection of the speaker into the world and the simultaneous construction of the speaker according to the world' (Hanks, 1996, p. 205).

In summary, a project that had started out as a way to compare children's conceptualizations of temporality as expressed in different languages became a project that was actually dealing with much more. The realization that the actual management of the activity frame within which references to time (and space and characters) also took place in time and was negotiated with the same multifunctional markers made clear that we were dealing with more than the mapping of temporal-

---

[4] Since we were dealing in the frog project with a fictional world of third-person characters, we didn't have to worry about the actual time dimensions between the telling and the told.

ity onto particular linguistic devices. This was the first turning point within the frog-book project that pointed explicitly to the genre activity that was under investigation: 'Narrative.'

So What Is Special About 'Narrative'?

Realizing that storytelling is a practice that requires more than tying events into temporal plot configurations, one may ask: What is it that makes narratives different and special when compared with other genres? Along the same lines, one may also ask how the learning task may be redefined with regard to the acquisition of narratives, or whether it is still possible to characterize the ability to tell stories in terms of special kinds of (linguistic) knowledge that the child has to learn.

I have tackled this very question in more detail elsewhere (Bamberg, 1999), so I will only briefly restate my basic line of argument: While it is possible to privilege narratives on structural grounds over other language games, such as argumentation or description, on functional grounds, they behave just like any other discourse genre. On structural grounds, the genre of narratives is distinguished not only by the way temporal and spatial relationships are constructed in a unifying fashion, but in addition, how these temporal and spatial domains (separately and in concert) orient toward a common third domain, namely, the configuration of character. In other words, temporal and spatial relationships are presented in a coordinated way to bring off a particular character constellation—usually one that presents characters as protagonists and antagonists, but also one that allows for 'character development'—in contrast to the epic, where characters remain 'the same' across time and space. Other language games (e.g., recipes, menus, descriptions, but even argumentations, or the answers of an eyewitness under cross-examination) do not allow for these kinds of complex character configurations.[5] Thus, the 'specialty' of narrative is that it can lend to characters the aura of stability and permanence on the one hand, and at the same time, it can give characters the potential to transform and change. No other genre, to the best of my knowledge, offers these types of constructive powers.

When it comes to the discursive function of narratives, narratives can be viewed like any other discourse: Stories are embedded in interaction. They are parts of interactional activities and locally accomplished projects, at least originally. This is the place where they are shared and come alive. They are typically occasioned by what is happening before and taken up on in subsequent turns. Speakers bid for the floor to tell a story; they attempt to 'make a point' (Labov & Waletzky, 1967/1997), and quite often they 'account' for one's own and/or others' social conduct as a matter of stake and interest (Potter, 1996). Stories typically make past actions accountable from a particular (moral) perspective for particular situated purposes. As Drew (1998, p. 295) argues:

> In the (interactional) circumstances in which we report our own or others' conduct, our descriptions are themselves accountable phenomena through which we recognizably display an action's (im)propriety, (in)correctness, (un)suitability, (in)appropriateness, (in)justices, (dis)honesty, and so forth. Insofar as descriptions are unavoidably incomplete and selective, they are designed for specific and local interactional purposes. Hence they may, always and irretrievably, be understood as doing moral work—as providing a basis for evaluating the "rightness" or "wrongness" of whatever is being reported.

In sum, narratives as discursive actions are parts of accounting practices in the way they are accomplished in everyday, mundane situations—nothing particularly fancy or special. They do not originate from or *in* speakers (and neither in speakers' minds nor brains), but in conversational settings where they have their functions and where they find their forms and contents. Since they are part of more general accounting practices, speakers position themselves and 'are positioned' in ways so that they themselves or others become implicated in ways analyzable by investigators.

---

[5] Testimonies of eyewitnesses are an interesting point in case: While the eyewitness herself may have a very concrete idea of what holds the character configuration together, the fragments that are exhibited in the interrogation in the courtroom may lead to a very different interpretation in the overhearing audience of judge and jury.

The ways in which characters are presented and the ways in which temporal and spatial relationships are orchestrated to present characters are reflective of speakers' positions as they are brought off in discourse. For this reason, it may be problematic to view the 'system' of temporal relationships (and for that matter the 'system' of spatial relationships) in narratives as independent from functional purposes. The construction of temporal and spatial relations in narrative requires an analysis that is coordinated with the ways speakers employ these 'systems' for positioning purposes. Along the same lines, it may be necessary to reformulate the acquisition task that is faced by the child: rather than 'cracking' each system independently and staring at it from the outside as a 'lone cognizer' and 'problem-solver,' the child is assisting him/herself by actively exploring and appropriating the systematicities in a framework of discourse and practice. Repeated use of form–function relationships as positioning practices ties the child into communal systems of identity displays—and this begins as early as children participate in interactive routines and practices. Simultaneously, these communal practices take place within scaffolding routines such as the use of variation sets in mother–child discursive practices (cf. Küntay & Slobin, 2002). Thus, the child emerges as a 'mindful' agent within situated communal practices, positioning him/herself and being positioned by others.

In summary, the activity of narrating is part of communal accounting practices just like any other interactive activity; as such, narrating is no different from other discourse activities. At the same time, the format of positioning characters in space and time with regard to one another lends an additional feature or quality to the activity of narrating. This feature can best be characterized as oscillating between constructing permanence and stability on the one hand and transformation and the possibility of development on the other (Bamberg, 2008). Whether and how these two sides of narrative activity can be connected and potentially become integrated is currently being debated (cf. Bamberg, 2006a, 2006b; Freeman, 2006; Georgakopoulou, 2006). Of special consideration in this debate is the role of interview techniques that seem to downplay and bleach out the potential of interactive accounting, thus creating situations where speakers seemingly engage in 'pure reflection'—as if speaking to themselves—and revealing their authentic selves. Without being able to further engage in this debate here, it should be noted that the potential of narrative for identity development has become of wide interest and controversy (see the special issue of *Narrative Inquiry*, 2006).

Relating Events in Time or in Narrative: From Cognition to Discourse

While the frog-book project originally started as a language acquisition project on temporality, the peculiarity of the elicitation material and the peculiarity of the storytelling responses we received quickly led to the realization that time is always tied to human purposes and genre activities. Thus, the price that was paid for using storytelling techniques was that temporality as a specific domain of form–function mappings became hopelessly (but also interestingly) intertwined with other domains, leading to the domain of human accounting practices—shot through with social values and situated moral work. In short, the frog-book project paved the way into the domain of discourse practices and the way such practices are at work in mundane, everyday interactive occurrences. However, the price paid turned out as a reward in a different way: Constructing characters in space and time positioned our participants and opened them up for analytic purposes way beyond the construction of events in time (or space). In other words, the frog-book project served as an eye-opener to the construction of selves and identities of speakers who engage in relating events in narrative. Although the story presented in the frog-book was just a harmless third-person account of a boy, a dog, and a frog, the subjective perspective from which these characters became positioned with regard to one another was conveyed in each telling, simultaneously revealing aspects of the self and identity of the narrators.

Taking this insight back to the language acquisition arena, it can be argued that it is necessary to reformulate the learning task in order to bring the never-ending process of self- and identity development into the process of language acquisition as well so as to see all three as intricately linked. Thus, participating in storytelling practices enables the young child to practice communal forms of accountability—from early on throughout the entire life span. When it comes to the consideration of what these practices are based on, that is, what types of prerequisites they require, I have previously argued that:

> These practices are not governed or influenced, at least not a priori, by representational (cognitive) frameworks (or schemata)… Rather, in the course of repeated participation in these practices representational processes are instantiated in and through the medium of conversation, potentially resulting in some common heuristics, which, if this is deemed theoretically or methodologically advantageous, can in turn be viewed as equivalents of 'linguistic knowledge.' (Bamberg, 2002, pp. 450f)

In other words, it may be more practical to consider cognitive schemata as the outcome or product of communicative practices (such as narrating) rather than their prerequisites. If we start from the assumption that the child's overarching accomplishment is his/her construction of an individual and social identity, and that participation in social practices is the central developmental mechanism for this accomplishment, cognition definitely will play an important role in it. However, cognition as a root metaphor that supposedly bootstraps children to their communal practices not only poses rationality over practices but also construes the child as an originally isolated organism (i.e., as situated 'outside' of social and communal practices)—from which point their development then could be argued to gradually *become* social. Within this framework, the development of Slobin's approach to 'thinking for speaking,' within which the child in acquiring a native language 'learns particular ways of thinking for speaking' (1996, p. 76), and in this kind of practice becomes sensitive to form-function pairings that are typologically pointing' the child to similar form-function pairings, becomes more fully understandable (see Küntay & Slobin, 2002; Slobin, 2000, 2003). And as Slobin puts it himself, culture and language co-construct each other in ongoing processes of speaking and engaging in cultural practices (Slobin, 2003, p. 187).

REFERENCES

Bamberg, M. (1985). *Form and function in the construction of narratives: Developmental perspectives.* Unpublished doctoral dissertation, University of California, Berkeley.
Bamberg, M. (1987). *The acquisition of narratives: Learning to use language.* Berlin: Mouton de Gruyter.
Bamberg, M. (1996). Perspective and agency in the construal of narrative events. In A. Stringfellow, D. Cahana-Amitay, E. Hughes, & A. Zukowski (Eds.), *Proceedings of the 20th annual Boston Conference on Language Development* (Vol. 1, pp. 30–39). Somerville, MA: Cascadilla Press.
Bamberg, M. (1997). Positioning between structure and performance. *Journal of Narrative and Life History, 7*, 335–342.
Bamberg, M. (1999). Identität in Erzählung und im Erzählen. Versuch einer Bestimmung der Besonderheit des narrativen Diskurses für die sprachliche Verfassung von Identität. *Journal für Psychologie, 7*, 43–55.
Bamberg, M. (2000). Language and communication—What develops? Determining the role of language practices for a theory of development. In N. Budwig, I. Uzgiris, & J. Wertsch (Eds.), *Communication: An arena of development* (pp. 55–77). Norwood, NJ: Ablex.
Bamberg, M. (2000). Critical personalism, language, and development. *Theory & Psychology, 10*, 749–767.
Bamberg, M. (2002). Literacy and development as discourse, cognition or as both? *Journal of Child Language, 29*, 449–453.
Bamberg, M. (2006a). Biographic-narrative research, quo vadis? A critical review of 'big stories' from the perspective of 'small stories.' In K. Milnes, C. Horrocks, N. Kelly, B. Roberts, & D. Robinson, (Eds.), *Narrative, memory and knowledge: Representations, aesthetics and contexts* (pp. 63–79). Huddersfield, UK: University of Huddersfield Press.
Bamberg, M. (2006b). Stories: Big or small? Why do we care? *Narrative Inquiry, 16*(1), 139–147.
Bamberg, M. (2008). Selves and identities in the making: The study of microgenetic processes in interactive practices. In, U. Müller, J. Carpendale, N. Budwig, & B. Sokol (Eds.), *Social life and social knowledge* (pp. 205–224). Mahwah, NJ: Lawrence Erlbaum Associates.

Berman, R. A., & Slobin, D. I. (1994). *Relating events in narrative.* Hillsdale, NJ: Lawrence Erlbaum Associates.

Drew, P. (1998). Complaints about transgressions and misconduct. *Research and Social Interaction, 31,* 295–325.

Freeman, M. (2006). Life "on holiday." In defense of big stories. *Narrative Inquiry, 16*(1), 131–138.

Georgakopoulou, A. (2006). Thinking big with small stories in narrative and identity analysis. *Narrative Inquiry, 16*(1), 122–130.

Hanks, W. (1996). *Language and communicative practices.* Boulder, CO: Westview Press.

Küntay, A., & Slobin, D. I. (2002). Putting interaction back into child language: Examples from Turkish. *Psychology of Language and Communication, 6,* 5–14.

Labov, W., & Waletzky, J. (1967/1997). Narrative analysis: Oral versions of personal experience. In J. Helms (Ed.), *Essays on the verbal and visual arts* (pp. 12–44). Seattle: University of Washington Press. (Reprinted in *Journal of Narrative and Life History, 7,* 3–38.)

Mayer, M. (1969). *Frog, where are you?* New York: Dial Books for Young Readers.

Narrative Inquiry (2006). Narrative: State of the art. (Special issue)

Potter, J. (1996). *Representing reality: Discourse, rhetoric and social construction.* London: Sage.

Slobin, D. I. (1973). Cognitive prerequisites for the development of grammar. In C. A. Ferguson & D. I. Slobin (Eds.), *Studies of child language development* (pp. 175–208). New York: Holt, Rinehart, & Winston.

Slobin, D. I. (1996). From "thought and language" to "thinking for speaking." In J. J. Gumperz & S. C. Levinson (Eds.), *Rethinking linguistic relativity* (pp. 70–96). Cambridge, UK: Cambridge University Press.

Slobin, D. I. (1997). The origins of grammaticizable notions: Beyond the individual mind. In D. I. Slobin (Ed.), *The crosslinguistic study of language acquisition: Vol. 5. Expanding the contexts* (pp. 265–323). Mahwah, NJ: Lawrence Erlbaum Associates.

Slobin, D. I. (2000). Verbalized events. In S. Niemeier & R. Dirven (Eds.), *Evidence for linguistic relativity* (pp. 107–138). Amsterdam: John Benjamins.

Slobin, D. I. (2001). Form-function relations: How do children find out what they are? In M. Bowerman & S. C. Levinson (Eds.), *Language acquisition and conceptual development* (pp. 406–449). Cambridge, UK: Cambridge University Press.

Slobin, D. I. (2003). Language and thought online: Cognitive consequences of linguistic relativity. In D. Gentner & S. Goldin-Meadow (Eds.), *Language in mind: Advances in the study of language and thought* (pp. 157–192). Cambridge, MA: The MIT Press.

10

Plot and Evaluation
Warlpiri Children's Frog Stories

EDITH L. BAVIN

La Trobe University

> I suggest that several different sorts of factors "conspire" to produce a range of frog story varieties. These varieties result from combined influences of linguistic structure, online processing, and cultural practices.
>
> **Dan I. Slobin (2004, p. 219)**

There is a story in how Dan Slobin influenced my research. Joan Bybee, my Ph.D. supervisor, was on leave at Berkeley; on one occasion when I was visiting her I was invited to participate in a workshop on crosslinguistic language acquisition research organized by Dan Slobin. At the time I was teaching at the University of Oregon but a job in Australia was possible. When he heard about this possibility Dan suggested it would be a great opportunity to work on the acquisition of an Australian indigenous language. This was the initiating event. It seemed highly unlikely at the time, but as the plot unfolded, which will not be detailed here, I eventually arrived as a naive field worker in Yuendumu in central Australia. Many field trips later I started to collect frog stories. Later I was fortunate to be able to visit Dan at Berkeley for one semester, and also to participate in a workshop run by Dan focusing on analyzing frog stories from a typological perspective. My research on Warlpiri was heavily influenced by Dan's work. He has remained a source of inspiration.

INTRODUCTION

This chapter is based on narratives I collected from Warlpiri children and adults while conducting research on the acquisition of Warlpiri. The narratives were collected using Mercer Mayer's (1969) book about a boy, a dog, and a frog, the well-known *Frog, where are you*, which has been widely used in research across language groups (e.g., Bamberg, 1987; Berman & Slobin, 1994; Strömqvist & Verhoeven, 2004).

Features of the Warlpiri language have been well described by Ken Hale, and others (Hale, 1982, 1983; Nash, 1986; Simpson, 1991). Properties that make the language of interest typologically are its pragmatically determined word order, ergative-absolutive case system, argument ellipsis (subject and object), the cross-referencing system for subject and object, and two classes of word (noun and verb) plus many particles. The acquisition of Warlpiri including the social context of acquisition has been discussed in other papers (Bavin, 1990, 1991, 1992, 1995, 1998). One paper on ellipsis (Bavin, 2000) and one paper on the use of locative expressions (Bavin, 2004) reported data from the frog stories on which the current chapter is based. The chapter is concerned with evaluation, that is, the narrators' interpretations of the events that make up the story.[1]

There is not a universal way of telling a story (Bauman, 1969). While some stories entertain, others teach appropriate behavior through a moral embedded in the story, or they socialize children to values of the culture (e.g., Minami & McCabe, 1995). Story structures differ across cultures; typical stories in western societies involve an initiating event and a series of events leading to a resolution (Labov & Waletsky, 1967), but this is not universal. The content of stories also differs across cultures; if it is culturally appropriate to guess at someone's emotional state it is likely that a story character's emotional state will be incorporated into a narrative. From the stories they hear, children learn about structure and content and, as shown in the comparisons of children's narratives reported in Berman and Slobin (1994), they construct their stories using the linguistic means available to them. Thus narratives are a valuable research tool, not only for identifying how adults speaking typologically different languages and from different cultures encode events, but also in revealing a child's developing knowledge of his/her language and culture.

In developing a story narrators present events from their own perspective; in so doing they reveal their interpretation of the events and their attitudes toward them (Bamberg & Damrad-Frye, 1991). They may add causal connections and assume emotions and mental states as well as intentions of the characters involved, and they may add evaluative comments or propose motivations for the events depicted in the series of pictures. These represent the evaluative function of narratives, as opposed to the referential (Labov & Waletzky, 1967). Berman (1996, p. 240) proposes a tripartite analysis of narrative texts: *narrative clauses*, the sequential elements which describe the events; *evaluative elements*, or interpretive elements, which reflect the perspective of the narrator as well as the subjective interpretation of events; *informative elements*, which contribute information about the external or physical circumstances. Differences in the use of evaluative devices across languages have been reported (Bamberg & Damrad-Frye, 1991; Küntay & Nakamura, 2004), and these elements are a major focus of the current chapter.

In their study on Japanese and Turkish frog stories Küntay and Nakamura (2004) reported that the overall number of evaluative devices used relative to story length did not differ greatly across their age groups (4- to 9-year-olds and adults); however, the adults, particularly the Turkish, used more elements for evaluative function than the children. Bamberg and Damrad-Frye (1991) also found more evaluative devices used by adults in their analysis of frog stories collected from English speakers. While young children use some evaluative expressions, they are used at the local level, in reference to specific events rather than being integrated into the narrative as a whole. More mature narrators integrate evaluation into the narrative, that is, they use evaluative elements globally (Bamberg and Reilly, 1996). Thus it is important to look at where and how narrators use evaluative elements in relation to their stories as a whole.

In the following sections I discuss the overall plot structure of the frog story as considered by Berman and Slobin (1994), and the framework for coding evaluative language used by Küntay and Nakamura (2004) in their analysis of Turkish and Japanese frog stories. I then discuss the Warlpiri frog story data in terms of overall plot, events encoded, and evaluative elements used.

PLOT STRUCTURE AND EVALUATION

Plot

Berman and Slobin (1994, p. 46) identified three main plot components of the frog story: the plot initiating event (the onset) in which the boy discovers that the frog has disappeared; the sustained search (unfolding of the plot), in which the boy and dog search for the missing frog, passing through a series of events; and the resolution, the boy's finding of the frog or another frog. To incorporate

---

[1] My sincere thanks to the story tellers. I gratefully acknowledge the help I received from Nancy Napanangka, Cecily Napanangka, Barbara Napaljarri, and the late Kay Napaljarri in collecting and transcribing the stories.

these components into a cohesive story the narrator must make inferences; for example, because the frog is seen climbing from the glass bowl in one picture and is not there in the next it can be assumed that the frog has escaped; when the boy and dog hold up some clothes and look into the bowl it is assumed they are searching for the frog; and it might be assumed their various encounters are related to finding the same or another frog. Another inference can be made at the end of the story when the boy is seen holding a frog: that he will take it back home. Other inferences can be drawn within each event comprising the search, as well as at the beginning and end of the story. The inferences relate to the speaker's perspective on the narrative.

Children do not necessarily include all three aspects of the plot in their stories. Aksu-Koç and Tekdemir (2004) report a developmental pattern in their analysis of Turkish frog stories: none of the 3-year-old participants mentioned all three of the plot components, half of the 4-year-olds included at least two, 75% of the 7-year-olds mentioned all three, and by 9 years of age all children packaged the three components cohesively.

Evaluative Elements

The elements used to capture the speaker's perspective on the events in narratives told from the book *Frog, where are you?* have been reported by a number of researchers (Bamberg & Damrad-Frye, 1991; Bamberg & Reilly, 1996; Küntay & Nakamura, 2004; Reilly, 1992). To compare the evaluative language used in the Turkish and Japanese frog stories told by 5- to 9-year-olds Küntay and Nakamura coded five categories of evaluative devices, based on Bamberg and Damrad-Frye's coding scheme (a–e below).

   a. Frames of mind: expressions that refer to mental and affective states, e.g., *happy, scared, surprised, to make angry*. In Warlpiri, emotion terms are nouns; these can be used to derive verbs as in *lani* 'fear' -> *lani-jarrimi* 'become frightened.'
   b. Hedges: distancing devices, uncertainty with respect to the truth of the proposition, e.g., *seems like, probably* and *I think*. Two relevant forms in Warlpiri are the particles *marda* 'maybe, perhaps' and *nganta* 'supposedly.'
   c. Negative qualifiers: highlight underlying expectations or discrepancies. Three negative forms in Warlpiri are *lawa* 'no, not, nothing,' *kula* 'negative auxiliary' (appearing in second position in a clause) and *wangu* 'not having.'
   d. Character speech: Direct and reported speech, attributed to story characters.
   e. Causal connectors: e.g., *because, in order to*.

Other features they considered included:

   f. Enrichment expressions: reveal the unexpected, e.g., *again* and *suddenly*; intensifiers; repetitions; connectives, e.g., *however*.
   g. Onomatopoeia.
   h. Evaluative remarks: These are often asides about the events, conveying the narrator's reflections.

In analyzing the Warlpiri stories, categories (a–d) were included in the analysis but causal connectors were not as only one example was identified (*marlaja* 'because'), from an adult.[2] Two other categories were added. First, value judgments: elements not included above that clearly presented the speaker's perspective. This category included intensifiers (such as *jarlu* 'really' as in *wiri jarlu*

---

[2] Only two children incorporated onomatopoeia. Repetition was not included because it is typical for Walpiri narrators to adopt a 'build up-style' (Bavin, 2004): Some information is provided, then it is repeated or partially repeated with a bit more information added, and so on. It is hard to distinguish this learned rhetorical style from an individual's use of repetition for evaluation.

'really big'), other qualifiers (such as *juku* 'straight, true, representing a constant state'), affect (*pardu*, the diminutive of affection), and exclamations. The second category added was inferencing: about kin relations among the frogs, and where the boy, dog, and frog were going. These draw on cultural knowledge. Some of the terms used to identify the frogs at the end of the story were *ngati* 'mother,' *kurdu* 'child,' *jaja* 'father,' and *ngawurru* 'sister.' Inferences were made about the frog's destination when he left the bowl, where the boy and dog were going, and whether the boy and dog were going home at the end (*ngurra-kurra,* camp-ALL 'to home').

THE WARLPIRI NARRATIVES

The Data

With the exception of the stories from the teenagers, all narratives were collected in Yuendumu, an indigenous community located in the center of Australia in desert terrain, 300 km northwest of Alice Springs. The teenagers told their stories sitting outside in a large park in Melbourne when on a school trip from their community. With few exceptions, the children and adults were tested sitting outside, where they are more comfortable. The locations included the school grounds, camps in the community, or a school room. All children attending school on the days narratives were collected were invited to participate. In addition, adult helpers identified other children in the community. The data collection took place over several years. Children and their parents often did not know their dates of birth; these were obtained and checked from health records in the clinic.

Warlpiri was the only language used with the children. The experimenter gave the book individually to each child to look through. For the younger children the book was held by the experimenter, who turned the pages. The experimenter pointed to the picture of the deer and asked the children to name it; if children did not provide a label the word *kuyu* 'meat/animal' was given. Then the children were asked to tell a really good story (*jimi ngurrju* 'story good'). The experimenter did not look at the pictures as the children spoke. Adult Warlpiri speakers helped to transcribe and to check the transcriptions. If the children spoke too quietly for an adult Warlpiri speaker to understand, or if a child used only single words for each picture, the data were not included.

Fifty-four Warlpiri stories were analyzed, four from adults and 50 from children aged from 4 to 10 years as well as a group of teenagers (13–15 years of age). In order to identify differences in the development of the plot and the use of evaluative language, the 50 non-adult Warlpiri participants from whom stories were collected were divided into five equal groups of 10. The age range and mean for each group are presented in Table 10.1. The adults were all mothers and some grandmothers, aged in their 40s and 50s.

In order to examine how much of the story content was included across age groups, 24 items were identified (see Table 10.2) and the number of these items included was calculated for each speaker. Also counted was the number of major plot components included in each story. Evaluative elements and inferences were also identified.

TABLE 10.1 Age, Story Items, Plot Components, and Search Statements by Group (10 per group)

Group	Age (mean)	Number of Events Included (mean)	Number of Children Incorporating 3 Plot Components	Number of Search Statements (mean)
1	4;10–5;11 (5.7)	9–16 (11)	2	0–3 (1)
2	6;0–7;10 (7.1)	7–20 (13.4)	2	0–3 (1.4)
3	8;0–8;8 (8.2)	7–20 (12.6)	5	0–5 (1.3)
4	8;9–10;7 (9.7)	8–21 (15.6)	5	0–11 (4)
5	13–16 (14)	14–24 (16.8)	9	3–9 (4.6)

TABLE 10.2 Main Events/Items Coded

1.	Introduction	13.	There is an owl
2.	Boy/dog sleeping/lying down	14.	The boy falls
3.	The frog leaves	15.	He climbs a hill/rock
4.	Boy/dog discover fog has left	16.	He holds onto a tree/deer
5.	They search inside	17.	The deer carried him
6.	The dog gets stuck	18.	& threw him to the water
7.	The dog falls/jumps	19.	The dog chases the deer
8.	The boy calls	20.	The dog and boy fall
9.	They see a hole/rabbit	21.	The boy warns dog to be quiet
10.	The bees chase the dog	22.	They climb log/are safe on tree
11.	Bee hive/sugarbag fell	23.	They see some frogs
12.	The boy climbs a tree	24.	The boy takes a frog

The Story Events

The first analysis determined which of the 24 story items identified were included in the stories. As shown in Table 10.1, there was diversity within each age group in how many of the 24 items were mentioned. While the children looked thoughtfully at all the pictures, not all of them spoke about the contents of each. In addition, the same number of items may have been included by different children but the amount of detail varied, both within and across age groups. For example, some children gave elaborate information on the boy falling and the boy and dog in the water, but not on the boy finding the frog, while others gave minimal information on the fall and more on the owl event. Some of the 24 elements identified were clearly more important than others as they were included by most of the children in a group. For the youngest, the 5-year-olds, no single item was included by all 10 children, but 80% included an introduction to the characters. As a group, the young children focused on *who* rather than *what* happened. For the 6- to 7-year-olds also, no single item was mentioned by all children, but nine included the boy/dog seeing the frogs at the end of the story, eight introduced the characters at the beginning of the story, and eight included the incident with the owl. All ten of the 8-year-olds included the introduction, and nine included the frogs at the end; the incident of the deer throwing the boy into the water was included by eight. These same three components were mentioned by all children in the 9-year-old group; in addition, the frog leaving was included by nine; discovering its absence, the bees chasing the dog, the boy climbing a tree, and the owl event were items included by eight. All the teenagers (group 5) included the following five items: the introduction, the discovery of the frog's disappearance, the owl event, climbing the log when in the water, and seeing the frogs at the end. Three other components were each included by nine children in the group: the frog's leaving, the initial search, and the dog falling from the window; another three items were included by eight: the boy's climbing a hill, being thrown to the water, and taking a frog at the end. In comparison, 14 of the story events listed in Table 10.2 were included by all four adults.

To summarize, from a skeleton story for the youngest group there was development to a more comprehensive story from the teenagers and adults. The older participants had more scope for integrating evaluative elements. The youngest children often just identified the characters as an introduction to the story; this was perhaps influenced by hearing adults talk about traditional paintings, which illustrate dreaming stories and the kin groups associated with the land depicted (Sutton, 1988). The kin system underlies the social and economic organization of the community and people's behavior to others depends on their kin (skin) group.

PLOT COMPONENTS

The narratives were coded for the three plot components. (See Table 10.1 for the summary.) To be counted as having included the initiating event, the story teller mentioned that the frog had left and the boy (or dog) could not see it; or that the boy (or dog) was no longer able to see it, the inference being that they could previously. For example, in (1) the narrator included the frog's leaving and the boy's discovery of this. It is a detailed account produced by the youngest teenager. Note the *rla* in both *nya-ngu-lu-rla* and *lawa-lu-rla* in the last two lines of this example is a dative bound pronominal, a cross-reference marker indicating they were looking for something:

(1) Wirriya manu jarntu-pala nyina-ja jarlji-kirli
　　boy and dog–DUSUBJ sit-Past frog-having
　　'A boy and a dog sat with a frog'
　　manu jarlji-ngki-lpa-jana nya-ngu
　　and frog-ERG-PASTIMPF-3PL:OBJ see-Past
　　'and the frog looked at them.'
　　Ngula nguna-ja-lku wirriya-ju
　　that one lie-PAST-now boy-FOC
　　'The boy lay down now'
　　manu jalji-ji wilypi:pardi-ja
　　and frog-FOC arise-PAST
　　'and the frog emerged.'
　　Yakarra:pardi-ja-lku wirriya-ju
　　arise-PAST-now boy-FOC
　　'The boy got up.'
　　Nya-ngu-lu-rla mulukunpu-rla
　　see-PAST- 3PL:SUBJ-DAT jar-DAT
　　'They looked for it in the jar.'
　　Lawa-lu-rla nya-ngu
　　no-3PLSUBJ-DAT see-PAST
　　'They didn't see it.'

In contrast, example (2) is from the narrative of a 5-year-old and example (3) from a 6-year-old. There is no overt mention of the frog leaving in (2), but the expression *lawa-lku* 'nothing now' implies something was there before. In (3) also the connection between the frog's leaving and the boy's discovery of this fact is indicated by the dative cross-reference marker *rla* on the imperfective *ka*. Without *rla*, the boy would be looking, not looking for something.

(2) Nya-nyi ka-pala prak-praku
　　look-PAST-IMPFV-DUSUBJ frog
　　'They (two) are looking at a frog.'
　　Wirriya ka-pala nguna-mi
　　boy IMPFV-DUSUBJ lie-NONPAST
　　'The boy is lying down.'
　　Lawa-lku
　　NEG-now
　　'Nothing now.'
(3) Praku-praku ka wiily:pardi-mi
　　frog IMPFV emerge-NONPAST
　　'The frog is getting up'
　　manu ya-ni ka
　　and go-NONPAST IMPFV

'and it's going.'
Yakarra:pardi-ja-lu, nya-nyi-lki ka-rla
arise-PAST-3PL:SUBJ, see-NONPAST-now IMPFV-DAT
'They got up, he's looking for it now.'

As can be observed in Table 10.1, only 2 of the 10 children in the youngest age group incorporated all three components of the plot adequately as defined by the criteria above. Three children of the 5-year-old group established the initiating event as did five of the 7-year-old group, six of the 8-year-old group and nine of the 9-year-old group. All of the teenagers did.

Two other components were necessary in the criteria established for the global level of story organization. A strict interpretation of *search* was taken in coding the narratives. To be counted as having included the second plot component, the narrator needed to have indicated that the boy/dog looked or called for the frog, but they were also required to indicate a sustained search. That is, at least a second example of looking or calling for the frog was required. If the narrator said, for example, that the boy picked up the boot or that he looked, this was not counted as meeting the criteria for a search. Nor was it enough to say the frog was not there or just that the dog entered the jar, or that the boy looked in a hole or climbed a tree. Table 10.1 shows the range in the number of search elements included by age group. In the youngest group three of the children, after the initial search event, inferred that the boy was looking for the frog but in the two youngest groups, only four children in each indicated a sustained search. Six of the 8-year-olds and seven of the 9-year-olds incorporated a sustained search. In the teenager group all but one narrator presented a sustained search. An example from a girl of 8;11 in group 4 is presented in (4). The example shows that the narrator is clear why the child and dog are seen in the picture picking up clothes and the frog's bowl.

(4) Jarlji-ka juurl:pinyi yatijarra ngurra-ngulu
 frog-IMPFV jump north home-ELAT
 'The frog is jumping north out of its home.'
 Nya-ngu-pala wirriya-jarra-ngku lawa jarli-ki
 see-PAST-DUSUBJ boy-DU-ERG NEG frog-DAT
 'The two boys couldn't see the frog.'
 manu maliki-rli nya-ngu-rla warru jarlji-ki
 and dog-ERG see-PAST-DAT around frog-DAT
 ngurra-kari ngurra-kari
 home-another home-another
 'And the dog looked around for the frog in other places.'
 wirriya-ngku-rla warru-rnu jarlji-ki .
 boy-ERG-DAT look-PAST frog-DAT
 'The boy looked for the frog.'
 Wangka-ja wirriya "Nyarrpara mayi"?
 Speak-PAST boy where-Q
 'The boy said, "Where is it?"'

Following the sequence in (4) the boy called out for the frog on three separate occasions through the ensuing events. The child incorporated direct speech as the child called the frog to come, and used the statement that the boy looked for the frog down in a hole and also *jarlji lawa juku* (frog NEG just, 'Still no frog'). Clearly the narrator connected the events into a search for the missing frog.

The third plot component, the resolution, was the finding of the frog. Seeing a frog and taking one was considered appropriate when coding the stories. Finding the frog was also acceptable. Several narrators only mentioned that the boy saw a frog (or frogs). This was not coded as a resolution because there was no indication that the boy had found his lost frog or that he had obtained another; it was necessary to say he picked one up and took it home, or that he carried one back. Of the 5-year-olds five children met the criteria, and eight of the 7-year-olds, six of the 8-year-olds, seven of the

9-year-olds, and eight of the teenagers. Overall, more children were successful in encoding this plot component than either the first or second. An example from a teenager is presented in (5).

(5) Nyan-ngu-palangu ngati-nyanyi manu jaji-nyanu
see-PAST-DUOBJ mother-POSS and father-POSS
manu kurdu-kurdu, wilki-pala manu jinta-kari-ji
and child-child seven and one-other-FOC
'They looked at them, the mother and father and children, 7 and one other.'
pina ka-ngu wardininyi-lki ngapa-wana
back IMPFV-PAST happy-now water-along
'They carried it back happy along the water.'

The teenagers were more likely to maintain the search theme than the younger children, with repeated examples of calling or looking for the frog and not finding it. For three teenagers, in particular, the most frequent ways in which this lack of success was conveyed was with the negative *lawa*, used alone, or in combination, *lawa juku* 'not yet'; less frequently it appeared with a verb form, *lawa-pala nyanu-rla* (NEG-DUSUBJ see-PAST-DAT 'They didn't see it'), or with *wangu* 'not having,' or the negative auxiliary *kula*. All four adults maintained the search theme, focusing on the child's attempt to find the frog and his encounters along the way. One adult story included 20 examples of the boy or dog looking for the frog or calling for it, another had 12 examples, another had 9 examples, and the fourth had 3 examples.

EVALUATIVE ELEMENTS

Not all categories used previously in analyzing evaluative functions were relevant in coding the Warlpiri data. The number of children in each group who used specific evaluative forms of language at least once is shown in Table 10.3.

All the participants with the exception of one child in the 7-year-old group and one in the 9-year-old group used at least one evaluative element at least once; the older children tended to use devices with greater frequency than the younger children. However, even in the two youngest age groups one child in each was quite prolific. One 5-year-old used four strategies: attributing mental states, hedges, negative qualifiers, and evaluative comments. One 6-year-old girl used five different evaluation devices at least once: attributing mental states, hedges, intensifiers, evaluative comments, future and inferences about kin and destination. Three children in the 8-year-old group used four elements at least once. One child in the 9-year-old group used six elements at least once, two used five at least once, and two used four elements at least once. In the teenage group one participant used six types at least once and three used five.

TABLE 10.3 Number of Children Using Types of Evaluative Elements

Evaluative Device	Mean Age of Group				
	5;7	7;1	8;2	9;7	14
Frames of mind: mental states	5	6	7	5	6
Hedges	2	3	2	5	6
Negative qualifiers	4	6	5	7	9
Character speech	1	1	4	5	4
Value	2	4	2	6	4
Future/irrealis	3	1	3	0	0
Inference: kin and/or destination	1	3	3	4	9

The fact that the older speakers included multiple examples of a type reflects evaluation at the global level. For example, the adults predominantly used direct speech, taking on the role of the main character. Most examples of character speech were questions about the location of the frog with some responses from the secondary characters. The second highest number of tokens was for the negative qualifiers, all related to the failure to locate the frog. Both of these high-use elements focus on the overall plot of the narrative. The irrealis marker and future marker were not used by the teenagers and adults, who focused on what happened, using the past tense. In the younger groups, however, several children predicted what would happen, for example, that the dog would fall, based on remembering the sequence of events from previewing the pictures.

Attributing mental states to the characters was used more than any other category by children in the youngest age group and was also the most frequently used element in terms of number of tokens, with hedges a close second. Fear was the mental state most frequently included. Most examples were about the boy's fear in relation to the owl, or vice versa; to most children the owl was scary. Others expressed fear in relation to the bees and dog. Some children used the inchoative form *lani-jarrimi* 'become afraid,' assuming the boy or dog became frightened of the owl (or bees); others used the causative verb (*lani-manu*) and an ergative form of the agent (for example, *kuurrkuupa-rlu* 'owl-ERG'). That is, there was variability in whether a child attributed cause or not to the owl/bees.

The 7-year-olds (group 2) incorporated negative qualifiers and mental states more than any other types of evaluative element. However, negative state elements did not focus on the search element much. The most frequently used, in tokens, was attributing a mental state to the characters. While one child said that the owl was frightened and another that the boy and dog were happy at the end of the story, other children in this group appeared concerned about the boy or dog being frightened by the owl or bees. Several children inferred where the boy and dog might be going, as in example (7). Negative state elements were used but did not focus on the search element as much as for the adults.

(7) wanti-ja-lku-pala jungu-juku ngapa-kurra
 fall-PAST-now-DUSUBJ true-just water-ALL
 kaninja-rra warnayarra-kurlangu-kurra.
 Down-DIR water snake-POSS-ALL
 'They fell down to the home of the water snake.'

For the 8-year-olds attributing a mental state to characters was the most frequently used evaluative element. Seven children in the group included at least one example. One child indicated that the dog became angry; another child said that the child became angry. However, fear was the predominant emotion expressed. More 9-year-olds used negative qualifiers than any other evaluative element although, in terms of number of examples, hedges and mental states were the most frequently used, with intensifiers (*jarlu* 'really') and other value terms the next most frequently used. In the hedges category five children expressed the view at least once that a character tried to do something (*puta* 'try'). In the mental states category fear was the most likely to be used, although one child stated that the boy got mad (*warrangu-jarrija*) when the dog fell from the window and broke the jar. Another child in group 4 used the Warlpiri equivalent of 'The boy kept a smile on his face' and another attributed a mental state to the frog.

Nine of the teenagers used negative qualifiers, and tokens in this category were clearly the most frequent. The teenagers seemed to focus on the search and not being able to find the frog. In addition, nine of the narrators made inferences about the kin relations among the frogs or destination of the boy and frog. Four teenagers used character speech, some with multiple examples. The use of character speech shows events are interpreted from the characters' perspective. In contrast to the teenagers and adults, only one child in the youngest group incorporated character speech; she used a very high-pitched voice as she imitated the boy calling to the frog in a hole.

While the number of children referring to mental states was fairly stable across the age span, the use of hedges increased, as did inferences. Many inferences referred to the boy going back home with the frog. This cyclic nature of journeys is evident in adults' stories and reflects the worldview of the Warlpiri people (Hale, 1986).

CONCLUSIONS

Children need knowledge of their language structures to encode events into a story, but to make a good story they also need to combine the elements into a cohesive whole; adding evaluation helps in this respect. Those children who hear stories frequently will be more familiar with the general style of story telling for the culture and more familiar with how a narrator may embellish a narrative to make it more interesting.

The youngest children in the current study clearly had knowledge of the basic structures of their language. In addition, all but one included some evaluation, one using four different means for elaborating the information perceived in the pictures. Similarly in the 6- to seven-year-old age groups all but one child used evaluative devices with some children using multiple examples of each. However, it was only with the 9-year-olds and teenagers that the overall structure of the story, the plot and details of the main events were clearly represented and evaluated by the majority of children in the group.

Similarities were found to other studies based on the frog story. However, one particularly interesting aspect about the Warlpiri stories was the inferencing based on cultural knowledge. A number of children spoke about the frog leaving to go to the water, or they reported that boy and dog fell to the frog's home, or the home of the water snake or crocodile. As Slobin (2004) states, several different sorts of factors "conspire" to produce a range of frog-story varieties. Language and cultural practices are influencing factors; age is another, but familiarity with the genre is also important. The two children in the 5- and 6-year-old groups who were prolific in the use of evaluative elements are from families in which the adults are good narrators and who support keeping Warlpiri strong as a language in times of cultural change.

REFERENCES

Aksu Koç, A., & Tekdemir, G. (2004). Interplay between narrativity and mind reading: A comparison between Turkish and English. In S. Strömqvist & L. Verhoeven (Eds.), *Relating events in narrative: Typological and contextual perspectives* (pp. 307–327). Mahwah, NJ: Lawrence Erlbaum Associates.

Bamberg, M. (1987). *The acquisition of narratives: learning to use language*. Berlin: Mouton de Gruyter.

Bamberg, M., & Damrad-Frye, R. (1991). On the ability to provide evaluative comments: Further explorations of children's narrative competencies. *Journal of Child Language, 18*, 689–710.

Bamberg, M., & Reilly, J. (1996). Emotion, narrative, and affect: How children discover the relationship between what to say and how to say it. *Journal of Narrative and Life History, 7*, 330–341.

Bauman, R. (1969). *Verbal art as performance*. Rowley, MA: Newbury House Publishers.

Bavin, E. L. (1990). Locative terms and Warlpiri acquisition. *Journal of Child Language, 17*, 43–66.

Bavin E.L. (1991). The acquisition of Warlpiri kin terms. *Pragmatics, 1*, 319–344.

Bavin, E. L. (1992). The acquisition of Warlpiri. In D. I. Slobin (Ed.). *The crosslinguistic study of language acquisition* (Vol. 3, pp. 309–372). Hillsdale, NJ: Lawrence Erlbaum Associates.

Bavin, E. L. (1995). Inflections and lexical organisation: Some evidence from Warlpiri. In H. Pishwa & K. Marold (Eds.) *The development of morphological systematicity* (pp. 39–53). Tübingen: Gunter Narr Verlag.

Bavin, E. L. (1998). Factors of typology in language acquisition: Some examples from Warlpiri. In A. Siewierska & J. Song (Eds.), *Case, typology and grammar* (pp. 37–55). Amsterdam/Philadelphia: John Benjamins.

Bavin, E. L. (2000). Ellipsis in Warlpiri children's narratives: An analysis of Warlpiri frog stories. *Linguistics, 38*, 569–589.

Bavin. E. L. (2004). Focussing on "where." An analysis of Warlpiri frog stories. In S. Strömqvist & L. Verhoeven (Eds.) *Relating events in narrative: Typological and contextual perspectives* (pp. 17–35). Mahwah, NJ: Lawrence Erlbaum Associates.

Berman, R. (1996). Narrative theory and narrative development: The Labov impact. *Journal of Narrative and Life History, 7,* 235–244.

Berman, R., & Slobin, D. I. (1994). *Relating events in narrative* (Vol. 1). Hillsdale, N.J.: Lawrence Erlbaum Associates.

Hale, K. (1982). Some essential features of Warlpiri verbal clauses. In S. Swartz (Ed.) *Papers in Warlpiri grammar: in memory of Lothar Jagst* (pp. 217–315). (Work Papers of SIL-AAB:Series A, 6) Darwin: SIL.

Hale, K. (1983). Warlpiri and the grammar of non-configurational languages. *Natural Language and Linguistic Theory, 1,* 5–47.

Hale, K. (1986) Notes on world view and semantic categories. In P. Muysken & H. van Riemsdijk (Eds.). *Features and projections* (pp. 233–254). Studies in generative grammar, 25, Dordrecht, The Netherlands: Foris.

Küntay, A., & Nakamura, K. (2004). Linguistic strategies serving evaluative functions. In S. Strömqvist & L. Verhoeven (Eds.), *Relating events in narrative: Typological and contextual perspectives* (pp. 329–358). Mahwah, NJ: Lawrence Erlbaum Associates.

Labov, W., & Waletzky, J. (1967). Narrative analysis: Oral versions of personal experience. In J. Helm (Ed.) *Essays on the verbal and visual arts* (pp. 12–44). Seattle: University of Washington Press. [Reprinted in *Journal of Narrative and Life History,* 3–38.]

Mayer, M. (1969). *Frog, where are you?* New York: Dial.

Minami, M., & McCabe, A. (1995). Rice balls and bear hunts: Japanese and North American family narrative patterns. *Journal of Child Language, 22,* 423–445.

Nash, D. (1986). *Topics in Warlpiri grammar.* New York: Garland Publishing.

Reilly, J. (1992). How to tell a good story: The intersection of language and affect in children's narratives. *Journal of Narrative and Life History, 2,* 355–377.

Simpson, J. (1991). *Warlpiri morphosyntax: A lexicalist approach.* Studies in Natural Language and Linguistic Theory. Dordrecht, The Netherlands: Kluwer.

Slobin, D. I. (2004). The many ways to search for a frog. In S. Strömqvist & L. Verhoeven (Eds.), *Relating events in narrative: Typological and contextual perspectives* (pp. 219–257). Mahwah, NJ: Lawrence Erlbaum Associates.

Strömqvist, S., & Verhoeven, L. (2004). *Relating events in narrative: Typological and contextual perspectives.* Mahwah, NJ: Lawrence Erlbaum Associates.

Sutton, P. (Ed.) (1988). *Dreamings: The art of Aboriginal Australia.* New York: Asia Society Galleries & George Braziller Publishers.

11

Clause Packaging in Narratives: *A Crosslinguistic Developmental Study*

RUTH A. BERMAN and BRACHA NIR-SAGIV

Tel Aviv University

My main difficulty in following the editors' guidelines was how to write a "short" paragraph about Dan's impact on my life and work.[1] Here goes my feeble attempt to apply one of the countless lessons I learned from Dan: When thinking for speaking (or writing), be "clear, processible, quick and easy, and expressive" (Slobin, 1977, p. 186). Since Dan urged me to look into acquisition of Hebrew when we first met at a coffee-shop in Berkeley in the 1970s, we have shared many good meals and much talk in Berkeley, Nijmegen, and Beth-Herut, along with workshops in crosslinguistic acquisition (1980), temporality (1981, 1986), and narrative development (1995). Both within and beyond these contexts, although I am the older, Dan was and is the wiser. I am indebted to him for having inspired my thinking and guided my research on form–function relations in language acquisition, development, and use. In the language shared by our parents' generation, my *broxe* 'blessing' to him in this well-deserved tribute from our community is *zol er zayn gezunt un shtark nokh lange yorn!*[2]

INTRODUCTION

This chapter follows from Berman and Slobin (1994) and is inspired by Slobin's ideas in the years before, during, and since the first "Frog Story" volume appeared. In *crosslinguistic perspective*, we aim to shed light on Slobin's question of "whether typological contrasts in rhetorical style found in frog stories are restricted to this limited genre of picture-elicited narratives intended for children" (2004a, p. 117). Slobin has addressed this issue in both depth and breadth, moving from children's oral narratives to the rhetorical style of novels, newspaper reports, and conversations (1996, 2000) and the "discourse effects of linguistic typology" in novels in different languages and in multilingual translations (2003a, 2004b). The present study is motivated by similar goals, but is restricted to three of the five languages in the original frog-book study—English, Hebrew, and Spanish—a slice of the many languages that Slobin has mastered and investigated.

In *developmental* terms, the chapter departs from Berman and Slobin's use of 9-year-olds as the oldest school-age participants. By taking middle childhood as the starting-point for our study, we focus on "later language development" (Berman, 2007), when the impact of "typological bootstrapping"

---

[1] This first paragraph is the first author's personal homage to Dan.
[2] 'He should be healthy and strong for many more years to come!'

(Slobin, 2001, p. 441) is already well in place. We found that children as young as 9 years of age may use all the forms we identified as playing a role in text-embedded syntax, the topic of this chapter. However, only the texts produced by high-school adolescents fully reflect the rhetorical options favored by literate adults in their speech community. This underscores another of Slobin's important insights: Linguistic forms may emerge in early childhood, but full realization of their rhetorical functions has a long developmental history.

In *genre*, this chapter deals with personal-experience narratives, rather than the fictive children's adventure story of the Frog Story. Its theme is not a search, but interpersonal conflict, recounting an incident in which the narrator had been involved in "problems between people." The texts examined here are written rather than oral, so that our concern is with "thinking for writing" (Slobin, 2003b).

In *topic*, our study departs from Slobin's research on contrastive rhetoric in narrative, which has focused on motion events (2003b) or "how people move" (2003a). Rather, we extend earlier analyses of "syntactic packaging" (Berman & Slobin, 1994) or "connectivity" (Berman, 1998) so as to examine inter-clausal *syntactic architecture*. This derives directly from the idea of *packaging* as "a kind of visual metaphor for the various ways in which situations can be analyzed into components and encoded in multi-clausal constructions" (Berman & Slobin, 1994, p. 538). Unlike purely structuralist analyses, this means that narrative clause-linkage is viewed as having *rhetorical effects* such as subordinating event components to a high point, conflating different phases of an event into a single event complex, and providing speaker-writers with control over the rhythm and tempo of the narratives that they construct.

CLAUSE PACKAGING

Our analysis of "contrastive rhetoric" focuses on the expressive options that narrators select for "relating events in narrative" by packaging them together in the texts they construct. To this end, we adopt the notion of "Clause Package" (CP) as an independently motivated device for analyzing units of text beyond the level of the single clause in both narrative and non-narrative discourse, spoken and written.[3] A CP is a text-embedded unit of two or more clauses connected by abstract linkage relations that are typically but not necessarily identified by syntactic criteria. Thus, within each CP, relations of clause-linkage are often explicitly marked by coordinating or subordinating conjunctions, but they may sometimes be inferred from the thematic progression of a text. As such, clause packaging departs from most linguistic analyses of "nexus" (Foley & Van Valin, 1984), "clause-combining" (Haiman & Thompson, 1988), or "clause complexes" (Matthiessen, 2002). Clause Packages also differ from traditional, pedagogically motivated notions such as a "T(erminable) Unit" (Hunt, 1965; Verhoeven & van Hell, in press), since they take account of how such units function in the text as a whole.[4] For example, we distinguish cases where lexical connectives like *and, so, but* function as grammatical markers of connectivity or as pragmatically motivated "utterance-introducers" (Berman, 1996) or as "segment-tagging" discourse markers (Ravid & Berman, 2006). Moreover, to delimit CP boundaries, we also take account of discourse-topic shift or maintenance—whether the speaker-writer is referring to a different aspect of the same topic or to a distinct topic.

Application of these criteria is illustrated in (1), from the narrative written by a Californian graduate school student.

---

[3] The idea of a "clause package" emerged in the framework of a crosslinguistic study in which the first author was principal investigator (PI) (Berman & Verhoeven, 2002; Katzenberger, 2004) and has been refined in studies by the second author (Nir-Sagiv, 2004; 2008).

[4] Although ostensibly conducted in the same framework as the present study, hence adopting the term "clause packaging," the analysis of Verhoeven and van Hell in fact considers only T-units.

(1) Excerpt from English Adult Narrative[5]
   CP1:
   1   *I experienced a brief conflict with a friend*
   2   *while in graduate school.*
   CP2:
   3   *My friend and I discussed an incident*
   4   *in which a fellow student was asked*
   5   *to leave the program*
   6   *because he had inappropriately obtained information for the upcoming qualification examination.*
   CP3:
   7   *My friend's perspective was*
   8   *that the individual was being treated too harshly.*
   9   *It was his view*
   10 *that a more thorough investigation plus a more lenient judgment may have been better.*

Clause Packages as so defined and illustrated provide the framework for our analysis of narratives produced by native speakers of three different languages.

DATA SOURCES AND ANALYSIS

Our data-base is taken from a large-scale crosslinguistic project on developing text construction abilities, in which schoolchildren, adolescents, and adults were asked to tell and write a story about an incident where they had been involved in interpersonal conflict and to give a talk and write an essay discussing the topic of "problems between people" (for details, see Berman & Verhoeven, 2002; Berman, 2005).[6] Below we consider 240 texts written in Californian English, Iberian Spanish, and Israeli Hebrew, 20 at each of four age groups: 9- to 10-year-old 4th graders (henceforth **G** for grade school), 12- to 13-year-old 7th graders (**Junior**-high), 16- to 17-year-old 11th-graders (**High**-school), and graduate school university students (**Adults**).

We defined five types of clause-linkage as representing different *functional configurations* of clause combining in discourse. The classification reflects our view of clause-linkage development as progressing from "flat" stringing of clauses via layering to nesting, rather than as a straightforward shift from linear to hierarchical.[7] And it involves a notion of "syntactic architecture" beyond syntax in the traditional sense, with content and structure treated together as indivisible facets of clause combining. By "architecture" we understand "formation or construction, whether the result of conscious act … or of a random disposition of the parts" (*Webster's Third New International Dictionary*), a definition that conjures up notions of building, of scaffolding, of design, and of esthetic (here, rhetorical) principles. The classification in (2) uses the familiar notions of *parataxis* and *hypotaxis* along with the less conventional terms, *isotaxis* and *endotaxis*, as (re-)defined for present purposes. And in deference to Slobin, we use spatial metaphors to lend transparency to these labels.

---

[5] Sample texts are divided into clauses, and standardized for spelling and punctuation.

[6] Collection of the English-language sample was supervised by Judy S. Reilly of San Diego State University, and in Spanish by Liliana Tolchinsky, University of Barcelona, with help from Melina Aparici. All participants in the study were monolingual native speakers.

[7] These categories disregard clause-internal structure and content. A text might manifest complex clause packaging and yet be "flat" in phrase structure.

(2) Five Types of Syntactic Architecture
   I   **Isotaxis** = 'equal organization': **isolating** (autonomous clauses)
   II   **Symmetric Parataxis** = 'side by side organization': **stringing** of clauses
   III **Asymmetric Parataxis** = 'partial equivalence': **dependent stringing**
   IV   **Hypotaxis** = 'one under the other': **layering** of clauses
   V   **Endotaxis** = 'one inside the other': **nesting** of clauses

Each CP was analyzed as a construction with a Main Clause (MC) as its "head," thus:

- **Level I: Isotaxis [ISO]**—(a) a Single clause with no internal architecture—a *bare CP*, and (b) the head Main Clause (MC) of any CP, isotactic with respect to the MCs of its neighboring CPs.
- **Level II: Symmetric Parataxis [PAR]**—Juxtaposed or Coordinated clauses with overt subject-marking, related by *symmetric stringing* either to the MC or to one or more other juxtaposed or coordinated clauses.[8]
- **Level III: Asymmetric Parataxis [AsPAR]**—clauses linked by *dependent stringing* (a) Coordinated clauses with same-subject ellipsis or verb-gapping, and (b) Complement clauses attached obligatorily to the MC.[9]
- **Level IV: Hypotaxis [HYPO]**—Relative and Adverbial clauses related to the MC by asymmetric *layering*.
- **Level V: Endotaxis [ENDO]**—Adverbial and Relative Clauses *nested* inside another clause.[10]

These types of clause-linkage are illustrated in (3) by the opening segments of high-school narratives in three languages.[11]

(3) Opening Segments of Three High-School Narratives:
   Hebrew [hH17]
   CP1: *Be-ofen klali ani loh mitxakexet be-ofen ishi imm yeladim le-itim krovot.* **[ISO]**
   'Generally speaking I don't often personally rub up against other kids.'
   CP2: *Ha-mikre <še-ani maclixa laxshov alav axshav>* **[ENDO]** *hu mikre* **[ISO=MC]** *še-bo ben kita sheli paga bi.* **[HYPO]** *Hu tipus koxani meod* **[PAR=MCJ]**[12] *ve-noheg lehitapel el yeladim.* **[AsPAR]**
   'The incident <I manage to think about now> is one where a kid in my class hurt my feelings. He's a very power-hungry type and tends to pick on kids.'
   English [eH02]
   CP1: *When I was in the seventh grade,* **[HYPO]** *I had a conflict with a boy* **[ISO=MC]** *who was in a few of my classes.* **[HYPO]**
   CP2: *As it turned out,* **[HYPO]** *his father was an executive vice-president at the company* **[ISO=MC]** *where my father worked.* **[HYPO]**
   CP3: *The boy was constantly giving me grief* **[ISO=MC]** *saying* **[AsPAR, NF]** *that <if I ever did anything>* **[ENDO]** *<to upset him>* **[HYPO]**> *he would have my father fired.* **[AsPAR]**

---

[8] We treat person-marking inflections as arguments, hence assigned to Level II symmetric parataxis. Inflectional marking of subject is across-the-board in Spanish, less so in Hebrew, as shown by children's symmetric parataxis by inflection in Spanish in (9) and by 3rd person pronoun in Hebrew in (7).
[9] This corresponds to Foley and Van Valin's (1984) 'co-subordination.'
[10] Each CP in the sample was specified, coded, and scored by two trained linguists, native speakers of the target languages, working separately to ensure reliability.
[11] Angled brackets mark center-embedded clauses; labels in square brackets indicate subject ID.
[12] MCJ stands for a main clause related by juxtaposition without overt markers to the head MC.

Spanish [sH11]
CP1: *Uno de los casos más importantes <que he vivido>* **[ENDO]** *<relacionado con el mundo del colegio, los estudiantes y todo su ambiente>,* **[ENDO]** *fue el caso de un alumno* **[ISO=MC]** *que era compañero mío* **[HYPO]** *e incluso éramos amigos.* **[PAR]**

'One of the most important incidents <that I have lived> <relating to the world of school, students, and its whole atmosphere> was the case of a student who was a classmate of mine and (we) were even friends.'

The syntactic architecture of the three excerpts in (3) is represented graphically in Figure 11.1.

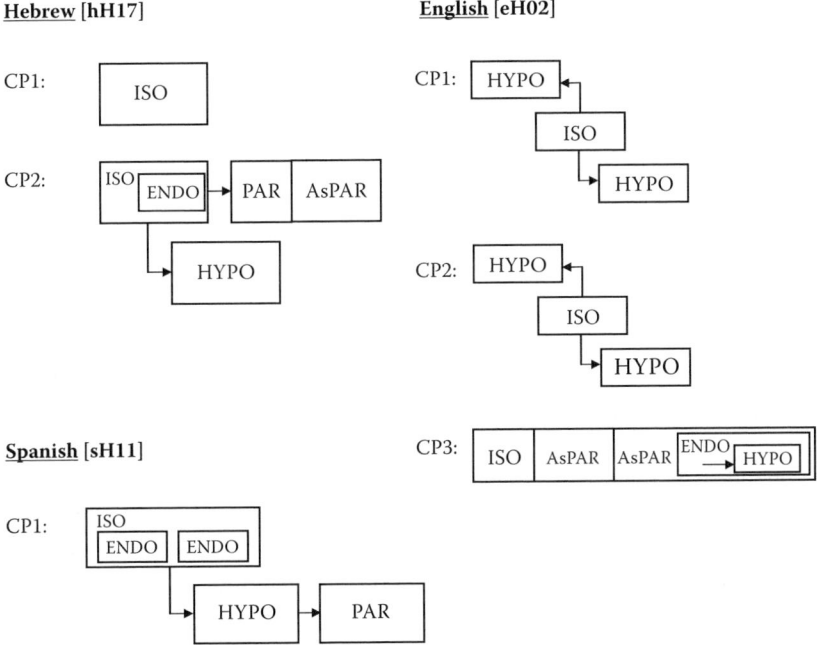

Figure 11.1 Syntactic architecture of high-school narrative openings in three languages.

Figure 11.1 shows that adolescent narratives vary in their syntactic architecture, from the initial isolating clause in the Hebrew text, via the largely hypotatic relationships in English, and Spanish preference for endotaxis. This variation proved indicative of both age-dependent development and general language-related differences.

CROSSLINGUISTIC AND DEVELOPMENTAL TRENDS

Our analyses refine and extend Berman and Slobin's (1994) findings for syntactic packaging in the oral narratives of children, the oldest of whom were at the age of the youngest here. First, as shown in Figure 11.2, *CP density,* measured by mean number of clauses per package, increases with age in all three languages.

The breakdown in Figure 11.2 reaffirms that with age, narrators package information more densely into a single unit of discourse processing. They combine clauses in more tightly cohesive constructions, showing that they can pre-plan longer stretches of output within narrower pieces of discourse (Hickmann, 2003). Across age-groups and languages, clause-linkage (in written personal-experience narratives) ranges from around two and a half to five clauses per CP, with the three languages differing significantly in this respect: Spanish shows greatest CP density (M=4.21), followed by English (M=3.16), and Hebrew (M=2.74).

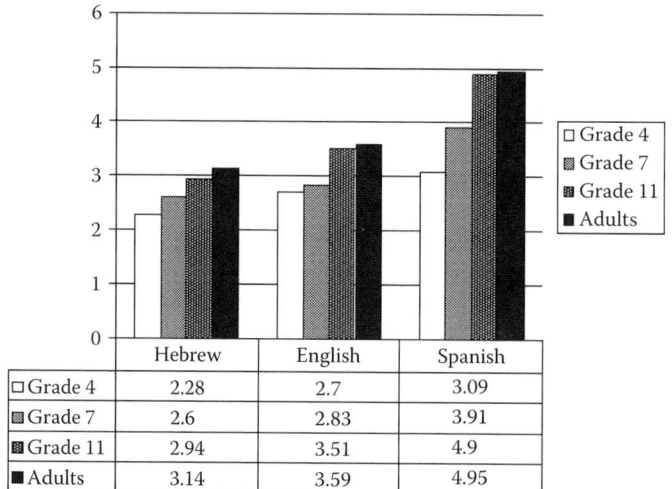

Figure 11.2 Mean number of clauses per Clause Package, by age and language [N = 20 per age-group in each language].

Crosslinguistic Comparisons

Analyses of the internal constituency of clauses packages in each language are consistent with these crosslinguistic differences in CP density. For example, typological differences between the three languages in same-subject ellipsis underlie contrasting use of coordinate and complement structures. Thus, while there was no significant difference in the extent to which the three languages relied on paratactic stringing (both symmetric and asymmetric), the languages differ in the *type* of stringing they prefer: Hebrew favors same-subject coordination, the bulk (85%) with ellipsis of the shared subject; English, as a subject-requiring language, deploys more pronominal type coordination; while Spanish favors different-subject coordination as an alternative to grammaticized same-subject inflectional marking. Spanish reliance on coordination with *different* subject nominals reflects a sophisticated "topic shifting" rather than a strictly sequential same-subject type of parataxis favored by Hebrew. These contrasting patterns underscore the idea that apparently similar surface forms in fact perform different functions in different languages.

CP-internal syntactic architecture reveals other language-specific *favored rhetorical options*, as follows: Spanish speaker-writers across the board use endotaxis or nesting (typically center-embedded relative and adverbial clauses) significantly more than the other two languages (Spanish, M=6.5; Hebrew, M=4.8; English, M=4.5).[13] In contrast, Hebrew speaker-writers favor isotaxis (Hebrew, M=12.58; English, M=3.86; Spanish, M=1.65), aligning syntactically autonomous clauses in a style that echoes classical Biblical Hebrew and Arabic (Johnstone, 1987; Ostler, 1987; Waltke & O'Connor, 1990). English lies between the two, relying far more on dependent stringing by complementation (English, M=14.5; Spanish, M=10.8; Hebrew, M=8.3) and on layering by nonfinite subordination (English, M=11.56; Spanish, M=9.62; Hebrew, M=4.18).

The favored rhetorical options we detected are illustrated by the sample texts in (4) to (6), narratives written by graduate school adults in their 20s and 30s, tagged for CP boundaries and type of clause packaging.

(4) Hebrew Woman's Narrative [hA16]
CP1: *birconi lixtov al mikre shel xoser hitxashvut be-lakoax.* **[ISO]**
'(It is) in-my-desire to-write about an incident of lack of consideration for a client.'

---

[13] Figures in parentheses give mean proportion of each type of linkage out of total clauses per text.

CP2: *lifney kama shanim avarnu le-dira* **[ISO=MC]** *še-loh haya ba aron bgadim.* **[HYPO]**
'Some years ago, we moved to an apartment that didn't have a wardrobe.'

CP3: *hizmanu aron ecel xevrat rehitim.* **[ISO]**
'We ordered a closet from a firm of furniture-makers.'

CP4: *bizman ha-hamtana menahel ha-shivuk haya nexmad ve-xaviv.* **[ISO]**
'During the period of <u>waiting</u>, the manager of <u>marketing</u> was very nice and friendly.'

CP5: *ax <kše-higia zman ha-harkava* **[ENDO]** *<še-kamuvan hitarex me'ever la-ta'arix <še-huvtax>>***[HYPO in ENDO=STACKED]**>, *ha-hitxamkuyot hayu merubot, davar* **[ISO=MC]** *še-garam li ogmat nefesh beshel ha-siba* **[HYPO]** *še-bgaday hayu mefuzarim ba-xeder be-hamtana la-aron.* **[HYPO]**
'However, when the time came for <u>assemblage</u> of the closet, that naturally extended beyond the due date promised, the <u>evasions</u> were many, which caused me much distress for the reason that my clothes were scattered all-over the-room in <u>anticipation</u> of the closet.'

CP6: *leaxar telefonim rabim ve-keasim merubim <leaxar še-higia markiv cair ve-xasar nisayon >* **[ENDO]** *< še-hirkiv madafim akumim>***[HYPO in ENDO=STACKED]**> *higia ha-markiv ha-menuse* **[ISO=MC]** *ve-hirkiv aron le-tiferet* **[AsPAR=COORD]**
'After numerous telephone-calls and many <u>wraths</u>, after (there) came a young, inexperienced assembler that assembled the shelves crooked, an experienced assembler arrived and assembled the closet superbly.'

CP7: *ota xevra loh tizke liroti shuv be-xanuta beshel ogmat ha-nefesh* **[ISO=MC]** *še hayta li* **[HYPO]**
'The said firm will not be-privileged to see me again in their store due to the distress that I had.'

Nearly half the CPs (3 out of 7) in this short Hebrew narrative consist of single clauses. We suggest that Hebrew might favor isotaxis because it is more "nominally" oriented than English or Spanish. Thus, Hebrew texts abound in verbless present tense constructions (the "nominal sentences" of traditional Hebrew grammars). And, as demonstrated by the underlined terms in the glosses in (4), strings that may constitute two or more predicating clauses in Germanic or Romance languages are often verbless in Hebrew. The language relies heavily on nominalizations of verbs and adjectives rather than on non-finite infinitives, participles, or gerunds (Berman, 1978), as a typical feature of sophisticated Hebrew narrative style (Ravid & Cahana-Amitay, 2005).

Compare this with the English-language text in (5).

(5) Californian Male Graduate Student's Narrative [eA05]
  CP1: I experienced a brief conflict with a friend **[ISO=MC]** while in graduate school. **[HYPO]**
  CP2: My friend and I discussed an incident **[ISO=MC]** in which a fellow student was asked **[HYPO]** to leave the program. **[AsPAR=CMP, NF]**
  CP3: The student had been asked **[ISO=MC]** to leave **[AsPAR=CMP, NF]** because he had inappropriately obtained information for the upcoming qualification examination. **[HYPO]**
  CP4: My friend's perspective was **[ISO=MC]** that the individual was being treated too harshly. **[AsPAR=CMP]** It was his view **[PAR=MCJ]** that a more thorough investigation plus a more lenient judgment may have been better. **[AsPAR=CMP]**
  CP5: It was my argument **[ISO=MC]** that the person had a previous history of questionable behavior **[AsPAR=CMP]** and that the school had an obligation **[AsPAR=CMP]**

CP5: to rigorously enforce its own policies **[AsPAR=CMP, NF]** as well as ensure its own reputation. **[AsPAR=CMP, NF]**
CP6: Over the next week this issue came up time and again with my friend and I. **[ISO]**
CP7: Somehow the issue became personalized **[ISO=MC]** in that we each thought **[HYPO]** that the other was being too judgmental and rigid. **[AsPAR=CMP]**
CP8: By week's end we both realized **[ISO=MC]** that we had misinterpreted **[AsPAR=CMP]** what the other was trying to say. **[HYPO]**
CP9: It was an understandable situation **[ISO=MC]** in which we each thought **[HYPO]** that the other was criticizing our perspectives and values as opposed to our point of view **[AsPAR=CMP]** but by week's end we were able to clarify everything **[PAR]** and end the misunderstanding. **[AsPAR=GAP]**
CP10: In summary, my friend and I misinterpreted <what was in fact an objective commentary> **[ENDO]** as a personalized criticism. **[ISO=MC]**
CP11: By talking everything over **[HYPO, NF]**, we were able to clear everything up **[ISO=MC]** and soothe the hurt feelings. **[AsPAR=GAP]**

Of the 37 clauses in the English narrative in (5), nearly a third are Complement clauses that we analyzed as dependent, asymmetric parataxis, and several are non-finite. Rhetorically, this reliance on complementation for syntactic stringing of clauses differs markedly from stereotyped chaining of complement clauses in the "so s/he said and I said" interchanges common to personal-experience narratives, particularly about interpersonal conflict. And here they are governed by sophisticated predicates such as *was asked, realized, thought* or by abstract nominals like *his view, my argument, an obligation,* and not only the *verba dicendi* typical of complement clause construction among younger children. Although Spanish and Hebrew have similar structural options of complementation, narrators in these languages rely less on this device than their English-speaking counterparts.

The text in (5) contains relatively few *non-finite* clauses, evidently due to individual stylistic choice: The narratives of some English-speaking adolescents and adults abound in non-finite clauses, while others use them sparingly. Across the sample, however, nonfinite subordination is far commoner for clause packaging in English than in Spanish and particularly Hebrew, where it is negligible compared with non-verbal nominalizations.

Consider next, the quite typical adult narrative written in Spanish in (6).

(6) Spanish Woman's Narrative [sA04][14]
CP1: *He vivido algunas situaciones en el colegio* **[ISO=MC]** *en las que no había nada de compañerismo.* **[HYPO]**
'(I) have lived [=experienced] some situations in school in which there was no companionship.'
CP2: *A lo mejor en un exámen yo no sabía algo* **[ISO=MC]** *y se lo preguntaba a un compañero* **[PAR]** *y éste no me hacía ni caso* **[PAR]**. *Mientras que <a mí cuando me preguntaban>* **[ENDO]** *les contestaba* **[PAR]** *o le acercaba mi exámen* **[PAR]** *para que lo vieran.* **[HYPO]**
'Probably on a test I didn't know something and (I) asked a friend about it, and that-one [=he] took no notice of me. Whereas, while (people) were asking me, (I) responded to them or (I) moved my test closer, so that (they) would see it.'
CP3: *También me he quedado con el dinero de alguna persona* **[ISO=MC]**. *En el vestuario de un gimnasio me he encontrado dinero* **[PAR]** *y <sabiendo* **[ENDO, NF]** *<que era de alguna de las personas>* **[HYPO in ENDO=STACKED]** *<que había allí>* **[HYPO in ENDO=STACKED]** *<en lugar de preguntar* **[HYPO, NF in ENDO=STACKED]** *>>>> me lo he quedado.* **[PAR]**

---

[14] This Spanish adult text is not a canonic narrative, but recounts personal experiences with the situations depicted in the video that served as a trigger to text elicitation.

'Also (I) have kept the money from some person. In the changing room of the gym, (I) have found some money, and knowing that (it) was of [=belonged to] some of the people that were there, instead of to-ask [=instead of asking], (I) kept it for myself.'

CP4: *He visto* **[ISO=MC]** *cómo niñas de mi clase han despreciado a otra* **[AsPAR=CMP]** *por querer simplemente* **[HYPO, NF]** *juntarse con ellas.* **[HYPO, NF]**
'(I) have seen how girls in my class have mocked another (girl) for to-want [=because of wanting] simply to-be-together with others.'

In marked contrast to the Hebrew text in (4), isotaxis here functions only in the main clauses of CPs, although the two texts are similar in rhythm and tempo. Thus, the Spanish text in (6) starts out relatively flatly, builds up to richly elaborated syntactic nesting in the two middle CPs, and then winds down again at the end. CP3 shows a multiple layering plus nesting of one clause inside another of a kind far commoner in Spanish than the other languages, even among adults. Unlike the English narrative in (5), the Spanish text contains few complements and non-finite predicates, the latter in a present-participle adverbial (*sabiendo*) or preposition-governed infinitives (*en lugar de preguntar, por querer, (por) juntarse*).

The three texts in (4) to (6) illustrate key features of contrastive rhetoric. First, the notion of "favored" rhetorical device is not absolute, but describes a *relative preference* for some over other of the options available in the target language. Thus, as can be seen by CP5 and CP6 in (4)—the story's "high point" (Labov, 1972)—mature Hebrew speaker-writers can and do use hypotaxis and endotaxis, and they also stack the two together when they wish—here, to recount the complicated series of events that constitute the main episodes. However, as noted, Hebrew speakers rely on these options far less than their peers in Spanish, with English lying in-between. Second, echoing another of Slobin's insights, the *same function* is expressed by different forms both developmentally and also across languages. All three languages possess similar repertoires for clause-linking—juxtapositioning, same and different subject coordination, complementation, adverbial and relative clauses. But they differ in the means they favor for expressing the rhetorical functions of stringing, layering, and nesting.

Age-Related Comparisons

Our analyses revealed a clear interaction between target language and age and level of schooling. For example, hypotactic "layering" increases significantly by age in all three languages; but in Spanish, this occurs more than in the other languages from as early as 4th grade, in English it increases significantly from 7th grade, whereas in Hebrew, hypotaxis is used across the group rather than as an occasional individual preference only from high school.

In general, the crosslinguistic trends we noted emerge even in the youngest age-group, becoming more marked from Grade 7 and especially from high school on. This underlines Slobin's recognition that young children not only know the linguistic forms of their native language, they also have a sense of its rhetoric. Yet it takes until adolescence and beyond for these preferences to consolidate, on the one hand, and to be flexibly varied across a range of alternative options (here, for clause packaging architecture), on the other.

Clause packaging also interacts with other facets of more advanced text construction abilities. The fact that high school emerged as a cut-off point between younger children and adults in syntactic architecture corresponds to findings from other domains in the crosslinguistic project, including: lexical density, diversity, and register in English (Nir-Sagiv, Bar-Ilan, & Berman, 2008); use of verb-tense and morphology in Hebrew (Berman & Nir-Sagiv, 2004); and devices for downgrading agency in Spanish (Tolchinsky & Rosado, 2005). Together, these findings underscore the close interconnection between general social cognitive developments and the flowering of rhetorical expressiveness in adolescence.

Finally, as predictable from Slobin's developmental credo, the *functions* of the same surface linguistic forms change across time. We illustrate this by narratives written by three children from the youngest age-group in (7) through (9).

(7) Story Written by Hebrew-Speaking 4th-Grade Boy [hG09]
    CP1: *xaver sheli loh haya xaver shel yeled axer.* **[ISO]**
          'My friend wasn't friends with another kid.'
    CP2: *ve-az pitom hu asa ito daf be-beyt ha-sefer* **[ISO=MC]** *ve-hu amar lo loh lihyot xaver sheli.* **[PAR]**
          'And then suddenly he did classwork with him at school and he told him not to be my friend.'
    CP3: *ve-az hu loh haya xaver sheli shavua shalem.* **[ISO]**
          'And then he wasn't my friend a whole week.'
    CP4: *ve-pitom hu haya xaver sheli ve-loh shelo.* **[ISO]**
          'And suddenly he was my friend and not his.'

This juvenile (though not atypical) 4th grade story consists mainly of isolated clauses, with each of the three non-initial CPs initiated by a discourse marking segment-tagger *and, and then, and suddenly*, similarly to the oral "Frog Story" narratives of 5- and 9-year-old Hebrew-speaking children (Berman, 1996; Berman & Neeman, 1994). The functions of these same forms differ when used by young children compared with more mature narrators. Among children, isolating clauses often constitute the entire narrative skeleton, with each step in the sequence of events presented separately, so that clause packaging serves to string situations one after another, as the story proceeds in time and verbal output, with no hierarchical pre-planning. In the Hebrew adult text in (4), the first few CPs likewise consist largely of clauses that are minimally strung together syntactically, but here, they serve the writer to set the background and specify the story-initiating event. From the high point on, the crux of her story is conveyed by densely linked packages of clauses, ending in a minimally layered final CP. This lends the text in (4) a hierarchically integrated rhythm and tempo by initial stringing of statements leading up to a high point and winding down again. Such flexible, globally motivated alternation is rare among children but common in more mature narratives that mark their story openings and closings as distinct in thematic content (Tolchinsky, Johansson, & Zamora, 2002) and in linguistic forms (Berman & Katzenberger, 2004), as well as in their clause-combining syntactic architecture.

Young Hebrew-speaking children can and do package clauses together by hypotaxis and occasional endotaxis, not only by parataxis. But, again unlike more proficient speaker-writers of the language, they do so locally, as a means of linking individual clauses, rather than subordinating clause packages to the over-arching organization of the text as a whole. A not dissimilar picture emerges in the (again quite typical) 4th-grade English-language story in (8), although this relies far more on asymmetric parataxis by complementation.

(8) Story Written by English-Speaking 4th Grade Boy [eg03]
    CP1: Me and my sister got a beanie baby at Children's Hospital. **[ISO]**
    CP2: We left them both on the day bed. **[ISO]**
    CP3: When we came back, **[HYPO]** we did not know **[ISO=MC]** which one was which, **[AsPAR=CMP]** so we started to fight about it. **[HYPO]**
    CP4: My sister gave me the wrong beanie baby **[ISO=MC]** and I said to Juliet **[PAR]** that mine had a wrinkle on his head. **[AsPAR=CMP]**
    CP5: So Juliet gave me the one **[ISO=MC]** she had in her hand. **[HYPO]**
    CP6: I took a marker **[ISO=MC]** and marked mine **[AsPAR= COORD]** and Juliet did not **[AsPAR=GAP]** so we know **[HYPO]** which one was which. **[AsPAR=CMP]**

Unlike the English adult text in (5), the complement clauses in (8) all follow linearly from their matrix clauses, not embedded inside one another or inside coordinate or subordinate clauses. And the matrix predicates are the basic *know, said*. Also in contrast to the adult text, this child's narrative contains no non-finite clauses, as a tightly woven means of subordinating one facet of a situation to another. While non-finite subordination does occasionally show up in the English 4th and 7th grade samples, it becomes a preferred rhetorical option for many English-speaking narrators only from high school on.

The Spanish child's text in (9) contrasts markedly with those of her Hebrew- and English-speaking peers: It contains several relative and adverbial clauses, its paratactic strings are often embedded in a layered fashion inside coordinate or subordinate clauses, and it contains an endocentric construction nested inside another, all mirroring the densely packaged rhetoric of Spanish narrative style. On the other hand, in the attitudes it expresses, in thematic content, and even in the linguistic forms it deploys (with occasional grammatical errors), this narrative remains clearly juvenile.

(9) Story Written by Spanish-Speaking 4th-Grade Girl [sG13]

    CP1: *El otro día mis amigas se pelearon* **[ISO=MC]** *y empezaron a hacerse burlas y cada vez más.* **[PAR]**
    'The other day my friends quarreled and began to play tricks and every time more.'

    CP2: *Entonces la °castigaron* **[ISO=MC]** *pero todavía no se han perdonada* **[PAR]** *y en la clase se pelean todos los días.* **[PAR]**
    'Then (they were) punished but still (they) have not forgiven one another and in class (they) quarrel every day.'

    CP3: *A mí no me gustan las peleas* **[ISO=MC]** *porque después empiezan* **[HYPO]** *y en mi clase he visto* **[PAR]** *que nunca se acaban.* **[AsPAR=CMP]**
    'I don't like quarrels because afterwards (they) begin and in my class (I) have seen that (they) never end.'

    CP4: *Pero me gustaría* **[ISO=MC]** *que lo arreglaran* **[AsPAR=CMP]** *porque somos compañeros* **[HYPO]** *y tenemos que llevarnos bien* **[HYPO]** *porque si no todos los años <que nos quedan>* **[ENDO]** *seguirán peleándose* **[HYPO]** *y eso a mí no me gusta.* **[HYPO]**
    'But I would like that (they) should get on because (we) are classmates and (we) should get on well because if not all the years that remain to-us (they) will-continue quarreling with one another and me, I don't like that.'

This Spanish girl's text is a dramatic demonstration of Slobin's notion of "typological bootstrapping." Just as Hebrew-speaking preschoolers find it quite natural to manipulate stem-internal vowel changes in alternating between past and present tense or between nouns and adjectives, and they inflect verbs and adjectives for gender and number agreement; just as young English speakers learn to manipulate the complex auxiliary alternations and the *wh-* marking systems of their language; so Spanish-speaking children early on demonstrate remarkable facility with layering and even nesting clauses as typologically preferred ways of clause packaging in their language.

This picture is confirmed by what we found for endotaxis across the sample: Spanish makes significantly more use of endotactic nesting than English or Hebrew and it exhibits the clearest developmental trend from grade school across adolescence in this respect. In English, and even more markedly in Hebrew, endotaxis increases somewhat as a function of age, but it remains a largely individual rhetorical preference, rather than an across-the-board typological feature of the language. This interaction between typology and development is particularly marked in the case of *stacking* ("X on hypotaxis"): multiple layering of clauses by incorporation of coordinate, complement, and/or subordinate clauses inside subordinates. Stacked clause packaging occurs significantly more in Spanish across the sample. And it shows a dramatic age-related increment in all three languages, being rare among the youngest children, rising significantly at junior high school age in Spanish, and from high school in English and Hebrew.

DISCUSSION

We hope to have shed light on *advanced syntax* from several novel perspectives. Development of clause packaging architecture involves more than the number of clauses packaged together in a single unit of text or a straightforward shift from isolating via coordinating to subordinating. Rather, syntactic architecture changes as constructions known to children from preschool age are used in new combinations to form more varied and complex clause packages. And typologically, the earliest and most accessible types of packaging reflect the favored rhetorical options of a given target language, by stringing, layering, or nesting.

The analytical framework we propose allows for a fine-tuning of the notion "syntactic architecture" by specifying the depth and distance of attached clauses within a CP.[15] Thus, complexity of clause-linkage relates critically to cases where coordinate, complement, and subordinate clauses depend not on the main clause but on each other. More fine-grained analyses are now under way to detail the nature of these attachments: in *amount*—the number of clauses attached to a given MC within a CP; *variety*—the number of different types of non-MCs within the CP; and *structure*—coordination by juxtaposition, different/same subject pronominalization/ellipsis; adverbial clauses inside, preceding, or following the MC, and types and positions of relative clauses. Of particular interest are constructions confined to adult texts, like relative clauses constructed on propositions rather than on NPs in English or non-finite gerundives in Hebrew. In addition, investigation of the interaction between phrase-level intra-clausal complexity and inter-clausal packaging might reveal a "trade-off" between the two across development and languages.

The notion of *preferred rhetorical options* was a leitmotif of this chapter. Here, across-group trends that we observed need to be hedged by considering individual differences. For example, not only was non-finite subordination favored significantly more in English than Spanish and especially Hebrew, within-group variation for this domain reflects a similar pattern. In Hebrew, variation is high across the sample, pointing to this as an individual choice; in Spanish, non-finites become a "group" option only for adults, hence are a highly sophisticated device; in English, non-finites are favored across the group from high school on, underlining the difference between developmentally constrained and typologically pervasive rhetorical preferences. Just as even very young children use most if not all of the structural options available in the target language, so will some though not all speaker-writers of a language deploy typologically less favored options in the course of text construction.

We conclude with a note on methodology and directions for future research. There is a rich literature on clause-combining in linguistics, but relatively little on discourse-embedded syntax in acquisition research. Our study was inspired by the procedures for crosslinguistic and developmental data elicitation that originated in Slobin's (1967, 1982) early work on acquisition of communicative competence, as extended to narrative discourse in the Frog Story studies (Slobin, 2004a). Following principles established for the Berman and Slobin (1994) study, our current crosslinguistic research relates to monologic texts based on a shared trigger, derived by similar instructions, and divided into clauses and clause packages by parallel procedures in different countries. This ensured close comparability of the analyses presented here for three languages across four age-groups. Further research along similar lines should be undertaken—of additional languages, oral as well as written narratives, and expository as well as narrative texts—as the basis for fresh insights into developing text construction abilities and contrastive rhetoric within and beyond the domain of clause packaging.

---

[15] Our notion of "depth" is not equivalent to position on a generative tree structure. Although the Main Clause is defined as the head of a CP, its associated clauses are not necessarily related by principles of X-bar structure.

REFERENCES

Berman, R. A. (1978). *Modern Hebrew structure*. Tel Aviv, Israel: University Publishing Projects.
Berman, R. A. (1996). Form and function in developing narrative abilities: The case of 'and.' In D. I. Slobin, J. Gerhardt, A. Kyratzis, & J. Guo (Eds.), *Social interaction, context, and language: Essays in honor of Susan Ervin-Tripp* (pp. 243–268). Mahwah, NJ: Lawrence Erlbaum Associates.
Berman, R. A. (1998). Typological perspectives on connectivity. In N. Dittmar & Z. Penner (Eds.), *Issues in the theory of language acquisition* (pp. 203–224). Bern: Peter Lang.
Berman, R. A. (2005). Introduction: Developing discourse stance in different text types and languages. *Journal of Pragmatics, 37* [Special issue on *Developing Discourse Stance across Adolescence*], 105–124.
Berman, R. A. (2007). Developing language knowledge and language use across adolescence. In E. Hoff & M. Shatz (Eds.), *Handbook of language development* (pp. 346–67). London: Blackwell Publishing.
Berman, R. A., & Katzenberger, I. (2004). Form and function in introducing narrative and expository texts: A developmental perspective. *Discourse Processes, 38*, 57–94.
Berman, R. A., & Neeman, Y. (1994). Development of linguistic forms: Hebrew. In R. A. Berman & D. I. Slobin (Eds.), *Relating events in narrative: A crosslinguistic developmental study* (pp. 285–328). Hillsdale, NJ: Lawrence Erlbaum Associates.
Berman, R. A., & Nir-Sagiv, B. (2004). Linguistic indicators of inter-genre differentiation in later language development. *Journal of Child Language, 31*, 339–380.
Berman, R. A., & Slobin, D. I. (1994). *Relating events in narrative: A crosslinguistic developmental study*. Hillsdale, NJ: Lawrence Erlbaum Associates.
Berman, R. A., & Verhoeven, L. (2002). Developing text production abilities across languages and age-groups. *Written Language and Literacy, 5*, 1–44.
Foley, W. A., & Van Valin, R. D. (1984). *Functional syntax and universal grammar*. Cambridge, UK: Cambridge University Press.
Johnstone, B. (1987). Parataxis in Arabic: Modification as a model for persuasion. *Studies in Language, 11*, 85–98.
Haiman, J., & Thompson, S. A. (Eds.) (1988). *Clause combining in grammar and discourse*. Amsterdam: John Benjamins.
Hickmann, M. (2003). *Children's discourse: Person, space, and time across languages*. Cambridge, UK: Cambridge University Press.
Hunt, K. W. (1965). Grammatical structures written at three grade levels. *NCTE research report #3*. Champaign, IL: NCTE.
Katzenberger, I. (2004). The development of clause packaging in spoken and written texts. *Journal of Pragmatics, 36*, 1921–1948.
Labov, W. (1972). *Language in the inner city*. Philadelphia: University of Pennsylvania Press.
Matthiessen, M. I. M. (2002). Combining clauses into clause complexes: A multi-faceted view. In J. Bybee & M. Noonan (Eds.), *Complex sentences in grammar and discourse: Essays in honor of Sandra A. Thompson* (pp. 235–319). Amsterdam: John Benjamins.
Nir-Sagiv, B. (2005, October). Grammatical constructions in narrative discourse: The case of clause packages. *New Directions in Cognitive Linguistics: First UK Cognitive Linguistics Conference*, Brighton.
Nir-Sagiv, B. (2008). *Clause packages as constructions in developing narrative discourse*. Unpublished doctoral dissertation, Tel Aviv University.
Nir-Sagiv, B., Bar-Ilan, L., & Berman, R. A., (2008). Vocabulary development across adolescence: Text-based analyses. In I. Kupferberg & A. Stavans (Eds.), *Language education in Israel: Papers in honor of Elite Olshtain* (pp. 47–76). Jerusalem, Israel: Magnes Press.
Ostler, S. E. (1987). English in parallels: A comparison of English and Arabic prose. In U. Connor & R. Kaplan (Eds.), *Writing across languages: Analysis of L2 texts* (pp. 169–185). Reading, MA: Addison Wesley. 169–185.
Ravid, D., & Berman, R. A. (2006). Information density in the development of spoken and written narratives in English and Hebrew. *Discourse Processes, 41*, 117–149.
Ravid, D., & Cahana-Amitay, D. (2005). Verbal and nominal expression in narrating conflict situations in Hebrew. *Journal of Pragmatics, 37* [Special issue on *Developing Discourse Stance Across Adolescence*, edited by R. A. Berman], 157–184.
Slobin, D. I. (1967). *A field manual for cross-cultural study of the acquisition of communicative competence*. Berkeley: University of California.
Slobin, D. I. (1973). Cognitive prerequisites for the development of grammar. In C. A. Ferguson & D. I. Slobin (Eds.), *Studies of child language development* (pp. 175–208). New York: Holt, Rinehart & Winston.

Slobin, D. I. (1977). Language change in childhood and history. In J. MacNamara (Ed.), *Language learning and thought* (pp. 185–214). New York: Academic Press.

Slobin, D. I. (1982). Universal and particular in the acquisition of language. In E. Wanner & L. R. Gleitman (Eds.), *Language acquisition: The state of the art* (pp. 128–170). Cambridge, UK: Cambridge University Press.

Slobin, D. I. (1996). From "thought and language" to "thinking to speaking." In J. J. Gumperz & S. C. Levinson (Eds.), *Rethinking linguistic relativity* (pp. 70–96). Cambridge, UK: Cambridge University Press.

Slobin, D. I. (2000). Verbalized events: A dynamic approach to linguistic relativity and determinism. In S. Niemeir & R. Dirven (Eds.), *Evidence for linguistic relativity* (pp. 107–138). Amsterdam: John Benjamins.

Slobin, D. I. (2001). Form-function relations: How do children find out what they are? In M. Bowerman & S. C. Levinson (Eds.), *Language acquisition and conceptual development* (pp. 406–449). Cambridge, UK: Cambridge University Press.

Slobin, D. I. (2003a). How people move. In C. L. Moder & A. Martinovic-Zic (Eds.), *Discourse across languages and cultures* (pp. 195–210). Amsterdam: John Benjamins.

Slobin, D. I. (2003b). Language and thought online: Cognitive consequences of linguistic relativity. In D. Gentner & S. Goldin-Meadow (Eds.), *Language in mind: Advances in the investigation of language and thought* (pp. 157–191). Cambridge, MA: The MIT Press.

Slobin, D. I. (2004a). The many ways to search for a frog: Linguistic typology and the expression of motion events. In S. Strömqvist & L. Verhoeven (Eds.), *Relating events in narrative*: Vol. 2. *Typological and contextual perspectives* (pp. 219–257). Mahwah, NJ: Lawrence Erlbaum Associates.

Slobin, D. I. (2004b). Relating events in translation. In D. Ravid & H. B. Shyldkrot (Eds.), *Perspectives on language and language development: Essays in honor of Ruth A. Berman* (pp. 115–130). Dordrecht, The Netherlands: Kluwer.

Tolchinsky, L., Johansson, V., & Zamora, A. (2002). Text openings and closings: Textual autonomy and differentiation. *Written Language and Literacy, 5,* 219–254.

Tolchinsky, L., & Rosado, E. (2005). The effect of literacy, text type, and modality on the use of grammatical means for agency alternation in Spanish. *Journal of Pragmatics, 37,* 209–238.

Verhoeven, L., & van Hell, J. G. (in press). Clause packaging in Dutch narrative and expository text writing in children and adults. *Discourse Processes* [special issue].

Waltke, B. K., & O'Connor, M. (1990). *A introduction to Biblical Hebrew syntax.* Winona Lake, IN: Eisenbrauns.

12

The Many Ways to Search for a Frog Story
On a Fieldworker's Troubles Collecting Spatial Language Data

RAPHAEL BERTHELE
University of Fribourg, Switzerland

> The challenge to the typological linguist is to find sets of variables that co-occur and to try to account for those co-occurrences. However, linguistic patterns don't occur in the abstract. They arise in the course of language in use.
>
> **Dan I. Slobin (2004, p. 253)**

INTRODUCTION[1]

This chapter is directly related to one of the first questions I asked Dan Slobin during my stay at Berkeley in summer 2001. At that time, inspired by the work on spatial language by Dan and his colleagues, I was in the process of preparing a study of motion events and static spatial relations on the border between Romance and Germanic languages. My goal was to investigate the non-standard varieties along the Swiss part of this border and to compare nonstandard and standard varieties with respect to the well-known distinction between satellite- and verb-framed languages (Talmy, 2000). Since the plan was to collect a sociologically stratified sample, including older and less literate informants, I was worried if picture stimuli would be the adequate means to elicit narratives. Dan told me that the frog story stimulus is perfectly appropriate for older informants, and showed me the transcripts of elderly informants, including his father's retelling in Yiddish. Eventually, I carried out my research project using the frog story as one of the stimuli, and indeed, most of the informants actually cooperated and produced good data. But not all of them did. A certain number of elicitation sessions in one particular alpine area, the Muotathal, surprisingly often turned into the fieldworker's nightmare. The principal goal of this contribution is to present a detailed analysis of the problems encountered in the field. My contribution has a rather personal flavor: The research reported here would have never seen the light if Dan Slobin had not passed on the spatial language virus to me. The only downside of being contaminated with this virus was my difficult encounters with some people in the field who were not at all amused about retelling a

---

[1] The author is greatly indebted to Şeyda Özçalışkan and Elena Lieven for their comments on earlier versions of this chapter.

children's book to a stranger. Consequently, I feel that this Festschrift is a good place to report both pleasure and pain Dan's charisma caused me.

In the first section, I briefly introduce the speech communities I have selected for my study. In the second section, I propose a taxonomy of elicitation problems based on my experience as a fieldworker. However, since most informants produced usable data even in the Alpine "problem area," there are results from the spatial language survey, which are presented briefly in the penultimate section. In the final section, I attempt to connect the seemingly unrelated findings from the preceding sections.

SPEECH COMMUNITIES

Language is a social practice, and the locus of language use is the speech community. The many different definitions and construals of the speech community in anthropological linguistics and sociolinguistics vary on a scale from relatively abstract notions of shared systems or shared sets of (variable) rules (Labov, 1972) to more concrete aggregates of people who actually interact on a more or less regular basis (Gumperz, 1968; Milroy, 1992). The major research objective of the study reported here is to compare different language varieties spoken by the speech communities that are situated more or less along the Romance–Germanic border in terms of their repertoire of spatial expressions (e.g., lexicon, constructions; see Table 12.1).

On the Romance side, I collected data from standard French and from three dialects of Romansh, a minority language in eastern Switzerland. On the Germanic side, I have collected data from four Swiss German dialects and Standard High German spoken by German informants. Native Swiss Germans are native speakers of a dialect, and the German standard language is acquired as an L2 after the dialect is learned. The speakers of the Romansh varieties are all bilingual in Romansh and (Swiss) German because of the minority status of Romansh. The German-speaking Sense and Wallis areas are directly located at the border to the francophone territories, and both cantons (Wallis, Fribourg) are officially bilingual in German and French. The Bern dialect is the dialect of the capital Bern and its surroundings, and the Muotathal dialect is the dialect of a valley in the central Swiss Alps.

I expect essential differences between standard (or near-standard) varieties and non-standard varieties of a language in both the usage culture and the ecolinguistic embedding. I believe that these differences affect the motion verb typology in ways that have so far been ignored in the field. In fact, one of the goals of my study is to show that predictions regarding the inventory and nature of spatial language repertoires that are based solely on genetic typology are insufficient and inadequate to study several varieties of the "same language." The main hypothesis is that spatial language typology only provides adequate results if it takes into account the particular usage patterns of dialectal

TABLE 12.1 Summary Table for Language Varieties and Their Location

Language Variety	Location	# of Frog Stories
Standard High German	Germany	20
Bern Swiss German	Western Switzerland	10
Wallis Swiss German	Southern Switzerland	4
Sense Swiss German	Western Switzerland	10
Muotathal Swiss German	Central Switzerland	26
Standard French	Western Switzerland	20
Sursilvan Romansh	Eastern Switzerland	10
Vallader Ladin Romansh	Eastern Switzerland	10
Surmiran Romansh	Eastern Switzerland	10

practice, its situatedness and cultural embedding. In a later section, I will provide some evidence along these lines. But before that, the next section will show that there is an even more fundamental problem, namely, that the linguistic elicitation tasks are not necessarily perceived in the same way across different speech communities.

I have chosen the Muotathal dialect as one of the varieties in my sample because it is spoken by probably the most traditional and conservative community of Switzerland. The village and its surrounding hamlets (with a total of about 3000 inhabitants) are located in an alpine valley that forms a dead end with no significant pass leading over the Alps and with hardly any local tourist industry. Although more and more of its inhabitants are going to school and work outside the valley, the local community remains characterized by dense and multiplex social networks. Multiplex networks consist of ties which are of multiple types. For example, a person's cousin may at the same time be his or her employee, neighbor, and godparent. Dense networks are networks with many such ties between virtually all members of the community (Milroy, 1992). This kind of social structure usually entails a high degree of loyalty to the local culture and community, which also is the case in the Muotathal, even among the younger generations. What it means for a non-native scholar to collect dialect data in such an area will be discussed in the following section.

A SIMPLE TAXONOMY OF ELICITATION FAILURES

Similar to many other linguistic studies on motion verbs, I used the frog story stimulus (Mayer, 1969). While collecting frog story data in different areas and languages, I had not encountered any major problems—not until I went to the Muotathal. During my first visit in 2002, I was accompanied by a friend of mine, Franz S., who is a native of the valley but left it many years ago because his plan was to become a professional DJ, a career which is highly incompatible with the local job market. We first went to see Franz's parents in order to enter the social network of the local community in the most natural way possible. After a nice lunch, I briefly explained what I was interested in. Swiss dialect speakers are generally proud of their dialect, and in virtually all informal and some more formal contexts, it is normal (in the normative sense) to use one's native dialect with other Swiss German natives. Thus, we were all comfortably speaking our respective dialects. When I finished my introductory remarks, my friend's 70-year-old father, who had been very hospitable and kind before, stood up, walked to the door, and said he had no time for such follies. I somehow had the impression that if I had not been his son's friend, he would have kicked me out of his house. Here we have the first category of failure, the most radical and staggering experience a fieldworker can have.

Type 1: "Get Lost Immediately!"—Informants Protect Their Negative Face

During the remainder of my data collection sessions in the area, I experienced further variants of this type of failure: One informant told me to immediately get lost when I knocked at his barn door, without even letting me finish my introductory remarks. Another informant, one of my friend's many cousins, simply waved his scythe with which he was cutting the hay, threateningly, and did not bother to take the cheroot out of his mouth when I started to explain my request.

Such outright rejection is rather uncommon, and it has an extremely demoralizing effect on the fieldworker's enthusiasm. I have to admit that there were moments when I thought about giving up and leaving the Muotathal spatial language to its scientifically unexplored status.

From a pragmatic point of view, this first type of failure most certainly relates to the notion of face. According to Brown and Levinson (2000) and Goffman (1967), we can distinguish between negative and positive face. Positive face is "the positive consistent self-image or personality (crucially including the desire that this self-image be appreciated and approved of)" (Brown & Levinson, 2000, p. 61). Negative face, on the other hand, is the "freedom of action and freedom from imposition" (i.e., the desire not to be imposed upon, intruded, or otherwise put upon; Brown & Levinson, 2000, p. 61).

It seems that in the tight-knit and relatively isolated community I was trying to elicit data from, we can observe a tendency toward a remarkably high need to protect negative face. In principle, any request in many different cultural and situational settings is a potential face threatening act, but usually the fieldworker can neutralize this threat by using positive politeness (i.e., by showing interest in the local people, their culture and language). It is particularly troubling that even informants who had close family ties to my friend Franz sometimes refused to cooperate—even in his presence.

Type 2: "Ask Chaplain Gwerder"—Protect Positive Face and Try to Convince Fieldworker to Ask Someone Else

The second type is much more common and can be experienced in many different speech communities. These are cases where negative face and its protection are not the main problem. On the contrary, the fieldworker often received a very hospitable reception, good food, and strong or not so strong local drinks, and a lot of very nice small talk took place. But nevertheless, the informants refused or tried to refuse to do the frog story task. Here, my assumption is that the potential informant tried to save his/her positive face, because s/he thought that the fieldworker or other people might express ridicule or disapproval of his/her narrative. There are several potential reasons why somebody might be afraid of losing his/her positive face in retelling a story: (1) the Low variety[2] problem (i.e., the speaker feels inferior because s/he is the speaker of a lower prestige dialect), (2) the dialect decay problem (i.e., the informant feels that s/he is not a good speaker of the "real," "good," "old" dialect any more), and (3) the bad storyteller problem (i.e., the informant thinks s/he cannot tell good stories).

As aforementioned, in the Swiss German context the use of dialect, even among complete strangers, is the unmarked choice. Thus (1) is unlikely to be expected in this context. Nevertheless, surprisingly, two of the Muotathal informants switched to Standard High German, even though both the fieldworker and they themselves were talking Swiss German exclusively until they started the narrative task (see the underlined stretches in example 1).

(1) *Es isch es hündli cho und s chind isch det gsässe und undefür isch ... und da drinne hed ... isch ... det isch jetzt e frosch drine.* <u>Am Abend ging er ins Bett</u> [...] <u>Das Kind ging</u> ... <u>Der Kleine ging ins Bett</u>. *De chlii isch is bett gangä.*
'There came a dog and the child sat there and below is ... and inside there has ... is ... there is now a frog inside. <u>In the evening he went to bed.</u> [...] <u>The child went</u> ... <u>The little one went to bed</u> ... The little one went to bed.'

Here, the observer's paradox (Labov, 1972, p. 109) seems to act in a way that is rather unusual given the relatively high sociolinguistic status of the dialects in German-speaking Switzerland.

A lot more common in the Swiss German context, and again particularly so in Muotathal, is the dialect decay problem (i.e., the feeling of the informants that their dialect is not the real, pure dialect any more due to their dialect leveling with neighboring dialects, or due to contact with the standard language). Oftentimes I was told to talk to Chaplain Gwerder, who is the author of a local dialect dictionary and the most prominent expert on local culture, history, and language. Some people did not understand why I wanted to record their very normal everyday dialect rather than the prototypical informant who "knows all the old words."

The third reason why somebody may be afraid of losing their (positive) face is the informant's feeling that s/he is a lousy storyteller. This is exemplified by the keeper of a newsstand on the main road of the village who tried to avoid doing the retelling task by offering to arrange for other people to do it instead of herself (see his response in example 2):

---

[2] Please cf. Ferguson's (1959) concept of diglossia, involving a High (prestige) and a Low variety.

(2) *Näi aso, das tun ich ned gäre, söl öpper andersch [...] ich wo niä gschichtäli verzelle, de nacher töönt das eso blööd [...] näi aso säich, he söll öpper verbiichoo, söll öpper anders. [Alfons, a local walks by] De Alfons söll doch schnäll e gschicht cho verzelle, de cha doch das.*
'Well no, I don't like to do this, someone else should [...] I never tell stories, and then this sounds so stupid [...] well no, bullshit, hey, someone please come here, someone else should. [Alfons walks by] It's Alfons who should come quickly and tell a story, he knows how to do this.'

This type of affirmation that people do not know how to tell stories was frequent among the Muotathal informants' excuses, and I started to doubt the generally assumed universality of narratives in all cultures of the world. However, Franz's mother, my first informant in the valley, added, after insisting on the fact that she had hardly ever told stories to her children, that her eldest daughter was the storyteller in the family (see example 3):

(3)
fieldworker: *Es goot drum, das mer die gschicht verzellt [...] es goot au überhaupt nid um richtig oder falsch, sondern drum, de dialekt z beschriibe.*
'This is about telling me this story [...] it is not about correctness at all, but about describing the dialect.'
informant: *Jo ich wäiss nüd.[...] ja ich cha, ich weis nöd, ich lise scho vil aber [...] ich cha jetzt doch nid ä gschicht machche [...].*
'Well, I don't know [...] yes I can, I don't know, I do read a lot but [...] I can't make a story now.'
Franz S.: *Es gaat nöd um schriftspraach, nume ums gschichtli verzelle.*
'This is not about the standard/written language, only about telling a story.'
fieldworker: *Aber si händ doch sicher, wo de franz en chliine gsii isch, im gschichte verzellt?*
'But you certainly told stories to Franz when he was a child?'
informant: *Äbe nid eso vil, da simmer am umbuue gsii, d Maria hed im mee, d schwöschter.*
'Not so much, we were transforming [the farmhouse] at that time, Maria has him more [=told him more stories], the sister.'
fieldworker: *De chönd si s jetzt noohole.*
'So you can make up for this now.'
informant: [laughs, and starts telling the story] *Äbe ja, de sött gläub is bett und...*
'OK then, this one should go to bed and …'

It goes without saying that the Muotathal is by no means the world's only non-narrative culture. There are collections of Muotathal sagas and legends, and during my days of field work in the valley, I had the pleasure to attend a couple of informal gatherings where stories were told and retold for the umpteenth time. And even more revealing, my friend Franz's mother herself, who, after she had eventually agreed to tell me the frog story, digressed from the narration when she saw the panel with the little boy looking for the frog in his boots, and she started to tell a real life story about a little boy who found a snake in his boot a couple of weeks ago. This type of digression is particularly frequent when using picture stimuli with elderly and less educated informants, and it represents another—although minor—obstacle on the fieldworker's thorny path to motion verb data.

Type 3: "This Does Not Make Sense!"—Refusal to Cooperate Due to Pragmatically Odd Task

From a pragmatic point of view, the elicitation of frog story narratives is not as unproblematic as it may seem at first sight. The informant's retelling of the story to a formerly unknown fieldworker actually involves a great deal of interactional awkwardness. It actually involves several problems: (1) telling a children's picture book not to a child, but to an adult, (2) who is not part of the community within which stories are usually told (family, friends, and neighbors), (3) who comes from a university outside the valley (=sociologically and geographically very far away), (4) who knows and masters "good language" a lot better than the informant, (5) who even seems to know a lot about "good dialect" more than the informant, (6), who already knows the story a lot better than the storyteller, (7) who is actually not really interested in the story, but in something else, and (8) this something else is supposed to be "science," and, not surprisingly, it is not only mountain farmers who question the importance of this type of scientific enterprise.

Indeed, the frog story task is quite odd. In most cases the telling of stories prototypically expands the common ground by carrying over propositional content from the speaker to the hearer. However, in this context, the speaker has to catch up with the hearer's profound knowledge of the propositional content. This informational awkwardness is clearly reminiscent of classroom settings; thus it should be no surprise at all that some of the informants feel uneasy about the whole setup.

Therefore, the retelling of the frog story to the fieldworker involves a considerable amount of ability to role play. As such, it turned out to be one of the best introductory remarks that the informant should try to tell the story pretending s/he is telling it to a child. But obviously, some informants simply are not willing or are unable to play this game because they think that it does not make sense to anybody involved. We find numerous very typical remarks in the recorded material that show how odd the task seems to be even to those who take part without or with only a little objection (see example 4).

(4) *Bewunderets dänk der frosch da drinnen und—und aabig isch ja und der mond schiint ja—ächch—und jetz isch er na uusecho und dä schlaaft und der hund isch uf der techchi oobe; sch nüüt für miich.*
'They obviously admire the frog inside and – and it's in the evening and the moon shines—alas—and now he came out and this one sleeps and the dog is on the blanket; this is nothing for me.'

This transcript from the very beginning of a frog story retelling shows a couple of features that indicate the informant's uneasiness with the task: The informant overtly states that she is ill-suited for this task (*this is nothing for me*). Moreover, discourse particles such as *dänk* 'obviously' and *ja* 'of course'[3] express the narrator's point of view that the propositions of her narration are trivial, self-evident, and/or already known to the interviewer.

The introduction of new referents with definite articles and demonstrative pronouns (*der frosch* 'this frog') suggests that the narrator is very much aware of the fact that the listener already knows the story and its protagonists. Similarly, the first mention of the main characters with personal pronouns instead of proper or generic names again alludes to the common knowledge that the retelling does not require a more fleshed out introduction of the characters. I assume that this marked way of introducing referents is due to the informant's perception of the unnatural setting in which the narration occurs.

Type 4: "There Is Another Dog Again, I Think." Cooperate Willingly, But Without Getting the Nature of the Task

Some informants cooperate ungrudgingly, but deliver unusable text. Typically, this type of informant takes a long look at the first panel of the picture book and then starts delivering a meticulous description of the figures and objects depicted. Even though the fieldworker tries to talk these informants into a more relaxed and more global way of talking about the events in the book, they insist on rendering a series of states, as in example 5:

---

[3] The English glosses have to be very approximate, since these particles are almost impossible to translate.

(5) *E Bueb ... ja er hed es Glas vorem zueche, weiss nid öb er öppis wott druss usse nä und es isch e Huend no druff obe. [...] Na isch er nüme drinne gsi. De Huend isch da aber au, ja de Grind is Glas inne gstreckt, gläbene ich, hed er. [...] Da isch au wieder e Huend und isch im Glas inne mit de Schnuure. Da hed er de Grind wieder im Glas inne.*
'A boy ... well he has a jar in front of him, don't know if he wants to take something out of it and there is a dog on top. [...] The dog is there too, yes, I think he stretched his head into the jar. [...] There is a dog again and he is in the jar with his muzzle. There he has the head in the jar again.'

The passage shows a number of characteristics: it uses static descriptions of states rather than linking the states depicted with dynamic motion verbs; thus the retelling makes it impossible to keep track of 'the same' referents in the course of the story (e.g., a 'new' dog is reintroduced via the indefinite article although it had already been talked about before). This way of 'retelling' the story as a series of states rather than overlapping and consecutive dynamic events is rather fruitless for the study of motion verbs since only very few motion verbs are actually used by the informants.

SUCCESSFUL ELICITATION

Even though the preceding sections document how difficult data elicitation can be in certain communities, it is important to keep in mind that the majority of potential informants, even in Muotathal, played the game and delivered good and usable narratives for the analysis. Actually, I decided to collect the highest number of frog story retellings in Muotathal, since an analysis of pilot data from different dialect areas provided preliminary evidence that the Muotathal dialect deviates more from Standard High German than other Swiss German dialects: Muotathal Swiss German, in the pilot data, seemed to be a satellite-framed language that does not exhibit a great deal of manner verb use. Thus, a larger and sociolinguistically stratified sample from Muotathal was collected to shed more light on this deviation from the typological prediction according to which satellite-framed languages are 'manner-salient' languages. In this section I will give a partial summary of the results of my study, mainly to be able to ask the final and quite essential question in the final section: whether and how the elicitation difficulties described in this section and the results of the spatial language analyses might be connected.

It is safe to assume that in the present volume it is quite unnecessary to introduce Talmy's (2000) motion verb typology and Slobin's (e.g., 1996 and 2004) groundbreaking empirical and theoretical contributions to the typology. One of the most important findings in the framework provided by Talmy and Slobin is that the use of verbs that lexically encode path information is more typical of certain languages than of others. Languages that canonically map the path onto the verb are called verb-framed languages. This is because in Talmy's paradigm, path verbs convey the framing event of the spatial scene described by the speaker (e.g., *sortir* 'exit,' *entrer* 'enter,' *descendre* 'descend,' *monter* 'ascend'). Languages that map the path onto any kind of particle in verb-sister position (i.e., in a satellite) are called satellite-framed languages. So far, it has been claimed that Romance languages belong to the verb-framed type (Talmy, 2000, p. 222), with occasional deviations that are claimed to be due to language contact (e.g., Schwarze, 1985). Since up to now nobody has worked on Romansh within this particular paradigm, one of the goals of this study was to find out whether Romansh belonged to the verb- or the satellite-framed type. Figure 12.1 shows the proportions of path verbs in relation to the total number of motion verbs used.

Clearly, there is a cline from standard French, with a high proportion of path verb use to Swiss German and Romansh with a very low proportion of path verb use. Romansh thus is not a verb-framed language, since it canonically maps the path information onto locative particles, just as English and German. Language contact with Swiss German obviously could be one explanation for this finding. Another argument advocated by Mair (1984; see also Berthele, 2004, 2006) is that Romansh simply maintained the Latin satellite-framed structure.

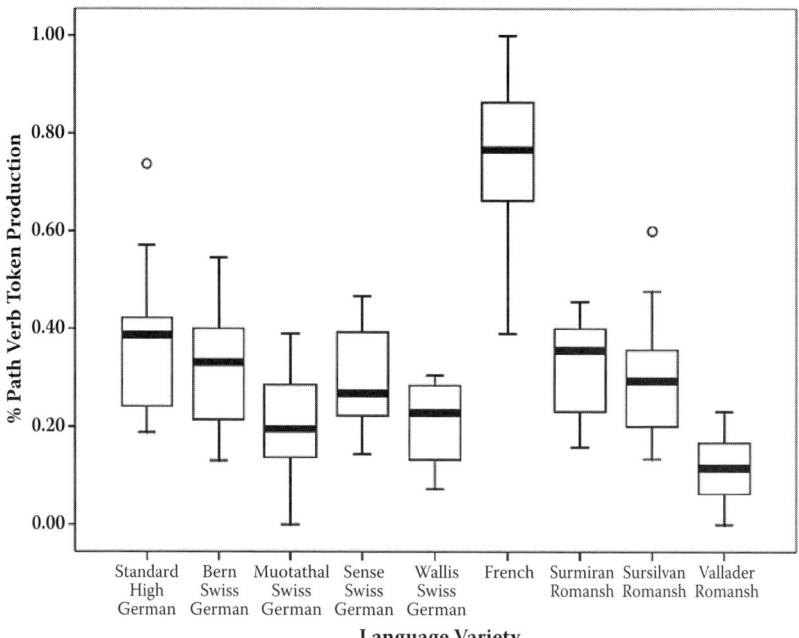

Figure 12.1 Proportional use of path verbs in the different language varieties. Percentages were computed by dividing each informant's total number of path verbs by the total number of motion verbs, separately in each language variety. The horizontal line indicates the median, boxes contain the middle 50% of the data, and the vertical lines represent the scattering of the values.

A one-way ANOVA showed significant differences in path verb use between the varieties in the sample ($F(8, 111) = 39.46, p < 0.01$). French speakers used significantly more path verbs than all other varieties in the sample (mean differences range between 0.44 and 0.64, $p < 0.01$, Scheffe). In addition, Muotathal Swiss German differed significantly from Standard High German (mean difference = $-0.17, p = 0.01$, Scheffe), and Muotathal Swiss German was at the lower end of the scale of path verb use.

According to Talmy (2000), if the verb slot does not carry the path information, it is expected to convey additional information about the co-events (e.g., information about manner of motion.). Thus, Figure 12.2 shows the proportion of manner verbs in the varieties in our sample.

Quite clearly, the French data match the prediction of low manner verb use in verb-framed languages. Standard High German also fits in nicely with Talmy's prediction that satellite-framed languages have a high rate of manner verb use. However, some undoubtedly satellite-framed languages such as Muotathal Swiss German and Romansh seem to use a great deal of neither path nor manner verbs (for a more detailed analysis of the data see Berthele, 2006). In fact, the language varieties differ reliably in their proportional use of manner verbs ($F(8, 111) = 11.39, p < 0.01$), also showing a significant difference between Muotathal Swiss German and the German standard language (Mean difference = $-0.16, p < 0.01$, Scheffe). And, in addition to the differences in manner and path verb use, particularly Muotathal and Vallader Ladin have overall rather low bilogarithmic type–token ratios (Herdan's Index) in the finite verb slot. Some of these results do not fit in with the general expectations and empirical findings in Talmy's and Slobin's work, which would predict many different descriptive manner verbs and thus high type–token ratios in the verb slot of satellite-framed languages (cf. the comparison of type-token ratios of motion verbs in Spanish and English texts in Slobin, 1996, p. 208).

If we take the whole sample of my study and correlate external sociolinguistic factors such as age, gender, and occupation (blue vs. white collar professions) with the dependent variables, type–token ratio, manner and path verb use, we find no significant correlations. Surprisingly, the dependent

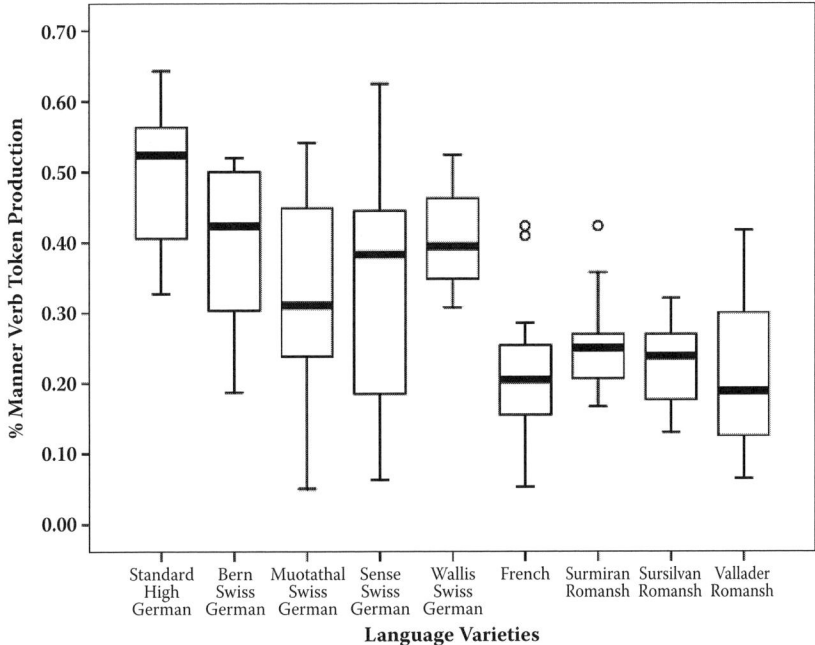

Figure 12.2 Proportional use of manner verbs in the language varieties in the sample. Percentages were computed by dividing each informant's total number of manner verbs by the total number of motion verbs, separately in each language variety.

variables show significant correlation with the estimated demographic size of the dialect or the standard language community (manner verbs: spearman's rho 0.162, $p < 0.05$; path verbs: Spearman's rho 0.635, $p < 0.01$; type–token ratio: spearman's rho 460, $p < 0.01$).[4] That is, the larger the speech community is, the higher the values of the type–token ratios, manner verbs, and the path verb variables are. For example, both Muotathal Swiss German and Valladar Ladin and Surmiran Romansh are small varieties spoken by far less than 10,000 speakers. Intermediate (i.e., relatively big) dialects such as Bern Swiss German or Sursilvan Romansh show intermediate values on the cline between high and low manner-salience. I assume that particularly the varieties spoken in small speech communities, such as Muotathal Swiss German or the smaller Romansh dialects, instantiate what Koch and Oesterreicher (1994, p. 591) call the 'language of proximity.' The 'language of proximity,' with its predominantly oral use, is also directly related to Givón's (1979) idea of pragmatic mode. The frequent use of semantically simple verbs, such as *come* and *go*, is a feature both of the pragmatic mode (Givón, 1979, p. 223) and of the language of proximity. Moreover, we predict low type–token ratios in the open class lexicon of the language of proximity (Koch & Oesterreicher, 1994, p. 591). However, this does not mean at all that dialects overall have restricted vocabularies. On the contrary, as the study by Snell-Hornby (1983, p. 76) shows, the verbal lexicon of German dialects can be quite elaborate. Therefore, my guess is that even though descriptive verbs (i.e., manner verbs) are available in the dialects as well, they tend only to be used if the manner of motion itself is an important part of the description of a motion event. Thus, also in Muotathal dialect manner verbs are almost categorically used in the frog story scene where the boy falls down from the tree (see example 6).

(6) *Und dr Büebl isch appem Baum appe trooled*
    'And the boy toppled down from the tree.'

---

[4] The size of the variety operationalized in an ordinally scaled variable, cf. Berthele, 2006, p. 84.

For most other motion events, general verbs of motion such as *come* and *go* do the job perfectly well. In the standard language, on the other hand, it is considered bad style if the speaker keeps using these generic verbs throughout longer narrative stretches. When I was explaining my research interests more precisely right after the elicitation procedure, a few Muotathal informants actually spontaneously remembered how the German teachers in school kept reminding the pupils to vary the lexicon and use 'different words' as much as possible. My hypothesis therefore is that small varieties share more features with the pragmatic mode, since they prototypically represent the language of proximity, a code that has undergone to a considerably lesser extent the processes of standardization that characterize the formation of European standard languages (Stein, 1997; see Berthele, 2006, p. 235 for a more detailed discussion).

SUMMARY AND DISCUSSION

There is one question that might arise when we consider the difficulties of data collection reported in the section above and the significantly deviant results of the analysis of verb use in this particular variety of Muotathal Swiss German: could it be that the informants felt so uneasy that their linguistic output is distorted and it does not show its "natural" patterns that would fit in better with the typological expectations? Alternatively, could it be that the observer's influence, for some specific cultural reason, is stronger in some places than in others? In order to answer this question we need to know what the unmonitored and spontaneous production of motion verb descriptions in this dialect looks like. There are unfortunately no corpora available of spontaneously spoken Swiss German. But at certain moments during elicitation, the informants were distracted during or after the narrative task and, as a result, some discussions among the locals could be recorded almost accidentally, just by not switching off the recorder. It makes little sense to run any statistical analyses based on transcripts of these recordings, but they nevertheless give a good feel for the variety these informants actually use, and they thus allow an approximate answer to the question of whether the elicited frog story narrations come close to the natural way of speaking Muotathal dialect. The following transcript from an informant talking about alpine dairy farming may serve as an illustration (see example 7):

(7) *Hellweid, hie sind's z alp, da chamer da unde vom Schache, äbe gägem bürgeli [...] ja s sisch e soo gsii, voränä isch ds huus dert bim gade änne gsii, und dernaa isch halt eisch e laui choo und ds huus und der gade, ds huus heds gnuu, und de isch e groosse aahore, und der säb isch blibe.*
'Hellweid (toponym), here they went to the alp, there one can down there from the Schachen (toponym), well towards the Bürgeli (toponym) [...] yes it was like this, before the house was there next to the barn, and then came an avalanche and the house and the barn, it took the house, and then there is a big maple tree, and that one stayed there.'

This passage illustrates the use of general verbs (e.g., *cho*, 'to come') even for dramatic events such as an avalanche rumbling down a mountain and destroying a house. The verb *sii* ('to be') is frequently used on this cline toward semantic depletion of the verb slot (e.g., *hie sind's z alp* = [literally] *here they are to the alp*; see Berthele, 2006, p. 130 for further discussion). In addition, the passage also shows the frequent doubling of the path or place particle as extensively described in Berthele (2004).

Hence, after listening to these additional spontaneous interactions, I assume that the patterns discovered in the frog story data indeed reflect more or less unmarked Muotathal Swiss German dialect. However, further research, which factors out the cultural variables that interact with the supposedly universally applicable task of retelling a picture book, is necessary to back up this claim. And it is likely that the picture book method has a certain number of side effects in particular speech communities. The kinds of problems discussed in this chapter are unlikely to occur in elicitation sessions with university students who are used to role play tasks, and who often have basic knowledge about methods used in social sciences. Thus, it is not surprising that no Muotathal informant who had benefited from higher education showed any kind of reluctance toward the task.

To sum up the problems and results laid out in the two previous sections, it seems as if there is a common underlying cultural factor which accounts for both the elicitation problems and the relatively deviant or typologically surprising spatial language data: our informants belong to tight-knit and multiplex social networks with a relatively high level of what early sociologists called "mechanical solidarity" (Durkheim, 1893), which basically means a high amount of cultural and everyday common ground. The language that fits in best with this social reality can be less explicit. Thus, my assumption is that orality fosters expressive economy which in turn entails low amounts of descriptivity in "accessory" domains such as the expression of manner. At the same time, speakers of such networks are less used to spontaneous and unfamiliar ways of interacting with non-members of the local community, and they are most certainly less accustomed to doing role plays such as the frog story task. If the linguistic patterns that emerge from the successful elicitation sessions represent and reflect the authentic language use within a dialect community, then the community presented in this chapter allows insights into the ways culture, language use, and language typology are intertwined, and shows that there is no valid way of doing use-based typology without taking into account external sociolinguistic factors.

REFERENCES

Berman, R. A., & Slobin, D. I. (1994). *Relating events in narrative: A crosslinguistic developmental study.* Hillsdale, NJ: Lawrence Erlbaum Associates.

Berthele, R. (2004). The typology of motion and posture verbs: A variationist account. In B. Kortmann (Ed.), *Dialectology meets typology. Dialect grammar from a cross-linguistic perspective* (pp. 93–126). Berlin: Mouton de Gruyter,.

Berthele, R. (2006). *Ort und Weg. Die sprachliche Raumreferenz in Varietäten des Deutschen, Rätoromanischen und Französischen.* Berlin: Mouton de Gruyter.

Brown, P., & Levinson, S. (2000). *Politeness. Some universals in language use.* Cambridge, UK: Cambridge University Press.

Durkheim, E. ([1893] 1973). *De la division du travail social. Etude sur l'organisation des sociétés supérieures.* Paris: Presses Universitaires de France.

Ferguson, Ch. A. (1959). Diglossia. *Word, 15,* 325–340.

Givón, T. (1979). *On understanding grammar.* New York: Academic Press.

Goffman, E. (1967). *Interaction ritual: Essays on face to face behavior.* Garden City, NY: Anchor Books.

Gumperz, J. (1968). The speech community. In D. L. Sils (Ed.), *International encyclopedia of the social sciences* (pp. 381–386). New York: Macmillan.

Koch, P., & Oesterreicher, W. (1994). Funktionale Aspekte der Schriftkultur. In H. Günther, & O. Ludwig, (Eds.), *Writing and its use: An interdisciplinary handbook of international research* (pp. 587–604). Berlin: Mouton de Gruyter.

Labov, W. (1972). *Language in the inner city. Studies in the Black English vernacular.* Philadelphia: University of Pennsylvania Press.

Mair, W. N. (1984). Transferenz oder autonome Bildung? Bemerkungen zum Problem der Partikelverben im Ladinischen, Friulanischen, Italienischen und Französischen. *Zeitschrift für Romanische Philologie, 100,* 408–432.

Mayer, M. (1969). *Frog, where are you?* New York: Dial Press.

Milroy, L. (1992). *Language and social networks.* Oxford, Cambridge, MA: B. Blackwell.

Schwarze, Ch. (1985). "Uscire" e "andare fuori": struttura sintattica e semantica lessicale. In Società Di Linguistica Italiana (Ed.), *Sintassi e Morfologia Della Lingua Italiana D'Uso. Teorie E Applicazioni Dscrittivi* (pp. 355–371). Rome: Bulzoni.

Slobin, D. I. (1996). Two ways to travel: Verbs of motion in English and Spanish. In S. A. Thompson & M. Shibatani (Eds.), *Grammatical constructions: Their form and meaning* (pp. 195–217). Oxford, UK: Oxford University Press.

Slobin, D. I. (2004). The many ways to search for a frog: Linguistic typology and the expression of motion events. In S. Strömqvist & L. Verhoeven (Eds.), *Relating events in narrative: Typological and contextual perspectives* (pp. 219–257). Mahwah, NJ: Lawrence Erlbaum Associates.

Stein, D. (1997). Syntax and varieties. In J. Cheshire & D. Stein (Eds.), *Taming the vernacular: From dialect to written standard language* (pp. 35–50). London: Longman.

Snell-Hornby, M. (1983). *Verb-descriptivity in German and English*. Heidelberg: Carl Winter.

Talmy, L. (2000). *Toward a cognitive semantics: Vol. 2. Typology and process in concept structuring*. Cambridge, MA: The MIT Press.

13

Between Frogs and Black-Winged Monkeys
Orality, Evidentials, and Authorship in Tzotzil (Mayan) Children's Narratives[1]

LOURDES DE LEÓN
Center for Higher Studies in Social Anthropology, Mexico

The expression of experience in linguistic terms constitutes thinking for speaking—a special form of thought that is mobilized for communication [...] in acquiring a native language a child acquires particular ways of thinking for speaking.

Dan I. Slobin (1996, p. 76)

Dan Slobin thinks in multiple languages as he speaks about Turkish, English, Spanish, Russian, or even a Mayan language. His marvelous mind has moved from speaking multilingually to thinking multilingually, filtering knowledge and experience through typologies of space, time, motion, signing, telling. I admire how he bravely challenges his own assumptions as he confronts them with yet another language, and another culture. I thank him for his inquisitive mind, and for his exquisite sensitivity in finding connections among the enormous diversity of languages of the world. In this multilingual dialogue he has created communities of thought across boundaries, languages, and cultures.

The present study is a tribute to Dan from Mayan Tzotzil children from the small village of Nabenchauk, Zinacantán, Chiapas, Mexico via the researcher and author. In the spirit of Dan's intellectual adventures, I dare here to test the use of *Frog, where are you?* as a method to explore narrative development in an oral culture. The exercise brings to the forefront such aspects of telling a story as text, context, and speaker's perspective, therefore highlighting the cultural assumptions of narrative production.

---

[1] I acknowledge the invaluable collaboration of José Apolonio Pérez and the staff and children of the state elementary school of Nabenchauk, Zin, Chiapas, Escuela Belisario Dominguez. I also acknowledge the always generous and loving support from the Vaskis family, especially from my goddaughter Cande (10 years old) who provided marvelous guidance about the ethnography of school children and their narrative life in Tzotzil. This study is part of a larger project, "The development of communicative competence in Tzotzil children," financed by CONACyT (México), Grant No. 42585.
I thank Sue Ervin-Tripp and Nancy Budwig for their thoughtful comments to a previous draft. Any misconceptions or errors remain my own responsibility.

INTRODUCTION

In the last decades, psycholinguists, sociolinguists, and linguistic anthropologists have devoted great attention to exploring children's narrative development.[2] In particular, Slobin's crosslinguistic project has broadened, in important ways, our understanding of the role language typologies play in children's narrative organization and design (Berman & Slobin, 1994; Slobin, 1991, 1996, 2000, 2003, 2004).[3] Berman & Slobin (1994) and associated researchers' comparative project on children's narrative development has brought together the largest set of typologically diverse languages (Bamberg, 1987, 1997a; Strömqvist & Verhoven, 2004). The authors have initially compared narratives produced from the wordless picture book *Frog, where are you?* (Mayer, 1969) in five languages (English, German, Spanish, Turkish, and Hebrew) spoken in culturally comparable urban environments. Gradual inclusion of typologically diverse minority languages from smaller scale cultures around the world (e.g., Australian Aboriginal, Eskimo, Mayan) has opened new questions of enormous theoretical and methodological value (Brown, 2000, 2004; Allen, Crago, & Pesco, 2006; Engberg-Pedersen & Trondhjem, 2004; Strömqvist & Verhoven, 2004; Wilkins, 1997).

The present chapter examines the contrast between elicited Frog Stories versus spontaneous oral stories produced by Tzotzil Mayan children in terms of how they design "real Tzotzil (Mayan)" narratives. Such stories are characterized by the inclusion of evidential particles related with direct and indirect reported speech. In fact, any piece of discourse produced in this oral culture—myth, dreams, gossip, narrative, or everyday conversation—is normally built with these particles (de León, 2000, 2005; Haviland, 1987, 1989, 1995; Laughlin, 1975). This chapter tests the methodological implications of elicitation in an oral culture, looks at the role of evidentials in the construction of narratives in Tzotzil Mayan, and finally evaluates the cultural implications of literacy and schooling in an oral culture.

STUDYING ELICITED NARRATIVES IN AN ORAL CULTURE

The present study was carried out in the hamlet of Nabenchauk, Zinacantán in the Southern state of Chiapas, Mexico, where Tzotzil Mayan is spoken by virtually the entire population. The community has about 3000 inhabitants, but the population of Tzotzil speakers sums up to around 250,000 over the Highlands of Chiapas. Ethnographic and linguistic research in this community has extended for over two decades.

Tzotzil is a mildly agglutinative language with VSO order with roots that are highly productive to derive different classes of words (e.g., verb, adjective, classifiers).

One of the main areas of study conducted by the researcher has dealt with early semantic and syntactic acquisition, as well as children's language socialization (de León, 1998, 1999, 2002, 2005). The present study focuses on the development of narrative abilities in children from 7 to 14 years old. It is based on a cross-sectional design with six children at each age group, and six adults.

The stories were jointly elicited by the researcher and a native male Tzotzil speaker who is a member of the community of study. José Apolonio Pérez is 22 years old, and has worked with some of the interviewed children as a teacher of a literacy project in Tzotzil carried out by an NGO that promotes literacy in the Mayan languages of the Highlands of Chiapas. All stories were elicited in dialogic interaction between the children and Pérez and with the presence and feedback in Tzotzil of the main researcher. Transcription was done by Pérez and jointly checked with him by the main researcher.

---

[2] For studies of narratives and children's discourse in the linguistic anthropology field see Ervin-Tripp and Mitchell-Kernan, 1977; Gumperz and Kyratzis, 2001; Hoyle and Adger 1998; Goodwin, 1990; Labov and Waltetzky 1967; Ochs and Schieffelin, 1979.

[3] See Berman and Verhoeven (2002), Blum-Kulka (2004), and Hickman (1996) for crosslinguistic studies in narrative development.

Methodological and Ethnographic Considerations

Tzotzil Mayan culture is primarily oral; the average amount of schooling for the population is through the early elementary school years and is done entirely in Spanish. Although in the last decade there has been an increasing interest in publications of written Tzotzil texts by native writers belonging to NGOs or to governmental institutions (López Calixto Méndez, 2000; *Sk'op ya'yeej*, 1998; *Snopobil*, 2003; Pérez López, 1998),[4] publications of the Bible (*Xch'ul C'op Jtotic Dios*, n.d.), and academic publications about Tzotzil oral literature (Laughlin, 1975, 1977; Laughlin & Karasik, 1988, 1996), literacy is reduced to a minority of intellectuals, catechists, and writers, and is not generalized as a cultural practice. The average level of elementary studies in the indigenous population is second grade. Furthermore, schooling is mostly in monolingual Spanish, which does not help in developing literacy in the native languages. The main family where the author has carried out ethnographic and linguistic research for over two decades is composed of six adults and four children living in the same household. Out of these 10 family members only two adults (mother and father) went to school up to second grade in the late 1970s. Currently one of four grandchildren attends fifth grade. Books are not read at home, with the exception of the only girl who attends school (de León, 2005). This is the average situation for Zinacantec families.

On the other hand, orality shows high vitality in this community. Children learn the language at home in a predominantly monolingual environment. Discourse genres are prolific from natural conversation, gossip, ritual, healing, old narratives, folktales (Haviland, 1977, 1987, 1989; see Laughlin, 1977; Laughlin & Karasik, 1988, 1996; Gossen, 1974a, 1974b). Narratives normally unfold in dialogic or multiparty interaction in culturally relevant encounters.

In sum, Tzotzil is spoken in everyday community life, with the exception of the school and the clinic, where doctors are Spanish speakers and require translators of Tzotzil. Whereas women are mostly monolingual in this Mayan language, men show some incipient bilingualism because they work in commerce and transportation. However, Tzotzil is mostly spoken at home.

Given the oral background of the community of study, elicitation of narratives with printed stimuli is not culturally natural, and required ethnographic adaptation. For this purpose, three complementary elicitation strategies were combined. After a conversation with each child about his family and everyday activities, we gave the children the Frog Story book to see it page by page, saying that we were going to ask them to tell what happened with the boy and his frog, shown in the book. Then we proceeded to ask him or her to (i) tell the Frog Story from the printed book, (ii) retell the Frog Story without the visual input, (iii) tell a spontaneous narrative based on retelling or on a personal experience.

Elicitation Procedures

Elicitation of the printed book *Frog, where are you?* was done with the format used in previous studies (Bamberg, 1987, 1997b; Berman & Slobin, 1994).[5] We started by asking children and adults to familiarize themselves with the book page by page, and then to tell the story of the boy, his dog, and his frog. The story was produced in dialogic interaction with backchannel turns from the interviewer, following cultural patterns of interaction.[6] After the participants told the elicited story, the interviewer asked them to tell what they remembered of the story without looking at the book. Finally, in order to prepare the children for a spontaneous narrative, we first asked if they wanted to tell a story told by their parents or grandparents. Some of these stories told mainly by elder people

---

[4] There is an ample list of publications in Chiapas indigenous languages of the NGO Sna Jtz'ibajom (The House of the Writer) coordinated by Robert M. Laughlin. The Centro de Estudios de Lenguas y Literaturas Indígenas and the Chiapas UNAM program have also published a large number of books, many of them resulting from state contests to promote writing in the native languages of the state.

[5] The frog-book project resulted in the Berman and Slobin volume (1994) which was based on children's (and adults') tellings of the book *Frog, where are you?* This wordless picture book contains 24 pictures in which a boy and his dog try to find their pet frog, who had run away from home.

[6] See Brown (2004) for a similar technique in neighboring Tzeltal Frog Stories.

are classified as *vo'ne k'op* ('old words') and have a sort of "fable" flavor, for example, why the jaguar got spots, or why the fox is smart, etc. (Laughlin, 1977, 1988, 1996; see Gossen, 1974a, 1974b for neighboring Tzotzil Chamula oral genres). Other stories are about supernatural creatures such as the *j'ik'al* "the black man" (black-winged monkey), a legendary being that scares people in the night and kidnaps women (Lopez Calixto Mendez, 2000; Haviland, n.d.), or the *jmakbe* "the boogie man," who steals and cuts people's heads off in the paths that lead to the woods, among others (see Laughlin & Karasik, 1988, 1996).

The open question for eliciting a spontaneous narrative went like this:[7]

1. ¿mi oy k'usi xa k'an xa lo'ilaj xlo'ilaj atot ame' mi amuk'tot amuk'tame' ta ana? ¿mi oy avayoj li vo'ne lo'iletike?
   Is there any story you would like to talk about, some story you have heard from your father, your mother, your grandfather, your grandmother. Have you heard "old stories"?

For some children this question triggered interest in telling stories they have heard at home; for some others it didn't. So we left the space open to have them talk. We then proceeded with a more specific question related to the supernatural beings of high cultural and social relevance such as the *j'ik'al* "the black man" (black-winged monkey) or the *jmakbe* "the boogie man." Here we asked if they had heard about these beings' appearances in the village.

2. ¿mi oy ava'ioj ali lo'ile iyul la iyilik li jmakbe/li j'ik'ale?
   Have you heard the story that some people (hearsay) saw the boogie man or the black-winged monkey?

This last strategy was used because in preliminary ethnographic research children showed a preference for talking about topics related to scary supernatural beings. Furthermore the main researcher conducted previous ethnographic research at the home of her 10-year-old goddaughter Cande about current home narratives at the time of the research, and school narratives that filtered into home talk, particularly at meal times. Among the main stories told at home during the research period (Oct.–Dec. 2004, Jan.–Dec. 2005) I recorded stories about Zapatistas passing by the village, deaths, thieves, car accidents, dangerous sports (such as jumping rope!), tragedies of countrymen working in the United States, the construction and collapse of a nearby major highway bridge, and stories about various supernatural beings that appeared frequently in everyday life. According to the gossip collected in several households I visited, the *jmakbe* "boogie man," in particular, was recurrently appearing to collect people's heads in the paths that led to the woods, because the "engineers building the highway needed a large collection of human skulls for the bridge." The *j'ik'al* "the black-winged monkey," also showed up on many occasions with several manifestations: sometimes like a huge black hen, some other times like a feathered monkey with wings (López Calixto, Mendez, 2000; de León, 2001, 2005; Haviland, n.d.). In general, scary stories dealing with fearful situations, dangers, and threats to life ("soul loss") were the recurrent ones and were interestingly consistent with the topic of "fear" which is very pervasive in Zinacantec child socialization, and in adult life (de León, 2002, 2005).

At the time of the data collection, one of the favorite stories children brought home from school was the story of an *anima* or dead person's soul (apparently a "dead teacher" who was wandering at school, and was trying to snatch children away).[8] The *"anima"* story was the one that triggered immediate involvement. We elicited it as follows:

---

[7] Tzotzil text is transcribed in practical orthography with symbols that are roughly equivalent to English except that j=/h/, x=/š/, and ' indicates glottal stop.
[8] I asked the school principal about this story and he said that one of the teachers told it to the children to discipline them through fear. However, according to the children, there was apparently another "dead soul" wandering outside the school, a presumed worker who fell into a ditch.

3. *¿mi oy ava'ioj li' ta eskuela ali lo'ile iyul la iyilik li anima?*
   Have you heard here at the school a story, so they say, that some (children) saw an *anima* (soul of dead person)?

Interestingly enough, the choice of a spontaneous story related to a scary personal experience was comparable to the well-known technique used in the study of narratives of personal experience and danger of death (Labov & Waletzky, 1967), which dealt with emotional experience and subjective involvement in the narrative process.

The present study examines two kinds of narratives: elicited Frog Stories, and spontaneous narratives elicited with questions (1) and/or (2), and/or (3). It was decided not to include free Frog Stories based on recollection, since the data turned out to be incomplete due to the fact that some children did not want to repeat the story, because they mostly did picture-description rather than building up a plot or they would just say a couple of sentences. There were some cases, however, where oral summaries were excellent, but that will be the topic of another paper.

CHILDREN'S NARRATIVE DEVELOPMENT: COGNITIVE VS. TYPOLOGICAL ISSUES

One central interest in crosslinguistic research in children's narrative development has been the relationship between typological resources and narrative construction (Berman & Slobin, 1994; Hickmann, 1996). Other studies have looked also at features of narrative design, which apparently respond to factors of cognitive development (McCabe & Peterson, 2001), or of expressions of metalinguistic development (Blum-Kulka, 2004; Hickman, 1993, 1996).

One major finding in Berman and Slobin's (1994) study is that the narratives in English, German, Hebrew, Spanish, and Turkish showed common developmental patterns across the five languages and also many patterns that were characteristic of the individual languages and typological groups of languages: "The exact same scene is described by speakers of all five languages in ways which are peculiarly suited to the perspectives most naturally encoded in each language" (Berman & Slobin, 1994, p. 17). Other studies with the same stimuli have found also a relation between typological patterns and rhetorical style (Brown, 2004; Engberg-Pedersen & Trondhjem, 2004). Regarding narrative development per se, Brown and Slobin found out that there are language-specific interactions between narrative organization and linguistic expression.

Narrative functions that are expressed by obligatory devices all appear early (by about age 3), but even by age 9 children have not fully acquired the narrative style of their language. In examining the evolution of narrative capacities from ages 3 to 12, the authors find a gradual evolution from spatially motivated linking of utterances as picture-by-picture description (3-year-olds) to interclausal sequential chaining of events (most 5-year-olds), increasing clausal chaining of partially elaborated events (most 9-year-olds), and finally a global organization of entire texts around a unified action/structure (some 9-year-olds and adults) (Berman & Slobin, 1994, p. 58).

The authors notice that for young children (3-year-olds) the salience of individual pictured scenes is what counts, rather than a structurally motivated hierarchy of narrative importance. They also note that around 9 years old "[the children's] perception of the narrative task is stereotypical, rather than constituting a vehicle for individual style and self expression" (Berman & Slobin, 1994, p. 69). Regarding adult narratives, the study indicates that there is not a particular type of narrative that can be characterized as an "adult model" (p. 78). Rather, the adults' accounts ranged from complex elaborated narratives that provide fine details of background and attendant circumstances to short, concisely encapsulated, and closely packaged narratives.

Hickman's (1996) work on discourse organization in children's narratives has argued that, even though all children must acquire the devices necessary for the construction of cohesive discourse, they have different problems to solve during the course of acquisition depending on the particular way in which subsystems in their native language are organized.

The present study explores how evidential resources in a Mayan language contribute to discourse cohesion. Although evidentials do not represent "subsystems" in a language but rather a general organizing principle for anchoring the locutionary status of the narrator, they are central in understanding the development of narrative construction in the language of the study.

Evidentials

Tzotzil and neighboring Tzeltal have been the object of several leading studies on discourse genres such as gossip, ritual language, conversation (Haviland, 1977, 1987, 1996), traditional narrative (Laughlin, 1977; Laughlin & Karasik, 1988, 1996), language games (Gossen, 1974a, 1974b; de León, 2005), pragmatics, and interaction (Brown & Levinson, 1978 for Tzeltal).

Studies of Tzotzil conversation and narrative have highlighted the important role evidentials play in this oral culture (Haviland, 1989; Laughlin, 1975). In particular, narratives are characterized by the prolific use of two evidential particles for reported speech: one is *xi* 'say,' which is used for direct reported speech; the other one is the evidential particle *la* 'hearsay,' which is used for indirect quotation (Haviland, 1989; de León, 2000, 2005). Direct quotation is a favored Zinacantec narrative device (Haviland, 1989, 1996, p. 274). Although it is achieved through a large collection of verbs of speaking, the most frequent by far in adult Tzotzil is *xi* 'say' (derived from the highly defective root *chi* 'say').[9] The indirect quotation particle *la* 'hearsay' accompanies declarative sentences to mark them as hearsay, or as propositions not directly attested by the speaker. Laughlin (1975, p. 201) writes that *la* is a "[p]article used primarily in narrative speech—e.g., gossip, folk tales, dreams—indicating object or action not directly perceived, or information for whose veracity the speaker assumes no responsibility." While declarative sentences with *la* are particularly appropriate to recounting myths, the clitic is also central to conversational contexts, used in a variety of functions such as quoting questions, commands, etc. (Haviland, 1995, p. 5).[10] A calculation of the relative frequency of the two particles in two narrative texts of about a total of 500 utterances was around five for indirect report to one for direct report (de León, 2000).

An example of the use of these two particles in a fragment of a folk tale is illustrated in example (1):

(1) **The Rabbit Tale** (Laughlin, 1977)[11]
   1. *Oy **la** j-kot t'ul ta la x-0-k'ot*
      EXIST **EVID** one-CL rabbit REL **EVID** ICP-3B arrive
      y-elk'an lo'bol
      3A-steal fruit
      They say there is a rabbit that goes [to the orchard] to steal fruit [...] (hearsay)
   2. *i-0-tal **la** j-kot 'ok'il.*
      CP-3B-come EVID one-CL coyote
      a coyote came (hearsay)
   3. *mi l-a-tal, ok'il? **xi la** ti t'ul=e*

---

[9] See Haviland (1998, p. 187, fn 12) for a more detailed anaylisis of xi. See Lucy (1993) on the Yucatec Mayan cognate ki, which he defines as a "metapragmatic presentational."

[10] Brown and Levinson (1978) report that the equivalent quotative particle in Tzeltal (lah) indicates that "[the] speaker avoids responsibility for believing in the truth of the utterance [...]. But it may also be used to distance the speaker from a command, by indicating (truly, or as a pretence) that it is a third-party command" (1978, p. 157).

[11] Abbreviations: 1 (first person), 2 (second person), 3 (third person), A (absolutive), ADJ (adjectival predicate), APL (applicative), ART (article), AUX (auxiliary), CL (clitic), CLAS (classifier), CP (completive aspect), DEM: (demonstrative), DIR (directional), E (ergative), EVID (evidential), EXIST (existential), ICP (incompletive aspect), INC (inchoative), INC (inclusive), INT (interrogative), P (positional root), PERF (perfect), PL (plural), PT (particle), RES (resultative), REL (relational).

     INT ICP-2B-come coyote s**ay EVID** ART rabbit=CLIT
     Have you come coyote? says the rabbit (hearsay)
  4. *l-i-tal,* ***xi la****.*
     ICP-1B-come, **say EVID**
     I came, he says (hearsay)
  5. *Aa, k'usi ch-a-pas?* ***xi la*** *ti 'ok'il=e.*
     Ah, what ICP-2A-do say **EVID** ART coyote=CLIT
     Ah, what are you doing? says the coyote (hearsay)
  6. *Mu k'usi ta j-pas,*
     NEG what ICP-1A-do
     I am not doing anything
  7. *yu'un l-i-tzak=e l-i-chuk=e,*
     because CP-2B-grab=CLIT CP-2B-tie=CLIT
     because he [the owner of the fruit] caught me and tied me up
  8. *xi la ti t'ul=e.*
     say **EVID** ART rabbit=CLIT
     says the rabbit (hearsay)
[…]

Jakobson has characterized evidentials on the basis of their property of articulating the speech event, the narrated event, and "the narrated speech event …, namely the alleged source of information about the narrated event" where notions of truth and validity are central (Jakobson, 1970 [1957], p. 4). The notion of reported speech lines up with that of evidential as "source of evidence" in the sense that both suggest forms of embedding speakers or, in other words, of transpositions of one locutionary space onto another one. In Tzotzil, the use of evidentials or reported speech particles involves decisions about allocating authorship, handling evidence, and knowledge through the projection of locutionary spaces.

In de León (2005) I show that acquisition starts around 2 years old with *xi* 'say' coming first followed by *la* 'hearsay.' Very young Tzotzil learners use it to attribute source of information, to transmit it, but also to manipulate it strategically. In this chapter, I will show how these two monosyllabic particles play a central role in the construction of child narratives in Tzotzil, and contrast to their lack of appearance in elicited Frog Stories.

A COMPARISON OF ELICITATION FROM PRINTED STIMULI VS. SPONTANEOUS NARRATIVES

In this section I will present results of the two elicitation tasks in order to compare the difference between elicitation from a printed visual stimuli from the Frog Story book vs. spontaneous narratives about current topics in the children's spontaneous everyday lives. The data are organized in four age groups of six participants each one: Group 1: 7–9 years old, Group 2: 10–11 years old, Group 3: 12–14 years old, Group 4: adults. Each age group had three males and three females.

I will start by showing that the number of clauses in elicited Frog Stories increased gradually by age (see Figure 13.1).

Figure 13.1 also shows that adult stories ranged from 25 to 156 clauses. The lowest number of clauses in one of the adults (25) was similar to the lowest number of clauses for the three children's age groups (N: 21, 30, 30). Figure 13.2 breaks up the number of clauses per adult. As shown, there is a large variation with a mean of 81.83 clauses for the six adult participants.

Berman and Slobin (1994, p. 78) pointed out that in their crosslinguistic study adult Frog Stories varied from short and encapsulated to elaborated and lengthy. The shortest story of participant #2 in Figure 13.2 was actually mere picture-description focused on specific details such as the shape and

182 CROSSLINGUISTIC APPROACHES TO THE PSYCHOLOGY OF LANGUAGE

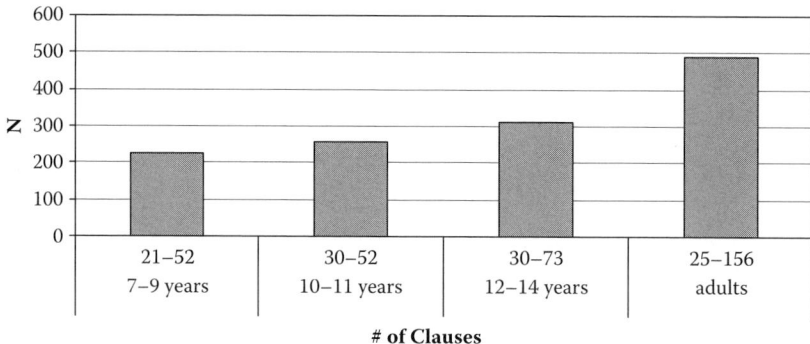

Figure 13.1   Total number of clauses in Tzotzil Frog Stories.

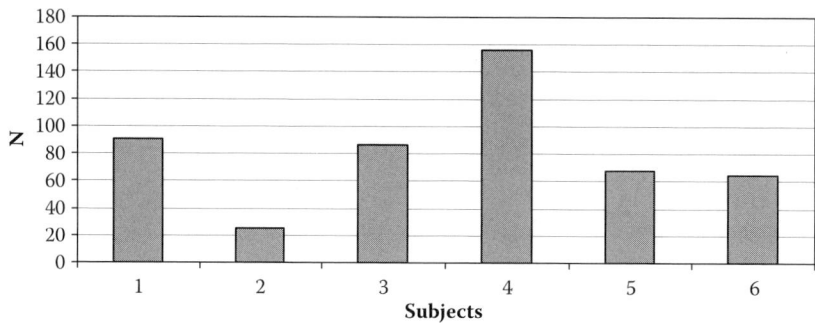

Figure 13.2   Number of clauses in adult Frog Stories.

orientation of the dog's tail, or the orientation of its gaze. Literacy did not play a specific role in the number of clauses per story since there was variation across all our participants. Figure 13.3 shows that our first three adults (1, 2, 3) were illiterate (Adult 1), or quasi-illiterate (Adults 2 and 3 with 1 year of elementary school), adults 3–6 had high school studies (adult 3), or higher education (adults 5 and 6) (see Figure 13.3). Schooling factors for adult participants were not addressed as a variable in the original design of the study, but apparently play some role which poses possible hypotheses that could be addressed in another study. One of these hypotheses suggests that increasing schooling orients the narrators to produce decontextualized stories without the here-and-now anchor provided by the reported speech evidentials persistently present in spontaneous oral narratives.

Figure 13.4 shows that Frog Stories produced in Tzotzil by the children and adults of the study tended to elaborate on picture-description with various degrees of cohesion and clause integration that increased by age.

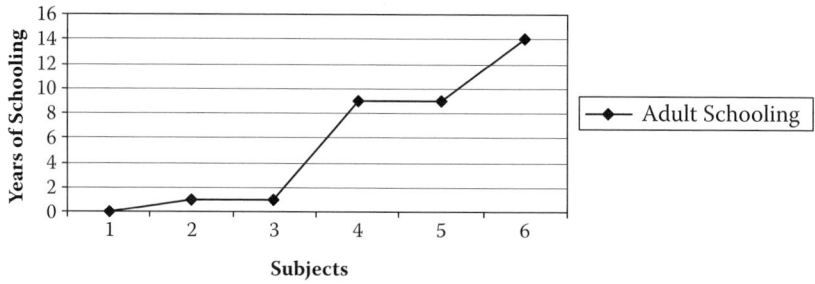

Figure 13.3   Schooling in adult participants.

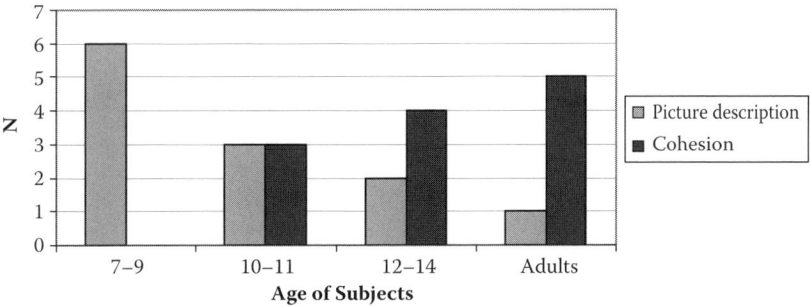

Figure 13.4 Picture description vs. narrative cohesion.

Stories based on picture-description had a rich elaboration of visual details through Tzotzil resources such as positional verbs or adjectives (*patal* "lying down with stretched limbs" (see example 2), *xojol* "inserted in ring like shaped cavity" (see example 3), *nujul* "face down," *tzukul* "upside down"; classifiers (*va'* 'standing on two feet' (example 3), *kot* 'standing on four feet' (see example 3)); directionals (*yalel* "downwards" (see example 2), *muyel* "upwards"), etc.

(2) (Xun Romin)
   te to`ox **pat-al** ta s-ba s-tem li k`ox krem s-k`el-oj
   there still **lie**-ADJ REL 3E-face 3E-bed Dem small boy 3E-see-PERF
   ***yalel**=e*
   downwards=CL
   The boy is there lying down with stretched limbs looking downwards

(3) (Xun Romin)
   *nach'-al ta bentana x-cha`-**va`-al**-ik x-chi`uk j-**kot***
   REL peeking at window 3E-two-**CLAS stand**-ADJ-PL 3E-with one-**CLAS**
   s-tz'i`=e tey **xoj-ol** li limet=e ta s-ni`
   3E-dog=CL there **inserted**-ADJ ART bottle=CL REL 3E-nose
   li tz'i`e v-a`i un
   ART dog=CL 2E-hear PT
   The two standing ones peeking out of the window with one (four-legged) dog, the bottle is inserted (ring-like object) in the dog's nose, do you understand?

The Tzotzil-oriented attention to visual details related to body posture, shape, or motion trajectory produced a range of child and adult "stories" that went from utterances linked by spatial features based on mere picture description to partial elaboration of events through clausal chaining with scant global integration, with one or two exceptions in the children's studies. In sum, narrative flow did not progressively increase by age, and was not present in all of the adults' stories (see Figure 13.4). Berman and Slobin (1994, p. 58) found that picture description was a characteristic of the stories produced by 3-year-olds of their study and that increasing clausal chaining and partial elaboration of events was present in most of the 9-year-olds. They noticed that the global organization of entire texts around a unified action/structure was already present in some 9-year-olds and in adults (1994, p. 58). Our data show that picture-description in our elicited stories is present in all the participants of the study. It is present in all stories of children from 7 to 9 years old and decreases gradually by age. One adult story consisted of only picture-description. It should be mentioned that those participants who did not focus exclusively on picture-description produced cohesive stories at some level of event integration, but global integration was not the norm.

In this chapter, cohesion is measured in terms of narrative flow and event integration. Within "cohesive" stories those that achieved a level of global integration were produced with the evidential *la* "hearsay," or were produced by two bilingual participants who did not use the evidential.

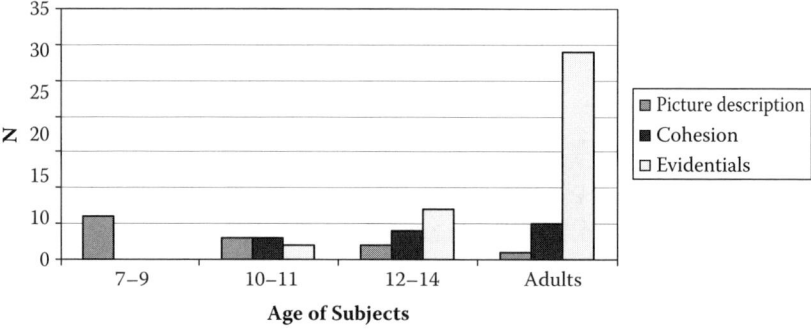

Figure 13.5 Cohesion and the use of the evidential *la* (hearsay).

Participants who used the evidential were one child in the 10–11-year-old age group, one child in the 12–14 age group, and one adult. Figure 13.5 shows the absolute number of uses of *la* 'hearsay' by these participants.

Interestingly enough, the stories with *la* 'hearsay' were overheard by these three narrators before they produced their own elicited story. By far, the best child story was produced by a 10-year-old child and her illiterate aunt who overheard the story from another family member, having been previously familiarized with the book. Example (4), shows a fragment of a Frog Story told by this 10-year-old girl (Cande). She started the first scene of her story from the back cover picture of the book where the boy appears calling his frog standing on a log. Here she starts by linking through inference this scene with the central theme of story "the lost frog," (line 1) inserting the evidential *la* "hearsay." She then links it with the first scene (line 2) saying the boy "has already found the frog," and then elaborates on the frog as going away again.

(4) Cande (10 years old: third grade)
   1. *li k'ox krem=e muy=em ta te' xchi'uk j-kot s-ts'i'*
      DET small boy=CL ascend-PERF REL tree with one-CLAS 3E-dog
      *yu' **la** ch'aval y-amuch, chapta xa li amuch=e*
      because **EVID** NEG 3E-frog shout already DET frog=CL
      The little boy climbed the tree with his dog because his frog was not there, he calls the frog (hearsay)
   2. *i-s-ta xa li y-amuch te xa s-tik'-oj*
      CP-3E-seek already DET 3E-frog LOC already 3E-put_in-PERF REL
      ta yav,
      container
      He has already found the frog. He (the frog) is already inserted in the container
   3. *ta s-k'el-ik xchi'uk s-tz'i*
      REL 3E-look-PL with 3E-dog
      and (the boy) looks at it with his dog
   4. *li k'ox krem=e vay-em xa xchi'uk s-tz'i amuch=e ta x-lok' xa*
      ART-small boy=CL sleep-PERF already with 3E-dog frog=CL REL 3E-go_out already
      The little boy is already asleep with his dog, the frog has already gone out

In her oral retelling of the story she inserts the evidential *la* "hearsay" in every clause. Her oral summary is perfectly cohesive and flows as freely as any Tzotzil spontaneous narrative.

(5) Oral summary of Frog Story by Cande
   1. *ali jun k'ox kreme oy **la** i-0-ch'ay, ali oy to'ox*

Hmm one small boy EXIST **EVID** ICP-3B-lose, hmm EXIST then
Hmm, there is a little boy that got lost (hearsay)
2. *li y-amuch s-tik'-oj la ta k'ox plastiko un av-a'i-un*
ART 3E-frog 3E-insert-PERF EVID REL small plastic PT 2E-hear -PT
His frog was inserted in the small plastic container (hearsay), do you understand?
3. *i-0-lok' la ech'el li amuch un=e (ch)ba s-ta*
ICP-go_out **EVID** DIR ART frog PT=CLIT ICP-AUX 3E-find
The frog went out (hearsay) to look for
4. *la x-chi'il-tak un*
EVID 3E-friends-PL PT
his friends (hearsay)

In example (6) I present a fragment of Cande's illiterate aunt telling the Frog Story in a totally free and integrated manner. The hearsay evidential provides an epistemic stance: the aunt comments upon emotional states of the protagonists; she also chains clauses with connectives, and achieves a global integration of the story. This story was told in interactive dialogue with her nephew, who had told it before she did.

(6) Fragment of Frog Story told by Cande's illiterate aunt (PV)
1. *k-al-tik ali oy la ali jun k'ox krem*
1B-say-PL hmm EXIST **EVID** hmm one small boy
Let's say that there is small boy (hearsay)
2. *te la te la vay-em*
DEM **EVID** DEM **EVID** dormir-PERF
sleeping there (hearsay)
3. *te la ali .ali jun la y-o`on vay-em-ik*
DEM **EVID** hmm hmm one **EVID** 3A-heart sleep-PERF-PL
ta s-tem
REL 3E-bed
There they say that they happily sleep in their bed (hearsay)
4. *pero ali xchi`uk la j-kot amuch*
But hmm with **EVID** one-CLAS frog
but with his frog (hearsay)
5. *ti amuch=e te la te la s-jun y-o`on*
ART frog=CLIT DEM **EVID** DEM **EVID** 3E-one 3A-heart
That frog is happy (hearsay)
6. *s-0-pat-an-oj ta s-ba s-tem*
ICP-3A-stand -PERF REL 3A-face 3A-bed
He (the frog) is standing (with stretched limbs) on the bed
7. *te i-0-vay-ik to`ox*
DEM CP-3B-sleep-PL still
There they were still sleeping
8. *lajeltza k'alal ali i-0-yul x-ch'ulel-ik=e*
finally when hmm ICP-3B-arrive 3A-soul –PL=CLIT
ch'abal xa amuch
no PT frog
finally when they woke up, the frog is not there anymore
9. *lok'-em xa ech'el*
go out-PERF already DIR
She went out.

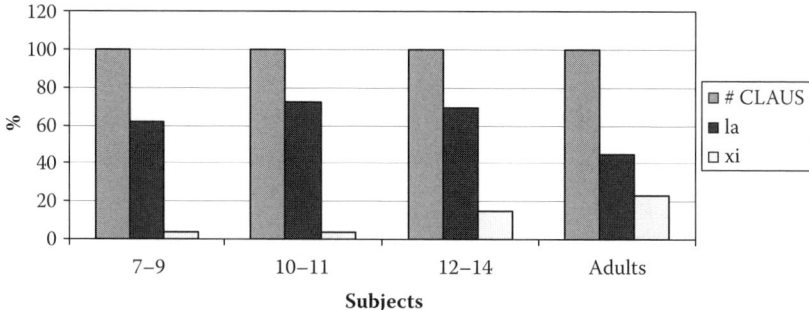

Figure 13.6 Evidentials in spontaneous narratives.

As we see there is repetition and elaboration of the emotional state of the boy and the frog as "being happy." The connective *lajeltza* "finally" and *k'alal* "when" (line 8) guides the narrative flow into the next event where the narrator chains event 1 (boy and frog sleeping) with event 2 (frog disappearing) after they both "wake up" ("their soul arrives"). We see here the chaining of clauses through the connective and a positioning of the narrator as the subjective author providing feelings and actions of the protagonists as hearsay. The story has an apparent "collective" author that brings the flavor of Tzotzil orality through eight tokens of the hearsay evidential. The oral texture of this story takes us to the spontaneous narratives that look very similar to this one.

All the spontaneous narratives produced by the participants of the study consistently had the evidential *la* "hearsay," with increasing use by age of the direct report *xi* "X says." Overall, results indicate that a "true Tzotzil narrative" requires, by design, the use of the evidential particles. The evidentials go along with cohesive discourse that flows through connectives and temporal and spatial integration. Figure 13.6 shows that all spontaneous "true Tzotzil stories" had the two reported speech evidentials. The data show that for every 100 clauses produced in each age group the evidential *la* "hearsay" is present in a rate over 60% for children and around 42% for adults. In their spontaneous narratives children are clearly behaving as true Tzotzil narrators in all age groups. It is interesting that children tend to produce a higher rate of the hearsay evidentials than adults. This may reveal their own epistemic stance toward the information presented in the narration as told by someone else. Authorship is presented as reporting what others said, which makes the narration look more legitimate, although the narrator is ultimately the author. The evidential for reported speech *xi* "X says" is used increasingly by each age group. Adult narratives have it in a rate of almost two hearsay particles for one direct report evidential.

Among spontaneous narratives, a popular one was about the supernatural being *j'ik'al* "the black-winged monkey.' There were several versions of it. In example (7) I present a fragment from a 10-year-old:

(7)
1. *s-0-bon-oj* **la** *sat jun vinik xi-ik k-a'i,*
   ICP-3E-paint-PERF **EVID** FACE one man say-PL 1A-heard
2. *x-chi'uk* **la** *y-ak'-oj-be k'uk'um kaxlan k'usi-tik, oy* **la**
   3E-with **EVID** 3E-give -PERF-APL feather hen what-PL EXIST **EVID**
3. *oy* **la** *s-k'uk'um kaxlan ta sat.*
   EXIST **EVID** 3E-feather hen REL face
   They say that a man painted his face, I heard them say it. They also say that he put on hen's feathers and other things, I heard people saying it, they also say that he had hen's feathers on his face.

Here the boy is apparently portraying a "fake" *j'ik'al* who paints his face and puts hen's feathers on his body and face. His use of the two evidentials attributes the information to others in a locutionary shift that is more of a strategy that allows space for authorship. It is clear that this is his own version. A similar strategic use of the evidential is presented in de León (2005) in a story produced dialogically with the author by Cande at the age of 4. The child is reporting the appearance of a *j'ik'al* in her house. A fragment is presented in (8).

(8) Cande (4 years old) retells the *j'ik'al* appearance at home
1. Cande; oy xk'ojk'on li' ta yutnae
   'You can hear the knocking inside the house.'
2. i' va'i ta yut na yu'un xa me j'ik'alun
   'It stood up there and then it turned into the black creature.'
   […]
3. LL; mi k'ux'elan li sate?
   'How do his eyes look?'
4. Cande; solel **la** ik'
   'They say that they are really black.'
5. LL; mi oy yok
   'Does it have feet?'
6. Cande; oy **la** a'a
   'It has indeed, so they say.'
   ali xonobe li' **la** k'alal li xonobe
   'His shoes go up to here.'
   [she shows a gesture by her knee]
   […]

The child goes on to elaborate the way the winged creature knocked at the door and entered laughing into the house. Although the incident itself was 'true' and intensely commented on by the family, she 'appropriated' it through her own story. I later showed her father the video recording of the story telling. He was a bit uneasy, but also very surprised and excited by the child's production. He pointed out that nobody had portrayed the *j'ik'al* as she did. From the point of view of the structure of the text, the child is skillfully transposing different authors (other quoted "tellers") through the use of the evidential *la* 'hearsay,' and *xi* (say); this makes her story an apparently collective enterprise, although she is the ultimate author.

By contrast, constructing a narrative out of a printed stimulus in this oral culture has varied outcomes depending on having overheard it before telling it, or having some literacy or schooling background. Stories of schooled narrators lacked the evidential and, although rich in visual detail, did not really achieve a global integration. Only bilingual schooled narrators produced a cohesive story, but without the evidential. Interestingly enough, their stories used, to a lesser degree than monolingual Tzotzil speakers, some Tzotzil expressive resources provided by the grammar of this Mayan language such as positional verbs (*xoj*: with head stuck in ring-like container (head of dog stuck in container), *patal*: lying with legs stretched forward (dog lying on bed)) or directionals to indicate motion trajectory. This was an unexpected finding and obviously begs for future attention.

CONCLUSIONS

Studies of narrative development have been traditionally done in cultures that are highly literate. Comparative studies that strive for crosslinguistic comparison depend on standard visual stimuli (printed or videotaped) that allows for control over cross-sectional data. The present study is framed within the same concern. It offers important crosslinguistic information about expressive resources in a Mayan language. Its value lies in directing our attention to the cultural context of the language being studied, providing critical information about aspects that contribute to methodological adequacy. It also brings to the surface unforeseen factors that contribute to defining a "true story" in terms of cultural relevance.

Orality is a dominant mode in Tzotzil, and evidentials are at its core. In reviewing published stories written by native Tzotzil writers we note that the reported speech evidentials presented here are not suppressed from the written version (de León, 2000; Lopez Calixto Méndez, 2000; *Sk'op ya'yeej Sna Jtzi'bajom*, 1998). In spite of this marked tendency, the study also reveals that literacy, bilingualism, and schooling can permeate ways of designing a story: decontextualization and displacement of the voice of the narrator as separated from the author. This effect can produce a range of results that go from picture-description to partial integration. Truly good stories were anchored in the here-and-now through epistemic resources and reported as heard in the oral texture of collective discourse.

The study also reveals that the notion of a book as a source for story telling is also a cultural artifact. It is of great interest, for educational purposes, to think about what schoolbooks offer to the children of the study. We certainly see that books are not culturally integrated into everyday discursive practices, and they don't trigger any specific "school register" (see Cazden, 1994; Michaels, 1991; Wolf, 1985). This is not surprising since schooling is entirely in Spanish in this community and there is no home literacy. In spite of achieving some level of literacy in Spanish, the children do not give indications of taking a cognitive metalinguistic leap that involves comprehension and production. Printed images in this community do not necessarily connect with the notion of "story" in literate cultures.

Several authors have argued that a central component of later language development is the attainment of literacy: "Thus, there is an ongoing, cyclical relationship between literacy and later language development, a process that is heavily supported by metalinguistic competence" (Nippold, 2004, p. 6). In this respect, Blum-Kulka notices that "[o]ral narratives have two essential features that make them crucial to the development of pragmatic competencies: as prime and early examples of connected discourse, linked to literate uses of language, and as social and cultural enactments of the narrative paradigm" (Blum-Kulka, 2004, p. 195; Bruner, 1986). This point seems to be unquestionable in literate cultures. However, the data presented here suggest that the apparent dependent link between literacy and later language development is not universal. Metalinguistic competence is certainly present in language development in Tzotzil but not directly or necessarily associated with literacy.

Data from the spontaneous narratives offered a clear picture of the development of evidentials as central in narrative development. In de León (2005), I show that children as young as 2 years old learn to frame reported speech with the evidential *xi* "X says," and then acquire *la* "hearsay." The data presented here show increasing use of both evidentials in the children's narratives. Hickman (1993, 1996, p. 207) considers the major developmental feature of speech representation to be the ways in which children learn to transform dialogues into narrative texts. She finds that children younger than 7 years old acquire resources for framing dialogue. Blum-Kulka (2004) also establishes a connection between framed speech and the transition from utterance to text: "[t]he case of speech representation further illustrates how the study of specific discursive phenomena may cut across the dividing lines of 'conversational' versus 'discursive literary skills'" (2004, p. 209). This process is indeed present in children's narrative development in Tzotzil, but only in the oral mode.

The elicitation of Frog Stories in Tzotzil confirms Slobin's slogan about "thinking for speaking" in an interesting way. Our illiterate participants were thinking as a result of the visual stimuli, making prolific use of spatial resources in their narratives, but "thinking and talking for descriptive purposes." They were also suppressing the evidentials, and this was a central piece of information in the study. This suppression reveals a way of "thinking for speaking," in this case "thinking for telling or describing in a specific mode." This leads us to a finer view of "speaking" which unpacks cultural assumptions that go with ways of thinking. Along this line, Slobin has recently expressed how culture permeates language: "culture and language co-construct each other in ongoing processes of speaking and engaging in cultural practices" (Slobin, 2003, p. 187).

In examining the development of narrative in an illiterate culture speaking a non-European language I have encountered two crucial issues in the study of crosslinguistic acquisition in cross-cultural contexts: cultural assumptions about methodologies and about language theories. The present study touches an important central question in the study of language acquisition: the inherently interactional context in which a language is learned and the fact that grammar surfaces in everyday discourse. In a recent paper, Küntay and Slobin (2002) eloquently bring this point upfront, highlighting several grammatical categories that can only be learned in discursive interaction, among them, evidentials:

> It is trivially obvious that linguistic categories such as case-marking, verbal inflections, word order, and evidentiality do not present themselves transparently to the child learner of a language. Both intuitively, and theoretically from a discourse-functional theoretical approach to language development (Budwig, 1995; Clancy, in press; DuBois, 2002), all these interesting components of the grammatical code come to the young learner in the give and take of everyday life, mostly embedded in early adult-child discursive interaction. However, as in most child language research, these "real" interactive events get reduced to textual transcripts that only represent interaction "in vitro." [...] "The tendency to decontextualize textual content or linguistic forms from discursive interactions troubles the entire field of child language, but it is accentuated in the study of the acquisition of non-Indo-European languages that have more recently come to the foreground of the field [...]." (Küntay & Slobin, 2002, p. 5)

Along this line, Bamberg (1997b, this volume) has argued that interactional "positioning" is central to narrative construction. Bamberg considers that the positioning of the narrator unites the pragmatics of narrating with the semantic organization of the narrative. "Positioning analysis may possibly best be understood as granting more centrality to the speaker active engagement in the construction process of narratives" (Bamberg, 1997b, p. 34; see also Wortham, 2000). The data presented here show that in a language like Tzotzil evidential particles grammaticize the positioning of the speaker in the process of constructing a narrative, which is interesting from the perspective of narrative production, in general.

The present study brings together several of Dan Slobin's visionary concerns about crosslinguistic acquisition. One of them is to examine a new language spoken by a small-scale culture under the light of major crosslinguistic endeavours about narrative development (Berman & Slobin, 1994; Strömqvist & Verhoven, 2004). Using a standardized method of elicitation I was able to confirm, by contrast, the nature of a "true narrative" in Tzotzil. Spontaneous narratives show how Tzotzil evidentials project locutionary spaces that emerge from situated, interactional oral discourse. By contrast, narratives stemming from printed stimuli do not, in general, achieve a full integration, but provide rich data about the grammar of space and time in this language. We encounter here a finer view of what "thinking for speaking" means under the light of a non-urban, small-scale culture as it uncovers the cultural implications of literacy and schooling. This is undoubtedly another central concern in Slobin's work which can be reformulated, in light of the present study, as "thinking for speaking in cultural modes."

REFERENCES

Allen, S. E. M., Crago, M. B., & Pesco, D. (2006). The effect of majority language exposure on minority language skills: The case of Inuktitut. *International Journal of Bilingual Education and Bilingualism*, 9(5), 578–596.

Bamberg, M. (1987). *The acquisition of narratives: Learning to use language*. Berlin: Mouton de Gruyter.

Bamberg, M. (1997a). A constructivist approach to narrative development. In M. Bamberg (Ed.), *Narrative development—Six approaches* (pp. 89–132). Mahwah, NJ: Lawrence Erlbaum Associates.

Bamberg, M. (1997b). Positioning between structure and performance. *Journal of Narrative and Life History*, 7(1–4), 335–342.

Bamberg, M. (this volume). Sequencing events in time or sequencing events in story-telling? From cognition to discourse—with frogs paving the way.

Berman, R. (2004). Between emergence and mastery. The long developmental route of language acquisition. In R. A. Berman, (Ed.), *Language development across childhood and adolescence* (pp. 9–34). Amsterdam/Philadelphia: John Benjamins.

Berman, R. A., & Slobin, D. I. (Eds.). (1994). *Relating events in narrative*. Hillsdale, NJ: Lawrence Erlbaum Associates.

Berman, R. A., & Verhoeven, L. (Eds.). (2002). Cross-linguistic perspectives on the development of text production abilities in speech and writing. *Written languages and literacy,* (5, Parts 1 and 2 (special issue), 1–44.

Blum-Kulka, S. (2004). The role of peer interaction in later pragmatic development. The case of speech representation. In R. A. Berman (Ed.), *Language development across childhood and adolescence* (pp. 191–210). Amsterdam/Philadelphia: John Benjamins.

Brown, P. (2000). 'He descended legs-upwards': Position and motion in Tzeltal frog stories. In E. Clark (Ed.), *Proceedings of the 30th Stanford Child Language Forum, 30,* 67–75. Stanford: CSLI.

Brown, P. (2004). Position and motion in Tzeltal frog stories: The acquisition of narrative style. In S. Strömqvist & L. Verhoeven, (Eds.), *Relating events in narrative: Typological and contextual perspectives* (pp. 37–57). Mahwah, NJ: Lawrence Erlbaum Associates.

Brown, P., & Levinson S. (1978). Universals in language usage: Politeness phenomena. In E. N. Goody (Ed.), *Questions and politeness* (pp. 55–289). Cambridge, UK: Cambridge University Press.

Bruner, J. (1986). *Actual minds, possible worlds.* Cambridge, MA: Harvard University Press.

Budwig, N. (1995). *A developmental-functionalist approach to child language.* Mahwah, NJ: Lawrence Erlbaum Associates.

Cazden, C. (1994). Situational variation in children's language revisited. In Biber D. & Finegan E. (Eds.), *Sociolinguistic perspectives on register* (pp. 277–293). New York: Oxford University Press.

Clancy, P. M. (2003). The lexicon in interaction: Developmental origins of preferred argument structure. In J. Du Bois, L. Kumpf, W. Ashby (Eds.), *Preferred argument structure: Grammar as architecture for function* (pp. 81–108). Amsterdam/Philadelphia: John Benjamins.

Cook-Gumperz, J., & Kyratzis, A. (2001). Child discourse. In D. Shiffrin, D. Tannen, & E. H. Hamilton (Eds.), *The handbook of discourse analysis.* Malden, MA: Blackwell.

de León, L. (1998). The emergent participant: Interactive patterns of socialization of Tzotzil (Mayan) children. *Journal of Linguistic Anthropology, 8*(2), 131–161.

de León, L. (1999). Verb roots and caregiver speech in Tzotzil Mayan acquisition. In L. Michaelis & B. Fox (Eds.), *Language, cognition, and function.* Stanford: Stanford Center for Language and Information.

de León, L. (2000). Detrás del texto. Estudio introductorio a López Calixto Méndez Mariano (pp. xi–xxv). *El Sombrerón: Jsemet Pixol.* San Cristóbal de las Casas, Chis: PROIMMSE-UNAM.

de León, L. (2001). Finding the richest path: The role of language and cognition in the acquisition of vertical path by Tzotzil (Mayan) children. In M. Bowerman & S. Levinson (Eds.), *Conceptual development and language acquisition.* Cambridge, UK: Cambridge University Press.

de León, L. (2002). El miedo y el espacio en la socialización infantil zinacanteca. In A. Breton, A, M. Becquelin, & M. H. Ruz, (Eds.), *Los espacios mayas: usos, representaciones, creencias* (pp. 505–539). México, Universidad Nacional Autónoma de México (Centro de Estudios Mayas) / Centro Francés de Estudios Mexicanos y Centroamericanos.

de León, L. (2005). *La llegada del alma: Lenguaje, infancia y socialización entre los mayas de Zinacantan.* México: Instituto Nacional de Antropología e Historia, CONACULTA, CIESAS.

de León, L. (2007). Parallelism, metalinguistic play, and the interactive emergence of Tzotzil (Mayan) siblings' culture. *Research on Language and Social Interaction 40*(4). Special issue edited by M. H. Goodwin, & A. Kyratzis.

Du Bois, J. W. (2002). Discourse and grammar. In M. Tomasello (Ed.). *The new psychology of language: Vol. 2. Cognitive and functional approaches to language structure* (pp. 47–87). Mahwah, NJ: Lawrence Erlbaum Associates.

Engberg-Pedersen, E., & Trondhjem, F. B. (2004). Focus on action in motion descriptions: The case of West Greenlandic. In S. Strömqvist & L. Verhoveven (Eds.), *Relating events in narrative* (Vol. 2, pp. 59–88). Mahwah, NJ: Lawrence Erlbaum Associates.

Ervin-Tripp, S., & Mitchell-Kernan, C. (1977). *Children's discourse.* New York: Academic Press.

Goodwin, M. H. (1990). *He-said-she-said. Talk as social organization among Black children.* Bloomington: Indiana University Press.

Gossen, G. (1974a). To speak with a heated heart: Chamula canons of style and good performance. In R. Bauman & J. Sherzer (Eds.), *Explorations in the ethnography of speaking* (pp. 389–413). Cambridge, UK: Cambridge University Press.

Gossen, G. (1974b). *Chamulas in the world of the sun: Time and space in a Maya oral tradition.* Cambridge, MA: Harvard University Press.
Halliday, M. A. K., & Hasan, R. (1976). *Cohesion in English.* London: Longman.
Haviland, J. B. (1977). *Gossip, reputation and knowledge.* Chicago: University of Chicago Press.
Haviland, J. B. (1987). Fighting words: evidential particles, affect and argument. *Proceedings of the 13th annual meeting of the Berkeley Linguistics Society.*
Haviland, J. B. (1989). Sure, sure: Evidence and affect. *Text, 9*(1), 27–68.
Haviland, J. B. (1995). Evidentials in Tzotzil conversation. "CONVERS" symposium, LSA Linguistic Institute, Albuquerque.
Haviland, J. B. (1996). Text from talk in Tzotzil. In M. Silverstein & G. Urban, (Eds.), *Natural histories of discourse* (pp. 45–80). Chicago: University of Chicago Press.
Haviland, J. B. (n.d.). "El Negro Cimarrón." Videotaped story of the *J'ik'al* ("Black winged-monkey") in http://anthro.ucsd.edu/~jhaviland/ link to Archivo de Lenguas de Chiapas, Seres sobrenaturales.
Haviland, J. B. (1977). *Gossip, reputation and knowledge.* Chicago: University of Chicago Press.
Hickman, M. (1993). The boundaries of reported speech in narrative discourse: Some developmental aspects. In J. Lucy (Ed.), *Reflexive language* (pp. 63–88). New York: Cambridge University Press.
Hickman, M. (1996). Discourse organization and the development of reference to person, space, and time. In P. Fletcher & B. MacWhinney (Eds.), *The handbook of child language* (pp. 194–218). Oxford: Blackwell Publishers.
Hoyle, S. & Adger, C. T. (1998). *Kids talk: Strategic language use in later childhood.* New York: Oxford University Press.
Jakobson, R. (1970) [1957]. Shifters, verbal categories, and the Russian verb. In R. Jakobson, *Selected writings: Vol. 2. Word and language* (pp. 130–147). The Hague: Mouton.
Kernan, K. T. (1977). Semantic and expressive elaboration in children's narratives. In S. Ervin-Tripp & C. Mitchell-Kernan (Eds.), *Child discourse* (pp. 91–102). New York: Academic Press.
Küntay, A., & Slobin, D. I. (2002). Putting interaction back into child language: Examples from Turkish. *Psychology of Language and Communication, 6,* 5–14.
Labov, W. (1972a). *Language in the inner city.* Philadelphia: University of Pennsylvania Press.
Labov, W. (1972b). *Sociolinguistic patterns.* Philadelphia: University of Pennsylvania Press.
Labov, W., & Waletzky J. (1967). Narrative analysis: Oral versions of personal experience. In J. Helm (Ed.), *Essays on the verbal and the visual arts* (pp. 12–44). Seattle: University of Washington Press.
Laughlin, R. (1975). *The great Tzotzil dictionary of San Lorenzo Zinacantán.* Washington, DC: Smithsonian Institution Press.
Laughlin, R. (1977). *Of cabbages and kings: Tales from Zinacantan.* Smithsonian Contributions to Anthropology No. 3. Washington, DC: Smithsonian Institution Press.
Laughlin, R. M., & Karasik, C. (Eds.) (1988). *People of the bat: Mayan tales and dreams from Zinacantan.* Washington, DC: Smithsonian Institution Press.
Laughlin, R. M., & Karasik, C. (Ed.), (1996). *Mayan tales from Zinacantan: Dreams and stories from the people of the bat.* Washington, DC: Smithsonian Institution Press.
López Calixto Méndez, M. (2000). *El sombrerón: Jsemet Pixol.* San Cristóbal de las Casas, Chiapas: PROIMMSE-UNAM.
Lucy, J. A. (1993). Metapragmatic presentationals: Reporting speech with quotatives in Yucatec Maya. In J. A. Lucy (Ed.), *Reflexive language.* (pp. 91–125). Cambridge, UK: Cambridge University Press.
Mayer, M. (1969). *Frog, where are you?* New York: Dial.
McCabe, A. & Peterson, C. (Eds.) (2001). *Developing narrative structure.* Mahwah, NJ: Lawrence Erlbaum Associates.
Michaels, S. (1991). The dismantling of narrative. In C. Peterson & A. McCabe (Eds.), *Developing narrative structure* (pp. 303–350). Mahwah, NJ: Lawrence Erlbaum Associates.
Nippold, M. A. (2004). Research on later language development: International perspectives. In R. Berman (Ed.), *Language development across childhood and adolescence* (pp. 1–8). Amsterdam/Philadelphia: John Benjamins.
Ochs, E., & Schieffelin, B. (1979). *Developmental pragmatics.* New York: Academic Press.
Pérez López, E. (1998). *El pájaro alferez: Alteres: te'tikal mut.* México: Instituto Nacional Indigenista.
Romaine, S. (1984). *The language of children and adolescents.* New York: Basil Blackwell.
Sk'op ya'yeej Sna Jtzi'bajom: Cuentos de Sna Jtz'ibajom. (1998). Mexico: Instituto Nacional Indigenista.
Slobin, D. I. (1985). Why study language crosslinguistically? In D. I. Slobin (Ed.), *The crosslinguistic study of language acquisition: Vol. 1. The data* (pp. 3–24). Hillsdale, NJ: Lawrence Erlbaum Associates.

Slobin, D. I. (1991). Learning to think for speaking: Native language, cognition, and rhetorical style. *Pragmatics 1*, 7–26.

Slobin, D. I. (1996). From 'thought and language' to 'thinking for speaking.' In J. Gumperz & S. C. Levinson (Eds.), *Rethinking linguistic relativity* (pp. 70–96). Cambridge, UK: Cambridge University Press.

Slobin, D. I. (2000). Verbalized events. A dynamic approach to linguistic relativity and determinism. In S. Dins Niemeier & R. Dirven (Eds.), *Evidence for linguistic relativity*. (Vol. 198) CILT. Amsterdam/Philadelphia: John Benjamins.

Slobin, D. I. (2003). Language and thought online: Cognitive consequences of linguistic relativity. In D. Gentner & S. Goldin-Meadow (Eds.), *Language in mind: Advances in the investigation of language and thought* (pp. 157–191). Cambridge, MA: The MIT Press.

Slobin, D. I. (2004). The many ways to search for a frog: Linguistic typology and the expression of motion events. In S. Strömqvist & L. Verhoeven (Eds.), *Relating events in narrative: Vol. 2. Typological and contextual perspectives* (pp. 219–257). Mahwah, NJ: Lawrence Erlbaum Associates.

Snopobil yu'un ololetik ta tsotsil. Creacion de niños tsotsiles (Chamula y Zinacantán) (2003). México: CONACULTA.

Strömqvist, S., & Verhoeven, L. (Eds.) (2004). *Relating events in narrative* (Vol. 2). Mahwah, NJ: Lawrence Erlbaum Associates.

Wilkins, D. P. (1997). The verbalization of motion events in Arrernte (Central Australia). In E. Clark (Ed.), *Proceedings of the 28th annual Child Language Research Forum* (pp. 295–308). Stanford: CSLI.

Wolf, D. P. (1985). Ways of telling: Text repertoires in elementary school children. *Journal of Education, 167*, 71–87.

Wortham, S. (2000). Interactional positioning and narrative self-construction. In M. Bamberg & A. McCabe (Eds.). *Narrative Inquiry 10*(1), 157–184.

Xch'ul C'op Jtotic Dios—Santa Biblia, Biblia en Tzotzil de Chenalho (n.d.). Traducción ecuménica: Católicos-Presbiterianos. México: Sociedad Bíblica de México.

14

Learning to Express Motion in Narratives by Mandarin-Speaking Children[1]

JIANSHENG GUO
California State University, East Bay

LIANG CHEN
The University of Georgia

[L]inguistic patterns don't occur in the abstract. They arise in the course of language in use.

Dan I. Slobin (2004, p. 253)

When I (Jiansheng Guo)[2] first went from China to Berkeley in 1986 to do my graduate studies in language acquisition, I was overwhelmed by Dan's enthusiastic energy, charismatic warmth, expansive knowledge, and capacious heart and mind. His sharp insights and never-ending interest in a wide range of intellectual issues across many disciplines were contagious, and forever exciting and stimulating. Dan consistently shows his students his trade-mark intellectual style by examining the issue from multiple directions and dimensions. He always approaches the understanding of language dialectically from both static and dynamic perspectives, never separating language use and language structure. He believes that "One cannot separate a theory of language *change* from a theory of language *structure*" (Slobin, 1977, p. 186). He begins with the research question about the universal character of language in language acquisition, but he addresses the issue ingeniously, by looking at the vast variations of languages and the dynamic nuances in language change and development. A philosophical and dialectical remark of his struck me in my first year at Berkeley, and has been engraved in my mind ever since: "In a remarkable way, language maintains a universal character across all of these continuing changes, so that the more it changes, the more

---

[1] Data transcription was supported by internal research grants to the first author from Victoria University of Wellington, New Zealand, and California State University, East Bay. We are grateful to Jianhua Yang from the Chinese National Institute of Educational Research for help with data collection, and to the teachers, children, and college students in Beijing for participating in the research. We also thank Katie Coleman from the University of Georgia for proofreading and language comments and Susan Ervin-Tripp and Nancy Budwig for their very helpful editorial comments that make the chapter more readable. The remaining errors and oversights, of course, are entirely ours.

[2] The beginning personal paragraph is written in the voice of the first author Jiansheng Guo.

sure we can be of what it is" (Slobin, 1977, p. 186). This motto has since inspired me to examine the complex and dynamic nature of any ostensibly simple and static phenomenon.

THEORETICAL BACKGROUND AND FOCUS OF THE STUDY

Thinking for Speaking

Slobin's dialectical approach to language has led him to develop one of his current major theoretical positions concerning the psychology of language, the hypothesis of *thinking for speaking* (Slobin, 1987, 1996a), which he formulates as follows (Slobin, 1996a).

> [T]he expression of experience in linguistic terms constitutes thinking for speaking—a special form of thought that is mobilized for communication. In the evanescent time frame of constructing utterances in discourse one fits one's thoughts into available linguistic frames. 'Thinking for speaking' involves picking those characteristics of objects and events that (a) fit some conceptualization of the event, and (b) are readily encodable in the language. (p. 76)

According to this hypothesis, the structures of utterances are a product of the thinking process at the time of communication, which is constrained by multiple factors. In this proposal, Slobin turns the traditional static approach toward conceptualizing the language and thought issue into a dynamic one. "The consequences of this shift from names of abstract entities to names of activities is to draw attention to the kinds of mental processes that occur during the act of formulating an utterance" (Slobin, 1996a, p. 71). Similarly, this proposal shifts our research focus from the deeply entrenched tradition of studying language competence (Chomsky, 1965), to an emphasis on studying the dynamic psychological and social processes of language in communication and discourse. Slobin (2004) states,

> [L]inguistic patterns don't occur in the abstract. They arise in the course of language in use… [H]abitual patterns of language use are shaped by ease of accessibility of linguistic forms—to producer and receiver, as well as by the dynamics of cultural and aesthetic values and the perspectives and communicative aims of the speaker. (p. 253)

Slobin's approach has proven to be extremely helpful for working on a thorny issue regarding the classification of Mandarin Chinese in motion event typology (Chen, 2005). In this chapter, we will illustrate how the shift in our research attention from static structural analysis to dynamic language use could shed fresh insight on this issue. In particular, we will examine the rhetorical style (Berman & Slobin, 1994; Slobin, 1996a, 2004) of Mandarin-speaking adults' use of motion expressions as a window onto the speakers' thinking for speaking. We will also examine how children develop such a rhetorical style.

Motion Expression Typology and Mandarin Chinese

According to Talmy's (1991, 2000) seminal work on the language typology of the linguistic expression of motion, the languages in the world can be divided into verb-framed languages and satellite-framed languages. Languages that encode path of motion in the main verb or verb root of a sentence are regarded as verb-framed (e.g., Spanish, Turkish, Hebrew), and those that encode path in the satellite elements (e.g., particles, prepositions, and other subordinate components of the main verb) are regarded as satellite-framed (e.g., English, Russian, German). Slobin (Berman & Slobin, 1994; Slobin, 1996b) applies this typological classification to the study of the rhetorical styles in motion expressions in the narratives based on the wordless picture book *Frog, where are you?* (Mayer, 1969). However, as more languages are studied, issues have arisen to challenge Talmy's dichotomous typology. Penelope Brown (2004) reports that Tzeltal, a Mayan language, can express path of motion in both main verbs and directional satellites, and consequently, Tzeltal could be classified as either language type. Zlatev and Yangklang (2004) report that Thai, a serial-verb language, allows juxtaposition of two main verbs with equal grammatical status in one clause, with one verb expressing path and the other expressing manner. To add to the problem, serial-verb languages are not a rare phenomenon, but rather are represented by a wide range of language families, such as Niger-Congo, Hmong-Mien, Mon-Khmer, Austronesian, Tai-Kadai, and Sino-Tibetan (Zlatev & Yangklang, 2004).

Mandarin Chinese, a Sino-Tibetan language, is a serial-verb language that poses a similar problem. The disagreement about the typological categorization of Mandarin in the linguistics literature is quite dramatic (Chen, 2005). Talmy (1991, 2000) classified Mandarin Chinese as a satellite-framed language, because (according to the traditional linguistic analysis) the second verb (V2), which expresses path in a serial verb (V1+V2) construction, is categorized as directional complement (Lü, 1980) or a complement in a verb compound (Chao, 1968; Li & Thompson, 1981). In Talmy's view, these complements are satellites. However, some Chinese linguists (Tai, 2003; Hsueh, 1989) argue that V2 in fact functions as the center of predication, even though it might not be analyzed as the main verb in surface syntax. Based on his painstaking illustration that V2 expresses foreground information while V1 expresses background information, which is just the opposite of the English verb+complement construction, Tai (2003) concludes that Mandarin should be considered a verb-framed language. So far, no clear and convincing argument has been made regarding whether V1 or V2 in the resultative verb compound (of which the directional verb compound is a subcategory) is the primary predicate (and therefore the verb head). Huang (1988) attempted to resolve this dispute with an extensive review, but could only settle with the tentative conclusion that it is "more likely to be right" (p. 309) that V1 is the primary predicate.

Slobin (2004) classified such languages as a third language type—the equipollently-framed languages—because path and manner are expressed by two linguistic forms that have roughly equal morphosyntactic status (see also Zlatev & Yangklang, 2004). In response to Slobin's proposal, Talmy (this volume) presents a list of detailed criteria for identifying the category of main verbs. Talmy approaches this issue by examining the relevant linguistic forms through a set of phonological, lexical, and syntactic distributional criteria. Although Talmy's detailed criteria deal with this thorny issue in a very sophisticated way, they raise a fundamental methodological question. Several of Talmy's criteria have to be determined by statistical data found in actual language use, i.e., performance, rather than by the researchers' native intuition, i.e., competence. In fact, Talmy (1985, 2000) invokes the concept of performance in his earlier work by using the term "characteristic" in discussing the two types of languages:

> Any language uses only one of these types ... in its most characteristic expression of Motion. Here, 'characteristic' means that: (i) It is *colloquial* in style, rather than literary, stilted, etc. (ii) It is *frequent* in occurrence in speech, rather than only occasional. (iii) It is *pervasive*, rather than limited, that is, a wide range of semantic notions are expressed in this type. (Talmy, 1985, p. 62)

According to this formulation, one must examine performance, rather than competence, to determine whether an expression pattern is characteristic of a language. This coincides, in spirit, with Slobin's (2004) call for the shift of our attention from typologies of language structures to "typologies of language use" (p. 253). Perhaps the study of speakers' spontaneous language use may provide better insight into this difficult issue of the typological classification of Mandarin than linguists' intuitions.

Child Language Development and Mandarin Chinese Motion Expressions

One of the key debates in child language development is between the "cognitive hypothesis" and the "language-specific hypothesis." The "cognitive hypothesis" (for general discussion of this position, see Cromer, 1976; Bowerman, 1976; Clark, 1977) claims that children come to the task of language learning with a pre-existent cognitive representation of the world. In the initial stage of language learning, children learn how to map the structures of the cognitive system onto the linguistic system. In contrast, the "language-specific hypothesis" (for general discussion of this position, see R. Brown, 1958; Bowerman, 1985, 1996; Gentner, 1982) claims that the language learning process is often under the "immediate influence ... of the *semantic structure of the input language*" (Bowerman, 1985, p. 1305), and such influence begins, as Bowerman (1985) argues, from the very beginning:

> I argue that children are prepared from the beginning to accept linguistic guidance as to which distinction ... they should rely on in organizing particular domains of meaning. (p. 1284)

The central issue in this debate is not whether the cognitive or linguistic structures do or do not play any role in child language development, since people on both sides would agree that both ultimately play a role. The crucial question in the debate is when and how each of the two factors exerts its influence on language development. Empirical studies of children's development of motion expressions do not seem to provide a clear picture regarding this debate. Choi and Bowerman's (1991) study of English and Korean children's motion verbs shows that such a typological influence could be effective at the onset of language development at the one-word stage. However, other studies seem to keep the door of the debate open. Hohenstein, Naigles, and Eisenberg (2004) found that both English- and Spanish-speaking children start to use similar types of verbs (*come, go, fall*) at age 2. Only with development do English-speaking children start to use more manner-specific verbs such as *hop* and *march*, and Spanish-speaking children start to use more path-specific verbs such as *bajarse* "descend" and *salir* "exit."[3] Hohenstein (2005) reports that, in eye-fixation experimental tasks involving video recordings of motion events, 7-year-old English- and Spanish-speaking children were influenced by their native language typology, but 3.5-year-olds were not. These disparities in findings may be due to the different methods of data collection and different types of data collected. But an alternative explanation might also be relevant. In these languages, the linguistic structures only allow speakers to express one kind of cognitive component with ease. In order to express the other kind of cognitive component, speakers have to resort to forms that significantly increase the processing load. In this situation, these languages do not provide enough freedom for young children to reveal their weak cognitive bias.

Mandarin Chinese may provide a unique testing ground to examine some possible early cognitive tendencies. The existence of the serial verb construction in Mandarin provides its speakers with three structural means of expressing motion: (1) use of both Manner and Path verbs in the verb phrase, (2) use of a Manner verb only, or (3) use of a Path verb only.[4] Linguistically, all structures are equally grammatical and natural. This structural feature helps eliminate the situation where children are forced to focus on either manner or path. Consequently, the study of Mandarin is conducive to the examination of the existence of any weak cognitive bias toward path or manner in motion expressions. If children, in the linguistically freer environment of Mandarin, still restrict themselves to the characteristic usage of the native language, then the "language-specific" hypothesis will receive stronger empirical support.

Focus of the Study

This study has two goals. First, it examines adult use of motion expressions in order to determine the typological classification of Mandarin Chinese. If the adult Mandarin speakers' speech shows a mixture of characteristics typically associated with both verb-framed and satellite-framed languages, then it gives supporting evidence that Mandarin Chinese is indeed an equipollently-framed language. Second, it examines the developmental path of Mandarin-speaking children's use of motion

---

[3] Admittedly, an alternative explanation for this convergence-first-and-divergence-later pattern of development is that the more general verbs shared by the young children in both languages are high frequency words, and hence are acquired earlier. Although it is an important issue, discussion of the specific interpretation of these results and their significance is beyond the scope of this chapter.

[4] Any of the three options may be followed by a Deictic verb (*lái* "come" or *qù* "go").

expressions, and uses it to explore the debate between the "language-specific" and "cognitive" hypotheses. If the characteristics of language use by the youngest age group show similar patterns as those of Mandarin-speaking adults, it will provide supporting evidence for the "language-specific hypothesis."

Elicited narrative data based on the "Frog Story" method (Bamberg, 1987; Berman & Slobin, 1994) will be used. Two of the four linguistic measures discussed by Slobin (1996b) in differentiating satellite- and verb-framed languages will be used for this study: (1) proportions of Manner and Path verbs both in token and type frequencies, and (2) proportion of mention of ground information in the motion expression clause. To accommodate the specific characteristics of Mandarin, measure (1) will be calculated using two additional measures: (a) the proportions of different types of verb constructions, and (b) the frequencies of the types and tokens of different types of motion verbs.

DATA COLLECTION AND CODING CATEGORIES

Subjects and Data

Twelve native Mandarin speakers were recruited from each of six age groups: 3-, 4-, 5-, 7-, and 9-year-old children and undergraduate college students (as adult participants). These research participants were recruited from a preschool, an elementary school, and two universities in Beijing, China.

Data were collected from individual children following the standard Frog Story data collection procedure. The picture book *Frog, where are you?* (Mayer, 1969) was shown to each participant page by page from the beginning to the end. Once all the pictures were shown, the researcher returned to the first page and asked each participant to tell the researcher a story based on the entire book. Each participant's oral narrative was tape recorded, transcribed, and coded for analysis.

Coding

Transcription and coding of data were done by Mandarin native speakers. Each set of transcription and codes was checked by at least two researchers for maximum agreement. The coding categories are described and illustrated below.

Motion Expressions A motion expression is defined as a clause that consists of at least one linguistic unit that expresses what Talmy (2000) calls translational motion, "in which the location of the Figure changes in the time period under consideration" (p. 25). Such translational motion events include (1a) movement between two macro-locations, (1b) posture changes, (1c) appearance or disappearance with respect to a ground, and (1d) the engagement or disengagement of a figure to or from a ground.[5] These expressions are included because they not only convey motion events, but also allow the use of the three verb constructions: Manner+Path, Manner alone, and Path alone. Motion expressions include both (1) agentive motion where the moving figure performs the action of motion coded by the Manner verb (V1), as shown in 1a, 1b, and 1c, and (2) caused motion, where the figure's movement is caused by another agent, and consequently the Manner verb (V1) encodes the other agent's action, rather than the one of the moving figure, as shown in 1d.

1a. 小狗跑到山上。
 xiǎo gǒu pǎo dào shān shàng.
 little dog run arrive hill top
 "The little dog ran to the hill."

---

[5] This category is what Talmy (2000, p. 38) refers to as the PUT category in the "mid-level" morphology.

1b. 小狗站起来。
xiǎo gǒu zhàn qǐ lái
little dog stand arise come
"The little dog stood up."

1c. 洞里钻出来一只小鼹鼠。
dòng lǐ zuān chū lái yì zhī xiǎo yànshǔ
hole inside squeeze exit come one CL[6] little mole
"From the hole, a little mole squeezed out."

1d. 小孩戴上帽子。
xiǎo hái dài shàng màozi
little child wear up hat
"The little child put on the hat."

Motion Verb Types Four general categories are identified for all motion verbs according to what component of the meaning of motion they convey: Manner verbs, Path verbs (non-deictic), Deictic verbs (indicating path), and Neutral verbs. Manner verbs are those that indicate what Talmy (2000) calls co-events of motion, including manner [in various relations to the motion event (Talmy, 2000, p. 42)] and cause (e.g., 掉 diào "fall/drop/come-off," 爬 pá "craw," and 踢 tī "kick"). Path verbs are those that indicate "the path followed … by the Figure object with respect to the Ground object" (Talmy, 2000, p. 25; e.g., 出 chū "exit," 上 shàng "ascend/up," 回 huí "return"). There are only two Deictic verbs indicating path in Mandarin, 来 lái "come" for motion approaching the speaker, and 去 qù "go" for motion away from the speaker. Neutral verbs are those verbs that do not express any notion of translational motion in the normal context. However, in the data, they are used in the V1 slot in the V1+V2 serial verb construction, and consequently acquire the function and meaning of Manner verbs (e.g., 弄 nòng "make/cause/get-something-into-the-state-of," 坐 zuò "sit," 趴 pā "lie on stomach").

Verb Constructions In Mandarin, the serial verb construction normally allows the following seven verb construction types: M+P+D (Manner+Path+Deictic), M+P (Manner+Path), M+D (Manner+Deictic), M (Manner), P+D (Path+Deictic), P (Path), and D (Deictic). Traditionally, the first component (V1) in the construction is considered the main verb, while the following components are the complement. Examples are given below:

2a. M+P+D (Manner+Path+Deictic)
他掉到河里去了
tā diào dào hé lǐ qù le
he fall reach river inside go PERF
"He fell into the water."

2b. M+P (Manner+Path)
他掉到水里
tā diào dào shuǐ lǐ
he fall reach water inside
"He fell into the water."

2c. M+D (Manner+Deictic)
他掉河里去了
tā diào hé lǐ qù le
he fall river inside go PERF
"He fell into the water."

2d. M (Manner)
鹿不停地往前跑

---

[6] Abbreviation glossing: ADVB = adverbial marker; CL = classifier; PERF = perfective marker.

lù bù tíng de wǎng qián pǎo
deer not stop ADVB toward front run
"The deer keeps running forward."

2e. P+D (Path+Deictic)
马蜂过来了
mǎfēng guò lái le
bee cross come PERF
"The bees came over."

2f. P (Path)
小孩出了家门
xiǎo hái chū le jiā mén
little child exit PERF home door
"The little child came out of the door of the house."

2g. D (Deictic)
一只野鹿来了
yì zhī yě lù lái le
one CL wild deer come PERF
"A wild deer came."

In the M+P+D or M+P constructions, Neutral verbs are also used in the M position. In these contexts, the Neutral verbs acquire some motion meaning with or without the aid of a following Path verb. Therefore, these Neutral verbs are coded as M in these constructions. Below are examples for each situation.

3a. Neutral verbs as M in M+P+D
他们俩站起来
tāmen liǎ **zhàn** qǐ lái
they two stand arise come
"They two stood up."

3b. Neutral verbs as M in M+P
他骑到鹿顶上
tā **qí** dào lù dǐng shàng
he ride reach deer peak top
"He rode onto the top of the deer's head."

3c. Neutral verbs as M in M
给那小孩垂鹿头上了
gěi nèi xiǎo hái **nòng** lù tóu shàng le
give that little child make deer head top PERF
"(It) got the little child onto the head of the deer."

In cases where the Deictic verb 来 lái "come" is used with a Path verb after it, 来 lái loses most of its deictic meaning and becomes a Manner verb. Such cases are included in the M category. This construction is quite rare; in this corpus, it only occurs when 来 lái is used with the Path verb 到 dào "reach/arrive." The following is an example.

4. Deictic verb as M in M+P
他们来到池塘边
tāmen lái dào chítáng biān
they come reach/arrive pond side
"They came to the side of a pond."

200 CROSSLINGUISTIC APPROACHES TO THE PSYCHOLOGY OF LANGUAGE

In the data, the locative coverb 在 zài "at" is also coded as P in M+P or M+P+D constructions. Although these uses of zài, strictly speaking, are not correct, the fact that even some adults used it that way indicates that this use is beginning to creep into the language. In example (5), below, the Path verb 到 dào "reach/arrive" should be used instead of 在 zài.

5. Locative coverb 在 zài "at" as P in M+P
   小狗把头伸在了瓶子里
   xiǎo gǒu bǎ tóu shēn <u>zài</u> le píngzi lǐ
   little dog BA head stretch at PERF bottle inside
   "The little doggie poked his head into the bottle."

Ground Information Ground information includes the source (e.g., 从洞里 cóng <u>dòng lǐ</u> "from <u>the hole</u>"), medium (e.g., 跑过<u>树林</u> pǎo guò <u>shùlín</u> "run through <u>the bush</u>"), and goal (e.g., 钻进洞里 zuān jìn <u>dòng lǐ</u> "squeeze into <u>the hole</u>") of motion that is expressed in the same clause with the motion verbs. Following Slobin's (1996b) practice, a clause is coded simply as plus-ground regardless of how many pieces of ground information it contains.

RESULTS

General

As shown in Table 14.1, a total of 1956 motion expressions have been identified across all age groups. Different age groups have quite comparable mean numbers of motion expressions per person, ranging from 25 to 29.

TABLE 14.1 Motion Expressions by Age Groups

	Motion Expressions/Person		
Age	Age Mean	Range	% of Total Utterance
3 yr	27	14–43	35%
4 yr	25	11–35	34%
5 yr	25	14–40	39%
7 yr	29	15–52	44%
9 yr	29	19–42	47%
Adult	29	13–44	40%

Language Type as Shown in Adult Speech

Distribution of different verb constructions used by adults is shown in Figure 14.1. On average, 71.5% of an adult's motion expressions contain both Manner and Path verbs (30.7% with a Deictic and 40.8% without a Deictic), 12.9% are Manner only constructions, with or without a Deictic, 10.6% are Path only constructions, with or without a Deictic, and 5.1% are Deictic constructions where Deictic verbs are used as a main verb.

As shown in Table 14.2, on average, each adult participant used more Manner verb types (including Manner and Neutral verbs) than Path verb types. On average, 55.2% of each participant's motion expressions contain ground information, with individual differences ranging from 38.5% to 80.8% (see Figure 14.7).

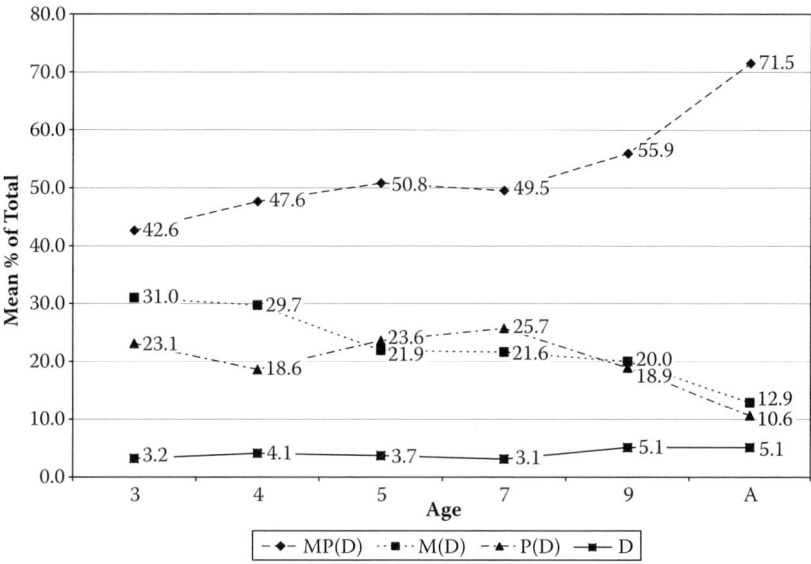

Figure 14.1 Motion verb construction types of age.

TABLE 14.2 Mean Adult Verb Types and Type/Token Ratios for Different Motion Verb Categories

Verb Category	# of Verb Types	T/T Ratio
Manner	10.6	1/1.9
Neutral	3.1	1/1.0
Path	7.1	1/3.1
Deictic	1.9	1/6.0

Developmental Trends Across Age Groups

Verb Constructions Figure 14.1 shows the mean percentages of different motion verb constructions across the six age groups, where the constructions with or without a Deictic verb are combined. Verb constructions consisting of both a Manner verb and a Path verb increase steadily with age, while those having only a Manner verb or only a Path verb decrease with age, with a clear drop between 9-year-olds and adults. The use of a Deictic as a main verb is low across all age groups, although it shows a slight increase with age.

Figures 14.2, 14.3, and 14.4 break down each construction type by the presence or absence of a Deictic verb in the construction. Figure 14.2 shows that the M+P+D construction is virtually steady across age groups, but the M+P construction increases drastically with age. Thus the increase of the M+P+(D) construction shown in Figure 14.1 is almost entirely due to the increase of the M+P construction. Figure 14.3 shows that, across all age groups, the majority of Manner verbs do not normally take Deictic verbs by themselves, and this tendency is most evident in adult speech. Figure 14.4 shows that the use of Deictic verbs in constructions containing a Path verb decreases with age, and in adult speech, the proportion of P constructions exceeds that of the P+D construction. Putting Figures 14.2, 14.3, and 14.4 together, it appears that speakers use Deictic verbs less frequently in motion constructions as they grow older.

Motion Verbs Figure 14.5 shows the developmental trend in the number of verb types from each of the four motion verb categories: Manner, Neutral, Path, and Deictic verbs. The mean Manner and

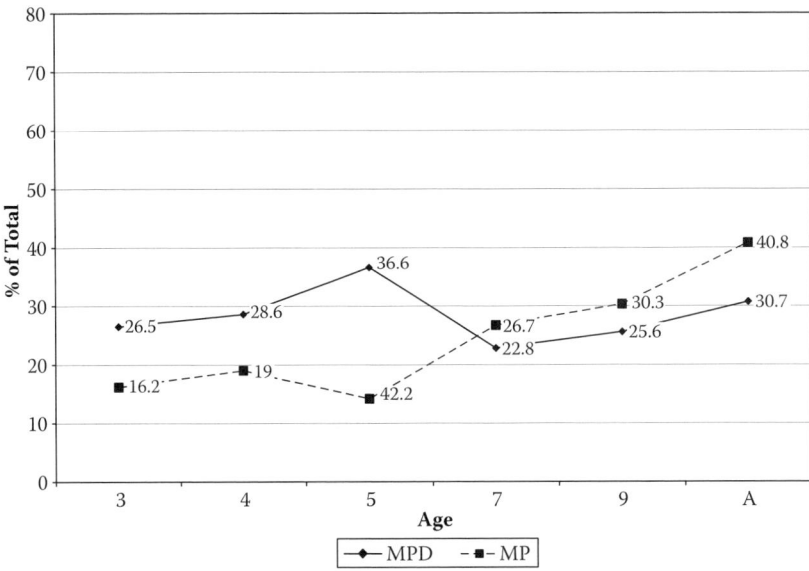

Figure 14.2 Breakdown of M+P+(D) constructions by deictic verb presence by age.

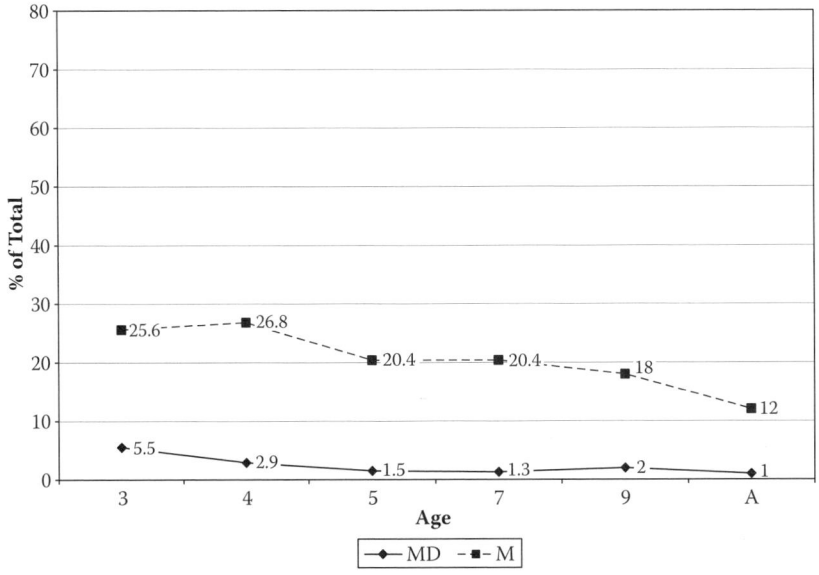

Figure 14.3 Breakdown of M+(D) constructions by deictic verb presence by age.

Neutral verb types are quite comparable among children aged 3 through 7, although there is a clear increase at age 9. In contrast, Path verb types show a steady increase across all age groups, from 4.9 for 3-year-olds to 7.1 for adults. Children use both Deictic verbs as early as 3 years of age. Figure 14.6 shows the developmental trend of the Type/Token ratios of the four motion verb categories. Type/Token ratios across all age groups are generally comparable for Manner and Neutral verbs, while the Path verb T/T ratio for 3-year-olds is higher than those of the other age groups. Type/Token ratios for Deictic verbs show a general decrease with age, but they are significantly higher than those of the other three categories for all age groups.

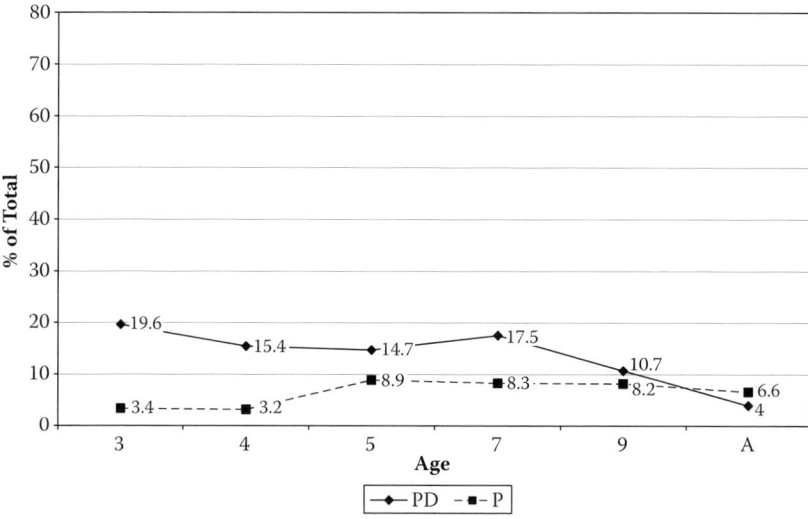

Figure 14.4 Breakdown of P+(D) constructions by deictic verb presence by age.

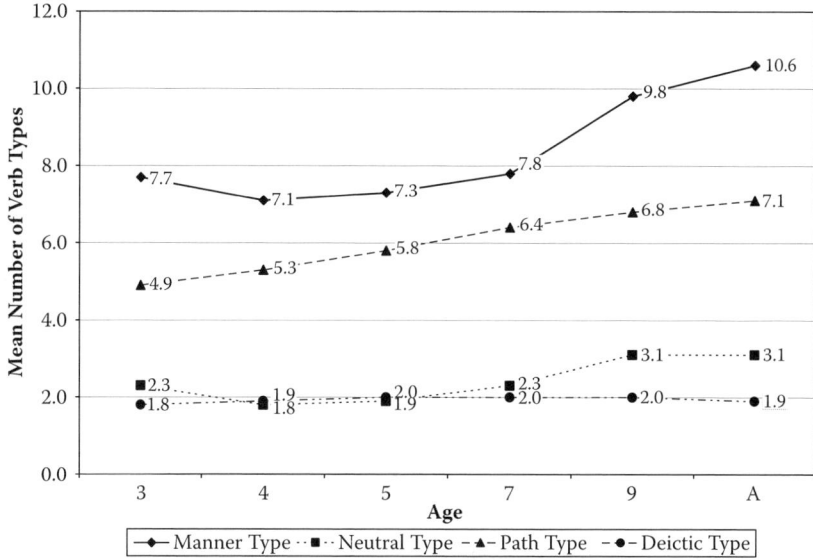

Figure 14.5 Development of verb types of different categories of motion verbs.

Ground Figure 14.7 shows that, among 3- to 7-year-old children, the mean percentages of plus-ground expressions are quite comparable, fluctuating between 34.9% and 41.4%. There is a clear increase between 7- and 9-year-olds (41.4% vs. 48.8%), and another one between the 9-year-olds and adults (48.8% vs. 55.2%).

THEORETICAL SIGNIFICANCE OF THE STUDY

Motion Event Typology of Mandarin

Previous studies (Naigles, Eisenberg, Kako, Highter, & Mcgraw, 1998; Özçalışkan & Slobin, 1999; Papafragou, Massey, & Gleitman, 2005; Slobin, 1996b, 2004) found that the typological characteristics

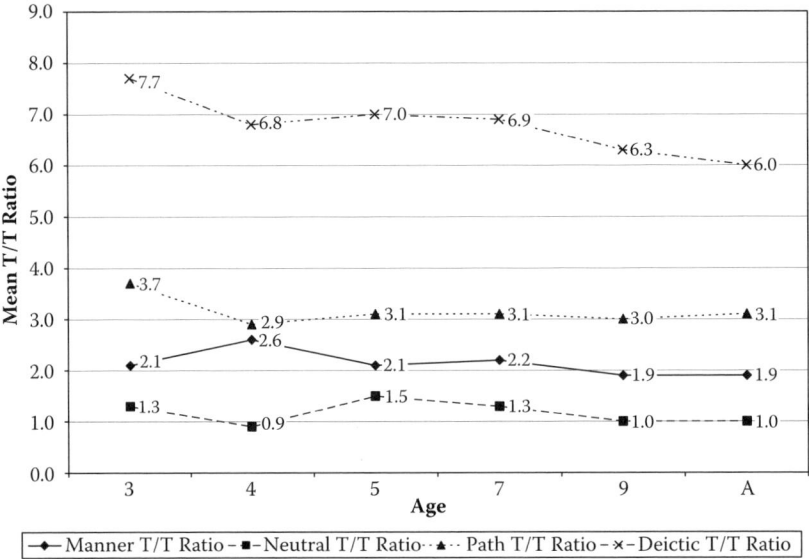

Figure 14.6 Development of type/token ratio of different categories of motion verbs.

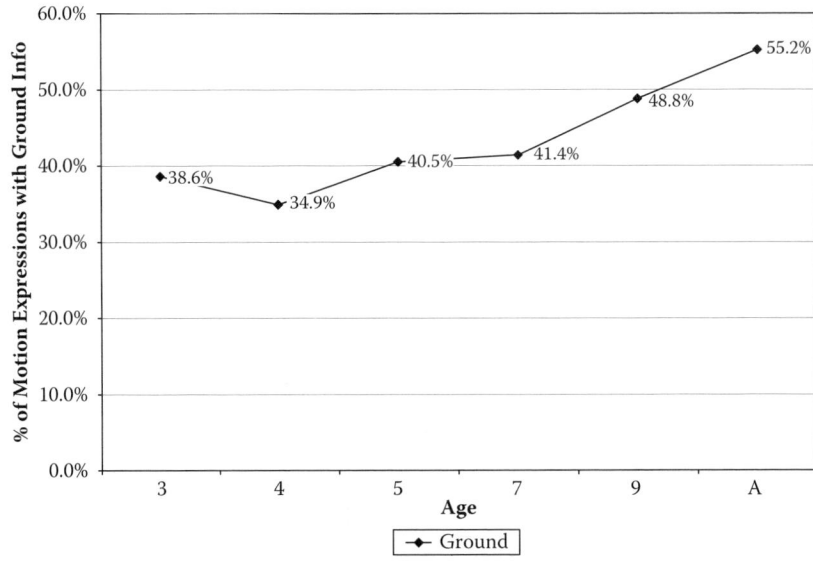

Figure 14.7 Development of % of motion expressions with ground information.

of languages exert a strong influence on speakers' choice of expressions of motion, either in naturalistic discourse or in experimental elicitations. Conversely, when linguistic analysis cannot determine the typological classification of a language, we might be able to infer that classification by examining native speakers' usage of the language. The studies mentioned above generally find that speakers of satellite-framed languages tend to use more Manner verbs than speakers of verb-framed languages, while speakers of verb-framed languages tend to use more Path verbs, in terms of both verb types and token frequencies. Results from this study show that Mandarin adult speakers use equal numbers of Manner and Path verb tokens. The majority of their motion expressions take the form of an M+P+(D) construction. M+(D) constructions occur with the same frequency as P+(D) constructions, so adults show no preference toward any one construction. By this measure, Mandarin sits right in the middle, showing no tendency toward either language type.

Measures of other aspects of Mandarin speakers' rhetorical style show a "split personality." The level of vocabulary diversity (measured by verb types) in each verb category seems to indicate that Mandarin sides with satellite-framed languages. When Manner and Neutral verb types are combined, they are almost twice as many as Path verb types. By this measure, Mandarin seems to tilt toward a satellite-framed language. But the frequency of plus-ground clauses points in another direction. Slobin (1996b) claims that speakers of satellite-framed languages use plus-ground expressions more frequently than speakers of verb-framed languages. On average, only 55.2% of each Mandarin-speaking adult's motion expressions included ground information. This is not only a far cry from the 82% found among English-speaking adults, but also well below the 63% found among speakers of Spanish (Slobin, 1996b), which is an exemplar verb-framed language. On this account, Mandarin is definitely included in the camp of verb-framed languages.

Putting things together, we have good reasons to infer that Mandarin Chinese indeed belongs to the third type, the equipollently-framed language (Slobin, 2004). This classification might explain why linguists have not reached a clear conclusion about the typological categorization of Mandarin within a dichotomous framework.

Development of Motion Expressions

Although young children's motion expressions appear to have a long way to go to catch up with those of adults in terms of the frequency of the M+P+(D) construction, children's rhetorical style seems to represent a prototype of that of adults. Even at 3 years of age, verb constructions resemble those of adults in order of frequency: M+P+(D), M+(D), P+(D), and D. From age 5 on, children's styles resemble those of adults in a very remarkable way in that proportions of M+(D) and P+(D) constructions are almost identical, showing the characteristic of an equipollently-framed language. This seems to support the "language-specific" hypothesis that children show strong native language influence in their language use very early in life.

However, 3- and 4-year-olds' data show some degrees of freedom in children's style. They use M+(D) constructions significantly more frequently than P+(D) constructions (31.0% vs. 23.1% for 3-year-olds and 29.7% vs. 18.6% for 4-year-olds). This shows that when linguistic structures allow them a choice, younger children seem to pay more attention to manner than path of motion. This finding indicates that children at early stages of development might not follow typical patterns of use for their native language entirely, although the evidence is not definitive or strong. This finding is similar to that of Hohenstein, Naigles, and Eisenberg (2004). Hohenstein et al. (2004) compared the production of motion verbs in young English- and Spanish-speaking children, and found that at age 2, the motion verbs used by children from both languages "are composed primarily of general path-conflating verbs produced in 'bare' intransitive sentences." Only by the end of the third year do English-speaking children start to diverge and follow their native language pattern. These results suggest that children tend to start with path of motion from early on, in spite of their language typology. However, the findings of the current study show that when given the choice, where the adults' frequency of Manner and Path verbs are comparable, young Mandarin-speaking children seem to lean more toward manner of motion, rather than path. Of course, the youngest children's utterances in the current study are at a much more advanced level than those children in Hohenstein et al.'s (2004) study. In order to draw more definitive conclusions, Mandarin data from comparable age groups are needed.

A somewhat surprising and puzzling finding from this study is that of the development of the Deictic verbs. By age 3, children's use of the two Deictic verbs 来 lái "come" and 去 qù "go" has reached the adult level in frequency in either the M+P+D, the M+D, or the P+D constructions. What children need to develop, as they grow older, is the use of motion expressions without the Deictic. It seems that young children find it difficult to use the motion expressions without a Deictic verb. This difficulty clearly violates Slobin's (2004) principle that it is *ease of processing* that constrains one's rhetorical style. Why are the constructions with more components easier for younger children than those with fewer ones? One possible explanation could be found in Karmiloff-Smith's (1979) insights about conceptual development and language acquisition. When young children first learn distinct conceptual functions, they need "to mark each function separately for a time in order to render the distinction tangible" (p. 95; cited in Slobin, 1985). Based on this insight, Slobin (1985) proposed the Operating Principle (OP): Maximal Substance, which states that "While you are mastering the linguistic expression of a Notion, mark that Notion with as much acoustic substance as possible, with maximal phonological separation of the form in question from adjacent speech units" (pp. 1202–1203). It is possible that the younger Mandarin speakers are still in the early stage of learning the conceptual element of deictic relations embedded in each motion expression, and therefore prefer to use explicit forms to indicate such a notion. As they grow older, and when this notion is fully acquired, it can be implicitly implied without any surface form. However, another explanation is also possible. Expressions with Deictic verbs, such as M+P+D, seem to be more colloquial, and those without Deictic verbs, such as M+P, seem to be more formal and literary. Therefore, the higher frequency of Deictic verbs among younger children could be due to the fact that most of their language input is limited to speech. As they get close to school age and have more exposure to written language that is read to them, they start to learn the more literary form of the motion expressions. A plausible and valid explanation for this phenomenon requires further research.

Conclusion and Future Research

The typological classification of Mandarin Chinese regarding expression of motion has caused much controversy. Based on linguistic analyses derived from linguists' intuitions, scholars have come up with opposing conclusions. However, following Slobin's wisdom, we tried to address this issue the other way around, by first examining speakers' rhetorical styles, and then considering language type. Adult Mandarin speakers' rhetorical styles in elicited narratives indicate that Mandarin Chinese is neither a satellite-framed nor a verb-framed language. Various measures of the characteristics of adult Mandarin speakers' rhetorical styles indicate that Mandarin indeed belongs to a third type, what Slobin (2004) calls the equipollently-framed type.

Mandarin-speaking children's rhetorical styles have already shown the overall prototype of these typological characteristics at age 3, showing some support for the "language-specific hypothesis." However, before the age of 5, young children show a tendency to favor manner over path, showing some evidence for the "cognitive hypothesis." Use of Deictics is already acquired by age 3, but acquisition of using motion constructions without the Deictics is not complete even at age 9. Further research is needed to investigate why expressions without a Deictic verb are harder to learn than those with one. This will require data from very early stages of language development so that it is possible to portray the developmental paths of these words and constructions from the very beginning. It is also necessary to examine the language input to determine whether adults or older peers use more Deictic verbs when they talk to younger children.

REFERENCES

Bamberg, M. (1987). *The acquisition of narratives: Learning to use language.* Berlin: Mouton de Gruyter.
Berman, R., & Slobin, D. (1994). *Relating events in narrative: A crosslinguistic developmental study.* Hillsdale, NJ: Lawrence Erlbaum Associates.
Bowerman, M. (1976). Semantic factors in the acquisition of rules for word use and sentence construction. In D. Morehead & A. Morehead (Eds.), *Normal and deficient child language* (pp. 99–179). Baltimore: University Park Press.
Bowerman, M. (1985). What shapes children's grammars? In D. Slobin (Ed.), *The crosslinguistic study of language acquisition: Vol. 2. Theoretical issues* (pp. 1257–1319). Hillsdale, NJ: Lawrence Erlbaum Associates.

Bowerman, M. (1996). The origins of children's spatial semantic categories: Cognitive versus linguistic determinants. In J. Gumperz & S. Levinson (Eds.), *Rethinking linguistic relativity* (pp. 145–176). Cambridge, UK: Cambridge University Press.

Brown, P. (2004). Position and motion in Tzeltal frog stories: The acquisition of narrative style. In S. Strömqvist & L. Verhoeven (Eds.), *Relating events in narrative: Typological and contextual perspectives* (pp. 37–57). Mahwah, NJ: Lawrence Erlbaum Associates.

Brown, R. (1958). *Words and things.* New York: The Free Press.

Chao, Y. (1968). *A grammar of spoken Chinese.* Berkeley: University of California Press.

Chen, L. (2005). *The acquisition and use of motion event expressions in Chinese.* Unpublished doctoral dissertation, University of Louisiana at Lafayette.

Choi, S., & Bowerman, M. (1991). Learning to express motion events in English and Korean: The influence of language-specific lexicalization patterns. *Cognition, 41,* 83–121.

Chomsky, N. (1965). *Aspects of the theory of syntax.* Cambridge, MA: The MIT Press.

Clark, E. (1977). Universal categories: On the semantics of classifiers and children's early word meanings. In A. Juilland (Ed.), *Linguistic studies presented to Joseph Greenberg.* Saratoga, CA: Anma Libri. [Reprinted in E. Clark, 1979. *The ontogenesis of meaning* (pp. 253–267). Wiesbaden: Akademische Verlagsgesellschaft Athenaion.]

Cromer, R. (1976). The cognitive hypothesis of language acquisition and its implications for child language deficiency. In D. Morehead & A. Morehead (Eds.), *Normal and deficient child language* (pp. 283–333). Baltimore: University Park Press.

Gentner, D. (1982). Why nouns are learned before verbs: Linguistic relativity versus natural partitioning. In S. Kuczaj (Ed.), *Language development: Vol. 2. Language, thought, and culture* (pp. 301–334). Hillsdale, NJ: Lawrence Erlbaum Associates.

Hohenstein, J. (2005). Language-related motion event similarities in English- and Spanish-speaking children. *Journal of Cognition and Development, 6*(3), 403–425.

Hohenstein, J., Naigles, L., & Eisenberg, A. (2004). Keeping verb acquisition in motion: A comparison of English and Spanish. In D. Hall & S. Waxman (Eds.), *Weaving a lexicon* (pp. 569–602). Cambridge, MA: The MIT Press.

Hsueh, F. (1989). The structure meaning of Ba and Bei constructions in Mandarin Chinese. In J. Tai & F. Hsueh (Eds.), *Functionalism and Chinese grammar* (pp. 95–125). South Orange, NJ: Chinese Language Teachers Association.

Huang, J. (1988). *Wo pao de kuai* and Chinese phrase structure. *Language, 64,* 274–311.

Karmiloff-Smith, A. (1979). *A functional approach to child language.* Cambridge, UK: Cambridge University Press.

Li, C., & Thompson, S. (1981). *Mandarin Chinese: A functional reference grammar.* Berkeley: University of California Press.

Lü, S. (1980). *Xiàndài hànyǔ bābǎi cí (Eight hundred words in modern Chinese).* Hong Kong: Shāngwù Yìnshūguǎn (Commercial Press).

Mayer, M. (1969). *Frog, where are you?* New York: Dial Press.

Naigles, L., Eisenberg, A., Kako, E., Highter, M., & Mcgraw, N. (1998). Speaking of motion: Verb use in English and Spanish. *Language and Cognitive Processes, 13*(5), 521–549.

Özçalışkan, S., & Slobin, D. (1999). Learning how to search for the frog: Expression of manner of motion in English, Spanish, and Turkish, *Proceedings of the 23rd Annual Boston University Conference on Language Development, 23,* 541–552.

Papafragou, A., Massey, C., & Gleitman, L. (2005). When English proposes what Greek presupposes: The cross-linguistic encoding of motion events. *Cognition, 98*(3), B75–B87.

Slobin, D. I. (1977). Language change in childhood and in history. In J. MacNamara (Ed.), *Language learning and thought,* (pp. 185–214). New York: Academic Press.

Slobin, D. I. (1985). Crosslinguistic evidence for the language-making capacity. In D. Slobin (Ed.), *The crosslinguistic study of language acquisition: Vol. 2. Theoretical issues* (pp. 1157–1256). Hillsdale, NJ: Lawrence Erlbaum Associates.

Slobin, D. I. (1987). Thinking for speaking. *Proceedings of the Annual Meeting of the Berkeley Linguistics Society, 13,* 435–444.

Slobin, D. I. (1996a). From "thought and language" to "thinking for speaking." In J. Gumperz & S. Levinson (Eds.), *Rethinking linguistic relativity* (pp. 70–96). Cambridge, UK: Cambridge University Press.

Slobin, D. I. (1996b). Two ways to travel: Verbs of motion in English and Spanish. In M. Shibatani & S. Thompson (Eds.), *Grammatical constructions: Their form and meaning* (pp. 195–220). Oxford, UK: Clarendon Press.

Slobin, D. I. (2004). The many ways to search for a frog: Linguistic typology and the expression of motion events. In S. Strömqvist & L. Verhoeven (Eds.), *Relating events in narrative: Typological and contextual perspectives* (pp. 219–257). Mahwah, NJ: Lawrence Erlbaum Associates.

Tai, J. (2003). Cognitive relativism: Resultative construction in Chinese. *Language and Linguistics, 4*(2), 301–316.

Talmy, L. (1985). Lexicalization patterns: Semantic structure in lexical forms. In T. Shopen (Ed.), *Language typology and syntactic description: Vol. 3. Grammatical categories and the lexicon* (pp. 57–149). Cambridge, UK: Cambridge University Press.

Talmy, L. (1991). Path to realization: A typology of event conflation. *Proceedings of the Annual Meeting of the Berkeley Linguistics Society, 17,* 480–519.

Talmy, L. (2000). *Toward a cognitive semantics: Vol. 2. Typology and process in concept structuring.* Cambridge, MA: The MIT Press.

Zlatev, J., & Yangklang, P. (2004). A third way to travel: The place of Thai and serial verb languages in motion event typology. In S. Strömqvist & L. Verhoeven (Eds.), *Relating events in narrative: Typological and contextual perspectives* (pp. 159–190). Mahwah, NJ: Lawrence Erlbaum Associates.

15

Typological Constraints on Motion in French and English Child Language

MAYA HICKMANN
CNRS & Université de Paris 8

HENRIËTTE HENDRIKS
University of Cambridge

CHRISTIAN CHAMPAUD
CNRS & Université de Paris 8

… in acquiring a native language, the child learns particular ways of thinking for speaking.

Dan I. Slobin (1996, p. 76)

INTRODUCTION

Ever since our student years, Dan Slobin has repeatedly demonstrated to all of us the indispensable role of comparative research in the study of language acquisition, showing us the way in his pioneering and persistent search for universal vs. variable aspects of child language. Although his initial aim was to generalize claims about universal mechanisms of language acquisition in the face of wide linguistic variation, evidence recurrently showed more and deeper crosslinguistic differences in child language over the years. This evidence, which was at first surprising and somewhat embarrassing, constituted the first step toward recent proposals suggesting that language particulars can massively or subtly influence cognitive functioning in many ways.

Most of what follows is directly inspired by Dan's recent research on linguistic relativity in spatial systems, particularly his proposal that language particulars shape our representations of motion. After a reminder of relevant typological contrasts, we present research concerning French vs. English child language, based on experimentally induced productions from 3 years on, and on spontaneous productions by children younger than 3 years of age. Findings suggest that typological factors strongly constrain language development and open new perspectives for future research concerning the relation between language and thought.

MOTION ACROSS LANGUAGES
Verb-Framing and Satellite-Framing

Spatial systems across languages display many striking variations (Gumperz & Levinson, 1996; Levinson, 2003; Levinson & Wilkins, 2006; Lucy, 1992; Nuyts & Pederson, 1997; Talmy, 2000), for example, in their means of expression, their focus on particular dimensions, their reliance on different reference systems, and their lexicalization patterns. With respect to motion, Talmy (2000) proposes a typological distinction between *satellite-* and *verb-framed* languages (e.g., Germanic vs. Romance). Thus, English (1) typically encodes manner in verb roots and path elsewhere, whereas French (2) encodes path in verb roots, marking manner by peripheral means or leaving it unexpressed:[1]

(1) to run up/down, across, away, back, into, out of …
(2) monter, descendre, traverser, partir, revenir, entrer, sortir … en courant
 ('to ascend, descend, cross, leave, return, enter, exit … by running.')

This typological contrast particularly concerns a large set of motion events that imply changes of location. In this respect, all spatial systems (as well as temporal-aspectual ones, see Klein, 1994) differentiate events that do or do not imply a state change. For example, the sentences in (3) necessarily mean that John's location has changed (roughly from 'here' to 'not here'), while those in (4) do not make such a commitment (presumably he ran within the same location). Manner verbs are used in both cases in English, whereas they typically describe motion within a given location in French (main verb in (4)), only serving as peripheral manner markings with location changes (subordinated gerund in (3)).

(3) John ran away. / Jean est parti en courant. ('Jean left by running.')
(4) John ran [in the woods]. / Jean a couru [dans les bois].

Note that most *prototypical* means of expressing motion events across languages can co-exist with other secondary options within a given language. Thus, French manner verbs can be combined with prepositional phrases marking goals and/or resulting locations as in (5), but such uses are more marked than the prototypical structures in (2) above (emphasis on resulting states, roughly 'He ran all the way to the other side'). In addition, some French verbs jointly lexicalize manner and path, e.g., *grimper* ('to climb up') implies a particular manner (using limbs) and direction (necessarily upwards).[2]

(5) Il a couru jusqu'à l'autre côté. ('He ran until the other side.')

Predominant framing properties run through each language, also affecting utterances about caused motion. Simple compact structures in English express cause among other aspects of motion, for example, intransitive and transitive uses of manner verbs with path satellites in (6). In contrast, French verbs do not typically lexicalize cause with other aspects of motion. Despite possible transitive uses of some manner or path verbs (e.g., *rouler la balle* 'roll the ball,' *monter la valise* 'ascend [=take-up] the suitcase,' *sortir le chien* 'exit [=take-out] the dog'), French provides distinct causative

---

[1] Literal translations of French examples are given whenever necessary.
[2] Most French manner+path verbs correspond to more marked uses (*dévaler* 'go down quickly' [higher register]). Note also that contemporary French displays remnants of an earlier system in old French (which was a full-fledged satellite-framed language), namely, some verbal prefixes that contribute spatial-temporal-aspectual markings (e.g., Latinate *a-, ex-, in-, trans-* in *accourir* 'to run to quickly,' *atterrir* 'to land,' *écrémer* 'to take cream off,' *emboîter* 'to fit into,' *traverser* 'to cross,' see Kopecka, 2006). Over centuries this sub-system has considerably reduced in size and productivity, now allowing only a few permissible combinations among a small set of elements, only few of which constitute independent lexical items (e.g., *courir* 'to run' is a lexical entry, but not *crémer*, which is derived from the noun *crème* 'cream').

constructions that are frequently used for caused motion (*faire* 'make' + infinitive) and that can combine cause with manner or path as in (7).[3] Furthermore, framing preferences also affect other domains beyond space. For example, in comparison to the English causative-resultative structure (8), French requires the spreading of information across clauses, such as the somewhat awkward and partial translations (9) and (10).

(6) The ball rolled across the street./He rolled the ball across the street.
(7) *faire rouler* 'make roll,' *faire glisser* 'make slide,' *faire monter* 'make ascend, *faire sortir* 'make exit,' *faire traverser* 'make cross' …
(8) She blew the paint dry.
(9) Elle a séché la peinture en soufflant dessus.
('She dried the paint by blowing on it.')
(10) Elle a soufflé sur la peinture pour la faire sécher.
('She blew on the paint to make it dry.')

Developmental and Cognitive Implications

Linguistic variation across spatial systems is presently at the center of a renewed debate concerning the role of language-specific determinants in development. Space indeed constitutes one of the most basic domains of behavior, assumed to involve universal perceptual/cognitive processes (Landau & Jackendoff, 1993). However, the considerable diversity that characterizes human languages clearly constrains our verbal representations of space, raising questions about the extent to which it might constrain children's language acquisition and their cognitive representations more generally.

Space Across Child Languages Crosslinguistic research has drastically renewed the study of language acquisition, enabling researchers to generalize claims about universals or to invalidate such claims in the light of strikingly different developmental patterns across languages. In this context, developmental research on space (see a review in Hickmann, 2003) has led to two types of claims. Some studies attribute recurrent developmental progressions across child languages to early pre-linguistic knowledge, assumed to be either innate or the result of early perceptual and conceptual activity, that provides a universal foundation for spatial cognition. However, a growing number of studies also report striking crosslinguistic differences in children's early and subsequent use of spatial language. In general, the findings show that children's language resembles more the adult system in their language group than the language of children of the same age but in typologically different language groups, suggesting the impact of language particulars on language acquisition.

Crosslinguistic variability has further led to the revival of the old debate between 'Whorfian' and 'anti-Whorfian' views (Gumperz & Levinson, 1996; Whorf, 1956). Whorfian approaches view language as partially but significantly structuring human cognition (Berman & Slobin, 1994; Bowerman, 1996, 2007; Bowerman & Choi, 2003; Choi & Bowerman, 1991; Levinson, 2003; Slobin, 1996, 2003, 2004, 2006). Anti-whorfian views argue that it does not affect non-linguistic cognition beyond its superficial impact on language use itself (Clark, 2003; Munnich & Landau, 2003).

Dan Slobin's Contribution Slobin's crosslinguistic research (1985) first highlighted universal mechanisms driving language acquisition, proposing that all children rely on general strategies (e.g., perceptually induced 'operating principles'), despite language particulars, that may also influence the acquisition process. He then showed that the impact of language particulars might go well beyond such differences, also affecting more deeply the course of language acquisition and even cognitive organization. For example, such factors influence attentional focus during

---

[3] Such constructions can also include additional peripheral information (e.g., *faire rouler la balle de l'autre côté de la rue* 'to make-roll the ball to the other side of the street,' *faire sortir le chien à coups de pied* 'to make-exit the dog by foot kicks [=kicking it]').

discourse organization (Berman & Slobin, 1994; Slobin, 1996, 2003, 2004, 2006). Speakers focus on details of motion and presuppose locations in satellite-framed languages (English, German, Turkish), whereas they provide more information about locations while presupposing the details of motion in verb-framed languages (Spanish, Hebrew). Although such language-specific effects might co-exist with the types of universal strategies proposed by Slobin's earlier writings, recurrent findings revealing striking crosslinguistic differences over a large developmental span now suggest that each language (or language family) influences on-line human cognitive processes in its own way. Although different means of expression are possible within a given spatial system, typological properties constrain which options are cognitively less costly, more accessible, and easier to learn for children, thereby influencing how they construct spatial representations.

Slobin (2004, 2006) attributes a major role to lexicalization patterns in order to account for crosslinguistic differences concerning motion. He proposes that languages can be placed along a continuum that characterizes the relative salience of manner in relation to motion. At the two extremes, manner information is either most salient because it is lexicalized in verb roots (satellite-framed languages) or least salient because it is peripheral (verb-framed languages). This proposal has proven to be an accurate predictor of how languages represent motion and a most useful tool to test the cognitive implications of such crosslinguistic differences, despite some debates concerning the details of Talmy's typology and/or of Slobin's claims (e.g., Filipović, 2002; Kopecka, 2006; Lemmens, 2002; Peyraube, 2006).

Although the spatial system of French has been described in some detail, few studies are available concerning this domain in French child language. Early results concern mostly children's production and comprehension of spatial prepositions in relation to static location, with little concern for motion and for a crosslinguistic perspective (e.g., Piérart, 1978; Verjat, 1991). Since the typological status of French is of particular interest for Talmy's and Slobin's proposals, we summarize below some of our research concerning voluntary and caused motion in French vs. English child language. We discuss first some experimentally elicited productions from the age of 3 years on, then earlier spontaneous productions.

In both sets of data we examined the following predictions, based on the typological properties of French and English, particularly their different lexicalization and grammaticalization patterns. Our general prediction was that, because utterance structure is generally more compact in English than in French, children learning English should encode more information about motion and their utterances should therefore be semantically "denser," irrespective of age and notwithstanding developmental progressions in utterance complexity. This general prediction can be further reformulated in terms of more specific predictions. French learners should encode motion information mostly in verb roots, while English learners should also do so by means of other devices. When describing voluntary motion, English learners should mention manner information more frequently than French learners, particularly by means of compact manner+path utterances. With respect to caused motion, English learners should compactly combine causality with other informational components (manner of motion, manner of causing motion, path) more frequently than French learners.

MOTION IN FRENCH AND ENGLISH AFTER THREE YEARS: EXPERIMENTAL DATA

Voluntary Motion

A first study (Hickmann, 2003) compared picture-elicited narratives produced by adults and children (4 to 10 years) in French (verb-framed) vs. English, German, and Chinese (satellite-framed). Although findings show similar developmental progressions across languages in children's ability to provide locations that spatially anchor discourse, striking crosslinguistic differences were also found in relation to motion at all ages. Predicates were least compact and varied in French, as a result of subjects' tendency to encode information only in verb roots focusing mostly on one type of information: path when describing changes of location (e.g., *partir* 'to leave') or manner when describing motion within a location (e.g., *voler* 'to fly'). Utterances combining these and other information types occurred only from 10 years on (e.g., manner+path in *grimper* 'to climb up'; cause+path in *faire descendre* 'to make descend'). In contrast, predicates were semantically denser and more varied in English (and in other satellite-framed languages), as a result of the frequent encoding of multiple information types by verb+satellites constructions (e.g., *to run up, down, into, away, to jump over, to pull down to, to chase away*).

In a second more controlled experiment (Hickmann, 2006), children narrated animated cartoons showing spontaneous displacements that systematically varied in terms of path and manner. English speakers of all ages compactly expressed both manner (in verb roots) and path (in satellites) with all event types (see (11) and (12)). In contrast, at all ages French responses frequently focused on path alone, although they were also age- and event-specific. Adults used verbs lexicalizing manner and path to describe upward motion (*grimper* in (13)), as well as path verbs with peripheral manner markings to describe crossing events (14). French children mostly used path verbs without manner markings for all events (15), but also produced several other response types: manner verbs without location changes (*nager dans la rivière* 'to swim in the river'), adverbial phrases marking terminal boundaries (*passer jusqu'à l'autre bout* 'to pass all the way to the other end'), or responses distributing path and manner across clauses (16). Developmental progressions also occurred in both languages, showing children's increasing ability to combine manner and path with age. English path particles were sometimes used by young children with semantically lean motion verbs (*to go up*) but with manner verbs at later ages (*to run up*). French showed an increasing use of path verbs with peripheral manner markings (subordinate gerunds). Nonetheless, the joint encoding of manner and path was less frequent in French with all event types and at all ages.

(11) The boy is swimming across the river. (4 years)
(12) A squirrel ran along and ran up a tree into a hole, then it climbed down the tree and ran off again. (6 years)
(13) J'ai vu un chat qui grimpait le long d'un pilone électrique […], le chat est redescendu […] avant de s'en aller. (Adult)
('I saw a cat that was climbing up along an electric pole […], the cat went back down […] before leaving.')
(14) Un garçon traverse la route en courant. (Adult)
('A boy crosses the road by running.')
(15) Il monte, après il redescend. […] Et puis il est reparti. (3 years)
('He goes up, then he goes back down. […] And then he went away.')
(16) […] elle fait du vélo […] puis elle traverse la voie ferrée. (5 years)
([…] 'she's bicycling. […] then she crosses the railway tracks.')

Caused Motion

In an experiment focusing on caused motion (Hickmann, 2007; Hickmann & Hendriks, 2006), adults and children (3 to 6 years) had to describe object displacements performed by the experimenter (e.g., putting a lid onto a pan or toys into a box; see Bowerman, 1996, 2007). French speakers used neutral prepositions (if any at all), but specific verbs expressing particular types of information (manner of attachment, spatio-functional disposition, entity properties, e.g., *accrocher* [*à*] 'to hook [at/to]'). In contrast, English speakers used relatively neutral verbs with specific particles and prepositions (e.g., *to put onto/into, to take off/out of*) and, when specific verbs occurred, they mostly marked posture (*to sit in*) or the manner of causing motion (*to push into, to pull out of*). French children also increasingly relied on verbs as their verbal lexicon expanded with age (e.g., *mettre sur le crochet* 'to put on the hook' vs. *accrocher* 'to hook').

In another experiment (Hickmann & Hendriks, 2005) adults and children (5 to 10 years) narrated animated cartoons in which a man displaced objects (e.g., rolling a ball down a hill). Several types of information were relevant: causality (CAUSE) and the manner of causing motion (ACTION of pushing or pulling); the manner of the objects' displacements (O-MANNER, roll or slide); the agent's manner of motion (A-MANNER, walk); the path followed by the agent and object (PATH, up, down, across, into). Given that this potential range of information could not be expressed within single clauses in any language, two predictions were made concerning speakers of all ages: (1) that they would have to be selective in what they would choose to encode and/or would organize varied information across clauses, and (2) that they would produce denser utterances in English as compared to French. At all ages the mean semantic density of utterances (mean number of components expressed) was higher in English than in French (two-three vs. one-two components) and it increased with age in French (but not in English), particularly with children's increasing use of subordinate clauses. CAUSE was as frequent in both languages. However, English speakers also expressed manner in main verbs (ACTION, O-MANNER) and PATH in other devices (e.g., (17) and (18)). In contrast, French speakers rarely expressed ACTIONS and distributed less information in more varied ways (e.g., (19) to (22)). Finally, the idiosyncratic uses in (23) to (25) illustrate young French children's difficulty in combining CAUSE with other types of information.

(17) *He pulls the suitcase down.*
(18) *He rolls the wheel across the street.*
(19) *Le pneu roule.* ('The tire is rolling.')
(20) *Il monte le paquet.* ('He is ascending the package.')
(21) *Il fait rouler le ballon.* ('He is making the ball roll.')
(22) *Il traverse la rue en tirant.* ('He is crossing the street pulling.')
(23) *Il fait pousser le paquet.* ('He makes push the package.')
    [instead of *pousser* 'push' or *faire avancer* 'make advance']
(24) *Il traverse le cheval.* ('He crosses the horse.')
    [instead of *faire traverser* 'make cross']
(25) *Il enroule la roue.* ('He wraps the wheel.')
    [instead of *faire rouler* 'make roll']

Summary

From 3 years on speakers produce denser utterances about motion in English than in French and they do not rely on the same devices nor focus on the same information across languages. When describing spontaneous motion, English speakers encode both manner (in verb roots) and path (in satellites). French speakers frequently focus on path alone (encoded in verb roots) at all ages, notwithstanding some peripheral marking of manner information (mostly adults) and verbs lexicalizing both path and manner (upward motion). With respect to caused motion, one study (acted-out object displacements) shows that information is encoded in English satellites but in French verbs, and that verb semantics differs in English vs. French (e.g., manner of causing motion vs. attachment). In another task (cartoons), English speakers combine cause and manner (verb roots) with path and other components (satellites), whereas French speakers express path (verbs) and distribute few other components elsewhere. Despite increasing semantic density in both languages, crosslinguistic differences occur at all ages, suggesting that typological properties constrain the locus and focus of motion information in verbal representations from 3 years on.

EARLY ACQUISITION PHASES: LONGITUDINAL NATURALISTIC DATA

We turn to analyses of corpus-based spontaneous productions in order to determine whether language-specific effects can also be observed during initial phases of acquisition. As summarized in Table 15.1, the database involves two French-speaking children (Clara, Grégoire) and two

TABLE 15.1 Summary of Data Base for All Children

	Clara French	Grégoire French	Sarah English	Adam English
Period 1				
Mean MLU	1,9	1,9	1,9	2,1
Mean Age	1;9	1;9	2;6	2;4
# of sessions	12	4	12	6
Period 2				
Mean MLU	3,3	3,2	3,1	3,4
Mean Age	2;9	2;3	3;5	3;2
# of sessions	8	5	12	12
Period 3				
Mean MLU	4,7	4,6	4,1	4,5
Mean Age	3;3	2;7	4;6	4;6
# of sessions	8	8	6	12
Period 4				
Mean MLU	5,3	4,9	n.a.°°	n.a.°°
Mean Age	4;1	3;4		
# of sessions	12	8		
# of utterances about motion	1134	1146	299	1909

° Ages are shown in years; months.
°° Not applicable (see Note 1).

English-speaking children (Sarah, Adam) during four developmental periods (P1 to P4) defined by mean length of utterance (mean MLU for P1 <2.5; for P2 = 2.5–4; for P3 = 4.1–5; for P4 >5).[4]

Verbs and Other Devices Encoding Motion

A first analysis examined children's utterances about motion to test our prediction that language-specific properties should invite them to encode motion information either in verb roots (French) or both in verbs and in other devices (English). Table 15.2 shows the most frequent motion verbs in the corpora. Children denote three types of events: *voluntary* motion (*go, come, run; aller* 'go,' *marcher* 'walk,' *sortir* 'exit,' *partir* 'leave'), *involuntary* motion without explicit causes (*fall; tomber* 'fall'), and explicitly *caused* motion in simple structures (*pick up, take off, put, push, bring; mettre* 'put,' *enlever* 'take off,' *pousser* 'push,' *apporter* 'bring') or in complex constructions (*make stand; faire tomber* 'make fall'). Transitive and intransitive uses of the same verb roots occurred in some cases, but more so in English (nine verb types, e.g., *fly, roll, stand* for voluntary and caused motion) than in French (only one verb type, *rouler* 'to roll').

With respect to other devices, a distinction was made between motion verbs that were used alone (e.g., (26)) and those that were accompanied by one or more additional devices contributing

---

[4] All available French recordings (collected by the authors) were analyzed. A comparable subset of the English recordings (from CHILDES) was selected as follows, particularly during age periods that provided many more sessions than in French. First, the most comparable (lowest) ages were selected in English within each period, since age was notably lower in French than in English for the corresponding mean MLUs of P1 to P3 (no English session corresponded to French P4). Second, a random selection among remaining files consisted of choosing every second or third file within each period. All utterances in the analyzed sessions were included with the exception of verbless utterances, which decreased after P1 for all children. Some fluctuations occurred, particularly for Grégoire's P4, where one file displayed a lower MLU, resulting in a slightly lower mean MLU. Although the volume of utterances analyzed varied across children (depending on session length), the total number of utterances about motion was comparable across languages.

TABLE 15.2 Most Common Verb Roots Used to Denote Motion Events*

Frequency Level	Event Type	English	French
> 450	Voluntary	go	—
	Caused	—	mettre ('put')
100–449	Voluntary	come	aller ('go')
	Involuntary	fall[intr]	tomber ('fall')
	Caused	put, take, *fall[trans]*	prendre ('take'), donner ('give')
51–99	Voluntary	drive, turn[intr]	partir ('leave'), monter ('ascend'), venir ('come')
	Caused	throw, turn[trans]	enlever ('take off')
31–50	Voluntary	walk, fly[intr], run	rouler[intr] ('roll'), sortir ('exit')
	Caused	push, bring, *fly[trans]*	faire ('make'[+Ca]), ranger ('to put away'), tourner ('turn'), *rouler[trans]* ('roll')
21–30	Voluntary	jump, sit, stand[intr]	marcher ('walk'), passer ('pass'), sauter ('jump'), rentrer ('enter'), descendre ('descend')
	Involuntary	*drop[intr], spill[intr]*	—
	Caused	spill[trans], park, drop[trans], *stand[trans]*	remettre ('put back'), tirer ('pull')
10–20	Voluntary	dance, step, swim, get[intr], *roll[intr], move[intr]*	revenir ('come back'), voler ('fly'), bouger ('move'), s'asseoir ('sit down'), faire du ski ('ski'), couler ('drip'), nager ('swim'), danser ('dance'), rattraper ('catch up with'), courir ('run'), s'en aller ('leave')
	Caused	knock, hang, move[trans], pick, *roll[trans], get[trans]*	

* Token frequencies are based on all corpora within each language. Verbs are shown in decreasing order within each frequency level and event type. Frequency levels are shown independently of transitive [trans] and intransitive [intr] uses of verbs (italics show [trans/intr] use-frequency under 10).

motion information ((27) to (31)): spatial prepositions and particles (*par* 'by/through,' *off, out*), as well as devices providing manner (*à quatre pattes* 'on all fours') or general locations (*dehors* 'outside'). As expected, Figure 15.1 shows that French-speaking children frequently used motion verbs alone (Clara 82%, Grégoire 81%), but English-speaking children did so less frequently (Sarah 39%, Adam 37%), more frequently combining motion verbs with other devices (Sarah 61%, Adam 63%).

(26) Elle va nager la voiture, hein? (Grégoire P3)
 ('It's going to swim the car, isn't it?')

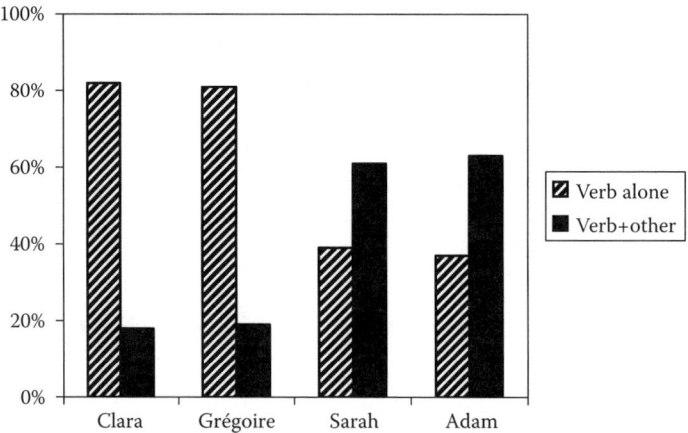

Figure 15.1 Joint use of verbs and other devices relevant to motion.

(27) Je passe par les fleurs. (Clara P3)
    ('I'm passing by/through the flowers.')
(28) Whoops the top fell off. (Sarah P3)
(29) See all the cats swim out. (Adam, P3)
(30) Il court à quatre pattes. (Grégoire P3)
    ('He's running on all fours.')
(31) Et pis dehors j'ai fait du poney dehors. (Grégoire, P2)
    ('And then outside I did [rode] pony outside.')

Semantic Content and Utterance Density

Utterances were further examined with respect to their semantic content. The list in (32) shows and illustrates all of the information components encoded by children in relation to motion: path (Pa), manner of motion (Mm), change of posture (Po), cause of motion (Cm), and manner of causing motion (Mc). General location was the only other type of information expressed.[5]

(32) Path of motion: direction (*up, monter* 'ascend'),
    boundaries (*into, entrer* 'enter'),
    deixis (*come, venir*) ...
    Manner of motion: *run, courir, à quatre pattes* 'on all fours' ...
    Change of posture: *sit down, s'asseoir* ...
    Cause of motion: *bring, faire tomber* 'make fall' ...
    Manner of causing motion: *pull, pousser* 'push' ...

Components expressed in verb roots are shown in Figure 15.2. In both languages CAUSE is most frequent, especially in one child's verbs (Clara 59% vs. Grégoire 39%, Sarah 38% and Adam 42%), while MANNER OF CAUSING MOTION is least frequent (8% to 12% for all children). PATH is as frequent in both languages (English 20%, French 24%). MANNER of motion tends to be more frequent

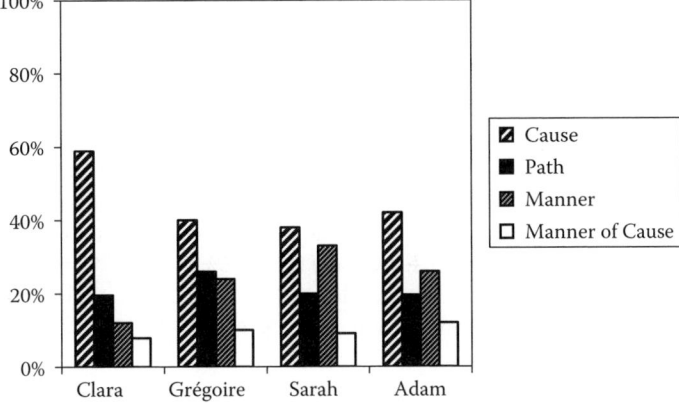

Figure 15.2   Motion information expressed in verb roots.

---

[5] Semantic coding was straightforward and highly reliable across two coders, with few disagreements, mostly concerning two types of cases that were resolved as follows: 1) *come/venir* were coded as marking deixis (path), *go/aller* as neutral verbs (no manner, no path); 2) since some French prepositional or adverbial phrases can be ambiguous (goals or locations, depending on verb semantics, verbal morphology, discourse inferences, e.g., *monter dessus* 'ascend on[it],' *courir dedans* 'run in[it]'), they were coded as locations not inherent to motion, unless they were clearly marked for path (*courir jusqu'à* 'run/go all the way to').

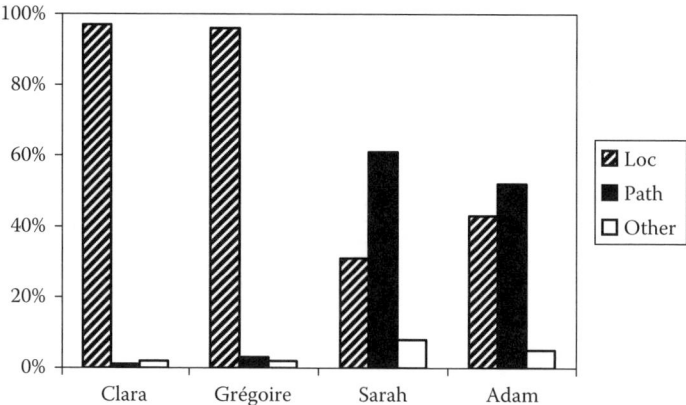

Figure 15.3 Motion information expressed outside of verb roots.

in English than in French (27% vs. 18%), although some individual differences occur in French, where manner verbs are more frequent for one child (Grégoire 28% vs. Clara 12%; for comparison Sarah 33%, Adam 26%). As shown in Figure 15.3, other devices rarely express any motion information in French (mostly location, Clara 97%, Grégoire 96%), whereas in English they frequently express path (Sarah 61%, Adam 52%) in addition to location (Sarah 31%, Adam 43%).

An overall measure of *utterance density* (UD) was calculated for all utterances that contained at least one of the five motion components listed in (32) above (regardless of their locus). As illustrated below (brackets show components), utterances fell into three groups (UD1, UD2, UD3+), depending on whether they expressed one component (*voler* 'fly' in (33)), two components (*fly* in (34)), or more (*push down* in (35)).

(33) Tiens celui-là i vole. (UD1 [Mm], Clara P2, 'Hey this one it flies.')
(34) I'm going fly a kite. (UD2 [Ca+Mm], Sarah, P3)
(35) I just pushed it down (UD3 [Ca+Mc+Pa], Sarah, P3)

As shown in Figure 15.4, semantic density is higher in English than in French. Most French utterances are UD1 (78%), fewer are UD2 (20%), and very few are UD3+ (2%). In comparison, more English utterances are UD2 (52%) and fewer are UD1 (38%), while UD3+ utterances are infrequent but nonetheless more frequent than in French (10%). This crosslinguistic difference holds at all ages and density shows no increase from P1 to P4: within each period, UD1 utterances are more frequent in French (e.g., 74% to 79%) than in English (25% to 41% in English).[6] Observed density levels hold for both children within each language, despite some individual differences. Density is low for both French children—and only slightly lower for Clara (UD1 82%, UD2 17%) than for Grégoire (UD1 74%, UD2 22%). Density is higher for both children in English, but Adam produces fewer UD1 utterances (35%) and more UD2 utterances (56%) than Sarah (UD1 62%, UD2 21%), who produces more UD3+ utterances (17%) than Adam (9%).

Higher utterance density in English is related to joint uses of verbs and other devices (see Figure 15.1 above). A further glance at information locus shows three ways in which specific components of motion (in (32) above) were encoded: only in verbs (V+X– in (36)), only in other devices (V–X+ in (37)), or in both (V+X+ in (38)). In French, the locus of information is clearly in verbs (V+X– 99%). This is less frequent in English (54%), where motion is also encoded in two more ways: verbs and other devices (V+X+ 35%) or other devices only (V–X+ 11%). This pattern clearly holds for all age periods in both languages. Thus, in French most utterances are V+X– for both children regardless of

---

[6] Across developmental periods, utterance density was remarkably stable in French, but tended to fluctuate in English, showing even an occasional decrease in density, partially related to variable proportions of utterances without any path or manner information (e.g., the neutral verb *go*).

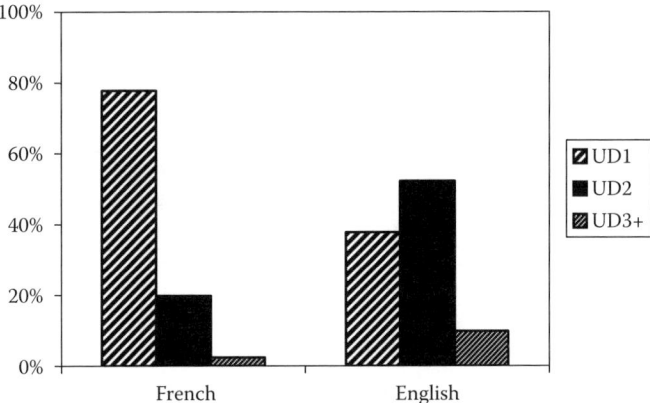

Figure 15.4 Overall utterance density for motion events.

age (99% to 100%). Similarly in English, regardless of age, children produce either V+X– (P1 55%, P2 55%, P3 54%) or V+X+ (P1 41%, P2 36%, P3 33%) utterances.

V+X– (36) a. They all dance. (UD1 [Ma], Sarah P3)
　　　　　b. Elle est partie. (UD1 [Pa], Clara P1)
　　　　　　('She has left.')
V–X+ (37) a. The mouse went up the clock. (UD1 [Pa], Sarah P3)
　　　　　b. Il va très vite. (UD1 [Ma], Clara P3)
　　　　　　('He is going very fast.')
V+X+ (38) a. I climb up the ladder. (UD2 [Ma+Pa], Sarah P2)
　　　　　b. Elle rentre à la pointe des pieds. (UD2 [Pa+Ma], Clara P4)
　　　　　　('She's entering at/on the tip of her feet.')

Finally, an unexpected result emerged in relation to the types of events that were denoted by children's motion verbs. Voluntary motion is overall more frequent than caused motion in English (57% and 38%), while the reverse tends to be true in French (42% and 52%). As shown in Figure 15.5, variations occur across ages. During P1, children focus more on voluntary motion than on caused motion in both languages (English 77% and 18%; French 62% and 25%). During P2 both event types are roughly as frequent (English 50% and 45%; French 45% and 46%). Thereafter, children talk less about caused motion in English (39%) than in French (P3=P4 57%) and the reverse is true for voluntary motion (English 56%, French 38%). Despite some individual differences during P2 (e.g., voluntary: Sarah 63%, Adam 48%, Grégoire 50%, Clara 32%), children increasingly talk about caused motion, but they do so more in French such as (39) and (40). We return to this result below. Recall that our predictions only concerned crosslinguistic differences in the density of utterances about motion.

(39) On met ça avant. (Clara P2)
　　　('One puts that before.' [wanting to put paint])
(40) Faut faire nager ma voiture. (Grégoire P3)
　　　('Must make swim my car.')

Summary

Young children learning English and French spontaneously talk about voluntary and caused motion to different degrees, but the results follow our predictions with both event types. French-speaking children use verbs to express motion information, but English-speaking children frequently associate

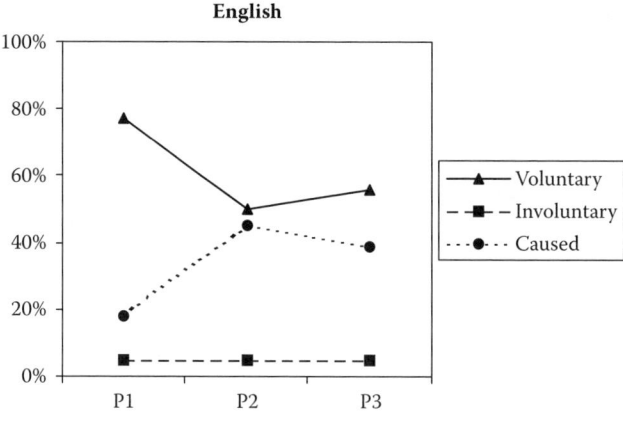

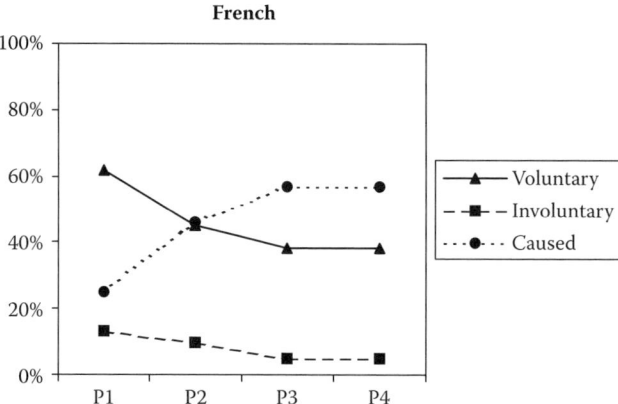

Figure 15.5 Types of motion events denoted.

verb roots with other devices. In both languages children express a variety of information components about motion (cause, path, manner), but they do so to different degrees and in different ways in the two languages. Manner verbs are more frequent in English than in French. Other devices frequently encode path in English, but rarely encode any motion information in French, where they almost exclusively express locations. Utterances are semantically denser in English, expressing more aspects of motion. These results hold for all periods, notwithstanding changes over developmental periods and individual differences.

CONCLUDING REMARKS

We examined how children talk about motion events in English and in French, predicting that typological properties (satellite- and verb-framing) should influence the semantic density of their utterances. Our general hypothesis was that utterance density should be higher in English than in French, irrespective of age (2 years to adulthood), event type (voluntary or caused motion), and situation (experimentally induced productions and early spontaneous productions). In summary, four main findings emerge.

First, as predicted, typological constraints on the locus of motion information in different languages determine the semantic density of children's utterances. Regardless of age and in all of the discourse situations examined, speakers express denser information in English than in French because they use easily accessible verb+satellite constructions to encode varied information about motion. For example, English speakers use such constructions to encode both the manner and the path of voluntary motion within one single clause. In contrast, French discourse is semantically less dense, because speakers have to use the main verb to express the path and/or cause of motion, and can only use less accessible peripheral devices to express manner (such as subordinate clauses). Accordingly, young children typically lexicalize path (with voluntary motion) or cause (with caused motion) in the verb and they rarely express manner. Thus, the relative complexity and accessibility of language structures for expressing certain semantic notions result in different degrees of salience for these notions in the discourse of children learning different languages.

Second, despite this crosslinguistic difference, the overall semantic density of children's utterances increases with age in both languages. In particular, children at 3 years of age tend to express less information about motion than children at later ages. Increasing semantic density presumably reflects the development of children's general cognitive capacity to simultaneously process multiple informational components, independently of the properties of the particular language they are learning. Not surprisingly, it is cognitively easier for all children to express only one semantic component of motion rather than more types of information. This is particularly clear in experimental situations specifically designed to invite them to encode more than one component.

A third finding, however, shows different developmental patterns in the encoding of manner and of path in children's discourse across languages. In particular, although manner is more frequent in English than in French, it increases with age in both languages, whereas path does not show such an increase in either language. Thus, our data show that manner information is infrequent in young children's discourse and strongly increases with age. Since manner in French is mainly expressed by peripheral devices, unless the main verb jointly expresses both manner and path (but this is not the prototypical pattern), such lexical items and constructions are harder to learn and therefore acquired late. In English, although the encoding of manner is more systematic than in French at all ages and with all event types, it nonetheless increases with age. Some of the utterances produced by the youngest English learners encode only path, while path+manner utterances increase with age. In line with this point, recall that spontaneous productions during early acquisition phases show no increase in semantic density across developmental periods in either language, as well as weaker language differences with respect to the expression of manner in comparison to experimentally induced productions from 3 years of age on.

Regardless of age, then, children encode path equally frequently in the two languages, expressing this component earlier and more systematically than manner. Therefore, in both languages, the increasing semantic density of children's utterances actually reflects their increasing encoding of manner. These findings suggest that path is more basic than manner as a result of more general and presumably universal factors. The general nature of location changes and their role in the construction of discourse representations may explain why this should be the case. With location changes, path provides the information that is necessary to locate entities at any point during unfolding discourse. In contrast, once introduced in discourse, general locations provide spatial anchors that can be entirely presupposed in subsequent utterances until a location change occurs in further discourse. As discussed above, it is precisely in relation to the manner of motion (rather than to its path) with location changes (rather than with motion within a given location) that predictions based on Talmy's and Slobin's proposals were expected to hold.

To summarize so far, general and presumably universal factors account for some findings, but only language-specific factors can account for others. General factors account for two findings: (1) young children's tendency to encode single information components and their increasing capacity to encode multiple components in both languages; (2) the more basic nature of path, explaining why in both languages young children encode path, rather than manner, when their utterances focus on only one component. However, only language-specific factors can account for why manner is more systematically encoded and utterance semantic density therefore higher in English at all ages. These different developmental rates follow from lexicalization and grammaticalization patterns in the two languages. Children acquiring French must learn a more complex system than those acquiring English in order to simultaneously express different aspects of motion. These findings are in line with studies of other child languages and they support the predictions that can be made on the basis of Slobin's proposal (e.g., Berman & Slobin, 1994; Choi & Bowerman, 1991; Slobin, 1996, 2004, 2006).

Finally, young children's utterances seem to focus on different types of motion—voluntary in English, and caused in French. This finding was not predicted, since our hypotheses only concerned the relative semantic density of children's utterances about (any type of) motion event in English vs. French, but not the relative frequency with which they would talk about different event types. One explanation might be that the distinction between voluntary and caused motion is more highlighted in French than in English. Whereas simple structures can express multiple aspects of both event types in English, French provides distinct constructions for caused motion (*faire* 'make' + infinitive). Causative constructions are quite productive and frequently the only way to represent motion produced by an external force (as distinct from motion spontaneously performed by an agent). Their frequent and sometimes quasi-obligatory use may therefore increase the salience of caused motion, despite the fact that they are difficult to learn. Related results have been observed in other verb-framed languages, showing for example an earlier distinction between voluntary and caused motion in Korean as compared to English (e.g., Choi & Bowerman, 1991).

In line with this account, early spontaneous productions show more transitive and intransitive uses of the same verbs in English.[7] In addition, children use causative constructions in French (but almost none in English) to represent motion, but also other events (e.g., *faire crier* 'to make scream,' Clara P3, *faire mouiller* 'to make [to/be] wet,' Grégoire P3). Our findings then suggest that the relative salience of information—particularly with changes of location—may result from different factors in a given language: the relative accessibility of some structures among other options expressing the same meaning; but also the highly-productive nature of some constructions expressing meanings that cannot be expressed otherwise (or at best only in rather awkward ways), distinctly differentiating some representations of motion from others (caused vs. voluntary).

In conclusion, our findings support the claim that typological properties constrain how speakers talk about motion from early acquisition phases to adulthood, inviting them to use different devices that focus their attention on different types of information. Assuming that these results are not merely due to sampling problems (particularly during early developmental phases), they show that general universal factors cannot alone account for language acquisition and language-specific factors have to be taken into account. As Slobin proposes, particular typological properties lead children to learn a particular way of 'thinking for speaking' when they acquire their native language. Among the aims to follow in the future in order to test this hypothesis, comparative research must further examine the timing of language-specific determinants by examining children's early language comprehension before the emergence of language. Despite its misnomer, we now know that the 'pre-linguistic' period is quite linguistic, even though it is mainly characterized by perceptual/receptive language skills (in addition to non-verbal concepts) before the emergence of productive language. A second question concerns the potential effects of language-specific factors on co-verbal and non-linguistic representations (e.g., gestures, non-verbal categorization, visual memory). This is a pressing challenge facing 'relativistic' approaches, since it is the only way to show that language particulars affect our cognitive organization beyond the production or comprehension of language itself. It is perhaps the most difficult challenge to meet in the context of current debates concerning the relation between language and cognition or, as Slobin puts it, between speaking and thinking.

REFERENCES

Berman, R. A., & Slobin, D. I. (Eds.). (1994). *Different ways of relating events in narrative: A crosslinguistic developmental study*. Hillsdale, NJ: Lawrence Erlbaum Associates.

---

[7] Some of these uses in English were rather idiosyncratic (e.g., transitive *fall*).

Bowerman, M. (1996). The origins of children's spatial semantic categories: Cognitive versus linguistic determinants. In J. J. Gumperz & S. C. Levinson (Eds.), *Rethinking linguistic relativity* (pp. 145–176). Cambridge, UK: Cambridge University Press.

Bowerman, M. (2007). Containment, support and beyond: Constructing topological spatial categories in first language. In M. Aurnague, M. Hickmann, & L. Vieu (Eds.), *Spatial entities in language and cognition* (pp. 177–203). Amsterdam: John Benjamins.

Bowerman, M., & Choi, S. (2003). Space under construction: Language-specific categorization in first language acquisition. In D. Gentner & S. Goldin-Meadow (Eds.), *Language in mind: Advances in the study of language and thought* (pp. 387–427). Cambridge, MA: The MIT Press.

Choi, S., & Bowerman, M. (1991). Learning to express motion events in English and Korean: The influence of language-specific lexicalization patterns. *Cognition, 41*, 83–121.

Clark, E. (2003). Language and representations. In D. Gentner & S. Goldin-Meadow (Eds.), *Language in mind: Advances in the study of language and thought* (pp. 17–24). Cambridge, MA: The MIT Press.

Filipović, L. (2002). *Verbs in motion expressions: Structural perspectives*. Unpublished doctoral dissertation. Cambridge University, Department of Linguistics.

Gumperz, J. J., & Levinson, S. C. (Eds.). (1996). *Rethinking linguistic relativity*. Cambridge, UK: Cambridge University Press.

Hickmann, M. (2003). *Children's discourse: Person, space and time across languages*. Cambridge, UK: Cambridge University Press.

Hickmann, M. (2006). The relativity of motion in first language acquisition. In M. Hickmann & S. Robert (Eds.), *Space across languages: Linguistic systems and cognitive categories* (pp. 281–308). Amsterdam: John Benjamins.

Hickmann, M. (2007). Static and dynamic location in French: Developmental and crosslinguistic perspectives. In M. Aurnague, M. Hickmann, & L. Vieu (Eds.), *Spatial entities in language and cognition* (pp. 205–231). Amsterdam: John Benjamins.

Hickmann, M., & Hendriks, H. (2005, July). Children's expression of caused motion in French and English. Paper presented at the IASCL conference, Berlin, Germany.

Hickmann, M., & Hendriks, H. (2006). Static and dynamic location in French and in English. *First Language, 26*(1), 103–135.

Klein, W. (1994). *Time in language*. London and New York: Routledge.

Kopecka, A. (2006). The semantic structure of motion verbs in French: Typological perspectives. In M. Hickmann & S. Robert (Eds.), *Space across languages: Linguistic systems and cognitive categories* (pp. 83–101). Amsterdam: John Benjamins.

Landau, B., & Jackendoff, R. (1993). What and Where in spatial language and spatial cognition. *Behavioral and Brain Sciences, 16*(2), 217–38.

Lemmens, M. (2002). Tracing referent location in oral picture descriptions. In A. Wilson, P. Rayson, & T. McEnery (Eds.), *A rainbow of corpora—Corpus linguistics and the languages of the world* (pp. 73–85). Munich: Lincom-Europa.

Levinson, S. C. (2003). Language and mind: Let's get the issues straight! In D. Gentner & S. Goldin-Meadow (Eds.), *Language in mind: Advances in the study of language and thought* (pp. 59–46). Cambridge, MA: The MIT Press.

Levinson, S. C., & Wilkins, D. P. (2006). *Grammars of space: Explorations in cognitive diversity*. Cambridge, UK: Cambridge University Press.

Lucy, J. (1992). *Language diversity and thought: A reformulation of the linguistic relativity hypothesis*. Cambridge, UK: Cambridge University Press.

Munnich, E., & Landau, B. (2003). The effects of spatial language on spatial representation: Setting some boundaries. In D. Gentner & S. Goldin-Meadow (Eds.), *Language in mind: Advances in the study of language and thought* (pp. 113–155). Cambridge, MA: The MIT Press.

Nuyts, J., & Pederson, E. (Eds.). (1997). *Language and conceptualization*. Cambridge, UK: Cambridge University Press.

Peyraube, A. (2006). Motion events in Chinese: A diachronic study of directional complements. In M. Hickmann & S. Robert (Eds.), *Space across languages: Linguistic systems and cognitive categories* (pp. 121–135). Amsterdam: John Benjamins.

Piérart, B. (1978). Genèse et structuration des marqueurs de relations spatiales entre trois et dix ans. In J. Costermans (Ed.), *Structures cognitives et organisation du langage, Cahiers de l'Institut de Linguistique, 5*(1–2), 41–59.

Slobin, D. I. (1985) Crosslinguistic evidence for the language-making capacity. In D. I. Slobin (Ed.), *The crosslinguistic study of language acquisition* (pp. 1157–1257). Hillsdale, NJ: Lawrence Erlbaum Associates.

Slobin, D. I. (1996). From 'thought to language' to 'thinking for speaking.' In J. J. Gumperz & S. C. Levinson (Eds.), *Rethinking linguistic relativity* (pp. 70–96). Cambridge, UK: Cambridge University Press.

Slobin, D. I. (2003). Language and thought online: Cognitive consequences of linguistic relativity. In D. Gentner & S. Goldin-Meadow (Eds.), *Language in mind: Advances in the study of language and thought* (pp. 157–191). Cambridge, MA: The MIT Press.

Slobin, D. I. (2004). The many ways to search for a frog: linguistic typology and the expression of motion events. In S. Strömquist & L. Verhoeven (Eds.), *Relating events in narratives: Vol. 2. Typological and contextual perspectives* (pp. 219–257). Mahwah, NJ: Lawrence Erlbaum Associates.

Slobin, D. I. (2006). What makes manner of motion salient? Explorations in linguistic typology, discourse, and cognition. In M. Hickmann & S. Robert (Eds.), *Space across languages: Linguistic systems and cognitive categories* (pp. 59–81). Amsterdam: John Benjamins.

Talmy, L. (2000). *Towards a cognitive semantics*. Cambridge, MA: The MIT Press.

Verjat, I. (1991). Le statut cognitif des marqueurs 'devant' et 'derrière' chez l'enfant français. *L'Année Psychologique, 91*, 207–230.

Whorf, B. L. (1956). *Language, thought and reality*. Cambridge, MA: The MIT Press.

16

Language and Affect
Japanese Children's Use of Evaluative Expressions in Narratives[1]

KEIKO NAKAMURA
Keio University

> There is a special kind of thinking that is intimately tied to language—namely, the thinking that is carried out, on-line, in the process of speaking...In my own formulation: the expression of experience in linguistic terms constitutes thinking for speaking—a special form of thought that is mobilized for communication...
>
> **(Slobin, 1996, pp. 75–76)**

My first meeting with Dan was in the spring of 1988, when I was busy visiting graduate programs in psychology. Over the past two decades, he has been an invaluable mentor and I have been constantly amazed by his strong dedication to his teaching and research. In particular, Dan's firm commitment to the crosslinguistic approach and his introduction of the Frog Story to the field as a methodological tool have influenced my own research on Japanese language development, especially my work on narratives. The study presented here is an extension of a paper on evaluative language use in Japanese and Turkish narratives (Küntay & Nakamura, 2004) and it focuses specifically on Japanese data.

INTRODUCTION

Over the past two decades, a growing body of research on language and affect has emerged. Although these studies have drawn from a variety of approaches and methodologies, they all strongly support the view that language and affect are closely intertwined. Across languages, different phonological, morphosyntactic, lexical, and discourse features are used to express one's attitudes, moods, and feelings. We know that both children and adults use language to signal how they feel, while also interpreting and responding to affective information in the language of others (Ochs & Schieffelin, 1986). Our linguistic ability to express our feelings seems to develop in an effortless manner. As Ochs and Schieffelin (1986) state, "beyond the function of communicating referential information, languages are responsive to the fundamental need of speakers to convey and assess feelings, moods, dispositions, and attitudes" (p. 9). But, how do children learn to express affective information?

---

[1] This research was supported by a Humanities Graduate Research Grant from the University of California, Berkeley.

There have been numerous developmental studies which examine the relationship between language and affect. We know that children's ability to talk about emotions develops early and has various consequences for interpersonal interaction and subsequent socio-emotional development (e.g., Bretherton, Fritz, Zahn-Wexler, & Ridgeway, 1986; Dunn, Brown, & Beardsall, 1991; Zahn-Waxler, Radke-Yarrow, & King, 1979). Researchers have also examined children's comprehension and production of lexical and grammatical expressions of affect in different cultures (e.g., Ochs, 1986; Schieffelin, 1986). These studies illustrate that across cultures, from an early age, children are able to use affective terms and grammatical constructions to express feelings, moods, attitudes, and dispositions.

Among the many research orientations to the topic of language and affect, sociolinguistic approaches have examined the role of affect in narratives (e.g., Labov & Waletsky, 1967; Schiffrin, 1987; Tannen, 1982). In particular, Labov and Waletsky (1967), in their seminal study of 600 personal narratives on near-death experiences, distinguished two major functions of narratives, namely (1) the referential function and (2) the evaluative function. While the referential components include information about the characters and the events of the story and are grounded in sequentiality and temporality, the evaluative components give meaning to the story by revealing the narrator's perspective and understanding of narrated events. Evaluative components can suspend the flow of the plot and give the story meaning by adding narrator reactions, judgments, and interpretations. This allows the speaker to convey affect by reflecting speaker attitudes, moods, and feelings.

There have also been a large number of studies that look at the development of evaluative devices in children's conversational narratives. Umiker-Sebeok (1979) found devices such as lexical intensifiers, references to emotional states, and comparators in preschoolers' intra-conversational narratives. She found that, between ages 3 and 5, the frequency of use and repertoire of evaluative devices increased. In a study with 2-year-olds, Miller and Sperry (1988) observed family interactions filled with talk about the affective states of family members, which they considered to be a narrative evaluation strategy. In addition, Peterson and McCabe (1983) reported that children use both lexical and phonological evaluative devices to convey evaluation in personal narratives. Furthermore, Hudson, Gebelt, Haviland, and Bentivegna (1992) reported that even young children employ different narrative structures when narrating experiences related to different emotional moods (e.g., happiness, anger, fear).

Evaluative devices are found not only in personal narratives that depict personal experiences in first-person voice but also in third-person narratives that depict the experiences of others. Bamberg and Reilly (1996) found that narrators creating elicited oral narratives employ considerable effort in expressing the significance of events from their own emotional and subjective point of view. As they argue, in order to tell a good story, narrators must infer and convey aspects of the story that are not obvious (e.g., intentions and feelings of characters, narrators' interpretations). In a study of evaluative devices used in elicited oral narratives, Bamberg and Damrad-Frye (1991) examined five different categories: references to characters' mental and affective states (frames of mind), character speech, hedges, negative qualifiers, and causal connectors as used by 5-year-old, 9-year-old, and adult speakers of American English. Adults, on average, used three times as many evaluative devices (relative to story length) as compared to 5-year-olds. Furthermore, Küntay and Nakamura (2004) conducted a comparison of evaluative devices used by Turkish and Japanese children and adults in elicited oral narratives. Even from an early age, children were socialized to use language- and culture-appropriate strategies to mark evaluative functions. While Turkish narrators used frames of mind, enrichment devices, and evaluative remarks, Japanese narrators relied heavily on character speech, frames of mind, enrichment devices, negative qualifiers, and onomatopoeia.

This study attempts to further explore the ability of children and adults to express affect by using culturally appropriate evaluative devices in narrative. In this study, the term "affect" is defined as a broader category than "emotion," to include feelings, attitudes, moods, and dispositions associated with persons and situations (Ochs & Schieffelin, 1986). During narrative construction, narrators express their feelings and attitudes toward various events and characters, as well as their own act of narration. Mastery of evaluative skills helps to convey affect and creates a more effective, coherent narrative.

Researchers such as Maynard (1993, 1999) have repeatedly commented that one cannot use Japanese without revealing one's personal attitude (e.g., toward the content of information and toward the addressee). This study will examine some of the evaluative devices in Japanese narratives which convey such affect, utilizing a developmental framework. How do Japanese children encode affective content into their narratives through the use of evaluative devices? The purpose of this study is to examine (1) what types of evaluative devices Japanese children and adults use in oral narratives and (2) how the usage of such evaluative devices changes with age. Research on this topic will add to the growing body of literature on affect in narratives across languages and cultures and help us to understand the process of narrative development.

METHOD

Participants

Seventy-six monolingual Japanese children and 16 monolingual Japanese adults participated in the study.[2] The children included seven 3-year-olds, seventeen 4-year-olds, seventeen 5-year-olds, nineteen 7-year-olds and sixteen 9-year-olds. All participants came from middle-class families living in the Tokyo and Kobe metropolitan areas.

Procedure

The task consisted of telling a story based on the 24-page wordless picture book *Frog, where are you?* (Mayer, 1969). This picture book has been used by Berman, Slobin, and their colleagues (Berman & Slobin, 1994) to identify different linguistic strategies used by narrators of different ages speaking different languages (e.g., Strömqvist & Verhoeven, 2004). Although the use of this storybook as a narrative-elicitation device limits the range of linguistic expressions that may be gathered, it provides researchers with an excellent way to collect and compare narratives from speakers of different ages and languages in their depiction of the same set of events.

The story is about a boy, a dog, and their pet frog. It begins with the boy and dog looking at their frog in a jar. While the boy and the dog are asleep, the frog escapes. The next morning, discovering that the frog has escaped, the boy and the dog start to look for it. During their search, they run into various animals in the woods and experience several incidents (e.g., being chased by bees, being pushed off a cliff by a deer). Eventually they are reunited with their frog. In order to tell the story successfully, the narrator must infer and convey aspects of the story which are not overtly available from the pictures (e.g., relationships between characters, emotions and mental states, such as fear, surprise) as well as provide intentions, motivations, and causal explanations for the characters' actions through the use of evaluative expressions.

The narrators were given time to look through the book and then asked to tell the story. All narratives were audiotaped and transcribed.

Coding

Coding categories for the evaluative devices were adapted from Bamberg and Damrad-Frye (1991). As Japanese differs from English in its types of evaluative devices, two coding categories were added, namely, *onomatopoeia* and *enrichment expressions*:[3]

---

[2] The data examined in this study are the same dataset examined in Küntay and Nakamura (2004), with an additional group of 3-year-olds.
[3] The seven coding categories examined in this study are not exhaustive in terms of possible evaluative devices. Other types of evaluative devices also need to be examined in the future (e.g., verb style shifts, passive vs. active voice, perspective-encoding through verbs of giving and receiving, use of auxiliary verbs and sentence-final particles encoding attitude).

- *Overall story length:* Children's narratives varied considerably in length. Therefore, proportional measures were used in order to make meaningful comparisons by controlling for variation in story length. Each clause in a complex sentence roughly represented one single event.
- *Evaluative devices*: A list of evaluative devices and their descriptions is provided below.
  - *Frames of mind* are expressions that refer to the mental and affective states of characters as inferred by the narrator, leading to audience interest and empathy.
  - *Emotion terms* are words used by the narrator to refer to a character's emotions (e.g., *kanashii* 'to be sad,' *okoru* 'to be angry').
  - *Affective behaviors* include descriptions resulting from emotions (e.g., *naku* 'to cry,' *warau* 'to laugh').
  - *Emotion verbs* are descriptions of action that initiate emotion in others (e.g., *bikkuri-saseru* 'to surprise,' *odokasu* 'to frighten').
  - *Mental state verbs* are verbs that attribute cognitive states, epistemic stances, or physiological states to the narrator or the characters (e.g., *omou* 'to think,' *kimeru* 'to decide').
- *Character speech* occurs when the narrator speaks for one of the characters, using direct or indirect speech. Character speech reflects a narrator's understanding of a character's feelings and intentions, adding immediacy and vividness to the story. Examples include direct character speech (e.g., *otoko no ko wa "shizuka ni!" to itta* 'The boy said "Be quiet!"') and indirect character speech (e.g., *otoko no ko wa inu ni shizuka ni suru yoo ni itta* 'The boy told the dog to be quiet'). Direct character speech is often accompanied by animated voice and prosody.
- *Negative qualifiers* reveal the narrator's expectations by depicting story circumstances or events that did not take place. All direct negations of states and actions were included in this category (e.g., *nai* 'don't have,' *inai* 'isn't (there),' *noborenai* 'can't climb').
- *Causal connectors* refer to the inferred motivation for an action, providing causal frameworks for the implicit relationships between temporally sequenced events (e.g., *kara* 'because,' *no ni* 'in order to').
- *Hedges* inform the audience about the narrator's uncertainty regarding the truth value of a specific proposition, such as lexical devices that suggest non-commitment to the truth value of the proposition (e.g., *moshikashitara* 'maybe,' *sukoshi* 'a little') and expressions that convey uncertainty on the part of the narrator in respect to the truth value of story elements (e.g., *omou* '(I) think').
- *Onomatopoiea* are Japanese mimetic expressions which help to attract the listener's attention by conveying information vividly. McVeigh (1996) describes the important role that onomatopoeia plays in the depiction of mental and emotional states in Japanese. Three different categories of mimetic expressions were included: (1) phenomimes, phonetic representations of phenomena perceptible by non-auditory senses, such as *kushakusha* 'all rumpled,' *guruguru* 'round and round'; (2) psychomimes, phonetic representations of psychological states (e.g., emotions), such as *mutto* 'sullen,' *gakkari* 'disappointed,' and (3) phonomimes, phonetic representations of sounds, such as *bunbun* 'buzz-buzz' (Martin, 1975).
- *Enrichment expressions* are adverbial phrases, which serve as intensifiers and emphatic markers (e.g., *totemo* 'very,' *itsumo* 'always'), drawing the listener's attention to a specific event. Adverbial phrases which reveal the unexpected or inferred nature of an action, such as *mata* 'again' and *kyuu ni* 'suddenly,' were also included, as well as connectives that preface unexpected events, such as *shikashi* 'however.'

All instances of evaluative devices were extracted from the data, and the relative frequency with which each evaluative device was used was assessed by dividing the frequency of production of an evaluative device across children within an age group by the total number of clauses produced in each age group. Further analysis included qualitative comparisons of the similarities and differences in children's use of evaluative devices across ages.

RESULTS

In order to be able to compare the use of evaluative devices across age groups, the overall story length for each age group was established, using the number of clauses as an indication of story length. The mean number of clauses was 31.1 for the 4-year-olds, 41.4 for the 5-year-olds, 51.0 for the 7-year-olds, 37.9 for the 9-year-olds, and 57.4 for the adults.[4] In general, with the exception of the 9-year-olds, there was a gradual increase in the number of clauses, thus the length of narratives with age.

As can be seen in Table 16.1, children did not differ in their overall use of evaluative devices across the different ages.[5] Children at all ages, as well as adults, consistently made attempts to employ evaluative devices in their narratives. One surprising finding was that the 9-year-olds used the fewest evaluative devices (relative to story length) as compared to the other age groups.[6]

Analyses of the narrative data revealed various age-related trends in the use of specific evaluative devices.

TABLE 16.1 Percentage of Clauses Containing Type of Evaluative Device in Japanese (by age)*

	4	5	7	9	Adults
Frames of mind	8.7	8.1	10.5	6.4	13.2
Character speech	9.8	10.1	7.4	5.3	5.1
Negative qualifiers	6.1	6.1	5.3	5.3	6.5
Causal connectors	2.8	1.0	3.9	2.0	3.7
Hedges	1.3	1.9	4.3	2.3	2.3
Onomatopoeia	3.6	3.3	3.1	2.2	1.0
Enrichment expressions	4.5	4.8	3.9	9.7	10.0
Total	36.9	35.2	38.5	33.2	41.9
Mean # of clauses	31.1	41.4	51.0	37.9	57.4

Note: From "Linguistic strategies serving evaluative functions: A comparison between Japanese and Turkish narratives" by A. Küntay & K. Nakamura, in S. Strömqvist & L. Verhoeven (Eds.), *Relating events in narrative, Volume 2: Typological and contextual perspective* (p. 341), 2004, Mahwah, NJ: Lawrence Erlbaum Associates. Copyright 2004 by Lawrence Erlbaum Associates, Inc.

* The percentages were computed by dividing the total number of evaluative devices children produced within an age group by the total number of clauses the same children produced in their narrative reproductions.

---

[4] Please note that the means presented here do not take into account individual variation, which would have been better reflected with a different form of statistical analysis.
[5] As there were only seven 3-year-olds who were able to construct coherent narratives, quantitative analyses were not conducted on the 3-year-old data.
[6] The poor performance of the 9-year-olds has been discussed in Küntay and Nakamura (2004). One possible factor is the boy:girl ratio (twelve boys: four girls), as boys tend to produce shorter, less elaborate narratives than girls. Another factor may be the fact that school-age children tend to be less engaged in the task, regarding it as a school task (something to be completed) rather than as a fun task (something to be creative with).

Frames of Mind

In general, with the exception of the 9-year-olds, the number of references to frames of mind increased with age.

Emotion Terms
Even 3-year-olds were able to describe basic emotions such as *kowai* 'to be scared' and *okoru* 'to be angry' (see examples 1 and 2, ages are indicated in parentheses).

(1) *kaeru* **kowai** *no*. (3;0)
    frog scared EP[7]
    'The frog **is scared**.'
(2) **okotteru** *no…kore*. (3;0)
    angry-PROG EP this
    'This (the frog) **is angry**.'

Narrators became more likely to make overt references to emotions and use a wider variety of emotion terms with increasing age. For example, while the 4-year-olds only used four emotion terms (*okoru* 'to be angry,' *yorokobu* 'to be happy,' *bikkuri suru* 'to be surprised,' *hazukashii* 'to be embarrassed'), adults used 14 emotion terms, which included complex emotions, such as *hotto suru* 'to be relieved,' *shinpai suru* 'to be worried,' and *tanoshii* 'to enjoy.'

(3) *inu ga* **shonbori-shiteru**. (5;0)
    dog SUBJ dejected-do-PROG
    'The dog **is dejected**.'
(4) *risu mitai na no ga dete-kite* **bikkuri shita**. (7;8)
    squirrel like one SUBJ come out-CONT surprise-do-PAST
    'Something like a squirrel came out and (the boy) **was surprised**.'

In general, references to emotions were used for different functions, either to attribute feelings as outcomes of actions, or to attribute feelings as motivations to act. Both of these helped to organize the sequence of actions into a coherent story. Preschoolers used references to third-person characters' emotional states in order to describe the local aspects of the story, such as those inferred from the characters' facial expressions. On the other hand, older child narrators, as well as adults, used references to emotional states to signal the relevance of individual story events from a more global storytelling perspective. Similar findings were reported for English-speaking narrators (Bamberg & Reilly, 1996).

Affective Behaviors
Even the youngest narrators were able to depict affective behaviors such as crying and laughing. The number of affective behaviors depicted did not change over time.

(5) **waratta**. (3;0)
    laugh-PAST
    '(He) laughed.'
(6) *de* **naiteru** *no*. (3;0)
    and cry-PROG EP
    'And (he)'s **crying**.'
(7) *bin o watte-shimatte maikeru wa jon o* **okorimashita**. (adult)
    jar DO break-end up-CONT Michael TOP John DO scold-PAST-POL

---

[7] Abbreviations for glosses: COND conditional; CONT continuative; COP copula; DO direct object marker; EP extended predicate; GEN genitive; IO indirect object marker; LOC locative; NEG negative; NONPAST nonpast; POT potential; PASS passive; PAST past; POL polite; PROG progressive; Q question; QUOT quotative; SUBJ subject marker; TOP topic marker.

'Since (the dog) ended up breaking the jar, Michael **scolded** John.'

Emotion Verbs This category included actions which trigger emotion in others, such as *bikkuri-saseru* 'to surprise someone.' The number of expressions in this category was relatively small and emotion verbs were used only by a few narrators.

(8) *maikeru wa fukuroo ni **odorokasarete** ochite-shimaimashita.* (adult)
    Michael TOP owl IO be surprised-PASS fall-end up-PAST-POL
    'Michael **was surprised** by the owl and ended up falling down.'

Mental State Terms Even the youngest narrators were able to use basic mental state terms, such as *omou* 'to think' and *wakaru* 'to understand' as well as expressions related to internal desires and hopes.

(9) *sorede otoko no ko ga nanka aru ka na to **omotteru** no.* (4;0)
    and then boy SUBJ something exist Q QUOT think-PROG EP
    'And then the boy **is thinking** "is there something (in this hole)?"'
(10) *jibun de **nobori-tagatteru** no.* (5;4)
    himself by climb-want-PROG EP
    '(He) **wanted to climb** (up) by himself.'

Narrators were also able to use mental state terms which indicated inner psychological and cognitive states (e.g., *to suru* 'to try').

(11) *hachi ga inu o kamoo **to shita**.* (4;0)
    bees SUBJ dog DO bite-try-PAST
    'The bees **tried** to bite the dog.'

Other mental state terms depicted the attentional levels of the characters (e.g., *ki ga tsuku* 'notice,' *mushi suru* 'ignore').

(12) *jibun wa hachi ni **chuui shita**.* (5;4)
    he TOP bees IO be careful-PAST
    'He **was careful** of the bees.'
(13) *otoko no ko wa **shiranpuri o shiteru** no.* (5;5)
    boy TOP ignoring DO do-PROG EP
    'The boy **is ignoring** (the dog).'

Basic physiological states included sleep, death, and various levels of consciousness. Even the 3-year-olds were able to depict simple physiological states, such as *itai* 'to be in pain.' With age, narrators became able to depict more complex physiological states.

(14) ***neteru**.* (3;0)
    sleep-PROG
    '(The boy)'s **sleeping**.'
(15) ***oboreteru**.* (3;6)
    drown-PROG
    '(He)'s **drowning**.'

Overall, the total number of types of frames of mind expressions increased steadily with age: 4-year-olds (15 types), 7-year-olds (22), and adults (41). As mentioned previously, frames of mind terms used by the 4-year-olds were limited to a handful of basic mental state and emotion terms, such as *omou* 'to think,' *hoshii* 'to want,' and *yorokobu* 'to be happy.' Adults, on the other hand, were able to use a wider range of expressions, such as *gokigen o toru* 'to get on someone's good side,' *kawaigaru* 'to treat fondly,' *yakusoku o suru* 'to promise,' and *kanshin suru* 'to be impressed.'

Metalinguistic comments, in which the narrators made comments and asked questions about details in their own stories, were also included in the analysis, and were commonly observed in all age groups.

(16) *kore nandaka **wakaranai** no.* (4;0)
 this what know-NEG EP
 '(I) **don't know** what this is.' (pointing)

Character Speech

The results show that use of character speech seems to decrease with age. Initially, Japanese children seem to rely heavily on character speech (e.g., in combination with animated tone of voice, exaggerated prosody, and intonation), while adults tend to use other types of evaluative devices. Character speech was the evaluative device used most frequently by the 4- and 5-year-old narrators. With the younger age groups, direct speech appeared frequently for both the human and animal characters:

(17) "***shiii!***" *tte iutteru.* (3;0)
 shhhh QUOT say-PROG
 '(He)'s saying "**shhhhh!**"'
(18) "***nani suru no yo!***" *tte iu no.* (4;11)
 what do EP QUOT say EP
 '(He) says "**What are (you) doing?**"'

Several younger children used direct character speech throughout their narratives (i.e., one quote for each picture), so that the whole narrative was in a dialogue format, as seen in the following excerpt:[8]

(19) *aa mogura datta!*   Hey, it's a mole!
 kaeru-san!   Frog!
 are doko itta no?   Hey, where did (you) go?
 waaa ita!   (scream) there's (an owl)!
 kyaa kowai!   (scream) (I'm) scared!
 nigero!   Run away!

Direct character speech decreased with age, and indirect character speech constituted a larger proportion of quoted speech for the older narrators:

(20) *otoko no ko wa inu ni **shizuka ni suru yoo ni** iikikasete ki no*
 man child dog quiet to do say-repeat-CONT tree
 uragawa o nozoki-komimashita. (adult)
 back DO look in-PAST-POL
 'The boy repeatedly told the dog to be quiet and peered around the back of the tree.'

Overall, the importance of character speech as an evaluative device seemed to decrease with age, as older narrators used other evaluative strategies.

---

[8] Parts in parentheses are ellipted in Japanese.

Negative Qualifiers

The number of negative qualifiers was approximately the same for all age groups. In general, the most common type of negative qualifier was a negation of state or existence, as in *inai* 'to not exist (animate)' and *nai* 'to not exist (inanimate).'

(21) *kaeru ga **inai**.* (3;0)
   frog SUBJ to be-NEG
   'The frog's **not (there)**.'
(22) *sorekara doko mo sagashita no ni nanni mo **nakatta** no.* (4;11)
   and then where also search-PAST but something also exist-NEG EP
   'And then (they) searched everywhere, but there **was nothing**.'

In addition, even the youngest children were able to use negations of action, such as *ochitenai* 'isn't falling' or *haitte-inai* 'isn't inside,' which reflect the narrators' expectations regarding anticipated actions.

(23) *kodomo ga hato ni tsuki-saserareru to omottara*
   child SUBJ pigeon IO poke-PASS QUOT think
   tsuki-saserare-nakatta. (4;0)
   poke-PASS-NEG-PAST
   'The child thought (he) was going to be poked by the pigeon, but (he) **was not poked**.'
(24) *kono iwa dare mo **notte-nai** no.*
   this boulder someone climb on-NEG EP
   'No one is (climbed up) on this boulder.'

With age, children become more skillful at encoding concepts related to negation of the character's ability, such as *noborenai* 'can't climb up.'

(25) *booshi **torenai** no.* (3;0)
   hat remove-POT-NEG EP
   '(He) **can't remove** (his) hat.'

Causal Connectors

The number of causal connectors did not show a clear developmental trend. While the mean number was relatively high for the 7-year-olds (M=3.9) and adults (M=3.7), it was much lower for the 5-year-olds (M=1.0) and 9-year-olds (M=2.0). There were strong individual differences in the use of causal connectors, especially among the younger children: only 4 of the seventeen 4-year-old narrators and 6 of the seventeen 5-year-old narrators used causal connectors. Furthermore, their choice of causal connectors was limited to *kara* 'because' and *yoo ni* 'in order to.' A larger proportion of the older narrators used causal connectors and they were able to use a larger variety of linguistic devices to mark causal relations. Almost all of the causal connectors expressed purpose by providing explicit motivations for a character's actions or behaviors.

(26) *okotteru ... nanka shita **kara**.* (4;6)
   angry-PROG something do-PAST because
   '(He)'s angry because (the dog) did something.'
(27) *kaeru o yonde-mita **kara** hachi ga dete-kimashita.* (9;3)
   frog DO call-CONT-try so bees SUBJ come out-PAST-POL
   '**Because** (he) tried calling the frog, bees came out.'

In many cases, causality was not expressed by an explicit causal connective, but was conveyed by a series of sequential clauses:

(28) *koomori ga dete kokechatta.* (3;0)
 bat SUBJ come out-CONT fall down-end up-PAST
 'A bat came out and (the boy) ended up falling down.'
(29) *Kukkii wa hachi no su o mitsukete oo-yorokobi.* (5;5)
 Cookie TOP bee GEN hive DO find-CONT very happy
 'Cookie found a beehive and was very happy.'

Children also used explicit and implicit causal markers that indicate physical causality:

(30) *sore de inu ga okkochite garasu ga warechatta no.* (5;5)
 and then dog SUBJ fall-CONT glass SUBJ break-end up-PAST EP
 'And then the dog fell and the glass ended up breaking.'
(31) *fukuroo-san ga tobi-dashite-kita kara dosuun-tte shita no.*
 owl SUBJ fly-out-come-PAST so thud-QUOT do-PAST EP
 '(The boy) fell with a thud because the owl came flying out.'

As discussed in Küntay and Nakamura (2004), Japanese narratives included a lower percentage of clauses with causal devices than the narratives produced by English-speaking children and adults (Bamberg & Damrad-Frye, 1991). In particular, the proportion of clauses explicitly combined with mental state terms was much lower in Japanese narratives. One possible explanation for this is that Japanese narrators may feel that it is not necessary to explicitly tie mental state expressions to causal connectives as such relations are implied, perhaps due to the Japanese cultural concept of *sasshi*, which means 'consideration for others.'[9]

Hedges

The number of hedges was relatively low in all age groups, with the only exception of the 7-year-olds. No clear developmental trend was found for either the number or the type of hedges children produced. For example, while the 4-year-olds used five types of hedges, including *moshikashitara* 'maybe' and *mitai na* 'like,' the adults also used only five types of hedges. Some of these overlapped with the forms used by the 4-year-olds, such as *deshoo* 'probably,' while others differed (e.g., *yoo da* 'seems'). The highest number of hedges appeared in the 7-year-olds' narratives, which was primarily due to the frequent use of hedges by only a few narrators within this age group, reflecting strong individual differences.

(32) **moshikashitara** *inu ga koko ni noborenai to* **omou**. (4;4)
 maybe dog here to climb-NEG-POT think
 '(I) **think** that **maybe** the dog cannot climb (up) here.'
(33) *wankun wa sakki no hako* **mitai na** *yatsu o kabutte shiranpuri o*
 dog TOP before box like thing DO wore-CONT ignore DO
 shiteru no. (5;5)
 do-PROG EP
 'The dog is wearing the box-**like** thing and ignoring (the boy).'

Overall, we found fewer hedges in Japanese narratives as compared to what has been reported for English-speaking children by Bamberg and Damrad-Frye (1991). The narrators in this study

---

[9] According to Ishii (1984), *sasshi* involves consideration for others through the perceptive understanding of messages from a minimal number of explicit cues.

seemed to feel that the narrative construction task was a formal one; they used long pauses, taking time to formulate what they were going to say. Although many researchers have reported that avoidance of direct assertions through the use of hedges is particularly important in Japanese society, where politeness is strongly valued, it is possible that there are genres in which hedges occur relatively infrequently (e.g., Maynard, 1990). Differences in genre (e.g., elicited narratives vs. personal narratives) may also explain why fewer hedges appeared as compared to Minami (1998), who reported frequent use of hedges in Japanese personal narratives.

Onomatopoiea

In general, young children used a wider variety of onomatopoeia than adults. Overall, 4- and 5-year-olds used nineteen and seventeen different types of onomatopoeia respectively, such as *bun-bun* 'buzz-buzz,' *doboon* 'splash,' and *kunkun* 'sniff-sniff.' With age, the variety of onomatopoeia decreased, with the 9-year-olds only using nine types. Adults tended to rely on other evaluative strategies in their narratives.

In general, the onomatopoeic expressions used by the children were phonomimes and phenomimes, with a small handful of psychomimes. Phonomimes included animal noises, or expressions depicting the falling noises of the dog, the deer, and the boy or the splashing sound of the water.

(34) *taoreru* **DOTTEN** *to.* (3;0)
 fall-NONPAST thud QUOT
 '(He)'s going to fall with a **thud**.'
(35) *shika okkotta **jabon**!* (3;9)
 deer fall-PAST splash
 'The deer fell "**splash**"!'

Examples of phenomimes, sound representations of phenomena perceptible by non-auditory senses describing the manner or appearance of a situation, included the following (see 36 and 37 below):

(36) *tori ga **zaa**! to dete-kite kodomo ga ochita*
 bird SUBJ swoop QUOT come out-CONT child SUBJ fall-PAST
 no. (4;11)
 EP
 'A bird came out with a swoop and (so) the child fell down.'
(37) *inu wa **noro-noro** aruite-iru.* (7;4)
 dog TOP slowly walk-PROG
 'The dog is walking **slowly**.'

A variety of phenomimes were used to express the wetness of the boy's clothes after he fell into the water.

(38) *oyoofuku wa **betobeto ni** nureta kedo kutsushita toka wa*
 clothes TOP sticky wet-PAST but socks etc. TOP
 nurenakatta no.
 wet-NEG-PAST EP
 'His clothes were wet and **sticky** but his socks and stuff didn't get wet.' (4;11)
(39) *sorede bisho-bisho ni natte "shii!"-tte shiteru no.* (4;7)
 and then drip-drip become-CONT "shhh" QUOT do-PROG EP.
 'And then (he) became **soaking wet** and is going "shhh!"'

Enrichment Expressions

The use of enrichment expressions increased with age. The 4-year-olds relied on a small number of adverbial expressions (e.g., *mata* 'again,' *itsumo* 'always').

(40) *kaeru-chan to wanwan **mada** neteru.* (3;0)
   frog and dog still sleep-PROG
   'The frog and dog are still sleeping.'

(41) ***mata** ana o miteru.* (4;8)
   again hole look-PROG
   '(The boy) is looking at the hole **again**.'

The older children were more skillful at using adverbs of manner, such as *shizuka ni* 'quietly.'

(42) *sorede **isshoo-kenmei** sagashitan dakedo inakatta.* (4;11)
   and then hard look-PAST but is-NEG-PAST
   'And then (the boy) looked as **hard as he could**, but (the frog) wasn't there.'

(43) *kaeru wa bin kara **shizuka ni** tobidashita.* (9;0)
   frog TOP jar from quietly jump out-PAST
   'The frog jumped out **quietly** from the jar.'

The older children and adults were able to use a wider range of adverbial expressions, which heightened a sense of drama, such as *totemo* 'very' and *hisshi ni* 'urgently.'

(44) *otoko no ko ga ana o nozoki nagara uta o utatte-itara **ikinari***
   man child SUBJ hole peer while song sing suddenly
   risu ga tobi-dashite kita. (7;7)
   chipmunk SUBJ jump out-CONT come-PAST
   'When the boy was singing as he was peering into a hole, **all of a sudden** a chipmunk came flying out.'

The older narrators were also able to use more complicated sentence constructions, including connectives such as *tokoro ga* 'however' and *kedo* 'but,' all of which expressed occurrences that defied expectations.

(45) ***sagashitemo sagashitemo** imasen deshita.* (9;3)
   look for-but look for-but be-NEG COP-PAST-POL
   '(They) looked and looked (for the frog) **but** (he) wasn't anywhere.'

(46) *sorede sagashite-itan dakedo mitsukaranakatta no.* (5;5)
   and then search-PROG-PAST but find-NEG-PAST EP
   'And then (they) were searching (for the frog), **but** (they) did not find him.'

Relative Frequencies of Evaluative Expressions

The relative frequencies of evaluative expressions, as seen in Table 16.1, changed with age. Although they may be shorter in length and simpler in story complexity, the narratives of the preschool children are affectively rich, with multiple evaluative devices. As stated previously, the number of evaluative devices used did not vary greatly between the different age groups. However, different age groups relied on different types of evaluative devices. Four-year-olds and five-year-olds used character speech more than any other evaluative device, followed by frames of mind and negative qualifiers. Seven-year-olds, however, used more frames of mind than character speech, although these, too, were followed by negative qualifiers. Nine-year-olds used many adverbial enrichment expressions, followed by frames of mind and causal expressions. Adults used frames of mind most often, followed by adverbial enrichment expressions and negative qualifiers. Two of the coding categories—hedges and causal expressions—showed no age-related trends.

DISCUSSION

In the results, we saw that many different types of evaluative devices are used by Japanese children and adults in their construction of elicited oral narratives. One question that emerges is how the usage of these evaluative devices changes with age. First, some of the evaluative devices used by older children and adults are linguistically more complex. For example, younger children tend to rely heavily on direct character speech, while older children and adults use a higher proportion of indirect character speech. While direct character speech involves the simple use of direct quotation with a quotative particle, indirect character speech involves the reformulation of a quotation into an embedded clause with a quotative particle.

Second, some changes are related to the acquisition of age-appropriate speech forms. For example, frequent use of onomatopoeia is often associated with baby talk. The 4- and 5-year-olds used many onomatopoeic forms; however, this decreased with age. Adults were less likely to use onomatopoeic forms and instead relied on strategies such as adverbial enrichment expressions.

Third, the use of some evaluative forms requires a greater depth of understanding of others' minds. Adults used the greatest number and diversity of frames-of-mind expressions. For example, regarding the number of types, adults were able to refer to a wider repertoire of both basic and complex emotions and attribute such emotions to various characters. The youngest children tended to limit themselves to basic emotions that were obvious from the pictures in the storybook (i.e., the facial expressions of the characters), while the adults were able to infer numerous emotions not only from the facial expressions of the characters, but also from other aspects of the story, such as the sequence of actions and the relationships between the characters.

One major limitation of this study is the need for paralinguistic analyses. Reilly (1992) examined paralinguistic evaluative elements such as narrators' gestures, facial expressions, and prosodic features in her analysis of linguistic evaluative devices used by American children (ages 3 to 11) in their oral narratives. She reported that while paralinguistic evaluative strategies were common in the young children's narratives, with increasing age, linguistic devices gained prominence. Furthermore, Reilly (2001), comparing the development of evaluation across two different languages in two different modalities, namely, spoken English and American Sign Language, reported that while both speaking and signing preschoolers rely heavily on paralinguistic strategies (e.g., vocal prosody, facial expression, gesture) to express evaluation, school-age children primarily convey evaluation linguistically. Similar observations were made with the Japanese children as they attempted to convey affect in their narratives. A re-analysis of the data may shed further light on how narrators learn to coordinate linguistic and paralinguistic strategies in their expression of affect.

Another important issue is how children are socialized to express affect in language. Most research on the socialization of emotive language has focused on talk about emotions in parent–child conversations and the subsequent ability of children to talk about emotions and understand the emotions of others at later ages (Dunn, Bretherton, & Munn, 1987; Dunn, Brown, & Beardsall, 1991). Such talk gives children a great deal of information about culturally appropriate ways of expressing and interpreting emotion. What we see in the narrative data is how children internalize cultural norms regarding affect expression in narratives. From an early age, children are exposed to the narrative style favored by their cultures and their caregivers (e.g., Heath, 1983; McCabe & Peterson, 1991; Minami, 1996; Minami & McCabe, 1995). Even preschoolers are able to tell stories using evaluative devices that are culturally appropriate (Küntay & Nakamura, 2004). For example, while Japanese child narrators rely heavily on onomatopoeia in their construction of narratives, Turkish narratives rarely contain sound symbolism devices. On the other hand, Turkish adult narrators often include subjective commentaries of ethical or aesthetic content, which reflect the narrator's point of view or opinion—a feature that is not found in Japanese narratives. In addition to talk about affect in parent–child interactions, children's books and book-reading styles may also be an invaluable source of language socialization for encoding affect in language.

This study has explored the ability of children and adults to express affect by using culturally appropriate evaluative devices in narrative. During narrative construction, narrators express their feelings and attitudes toward various events and characters. Mastery of evaluative strategies helps affect to create a more effective, coherent narrative. Japanese children and adults use a variety of culturally appropriate evaluative devices in their oral narratives to provide affective information for the listener. With age, speakers are able to choose from a wider range of evaluative strategies, leading to changes in patterns of usage.

REFERENCES

Bamberg, M., & Damrad-Frye, R. (1991). On the ability to provide evaluative comments: Further explorations of children's narrative competencies. *Journal of Child Language, 18*, 869–710.

Bamberg, M., & Reilly, J. (1996). Emotion, narrative, and affect: How children discover the meaning of what to say and how to say it. In D. I. Slobin, J. Gerhardt, A. Kyratzis, & J. Guo (Eds.), *Social interaction, social context, and language: Essays in honor of Susan Ervin-Tripp* (pp. 329–341). Mahwah, NJ: Lawrence Erlbaum Associates.

Berman, R., & Slobin, D. I. (1994). *Relating events in narrative: A crosslinguistic developmental study.* Hillsdale, NJ: Lawrence Erlbaum Associates.

Bretherton, I., Fritz, J., Zahn-Waxler, C., & Ridgeway, D. (1986). Learning to talk about emotions: A functionalist perspective. *Child Development, 57*, 529–548.

Dunn, J., Bretherton, I., & Munn, P. (1987). Conversations about feeling states between mothers and their young children. *Developmental Psychology, 23*, 132–139.

Dunn, J., Brown, J., & Beardsall, L. (1991). Family talk about feeling states and children's later understanding of others' emotions. *Developmental Psychology, 27*(3), 448–455.

Heath, S. B. (1983). *Ways with words: Language, life, and work in communities and classrooms.* Cambridge, UK: Cambridge University Press.

Hudson, J. A., Gebelt, J., Haviland, J., & Bentivegna, C. (1992). Emotion and narrative structure in young children's personal accounts, *Journal of Narrative and Life History, 2*(2), 129–150.

Ishii, S. (1984). Enryo-sasshi communication: A key to understanding Japanese interpersonal relations. *Cross Currents, 1*(11), 49–58.

Küntay, A., & Nakamura, K. (2004). Linguistic strategies serving evaluative functions: A comparison between Japanese and Turkish narratives. In S. Strömqvist & L. Verhoeven (Eds.), *Relating events in narrative: Vol. 2. Typological and contextual perspective* (pp. 329–358). Mahwah, NJ: Lawrence Erlbaum Associates.

Labov, W., & Waletsky (1967). Narrative analysis: Oral versions of personal experience. In J. Helm (Ed.), *Essays on verbal and visual arts* (pp. 12–44). Seattle: University of Washington Press.

McCabe, A., & Peterson, C. (Eds.). (1991). *Developing narrative structure.* Hillsdale, NJ: Lawrence Erlbaum Associates.

McVeigh, B. (1996). Standing stomachs, clamoring chests and cooling livers: Metaphors in the psychological lexicon of Japanese. *Journal of Pragmatics, 26*, 25–50.

Martin, S. (1975). *A reference grammar of Japanese.* Tokyo: Tuttle.

Maynard, S. (1990). *An introduction to Japanese grammar and communication strategies.* Tokyo: The Japan Times.

Maynard, S. (1993). *Discourse modality: Subjectivity, emotion and voice in the Japanese language.* Amsterdam/Philadelphia: John Benjamins.

Maynard, S. (1999). *Jooi no gengogaku.* Tokyo: Kurosio Shuppan.

Mayer, M. (1969). *Frog, where are you?* New York: Dial Press.

Miller, P., & Sperry, L. (1988). Early talk about the past: The original and conversational stories of personal experience. *Journal of Child Language, 22*, 423–45.
Minami, M. (1996). Japanese children's personal narratives. *First Language, 16*, 339–363.
Minami, M. (1998). Politeness markers and psychological complements: Wrapping-up devices in Japanese oral personal narratives. *Narrative Inquiry, 8*(2), 1–20.
Minami, M., & McCabe, A. (1995). Rice balls and bear hunts: Japanese and North American family narrative patterns. *Journal of Child Language, 22*, 423–45.
Ochs, E. (1986). From feeling to grammar. In B. Schieffelin & E. Ochs (Eds.), *Language socialization across cultures* (pp. 251–272). Cambridge, UK: Cambridge University Press.
Ochs, E., & Schieffelin, B. (1986). Language has a heart. *Text, 9*(1), 7–25.
Ogino, M., & Kobayashi, H. (1999). Gengo kakutoku no shoki hattatsu [Early development in language acquisition]. In S. Kiritani (Ed.), *Kotoba no kakutoku [Language acquisition]* (pp. 71–116). Kyoto, Japan: Minerva Shobo.
Peterson, C., & McCabe, A. (1983). *Developmental psycholinguistics: Three ways of looking at a child's narrative.* New York: Plenum.
Reilly, J. S. (1992). How to tell a good story: The intersection of language and affect in children's narratives. *Journal of Narrative and Life History, 2*, 355–377.
Reilly, J. S. (2001). From affect to language: Development of evaluation in narratives in spoken English and American Sign Language. In L. Verhoeven & S. Strömqvist (Eds.), *Narrative development in a multilingual context* (pp. 399–417), Amsterdam: John Benjamins.
Schieffelin, B. (1986). Teasing and shaming in Kaluli children's interactions. In B. Schieffelin & E. Ochs (Eds.), *Language socialization across cultures* (pp. 165–181). New York: Cambridge University Press.
Schiffrin, D. (1987). *Discourse markers.* Cambridge, UK: Cambridge University Press.
Slobin, D. I. (1996). From 'thought to language' to 'thinking for speaking.' In J. J. Gumperz & S. C. Levinson (Eds.), *Rethinking linguistic relativity* (pp. 70–96). Cambridge, UK: Cambridge University Press.
Strömqvist, S., & Verhoeven, L. (Eds.). (2004). *Relating events in narrative: Vol. 2. Typological and contextual perspectives.* Mahwah, NJ: Lawrence Erlbaum Associates.
Tannen, D. (1982). Oral and literate strategies in spoken and written narratives. *Language, 58*(1), 1–21.
Umiker-Sebeok, J. (1979). Preschool children's intraconversational narratives. *Journal of Child Language, 6*, 91–109.
Zahn-Waxler, C., Radke-Yarrow, M., & King, R. (1979). Child rearing and children's prosocial initiations towards victims of distress. *Child Development, 48*, 319–330.

17

Rethinking Character Representation and Its Development in Children's Narratives

AGELIKI NICOLOPOULOU

Lehigh University

Once upon a time there were two researchers who had a theory that they kept in a jar. And one night, while they were asleep, the theory ran away. When they woke up, and found that they had no theory anymore, they went out on a search into the Grove of Academe. ... They weren't sure which one was the right theory, but they picked a lively one and hoped for the best. They went back home to write a book.

Ruth Berman and Dan I. Slobin (1994, p. 643)

I was fortunate to have Dan Slobin as one of my mentors. While he was never officially my advisor, I took all the graduate courses Dan offered while I was at Berkeley and participated in many informal intellectual gatherings at his home in the Berkeley hills. Following the practice of one of his own mentors, Jerome Bruner, Dan used to invite the developmental students to his home for lively discussions in connection with graduate seminars or visits by scholars from elsewhere—thus giving us opportunities for the "legitimate peripheral participation" that graduate apprenticeship requires. Since leaving Berkeley, I've continued to be educated and intellectually stimulated by his work and the intellectual sensibility informing it.

In all these contexts, Dan has valuably taught by example as well as instruction—the example of a scholarly perspective that is wide-ranging, interdisciplinary, imaginative, and open to new ideas and at the same time solidly grounded, analytically acute, and theoretically and methodologically rigorous. In a style captured by the quotation above, he has always encouraged us to follow theoretical and empirical puzzles where they take us, using theoretical models and research paradigms to solve problems rather than being trapped by them.

In many respects, this is the kind of path I have followed in my own work on narrative. That wasn't a prominent subject for me as a graduate student, but I stumbled over it later in the course of pursuing other problems, and over the years I have become increasingly aware of the importance of understanding narrative and its role in children's experience and development. Of course, my own interest in narrative has been part of a wider burst of narrative research in psychology, education, and related fields. But I'm convinced that some crucial dimensions of narrative have remained insufficiently explored, and that part of the problem lies in the limitations of the theoretical and methodological resources we've been using. So in the spirit of Dan Slobin, I will try to consider where we stand in our pursuit of this elusive quarry and how we might find more lively theories to help us out.

INTRODUCTION

Researchers have mainly conceptualized narratives as temporally and causally connected sequences of events (e.g., Nelson, 1996), but all of us know that narratives take on more meaning and become more powerfully absorbing when they also include vivid, effective, and engaging depictions of characters. Both children and adults are drawn into stories—as listeners, readers, and tellers—in large part through their engagement and identification with characters. In his comprehensive overview of narrative research, Toolan (2001, p. 81) argued that "[c]haracter, and everything it entails in the way of deep insight into the minds of imagined others, their uniqueness of motive and difference of worldview, is often what most powerfully attracts readers to novels and stories" (cf. Culler, 1975, p. 230). Children's fascination with characters in narratives, which often includes imaginative identification, has not escaped the notice of parents, teachers, and other adults who interact with them on a regular basis. And the characters that interest children in stories read or told to them, or that they see in TV cartoons and other forms of popular culture, help to shape their own representation and use of characters in the narratives they compose and those they enact in pretend play.

These everyday observations have been confirmed by richly detailed ethnographic studies of young children ranging from ages 2 to 6 (e.g., Miller, Hoogstra, Mintz, Fung, & Williams, 1993; Rowe, 1998; Wolf & Heath, 1992). In all these studies, children's imaginative engagement with characters in stories that were read or told to them helped to draw children into the stories, deepened their involvement and excitement, and facilitated a process of narrative appropriation, retellings, and pretend play re-enactments in which they enhanced their linguistic, cognitive, and emotional skills. Identification with characters in narratives seems to begin as early as 2 years and becomes even stronger by 4 or 5 years.

This picture is further corroborated by analyses of 3- to 5-year-old children who participated in their preschool classrooms in a regular storytelling and story-acting practice initiated by the teacher/researcher Vivian Paley (e.g., Paley, 1986, 1988, 1990). Paley's ethnographic accounts as well as research by others (e.g., Nicolopoulou, 1996, 1997b, 2002; Nicolopoulou & Richner, 2007; Nicolopoulou, Scales, & Weintraub, 1994; Richner & Nicolopoulou, 2001) have demonstrated that children participate enthusiastically in this narrative practice; that it promotes their learning and development in a range of domains; and that the children use this narrative activity to explore themes that concern them, to make sense of the world, and to help define important elements of their own identities. In constructing their narratives, the children draw characters and other elements from a wide range of sources including fairy tales, children's books, and TV as well as the stories of other children and their own everyday experiences. However, this is not a matter of simple imitation and passive absorption. Children are selective in their choice of characters, often develop strong attachments to certain characters or types of characters, and invest considerable effort in putting their own stamp on the ways they use and portray these characters.

None of this may sound surprising. But despite the importance we all attribute to character and its portrayal, it has received surprisingly little systematic attention in developmental research on narrative. The present chapter argues that this puzzling neglect of character representation in narrative research is unfortunate and damaging, considers some current efforts to capture this dimension of narrative, and begins to outline an approach that can help us take these efforts further and deeper. The main focus will be on children's construction and use of characters in their own narratives, but many of the issues addressed are also relevant to children's comprehension of and responses to the narratives of others.

NARRATIVE RESEARCH AND CHARACTER

Developmental research on narrative has flourished during the past several decades, but relatively little has focused directly on children's portrayal and use of characters. Part of the reason is that since the 1970s most of this research has been dominated by various types of formalist analysis—that is, it tends to focus more or less exclusively on the formal structure of narratives and to neglect both their symbolic content and the ways that children *use* narrative for diverse modes of symbolic action, not least in the construction of reality and identity (for a critical overview, see Nicolopoulou, 1997a). Thus, the analysis of plot structure and its development has predominated, and when attention has been paid to character representation, this has often emerged as a by-product of research focusing on plot structure.

Episodic Structure Analysis and Characters as Intentional Agents

One important example of this subordination of character to plot is the extensive body of work on the episodic structure of narratives. In particular, story grammar analysis (e.g., Stein, 1988) argues that a well-formed story conforms to a particular type of episodic structure, organized around the goal-directed activity of a main protagonist who reacts to an initiating event or state of lack and attempts to change it. This conception of plot structure in effect highlights one aspect of the mental life of characters, or at least the main character, namely goal-directedness or intentionality, whether this is inferable from the plot or explicitly indicated in the story. Mostly in response to questions raised by theory of mind research, some narrative researchers have therefore asked *when* children actually begin to depict characters as having thoughts, beliefs, feelings, hopes, goals, intentions, and plans that frame and motivate their goal-directed activity—in other words, when children begin to portray characters as mental agents. The usual criterion is explicit mention or description of such inner mental states, and on this basis narrative researchers broadly agree that children do not portray characters as mental agents with much frequency until around 8 or 9 years of age (e.g., Berman & Slobin, 1994; Leondar, 1977; Shapiro & Hudson, 1991; Stein, 1988; Stein & Albro, 1997). In a typical finding, Stein (1988, p. 296) concluded that very few young children use narrative "to explore internal states, motivation, and thinking of their story characters." From this perspective, character portrayals by younger children are analyzed less in their own terms than in terms of characteristics that they do *not* (yet) possess.

A partial exception to this pattern can be found in some work by Stein, Trabasso, and associates which suggests that children begin to represent the inner worlds of characters a bit earlier (e.g., Trabasso & Stein, 1994; Trabasso, Stein, Rodkin, Munger, & Baughn, 1992), but this qualification results mainly from the use of less demanding and more indirect criteria (see Nicolopoulou & Richner, 2007). And even indirectly, this analysis addresses only one aspect of characters' inner mental life—namely, intentionality or goal-directed activity. When narrative researchers have looked for explicit and richly developed portrayals of characters' inner mental life in children's narratives, they have generally not found these with much frequency until middle childhood—that is, 8–9 years. However, there is a puzzling discrepancy between this prevailing consensus in narrative research and the findings of an increasing body of research on young children's social understanding and their theories of mind indicating that young children, even 4-year-olds, regularly employ a mentalistic conception of the person, attributing to others mental states such as thoughts, beliefs, intentions, desires, and emotions that are used to explain and predict people's actions and interactions (see Nicolopoulou & Richner, 2007).

Seeking Earlier Precursors to Mentalistic Character Portrayals

As part of one effort to resolve or minimize this age discrepancy, Benson (1996, 1997) analyzed narratives by 4-, 5-, and 6-year-olds looking for early precursors to a full-blown mentalistic conception of the person. She found that even the youngest children included some references to characters' internal states (e.g., sensations/perceptions, volitions, cognitions) and to psychological causation (e.g., internal states used either as antecedents or consequents of actions and events). Similar results were found by two studies from a different line of research that examined stories by English-speaking (Bamberg & Damrad-Frye, 1991) and by Japanese- and Turkish-speaking (Küntay and Nakamura, 2004) populations, respectively, to measure the frequencies with which narrators at different ages included descriptions of characters' "frames of mind"—i.e., emotional states or reactions (e.g., happy, sad, angry, scared) or other internal mental states (e.g., thinking, being interested in something). Even some of the youngest children (5-year-olds in the first study and 4-year-olds in the second) offered such descriptions in at least some of their stories, although the frequencies varied among the different populations, and between early childhood and adulthood the proportions of narrative clauses describing characters' frames of mind generally tended to increase with age in all three populations, but usually not in a linear fashion.

Although these results are suggestive in some respects, they do not yet provide a clear picture of young children's developing conceptions of mental agency or the ways that these are expressed in construing and portraying characters. The types of internal states included in these studies were a mixed bag, ranging from simple sensations and emotions to higher-order cognitions, thoughts, plans, and complex feelings, and there was no systematic effort to draw distinctions between them. Also, some of Benson's categories seem questionable as inner mental states (e.g., relationships and being asleep or awake), and it is not clear how much these categories contributed to her overall results. Nor have the aggregations of these various traits been integrated into coherent pictures of how children at each age portray and relate the characters in their narratives. Only a more carefully delineated and theoretically motivated typology of children's conceptions of the person would allow us to capture the full range of children's developing abilities and inclinations for character representation.

Character Representation and Its Development in Narrative Research: Summing Up and Looking Ahead

This overview has necessarily been brief, incomplete, and schematic. But it highlights some persistent gaps and limitations in the treatment of character representation by most narrative research. In accord with its predominantly formalist orientation, developmental research on narrative has focused mostly on linguistic or plot structure and has paid relatively little systematic attention to the narrative construction, understanding, and use of characters by children and adults. Some tendencies that appear to be exceptions actually help to prove the rule, since they focus only on certain traits of characters with a fairly direct bearing on plot structure, such as goals and intentions that move the plot or characters' thoughts and feelings that express attitudes toward and evaluations of events in the plot. Even in its own terms, this body of research has not been able to give us a clear, coherent, and systematic developmental picture of when and how children portray characters as mental agents—and has found it difficult to overcome some perplexing discrepancies between its own findings and relevant findings from theory of mind research. And, taken in isolation, these elements of character representation cannot fully capture the characters portrayed in narratives and the changing emphases in children's narrative construction, delineation, and use of characters over the course of development. The child's conception of the *mind*, as defined by this research and most theory-of-mind perspectives, is only one element in the child's conception of the *person*.

More generally, the narrow range of questions about the portrayal and use of characters that are systematically posed by most current research leaves out or inadequately explores a host of important issues that ought to concern developmental research on narrative. Some other questions, familiar from broader perspectives and problematics in narratology, would include the symbolic and emotional significance of narrative characters, which *kinds* of characters children (and adults) choose to represent in narratives, whether and to what extent they differentiate and individualize characters and endow them with depth and personality, and—not least—how they handle the *relationships* between different characters within narratives.

Indeed, given the fact that there is a tendency for much current research to approach character as a by-product of studying plot structure, it is ironic that little systematic attention has been paid to the ways that children's developing conceptions of the person and their expression in character representation might affect the development of plot structure, narrative genres, and modes of narrative coherence. Researchers have properly devoted considerable attention to the developing strategies by which *events* are related in narrative, but it is also important to understand the complex and shifting strategies employed to relate *characters* in narrative. Children's mastery of episodic structure is certainly a key element in their efforts to achieve narrative coherence, but their construction and use of characters is also an important dimension of these efforts. Both for understanding narrative development itself and for understanding the role of narrative in the broader context of children's experience and development, narrative research needs to pay more sustained, systematic, comprehensive, and sophisticated attention to character representation.

TAKING CHARACTER MORE SERIOUSLY: SOME STEPS TOWARD AN ORIENTING FRAMEWORK

Advancing our understanding of character representation and its development requires overcoming methodological as well as theoretical limitations. Most research on children's narrative development has used narratives elicited by adults in socially isolated experimental settings, employing techniques that constrain children's narrative initiative and flexibility—especially in their selection, portrayal, differentiation, and coordination of characters. For example, children are usually presented with pre-selected story formats, often including pre-selected characters, in wordless picture books, picture sequences, story-topics, or story-stems. Although there are good justifications for many of these methodological choices, it can be argued (e.g., Nicolopoulou, 1996; Richner & Nicolopoulou, 2001) that the kinds of material generated by these procedures do not fully capture young children's actual and potential narrative abilities. In particular, less constraining and more engaging elicitation techniques can help produce a richer and more illuminating picture of character representation and its development in children's narratives.

However, the more difficult and essential challenges that need to be addressed are conceptual and theoretical. What follows is a quick and partial overview of some key theoretical resources and orienting perspectives on which further research in this area can build.

What the Narratologists Can and Can't Tell Us

Developmental research on character representation cannot simply take over ready-made models from narratology, because the theoretical approaches to character offered by narratologists also tend to be fragmentary and underdeveloped (for further discussion of this point, see Culler, 1975; Rimmon-Kenan, 1983; Toolan, 2001). One reason is that structuralist theories, which have predominated within narratology, tend to view characters as abstract elements in the articulation of a larger formal design. At best, these approaches tend to dissolve particular characters within classes of characters or roles. For example, Propp's (1968) influential structural analysis of the folktale subordinated characters to a set of general categories or roles—the donor, the villain, the hero, the helper, the false friend, and so on—that fulfill specific functions within the overall structure of the plot. Greimas (1977) identified a smaller set of basic categories or types of character, termed *actants*, that he argued operate as interrelated pairs of roles. Nevertheless, it is worth noting that even these severely structuralist approaches in narratology view the portrayal of character types and the relations between them as a key dimension of narrative structure, rather than viewing this structure purely in terms of interconnected sequences of events.

Other narratologists have emphasized the need for richer, more differentiated, and more developmentally sensitive approaches to character representation. Rimmon-Kenan (1983) argued that we should consider character and plot as interdependent and analyze the forms of this interdependence. With respect to the representation of characters, Rimmon-Kenan proposed focusing on three criteria: *complexity*, ranging from allegorical types or caricatures to the complex multi-layered characters we encounter in major novelists; capacity for *development*, ranging from static characters to those whose dynamic transformations are portrayed in the text; and degrees of *penetration into the inner life*. In order to follow up these very useful heuristic guides offered by Rimmon-Kenan, one necessary step would be to go beyond the separate axes proposed here and delineate the concrete ways in which these different features are integrated in concrete character portrayals. As Bruner (1986, pp. 38–39) usefully put it, a narrative character "is not a bundle of autonomous traits but" (to a greater or lesser degree) "an organized conception" or "gestalt," organized in turn by one of "the different ways that we construe 'personhood'" in narrative.

One such "morphology" of personhood, offered by the philosopher Amélie Rorty (cited in Bruner, 1986, pp. 39–40) on the basis of a critical overview of western literature, distinguishes characters, figures, persons, selves, and individuals. The use of these different conceptions of personhood entails different implications for characters' "powers of action," "relations to one another," "properties and proprieties," and other qualities. Furthermore, such conceptions of the person have an inescapable sociocultural dimension: "our conception of society's proper strictures and freedoms will vary with our conceptions of ourselves as characters, persons, selves, individuals" (p. 40). We therefore must understand these representations of character as situated in and interacting with circumstances, action, plot, and context.

Bruner: The "Dual Landscape" of Narrative and the "Morphology" of Persons

As part of his ambitious program for a cultural turn in developmental psychology, Bruner (1986) has advanced a provocative and influential approach to narrative that synthesizes elements from a wide range of sources in psychology, narratology, philosophy, and literary theory, including some of the ones just discussed. Narrative, he has argued, is a resource we employ not only to portray but also to make sense of human experience, our own and that of others; to a great extent, we render it intelligible by narrativizing it, by ordering and representing it in narrative form (Bruner, 1986, pp. 11–43). In Bruner's model, the underlying structure of a fully formed narrative involves integrating plot, setting, character, and consciousness within a "dual landscape" of action and consciousness (Bruner, 1986, p. 14). The landscape of action consists of "arguments of action: agent, intention or goal, situation, instrument, something corresponding to a 'story grammar.'" And the landscape of consciousness conveys "what those involved in the action know, think, or feel, or do not know, think, or feel." Powerful and gripping narratives must construct these two landscapes simultaneously and integrate them effectively.

This integration is accomplished in different ways within the framework of various culturally available narrative genres that individuals need to master, employ, and elaborate. As Feldman, Bruner, Kalmar, and Renderer (1993) have argued, narrative genres embody constitutive mental models with distinctive conceptions of character, of the mental life of characters, of relations between characters, and of relations between characters and events. In order to grasp and analyze these underlying conceptions, we need a theoretically informed "'morphology' of persons" (Bruner, 1986, p. 39) with which to interpret the developing representations of personhood in narrative. Feldman and Bruner (e.g., Feldman et al., 1993) have applied this analytic perspective to the stories of 10-year-olds, adolescents, and adults. The challenge remains to apply it to character representation and its development in the narratives of younger children.

SOME POSSIBLE DIRECTIONS FOR FUTURE RESEARCH: THREE CONCRETE EXAMPLES

How can we most effectively follow up these suggestions? As a first step toward a response, let me offer three examples of my own research (partly conducted in collaboration with Elizabeth Richner) that highlight different but interrelated aspects of children's construction and use of characters in their narratives.

The three studies discussed below analyzed about 600 stories freely composed by 3- to 5-year-old English-speaking children, predominantly from middle-class families, participating in a version of the storytelling and story-acting practice pioneered by Paley (e.g., 1986, 1988, 1990) that was a daily activity in their preschool classrooms. (For various technical reasons, the precise number of stories analyzed in each study varied very slightly.) Thirty children were selected from those attending four half-day mixed-age nursery classes in a preschool/elementary school in western Massachusetts observed over a period of several years (two classes from 1992–1993 and two from 1994–1995) to obtain a sample equally divided between boys and girls and between 3-, 4-, and 5-year-olds. At a certain period during the day, any child who wished could dictate a story to a teacher, who recorded it as the child told it. At the end of the day, each of these stories was read aloud to the entire class during group time, while the author and other children, whom the author chose, acted out the story. In this practice, therefore, the children's storytelling was voluntary, self-initiated, and relatively spontaneous: the stories were neither solicited directly by adults nor channeled by props, story-stems, or suggested topics. In particular, no restrictions were placed on children's selection, portrayal, and use of characters.

Furthermore, in contrast to the artificial situations that predominate in much research on young children's narratives, the children's storytelling and story-acting were embedded in the shared public setting of the classroom miniculture and the children's everyday group life, a context that also provided the children with extensive opportunities for narrative sharing, experimentation, and cross-fertilization. There is strong evidence that these conditions lead children to produce narratives that are richer, more ambitious, and more illuminating than when they compose them in isolation from their everyday social contexts and in response to agendas shaped directly by adults (Nicolopoulou, 1996, 2002). The quality of this material was enhanced by the fact that children's participation in this type of storytelling and story-acting practice significantly promoted the development of their narrative skills (Nicolopoulou, 2002).

The Narrative Representation of Characters as Mental Agents: From Actors to Agents to Persons in Young Children's Narratives

As Bruner and others have correctly emphasized, a key requirement for studying the narrative construction of reality and identity is a sophisticated and theoretically informed "morphology of persons" (Bruner, 1986, p. 39) with which to analyze developing conceptions of the person and the ways that these are manifested in the construction and construal of narrative characters by children and adults. We sought to use both methodological and conceptual innovations to deepen and refine the prevailing understanding of one aspect of this problem, namely, the process by which children come to represent characters as mental agents. In doing so, we also hoped to address some puzzling discrepancies, mentioned earlier, between relevant findings reported by developmental research in narrative and in social cognition.

Since no suitable theoretical model was readily available to capture the increasing depth and complexity of children's character representations, we constructed a developmental typology that drew on a range of sources in narrative and social cognition research, philosophy, and narratology. Loosely adapting the classification offered by Rorty (1988), we proposed three basic levels of character representation: from actors to agents to persons. These basic categories were further elaborated to yield an 8-level typology (for greater detail, see Nicolopoulou & Richner, 2007).

Actors are essentially non-mentalistic characters, described exclusively in terms of externally observable actions and characteristics. *Agents* are depicted as having rudimentary psychological capacities including abilities to perceive, feel, and communicate; to respond physically or emotionally to events and/or other characters; or to manifest intentions-in-action (as opposed to prior intentions). *Persons* are explicitly portrayed as having more complex representational beliefs, desires, intentions, and emotions that motivate or direct action. In its highest levels, our category of "persons" corresponds roughly to what most theory-of-mind researchers would regard as a full mental agent.

Using this typology, we analyzed the portrayal of characters in 617 spontaneous stories composed by 30 children (10 each at 3, 4, and 5 years) in the storytelling and story-acting practice just described. Results indicated a clear developmental progression along the lines hypothesized by our typology. Children's representation of characters shifted from almost exclusively physical and external portrayals of actors at 3 to increasing inclusion of agents with rudimentary mental states at 4 and of persons with mental representational capacities at 5 (for a fuller presentation of these results, see Nicolopoulou & Richner, 2007). At the same time, certain features of character representation were linked with the children's use of different narrative genres, and girls and boys tended to favor different genres, so that there were some gender-related differences in the overall developmental trajectories followed by girls' and boys' stories. These findings provide a more precise and differentiated developmental picture of the emergence of mentalistic character representations than previous narrative research, and they also suggest some possibilities for closer and more systematic integration between narrative and social cognition research on these issues.

From Conceptions of the Mind to Conceptions of the Person: Toward a More Comprehensive and Socioculturally Informed Approach

By itself, however, studying the emergence of more mentalistic portrayals of characters captures only one aspect of the development of children's conceptions of the person as these are expressed, constructed, and elaborated in their narratives. Not only are conceptions of the person not simply reducible to conceptions (or folk theories) of the mind, but it is also important to grasp the ways in which images of the person are inextricably and reciprocally linked to images of social relations and the social world. Furthermore, narrative research needs to examine whether and how modes of character representation by different sets of children express *distinctive* conceptions of the person in ways that are socioculturally patterned. (For a more extended treatment of these issues, see Richner & Nicolopoulou, 2001.)

We pursued these questions in a separate study (Richner & Nicolopoulou, 2001) that analyzed the same body of young children's spontaneous stories using conceptual tools designed to capture the multiple, culturally mediated, and socially situated character of young children's conceptions of the person and their development. Our analysis indicated that the girls and boys in these preschool classes constructed and elaborated two predominant gender-related narrative genres which embodied and expressed contrasting images of social relations and of the social world and, correspondingly, quite distinctive conceptions of the person. (To borrow loosely from Greimas's [1977] terminology, within each of these genres narratives tended to be organized around different systems of *actants*—i.e., of interrelated character types and their connections.) Within the framework of the *family/group genre*, the girls portrayed and developed a conception of the person as essentially *socially embedded and interdependent*. Within the framework of the *heroic-agonistic genre*, the boys portrayed and developed a conception of the person as essentially *separate and conflictual*.

These results accorded with the main thrust of findings from some previous studies (e.g., Nicolopoulou, 1997b; Nicolopoulou, Scales, & Weintraub, 1994), but this analysis allowed us to delineate these gender-related character representations in greater depth and detail and also to map their *developmental pathways* across the 3–5 age period. Each model of personhood remained fundamentally consistent for each gender with increasing age, but within each of these frameworks the model of personhood was also developed considerably in depth and complexity. In the girls' stories, the socially embedded and interdependent person, while still acting in the context of a cohesive group marked by networks of stable, harmonious, and predominantly "given" relationships, became an increasingly *individuated and self-consciously responsible* group member. In the boys' stories, the separate and agonistic person, originally portrayed as an extremely isolated and transitory locus of disconnected actions, became an increasingly *stable, autonomous, and self-conscious mental agent*, at times capable of alliances and leadership as well as conflict. In both models, this developmental transformation in the portrayal of the person was bound up with a transformation in the symbolic landscape of social relationships portrayed in the stories.

Beyond their direct significance, these results supported the larger argument that more interpretive and socioculturally sensitive analyses of young children's narratives, of the type proposed and employed in this study, can offer powerful tools for investigating children's character representation and its development in ways that do justice to their richness, complexity, and diversity.

Reconsidering "Main Character": How Do Children Actually Construct, Use, and Coordinate Central and Secondary Characters?

Developmental research on character representation also needs to examine systematically the ways that children (and adults) *use* and *coordinate* characters as part of their larger strategies for constructing narratives and achieving narrative coherence. One piece of this puzzle is children's construction and use of main characters. A great deal of narrative research assumes, explicitly or in effect, that "well-formed" and coherent children's narratives are organized around the goal-directed activity of a single main character. However, surprisingly little research has directly addressed the questions of whether and when children actually portray a single main character in their narratives and, when they do, how they use main characters and relate them to other characters. (As noted earlier, many studies effectively foreclose or obscure these questions by presenting children with story formats that already specify the characters, and often a main character, in advance.)

The few studies in this area (Bamberg, 1986; Karmiloff-Smith, 1985; McGann & Schwartz, 1988) are inconclusive about the defining features of main character and the age at which children begin to mark a main character. But they share a focus on examining children's awareness or recognition of main characters, using mainly linguistic criteria, rather than on systematically reconstructing children's own conceptualizations of main character. Nor have they attempted a developmental analysis of the ways that children used main characters in their narratives or related them to other characters.

In an analysis based on the same body of preschoolers' spontaneous stories described earlier, two of my graduate students and I (Nicolopoulou & Ilgaz, 2006; Nicolopoulou & Richner, 1999) have constructed a theoretically and empirically informed developmental typology with which to address these questions. Preliminary results indicate that when children are given the opportunity to compose their own stories with no restrictions on topics or character selection, they do not necessarily organize their stories around a single major protagonist. However, main characters did appear with increasing frequency over the 3–5 age span. The 3-year-olds very rarely showed the ability or inclination to distinguish main characters from other characters. By 4 and 5 years the inclusion of main characters in narratives became increasingly frequent.

More important, however, our research so far has already made it clear that the problem needs to be reframed, because it is not sufficient to focus simply on the presence or absence of main characters in children's narratives. This captures only one aspect of a larger process. Instead, narrative researchers should ask when and how children come to differentiate *central* characters (which may be single or clustered) from *secondary* or *peripheral* characters and what narrative strategies they use to *connect* and *coordinate* these different characters. Our findings indicate a gradual and complex developmental process in these respects. It was not until age 5 that most children mastered the ability to construct substantial proportions of their stories around interrelated sets of stable, continuous, and differentiated characters and the interactions between those characters. Furthermore, girls and boys used different predominant strategies to construct and coordinate central and secondary characters, linked to distinctive gender-related narrative genres that organized and oriented their stories, so the developmental trajectories manifested in their narratives were significantly different. This research is still in an exploratory stage, but the results suggest that further inquiry along these lines would be fruitful and illuminating.

CONCLUDING REMARKS

As I have tried to convey in this chapter, character representation and its development remain a surprisingly unexplored area in developmental research on narrative. And this neglect is unfortunate, because the selection, portrayal, construal, and coordination of characters add up to a crucial dimension of narrative experience for both children and adults—one that is also inextricably linked to other dimensions of narrative that have received more attention, including plot structure and the strategies by which narrative coherence is constructed and maintained. Developing more systematic, probing, and sophisticated theoretical and methodological tools for analyzing character representation can thus enrich our understanding of narrative development in a range of domains, and I have tried to outline some resources and exploratory efforts on which this research enterprise might usefully draw. In the spirit of the quotation at the head of this chapter, we should follow up these leads and see where they take us.

REFERENCES

Bamberg, M. (1986). A functional approach to the acquisition of anaphoric relationships. *Linguistics, 24,* 227–284.

Bamberg, M., & Damrad-Frye, R. (1991). On the ability to provide evaluative comments: Further explorations of children's narrative competence. *Journal of Child Language, 18,* 689–710.

Benson, M. S. (1996). Structure, conflict, and psychological causation in the fictional narrative of 4- and 5-year-olds. *Merrill-Palmer Quarterly, 42,* 228–247.

Benson, M. S. (1997). Psychological causation and goal-based episodes: Low-income children's emerging narrative skills. *Early Childhood Research Quarterly, 12,* 439–457.

Berman, R., & Slobin, D. I. (Eds.). (1994). *Relating events in narrative: A crosslinguistic developmental study.* Hillsdale, NJ: Lawrence Erlbaum Associates.

Bruner, J. (1986). *Actual minds, possible worlds.* Cambridge, MA: Harvard University Press.

Culler, J. (1975). *Structuralist poetics: Structuralism, linguistics, and the study of literature.* Ithaca, NY: Cornell University Press.

Feldman, C., Bruner, J., Kalmar, D., & Renderer, B. (1993). Plot, plight, dramatism: Interpretation at three ages. *Human Development, 36,* 327–342.

Greimas, A. J. (1977). Elements of a narrative grammar. *Diacritics, 7,* 23–40.

Karmiloff-Smith, A. (1985). Language and cognitive processes from a developmental perspective. *Language and Cognitive Processes, 1,* 61–85.

Küntay, A. C., & Nakamura, K. (2004). Linguistic strategies serving evaluative functions: A comparison between Japanese and Turkish narratives. In S. Strömqvist & L. Verhoeven (Eds.), *Relating events in narrative: Typological and contextual perspectives* (pp. 329–358). Mahwah, NJ: Lawrence Erlbaum Associates.

Leondar, B. (1977). Hatching plots: Genesis of storymaking. In D. Perkins & B. Leondar (Eds.), *The arts and cognition* (pp. 172–191). Baltimore: The Johns Hopkins University Press.

McGann, W., & Schwartz, A. (1988). Main character in children's narratives. *Linguistics, 26,* 215–233.

Miller, P. J., Hoogstra, L., Mintz, J., Fung, H., & Williams, K. (1993). Troubles in the garden and how they get resolved: A young child's transformation of his favorite story. In C.A. Nelson (Ed.), *Memory and affect in development. The Minnesota Symposia on Child Psychology* (Vol. 26, pp. 87–114). Hillsdale, NJ: Lawrence Erlbaum Associates.

Nelson, K. (1996). *Language in cognitive development: The emergence of the mediated mind.* New York: Cambridge University Press.

Nicolopoulou, A. (1996). Narrative development in social context. In D. I. Slobin, J. Gerhardt, J. Guo, & A. Kyratzis (Eds.), *Social interaction, social context, and language: Essays in honor of Susan Ervin-Tripp* (pp. 369–390). Mahwah, NJ: Lawrence Erlbaum Associates.

Nicolopoulou, A. (1997a). Children and narratives: Toward an interpretive and sociocultural approach. In M. Bamberg (Ed.), *Narrative development: Six approaches* (pp. 179–215). Mahwah, NJ: Lawrence Erlbaum Associates.

Nicolopoulou, A. (1997b). Worldmaking and identity formation in children's narrative play-acting. In B. D. Cox & C. Lightfoot (Eds.), *Sociogenetic perspectives on internalization* (pp. 157–187). Mahwah, NJ: Lawrence Erlbaum Associates.

Nicolopoulou, A. (2002). Peer-group culture and narrative development. In S. Blum-Kulka & C. E. Snow (Eds.), *Talking to adults: The contribution of multiparty discourse to language acquisition* (pp. 117–152). Mahwah, NJ: Lawrence Erlbaum Associates.

Nicolopoulou, A., & Ilgaz, H. (2006, June). Further explorations on the development of main character in preschoolers' spontaneous stories. Paper presented at the annual meeting of the Jean Piaget Society, Baltimore, MD.

Nicolopoulou, A., & Richner, E.S. (1999, July). The development of main character in young children's narratives. Poster presented at the triennial meeting of the International Association for the Study of Child Language, San Sebastián, Spain.

Nicolopoulou, A., & Richner, E. S. (2007). From actors to agents to persons: The development of character representation in young children's narratives. *Child Development, 78*, 412–429.

Nicolopoulou, A., Scales, B., & Weintraub, J. (1994). Gender differences and symbolic imagination in the stories of four-year-olds. In A. H. Dyson & C. Genishi (Eds.), *The need for story: Cultural diversity in classroom and community* (pp. 102–123). Urbana, IL: NCTE.

Paley, V. G. (1986). *Mollie is three: Growing up in school*. Chicago: The University of Chicago Press.

Paley, V.G. (1988). *Bad guys don't have birthdays: Fantasy play at four*. Chicago: The University of Chicago Press.

Paley, V. G. (1990). *The boy who would be a helicopter: The uses of storytelling in the classroom*. Cambridge, MA: Harvard University Press.

Propp, V. (1968). *Morphology of the folktale*. Austin: University of Texas Press. [Original work published in Russian in 1928.]

Richner, E. S., & Nicolopoulou, A. (2001). The narrative construction of differing conceptions of the person in the development of young children's social understanding. *Early Education & Development, 12*, 393–432.

Rimmon-Kenan, S. (1983). *Narrative fiction: Contemporary poetics*. London: Routledge.

Rorty, A. O. (1988). *Mind in action: Essays in the philosophy of mind*. Boston: Beacon Press.

Rowe, D.W. (1998). The literate potentials of book-related dramatic play. *Reading Research Quarterly, 33*, 10–35.

Shapiro, L. R., & Hudson, J. A. (1991). Tell me a make-believe story: Coherence and cohesion in young children's picture-elicited narratives. *Developmental Psychology, 27*, 960–974.

Stein, N. L. (1988). The development of children's storytelling skill. In M. B. Franklin & S. S. Barten (Eds.), *Child language: A reader* (pp. 282–297). New York: Oxford University Press.

Stein, N. L., & Albro, E. R. (1997). Building complexity and coherence: Children's use of goal-structured knowledge in telling stories. In M. Bamberg (Ed.), *Narrative development: Six approaches* (pp. 5–44). Mahwah, NJ: Lawrence Erlbaum Associates.

Toolan, M. J. (2001). *Narrative: A critical linguistic introduction* (2nd ed.). London: Routledge.

Trabasso, T., & Stein, N. L. (1994). Using goal-plan knowledge to merge the past with the present and the future in narrating events on line. In M. M. Haith, J. B. Benson, R. J. Roberts Jr., & B. F. Pennington (Eds.), *The development of future-oriented processes* (pp. 323–349). Chicago: The University of Chicago Press.

Trabasso, T., Stein, N. L., Rodkin, P. C., Munger, M. P., & Baughn, C. R. (1992). Knowledge of goals and plans in the on-line narration of events. *Cognitive Psychology, 7*, 133–170.

Wolf, S. A., & Heath, S.B. (1992). *The braid of literature: Children's worlds of reading*. Cambridge, MA: Harvard University Press.

18

Motion Events in English and Korean Fictional Writings and Translations

KYUNG-JU OH

Cambridge, Massachusetts

> It should be evident that one cannot escape the influence of language while in the process of formulating or interpreting verbal messages.
>
> **Dan I. Slobin (2000, p. 107)**

Dan Slobin was an incredibly supportive teacher and a generous mentor when I was a graduate student at Berkeley. This chapter is based on one of my dissertation chapters (Oh, 2003) that was directly influenced by Dan's work on motion events in fiction writings and their translations.

INTRODUCTION

The last two decades saw "motion events" becoming an exciting test field for crosslinguistic research. A relatively clear typology that crosscuts cultures makes this an exciting area to explore to examine the relation between language and thought.

A "motion event" (defined here as the movement of an entity changing its location from one point in space to another) is composed of various semantic/conceptual elements, including "motion" (change of location through movement), "figure" (the moving entity), "path" (the trajectory through which the figure moves), and "manner" (the way in which the entity moves). Languages tend to adopt one of two major patterns in terms of how path of motion—the core element of a motion event according to Talmy (2000)—is "lexicalized" (that is, in which grammatical category of words it is typically expressed). In some languages, "satellites"—grammatical elements (e.g., *up, across, into*) associated with verbs—are the preferred means for expressing path. In others, it is the main verb (e.g., *ascend, cross, enter*). Languages that express path mainly in satellites are called satellite-framed languages (S-languages, hereafter), and those which typically express path in verbs are called verb-framed languages (V-languages). Each of these two contrasting groups of languages encompasses a wide range of languages spoken in diverse cultures: S-languages include English, German, Mandarin Chinese, and French, and V-languages include Spanish, Turkish, Japanese, and Korean (Talmy, 1985, 2000).[1]

In S-languages, in which the main verb is open to express semantic elements other than path, manner of motion seems to receive more attention in verb use. In numerous crosslinguistic studies, Slobin

---

[1] Note that this typology is based on what the predominant pattern in the language is, rather than what is grammatical in the absolute sense. Thus, although path sometimes is expressed in verbs in English, English is considered an s-language because path is typically expressed in satellites in this language.

253

and his colleagues (Berman & Slobin, 1994; Özçalışkan & Slobin, 1999; Slobin, 1996, 2000) found that speakers of S-languages produce verbs expressing manner of motion at a higher frequency and in greater variety when they describe motion events. This finding was repeatedly supported by other researchers as well (e.g., Naigles, Eisenberg, Kako, Highter, & McGraw, 1998). Based on this, Slobin (1996, 2004) proposed that S-languages tend to be more highly "manner-salient" than V-languages, and that speakers of S-languages may habitually pay more attention to manner of motion than V-language speakers do during online language processing. In support of this hypothesis, S-language speakers were found to include more manner information than V-language speakers when they verbally recalled motion events that had been presented to them in written texts (Slobin, 2000).

However, in the studies cited above, only verb use was considered in the analysis. More recently, researchers began attending to alternative linguistic means to express manner of motion as well as verbs. Naigles et al. (1998) reported that V-language speakers used more adverbials of manner than S-language speakers in motion-event description tasks, and that these "compensate" for V-language speakers' less frequent use of manner verbs. On the other hand, in another study involving fiction writings and their translations, Özçalışkan and Slobin (2003) and Slobin (2005) suggested that V-language speakers and writers do not use alternative manner expressions frequently enough to compensate for their less frequent use of manner verbs.

The present study adopts the approach of Özçalışkan and Slobin (2003) and examines how manner verbs and other types of manner expressions are used in fictional motion-event descriptions by well-known authors and in their translations by professional translators. If professional writers are considered highly skilled craftsmen of a particular language, this study should illustrate how manner of motion is expressed in a language at its best. If the goal of translators is to faithfully convey the meaning of the original text in good sentences in the target language, their work should offer insights into the potential of a given language to express particular types of manner of motion described in another language.

METHOD

Novels and short stories from ten English/American authors and ten Korean authors, as well as their translations into the other language by different translators, were selected as a sample. All of the original authors are relatively well-known and respected writers in their own language communities. Aside from this restriction, the selection was made largely based on the availability of both the originals and their translations in libraries in the San Francisco Bay Area. A list of the original authors, original writings, and translators that were sampled for the study is presented in Table 18.1.

Ten motion-event descriptions—defined here as descriptions of movement of a character or characters between two points in space—were collected from each original author by randomly opening a page and finding the first motion-event description from an arbitrarily chosen point on the page. Only explicitly expressed motion events, not implications of motion (as those in which a character is described as being at one place in one paragraph and then being at another place in the next), were included in the sample, although it is possible that there is a crosslinguistic and/or cross-cultural difference in terms of how often actual processes of location change are explicitly described. After all the motion event samples were collected from the original works, the equivalent parts were identified in their translations. This generated a total of 400 motion-event descriptions.

The two independent variables of the present study are "presentational language" and "source language." Presentational language refers to the language in which the texts are presented at the surface level, and source language refers to language in which the texts were originally composed. Each of the two independent variables has two conditions, English and Korean. This results in a total of four different conditions. For example, a text originally composed in English would belong to a condition in which English is the presentational language and the source language. The Korean translation of the same text would belong to a condition in which Korean is the presentational language and English is the original language.

Particular analyses made in this study are explicated in the following subsections.

TABLE 18.1   List of the Sources of the Sample

Original Language	Author	Title	Translator	Type of Writing
Korean	Choi In-hoon	Kwangcang (Plaza)	Kevin O'Rourke	Novel
	Kim Tong-ri	Saban ui sipcaka (The cross of Saphan)	Sol Sun-bong	Novel
	Park Kyung-ri	Thoci	Anita Tennant	Novel
	Yi Chong-jun	Janinhan tosi (The cruel city)	Choe Yong	Novel
	Yi Mun-yol	Kumsico (The golden phoenix)	Suh Jr-moon	Novella
	Ch'ae Man-shik	Leydimeyidulaypu (A ready-made life)	Kim Chong-un & Bruce Fulton	Short story
	Kim Sung-ok	Sewul, 1964, kyewul (Seoul, 1964, winter)	Peter Lee	Short story
	O Young-su	Meyali (The echo)	Hong Myong-hui	Short story
	Park Wan-so	Naui kacang nacong cinin kes (My last possession) & Eytten yaman (A certain barbarity)	Chun Kyung-ja	Short story
	Yun Heung-gil	Hwanghonui cip (The house of twilight)	Martin Holman	Short story
English	Ernest Hemingway	*For whom the bell tolls*	Kim Byung-kil	*Novel*
	Carson McCullers	*The ballad of the sad café*	Ahn Dong-rim	Novella
	George Orwell	*1984*	Han Chi-hui	Novel
	John Steinbeck	*Grapes of wrath*	Maeng Hoo-bin	Novel
	Virginia Woolf	*The years*	Kim Soo-jung	Novel
	John Cheever	The bridgadier and the golf widow	Moon Sang-tuek	Short story
	Bernard Malamud	The magic barrel	Ryo Seok-ki	Short story
	O. Henry	The cop and the anthem, The romance of a busy broker, After twenty years.	Kim Ki-toek	Short story
	James Purdy	Good night, sweetheart	Kang Bong-sik	Short story
	John Updike	Flight, Pigeon feather	Lee Jae-ho	Short story

Manner Verb Use

Manner was defined as "motor pattern modulating movement of protagonist, rate, degree of effort, etc." (Slobin, 1998, p. 2). Manner verbs included verbs or deverbal nouns that contain information regarding manner of motion. Repetition of the same verb within a description was ignored. Across the four conditions of this study, the mean frequencies of manner verbs per motion event description were obtained.

Alternative Manner Expressions

Manner of motion can also be expressed in adverbs, adjectives, phrases, clauses, or sentences that described the physical characteristics of the movement itself. The following examples illustrate some of these cases:

   Physical characteristics of movement by adverbs: *He walked <u>briskly</u> and <u>erectly</u>.* (Malamud)
   Physical characteristics of movement by adjectives: *Miss Amelia crossed the porch with two <u>slow, gangling</u> strides.* (McCullers)
   Physical characteristics of movement by adverbial phrases: *With her basket on her arm she walked down...<u>with the swaying movement of a woman with child</u>.* (Woolf)
   Physical characteristics of movement by separate clauses: *<u>Bending under the weight of the packs</u>,...they climbed...in the pine forest that covered the mountainside.* (Hemingway)

   Manner can also be indicated through "internal state or physical condition of a moving entity," "features of the physical setting that could influence manner of motion" (Özçalışkan & Slobin, 2003), or other relevant features that allow readers to infer manner of motion further than what was already explicitly expressed in other parts of the description. Some examples include:

> Internal state of moving entity: *He walked down stairs, <u>depressed</u>.* (Malamud)
> Features of the physical setting that could influence manner of motion: *Then Crosby....began to edge...down the <u>slippery</u> steps.*(Woolf)
> Relevant features that allow readers to infer manner: *<u>There was a heavy tramp of boots in the passage</u>. The steel door <u>swung open with a clang</u>. O'Brien walked into the cell.* (Orwell)

A word or a group of words that describes the same quality of manner was considered as one manner expression. Across the four language conditions, the mean frequencies of such manner expressions per motion event description were counted for each condition.

In order to maintain consistency of coding, one coder (the author) coded all the data. To appraise reliability of coding, a second coder coded 15% of the data. The final agreement rate reached 89.7%.

Descriptions Containing Manner Information

The number of manner expressions is not in itself a definite indicator of how much manner is elaborated or how much cognitive attention is paid to manner. A vivid verb can express as much as, or even more than, a string of manner words. As a rough indicator of how much attention writers/translators of different languages pay to manner of motion, the frequency of descriptions containing at least one manner expression (regardless of its type) was counted. Among all the descriptions with manner information, the number of descriptions of the following three types was also counted in order to study preferred means of expressing manner in the two languages: (1) descriptions with at least one manner verb but no other alternative manner expressions, (2) descriptions with both a manner verb and alternative manner expressions, and (3) descriptions with alternative manner expressions but no manner verbs.

Translation of Manner Expressions

Making an objective decision regarding whether or not a particular manner expression was conveyed properly in its translation is not a simple task. In this study, straightforward quantitative analyses were devised to appraise how manner information is translated across the two typologically different languages. First, whether or not a trace of a manner verb could be found in translation was considered. Furthermore, in what linguistic category—a manner verb, an alternative expression, or a combination of the two—the meaning of the original manner verb could be found in the translated sentence was considered. If use of alternative expressions compensates for relatively sparse use of manner verbs in Korean (and in other V-languages), most English manner verbs would be translated into Korean either as manner verbs, alternative manner expressions, or combinations of both. Conversely, if much of the manner information in English manner verbs is not translated into Korean, it would indicate that manner is more likely to be neglected in Korean. Considering that information tends to be lost in translation in general, translations of Korean manner verbs to English were also considered for comparison.

Examining how all manner expressions are treated in translation is much more problematic. One "manner expression" (a verb, an adverb, or a clause/sentence/group of sentences that bears an implication for manner of motion) often does not describe a particular manner of motion by itself, but rather does so together with other expressions. Judgments regarding whether such expressions were translated can be highly subjective because they carry incomplete information. Nevertheless, an effort was made to determine whether or not such alternative manner expressions were translated.

RESULTS

Manner Verb Use

Table 18.2 presents the mean number of manner verbs per motion-event description in each language condition.

A two-by-two ANOVA (source × presentational language) revealed a significant main effect of source language ($F(1, 396) = 3.601$, $p = 0.025$), with texts originally written in English containing more manner verbs than texts originally written in Korean, and a significant main effect of presentational language ($F(1, 396) = 6.250$, $p = 0.003$), with texts presented in English containing more manner verbs than texts presented in Korean. No significant interaction between source and presentational language was detected. Planned pair-wise comparisons revealed that English original texts contain significantly more manner verbs than Korean originals ($F(1, 198) = 14.881$, $p = 0.000$). The differences between English originals and their Korean translations ($F(1, 198) = 4.845$, $p = 0.029$), and between Korean originals and their English translations ($F(1, 198) = 3.906$, $p = 0.050$) were also significant.

English texts contained not only a higher frequency of manner verbs but also a larger variety of them. Lists of English and Korean manner verbs are presented in Table 18.3.

TABLE 18.2 Mean Number of Manner Verbs per Motion-Event Description by Condition

		Presentational Language		
		English	Korean	Mean
Source Language	English	0.98 (0.876)	0.72 (0.792)	0.85 (0.843)
	Korean	0.78 (0.970)	0.54 (0.731)	0.66 (0.865)
	Mean	0.88 (0.927)	0.63 (0.766)	

Standard deviations are provided in parentheses.

TABLE 18.3 Manner Verbs Appearing in the Sample Texts

Source Language	Presentational Language	
	English	Korean
English	burst, charge, chase, climb, dash, drop, flee, fling, halt, hike, hobble, hurry, jerk, march, moon, pull oneself, quicken, race, run, rush, sail, saunter, sidle, sink, slid, slip, slow, sneak, spring, step (take steps), stride, stroll, strut, stumble, swagger, walk, wander, be dumped, be carried, be harried 40 types	Ccochta 'chase,' caechokhada 'hurry,' cellumkerita 'limp,' celttwukkerita 'limp,' heychita 'push (one's way),' kenilta 'stroll around,' ketta 'walk,' kita 'crawl,' kkulta 'drag,' nalta 'fly,' nalttwuita 'bounce about,' naepaengkaechita 'throw,' nucchuta 'slow,' panghwanghata 'wander,' ppacienakata 'escape,' talita 'run,' thwita 'spring,' tomangchita 'flee,' tolcinhata 'dash,' ttwuichie-(used only with other verbs) 'run,' ttwuita 'run,' kilul chca kata 'find one's way' 22 types
Korean	climb, creep, dash, drag, fall, flee, fling, fly, hurry, jump, plop, run, rush, saunter, slacken, slip, slow, shot, stagger, steal, step (take a step, footsteps), stride, toddle, toss, walk, wander, thread one's way 27 types	ana(olita) 'pick (up),' cicheyhata 'slacken,' cwulhangrangchita 'run away,' chyepakta 'fling,' heymaeta 'wander,' mulupkelum 'knee-walking,' naetatta 'shot,' ketta 'walk,' kelumma 'toddle,' kkulta 'drag,' picipko(tulekata) 'push (in),' sesengita 'hover,' talita 'run,' tencita 'throw,' thada 'moving via rope or other devices,' titta 'step,' ttuta 'slacken,' tomangchita 'flee,' ttelecita 'fall,' twiskelumchita 'walk backward,' ttwuita 'run, jump,' tempyetulta 'attack forward,' pal ul ttey nohta 'take steps' 23 types
	Total for all English texts: 54 types	Total for all Korean texts: 40 types

Alternative Manner Expressions

Table 18.4 presents the mean number of alternative manner expressions—manner expressions other than manner verbs—per motion-event description.

Even though texts translated into Korean and texts originally written in Korean contained more alternative manner expressions than their English counterparts, these differences were not statistically significant. A two-by-two ANOVA (presentational language × source) revealed no significant main effect of source or presentational language, or interactions between the two. In planned pairwise comparisons, no significant difference was found between the English original texts and the Korean original texts, between the English originals and their translations to Korean, or between the Korean originals and their translations to English.

When all manner expressions—both manner verbs and alternative expressions—were compared, English texts (i.e., English originals and English translations of Korean originals) contained more manner expressions than Korean texts (i.e., Korean originals and Korean translations of English originals). However, no statistically significant differences were detected between any two conditions among the four. Mean numbers of all manner expressions are presented in Table 18.5.

Descriptions Containing Manner Information

In the previous subsection, the number of manner expressions was considered. In this section, the number of descriptions (out of 100 descriptions in each condition) that contain manner information is considered.

The number of cases that contained manner expressions (verb or alternative) in each condition is presented in Table 18.6.

Chi-square analyses indicated a significant association between language conditions and use of manner expressions (χ^2 (3) = 8.264, p = 0.041). Source language was significantly associated with presence/absence of manner information (χ^2 (1) = 7.580, p = 0.006). More descriptions originally written in English contained manner expressions (83 descriptions in the English original texts and 78 descriptions in their English to Korean translations, totaling 161 descriptions) than descriptions

TABLE 18.4 Mean Number of Alternative Manner Expressions

		Presentational Language		
		English	Korean	Mean
Source Language	English	0.85 (1.239)	0.96 (1.163)	0.91 (1.197)
	Korean	0.81 (1.098)	1.02 (1.247)	0.92 (1.172)
	Mean	0.83 (1.161)	0.99 (1.203)	

Standard deviations are provided in parentheses.

TABLE 18.5 Mean Number of All Manner Expressions (Manner Verbs and Alternative Expressions)

		Presentational Language		
		English	Korean	Mean
Source Language	English	1.83 (1.676)	1.68 (1.550)	1.76 (1.612)
	Korean	1.59 (1.764)	1.56 (1.678)	1.58 (1.717)
	Mean	1.71 (1.721)	1.62 (1.612)	

Standard deviations are provided in parentheses.

TABLE 18.6 Distribution of Manner Information Across Different Linguistic Means

	Number of Descriptions With No Manner Expressions	Number of Descriptions With Manner Information			
		Manner Verbs Only	Manner Verbs + Alternative Expressions	Alternative Expressions Only	Sum
English Original	17	37	32	14	83
English to Korean	22	20	34	24	78
Korean to English	32	15	39	14	68
Korean Original	31	10	33	26	69

originally written in Korean (69 descriptions in the Korean original tests and 68 descriptions in their English translations, totaling 137).

When the analysis was conducted on the original texts only (without including their translations), the same pattern was found. The English original texts contained more descriptions with manner expressions than the Korean original texts (χ^2 (1) = 7.219, p = 0.007).

Presentational language was not significantly associated with presence/absence of manner information. Differences between English original texts (83 descriptions containing manner expressions) and their Korean translations (78 descriptions containing manner expressions), or those between Korean originals (69 descriptions containing manner expressions) and their English translations (68 descriptions containing manner expressions) were not statistically significant.

When the distribution of motion-event descriptions across three different ways of expressing manner (by manner verb, by a manner verb and additional expressions, and by additional expressions only) was considered, English texts had a higher proportion of descriptions in which manner was expressed through verbs only than the Korean texts. Both source (χ^2 (2) = 10.938, p = 0.004) and presentational language (χ^2 (2) = 12.172, p = 0.002) had significant associations with the distribution of motion-event descriptions across the three different ways of expressing manner being considered here. The association between language condition and distribution of manner information was significant when the English originals and the Korean originals were considered (χ^2 (2) = 17.989, p = 0.000) and when the English originals and their Korean translations were considered (χ^2 (2) = 7.614, p = 0.022), but not when the Korean originals and their English translations were considered.

Translation Of Manner Expressions

Table 18.7 presents how manner verbs were translated across the two languages. It shows that more manner verbs were translated to manner verbs in the Korean-to-English translations than in the English-to-Korean translations. By contrast, fewer manner verbs were translated to alternative manner expressions (either alone or used together with a manner verb) in the Korean-to-English translations than in the English-to-Korean translations. Furthermore, manner information expressed in manner verbs in the original language was less likely to be completely lost in the Korean-to-English translations (19%) than in the English-to-Korean translations (34%).

TABLE 18.7 Translations of Manner Verbs

	Manner Verbs Only	Manner Verbs + Alternative Expressions	Alternative Manner Expressions Only	Not Translated	Others*
English to Korean	45% (44)	8% (8)	13% (13)	34% (33)	0% (0)
Korean to English	65% (35)	4% (2)	2% (1)	19% (10)	11% (6)

* "Others" represents cases in which a manner verb and an alternative manner expression accompanying it, as a whole, were translated into another manner verb and an alternative manner expression.
Absolute frequencies are provided in parentheses.

When an attempt was made to determine whether alternative manner expressions (other than manner verbs) were translated, fewer such manner expressions were found to be abandoned in the Korean-to-English translations (20 out of 156, 12.8%) than in the English-to-Korean translations (33 out of 183, 18%). When all manner expressions were counted, 33 manner expressions in the English descriptions were not translated compared to 20 in the Korean originals.

DISCUSSION

Fiction writings of professional writers in English (S-language) and Korean (V-language), and their translations to the other language, were examined in this study, with a focus given to the way in which manner of motion is described.

The results of this study confirm the richness of the repertoire of manner verbs in S-languages as compared with V-languages. The English original motion-event descriptions sampled in this study contained a greater number and wider variety of manner verbs than the Korean original sample. In addition, the English translations contained more manner verbs than their Korean originals, while the Korean translations contained fewer manner verbs than their English originals.

This study also indicates the importance of adverbs, separate clauses, and sentences in V-languages for describing and indicating manner of motion. When such alternative expressions and manner verbs were counted, no significant difference was found across the two languages in the overall number of manner expressions. Korean speakers' heavy reliance on these alternative expressions (in place of manner verbs) was also reflected in the way manner verbs were translated between English and Korean. As can be seen in Table 18.7, in the English-to-Korean translations, 21% of English manner verbs were translated into alternative manner expressions ("manner verbs + alternative expressions" or "alternative manner expressions only"), as opposed to 6% of manner verbs in the Korean-to-English translations.

Many of the "alternative manner expressions" included in the Korean sample were what are called ideophones—words that imitate what they express in their sounds. Slobin (2004) and Ibarretxe-Antuñano (2003) observed that some V-languages, while lacking rich manner verb vocabulary, may benefit from a variety of ideophones. In fact, the data collected for the present study contained quite a few such ideophones, some of which offer vivid and detailed information regarding manner. (See Table 18.8 for the ideophones found in the Korean sample.)

Thus, it appears that, when skilled writers of Korean compose written sentences with the goal of being expressive and/or conveying particular information written in another language, they use various linguistic means to *supplement* the scantiness of manner verbs in their language (both in frequency and type).

Whether or not this *compensates* for the scarcity of manner verbs adequately is another question, and a much more difficult one to tackle as it is hard to make a precise comparison between a Korean sentence and an English sentence in terms of the amount of manner information they contain. This study addresses this matter only indirectly. When the number of descriptions containing any manner information was counted as an indicator of attention to manner, a higher proportion of English descriptions than Korean ones contained manner information. Even in translation, manner of motion expressed in the original text was more likely to be ignored when the text was translated from English to Korean than the other way around. Table 18.6 indicates that among the 83 English original descriptions that contained manner information, 5 of them (approximately 6%) lost all trace of manner in their Korean translations. Only one such case (approximately 1.4%) was identified in the Korean-to-English translations. In the English-to-Korean translations, 34% of manner verbs were completely ignored and not translated at all, compared to 19% in the Korean-to-English translations. When all manner expressions were counted, as discussed in Results, 33 manner expressions in the English descriptions were not translated as compared to 20 in the Korean originals. Although these numbers may not be dramatic, they reflect a consistent trend.

TABLE 18.8 Ideophones Identified in Korean Texts

Korean Ideophone	English Gloss (according to Si-sa Elite Concise Korean-English Dictionary, 1995)
esulleng esulleng	(used with 'walk') stroll [ramble] about; saunter [lounge] along; walk at a leisurely pace
sengkum sengkum	with long steps. | (together with 'walk') stride (along); take [walk with] long [big, large, great] steps [strides]
ussuktaemye (ussuktaeta)	raise [draw up] one's shoulders in pride; swagger; bluster; hold one's head high
whik	(1) suddenly; abruptly; with a jerk; quickly (2) whizzing; whistling; with a whistle [whiz(z)] (3) with full force; with all one's strength
hekepcikep	in a hurry [flurry]; hurry-scurry
hwicheng hwicheng (hwicheng-kerita)	(1) yield; give; bend; be pliant [pliable, flexible, supple] (2) be unsteady; reel; be shaky; be groggy …|(with 'walk') walk unsteadily; shamble along
Esil esil	Not listed
pitul pitul	totteringly; staggeringly; reelingly; falteringly; waddlingly| (with 'walk') stagger [shamble, dodder] along; walk with tottering steps
pisil pisil	Same as pisul pisul (pisul pisul: totteringly; staggeringly; reelingly; falteringly|(with 'walk') dodder along; walk with faltering steps)
sulkum sulkum	stealthily; sneakingly; furtively; covertly; quietly
salkum salkum	stealthily; quietly; sneakingly; furtively; secretly; surreptitiously …| (with 'walk') walk noiselessly [stealthily]; sneak [skulk] about

Thus, it appears that, in spite of the availability of "alternative manner expressions" in Korean, Korean speakers still seem to pay less attention to manner than English speakers.

CONCLUSIONS

The results of this study showed that various alternative manner expressions are available to, and utilized by, Korean writers to express manner of motion. However, Korean still seems to remain a "low-manner-salient" language, as more of the Korean original descriptions lacked manner information than the English originals, and manner information was more likely to be lost in the English-to-Korean translations than in the Korean-to-English translations.

Ideophones and other alternative manner expressions are not essential grammatical components of a sentence as the main verb is. Such optional elements many not have as much influence on thinking for speaking as patterns involving central components of a sentence.

Slobin was right when he said that "[o]ne does not seem to be able to escape the influence of one's language while in the process of formulating or interpreting verbal messages" (2000, p. 107). In fact, it does not seem to be easy to escape the influence of the lexicalization pattern of one's language, even with the aid of other resources available in the language.

REFERENCES

Berman, R. A., & Slobin, D. I. (1994). *Relating events in narrative: A crosslinguistic developmental study*. Hillsdale, NJ: Lawrence Erlbaum Associates.

Ibarretxe-Antuñano, I. (2003). What translation tells us about motion: A contrastive study of typologically different languages. Unpublished manuscript, Universidad of Deusto, Spain.

Naigles, L., Eisenberg, A., Kako, E., Highter, M., & McGraw, N. (1998). Speaking of motion: Verb use in English and Spanish. *Language and Cognitive Processes, 13,* 521–549.

Oh, K. (2003). *Language, cognition, and development: Motion event descriptions in English and Korean*. Unpublished doctoral dissertation, University of California, Berkeley.

Özçalışkan, S., & Slobin, D. I. (1999). Learning 'how to search for the frog': Expression of manner of motion in English, Spanish, and Turkish. In A. Greenhill, H. Littlefield, & C. Tano (Eds.), *Proceedings of the 23rd Annual Boston University Conference on Language Development* (pp. 541–552). Somerville, MA: Cascadilla Press.

Özçalışkan, S., & Slobin, D. I. (2003). Codability effects on the expression of manner of motion in English and Turkish. In A. S. Özsoy, D. Akar, M. Nakipoglu-Demiralp, E. E. Taylan, & A. Aksu-Koç (Eds.), *Studies in Turkish linguistics* (pp. 259–270). Istanbul: Bogaziçi University Press.

Si-sa Elite Concise Korean-English Dictionary (1995). Seoul, Korea: Si-sa-yong-o-sa.

Slobin, D. I. (1996). From "thought and language" to "thinking for speaking." In J. J. Gumperz & S. C. Levinson (Eds.), *Rethinking linguistic relativity* (pp. 70–96). Cambridge, UK: Cambridge University Press.

Slobin, D. I. (1998). *Coding of motion events in narrative texts.* Unpublished manuscript, University of California, Berkeley.

Slobin, D. I. (2000). Verbalized events: A dynamic approach to linguistic relativity and determinism. In S. Niemeier & R. Dirven (Eds.), *Evidence of linguistic relativity* (pp. 107–138). Amsterdam/Philadelphia: John Benjamins.

Slobin, D. I. (2004). The many ways to search for a frog: Linguistic typology and the expression of motion events. In S. Strömqvist & L. Verhoeven (Eds.), *Relating events in narrative: Typological and contextual perspectives* (pp. 219–257). Mahwah, NJ: Lawrence Erlbaum Associates.

Slobin, D. I. (2005). Relating narrative events in translation. In D. Ravid & H.B. Shyldkrot (Eds.), *Perspectives on language and language development: Essays in honor of Ruth A. Berman* (pp. 115–130). Dordrecht, the Netherlands: Kluwer.

Talmy, L. (1985). Lexicalization patterns: Semantic structure in lexical forms. In T. Shopen (Ed.), *Language typology and syntactic description: Vol. III. Grammatical categories and the lexicon* (pp. 56–149). Cambridge, UK: Cambridge University Press.

Talmy, L (2000). *Toward a cognitive semantics: Vol. II. Typology and process in concept structuring.* Cambridge, MA: The MIT Press.

19

Learning to Talk About Spatial Motion in Language-Specific Ways

ŞEYDA ÖZÇALIŞKAN
Georgia State University

> One cannot make claims about the acquisition or use of a grammatical form without situating it typologically, in a network of interactive psycholinguistic factors.
>
> **Dan I. Slobin (1997, p. 35)**

*M*y initial acquaintance with Dan was at the University of California, Berkeley, where I studied as a graduate student under his supervision. He introduced me to the field of spatial language and cognition, and we worked on several projects together, examining crosslinguistic variation in the expression of spatial motion. Dan has been a wonderful mentor and an insightful collaborator ever since. Looking back, I still miss all the stimulating conversations we had back at Berkeley, with the topics ranging from the (im)possibilities of encoding manner in verb-framed languages, to reminiscences about life in İstanbul, Turkish music and politics. Dan has been a key figure in my intellectual development, and I feel very fortunate to have had the chance to be one of his doctoral students.

Spatial motion is a domain that shows wide variation in linguistic expression across different languages of the world, but this variation can be explained by a finite set of universal patterns (Talmy, 2000). As such, it provides a useful realm to observe universal vs. language-specific patterns in children's early use of language. This chapter examines developmental changes in children's talk about spatial motion in a comparison between English and Turkish, two languages that show typologically distinct patterns in their expression of motion. The chapter focuses on the manner and path components of motion, and provides a detailed account of how children express each of these motion components in the two languages over developmental time.

TYPOLOGY OF MOTION EVENTS

Talmy (2000) defines a motion event as composed of a *framing event* and a *co-event*. The framing event provides the schematic structure for the event and has four components: a moving *figure*, a physical *landmark* with respect to which the figure moves, an activating process, namely, *motion*, and a *path* that relates the figure to the landmark. The *co-event* elaborates or motivates the framing event, and its encoding is optional. One such co-event is the *manner event*, which encodes the manner in which the motion is carried out (*running, crawling*). Of the four components of the framing event, Talmy defines path as the core feature of the event, and divides the world's languages into two groups based on their expression of path information: verb-framed languages (V-languages) typically encode path in the main verb (*exit, enter*), whereas satellite-framed languages (S-languages) typically express path in a satellite associated with the main verb (go *out*, go *down*).

Differences in the lexicalization of path (inside *vs.* outside the verb) have consequences for whether path or manner of motion is frequently mentioned by speakers of each language type. The preference of S-language speakers to express path by satellites leaves the main verb available for manner information. Since the main verb is the obligatory core of a predicate, this gives S-language speakers an easily codable linguistic option to convey manner. As an outcome, S-language speakers develop a habitual pattern of encoding manner (Slobin, 2000). In contrast, because V-language speakers typically express path in the main verb, they have to use subordinate grammatical constructions, such as gerunds (e.g., *exit running*) or adverbs (e.g., *exit hastily*) to convey manner when necessary. However, since such constructions add an extra processing load, V-language speakers are less likely to express manner in their expression of motion (Slobin, 2004).

Earlier research with adult speakers focused mainly on manner of motion and supported the typological dichotomy, with S-language speakers encoding manner more extensively than V-language speakers across different languages of the world (Gennari, Sloman, Malt, & Fitch, 2002; Naigles, Eisenberg, Kako, Highter, & McGraw, 1998; Oh, 2003; Özçalışkan, 2004, 2005; Özçalışkan & Slobin, 2003; Papafragou, Massey, & Gleitman, 2002). Thus, adults speaking different languages followed the typological patterns characteristic of their language.

HOW DO CHILDREN LEARN TO TALK ABOUT MOTION IN TYPOLOGICALLY DISTINCT WAYS?

The crosslinguistic variation observed in adults' speech about motion raises several important questions for language learning, one of which is how early this variation is learned by children exposed to typologically different languages. Do children begin with a set of conceptual primitives that are universal and simply map spatial words onto these concepts at the beginning? Or are the child's earliest concepts of motion already influenced by the language the child is learning, thus show language-specific patterns? Previous research presents inconclusive evidence. Some researchers argue for the existence of conceptual primitives that are universally applicable (Zheng & Goldin-Meadow, 2002), while others claim that children's earliest spatial concepts are already influenced by the language the child is learning (Choi & Bowerman, 1991). Thus, the question about children's earliest motion expressions and whether they reflect universal or language-specific patterns remains unresolved.

Earlier research on children's talk about motion mainly centered on the manner and path components of motion and looked at children's production of motion verbs conveying either of these two components. One set of studies provided evidence for an early effect of language on children's motion descriptions, showing greater manner verb use by S-language speakers than V-language speakers (Oh, 2003; Özçalışkan, 2007; Özçalışkan & Slobin, 1999; Papafragou et al., 2002). In contrast, another study, which examined the types of verbs produced by children who had never been exposed to a usable conventional language model,[1] showed an early preference for path verbs and suggested that path might be a conceptual primitive before children learn to talk about motion in language-specific ways (Zheng & Goldin-Meadow, 2002).

Most of these earlier studies focused almost exclusively on motion verbs, leaving linguistic forms other than the verb mostly unexplored. However, each language type provides multiple linguistic options (e.g., verbs, particles, adverbials, prepositions) to the young language learner to encode manner and path; and it is possible that at early ages, children can rely on forms other than the verb to

---

[1] The children in the Zheng and Goldin-Meadow study included deaf Chinese and American children, who had never been exposed to a sign language by their hearing parents. These children nonetheless developed spontaneous gesture systems that had language-like structure at many levels, and the study was based on what children conveyed in their gestures.

convey the manner and path dimensions of motion in either language type. Thus, a more systematic analysis of linguistic forms other than the verb to convey the two components of motion is necessary to draw stronger conclusions about the universality or language-specificity of children's early motion descriptions.

As a step in this direction, this chapter examines developmental changes in children's talk about motion in English (an S-language) and Turkish (a V-language). It aims to identify which linguistic forms children use to convey the two components of motion—manner and path—in the two languages, and how their use of each form changes over developmental time. My prediction is that even if we would observe crosslinguistic differences in children's use of manner and path verbs at early ages—with English speakers using more manner and Turkish speakers using more path verbs—these differences might be offset by children's use of lexical items other than the verb. That is, English-speaking children would use the verb to express manner, but at the same time, would rely more heavily on particles and prepositions to convey path of motion than Turkish speakers. As a corollary to this, Turkish-speaking children would use the verb to express path, but might produce more adverbials than English speakers to convey the manner dimension. Thus, children speaking either language type could express manner and path at comparable rates, but only by using different linguistic means. The differences in the mapping strategies for path of motion (inside *vs.* outside the verb) might also lead to further differences between the two languages. If English speakers would indeed rely more heavily on path satellites to express path information, they would also be more likely to produce motion descriptions with more complex paths (i.e., with multiple path satellites) than Turkish speakers.

I examined these predictions by studying the narratives produced by English (S-language) and Turkish (V-language) speakers. The participants included 30 monolingual English-speaking and 30 monolingual Turkish-speaking children, at the mean ages 3;8 (*range* = 3;01–4;03), 5;6 (*range* = 5;02–6;01), and 9;6 (*range* = 9;01–10;01), with 10 participants in each age and language group, along with 10 adult native speakers of each language ($M = 2\,0$, *range* = 18–40). The English and the Turkish data were collected in San Francisco and Istanbul, respectively.[2] Participants came from middle-class families with literate backgrounds.

Participants were interviewed individually, using a picture book, *Frog, where are you?* (Mayer, 1969). They were asked to look through the entire book and tell a story, looking at the pictures. All responses were audiotaped and transcribed. For this study, I extracted all motion descriptions from the transcriptions and analyzed them in terms of the different types of semantic elements (manner, path) conveyed by the different linguistic forms (verbs, adverbs, particles, prepositions).

Each motion verb was categorized either as manner or path. Manner verbs encoded either the motor pattern (*dog runs away*), or the rate of motion (*gopher pops out*), or the degree of effort involved in the motion (*deer throws them off*). Path verbs encoded only the direction of motion (*owl exited from the hole*). Type and token frequencies of verbs used to express manner and path were compared by two-way ANOVAs, with age and language as the between subject factors. I also computed the frequency of linguistic forms other than the verb that conveyed manner (*owl exits rapidly*) or path (*owl flies out*) information in each language, and analyzed differences by chi-square or one- (language) or two-way (language × age) between subjects ANOVA comparisons, as appropriate. Further analysis involved computing the number of path satellites attached to a single verb of motion in each language. Each motion description was coded as having either zero (*he climbs*), one (*he climbs up*), or two or more path satellites (*he climbs up into the hole*). Scores were compared by two-way ANOVAs, with age and language as the between subject factors, separately for events with zero, one, or two-or-more path satellites.

In the remainder of the chapter, I will present the results of this analysis, focusing first on manner and then on path of motion. I will discuss the expression of each motion component first in the verb and then in a linguistic element outside the verb (e.g., particle, adverbial), and show how

---

[2] The data were collected by Tanya Renner, Virginia Marchman (English), and Ayhan Aksu-Koç (Turkish) as part of a crosslinguistic project on narrative development (Berman & Slobin, 1994).

the expression of a motion component in *vs.* outside the verb varies by the language and age of the child. In the last section, I will focus on a subcategory of motion events, namely, events that involve traversal of a spatial boundary, which places additional constraints on the expression of manner and path in V-languages, and show how early children are attuned to tighter restrictions in the lexicalization of motion in the two languages.

HOW DO CHILDREN EXPRESS MANNER IN ENGLISH AND TURKISH?

Expressing Manner in the Verb

English and Turkish speakers differed in their preference to use manner verbs in the main verb position ($F(1, 72) = 41.57$, $p < 0.001$). As Figure 19.1 shows, English speakers used more manner verbs than Turkish speakers at all ages (Scheffé, $ps < 0.05$), and this difference was present as early as age 3 (see examples 1 to 6 for crosslinguistic differences in speakers' choice of motion verbs—with English speakers typically expressing manner in the verb, as shown in examples 1, 3, 5).[3]

The frequency of manner verb use also changed over time ($F(3, 72) = 9.49$, $p < 0.001$), with adult speakers producing more manner verbs than the 3-year-olds in both English and Turkish (Scheffé, $ps < 0.05$). However, no such reliable difference was observed between the 3-, 5-, and 9-year-olds in either language. Thus, children remained relatively stable in their production of manner verbs over time in both English and Turkish.

(1) (3;4) *He climbed a tree.*
(2) (3;7) *Çocuk agac-a çık-mış.*
          child tree-DAT ascend-PAST
          'Child ascended to the tree.'
(3) (5;2) *The dog ran out of the window.*
(4) (5;4) *Köpek düş-üyor cam-dan.*
          dog fall-PRESENT window-ABL
          'The dog is falling from the window.'

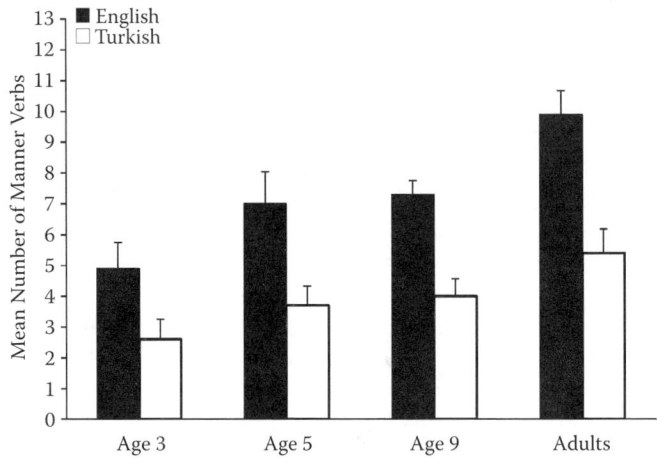

Figure 19.1 Mean number of manner verbs produced by English and Turkish speakers.

---

[3] List of abbreviations: ABL: ablative (from), CONV: converb, DAT: dative (to), NOM: nominalization, POSS: possessive, PLU: plural, PAST: past tense, PRESENT: present tense.

(5) (9;9) *They climbed over the log.*
(6) (9;11) *Kütüg-ün üst-ü-ne çık-ıyor-lar.*
 log-POSS top-POSS-DAT ascend-PRESENT-PLU
 'They are ascending to the log's top.'

The crosslinguistic difference was also evident in the diversity of the manner verb lexicon. As can be seen in Table 19.1, English speakers used a greater variety of manner verbs than Turkish speakers in their motion descriptions ($F(1,72) = 26.08, p < 0.001$), and this difference was reliable for each age group (Scheffé, $ps < 0.05$), with the only exception of the 3-year-olds, who had a very limited manner verb lexicon in both languages.

Speakers' manner verb lexicon also increased over time ($F(3,72) = 14.87, p < 0.001$), with adult speakers producing a greater variety of manner verbs than the 3-year-olds in both English and Turkish (Scheffé, $ps < 0.05$). However, no such reliable difference was observed between the 3-, 5-, and 9-year-olds. Thus the extent of children's manner verb lexicon remained unchanged over time.

The above analysis clearly shows that Turkish speakers do not routinely express manner in the main verb, which is a slot typically reserved for path information in V-languages. This still leaves Turkish speakers the option of conveying manner in a subordinate clause attached to a main path verb, such as *eve koşarak gir* 'house-to running enter.' Interestingly, however, children's motion

TABLE 19.1 Types of Manner Verbs Used by English and Turkish Speakers[a]

	English	Turkish
Ages 3;1–4;3		
List of verbs	chase, climb, fly, jump, knock, run, splash, step, swim, throw	at 'throw,' atla 'jump,' it 'push,' kaç 'run away,' kay 'slip,' sallan 'swing,' tırman 'climb up,' uç 'fly,' yüz 'swim'
Total verb type	10 types	9 types
Mean verb type (SD)	2.8 (1.6)	1.7 (1.3)
Ages 5;0–6;1		
List of verbs	bam, chase, climb, crawl, creep, fly, hop, jump, knock, lift, pop, pull, push, race, run, rush, sneak, splash, step, swim, throw, walk	at 'throw,' atla 'jump,' bat 'sink,' kaç 'run away,' kovala 'chase,' koş 'run,' saldır 'attack,' uç 'fly,' üşüş 'gather running,' yürü 'walk,' yuvarla 'roll,' yüz 'swim'
Total verb type	22 types	12 types
Mean verb type (SD)	4.7 (2.1)	2.9 (1.4)
Ages 9;1–10;0		
List of verbs	buck, chase, climb, drop, dump, fly, jump, run, poke, pop, push, sneak, stumble, swoop, throw, tip, walk	at 'throw,' atla 'jump,' dolaş 'wander,' fırlat 'throw,' kaç 'run away,' kovala 'chase,' koş 'run,' tırman 'climb up,' uç 'fly,' yürü 'walk,' yüz 'swim'
Total verb type	17 types	11 types
Mean verb type (SD)	4.9 (0.88)	3.5 (1.5)
Adults		
List of verbs	bump, chase, crawl, creep, climb, deposit, drop, escape, flap, fly, hit, hop, jump, knock, limp, plummet, pop, ride, run, slip, sneak, splat, step, sulk, swarm, throw, tiptoe, tumble, walk, wander	adım at 'step,' at 'throw,' fırla 'dash,' dolan 'wander,' kaç 'run away,' kovala 'chase,' koş 'run,' saldır 'attack,' sıyrıl 'sneak out,' tırman 'climb up,' uç 'fly,' yuvarlan 'rol,' yürü 'walk,' zıpla 'bounce'
Total verb type	30 types	14 types
Mean (SD)	7.1 (1.8)	4.1 (1.8)

[a] Total verb type refers to the total number of different verbs produced across all participants within an age group and mean verb type refers to the average number of verb types produced by a participant within an age group.
SD = standard deviation

descriptions contained no instances of 'path-verb + subordinate-manner-verb' constructions in either language. Moreover, the incidence of such constructions was quite rare among adult speakers; there were only two adults, one per language, who produced a total of three 'path-verb + subordinate-manner-verb' constructions. Thus, the analysis clearly shows that Turkish speakers do not typically express manner in the verb, be it a main verb or a subordinate verb. However, the question still remains as to whether Turkish speakers omit manner altogether from their motion descriptions or whether they would opt to use lexical items other than the verb to convey manner of motion.

Expressing Manner Outside the Verb

English and Turkish speakers both use adverbials (*enter rapidly, hızla gir* 'rapidly enter') to express manner outside the verb. The use of adverbials is not constrained by the lexicalization patterns of either language type, making them equally accessible to speakers of both languages. However, given that the main verb is typically reserved for expressing path in Turkish, Turkish speakers may rely more heavily on adverbials to convey manner than English speakers.

As Table 19.2 shows, children speaking either English or Turkish very rarely used adverbials to encode manner, showing no reliable differences between the two languages. However, there were significantly more adult speakers in Turkish than in English who used adverbials to convey manner ($X^2(1) = 7.27, p < 0.01$). Moreover, Turkish adults produced manner adverbials at higher frequencies than English-speaking adults ($F(1, 18) = 10.87, p < 0.01$; see examples 7–10, adverbials are underlined).

(7) (3;11) *Or-dan çık-ıyor uslu uslu.*
There-ABL exit-PRESENT quietly quietly
'From there he exits <u>quietly</u>.'

(8) (5;0) *Yavaş yavaş yürü-yormuş.*
Slowly slowly walk-PAST
'He was walking <u>slowly</u>.'

(9) (9;1) *Sessizce kurbaga kavanoz-un-dan çık-arak kaç-tı.*
Quietly frog jar-POSS-ABL exit-CONV escape-PAST
'The frog <u>quietly</u> exited from its jar and escaped.'

(10) (adult English speaker) *The bees are now coming out <u>in full force</u>.*

In summary, the expression of manner of motion shows strong crosslinguistic differences. English speakers use higher token and type frequencies of manner verbs than Turkish speakers. However, at the same time, speakers of both languages rarely use adverbials to add manner to their descriptions until adulthood. Thus, at the early ages, children mainly rely on verbs to convey manner of motion in both languages, and English speakers express manner more extensively than Turkish speakers beginning from age 3;8.

TABLE 19.2 Use of Adverbials Encoding Manner in English and Turkish

Age	English		Turkish	
	Number of Participants	Number of Instances	Number of Participants	Number of Instances
3;1–4;3	0	0	2	2
5;0–6;1	0	0	4	4
9;1–10;0	0	0	4	4
Adults	2	2	9	18

HOW DO CHILDREN EXPRESS PATH IN ENGLISH AND TURKISH?

Expressing Path in the Verb

English and Turkish speakers differed in their preference to use path verbs in the main verb position ($F (1, 72) = 62.76, p < 0.0001$). As Figure 19.2 shows, Turkish speakers used more path verbs than English speakers at all ages (Scheffé, $ps < 0.05$), and this difference was observable by age 3;8. However, speakers' use of path verbs did not change over time ($F (3,72) = 2.60$, ns). Thus, children and adults speaking either language remained relatively stable in their overall production of path verbs.

The crosslinguistic difference was also evident in the diversity of the path verb lexicon. As Table 19.3 illustrates, Turkish speakers produced more path verb types than English speakers in their motion descriptions ($F (1,72) = 47.90, p < 0.001$), and this difference was reliable for each age group (Scheffé, $ps < 0.01$), with the exception of the 9-year-olds.

Speakers' path verb lexicon also increased over time ($F (3,72) = 10.75, p < 0.001$), with adult speakers producing a greater variety of path verbs than the 3-year-olds in both English and Turkish (Scheffé, $ps < 0.05$). However, no such reliable difference was observed between the 3-, 5-, and 9-year-olds. Thus the children remained relatively stable in their extent of path verb lexicon over time in both languages.[4]

These results show that English speakers are less likely than Turkish speakers to express path of motion in the verb. However, both languages, English in particular, also use grammatical forms other than the verb to convey path. Consequently, I asked whether these non-verb forms make any difference in the expression of path information in the two languages. One factor that makes path differ from manner is that path constitutes the core feature of a motion event, while manner is optional (Slobin, 2004; Talmy, 2000). Therefore, English speakers might use lexical items other than the verb more extensively, and speakers of both languages might be equally likely to express path in their motion descriptions.

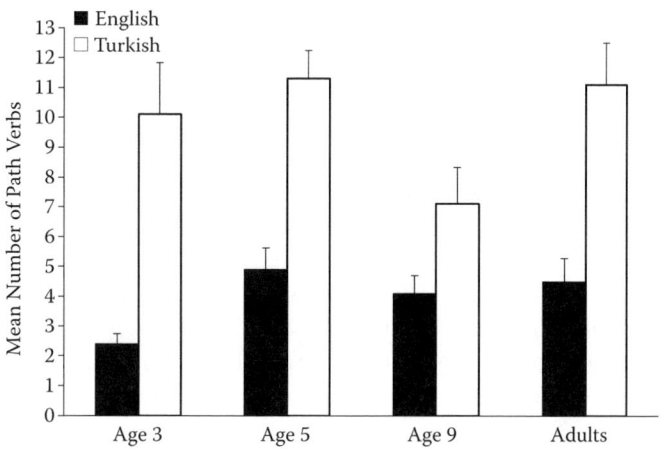

Figure 19.2   Mean number of path verbs produced by English and Turkish speakers.

---

[4] Speakers of both languages also used a small number of other verbs (*go, get, move*) that conveyed neither manner nor path information. They produced these verbs at roughly comparable rates, with no reliable differences between the two languages.

TABLE 19.3 Types of Path Verbs Used by English and Turkish Speakers[a]

	English	Turkish
Ages 3;1–4;3		
List of verbs	come, fall	çık 'exit/ascend,' düş 'fall,' gel 'come,' gir 'enter,' in 'descend,' kon 'land'
Total verb type	2 types	6 types
Mean verb type (SD)[b]	1.3 (0.48)	2.8 (1.03)
Ages 5;0–6;1		
List of verbs	come, fall	bin 'mount,' çık 'exit/ascend,' dön 'return,' düş 'fall,' gel 'come,' gir 'enter,' in 'descend,' uzaklaş 'move away'
Total verb type	2 types	8 types
Mean verb type (SD)	1.9 (0.32)	3.8 (1.03)
Ages 9;1–10;0		
List of verbs	come, fall, follow, land	çık 'exit/ascend,' düş 'fall,' gel 'come,' gir 'enter,' peşine düş 'follow,' peşine takıl 'follow,' takip et 'follow'
Total verb type	4 types	7 types
Mean verb type (SD)	2.0 (0.82)	2.6 (0.97)
Adults		
List of verbs	approach, come, depart, fall, follow, land, leave	aş 'go over,' ayrıl 'leave,' çık 'exit/ascend,' dön 'return,' düş 'fall,' gel 'come,' gir 'enter,' in 'descend,' izle 'follow,' peşine düş 'follow,' peşine takıl 'follow,' uzaklaş 'move away,' yaklaş 'approach'
Total verb type	7 types	13 types
Mean verb type (SD)	2.7 (1.06)	4.5 (1.35)

[a] Total verb type refers to the total number of different verbs produced across all participants within an age group and mean verb type refers to the average number of verb types produced by a participant within an age group.
[b] SD = standard deviation

Expressing Path Outside the Verb

English and Turkish speakers rely on different linguistic means to express path outside the verb. English mainly uses verb particles (*bees swarm out, boy climbs up*) and prepositional phrases (*owl pops out of the hole, boy falls into the water*), while Turkish uses noun phrases with directional suffixes (*kavanoz-dan kaç* 'jar-ABL escape,' *agac-a çık* 'tree-DAT ascend') and postpositions (*dışarı dogru çık* 'outside towards exit') to convey path outside the verb.

A close examination of path expressions outside the verb (i.e., path satellites) in the two languages showed that both English and Turkish speakers used path satellites quite extensively, with mean frequencies of 12.5 for the English and 9.7 for the Turkish speakers across the different ages. Nonetheless, as can be seen in Table 19.4, overall, English speakers produced more path satellites than Turkish speakers ($F (1, 72) = 9.18$, $p < 0.01$), even if this difference was only reliable for the 9-year-olds (Scheffé, $p = 0.01$).

Speakers' use of path satellites also changed over time ($F (3, 72) = 13.22$, $p < 0.001$), with adult speakers producing significantly more path satellites than the 3-year-olds in both languages (Scheffé, $ps < 0.01$). However, no such reliable difference was observed between the 3-, 5-, and 9-year-olds in either language. In other words, children remained stable in their production of path satellites over time.

In summary, English and Turkish speakers showed both similarities and differences in their expression of path of motion. Turkish speakers typically encoded path in the verb, using higher token and type frequencies of path verbs than English speakers. On the other hand, both languages encoded path information outside the verb quite frequently. This is not a surprising finding given

TABLE 19.4 Mean Number of Path Satellites

Age	English (SD)	Turkish (SD)
3;1–4;3	8.3 (3.5)	7.4 (2.6)
5;0–6;1	12.4 (5.8)	9.3 (4.1)
9;1–10;0	12.1 (2.9)	7.8 (4.1)
Adults	17.0 (4.2)	14.3 (4.4)
TOTAL	12.5 (5.1)	9.7 (4.6)

that path constitutes an obligatory component of a motion event, and any further specification of path requires the use of path expressions other than the verb, which only conveys limited path information.

However, even though both English and Turkish speakers were equally likely to produce path satellites in their motion descriptions, the way in which they packaged these path satellites showed robust crosslinguistic differences. As can be seen in Figures 19.3A to 19.3D, English speakers were more likely to attach one ($F(1, 72) = 3.4$, $p = 0.06$) or two-or-more ($F(1, 72) = 16.36$, $p < 0.001$) path satellites to a single verb of motion than Turkish speakers, and this crosslinguistic difference was observable at almost each age (Scheffé, $ps < 0.05$). The opposite was true for events with zero path satellites; Turkish speakers produced significantly more event descriptions without any path satellites than English speakers ($F(1, 72) = 42.24$, $p < 0.001$), and this difference was also reliable at each age (Scheffé, $ps < 0.01$). Thus, overall, English speakers produced event descriptions with more complex paths (i.e., with greater number of path satellites) than Turkish speakers.

Speakers also produced more motion descriptions with zero ($F(3, 72) = 3.02$, $p < 0.05$), one ($F(3, 72) = 7.52$, $p < 0.001$), or two-or-more ($F(3, 72) = 16.06$, $p < 0.001$) path satellites over time, with adult speakers differing significantly from the 3-year-olds (Scheffé, $ps < 0.001$) in both languages.

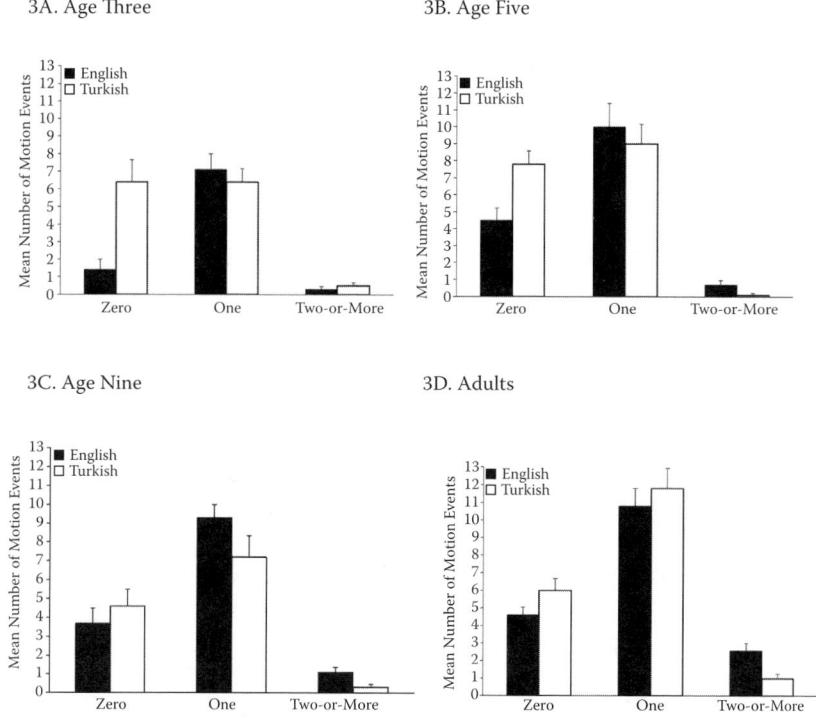

Figure 19.3 Mean number of motion event descriptions with zero, one, or two-or-more segments produced by 3- (A), 5- (B), 9-year-old children (C) and adult speakers (D).

However, no such reliable difference was observed between the 3-, 5-, and 9-year-old children in either language in terms of their expression of motion events with different path satellites. Sample descriptions with zero (11), one (12), and two-or-more (13, 14) path satellites are provided below (each path satellite is underlined).

(11) (3;9) *Düş-üyor çocuk*
            Fall-PRESENT child
            'The child is falling.'
(12) (3;9) *All the bees are flying <u>out of the honey</u>.*
(13) (5;8) *They walk <u>over</u> <u>to the log</u>.*
(14) (9;11) *He tips him <u>off</u> <u>over a cliff</u> <u>into the water</u>.*

In summary, even though English and Turkish speakers were equally likely to use path satellites in their motion descriptions, they nonetheless differed in the complexity of their path expressions. Turkish speakers showed a greater tendency to describe events without any path elements (except for the verb, which encoded path), whereas English speakers were more likely to attach multiple path satellites to a single verb of motion.

TIGHTENING THE CONSTRAINTS ON LEXICALIZATION: HOW DO CHILDREN EXPRESS BOUNDARY-CROSSING EVENTS IN ENGLISH AND TURKISH?

The above analysis clearly shows that English and Turkish speakers differ in their expression of manner and path, with English speakers *typically* conveying manner and Turkish speakers *typically* conveying path in the main verb of a clause describing motion. Interestingly, however, Talmy's typological dichotomy does not apply equally to the lexicalization of *all* motion events. In fact, in V-languages, speakers can use manner verbs as the main verb when expressing continuous events such as *running toward a house* or *strolling in the park*. It is only in describing motion events that involve the crossing of a spatial boundary (i.e., motion into/out of/over a bounded region) that V-language speakers are *required* by their language to use a path verb (*enter, exit*) to mark the change of location (Slobin & Hoiting, 1994). Thus, the true typological dichotomy is said to be restricted to motion events that highlight the moving figure's traversal of a spatial boundary.

Accordingly, I next asked how early children would observe the additional constraints boundary crossing imposes on the expression of manner and path in a V-language such as Turkish. Using the same dataset, I examined children's descriptions of four scenes from the frog storybook, each of which conveyed motion across a spatial boundary. These scenes included frog's exit from a jar, bees' exit from a hive, groundhog's exit from a hole, and owl's exit from a nest. Given the constraints in lexicalization, I expected Turkish speakers to use exclusively path verbs and English speakers to use either manner or path verbs in describing these four boundary-crossing events.

First looking across the different ages, I found that 85% of the Turkish speakers (34/40) used path verbs to describe boundary-crossing events, in contrast to only 15% of the English speakers (16/40), thus marking a significant crosslinguistic difference ($\chi^2(1) = 15.41, p < 0.001$). The pattern was reversed for manner verbs, with significantly more English speakers using manner verbs to describe boundary-crossing events than Turkish speakers (24 *vs.* 2; $\chi^2(1) = 25.13, p < 0.001$). The patterns were the same for the frequencies with which each verb type was produced. Turkish

TABLE 19.5 Distribution of Boundary-Crossing Events by Verb Type

		Manner Verb		Path Verb	
		Number of Participants	Number of Events	Number of Participants	Number of Events
Ages 3;1–4;3	English	2	3	3	5
	Turkish	0	0	7	11
Ages 5;0–6;1	English	7	7	6	8
	Turkish	0	0	9	20
Ages 9;1–10;0	English	7	9	2	3
	Turkish	0	0	8	19
Adults	English	8	10	5	6
	Turkish	2	2	10	27

speakers described 96% of the boundary-crossing events with path verbs (77/80), whereas English speakers were equally likely to use either manner (29/80) or path verbs (22/80) to describe boundary-crossing events.[5] Thus, in line with my expectations, Turkish speakers relied almost exclusively on path verbs to describe boundary-crossing events, while English speakers displayed a more distributed pattern of verb choices.

Next, looking at the developmental changes in children's descriptions of boundary-crossing events, I found evidence for early attunement to language-specific patterns. As can be seen in Table 19.5, Turkish-speaking children relied exclusively on path verbs to describe boundary-crossing events from age 3 to age 9. It was adult Turkish speakers who added a few manner verbs to their repertoire, while still relying predominantly on path verbs to describe such events. In contrast, English-speaking children initially used both manner and path verbs to describe boundary-crossing events, but increased their manner verb use steadily over time, with a considerable increase at age 5;6.[6]

The developmental patterns were the same for the types of verbs speakers used to describe boundary-crossing events. As Table 19.6 shows, at all ages, Turkish-speaking children used only a single verb type that encoded path (*çık* 'exit') to describe all four boundary-crossing events. Adult Turkish speakers added two manner verbs to this list, both of which encoded ballistic, instantaneous motion (*fırla* 'dash,' *sıyrıl* 'sneak'). In contrast, English speakers used a variety of manner verbs across the different ages to describe boundary-crossing events. The diversity of their verb lexicon also increased with age, with a considerable expansion at age 5;6. Sample boundary-crossing descriptions are presented in examples 15 to 20.

(15) (3;1) *An owl flew out of here.*
(16) (4;0) *Kuş çık-ıyor yuva-dan.*
 Bird exit-PRESENT nest-ABL
 'Bird exits from the nest.'
(17) (5;10) *In the middle of the night his frog creeped out of its jar.*

---

[5] In describing boundary-crossing events, English-speaking children occasionally used the verb *get*—which conveyed neither manner nor path information—typically along with a particle (*get out*). The use of this verb did not change over time.

[6] English and Turkish speakers also rarely used lexical options other than the verb to encode manner in their boundary-crossing descriptions. One adult English speaker (example 10) and two Turkish-speaking children were the only participants who used adverbials to add manner to their boundary-crossing descriptions (examples 7, 9).

(18) (5;3) *Kurbaga kavanoz-dan çık-ıyor.*
Frog jar-ABL exit-PRESENT
'Frog exits from the jar.'
(19) (9;10) *A gopher popped his head out.*
(20) (9;5) *Bur-dan köstebek çık-mış birtane.*
Here-ABL gopher exit-PAST one
'One gopher exits from here.'

TABLE 19.6 Types of Verbs[a] Used by English and Turkish Speakers in Boundary-Crossing Descriptions

Age	3;1–4;3	5;0–6;1	9;1–10;0	Adults
English	come (out)	come (out)	come (out)	come (out)
	fly (out)	fly (out)	fly (out)	fly (out)
	climb (out)	creep (out)	climb (out)	climb (out)
		pop (out)	pop (out)	pop (out)
		sneak (out)	sneak (out)	sneak (out)
		jump (out)	jump (out)	step (out)
		hop (out)		tiptoe (out)
		crawl (out)		crawl (out)
				swarm (out)
Turkish	çık 'exit'	çık 'exit'	çık 'exit'	çık 'exit'
				fırla 'dash'
				sıyrıl 'sneak'

[a] Come and çık 'exit' are path verbs; climb, crawl, creep, fly, hop, jump, pop, sneak, step, swarm, tiptoe, fırla 'dash,' and sıyrıl 'sneak' are manner verbs.

In summary, English and Turkish speakers showed robust differences in describing motion events that involve traversal of a spatial boundary. Turkish-speaking children showed a uniquely V-language pattern, relying exclusively on path verbs, while English-speaking children used both manner and path verbs to describe boundary-crossing events. These findings clearly show early attunement to the constraints in the lexicalization of boundary-crossing events in V-languages.

LEARNING TO EXPRESS MOTION EVENTS IN ENGLISH AND TURKISH: CONCLUDING REMARKS

In this chapter, I explored how children exposed to typologically distinct languages learn to talk about spatial motion in language-specific ways, in a comparison between English (S-language) and Turkish (V-language). More specifically, I examined whether children, in addition to motion verbs, would also rely on lexical options other than the verb to convey the manner and path components of motion, thus conveying these two components at comparable rates in the two languages. I found evidence for early sensitivity to language-specific patterns in children's use of motion verbs: English-speaking children used the verb mainly to convey manner and Turkish-speaking children used the verb mainly to convey path of motion, beginning from age 3. The patterns became even stronger in the description of boundary-crossing events, with Turkish-speaking children showing an exclusive preference for path verbs.

However, children's expression of manner and path in a lexical item other than the verb presented a more complex picture. Turkish-speaking children did not opt to express manner outside the verb, which resulted in lower rates of manner expression in Turkish as compared to English. In contrast, English-speaking children expressed path outside the verb routinely, and thus conveyed path information at comparable rates to Turkish speakers. But why do children rely on lexical items outside the verb to express path, but not manner?

Several non-mutually exclusive explanations are possible. First of all, as suggested by Talmy (2000), unlike manner, path constitutes the core feature of a motion event, and thus is more likely to be encoded in any language. Because English speakers reserve the verb for manner information, they have to rely on other lexical items to convey path of motion. This, in turn, leads to a greater expression of path outside the verb in English.

This is in fact bolstered by the fact that it was not only English but also Turkish speakers who relied extensively on lexical items outside the verb to convey path information. The inflectional morphology of Turkish—which allows easy encoding of path outside the verb—might have increased Turkish speakers' tendency to include additional path information, leading to extensive use of path satellites in Turkish similar to English. Thus, the morpho-synactic configuration of a language may also act as an important factor in explaining typological patterns (see also Ibarretxe-Antuñano, 2004; Slobin, 2004).

Even though both English and Turkish speakers used path satellites extensively, they differed in the number of path satellites they attached to a single verb of motion. A similar pattern was observed among adult speakers (Slobin, 2004): V-language speakers used a series of separate clauses—each with a separate motion verb—to describe the path components of a motion trajectory, while S-language speakers used a series of path satellites attached to a single verb of motion to describe the same motion trajectory, which, according to Slobin (1996), was an outcome of the boundary-crossing constraint in V-languages. That is, following the patterns of a V-language, Turkish speakers in this study had to introduce a new motion predicate every time they expressed motion across a boundary. This, in turn, might have decreased their chances of accumulating more than one path satellite per verb, leading to fewer descriptions with complex paths in Turkish than in English.

In summary, children showed early attunement to the lexicalization patterns of their native language, suggesting that children's earliest spatial concepts might already be influenced by the semantic organization of their language. However, the question still remains as to whether variation in linguistic expression has cognitive correlates, leading to different mental imagery in the conceptualization of motion events. Future research is needed to unravel the link between variation in linguistic expression and variation in conceptualization of motion in typologically distinct languages.

REFERENCES

Berman, R. A., & Slobin, D. I. (1994). *Relating events in narrative: A crosslinguistic developmental study.* Hillsdale, NJ: Lawrence Erlbaum Associates.

Choi, S., & Bowerman, M. (1991). Learning to express motion events in English and Korean: The influence of language-specific lexicalization patterns. *Cognition, 41*, 83–121.

Gennari, S. P., Sloman, S. A., Malt, B., & Fitch, T. (2002). Motion events in language and cognition. *Cognition, 83*, 49–79.

Ibarretxe-Antuñano, I. (2004). Language typologies in our language use: The case of Basque motion events in adult oral narratives. *Cognitive Linguistics, 15*(3), 317–349.

Mayer, M. (1969). *Frog, where are you?* New York: Dial Press.

Naigles, L., Eisenberg, A., Kako, E., Highter, M., & McGraw, N. (1998). Speaking of motion: Verb use by English and Spanish speakers. *Language and Cognitive Processes, 13*(5), 521–549.

Oh, K. (2003). *Language, cognition and development: Motion events in English and Korean.* Unpublished doctoral dissertation in psychology, University of California, Berkeley.

Özçalışkan, Ş. (2004). Encoding the manner, path and ground components of a metaphorical motion event. *Annual Review of Cognitive Linguistics, 2*, 73–102.

Özçalışkan, Ş. (2005). Metaphor meets typology: Ways of moving metaphorically in English and Turkish. *Cognitive Linguistics, 16*(1), 207–246.

Özçalışkan, Ş. (2007). Metaphors we move by: Children's developing understanding of metaphorical motion in typologically distinct languages. *Metaphor and Symbol, 22*(2), 147–168.

Özçalışkan, Ş., & Slobin, D. I. (1999). Learning 'how to search for the frog': Expression of manner of motion in English, Spanish, and Turkish. In A. Greenhill, H. Littlefield, & C. Tano (Eds.), *Proceedings of the 23rd Annual Boston University Conference on Language Development* (pp. 541–552). Somerville, MA: Cascadilla Press.

Özçalışkan, Ş., & Slobin, D. I. (2003). Codability effects on the expression of manner of motion in English and Turkish. In A. S. Özsoy, D. Akar, M. Nakipoglu-Demiralp, E. E. Taylan, & A. Aksu-Koc (Eds.), *Studies in Turkish linguistics* (pp. 259–270). Istanbul, Turkey: Bogaziçi University Press.

Papafragou, A., Massey, C., & Gleitman, L. (2002). Shake, rattle, 'n' roll: The representation of motion in language and cognition. *Cognition, 84,* 189–219.

Slobin, D. I. (1996). Two ways to travel: Verbs of motion in English and Spanish. In M. Shibatani & S. A. Thompson (Eds.), *Essays in semantics* (pp. 195–217). Oxford, UK: Oxford University Press.

Slobin, D. I. (Ed.). (1997). *The cross-linguistic study of language acquisition: Vol. 5. Expanding the contexts.* Mahwah, NJ: Lawrence Erlbaum Associates.

Slobin, D. I. (2000). Verbalized events: A dynamic approach to linguistic relativity and determinism. In S. Niemeier & R. Dirven (Eds.), *Evidence for linguistic relativity* (pp. 107–138). Amsterdam: John Benjamins.

Slobin, D. I. (2004). The many ways to search for a frog: Linguistic typology and the expression of motion events. In S. Strömqvist & L. Verhoeven (Eds.), *Relating events in narrative: Typological and contextual perspectives* (pp. 219–257). Mahwah, NJ: Lawrence Erlbaum Associates.

Slobin, D. I., & Hoiting, N. (1994). Reference to movement in spoken and signed languages: Typological considerations. *Proceedings of the 20th Annual Meeting of the Berkeley Linguistics Society* (pp. 487–505).

Talmy, L. (2000). *Toward a cognitive semantics: Vol. II. Typology and process in concept structuring.* Cambridge, MA: The MIT Press.

Zheng, M., & Goldin-Meadow, S. (2002). Thought before language: How deaf and hearing children express motion events across cultures. *Cognition, 85,* 145–175.

20

Learning to Tell a Story of False Belief
A Study of French-Speaking Children

EDY VENEZIANO, LAETITIA ALBERT, and STÉPHANIE MARTIN

Université Paris–CNRS Descartes

> ...the activity of thinking takes on a particular quality when it is employed in the activity of speaking.
>
> **Dan I. Slobin (1987, p. 435)**

Dan Slobin's work has been very influential on the thinking of the first author since her student years, and was an important point of reference in Mimi Sinclair's Geneva-based Genetic Psycholinguistics group where she worked for many years. What fascinated and interested the group was the importance Slobin assigned to thinking processes in language acquisition and functioning. The present work situates itself within two main strands of Dan's influential research in this area, namely, (1) the complex relations between language and cognition and (2) the study of narrative development as a particularly privileged vantage point from which to study these relations.

INTRODUCTION

Earlier studies on children's capacity to tell a story out of wordless pictures (as in the "Frog Story" studies, e.g., Berman & Slobin, 1994; Strömqvist & Verhoeven, 2004) show that preschoolers can organize their storytelling to reflect the successive unfolding of events on the action/behavioral level, but expression of the reasons for events is still scarce at 6 years and increases only gradually until 9 to 10 years of age (e.g., Bamberg, 1994; Bamberg & Damrad-Frye, 1991; Berman & Slobin, 1994; Berman, 2004). Moreover, even if some 4- to 5-year-olds may attribute mental states to the character of a single picture "story" (Bokus, 2004; Richner & Nicolopoulou, 2001), references to beliefs within a structured narrative are still rather uncommon at 6 to 7 years. It is mainly around 8 to 9 years that children start to use the characters' mental states to explain their behaviors (Bamberg, 1994; Bamberg & Damrad-Frye, 1991; Berman & Slobin, 1994), while it is even later that they explicitly let know that a character has a false belief about the state of the world or about the intentions and mental states of other characters (Aksu-Koç & Tekdemir, 2004; Bamberg & Damrad-Frye, 1991; Küntay & Nakamura, 2004; Veneziano & Hudelot, 2006) and that different points of view on the same event are attributed directly to different characters, recognizing explicitly that people can interpret the same information differently, a hallmark that mental life is interpretive (e.g., Lalonde & Chandler, 2002).

The research reported in this chapter explores whether there is an impassable developmental threshold for the late appearance of children's expression of the mental stances of characters in their narratives. To this effect, the present study introduced two features intended to facilitate the expression of these aspects. One was the choice of the "Stone Story."[1] This is made up of five wordless pictures whose sequence highlights the fact that the two characters have different viewpoints on one of the key events, something that leads to a misunderstanding between them. This characteristic of the story could promote the expression of multiple perspectives and a relativistic account of reality. The other feature was the use of intervention procedures intended to help children to focus their attention on the expression of causal connections. For one group of children the intervention consisted in a Piagetian-type of scaffolding,[2] and for another group in a narrative told by the experimenter mentioning the reasons of events and their connections in the overall story. The intervention occurred *after* children had produced an initial narrative and before they were asked to retell the story. For each child, the first narrative (before intervention) and the second narrative (after intervention) were compared to examine the effect of the intervention on the expression of the mental stances of the characters (in particular, the characters' beliefs and their impact on behavior). We supposed that by focusing young children's attention on evaluative discourse, their mentalistic orientation would improve. Indeed, Eaton, Collis, and Lewis (1999) have shown that even some 5-year-olds talk about the internal states of the characters for explanatory purposes when they tell their story piecemeal by successively answering questions about the characters' internal states. Would the intervention procedures used in this study have a positive influence on children's expression of beliefs and false beliefs of the characters even in their single-speaker's narratives? In that case, would the new mind-oriented account of events be ephemeral or persist over time? And, would the progress be related to children's performance on first-order "false belief" tasks that provide cognitive measures of theory of mind?

If children add mentalistic content to the narratives they produce after intervention, talking about beliefs and expressing multiple perspectives on the same event, the reasons for the poverty of these expressions in their first narratives must be looked at differently and elsewhere than in cognitive limitations in theory of mind. The comparison of the different narrations produced by the same children at different times and the relation between the expression of mind-related accounts and children's performance on theory of mind tasks will contribute to our understanding of the nature of the variables involved in the limited mind-oriented references found in narratives of young children.

METHOD

Subjects

Sixty French-speaking children (30 girls and 30 boys) aged 6;0 to 7;8 years (mean age: 6;8 year, s.d.: 4 months), attending elementary schools in Paris and its suburbs, participated in the study.

Materials

The "Stone Story," part of a collection of short picture-series stories for young children (Furnari, 1980), was used for data collection. It consists of five pictures with no text (see Appendix 1). The first depicts the "greeting" exchanged between two characters, referred to here as P1 and P2. The second shows the accidental stumbling of P1 on the stone, leading P1 to push P2 (the "first push"). The third

---

[1] The Stone Story is one of two stories used in a research project on which the first author collaborated. The project, coordinated by V. Laval of the University of Poiters, benefited from grant 02 3 0615 of the ACI program of the French Ministry of Research.
[2] The scaffolding procedure used in this study is a modified version of the scaffolding procedure used in the research mentioned in footnote 1.

picture shows P2 pushing back P1. The fourth picture depicts P1 crying and pointing backwards to the stone. The fifth shows P2 helping P1 to get back on his feet.

The story can be narrated at the simple descriptive level stating the succession of events, as in the following example:

(1) (KEN 6 ;2)
"*C'est des enfants/i s'disent salut/ après i s'bagarrent et l'autre enfant d'abord …/il tape/ après c'est l'autre enfant /après l'autre enfant i pleure.*"
'It is two children/they say hi/then they fight and the other child at first … /he hits/then it is the other child/then the other child cries.'

However, the story can also be told in a more elaborate manner where the first "push" is viewed as an accidental, physically caused event by P1 and as an intentionally caused one by P2, thus attributing to P2 a false belief about the state of mind of P1. Moreover, picture 4 can be interpreted within this overall framework as the time of the dissipation of the misunderstanding where P1 explains retroactively the reasons for the first push:

(2) (NAT 6;6)
"*(…) c'est deux garçons qui sont amis (…)/celui à la salopette bleue **trébuche** contre une pierre (…) et pousse (…) celui au short **et alors celui au short croit qu'il l'a fait exprès donc** il pousse celui à la salopette mais après **le garçon à la salopette lui dit que c'était à cause de la pierre**/donc le garçon en short **a compris qu'il s'était trompé**/donc ils redeviennent amis.*"
'(…) it is two boys who are friends (…)/the one in the blue overalls **stumbles** against a stone (…) and <u>pushes</u> (…) the one in shorts and then the one in shorts **thinks he did it on purpose so** he pushes the one in the overalls but then **the boy in the overalls tells him that it was because of the stone**/so the boy in shorts understood that **he had been mistaken**/ so they become friends again.'

Procedure

Narratives about the Stone Story were requested at different times. At the beginning, children were presented with the five pictures one at a time, ending up with the whole set laid down in front of the children, who were allowed to look at it for up to two minutes. If they wished, the children could see the pictures again for a maximum of two minutes, three times at most. When the child was ready to tell the story, the pictures were removed from sight.[3]

After their *first narrative* children were randomly assigned to one of three conditions:

a) The *scaffolding* condition (29 children): The experimenter systematically asked the children four questions while the pictures were visible: "How come that" (1) P1 pushes P2; (2) P2 pushes back P1; (3) P1 shows the stone, and (4) P2 helps P1 to get back on his feet?
b) The *model* condition (21 children): The experimenter told a story to the children (see Appendix 2) while the pictures were visible. The experimenter introduced the story by saying: "Very good. That was a very nice story. Now it's my turn to tell you the story. Listen carefully."
c) The *simple repetition* (control) condition (10 children): Children were asked to play a "memory" game with pairs of the five pictures of the Stone Story and four additional pairs of pictures constructed by some transformations of the original pictures.

---

[3] This mode of presentation was designed with the collaborative project mentioned in footnote 1.

To examine the effect of the interventions, children of all three groups were then asked to tell the story once again (the *second narrative*). As was the case for the first narrative, here also the children told their story without having the pictures in front of them. Moreover, in order to examine the stability of the eventual effects of the interventions, children of the two experimental groups (15 from the scaffolding and 11 from the model conditions) were seen again one week later. They were shown the same five pictures and asked to tell the experimenter the story again under the same conditions (the *third narrative*).

All the interviews were audio-recorded and transcribed *verbatim*.

Analysis of the Data

We focus here on three measures of children's evaluative talk: (1) the attribution of *internal states* to the characters with particular attention to epistemic states; (2) the expression of the conditions that render P2's belief a *false belief* leading to the misunderstanding; (3) the retroactive explanation of the first push serving to *rectify the false belief* of P2 and leading to the resolution of the misunderstanding.

Attribution of Internal States to the Characters

Four types of internal states were distinguished:

1. *Physical* sensations, including perceptions, for example:
   (3)
   a. "*il s'est fait **mal***" (SOP 6;7)
      'he **hurt** himself'
   b. "*il **a pas vu** qu'il y a une pierre*" (PUL 6;11)
      he **didn't see** that there is a stone

2. *Emotional* states, for example:
   (4)
   a. "*y en a un qui est **fâché**"* (CHA 6,6)
      'there is one who is **angry**'
   b. "*ils sont **contents**"* (BRA 6;9)
      'they are **happy**'

3. *Intentional* states of the characters, for example:
   (5)
   a. "*y en a un qui **veut** lui faire un câlin*" (STE 6;11)
      'there is one who **wants** to hug him'
   b. "*il le pousse sans faire exprès*" (JAN 6;11)
      'he pushes him **not on purpose**'

4. *Epistemic* states referring to beliefs, thoughts, or knowledge of the characters, either about the state of the world (example 6a) or about the other character's internal state (example 6b), in the latter case constituting a mental state attribution of second order:
   (6)
   a. "*il **ne savait pas** qu'il avait trébuché*" (JAN 6;11)
      'he **didn't know** that he had stumbled'
   b. "*il **croit qu'il l'a fait exprès** de le pousser*" (CHA 6;6)
      'he **believes that he did it on purpose** to push him'

The False Belief (FB)

The explicit expression of a false belief (FB) has been identified when children not only attribute to P2 the belief that the push by P1 was intentional (a second order belief coded by "epistemic states"), but when they also explain that the same first push was accidental, thus creating the conditions establishing that P2's belief about the intentions of P1 is a *false belief*:

(7)
*"celui à la salopette **il trébuche sur une pierre et puis il a poussé** celui au short/ et celui au short **il croit qu'il a fait exprès** "* (BAP 6;9)
'the one in the blue overalls **he stumbles on a stone and then he has pushed** the one in shorts/ and the one in shorts **he thinks that he has done it on purpose**.'

Rectification of False Belief (RFB) With the rectification of the false belief (RFB), the two different points of view are attributed explicitly to the two characters, one of them seeing the event as accidental (P1) and the other as intentionally caused (P2). The RFB was coded when, after the attribution to P2 of the false belief about P1's intentions, children had P1 communicate the unintentional nature of his first push to P2, using either direct speech, as in example 8, or indirect speech, as in example 9:

(8) (AME 6;7, for whom the FB had been coded)
*"**je t'ai pas poussé** euh/ **j'ai trébuché sur une pierre** "*
'**I didn't push you/ I stumbled on a stone**'
(9) (STE 6;11, for whom the FB had been coded)
*"après l'autre **il lui dit qu'il a pas fait exprès de le pousser**"*
'afterwards the other **tells him that he hasn't pushed him on purpose**'

Theory of Mind Tasks All children were presented with two classic tests of theory of mind, the "deceptive box" test, using a tube of *Smarties* with a pen inside (Perner, Leekam, & Wimmer, 1987) and the "unexpected transfer" test of Maxi and the chocolate (Wimmer & Perner, 1983). The tests were considered passed if the children provided the expected answers to the following three questions: (1) the "belief" question (*Smarties*: "What will Paul say when he sees the box?"; *Maxi*: "Where is Maxi going to look for the chocolate?"), (2) the "reality" question (*Smarties*: "What is in fact inside the box?"; *Maxi*: "Where is in fact the chocolate?"), and (3) the "memory" question (*Smarties*: "When you saw the box, what did you say there was inside it?"; *Maxi*: "Where had Maxi placed the chocolate?").

RESULTS

First and Second Narratives

Table 20.1 presents the number of children attributing any type of internal state, epistemic states, the false belief, and the rectification of the false belief to the story characters in their *first* and their *second* narratives, according to the condition they underwent in between the two narrations.

In the first narrative, none of the children, in any of the three groups, expressed any epistemic states, the false belief or the rectification of the false belief.

On the other hand, across the three groups, about one-third of the children (37%) expressed at least one non-epistemic internal state, mostly of the emotional (*fâché* 'angry,' *content* 'happy') and physical types (avoir *mal* 'ache'), and some of the intentional type (*sans faire exprès* 'not on purpose'). Some of our 6- to 7-year-olds could thus attribute internal states to the characters but not of the epistemic type, pointing clearly to a specific difficulty in dealing with these kinds of internal states. Before the intervention phase, the three groups of children did not show any significant differences on the measures considered here.[4]

---

[4] None of the children expressed epistemic states, attributed a FB or rectified it and the one-sample chi-square test applied to the number of children that in each group mentioned at least one internal state was not significant: $\chi^2 (2) = 1.56$ n.s.

TABLE 20.1 Percentages of Children Producing Internal States, Epistemic States, False Belief, and Rectification of False Belief in First and Second Narratives, According to the Two Experimental Conditions

Expression of	Narrative	Scaffolding Group (N=29)	Model Group (N=21)	Control Group (N=10)	Total (N=60)
All types of Internal States[a]	First Narrative	38%	43%	20%	37%
	Second Narrative	62%	71%	0%	55%
Epistemic States[b]	First Narrative	0%	0%	0%	0%
	Second Narrative	41%	57%	0%	40%
False Belief	First Narrative	0%	0%	0%	0%
	Second Narrative	21%	43%	0%	25%
Rectification of False Belief	First Narrative	0%	0%	0%	0%
	Second Narrative	14%	29%	0%	17%

[a] The figures are the percentages of children who attributed at least one internal state.
[b] The figures are the percentages of children who attributed at least one epistemic state.

How do these same children tell the story *after* intervention? While none of them mentioned epistemic states, P2's false belief, or its rectification by P1 in their first narrative, quite a few of them did so in their second narrative. For both experimental groups taken together (scaffolding and model groups), the number of children who mentioned at least one epistemic state, the false belief and its rectification showed a significant increase from the first telling.[5] The number of children who improved in these measures from the first to the second narrative increased also in each of the experimental groups. However, in the scaffolding group, the change in the number of children expressing the RFB did not reach significance.[6]

In contrast to these improvements in the experimental conditions, children in the control group (repetition only) showed no improvements on any of the measures.

It should also be noted that concerning the reference to any kind of internal state, no significant changes were found in any of the conditions, both in the number of children producing at least one of them, and in the overall number of internal states produced before and after intervention.[7]

The next question was whether one intervention procedure (scaffolding or model) would prove more effective than the other in leading children to produce mind-oriented narratives.

In fact, none of the measures reported here showed a significant difference between the two experimental conditions, i.e., intervention by scaffolding and by the telling of a story model.[8]

---

[5] Results of the 2 × 2 chi-square tests (corrected for continuity) applied to the number of children mentioning at least one epistemic state, expressing the false belief or its rectification, before and after intervention, in the experimental conditions taken together, are as follows. For epistemic states: $\chi^2 (1) = 29.01$, $p<<0.001$; for FB: $\chi^2 (1) = 15.37$, $p<<0.001$; for RFB: $\chi^2 (1) = 9.0$, $p<0.01$.

[6] Results of the 2 × 2 chi-square tests (corrected for continuity) applied to the number of children mentioning at least one epistemic state, expressing the false belief or its rectification, before and after intervention, in each of the two experimental groups, are as follows. For the scaffolding group: for epistemic states: $\chi^2 (1) = 12.71$, $p<<0.001$; for FB: $\chi^2 (1) = 4.65$, $p<0.05$; for RFB: $\chi^2 (1) = 2.42$, $p=0.12$. For the model group: for epistemic states: $\chi^2 (1) = 14.12$, $p<<0.001$; for FB: $\chi^2 (1) = 9.05$, $p<0.01$; for RFB: $\chi^2 (1) = 4.86$, $p<0.05$.

[7] Results of the 2 × 2 chi-square tests (corrected for continuity) applied to the number of children mentioning at least one internal state of any kind, before and after intervention are as follows. In the scaffolding group: $\chi^2 (1) = 2.48$; in the model group: $\chi^2 (1) = 1.54$; in the control group: $\chi^2 (1) = 0.55$. Similar results are obtained for the number of internal states.

[8] Results of the 2 × 2 chi-square tests (corrected for continuity) applied to the number of children mentioning at least one epitemic state, expressing the false belief or its rectification, before and after intervention, according to the experiment group, are all nonsignificant: for internal states, $\chi^2 (1) = 0.0013$; $\chi^2 (1) = 0.0013$; for epistemic states: $\chi^2 (1) = 0.663$; for FB: $\chi^2 (1) = 1.89$; for RFB: $\chi^2 (1) = 0.867$.

TABLE 20.2 Percentages of Children[a] Producing Internal States, Epistemic States, False Belief and Rectification of False Belief in Second and Third Narratives, According to the Two Experimental Conditions

Expression of	Narrative	Scaffolding Group (N=15)	Model Group (N=11)	Total (N=26)
All types of Internal States[b]	Second Narrative	60%	82%	69%
	Third Narrative	67%	82%	73%
Epistemic States[c]	Second Narrative	40%	55%	46%
	Third Narrative	47%	55%	50%
False Belief	Second Narrative	27%	36%	31%
	Third Narrative	33%	45%	38%
Rectification of False Belief	Second Narrative	20%	36%	27%
	Third Narrative	17%	36%	31%

[a] The figures in this table concern only the children who were retested for stability.
[b] The figures are the percentages of children who attributed at least one internal state.
[c] The figures are the percentages of children who attributed at least one epistemic state.

The Third Narrative

In order to examine the long-term effect of the two interventions (scaffolding and model), children's mind-oriented expressions in the second narrative were compared with those in the third narrative obtained one week later from the same children. A subgroup of children, 15 from the scaffolding and 11 from the model conditions, participated in this test of stability. The results are presented in Table 20.2.

In the third narrative, the performance of these children remained stable for the production of epistemic states, false belief and rectification of false belief, and even some children who had not expressed the FB or the RFB in their second narrative did so in their third (one child in the scaffolding and one child in the model groups added the FB, while one child in the scaffolding group added the RFB). Only one child no longer mentioned the false belief he had expressed in the second narrative (in the scaffolding group).

The Relation Between Theory of Mind Tasks and Theory of Mind in the Narratives

Among the 60 children across the three conditions, 43% passed both ToM tasks, 50% passed only one of the two tasks, and 7% passed neither of the two. Moreover, 92% succeeded in the "deceptive box" test, while only 45% succeeded in the "unexpected transfer" task. To examine the relationship between children's false belief performance in the cognitive tasks and in the narratives, the 50 children of the two experimental conditions were retained, given that only these children produced mind-oriented narratives after intervention. Children were assigned to one of three categories according to their performance in the ToM tasks (that is, whether they passed both items, only one item, or neither of the two). Then, for each of these three groups, the number of children expressing epistemic states, the false belief or the rectification of the false belief in their second narrative was noted (none of them had done it in the first narrative). These data are presented in Table 20.3. They show that children who expressed at least one epistemic state, the false belief or the rectification of the false belief in their second narrative tend to be found more often among the children who succeeded in both ToM tasks, although only the connection to RFB reaches significance.[9]

---

[9] Results of 2 × 3 chi-square tests applied to the number of children mentioning at least one epistemic state, expressing FB or RFB in the second narrative, according to the three categories of success in ToM tasks, are as follows: for epistemic states: $\chi^2 (2) = 1.94$, $p=0.37$; for FB: $\chi^2 (2) = 4.45$, $p<0.108$; for RFB: $\chi^2 (2) = 5.98$, $p=.05$.

TABLE 20.3 Relationship Between Children's Performance on ToM Tasks and Expression of Epistemic States, FB and RFB in the First and Second Narratives[a]

		Number of ToM Tasks Passed		
		0	1	2
Expression of	Narrative	(N = 4)	(N = 23)	(N = 23)
Epistemic States[b]	First Narrative	0%	0%	0%
	Second Narrative	25%	35%	52%
False Belief	First Narrative	0%	0%	0%
	Second Narrative	0%	22%	43%
Rectification of False Belief	First Narrative	0%	0%	0%
	Second Narrative	0%	9%	35%

[a] The figures in this table concern only the children in the two experimental conditions.
[b] The figures are the percentages of children who attributed at least one epistemic state.

Linguistic Expression of the Second-Order Belief

When children expressed P2's belief about the intention of P1 (a second-order belief that is a necessary component of the expression of false belief as defined here), all of them expressed it in a relatively complex completive sentence structure. In French, this sentence structure requires present or imperfect tense in the principal clause, past perfect or pluperfect tense in the subordinate clause, and the subject in the principal clause to be different from that of the subordinate (see examples 6b and 7). In order to examine whether linguistic structural complexity may have affected children's expression of this component of false belief, children's overall use of this kind of completive sentence structures was analyzed. The main purpose was to see whether children who didn't express P2's second-order belief in any of their narratives produced nevertheless completive structures for other purposes.

Among the 42 children (70% of all participants) who did not express any second order belief across narratives, 52% of them used at least a completive structure of the kind mentioned above for other purposes:

(12) (PAU 6;11)
Child: *je crois qu'ils sont fachés.*
'**I think that they** are angry.'

DISCUSSION

In their first narrative, children aged 6 to 7 years did refer to the characters' internal states, but these concerned mostly physical sensations, emotional and intentional states. None of the children referred to the characters' epistemic states, to P2's false belief, or to the rectification of the false belief. It seems that we can thus conclude that, within the confines of the testing situation, and like similar studies (e.g., Aksu-Koç & Tekdemir, 2004; Berman 2004; Veneziano & Hudelot, 2006), 6- 7-year-olds do not take on spontaneously a mind-oriented approach to storytelling. Thus, contrary to what we expected, the particular nature of the story selected for this study, one which lends itself to an interpretation in terms of a misunderstanding between the characters, failed to promote mind-oriented narratives in children of this age.

However, some of the children who experienced the scaffolding or model interventions, but none of those who were simply asked to retell the story, adopted the mind-oriented approach in their second narrative, thus revealing an unexpected competence in this domain. When given the opportunity to think about causal connections, or after hearing a story containing causal links and belief attributions, a sizeable number of children proved able to talk about intentions and beliefs about intentions, they could make clear that P2 held a false belief, while some even resolved the misunderstanding by a retroactive explanation of the first push. Results for stability across time clearly show that improvements in mind-oriented measures are not simply the result of the immediately previous conversation or of the story just heard from the adult. The fact that children maintained their mind-oriented approach one week later, and that some even showed it then for the first time, indicates that a good number of children genuinely improved their approach to the telling of this story.

How to explain the scarcity of mind-oriented content in children's first narratives and the improvements in narratives produced after interventions? It could be that young children do not yet appreciate the pragmatic necessity of talking about these features (e.g., Poulsen et al., 1979) and that the scaffolding and model procedures might simply have helped children understand that the expected narrative is a mind-oriented one. According to this interpretation, children have the ability to take a mind-oriented approach, but they do not consider it relevant for narrative purposes. Although this interpretation could account for some of the results, it does not explain why none of the children supposed to have a richer understanding of the story relations, talk about them in their first narrative, nor why only some of the children take a mind-oriented approach after the intervention procedures.

However, it could also be that the poverty of mind-oriented discourse in children's first narratives is due to cognitive and linguistic loads involved in processing the story pictures and in *thinking with a view to narrating*. Indeed, if it is true that "the activity of thinking takes on a particular quality when it is employed in the activity of speaking" (Slobin, 1987, p. 435) and that "components which must be attended to in thinking for speaking must also be mentally stored for future speaking" (Slobin, 2003, p. 178), the mobilization of children's narrative resources might interfere with their conceptualization of the story. It might also be the case that, given all of the above, children may experience difficulties in integrating the various competences involved in the task, abilities that are not completely mastered at these ages. Indeed, telling an uninterrupted story out of pictures is a complex task requiring cognitive resources at different levels. There is the interpretation load of the pictures, the thinking for narrating that requires coherence, cohesion, and "decontextualizability" (Sawyer, 2003), the communicative constraints that require taking into account the interlocutor and the goals of storytelling, and also the fact that children have no personal involvement in the story and thus need to invest the characters with motivations and beliefs that are extraneous to their immediate mental world. Under these conditions, the cognitive and linguistic resources mobilized for constructing a narrative might leave little leeway for children to apprehend and explicitly express the characters' epistemic states, particularly when these involve false beliefs (e.g., Aksu-Koç & Tekdemir, 2004) or different points of view on the same situation.

Both the model and the scaffolding conditions reduce processing loads. The story model incurs this reduction by presenting all the needed story elements in a predigested, ready-made form. The scaffolding condition does so by having children reflect about causal connections in a piecemeal fashion, an activity that may lead them to think about the epistemic and intentional states of the characters that provide coherence at the local (explaining the isolated events) and global (integrating several events and their explanations) levels.

Thus, children who did not produce mind-oriented first narratives may have had the cognitive tools for talking about mental states but the complexity of the task prevented them from talking explicitly about mental features, which are themselves still fragile and undergoing development at this age (e.g., Chandler, 2001). However, when the complexity of the storytelling task is reduced by intervention procedures, children can draw upon these competences.

Why, then, are some children not affected by the intervention procedures? Is it because those children have not yet sufficiently mastered the complexity of the linguistic structure needed to express the second-order belief of P2 (a necessary component of false belief)? This does not seem to be the case. Our results indicate that the absence of second-order belief attribution cannot be imputed to the linguistic complexity needed for its expression, since children who use completive structures either for narrating purposes or in conversation with the experimenter, do not attribute any kind of epistemic state to the characters. Is it because these children have not yet fully mastered the basic concepts of theory of mind? Our results suggest that the cognitive mastery of first-order ToM, as instantiated by the False Belief tasks, may in part be involved, since those children who passed both ToM tasks are those who improved most. Moreover, children who failed on both tasks did not improve their expression of the false belief nor of its rectification. Success in first-order ToM tasks is not sufficient, however, since children may pass both tasks and yet not tell a mind-oriented narrative after intervention. Larger sample sizes in the different ToM categories might help clarify this issue in future research. However, success in first-order FB tasks may not be sufficient. For this story, coding false belief requires children to present two different visions of the same event, and with the rectification of the false belief (RFB), the two different points of view are attributed directly to the two characters, one of them seeing the event as accidental (P1) and the other as intentionally caused (P2). The co-existence of these two different points of view of the *same* event evidences an interpretive level of theory of mind (e.g., Carpendale & Lewis, 2006; Lalonde & Chandler, 2002), according to which knowledge is *"relativistic"* (Veneziano & Hudelot, 2006) since it depends on the mental constructions of the people involved. Moreover, the viewpoint of P2 in this context is a second-order belief and not simply a first-order one. In future research, second-order False Belief tasks should be administered as well to better clarify the influence of cognitive development on children's narrative expression.

Several other factors could also explain individual differences. Two are particularly worth considering in future research. One concerns children's level of comprehension of the story independently of the explicit expression of the story elements. That is, children should be given the opportunity to manifest their understanding of the reasons of events and of the characters' mental stances with a minimum of talk in narrative form. The other variable concerns children's participation in the scaffolded conversations during intervention. Some of the individual variation in the second narratives could be due to the more or less active participation of the children in the scaffolded interactions. Children who offered mind-oriented elements in answer to the adult's questions during the scaffolding phase could produce these elements in their second narrative more easily than children who did not provide answers.

Finally, in considering the impact of different kinds of interventions, future research should consider more carefully the way children express their mental attributions and how they knit them into the overall plot. Although the scaffolding and the model interventions led a comparable number of children to take on a mind-oriented approach to narration, the general impression is that the narratives of children who participated in the scaffolding procedure were more coherent and cogently structured. This difference might reflect a deeper understanding of the more subtle intricacies of the story plot by children who participated in the scaffolding than in the model procedure, due to the fact that the piecemeal conversation on the reasons of events offers greater opportunities for thinking that is directly encoded in overt speaking.

APPENDIX 1: THE STONE STORY PICTURES

APPENDIX 2: MODEL STORY

Deux copains se disent bonjour de loin. Le garçon à la salopette va vers le garçon au short mais, comme il ne voit pas qu'il y a une pierre par terre, il trébuche sur la pierre et comme ça il pousse le copain. Le garçon avec le short croit alors que son copain a fait exprès de le pousser et il repousse le copain. Le copain avec la salopette tombe parterre et pleure. Il se dit que son ami doit avoir pensé qu'il avait fait exprès de le pousser. Alors il lui montre la pierre derrière et lui dit que c'était à cause de la pierre qu'il l'avait poussé au tout début. Le copain avec le short comprend qu'il s'était trompé; il aide alors son copain à se relever et ils redeviennent amis.

Two pals greet each other from a distance. The boy in overalls goes toward the boy in shorts but, as he doesn't see a stone on the ground, he stumbles on the stone and in this way he pushes his pal. The boy in shorts thinks that his friend has pushed him on purpose and so he pushes him back. The pal in overalls falls and cries. He says to himself that his friend must have thought he pushed him on purpose. At that point he shows his pal the stone and tells him that it was because of that stone that he had pushed him earlier. The pal in shorts understands that he had been mistaken. He helps his pal get back on his feet and they become friends again.

REFERENCES

Aksu-Koç, A., & Tekdemir, G. (2004). Interplay between narrativity and mindreading: A comparison between Turkish and English. In S. Strömqvist & L. Verhoeven (Eds.), *Relating events in narrative: Typological and contextual perspective* (pp. 307–327). Mahwah, NJ: Lawrence Erlbaum Associates.

Bamberg, M. (1994). Development of linguistic forms: German. In R. A. Berman & D. I. Slobin (Eds.), *Relating events in narrative: A crosslinguistic developmental study* (pp. 189–238). Hillsdale, NJ: Lawrence Erlbaum Associates.

Bamberg, M., & Damrad-Frye, R. (1991). On the ability to provide evaluative comments: Further explorations of children's narrative competencies. *Journal of Child Language, 18*(3), 689–710.

Berman, R. (2004). The role of context in developing narrative abilities. In S. Strömqvist & L. Verhoeven (Eds.), *Relating events in narrative: Typological and contextual perspectives* (pp. 261–281). Mahwah, NJ: Lawrence Erlbaum Associates.

Berman, R., & Slobin, D. I. (1994). *Relating events in narrative: A crosslinguistic developmental study.* Hillsdale, NJ: Lawrence Erlbaum Associates.

Bokus, B. (2004). Inter-mind phenomena in child narrative discourse. *Pragmatics, 14*(4), 391–408.

Carpendale, J., & Lewis, C. (2006). *How children develop social understanding.* Malden, MA: Blackwell.

Chandler, M. (2001). Perspective taking in the aftermath of theory-theory and the collapse of the social role-taking enterprise of the social role-taking literature. In A. Tryphon & J. Vonèche (Eds.), *Working with Piaget: In memoriam–Bärbel Inhelder* (pp. 39–63). Hove, UK: Psychology Press.

Eaton, J. H., Collis, G. N., & Lewis, V. A. (1999). Evaluative explanations in children's narratives of a video sequence without dialogue. *Journal of Child Language, 26*, 699–720.

Furnari, E. (1980). *Esconde-esconde para crianças de 3 a 5 años.* São Paulo, Brasil: Editora Ática.

Küntay, A.C., & Nakamura, K. (2004). Linguistic strategies serving evaluative functions: A comparison between Japanese and Turkish narratives. In S. Strömqvist & L. Verhoeven (Eds.), *Relating events in narrative: Typological and contextual perspective* (pp. 329–358). Mahwah, NJ: Lawrence Erlbaum Associates.

Lalonde, C. E., & Chandler, M. J. (2002). Children's understanding of interpretation. *New Ideas in Psychology, 20*(2–3), 163–198.

Perner, J., Leekam, S. R., & Wimmer, H. (1987). Three-year-olds' difficulty with false belief: The case for a conceptual deficit. *British Journal of Developmental Psychology, 5*(2), 125–137.

Poulsen, D., Kintsch, E., Kintsch, W., & Premack, D. (1979). Children's comprehension and memory for stories. *Journal of Experimental Child Psychology, 28*, 379–403.

Richner, E. S., & Nicolopoulou, A. (2001). The narrative construction of differing conceptions of the person in the development of young children's social understanding. *Early Education & Development, 12*, 393–432.

Sawyer, R. K. (2003). Coherence in discourse: Suggestion for future work. *Human Development, 46*, 189–193.

Slobin, D. I. (1987). Thinking for speaking. *Proceedings of the Thirteenth Annual Meeting of the Berkeley Linguistics Society* (pp. 435–444).

Slobin, D. I. (2003). Language and thought online: Cognitive consequences of linguistic relativity. In D. Gentner & S. Goldin-Meadow (Eds.), *Language in mind: Advances in the investigation of language and thought* (pp. 157–191). Cambridge, MA: The MIT Press.

Strömqvist, S., & Verhoeven. L. (Eds.). (2004). *Relating events in narrative: Typological and contextual perspectives.* Mahwah, NJ: Lawrence Erlbaum Associates.

Veneziano, E., & Hudelot, C. (2006). Etats internes, fausse croyance et explications dans les récits: Effets de l'étayage chez les enfants de 4 à 12 ans. *Langage et l'Homme, 41*(2), 119–140.

Wimmer, H., & Perner, J. (1983). Beliefs about beliefs: Representation and constraining function of wrong beliefs in young children's understanding of deception. *Cognition, 13*, 103–128.

Part III

Theoretical Perspectives on Language Development, Language Change, and Typology

Introduction

ELENA LIEVEN
Max Planck Institute for Evolutionary Anthropology and University of Manchester

> There can be no disagreement that aspects of the capacity to acquire and use language are inherited: this is a general truth about species-specific behaviour. But the structure of language arises in two diachronic processes: biological evolution and ever-changing processes of communicative interaction. The structure of language could not have arisen in the genetically determined brain architecture of an individual ancestor alone, because language arises only in communication between individuals. That is, after all, what language is for. As soon as we free ourselves from this confusion of levels of analysis—the individual and the social—many of the puzzles of language structure appear to have solutions beyond divine intervention or genetic determinism. The traditional attempt to account for linguistic structure is rather like trying to locate the law of supply and demand in the mind of the individual producer and consumer, or the shape of a honeycomb in the genetic structure of the individual bee.
>
> **Dan I. Slobin (2001, p. 109)**

The chapters in this section address, in one way or another, the major theoretical issues with which Slobin's research has been concerned: the nature of the precursors to language development—innate or not—the relationship between diachronic and synchronic language change, and the psychological processes involved in learning and using language were major concerns for many years. Subsequently his interests in the interplay between cognition, typology, and language use and the acquisition of sign languages have both developed into major research programs. As a result, there are major overlaps between what appears in this section and papers appearing in other sections of this book. However, in this section these theoretical issues are addressed more directly. In brief overview, all the authors ask 'what is language?' and 'what are the processes underlying its learning and use?'

In the mid-1960s, Slobin provided a radically different theoretical approach to the study of children's language acquisition. His 'operating principles' approach suggested that children were equipped with a number of cognitive-linguistic 'strategies' that allowed them to break into any language. In his attention to variation between languages, to processing demands, and to development, this approach provided both a major challenge to the highly abstract, algorithmic approach of Chomsky and his followers and a welcome emphasis on the empirical realities of the problem. Whatever children bring to language acquisition, whether innate and linguistically encapsulated, or more cognitively based, they have to learn from what they hear. While the range of languages available for children to learn from was often cited as a rhetorical argument for the necessity of a highly abstract Universal Grammar, Slobin was the first to seriously address the implications of this typological variation for a psychologically realistic theory of language acquisition. The fact that children learning languages other than English are presented with a range of factors such as greater variation in syntactic word order, and much richer and very different types of morphology should be studied in depth before stating ex ante that one set of universals would suffice in accounting for the learning of every language (Slobin, 1973, 1985).

In different ways the articles by Givon and Savage-Rumbaugh, Van Valin, Bever, Klein, Bybee and Sweetser address these issues. Givon and Savage-Rumbaugh's chapter follows in the tradition of studying human-enculturated apes to see how close their cognitive and communicative skills are to those of young children. They report attempts to test a 'language-trained' bonobo ('pygmy chimpanzee'), named Panshiba, on a number of language and cognitive tasks. Both this and much other research suggests that while non-human primates have the rudiments of the various skills that make up the language learning capacity, they come together in humans in a way that allows cultural learning to take off, with the leading role being played by the development of social cognition and intention reading (Tomasello & Call, 1997; Tomasello, Carpenter, Call, Behne, & Moll, 2005). It is the particular form of human sociality that provides the basis for the evolution of language and for diachronic language change.

The other chapters that address the question of what language-specific skills may underpin the human language capacity make a range of very different proposals. Van Valin presents an explicit attempt to provide a grammar of the adult language that children can work toward on the basis of cognitive and interactive universals (his Role and Reference Grammar). He addresses the question of whether the specifically human capacity for language arises from a Chomskian-type 'syntax module' or whether one could develop a theory of Universal Grammar, i.e., one that genuinely takes account of typological variation, but is founded on the fundamentals of interaction between human beings: what is new, what is given, and what needs to be represented and talked about.

In contrast, Bever retains a role for an innate Universal Grammar and for some version of 'deep structure,' because he accepts the 'poverty of the stimulus' argument. On the other hand, his own work and that of many others has shown that much of sentence comprehension and production takes place by operating on the surface structure of the sentence, using various processing strategies of the type suggested by Slobin and many others. Bever suggests that one very important strategy is the use of the canonical surface form of the language (e.g., for English, NP V [NP]). He argues that while almost all on-line language analysis can be explained by these processing biases, we process everything twice, once on-line as the message unfolds and once when the full sentence is available, using an abstract, Chomskian-type grammar. This, he suggests, is the only way to take care of garden path type problems that arise from using surface templates. An example of an on-line processing constraint comes from an early set of pioneering experiments Bever conducted with Slobin (Slobin & Bever, 1982) on children's understanding of word order in a range of languages. These early experiments, together with Slobin's operating principles, provided the basis for the attempt by Bates and MacWhinney (1987) to quantify the cues available to children and their relative strength in different languages in the Competition model .

Whereas Van Valin presents a whole grammar and Bever retains some version of a Chomskian grammar, Klein's article is an analytic critique of approaches to the problem of linguistic innateness and universal grammar. He points out that the 'language faculty' is not unitary and includes at least fundamental abilities to construct, copy, and communicate. He suggests that we should concentrate on looking for interesting properties of linguistic systems that have pervasive consequences for the organization of languages. His suggestion for one such linguistically specific universal is finiteness: the anchoring of the sentence 'base' with its arguments to the topic component. However, he maintains that we should study linguistic phenomena such as finiteness in their own right as properties of languages rather than thinking that we can go back to see how they might reflect a Universal Grammar faculty, let alone anything about the way in which language is represented in the brain. Thus although finiteness fundamentally involves grounding utterances for hearers (see, for instance, Langacker, 1987, on grounding) and in this sense has its roots in human sociality, it is interesting that developing the 'machinery' to mark finiteness in a particular language is certainly a protracted task for children. An example is the long period of so-called 'optional infinitive' use by children learning Dutch, German, and English. Note, however, that this is closely related to the structure of the language that children are hearing (Wijnen, Kempen, & Gillis, 2001; Freudenthal, Pine, Aguado-Orea, & Gobet, 2007). In support of Klein's emphasis on the crucial importance of finiteness to human syntax, a number of researchers, including Rispoli in his chapter, have argued that the emergence of finiteness constitutes a major breakthrough in children's syntactic development (see, for instance, Jordens, 2002).

Bybee, in her answer to the question of where grammar comes from, is much closer to where, I suspect, Slobin currently stands on this issue. She argues that grammar comes from history and human interaction. Slobin has always emphasized the importance of language change to understanding what language is and the processes that might be involved in learning and using it. Although he has moved away from the direct relationship between language learning and language change that he outlined in his brilliant article (Slobin, 1977) 'Language change in childhood and history,' his work has always been strongly influenced by the insights of diachronic linguistics. An example is the very influential article with Bybee on children's past tense over-regularizations, which, like the Rispoli and Menn chapters, used errors as a window on the processes which affect children's learning (Bybee & Slobin, 1982). In their emphasis on type and token frequency, analogy, and sound salience they addressed many of the processes also involved in the ways in which words grammaticize into morphemes. This process, which is pervasive in the history of languages, has major theoretical importance since it moves content words in a language toward becoming grammatical morphemes and thus into the so-called 'functional categories' of UG. A similar process can be seen in the way that word order changes occur in the history of a language (compare, for instance, syntactic word order in Old English and Modern German with that of Modern English). The implication is, as both Bybee, here and elsewhere (Bybee & Hopper, 2001; Bybee, 2003), Slobin (1997a), and many others have consistently argued, that grammar is created during communicative interaction between humans and, therefore, syntactic 'machinery' is a constantly fluid and changing set of processes rather than a pregiven, modular 'faculty.'

Sweetser's analysis of the similarities and differences between spoken language, sign language, and co-speech gesture also indicates that we should be thinking in terms of continua rather than encapsulated, and completely separate, systems. She critically examines traditional claims for the difference between sign systems and gesture: for instance, that the former are analytic, conventional, and the subject of conscious monitoring while the latter is iconic and unconscious. She argues that while these contrasts indeed form two ends of a continuum, it *is* a continuum rather than an absolute dichotomy. In her view of sign languages as both fully conventional in the same way as spoken languages but also as containing more iconicity, she comes to very similar conclusions as Slobin has in his work on sign languages (Hoiting & Slobin, 2007) and in the development of the Berkeley Transcription System for sign language research (Hoiting & Slobin, 2002). The implication of both Bybee and Sweetser's chapters is that, in actual language use, dichotomies that are proposed on the basis of theoretical considerations often turn out to be clines.

This central emphasis on 'language-in-action' is also reflected in the ways that errors can be used as a guide to both the structure of underlying representation and to the on-line processes required to produce an utterance. Many of Slobin's early hypotheses about the nature of the 'operating principles' available to the 'Language Making-Capacity' (LMC) of the child (Slobin, 1985, p. 1158) were based on the errors that children made. It can be difficult to identify the causes of omission errors, for instance, whether they arise from 'ungrammatical' representations or from on-line, temporary production problems. But systematic errors of commission can be an extremely important guide to the nature of the underlying linguistic representations of the speaker. To give just one example from the many in Slobin's work, he argued, in an early analysis of the overgeneralization of the feminine accusative marker by Russian-speaking children (Slobin, 1966; see also Slobin, 1997b, pp. 6–8) that they were using the least multifunctional and most consistent inflection available. This particular form was the only accusative inflection that was not homophonous with inflections in other parts of the case, person, and number paradigms. Slobin suggested that this was an example of the operating principle: Underlying semantic relations should be marked overtly and clearly, i.e., that children will learn such unique form-function mappings earlier other things being equal (Slobin, 1979).

The chapters by Rispoli and Menn are detailed examples of the ways in which errors of commission can be used to identify the underlying linguistic system with which the speaker is operating, in the case of Rispoli, language learning children and in the case of Menn, adults with acquired aphasia. Rispoli, in his chapter, analyzes the errors that occur in children's learning of the personal pronoun paradigm of English (e.g., *Her did it, Him is nice*) to predict the relationship between the development of finiteness marking and the expansion of the pronoun paradigm—arguing that both factors are required to explain individual differences between children in the development of the paradigm and that these errors are relatively rare even in children who make them at all. Here, errors are used to develop a theory of the underlying relations between different parts of the child's linguistic representations. Menn, in an overview of the different types of speech production errors made by aphasic patients, uses the patterns of errors found crosslinguistically to critique current ideas of morphological and syntactic 'simplicity.' Here errors are used to extend our understanding of the interplay between linguistic representation and the processing requirements of 'language in action.'

The final set of chapters in this section takes up Slobin's work on the semantics of motion verbs that was initially inspired by Talmy's (1985, 1988) fundamental question as to why languages grammaticize some cognizable aspects of the world and not others—a question not unrelated to the issues raised by Sweetser of what can/does appear in linguistic systems as opposed to co-speech gestures. Here too, we can see fundamental questions about what language is. Is language a reflection of universals of human cognition (as Slobin argued at earlier stages in his approach to this issue, Slobin, 1985) or, alternatively, is cognition affected by language, as he has argued more recently in his discussion of grammaticization (Slobin, 1997a, p. 296) and of 'thinking for speaking' (Berman & Slobin, 1994; Slobin, 1996). One important focus for this question has been Talmy's typology of motion events and their expression in different languages (Talmy, 1991), which many of the chapters in Section 2 also address in the context of narrative studies. In this section, the chapters address Slobin's proposed amendment to Talmy's binary division between verb-framed and satellite-framed by proposing a category of 'equipollently framed' language type and are an ongoing example of the way that scientific discourse progresses. First Talmy himself presents a challenge to the necessity for Slobin's category of equipollency with a detailed analysis of Atsugewi verb complexes, serial verb constructions in Mandarin, and the way in which both manner and path are expressed outside the main verb in Jaminjong. Next Ibarretxe Antuñano, in an analysis of fourteen languages, suggests that languages can be placed on a cline of how elaborated path description typically is, and that this can be orthogonal to whether they are verb-framed, satellite-framed, or equipollent. Kopecka, using a diachronic perspective, demonstrates how French has moved from being a satellite-framed to a verb-framed pattern over the last 800 years through the loss of productivity of verb prefixes. This surely also argues for a cline rather than a dichotomy. Finally, Sampaio, Sinha, and Sinha point out that conflation of either path or manner onto the verb is only one type of possible mapping process from conceptualization to expression. They show that there is also a process of distribution in the semantics of space and motion where one conceptualization is mapped to more than one element. They argue that the verb-framed versus satellite-framed distinction may apply less well to languages as a whole than to particular constructions (e.g., the 'basic motion construction' in which figure but not ground is expressed by contrast with a 'fully specified motion construction' in which both path and ground can be expressed, for instance, by adpositional elements). For languages as a whole, they too suggest that these distinctions are better seen as tendencies or mapping preferences rather than dichotomies.

CONCLUSION

In the course of his research career, Slobin has made a number of original research proposals that have been seminal in guiding subsequent research: 'operating principles,' 'basic child grammar,' 'thinking for speaking,' to name three of the most influential. They have led to a vast range of important research. His ideas have been not only theoretically bold but also rooted in empirical reality. He has constantly drawn attention to the necessity of having a theoretical account of linguistic representation, one that is psychologically real as well as typologically sensitive. He has always recognized the tension between an account that highlights the 'semi-detachment' of form from function in some aspects of language structure and one that attempts to cope with the pervasiveness of semantic and pragmatic function in how language is structured and changes. More important, he has always been willing to change his mind and to rethink his ideas when theoretical arguments and/or data suggest it. As a result he has inspired generations of scholars to do research that is simultaneously theoretically driven and empirically grounded.

REFERENCES

Bates, E., & MacWhinney, B. (1987). Competition, variation, and language learning. In B. MacWhinney (Ed.), *Mechanisms of language acquisition* (pp. 157–193). Hillsdale, NJ: Lawrence Erlbaum Associates.

Berman, R., & Slobin, D. I. (1994). *Relating events in narrative: A crosslinguistic developmental study*. Hillsdale, NJ: Lawrence Erlbaum Associates.

Bybee, J. (2003). Cognitive processes in grammaticalization. In M. Tomasello (Ed.), *The new psychology of language* (Vol. II, pp. 145–167). Mahwah, NJ: Lawrence Erlbaum Associates.

Bybee, J., & Hopper, P. (2001). *Frequency and the emergence of language structure*. Amsterdam: John Benjamins.

Bybee, J. L., & Slobin, D. I. (1982). Rules and schemas in the development and use of the English past tense. *Language, 58*(2), 265–289.

Freudenthal, D., Pine, J., Aguado-Orea, J., & Gobet, F. (2007). Modelling the developmental patterning of finiteness marking in English, Dutch, German and Spanish using MOSAIC. *Cognitive Science, 31*, 311–341.

Hoiting, N., & Slobin, D. I. (2002). Transcription as a tool for understanding: The Berkeley Transcription System for sign language research (BTS). In G. Morgan & B. Woll (Eds.), *Directions in sign language acquisition* (pp. 55–75). Amsterdam/Philadelphia: John Benjamins.

Hoiting, N., & Slobin, D. I. (2007). From gestures to signs in the acquisition of sign language. In S. Duncan, J. Cassell, & E. T. Levy (Eds.), *Gesture and the dynamic dimension of language: Essays in honor of David McNeill* (pp. 51–65). Amsterdam/Philadelphia: John Benjamins.

Jordens, P. (2002). Finiteness in early child Dutch. *Linguistics 40*, 687–765.

Langacker, R. (1987). *Foundations of cognitive grammar* (Vol. 1). Stanford, CA: Stanford University Press.

Slobin, D. I. (1966). The acquisition of Russian as a native language. In F. Smith & G. A. Miller (Eds.), *The genesis of language: A psycholinguistic approach* (pp. 129–148). Cambridge, MA: The MIT Press.

Slobin, D. I. (1973). Cognitive prerequisites for the development of grammar. In C. Ferguson & D. Slobin (Eds.), *Studies of child language development* (pp. 175–208). New York: Holt, Rinehart & Winston.

Slobin, D. I. (1977). Language change in childhood and history. In J. Macnamara (Ed.), *Language learning and thought* (pp. 185–214). New York: Academic Press.

Slobin, D. I. (1979). *Psycholinguistics* (2nd ed.). Glenview, IL: Scott Foresman.

Slobin, D. I. (1985). Crosslinguistic evidence for the language-making capacity. In D. I. Slobin (Ed.), *The crosslinguistic study of language acquisition: Vol. 2. Theoretical issues* (pp. 1157–1256). Hillsdale, NJ: Lawrence Erlbaum Associates.

Slobin, D. I. (1996). From 'thought' and language' to 'thinking for speaking.' In J. Gumperz & S. Levinson (Eds.), *Rethinking linguistic relativity* (pp. 70–96). Cambridge, UK: Cambridge University Press.

Slobin, D. I. (1997a). The origins of grammaticizable notions: Beyond the individual mind. In D. I. Slobin (Ed.), *The crosslinguistic study of language acquisition: Vol. 5. Expanding the contexts* (pp. 265–323). Mahwah: NJ: Lawrence Erlbaum Associates.

Slobin, D. I. (1997b). The universal, the typological and the particular in acquisition. In D.I. Slobin (Ed.), *The crosslinguistic study of language acquisition: Vol. 5, Expanding the contexts* (pp. 1–39). Mahwah: NJ: Lawrence Erlbaum Associates.

Slobin, D. I. (2001). Form/function relations: How do children find out what they are? In M. Bowerman & S. Levinson (Eds.), *Language acquisition and conceptual development* (pp. 406–449). Cambridge, UK: Cambridge University Press.

Slobin, D. I., & Bever, T. G. (1982). Children use canonical sentence schemas —a crosslinguistic study of word order and inflections. *Cognition, 12*(3), 229–265.

Talmy, L. (1985). Lexicalization patterns: Semantic structure in lexical forms. In T. Shopen (Ed.), *Language typology and syntactic description* (Vol. 3, pp. 57–149). Cambridge, UK: Cambridge University Press.

Talmy, L. (1988). The relation of grammar to cognition. In B. Rudzka-Ostyn (Ed.), *Topics in cognitive linguistics* (pp. 165–205). Amsterdam: John Benjamins.

Talmy, L. (1991). Path to realization: A typology of event conflation. *Proceedings of the annual meeting of the Berkeley Linguistics Society, 17*, pp. 480–520

Tomasello, M., & Call, J. (1997). *Primate cognition*. Oxford, UK: Oxford University Press.

Tomasello, M., Carpenter, M., Call, J., Behne, T., & Moll, H. (2005). Understanding and sharing intentions: The origins of cultural cognition. *Brain and Behavioral Sciences, 28,* 675–735.

Wijnen, F., Kempen, M., & Gillis, S. (2001). Bare infinitives in Dutch early child language: An effect of input? *Journal of Child Language, 28,* 629–660.

21

Can Apes Learn Grammar?
A Short Detour Into Language Evolution[1]

T. GIVÓN
University of Oregon

SUE SAVAGE RUMBAUGH
The Great Apes Trust

Something about this interaction of early experience, rate of growth and inherent structure makes it very easy for children to acquire—even invent—language, while apes can only approach the rudiments of these accomplishments with strenuous efforts of both animal and trainer.

Dan I. Slobin, (1997, p. 142)

INTRODUCTION

Over the years, Dan Slobin's work has touched repeatedly on the classical developmental triangle of language acquisition, diachronic change, and language evolution. A striking thing about Dan has always been his willingness, indeed his eagerness, to change his mind, nowhere more conspicuously than in his reflections upon the interaction between the three developmental domains. In the 1970s, Dan pioneered the idea of a close parallelism between first language acquisition and diachronic change (Slobin, 1977). In the 1980s he rejected this idea for lack of demonstrable shared mechanisms (Bybee & Slobin, 1982; Slobin, 1985, 1994, 2002). In the same vein, he has also come to reject the recapitulationist parallelism, attractive to many of us, on general biological grounds (e.g., Lamendella, 1976, 1977; Bickerton, 1981, 1990; Givón, 1979, 2002; see also Gould, 1977), between child language development and language evolution (Slobin, 2002).

Parallelism—or analogy—is a curious construct in science, a pragmatic gambit, a gamble. Rather than full identity, analogy entails a pattern of *both* similarities and differences. In construing an analogy between two domains, one is thus burdened with having to decide which counts more— their similarities or their differences. An eminently reasonable take on our three-way developmental

---

[1] We are indebted to the National Institute of Health (National Institute of Child Health and Human Development) for financial support and encouragement [grant number HD-0060016-32A1]; to the Language Research Center, Georgia State University, for support and encouragement; to Liz Rubert-Pugh for the most competent and cooperative research assistance; and to Duane Rumbaugh for much intellectual stimulation. Above all, we shall forever remain indebted to *The Guys*—Kanzi, Panbanisha, and Nyota—for being such stimulating, entertaining, and challenging kin.

parallelisms is that, like all analogies (or metaphors), they are only useful as long as they can teach us something we don't yet know (i.e., for as long as one domain can shed light on another; Givón, 2002). It is in this spirit that the present study of teaching grammar to apes was undertaken.[2]

The research project the preliminary results of which are reported here was motivated initially by the possibility that a broad parallelism did indeed exist between the course of natural language development—both first and second—and language evolution, namely, the dependence of the acquisition of grammar on prior acquisition of a well-coded lexicon containing non-concrete items (Givón, 1979, 1990). That is, broadly speaking, grammatical communication invariably develops from pre-grammatical (pidgin) communication (Givón, 1979, 1990, 2002, 2005). The question we asked was: if apes (bonobos) had previously acquired command of a well-coded lexicon of nouns and verbs, and a rudimentary pidgin communication (Savage-Rumbaugh et al., 1993; Savage-Rumbaugh & Lewin, 1994), can they then, as do humans, also acquire grammar? With 'grammar' understood here is the sense used by adaptive-functional linguists—the *communicative use* of grammatical morphology and syntactic constructions.

We envisioned using traditional methodological constraints, so that the presence or absence of grammar can be assessed via *minimal-contrasts* (controlled stimuli sets), by either (i) contrasting the presence of a grammatical element vs. its absence (*subtraction*), or (ii) contrasting the presence of one grammatical element with the presence of another (*substitution*). Originally, we also envisioned instruction and testing of both production and comprehension, with at least two adult apes and a growing juvenile. However, for reasons beyond our control, our subject pool shrank to one adult female bonobo (Panbanisha, henceforth PB), and instruction and testing were confined to *comprehension* of oral English.

There are obvious differences between PB's pre-grammatical communication and human pidgin, differences that would easily impel a careful critic to reject our project as hopeless. PB's previous lexical knowledge and spontaneous communicative behavior, including lexical proficiency in both the lexigram board[3] and oral English, involved only *concrete* vocabulary. But the historical creation of grammar by adult humans depends crucially on pre-acquired *abstract* vocabulary: grammar is a highly abstract entity that did not historically spring directly from concrete vocabulary (Givón, 2005).

What is more, grammar is an *automated* speech-processing device that arises and is normally used by humans only at *high performance speed*, namely, during fluent communication (Givón, 1979, 1989, 2005). In natural, grammar-coded, oral human communication and in speech addressed to children, typically two to three words fall under one clausal intonation contour, and each intonational clause is processed, on the average, in 1–2 seconds (Chafe, 1994; Barker & Givón, 2002). In contrast, the symbolic lexical instrument available for communicative production with our apes, the lexigram board, entails extremely slow communication, with each word produced as a separate gesture ('intonation contour'), even when a 2- or 3-word clause is eventually interpreted or intended. The communicative rhythm of lexigram-using bonobos thus resembles that of human children at the pre-grammar *one-word stage* (children aged about 1 year; Bloom, 1973; Scollon, 1976). The problem becomes even greater if we consider some recent work that shows that children produce sentence-like constructions at the one-word stage using gesture and speech together (e.g., Goldin-Meadow & Butcher, 2003; Özçalışkan & Goldin-Meadow, 2005). Finally, three crucial features characterize adult human grammaticalized communication and set it apart from non-human communication: multi-propositional discourse coherence, a preponderance of declarative speech-acts, and spatially or temporally displaced referents. In sharp contrast, ape communication is overwhelmingly *mono-propositional* and *manipulative* and involves *non-displaced referents*.

---

[2] In the spirit of adventuresome analogy, it is perhaps of interest that the project of teaching grammar to apes was funded by the National Institute of Child Development.

[3] The lexigram board is a plastic board on which abstract symbols that stand for nouns and verbs are printed. The apes communicate by pointing to individual symbols. In a more advanced version of the lexigram board, the sound of the appropriate English word is produced electronically when the ape touches the symbol.

Given the combination of all these factors, we decided that the best course was to instruct and test the apes for their ability to understand words of an abstract, rather than a concrete nature (what has been called '*pre-grammar*'; Bickerton, 1981, 1990; Givón, 1979, 1985, 1989, 1995). That is, we decided to test them with the prerequisite early stage, which, according to our prediction, preceded the development of grammar in humans. Our reasoning was that if the apes are shown to be incapable of acquiring the cognitively more transparent pre-grammar, it is unlikely that they would acquire grammar.

PRE-GRAMMAR SYSTEMS

In the set of experiments reported here, we investigated four 'pre-grammatical' systems, all parts of the grammar of the Noun Phrase, or, from a functional-adaptive perspective, part of the grammar of referential coherence. We reasoned that we could investigate this more concrete domain of grammar through the use and comprehension of words that function as noun modifiers in the NP. We planned to extend the investigation later on to the much more abstract domain of the grammar of the Verb Phrase. In each grammatical sub-domain, we relied on lexical vocabulary that was already known to the ape (PB), and then combined it with teaching and testing new vocabulary embedded in the appropriate syntactic constructions and communicative tasks. We chose systems that could be tested with short multiword utterances, that required some degree of abstraction, and, importantly, that have been shown to be frequent precursors to grammaticized markers in languages. The four systems we studied and the reasons we chose them are presented below.

1. The proximate and distal demonstratives 'this' and 'that': The distal demonstrative (English 'that') is almost universally the pre-grammar source of the definite article (English 'the'). The proximate demonstrative (English 'this') is one of the two common sources for the indefinite article (English 'a') (Wright & Givon, 1987).
2. The numerals/quantifiers 'one,' 'two,' 'three,' 'all': The numeral 'one' in a quantifying NP construction is the most common source of the indefinite article (English 'a') (Givon, 1981). The quantifier 'all' in a quantifying NP construction is sometimes a source of plural markers in human grammars (see, for instance, Sankoff & Brown, 1976).
3. Color adjectives as restrictive noun modifiers: Restrictive adjectives as noun modifiers in the noun phrase (NP) are one of the simplest syntactic constructions found universally. Color adjectives are the kind most likely to appear in such a construction (Dixon, 1972). Adjectives in such a construction are used to differentiate between entities that are otherwise similar or even identical—except for the feature coded by the adjective.
4. The use of a spatial preposition in prepositional phrases: Concrete spatial prepositions are one of the common sources of more abstract directional, dative, benefactive, or direct-object case-markers in human language (Heine, Claudi, & Huennemeyer, 1991; Givon, 2001).

INSTRUCTIONAL AND TESTING METHODOLOGY

General Design

For each aforementioned system, we created a physical environment that was sufficiently familiar and amenable to PB, with respect to which all communicative trials and, later, testing trials were conducted. For reasons that are extraneous to this project, only one person was allowed to interact at close quarters with PB. That person—Elizabeth Rubert-Pugh—became the research assistant (RA) for the project, executing all instructional and testing trials and recording the results. Both instructional and testing trials were done in informally randomized trial blocks that were interspersed with other communicative activities and/or distractions. We will report the exact formula of the trials for each of the four systems separately. It should be noted that it was not always possible to engage PB's attention to be able to carry out balanced numbers of trials in different conditions or across sessions.

INSTRUCTION AND TESTING SESSIONS FOR THE FOUR SYSTEMS

Demonstrative Modifiers

(a) Instructional Trials The instructional sessions were a bit less structured than the testing sessions. The RA arranged two identical objects one right next to where she and PB were located, the other about 10 feet away. The RA would then point to either the near object (This x) or the far object (That x) and first tell PB: "Now Liz is going to touch/handle *This x*," then touch/handle it; or "Now Liz is going to touch/handle *That x*," then touch/handle it. The RA would then ask PB: "Panbanisha, can you now touch this/that x?" PB's reaction was then recorded. If it was correct (This = near; That = far), the RA praised PB. These instructional trials were interspersed with other activities.

A wide range of concrete objects were used in these trials, objects whose names were all familiar to PB. The most common objects were umbrella, can opener, towel, collar, celery, hat, wipe, balloon, string, cooler, chalk, bowl, soap, toothbrush, paint, chow, bubbles, carrot, potato, backpack, plastic bag, shirt, milk, hammer, clay, paper, mirror, water, trash, rock, brush, toothpaste. The instructional trials and other interspersed activities were also used to reinforce PB's familiarity with the names of these objects. These instructional activities lasted for approximately 4 months, from August to December 2002. The testing trials took place in the following month, January 2003.

(b) Testing Trials I (With Physical Pointing Cues) In these trials, the RA stood or sat next to PB, with one of two identical objects near them (within 2 feet) and the other removed (approximately 10 feet away). The same array of familiar objects was used alternately. In each trial, the RA commanded PB: "Panbanisha, touch *THIS/THAT x*." During that command, the RA *pointed* to the object and also *looked* at it. PB's response was then recorded. Some other activity is interspersed, then the next trial (Table 21.1).

Three such testing sessions with pointing were conducted with 2- to 6-day intervals in January 2003. PB's response in each trial was recorded 'correct' if she got up, went over and touched the far object following a 'that' instruction, or if she touched the near object following a 'this' instruction. No other response was produced by PB in the test trials. Since the task presented a binary choice, chance performance was 50%.

(c) Testing Trials (Without Physical Pointing) The procedure here was identical to that in (b) above, except that the RA wore dark glasses and did not point with her head or hand toward the object. Six separate trial sessions were conducted at 2-day intervals (Table 21.2).

TABLE 21.1 Results (With Physical Pointing)

Session	Demonstrative	Correct	Incorrect	Total
I	THIS	4	0	4
	THAT	3	0	3
II	THIS	4	0	4
	THAT	5	0	5
III	THIS	3	0	3
	THAT	3	0	3

TABLE 21.2 Results (Without Physical Pointing)

Session	Demonstrative	Correct	Incorrect	Total
I	THIS	3	0	3
	THAT	2	2	4
II	THIS	3	0	3
	THAT	0	3	3
III	THIS	2	0	2
	THAT	2	0	2
IV	THIS	3	0	3
	THAT	0	3	0
V	THIS	3	0	3
	THAT	0	3	3
VI	THIS	3	0	3
	THAT	0	3	3

(d) Interpretation When gestural pointing cues (with hand and/or head/eyes) were used, PB understood deictic pointing without any difficulty in 100% of the trials. When physical gestures were removed, however, her understanding of the distal verbal deictic 'that' went down to chance in session 1 and to always incorrect in sessions IV–VII, with the exception of only one session where she was correct on both trials.

However, chance level performance with a two-variable contrast should be 50%, and PB rejected the distal interpretation of 'that' in favor of the proximate interpretation 100% of the time, way beyond the expected chance level. In view of this, one must interpret her 100% correct performance on the 'this' trials as a mere *default preference*, in the absence of gestural cues, for the conveniently located nearby object rather than as real understanding of the verbal cue 'this.' That is, in 4 months of instruction we succeeded, indeed rather quickly (preliminary tests in August 2002 already indicated this), in teaching PB *deictic gestural pointing*. But after 4 months of instruction we still failed to teach her the communicative value of the verbal ('symbolic') labels 'this' and 'that.' However, it should be noted that very young children probably do not make a clear distinction between *this* and *that* and that, in fact, distinctive use of these terms is highly contextually determined (Clark & Sengul, 1978; Garton, 1983).

Numerals and Quantifiers

(a) Instruction Sessions Daily instructional sessions were carried out for 25 days in March and February 2003. Structured informally, the sessions typically involved:

(i) The RA (Liz) placing a set of ten (10) identical objects in a bin in front of PB.
(ii) The RA demonstrating to PB while saying:
"Panbanisha, now Liz is taking *ONE/TWO/THREE/ALL* x's from the bin.
Now Liz is going to put *it/them* back."
(iii) The RA replaces the objects, randomizing them carefully in the bin. Then asking PB:
"Now, Panbanisha, I want you to get *ONE/TWO/THREE/ALL* x's from the bin."

PB was praised every time she took the 'correct' number (same number as the RA in the demonstration). She was corrected if her performance varied from the RA's, and verbal reinforcement of the correct number was then given.

(b) Testing Sessions Two testing sessions were performed, each separated by a 2-week period, immediately following the instruction sessions. The physical environment was the same as in the

TABLE 21.3   Results of Numeral/Quantifier Test

Session	Numeral	Correct	Incorrect	Total	% Correct
I	ONE	3	1	4	75%
	TWO	4	0	4	100%
	THREE	2	2	4	50%
	ALL	4	0	4	100%
II	ONE	4	0	4	100%
	TWO	3		4	75%
	THREE	0	4	4	0%
	ALL	4	0	4	100%

teaching sessions (a) above. The verbal request formulas were likewise the same. The presentation of numerals/quantifiers was randomized informally. A correct response was counted when PB replicated the actions of the RA. All other responses were counted as incorrect. Since there were four numerals/quantifiers to choose from, we consider chance performance to be 25% (Table 21.3).

(c) Interpretation   It was not possible to do the required number of trials that would allow for statistical testing and the results are therefore statistically inconclusive. Further, we did not test verbal instructions without prior demonstration, so we cannot claim PB has acquired the comprehension of the numeral/quantifier verbal labels. The results are nonetheless coherent in terms of PB's cognitive capacity to understand quantification. At the two salient extremes of the quantification scale—ONE/TWO and ALL—PB performs best (75%–100%). At the middle point of the highest numeral (THREE) she performed the worst (50%–0%). Such results are consonant with Dahaene's (1997) reported cross-species data. Dahaene reports that animals and young children tend to have no trouble learning the lowest numerals 1–4, and a generalized concept of 'many,' but otherwise have a very elastic counting system that is sensitive to contextual relevance.

Modifying Color Adjectives

(a) General Design   We chose four colors, red, green, black, and white, which constitute the top of the Berlin and Kay's (1969) universal color scale for humans. These color words had not been previously taught to the apes, and had been put on the lexigram board.

(b) Instructional Sessions   Instructional sessions took place over about 6 weeks (May–June 2003). Sets of 8–12 small objects were placed in front of PB by the RA. The objects were identical in all ways except that 2–3 members of each set were *white, black, green,* or *red* in color. Other objects, all known to PB, were also placed in the immediate environment, for potential interaction with the selected colored objects. The demonstration verbal formula used during instructional trials was, "Now Liz is going to get a *WHITE* dog. The *WHITE* dog is going to bite Nathan. Panbanisha, can you make the *WHITE* dog bite Nathan?"[4]

(c) Testing After Prior Demonstration   The earlier testing sessions incorporated prior demonstration by the RA. The physical environment and sets of colored objects were the same as in (b) above. The general verbal instruction formula was, "Now Liz is going to get a *RED* dog and put it inside the shoe. Panbanisha, can you get a *RED* dog?" Six testing sessions were conducted every 1–2 days in June and July 2003 (Table 21.4).

(d) Testing Without Prior Demonstration   The physical environment and test objects were the same as in (c) above, but the test requests to PB were presented directly, without prior

---

[4] Nathan is a toy dog.

TABLE 21.4 Results of Testing for Color Adjectives After Prior Demonstration

Session	Adjective							
	White		Black		Red		Green	
	C	I	C	I	C	I	C	I
I	2	1	1	1	2	0	0	1
II	1	1	2	0	1	1	0	1
III	1	1	2	0	2	0	0	1
IV	0	1	2	1	0	2	0	2
V	2	0	0	2	1	1	0	2
VI	1	1	0	3	1	0	1	0
Total:	6	5	7	7	7	4	1	7
Total C:	6/11		7/14		7/11		1/8	
% C:	54%		50%		63%		12%	

C: correct, I: incorrect

demonstration by the RA in order to see whether the color names had been retained over time. There were six testing sessions of this type on successive days in July 2003 (Table 21.5).

(e) Interpretation First, only with the adjective 'green' does PB's performance (22% correct) fall to the level of chance (1/4 = 25%). So at the comprehension level, PB is capable of learning the use of the English *restrictive ADJ-N* construction. That is, she can learn to discriminate between objects that are identical/similar except for a single feature: color.

Second, the scale of percent correct performance follows, in the main, Berlin and Kay's (1969) observation for the probability of human cultures having distinct verbal labels for colors:

BLACK/WHITE > RED > BLUE/GREEN
(50–70%)   (36%)   (22%; chance)

TABLE 21.5 Results of Testing for Color Adjectives Without Prior Demonstration

Session	Adjective							
	White		Black		Red		Green	
	C	I	C	I	C	I	C	I
I	0	2	0	1	2	0	0	1
II	1	0	1	0	1	0	1	2
III	0	1	0	1	0	1	0	1
IV	1	1	1	0	0	2	1	1
V	2	0	2	0	1	1	0	1
VI	1	1	1	0	0	3	0	1
Total:	5	5	5	2	4	7	2	7
Total C:	5/10		5/7		4/11		2/9	
% C:	50%		71%		36%		22%	

C: correct, I: incorrect

One may, tentatively, conjecture that the adaptive pressure for apes' color distinctions follows the same pattern observed for humans, at the very least at the top of the color scale, and that PB's performance reflects this.

Spatial Prepositions

(a) General Design   We taught and tested PB on five spatial English prepositions: 'on top of,' 'under,' 'inside,' 'next to,' and 'away from.' For our instructional and testing sessions, we constructed a 2-foot square plywood box standing on two 6-inch props. The box was closed on five sides, with the open side facing PB and the RA at a distance of about 3 feet. Familiar small objects were then placed in various spatial relations to the box. The demonstration by the RA placed the object in the following target positions:

'on top of' = on top of the box and visible to PB
'under' = in the 6-inch space under the box
'inside' = inside the box, on the box's floor and visible to PB
'next to' = adjacent to the box on the right-hand side and visible to PB
'away from' = about 10 feet away from the box, to the right and back, visible to PB. Chance performance level was thus set at 1/5 (20%).

(b) Instructional Sessions   Informal multiple instructional sessions were conducted over 4 months, from September 2003 to January 2004. The general formula for instruction involved demonstration by the RA, request for performance by PB, corrections and re-demonstration by the RA, and praise for correct performance. Typical verbal formulas were "Now Panbanisha, Liz is putting the dog *INSIDE* the box. *INSIDE* the box. Can you now put the dog *INSIDE* the box?"

(c) Testing Following Demonstration   The physical environment and verbal instruction procedures in this set of testing session were identical to (b) above, with request for performance directly following a demonstration by the RA. Seven separate testing sessions were conducted in January 2004 at 12-hour intervals (Table 21.6).

The results of this test can be viewed as reflecting PB's understanding of distinct spatial relations and her ability to imitate the RA's immediately preceding demonstration. Her performance

TABLE 21.6   Results of Tests for Prepositions Following Demonstration

Session	Inside		On Top Of		Under		Next To		Away From	
	C	I	C	I	C	I	C	I	C	I
I	2	0	1	0	1	0	0	2	1	0
II	2	0	1	0	1	0	0	2	1	0
III	1	0	1	0	1	0	0	1	1	0
IV	1	0	1	0	1	0	0	1	1	0
V	1	1	2	0	1	0	1	0	2	0
VI	2	0	1	0	1	0	1	1	2	0
VII	1	1	1	0	1	0	1	1	2	0
Total:	10	2	8	0	7	0	3	8	10	0
Total C:	10/12		8/8		7/7		3/11		10/10	
% C:	83%		100%		100%		27%		100%	

C: correct, I: incorrect

TABLE 21.7 Result of Testing for Prepositions Without Prior Demonstration

Session	Preposition									
	Inside		On Top Of		Under		Next To		Away From	
	C	I	C	I	C	I	C	I	C	I
I	0	2	2	0	1	0	0	1	2	0
II	2	0	0	1	1	0	0	2	1	0
III	1	0	1	2	2	0	0	1	0	2
IV	1	1	0	0	2	1	1	0	0	1
V	1	0	1	1	2	0	1	0	0	1
VI	1	0	2	0	1	2	0	1	1	0
Total:	6	3	6	4	9	3	2	5	4	4
Total C:	6/9		6/10		9/12		2/7		4/8	
% C:	66%		60%		75%		28%		50%	

C: correct, I: incorrect

is essentially at the level of 80–100% correct on four of the five spatial relations. The only one that seems to perplex her consistently is 'next to.' An analysis of her mistakes shows that they distribute rather coherently: four 'under' and four 'on top of.' In other words, PB seems to interpret 'next to' as *outside* the box but still near enough. She then distributes her responses equally to the three plausible candidates: 'on top of' (four mistakes), 'under' (four mistakes) and 'next to' (three correct responses).

(d) **Testing Without Prior Demonstration** Six testing sessions were conducted on consecutive days in March 2004. The verbal request frames were the same as in (b) and (c) above but without the prior demonstrations by the RA (Table 21.7).

(e) **Interpretation** With chance performance being again 1/5 (20%), the results in the main hold up the trend observed in the test following prior demonstration in Table 21.6 above. For four of the five prepositions, the same ones as in Table 21.6, PB performed above chance (50–75%). For the same preposition, for which she flunked the cognitive imitation (i.e., 'next to'), PB produced correct responses at a rate of 28%, which places her performance almost at chance (~20%). Again in the absence of conclusive inferential statistics, the results nonetheless suggest, albeit tentatively, that it is possible to teach apes the verbal labels of concrete spatial relations—provided the spatial relation is cognitively transparent to them.

GENERAL DISCUSSION

PB can learn referential deixis with pointing though not without. She can learn *one/two/all* but not 'three.' She can learn *white/black/red* but not 'green' and she can learn *in/on/under/away from* but not 'next to.' This may not be very different from children in the one-word stage or just moving into multi-word speech. But eventually children extract this information for themselves—or create it in the case of a pidgin —however, there is very little sign that PB would succeed in doing this despite extensive and explicit training.

For reasons beyond our control, many other features of pre-grammar we intended to investigate could not be tested. Chief among these were pre-grammar of verb phrases (tense-aspect-modality, negation, subject/object pronouns), high-speed communication, abstract lexical vocabulary, multi-propositional coherence in discourse, declarative speech-acts, and temporal and spatial displacement from the immediate speech situation. These features are usually associated, often as *prerequisites*, with grammaticalized human communication. The latter three are always found in 'pre-grammatical' human communication, be it child pidgin, second language pidgin, or in patients with Broca's aphasia. However, all six features are absent in either natural or human-induced ape communication.

Our results, as of now, tend to point to a rather pessimistic view of whether it is meaningful to talk about grammar in apes, either at the comprehension level (Savage-Rumbaugh et al., 1993) or at the production level (Greenfield & Savage-Rumbaugh, 1991). The adaptive pressure, communicative goals, and cognitive prerequisites for grammar, which were noted above, are altogether missing in both natural and human-induced ape communication.

Grammar is not just the acquisition of *complex abstract structures*, but perhaps primarily the codification of highly sophisticated and rather abstract communicative functions—together with their associated complex/abstract structures. The communicative goals associated with grammar have to do, most likely, with *third-order representation* of the *epistemic and deontic mental states of one's interlocutor*, the so-called 'Theories of Mind' (Givón, 2002, 2005).[5] This entails rapid *perspective shifting* during communication (MacWhinney, 2002), and, we suspect, is akin to what Slobin (1997, p. 265) means by "beyond the individual mind." Given that the adaptive pressure, the neurocognitive prerequisites, and the highly abstract communicative goals associated with grammar have not been demonstrated in apes, it is not clear that the concept 'grammar' is all that meaningful, or useful, in discussing ape communication (Tomasello & Call, 1997).

We did our best to teach one ape—the highly intelligent, sweet-tempered, and relatively cooperative Panbanisha—some rudimentary pre-grammatical communicative devices. The fact that such an endeavor already raised great difficulties suggests, at the very least, that we exercise a certain measure of caution in imputing various grammatical competences to the apes.

REFERENCES

Barker, M., & Givón, T. (2002). The pre-linguistic origins of language processing rates. In T. Givón & B. Malle (Eds.), *The evolution of language out of pre-language*, TSL 53. Amsterdam: John Benjamins.
Berlin, B., & Kay, P. (1969). *Basic color terms*. Berkeley, CA: University of California Press.
Bickerton, D. (1981). *The roots of language*. Ann Arbor, MI: Karoma.
Bickerton, D. (1990). *Language and species*. Chicago: University of Chicago Press.
Bloom, L. (1973). *One word at a time: The use of single-word utterances before syntax*. The Hague: Mouton.
Bowerman, M. (1973). *Early syntactic development*. Cambridge, UK: Cambridge University Press.
Bybee, J., & Slobin, D. I. (1982). Why small children cannot change language on their own: Suggestions from the English past tense. In A. Ahlqvist (Ed.), *Papers from the 5th International Conference on Historical Linguistics*. Amsterdam: John Benjamins.
Chafe, W. (1994). *Discourse, consciousness and time: Displacement of conscious experience in speaking and writing*. Chicago: University of Chicago Press.
Clark, E., & Sengul, C. J. (1978). Strategies in the acquisition of deixis. *Journal of Child Language*, 5, 457–475.
Dahaene, S. (1997). *The number sense: How the mind creates mathematics*. Oxford, UK: Oxford University Press.
Dixon, R. M. W. (1972). Where have all the adjectives gone? In R. M. W. Dixon (Ed.), *Where have all the adjectives gone and other essays on semantics and syntax*. The Hague: Mouton.
Garton, A. (1983). An approach to the study of determiners in early language development. *Journal of Psycholinguistic Research*, 12, 513–525.
Givón, T. (1979). *On understanding grammar*. New York. Academic Press.
Givón, T. (1981). On the development of the numeral 'one' as an indefinite marker. *Folia Linguistica Historica*, 2(1), 35–53.

---

[5] First-order representations are of 'external' experience of either entities ('dog,' 'chair'), states ('the banana is in the box,' 'the box is red'), or events ('Kanzi ate the banana'). Second-order representations are of one's own mental constructs ('I saw Kanzi,' 'I want to leave,' 'I know that PB is outside'). Third-order representations are of the mental construct of one's interlocutor ('PB saw Kanzi,' 'Kanzi wants to leave,' 'PB knows that Kanzi is outside').

Givón, T. (1985). Iconicity, isomorphism and non-arbitrary syntax. In J. Haiman (Ed.), *Iconicity in syntax*. Amsterdam: John Benjamins.

Givón, T. (1989). *Minds, code and context: Essays in pragmatics*. Hillsdale, NJ: Lawrence Erlbaum Associates.

Givón, T. (1990). Natural language acquisition and organized language teaching. In H. Burmeister & P. Rounds (Eds.), *Proceedings of the 10th Second Language Research Forum (SLRF)*. Eugene: University of Oregon.

Givón, T. (1995). *Functionalism and grammar*. Amsterdam: John Benjamins.

Givon, T. (2001). *Syntax*, (Vol. 1, Chs. 5,6). Amsterdam: John Benjamins.

Givón, T. (2002). *Bio-linguistics: The Santa Barbara lectures*. Amsterdam: John Benjamins.

Givón, T. (2005). *Context as other minds: The pragmatics of sociality, cognition and communication*. Amsterdam: John Benjamins.

Goldin-Meadow, S., & Butcher, C. (2003). Pointing toward two word speech in young children. In S. Kita (Ed.), *Pointing: Where language, culture, and cognition meet* (pp. 85–107). Mahwah, NJ: Lawrence Erlbaum Associates.

Gould, S. J. (1977). *Ontology and phylogeny*. Cambridge, MA: Harvard University Press.

Greenfield, P. M., & Savage-Rumbaugh, E. S. (1991). Imitation, grammatical development and the invention of protogrammar by an ape. In N. A. Krasnegor, D. M. Rumbaugh, R .L. Schiefelbusch, & M. Studdert-Kennedy (Eds.), *Biological and behavioral determinants of language development*. Hillsdale, NJ: Lawrence Erlbaum Associates.

Heine, B., Claudi, U., & Huennemeyer, F. (1991). *Grammaticalization: A conceptual framework*. Chicago: University of Chicago Press.

Lamendella, J. (1976). Relationship between ontogeny and philogeny of language: A neo-recapitulationist view. In S. R. Harnad, H. D. Stelkis, & J. Lancaster (Eds.), *The origins and evolutions of language and speech*. New York: New York Academy of Science.

Lamendella, J. (1977). *Neuro-functional foundations of symbolic communication*. San Jose, CA: San Jose State University.

MacWhinney, B. (2002). The gradual emergence of language. In T. Givón & B. F. Malle (Eds.), *The evolution of language out of pre-language* (pp. 231–263). Amsterdam: John Benjamins.

Özçalıskan, S., & Goldin-Meadow, S. (2005). Gesture is at the cutting edge of early language development. *Cognition*, 96(3), B101–B113.

Sankoff, G., & Brown, P. (1976). The origins of syntax in discourse: A case study of Tok Pisin relatives. *Language*, 52(3), 631–666.

Savage-Rumbaugh, E. S., Murphy, J., Sevcik, R. A, Brakke, K. E., Williams S. L., & Rumbaugh, D. M. (1993). *Language comprehension in ape and child*, (Serial no. 223, Monographs of the Society for Research in Child Development). Chicago: University of Chicago Press.

Savage-Rumbaugh, S., & Lewin, R. (1994). *Kanzi: The ape at the brink of the human mind*. New York: Wiley & Sons.

Scollon, R. (1976). *Conversations with a one-year old*. PhD dissertation, University of Hawaii at Manoa.

Slobin, D. I. (1977). Language change in childhood and history. In J. Macnamara (Ed.), *Language learning and thought*. New York: Academic Press.

Slobin, D. I. (1985). Crosslinguistic evidence for the language making capacity. In D. I. Slobin (Ed.), *The crosslinguistic study of language acquisition: Vol. 2. Theoretical Issues*. Hillsdale, NJ: Lawrence Erlbaum Associates.

Slobin, D. I. (1994). Talking perfectly: Discourse origins of the present perfect. In E. Pagliuca (Ed.), *Perspectives on Grammaticalization*. Amsterdam: John Benjamins.

Slobin, D. I. (1997). The origins of grammatical notions: Beyond the individual mind. In D. I. Slobin (Ed.), *The crosslinguistic study of language acquisition: Vol. 5. Expanding the context* (pp. 265–323). Mahwah, NJ: Lawrence Erlbaum Associates.

Slobin, D. I. (2002). Language evolution, acquisition and diachrony: Probing the parallels. In T. Givón & B. Malle (Eds.), *The evolution of language out of pre-language*, TSL 53. Amsterdam: John Benjamins.

Tomasello, M., & Call, J. (1997). *Ape cognition*. Oxford, UK: Oxford University Press.

Wright, S., & Givon, T. (1987). The pragmatics of individual reference. *Studies in Language*, 11(1), 1–33.

22

Some Remarks on Universal Grammar[1]

ROBERT D. VAN VALIN, JR.
*Heinrich Heine University Düssseldorf and
University at Buffalo, The State University of New York*

> My position is that language acquisition is guided by innate structural principles, some of which are unique to this particular task, and some of which are more general. The position advocated here can thus be characterized by such terms as 'nativist', 'constructionist', 'interactionist', 'cognitive', 'structuralist'.
>
> **Dan I. Slobin (1979, p. 76)**

Dan Slobin has been a good friend and an intellectual inspiration for many years. Through attending his seminars and in the course of many stimulating conversations I have been challenged by Dan on many fronts, and I have always come away enriched by his insights and wisdom.

INTRODUCTION

The cognitivist view of language acquisition, of which Dan Slobin was one of the pioneers and leading exponents, takes the position that the inborn rich cognitive endowment of human beings underlies their acquisition of language, not an autonomous language acquisition device [LAD]. The LAD, as posited in Chomsky (1965 and subsequent work), contains the abstract principles which constrain the form of a possible human language and make acquisition possible. Since a child can learn any human language, these principles must be universally valid, and therefore the LAD is also the locus of linguistic universals, that is, it is also a universal grammar [UG]. If, however, one posits that acquisition takes place without an autonomous LAD, what is the status of universal generalizations in a cognitive model? What could UG be without the LAD? Does UG exist? This leads to a truly fundamental question: are there universal syntactic generalizations that could constitute something like a UG? This chapter will address these issues, arguing that UG is an epiphenomenon derived from generalizations over language-specific constructions, and that there are no universal syntactic generalizations which are not reducible to or strongly motivated by universal semantic or pragmatic principles. We first discuss the issue of language acquisition without a LAD, then address the question of the existence of syntactic universals. Conclusions are in the final section.

---

[1] This chapter was written while the author was a visitor at the Max Planck Institute for Human Cognitive and Brain Sciences. I would like to thank W. Tecumseh Fitch, Anja Latrouite, and Richard Weist for comments on an earlier draft.

LANGUAGE ACQUISITION WITHOUT A LAD

The debate over the mechanisms underlying the acquisition of language by children has raged for decades, triggered by Chomsky's review of Skinner (1959). Chomsky's position has been consistently that the core grammatical structures are abstract and unmotivated by communicative or processing concerns and are therefore unlearnable based on the linguistic data to which the child is exposed. Consequently, the grammar is given in advance in an abstract form (the LAD), and the task of the child is to adapt it to the language she is exposed to. The actual content of the LAD has changed considerably over the years, from the formal principles organizing a grammar, to actual grammatical principles subject to parametric variation, and to, in recent work (Hauser, Chomsky, & Fitch, 2002; Chomsky, 2005), just the principle of recursion. While it was relatively clear what the task of the child was in the earlier conceptions of the LAD, it is less clear how a LAD, which just contains the principle of recursion, makes acquisition possible, since the vast majority of grammatical phenomena would fall outside of the 'narrow syntax' it defines and would be a property of the interface representations (Phonetic Form and Logical Form) and non-linguistic cognition; such interface phenomena would have to be learned based on the linguistic input. Hence the bulk of acquisition is left unaccounted for; in other words, the grammatical periphery dwarfs the grammatical core. It should be noted that Pinker and Jackendoff (2005) defend the traditional, richer theory of the LAD against the most recent Chomskyan conception of it; Fitch, Hauser, & Chomsky (2005) offer a spirited rejoinder.

Nevertheless, the basic claim remains that the LAD, an autonomous mental 'organ' composed of autonomous syntactic principles, is a necessary condition for the possibility of language acquisition. Autonomy, not innateness, is the key concept. As Chomsky (1975) noted, the question is not whether language is innate and unique to humans, but rather *how* it is innate, and his claim from the early 1960s until recently has been that it is the set of uniquely linguistic syntactic principles that characterizes how language is innate in humans. And because a child can learn any human language, these principles must be valid for all languages, that is, they must be universal. Hence the LAD is also a UG.

Slobin (1973) proposed an alternative conception of language acquisition, one in which cognitive principles play a key role. These cognitive principles are not abstract syntactic principles, but are concrete perceptual and cognitive principles that are relevant in many instances beyond language. He further developed his operating principles in his 1985 paper, 'Crosslinguistic evidence for the language-making capacity,' and there have been a number of proposals from other psycholinguists, such as Schlesinger (1982), Bruner (1983), Karmiloff-Smith (1992), Braine (1992, 1994), and Tomasello (2003), along similar lines. Braine (1992, 1994) argues for the following preconditions (1) to language learning (1992, p. 80).

(1) Preconditions to language learning:
    a. A cognitive architecture for an initial learning mechanism for concepts and relations.
    b. An account of the kinds of input delivered by sensory systems to the learning mechanism.
    c. 'Kantian-type framework categories,' including 'ontological categories' such as object, place and event, 'predicate' which comprises concepts (including properties) and relations, and 'argument' which refers to instances of concepts or entities related by relations.

The first two points refer to general cognitive processes; it is the third point which is most relevant here. Braine argues that there must be a system of mental representation that human beings have in which notions like 'object,' 'place,' and 'event' are represented and manipulated. This representational system is non-linguistic; it is, according to Braine, part of the initial cognitive endowment and is used in cognitive processes in many domains. Of particular importance is the idea that objects and their properties and objects and the relations among them are represented in terms of predicates (properties, relations) and arguments (objects). Braine (1990, 1993) calls this representation a 'natural logic' and argues that it is a fundamental component of human cognitive processes in many domains.

Slobin, Braine, and Bruner portray the initial cognitive endowment of human beings as very rich and structured. Bruner (1983) emphasizes that human infants are capable of highly focused analysis and reasoning in abstract domains and are also strongly predisposed to goal-directed activity, including communicative social interaction with other humans. Tomasello (2003) argues that the recognition that other humans have mental states and the desire to manipulate others' attention are powerful motivations for infants to learn to communicate and to master language. Another important aspect of this initial cognitive endowment is the set of general principles of rational human behavior discussed by Grice (1975), which apply to both linguistic and non-linguistic cognition. One could argue that the principle of recursion itself is not a uniquely linguistic principle, since recursion is found in other cognitive domains and is a necessary part of Braine's system of mental representation and reasoning. If this is the case, then either the last uniquely linguistic principle in the LAD vanishes, or one is forced to claim that recursion is represented at least twice cognitively, once in the LAD and once for other cognitive domains, a solution that would require considerable empirical evidence to justify, given its prima facie problematic nature.

It would be impossible in the context of a short chapter like this to demonstrate how these principles make acquisition possible (Tomasello, 2003, is an entire book devoted to this task), but one example can be given to illustrate how it is possible to go from cognitive principles that are not strictly linguistic to linguistic structure. Braine (1992) gives an explicit account of how basic clause structure could be developed on the basis of (1). He begins by specifying a set of (innate) developmental primitives (1992, p. 90), as listed in (2).

(2) Developmental primitives:
   a. A learning mechanism that uses the 'old-rules-analyze-new-material' principle.
   b. Semantic categories such as 'argument' and 'predicate,' including ontological categories, for example 'object,' 'place,' 'action,' and 'event.'
   c. A tendency to classify words and phrases, not already classified, as referring to instances of the categories in (b).

The semantic categories of 'argument' and 'predicate' are derivative of the 'natural logic' categories mentioned in (1c). Neither of the primitives in (2a) or (2b) is unique to language. The learning process postulated by Braine (1992) is summarized in (3).

(3) Learning process:
   a. Child begins to parse sentences based on the semantic categories in (2b), yielding (for English) a parse tree like the one on the left in Figure 22.1.
   b. Encountering new sentences which do not fit the semantic prototypes (e.g., *The situation justified the measures*), the child applies the principles in (2a) and (2c) and assimilates such propositions to the patterns arrived at by principle (2b).
   c. Syntactic categories are generalized from semantic ones (noun from 'object,' verb from 'predicate,' adjective from 'property,' etc.).
   d. Result is a semantically based yet syntactic representation of clause structure, as in the right tree structure in Figure 22.1.

There is no need to posit either syntactic categories or basic principles of phrase structure in the LAD, because Braine's account shows how they can be developed on the basis of information in the input and the 'natural logic' system of mental representation. This is obviously only the first step in the acquisition of phrase structure, but it is a momentous one, since it involves the crucial leap from cognitive categories to strictly linguistic ones. Further examples of the application of cognitive

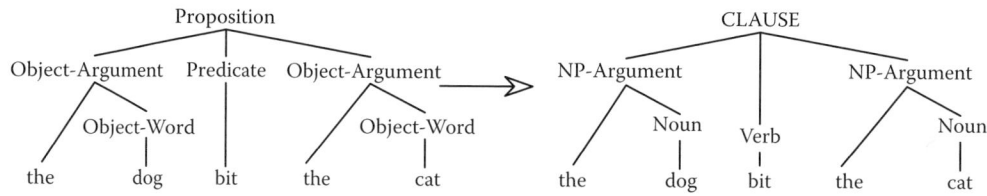

Figure 22.1 Transition from analysis in terms of ontological categories to syntactic categories.

principles to the acquisition of syntax can be found in Van Valin and LaPolla (1997, Epilog and the references therein) and Tomasello (2003), among others.

It is somewhat ironic that Chomsky's most recent position (Hauser, Chomsky, & Fitch, 2002; Fitch, Hauser, & Chomsky, 2005) is much closer to the position advocated by Slobin all along. By reducing the LAD/UG to the principle of recursion, most grammatical phenomena must be accounted for through the interplay of the linguistic faculty with other cognitive systems. Hence the kind of principles advocated by Slobin would now be part of the Chomskyan acquisition mechanism.

If it is the case that an autonomous LAD composed of abstract syntactic principles is not required for language acquisition, then what is the status of linguistic universals and UG?

THE NATURE OF UNIVERSALS

The generative notion of UG is a set of purely syntactic principles, which, in the Minimalist Program (MP; Chomsky, 1998, 2001), are invariant across languages; they constitute what is known as 'narrow syntax.' This crucially presupposes that there are in fact universally valid syntactic principles, and it is not at all obvious that this is the case. Three candidates for universal principles in the MP are MERGE, MOVE, and AGREE. MERGE joins two categories together to create a phrase. MOVE takes a category, copies it, and merges the copy into a higher position in the tree. AGREE involves checking features on two syntactic elements, e.g., subject-verb agreement. All of these would seem to be fundamental and essential grammatical operations in human language, but there is good reason to be skeptical about the universal validity of each of them, when facts from relevant languages are examined. MERGE takes two elements, a noun and a determiner or a noun phrase and a preposition, and forms a phrase, in these cases a noun phrase or a prepositional phrase. It is an essential part of MERGE that the two elements are structural sisters in the resulting structure. In many languages, especially Australian Aboriginal languages such as Dyirbal (Dixon, 1972), there is no requirement that elements which constitute what corresponds to a noun phrase or a verb phrase in familiar languages occur contiguous to each other; rather, the words in a sentence can occur in any possible order. This is illustrated in (4) from Dyirbal (all possible orders are grammatical).

(4) a. Baŋgul   yaṛaŋgu   balan   dyugumbil-Ø   buṛan.
       DET.ERG   man-ERG   DET.ABS   woman-ABS   saw[2]
    b. Dyugumbil baŋgul buṛan balan yaṛaŋgu.
    c. Yaṛaŋgu dyugumbil balan baŋgul buṛan.
       (all possible orders are grammatical)
       'The man saw the woman.'

The relevant point about these examples is that the determiner modifying a noun need not occur adjacent to the noun it modifies, and the verb can stand in any position with respect to the two noun phrase arguments. Only (4a) could be generated by MERGE; neither of the other two could be, nor could the majority of the other possible grammatical forms of this sentence. MOVE is posited

---

[2] Abbreviations: ABS 'absolutive case,' DET 'determiner,' ERG 'ergative case.'

to account for the phenomenon of displacement in human languages[3]; Chomsky (1998) characterizes displacement as a situation in which "the surface phonetic relations are dissociated from the semantic ones" (p. 35). As an example, consider a simple question like *What did you see?* The question word '*what*' is interpreted as the direct object of *see*, but it does not occur in the normal direct object position, that is, immediately following the verb. This is an instance of displacement. There are languages which lack displacement, such as Lakhota, a Siouan language of North America. The most obvious example of displacement is questions like the one discussed above, and in Lakhota the question word occurs in the same position as a non-question word noun phrase. This is illustrated in (5).

(5) a. Wičháša   ki   wíyą   ki   wayáke.
       man   the   woman   the   saw
       'The man saw the woman.'
    b. Wičháša   ki   tuwá   wayáka   he?
       man   the   who   see   Question
       'Who did the man see?'

Unlike English, the question word does not appear in the beginning of the sentence, and therefore there is no justification for positing the operation MOVE in Lakhota questions. In fact, there is no motivation for it anywhere in the grammar of the language (see Van Valin, 1987, 2003). In Chomsky's terms, there are no examples of the surface phonetic relations being dissociated from the semantic ones in the language. Hence, if there are languages without displacement, then there are languages in which there is no justification for claiming that MOVE exists in the grammar of those languages. Finally, AGREE involves checking inflectional features, such as person and number marking on a verb with the inherent person and number features of the subject. This is clearly an important grammatical operation in many languages, but there are languages (e.g., Thai, Mandarin Chinese) which have no inflectional morphology whatsoever and which exhibit no agreement phenomena at all. There is no empirical justification for postulating AGREE as part of the grammar of these languages. In sum, there are languages in which none of these three syntactic principles operates, and therefore they cannot be considered to be universal. It should be noted that it has recently been argued by Everett (2005) that there are languages which lack recursion in their syntax.

Advocates of the universality of these operations would reply as follows. MERGE applies in Dyirbal to generate (4a) only; all of the other variants are merely phonological variants generated by rules in Phonetic Form. Hence Dyirbal and languages like it are not a counterexample to the universality of MERGE. Languages like Lakhota do indeed have MOVE, just not overtly; it either operates in Logical Form after the structure is phonologically interpreted or involves the displacement of a phonologically null element. Hence it only appears that MOVE does not apply in such languages. Finally, the only difference between languages like Thai and Mandarin Chinese, on the one hand, and English, on the other, is that the morphemes carrying the agreement features are phonologically overt in English but phonologically null in the other languages. AGREE operates in these languages, even if there is no phonological indication of it. Thus, the claim of universality for these operations depends crucially on particular theoretical analyses and the existence of an extensive inventory of phonologically null elements, not on facts about languages.

Are there any purely syntactic principles which are universal? If by 'universal syntactic principles' is meant syntactic generalizations which are not reducible to, or strongly motivated by universal semantic or pragmatic principles, then the answer is 'no.' If, on the other hand, the question is, 'are there any universal grammatical properties of languages?' then the answer is 'yes.' Van Valin and LaPolla (1997) argue that there is a direct correlation between the degree of semantic motivation of a grammatical phenomenon and its potential universality: the higher the degree of semantic

---

[3] In Chomsky (2005) MOVE is merged with MERGE, which now comes in two varieties: external MERGE (traditional MERGE) and internal MERGE (traditional MOVE).

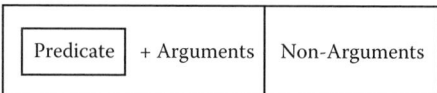

Figure 22.2   Basic distinctions underlying the layered structure of the clause.

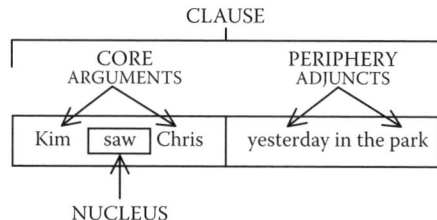

Figure 22.3   The layered structure of a simple English sentence.

motivation, the more likely it is to be universal or show very little crosslinguistic variation. In the remainder of this section, three examples of universal principles will be given, and they are all semantically motivated.

The first concerns universals of clause structure. While there are very good grounds for believing that the kind of phrase structure assumed for languages like English is not universal (see the Dyirbal examples in (4); Van Valin & LaPolla, 1997, pp. 17–25), there are nevertheless universal features of clause structure. All languages make two fundamental distinctions: the first is between predicating and non-predicating elements, and the second is among the non-predicating elements; some are semantically related to the predicate and others are not. In other words, all languages make the following contrasts: predicate vs. argument vs. adjunct. This is reflected syntactically in what in Role and Reference Grammar [RRG] (Van Valin, 2005) is called 'the layered structure of the clause.' The predicate is housed in the syntactic 'nucleus,' the nucleus plus the arguments of the predicate constitute the 'core' of the clause, and adjuncts occur in a periphery. This is illustrated in Figure 22.2, and these distinctions may be represented graphically for a simple English sentence as in Figure 22.3.

The semantic motivation for these syntactic units is summarized in Table 22.1.

These distinctions apply as readily to fixed word order languages like English as they do to free word order languages like Dyirbal, no matter what the order in a variant of (4) is; 'the man' and 'the woman' are core arguments, and 'see' is the predicate in the nucleus, just as in their English translation equivalents. The reason for this is that they are semantically motivated distinctions. And what is the ultimate motivation for the predicate vs. argument contrast? One of the fundamental functions of language is reference and predication, and because of this languages have to distinguish predicating from referring expressions, and this is reflected in the distinctions in Figures 22.2 and 22.3 and Table 22.1. Thus although the nucleus vs. core vs. periphery distinction is a true syntactic universal, it is semantically motivated.

The second phenomenon to be examined is reflexive binding, as illustrated in (6).

TABLE 22.1   Semantic Notions Underlying the Syntactic Units of the Layered Structure of the Clause

Semantic Element(s)	Syntactic Unit
Predicate	Nucleus
Argument in semantic representation of predicate	Core argument
Non-arguments	Periphery
Predicate + Arguments	Core
Predicate + Arguments + Non-arguments	Clause (= Core + Periphery)

(6) a. John looked at himself in the mirror.
    b. *Himself looked at John in the mirror.
    c. *John asked Mary to help himself (acceptable in Icelandic and many other languages).

Since reflexive constructions of this type involve two independent elements, the antecedent and the reflexive element, there are two fundamental issues to be resolved with respect to them: (1) what is the hierarchical relationship between them? and (2) what is the syntactic domain in which they both must occur? The answer to the second question must be syntactic in nature, but the answer to the first need not be. Semantic answers to the first question have been proposed in Jackendoff (1972, 1992), Van Valin and LaPolla (1997), and Van Valin (2005), among others, and the essence of the semantic answer is simple: the more agent-like argument binds the more patient-like argument, and not the other way around. This is exemplified in the contrast between (6a) and (6b). Why should this be the case universally? The answer follows directly from the meaning of the reflexive construction itself: a participant acts on him- or herself.[4] What about the syntactic domain question? Example (6c) is ungrammatical in English but grammatical in Icelandic and many other languages, and the issue of whether a reflexive element is 'too far' from its antecedent is not a semantic issue, since (6c) does satisfy the basic semantic requirement on reflexivization. Because the constraint on the syntactic domain of reflexivization is not a semantically motivated restriction, it is to be expected that there would be considerable crosslinguistic variation, and there is, as the variable grammaticality of (6c) across languages illustrates.

The final phenomenon is control, in which an argument in the main clause supplies the interpretation of a missing argument in a dependent clause. This is illustrated in (7).

(7) a. John persuaded Mary to wash the dishes.
    b. John promised Mary to wash the dishes.

The noun phrases *John* and *Mary* are constituents of the main clause, and the infinitival complement has no subject argument; one of the main clause noun phrases, the controller, supplies the interpretation of the missing subject. In (7a) *Mary* is the controller (i.e., the one who will wash the dishes), while in (7b) *John* is the controller. Is this the case in other languages as well? If so, why should the controller choice be the same across languages? Van Valin (2005, pp. 241–243) looked at these phenomena in Dyirbal (Australia; syntactically ergative, free word order), Sama (Philippines; syntactically ergative, fixed word order), Lakhota (North America; syntactically accusative), and Acehnese (Indonesia; syntactically split-intransitive), and found that in every instance, verbs meaning 'persuade' show the pattern in (7a) and verbs meaning 'promise' show the pattern in (7b), despite the manifest syntactic differences among the languages. This suggests strongly that the motivation for this pattern is semantic, not syntactic, and this seems to be the case. Verbs that take the (7a) pattern not only include verbs like *persuade*, *tell*, and *order*, but also physical verbs like *force* and *make*. Why should this be so? These are all causative verbs, with the causing action being either verbal (as with *tell* or *order*) or physical (as with *force*). In a causative event, one participant acts on another with the intention of causing the other participant to do some action or have a particular mental state. This may be represented as in Figure 22.4.

$$X \xrightarrow[\text{VERBAL}]{\text{PHYSICAL}} Y \xrightarrow{\text{DO}} Z$$

Figure 22.4 Structure of causative event.

---

[4] This is, of course, an oversimplification, but it reflects the core case of reflexivization. See Van Valin (2005), §§5.3, 7.5, for a discussion of a wide range of cases from a number of languages.

If the verb describes a causative event, then it will be participant Y that does Z, as in (7a); if the event is not causative, then this structure does not apply and X does Z, as in (7b).[5] Regardless of the syntactic type of the language, the patterns in (7a) and (7b) hold universally, and the explanation for them is semantic.

In this section it has been argued that there is good reason to doubt the universal validity of any purely syntactic principle; however, there are universally valid grammatical phenomena, which are motivated strongly by semantic principles. Since a primary function of language is to convey meaning from one interlocutor to another, it is hardly surprising, then, that the truly universal features of the grammars of human languages are semantically driven.

CONCLUSION: THE ALLURE AND ILLUSION OF UNIVERSAL GRAMMAR

The idea of a universal grammar goes back a long way, as Chomsky (1966) showed, and the prospect of capturing the universally valid features of human language has a tremendous intellectual allure. Positing a universal grammar is an attempt to explain why there are any universally valid features at all. Moreover, it appears to provide an answer to what Chomsky calls the poverty of the stimulus problem (i.e., the alleged underdetermination of the output of language acquisition by the input) if it is assumed that every human being has a copy of UG in his/her head that serves as a LAD. It is not clear at all, however, how a LAD consisting solely of the property of recursion solves the alleged poverty of the stimulus problem. Thus, the question this chapter addresses, does UG exist? actually deals with two quite different notions of UG: UG as a compilation of universally valid features of human languages (henceforth 'UG_{HL}') and UG as a mental construct (henceforth 'UG_{LAD}').

UG_{LAD} makes a crucial assumption that has already been discussed: the relevant universal notions are abstract, purely syntactic principles and categories which are not motivated by any communicative or processing concerns. If this is the case, then it is truly mysterious why such principles show up in all languages, unless they are part of a UG_{LAD}. After all, why should children consistently hit upon the same communicatively unmotivated analyses? Given this assumption, positing a UG_{LAD} is the only plausible explanation. But if one rejects this assumption and adopts the perspective argued for in this chapter and the one advocated by Slobin, the picture that emerges is entirely different. The fact that universals exist is a consequence of their semantic underpinnings. Clauses in all languages have a nucleus-core-clause layered structure, because this follows from the fundamental semantic opposition among predicates, arguments, and adjuncts, not because there is an abstract syntactic principle specifying it. Reflexive and control constructions work the way they do across languages because of the semantics of the constructions, not because of any abstract syntactic principles. Hence they are learnable. The rich cognitive endowment that children are born with plays a crucial role, as discussed in the section above. Braine's account of the learning of clause structure in (1)–(3) yields a structure that is in fact very close to the basic nucleus-core clause structure. In the right-hand tree in Figure 22.1, what is labeled 'clause' is actually the core, in RRG terms, and the syntactic label for the node containing the verb is 'nucleus,' yielding the fundamentals of the layered structure of the clause.

If it is the case that what children are learning are meaningful constructions and communicatively motivated categories and principles rather than meaningless and communicatively unmotivated abstract syntactic principles, then the poverty of the stimulus problem simply evaporates.[6] Information of all types, phonological, semantic and pragmatic, can play a crucial role in the acquisition of syntax; children learn language in an information-rich environment. Van Valin (1994) argued, for example, that subjacency, long a prime example of the poverty of the stimulus, is in fact learnable,

---

[5] See Van Valin (2005, p. 243) for a more technical formulation of the generalization.
[6] Slobin has often referred to this as the 'poverty of the imagination problem,' i.e., 'I can't imagine how this could be learned, so it must be part of the LAD.'

given an analysis in terms of the interaction of pragmatics and syntax, rather than in terms of abstract syntactic principles alone. It goes without saying that children pay attention to the language in their environment, to the language that is directed at them, despite Chomsky's claims to the contrary. They have no other input; they have the language to which they are exposed and the kinds of cognitive principles proposed by Slobin and others. In particular, they have no universal linguistic principles in their heads guiding acquisition. When children produce structures during acquisition for which there is no obvious model in the input, it does not follow at all that they are ignoring the input or that they have misidentified the language in terms of the possibilities that UG_{LAD} permits. A much discussed example of this is the production by some English-speaking children of long-distance WH-questions with a medial WH-word (e.g., *Who do you think who the cat chased?*) (Thornton, 1995), a feature of adult German and Hungarian but not adult English. This is not a case of these children thinking they are learning German or Hungarian. Rather, as Van Valin (1998) argues, these structures result from children attempting to mark a distinction overtly, which adult English speakers do not in fact mark morphosyntactically. They are making a reasonable hypothesis based on the data to which they are exposed, which turns out to be wrong.

So, does Universal Grammar exist? Yes and no. UG_{LAD} does not exist. UG_{HL} does exist, but as an abstraction, a convenient fiction, not as a part of any speaker's linguistic competence. It is the result of abstracting over language-specific constructions and other phenomena. Chomsky has claimed for the past 25 years that constructions are epiphenomenal and only the parameterized principles of UG_{LAD} are real, but the reality is more or less the opposite: UG_{LAD} doesn't exist, and UG_{HL} is an epiphenomenon generalized from the properties of language-specific constructions. UG_{HL} resides in linguists' theories, not in the heads of speakers.

REFERENCES

Braine, M. D. S. (1990). The 'natural logic' approach to reasoning. In W. F. Overton (Eds.), *Reasoning, necessity and logic*. Hillsdale, NJ: Lawrence Erlbaum Associates.
Braine, M. D. S. (1992). What sort of innate structure is needed to 'bootstrap' into syntax? *Cognition, 45*, 77–100.
Braine, M. D. S. (1993). The mental logic and how to discover it. In J. Macnamara & G. Reyes (Eds.), *The logical foundations of cognition* (pp. 241–263). Oxford, UK: Oxford University Press.
Braine, M. D. S. (1994). Is nativism sufficient? *Journal of Child Language, 21*, 9–31.
Bruner, J. (1983). *Child's talk: learning to use language*. New York: Norton.
Chomsky, N. (1959). Review of Skinner, *Verbal behavior. Language, 35*, 26–58.
Chomsky, N. (1965). *Aspects of the theory of syntax*. Cambridge, MA: The MIT Press.
Chomsky, N. (1966). *Cartesian linguistics*. New York: Harper & Row.
Chomsky, N. (1975). *Reflections on Language*. New York: Pantheon.
Chomsky, N. (1998). Minimalist inquiries: The framework. *MIT Occasional Papers in Linguistics, 15*.
Chomsky, N. (2001). Derivation by phase. In M. Kenstowicz (Ed.), *Ken Hale: A life in language* (pp. 1–52). Cambridge, MA: The MIT Press.
Chomsky, N. (2005). Three factors in language design. *Linguistic Inquiry, 36*, 1–22.
Dixon, R. M. W. (1972). *The Dyirbal language of north Queensland*. Cambridge, UK: Cambridge University Press.
Everett, D. L. (2005). Cultural constraints on grammar and cognition in Pirahã. *Current Anthropology, 46*, 621–646.
Fitch, W. T., Hauser, M. D., & Chomsky, N. (2005). The evolution of the language faculty: Clarifications and implications. *Cognition, 97*, 179–210.
Grice, H. P. (1975). Logic and conversation. In P. Cole & J. Morgan (Eds.), *Syntax & Semantics: Vol. 3. Speech acts* (pp. 41–58). New York: Academic Press.
Hauser, M., Chomsky, N., & Fitch, T. (2002). The faculty of language: What is it, who has it, and how did it evolve? *Science, 298*, 1569–1579.
Jackendoff, R. (1972). *Semantic interpretation in generative grammar*. Cambridge, MA: The MIT Press.
Jackendoff, R. (1992). Madame Tussaud meets the binding theory. *Natural Language and Linguistic Theory. 10*, 1–31.

Karmiloff-Smith, A. (1992). *Beyond modularity*. Cambridge, MA: The MIT Press.

Pinker, S., & Jackendoff, R. (2005). The faculty of language: What's special about it? *Cognition, 95*(2), 201–236.

Schlesinger, I. (1982). *Steps to language: Toward a theory of language acquisition*. Hillsdale, NJ: Lawrence Erlbaum Associates.

Slobin, D. I. (1973). Cognitive prerequisites for the development of grammar. In C. Ferguson & D. Slobin (Eds.), *Studies of child language development* (pp. 175–208). New York: Holt, Rinehart & Winston.

Slobin, D. I. (1979). *Psycholinguistics* (2nd ed.). Glenview, IL: Scott Foresman and Company.

Slobin, D. I. (1985). Cross-linguistic evidence for the language-making capacity. In D. Slobin (Ed.), *The crosslinguistic study of language acquisition*: (Vol. 2, pp. 1157–1256). Hillsdale, NJ: Lawrence Erlbaum Associates.

Thornton, R. (1995). Referentiality and WH-movement in child English: Juvenile D-linkuency. *Language Acquisition, 4*, 139–175.

Tomasello, M. (2003). *Constructing a language*. Cambridge, MA: Harvard University Press.

Van Valin, R. (1987). The role of government in the grammar of head-marking languages. *International Journal of American Linguistics, 53*, 371–397.

Van Valin, R. (1994). Extraction restrictions, competing theories and the argument from the poverty of the stimulus. In S. Lima et al. (Eds.), *The reality of linguistic rules* (pp. 243–259). Amsterdam/Philadelphia: John Benjamins.

Van Valin, R. (1998). The acquisition of WH-questions and the mechanisms of language acquisition. In M. Tomasello (Ed.), *The new psychology of language: Cognitive and functional approaches to language structure* (pp. 221–249). Mahwah, NJ: Lawrence Erlbaum Associates.

Van Valin, R. (2003). Minimalism and explanation. In J. Moore & M. Polinsky (Eds.), *Explanation in linguistics* (pp. 281–297). Stanford: CSLI.

Van Valin, R. (2005). *Exploring the syntax-semantics interface*. Cambridge, UK: Cambridge University Press.

Van Valin, R., & LaPolla, R. (1997). *Syntax: structure, meaning & function*. Cambridge, UK: Cambridge University Press.

23

The Canonical Form Constraint
Language Acquisition Via a General Theory of Learning

THOMAS G. BEVER
University of Arizona

"Poppa, Will you Stop That!"...."Sure."

Dan I. Slobin (1978, p. 52)

BACKGROUND

In the early 1970s, Dan Slobin acquired substantial funding to test the development of language comprehension strategies in several languages—English, Italian, Serbo-Croation, Turkish. This represented the intersection of our interests: his in developing a comprehensive theory of language acquisition, mine in the idea that early stages of acquisition depend on the creation of statistically supported behavioral strategies that short-cut syntactic knowledge. My laboratory's original finding was in English, based on a set of studies that had children act out simple sentences with puppets (a collaborative study with Jacques Mehler and Virginia Valian). Typical performance data showed that at age 2, children use a simple strategy that focuses primarily on the exact sequence Noun Phrase+Verb, interpreting that as Agent+Verb. By age 3–4, they rely both on a more elaborated analysis of word order and semantic meaning. Thus, at age 2, children interpret declarative and object cleft sentences, along with semantically unlikely sentences above chance: in these constructions, the noun immediately before the verb is in fact the agent. By age 4 their performance depends on two strategies (1):

(1) a. NV(N) = Agent, predicate (patient)
   b. Animate nouns are agents, inanimate nouns are patients.

(1a) represents a shift from assigning the noun immediately before the verb as agent to assigning the *first* noun in the overall sequence as agent. This maintains correct performance on simple declarative sentences, but a decrease in performance on sentence types in which the first noun phrase is not the agent (object clefts and passives). Typical data are summarized in Table 23.1.

The emergence of the two kinds of strategies accounts for the decrease in performance on semantically reversible sentences that violate the normal order of English (1a). The emergence of reliance

TABLE 23.1 Percentage Correct Interpretations of Simple Sentences by Children (Children Make Small Puppets Act Out Short Sentences. The Primary Measure Is Which Noun Is the Agent and Which the Patient: Chance Performance Is 50%)

	Age 2	Age 4
Semantically Reversible		
The dog bit the giraffe	90%	98%
It's the giraffe that the dog bit	87%	43%
The giraffe got bit by the dog	52%	27%
Semantically Irreversible		
The dog ate the cookie	92%	96%
The cookie ate the dog	73%	45%
The cookie got eaten by the dog	55%	85%

on semantic information accounts for the increase in performance on sensible sentences *(the dog ate the cookie)*, and the decrease in performance on semantically odd sentences *(the cookie ate the dog)*. The reliance on semantic factors at age 4 also can override the word order strategy, leading to correct performance on irreversible passives *(the cookie got eaten by the dog)*.

Although I was an interloper in the language acquisition enterprise, Dan embraced the idea of early childhood language processing strategies, and immediately asked the following questions: are the strategies universal? If so, do they differ in importance for each language? It is important (and amusing) to remember that before Dan focused his major research program on language acquisition, he was a charter member of George Miller's original psycholinguistics platoon, devoted to demonstrating the 'psychological reality' of transformational grammar (in its 'syntactic structures' manifestation of the day): a typical result was that passive sentences are harder to process than actives, presumably due to the additional, 'passive' transformation (Miller, 1962). In that role, Dan showed that in fact passive sentences are not harder than actives if they are semantically irreversible, i.e., adults follow the childhood strategy (1b) above (Slobin, 1966). This finding of Dan's had played a role in prompting me to think about processing strategies as distinct from rule-based syntactic computations (Bever, 1970). My idea was that children learn these strategies, based on their 'cue validity' in child-directed speech. I never went as far over the statistical cliff into an agrammatical abyss, as emerged in the later writings of Liz Bates and Brian MacWhinney, but the idea of separate-but-equal processing and rule systems became a constant theme in my language science program, even persisting today. Dan himself wrote about the processing issue in his foundational, short and brilliant introduction to psycholinguistics—based on the notes he wrote to help his students in the first post-transformational grammar course in modern psychology of language.

We all know that Dan Thinks Big. He was intrigued by the possibility that semantic and syntactic strategies are themselves learned, and continue to override syntactic processing, even in adulthood. So, Big Thinking in this case led to a month-long 'working' conference to develop the crosslinguistic materials and experimental methods to be used in the study. The conference brought together several professors (me, Dan, Sue Ervin-Tripp, Eve Clark) and graduate students (including a surprise visit from Liz Bates). There was nothing really special about a working conference, except that it was for a full month and its location was set in the dramatic hills just above Dubrovnik. This was at a time when Yugoslavia was still behind the Plastic Curtain. Enough said.

The resulting project involved long and complicated management, which Dan and students slogged through; and this is what we found in the end (Slobin and Bever, 1982):

(2) a. Children acquire processing strategies adaptive to the statistical regularities in the structure of their own language. Thus, in English what develops is sensitivity to word order, in Turkish, sensitivity to patient-recipient inflectional markers, and in Italian and Serbo-Croation, a mixture of the two kinds of linguistic signals.
   b. There is *some* acquired tendency for initial nouns to be taken as agents when the stimuli violate general syntactic properties of the language.

Let me now turn to an important and lasting theoretical implication of these findings: the necessity of a canonical form to make languages learnable, and how that constraint filters computationally possible languages to actually attested languages.

DO ADULTS USE A DERIVATIONAL AND RECURSIVE GRAMMAR?

The basic puzzle of acquisition is set by the undeniable fact of 'the poverty of the stimulus,' the fragmentary and often ungrammatical language, which children hear from their caretakers. No doubt there are many subtle cues, even subtle feedback when the child makes a linguistic error, but only a highly pre-tuned and hypothesis-forming system could make use of them to develop knowledge of syntactic rules and architectures. Of course, the first question is, *do speakers actually develop a generative grammar, or only a simulation of it?* This is the original question about psychological reality of grammar—if adult speakers do not actually use grammatical knowledge as part of their language behavior, we do not have to worry about how children might learn it. Fifty years of linguistic and psycholinguistic research and intuition have established the following facts about adult language behavior (3):

(3) a. Syntactic processes are indeed 'psychologically real,' that is, sentence level syntax plays a causal role in representations used in language comprehension and production.
   b. Syntactic processes are recursive and derivational: they range over entire sentences in a 'vertical' fashion (as opposed to serial) with successive re-applications of processes to their output. These properties have been true of every variant of generative grammar, from Syntactic Structures (Chomsky, 1957) to the Minimalist Program (Chomsky, 1995).
   c. Sentence behavior is instant and 'horizontal'—speakers believe that they comprehend and produce meaningful sentences simultaneously with their serial input or output. Comprehension certainly does not wait until the end of each sentence: production of a sentence does not wait until it is entirely formulated.

These three observations set a conundrum (4):

(4) a. Sentence processing involves complex computation of syntax with whole sentences as domain—*it is vertical*.
   b. Language behavior proceeds serially and incrementally—*it is horizontal*.

Standard processing models deal with one or the other side of the conundrum. Models which assign syntactic derivations as an initial stage of comprehension and production account for (4a) but not so well for (4b). Models which assign meaning via pattern recognition and completion account for (4b) but not for (4a) at all well.

Recently, Dave Townsend and I rehabilitated the classic comprehension model of analysis by synthesis to provide at least a logical solution to the conundrum (Halle & Stevens, 1962; Townsend & Bever, 2001). In this view, people understand everything twice, once by way of initial perceptual strategies such as (1a) and (1b), once by the assignment of a syntactic derivation. The analysis by synthesis architecture lays out the two processes as proceeding in time. First the perceptual patterns assign likely interpretations to sentences, using something like a pattern completion system in which initial parts of a serial string automatically trigger a complete template. Second, the initially assigned potential meaning triggers (and constrains) a syntactic derivation. Another way of stating this is that the two ways of accessing meaning and structure converge, roughly at the ends of major syntactic units. That is, as we put it, *we understand everything twice.*

In our book, we adduced a wide range of intuitive and experimental evidence supporting this view of comprehension, reviewing more than 500 references. Some examples include the following:

(5) a. The NVN template in English is extremely powerful and ineluctable. It explains the unacceptability of reduced relative sentences (e.g., 'the horse raced past the barn fell'; compare with 'the horse ridden past the barn fell').[1]
 b. We can recognize sequences as forming sentences using the initial perceptual patterns, only to subsequently realize that they are nonsense (e.g., 'More people went to Russia last year than I have').
 c. Processing is unevenly distributed across sentences, with the greatest load just at the end of major units (first demonstrated in Bever, 1970, later re-minted by Carpenter and Just, 1975 as 'end of clause wrap up').
 d. Empty categories are assigned to sentences in the temporal order that they are assigned derivationally: WH-trace, NP-trace, PRO.
 e. Full derivations that specify minor details of phrase structure are not available until a sentence is just completed.
 f. Semantic information can become available before syntactic information in a sentence.
 g. Discourse context processes can influence early semantic interpretation, but not syntactic assignments.
 h. Broca's aphasics can discriminate the grammaticality of sentences they cannot understand.
 i. Brain imaging studies show an early and late process, the first associated with assignment of surface patterns, the second with derivational syntactic assignments.

We adduced a full range of existing and new facts to support the model, indeed to support several of the surprising features. The reader is invited to consult the book for a full description (Townsend & Bever, 2001). Here I focus on one case study, the comprehension of syntactic passives (see 6).

(6) a. Athens was attacked.
 b. Athens was ruined.

Classically, the passive form of verbs can be differentiated into 'syntactic' vs. 'lexical' passives. Lexical passive participles (e.g., ruined) distribute in the same way as normal (stative) adjectives, motivating their categorization as lexically coded, stative-like adjective forms (see examples in 8). This motivates the decision that lexical passives are coded in the lexicon as separate lexical items. Thus the derivation of a sentence with a lexical passive, participle (e.g., 8a), is like that of a corresponding adjectival sentence (8 d).

(7) a. *Athens was quite attacked.
 b. *Athens looked attacked.
 c. Athens was being attacked.

(8) a. Athens was quite ruined.
 b. Athens looked ruined.
 c. *?Athens was being ruined.

---

[1] NVN = Noun Verb Noun; NP = Noun phrase.

d. Athens was quite large.

Syntactic passive participles (e.g., 'attacked' in 7c) do not pattern as adjectives (cf. 7a and 7b), but are analyzed as part of a true passive construction with a derivation. The corresponding surface forms from a derivation of syntactic passives in a theory that includes traces from movement look schematically like that in (9a), in contrast with lexical passive constructions that do not include a trace.

(9) a. Athens was attacked. [t-Athens]
  b. Athens was ruined.

Various studies have shown that there is some evidence that the trace is actually present in the mental representation of sentences with syntactic passives, and not present in sentences with lexical passives. Typical studies show that shortly after the trace, the antecedent of the trace is more salient, e.g., in a word probe paradigm. That is, there is a classic kind of psychological demonstration of the 'reality' of syntactic passive trace. At the same time, the evidence suggests that the trace does not acquire its force in the representation immediately, but only after about a tenth of a second (McElree & Bever, 1989; Bever & Sanz, 1997).

These facts are given a handy explanation in the analysis by synthesis model. On that model, both kinds of 'passives' are initially understood via a variant of the canonical sentence schema for English:

(10) N V (N) => agent/experiencer action/predicate

That schema initially misassigns 'attacked' as an adjective, part of a predicate phrase. That analysis, while syntactically incorrect, is sufficient to access a form of semantic information—modeled on the semantic interpretation schema for lexical passive adjectives. Thus, an initial comprehension of the sentence can be based on a syntactic misanalysis, which is eventually corrected by accessing the correct derivation. This sequence also explains the fact that the evidence for the trace appears only after a short time has passed.

The psycholinguistic experimental literature of the last two decades is rife with controversy over how quickly and effectively statistically reliable information is assigned during comprehension. Much of this controversy has been couched under the rubric of proving or disproving that connectionist associative models can account for language behavior without recourse to linguistic derivational rules. Often the researchers argue past each other or about different examples. While not a lot of light has come out of these efforts, they have documented that comprehenders are indeed sensitive to a wide range of statistically grounded information early in their comprehension. At the same time, experiments like the preceding ones on trace also demonstrate that derivational structures are assigned as part of the comprehension process. Thus, the 'inelegance' of the analysis-by-synthesis model in postulating two kinds of overlapping computational operations captures an evident fact that this is how people do it.

Aside from time consuming and often inconclusive experimental investigations, this model explains a number of simple and well known facts. Consider the following examples.

(11) a. The horse raced past the barn fell.
  b. More people have gone to Russia in the last decade than I have.

Our intuitions about each of these cases exemplify a different aspect of the analysis by synthesis model. The first (11a) reflects the power of the canonical form strategy in English, which initially treats the first six words as a separate sentence (Bever, 1970). This sentence is often judged ungrammatical by native speakers until they see some parallel sentences of the same formal structure or related to it:

(12) a. The horse ridden past the barn fell.
   b. The horse that was raced past the barn fell.
   c. The horse racing past the barn fell.

The example is pernicious in part because of the canonical form constraint, but also because recovering from the mis-analysis is itself complex: the correct analysis in fact includes the proposition that 'the horse raced' (i.e., was caused to race). Thus, as the comprehender re-works the initial mis-parse, the correct analysis reinforces the incorrect surface analysis on which 'the horse' is taken to be the subject of the embedded verb. This seduces the comprehender back into the mis-parse.

The second example above (11b, due to Mario Montalbetti) is the obverse of the first example. In the second example, the comprehender thinks at first that the sentence is coherent and meaningful, and then realizes that in fact it does not have a correct syntactic analysis. The initial perceptual organization assigns it a schema based on a general comparative frame of two canonical sentence forms—'more X than Y,' reinforced by the apparent parallel structure in X and Y ('… have gone to Russia… I have'). On the analysis-by-synthesis model, this superficial initial analysis gains entry to the derivational parse system, which then ultimately blocks any coherent interpretation.

I do not expect to have convinced the reader of our model via such simplified examples alone. In our book, we organize a range of experimental and neurological facts in support of the general idea that an early stage of comprehension rests on frequent statistically valid patterns, followed by a more structurally complete assignment of a syntactic derivation.

An important consequence of the model for linguistics is that it requires certain universal features of actual languages in order to work. Most important is the otherwise surprising fact that actual languages have a characteristic set of statistically grounded structural patterns at each level of representation. It further requires that complex constructions with intricate derivations be functionally homonymous with simpler constructions in ways that allow the simpler constructional analysis to convey the more complex meaning at an initial pre-derivational stage of processing. In the next sections, I will develop the implications of this for language learning and linguistic universals and relate it to cognitive science in general.

ANALYSIS BY SYNTHESIS IN LANGUAGE ACQUISITION

The model is inelegant in the sense that it solves the conundrum by fiat—sentence processing is both complex and fast because it is simultaneously handled by two systems, one fast and sometimes wrong, one slow but ultimately correct. Our achievement was not to create an elegant solution to the conundrum, but rather to show that humans solve it inelegantly. This model unites two historically competing observations in the cognitive sciences about the mind (13):

(13) a. Everything we do is based on habits.
   b. Everything (important) we do is based on symbolic computations.

These two insights have alternately dominated scientific dogma about the mind for two centuries. The analysis-by-synthesis model is an architecture that shows how the two insights might be integrated together in adult behavior. A corresponding model holds for the acquisition of complex behaviors, such as language. On that model, the child alternates (logically) between formulating statistical generalizations about the language, and formal derivational processes that account for those generalizations. The evidence from Slobin & Bever (1982) supports the first idea, while the child's ultimate mastery of the structure of language supports the second idea. In today's zeitgeist, many researchers are exploring the extent to which child-directed speech offers helpful statistical regularities that might guide the infant and child toward language, and also the extent to which infant pattern learning strategies might presage and facilitate language learning. Such recent research shows that the infant is indeed a good extractor of certain kinds of patterns, and that child-directed speech actually has many statistically grounded properties, which lead toward (but not all the way to) correct syntactic analyses (e.g., Curtin et al., 2005, for segmentation; Golinkoff 1975; Golinkoff et al., 2005; Mintz, 2002, 2003, 2006; Redington & Chater, 1998; Redington et al., 1998; Brent, 1996; Cartwright & Brent, 1997; Gerken, 1999). At the same time, there is now considerable research showing that infants are quite good at drawing statistical inference from the presentation of serial strings with various kinds of structure (Saffran et al., 1996; Saffran, 2001, 2003; Gomez & Gerken, 1999; Marcus et al., 1999); older children also show statistical sensitivity in developing grammatical and lexical ability (Bates & MacWhinney, 1987; Gillette et al., 1999; Moerk, 2000; Yang, 2006; Naigles & Hoff-Ginsburg, 1998).

At the same time, there are various schemes proposed as to how a richly endowed innate structural scheme might arrive at a correct grammar with very impoverished input data—the dominant acquisition scheme within the framework of generative grammar is 'parameter setting': this is the idea that all languages can be described by a set of parameters (e.g., right vs. left branching, Np V Np vs. Np Np V, prodrop vs. no prodrop)—by hypothesis, the child has the set innately, each with a default setting: the child's task in learning his/her language is to learn which parameters in his/her language have a non-default setting (Lightfoot, 1991; Pinker, 1984; Fodor, 1998, 2001; Fodor & Sakas, 2004).

My hypothesis and that of a few others who accept the idea that children in fact acquire generative grammar (e.g., Gilette et al., 1999; Gleitman, 1990; Papafragou et al., 2007) is that neither kind of scheme alone is adequate to the facts. On this view, acquisition is as inelegant as adult language behavior—it involves both formation of readily available statistical generalizations and the availability of structures to rationalize violations of those generalizations. This view converges onto a traditional view of learning—hypothesis formation and rejection/refinement of the hypothesis based on further data (Karmiloff-Smith & Inhelder, 1973).

This view requires that the child be presented with overwhelming statistical regularities in the language s/he hears, in order to facilitate the formation of statistical generalizations. This requirement explains several computationally eccentric facts about attested languages (14):

(14) a. Each language has a canonical surface form: In English this is essentially NP V (NP) (it can differ by language and is not always serial, as in Slobin & Bever, 1982).
b. Statistically, the canonical form has a dominant interpretation in semantic relations: In English this is NP V (NP) = Agent/experiencer, predicate, patient.
c. The canonical form interpretation is violated in a set of minority constructions: In English, this includes passives, raising, unaccusatives, middle constructions.
d. The minority constructions that violate the form can nonetheless be approximately correctly interpreted by application of the canonical form interpretation. (This is exemplified in the initial stages of comprehending passives, discussed above in examples (6)–(9).)

None of these properties follows directly from the computational architecture of grammar. Yet they are characteristic of languages. In English, the first property (14a) has been noted as the result of rule 'conspiracies,' which guarantee that sentences have the same surface form regardless of their thematic relations and derivation. In the case of English, the vast majority of sentences and clauses have a canonical form in which there appears to be a subject preceding a verb:

(15) a. The boy hit the ball.
b. The ball was hit by the boy.
c. It is the boy who hit the ball.
d. The boy was happy.
e. The boy seemed happy.
f. The boy was easy to see.
g. It was easy to see the boy.
h. Who saw the boy?
i. Who did the boy see?
j. Visiting relatives can be a nuisance.

The notion of such conspiracies is not novel, be it in syntax or phonology (cf. Ross, 1972, 1973a, b). In traditional derivational terms there has to be some kind of constraint on derivations such that they almost all end up with the same general surface form. This is despite the computational fact that each underlying or logical form could be reflected in a unique surface sequence. On our interpretation, such computationally possible languages will not be learned because they make it hard for the language learning child to develop an early statistically based pattern that it can internalize and use for further stages of acquisition.

This facilitates the formation of a surface schema based on statistical dominance of the pattern. The second property above (14b) relates that schema to a standard semantic interpretation. The third property is particularly important if the child is to discover that there are actual derivations in which a given surface form can express different patterns of thematic relations. The fourth property contributes further to the child's ability to interpret sentence types for which it does not yet have a syntactic analysis. For example, raising (16a) or passive constructions such as (16c) can be interpreted via a schema based on a simple preterite construction (16b and 16d).

(16) a. Harry seemed/looked/happened-to-be happy.
b. Harry was happy.
c. Harry was hit (by Bill).
d. Harry was happy (about Bill).

The combination of these characteristics guarantees that the child can transcend the 'poverty of the stimulus' problem—the child can create and then analyze his/her own set of form/meaning pairs based on these generalizations. In addition, this solves an important problem for any learning scheme, namely, the problem of how children understand sentences for which they do not yet have a correct syntactic analysis (Valian, 1999). The idea that the child maintains a list of grammatically unresolved sentences is unsatisfactory because any given list is heterogenous unless it is given some kind of prior ordering and structure. The analysis-by-synthesis model suggests that they rely on statistical patterns and occasional false analyses to generate an internal bank of meaning/form pairs which present a constant puzzle for coherent derivational analysis.

The example-generating role of such internalized patterns cannot be overemphasized. To some extent it mitigates the 'poverty of the stimulus' the fact that the child receives sporadic, errorful, and limited input to work with. It allows the child to generate new exemplars of acquired patterns, thereby expanding its internal data bank of slightly different meaning-form pairs to be analyzed syntactically. This partially resolves, or at least clarifies the problem of how children access positive and negative feedback as guides to their emerging syntactic abilities, even if they treat each sentence initially as a unique item. On this view, the child can attempt derivation of a construction based on a subset of sentences of a given general pattern, and then 'test' the derivational structure on other sentences of a similar pattern. (Choinard & Clark, 2003; Dale & Christiansen, 2004; Golinkoff et al., 2005; Lieven, 1994; Moerk, 2000; Morgan et al., 1995; Saxton, 1997; Valian, 1999).

Another important fact is that children know about the difference between how they talk and how they should talk grammatically. There are numerous anecdotes reporting this awareness. Slobin (1978) reported extended interviews with his child demonstrating a similar sensitivity: 'she rarely uses some of the [strong] verbs correctly in her own speech; yet she is clearly aware of the correct forms.' He reports the following dialogue at 4;7 (pp. 52–53).

Dan: Did Barbara read you that whole story?
...
Heida: Yeah
...
and
...
mama this morning after breakfast, read ('red')

Dan: You don't know when she what?
Heida:
...
she readed the book
...
Dan: M-hm
Heida: That's the book she read. She read the whole, the whole book.
the whole book
...
I don't know when she readed ('reeded')
...
Dan: That's the book she readed, huh?
Heida: Yeah
...
read! (annoyed)
Dan: Barbara readed you Babar?
Heida: Babar, yeah. You know cause you readed some of it too
...
she readed all the rest.
Dan: She read the whole thing to you, huh?
Heida: Yeah,
...
nu-uh, you read some.
Dan: Oh, that's right; yeah, I readed the beginning of it.
Heida: Readed? (annoyed surprise) Read!
Dan: Oh, yeah -read.
Heida: Will you stop that Papa?
Dan: Sure

Heida's complaint shows that she was aware of the distinction between the correct sentence form and his own dependence on forming the past tense with the regular ending. Awareness of this kind is consistent with the view here that the child develops statistical patterns as part of the overall acquisition process, of which s/he himself can be aware.

These facts and considerations offer an explanation for the set of peculiar facts above (14)—peculiar in the sense that the computational architecture of syntax does not in itself require any of the properties (14a)–(14d). Rather, those properties are functional if language learning is to proceed based on the formation of generalizations, and the subsequent analysis of syntactic derivations for sentences described by those generalizations. That is, those properties exist in attested languages because they make language learnable, using a general hypothesis formation procedure.

There are also implications for linguistic universals that have been taken to be part of universal grammar. A particularly clear example is the Extended Projection Principle (EPP, Svenonious, 2002; McGinnis & Richards, in press). This was first noted as the structural/configurational requirement that sentences in English and a few other languages must always 'look' as though they have subjects, even when the subject NP is clearly without semantic content (17) (cf. Lasnik, 2001; Epstein & Seely, 2002; Richards, 2003, for a general description).

(17) a. 'It' is raining.
b. 'There' are three men in the room.
c. 'It' surprised us that John left.
d. 'Es' geht mir gut.
e. 'Il' pleut.

The EPP is an embarrassment to syntactic theory, especially in the minimalist framework, because it simply has to be stipulated, rather than following from a minimal set of structure building principles. But, we can see that it actually can be interpreted as the instantiation of the canonical form constraint, not a structural principle, but a fact of attested languages that plays a role in their learnability.

Of course, a proposal like this requires fuller investigation to check out all the scientific nooks and crannies. Most important, I have not elaborated the general learning theory here in enough detail to be convincing on its own. But this discussion serves as an outline of how a simplified model of language acquisition, based on a general model of human learning, can explain universal properties of attested languages, including some properties that have been taken to be structural. When Slobin decided to explore the question of the child's acquisition of canonical forms in different languages, it began a scientific journey that showed the universality of such a stage. That, in turn, has licensed consideration of how such statistical generalizations in attested languages might be explained by a general acquisition theory, which develops not only those generalizations but also arrives at a structural knowledge involving derivations. That acquisition theory in turn can explain why many computationally possible languages do not exist. It also explains some specific apparent structural features of language. It explains the overwhelming feature of languages as used, displaying canonical forms with a canonical pattern of thematic relations, which nonetheless also have specific exceptions to those patterns.

REFERENCES

Bates, E., & MacWhinney, B. (1987). Competition, variation and language learning. In B. MacWhinney (Ed.), *Mechanisms of language acquisition* (pp. 197–193). Hillsdale, NJ: Lawrence Erlbaum Associates.

Bever, T. (1970). The cognitive basis for linguistic structures. In J. Hayes (Ed.), *Cognition and the development of language* (pp. 279–362). New York: John Wiley & Sons.

Bever, T., & Sanz, M. (1997). Empty categories access their antecedents during comprehension. *Linguistic Inquiry, 28,* 68–91.

Brent, M. R. (1996). *Computational approaches to language acquisition.* Cambridge, MA: The MIT Press.

Carpenter, P. A., & Just, M. A. (1975). Sentence comprehension. *Psychological Review, 82,* 45–73.

Cartwright, T. A., & Brent, M. R. (1997). Syntactic categorization in early language acquisition: Formalizing the role of distributional analysis. *Cognition, 63*(2), 121–170.

Chomsky, N. (1957). *Syntactic structures.* The Hague: Mouton.

Chomsky, N. (1995). *The minimalist program.* Cambridge, MA: The MIT Press.

Chouinard, M. M., & Clark, E. V. (2003). Adult reformulations of child errors as negative evidence. *Journal of Child Language, 30,* 637–669.

Curtin, S., Mintz, T., & Christiansen, M. (2005). Stress changes the representational landscape: Evidence from word segmentation. *Cognition, 96,*(3), 233–262.

Dale, R., & Christiansen, M. H. (2004). Active and passive statistical learning: Exploring the role of feedback in artificial grammar learning and language. *Proceedings of the 26th Annual Conference of the Cognitive Science Society, 26,* 262–267.

Epstein, S., & Seely, D. (2002). *Derivation and explanation in the minimalist program.* Malden, MA: Blackwell Publishing.

Fodor, J. (1998). Unambiguous triggers. *Linguistic Inquiry, 29,* 1–36.

Fodor, J. D. (2001). Setting syntactic parameters. In M. Baltin and C. Collins (Eds.), *The handbook of contemporary syntactic theory* (pp. 730–738). Oxford, UK: Blackwell Publishers.

Fodor, J. D., & Sakas, W. G. (2004). Evaluating models of parameter setting. In A. Brugos, L. Micciulla, & C. E. Smith (Eds.), *BUCLD 28: Proceedings of the 28th Annual Boston University Conference on Language Development* (pp. 1–27). Somerville, MA: Cascadilla Press.

Gerken, L. A. (1996). Phonological and distributional cues to syntax acquisition. In J. Morgan & K. Demuth (Eds.), *Signal to syntax: Bootstrapping from speech to grammar in early acquisition* (pp. 411–426). Mahwah, NJ: Lawrence Erlbaum Associates.

Gillette, J., Gleitman, L., Gleitman, H., & Lederer, A. (1999). Human simulation of vocabulary learning. *Cognition, 73,* 35–176.

Gleitman, L. R. (1990). The structural sources of verb meanings. *Language Acquisition: A Journal of Developmental Linguistics, 1*(1), 3–55.

Golinkoff, R. M. (1975). Semantic development in infants: The concepts of agent and recipient. *Merrill-Palmer Quarterly, 21,* 181–193.

Golinkoff, R., Pence, K., Hirsh-Pasek, K., & Brand, R. (2005). When actions can't speak for themselves: Infant-directed speech and action may influence verb learning. In D. Massaro, R. Calfee, J. Sabatini, & T. Trabasso (Eds.), *From orthography to pedagogy: Essays in honor of Richard L. Venezky* (pp. 63–79). Mahwah, NJ: Lawrence Erlbaum Associates.

Gómez, R. L., & Gerken, L. A. (1999). Artificial grammar learning in one-year-olds leads to specific and abstract knowledge. *Cognition, 70,* 109–135.

Halle, M., & Stevens, K. N. (1962). Speech recognition: A model and a program for research. RLE Reports: Reprinted in J. A. Fodor & J. J. Katz, (Eds.), *The structure of language: Readings in the philosophy of language.* Englewood Cliffs, NJ: Prentice-Hall.

Karmiloff-Smith, A., & Inhelder, B. (1973). If you want to get ahead, get a theory, *Cognition, 3,* 195–212.

Lasnik, H. (2001). A note on the EPP. *Linguistic Inquiry, 32,* 356–362.

Lieven, E. (1994). Crosslinguistic and crosscultural aspects of language addressed to children. In C. Galloway & C. J. Richards (Eds.), *Input and interaction in language acquisition* (pp. 56–74). New York: Cambridge University Press.

Lightfoot, D. (1991). *How to set parameters.* Cambridge, MA: The MIT Press.

Marcus, G. F., Vijayan, S., Bandi Rao, S., & Vishton, P. M. (1999). Rule-learning in seven-month-old infants. *Science, 283,* 77–80.

McElree B., & Bever, T. (1989). The psychological reality of linguistically defined gaps. *Journal of Psycholinguistic Research, 18,* 21–35.

McGinnis, M., & Richards, N. (Eds.). (in press). *Proceedings of the EPP/Phase Workshop.* Cambridge, MA: MIT Working Papers in Linguistics.

Miller, G. (1962). Some psychological studies of grammar. *American Psychologist, 17,* 748–762.

Mintz, T. H. (2002). Category induction from distributional cues in an artificial language: Grammatical categories in speech to young children. *Cognitive Science, 26*(4), 393–424.

Mintz, T. H. (2003). Frequent frames as a cue for grammatical categories in child directed speech. *Cognition, 90*(1), 91–117.

Mintz, T. H. (2006). Finding the verbs: Distributional cues to categories available to young learners. In K. Hirsh-Pasek & R. M. Golinkoff (Eds.), *Action meets word: How children learn verbs* (pp. 31–63). New York: Oxford University Press.

Moerk, E. L. (2000). *A first language taught and learned.* Baltimore: Brookes Publishing.

Morgan, J. L., Bonamo, K. M., & Travis, L. L. (1995). Negative evidence on negative evidence. *Developmental Psychology, 31,* 180–197.

Naigles, L. R., & Hoff-Ginsberg, E. (1998). Why are some verbs learned before other verbs? Effects of input frequency and structure on children's early verb use. *Journal of Child Language, 25*(1), 95–120.

Papafragou, A., Cassidy, K., & Gleitman, L. (2007). When we think about thinking: The acquisition of belief verbs. *Cognition, 105,* 125–165.

Pinker, S. (1984). *Language learnability and language development.* Cambridge, MA: Harvard University Press.

Redington, M., & Chater, N. (1998). Connectionist and statistical approaches to language acquisition: A distributional perspective. *Language and Cognitive Processes, 13*(2–3), 129–191.

Redington, M., Chater, N., & Finch, S. (1998). Distributional information: A powerful cue for acquiring syntactic categories. *Cognitive Science, 22*(4), 425–469.

Richards, N. (2003). Why there is an EPP. *Gengo Kenkyu, 123,* 221–256.

Ross, J. (1972). The category squish: Endstation Hauptwort. In P. Perntau et al. (Eds.), *Chicago Linguistic Society, 8,* 316–328.

Ross, J. (1973a). A fake NP squish. In C. Bailey & R. Shuy (Eds.), *New ways of analyzing variation in English* (pp. 96–140). Washington, DC: Georgetown University Press.

Ross, J. (1973b). Nouniness. In O. Fujimura (Ed.). *Three dimensions of linguistic theory* (pp. 137–257). Tokyo: TEC Corporation.

Saffran, J. R. (2001). Words in a sea of sounds: The output of infant statistical learning. *Cognition, 81*(2), 149–169.

Saffran, J. R. (2003). Statistical language learning: Mechanisms and constraints. *Current Directions in Psychological Science, 12,* 110–114.

Saffran, J. R., Aslin, R. N., & Newport, E. L. (1996). Statistical learning by 8-month-old infants. *Science, 274,* 1926–1928.

Saxton, M. (1997). The contrast theory of negative input. *Journal of Child Language, 24,* 139–161.

Slobin, D. I. (1966). Grammatical transformations and sentence comprehension in childhood and adulthood. *Journal of Verbal Learning and Verbal Behavior, 20,* 120–136.

Slobin, D. I. (1978). A case study of early language awareness. In A. Sinclair, R. Jarvella, & W. J. M. Levelt (Eds.), *The child's conception of language* (pp. 45–54). Heidelberg, Germany: Springer-Verlag.

Slobin, D. I., & Bever, T. G. (1982). Children use canonical sentence schemas: A crosslinguistic study of word order and inflections. *Cognition, 12,* 229–265.

Svenonius, P. (2002). *Subjects, expletives and the EPP.* New York: Oxford University Press.

Townsend, D., & Bever, T. G. (2001). *Sentence comprehension.* Cambridge: The MIT Press.

Valian, V. (1999). Input and language acquisition. In W. C. R. T. K. Bhatia (Ed.), *Handbook of child language acquisition* (pp. 497–530). New York: Academic Press.

Yang, C. (2006). *The infinite gift.* New York: Scribner.

24

Finiteness, Universal Grammar, and the Language Faculty[1]

WOLFGANG KLEIN

Max Planck Institute for Psycholinguistics (Nijmegen)

This is excellent research, but it's so terribly boring.

Dan I. Slobin (personal communication)

KANTIAN QUESTIONS

Die menschliche Vernunft hat das besondere Schicksal in einer Gattung ihrer Erkenntnisse: daß sie durch Fragen belästigt wird, die sie nicht abweisen kann, denn sie sind ihr durch die Natur der Vernunft selbst aufgegeben, die sie aber auch nicht beantworten kann, denn sie übersteigen alles Vermögen der menschlichen Vernunft (Immanuel Kant, 1781).[2]

If it is indeed the fate of the human mind to be haunted by questions which, by its very nature, it is not able to answer, then the study of human language has to offer some good candidates for such questions, for instance

– *What is the origin of language?*

Our species is the only one which nature, or God, has endowed with this remarkable gift. How and when did it come into existence?

– *Is there a 'Universal Grammar'?*

Do the many linguistic systems that mankind has developed over the millenia share some properties above and beyond the obvious ones, for example, that they have a lexicon and a grammar?

– *What is the relationship between language and the mind?*

---

[1] The editors asked us to begin with a short paragraph, briefly stating our relationship with Dan and the way in which this work is influenced by him or related to his work and interest. How can one explain 30 years of friendship and continuous discussion in a short paragraph? So, I thought I would simply try to write something in which the traces of this are found everywhere—and which Dan enjoys. —I wish to thank Christine Dimroth and Clive Perdue for helpful discussions. Thanks also to Leah Roberts who checked my English.

[2] 'Human reason, in one sphere of its cognition, is called upon to consider questions, which it cannot decline, as they are presented by its own nature, but which it cannot answer, as they transcend every faculty of the mind' (Kritik der reinen Vernunft, first sentence, translated by J. M. D. Meiklejohn).

We are the only 'speaking animal'—but we are also the only one who is able to divide by 17, to compose a symphony, or to put together a *Festschrift*. How is the gift of language related to these other talents?

These questions have been with us since the days of the Greek philosophers; they have been and still are the object of vivid discussion. But we are still very far from a generally accepted answer. Are they indeed of the Kantian type—that is, questions whose answer is beyond our intellectual capacities, just as algebraic topology is beyond the intellectual capacities of the average cow? This may well be. But there may be less dramatic reasons, for example, the lack of reliable empirical evidence. This holds obviously for the first question, the origin of language; the evidentiality marker that could mark the weakness of the evidence on this issue must still be invented. Maybe just this fact renders the question so popular. When the Societé de Linguistique de Paris was founded in 1866, it stated in its constitution:

> **Article 2**. La Société n'admet aucune communication concernant, soit l'origine du langage, soit la création d'une langue universelle. [The society does not admit any discussion on the origin of language or on the creation of a universal language]

But more than a century later, discussions are as vivid as ever, and the evidence is almost as thin as ever.

It is less obvious but no less true that our empirical knowledge about most of the world's about 6000 existing languages is quite limited. For how many of these do we have reliable descriptions? Let us assume that three grammars and three dictionaries suffice for a reliable description. Over the years, I have asked numerous colleagues how many languages meet this criterion. Estimates vary, but they go hardly beyond 100. This means that at most, 3 percent of the world's languages are well-described, 97 percent are not. Therefore claims about universal traits of human languages must be considered with caution.

But the main problem with the linguistic 'Kantian questions' are fundamental conceptual unclarities. What is 'language,' whose origin, whose universal properties, whose relation to the mind are at issue? Saussure once made a three-fold distinction, which is found in a great deal of later linguistic work. There is, first, 'la faculté de langage'—the language faculty, with which, pathological cases aside, we are all born. Second, there is 'la langue,' that is, the individual linguistic system such as Tzeltal or Chinese. And finally, there is 'la parole'—the product of linguistic knowledge in actual communication. Obviously, the question of the origin of language varies considerably with the notion of language at stake. It may well be that the necessary changes in our brain and other parts of our physiology occurred many thousand years before the first linguistic systems were created in some complex social activity. Similarly, very different components of the mind come into play, depending on whether we relate the mind to the 'language faculty,' to a particular linguistic system, or to actual communication.

In fact, the situation is more complicated. Consider the 'language faculty' whose study is considered by many to be the core task of linguistics. Under this view, it is not the structural or functional properties of specific linguistic systems which are at the heart of our endeavors, but the language faculty behind those properties. But does it really make sense to speak of the language faculty? It appears to me that here, too, at least a three-fold distinction must be made. There is, first, the capacity to construct a linguistic system—and that's what our ancestors had to do in the first place, as soon as their brain and other parts of their body, eyes, ears, larynx, hands, were ready for it. This capacity is not the same as the capacity to copy a linguistic system—and that's what we have to do in first or second language acquisition.[3] These two capacities are related but surely not identical. The types of social activities in which they operate are partly different, and so are probably the parts of our brain that are involved in them. It is one thing to learn that [rir] means 'to give audible

---

[3] Note that this is not the capacity to copy 'the input' but the regularities of the linguistic system which underlies the input.

expression to an emotion (as mirth, joy, derision, embarrassment, or fright) by the expulsion of air from the lungs resulting in sounds ranging from an explosive guffaw to a muffled titter and usually accompanied by movements of the mouth or facial muscles and a lighting up of the eyes' (according to *Websters' Third*), and another thing to invent a sound sequence or a gesture which among a group of people evokes a certain idea, a certain concept. There is, third, the capacity to use a linguistic system, once stored in the head, for communicative and other purposes. Note that we speak here of the capacity to use a linguistic system, not the actual use itself—'parole' or 'performance.' This capacity involves, for example, the integration of information encoded by the system and information that comes from context.

In other words, it is misleading to say 'There is a language faculty.' There are several such faculties—at least what we might call the Construction Faculty, the Copying Faculty, and the Communication Faculty. They share many characteristics, but they also differ in essential respects. They may well have different origins in the history of our species, and they may well bear different relations to what we consider to be the mind.

They also give rise to different interpretations of the notion 'Universal Grammar.' It may have taken the Construction Faculty a long time to develop particular structural devices, for example, subordination or, at a still later stage, extractions from subordinate structures. Should we understand by 'Universal Grammar' the set of structures which is shared by all linguistic systems developed up to a certain time, or should we rather see it as the set of features which are, so to speak, in the reach of the Construction Faculty, even if they are not found in all linguistic systems—perhaps not in a single linguistic system existing right now? In the words of the Scholars, does Universal Grammar consist of 'universalia actu' [an operative universal] or of 'universalia potentia' [a potential universal]?

How can all of this be related to the mind? The heated debates about the modularity of mind some years ago often give the impression that people know what they speak about when they argue that the mind is modular or not. But what, then, is the mind? The *Encyclopedia Britannica* 15th edition characterizes the human mind as 'the complex of faculties involved in perceiving, remembering, considering, evaluating, and deciding.' If it is correct, then 'the mind' is surely not something specifically human: cats and mice, too, perceive, remember, consider, evaluate, and decide. It appears to me that any attempt to determine the relationship between 'language' and 'the mind' is a hopeless enterprise. What we can do, perhaps, is to look at characteristic properties of linguistic systems, in particular, properties which are shared by all known linguistic systems, and ask how these are related to other capacities that appear to be unique to our species.

In this chapter I will have a look at such a property—finiteness, in the sense of 'finite' vs. 'non-finite' verb forms. This is perhaps an unexpected choice. Finiteness is not among the foremost candidates for a linguistic universal; in fact, a number of languages are generally considered to have no finite verbs, and hence no finiteness at all. But this reasoning may be premature. There are four reasons why I have chosen finiteness, rather than, for example, the distinction between nouns and verbs or recursive devices.

1. Finiteness is not what one might call a 'trivial universal,' such as the fact that all linguistic systems (a) couple sounds or gestures with meaning in (b) either elementary expressions ('lexicon') or complex expressions (brought forth by grammatical rules). These are indeed observed in all human languages, but they are also found in programming languages or flag codes.
2. All attempts to define non-trivial syntactic universals, for example, universal constraints on transformations, have not turned out to be very successful so far.
3. It is not trivial how finiteness could be related to other 'parts of our mind.' All known languages can express temporal and spatial relations, and all known languages have devices to relate the meaning of many expressions to the here-and-now of the speech situation. But temporality, spatiality, or deictic anchoring are also found in other domains of our cognition. It is also clear that compound linguistic expressions exhibit a 'hierarchical' structure, as described in terms of parts of speech, constituent structure, etc.; but other areas of human

cognition and action exhibit hierarchical structures as well, for example, composing a string trio or preparing a seven-course dinner. This is not true for finiteness, and therefore it might indeed be a purely linguistic universal.
4. Recent work in language acquisition has shown that the finiteness distinction plays an important role in the structure of early utterances in first as well as in second language acquisition (e.g., Dimroth & Lasser, 2002).

FINITENESS

Finiteness as an Inflectional Category

The notion of finiteness goes back to Priscianus' *Institutiones grammaticae*. He distinguished between expressions (verbs as well as nouns) which only specify general properties of objects or actions—bare lexical items, as it were—and expressions which apply to a concrete case. The meaning of these latter expressions is somehow 'delimited,' whence the term *finitum*. The original distinction is not particularly clear, and 1500 years of research has not really changed this, except that the term is no longer used for nouns. Finiteness is one of those notions that is used by everybody and understood by nobody. David Crystal (in Bright, 1992, IV, 299), for example, characterizes it as follows:

> **finite** Characteristic of a verb or construction that can occur on its own in an independent clause, permitting formal contrasts of tense and mood; contrasts with a **non-finite** verb or construction, which occurs on its own only in a dependent clause, and which lacks tense and mood contrasts; examples are infinitives and participles.

This definition mirrors the common understanding that finiteness is an inflectional category of the verb. Typically, it is not defined but introduced by means of some characteristic examples: *amor, amabis, amavisti* are finite, whereas *amare, amata, amavisse* are non-finite; and then, the intelligent student is supposed to generalize. And the intelligent student normally concludes that finiteness is an inflectional category of the verb.

This idea faces at least two substantial problems. First, the distinction between finite and non-finite is also made for languages in which it is hardly ever marked on the verb. English, the drosophila of linguistics, is a good example. With very few exceptions, such as *has* or *swam*, all finite forms can also be non-finite; and similarly, with the exception of the present participle and some irregular forms, such as *swum*, all non-finite forms can also be finite. Nevertheless, everybody considers *left* in *He left* as finite, and as non-finite in *He has left*. Some modal verb forms, such as *ought* or *can*, are unfailingly considered as finite, although they are not inflected all. Hence, finiteness cannot just be an inflectional category of the verb. Verb morphology is just one way to encode it.

Second, there are numerous syntactic, semantic, and pragmatic phenomena which go with finiteness. The most obvious of those is the 'Finiteness restriction':

(1) Finiteness restriction
A syntactically complex verb form can contain several non-finite forms but maximally one finite form.

In German, for example, it is possible to say *Er muss tanzen können*, whereas the English counterpart *He must can dance* is strictly forbidden. The restriction is not semantic: *He must be able to dance* is easily possible. But *can* is finite, and *must* is finite, and hence, the combination *He must can dance* is impossible. What is the reason for this restriction?

There are many other 'finiteness phenomena,' and in what follows, I will go through some of them. Examples are mostly from German because it has a relatively clear and consistent marking of finiteness.

Syntactic Properties of Finiteness

There is a long-standing discussion about the basic word order in German—is it SOV or SVO? The facts are relatively clear and can, minor complications aside, be described by three rules:

(2) Basic word order
   a. In declarative clauses, the finite verb is in second position.
   b. In subordinate clauses, the finite verb is in final position.
   c. In yes/no questions and in imperatives, the finite verb is in initial position.

Since the basic word order is usually determined with respect to declaratives, immediate observation speaks for SVO. But note that all three rules in (2) are only correct with reference to the finite verb: a sentence can have many verbs, but only one finite verb, and this one is decisive. Now, a finite verb such as *kam [came] or schlief [slept]*, merges a finite component, abbreviated fin, and a lexical component, abbreviated V (the latter specifying its argument structure and its descriptive properties). When fin and V are separated, then it is easy to see that fin is relevant for word order:

(3) a. *Gestern ist Isolde zum ersten Mal gekommen.*
       Yesterday has Isolde for the first time come.
    b. *..., obwohl Isolde gestern zum ersten Mal gekommen ist.*
       ..., although Isolde yesterday for the first time come has.
    c. *Ist Isolde gestern zum ersten Mal gekommen? Sei nicht traurig!*
       Has Isolde yesterday for the first time come? Be not sad!

Hence, German is neither SOV nor SVO—it is 'fin-second'; the verb as a carrier of lexical information is irrelevant in this regard. Similarly, subordinate clauses are 'fin-last'; yes-no-questions and imperatives are 'fin-first.'[4] This points to another important fact: there appears to be a close connection between finiteness and the illocutionary role of the clause: A sentence can only express an assertion when fin is in second position.[5]

A second syntactic property that goes with finiteness is 'licensing,' i.e., the fact that some element can only show up if some other element is present. In German, finiteness functions as a licensor for the grammatical subject as well as for expletive elements.[6]

(4) Licensing
   a. No explicit grammatical subject without finiteness.
   b. No expletive element without finiteness.

There are a few exceptions to (4a), for example:

---

[4] Note that this entire reasoning applies analogously under the assumption that, on some deeper level of description, the word order is SOV, and then V is 'moved' into its various positions. In this case, what is moved is fin, and if it so happens that fin and the lexical component of the verb are realized in one morphological form, then both components are 'moved.'

[5] This does not mean that sentences with fin in second position are necessarily assertions. First, there may be other markers (such as a wh-word) that lead to a different illocutionary role, and second, the position of fin must be accompanied by an intonational fall at the end.

[6] Neither the term 'subject' nor the term 'expletive' is clearly defined across languages (in fact, not even within languages); therefore, the following two constraints should be read with some caution: there may well be items called 'expletive' which need no such licensing (Nigel Duffield pointed out this problem to me). This, incidentally, is a very general problem of cross-linguistic claims. Consider, for example, the 'Binding principles' of generative grammar, which, subject to parameterized variation of the notion 'governing category,' are supposed to be universals. Thus, binding principle A states that anaphors are bound by their governing category. In English, anaphors are words such as himself or each other. But I am not aware of a language-independent definition of 'anaphor' (except that it is an element which is bound by its governing category—which would render the principle circular).

(5) *Ich eine Krawatte tragen—niemals!*
    I wear a necktie—never!

Sentences like (5) have a peculiar flavor. They describe a state of affairs without either taking a stand on its truth, as in an assertion, or challenging someone else to do this, as in a question, or instructing someone to do something which would make it true, as in an imperative: They raise a topic but lack an illocutionary role.

How could finiteness be related to the presence of an expletive element or a grammatical subject? It could be a matter of the argument structure, i.e., finiteness introduces a new argument variable that is required for the subject or for the expletive; or it could have to do with the informational status of expletives and grammatical subjects. At least in the case of the subject, the first hypothesis is not plausible: the grammatical subject clearly fills an argument variable provided by the non-finite component of the verb, for example, the agent, if the lexical verb is agentive. But typically, the grammatical subject not only matches one of the verb's argument slots, it also has *topic status* in the utterance. Similarly, expletive elements typically lead to a particular information structure. Thus, the two licensing constraints appear to be connected to what counts as 'topic information' in the utterance: there is no 'topic slot' without finiteness.

We may sum up these observations in two points:

1. Finiteness is not just an issue of verb inflection; it is deeply rooted in the way in which utterances are structured. We must distinguish between the 'finiteness' and the way in which it is encoded in a particular language, e.g., by verb inflection.
2. Finiteness is connected to the 'illocutionary status' of the sentence and the 'topic-status' of constituents.

Semantic Properties of Finiteness

Specific and Non-Specific Interpretation of Noun Phrases

Indefinite noun phrases such as *a castle, three castles* can have both a specific and a non-specific reading. Some verbs enforce a specific reading, when the noun phrase is in object position; other verbs do not resolve the ambiguity regarding specificity:

(6) a. *Marke kaufte ein Schloss.*
       'Marke bought a castle.'
    b. *Marke suchte ein Schloss.*
       'Marke looked for a castle.'

In (6b), Marke may have tried to find a particular castle, for example, one in which he suspects Tristan and Isolde are hidden; or he may have tried to find something which meets the properties of being a castle. In (6a), only the first reading is available. Since the two utterances only differ in the lexical meaning of the verbs *kaufen* 'buy' and *suchen* 'search,' the difference in the NP interpretation is usually related to the difference between these two lexical verbs. Quine, who first studied this phenomenon, dubbed verbs of the type *kaufen* as transparent, and verbs of the type *suchen* as opaque. Note now that *kaufte* and *suchte* in (6) are finite, hence, they include V, the carrier of lexical content, as well as fin. When the verb is not finite, the difference disappears:

(7) a. *Es ist teuer, ein Schloss zu kaufen.*
       'It is expensive to buy a castle.'
    b. *Ein Schloss zu kaufen, passiert einem ja nicht sehr oft.*
       'To buy a castle, does not happen very often to you.'

Here, the direct object has a specific as well as a non-specific reading, although the verb is transparent. The difference shows up again, if the indefinite noun phrase is in the scope of some 'higher' transparent or opaque finite verb (note that the lexical character of the non-finite verb, here *kaufen*, is irrelevant):

(8) a. *Marke gelang es, ein Schloss zu kaufen.*
   'Marke succeeded to buy a castle.'
   b. *Marke wünschte, ein Schloss zu kaufen.*
   'Marke wished to buy a castle.'

In other words, finiteness is somehow crucial for specific interpretation of indefinite noun-phrases. Consider now (9):

(9) a. *Dreimal hat Marke ein Schloss gekauft*
   'Three times has Marke a castle bought.'
   b. *Marke hat ein Schloss dreimal gekauft.*
   'Marke has three times a castle bought.'

In (9a), three different times in the past are talked about. About each of them, it is said that Marke bought a castle at that time. There is a t_1-castle, a t_2-castle, and a t_3-castle bought by Marke. It could be the same castle, but it need not. This means that 'specificity' is relative to the times about which something is said—it is relative to 'topic times,' in other words. We may state this as a restriction on the interpretation of indefinite noun phrases:

(10) Indefinite specificity reading
   'Specific' means 'unique with respect to a topic time.'

In (9b), the adverbial is in a different position. The assertion relates to a—possibly very long—time in the past, which is assumed to include three castle-buying situations. But there is only one topic time, and therefore, the castle is normally understood to be the same: Since 'specific' means 'unique with respect to the topic time,' there is only one entity since there is only one topic time.

How is this connected to finiteness? Non-finite constructions such as *to buy a castle* selectively describe a buying situation (omitting the buyer). But they do not link this situation to some topic time, and no assertion is made that such a buying situation obtains at such a time. Hence, the term *a castle* is not confined to a specific reading: it is not 'topic time unique.' In brief: No finiteness—no topic time, and no topic time—no specificity. Somehow, finiteness links the descriptive content of the entire sentence to the topic time.

Tense Traditionally, tense is often connected to finiteness. But what is tense? Under its received definition, it is a deictic time-relational category of the verb, whose function is to locate the situation described by the clause to the time of utterance. Thus, in *The Pope was ill*, his being ill is placed into the past; in *The Pope is ill*, it is said to encompass the time of utterance; and in *The Pope will be ill*, it is in the future. This seems so obvious that one is almost embarrassed to mention it. But in fact, it cannot be correct in general. Consider (11):

(11) (*Why didn't the Pope give an audience yesterday?*)—*He was ill.*

This does not assert that his illness precedes the time of utterance; it could as well include it, that is, he could still be ill. And in *The Pope was dead*, it is almost certain, even for the Pope, that he is still dead at the moment of speech—a function which is normally assigned to the present tense.

The function of the preterite is rather to assert (or to ask) something about some particular time span in the past, and about this 'topic time,' it is said that he was ill. The 'time of the situation'— the time at which the state of affairs described by the non-finite component obtains—can be much longer; but nothing is said about that. In other words, tense serves to mark whether the topic time precedes, contains, or follows the time of utterance. The time of the situation in turn may precede, contain, or follow the topic time. I think it is this relation between topic time and situation time that underlies the traditional notion of (grammatical) 'aspect.'

If finiteness introduces a topic time, and if tense imposes a temporal restriction on how the topic time is situated relative to the here-and-now, it should not be surprising that tense and finiteness can be clustered in one form, and this is indeed what happens in many languages.

Prosodic Properties of Finiteness

If we want to describe what some expression contributes to the meaning of the entire construction in which it appears, then it often helps to contrast this expression to some other expression by intonation. What happens when the highlighted expression is a finite verb, which merges V with fin:

(12) *Tristan LAG auf dem Sofa.*
    'Tristan was lying on the sofa.'

Intuitively, the contrast can go in three directions:

(13) a. *(Er saß nicht auf dem Sofa). – Er lag auf dem Sofa.*
       'He was not sitting on the sofa.' 'He was lying on the sofa.'
    b. *(Er liegt nicht auf dem Sofa). – Er lag auf dem Sofa.*
       'He is not lying on the sofa.' 'He was lying on the sofa.'
    c. *(Er lag nicht auf dem Sofa). – Doch, er lag auf dem Sofa.*
       'He was not lying on the sofa.' 'Oh yes, he was lying on the sofa'

In (13a), the highlighting targets the lexical meaning of the bare verb *lieg* 'lay'-, in contrast to *sitz* 'sit'-. In (13b), the highlighting targets the tense component of *lag*; the topic time is in the past, rather than right now. The most interesting case, though, is (13c): the contrast is between 'his lying on the sofa is not asserted - is asserted.' Thus, fin is the carrier of tense and of assertion: it relates the descriptive content of the sentence, as described by its non-finite part ('Tristan lay on the sofa') to a topic time, and it asserts that this descriptive content—the mere proposition, so to speak—obtains at that time.

Not all sentences with a finite verb express an assertion. Other illocutionary roles may come into play, for example, questions or imperatives, in which, as we have seen, fin has a different position and perhaps a different intonation. Or else the assertion is somehow overruled by higher functional elements, which give the clause a different status, for example, in temporal clauses or in relative clauses. These important issues will not be pursued here. Instead I will try to put the core notion of topic time into a somewhat wider perspective. So far, it has been assumed that fin relates the 'bare proposition' to the topic time: is it just the topic time, or are there other topic components which play a role in connection with fin?

The Topic Situation

Is the following assertion, uttered here and now, true or false?

(14) *Es gab keinen Wein mehr.*
    'There was no more wine.'

Even if you know German perfectly well, and even if you know what the world is, was, and will be like—maybe even what all possible worlds are like—you are not able to answer this question. To achieve this, you must know about which situation the person who utters (14) is talking. Depending on this information, the answer is 'yes' or 'no.' Every assertion is relative to a topic situation. The topic time is but one of the parameters which fix this topic situation; others are the place talked about, the entity talked about (often encoded as grammatical subject), or even the world talked about (real world vs. some fictitious world). The necessary information about the topic situation may come from context, but also from the utterance itself; in this case, the 'topic-hood' is often marked, for example, by position, by special particles, or perhaps by other devices.

Finite Utterance Organization

Our observations so far lead to an incipient picture of the role of finiteness. For an utterance to fulfill an illocutionary function, such as making an assertion, it must encode three meaning components:

1. A topic component. It minimally includes a 'topic time'; it is plausible that it also contains a 'topic world' and a 'topic place.' Optionally, other elements can be added, for example, a 'topic entity,' typically realized by the grammatical subject.
2. A (non-finite) sentence base. Minimally, this is a (non-finite) lexical verb, whose argument slots are filled appropriately. Other elements, such as adverbials, particles can be added.
3. A linking component. It relates the sentence base to the topic component, for example, by indicating that the former holds at the latter. This is the function of 'finiteness.' The exact type of linking requires additional means, for example, the choice of a particular position or intonational cues.

These components can be encoded in different ways. In many languages, finiteness and topic time are jointly expressed by verb inflections. Similarly, finiteness and the 'topic world' can be brought together by verb inflection—resulting in the category of mood (cf. Crystal's definition from page 336). But languages may have very different devices, grammatical as well as lexical, in which they encode this overall structure.

If this picture is essentially correct, then it suggests explanations of a number of facts which initially seem unrelated and which otherwise are completely mysterious, such as the reason why subjects and expletives typically must be licensed by finiteness, or why specific readings of noun phrases depend on finiteness. It is also completely in line with the 'finiteness restriction' stated on page 336: there is only one such linking between topic component and descriptive content in a sentence. It also raises a number of problems, for example, about the role of finiteness in subordinate clauses. I will not follow up these problems here but return to the Kantian questions from page 333.

FINITENESS AND UNIVERSAL GRAMMAR

Finiteness is a not peripheral property of some inflectional systems; it is a fundamental organizational principle of human languages with numerous important consequences in syntax, semantics, and pragmatics. This principle can be 'language-specific' in one of two ways: it is either

(a) specific to linguistic systems, in contrast to other manifestations of the human mind, or
(b) specific to particular languages or universal.

As was pointed out in the first section, there is no agreement on what the human mind is and what its various manifestations are. But we can look at some other activities, which we feel are uniquely human, and ask whether they involve a similar organizational principle. In all cases I can think of, the answer is negative. Consider, for example, the ability to divide by seven, the ability to cook pea soup, the ability to design a tuxedo, the ability to play straw poker (whatever this is), and so on. I see no evidence that organizational principles similar to finiteness are found in these activities. There is one potential exception—pointing, in the sense of intentionally directing another person's attention to some object or action in the environment and thus somehow introducing a 'topic.' But pointing alone does not have the organizational power of finiteness. As an organizational principle, finiteness is specific to linguistic systems.

Is it found in all human languages? Most structural universals are fairly trivial: linguistic systems consist of expressions, which combine sounds, gestures, or some other 'carrier' with meaning that can be simple or compound. There are other, less trivial candidates like recursion and, as a consequence, the possibility of constructing infinitely many sentences. I think that this possibility may be a bit overrated: after all, each apple tree is 'recursive,' because each branch can have another branch. But recursion is often considered to be a highlight of human language, in contrast to other communicative systems. Imagine now a language English,° which is exactly like English except that it lacks subordination and other recursive devices. Would we say that English° is not a human language? I think not: it is still a product of the human language faculty, although its structural and communicative potential is reduced. In fact, it may have taken many millenia in the history of mankind before the first devices that make recursion possible were created. Thus, recursion, finiteness, and perhaps other principles are something like 'universalia potentia'—organizational principles which the human language faculty is able to construct, copy, and process.

The notion of Universal Grammar can be construed in at least two ways. It can be a set of structural or functional properties that are found in all linguistic systems; or it is a set of constraints that state which properties are excluded from such systems, that is, which are beyond the range of what our language faculties can construct, copy, or use. Both notions of Universal Grammar lead to serious problems as soon as we go beyond the trivial. I think we should therefore stop the quest for Universal Grammar and be happy to look for non-trivial and 'interesting' principles which underlie the design of linguistic systems—interesting in the sense that they are not marginal properties of a particular language but have numerous consequences for the syntax, semantics, and pragmatics of many linguistic systems. Finiteness is such a principle.

We may call such principles elements of 'Universal Grammar,' because they are somehow fundamental to the structure of human languages. Or we may simply call them 'important principles of linguistic systems.'[7] In any case, this is only a matter of terminology.

UNIVERSAL GRAMMAR AND THE HUMAN LANGUAGE FACULTY, OR: THE PROPERTIES OF THE BREAD ARE NOT THE PROPERTIES OF THE BAKER

Suppose that there are indeed principles of Universal Grammar beyond the obvious, of which finiteness may be one. What does this mean for our understanding of the human language faculty? The answer, I believe, is: close to nothing. There are two reasons. First, there is not one language faculty—there are several, and the question of how universal, language-specific principles are related to the 'language faculty' is a different one, depending on whether we mean the Construction Faculty, the Copying Faculty, or the Communication Faculty.

The second reason why non-trivial universal principles do not tell us very much about the human language faculties is very different. In linguistics, it has become common to set 'Universal Grammar' and the 'language faculty' in parallel. In Chomsky's words:

> the language organ is the faculty of language (FL); the theory of the initial state of FL, an expression of the genes, is universal grammar (UG); theories of states attained are particular grammars; the states themselves are internal languages, 'languages' for short. (Chomsky 2002, p. 64)

---

[7] Other 'important principles' are, as we have argued in Klein and Perdue (1997), for example, 'Focus last' or 'Agent first.' In contrast to finiteness, they are already found in very elementary learner systems.

This is what one might call the 'Structural Analogy Fallacy.' Universal properties of linguistic systems, just like specific properties of linguistic systems, are a product of our linguistic faculties, and we must never confuse the properties of a product with the properties of its producer. Here, as elsewhere, the relation between product and producer is one of causation, rather than of structural similarities. This also applies when the product itself is a capacity that can be used to bring forth other products. Thus, the capacity to process linguistic knowledge and to use it for communicative and other purposes—the Communication Faculty—is a product of the Construction Faculty and the Copying Faculty, and at the same time, it allows these faculties to do more of their job.

My mother's apple pie, an old-fashioned wig, and Michelangelo's 'David' have something in common—they all are hand-made. No analysis of all of these and similar objects tells us much about the shape of the hands, or the neural mechanism that controls them. In this case, the products are artifacts. But the same considerations apply to 'natural' products. Chlorophyll is green, but the genetic information which leads to its production in plants is not green. Linguistic systems share properties of artifacts and natural products, and opinions are at variance as to how the relation between both sides should be seen; but in any case, they are products. Finiteness is a property of these products. It is neither in the mind nor in the brain, although the human brain brings about linguistic systems, which, in turn, make finite constructions possible. It is a property of utterances, brought about by the ability to integrate the expressions into the flow of discourse and to invent or copy grammatical and lexical devices which encode this integration.

CONCLUSIONS

When we say that our species is the only one born with the 'language faculty,' then this means that there are several components in the human brain, whose joint effort allows us

- to construct systems of linguistic knowledge,
- to copy linguistic knowledge from others, including its storage in the brain, and
- to integrate this knowledge into the flow of ongoing information.

Each of these capacities involves many subcomponents, such as memory access and motor control, and each of these may be affected, with specific results for the interaction.[8] They also may change in different ways over the life span. Adult second language learners maintain the ability to pair sounds or gestures with meanings, and they maintain the ability to form complex expressions—at least for a long time. But their ability—and perhaps their willingness—to do this in exactly the same way as is done in the input diminishes over time. Adults do it, but like Frank Sinatra, they can say 'I did it my way.' Age appears to affect the Copying Faculty much more than the Construction Faculty. This suggests that to some extent, different parts of the brain are involved in both faculties. It is even more obvious that the Communication Faculty requires different neural activities, for example, all of those that are needed to monitor and integrate contextual information.

All three language faculties are products of our brain—products which in turn bring forth other products, namely, linguistic systems or, in the case of the Communicative Faculty, utterances that are integrated into the flow of discourse. Many of the brain components, which produce these three capacities, are also involved in other tasks which our species is able to achieve, such as playing dominoes, creating religions, and frying eggs. Each of these non-linguistic abilities is a product of the

---

[8] Thus, if a subcomponents drops out, for example, due to a genetic deficit, then this does not say very much about the three language faculties in their entirety. If a spark-plug does not work, then the car does not work, or does not work properly. But the spark-plug is but a little component in a complex machine.

human brain. It appears to me that it is not only an ill-defined but also a relatively fruitless task to compare these products of the human brain with one of its other products—linguistic knowledge.[9]

These considerations have a number of substantial consequences. First, it should be clear that principles of Universal Grammar tell us practically nothing about the human language faculties, just as little as the in-depth and comparative study of bread and cake tells us little about the brain and the hand of the baker. Even if it could be shown that all breads have a crust, this does not mean that the baker has a crust.

Second, just as the study of the baker's hand and brain tells us little about the bread and the cake, physiological research, in particular brain research, tells us little about the structure of human languages. It is interesting in its own right, but it sheds no light on the way in which finiteness, or whichever important organizational principle, helps to structure utterances, let alone on questions such as how Chinese argument structure or Inuktitut verb inflection is organized. This does not mean that research on the 'language side' of the brain is irrelevant. It is just a different issue. It can tell us where certain types of linguistic knowledge are stored and how they are activated under specific conditions. But it cannot tell us anything about this linguistic knowledge itself. Religious systems are also stored somewhere in the brain, and they are accessed under specific conditions; but studies on location and processing of religious beliefs in the left temporal lobe, or wherever else, do not really inform us about these beliefs. It is one thing to believe whether Virgin Mary went straight to heaven, the only infallibility decision of a Pope so far, and another to know where this belief is stored in the cells and how it is processed as need arises.

Third, if we want to understand the various human language faculties, the 'producers' rather than their products, then we should investigate them 'on the job'—that is, when they create linguistic knowledge, a case that is rarely observed in our times; when they copy linguistic knowledge, a case that is regularly observed in language acquisition; and when they integrate linguistic knowledge into the flow of information, and that's what we do every day when we speak and listen.

In the first place, however, the linguist should be pleased to study the many structural and functional properties of linguistic systems, what they have in common and what they do not share, how they are processed, and how they are acquired. And in view of the little we really know about all of these issues, studying any of them should be enough of a challenge.

REFERENCES

Blom, E. (2001). *From root infinitive to finite sentence*. Phil. dissertation: Utrecht.
Bright, W. (Ed.). (1992). *International encyclopedia of linguistics*. Oxford, UK: Oxford University Press.
Chomsky, N. (2002). *On nature and language*. Cambridge, UK: Cambridge University Press.
Dimroth, C., & Lasser, I. (Eds.). (2002). Finite options. How L1 and L2 learners cope with the acquisition of finiteness. Berlin, New York: Mouton de Gruyter [Special issue of *Linguistics*, 40–44].
Klein, W., & Perdue, C. (1997). The basic variety, or: Couldn't natural languages be much simpler? *Second Language Research 13*, 301–347.
Lasser, I. (1997). Finiteness in adult and in child language. *MPI Series in Psycholinguistics* (Vol. 8). Nijmegen: Max Planck Institute for Psycholinguistics.

---

[9] I believe, incidentally, that 'real' languages such as Latin or Yiddish are only a special case of the many manifestations of the human language faculties. The normal cases are 'learner varieties,' i.e., much less elaborate systems. Most people all over the world develop several such systems, and the fact that they are not counted as 'languages' because they are imperfect replications of what is spoken in their environment is no reason to exclude them from the linguistic systems which the human language faculties are able to bring about.

25

Grammaticization
Implications for a Theory of Language

JOAN BYBEE
University of New Mexico

> ... the study of language in its unstable or changing phases is an excellent tool for discovering the essence of language itself.
>
> **Dan I. Slobin (1977, p. 185)**

Dan Slobin's breadth of interest and expertise has been one important factor in determining the importance of his contributions to the understanding of language. Particularly important has been his ability to draw upon both child language and language change as sources of evidence for the nature of language. In the paper quoted above he outlined a number of general principles of language that emerged from an examination of language change and language acquisition. He did not, however, subscribe to the generally accepted view that children are responsible for language change; rather, in characteristic fashion, he was able to see beyond the superficial similarities to identify the core issues: language change and language acquisition are distinct processes and while they interact, the second does not cause the first. In Bybee and Slobin (1982a), we reported on differences between the errors that children make in using the English past tense (from Bybee and Slobin, 1982b) and typical change in morphological systems, concluding that young children are not the source of these changes. Later, in a 1997 chapter, Slobin presented arguments against the proposal that grammaticizable notions are innate (see discussion below).

In this chapter, I follow up on the view that language change tells us about the nature of language. In particular, I focus on the idea that careful study of the process of grammaticization reveals that we must revise our ideas about the nature of grammar. By examining recent proposals from the generative theorists on grammaticization, I uncover certain assumptions about grammar that grammaticization research reveals to be in error.

GRAMMATICIZATION

Research into grammaticization in the 20th century began in the 1970s in the context of Greenberg's typological research, where it became clear that grammatical markers in related and unrelated languages could be compared in terms of where they were positioned on certain paths of change (Greenberg, 1978). Givón (1979, and elsewhere) explored these crosslinguistic paths of change, which suggested to him a view of grammar and its evolution that was quite distinct from the generative view.

Grammaticization research began to flourish in the 1980s with the publication of books by Lehmann (1982), Heine and Reh (1984), and Bybee (1985). In these works certain general trends were documented across languages, which raised numerous questions about the development and nature of grammar. Later works probed the mechanisms and factors that contributed to the development and change of grammar. The factors identified were metaphor (Heine, Claudi, & Hünnemeyer, 1991), pragmatic inference (Traugott, 1989), generalization and frequency increase (Bybee, Perkins, & Pagliuca, 1994). These works all emphasized that the processes contributing to grammaticization are operative when language is being used (see Bybee, 2003a, for an overview). In his unpublished comments at the end of the Grammaticalization Symposium held in Eugene, Oregon, in 1989, Dan Slobin remarked that grammaticization theory, as being practiced by the participants in the symposium, constituted a psycholinguistic theory of language use.

Indeed, the researchers in this group (see Traugott & Heine, 1991) were largely self-identified as 'functionalists' and viewed their research as a major contribution to the understanding of the nature of grammar. What grammaticization revealed for these researchers (myself included) is that grammar is mutable and variable; it is formed gradually from lexical material obscuring the distinction between lexicon and grammar. The changes that define grammaticization affect the phonology, syntax, semantics, and pragmatics of constructions. As a result, the research of this functionalist group centered on understanding the semantic changes that characterize grammaticization perhaps even more than the morpho-syntactic changes. In all of this work a tight connection is seen between the changes in form, meaning, and context. Given the importance of pragmatics, it seems necessary to view the change process as occurring while language is used. Given the importance of gradual rises in frequency of use, and changes in relative frequency among related uses, it seems necessary to view change in cognitive representations (i.e., grammar) as a reflection of changes in usage. Thus a view of language emerges which takes grammar and usage to be intimately intertwined. In this research, then, the new information about grammaticization is taken to inform a general theory of language, and indeed, it suggests a very different view of language than that offered by generative linguistics (Bybee, 2006). It suggests a Usage-Based Model of language (Langacker, 1988; Barlow & Kemmer, 2000; Bybee, 2001).

Generative linguists have only much more recently addressed grammaticization and how the phenomenon would be viewed in their framework (Roberts & Roussou, 2003; van Gelderen, 2004). Anyone who started studying grammaticization from the functionalist point of view will be very disappointed with the generativist account, as it addresses only a very small portion of the total phenomenon, focusing as it does on the changes in category and constituency while taking semantic, pragmatic, and phonological change to be peripheral, sometimes accidental or random concomitants of change. The other disappointment comes in the so-called 'explanatory' principles, which appear to be fairly ad hoc principles designed primarily to get grammaticization to move in the right direction. The problem with generative grammar vis-à-vis grammaticization is not that the researchers investigating this topic are not clever enough, but rather that many of the most basic assumptions of structuralism and generative grammar are incompatible with the facts of grammaticization. That is why the functionalist researchers have changed their view of grammar when confronted by the facts of grammaticization.

In the following sections, I will discuss differences between the functionalist view of grammaticization and that of the generativists, demonstrating which of the basic assumptions of generative grammar must be abandoned in order to have a coherent theory of language as well as a coherent theory of the creation and change of grammar.

GRADUALNESS

Language change is gradual and produces periods of variation as innovative and conservative patterns are used alongside one another. If grammars are conceived of as discrete, as they are in generative theory, the gradualness of language change presents a problem. One approach to this problem is to distinguish usage from grammar; usage may change gradually, but grammar change is abrupt. Thus King (1969) lays out the program for a generative theory of change:

> Within generative grammar, change is regarded as change *in competence*, not just change in performance. Change occurs because the grammar of the language has changed, and the largely random effects of performance have nothing to do with it. (italics in original, p. 15)

A related approach assumes that small changes accrue by rule addition at the end of the grammar, followed by a radical restructuring during the acquisition process (Andersen, 1973; Lightfoot, 1979, 1991; Roberts & Roussou, 2003). In this view, adult grammars cannot change, so grammar change is only possible during the language acquisition process. Other approaches blur the notion of a discrete grammar: Harris and Campbell (1995) allow the grammar to contain more than one analysis of a given structure, even in the individual speaker. Thus while they take reanalysis to be abrupt, they allow intermediate stages of overlapping analyses.

The functionalists studying grammaticization do not assume the discreteness of grammar, but rather study the facts of the process either without making any claims about the nature of grammar or letting the process itself reveal the properties of grammar. The gradualness of change in the phonetic, morpho-syntactic, and semantic/pragmatic properties of grammaticizing constructions provides a view of grammar as dynamic, variable, and always susceptible to change. In this view the cognitive organization of language is highly influenced by experience with language; forms and constructions that are used frequently have stronger representations and those that are used less have weaker representations. Thus usage and grammar are not separate and the nature of the representation can change over time, even in adults (Bybee, 2006).

The strong link between phonetic and morpho-syntactic form and meaning and context suggests a construction-based grammar where form and meaning are directly associated. Thus the first notion generativists have to abandon to understand grammaticization is the notion of a discrete grammar built on abstract, symbolic units and relations. The nature of the grammaticization process reveals that construction frames and even specific instances of constructions are represented cognitively. In the grammaticization process a specific instance of a construction, with lexical material in it, changes phonetically, semantically, pragmatically, and morpho-syntactically to become a new construction. For instance, the *be going to* construction was in Shakespeare's time only one lexical instance of a general purpose-clause construction (e.g., *They are going/ journeying/riding to see the Queen*). But now in its intention/future sense (*It is going to rain*), it is a different construction and restricted to the one verb, *go*. The only way the instance of the purpose construction with *go* in it could have accrued new pragmatic, semantic, and other properties was for that instance of the construction to have a representation in memory. This fact suggests a grammar that represents very specific information about constructions and the lexical material used in them (see also Langacker, 1988).

The gradualness of change also suggests that cognitive representations change as usage patterns change, even if these changes are only increases or decreases in frequency. Such changes in usage patterns can occur as adults use language; thus not all linguistic change is to be attributed to child language acquisition, as we shall see in the next section.

UNIDIRECTIONALITY

One focus of work on grammaticization is the identification of paths of change and the verification of their crosslinguistic validity. On a general level, the directionality of change is always from lexical to grammatical meaning and from independent lexical item to grammatical word—either auxiliary, clitic, or particle—and further to affixation. In addition, a number of more specific semantic paths of change have been identified (Givón, 1979; Lehmann, 1982; Heine & Reh, 1984; Heine, Claudi, & Hunnemeyer, 1991; Bybee, Perkins, & Pagliuca, 1994). When used in constructions with nouns, body part terms become spatial adpositions, demonstratives become determiners, the word for 'one' becomes an indefinite article; when used in constructions with verbs, pronouns become agreement markers, a phrase indicating movement toward a goal becomes future, as do verbs signaling volition, a verb meaning 'finish' becomes a perfect and then perfective or past, a phrase meaning 'be located at' becomes a progressive, and so on. All of these paths and many more have been abundantly documented across languages, while reverse travel on one of these paths is either completely missing from the record or rarely seen (Norde, 2001).

Janda (2001) discusses at length the problem that unidirectionality poses for the hypothesis that children change language in the acquisition process. Since language change continues in the same direction generation after generation, the puzzle for generative theory is how children know in what direction the change is traveling, since they only have access to synchronic data. Roberts and Roussou (2003) pose the problem this way: in a generative theory, diachronic change should be a random walk through parameter space, with no inherent directionality. Yet the strong directionality of grammaticization cannot be denied. Thus other factors have to be sought to account for directionality.

Here is another case where the facts of language change should lead to a change in theoretical perspective. The problem of unidirectionality is solved by simply looking for other sources of language change than parameter setting or reanalysis by children. Indeed, as I discuss below, the types of change that are part of the grammaticization process are very unlikely to be initiated by children and more likely to be set in motion by speakers who have already acquired the language and use it in their everyday interactions.

In Bybee (2003b) I have discussed the major mechanisms of change in grammaticization as processes that occur while language is being used. Increases in frequency of use heighten and accelerate these processes as the mechanisms apply over and over again. Phonetic reduction is the result of the automatization of the neuromotor routine due to repetition. Semantic bleaching is like habituation—the increased frequency of the use of a grammaticizing expression robs it of its semantic force, making it appropriate in more contexts, which increases its frequency even more. At the same time, the expression comes to be viewed as a single unit, losing its internal structure and its relations to the lexical items and constructions from which it originated. The pragmatic inferences that go with the expression are repeated, and through repetition become conventionalized as part of the meaning of the new construction. This account emphasizes the role of repetition, gradual changes in usage patterns, gradual change in both implications and meaning, and expansion to new contexts.

The inherent directionality of grammaticization is directly related to the mechanisms of change that propel the process, and these mechanisms are all parts of language use. Changes related to increases in frequency all move in one direction and even decreases in frequency do not condition reversals: there is no process of de-automatization or de-habituation, subtraction of pragmatic inferences, etc. Once phonetic form and semantic properties are lost, there is no way to retrieve them. Thus grammaticization is unidirectional. However, that does not mean that the process does not sometimes get stalled. There is not much discussion of this phenomenon in the literature either because it is rare or because researchers have focused their attention more on clear cases that proceed to completion. However, there are some cases in which change is not progressing as steadily as would be predicted. For instance, the Present Perfect in American English seems to be used less by younger speakers than by older ones. Even if it were to fall into disuse, and decrease in frequency, it would not retrace its steps back to a resultative or possessive construction; it would simply be replaced gradually by another form.

The mechanisms of change that are operative during language use can occur in the speech of adults or children. However, very young children are less likely to be the moving force behind these changes: the type of phonetic change that occurs in grammaticization often creates segments and sequences that are more difficult to perceive accurately and produce, rather than those that are easier to produce. For instance, the contraction of the negative in *didn't, couldn't, wouldn't,* and *shouldn't* in American English is actually very difficult to produce, involving as it does, a glottal stop and syllabic nasal. This is not likely to be the work of very young children. Similarly, habituation requires extensive exposure to forms and constructions, and acquiring and making appropriate pragmatic inferences are processes that require a fairly mature understanding of inter-speaker relationships. However, this is not to say that the acquisition process has no effect on grammaticization: indeed, usage patterns and meanings that have become rare among adults may not be acquired at all by children, e.g., *may* as indicating permission is losing the competition with *can*.

The second notion that generativists have to give up to understand grammaticization is the notion that only children can change grammar and thus language (Croft, 2000). Adult grammars change too. Even though some researchers define grammaticization as reanalysis (Clark, 2006), whether or not reanalysis is regarded as a major factor in change depends upon one's view of grammar. Reanalysis is particularly emphasized by researchers who are interested more in the morpho-syntactic properties of change. Once the big picture is in view, and the phonetic, pragmatic, semantic, and usage changes are considered, the role of reanalysis appears to be quite minor. In a usage-based grammar, the notion is hardly needed, or if used at all, change must be viewed as multiple mini-reanalyses (Haspelmath, 1998).

The argument that some notion of reanalysis is needed results from the fact that, for instance, if an item is clearly a verb at one stage (OE *cunnan* 'to know') and clearly an auxiliary (Present Day English *can*) at a later stage, reanalysis must have taken place. But isn't this just the linguist's point of view? Was there really some point at which a new generation reanalyzed *can* as an auxiliary? The facts show that the change was very gradual and manifested mainly by changes in relative frequency over time (Bybee, 2003b). It is well-known that auxiliaries retain some of the properties of verbs, leading to lengthy arguments about their synchronic status (Heine, 1993). Thus reanalysis is just the linguist's post hoc description of a process that is actually quite gradual and more complex than the term 'reanalysis' suggests.

GRAMMATICIZABLE CATEGORIES

At first generative grammarians were not interested in the content of grammaticized categories. Chomsky (1957) asserted that there was nothing interesting to be said about the meanings of inflectional categories. In contrast, cognitive-functional linguists have taken on the question of what constitutes a grammaticizable notion. Bybee (1985) addresses this issue with respect to inflectional categories identifying semantic and usage factors that help to explain the content of these categories. Talmy (1985, 1988) takes on a broader array of notions expressed grammatically through derivation, particles, and other means. Talmy sees the content of these categories as part of a design feature of language in which lexicon is distinguished from grammar and one can posit that the latter specifies 'an innate inventory of concepts available for serving a structuring function in language' (Talmy, 1988, p. 197). Slobin earlier endorsed a similar position (Slobin, 1985). It is a testament to his intellectual openness that he later argued against this position. Slobin (1997) examines such claims more carefully and, armed with data on grammaticization across languages, concludes that the evidence is lacking for a set of grammatical morphemes in each language that is mapped onto a universal and limited set of semantic notions.

Slobin considers a number of semantic domains in a variety of languages to argue that there is not a consistent mapping of semantic notions onto grammatical expressions either within or across languages. First he points out that various notions in the modal domain have a variety of expression types in English. The classic modal auxiliaries, e.g., *may, can, must, should*, etc., have a well-known set of behavioral properties that identify them as a class (taking the negative without *do*, inverting for questions, etc.). However, very similar notions in English can be expressed with items outside this class, such as the expressions *have to, got to* which take *do* for questions and do not invert with the subject.

Next Slobin presents a number of examples from different semantic domains showing that what is expressed grammatically in one language may have lexical expression in another. For instance, the modal notions equivalent to those expressed by auxiliaries in English are expressed by full verbs in Spanish, the equivalent of Mandarin numeral classifiers are nouns in English, and so on.

Another way to address this question is to ask if there is a finite, universal set of grammatical meanings that may be exploited in the languages of the world. The examination of a wide range of languages, such as that used in Bybee, Perkins, and Pagliuca (1994), turns up a negative answer. There is no pre-specified set of grammaticizable notions any more than there is a finite set of phonetic segments that occurs in the languages of the world (Port & Leary, 2005). Instead, we must think of the factors or mechanisms of change that lead to the evolution of grammatical meanings. As in a complex system, once these mechanisms are put into action on the existing lexical material of a language, categories will emerge (Holland, 1998). In many cases these categories will mirror those found in other languages, but we cannot rule out the possibility of novel developments. For example, some languages have categories that correspond to their particular environments: the Nicobarese language (spoken on an island) has an affix that means 'toward the sea' and a contrasting one that means 'inland to the jungle'; these contrast with two other affixes that indicate the direction to the left or right as one faces the sea (Braine, 1970). Karok (a Native American language of California) has a set of derivational suffixes expressing direction that reference deictic points such as 'here' and 'there' but also relative locations that reference up and down river, up and down hill (Bright, 1957). For instance, the suffix *–rupu* means 'hence downriverward' and contrasts with *–ra:* 'hither from downriver'; these in turn contrast with *–ro:vu* 'hence upriverward' and *–várak* 'hither from upriver.'

Thus the evidence for an innate set of 'functional categories'—such as past, perfective, subjunctive—looking for grammatical expression as proposed by Roberts and Roussou (2003) is simply not available. The crosslinguistic diversity demonstrates that some other mechanism besides innate endowment must account for the crosslinguistic similarity in grammatical notions. The content of grammaticized categories can be explained through a combination of cognitive and discourse/functional considerations. Examining paths of grammaticization shows how these factors interact to produce grammatical meaning. Paths of change show that the development of grammatical meaning is slow and gradual; while some grammatical notions are very similar across languages, they all exhibit language-particular features of nuance, inference, and distribution (see Bybee & Pagliuca, 1987). If functional categories were innately specified, then grammaticization would occur abruptly as children fit lexical items to grammatical slots and grammatical meaning would be the same even in detail across all languages.

Moreover, Slobin (1994, 1997) notes that some of the meanings for grammatical categories are such that they are not available to very young children. The common change of deontic meaning to epistemic is not likely to be accomplished by children, since the expression of epistemicity is such a late acquisition for children. Epistemicity is a domain that is only relevant in interpersonal communication; it has no independent status in cognition, as, say, shapes and motion do. Thus Slobin says:

> On closer inspection, crosslinguistic diversity in patterns of grammaticization points to adult communicative practices as the most plausible source of form-function mappings in human languages, rather than prototypical events in infant cognition. (1997, p. 276)

Similarly, the important role of pragmatic inference in shaping grammatical meaning (Traugott, 1989; Traugott & Dasher, 2002) points to adults as the innovators, since it often takes children years to acquire the ability to make appropriate inferences.

Thus, the third notion that generativists have to give up is the notion that crosslinguistic similarities can be accounted for by innate universals. Languages are products of their history. Languages are constantly changing; there is nothing static or given about their structures (Hopper, 1987) that would suggest innately specific structure or categories.

The absence of innate universals does not mean that child language acquisition plays no role at all in the innovation or propagation of change. However, the role of children must be assessed carefully and not just assumed. Parallels between ontogeny and phylogeny have been pointed out in the literature. Slobin (1994) discusses the parallels between children's acquisition of the Present Perfect in English and its development diachronically. A careful look at the discourse contexts in which children work out the functions of the Present Perfect shows some parallels with the contexts in which it begins to take on its present-day functions. In addition, the order in which uses of the Present Perfect develop for children is similar to the diachronic order: for instance, children use the resulting state meaning of the Present Perfect before the perfect of experience and the continuative perfect and this reflects the order of development diachronically. However, Slobin notes that children start with the notions that are concrete and anchored in the present because these notions are cognitively the most simple, natural, and accessible. Similarly, in diachrony, the most concrete notions constitute the starting points for grammaticization because the material the process works on comes from the basic lexicon. The parallel here between ontogeny and phylogeny is the correspondence between two processes that may be only superficially similar.

An aspect of change in which transmission to a new generation may play a role concerns the change in relative usage frequencies among competing forms or competing meanings. Infrequent uses or forms may fail to become part of the new generation's productive repertoire. The more frequent forms will increase their domains to make up for this loss. After several generations, a form or a use may simply not occur anymore. In this way, for instance, the future/obligation modal *shall* is in the process of becoming obsolete in American English, especially for younger speakers. At the same time, the frequency of *will, be going to,* and other expressions becomes more frequent. Such changes can occur among adults as well, but the complete loss of forms and uses requires a new generation.

TRIGGERING EXPERIENCES AND ECONOMY PRINCIPLES

The account I gave above of the grammaticization process depicted it as occurring while people use language. The causal mechanisms, e.g., the neuromotor automatization that leads to phonetic reduction, habituation that gives rise to semantic bleaching, pragmatic inferencing that adds meaning from context, and categorization that allows constructions to expand their applicability, are all domain-general cognitive processes that apply in language use as well as in other cognitive activities. These mechanisms contribute to the explanation of the process of grammaticization and its directionality. In contrast, in the generative accounts, these causal mechanisms are not available, so other causes must be sought. Recall that in these theories, since language change is grammar change, reanalysis or change in parameter settings is viewed as what must be explained.

The generative accounts that I have examined (Lightfoot, 1979, 1991; Roberts & Roussou, 2003; van Gelderen, 2004) all view the grammar as simpler or more economical after grammaticization has taken place. Thus principles of economy must be proposed as evaluation metrics applied by the child in the acquisition process. In addition, Roberts and Roussou identify, for each change they discuss, other changes that serve as triggers for the actual parameter change. Of course, both principles and triggers themselves need explanations. It is important to note also that all of these accounts view the semantic and pragmatic changes that occur in grammaticization as independent of, or in some cases, the result of the grammatical reanalysis.

Lightfoot (1979) analyzes the development of the class of modal auxiliaries (*may, can, must, will, shall, might, could, would, should*) from verbs in the history of English by postulating two stages to the change: First, a series of 'apparently isolated changes took place early in the history of English' (p. 101). These include the following: (i) the pre-modals lost their ability to take direct objects (so that sentences such as *I can music* became rare and disappeared); (ii) the class of verbs that the modals come from (the Preterite-Present verbs) was already inflectionally anomalous and this class lost some of its members; (iii) the past tense forms of these verbs began to lose their past tense meaning (*should* and *would* come to be used as hypotheticals indicating present or future); and (iv) a new infinitive marker *to* developed.

Lightfoot claims that these changes made it increasingly difficult to analyze these changing verbs (or 'pre-modals') as verbs. He proposes a Transparency Principle by which reanalysis is called for when the surface behavior strays too far from the underlying categorization of items. As a result, in the second stage, in the middle of the sixteenth century, these erstwhile verbs were reanalyzed by a generation of speakers as 'modals,' creating a new category in the grammar of English. As a result of this reanalysis, the new modals lost their infinitive forms (disallowing two modals in the same clause, as in *She shall can do it*, which formerly was possible), and they lost their *–ing* forms. In addition, the pattern of negation by which the negative follows the verb, formerly possible with all verbs, became restricted to the modals and other auxiliaries and the pattern for questions in which the verb inverts with the subject, formerly possible with all verbs, became restricted to the modals and other auxiliaries.

In an extensive review of this analysis, Frans Plank (1984) points out two major problems: first, none of the changes that lead up to the reanalysis or result from it occur at the same time for all the modals. All the changes going on take place slowly and gradually and at different rates for different modals. This fact argues against an abrupt reanalysis by which the category is suddenly created in the grammar. Second, Plank argues that a prime motivator for the changes Lightfoot discusses is semantics and these are not isolated changes at all. As early as the Old English period, the modals had begun a process of semantic bleaching or generalization that eventually made them too weak to be used as main verbs in infinitive or gerund forms.

In addition, the changes that led to the development of the negation and question patterns took place gradually over about two centuries. Ogura (1993) and Bybee (2003c) document the gradual development of the periphrastic *do* that was necessary for the negation and question patterns to become categorical. Both of these studies show a gradual diffusion of the *do* pattern over two centuries. The gradualness of all of these changes makes an abrupt reanalysis within one generation seem implausible.

Lightfoot's (1991) analysis of the development of the class of modals changes some of the details of his 1979 analysis and uses the terminology of parameter setting, but the basic principle of disassociating the syntactic changes from the semantic ones remains, as does the claim that reanalysis is abrupt. In addition, he points to morphological changes as triggering the parametric change, as do Roberts and Roussou (2003), to whose views we now turn.

Roberts and Roussou (2003) discuss a number of changes in the history of English, Greek, and Romance languages. Like Lightfoot, these authors note that parameter change is an aspect of the process of parameter setting during language acquisition. In the cases they discuss, a parameter change occurs when other changes create syncretism, which is the loss of morphological distinctions, such as between indicative and subjunctive. They propose a preference for a one-to-one mapping between features and lexical items. When a morphological marking is obscured by change, such as the loss of an infinitive suffix, or the loss of the subjunctive/indicative inflection, some other lexical item is mapped onto the innate function. For instance, they propose that the English modals developed because of the loss of the infinitive suffix. Thus a sentence such as *nat can we seen* 'we cannot see' in which the *–n* on *see* is the infinitive marker becomes *nat can we see* with the loss of the suffix. The resulting sentence appears then to have two main verbs, so the first, *can*, is reanalyzed as a functional category in <T(ense)>. In their account, the loss of the suffix triggers the change of *can* from a verb to an auxiliary, a parametric change.

Among the changes that Roberts and Roussou discuss, quite a number have the loss of morphology, especially inflection, as the cause. A case in point is their view that the loss of the infinitive suffix in English led to parametric change. Citing the loss of morphology as a cause for syntactic change is traditional in historical linguistics (Vennemann, 1975); the assumption is that sound change is responsible for this loss and the loss creates intolerable ambiguity about underlying structure. In grammaticization theory, however, the loss of inflectional categories is simply the end point of the grammaticization process. Such phonetic loss simply parallels the loss of meaning in the inflections; the meaning is so eroded and bleached that it no longer serves a clear function. By the time this happens, alternate means of expressing the same notions have already emerged. Languages do not go through phases of dysfunction because some element has been wiped out by phonetic change, followed by prophylactic measures that reestablish functionality. Change is normal and is ongoing at all times.

In terms of explanation, then, grammaticization provides a much richer framework for understanding syntactic change, as well as semantic, pragmatic, and morphological change. When we take the long view of grammaticization as a process that might have to be tracked over millennia, a process that is constantly at work in language, then the idea that certain dysfunctions develop and are abruptly remedied begins to sound implausible. In addition, the postulation of various principles—the Transparency Principle (Lightfoot, 1979), the Economy Principle (van Gelderen, 2004), the dispreference for syncretism (Roberts & Roussou, 2003)—gets us nowhere, since neither these principles themselves nor the processes that produce the alleged violations of these principles are explained.

GRAMMATICIZATION AS A THEORY OF LANGUAGE

Some critics of 'grammaticization theory' argue that grammaticization is not a single process, but the result of the correspondence among multiple processes of change that also occur independently of one another—an epiphenomenon (Campbell, 2001; Newmeyer, 1998). Some supporters of grammaticization as a theory of language also argue that the process itself has multiple components, which typically occur independently, but also happen to coincide in some cases (Hopper, 1991). In fact, this is precisely what I have been arguing here: grammaticization, like grammar, is emergent from language use. It does not matter whether grammaticization is considered one process or multiple processes acting together, grammaticization describes the long, gradual phenomenon of the creation, development, and loss of grammar. In Bybee (2003b), I argue that the various parts of the grammaticization process have in common the fact that frequency of use is necessary for the changes to progress. Frequency of use is one of the major links among the changes that occur in phonology, morphology, syntax, semantics, and pragmatics.

Newmeyer (1998) goes so far as to claim that there can be no such thing as a diachronic process. His argument, like that of Janda (2001) discussed above, is based on the assumption that change only occurs in the language acquisition process. He argues against a putative practice of treating diachronic change in terms of the forms that change as if speakers were not involved. This is of course either a straw man or a deep misunderstanding of the approach taken to grammaticization in works by Bybee, Traugott, Haiman, Heine, and Hopper. The postulation of metaphor, pragmatic inference, semantic bleaching, neuromotor automatization, and conventionalization all require the human mind as the major participant in speech events where change occurs.

Another criticism is that there is no such thing as 'grammaticization theory' (Newmeyer, 1998). On this I beg to differ. The phenomenon itself gives rise to a general theory of language essentially equivalent to what has come to be called Usage-Based theory. As a diachronic theory of language, grammaticization theory predicts future development and aids in the reconstruction of past developments. More importantly, it gives rise to a set of hypotheses that explain why languages have grammar. The word 'explain' is not used lightly here—by examining thoroughly the process by which the categories and constructions of grammar arise, we eventually arrive at an understanding of why grammar exists.

On the synchronic plane, the phenomenon of grammaticization points to general properties of language that require a view very different from the generative one and hence a competing theory. First, grammar is not autonomous from semantics or pragmatics. Without meaning, no grammar would develop. Second, grammar is derived quite directly from usage and distributions that occur in natural use. Third, cognitive representations of language are dynamic, changing all the time as they respond to new experience, to frequency increases and decreases. Fourth, no specifically linguistic feature is innate; all derive from domain-general processes. Finally, crosslinguistic similarities are due to the fact that the same mechanisms apply when people use language in different social and cultural settings. These postulates, arising directly from observations of the process of grammaticization, do indeed constitute the basis for a theory of language.

REFERENCES

Andersen, H. (1973). Abductive and deductive change. *Language, 49*(4), 765–793.
Barlow, M., & Kemmer, S. (Eds.). (2000). *Usage-based models of language*. Stanford: CSLI.
Braine, J. C. (1970). *Nicobarese grammar (Car dialect)*. Doctoral dissertation, University of California at Berkeley.
Bright, W. (1957). *The Karok language* (Vol. 13). Berkeley: University of California Publications in Linguistics.
Bybee, J. (1985). *Morphology: A study of the relation between meaning and form*. Philadelphia: John Benjamins.
Bybee, J. (2001). *Phonology and language use*. Cambridge, UK: Cambridge University Press.
Bybee, J. (2003a). Cognitive processes in grammaticalization. In M. Tomasello (Ed.), *The new psychology of language* (Vol. II, pp. 145–67). Mahwah: Lawrence Erlbaum Associates.
Bybee, J. (2003b). Mechanisms of change in grammaticization: The role of frequency. In R. Janda & B. Joseph (Eds.), *Handbook of historical linguistics* (pp. 602–623). Oxford: Blackwell Publishers.
Bybee, J. (2003c, August). The development of the category of auxiliary in English. Paper presented at the International Conference on Historical Linguistics, Copenhagen.
Bybee, J. (2006). From usage to grammar: The mind's response to repetition. *Language, 82*, 711–733.
Bybee, J., & Pagliuca, W. (1987). The evolution of future meaning. In A.G. Ramat, O. Carruba, & G. Bernini (Eds.), *Papers from the VIIth International Conference on Historical Linguistics* (pp. 109–122). Amsterdam: John Benjamins.
Bybee, J., Perkins, R., & Pagliuca, W. (1994). *The evolution of grammar: Tense, aspect and modality in the languages of the world*. Chicago: University of Chicago Press.
Bybee, J., & Slobin, D. I. (1982a). Rules and schemas in the development and use of the English past tense. *Language, 58*, 265–289.
Bybee, J., & Slobin, D. I. (1982b). Why small children cannot change language on their own: Evidence from the English past tense. In A. Alqvist (Ed.), *Papers from the Fifth International Conference on Historical Linguistics* (pp. 29–37). Amsterdam: John Benjamins.
Campbell, L. (2001). What's wrong with grammaticalization? In L. Campbell (Ed.), *Grammaticalization: A critical assessment*. Special issue of *Language Sciences, 23*(2–3), 113–161.
Chomsky, N. (1957). *Syntactic structures*. The Hague: Mouton.
Clark, B. (2006). Review of E. van Gelderen, *Grammaticalization as economy*. *Journal of Germanic Linguistics, 18*(1), 71–84.
Croft, W. (2000). *Explaining language change*. Harlow, UK: Long Linguistics Library.
Givón, Talmy. (1979). *On understanding grammar*. New York: Academic Press.
Greenberg, J. (1978). How does a language acquire gender markers? In J. Greenberg, C. Ferguson, & E. Moravcsik (Eds.), *Universals of human language* (Vol. III, pp. 47–82). Stanford: Stanford University Press.
Harris, A. C., & Campbell, L. (1995). *Historical syntax in cross-linguistic perspective*. Cambridge, UK: Cambridge University Press.
Haspelmath, M. (1998). Does grammaticalization need reanalysis? *Studies in Language, 22*(2), 315–351.
Heine, B. (1993). *Auxiliaries: Cognitive forces and grammaticalization*. New York: Oxford University Press.
Heine, B., Claudi, U., & Hünnemeyer, F. (1991). From cognition to grammar: Evidence from African languages. In E. C. Traugott & B. Heine (Eds.), *Approaches to grammaticalization* (Vol. 1, pp. 149–187). Amsterdam: John Benjamins.
Heine, B., & Reh, M. (1984). *Grammaticalization and reanalysis in African languages*. Hamburg, Germany: Buske.
Holland, J. H. (1998). *Emergence: From chaos to order*. New York: Basic Books.
Hopper, P. J. (1987). Emergent grammar. *BLS, 13*, 139–157.
Hopper, P. J. (1991). On some principles of grammaticization. In E. C. Traugott & B. Heine (Eds.), *Approaches to grammaticalization* (Vol. 1, pp. 17–35). Amsterdam: John Benjamins.
Janda, R. D. (2001). Beyond 'pathways' and 'unidirectionality': On the discontinuity of language transmission and the counterability of grammaticalization. In L. Campbell (Ed.), *Grammaticalization: A critical assessment*. Special issue of *Language Sciences, 23*(2–3), 265–340.
King, R. D. (1969). *Historical linguistics and generative grammar*. Englewood-Cliffs, NJ: Prentice Hall.
Langacker, R. W. (1988). A usage-based model. In B. Kudzka-Ostyn (Ed.), *Topics in cognitive linguistics* (pp. 127–161). Amsterdam: John Benjamins.
Lehmann, C. (1982). *Thoughts on grammaticalization: Vol. 1. A programmatic sketch*. (Arbeiten des Kölner Universalien-Projekts 48). Köln: Universität zu Köln. Institut für Sprachwissenschaft.

Lightfoot, D. (1979). *Principles of diachronic syntax*. Cambridge, UK: Cambridge University Press.
Lightfoot, D. (1991). *How to set parameters: Arguments from language change*. Cambridge, MA: The MIT Press.
Newmeyer, F. J. (1998). *Language form and language function*. Cambridge, MA: The MIT Press.
Norde, M. (2001). Deflexion as a counterdirectional factor in grammatical change. In L. Campbell (Ed.), *Grammaticalization: A critical assessment*. Special issue of *Language Sciences, 23*(2–3), 231–264.
Ogura, M. (1993). The development of periphrastic *do* in English: A case of lexical diffusion in syntax. *Diachronica, X*, 1.51–85.
Plank, F. (1984). The modals story retold. *Studies in Language, 8*(3), 305–364.
Port, R. F., & Leary, A. P. (2005). Against formal phonology. *Language, 81*(4), 927–964.
Roberts, I., & Roussou, A. (2003). *Syntactic change: A minimalist approach to grammaticalization*. Cambridge, UK: Cambridge University Press.
Slobin, D. I. (1977). Language change in childhood and in history. In J. Macnamara (Ed.), *Language learning and thought* (pp. 185–214). New York: Academic Press.
Slobin, D. I. (1985). Crosslinguistic evidence for the language-making capacity. In D. I. Slobin (Ed.), *The crosslinguistic study of language acquisition: Vol. 2. Theoretical perspectives* (pp. 1157–1256). Hillsdale, NJ: Lawrence Erlbaum Associates.
Slobin, D. I. (1994). Talking perfectly: Discourse origins of the Present Perfect. In W. Pagliuca (Ed.), *Perspectives on grammaticalization* (pp. 119–133). Amsterdam: John Benjamins.
Slobin, D. I. (1997). The origins of grammaticizable notions: Beyond the individual mind. In D. I. Slobin (Ed.), *The crosslinguistic study of language acquisition: Vol. 5. Expanding the contexts* (pp. 1–39). Mahwah, NJ: Lawrence Erlbaum Associates.
Talmy, L. (1985). Lexicalization patterns: Semantic structure in lexical forms. In T. Shopen (Ed.), *Language typology and syntactic description: Vol. 3. Grammatical categories and the lexicon* (pp. 36–149). Cambridge, UK: Cambridge University Press.
Talmy, L. (1988). The relation of grammar to cognition. In B. Kudzka-Ostyn (Ed.), *Topics in cognitive linguistics* (pp. 165–206). Amsterdam: John Benjamins.
Traugott, E. C. (1989). On the rise of epistemic meanings in English: An example of subjectification in semantic change. *Language, 65*, 31–55.
Traugott, E. C., & Dasher, R. B. (2002). *Regularity in semantic change*. Cambridge, UK: Cambridge University Press.
Traugott, E. C., & Heine, B. (Eds.). (1991). *Approaches to grammaticalization* (Vols. 1 and 2). Amsterdam: John Benjamins.
van Gelderen, E. (2004). *Grammaticalization as economy*. Amsterdam: John Benjamins.
Vennemann, T. (1975). An explanation of drift. In C. N. Li (Ed.), *Word order and word order change* (pp. 269–305). Austin: University of Texas Press.

26

What Does It Mean to Compare Language and Gesture? Modalities and Contrasts

EVE SWEETSER
University of California, Berkeley

> Perhaps we keep finding iconicity because there is no other way for a semiotic system to be created and used by human beings without a close fit between form and function. After all, is it possible to make a mold for a statue that does not conform to the shape and dimensions and substance of the statue?
>
> **Dan I. Slobin (2005, p. 321)**

*I*n this chapter I would like to reexamine some of the traditional dichotomies between language and gesture. In order to do so, it will be necessary to consider a three-way contrast—spoken languages, signed languages, and gesture. Without this three-way comparison, we risk collapsing contrasts between visual and auditory media with contrasts between linguistic structure and co-linguistic gestural structure. Such a comparison clearly belongs in this volume because Dan Slobin's work on Thinking for Speaking has provided a crucial impetus to the research which feeds my new evaluation—both his own work on spoken and signed language, and the new perspectives on co-speech gesture which have been inspired by that work, not to mention his general intellectual influence on my work for the last 30 years. Dan has never been never afraid to cross boundaries between modalities—or to be skeptical about accepted dichotomies. So I hope readers will see this chapter as being in his tradition.

Returning to our topic: what kinds of contrasts are there between language and gesture? First of all, many researchers agree that language is *conventional*, while spontaneous co-speech gesture is *non-conventional and flexible* (though "quotable gestures" are conventional). In gesturing about a tree, for example, a gesturer might trace the fat tube of the trunk with two "C" hands forming a circle, while another gesturer might hold up a forearm as trunk with fingers as branches. Neither would be "wrong," and indeed they might successfully highlight different aspects of the tree's structure. However, Hong Kong Sign Language conventionally and lexically represents TREE in the first way, while the American Sign Language lexical sign for TREE is based on the second strategy. Neither language's word for TREE is correct in the other language.

Similarly, there seems some consensus that language is *compositional, discrete, and analytic*, while gesture is *global and synthetic*. Further, as McNeill (1992, 2005) and others have documented, language is a more *consciously* monitored channel relative to gesture. Speakers are often unaware of gesturing at all, while non-sleeping language-users are aware at least of whether they are producing linguistic forms, even if they cannot be conscious of each lexical and morphological choice involved in production. Overall there are also general feelings that language is somehow *abstract*, while gesture is *"concrete"* not only in physical performance (we move concrete body parts in space when we gesture) but in the kinds of imagery used and meanings represented.

An obvious question is, to what extent these contrasts are contrasts between modalities (aural/oral vs. visual/gestural), and to what extent they are contrasts between Language (linguistic structure) and Non-Language. It seems plausible, for example, to assume that conscious monitoring is a characteristic of the primary linguistic channel, whatever channel that is. Signers know that they are signing, as surely as speakers know that they are speaking, even though signers and speakers alike may be unaware of ancillary non-linguistic actions—such as scratching their heads, or even iconic co-speech gestures. Full conventionality likewise seems prima facie to be a characteristic of the linguistic channel per se, and not of one modality or the other (though there will be more discussion of quotable gestures below). There may be more than one iconic gesture which can be used to express a particular concept, but (as we saw above with the ASL and HKSL signs for TREE) only one is the conventional sign for some particular meaning in a particular signed language.

Concreteness might initially seem more likely to be a characteristic of the medium rather than of Language vs. Gesture. That is, a linguistic sign is as much a concrete action as a gesture accompanying spoken language. And because of the heavily iconic nature of the visual/gestural medium, in many cases signed languages indicate abstract meanings metonymically or metaphorically. The ASL sign for TIME involves directing the dominant hand toward the back of the non-dominant hand's wrist—this sign is iconic for a wrist-watch, and thus metonymic for the time which a watch measures. The ASL time-line (paralleled in other signed languages as well as in many spoken-language gesture systems) metaphorically maps space onto time: the space in front of the signer maps onto future time, the front of the signer's body onto the present, and the space behind the signer onto the past.

Analyticity is perhaps the most complex issue. The claim is of course that it is a characteristic of Language. Complex linguistic communication depends on the fact that putting signs together produces a meaning which is conventionally related to the conventional meanings of the individual signs. Compositionality in morphology and syntax are generally seen as the most basic requirement of full Language—nor shall I question this. But, as we shall see, gesture can be complex and compositional too.

Let us examine these issues in turn. Part of my argument will be that since gesture is a very heterogeneous category, different subcategories of gesture may in fact relate differently to these parameters. We will also need to keep in mind that speakers' gesture processes are themselves multimodal. Although an English speaker saying *Oh* or *Ow* is using a learned linguistic form, a scream is something a baby does not have to learn; it is a vocal gesture (Liddell 2000, 2003).

Throughout my discussion, I shall be using the Mental Spaces framework and Blending theory of Fauconnier and Turner (Fauconnier, 1998; Fauconnier & Turner, 1996, 2001) as background to this work. This framework underlies work on ASL by Liddell (1995, 1998, 2000, 2003), Taub (2001), and Dudis (2004), and also some recent work on gesture (Sweetser, 1998, 2003; Parrill & Sweetser, 2004; Sizemore & Sweetser, 2008). Blending theory has been a crucial tool in furthering our understanding of metaphor and iconicity, in spoken and signed languages and in gesture.

ANALYTICITY AND COMPOSITIONALITY

Let us reexamine McNeill's classic example of the gesture about the tree being bent back (McNeill, 2005, chap. 1; McNeill, 2000), which is represented by a hand apparently grasping an invisible something and bending it backwards. Crucially, says McNeill, it's the *whole* gesture that maps globally onto the whole represented situation, not compositional bits of the gesture that get composed into a whole meaning. When we compare this with the treatment of signed language we can see that similar issues arise there. For example, in the ASL sign for TREE, the entire hand and forearm map onto the shape of a tree, with the extended fingers as branches. On the other hand, it is only the global mapping which determines the match with a tree: in another context, one of those branch-representing extended fingers, the index finger, can represent a standing person; or the index and middle fingers extended downward can represent a bipedal animal walking (so here the index finger represents a leg). Yet these mappings are not "global" in the sense of being unanalyzed: Taub (2001) enumerates the mappings between the 5 hand and the imagined tree, in describing the TREE sign. The fingers are the branches, the arm is the trunk, the non-dominant arm (which is horizontal below the elbow of the "tree" hand) is the ground, and so on. And it is normal to think of hand shape, location, and motion as independent components of an ASL sign. But this kind of structure happens often in gesture as well. It happens perhaps most in conventional "quotable" gestures; Kendon's (2004) analyses of hand shapes' meanings and Calbris' (1990) analyses of French quotable gestures have shown meanings attributed separately to hand shape, location, and so on. In short, either gesture is (at least sometimes) more compositional than we had thought, or signed languages are less so.

McNeill's major point, however, is that the meaning of the bent-back hand as an agent bending over a tree is dependent on the larger discourse—it is top-down, rather than bottom-up interpretation, "global" in the sense that the meaning of the whole (a tree being bent back) is what gives meaning to the parts (the hand shape and the motion). This is a very important point. However, in itself it does not automatically establish that gesture is more synthetic or more global in its interpretation than language is. One of the most difficult problems for language processing systems has always been how to get the right "top-down" interpretive components into place for understanding texts, which are by no means interpretable entirely by taking the meanings of the pieces and composing them to get a meaning for the whole. Context is crucial in linguistic interpretation. Signed language "classifiers" are a case in point. In ASL, an extended index finger may represent different long thin things, depending on the need—or it may be a deictic point to a locus, rather than iconically representing anything; the signer's addressee will know what is represented from the context.

The question we should be asking, then, is whether the top-down meaning structure seen in gesture is different in kind from the sort of discourse-dependence and top-down interpretation which happens all the time in spoken and signed languages. My feeling is that yes, it is different—and that the difference lies primarily not in what is *present* in gesture, but in what is *absent* from it: the *incompleteness* of co-speech gesture. That is, since co-linguistic gesture presumes that the primary information channel is the linguistic one, there is no pressure for content-expressing gesture to represent the described situation as fully as in language. Of course *all* representations are incomplete: perhaps ironically, one of the few points on which formalist, functionalist and cognitivist linguists have converged in the last 20 years is that language never does more than give small but effective prompts toward construction of much richer cognitive structures. But I mean something specific here, by *incomplete*: I mean that the speaker/signer does not intend co-linguistic gesture to do the "full job" of prompting the desired cognitive representation. Although gestural iconic depiction can be quite rich, it does not attempt to "cover the ground" of the content—there is no reason for it to be complete. Naturally, then, gesture needs context from the primary communicative channel to be understood, while the linguistic channel, though often comparatively sparse in its cueing of representations, is charged with cueing mental structures covering the full content described—and hence needs less *content* context from other channels. Of course, language may often require facial expression and (vocal or non-vocal) gestural cueing to create the relevant *discourse* context—more on this later.

CONCRETENESS

It is not always clear exactly what analysts mean when they say that gestures are more concrete than language. Spoken language is a set of muscularly performed routines, which are physically experienced by the auditory systems of listeners. Signed language is another set of muscularly performed routines, this time performed by most of the same muscles (arms, hands, face, body core) which are involved in gesture. However, one thing that "more concrete" *could* mean in this context is that there is iconic structure involving what Liddell (1995, 1998, 2000, 2003) calls a *grounded blend*—one input to the blend is the physical structure of the Real Space of the speaker's body in the communicative setting. The English word *drive* does not involve this kind of Real-Space blend, but the ASL sign DRIVE does: it involves two hands grasping an imaginary steering wheel—the real physical presence of the two grasping hands in Real Space is blended with an imagined driving scenario involving a steering wheel. And gestural representations of driving canonically also involve such blends (LeBaron & Streeck, 2000).

In that case, however, there is no absolute line dividing such structures in signed languages from the ones found in gesture—or indeed, dividing those structures from vocal mimicry, where accent or tone of voice iconically represents accent or tone of voice. And perhaps that makes sense—the problem may lie in the fact that such vocal mimicry was not among the phenomena primarily considered by those who labeled gesture more "concrete" than language. Some new questions which need examination, therefore, would seem to be in what ways auditory Real-Space blends are different from visual ones, or how more conventional Real-Space blends differ from more flexible unconventional ones. Very little systematic work has been done on auditory Real-Space blends, which are a potentially rich domain for research, as Liddell has suggested.

It should be noted, in approaching these questions, that deictic aspects of gesture are "concrete" in the sense of involving Real-Space blends: displaced gestural deixis (cf. Hanks, 1990; Haviland, 1993, 2000; Levinson, 2003; Kita, 2003) allows a speaker/gesturer to point in the Real Space *as if* she were in an imagined space. A speaker might say *Go into my office and the light switch is over here on the left, next to the door*—gesturing to the left, although in English there is no need for the Real-Space gesture to be directionally aligned with the actual space of the described office. In this respect, however, deixis is different from iconicity: it is inherently linked to the Real Space, even in spoken language, and even when there is nothing iconic about the forms used (pronouns and words like *this* or *that* do not iconically represent their meaning). One can only interpret deictic forms via knowing who, where, and when a Speaker is—that is, by identifying her Real Space. Of course, spoken-language deictic forms refer to the Real Space more implicitly, in a less profiled manner—they *refer* to the profiled entity (for example, *that* thing) via its place in a network relating it to the Real-Space speaker—while gesture and signed language both seem to explicitly make use of the Real Space, pointing physically in it.

We should also want to know, therefore, how different deictic Real-Space blends are from iconic ones—and what cognitive difference it makes to access Real-Space blends more explicitly, as opposed to more implicitly. None of this seems likely to give us a simple, unified "gesture versus language" picture of the world.

CONVENTIONALITY

Much co-speech gesture is more flexible and less conventional than speech. But not all. The reason why we distinguish conventional co-speech gestures from language, in spoken communities, is the difference in medium, not the difference in conventionality. We know that "emblems" or "quotable gestures" (Kendon, 1990, 2004) are just as conventional as linguistic signs. When an English speaker holds up a hand in the "F" hand shape (thumb and index forming a circle, the other fingers extended), other English speakers know that this conventionally means "perfect, just right." This gesture is even polysemous in a rather predictable pattern paralleling linguistic polysemy: it could mean "I'm fine," "(you did a) Fine job," or "(the situation is) Perfect or precisely right," among other things. No accompanying speech is needed—the form carries conventional meaning independently. Speakers of other languages, I am told, may conventionally ascribe other unrelated meanings to the same gesture—in some cases, objectionable and insulting meanings. Coming to signed languages, of course many analysts have pointed out (Liddell, 2000, 2003 in particular) that signers gesture; but we would not be able to talk about "quotable gestures" as a special category in signed languages, since the language consists precisely of a range of conventional signs performed solely in the visual-gestural medium.

Returning to the distinction between "flexible" non-lexicalized gestures and conventional linguistic forms, it should be noted that conventionality by its very nature limits the relationship of the form to one particular contextual meaning. You can't have a separate conventional form for every shape of every individual object or path that you encounter. So an unconventional iconic form might be uniquely capable of expressing some particular detailed meaning. Also, it is easier to learn conventional form-meaning correspondences when they have some compositional regularity (a regular past tense is simpler to acquire than an irregular one). There is an extra profit to formal analyticity if it gives the learner regularity and productivity. Together with the *incompleteness* of co-speech gestural representation, this may help to account for perceived differences of globality vs. analyticity between more and less conventionalized forms—and hence between flexible co-speech gesture and language.

It remains somewhat of a mystery exactly how conventionalization affects the meaning of human symbolic forms. Our understanding of ritual, for example, would suggest that repeated and conventional Real-Space blends can have cognitive power which derives precisely from their conventionality. Perhaps some of the same forces are involved when a child demands a fourth sequential reading of the same story, despite having heard it dozens of times before. On the other hand, clichés lose the communicative power associated with "freshness" and innovation, as they become conventionalized larger units; they may (Bybee, 2007) show reduced phonological structure in production, and increasingly "subjective" or discourse-related meaning, as well. Linguists don't know how to make sense of both these two facts together; but at any rate they seem to fit into a broader psychological framework that includes both habituation and dishabituation as responses to stimulus repetition.

Flexible co-speech gesture shows strong conventional aspects as well as flexibility, however: there are culture-specific regularities in how people gesture about both concrete and abstract domains. Local catchments arise in any speaking/gesturing group—that is, speakers pick up each other's gestural uses for particular meanings (cf. LeBaron & Streeck, 2000; McNeill & Duncan, 2000) and re-use them. McNeill's well-known Snow White experiment (McNeill, 1992) showed how speedy this process is and how fast it can become "language-like" or symbolic in character; see also Goldin-Meadow (1993, 2003). Metaphor and iconicity can be conventional and culture-specific, both in language and in gesture. One classic iconic example, cited above, is the difference between the ASL sign for TREE (which uses the hand and arm as an iconic symbol of a tree, with the fingers as the branches) and the Hong Kong Sign Language sign for TREE, which uses the two hands to "trace" the form of a round vertical trunk. When we use the term *motivation*, we typically mean that iconicity or productivity is present along with convention, in defining a particular form-meaning relationship.

In metaphor as well, culturally specific metaphors will be conventionally represented in gesture. Núñez and Sweetser (2006) describe how speakers of Aymara (a language of the Andean highlands) gesture forward when referring to the past and backward when referring to the future, gestural structures which reflect their unusual cultural and linguistic metaphors for time. Speakers of English (and the many other languages where the future is metaphorically in front of the speaker) gesture in the opposite directions (cf. Lakoff & Johnson, 1980, 1999, on more general cognitive models of metaphor in language).

We further know from McNeill (1992), McNeill and Duncan (2000), and others that speakers of different languages regularly co-time their gestures with their speech in different language-specific patterns. We even know that they represent or leave unspecified different aspects of meaning, in the gestural medium, depending on their language; Spanish speakers do not tend to represent manner of motion in the same way that English speakers do, in describing motion scenes. This parallels the differences between the relevant linguistic structures, where Spanish speakers tend to omit description of manner (which is not normally part of the lexical verb meaning in Spanish), while English speakers include it naturally because their lexical verbs include manner (see Slobin, 1987, 1996, 2000).

Of course, no care-giver ever says to a child "don't put the stroke of your gesture on the object, put it on the verb" or "put in manner of motion in your gesture"—because of course the care-givers are themselves unconscious of the relevant patterns. (Care-givers also cannot overtly instruct children in many aspects of linguistic grammar, for the same reason.) Yet we know little about exactly how different culture-specific gestural patterns affect hearers/viewers, outside the world of emblems (which have been a focus for manuals and tourist advice since long before De Jorio or Desmond Morris (cf. Kendon, 2004)). How exactly do an Anglo-American gesturer's co-timing system and manner system communicate *differently* with a Chinese or a Spanish speaker/gesturer than with a fellow English-speaker/gesturer? It does not seem that everyday speakers can consciously put a finger on the differences in patterns at the level of co-timing—though it does seem that a large gesture space makes gesture salient to members of smaller-gesture-space cultures, who then say (e.g.) that Italians "gesture a lot"; conversely, Italians may feel that English speakers don't gesture much.

And where are the universals in gesture structure? To take one specific example, discussed in Sizemore and Sweetser (2008), Anglo-American speakers regularly represent the progress of non-deictic processes either horizontally across the body (left-to-right or right-to-left), or outward from the body, or both (diagonally). (Deictic motion processes are mapped onto directional gestures which fit the deictic viewpoint taken.) Thus, it is possible to gesture toward oneself as one describes deictic motion toward oneself (when saying *She came up to me*, for example). But when describing how to get a degree at Berkeley, or how to dial a telephone number, the gestures will move to locations progressively farther outward from the speaker's body (not toward the body) as the speaker mentions progressively later stages in the process. Is this a culture-specific fact about English gesturers, or is it more general? In my view, it is a potentially more general phenomenon, worthy of comparative crosscultural investigation; I believe it may stem from the fact that gesture is inherently, necessarily viewpointed in a way that speech is not. Not only is it produced *by someone*, as speech is (providing an essential deictic base for speech also), but it is produced in motion which necessarily emanates *from* the trunk of the body—from the unextended rest position of the arms, for example—to farther extended locations. The trunk is a source of bodily gestural motion.

We therefore need more systematic examination of conventional aspects of gesture, as well as of less conventional aspects of language, to distinguish the effects of conventionality from those of (for example) analyticity. And we need to keep in mind that motivation coexists with convention at every level of language and gesture: iconic motivation is not deterministic, but necessarily chooses particular aspects of the two mapped domains to highlight, as in HKSL TREE (outlining the trunk) and ASL TREE (the hand/forearm representing the tree).

ICONICITY, ANALYTICITY, AND CONVENTION

We have said that there are reasons why more iconic structures may indeed be more "global" or "top-down" than less iconic ones. Both gesture and signed languages centrally involve Real-Space iconic mappings in a way that spoken language does not. That is, they both involve capitalizing on interpretation of motion or location in Real Space as meaningful in the domain of expressed content. They therefore cannot have quite as analytic form-meaning relationships as spoken languages, in general. McNeill's "bending back the tree" example, mentioned above, is such a case: as we have said, you have to know the meaning of the whole in order to know the meaning of the parts. For gesture, we have suggested that incompleteness of gestural representation is another reason for globality in interpretation.

However, gesture does seem to have analytic dimensions, or at least, separable parameters of iconic meaning. For example, take Cienki's (1998) examples of gestures accompanying phrases like *good grade* and *do the right thing* versus *bad grade* and *cheat*: the speaker gestured higher for *good grade* and lower for *bad grade*, higher for *do the right thing* and lower for *cheat*. It is clear that the HEIGHT of the location of the gesture corresponds to positive value on an abstract scale, whether of grades or of morality. Clearly this is not the sole meaning of vertical location of gestures, which could also be locating imagined entities in physical space; in language, too, the words *high* and *low* primarily mean literal height, and only secondarily abstract metaphorical moral or grade "height."

But regularly and conventionally, just as with language, the up-down location of a gesture is in itself a parameter distinct from shape of the hand, or even identity of the scale which may be involved.

Force-dynamic structures such as gestural ones are perceived "as wholes"—grasping something, pointing at something. But they are also necessarily parametrically analyzable, presumably by the parameters involved in experientially differentiating them from each other (direction, location, and hand shape, for example). The fact that these parameters are co-performed with each other (a hand has to have both location and hand shape at every moment) long masked their separability as analytic parameters in signed languages, but of course linguists now accept that two signs can differ just by motion, or just by hand shape, or just by location. (Similarly, morphemes with suprasegmental or discontinuous forms in spoken languages were late in being recognized, just because you couldn't neatly assign each of them to a unique temporally adjacent subsequence of the written representation.) But much of the same analytic apparatus developed for cotemporal performance in signed languages is used in description of gesture, where hand shape is regularly noted (and potentially generalized over) independently of hand location.

And on the other hand, we can examine a spoken-language iconic example for comparison. Taub (2001) compares ASL iconicity with that of English sound-symbolic words such as *ding, pow, bang*, or *meow*. She notes that the English phonetics of *ding* have an abrupt onset (d) followed by a gradual offset (spelled "ng"); and that the high front vowel I has higher frequency of a crucial formant than, for example, O. Actual ringing of a bell produces a spectrogram with an abrupt onset and a gradual offset. And of course some bells have higher pitches than others —and indeed *ding, ding* represents a higher-pitched bell than *dong, dong*.

Now, that doesn't mean that we can simply say that "d" on its own, in isolation, represents the start of a bell-stroke, or "ng" the latter part of the stroke—these mappings have iconic naturalness *within* the larger form. (The same point can be made with respect to the "m" and "w" of *meow*, and so on.) *Dig* and *dog* both start with the same phoneme as *ding* and *dong*, and are contrastive by the same I vs. O vowel contrast: but their initial d does not refer to abrupt sound onset, nor is their I: O contrast interpreted as referring to pitch difference. So the iconic interpretation of the linguistic form *ding* is in a sense necessarily global, in that the individual (phonemic-level) submappings exist by coherence with each other as parts of the broader morpheme-level iconic mapping. We can identify specific parameters and segments and their mappings to specific parameters and aspects of the meaning—but such identification is necessarily relative to the whole mapping of form onto meaning. More of signed language is like this than spoken language; and a great deal of gesture is recognized by analysts to be like this.

For example, take a gesture of handing something to someone—an outstretched palm-up hand, perhaps with the thumb above the palm helping to "hold" the invisible surrogate object. Except as a part of the movement outward from the gesturer's body, it would not necessarily be interpreted as "giving"—it would just be "holding," or perhaps something else entirely. And further, the motion has to occur in the right temporal sequence: that is, as a single global motion from close to the speaker to a location closer to the imagined recipient. Movement in the opposite direction would either invert the meaning (someone giving the gesturer something), or make it meaningless. Location at specific points along the path of giving, without the global motion—and in particular, if the points were not in sequence!—would no longer convey the "giving" meaning. This is as true of gesture as it is of the ASL sign GIVE, which is based on the same iconic structure. *Temporal* and *aspectual* structure, like topological structure, have to be mapped "whole" (globally), in iconic mappings—it is the *entire* motion of the hand in this iconic gesture which maps onto the *entire* motion of giving an object to someone.

So what we are really seeing, in language and in non-language, in visual and in auditory media, is that iconicity has a special character. Iconic structures necessarily involve global synthetic mappings, because both the represented and the representing spaces consist of image-schematic structure which is perceived that way. (A cat's meow, or the sound of a bell, comes as a whole—you never get just the onset or just the end.) That does not of course mean there is not analyzable sub-structure—which may be quite systematically mapped too. This special character of iconicity is, then, in my view necessarily a factor in how analytic structure can be interpreted.

THE HETEROGENEITY OF GESTURE

As many analysts at different times have noted, gesture is extremely heterogeneous. So it doesn't make sense to attribute some particular degree of "iconicity" or "conventionality" to gesture in general. Some gestures are extremely conventional (so-called "emblems"), while others are not. Some are highly decomposable analytically—in particular, those built on broad parametric construals of Real-Space blends, such as GOOD IS UP or ABSTRACT IS UP, or ONGOING PROCESSES ARE FORWARD MOTION—while others may not be.

Different kinds of blends are involved in different classes of gestures. Discourse interactional gestures (including quotables like nods) are distinct in character from representational content gestures (Bavelas, Chovil, Lowrie, & Wade, 1992; Kendon, 1995). Sizemore and Sweetser (2008) argue that interpersonal gestures are inherently structured by the establishment of personal, interpersonal, and extrapersonal spaces, which allow us to interpret (for example) gestures into the interlocutor's personal space as having discourse-regulating functions. This brings a pervasive deictic character into interpersonal gesture. Content-related gestures, literal or metaphoric, often show more depictive and iconic character, though deictic structure is crucial to their interpretation as well (as in realizing that processes are depicted as motion AWAY from the gesturer).

As has frequently been observed, a single gesture may cross these lines. Beats, the prosodic gestures which have hardly been discussed in this chapter, are readily superimposed on both content and interpersonal gestures, often without changing the location and hand shape involved in those gestures; speakers may point and "beat" simultaneously, or make beats with a hand which is iconically representing the shape of an object. Similarly, Liddell's (2003) topic-maintenance "buoys" hold loci and may retain hand shape from content gestures. And in Furuyama's (2000) "imaginary origami-folding" task, when speakers reached into their interlocutors' personal gesture spaces to manipulate imagined origami paper, this gesture did indeed clearly combine representational content (depicting origami-folding) with discourse interaction; reaching into the interlocutor's space to "fold paper" clearly marks shared focus, in a way that an analogous gesture in the speaker's own gesture space would not have. As Smith (2003) and Engle (2000) have shown, it is not only imagined but real objects in the environment which can be incorporated into gestural structure, so that some gesture involves object manipulation of *visible surrogates* (there is a scene in the movie *Bend It Like Beckham* wherein one character explains the "offside" rule in soccer to another by using table implements such as a salt shaker to represent the relevant soccer field situation).

Sign language also has deictic and iconic features which are not as pervasively present in spoken languages (with the important exception of sound symbolic structures, noted above). As an example of both of these simultaneously, a palm-out hand in ASL can (as in gesture) represent a protective barrier for the speaker, while a palm-inward hand represents a protective barrier on someone else's behalf, perhaps against the speaker. The use of the hand to represent a two-dimensional barrier is iconic, as the hand is saliently two-dimensional when open. The directionality is deictic; the body is a deictic center, and the hand is naturally adapted to push things *away* from that center with the palm outward.

However, signing does *not* to my knowledge incorporate into its linguistic structure actions like those of the origami folders who reached into their interlocutors' space to manipulate the imagined paper developed by those interlocutors. Nor do conventional sign forms "reach into" the interlocutor's space as Sizemore and Sweetser's gesturers consistently did (Sizemore & Sweetser, 2008). This is not to say that signers couldn't do such things in co-sign gesture—as has been pointed out, signers clearly do gesture, even though analysts may disagree as to exactly which components of their motions are linguistic and which are gestural. Similarly, signed languages appear to have special constraints with respect to representing motion past a boundary, which are not there in gesture: a gesturer can say *ran into the room* and gesture with the moving hand right past a boundary hand, while a signer of ASL or ASN has to separately represent the running and the boundary crossing (Slobin & Hoiting, 1994). So another very important area of research is the examination of the precise constraints imposed on linguistic forms—as opposed to those imposed on gesture.

I do not claim to have redefined the characteristics of the Language-Gesture distinction or the Auditory-Visual one in this discussion. Rather, what I hope to have achieved is a rethinking of the problems involved in such definitions. It is important to note potential relationships between primary informational channel and completeness or analyticity—or between iconicity (with its global mappings) and real-space blending—and consider the consequences of such relationships. It is also important to break down traditional binary contrasts such as iconic vs. non-iconic as well as iconic vs. conventional—spectrums need to replace some binary oppositions, and more orthogonality needs to be recognized between classifications such as iconicity and conventionality.

REFERENCES

Bavelas, J., Chovil, N., Lowrie, D. A., & Wade, A. (1992). Interactive gestures. *Discourse Processes, 15*, 469–489.

Bybee, J. (2007). *Frequency of use and the organization of language*. Oxford, UK: Oxford University Press.

Calbris, G. (1990). *The semiotics of French gesture*. Bloomington: Indiana University Press.

Cienki, A. (1998). Metaphoric gestures and some of their relations to verbal metaphoric expressions. In J.-P. Koenig (Ed.), *Discourse and cognition* (pp. 189–204). Stanford CA: CSLI Publications.

Dudis, P. G. (2004). Body partitioning and real-space blends. *Cognitive Linguistics, 15*(2), 223–238.

Engle, R. A. (2000). Towards a theory of multimodal communication: Combining speech, gestures, diagrams and demonstrations in instructional explanations. Ph.D. dissertation, School of Education, Stanford University.

Fauconnier, G. (1998). Mental spaces, language modalities, and conceptual integration. In M. Tomasello (Ed.), *The new psychology of language* (pp. 251–279). Mahwah, NJ: Lawrence Erlbaum Associates.

Fauconnier, G., & Turner, M. (1996). Blending as a central process of grammar. In A. Goldberg (Ed.), *Conceptual structure, discourse and language* (pp. 113–130). Stanford: CSLI.

Fauconnier, G., & Turner, M. (2001). *The way we think*. New York: Basic Books.

Fillmore, C. J. (1997 [1971]). *Lectures on deixis*. Stanford CA: CSLI Publications (originally published by Indiana University Linguistics Club).

Furuyama, N. (2000). Gestural interaction between the instructor and the learner in origami instruction. In D. McNeill (Ed.), *Language and gesture* (pp. 99–117). Cambridge, UK: Cambridge University Press.

Goldin-Meadow, S. (1993). When does gesture become language? A study of gesture used as a primary communication system by deaf children of hearing parents. In K. R. Gibson and T. Ingold (Eds.), *Tools, language and cognition in human evolution* (pp. 63–85). New York: Cambridge University Press.

Goldin-Meadow, S. (2003). *Hearing gesture*. Cambridge, MA: Harvard University Press.

Hanks, W. F. (1990). *Referential practice: Language and lived space among the Maya*. Chicago: University of Chicago Press.

Haviland, J. B. (1993). Anchoring, iconicity and orientation in Guugu Yimithirr pointing gestures. *Journal of Linguistic Anthropology, 3*, 3–45.

Haviland, J. B. (2000). Pointing, gesture spaces and mental maps. In D. McNeill (Ed.), *Language and gesture* (pp. 13–46). Cambridge, UK: Cambridge University Press.

Kendon, A. (1990). Gesticulation, quotable gestures and signs. In M. Moerman & M. Nomura (Eds.), *Culture embodied* (pp. 53–77). Osaka: National Museum of Ethnology.

Kendon, A. (1995). Gestures as illocutionary and discourse markers in Southern Italian conversation. *Journal of Pragmatics 23*, 247–279.

Kendon, A. (2000). Language and gesture: Unity or duality? In D. McNeill (Ed.), *Language and gesture* (pp. 47–63). Cambridge, UK: Cambridge University Press.

Kendon, A. (2004). *Gesture: Visible action as utterance*. Cambridge, UK: Cambridge University Press.

Kita, S. (Ed.). (2003). *Pointing: Where language, culture and cognition meet*. Mahwah, NJ: Lawrence Erlbaum Associates.

Lakoff, G., & Johnson, M. (1980). *Metaphors we live by*. Chicago: University of Chicago Press.

Lakoff, G., & Johnson, M. (1999). *Philosophy in the flesh: The embodied mind and its challenge to Western thought*. New York: Basic Books.

LeBaron, C., & Streeck, J. (2000). Gestures, knowledge and the world. In D. McNeill (Ed.), *Language and Gesture* (pp. 118–138). Cambridge, UK: Cambridge University Press.

Levinson, S. (2003). *Space in language and cognition: Explorations in cognitive diversity*. Cambridge, UK: Cambridge University Press.

Liddell, S. (1995). Real, surrogate and token space: Grammatical consequences in ASL. K. Emmorey & J. Reilly (Eds.), *Language, gesture and space* (pp. 19–41). Hillsdale, NJ: Lawrence Erlbaum Associates.

Liddell, S. (1998). Grounded blends, gestures, and conceptual shifts. *Cognitive Linguistics, 9*(3), 283–314.

Liddell, S. (2000). Blended spaces and deixis in sign language discourse. In D. McNeill (Ed.), *Language and gesture* (pp. 331–357). Cambridge, UK: Cambridge University Press.

Liddell, S. (2003). *Grammar, gesture and meaning in American Sign Language*. Cambridge, UK: Cambridge University Press.

McNeill, D. (1992). *Hand and mind*. Chicago: University of Chicago Press.

McNeill, D. (Ed.). (2000). *Language and gesture*. Cambridge, England, UK: Cambridge University Press.

McNeill, D. (2005). *Gesture and thought*. Chicago: University of Chicago Press.

McNeill, D., &. Duncan, S. D. (2000). Growth points in thinking for speaking. In D. McNeill, *Language and gesture* (pp. 141–161). Cambridge, UK: Cambridge University Press.

Nuñez, R., & Sweetser, E. (2006) Aymara, where the future is behind you: Convergent evidence from language and gesture in the crosslinguistic comparison of spatial realizations of time. *Cognitive Science, 30*, 410–450.

Parrill, F., & Sweetser, E. (2004). What we mean by meaning: Conceptual integration in gesture analysis and transcription. *Gesture, 4*(2), 197–219.

Sizemore, M., & Sweetser, E. (2008). Personal and interpersonal gesture spaces: Functional contrasts in language and gesture. In A. Tyler, Y. Kim, and M. Takada (Eds.), *Language in the context of use: Cognitive and discourse approaches to language and language learning.* Berlin: Mouton de Gruyter.

Slobin, D. I. (1987). Thinking for speaking. In J. Aske et al. (Eds.), *Proceedings of the 13th annual meeting of the Berkeley Linguistics Society* (pp. 435–445). Berkeley: The Berkeley Linguistics Society.

Slobin, D. I. (1996). From 'thought and language' to 'thinking for speaking.' In J. Gumperz & S. C. Levinson (Eds.), *Rethinking linguistic relativity* (pp. 70–96). Cambridge, UK: Cambridge University Press.

Slobin, D. I. (2000). Verbalized events: A dynamic approach to linguistic relativity and determinism. In S. Niemeier & R. Dirven (Eds.), *Evidence for linguistic relativity* (pp. 107–138). Amsterdam: John Benjamins.

Slobin, D. (2005). Linguistic representations of motion events: What is signifier and what is signified? In C. Maeder, O. Fischer, & W. Herlofsky (Eds.), *Iconicity inside out: Iconicity in language and literature 4*. Amsterdam/Philadelphia: John Benjamins.

Slobin, D. I., & Hoiting, N. (1994). Reference to movement in spoken and signed languages: Typological considerations. *Proceedings of the 20th annual meeting of the Berkeley Linguistics Society* (pp. 487–505). Berkeley: The Berkeley Linguistics Society.

Smith, N. (2003). Gesture and beyond. Honors thesis, Program in Cognitive Science, University of California at Berkeley.

Sweetser, E. (1998). Regular metaphoricity in gesture: boldily-based models of speech interaction. In CD-ROM *Proceedings of the 16th International Congress of Linguists*, Paris, July 1997.

Sweetser, E. (2003). Literal and metaphorical viewpoint in gesture. Paper presented at the 8th International Cognitive Linguistics Conference, University of La Rioja, Spain, July 2003.

Taub, S. F. (2001). *Language from the body: Iconicity and metaphor in American Sign Language*. Cambridge, UK: Cambridge University Press.

27

On Paradigms, Principles, and Predictions

MATTHEW RISPOLI

University of Illinois at Urbana-Champaign

The capacity to create paradigms is central to the LMC.

Dan I. Slobin (1985, p. 1213)

This Festschrift contribution discusses paradigms. Infants and toddlers must discover the grammatical distinctions that will be important for building paradigms in their language and they must learn to incorporate the choices afforded by the paradigms into the sentences they produce. This was the perspective that pervaded the thinking of many minds devoting their time and attention to the problem of language development in the late 1980s at the University of California, Berkeley. At the center of this group, both challenging and guiding us, was Dan Slobin. This chapter is also about principles and prediction. As we shall see, Dan Slobin's forays into understanding the development of paradigms led to some initial principles. This chapter seeks to move us beyond principles to a level of prediction about the behavior of individual children.

Paradigms are at the center of what we mean by morphosyntax. The closed class morphemes of a language form a network or system of interrelationships by virtue of the fact that they are both similar to one another and that they contrast with one another. They are similar to one another by virtue of the grammatical features they share in common. They also contrast with one another. Consider for example, the forms of the auxiliary Be seen in the two sentences; (a) I am running, and (b) He is running. The forms am and is have tense in common. They are both present tense forms. However, they also contrast. The form am specifies a first person singular subject, whereas the form is specifies a third person singular subject. From the child's point of view, it is best if this network is matched by an isomorphic set of morphemes. That is, each feature in the paradigm would have its own corresponding morpheme. When the morphemes combine within a word in a string-like fashion to express the inflectional properties of a noun, verb, or adjective, we refer to this arrangement as agglutination. Languages like Turkish, which Dan Slobin studied in the 1970s, are fairly transparent in the relationship between a grammatical feature and the morpheme which expresses it. However, there are many languages in which the relationship between feature and morpheme is not one to one, but many to one. That is, several features combine in a single morpheme that expresses that specific combination. Such systems are called fusional, and English is one of these languages. In the prior English example am and is are similar in tense but contrast in person. However, one cannot separate am into two morphemes, one for tense and one for person. Consider the English third person singular agreement present tense suffix that appears on verbs (e.g., Sam want-s a ball). This morpheme expresses agreement in one and only one tense (it is not found in the past tense) and the person-number feature is a combination of third person AND singular. Crosslinguistically, paradigms express a rather limited set of grammatical features (tense, aspect, person, number, and gender are among a group of about twenty that recur in historically unrelated languages). However languages vary in the degree to which the features are expressed: from one-to-one isomorphism to extreme forms of many-to-one mapping, where combinations of several features are expressed in a single morpheme

Dan Slobin suggested several principles that governed the acquisition of paradigms (Slobin, 1985). Let me try to boil them down to a basic three. The first principle of the crosslinguistic perspective on paradigm acquisition is: (A) when isomorphism is extensive in a paradigm, as in agglutinating languages like Turkish, the child has an easier time learning it. The second principle is that (B) when isomorphism is lacking, as in fusional languages like English, confusion arises, as seen in the form of error. The third principle is that (C) the resulting confusion is never total chaos, but actually contains kernels of order. It is the third principle that makes life interesting for developmental psycholinguists, for errors give them insight into the mechanisms by which paradigms are learned.

The essence of science is prediction. At a very broad level, these three principles are predictive. Children learning agglutinative languages will make fewer errors than children learning fusional languages. But you can't extract predictions from these principles much beyond this general level. That is because the principles refer to languages, not children. As every developmental psycholinguist knows, we can speak of the "English-speaking child," but such talk covers a vast array of individual differences among the millions of children learning English as a first language. If the essence of science is prediction, shouldn't we be trying to predict what children will do? The answer to my mind is an unequivocal YES! In this way, we can harness the power of statistics to sort out patterns that are common among all children learning a language, and patterns that are individual to children. Both components are necessary to make predictions about what a child will do. Let's take a concrete example of a specific error and show how we can make predictions in a longitudinal framework.

The errors children make while learning the personal pronoun paradigm of English are a microcosmic demonstration of Principle C. The learning process is replete with never-total-chaos effects. These effects have been explored in greatest detail within a subset of the English pronominal system, the third person, case distinct personal pronoun paradigm (Loeb & Leonard, 1991; Moore, 1995, 2001; Pelham, 2000; Rispoli, 1994; Wexler, Schütze, & Rice 1998; Rispoli, 1998b; Pine, Rowland, Lieven, & Theakston, 2005). One can find similar effects in the first and second person pronouns (Budwig, 1989; Rispoli, 1998a). Linguistically, however, the first and second person pronouns refer to the speaker and listener, not entities outside of the axis of discourse. The subset forms a coherent unit in that the singular pronouns are gendered, but this gender distinction is neutralized in the plural. Thus the third person pronouns make a paradigmatically coherent subset. In addition, research has concentrated on the case distinct pronouns (this excludes the neuter singular), because researchers are naturally interested in the parts of the system that will give rise to error. Future research may well uncover more information about how paradigms are acquired by expanding to include more pronouns. For now, however, the case distinct third person pronouns seem to provide a well-defined and theoretically justified entrée into understanding the mechanisms of paradigm acquisition.

Without a doubt, the most prevalent pattern of pronoun case error is the overextension of the objective case form for the nominative and genitive forms (Gruber, 1967; Huxley, 1970; Rispoli, 1994; Thornton, 2002). I have termed this pattern "stereotypic" (Rispoli, 2000), because we have come to expect it, and because we have become so used to seeing it that we sometimes fail to notice the full diversity of errors involved in learning the case forms of these pronoun paradigms. But even within the realm of what might be considered the stereotype, we find interesting and informative variation. It is clear that the feminine singular is the locus of more replacements of the nominative case form than the masculine singular: there are a lot more her for she errors than there are him for he errors (Moore, 1995, 2001; Pelham, 2000; Rispoli, 1994; Rispoli, 1998b; Pine et al., 2005). I have suggested that this is because the feminine paradigm has both a suppletive nominative she and two oblique cells (objective and genitive) occupied by one word form her, and I have called this the double-cell effect (Rispoli, 1998b). No other personal pronoun is structured in this way, and her for she errors are reliably the most frequent of all the third person pronoun case errors.

There is converging evidence from independent research teams that pronoun case errors decrease as children incorporate finiteness into sentence production on a reliable and consistent basis (Loeb & Leonard, 1991; Rispoli, 2005; Wexler, Schütze, & Rice, 1998). Some claims to this effect have been stated in an overly strong manner. Schütze and Wexler (1996), for example, claimed that there is a tight association between nominative case error and unmarked, non-finite verb forms. However, when subjected to rigorous tests of association, the evidence for this hypothesis evaporates (Charest & Leonard, 2004; Pine, Joseph, & Conti-Ramsden, 2004; Pine et al., 2005; Rispoli, 1999). On the other hand, there is no doubt that the incidence of pronoun case error decreases as finiteness markers become more prevalent in sentence production.

There is good reason to believe that the negative relationship between finiteness and pronoun case error is heteroskedastic. In statistics, a variable is heteroskedastic if it lacks a constant variance. If one tries to predict the rate of pronoun case error based on finiteness alone, variance in the rate of pronoun case is far from constant. The variance in pronoun case error rates is orders of magnitude greater at the low end of the finiteness continuum than at the high end of the continuum (Rispoli, 2005). In other words, there are plenty of children at low levels of finiteness who have little or no pronoun case error as well as others at the same low level of finiteness marking with much higher rates of error. So, what keeps the children who have not acquired finiteness from making an enormous number of pronoun case errors? This is not just an esoteric question, for it gets at scientific essentials. Understanding error is important, and not being able to predict who will err and who will not means that our discipline lacks explanatory constructs.

The answer proposed in Rispoli (2005) was that variation in pronoun case error rates was additionally related to paradigm expansion. The more limited the expansion of the paradigm, the less likely pronoun case error becomes. Rispoli (2005) introduced a measure of pronoun paradigm expansion, SDpro (standard deviation of attempts at pronominal cells across the paradigm). Details for the calculation of SDpro are given in Rispoli (2005), but I shall review them here. SDpro tells us whether a child's attempts to express feature combinations in each cell of the paradigm are highly deviant from the mean (resulting in a high SD value), or very close to the mean (resulting in a low SD value). A high SD value indicates that the child is attempting to express the feature combinations of a limited number of cells, while neglecting other cells. This is considered as high concentration of attempts in a limited number of cells, hence limited paradigm expansion. A low SD value indicates that the child attempts to express the feature combinations in all or most cells with roughly similar frequencies (hence the value in each cell is not too deviant from the mean). This results in a low concentration of attempts in any one cell and more equal attempts across the cells of the paradigm, hence more elaborate paradigm expansion.

Let us use two examples from a 27-month-old child's data to illustrate the calculation and the concepts SDpro represents. Table 27.1A shows a very limited pronoun paradigm. The frequencies in each cell are converted to percentages of the total output (shown in parentheses). The observed percentage in a cell minus the mean percentage (11%) of the 9 cells is the deviation score of that cell (e.g., (.87–.11)). The deviation scores are squared (e.g., (.87–.11)^2), the squared deviation scores are summed and this sum is then divided by the number of cells minus 1 (i.e., 8) giving the variance. In this example the sum of the squared deviation scores is .65 and the variance is .082. The standard deviation is simply the square root of the variance, in this example .29 (the maximum SDpro is .316). The reason why we have a limited paradigm with a high concentration of productions on a single

TABLE 27.1A Pronoun Productions of a 27-Month-Old with a Limited Paradigm

	Masculine	Feminine	Plural
Nominative	26 (.87)	3 (.05)	0
Objective	3 (.05)	0	0
Genitive	2 (.03)	0	0

TABLE 27.1B Pronoun Productions of a 27-Month-Old with an Expanded Paradigm

	Masculine	Feminine	Plural
Nominative	14 (.10)	43 (.30)	1 (.01)
Objective	3 (.02)	25 (.18)	3 (.02)
Genitive	2 (.01)	36 (.26)	0

cell is because the child's attempts primarily focus on the cell of the masculine nominative (87%). Table 27.1B presents a relatively more expanded paradigm. The lower concentrations of the child's productions across the paradigm yield a lower SDpro of .12. Note that SDpro values are logically independent of error rate, because both correct productions and pronoun case errors are counted (errors are not indicated in Tables 27.1A and 27.1B). Now that we have reviewed how SDpro is calculated, we can discuss its relevance.

Rispoli (2005) is a departure from prior research in that it proposes a new causal model of pronoun case error. The model posits two causal factors, finiteness in sentence production and paradigm expansion, not just one, finiteness, as prior attempts to explain variation in pronoun case error rates have done (Schütze & Wexler, 1996). These two factors interact to increase or decrease the likelihood of pronoun case error. Pronoun case error is extremely unlikely after the child has mastered the marking of finiteness. The Rispoli model shares this aspect in common with more formal linguistic approaches such as Schütze and Wexler (1996). However, even when the child is far from the mastery of finiteness, the child is only at serious risk for pronoun case error when the paradigm is ambitiously over-expanded. This aspect of the model is unique. Rispoli (2005) provided support for this model with a large cross-sectional sample of children ranging in age from 24 to 48 months. A longitudinal test of the hypothesis is necessary. To truly test the hypothesis with longitudinal data both finiteness and paradigm expansion must be conceptualized as dynamic and changing.

In this contribution celebrating Dan Slobin's career and contributions, I would like to take an initial step in testing the two-factor model of the causation of the stereotypic pronoun case errors with longitudinal data. I ask a basic question. Is the initial state of paradigm expansion related to the direction of change in pronoun case error? It should be according to the two-factor causal model of pronoun case error. Children with limited paradigms (high SDpro) should not be making pronoun case errors initially. These children are close to ceiling at SDpro. These children have practically no place to go but to further expand the paradigm. So, we would expect these children's pronoun case error rates either to increase over time or to stay constant at zero. Children with expanded paradigms (low SDpro) are jumping off at an increased risk for pronoun case error. It is these children who should start out with more stereotypic pronoun case error. Over time, their rate of pronoun case error should decrease. Again, this is a very simple first step at testing the two-factor causal model of pronoun case error on longitudinal data. In fact, it is a baby step, in that I am not testing the relationship between finiteness and pronoun case error. That is because paradigm expansion is the novel and controversial part of the hypothesis.

The data are from 10 typically developing children. Two hours of language sample were taken every 3 months from 21 to 33 months of age. Their production of the case-distinct third person paradigm (third singular masculine he, him, his, feminine she, her, her and plural they, them, their) (Rispoli 2005) was tracked until it reached the following criterion: a minimum of 25 spontaneous and independent sentences with pronouns. The criterion was reached by all 10 children at 27 months. With 25 spontaneous and independent sentences, there is a reasonable denominator for calculating both SDpro and stereotypic pronoun case error, which is the overextension of the objective forms, him, her, and them. I am only interested in stereotypic error in this chapter, because the Schütze and Wexler (1996) model predicts a correlation between finiteness and the stereotypic error. There are other types of pronoun case error, but they are not at issue in this investigation.

TABLE 27.2 SDpro and Stereotypic Error Rates at 27, 30, and 33 Months

	27 mo		30 mo		33 mo	
Child	SDpro	Stereotypic Error	SDpro	Stereotypic Error	SDpro	Stereotypic Error
M6	.29	0	.25	0	.28	0
M8	.29	0	.19	.01	.12	0
M13	.26	0	.16	.13	.11	.21
F13	.18	0	.11	0	.14	.01
F18	.15	0	.18	0	.24	0
F15	.14	.03	.10	.01	.09	0
F1	.13	.38	.15	0	.09	0
F5	.12	.12	.11	0	.11	.02
F4	.12	.01	.09	0	.12	0
F17	.08	.06	.13	.02	.19	.03

Table 27.2 reports the SDpros at 27, 30, and 33 months, and the stereotypic error rates at the same times. The children are arranged by SDpro score at 27 months starting from the highest SDpro (limited paradigm) and moving downward to the lowest SDpro (expanded paradigm). Visual inspection readily shows that at 27 months there was a relationship between SDpro and the stereotypic error rate. Children with SDpro lower than .15 were already making stereotypic errors. The relationship between the SDpro and stereotypic error rate at 27 months was in fact quite strong, Spearman $\rho = -.81$, $p < .01$. Moreover, the SDpro at 27 months was related to the magnitude and direction of change in the stereotypic error rate between 27 and 30 months, Spearman $\rho = -.80$, $p < .01$. The SDpro at 27 months was moderately related to the average change in the stereotypic error rate between 27 months and 33 months, $\rho = -.69$, $p < .05$.

SDpro helps explain individual developmental profiles in the course of pronoun case acquisition of the 6-month period of 27 to 33 months. Two girls, F1 and F5, with broad paradigms at 27 months, decreased their stereotypic error rates rapidly in 3 months time. In contrast, some of the children with limited paradigms at 27 months, such as M13, actually showed subsequent increases in the stereotypic error rate, going from no stereotypic error to a stereotypic error rate of .20 at 33 months. Thus F1 and M13 represent two radically different paths in the development of pronoun case. F1 begins with a broad paradigm and runs into trouble with pronoun case. This girl's pronoun case errors are seen early, at 27 months. In contrast, M13 begins with a limited paradigm and subsequent expansion of the paradigm is accompanied by pronoun case error. This boy's errors emerge at 30 months of age and increase at 33 months of age.

Rispoli (2005) predicted that those children who follow a path of development characterized by relatively slow paradigm expansion might be able to avoid pronoun case error altogether. From Table 27.2 one can see that two children, M6 and F18, produced no stereotypic pronoun case errors in 6 hours of sample taken over 6 months. M6 had a high SDpro at 27 months (.29) and the paradigm remained highly limited over 6 months. F18 began with a moderate SDpro at 27 months (.18) and she actually pruned her paradigm back over the next 6 months to an SDpro of .24. These two children may well represent the predicted path that avoids error.

It should also be pointed out that paradigm expansion cannot predict all the variation in stereotypic pronoun case error in these data. The increase in paradigm expansion for M8 and F13 resulted in a very small increase in error rate. This suggests that other factors may be playing a role. Future research should be directed at uncovering these factors.

The phenomenon of pronoun case error is a microcosm of morphosyntactic development. It is a clear case of principle C, a never-total-chaos phenomenon. I would argue that we have made substantial progress in understanding pronoun case error. Except for those scientists who are fanatically committed to one-dimensional explanation, I think all would agree that several dimensions are needed to understand these errors. Rispoli (1994) pointed out that there was more than just the stereotypic overextension of the oblique form contained in the totality of pronoun case error. The phonological microstructure of the personal pronoun paradigms do account for variation in error rates. Rispoli (1994) suggested that mechanisms of paradigm building were implicated in the direction, magnitude, and variety of pronoun case errors. Strong relationships, both negative and positive, between sub-categories of pronoun case error were established empirically (Ogiela, 1995; Rispoli, 1994; Rispoli, 1998a, 1998b; Schuele, Haskill, & Rispoli, 2005). The general relationship between pronoun case errors and growth in finiteness has been examined in depth (Loeb & Leonard, 1991; Rispoli 2005; Schütze & Wexler, 1996; Wexler et al., 1998). With the introduction of SDpro in Rispoli (2005), claims about the influence of paradigm building can now be tested with much greater precision. SDpro will advance us toward the goal of predicting which children will make pronoun case errors and when. I am certain that we are closer to solid prediction today than we were 10 years ago. Let there be no mistake, the ability to predict pronoun case errors should be our goal, for prediction is the essence of science. In the new millennium, our corner of developmental science, developmental psycholinguistics, will stand or fall depending on whether we can move from the broad principles of Dan Slobin's generation to precise and accurate prediction.

REFERENCES

Budwig, N. (1989). The linguistic marking of agentivity and control in child language. *Journal of Child Language, 16,* 263–284.

Charest, M., & Leonard, L. (2004). Predicting tense: finite verb morphology and subject pronouns in the speech of typically-developing children and children with specific language impairment. *Journal of Child Language, 31,* 231–246.

Gruber, J. (1967). Topicalization in child language. *Foundations of Language 3,* 37–65.

Huxley, R. (1970). The development of the correct use of subject personal pronouns in two children. In G. Flores d'Arcais & W. Levelt (Eds.), *The development of the correct use of subject personal pronouns in two children. Advances in Psycholinguistics* (pp. 141–165). Amsterdam: North Holland.

Loeb, D., & Leonard, L. (1991). Subject case marking and verb morphology in normally developing and specifically language impaired children. *Journal of Speech and Hearing Research, 34,* 340–346.

Moore, M. (1995). Error analysis of pronouns by normal and language-impaired children. *Journal of Communications Disorders, 28,* 57–72.

Moore, M. (2001). Third person pronoun errors by children with and without language impairment. *Journal of Communications Disorders, 34,* 207–228.

Ogiela, D. (1995). *Pronoun case errors in specifically language impaired and normally developing children.* Unpublished master's thesis. Purdue University, West Lafayette, Indiana.

Pelham, S. (2000). *The curious case of pronouns: explaining children's usage.* Unpublished master's thesis. University of Kansas, Lawrence.

Pine, J., Joseph, K., & Conti-Ramsden, G. (2004). Do data from children with specific language impairment support the agreement/tense omission model? *Journal of Speech, Language and Hearing Research, 47,* 913–923.

Pine, J., Rowland, C., Lieven, E., & Theakston, A. (2005). Testing the agreement/tense omission model: Why the data on children's use of non-nominative 3psg subjects count against the ATOM. *Journal of Child Language, 32,* 269–289.

Rispoli, M. (1994). Pronoun case overextension and paradigm building. *Journal of Child Language, 21,* 157–172.

Rispoli, M. (1998a). Me or my: Two different patterns of pronoun case errors. *Journal of Speech and Hearing Research, 41,* 385–393.

Rispoli, M. (1998b). Patterns of pronoun case error. *Journal of Child Language, 25,* 533–554.

Rispoli, M. (1999). Case and agreement in English language development. *Journal of Child Language, 26,* 357–372.

Rispoli, M. (2000). Towards a more precise model of pronoun case error: A response to Schütze. *Journal of Child Language, 27,* 707–714.

Rispoli, M. (2005). When children reach beyond their grasp: Why some children make pronoun case errors and others don't. *Journal of Child Language, 32,* 93–116.

Schuele, C., Haskill, A., & Rispoli, M. (2005) What's /der/?: An anomalous error in a child with SLI. *Clinical Linguistics and Phonetics, 19*, 89–107.

Schütze, C., & Wexler, K. (1996). Subject case licensing and English root infinitives. In A. Stringfellow, D. Chana Amitay, E. Hughes, & A. Zukowski, (Eds.) *Proceedings of the 20th Annual Boston University Conference on Language Development* (pp. 670–681). Somerville, MA: Cascadilla Press.

Slobin, D. I. (1985). Crosslinguistic evidence for the language making capacity. In D. I. Slobin (Ed.), *The crosslinguistic study of language acquisition: Vol. 2. Theoretical issues* (pp. 1157–1319). Hillsdale, NJ: Lawrence Erlbaum Associates.

Thornton, R. (2002). Let's change the subject: Focus movement in early grammar. *Language Acquisition, 10*, 229–271.

Wexler, K., Schütze, C., & Rice, M. (1998). Evidence for the Agr/Tns omission model. *Language Acquisition, 7*, 317–344.

28

Child Language, Aphasia, and General Psycholinguistics[1]

LISE MENN

University of Colorado

One cannot make claims about the acquisition or use of a grammatical form without situating it typologically, in a network of interactive psycholinguistic factors.

Dan I. Slobin (1997, p. 35)

INTRODUCTION: DEFINING 'SIMPLICITY'

The language of children and of people with aphasia (along with others at considerable remove from the ideal speaker-hearer) is in some sense simpler than the language of fully fluent adults without brain damage who are speaking in their habitually used native tongue; in plainer words, it is simpler than the language of normal speakers.[2] But in what sense is it simpler?

We need to know what is simple for the mind to process because we expect that this will tell us about the nature of the mind and how it works; so this implies that we should be looking for a psycholinguistic approach to the problem. What does 'simple' mean psycholinguistically? The cross-linguistic data in this chapter show that our intuitions about simplicity in morphology and syntax are not adequate, nor are our predictions based on existing linguistic theories. I propose a definition of simplicity for aphasia that is based on the kinds of errors we find in aphasic speech: Whatever error form the aphasic speaker uses is simpler for her *at that moment* than the correct target form. Although some errors fall into patterns that can be accounted for by our intuitions about morphological and syntactic complexity, the classic idea that a single dimension of simplicity in morphosyntax can describe how both child language and aphasic language differ from normal adult language does not work. Yet there are significant resemblances between (some) child speech patterns and (some) aphasic speech patterns. Leheckova (2001, p. 179) gives a typical statement for Czech: "the forms most available to aphasics tend to correlate with the earliest acquired forms and the most frequent ones."

---

[1] Thanks to Bill Bright, Michael Gottfried, Alice Healy, Patrick Juola, Brian MacWhinney, Jean-Luc Nespoulous, Beverley Wulfeck, and the editors of this volume for references, corrections, and helpful suggestions. I dedicate this chapter to the memory of my husband and colleague Bill Bright, who encouraged all my work (and edited almost all of it) with love for over 20 years.

[2] I will use the term 'normal' in the sense defined here. While it is now usual in developmental studies to say 'typical,' that term is not adequate for aphasia research.

How can these correlations—as well as the fact that that they are imperfect—be explained? I will try to do this in terms of the 'network of interactive psycholinguistic factors' that Slobin proposed. Using such a framework, we will look at fascinating errors in picture descriptions and narratives produced by aphasics across several languages. These errors are important because they have to be explained by the interaction of moment-to-moment events during speech production, a time scale not usually discussed in either child language or aphasiology. These data, combined with what is already known about the process of language production in normal adults, give us a picture of the brain as an arena of intense competition between potentially relevant words and grammatical structures, an arena in which morphology, syntax, lexicon, phonology, and semantics interact at a furious pace in the course of producing each utterance.

DAN SLOBIN'S CONTRIBUTION TO APHASIA RESEARCH

Why should there be an aphasia chapter in a Slobin Festschrift? Well, Dan has published some lovely papers on aphasia in Turkish (e.g., Slobin, 1991), but the main reason is that comparative aphasiology (Liz Bates' term for the field) only got off the ground after Dan's Berkeley Crosslinguistic Acquisition Project showed how international teams could be organized and what they could contribute. His organizational strategy was the model for the international Cross Language Aphasia Study (CLAS) group that produced the Menn and Obler (1990b) volumes and subsequent publications, including the University of Montreal CLASNET working paper series edited by Jarema and Nespoulous beginning in 1995. If Liz were still with us, there would have been two comparative aphasiology chapters in this book, because Slobin's work was the inspiration for her group as well, even though our approaches were different—hers was based on experimental techniques, while mine is based on the traditions of linguistic fieldwork and the observational studies of Roger Brown. The result, fortunately, has been that the two groups' crosslinguistic results have been independent, complementary, and convergent. This chapter draws on data from both bodies of work, and from other sources in comparative aphasiology.

The aphasia corpora that I review look dramatically different from child language materials, but approaching both types of data from the viewpoint of online production might reveal unexpected similarities.

DEFINING SIMPLICITY

In the 1960s, thanks to tape recordings and the development of experimental methods to study language comprehension, production, and judgment (Caramazza & Zurif, 1978; Gleason, 1982), we began to understand that adult aphasias do not regress to a childlike or infantile state of language. This means that we cannot equate 'simpler' with what is learned earlier, and the reason we cannot do it is that the neural networks change over the course of development. What infants do first must be what is simplest for them at the time they start learning, but as they learn, what is simplest evidently keeps changing.

So we try again. As a first approximation to an operational definition of 'simple' language for adults who do not have brain damage, consider the landmark experimental study by Blackwell and Bates (1995). They showed that normal speakers under sufficient competing task stress start to have difficulty processing grammatical morphemes. (This is a defining symptom of the variety of aphasia known as agrammatism; we'll say more about the variety of aphasias shortly.) This tells us that, for normal speakers, understanding a sentence that requires only understanding word order and content words is easier than understanding a sentence that requires processing English grammatical morphemes (e.g., a semantically reversible passive-voice sentence).

Now let's consider the phenomenon alluded to in the title of a paper by Nespoulous and Lecours (1989, English version Nespoulous et al. 1998): *Pourquoi l'aphasique peut-il dire: "Je ne peux pas le dire" et pas "Elle ne peut pas la chanter?"* 'Why can the aphasic person say "I can't say it" but not "She can't sing that?"' What sort of language processing mechanism finds 'I can't say it' simpler than 'She can't sing that'? It must be a mechanism that is affected not just by independently retrieving syntactic structures and the words that go into them, as in a standard production model. This is because these two structures are identical and the words in them are all very frequent. It must be the case that the production process is also affected by the *likelihood that those particular words will be used in that particular structure*.

Frequency, as we shall see, must also be at least part of the key to answering the question posed by Nespoulous and Lecours, but, in addition to the frequency patterns built up by the speaker's history of language use, 'what is easier' in aphasic language production is highly dependent on the speaker/hearer's cognitive and emotional state at the moment of production. This applies to normal speakers, too; that is why we all make speech errors.

THE VARIETIES OF APHASIA

As we said at the outset, aphasia is defined as an adult acquired language disorder due to localized brain injury, but there are many varieties of aphasia, which differ in ways that we are still exploring. The infant brain is already differentiated anatomically and functionally; the adult brain has become further specialized, reflecting both maturation and experience. Even people who all have the same native language(s) may have stored their language information in somewhat different brain areas. Not only does injury to different parts of the brain produce different patterns of disordered language, but even injuries that look quite similar may produce rather different patterns of language breakdown (Caplan 1988).

The aphasias are traditionally divided into non-fluent and fluent syndromes. Mary Hyde, the statistician of Harold Goodglass's research team at the Boston VA Medical Center, used to say that people with non-fluent aphasia are like beginning second-language learners, talking in nouns and short familiar phrases with minimal grammar, while those with fluent aphasia are like people who once learned a second language and have now forgotten much of the vocabulary, while remembering the function words and the basic syntactic structures. This is not a bad analogy for a rough mental picture, certainly no worse than calling early child language 'telegraphic.'

Here is a somewhat better approximation for present purposes: all speakers with aphasia show some problems in finding words (i.e., lexical retrieval). Aphasic people who have been characterized as having *anomic aphasia* show deficits primarily in lexical retrieval, often worse for nouns than for verbs or other parts of speech; they are fluent except for their word-finding pauses. Those with *agrammatic Broca's aphasia*, the most-studied non-fluent aphasia, show deficits in lexical retrieval (most often worse for verbs and certain functors than for nouns), in producing complex syntactic structures, and usually in comprehension of complex syntax as well; their speech is almost always slow and effortful. People with *Wernicke's aphasia* show severe deficits in lexical retrieval, and in the comprehension of words and syntactic structures; they are notable for fluent production of semantically empty or uninterpretable, superficially well-formed speech (see, e.g., Berndt, 2001; Kent, 2003; Frawley, 2003).

BACK TO DEFINING SIMPLICITY: WHICH WAY IS DOWN?

What does 'simpler' mean in terms of morphology, syntax, and semantics? Several dimensions seem intuitively reasonable: simpler sentences use words and grammatical morphemes of higher frequency, have no embedding, are short, etc. But the more experience we have with sentences children use, with the language addressed to children and to foreigners, with speech errors, and with aphasic language, the more problems arise. For example, in most languages, aphasic verb tense production errors are, as one might expect, substitutions of present tense for past tense—but the reverse seems to be true for at least some agrammatic aphasic speakers of Arabic (Mimouni & Jarema, 1997), Polish (Jarema & Kądzieława, 1990), and Korean (Halliwell, 2000).

As a linguist, I feel that most purely linguistic approaches to aphasia apply only to a small subset of aphasic language difficulties. Suppose we put introspection and linguistic theories aside, and take a psycholinguistic stance. Assume that whenever imperfect speakers (that's all of us!) make an error, what we have produced is simpler than the probable target form, *for that speaker, at that moment*. Then, to come up with hypotheses about the sources of difficulty, one needs to examine that production in context, using basic psycholinguistic and data processing concepts, such as activation of items stored in memory, competition among possible responses to a stimulus, inhibition of one possible response by another, information, and redundancy.

THE PSYCHOLINGUISTICS OF PRODUCTION

Consider what is already known from experimental work with normal speakers about retrieving words, about constructing phrases and clauses, and about the interactions that plausibly go on during psycholinguistic processing. In the generally accepted type of production model (e.g., Bock & Levelt, 1994), word forms (lexemes) and word meanings (lemmas) are represented as linked 'nodes' in neural networks, with each meaning most tightly linked to its own forms. When nothing linguistic is happening (the *resting state*), nodes have a low (sub-threshold) level of activation. During comprehension or production of a word, the node that represents it becomes activated for a while—it 'lights up,' then fades over time, with the time scale depending on what kind of node it is. However, each time a word (or a structure) is heard, read, or used, the long-term resting state of the corresponding node also gets a little higher.

When the internal desire to express a concept or some external stimulus arouses a node above its threshold level, some activation spreads from the aroused node to the ones it is linked to. Activations to a given node that have been spread from multiple source nodes can add up so that they bring its total activation above threshold level. In many models, there may also be inhibitory signals from other aroused nodes; these inhibitory signals reduce the activation level of the nodes they are linked to.

Suppose, for example, we want to describe a large piece of living-room furniture that can seat three or more people. This concept will arouse all of the applicable words (*couch, sofa, divan, davenport*) to varying degrees, depending largely on which of these terms we have heard or used most often. The most frequent one will have the highest resting level, but if we have just heard one of the others (or even a word that sounds like it), that term may have enough total activation for the concept to arouse it to the same extent as the most frequent term. We want to say just one of them, and whichever one is most highly activated will be produced. However, if the activation levels of two of them are very close, those two compete to be said.

Let's assume that choosing a word to refer to an object normally inhibits the competing words for the same object. This inhibition will reduce the likelihood that we might end up trying to say two or more words at the same time. But sometimes this seems to happen nonetheless, leading to speech errors that are called *blends*, as in *at the end of today's lection* (*lecture* blended with *lesson*) (Garrett corpus, cited in Butterworth, 1982).

When we speak, structures, words, and grammatical morphemes become aroused in our minds in several steps, starting from the pre-verbal conceptual message to be conveyed. The claim that structures as well as words can be aroused is well-supported by the Bock group's work on structural priming (e.g., Bock, 1986; Bencini & Goldberg, 2000). For example, hearing a structure such as a prepositional phrase makes it more likely that hearers will use the same structure in their next utterance, even when the specific words and the semantics they produce are quite different. This finding now has successfully been applied to young children's language use and learning (Savage et al., 2003, 2006; Huttenlocher, 2004).

Just as we usually only want to use one word to refer to a given item, we only want to produce one of the possible semantically and pragmatically appropriate structures. For example, we don't want to say *Give me that* and *Give that to me* simultaneously. But both candidate structures may well be activated. How can one of them emerge as the winner? As with words, there is competition among the aroused structures, and probably inhibition of all but one well-formed winner. Evidence for competition is again found in blending errors, specifically phrasal blends, where one or more words from one of the competing structures end up being put into another structure. Here is an example from my collection, produced at the dinner table: "Oh, help all you want," a blend of "Take all you want" and "Help yourself." Exciting work on modeling the role of competition in lexical retrieval and sentence production that can explain the aforementioned blending errors has emerged in recent years (e.g., Cohen & Dehaene, 1998; Dell et al., 1997; Gordon & Dell, 2003; Gotts & Plaut, 2004; Martin et al., 1998; Martin & Dell, 2004).

COMPETITION IN APHASIC SPEECH PRODUCTION

Competition and attempted inhibition are rampant in the output of some aphasic speakers. Example (1) shows a struggle with choosing the subject NP and a complementizer (from an unpublished transcript of my moderately agrammatic co-author SK (Kleinman & Menn, 1999). SK was attempting what was for her a very complex structure, a negative predication in the first clause of a conditional. I have underlined her attempts at choosing a subject NP for the first clause and a complementizer to link the two clauses:

(1) *If you uh/we/you/if I ... (s)tranger, or doctor that the/like the/that uh no smile no no, I 'fraid.*
'If there was/you were a stranger or a doctor that didn't smile, I was afraid.'

Almost any transcript of moderate length from an agrammatic aphasic speaker whose disorder is of comparable severity will provide similar examples of competing alternative responses.

Here is a concurring introspective report from an agrammatic aphasic French speaker, M. 'Clermont' (rendered into grammatical French, checked for content accuracy with M. Clermont, and translated by Jean-Luc Nespoulous):

> ... whenever I have to produce a grammatical word, even though I know perfectly well that it is a preposition or an article ... that I need, several of them come up in my mind and I never know for sure which one to produce (Nespoulous et al., 1988).

Crosslinguistic data help us define the parameters of this competition among simultaneously aroused words and structures. The Bates group looked experimentally at the effects of paradigm complexity in the production of the definite article across English (one form, *the*), Italian (nine forms marked for gender and number, e.g. *il, la, le, gli*), and German (six forms for 16 gender, number, and case slots; see example below). Here is their analysis of a German speaker's struggle to choose among the forms of the German definite article (Bates et al., 1991 p. 9):

> Patients who are struggling to produce the right function word in an obligatory slot (e.g., production of articles in German) often go through a process of successive approximation and self-correction that is highly reminiscent of the word-finding episodes that are so often reported for both fluent and nonfluent aphasics (e.g., *die ... der ... das ... die ... den .. den Hund*).

The struggle to find the right form suggests that activation has spread through most or all of the paradigm of the definite article, and that the information about the number, gender, and case of the noun that the article must agree with is too weak or too slow to boost the activation of the correct form above the activation of its competitors.

The Bates group also found that German agrammatic aphasic speakers omitted definite articles less frequently than speakers of the other two languages, reflecting the high information value of these articles in German. However, they made more substitution errors than aphasic speakers of Italian did; Bates and Wulfeck (1989, p. 344) report that the average number of substitution errors for definite articles was 17% for German speakers with Wernicke's aphasia, 16% for German speakers with Broca's aphasia, but a dramatically lower 2.7% for Italian speakers with Wernicke's aphasia and 7.5% for Italian speakers with Broca's aphasia. Notice the differences across aphasic groups; there are also differences in the types of forms that they substitute when they make errors. Speakers with Broca's aphasia use more high-frequency or unmarked forms, while those with Wernicke's aphasia use more low-frequency or highly marked substitutions (Bates et al., 1991, p. 4; Slobin, 1991).

From data restricted to agrammatic Broca's aphasia but across a larger set of languages and structures, the statement that larger paradigms (and therefore larger sets of simultaneously aroused word forms) yield more substitution errors is borne out (Menn & Obler, 1990a in Boyce, Menn, & Obler, 1990b, pp. 1381–1382):

> The simpler the paradigm, the fewer the errors ... Speakers of Japanese, with its minimal paradigms, have essentially no verb errors and few content-verb omissions, but speakers of [Icelandic, Hindi, Hebrew, Finnish, and the Slavic languages] as well as the other Germanic languages and Romance languages, with complex paradigms, show many ... a model in which the different forms of the paradigm compete with one another for the output slot ... would be highly compatible with the findings that, in experimental studies of paradigms, inflected forms prime [i.e. arouse] one another in normal speakers of highly-inflected languages like Welsh. (Boyce, Browman, & Goldstein, 1987)

PREDICTABILITY AND ITS EFFECTS ON PRODUCTION

Bates et al. invoke the notion of *information* to help account for aphasic errors, mainly because more information leads to increased error rates, suggesting that the processing involved is more complex. More specifically, when there are more paradigmatic competitors and more competing complex rules, there is also more information that has to be processed to choose the correct word or morpheme. On the other hand, the more *redundant* (i.e., probable) a word that one is about to say is, the less information it carries. This is why the relative frequency of a collocation (i.e., the statistical probability that several words appear together) is important. The more several words of a phrase appear together, the more one can expect the rest of the phrase to appear as well and the greater the ease with which one can predict what comes next. For example, a native English speaker can easily complete the statement: "It's not the heat, it's the …."

The best-known attempt to model such data for child language and aphasia is the Competition Model (e.g., Bates & MacWhinney, 1989). In the Competition Model, the key notion is that a word or a morpheme is a potential cue to what is likely to come next, but some cues are more helpful than others, either because they are easier to perceive (and learn), or because they give more reliable information about what the next morpheme, word, or structure might be. Other things being equal, cues that are more reliable and more likely to be present when needed also have higher Cue Validity (see Bates & MacWhinney, 1989, pp. 41 ff. for a fuller statement). For example, encountering the definite article *the* in English tells you with nearly 100% validity that you are starting a noun phrase and that therefore a noun is coming up soon; it also tells you that the probability that the next word is a noun (*the girl*) is high, the probability that it is an adjective (*the next girl*) is substantial, and the probability that it is a verb or a preposition is barely above zero. Encountering *the* does not, however, tell you whether the upcoming noun will be singular or plural; in contrast, encountering the definite article form *las* in Spanish tells you that the next noun will be both plural and feminine.

The likelihood that a particular set of words will be used together in a particular order is key to understanding why the aphasic person is more likely to say *I can't say it* than *She can't sing that*. Each word in the phrase predicts the next one more strongly in *I can't say it* than in *She can't sing that*. (Note: grammar is not the only factor; speaking about one's own frustrations is emotionally loaded. Emotional arousal seems to increase the accessibility of words (Menn et al., 1998, 1999), and may also affect the accessibility of some grammatical structures.)

For another example of the effect of sequence probability, consider the pair of number errors in Example (2), from an agrammatic Dutch speaker narrating the "Cookie Theft" story in Kolk et al. (1990, p. 271).[3] The picture shows one boy and one girl stealing cookies, but the aphasic Dutch description has both nouns in the plural.

(2) *En binnen jongens en meisjes pakken iets*
'And inside boys and girls are taking something.'

I suggest that the phrase 'boys and girls,' so often used to address or describe groups of school children, is more common than the phrase 'a boy and a girl.' If this is also true in Dutch, then collocation frequency explains these unusual substitutions of plural for singular.

Examples (3) and (4) are from English agrammatic speakers, and also show the priming effect of high sequential probabilities.

(3) *forgot the wash the dishes*
'forgot that she was washing the dishes' (Menn, 1990, p. 157)
(4) *I like the go home.*
'I'd like to go home.' (SK, unpublished data)

Once they have chosen the definite article to follow *forget* or *like*, these agrammatic speakers are in trouble; both plug in familiar phrases (*wash the dishes, go home*) with appropriate semantic content, but in forms that cannot follow *the*. These utterances are difficult to explain in grammatical terms, because they show the article being substituted for the infinitive marker, and, even more strikingly, because the collocation 'V+the' goes across the major syntactic boundary between the verb and what should be the start of its NP object.

The collocation 'give to' seems to be dominating the two attempts at a dative construction in (5); but here I am less sure that sequential prediction alone will account for the error, and I present them as puzzles:

(5) *And the boy give to a cookie—the boy give to girl a cookie.* (Menn, 1990, p. 157)

COMPETING WORD ORDERS

In the Germanic languages other than English, there is a strong constraint: if a finite verb is used in a main clause, it must be the second constituent. This means that if something other than the subject is the first constituent, the subject must follow the verb, leading to two main-clause patterns:

---

[3] The Cookie Theft picture from the Boston Diagnostic Aphasia Examination (Goodglass & Kaplan, 1973, 1983; Goodglass, Kaplan, & Baressi, 2001), briefly, shows a typical American kitchen of 20–30 years ago: a woman is washing dishes, but she appears to be daydreaming, since she's wiping a dish and staring into space while water overflows the sink and splashes onto the floor near her feet. Meanwhile, behind her back, a boy of about 9 is climbing on a teetering stool to reach into a jar labeled 'COOKIES' sitting on a high shelf in a cupboard; a girl of about the same age is standing next to the stool, one hand reaching up and the other covering her mouth; she might be whispering to him, trying not to laugh, or cramming a cookie into her mouth.

Subject-Verb-(X) and Y-Verb-Subject. The X and Y constituents can be virtually anything, very often temporal or spatial adverbs (clause-coordinating conjunctions don't count as constituents of the clause). English has vestiges of this pattern in sentences like "Along came a spider." Comrie (1990) examined the CLAS data from Dutch (Kolk et al., 1990), German (Stark & Dressler, 1990), Icelandic (Magnúsdóttir & Thráinsson, 1990) and Swedish (Ahlsén & Dravins, 1990), and noted that two patients, whose utterances are given in examples (6)–(9), showed extensive (but not 100%) violations of this constraint, while the other six showed occasional errors:

Swedish case 1 (lines 43a and 24a in Ahlsén & Dravins, 1990, pp. 579, 582)

(6) *sen äter han mat*
 'then eats he food'
(7) *sen har tar en famn säd*
 'then he takes an armful of corn'

Icelandic Case 2 (lines 37a and 74a, Magnusdottir & Thrainsson, 1990, p. 526, 542)

(8) *svo hugsaði han*
 'then thought he'
(9) *svo han sofnaði aftur*
 'then he fell asleep again'

An approach to this pattern is to consider both SV(X) and YVS as constructions (Goldberg, 1995), with the 'basic' SVX having a higher resting level of activation. If a 'Y' word or constituent is activated enough to be spoken first, it should inhibit the SVX construction and activate the YVS construction, but in aphasia, this on-line interaction is impaired.

Aphasic transcripts, like normal speech error corpora, yield other examples of blends of competing structures. Example (10) is a blend at the clausal level, from a German Cookie Theft elicitation (Stark & Dressler, 1990, p. 380, line 48a):

(10) *Und es rinnt der Hahn über*
 'And the faucet is overflowing'

The ingredients of this blend are presumably as follows:

(10a) *Es rinnt der Hahn*   and   (10b) *Es rinnt das Wasser über*
 'The faucet is running'   'The water is running over'

Kolk et al. (1990) have a semantically based blend that was repeated three times in the course of Case 2's personal narrative (p. 261, lines 8, 11, 12), which is a blend of *langzamerhand* 'slowly' + *langzaam maar zeker* 'slow but sure.'

(11) *langzamerhand maar zeker*
 'slowly but sure'

CONCEPTUAL PRIMING: SEMANTICALLY RELATED WORDS AND PHRASES IN COMPETITION

Error data from English speakers with various types of aphasia who are describing a series of 50 household scenes, both probable and improbable, illustrate the importance of moment-by-moment factors in speech production (Menn, 2000; for more examples, see Menn et al. 2005; Menn &

Gottfried, 2007). Items from a particular brightly patterned suite of furniture (couch/sofa, armchair, footstool/ottoman) recur in the picture series, and this apparently fosters category-specific perseverative errors—in this case, the category of furniture. Example 12 shows an attempted description of a picture of a footstool behind an armchair produced by a man with fairly well-recovered Broca's aphasia (tested as having anomic aphasia).

(12) *The - th' sofa is - and the - <u>lonje (lounge)</u> was uh back of the <u>sofa</u> ....*

In the Bock-Levelt model of speech production, the arousal of lexical items for language production begins with the concepts to be conveyed. These then activate the semantic and syntactic information (the lemma) for these concepts. However, this activation may persist and spread instead of fading away properly. In (12), *sofa* and *lounge* were incorrectly used for *chair* and *footstool*. These words presumably were aroused where they were not appropriate by activation that spread to them from the related concepts of the pieces of furniture that are actually in the stimulus picture, and by additional activation from having seen the sofa and other articles of furniture in previous stimulus pictures.

Conceptual priming may also arouse phrasal structures, as we see from comparing (13) and (14). A stimulus picture was correctly described by a man with anomic aphasia as follows:

(13) *it's a chair turned around backwards ... table <u>set for one</u>.*

Many items later, he described a table with its chair turned away from it and with nothing on it as:

(14) *a table <u>set for two</u> but chair's on the wrong way.*

This speaker was presumably trying to contrast the table set for one with the new picture of the bare table, but it seems that he was defeated by persisting arousal of the 'set for X' construction.

Conceptual priming also operates in choosing functors, even definite articles. In German, telling 'Little Red Riding Hood' places interesting strains on article gender choice, for two reasons. First, both 'girl' (*das Mädchen*) and 'Little Red Riding Hood' (*das Rotkäppchen*) are formed with the diminutive suffix *-chen*, which makes them grammatically neuter, though they are semantically feminine. Since they are grammatically neuter, they require the neuter article *das* in the nominative and accusative cases, rather than the feminine form *die*. Second, when the wolf (masculine, *der Wolf*) impersonates first Red Riding Hood while knocking at the grandmother's door, and then the grandmother while lying in bed, we get another layer of conceptual complexity. Inhibiting the spread of activation from the semantically aroused feminine *die* to *Rotkäppchen* and *Wolf* evidently becomes an almost impossible task for the German agrammatic aphasic patient, Herr 'Meyer' (Stark & Dressler, 1990, p. 415–417, lines 23, 32, and 39):

(15) *Und die Grossmutter hm ... Die Wolf klopfen an und die Grossmutter ah sagt. Ah die-die Wolf sagt: "Rotkäppchen."*
'And the grandmother hm ... The(f.) wolf knocks and the grandmother, ah, says. Ah, the(f.) – the(f.) wolf says: "Little Red Riding Hood".'
(16) *Und die Grossmutter in ... die die Wolf sagt "Damit ich besser hören kann."*
'And the grandmother in ... the(f.) the(f.) wolf says "I can hear you better with them."'
(17) *Und der Wolf frisst die Rotkäppchen.*
'And the(m.) wolf eats the(f.) Little Red Riding Hood.'
(German requires the article before this name.)

In Dutch (Kolk et al., 1990, pp. 277–278, lines 150–151, 159), the folktale genre expectations, combined with the sequential expectations of what is likely to come after 'wicked,' cause lexical competition that the agrammatic aphasic participant, Mr. 'Heck,' cannot control. You can see evidence of this in examples (18) and (19), where the wicked wolf becomes a wicked witch and a wicked fairy.

(18) *Midden in het bos pakte de heks nee wolf en Roodkapje is opgegeten.*
 'In the middle of the forest the witch, no, wolf caught and Little Red Riding Hood has been eaten up.'
(19) *de boze fee de boze wolf in het bed, ja.*
 'the wicked fairy, the wicked wolf in the bed, yes.'

Finally, although nouns in isolation are usually given in the nominative (more formally, nominative appears to be the default case in case-marking languages), message-level arousal can sometimes choose an appropriate case semantically. In Example 20, one of several instances from a severely agrammatic Serbo-Croatian case (Zei & Sikić, 1990, p. 937, line 15), we find an accusative for Little Red Riding Hood's destination, without production of a subject, verb, or a preposition.

(20) *i sumu* (ACC)
 'and forest'

A correct genitive is even supplied (p. 946, line 66) without its governing preposition:[4]

(21) *patkea kosare* (GEN)
 'ducks [out of] basket'

DISCUSSION

This chapter presents a psycholinguistic approach to characterizing aphasic speech errors. I argue that the production of a syntactically, semantically, and pragmatically appropriate utterance requires sufficient arousal (i.e., above internal noise and above a threshold for response) of many structural layers, from overall clausal structure down to the word, morpheme, and phoneme levels. This process may be both helped and hindered by activation that spreads from one item to another that is frequently associated with it. The original activation may come from pragmatic focus on new or emotionally charged referents (Bock & Warren, 1985; Menn et al., 1998, 1999), from previous elements that were heard or produced, and also possibly from items that were aroused but not produced. Or it may come from unrecoverable sources, because even content-irrelevant context information can be eerily maintained and used—for example, producing better performance on a task if it is tested in the same place where it was learned (e.g., on land vs. underwater; Godden & Baddeley, 1975).

Often, of course, the aphasic speaker omits a word or gives no response to a stimulus. This could be caused by insufficient activation of any response, or by too much mutual or top-down inhibition of whatever morphemes, words, or constructions have been aroused.

We often see what looks like extraordinary competition within what is produced, with the details depending on syndrome, severity, and the particular type of construction or morpheme. Perseverations, strings of attempted self-corrections, and blends are present in non-fluent and fluent output alike, in functors and in content words, as far as the data extend. Some of these errors appear pragmatically based, some semantically based; some seem to be from spreading activation through a paradigm, and some from spreading activation through sequential (syntagmatic or construction-based) linkages. Although a huge amount of computational work needs to be done to

---

[4] It is also possible that the semantic/syntactic representations (lemmas) for the missing verbs and prepositions were aroused and then activated these case-marked noun forms, even though they were not able to activate their own phonological forms (lexemes).

model these data, sequential probability derived from clausal, phrasal, and morpheme-sequence predictability appears to play a major role in determining output patterns, as does the arousal of an item earlier in the particular discourse.

CONCLUSION: TOWARD A PSYCHOLINGUISTIC DEFINITION OF SIMPLICITY

What does this bottom-up psycholinguistic viewpoint say about the problem of 'simplicity' across speakers of varying abilities? What's 'simple' to produce has to be a structure—a word or a construction—that is easily activated above the response threshold in the context where it is needed, and that is considerably stronger than its competitors. As we have seen, cue strength and cue validity, the static components of the Competition Model, are clearly part of this picture; but the role of constructions and of the verbal and non-verbal context has also been highlighted. For colleagues studying child language in a construction-based framework, aphasic data showing the contribution of sequential probability to simplicity should be an unsurprising corroboration of what they are doing already. But the dramatic effect of prior occurrences of related material—in clinical terms, the perseveration of prior responses—may be less familiar.

When my aphasic study participants ask me what I am trying to find out, I answer them honestly: 'I am trying to figure out what makes some sentences harder than others.' It is more than a lifetime's work, for all of us. But the question cannot be answered in general. It has to be qualified: for whom, speaking what language, of what type, and in what immediate social, physical, linguistic, and emotional context.

The fact that the frequency of particular words occurring together in particular constructions plays a role in speech production brings us back to an important theme in Dan's work: if we compare the linguistic behavior of adults with acquired language disorders to the linguistic behavior of children, we can learn something about how development changes the way the brain deals with language. Since languages differ, learning different languages should, to some extent, form the brain's language faculty differently. Some differences might be trivial, no more than the difference between storing *dog*, *hund*, *inu*, or *sobaka*, with somewhat different distributions of canine examples and personal encounter histories. Differences might be deeper if the languages being processed have very different syntactic or morphological structures. This is because—as Dan's 'thinking for speaking' hypothesis emphasizes—the brain gets good at doing what it has to do frequently.

REFERENCES

Ahlsén, E., & Dravins, C. (1990). Agrammatism in Swedish: Two case studies. In L. Menn & L. K. Obler (Eds.), *Agrammatic aphasia* (pp. 545–622). Amsterdam: John Benjamins.

Bates, E., & Devescovi, A. (1989). Crosslinguistic studies of sentence production. In B. MacWhinney & E. Bates (Eds.), *The cross-linguistic study of sentence processing* (pp. 225–253). Cambridge, UK: Cambridge University Press.

Bates, E., and MacWhinney, B. (1989). Functionalism and the competition model. In B. MacWhinney & E. Bates (Eds.), *The cross-linguistic study of sentence processing* (pp. 3–73). Cambridge, UK: Cambridge University Press.

Bates, E., & Wulfeck, B. (1989). Crosslinguistic studies of aphasia. In B. MacWhinney & E. Bates (Eds.), *The cross-linguistic study of sentence processing* (pp. 328–374). Cambridge, UK: Cambridge University Press.

Bates, E., Wulfeck, B., & MacWhinney, B. (1991). Crosslinguistic research in aphasia: An overview. *Brain and Language, 41*, 123–148.

Bencini, G. M. L., & Goldberg, A. E. (2000). The contribution of argument structure constructions to sentence meaning. *Journal of Memory and Language, 43*, 640–651.

Berndt, R. (Ed.) (2001). *Language and aphasia. Handbook of neuropsychology* (Vol. 3.) Amsterdam: Elsevier Science.

Blackwell, A., & Bates, E. (1995). Inducing agrammatic profiles in normals: Evidence for the selective vulnerability of morphology under cognitive resource limitation. *Journal of Cognitive Neuroscience, 7,* 228–257.

Bock, J. K. (1986). Syntactic persistence in language production. *Cognitive Psychology, 18,* 355–387.

Bock, K., & Levelt, W. (1994). Grammatical encoding. In M. A. Gernsbacher (Ed.), *Handbook of psycholinguistics* (pp. 945–984). San Diego, CA: Academic Press.

Bock, J. K., & Warren, R. K. (1985). Conceptual accessibility and syntactic structure in sentence formulation. *Cognition, 21,* 47–67.

Boyce, S., Browman, C. P., & Goldstein, L. (1987). Lexical organization and Welsh consonant mutations. *Journal of Memory and Cognition, 26,* 419–452.

Butterworth, B. (1982). Speech errors: Old data in search of new theories. In A. Cutler (Ed.), *Slips of the tongue and language production.* Berlin: Mouton.

Caplan, C. (1988). The biological basis for language. In F. J. Newmeyer (Ed.), *Linguistics, The Cambridge Survey: Language: Vol. 3. Biological and social aspects.* Cambridge, UK: Cambridge University Press.

Caramazza, A., & Zurif, E. (1978). *Language acquisition and language breakdown.* Baltimore: Johns Hopkins University Press.

Cohen, L., & Dehaene, S. (1998). Competition between past and present: Assessment and interpretation of verbal perseverations. *Brain, 121,* 1641–1659.

Comrie, B. (1990). Word order in the Germanic languages—subject-verb or verb-second?: Evidence from aphasia in Scandinavian languages. In L. Menn & L. K. Obler (Eds.), *Agrammatic aphasia* (pp. 1357–1364). Amsterdam: John Benjamins.

Dell, G. S., Burger, L. K., & Svec, W. R. (1997). Language production and serial order: A functional analysis and a model. *Psychological Review, 104,* 123–147.

Frawley, W. (Ed.). (2003). *International encyclopedia of linguistics* (2nd ed.). New York: Oxford University Press.

Gleason, J. B. (1982). Converging evidence for linguistic theory from the study of aphasia and child language. In L. K. Obler & L. Menn (Eds.), *Exceptional language and linguistics* (pp. 347–356). New York: Academic Press.

Godden, D. R., & Baddeley, A. D. (1975). Context-dependent memory in two natural environments: On land and underwater. *British Journal of Psychology, 66,* 325–331.

Goldberg, A. (1995). *Constructions: A construction grammar approach to argument structure.* Chicago: University of Chicago Press.

Goldsmith, J. (2001). Unsupervised learning of the morphology of a natural language. *Computational Linguistics, 27,* 153–198.

Goodglass, H., & Kaplan, E. (1973). *Boston diagnostic aphasia examination.* Philadelphia: Lea & Febiger. [Revised editions 1983, 2001.]

Gordon, J. K., & Dell, G. S. (2003). Learning to divide the labor: An account of deficits in light and heavy verb production. *Cognitive Science, 27,* 1–40.

Gotts, S. J., & Plaut, D. C. (2004). Connectionist approaches to understanding aphasic perseveration. *Seminars in Speech and Language, 25,* 323–348.

Halliwell, J. (2000). Korean agrammatic production. *Aphasiology, 14,* 1187–1203.

Huttenlocher, J., Vasilyeva, M., & Shimpi, P. (2004). Syntactic priming in young children. *Journal of Memory and Language, 50,* 182–195.

Jarema, G., & Kadzieława, D. (1990). Agrammatism in Polish: A case study. In L. Menn & L. K. Obler (Eds.), *Agrammatic aphasia* (Vol. II, pp. 817–894). Amsterdam: John Benjamins.

Kent, R. (Ed.). (2003). *MIT encyclopedia of communication disorders.* Cambridge, MA: The MIT Press.

Kleinman, S., with Menn, L. (1999). Shirley says: Living with aphasia. http://spot.colorado.edu/~menn/Shirley4.pdf.

Kolk, H., van Grunsven, M., & Keyser, A. (1990). Agrammatism in Dutch: Two case studies. In L. Menn & L. K. Obler (Eds.), *Agrammatic aphasia* (pp. 179–220). Amsterdam: John Benjamins.

Lehečkova, H. (2001). Manifestation of aphasia symptoms in Czech. *Journal of Neurolinguistics, 14,* 179–208.

MacWhinney, B. (1987). The competition model. In B. MacWhinney (Ed.), *Mechanisms of language acquisition* (pp. 249–308). Hillsdale, NJ: Lawrence Erlbaum Associates.

MacWhinney, B., & Bates, E. (Eds.). (1989). *The cross-linguistic study of sentence processing.* Cambridge, UK: Cambridge University Press.

Magnúsdóttir, S., & Thráinsson, H. (1990). Agrammatism in Icelandic: Two case studies. In L. Menn & L. K. Obler (Eds.), *Agrammatic aphasia* (pp. 443–544). Amsterdam: John Benjamins.

Martin, N., & Dell, G. S. (2004). Perseverations and anticipations in aphasia: Primed intrusions from the past and future. *Seminars in Speech and Language, 25,* 349–362.

Martin, N., Roach, A., Brecher, B., & Lowery, J. (1998). Lexical retrieval mechanisms underlying whole-word perseveration errors in anomic aphasia. *Aphasiology, 12,* 319–333.

Menn, L. (1990). Agrammatism in English: Two case studies. In L. Menn & L. K. Obler (Eds.), *Agrammatic aphasia* (pp. 117–178). Amsterdam: John Benjamins.

Menn, L. (2000). Studying the pragmatic microstructure of aphasic and normal speech: An experimental approach. In L. Menn & N. Bernstein Ratner (Eds.), *Methods for studying language production* (pp. 377–401). Hillsdale, NJ: Lawrence Erlbaum Associates.

Menn, L., & Gottfried, M. (2007). Aphasic errors in expressing location: Implications for production models. *MIT Working Papers in Linguistics, 53,* 305–351.

Menn, L., Kamio, A., Hayashi, M., Fujita, I., Sasanuma, S., & Boles, L. (1999). The role of empathy in sentence production: A functional analysis of aphasic and normal elicited narratives in Japanese and English. In A. Kamio & K. Takami (Eds.), *Function and structure.* Amsterdam: John Benjamins. [Also CLASNET Working Papers #1, Centre de recherche, Centre hospitalier Côte-des-Neiges, Montreal, 1995.]

Menn, L., & Obler, L. K. (1990a). Conclusion: Cross-language data and theories of agrammatism. In L. Menn & L. K. Obler (Eds.), *Agrammatic aphasia* (Vol. II, pp. 1369–1389). Amsterdam: John Benjamins.

Menn, L., & Obler, L. K. (1990b). *Agrammatic aphasia: A cross-language narrative sourcebook.* Amsterdam: John Benjamins.

Menn, L., Reilly, K. F., Hayashi, M., Kamio, A., Fujita, I., & Sasanuma, S. (1998). The interaction of preserved pragmatics and impaired syntax in Japanese and English aphasic speech. *Brain and Language, 61,* 183–225.

Mimouni, Z., & Jarema, G. (1997). Agrammatic aphasia in Arabic. *Aphasiology, 11,* 125–144.

Nespoulous, J.-L., Code, C., Virbel, J., & Lecours, A. R. (1998). Hypotheses on the dissociation between "referential" and "modalizing" verbal behaviour in aphasia. *Applied Psycholinguistics, 19,* 311–331.

Nespoulous, J.-L., Dordain, M., Perron, C., Ska, B., Bub D., Caplan, D., Mehler, J., & Lecours, A. R. (1988). Agrammatism in sentence production without comprehension deficits: Reduced availability of syntactic structures and/or of grammatical morphemes. A case study. *Brain and Language, 33,* 273–295.

Nespoulous, J.-L., & Lecours, A. R. (1989). Pourquoi l'aphasique peut-il dire: "Je ne peux pas le dire" et pas "Elle ne peut pas la chanter"? (De l'intérêt des dissociations verbales dans l'étude du comportement verbal des aphasiques). *Cahiers du Centre Interdisciplinaire des Sciences du Langage, Mélanges offerts à J. Verguin.* Toulouse: Université de Toulouse-Le Mirail.

Savage, C., Lieven, E., Theakston, A., & Tomasello, M. (2003). Testing the abstractness of children's linguistic representations: Lexical and structural priming of syntactic constructions in young children. *Developmental Science, 6,* 557–567.

Savage, C., Lieven, E., Theakston, A., & Tomasello, M. (2006). Structural priming as implicit learning in language acquisition: the persistence of lexical and structural priming in 4-year-olds. *Language Learning and Development, 2,* 27–49.

Slobin, D. I. (1991). Aphasia in Turkish: Speech production in Broca's and Wernicke's patients. *Brain and Language, 41,* 149–164.

Slobin, D. I. (Ed.). (1997). *The crosslinguistic study of language acquisition: Vol. 5. Expanding the contexts.* Mahwah, NJ: Lawrence Erlbaum Associates.

Stark, J. A., & Dressler, W. (1990). Agrammatism in German: Two case studies. In L. Menn & L. K. Obler (Eds.), *Agrammatic aphasia* (Vol. I, pp. 281–442). Amsterdam: John Benjamins.

Zei, B., & Sikić, N. (1990). Agrammatism in Serbo-Croatian: Two case studies. In L. Menn & L. K. Obler (Eds.), *Agrammatic aphasia* (Vol. II, pp. 895–974). Amsterdam: John Benjamins.

29

Main Verb Properties and Equipollent Framing[1]

LEONARD TALMY

Department of Linguistics and Center for Cognitive Science
University at Buffalo, State University of New York

> The world does not present "events" to be encoded in language. Rather, experiences are filtered—(a) through choice of perspective, and (b) through the set of options provided by the particular language—into verbalized events.
>
> **Ruth Berman & Dan I. Slobin (1994, p. 9)**

It has been a pleasure adding my chapter to the others in this volume to acknowledge and thank Dan Slobin for his immense contribution. Dan's work has closely interacted with my own over the decades, from the typology of Motion, to the structure of spatial conceptions, to the semantics of grammar. In this Festschrift for him, I would like to thank him for his pivotal ideas in these and more areas. We have agreed on much and, where we have disagreed, each has often used the other's objections as a springboard for further developments, sometimes through several cycles, as in the case of the present chapter. Best of all, our linguistic interactions have taken place within a friendship that has also spanned the decades.

INTRODUCTION

This chapter[2] argues against too free a use of 'equipollent framing' as proposed by Slobin. Instead, it proposes an expanded set of criteria for main verb status, and finds them applying to languages that Slobin had considered to be equipollently framed.

The background is that Talmy (1991, 2000b, ch. 3, pp. 213–288) had proposed that languages fall into two main types on the basis of where the Path is represented in a sentence expressing a Motion event —or, more generally, where the 'core schema' is represented in a sentence expressing a 'macro-event.' In this two-category typology, if the Path is characteristically represented in the main verb or

---

[1] My thanks to Jiansheng Guo for comments on the chapter, to James Matisoff for information on Lahu, and to these two as well as to Lian-Cheng Chief for information on Mandarin. None of them is responsible for my errors and oversights.

[2] This chapter as published in the present volume has, for reasons of space, been shortened from the original version prepared for this Festschrift. The full original version can be accessed on Leonard Talmy's website: http://linguistics.buffalo.edu/people/faculty/talmy/talmyweb/index.html That full version, in turn, is a revision and expansion of one portion within Talmy (2005).

verb root of a sentence, the language is 'verb framed,' but if it is characteristically represented in the satellite and/or preposition, the language is 'satellite framed.' A satellite is a constituent in construction with the main verb (root) and syntactically subordinate to it as a dependent to a head. Another semantic component, the co-event—usually the Manner or the Cause of the Motion—might then characteristically show up in a particular constituent other than the one occupied by the Path. Note that this concept of framing type makes no appeal to the presence versus absence of a co-event or its characteristic location, but only to the characteristic location of the Path, which unlike the co-event is seen as criterial to a Motion sentence.

Subsequently, several studies (e.g., Delancey, 1989; Slobin and Hoiting, 1994; Schultze-Berndt, 2000; and Zlatev and Yangklang, 2004) either suggested or were noted by others as suggesting that certain languages do not neatly fit either category of the proposed typology. The main problem claimed was that the cited languages did not clearly assign either main verb status or satellite status to the constituent expressing Path. Where linguists considered together both the constituent expressing Path and the constituent expressing the co-event, they judged that the languages did not privilege either of these constituent types as being the main verb or some other kind of head or dominant category, nor mark the other constituent type as being a satellite or other kind of dependent or subordinate category. Slobin (2004) then proposed classifying such languages together in a third category of 'equipollently framed' languages within a now expanded typology.

To lay the ground for any challenge or constraint on this idea, we first observe that Slobin's (2004) concept of equipollent framing can be analyzed as actually comprising two distinguishable properties, ones that seemingly are often conflated. One property builds directly on the original basis I proposed for framing: whether the Path shows up in the main verb (root) or in a satellite/preposition—for short, main verb or satellite. In terms of this property, equipollence is claimed if it is unclear whether the constituent type that the Path characteristically appears in is either the main verb or a satellite. But the constituent expressing the Path along with the constituent expressing the co-event are together seen as forming all or most of a complex that does serve something like a main verb function. This circumstance could occur in several ways.

One way is that the constituent expressing the Path has no clear lexical category in its own right, but typically co-occurs with one or more other constituents, all of them together seeming to constitute a full main verb complex. This pattern has been thought to occur in certain polysynthetic constructions, such as the bipartite verb stems as described for Klamath in Delancey (1989)—addressed below in section 3. Another way is that the constituent expressing the Path might well have a lexical category, that of a verb, but is not *the* main verb—rather, only one of two or more verbs in the sentence that together again seem to constitute the full main verbal complex. This pattern has been thought to occur in certain serial verb constructions—treated below in section 4. In this paper, the term equipollence will be applied only to patterns like these that the first property pertains to.

The second property often associated with the notion of equipollent framing, but distinguishable from the first, is that the constituent expressing the co-event is judged to be a grammatical peer of the constituent expressing the Path. This circumstance could occur in the two just-cited patterns in which the two constituents together function like a main verb complex. In the Klamath bipartite verb stem, both constituents would be equally indeterminate with respect to lexical category, and in a serial verb construction, both constituents would equally be verbs. But since these patterns can already be addressed under the first property, they might have diminished relevance here. More importantly, the second property also holds in a construction where a third constituent functions as the true main verb, while the Path constituent and the co-event constituent, either singly or jointly, are outside any main verb designation. This circumstance might well occur among the co-verbs of Jaminjong—as discussed in section 5—and does occur in the polysynthetic constructions of Atsugewi (section 3).

Thus, any challenge to the existence or extent of equipollent framing hinges on whether, in the languages at issue, the Path constituent can be argued as having (predominantly) either main verb status or satellite status. Where both the Path constituent and the co-event constituent are considered together—and where these two are not both subordinate to a third verb constituent—any challenge to equipollence hinges on whether one of the two constituents can be argued as having (predominantly) main verb status while the other has satellite status. Accordingly, any inquiry into what constitutes main verb status can abet such challenges, and this is what is undertaken next.

AN EXPANDED SET OF CRITERIA FOR JUDGING MAIN VERB STATUS

It can be stated at the outset that there is nothing in principle the matter with extending the original framing typology to include a third category of indeterminate framing, that is, Slobin's equipollently framed category. In so far as such an indeterminate condition may occur, it would seem that the proposed form of equipollence is the right way to view it. The proposal here, though, is that the criteria used for judging main verb status have been too few, and that an expanded set of criteria might show a broader tendency among languages seen as candidates for equipollence, in fact to privilege one of the constituent types in question with main verb status. If so, then true equipollent framing might be rarer than proposed, perhaps even non-occurrent, and if occurrent, possibly an unstable stage that a language tends to transition out of with relative diachronic speed.

In (1) is an expanded set of proposed factors that tend to indicate that a language treats a particular constituent type as its main verb or verb root. Quite possibly none of these factors is criterial for main verb status. Rather, different subsets of the factors apply to a specific constituent type in different languages, with no individual factor emerging as crucial. The more factors that converge on a particular constituent type in a language, the more that that constituent type is being privileged with main verb status. Some languages exhibit what can be considered a split system of main verb status in that one subset of the factors applies to one constituent type, while another subset of factors applies to another constituent type.

(1) Factors that tend to mark a particular constituent type as the main verb (root)
Of two constituent types in a language that can be considered for having main verb status, one of them ranks higher for that status:
  a. Morphology
     if it can take inflections or clitics for such semantic categories as tense, aspect, mood, evidentiality, negation, causation, voice, transitivity, or the person, number, and gender of the subject (and object).
  b. Syntax
     if it functions as a head directly or nestedly in a construction with such other sentence constituents as: adverbs; particles for place, time, aspect, quantity, negation, etc.; or a subject or object nominal.
  c. Co-occurrence patterns
     if its presence is required across a range of construction types, while the other constituent type need not or can not be present in some of those construction types.
  d. Class size
     if it has more morpheme members or is open-class while the other constituent type has fewer morpheme members or is closed-class.
  e. Phonology
     e1. if its morpheme members have a greater average phonological length.
     e2. if its morpheme members vary over a greater range of phonological length or pattern.
     e3. if its morpheme members include phonemes ranging over a greater portion of the phonemic inventory of the language.
  f. Semantics
     f1. if the meanings of its member morphemes tend to have more substantive content, greater specificity, and a greater number of more varied conceptual components

associated together in more intricate relationships, while those of the other constituent type tend to have less of these.

f2. if the meanings of its member morphemes range over a greater variety of concepts and types of concepts and trail off into more outlying conceptual areas, while those of the other constituent type tend to fit a more stereotyped semantic category.

f3. if it seems to contribute the criterial component of 'actuation' to the proposition that is otherwise represented by the sentence.

Before using them to help resolve less clear cases, the factors in (1) can be checked out for English. Here, all the factors except the (1e) phonological ones seem to hold. To illustrate, we can consider for main verb status the constituent type instantiated by the morpheme *roll* and the constituent type instantiated by the morpheme *down* in the sample sentence *My neighbor seldom rolls down his shades*. The former constituent type ranks higher for main verb status first because it exhibits factor (1a)—e.g., here taking the inflection *-s* representing present tense, habitual aspect, and indicative mood, as well as third person and singular number for the subject. The constituent type here instantiated by *down* does not take inflections. The former constituent type also exhibits factor (1b). Here, for example, *roll* is the head of the construction it forms with *down*, not vice versa. And it further functions as the head of constructions—involving various degrees of nesting—that it forms with the temporal particle *seldom*, with the object nominal *his shades*, and with the subject nominal *My neighbor*. *Down* does not do any of these. The former constituent type further exhibits factor (1c) in that some representative of it must be present in a range of sentence types, whereas the constituent type here represented by *down* can or must be excluded from many of those sentence types. By contrast, the reverse pattern – that is, sentence types in which the *down* type of constituent must be present, while the *roll* type of constituent is optional or blocked —is minimal at best. The former constituent type additionally exhibits factor (1d) in that it is an open class with hundreds of morpheme members, whereas the constituent type here represented by *down* is a closed class with only a few dozen members. Finally, the former constituent type exhibits all three parts of factor (1f). Its member morphemes on average have greater and more specific semantic content, with more semantic elements of different types together—as *roll* here does relative to *down*. They also range over a greater variety of meanings—as, say, *roll, burrow*, and *gush* do relative to *down, out*, and *across*—where the latter tend to fill out a more stereotyped semantic category of path. (To be sure, the greater specificity and range of the former constituent type accords with its greater class size, though, in principle, these two factors need not be correlated). And last, they provide the actuating or dynamizing feature for a proposition—as *roll*, but not *down*, does in the example sentence.

Note that the factors in (1) are on purpose formulated generically, not in terms of Motion or any of its components such as Path or Manner. The reason is that main verb status should be independently based on properties neutral to the issue that prompted its explication. A quick look at Spanish might illustrate the need to emphasize this point. Consider a sentence like *La botella entró flotando a la cueva*, 'The bottle entered floating to the cave'—that is, "The bottle floated into the cave." The constituent type here instantiated by *entró*—let's call it constituent type 1—ranks higher for main verb status than the constituent type here instantiated by *flotando*—let's call it constituent type 2—with regard at least to the first three factors of (1). Thus, constituent type 1 takes many of the inflections indicated in (1a), while constituent type 2 takes none of them. It has more of the syntactic head properties of (1b) than constituent type 2. And it has the cooccurrence privileges of (1c): it must occur across a range of construction types for which constituent type 2 is only optional. Assuming as for English that any (1e) phonological differences between the two constituent types are negligible, what about the class size and semantic properties of factors (1d) and (1f)? Consider the findings if we were to allow the approach of limiting the examination to characteristic Motion-expressing sentences, and hence of limiting constituent type 1 to morphemes expressing Path and constituent type 2 to morphemes expressing Manner. Constituent type 1 would now be smaller in class size than constituent type 2, since the former would range only over those morphemes expressing basic Paths (Path verbs), while the latter would cover the rather larger group of morphemes expressing Manner

(Manner verbs). And with respect to the semantic factor (1f), the Paths expressed by the morphemes of constituent type 1 would be semantically rather spare and stereotyped, while the Manner-expressing morphemes of constituent type 2 would cover a more varied and more intricate set of meanings. For these two factors, then, constituent type 2 would rank higher in main verb status than constituent type 1. However, (1) is deliberately set up to address the entire morpheme complement of each of the two constituent types under comparison, not just some subset of that complement. On that basis, one would need to consider all the morphemes that can serve as constituent type 1, not just the Path verbs, as well as all the morphemes that can serve as constituent type 2, not just the Manner verbs. It is not certain how this intended comparison would turn out for Spanish under a full analysis, but it is likely that the class size and semantic diversity of the two constituent types would at least be more comparable, and perhaps tilted in favor of constituent type 1.

MAIN VERB CRITERIA APPLIED TO POLYSYNTHETIC CONSTRUCTIONS

Let me now apply the factors in (1) to Atsugewi, a Hokan language of northern California and the language of my fieldwork. Atsugewi is a polysynthetic language, that is, the core of the sentence is a complex constituent in turn consisting of a number of morphosyntactically distinguishable constituents that occupy distinct position classes in a specific sequence relative to each other, all of them morphologically bound. This constituent as a whole gains some ranking as main verb in that it takes many of the kinds of inflections listed under factor (1a), and it relates syntactically to other sentence constituents much as described under factor (1b). On this basis, I call this polymorphemic constituent a 'verb complex.' But what about the distinct constituent types within this verb complex? Might one of them exhibit enough of the remaining factors to merit status as the main verb root of the complex? The evidence below converges on just such a conclusion.

Delancey's (1989) analysis of Klamath, a Penutian language geographically near Atsugewi, stands as the main claim to equipollent framing within a polysynthetic verb. I am not familiar enough with Klamath to raise questions about its analysis directly. However, Delancey's paper cites Atsugewi as behaving in a way similar to Klamath, and proposes an areal basis for such similarity. But the conclusion below that Atsugewi does single out and privilege a particular bound constituent type as the verb root at least removes Atsugewi from Delancey's claim. In turn, it suggests another look at Klamath from the present perspective, with the possibility that some of the arguments advanced here for Atsugewi might apply to Klamath as well and diminish its claim as an exemplar of equipollence.

In one of its most characteristic patterns, an Atsugewi verb complex that expresses a Motion event has at its center a tripartite stem, that is, a stem consisting of three distinct constituent types, all of them bound morphemes (themselves in turn surrounded by potentially numerous derivational and inflectional affixes). The first of the three constituent types has morpheme members that prototypically refer to the kind of immediately prior event that caused the Motion event—what I label as the 'Cause'—or to what can simply be taken as the Instrument. The central constituent type has morpheme members that prototypically refer to the kind of object or material that functions as the Figure of the Motion event. The third constituent type has morpheme members that prototypically refer to the combination of a particular Path and type of Ground object within the Motion event.

Of these three constituent types, the central one referring to the Figure ranks highest for status as main verb root under the remaining factors in (1). Thus, to start with factor (1d) concerning class size (with factor (1c) reserved for later), the Figure-specifying constituent type has hundreds of morpheme members—and there is some evidence that new morphemes can be more easily added to this type, so that it has some claim to open-class status. By contrast, the Cause-specifying constituent type has only about two dozen members, while the Path+Ground-specifying constituent type has only some fifty members, both constituent types being clearly closed-class.

The Figure-specifying constituent type also ranks higher on all three phonological properties in factor (1e). First, the morphemes of this constituent type average a greater length and, second, they vary more in pattern than those of the other two constituent types. Thus, the Figure-specifying morphemes range from having no vowel and consisting of from one to three consonants, to having one vowel with various numbers of consonants on either end, to having two vowels with varying numbers of consonants at either end and in the middle. But the Cause-specifying morphemes are mostly CV (i.e. consonant vowel) in shape, the main divergences being that two of the forms add a continuant consonant after the first C, and two add one after the V. And the Path+Ground-specifying morphemes are mostly VCC or CVC in shape. In addition, the Figure-specifying morphemes have virtually no constraints on the phonemes that can occur in them. But the Cause-specifying morphemes can include stops only from the plain series, not from the glottalized or aspirated series; of the phonemically distinct dentals 'r/l/n,' they can morphophonemically include only r; and they lack the phoneme 'q.' As for the Path+Ground-specifying morphemes, the vowel that occurs in them is preponderantly 'i,' and none of the three 'q' stop phonemes occurs in them.

Considering for now only the first two semantic properties under factor (1f), the Figure-specifying constituent type again ranks higher than the other two constituent types. With regard to property (1f1), some of the Cause-specifying morphemes do refer to relatively contentful Instruments, such as the wind or buttocks. Likewise, some of the Path+Ground-specifying suffixes refer to relatively contentful Ground objects, such as liquid, a container, or someone's face or head. But many of the Figure-specifying morphemes have a still greater specificity, intricacy, and amount of content. Examples include a morpheme referring to a linear flexible object suspended from one end (e.g., a sock on a clothesline, a killed rabbit suspended from one's belt, a flaccid penis) and a morpheme referring to fabric that gets bunched up or unbunched in the process of moving (e.g., curtains getting opened, a sock getting put on). And, with respect to property (1f2), the Figure-specifying morphemes appear to cover a wider range of concepts. For instance, beyond the previous two examples, the kinds of Figure they refer to range from charcoal lumps, to anatomically contained fluid, to a water-borne canoe gliding lengthwise. True, the Cause-specifying morphemes have a certain range of their own, covering natural forces, a linear object engaged in various actions, body parts, and sensory stimuli. But they basically cover only these four semantic domains and make only a few distinctions within each of them. And what the Path+Ground morphemes specify for the Ground is for the most part a geometric type of schema.

Let me return now to the factor of co-occurrence patterns in (1c). The largest class of Figure-specifying morphemes must occur in the tripartite stem described at the outset—that is, they must be directly preceded by a Cause-specifying morpheme and followed by a Path+Ground-specifying morpheme. But there is also a class of Figure-specifying morphemes that, while still requiring a Cause morpheme on the left, can occur without a Path+Ground morpheme on the right. Further, there is another class of Figure-specifying morphemes that requires a Path+Ground morpheme on the right, but that refuses any Cause morpheme on the left. Thus, Figure-specifying morphemes occur across a certain range of construction types, across which the other two constituent types either do or do not occur. To round out the picture a bit, there are several additional classes of morphemes that occupy the same position class as the Figure-specifying morphemes but that do not specify the Figure. Some of these classes follow each of the three patterns of requirement or refusal just cited for different classes of Figure-specifying morphemes. In addition, one class can occur by itself—with neither the Cause nor the Path+Ground constituent type accompanying it. By contrast, neither the Cause constituent type nor the Path+Ground constituent type can occur by itself in a verb complex. And the two of them cannot occur together without a Figure-specifying constituent or one of its semantic alternatives occurring between them. The upshot of this set of co-occurrence patterns is that the constituent type that specifies the Figure (or certain semantic alternatives) is criterial to the verb complex, whereas the other two constituent types are not.

There is one more pattern involving co-occurrence that privileges the Figure-specifying constituent type. In a special construction, a Figure-specifying morpheme of the class that otherwise requires both a Cause morpheme and a Path+Ground morpheme can be removed from the verb complex entirely, placed in front as a frozen form, and set in construction with a new generic (or light) verb that now takes all the inflections. For example, the morpheme *-qput-* that refers to 'dirt' as a Figure, and that usually occurs at the center of a tripartite stem within a verb complex referring to dirt as moving or located, can also occur before a 'be' verb in a construction that means 'for there to be dirt present/in occurrence.' Neither of the other two constituent types can take part in such a construction. Thus, both within the verb complex and outside it, the Figure-specifying constituent type is singled out as the survivor across a range of construction types and so, by factor (1c) is once more accorded higher ranking for verb status.

Because of its high ranking on factors (1c) through (1f), the Figure-specifying constituent type (and its semantic alternatives) functions as the main verb to the greatest degree – more than any other constituent type. Since it is a bound morpheme within a polymorphemic word, my practice has been to term it the main verb root. Accordingly, the Cause-specifying constituent type can now be definitively treated as a prefix and the Path+Ground-specifying constituent type as a suffix. With appeal to the semantic property in (1f3), the Figure-specifying constituent type can now, as main verb root, be considered to actuate the multi-affixal verb complex it is in. (This in turn—as the whole-word constituent on the sentence level that functions as the verb on the basis of factors (1a) and (1b)—actuates the sentence as a whole). It is because the Figure-specifying morphemes in Atsugewi behave like the main verb root that I originally cited Atsugewi as an example of a third major type within my Motion-actuating typology. Namely, this is the type where, of the various semantic components within a Motion event, it is the Figure that characteristically appears in the main verb root along with 'fact of Motion.' (Presumably similar arguments could be made for Navajo as another example of this type).

For these reasons, the Figure-specifying morphemes have been consistently glossed in my work as verbs, not, say, simply as nominals that refer to the Figure. For example, *-qput-* is glossed as 'for dirt to move/belocated'—not, say, simply as 'dirt.' That is, the dynamizing semantic component of 'fact of Motion' is incorporated directly within the meanings of these morphemes.

By the same token, the other two constituent types have consistently *not* been glossed as verbs. For example, the Cause-specifying prefix *ca-* has been glossed either as an adverbial clause, 'as the result of the wind blowing on the Figure'—or simply as a prepositional phrase, 'from the wind'—but not as a verb form like 'for the wind to blow.' Likewise, the Cause prefix *ma-* has been glossed basically as the adverbial clause 'as the result of one's feet acting on the Figure'—or, in an agentive sentence, as 'by acting on the Figure with one's feet'—or simply as the instrumental phrase 'with one's feet.' But it has not been glossed as a verb form such as 'to do with the feet' or 'to act with the feet'—a kind of gloss that appears in other works that seem to be describing something comparable to a Cause morpheme.

Comparably, the Path+Ground-specifying suffixes have been glossed as prepositional phrases. For example, *-ic't* has been glossed as 'into liquid,' not as a verb form like 'move into liquid.' One place that this becomes an issue is for the Atsugewi morphemes for possession and change of possession. These morphemes belong to the exact same constituent type as the unproblematic Path+Ground suffixes and can occur in its position class with roughly the same sets of surrounding morphemes. But in some other treatments, apparently comparable morphemes are glossed like verbs as 'have' or 'give,' inconsistently with the glossing of other morphemes in the same constituent type. In my work, however, the relevant Atsugewi suffixes *-ahn* and *-ay* are glossed respectively as 'in one's possession' and 'into someone's possession' that is, in the same prepositional phrase mold as the other members of the same constituent type (see Talmy 2000b, ch. 4 for a more elaborate discussion of such issues). The point here is that once a particular constituent type has been identified as a verb root and other constituent types complementarily fall into place for their respective semantic-syntactic roles, then it is best to give a consistent form of glossing to the morphemes of each constituent type—a form that corresponds to the semantics of that type.

The conclusion from all the preceding, then, is that Atsugewi does not have equipollent framing. First, it has a definite main verb root—there is nothing indeterminate here—a root that in a Motion event happens to express the Figure. Next, Path is expressed in a satellite, subordinate to the main verb root, specifically, in the suffix immediately following the main verb root. Thus, by the original principle determining framing type, Atsugewi is a satellite-framed language. Lastly, both the Path and the co-event, in particular its Cause type, are equally expressed in satellites subordinate to the main verb root. Thus, together, they do not comprise all or even part of some complex that functions like a main verb. Rather, since they are both wholly outside the main verb root and relate to it as dependants to a head, they exhibit co-satellite or co-subordinate status—a status stipulated earlier as distinct from equipollence. Perhaps further research should examine whether, in accordance with some additional set of factors, two such co-satellites in turn exhibit some kind of asymmetry in syntax, semantics, phonology, etc. between themselves, with one more dominant and the other more subordinate, or instead exhibit a kind of coequality. But even any uncovered coequality at this level should not be identified with the equipollent framing that was proposed as a new framing type.

Finally, then, Atsugewi can be considered to have a split system in its conferral of main verb status. The multi-affixal verb complex as a higher-level constituent type, exhibiting the first two factors of (1), acts as the main verb relative to the other major constituent types in the sentence. At the same time, the simplex constituent type within the verb complex that specifies the Figure (or its alternatives) exhibits the remaining four factors of (1), and so can be considered to function as the verb root within the main verb complex—what I have dubbed the 'main verb root.' It is because of polysynthetic languages like Atsugewi that my work on the Motion-actuating typology from the outset stressed the need—insofar as verbal constituents were being considered—to use the verb *root* for cross-linguistic comparisons. It is the Figure-expressing main verb root within the polysynthetic verb complex of Atsugewi that is to be compared with the Path-expressing verb root within the inflected verb form of Spanish, and with the Manner- or Cause-expressing mono-morphemic V1 in an isolating language like Mandarin.

MAIN VERB CRITERIA APPLIED TO SERIAL VERB CONSTRUCTIONS

Another case to which Slobin (2004) applied his concept of equipollent framing was serial verb constructions. Although I am not as familiar with serial verbs as with polysynthesis, I can present some evidence counter to equipollent framing among them.

First, Matisoff, in his (1973, 1991) treatment of the Tibeto-Burman language Lahu, describes a characteristic construction, one that includes the representation of Motion events, in which up to five verbs can be concatenated within distinct position slots. He is clear, though, that the verb occurring in one of those position slots is the main verb, the 'head,' while the others—what he terms 'versatile verbs'—are semantically subordinate to the head verb and occupy pre-head and post-head position slots. (All these versatile verbs can also occur as main verbs.) Most of the factors in (1) appear to correlate with Matisoff's analysis and might be the basis for it. Without going through them all here, we can note that factor (1d) pertaining to class size seems to apply. Thus, the head position can be occupied by any of the hundreds of verbs in the language, including those referring to Manner or Cause in an expression of Motion. But the pre-head class of versatile verbs has only some dozen members; the 'juxtacapital' class of versatile verbs that immediately follows the head, and that represents the Path in a Motion expression, again has only some dozen members; the 'medial' class of versatile verbs that comes next has some fifteen to twenty members; the 'caudal' class of versatile verbs that comes last has some eight members; and the 'variable' class of versatile verbs, which can occur in several positions relative to the preceding classes, has eight members.

Or, further, we can note how factor (1c) pertaining to co-occurrence patterns might come into play. First, we need to observe that some of the versatile verbs have very similar meanings as a head and as a subordinate to a head—like the form with the meanings 'begin' and 'begin to,' respectively. But other versatile verbs have quite divergent meanings in the two roles—like the form that means 'send on an errand' as a head verb and 'cause to' as a subordinate. Now, a sentence can have just a single verb. But if this verb is one of the versatile verbs, the meaning that emerges is always that of its head role, never that of its subordinate role. Thus, the 'head' constituent type within a serial verb construction is the one that survives across a range of construction types, and, by factor (1c), thus gains additional main verb status. Thus, Matisoff's description stands as one counterexample to equipollent framing in a serial verb language.

I turn now to Mandarin, another language with a serial verb construction that can represent a Motion event as well as its semantic generalizations, using what some have proposed as equipollent framing. When representing such events, typically, the verb in the first position of the series, which can be designated as V1, represents the Co-event—either Manner or Cause. The verb in the second position, or V2, represents the Conformation component of Path. And a third verb or V3 can be present representing the Deixis component of Path. The verbs that can occur in each of the three positions of the series generally belong to different sets. The procedure proposed here is to compare the verbs in each such set—when in fact used in one position of the serial construction—with the same verbs when used as the sole verb in a sentence without a serial construction. This latter will here be designated as V0 —that is, V followed by a zero. To help in this comparison, I propose the principle in (2), which can be used in conjunction with the factors in (1) to suggest different degrees of main verb status.

(2) Principles for the degree of overlap of two otherwise distinguishable constituent types
  If a language has two syntactically distinguishable constituent types that share some but not all of their morpheme members, then:
  a. the degree of their divergence as distinct constituent types correlates with:
    a1. the proportion of non-overlap of their respective morpheme memberships and—for morphemes within the overlap—
    a2. the proportion of morphemes whose meanings differ in the two constituent types and
    a3. the degree of such differences in meaning.
  b. a morpheme within the overlap that has basically the same meaning in both constituent types can seem to belong either to a meta-category that spans both constituent types or to the dominant category type even when functioning syntactically in the other type.

These characteristics tend not to hold for a morpheme outside the overlap or a morpheme within the overlap that has distinct meanings in the two constituent types

These principles can be initially checked out in English. As a backdrop, first note that there is virtually complete overlap between some pairs of syntactically distinguishable constituent types, such as the nouns that can occur in subject NPs and the nouns that can occur in object NPs. And there is a complete disjunction between other pairs, such as between determiners and auxiliaries. But now consider two other syntactically distinguishable constituent types: prepositions, which are in construction with a nominal, and satellites, which are in construction with the verb. With respect to property (2a1), there is much overlap in the morphemic memberships of these two constituent types, but at the same time each type has morphemes not occurring in the other. Thus *in, on, off, up, down, across, along, through,* and *around* can all function either as satellites or as prepositions. But *away, back, ahead, forth, apart,* and *together* function only as satellites. On the other hand *of, from, at, towards, beside, among,* and (in standard English) *with* function only as prepositions. With respect to property (2a2), among the morphemes serving for both constituent types, many have similar senses in both usages. An example is *in* which has a comparable meaning when functioning as a preposition, as in *She is in the room*, and when functioning as a satellite, as in *She hurried in*. But other morphemes have distinct senses. Thus, *over* as a satellite includes the sense 'rotationally about a horizontal axis,' as in *The pole fell over,* but this sense is absent in the prepositional usage of the form. With respect to property (2a3), the semantic divergence between prepositional and satellite usages in such cases seem in general not to be very great. For example, the satellite senses and the prepositional senses of *over* can be fairly readily linked (see Brugmann, 1981). The two constituent types, therefore, can be judged to be neither identical nor unrelated, but rather partially overlapping and hence moderately distinct. Finally, with respect to property (2b), to a speaker with some syntactic sensitivity, a form like *in* with its comparable meaning in both usages might seem to belong to some meta-preposition/satellite category, or might seem, for example, to be a preposition even when functioning as a satellite as in *She hurried in*. But forms like *apart* and *of* would unambiguously be taken to be either a satellite or a preposition, respectively. And a form like *over* with its diverging senses might be starting to seem like having a foot in two different categories.

Other types of partial overlap can be found across languages. For example, one other type seems to hold in at least some noun-incorporating languages, such as Caddo, between their independent nouns, as one constituent type, and their incorporated nouns, as a second constituent type.

Returning to Mandarin, first of all, there might be some evidence that V1 ranks higher than V2 for main verb status on the basis of factors (1b, c, d, and f)—that is, on the basis of certain forms of syntactic, co-ocurrence, class size, and semantic behavior. For example, in terms of factor (1d) pertaining to class size, the set of forms that can occur as V1 might be significantly larger in size than the set able to occur as V2. But the following discussion appeals only to the principles in (2) so that their function can be seen. In broad strokes, the basic observation is that V1 is always taken as a main verb, and that a V2 is equally taken as a main verb if it can also appear elsewhere by itself as a V0 with the same meaning, but is otherwise taken as a satellite subordinate to V1. What follows is the finer-grained analysis.

With respect to property (2a1), it looks like there might be a greater overlap in morphemic membership between the V1 and V0 constituent types than between the V2 and V0 constituent types. If so, the class of first-position verbs may be more of a piece with the class of solo verbs, while the class of second-position verbs would show more divergence from the class of solo verbs. Moreover, in terms of property (2a2) across the overlapping portions of morpheme memberships, the morphemes that can function both as V1 and as V0 seem to have basically the same meanings across both usages, whereas a number of the morphemes that can function both as V2 and as V0 have divergent meanings across the two usages.

The V2/V0 overlap can be illustrated with morphemes first that do, and then that do not, have the same semantic content across the two usages. The form *jìn* refers to 'motion into' both as a V2, as in (3a), and as a V0, as in (3b).

(3) a. *Tā zǒu jìn le gōng-yuán.*
    she/he walk enter PERF park
    'She/He walked into the park.'
   b. *Tā jìn le gōng-yuán.*
    she/he enter PERF park
    'She/He entered the park.'

If now *jìn* is replaced by *guò*, the sentence corresponding to (3a), shown in (4a), can translate as 'She/He walked past/across the park.' Here, the new form in its V2 usage represents a fairly common path concept. But when *guò* appears as the V0 in a sentence corresponding to (3b), shown in (4b), the sentence does not correlatively mean 'She/He passed/crossed the park.' Rather, it indicates that the subject's movement was one within a succession of movements being observed from some distance by someone else. Further, the subject's path now tends to be that of passing to one side, rather than crossing—though the latter is in principle possible—largely because the Ground object, the park, is being conceptualized as a point due to observation from a distance. Thus, *guò* as a V2 functions semantically as one of a familiar series of Path specifiers, whereas it has certain semantic idiosyncracies as a V0: a case of semantic divergence.

(4) a. *Tā zǒu guò le gōng-yuán.*
    she/he walk pass PERF park
    'She/He walked past/across the park.'
   b. *Tā guò le gōng-yuán.*
    she/he pass PERF park
    'She/He was observed to pass the park as part of a longer route.'

Talmy (2000b, pp. 213–288) argues that where a language characteristically represents Path, it usually also represents certain other semantic categories, including aspect. And, indeed, the V2 slot in Mandarin is the characteristic constituent type not only for the representation of Path, but also for that of aspect. But, in terms of property (2a3), those morphemes expressing aspect in their V2 usage generally seem to express meanings there that are more divergent from those in their V0 usage than in the case of the Path morphemes. Thus, in their V2 usage, both *hǎo* and *wán* mainly express the aspectual concept 'to completion.' But in their V0 usage, although these forms can express comparable meanings, they tend instead to express quite distinct meanings. As a V0, *hǎo* usually means 'be good,' while *wán* is usually used to refer to something like 'be all for nothing/be done for.' Moreover, the same *guò* already seen above can also appear as a V2 to express the so-called 'experiential' aspect 'to have already/ever V-ed'—a meaning quite divergent from that in its V0 usage.

And now we come to the main point of the discussion based on (2). The semantic and syntactic properties of a morpheme covered under principle (2b) seem largely to determine a native speaker's sense of the lexical category of that morpheme in its V2 usage—specifically, whether the morpheme is functioning as a verb or as a satellite there. And this assignment in turn determines whether the V1-V2 construction exhibits equipollent framing or satellite framing. In particular, if the meaning of a morpheme in its V2 usage is basically the same as its meaning in its V0 usage, a speaker tends to regard the morpheme in its V2 usage as a verb having some prominence, roughly coequal with that of the V1 verb. The basis for this sense seems to be that even in its V2 usage, the morpheme is still associated with its capacity to stand alone as a full main verb in its V0 usage. But if a morpheme has divergent meanings in its V2 and V0 usages, the speaker tends to regard the V2 form as more subordinate than the V1 verb, hence, as a satellite to it. The basis for this impression might be that the morpheme in its V2 usage, semantically decoupled from the V0 usage, is not associated with any full main verb function, and instead is ascribed membership in some non-verb-like lexical category, now subordinate to the V1 which retains its verb status.

I, most recently, consulted with Lian-Cheng Chief, a native speaker of Mandarin from Taiwan (and a student of mine) on these issues, and his judgments generally accord with the preceding summary. Thus, his judgment about the V1 and V2 in sentence (3a) is that he cannot tell which of them, if either, is functioning as a sole main verb. In fact, they both seem equally verb-like to him, each introducing a separate verbal concept—first walking, then entering. This, then, is the first instance of what might be genuinely equipollent framing in the entire discussion so far.

But in the counterpart sentence in (4a) that contains *guò* instead of *jìn*, Chief's judgment is that the V1, *zǒu* is definitely the main verb, while the V2 *guò* is subordinate to it. The verbal concept of walking introduced by the V1 is not succeeded by another verbal concept introduced by the V2 but rather continues, with the V2 simply indicating where the walking takes place. Comparably, when the V2 is one of the aspect-specifying morphemes, Chief's judgement is clearly that the V1 is the main verb and that the V2 is a satellite.

Perhaps as a development in progress, the aspect-specifying forms that occupy the V2 position might together be coming to form a distinct lexical class, a class that is intrinsically more satellite-like in character. In fact, if a morpheme in the V2 position expresses aspect even moderately, the morpheme tends to become classed together with fully aspectual V2 morphemes and, accordingly, to seem to function as a satellite rather than as a verb. For example, the morpheme *zhòng* as a main verb in V0 position, as in (5b), means for a propelled object to hit rather than miss a target at which it has been aimed. In the V2 position, as in (5a), its meaning is quite comparable. Accordingly, it might have retained its character as a verb in the V2 position much as *jìn* does. However, its V2 use as in sentences like (5a) suggests something aspectual—a fulfilment or completion of the goal of aiming. This then seems to trigger its assimilation to the class of fully aspectual V2 forms and, hence, to a more satellite-like function. Thus, Chief judges that the V1 in (5a) is the main verb and the V2 is a subordinate form.

(5) a. *Tā shè zhòng le mù-biāo.*
    she/he shoot hit PERF target.
    'She/He shot (an arrow) and hit the target.'
   b. *Jiàn zhòng le mù-biāo.*
    arrow hit PERF target.
    'The arrow hit the target.'

Thus, of all the V1V2 serial constructions considered in this discussion of Mandarin, only the one with *jìn* in (3a) is a candidate for showing equipollent framing. In all the other constructions, the V2 emerges as subordinate to the V1 in what can be construed as the relation of a satellite to a main verb as head. Since the V2 forms in these constructions have expressed Path or its extension to aspect, these constructions show satellite framing.

MAIN VERB CRITERIA APPLIED TO COVERB CONSTRUCTIONS

Slobin (2004) has also applied the notion of equipollent framing to Jaminjong, a language in which both the constituent expressing Path and the constituent expressing the co-event are outside the constituent generally regarded as the main verb (see also Schultze-Berndt, 2000). As argued in the first section, this fact alone should exempt the first two constituents from equipollent status and at best accord them co-satellite or co-subordinate status. But a closer analysis of Jaminjong should come first, with these conclusions about framing returned to later.

We can apply the factors of (1) for main verb status to Jaminjung. Though my knowledge of it is still quite limited, Jaminjung seems to represent another kind of split system. A certain constituent type in the language takes the kinds of inflections outlined in factor (1a). It may exhibit some of the syntactic privileges of factor (1b) (though this needs clarification). And it is apparently the criterial constituent type in a sentence, having to be present while other constituent types need not be, in accord with the co-occurrence properties of factor (1c). On these bases, this constituent type is generally seen as the main verb, and it will here be referred to as such.

However, with respect to factor (1d), this constituent type is closed-class, with rather few morphemes as members. And with respect to the first two semantic properties of factor (1f), the meanings of the morphemes in this constituent type seem to be rather generic and to remain within rather stereotyped semantic limits.

On the other hand, there is another constituent type—or perhaps a family of related constituent types—often occurring in construction with the first type, that is open-class with many member morphemes, morphemes that have a wide range of rather specific meanings. This other constituent type thus exhibits at least two of the factors for main verb status, (1d) and (1f). (Whether it also exhibits the greater phonological freedom of factor (1e) still needs assessment). Perhaps for these reasons, this constituent type has been termed the 'coverb.'

Now, with regard to framing, Slobin has focused on two groups of coverbs, one expressing Path and another Manner, which can both occur together in a sentence along with the main verb. But it should be noted that the path coverbs apparently tend to express the geometrically more intricate Conformation part of the Path component. On the other hand, it is the main verb that expresses the Deictic part of the path component or, more generally, to express unbounded extended paths, the type that are covered under the 'ALONG' case of the 'Motion-aspect formulas' that are proposed as universal in Talmy (2000a, pp. 177–254). Thus, the main verb constituent type includes morphemes with such meanings as: 'go,' 'come,' 'take,' 'bring,' 'proceed away from,' 'procede toward,' and 'follow along after.' On the face of it, within my Motion-framing typology, Jaminjung would appear to belong to the verb-framed type. True, not many Path distinctions are marked within the main verb. But such a pattern was already proposed and exemplified under my Motion-actuating typology as 'Motion plus a minimally differentiated semantic component,' and can as readily be applied here.

Any accompanying Path coverb would then provide additional Path specifications as part of a fuller distributed Path representation.

The whole pattern seems rather comparable to that seen in Japanese or Korean. In those languages, Motion sentences often have a deictic 'come'/'go' verb root as main verb, accompanied by verb roots in a gerundive or bound form that express Manner and/or the Conformation part of Path. The main difference is that in Japanese and Korean the Conformation-specifying roots (and, for that matter, the Manner-specifying roots) can also occur as main verbs, whereas in Jaminjong they cannot.

If this interpretation holds, then the possibility of equipollent framing for Jaminjong simply disappears: this is a verb-framed language. As in Atsugewi, the Path constituent and the co-event constituent are both syntactically subordinate to the main verb as head, and so together exhibit co-satellite status or co-subordinate status.

A question raised for Atsugewi above could be pursued here as well. One could look further into the co-satellite status of the coverb expressing Path Conformation and the coverb expressing Manner to see whether a coequal pattern or a dominant versus subordinate pattern holds across these two types of non-main-verb constituents. And this question could be pursued equally for Jaminjung, Japanese, and Korean. But that would involve a further layer of phenomena, one not included under the original framing typology.

CONCLUSION

To sum up, this chapter has first argued that the concept of equipollent framing should only be applied to cases where a constituent expressing Path and a constituent expressing the co-event together serve most or all of a main verb-like function in a sentence, not where they are both outside a third constituent that does function as a main verb. In the latter case, the two constituents show co-satellite status or co-subordinate status, but not equipollent framing. Second, even in the applicable cases, actual equipollence in framing emerges as a seemingly much rarer phenomenon than previously claimed. The arguments against the claimed cases of equipollence are based on an expanded set of criteria for main verb status, and on principles for the assignment of lexical category.

REFERENCES

Berman, R., & Slobin, D. I. (1994). *Relating events in narrative: A crosslinguistic developmental study*. Hillsdale, NJ: Lawrence Erlbaum Associates.

DeLancey, S. (1989). Klamath stem structure in genetic and areal perspective. *Papers from the 1988 Hokan-Penutian languages workshop*, 31–39. Eugene, OR: University of Oregon Press.

Matisoff, J. A. (1973). *The grammar of Lahu*. UCPL no. 75. Berkeley: University of California Press.

Matisoff, J. A. (1991). Areal and universal dimensions of grammatization in Lahu. In E. C. Traugott and B. Heine (Eds.), *Approaches to Grammaticalization* (Vol. II, pp. 383–453). Amsterdam: John Benjamins.

Schultze-Berndt, E. (2000). Simple and complex verbs in Jaminjung: A study of event categorisation in an Australian language. *MPI Series in Psycholinguistics, no. 14*. Wageningen, Netherlands: Ponsen and Looijen.

Slobin, D. I. (2004). The many ways to search for a frog. In S. Strömqvist and L. Verhoeven (Eds.), *Relating events in narrative typological and contextual perspectives* (pp. 219–257). Hillsdale, NJ: Lawrence Erlbaum Associates.

Slobin, D. I., & N. Hoiting (1994). Reference to movement in spoken and signed languages: Typological considerations. *Proceedings of the Twentieth Annual Meeting of the Berkeley Linguistic Society Berkeley*: Berkeley Linguistics Society, 487–505.

Talmy, L. (1972). *Semantic Structures in English and Atsugewi*. Unpublished Doctoral Dissertation in Linguistics: University of California, Berkeley, CA.

Talmy, L. (1985). Lexicalization patterns: semantic structure in lexical forms. In Timothy Shopen (Ed.) *Language typology and syntactic description: Vol. 3. Grammatical categories and the lexicon* (pp. 57–149). Cambridge, UK: Cambridge University Press.

Talmy, L. (1991). Path to realization: A typology of event conflation. *Papers of the Seventeenth Annual Meeting of the Berkeley Linguistics Society* (L. A. Sutton, C. Johnson, and R. Shields, Eds.) (pp. 480–520). Berkeley: Berkeley Linguistics Society.

Talmy, L. (2000a). *Toward a cognitive semantics*: Vol. I. *Concept structuring systems* (pp. i–viii, 1–565). Cambridge: The MIT Press.

Talmy, L. (2000b). *Toward a cognitive semantics*: Vol. II. *Typology and process in concept structuring* (pp. i–viii, 1–495). Cambridge: The MIT Press.

Talmy, L. (2005). Interview: A windowing onto conceptual structure and language. Part 1: Lexicalisation and typology. [Written interview by Talmy on his work conducted by Iraide Ibarretxe] *Annual Review of Cognitive Linguistics, 3*, 325–347.

Zlatev, J., and Y. Peerapat (2004). A third way to travel. The place of Thai in motion-event typology. In Sven Strömqvist and Ludo Verhoeven (Eds.), *Relating events in narrative, typological and contextual perspectives* (pp. 159–190). Hillsdale, NJ: Lawrence Erlbaum Associates.

30

Path Salience in Motion Events

IRAIDE IBARRETXE-ANTUÑANO

University of Zaragoza

> Because path is an obligatory component of motion-event expressions, we can't compare languages in terms of the accessibility of path as a category: without a path verb or satellite or other path element, there is no motion event. However, languages differ with regard to the canonical segmentation of paths as well as the relative ease of building complex-path constructions. They also present an array of path elements going beyond the division into verb versus satellite. These differences are only partially determined by the Talmian typology.
>
> **Dan I. Slobin (2004, p. 238)**

The first time I met Dan was in Berkeley, in 2000, during my first year as a post-doc in the Linguistics Department. After a whole semester attending courses on theoretical linguistics, I was ready for something more 'practical.' Eve Sweetser told me about a professor in the Psychology Department, who worked on motion—an area I wanted to explore at the time. His name rang a bell but I didn't have the slightest clue about who or how this person was, so I imagined that I was going to meet a typical professor: very nice but too busy to hear yet another person mumbling about her research. What I found was just the opposite. Dan was very friendly and really enthusiastic about the possibility of adding Basque to the Frog Story database. When I came back to Berkeley after the summer, we started to work together, and those meetings marked the beginning of a whole new world in my research career. It is difficult to summarize in just one paragraph what Dan means for me and my research. His influence in my work is evident, but perhaps the lesson that he has taught me best, or in other words, the reason for which I admire Dan, is his combination of talent, knowledge, accessibility, and readiness to learn new things. Thanks Dan, for everything!!!

PROBLEMS IN LEXICALIZATION PATTERNS

Theoretical work on the linguistic organization of motion events has shown that this domain can be described by a limited set of underlying universal patterns, but that it is also construed in different ways in different languages. According to Talmy (1991, 2000), the world's languages can be divided into two main typological groups, verb-framed and satellite-framed, in terms of the way the core feature of a motion event, i.e., path, is expressed linguistically, and in the way languages express the components of a complex event. These lexicalization differences are directly reflected in the online use of language, and consequently, speakers of verb-framed and satellite-framed languages differ in their rhetorical styles when describing the same motion event (Slobin, 2000, 2004). These different patterns have important effects on the relative codability of the semantic domains that constitute the components of a motion event and speakers 'filter' their experience through language for purposes of speaking (Berman & Slobin, 1994, p. 9; Slobin, 2000, 2004). Thus, higher codability of a domain in a language leads to a wider expression of that domain by speakers of that language.

In recent years, there has been an increasing number of studies discussing Talmy's two-way typology and Slobin's 'thinking for speaking' hypothesis in a wide variety of languages. This, of course, indicates that Talmy's and Slobin's theories are useful tools for typological analysis. However, these studies have also pointed out that these models give rise to certain problems and limitations, since they do not fully account for some of the characteristics of these languages in the expression of motion.

According to some authors (e.g., Ameka & Essegbey, in press; Slobin & Hoiting, 1994; Slobin, 2004; and Zlatev & Yangklang, 2004), one of the main shortcomings of Talmy's theory is that some languages do not seem to fit in his binary typology. In these languages, the notions of *main verb* and *satellite*—the distinguishing means to express path in Talmy's dichotomy—are not at all evident or that useful. One of the possible solutions is the addition of a third type of lexicalization pattern. Slobin (2004, pp. 247–249), for instance, proposes what he calls an *equipollently–framed* category; this would cover all those languages that present problems for the original typology, that is, languages in which manner and path are expressed by equivalent grammatical forms.

Another problem that Talmy's theory does not seem to take into account is the fact that languages that share the same lexicalization pattern, and therefore, a similar habitual expression of motion, show a different degree of detailed elaboration of semantic components. In other words, languages might belong to the same group, but this does not imply that they characterize the motion event in the same way, both qualitatively and quantitatively. Consequently, there is *intra-typological variation*. For example, Spanish and Japanese are both verb-framed languages but their elaboration of the semantic component of manner of motion is quite different. Japanese, thanks to its large lexicon of mimetics (Hamano, 1998; Kakehi et al., 1996), describes this semantic component much more often and in much more detail than Spanish (Ohara, 2003; Sugiyama, 2005). A similar situation is found in the case of the semantic component of path. Spanish and Basque are both verb-framed languages but it has been shown (Slobin, 1996; Ibarretxe-Antuñano, 2004a, 2004b) that Spanish tends to limit the description of path to the verb (e.g., *descend*), while Basque generally offers a more detailed characterization of this semantic component (e.g., *descend from the cliff down to the river*). As a solution, it has been suggested that it is more useful to rank languages on a *cline of semantic component saliency* rather than to assign them to one of the typological categories (Slobin, 2004; Ibarretxe-Antuñano, 2004b, 2004c, in press).

In this chapter, I explore the issue of intra- and inter-typological variation in verb-framed, satellite-framed, and equipollently-framed languages with respect to the path component. It is argued that languages vary in the degree of detailed description with respect to the component of path independently from the lexicalization pattern they belong to. Therefore, I propose a *cline of path salience* that cross-cuts the three lexicalization patterns and classifies languages along a continuum between two ends: high-path-salient languages and low-path-salient languages. Table 30.1 summarizes the languages I use in this study, as well as their typological classification, as provided by the language researcher, and their data sources.[1]

As shown in Table 30.1, my language corpus consists of 14 verb-framed, 6 satellite-framed, and 4 equipollently-framed languages. Although data from these languages are drawn from different studies, they are suitable for this comparative analysis for two reasons: they have been (i) elicited using the wordless picture book, *Frog, where are you?* (Mayer, 1969), and (ii) analyzed following the procedure proposed in Berman & Slobin (1992) and Slobin (1996).

---

[1] I would like to thank the following people for providing me with useful data for this analysis: R. Berthele, T. Cadierno, L. Chen, S. Selimis, D. Slobin, M. Tanangkingsing, and J. Zlatev.

TABLE 30.1 List of Languages and Their Sources

Language	Typological Group	Source
Arrernte	Verb-framed	Wilkins, 2004
Basque	Verb-framed	Ibarretxe-Antuñano, 2003a, b, 2004a, b, c, in press
Cebuano	Verb-framed	Huang & Tanangkingsing, 2005; Tanangkingsing, 2004
Chantyal	Verb-framed	Noonan, 2003
Danish	Satellite-framed	Cadierno, 2004; Cadierno & Ruiz, 2006
English	Satellite-framed	Slobin, 1996
Ewe	Equipollently-framed	Ameka & Essegbey, in press
French	Verb-framed	Berthele, 2006
German	Satellite-framed	Berthele, 2006; Slobin, 1997
Hebrew	Verb-framed	Berman & Neeman 1994; Slobin, 1997
Icelandic	Satellite-framed	Ragnarsdóttir & Strömqvist, 2004
Japanese	Verb-framed	Kita, p.c.; Satoh, 2001
Malay	Verb-framed	Huang & Tanangkingsing, 2005
Mandarin Chinese	Equipollently framed	Chen, 2005
Saisiyat	Verb-framed	Huang & Tanangkingsing, 2005; Tanangkingsing, 2004
Spanish	Verb-framed	Slobin, 1996; & my own analysis (CHILDES Frog Stories)
Squliq	Verb-framed	Huang & Tanangkingsing, 2005
Swedish	Satellite-framed	Ragnarsdóttir & Strömqvist, 2004
Swiss German	Satellite-framed	Berthele, 2004, 2006
Tagalog	Verb-framed	Huang & Tanangkingsing, 2005
Thai	Equipollently-framed	Zlatev & Yangklang, 2004
Tsou	Equipollently-framed	Huang & Tanangkingsing, 2005
Turkish	Verb-framed	Aksu-Koç, 1994; & my own analysis (CHILDES Frog Stories)
West Greenlandic	Verb-framed	Engberg-Pedersen & Blytmann Trondhjem, 2004

INTRA- AND INTER-TYPOLOGICAL VARIATION IN PATH OF MOTION

In order to establish whether there is any kind of intra- and inter-typological variation in these languages, I will focus this analysis on speakers' descriptions of three complementary areas: (1) path and verbs, (2) path, verbs, and complements, and (3) path and event granularity.

Path and Verbs

One important piece of evidence that Slobin (1996) uses to demonstrate that satellite-framed languages describe path in more detail than verb-framed languages do is to count the number of verbs that appear alone or with a path satellite (English *fall* or *fall down* or Spanish *caer* 'fall') and the number of verbs that are accompanied by some path complement (English *fall down into the river* or Spanish *caerse al río* 'fall to the river'). Slobin calls the former 'minus-ground verbs' and the latter 'plus-ground verbs.' Let us see how the languages in my data behave with respect to this diagnostic test.

As shown in Table 30.2, there seems to be a cline of path elaboration in these languages. At the one end there are languages like Chantyal, Basque, Swedish,[2] Icelandic, English, and Danish—which

---

[2] Ragnarsdóttir and Strömqvist (2004, p. 126) divide motion descriptions into three groups: verb only, verb+particle/adverb, and verb + PP. Since they do not use the notion of satellite, the second group includes both cases of what Slobin would call minus-ground clauses (verbs+satellites) and cases of plus-ground clauses (verbs+adverbs); such motion descriptions are not included in Table 30.2 for Swedish and Icelandic and that is the reason why the percentages do not add up to 100% for these two languages. It is for this reason that we include information about the first and third categories only, which correspond to Slobin's (1996) bare verbs (verbs without any type of locative information, including satellites) and verbs+some path information categories, respectively. The second group in Icelandic is 15% and in Swedish 46%.

TABLE 30.2 Minus-Ground and Plus-Ground Verbs

Language	Minus-Ground	Plus-Ground
Chantyal[v]	0%	100%
Basque[v]	11,86%	88,14%
Swedish[s]	12%	42%
Icelandic[s]	14%	71%
English[s]	18%	82%
German[s]	26%	74%
Turkish[v]	27,27%	72,72%
Danish[s]	29,51%	70,49%
French[v]	31%	69%
Spanish[v]	37%	63%
Malay[v]	42%	58%
Mandarin Chinese[e]	48%	52%
Thai[e]	51%	49%
Tsou[e]	52%	48%
Tagalog[v]	55%	45%
Cebuano[v]	59%	41%
West Greenlandic[v]	60%	40%
Saisiyat[v]	61%	39%
Squliq[v]	64%	36%

[v]: verb-framed, [s]: satellite-framed, [e]: equipollently-framed

prefer to add path elements to the verb, and use minus-ground verbs less than 20% of the time. At the opposite end, we find languages like West Greenlandic, Saisiyat, and Squliq, which follow the opposite strategy and prefer to use minus-ground verbs more often (~60%) than plus-ground verbs, (~40%). Finally, there are some languages, such as Mandarin Chinese, Thai, Tsou, and Tagalog, that occupy the middle area and use minus-ground and plus-ground verbs at equal rates (~50%).

Three preliminary conclusions can be drawn from Table 30.2: (i) there is a clear continuum in the elaboration of path; (ii) languages within the same typological group describe path in different degrees of elaboration; that is, there is intra-typological variation; and (iii) languages from the three different lexicalization groups are situated at various points in this continuum according to the degree of path elaboration; that is, there is inter-typological variation.

Path, Verbs, and Complements

After the analysis of clauses, Slobin presents a more realistic narrative description of motion that includes more than just source and goal. As he argues, narrators in real narratives "need not limit a path description to a single verb and its adjuncts … [they] may present a series of linked paths or a path with way-stations" (1996, p. 202). In order to do so, he proposes a new unit of analysis, what he calls a 'complex path' or 'journey,' which is an extended path that includes milestones or subgoals, situated in a medium.

According to Slobin, in verb-framed languages, complex paths are not very common, and the verb is usually accompanied by just one piece of path information (Spanish *se cayó al río* 'he fell [down] to the river'). In satellite-framed languages, on the other hand, complex paths are common and verbs often include more than one path segment (English: *fell down from the cliff into the river*). Table 30.3 summarizes the results from some of the languages in my corpus.

As shown in Table 30.3, the use of one or several path complements in these languages is quite different and independent from the typological group they belong to. Languages within the same typological group such as Chantyal and Cebuano show radically different behaviors. In the former

TABLE 30.3 Path Elements per Verb

Language	Path Elements per Verb	Number of Path Elements per Verb		
		One	Two or +	Total
Basque[v]	Several	32	20	52
Turkish[v]	Several	24	8	32
Danish[s]	Several	(11)	(5)	(16)
Spanish[v]	Usually one	42	2	44
Mandarin Chinese[e]	One	594	1	595
Thai[e]	Extrictly one	81	1	82
West Greenlandic[v]	One	96	2	98
Chantyal[v]	Several	—	—	—
English[s]	Several	—	—	—
Cebuano[v]	One	—	—	—
Ewe[e]	One	—	—	—
Saisiyat[v]	One	—	—	—
Tzeltal[v]	Strictly One	—	—	—

[v]: verb-framed, [s]: satellite-framed, [e]: equipollently-framed; Danish data correspond to the deer scene only. The second column describes how many path elements per verb are usually found in these languages, and the third column contains the number of path clauses per verb only in those languages where this information was available.

group it is possible to express several path complements with a single verb of motion, while in the latter group it is possible to express only one path element per verb.

If we look at the data from those languages with information about the number of path elements per verb, we also see some variation. In the case of West Greenlandic, there are only two examples where the plus-ground verb has more than one path element as illustrated in (1). In the serial-verb languages, like Chinese and Thai, there is only one single example with more than one path segment, as shown in examples (2) and (3), respectively.

(1) *nakkaqaaq igalasserfimminngaanniit nunamut*
    fall-down.intensity.ind:3sg window-frame.abl ground.all[3]
    'It falls from the window frame onto the ground'
(2) *Mifēng cóng fēngcháo lǐ xiàng wài fēi-chū*
    Bee from beehive in toward outside fly-exit
    'Bees flew out from the beehive'
(3) *Tok1 caak1 huua4-kwaaN0 loN0 paj0 naj0 heew4*
    fall-from-deerhead-fall-go-in-pond
    'He falls from the deer head and into the pond'

In Spanish, the use of complex paths is also quite restricted. Out of the 44 cases of plus-ground verbs, only 2 have more than one path complement, as illustrated in (4).

(4) *El perro ... hace un movimiento tal que se precipita al suelo desde la ventana*
    'The dog ... makes a movement such that he plummets to the ground, from the window'

The number of path complements attached to plus-ground verbs is higher in Turkish. Of the 32 plus-ground examples, 8 have more than one path complement, as shown in (5):

---

[3] List of abbreviated morphemes: abl = ablative; abs = absolutive; acc = accusative; adn = adnominal; all = allative; ben = benefactive; dat = dative; det = determiner; ger = gerund; ind = indicative; indf = indefinite; inst = instrumental; loc = locative; perf = perfective; pl = plural; sg = singular.

(5) *Ve ikisi birlikte kayalıktan göle düstüler*
    and two together rock.abl lake.dat fall.past.pl
    'And the two together fell to the lake from the rock'

Basque is the language with more complex paths in this subgroup: in Basque 20 out of the 52 plus-ground verbs have more than one path complement (see examples 6–8).

(6) *Eta kristalezko ontzitik kanpora irtetea lortu zuen*
    and glass.inst.adn jar.abl outside.all exit.ger.det obtain.perf aux
    'And (the frog) managed to come out of the jar'
(7) *Bapatean Txuri txakurra leihotik behera joan zan*
    suddenly txuri dog.abs window.abl below.all go.perf aux
    'Suddenly, Txuri the dog went down from the window'
(8) *Danak amildegitikan behera erori zian ibai batera*
    all.abs cliff.abl.loc below.all fall.perf aux river one.all
    'All of them fell from the cliff down into the river'

Examples (6) and (7) have two path complements each: *ontzitik* 'from the jar' and *kanpora* 'to the outside,' and *leihotik* 'from the window' and *behera* 'to the ground,' respectively. Example (8) has three path complements: *amildegitikan* 'from the cliff,' *behera* 'to the ground,' and *ibai batera* 'to a river.' This type of construction, where the same verb occurs with at least two path complements, one for the source and one for goal, is very common in Basque. In fact, it has been argued that the expression of source and goal of a translational motion in the same clause as in *leihotik behera* 'from the window to the ground' and *amildegitikan behera* 'from the cliff to the ground' is a pervasive tendency in Basque. Ibarretxe-Antuñano (2004a, 2004b, in press) proposes that these sentences are cases of what she calls the 'Complete Path construction,' that is, the tendency to linguistically express in the same clause both the source and goal of the same motion event, even in cases where one of the components—usually the goal—is pleonastic (i.e., redundant). Notice that in (6) and (8) the information lexicalized in the goals *kanpora* 'to the outside' and *behera* 'to the ground' is 'repeated' in the verbs *irten* 'exit' and *erori* 'fall,' respectively. These Complete Path constructions are used in all types of directional motion (outward as in (6) or downward as in (7) and (8)), in different types of discourse genres (novels, spontaneous speech, experiments; Ibarretxe-Antuñano, in press), and even metaphorically (*hitzetik hortzera* 'from the word to the tooth'; in this expression the focus is on the short distance between these two elements, which is metaphorically understood as 'immediately'; Garai & Ibarretxe-Antuñano, 2002).

In this respect, Basque behaves differently from other verb-framed languages such as Hebrew or Spanish, where the incidence of this type of construction is quite rare. Berman and Neeman (1994), for instance, observed that Hebrew narrators do not use complex paths at all and hardly mention source or goal. Similarly, Slobin (1997) points out that the use of complex paths disappears after the age of 5 in Spanish and is replaced by static descriptions. Nevertheless, some verb-framed languages are very similar to Basque. Noonan (2003) reports a similar path elaboration in Chantyal, and Aksu-Koç (1994) and Özçalıskan (this volume) also point out that extended paths are not only frequent in Turkish but also increase with age.

Complex path constructions do not seem to appear in equipollently-framed languages; the representative examples of such languages in this corpus do not show any instance of more than one path element per verb. Satellite-framed languages, on the other hand, widely use this construction. Muotathal frequently uses prepositional phrase + adverb constructions, such as *uuse* 'outside,' *ine* 'inside' and *abbe* 'below' (Berthele, 2006, pp. 160–170). In sum, these results support our hypothesis that there is a continuum in the description and elaboration of path in the world's languages, independent of their typological group.

Path and Event Granularity

The final test I use to examine path elaboration in different languages is 'event granularity.' As Slobin (1996, p. 203) argues, languages may differ in the way they structure complex paths, but it is also necessary to look at the content of the narrative, at what is narrated, and see whether speakers of these languages express the same degree of event granularity, namely, the same degree of detailed description for an event. In order to test this possibility, Slobin chooses the 'deer scene' in the Frog Stories. This is a very rich and complex scene that depicts how the boy and the dog fall down from the cliff. It can be divided into six different narrative segments or subscenes: (i) deer starts to run, (ii) deer runs, carrying the boy, (iii) deer stops at a cliff, (iv) deer throws the boy (off the antlers/down); (v) boy and dog fall, and (vi) boy and dog land in water.[4]

The goal of this test is to see whether narrators who do not use a detailed description of path elements would nonetheless employ other strategies to provide path details (Slobin, 1996). The fact that a given language does not use clause-compacting (i.e., one verb with several paths) does not mean that it cannot show the same degree of event granularity; this language might use separate clauses but offer the same information in the end. Therefore, it is necessary to see how many of the six segments in the deer scene are mentioned in these languages. The results are summarized in Table 30.4.

Table 30.4 shows that languages such as Tagalog, Spanish, and Hebrew prefer to mention fewer than three segments of the deer scene most of the time, whereas languages such as Chinese, Basque, Ewe, Chantyal, and Squliq follow the opposite strategy and usually mention more than three segments. This variation adds further support to the results in the previous sections: (i) languages from the same typological group use different numbers of segments (Hebrew vs. Basque), and (ii) languages from different typological groups use similar numbers of segments (Chinese and Basque) to describe the same scene.

TABLE 30.4 Event Segmentation in the Deer Scene

Language	+ 3 segments	Mean #
Tagalog[v]	17%	1.8_4
Romance[v] (French, Portuguese, Spanish)	30%	2.1_4
Semitic[v] (Hebrew)	30%	2.0_4
Cebuano[v]	30%	2.2_4
Malay[v]	50%	2.5_4
Saisiyat[v]	60%	2.6_4
Slavic[s] (Polish, Russian, Serbo-Croatian)	76%	2.8_4
Thai[e]	80%	3.0_4
West Greenlandic[v]	80%	4.2_6
Tsou[e]	83%	3.1_4
Germanic[s] (Dutch, English, German, Icelandic, Swedish)	86%	3.0_4
Chinese[e]	92%	3.5_4
Basque[v]	93%	$4.4_6/3.1_4$
Arrernte[v]	100%	7.8_6
Ewe[e]	100%	—
Chantyal[v]	100%	4.0_6
Squliq[v]	100%	3.6_4

[v]: verb-framed, [s]: satellite-framed, [e]: equipollently-framed. Percentages are calculated as follows: number of speakers who mention 3 or more segments divided by the total number of speakers.

---

[4] Slobin (1997) reduces the six segments down to four. Since data sources in this chapter make use of both systems, the number of segments used in the calculation of the mean number is indicated in the third column in Table 30.4.

CONCLUSIONS: PATH SALIENCE CLINE AND POSSIBLE EXPLANATIONS

As Slobin (2004, p. 238) argues, languages cannot be compared on the basis of their accessibility to the semantic component of path. Path is the main component of a motion event, and as such, must be present in one form or another in the description of a motion event. However, languages can be compared on the basis of their degree of elaboration of path. Some languages describe this semantic component more often and in much more detail than others. Slobin attributes these differences to the type of lexicalization pattern; satellite-framed languages tend to include more information about path than verb-framed languages.

In this chapter, I have shown that the degree of elaboration of path is not strictly subject to the type of lexicalization pattern. Languages that belong to the same typological group can show completely different approaches toward the description of this semantic component. Based on the data discussed above, I propose a cline of path salience that cross-cuts the three lexicalization patterns and classifies languages along a continuum between two ends: high-path-salient languages and low-path-salient languages. The former offers rich and frequent descriptions of path, while the latter provides poor elaborations of this component. Figure 30.1 presents the position of each language along this continuum.

Once the path salience cline has been established, the next step is to propose possible explanations for both intra- and inter-typological variation. That is, it is necessary to investigate what makes some languages high-path-salient and others low-path-salient. I argue that there is a relation between path salience and the structural, discursive, and typological characteristics of each language, such as space and motion lexicon, word order, verb omission, redundancy, language orality, and culture. In order to understand how these factors contribute to the degree of path description, it is important to bear in mind the following: (i) this is an open list, that is, more factors will be included in future research, (ii) not all factors must be present at once in a given language, and (iii) not all languages should have the same number or type of factors to be classified as high- or low-path-salient. My hypothesis is that the more factors a language has the more likely that language is high-path-salient and occupies a closer position to the high-path-salient end of the cline. Due to space constraints, I cannot develop each of these factors in great detail, and therefore, I only offer a brief sketch of each contributing factor.

One of the possible factors is related to the linguistic devices that these languages provide for encoding different aspects of movement and location. Languages with high-path salience often come with rich lexical and morphological resources. Basque, for example, has five locative cases and more than 30 locative nouns or postpositions (Ibarretxe-Antuñano, 2001). Arrernte relies on an extensive case system and a special motion-devoted category of verbal inflections called the 'category of associated-motion' (Koch, 1984; Wilkins, 1991, 2004). Chantyal uses a rich set of directionals and case marking morphology (Noonan, 2003). The hypothesis that languages with rich linguistic resources for expressing motion tend to provide more details about path is supported by studies comparing Swedish and Icelandic (Ragnarsdóttir & Strömqvist, 2004; Strömqvist et al., 1995). Icelandic offers a higher proportion of path specification than Swedish. According to these studies, a contributing factor that may partly explain this difference is the presence of a case system in Icelandic and the lack of such a system in Swedish. Languages with low-path salience, on the other hand, often lack

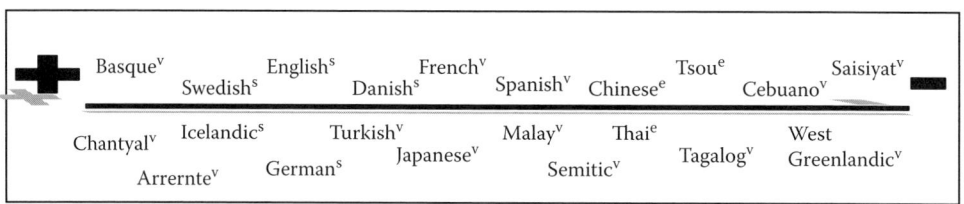

Figure 30.1 Path salience cline. ᵛ: verb-framed, ˢ: satellite-framed, ᵉ: equipollently-framed.

these elaborate systems. Squliq, for instance, does not have a distinct locative case, and Saisiyat has one single locative case particle *ray* that functions as source, goal, and location (Huang & Tanangkingsing, 2005).

The second explanatory factor has to do with word order. Verb-final languages are more prone to be high-path-salient than verb-initial languages. In my corpus, languages such as Basque, Chantyal, Japanese, and Turkish are verb final, whereas languages such as Saisiyat, Squliq, Tsou, and Tagalog are verb initial. For our purposes, what really matters about word order is the position of the verb in the sentence and the role it plays as carrier of path information. In verb-final languages, the verb goes at the end, and all those complements that provide and specify details about path occur sequentially before the verb. The semantic-pragmatic consequences of this ordering are clear: by the time the verb is produced—if it is at all, as discussed below—the complements have already provided all the necessary information about the motion event. In verb-initial languages the situation is the opposite. The first element that provides information about path is the verb itself; the complements seem unnecessary because the relevant information about path is already anticipated by the verb (Zlatev & Yangklang, 2004).

The third factor is related to the degree of tolerance for verb omissions.[5] High-path-salient languages are more likely to allow verb omissions than low-path-salient languages. Danish, for example, allows the omission of the main lexical verb and uses a modal verb instead when expressing direction toward a given goal, as in *I morgen skal jeg på universitet* (tomorrow shall I to the university) 'Tomorrow I will (go) to the university.' Basque is even more permissive with verb omission, and in some motion clauses, there is no need for the verbal element to be mentioned, just the goal complement, as in *Beste euskaldunentzat bukaturik utzi nuena Italia aldera baino lehen* (other basque.ben finished leave.perf aux.what Italy side.all before) 'What I left finished for other Basques before I (went) to Italy.' In low-path-salient languages such as Thai and West Greenlandic, on the other hand, it is not possible to omit the verb; not only is the verb an obligatory part of the clause but also the carrier of all the necessary semantic information for the description of the motion event. That is why Thai and West Greenlandic speakers seem to concentrate particularly on the verbs and omit nominal path specification (see Zlatev & Yangklang, 2004; Engberg-Pedersen & Blytmann Trondhjem, 2004).

The fourth factor concerns the existence of dummy verbs. The semantic load of these verbs is usually poor or very general, and when accompanied by path complements they are used for the description of motion events. High-path-salient languages are more likely to employ dummy verbs in motion constructions than low-path-salient languages. The verb 'be' is a typical candidate for these situations. For example, the Swiss German dialect Muotathal frequently uses the verb *sein* with a path complement in the accusative, as in *Und da isch e uffen baumstumpe* (and there is he onto.a.acc stump) 'And there he goes over the stump' (Berthele, 2006, pp. 114–129; see also his discussion of the Swiss German dummy verb *ga* 'go'). In Basque, the verb *izan* 'be' used in conjunction with the locative, allative, or ablative case is equivalent to saying a locative, goal, or source verb, as in *Izan zara ikastolara?* (be aux school.all) 'Did you go to school?' (see Zamarripa, 1913, p. 115).

The fifth factor is related to cultural systems. High-path-salient languages are more likely to possess cultural systems in which space and motion play a more important role than low-path-salient languages. Cultural values seem to exert enormous influence on the perception and description of specific domains of experience. Authors such as Wilkins (2004) and Bavin (2004) have argued that cultural factors are directly linked to the way space and motion are described in Arrernte and Warlpiri, respectively. Central Desert aboriginal communities show detailed attention to motion, paths, journeys, and orientation in space, and accordingly, this is reflected in their descriptions of motion events.

---

[5] I prefer to use the term *verb omission* because it covers not only cases of syntactic and pragmatic omissions of the verb or part of the VP, what is usually known as ellipsis or gapping (see Lappin, 1996; Lobeck 1995; Wilson, 2001), but also cases where the verb is simply omitted without any previous syntactic or pragmatic antecedent (see Ibarretxe-Antuñano, in press).

The sixth factor has to do with the concept of conceptually oral vs. conceptually written languages. Koch & Oesterreicher (1985) and Oesterreicher (2001) argue that languages—regardless of their form of communication (oral or written)—are consistently characterized by a number of morpho-syntactic, semantic, and pragmatic properties that are always present in the speakers' (oral or written) use of the language. It is usually argued that written language is stylistically very different from oral language. However, according to Koch and Osterreicher, languages will preserve some of their intrinsic characteristics as conceptually oral or written languages in both types of communication. For example, conceptually oral languages are characterized by elliptic constructions, congruence violations, low type-token ratios in the lexicon, redundancy, lexical variation, hyperbolic expressions, turn-taking signals, and self-corrections. In a conceptually oral language, these characteristics would appear in both oral and written texts. Conceptually oral languages are more likely to be high-path-salient than conceptually written languages because, due to their linguistic characteristics, these languages are allowed to express path elements several times within the same clause and to elide other elements much more freely than conceptually written languages. In other words, path descriptions that might be regarded as redundant or even ungrammatical in conceptually written languages are accepted in conceptually oral languages. A piece of evidence for these differences can be drawn from the analysis of path descriptions in the Swiss dialect Muotathal, which is a conceptually oral language and Standard High German, which is a conceptually written language (Berthele, 2004). The former not only scores higher in the description of path elements than the latter, but also shows a great deal of redundancy in the information provided by the verb. Adpositional phrases and particles, as illustrated in the example *dä ghiid usem fänschter usen obbenabbe* (that.one falls from.the.dat window out from.top.to.down), can also be included in this category. In connection with this factor, it is important to notice that languages in which the process of standardization is a relatively recent phenomenon are more likely to be conceptually oral languages, and therefore, high-path-salient. This hypothesis is confirmed by the situation of Basque and the Swiss dialects. In both cases, there is a situation of diglosia between the standard variety, Euskara Batua and Standard High German, respectively, and the different dialects spoken in these countries (Berthele, 2006; Euskaltzaindia, 1977; Goikoetxea Arrieta, 2003; Zuazo, 2001). Further support for the link between orality and high-path salience is found in the work of Sampaio et al. (2003) on Amondawa (Tupi Guaraní), a purely oral language that shows a relative constructional freedom in motion events.

In this chapter, I have argued that languages, regardless of their typological classification, can be classified along a cline of path salience. The position of each language on this scale depends on how accessible, frequent, and easy to process path devices are in each language, and can be explained by means of linguistic, discursive, and cultural factors. The typological classification of languages with respect to the description of motion events has to take into account not only how semantic components conflate in a given language, but also the degree of elaboration of these semantic components. Future research should tell us whether the cline of path salience proposed in this chapter can be considered a parameter for typological classification. In order to support this hypothesis, more typologically different languages should be added to this corpus, as well as more diverse types of data, not just orally elicited data as in Frog Stories. The list of interrelated factors is another area that should be expanded in future investigations.

REFERENCES

Aksu-Koç, A. (1994). Development of linguistic forms: Turkish. In R. Berman & D. I. Slobin (Eds.), *Relating events in narrative* (pp. 329–388). Hillsdale, NJ: Lawrence Erlbaum Asssociates.

Ameka, F., & Essegbey, J. (in press). Serialising languages: Satellite-framed, verb-framed, or neither. In L. Hyman & I. Maddieson (Eds.), *African comparative and historical linguistics: Proceedings of the 32th annual conference on African linguistics*. Lawrenceville, NJ: Africa World Press.

Bavin, E. L. (2004). Focusing on 'where.' An analysis of Warlpiri frog stories. In S. Strömqvist & L. Verhoeven (Eds.), *Relating events in narrative: Typological and contextual perspectives* (pp. 17–35). Hillsdale, NJ: Lawrence Erlbaum Associates.

Berman, R., & Neeman, Y. (1994). Development of linguistic forms: Hebrew. In R. Berman & D. I. Slobin (Eds.), *Relating events in narrative* (pp. 285–328). Hillsdale, NJ: Lawrence Erlbaum Associates.

Berman, R., & Slobin, D. I. (1994). *Relating events in narrative*. Hillsdale, NJ: Lawrence Erlbaum Associates.

Berthele, R. (2004). The typology of motion and posture verbs: a variationist account. In B. Kortmann (Ed.), *Dialectology meets typology* (pp. 93–126). Berlin: Mouton de Gruyter.

Berthele, R. (2006). *Ort und Weg. Eine vergleichende Untersuchung der sprachlichen Raumreferenz in Varietäten des Deutschen, Rätoromanischen und Französischen*. Berlin: Mouton de Gruyter.

Cadierno, T. (2004). Expressing motion events in a second language: A cognitive typological approach. In M. Achard & S. Neimeier (Eds.), *Cognitive linguistics, second language acquisition and foreign language pedagogy* (pp. 13–49). Berlin: Mouton de Gruyter.

Cadierno, T., & Ruiz L. (2006). Motion events in second language acquisition. *Annual Review of Cognitive Linguistics, 4*, 183–216.

Chen, L. (2005). *The acquisition and use of motion event expressions in Chinese*. Unpublished doctoral dissertation, University of Louisiana, Lafayette.

Engberg-Pedersen, E., & F. Blytmann Trondhjem. (2004). Focus on action in motion descriptions. The case of West-Greenlandic. In S. Strömqvist & L. Verhoeven (Eds.), *Relating events in narrative: Typological and contextual perspectives* (pp. 59–88). Hillsdale, NJ: Lawrence Erlbaum Associates.

Euskaltzaindia. (1977). *Euskararen liburu zuria-El libro blanco del euskara*. Bilbao: Euskaltzaindia.

Garai, K. J., & Ibarretxe-Antuñano, I. (2002). From X to Y: The 'complete path' construction in Basque. *Odense Working Papers in Language and Communication, 23*, 289–311.

Goikoetxea Arrieta, J. L. (2003). *Euskalkia eta hezkuntza: Dakigunetik ez dakigunera euskal diglosia erazian*. Bilbo: Euskaltzaindia/IKER.

Hamano, S. (1998). *The sound-symbolic system of Japanese*. Stanford: CLSI Publications.

Huang, S., & Tanangkingsing, M. (2005). Reference to motion events in six Western Austronesian languages. Towards a semantic typology. *Oceanic Linguistics, 44*(2), 307–340.

Ibarretxe-Antuñano, I. (2001). *An overview of Basque locational cases: old descriptions, new approaches*. (International Computer Science Institute Technical Report No. 01–006). Retrieved December 21, 2005, from ICSI webpage. Access: http://www.icsi.berkeley.edu/cgi-bin/pubs/publication.pl?ID=001193

Ibarretxe-Antuñano, I. (2003a). What translation tells us about motion: a contrastive study of typologically different languages. *International Journal of English Studies, 3*(2,) 151–176.

Ibarretxe-Antuñano, I. (2003b, July). Path in Basque. Paper presented at the 8th International Cognitive Linguistics Conference, University of La Rioja, Spain.

Ibarretxe-Antuñano, I. (2004a). Motion events in Basque narratives. In S. Strömqvist & L. Verhoeven (Eds.), *Relating events in narrative: Typological and contextual perspectives* (pp. 89–111). Hillsdale, NJ: Lawrence Erlbaum Associates.

Ibarretxe-Antuñano, I. (2004b). Language typologies in our language use: the case of Basque motion events in adult oral narratives. *Cognitive Linguistics, 15*(3), 317–349.

Ibarretxe-Antuñano, I. (2004c). Dicotomías frente a continuos en la lexicalización de los eventos de movimiento. *Revista Española de Lingüística, 34*(2), 481–510.

Ibarretxe-Antuñano, I. (in press). Basque: Going beyond verb-framed typologies. *Linguistic Typology*.

Kakehi, H., Tamori, I., & Schourup, L. (1996). *Dictionary of iconic expressions in Japanese*. Berlin: Mouton de Gruyter.

Koch, H. (1984). The category of 'associated motion' in Kaytej. *Language in Central Australia, 1*, 23–34.

Koch, P., & Oesterreicher, W. (1985). Sprache der Nähe-Sprache der Distanz. Mündlichkeit und Schriftlichkeit im Spannungsfeld von Sprachtheorie. *Romanistisches Jahrbuch, 36*, 15–34.

Lappin, S. (1996). The interpretation of ellipsis. In S. Lappin (Ed.), *The handbook of contemporary semantic theory* (pp. 145–175). Oxford, UK: Blackwells.

Lobeck, A. (1995). *Ellipsis. Functional heads, licensing, and identification*. Oxford: Oxford University Press.

Mayer, M. (1969). *Frog, where are you?* New York: Dial Press.

Noonan, M. (2003). Motion events in Chantyal. In E. Shay & U. Seibert (Eds.), *Motion, direction, and location in languages. In honor of Zygmunt Frajzyngier* (pp. 211–234). Amsterdam/Philadelphia: John Benjamins.

Oesterreicher, W. (2001). Historizität-Sprachvariation, Sprachverschiedenheit, Sprachwandel. In M. Haspelmath et al. (Eds.), *Language typology and language universals. An international handbook* (pp. 1554–1595). Berlin: Mouton de Gruyter.

Ohara, K. H. (2003, July). Manner of motion in Japanese: not every verb-framed language is poor in manner. Paper presented at the 8th International Cognitive Linguistics Conference, Universidad de La Rioja, Spain.

Ragnarsdóttir, H., & Strömqvist, S. (2004). Time, space and manner in Icelandic and Swedish. In S. Strömqvist & L. Verhoeven (Eds.), *Relating events in narrative: Typological and contextual perspectives* (pp. 113–141). Hillsdale, NJ: Lawrence Erlbaum Associates.

Sampaio, W., da Silva, V., & Sinha, C. (2003, July). Mixing and mapping: Motion and manner in Amondawa (Uru-eu-uau-uau). Paper presented at the 8th International Cognitive Linguistics Conference, University of La Rioja, Spain.

Satoh, K. (2001). Thinking for speaking in Japanese narrative. *Proceedings of the 1st Seoul International Conference on Discourse and Cognitive Linguistics. Perspectives from the 21st century* (pp. 71–82). Seoul, Korea.

Slobin, D. I. (1996). Two ways to travel: Verbs of motion in English and Spanish. In M. Shibatani & S. A. Thompson (Eds.), *Grammatical constructions. Their form and meaning* (pp. 195–219). Oxford, UK: Clarendon Press.

Slobin, D. I. (1997). Mind, code, and text. In J. Bybee, L. Haiman, & S. A. Thompson (Eds.), *Essays on language function and language type: Dedicated to T. Givón* (pp. 437–467). Amsterdam/Philadelphia: John Benjamins.

Slobin, D. I. (2000). Verbalized events: A dynamic approach to linguistic relativity and determinism. In S. Niemeier & R. Dirven (Eds.), *Evidence for linguistic relativity* (pp. 107–138). Berlin: Mouton de Gruyter.

Slobin, D. I. (2004). The many ways to search for a frog: Linguistic typology and the expression of motion events. In S. Strömqvist & L. Verhoeven (Eds.), *Relating events in narrative: Typological and contextual perspectives* (pp. 219–257). Hillsdale, NJ: Lawrence Erlbaum Associates.

Slobin, D. I., & Hoiting, N. (1994). Reference to movement in spoken and sign languages: Typological consideration. *Proceedings of the twentieth annual meeting of the Berkeley Linguistics Society* (pp. 487–503).

Strömqvist, S., Ragnarsdóttir, H., Engstrand, O., Jonsdóttir, M., Lanza, E., Leiwo, M., et al. (1995). The internordic study of language acquisition. *Nordic Journal of Linguistics, 18*, 3–29.

Sugiyama, Y. (2005). Not all verb-framed languages are created equal: The case of Japanese. *Proceedings of the thirty-first annual meeting of the Berkeley Linguistics Society*.

Talmy, L. (1991). Path to realization: A typology of event conflation. *Proceedings of the seventeenth annual meeting of the Berkeley Linguistics Society* (pp. 480–519).

Talmy, L. (2000). *Toward a cognitive semantics*. Cambridge, MA: The MIT Press.

Tanangkingsing, M. (2004). A study of motion events in Saisiyat and Cebuano. In M. Achard & S. Kemmer (Eds.), *Language, culture, and mind* (pp. 199–210). Standford: CSLI Publications.

Wilkins, D. (1991). The semantics, pragmatics and diachronic development of 'associated motion' in Mparntwe Arrernte. *Buffalo Papers in Linguistics, 1*, 207–257.

Wilkins, D. (2004). The verbalization of motion events in Arrernte. In S. Strömqvist & L. Verhoeven (Eds.), *Relating events in narrative: Typological and contextual perspectives* (pp. 143–157). Hillsdale, NJ: Lawrence Erlbaum Associates.

Wilson, P. (2001). Ellipsis. In J. Verschueren, J.-O. Ostman, J. Blommaert, & C. Bulcaen (Eds.), *Handbook of pragmatics* (pp. 1–26). Amsterdam/Philadelphia: John Benjamins.

Zamarripa, P. (1913). *Manual del Vascófilo*. Bilbao: Wilsen.

Zlatev, J., & Yangklang, P. (2004). A third way to travel. The place of Thai in motion-event typology. In S. Strömqvist & L. Verhoeven (Eds.), *Relating events in narrative: Typological and contextual perspectives* (pp. 159–190). Hillsdale, NJ: Lawrence Erlbaum Associates.

Zuazo, K. (2001). *Euskararen sendabelarrak*. Irun, Spain: Alberdaina.

31

Continuity and Change in the Representation of Motion Events in French[1]

ANETTA KOPECKA

Max Planck Institute for Psycholinguistics, Nijmegen, the Netherlands

Each type of lexicalization pattern engenders a type of style.

Dan I. Slobin (1997, p. 443)

I met Dan Slobin for the first time about 6 years ago during my postgraduate studies at the University of Lyon when he gave a talk entitled "Talking about motion events in two types of languages." Coincidentally, the two language types were also the ones competing in my own mind: my native satellite-framed language, Polish, and my academic verb-framed language, French. The crosslinguistic research presented by Dan Slobin at that time inspired the development of my own research. In my comparisons of Polish and French, one of the topics that I became particularly interested in was the typological complexity of Modern French, which contrasts with the typological regularity of Polish, and the diachronic sources of this complexity. It was Dan Slobin's enthusiastic encouragement that gave me confidence to pursue this topic further.

The present chapter is dedicated with gratitude to Dan Slobin. It is a continuation of the above diachronic investigation and draws from his research on the impact of the typology of motion events on rhetorical style in narrative.

INTRODUCTION

The linguistic representation of motion events and its impact on cognitive processes have been one of the main research topics explored in recent studies on crosslinguistic differences. This research has been widely influenced by the typology of motion events proposed by Talmy (1991, 2000), who divides languages into two types as satellite-framed and verb-framed, depending on whether they lexicalize path of motion in a verb satellite and manner of motion in the main verb (*run in*, *run out*), or lexicalize path in the main verb and manner periphrastically, in a gerund or other adverbial expression (*enter running*, *exit running*). The crosslinguistic research carried out by Slobin (e.g., 1991, 1996a, 1996b, 1997) and Berman and Slobin (1994) has opened new research perspectives, showing how such typological differences influence various activities mediated by language,

---

[1] I would like to thank Benjamin Fagard for his valuable help with the analysis of the Old French data and his careful reading of this chapter. Any errors in interpretation of these data are solely mine. I am also grateful to Elena Lieven and Şeyda Özçalışkan for helpful comments and suggestions on this chapter.

including speaking, listening, and translating, and how speakers of typologically distinct languages attend to different dimensions of motion events (path vs. manner). In particular, Slobin (1996a, 1996b, 2004) examined the impact of this typology on rhetorical style in narratives in both satellite- and verb-framed languages, showing that depending on whether manner is expressed in the main verb or optionally, in an adverbial, languages differ in their 'habitual style of expression' with respect to this specific dimension of motion. For example, in a study of novels and their translations between English (a satellite-framed language) and Spanish (a verb-framed language), he found that only half of the English manner verbs were translated into manner verbs in Spanish, whereas in the other half manner information was omitted. On the other hand, the translations from Spanish to English exhibited addition of manner information when such information was not overtly expressed in the source language. Furthermore, the study has shown that English elaborates path in a more detailed fashion than Spanish, leaving the scene setting to be inferred, whereas Spanish, on the contrary, allocates more attention to static descriptions and tends to leave path to be inferred. These results show that the translations between the two language types follow the characteristic pattern of the target rather than the source language, and differ in both rhetorical style and vividness of motion descriptions (e.g., Slobin, 2004).

This chapter analyzes such typological variation at the intra-linguistic level, using a diachronic perspective. It aims to show that French has shifted from a satellite- to a verb-framed pattern through the loss of productivity of verb prefixes and particles encoding path, and examines the consequences of this shift on rhetorical style in narratives. For this purpose, I present a comparative text-based study of linguistic representations of motion events based on translations of short narratives from Old to Modern French and investigate how the two dimensions of motion events, namely, path and manner, are elaborated in medieval narratives and their contemporary translations.

FROM A SATELLITE- TO A VERB-FRAMED PATTERN: A TYPOLOGICAL SHIFT IN FRENCH

According to the typology of motion events, French, like all other Romance languages, is *verb-framed*, expressing path typically in the main verb and manner in a gerund, in contrast to *satellite-framed* languages, such as Germanic and Slavic languages, which express path in a satellite (a particle or a prefix) and manner in the main verb (Talmy, 1985, 1991, 2000). Recent research (Kopecka, 2006, in press) has shown that the verb-framed pattern in French evolved from a satellite-framed pattern through the lexical fusion of verb prefixes and verb stems, and, more generally, that French has shifted from a satellite- to a verb-framed pattern through the loss of productivity of verb prefixes.

In particular, although Old French had a few verbs expressing path of motion (e.g., *monter* 'to go up,' *passer* 'to pass'), its common strategy for conveying path information was to use verb prefixes, as in Slavic languages, and verb particles, as in Germanic languages. Old French had about 10 verb prefixes, including *a-* 'to, toward,' *de-* 'from, off,' *é-* 'out,' *en-* (Lat. *in*) 'in, into,' *par-* 'by, all over,' *re-* 'back, again,' *tres-* 'across, through,' and as many verb particles, including *ariere* 'back,' *amont* 'up,' *aval* 'down,' *en* (Lat. *inde*) 'away,' *fors* 'out,' *jus* 'downward, down below,' and *sus* 'upward, up above.' All these prefixes and particles could be combined in a prolific way with verbs of motion; they could combine not only with manner verbs (e.g., *parcorir* 'to run through,' *tresvoler* 'to fly across'), but also with the existing path verbs (e.g., *parmonter* 'to climb up,' *trespasser* 'to pass across'), adding a further dimension to the meaning of the verb. However, the productivity of prefixes and particles has weakened over the centuries, engendering a typological change in French in the expression of motion. Thus, whereas some satellite-framed constructions have been maintained in Modern French, many others either have shifted pattern or have been lost. In order to illustrate this change, the next few paragraphs will provide examples of a change in some prefix-verb constructions (see

Kopecka, 2006, in press, for more detailed analysis of the typological shift in French and the ensuing typological complexity of the modern language).

The first phenomenon that has contributed to the typological change in French is the shift of some prefixed verbs of motion from a satellite-framed pattern to either a verb-framed or a hybrid pattern through the lexical fusion of verb prefixes with verb stems.

The examples in (1) illustrate the shift of two originally prefixed verbs of motion, *arriver* 'to arrive' and *éloigner* 'to move away,' toward the verb-framed pattern. In Old French, these verbs also existed in their simple, non-prefixed form and conveyed the meaning of non-telic paths. However, following the loss of the lexical autonomy of these simple forms, the prefix and the verb root fused lexically to form a monomorphemic path verb, which conveys a telic path.

(1) Old French　　　　　　　Modern French
   a.　*a-river*　　　　　　　*arriver*
       toward-sail along　　to arrive
   b.　*e-loignier*　　　　　　*éloigner*
       away-move　　　　　to move away

The examples in (2) show the shift of two other prefixed verbs, *affluer* 'to flow toward' and *déferler* 'to spread out,' toward a hybrid pattern. As was the case for the verbs illustrated above, these verbs also had simple, non-prefixed forms. Their primary function was to convey manner of motion. As the simple forms lost their autonomy, the prefix and the verb root merged to form a semantically 'hybrid' verb conflating both path and manner of motion in one lexical item.

(2) Old French　　　　　　　Modern French
   a.　*a-fluer*　　　　　　　*affluer*
       toward-flow　　　　　to flow toward
   b.　*dé-ferler*　　　　　　　*déferler*
       off-spread　　　　　　to spread out

It may be noted that, while for many verbs the lexical fusion illustrated in (1) and (2) occurred at a very early stage of the language, sometimes even in Latin (e.g., *descendre* 'to descend'), many other verbs have never fused with prefixes they formerly combined with (e.g., *ac-courir* 'toward-run').

The second phenomenon that has contributed to the typological change in French is the loss of the ability of certain motion verbs to combine with path prefixes. In Old French, the majority of motion verbs, and particularly manner verbs, could freely combine with path prefixes. This was, for example, the case for verbs like *couler* 'to flow,' *flotter* 'to float,' *nager* 'to swim,' and *voler* 'to fly,' as illustrated in (3). However, similar to many other verbs of motion encoding manner, these four verbs no longer combine with path prefixes. As a consequence, Modern French has to use a verb-framed pattern to describe similar events, encoding path in the main verb and manner periphrastically, in a gerund or in some other adverbial expression.

(3) Old French　　　　　　　Modern French
   a.　*a-couler*　　　　　　　*s'approcher en coulant*
       toward-flow　　　　　to approach flowing
   b.　*a-floter*　　　　　　　　*s'approcher en flottant*
       toward-float　　　　　to approach floating
   c.　*tres-nagier*　　　　　　*traverser à la nage*
       across-swim　　　　　to cross at a swim
   d.　*tres-voler*　　　　　　　*traverser en volant*
       across-fly　　　　　　to cross flying

The process of lexical fusion and, perhaps more crucially, the loss of free prefix-verb combinations significantly decreased the use of the satellite-framed pattern in favor of the verb-framed pattern, leaving only a few residual cases in the modern language (Kopecka, 2006). This typological development has had a crucial effect on the internal system of the language in general, and on the representation of motion events in particular. The next sections will examine the consequences of this change for the rhetorical style of narratives. To this end, we will apply the translation method used by Slobin at the crosslinguistic level to investigate the intra-linguistic implications of this change for narratives by looking at translations from Old French into Modern French. Our aim is to examine the extent to which Old and Modern French differ in their linguistic elaboration of path and manner of motion.

LEXICALIZATION PATTERNS IN TRANSLATION: FROM OLD INTO MODERN FRENCH

The study presented here is based on short narratives from the 12th and 14th centuries and their translations into contemporary French. Note that the end of the 13th century corresponds to the development of Old French into Middle French. I will refer to this medieval stage of the language as Old French. For the purpose of this study, I selected four narratives called *fabliaux*, which are humorous tales about noble society that used to be performed orally by *jongleurs* 'jugglers' (Leclanche, 2003). These texts are therefore notable for their vernacular style; they are also translated in a colloquial rather than a literary style. This presents an advantage for a typological study such as this, since the colloquial style makes use of the most characteristic patterns of the language (Talmy, 2000). Furthermore, these texts contain relatively frequent descriptions of motion, which served as the main motivation for their choice for the present study.

A total of 144 sentences depicting motion events was extracted from the original texts, resulting in a total of 183 verb clauses. All of the sentences contain intransitive verbs, depicting the autonomous motion of animate actors. Table 31.1 presents the frequency distribution of the patterns found in the four narratives in Old French (henceforth OF) and the patterns used in their translation into Modern French (henceforth MF).

Two main patterns were identified in OF: a verb-framed pattern (e.g., *il entra en une voiete* 'he entered a little path') with 67 occurrences and a satellite-framed pattern (e.g., *de la cuve sailli lués fors* 'he jumped out of the bath') with 62 occurrences. The satellite-framed pattern includes 32 constructions with a manner verb and 30 constructions with the general motion verb, *aler* 'to go.' Note that among all the verbs of motion, *aler* could combine with the greatest variety of path satellites, in particular verb particles (cf. Buridant, 2000, p. 543). In OF, there is also a mixed pattern consisting of the combination of a path verb (conveying a telic meaning) with a path satellite. In Table 31.1, I refer to this type of construction as verb-/satellite-pattern (e.g., *trespassee la charier* 'across-passed

TABLE 31.1 Lexicalization Patterns in Intra-Linguistic Translation: Frequency of Different Typological Patterns Used in Old French and Modern French Texts

Old French	Modern French						
	V-Pattern	V-/S-Pattern	S-Pattern	V+PP$_{ground}$	Hybrid Pattern	Other	Total
V-pattern	60		1	2	4		67
V-/S-pattern	23	1					24
S-pattern	46		13		3		62
V + PP$_{ground}$	11		1	14	2		28
Other						2	2
Total	140	1	15	16	9	2	

V-pattern = verb-framed pattern, S-pattern = satellite-framed pattern, V-/S-pattern = verb-/satellite-pattern, PP = prepositional phrase, V= verb

the path'). This pattern was quite common in OF and represents 24 occurrences in the OF data. In addition, there are 28 verb clauses that encode path in a prepositional phrase together with a reference object, called 'ground' (e.g., *a cort ala* 'went at the court'),[2] and two clauses that use nouns to convey the meaning of motion (e.g., *chevauchée* 'a ride').

In sum, it appears that both verb-framed and satellite-framed patterns are equally distributed in the OF narratives. Nevertheless, although there is not a strong preference for the use of a satellite- or a verb-framed pattern, we note that path satellites enjoy a very wide distribution, as they occur not only with manner verbs and the verb *aler*, but also with path verbs.

If we consider the patterns used in the translation into MF, at first glance, we may note a greater overall variety of patterns, due to the fact that the hybrid pattern (e.g., *affluer* 'to flow toward') developed relatively recently. However, there are two other observations to be made. First, there is an overall expansion in the use of the verb-framed pattern (140 tokens in MF vs. 67 tokens in OF), and a correspondingly significant diminution in the use of the satellite-framed pattern (15 tokens in MF vs. 62 tokens in OF). The second observation concerns the combination of path satellites with path verbs (i.e., verb-/satellite-pattern). Whereas in OF this was a possible coding strategy, in MF such combinations are essentially no longer in use; thus, as Table 31.1 shows, only one such construction was used in the translation to MF.

TYPOLOGICAL CONTRAST IN RHETORICAL STYLE: FROM OLD INTO MODERN FRENCH

The typological variation between OF and MF in terms of the use of the verb-framed or the satellite-framed pattern has crucial consequences for the way motion events are described in narratives. In this section, we will examine the discourse effects of this variation. Special attention will be given to the use of the satellite-framed constructions in medieval texts and their translation into modern texts, and to the ensuing differences in the linguistic representation of path and manner of motion.

Path of Motion in Intra-Linguistic Translation

As we have seen, OF had various means for conveying path of motion, including verbs and satellites (i.e., prefixes, particles). More interestingly, it was possible not only to combine path verbs with path satellites, but also to accumulate several path satellites around the same verb. This combinatorial strategy allowed the elaboration of complex paths with a single manner verb or a general verb of motion in OF, which, as we will see, is represented in a very distinct way in MF.

Consider the set of satellite-framed examples in OF in (4)–(7). In all of the sentences, we note the use of the same manner verb *tourne* 'he turns/moves round' describing motion without change of location. As for the path, it is indicated in different satellites, the morphosyntactic density of which increases from (4) to (7). In examples (4) and (5), path is expressed in one element: the particle *en* 'away' and the prefix *re-* 'back,' respectively. In example (6), both the particle *en* and the prefix *re-* occur in the same clause and function as two satellites of the same verb. Finally, example (7) features an additional particle, *ariere* 'backward' (similar to *re-*), so that the meaning of path is distributed across three different satellites—*en*, *re-*, and *ariere*—that are all combined with the same verb of motion.

This accumulation of path expressions illustrates the 'grammatical freedom' of OF, which is also characteristic of orally performed texts (Fleischman, 1990), and shows how the repetition fulfills a pragmatic (rather than grammatical) function in that it serves to foreground path information. In particular, these sentences describe a long episode where the protagonist, a squire, goes back and forth between his lord and a priest, who use him as a negotiator. As the negotiations drag on, the

---

[2] These prepositional phrases express either source- or goal-oriented motion, without indicating the change of state.

squire walks back and forth all night, repeating the same journey again and again. The accumulation of path expressions and, crucially, the recurrence of the same information related to the backward motion expressed by the prefix *re-* and the particle *ariere* appear to emphasize the protagonist's back-and-forth movement.

(4) *Dont s'en va cius et si s'en tourne,*
'And so he goes off and turns back'
Dusc'a la cambre ne sejourne (…).
'up to the room right away (…).' (Leclanche, 2003, p. 42)

(5) *Retourne tost, si di au prestre*
'Go back quickly and tell the priest'
Qu<e> il le me voist sans atente (…)
'to send her to me without delay (…).' (Leclanche, 2003, p. 48)

(6) *Puis s'en retourne et se couche;*
'Then he goes back to bed'
son cief envolepe et sa bouche
'he covers his entire head'
li escuiers, qui fu lassés.
'so tired is the squire.' (Leclanche, 2003, p. 42)

(7) *Dont s'en retourne chieus arriere,*
'And so he goes back'
Triste et mournes; sans areste.
'gloomy and exhausted, without delay.'
Au prestre vint, drecha la tieste,
'He comes to the priest, raises his head'
Si li dist (…).
'and says to him (…).' (Leclanche, 2003, p. 68)

Interestingly, when we compare translations of these different path expressions into MF in (4') to (7'), we see that the same verb *retourne* 'goes back' is used to translate all four verb constructions displayed in OF. Thus, in contrast to OF, where the aforementioned 'grammatical freedom' permits the accumulation and repetition of rich resources for expression of path, in MF this strategy is no longer felicitous. The resulting difference is that MF is less expressive with respect to this particular information.

(4') *L'écuyer s'en va;*
'The squire goes away';
il retourne sans traîner à la chambre (…).
'he goes back right away to the room.' (Leclanche, 2003, p. 43)

(5') *Retourne immédiatement dire au prêtre de m'envoyer la dame*
'Go back immediately and tell the priest to send me the lady'
sans attendre (…).
'without delay.' (Leclanche, 2003, p. 49)

(6') *Puis, fatigué, il retourne se coucher et se couvre*
'Then, tired, he goes back to bed and covers himself'
jusqu'aux yeux.
'up to his eyes.' (Leclanche, 2003, p. 43)

(7') *Sombre, abattu, l'écuyer retourne alors tout droit chez le prêtre,*
   'Gloomy, exhausted, the squire goes right back to the priest,'
   il relève la tête et lui dit (…).
   'he raises his head and says to him (…).' (Leclanche, 2003, p. 69)

More interestingly, from a typological perspective, besides the common repetition of path information illustrated above, the rich system of path satellites in OF and the possibility of compacting several path components into the same verb clause allow for more elaborate descriptions of path, thus emphasizing the progression of motion. Consider the sentence in (8) that describes a journey in great detail:

(8) *Si v<ont> aval par une sente*
   'They go down along a path'
   En un gardin, sor un vivier,
   'in a garden, over a fishpond,'
   A le maizon au chevalier (…).
   'to the house of the knight (…).' (Leclanche, 2003, p. 110)

There is a single verb of motion *vont* 'they go' and several elements describing the journey, such as *aval* 'down,' *par* 'by, along,' *en* 'in,' *sor* 'above, over,' and *a* 'to,' are attached to this verb. This information flow thus represents a complex path with its successive segments, including the downward motion (*aval*), the medium or the location passed along the path (*par, en, sor*), and the goal (*a*). When we look closely at the translation of this journey into MF, we note that, even if all the ground elements are expressed, path of motion is represented in a notably different way.

(8') *Ils descendent par un sentier dans un parc qui longe un vivier,*
   'They descend along a path in a park which stretches along a fishpond,'
   jusqu'à la demeure du chevalier (…).
   'up to the knight's residence (…).' (Leclanche, 2003, p. 111)

First, we note that the translation into MF makes use of the verb *descendent* 'descend/go down' to describe the protagonists' downward motion, which is expressed in the medieval text by a general verb of motion and a particle (*vont aval* 'go down'). The use of the path verb in MF appears to have consequences for how further segments of the path are represented. Thus, the modern text restructures the path in that it interprets *sor un vivier* 'over a fishpond' not as a segment of the path, but as a scene setting. Indeed, *sor un vivier* is translated by a relative clause with a path verb, as *qui longe un vivier*, which means 'which stretches along a fishpond' and refers to the location of the garden. By doing so, the translation into MF changes the semantic structure of the event. That is, in contrast to the OF example, which represents the path as a whole journey with its successive portions and therefore emphasizes the progression of the movement, the translation into MF allocates more attention to the setting where the event takes place.

Note that the greater use of verbs, as in example (8'), constitutes a pervasive pattern in MF, not only to translate a meaning conveyed by a particular satellite in OF, but also to segment the path into further sub-events. Consider the following sentence and its translation into MF. The medieval text describes the event by means of two typologically distinct coding strategies. We see, first, a general verb of motion combined with a path satellite—*s'en vont* 'they go away'—to express the departure, and second, two path verbs—*passent* 'they pass by' and *vienent* 'they come to'—to express the medium and the end point of the journey, respectively. Note that the medial verb *passent* encompasses two different ground elements, *l'uis* 'the door' and *le planchier* 'the room.'

(9) *Dont s'en vont maintenant andui*
  'And so now they both go off'
  Et passent l'uis et le planchier
  'and pass through the door and the room'
  Tant k'il vienent au chevalier
  'and come to the knight'
  Qui se gisoit desor sa coute.
  'who was lying on his coverlet.' (Leclanche, 2003, p. 76)

In contrast to the medieval text that encodes these two elements as a continuous path with one verb, the modern translation in (9') expresses these two ground elements in two different clauses, each with a different verb—*passent la porte* 'they pass by the door' and *traversent la salle* 'they cross the room'—thereby dividing the medial path into two different segments.

(9') *Tous deux partent aussitôt, passent la porte,*
  'They both leave right away, pass through the door,'
  traversent la salle et parviennent au chevalier
  'cross the room and come to the knight'
  qui était allongé sur sa couette.
  'who was lying on his coverlet.' (Leclanche, 2003, p. 77)

As noted by Slobin (1997), a descriptive strategy such as this, which consists of the use of two (or more) verbs that divide the path into segments, has an effect on the narrative style, because it slows the narrative tempo. In example (8), the apparent progress of the protagonists along the path is slowed by the emphasis on the successive path segments by means of individual verbs.

Manner of Motion in Intra-Linguistic Translation

In the medieval narratives, the preferred means of conveying manner information is the use of a finite main verb in a satellite-framed pattern (32 tokens). Manner information is elsewhere conveyed by modifiers such as adverbs, noun phrases, and prepositional phrases, which occur with path verbs in the verb-framed pattern (12 tokens) and, occasionally, with the generic verb of motion *aler* 'to go' in the satellite-framed pattern (4 tokens). Although OF did have gerundive forms, no gerunds depicting manner occur in the present data.[3] In this section, we will focus on the translation of manner verbs occurring in the satellite-framed pattern only. Constructions with a manner verb represent 56% (32 tokens) of the satellite-framed pattern in the medieval data. The remaining 48% (30 tokens) representing this pattern are constructed with the general verb of motion *aler* 'to go.'

As shown in Table 31.2, three different patterns have been used to translate the satellite-framed pattern with a manner verb from OF into MF: a verb-framed, a satellite-framed, and a hybrid pattern. Of the three patterns, the verb-framed pattern was the one most frequently chosen to translate the S-pattern from OF, with 21 tokens in total. It is important to note that of these 21 tokens, 18 omit manner information. As for the original satellite-framed pattern, it is represented in MF by the same type of construction in only 8 tokens.

The greater frequency of use of the verb-framed pattern in translation and the ensuing omission of manner have crucial consequences for the representation of motion events in narratives. Consider the sentence in (10), describing a journey of the protagonist on a horse along a heath:

---

[3] In Old French, gerunds had similar forms to present participles and are therefore sometimes difficult to distinguish. According to Fournier (2002), the modern form of gerunds composed of the preposition *en* and the participial form of the verb (e.g., *en courant* 'running') came into more systematic use only in the 18th century.

TABLE 31.2 Translation of Manner + Satellite Constructions from Old into Modern French

Old French	Modern French					Total
	V-Pattern		S-Pattern		Hybrid Pattern	
	V_{path}	$V_{path}+Adv_{manner}$	$V_{manner}+Sat_{path}$	$V_{go}+Sat_{path}$	$V_{path\ \&\ manner}$	
S-pattern $V_{manner}+Sat_{path}$	18	3	8	1	2	32
Total	21		9		2	

Sat = satellite, Adv = adverbial expression, V= verb

(10) *Mout chevauca pensivement*
  'He was riding very pensively,'
  Jouste en pendant, lés un laris (…).
  'near a slope, along a heath (…).' (Leclanche, 2003, p. 4)

There is a single verb, *chevauca* 'he was riding' describing manner of motion, which specifies the means used for the journey (i.e., a horse). Path of motion is expressed by the preposition, *lés* 'along.' The translation of this sentence into Modern French, however, shows the use of a different construction type, namely, the verb-framed pattern, as shown in (10').

(10') *Absorbé dans ses pensées, il longeait un escarpement, à l'orée*
  'Lost in his thoughts, he followed a slope, on the edge'
  d'une lande (…).
  'of a heath (…).' (Leclanche, 2003, p. 5)

Note that path of motion is now expressed in a finite verb *il longeait* 'he went along/followed,' whereas manner is omitted. In fact, by conveying path alone, the translator leaves the reader to infer manner—namely, the fact that the protagonist is riding a horse—from the context. This can be inferred to the extent that a few lines earlier we have been told that the main protagonist is a knight coming back from a tournament. Based on this previous information we may infer that he is traveling on a horse (see example 11).

(11) *C'est l'histoire d'un chevalier qui revenait en piteux état*
  'This is the story of a knight who was returning in a pitiful state'
  d'un tournoi (…).
  'from a tournament.' (Leclanche, 2003, p. 5)

Since the information about the manner of travel can be inferred from the identity of the protagonist, the translator leaves the manner information unexpressed in the description of the event itself. However, the data reveal several examples where manner information is lost in translation, and where such information could be noteworthy and relevant for the visual representation of the event. This is particularly striking in the translation of imperative sentences, like the one illustrated in (12). Before analyzing this example, it will be helpful to contextualize this specific episode. This is a story of a young boy who is in the service of a lord and secretly in love with his lord's wife. While the lord is away, the young boy confesses his affection to the young woman, but she, fearing her husband's prompt arrival, orders him to leave:

(12) *Beaus sire, car vos en alez!*
  'Dear sir, go away!'
  Fuiez de ci, alez la fors!
  'Flee from here, go outside!' (Leclanche, 2003, p. 166)

We may note the use of three motion expressions with the verb *alez* 'go' occurring twice with two different verb particles, *en* 'away' and *fors* 'outside,' and, more importantly, one manner verb, *fuiez* 'flee.' The use of this manner verb is most likely to be motivated by the gravity of the situation, as it implies *running away from danger*. However, when we look at the translation to MF in (12'), this verb is simply interpreted by a path verb *partez* meaning 'go away, leave,' which does not suggest any imminent danger. This difference between OF and MF may lead to a different interpretation of the event, such that in MF we may conclude that the woman is rejecting the boy, while the medieval text suggests that she is concerned for his safety.

(12') *Mon beau monsieur, retirez-vous!*
'My dear sir, take your leave!'
Partez d'ici! Dehors!
'Leave! Outside!' (Leclanche, 2003, p. 167)

A further example drawn from a different narrative is illustrated in (13). Similar to (12), this example depicts a lively and furtive event that takes place during the absence of the lord of a household. In the medieval text, we note the use of a manner verb *sailli* 'he jumped,' which is reinforced by a manner adverb *lués* 'right away.' Path of motion is expressed in the particle *fors* 'out.'

(13) *Et quant cil en ot fait son plain,*
'And when he had had his fill,'
De la cuve sailli lués fors
'he jumped right out of the bath,'
A un drap essuie son cors,
'dried off his body with a towel'
O la dame couche en un lit.
'and lay in the bed with the lady.' (Leclanche, 2003, p. 206)

In the translation of the event in (13'), there is no mention of the way the main character performs these actions. The whole event, with all its manner nuances, is interpreted with the verb *il sortit* 'he went out.' That is, not only the manner expressed by the verb, but also the manner expressed by the adverb is omitted in the translation.

(13') *Et quand il eut eu tout ce qu'il voulait, il sortit de la cuve,*
'And when he was satisfied, he got out of the bath,'
se sécha le corps avec une serviette
'dried his body with a towel,'
et se mit au lit avec la dame.
'and got into bed with the lady.' (Leclanche, 2003, p. 207)

Overall, as shown in examples (10) to (13), the description of motion events is more vivid and detailed in OF than it is in MF. The source texts depict manner by emphasizing subtle nuances of the events, whereas the target texts limit their descriptions to information about change of location, omitting the manner dimension of these events.

CONCLUSION

Taking a diachronic perspective on typological variation, this chapter has considered the shift from a satellite- to a verb-framed pattern in French, and examined the resulting stylistic differences between Old and Modern French.

As we saw in the introduction, the main distinction between the verb-framed and the satellite-framed pattern involves the expression of path of motion, that is, whether path is expressed in the main verb or in a verb satellite. The study has shown that Old French had several micro-systems to express path of motion such as verbs and verb satellites, with a rich system of prefixes and particles. By contrast, in Modern French, while some satellites have been maintained in the language, the dominant strategy for the expression of path is the verb. That is, although Old and Modern French do not represent *opposite poles* of a typological cline, they differ significantly in the use of these patterns in discourse, as shown by the study of medieval narratives and their contemporary translations. In contrast to Old French, where satellite-framed constructions were used extensively in the description of motion events, Modern French exhibits a considerably decreased use of satellite-framed constructions in favor of verb-framed constructions.

From a crosslinguistic perspective, such structural differences have been shown to be a determining factor for differences in the elaboration of both path and manner of motion in narratives and their translations (e.g., Slobin, 1996a, 1996b, 1997, 2004). Similar to these crosslinguistic studies, the present study shows that the typological differences between Old and Modern French lead to noticeably distinct ways of describing motion events. The analysis has shown that Old French could accumulate several satellites around a single verb, and hence provide more elaborate descriptions of path emphasizing the progression of motion. In contrast, Modern French expresses the same path information in separate verbs, some of which occur in relative clauses, and puts more emphasis on physical settings of a given event. Furthermore, the descriptions of motion are more vivid in the medieval texts, since manner of motion could be expressed easily in the main verb in satellite-framed constructions. In the contemporary translations, on the other hand, manner information is frequently omitted because its expression is optional in verb-framed constructions.

While much remains to be understood about the causes and consequences of the typological change observed in French, the cases discussed here provide evidence for the structural reorganization of path and manner expression and, importantly, point to differences in the types of information elaborated on in Old and Modern French. Further research will need to investigate these differences in more detail and to assess the cognitive processes involved in the conceptual reorganization of the domain of motion events in French.

REFERENCES

Berman, R., & D. I. Slobin, (Eds). (1994). *Relating events in narratives: A crosslinguistic development study.* Hillsdale, NJ: Lawrence Erlbaum Associates.

Buridant, C. (2000). *Grammaire nouvelle de l'ancien français.* Paris: Sedes.

Fleischman, S. (1990). *Tense and narrativity. From medieval performance to modern fiction.* London: Routledge.

Kopecka, A. (2006). The semantic structure of motion verbs in French: Typological perspectives. In M. Hickmann & S. Robert (Eds.), *Space in languages: Linguistic systems and cognitive categories* (pp. 83–101). Amsterdam: John Benjamins.

Kopecka, A. (in press). From a satellite- to a verb-framed pattern: A typological shift in French. In H. Cuyckens, W. De Mulder, & T. Mortelmans (Eds.), *Variation and change in adpositions of movement.* Amsterdam: John Benjamins.

Leclanche, J.-L. (Ed.), (2003). *Chevalerie et grivoiserie. Fabliaux de chevalerie.* Published, translated, presented, and annotated by Jean-Luc Leclanche. Paris: Champion Classiques.

Slobin, D. I. (1991). Learning to think for speaking: Native language, cognition, and rhetorical style. *Pragmatics 1,* 7–26.

Slobin, D. I. (1996a). Two ways to travel: verbs of motion in English and Spanish. In M. Shibatani & S. A. Thompson (Eds.), *Grammatical constructions: Their form and meaning* (pp. 195–217). Oxford, UK: Oxford University Press.

Slobin, D. I. (1996b). From "thought and language" to "thinking for speaking." In J. Gumperz & S. Levinson (Eds.), *Rethinking linguistic relativity. Studies in the social and cultural foundations of language* (pp. 70–96). Cambridge, UK: Cambridge University Press.

Slobin, D. I. (1997). Mind, code, & text. In J. Bybee, J. Haiman, & S.A. Thompson (Eds.), *Essays on language function & language type* (pp. 437–467). Amsterdam: John Benjamins.

Slobin, D. I. (2004). Relating narrative events in translation. In D. D. Ravid, & H. Bat-Zeev Shyldkrot (Eds.), *Perspectives on language and language development. Essays in honor of Ruth A. Berman* (pp. 115–129). Dordrecht: Kluwer Academic Publishers.

Talmy, L. (1985). Lexicalization patterns: Semantic structure in lexical form. In T. Shopen (Ed.), *Language typology and syntactic description: Vol. 3. Grammatical categories and the lexicon* (pp. 36–49). Cambrige, UK: Cambridge University Press.

Talmy, L. (1991). Path to realization: A typology of event conflation. *Proceedings of the seventeenth annual meeting of the Berkeley Linguistics Society* (pp. 480–519). Berkeley: Berkeley Linguistics Society.

Talmy, L. (2000). *Toward a cognitive semantics: Vol. 2. Typology and process in concept structuring*. Cambridge, MA: The MIT Press.

32

Mixing and Mapping
Motion, Path, and Manner in Amondawa[1]

WANY SAMPAIO
Federal University of Rondônia, Brazil

CHRIS SINHA and VERA DA SILVA SINHA
University of Portsmouth, UK

For more than thirty years our linguistic, psychological, and philosophical disciplines have sought to replicate themselves in the mind/brain of the child. The modules that are postulated often have names that evoke suspicion: they are the names of our own academic fields (linguistics, mathematics, physics, biology) or subfields (closed-class morphemes, grammaticizable notions). Could God or evolution have anticipated the academic and intellectual organization of late twentieth-century America?

Dan I. Slobin (1997, p. 266)

Dan Slobin's work has been an inspiration from my[2] first encounters with psycholinguistics as an undergraduate. I first met him some 30 years ago, when I was a research assistant on the Bristol Language Development Project, which was strongly influenced by Dan's crosslinguistic language acquisition project at Berkeley in the 1970s. From then until the present, I have been indebted to him, not just for his remarkable studies, but for the way his work exemplifies three fundamental lessons of method. The first is that if you want to understand the psychology of language, you have to understand language and linguistics. Dan Slobin's achievement has been to transform the 'border' sub-discipline of psycholinguistics into a truly interdisciplinary psychology of language, and in doing so he has contributed enormously to both psychology and linguistics. The second is that to understand language, you have to study languages. The transformation, in the last two decades or so, of the psychology of language into a comparative discipline may not have been

---

[1] Our most important thanks go to the Amondawa community, for sharing their language with us. We wish especially to thank Chief Tari Amondawa and Arikan Amondawa, who is the indigenous teacher in the village school. The fieldwork which forms the basis for this study was conducted by Wany Sampaio and Vera da Silva Sinha, who have spent many years studying the Amondawa language and culture, and sharing part of their lives with the community. Support for this study was provided by the European Union, as part of the collaborative project 'Stages in the Evolution and Development of Sign Use' under the NEST/Pathfinder program 'What It Means to Be Human'; by the Brazilian National Research Council (CNPq); and by the Federal University of Rondônia and the University of Portsmouth. We thank Jordan Zlatev and the editors of this volume for their helpful comments on previous drafts of this chapter.

[2] This paragraph is written in the voice of co-author Chris Sinha.

Dan's work alone, but he has undeniably been its leading proponent. The third is that our science is one with a longer tradition than is often acknowledged by contemporary theorists. There is no researcher with a more encyclopedic knowledge of this tradition than Dan. His awareness of it has informed his healthy skepticism toward claims from various quarters to newly minted monopolies on truth. There are few researchers who embody the combination of depth and breadth of knowledge of both past and contemporary research, and Dan Slobin is one of them. This chapter builds, with gratitude and affection, on his recent work on the typology of motion events.

INTRODUCTION

Amondawa is a Tupi Kawahib language (Tupi—Tupi Guarani—Tupi Kawahib) closely related to the other Kawahib languages (Diahoi, Karipuna, Parintintin, Tenharim, Uru-eu-uau-uau) of Amazonia. Much of the following analysis is therefore also applicable to those languages. The name 'Amondawa,' as is the case for many of the indigenous languages of Brazil, is not the original self-designation of the Amondawa people, but it has now been adopted as such. The community consists of some 150 people, all living in one village in Rondônia state, in the North Western Amazonian region of Brazil. The community experienced first official contact in 1984. All community members speak Amondawa, and while most also speak some Portuguese, Amondawa continues to be acquired as the first language, and is the language of instruction in the indigenous school of the community.

The Amondawa language is characterized by a complex system of 4-person/2-number/2-gender verbal prefixes. The verbal system is also marked in terms of an accusative-ergative distinction, based on the semantic distinction of control vs. non-control of action by the subject. Grammatical subjects which are semantically conceptualized as having deliberative control of action (animate human agents) are grammatically Agentive in transitive constructions, while non-control grammatical subjects are Patients in ergative-intransitive constructions. Word order is variable, based on the control/non-control distinction, the semantic distinction between human and non-human agents and patients, and the number of semantic roles specified in the construction. The examples we give below include verb- and subject-initial strings. Phonological and lexical reduplication are frequent in Amondawa, and demonstratives and other elements need not be adjacent to nouns (Sampaio and da Silva, 1998; Sampaio, 1999).

We present an analysis of the organization of motion events in the Amondawa language, in terms of the mapping of the semantic specification of **path** and **manner** to morpho-syntactic expression. We base this analysis on the distinction proposed by Talmy (1983, 1985, 1991) between **verb-framed** and **satellite-framed** languages, its extension by Slobin (2004) to encompass a third, **equipollent** type, and the complementary typological-discursive analysis proposed by Slobin (2000, 2004, 2006) of crosslinguistic differences in **manner salience**. As comparators for Amondawa, we refer to Brazilian Portuguese (BP) as a typical verb-framed language, English (E) and Dutch (NL) as typical satellite-framed languages, and French (F) as a language claimed by Pourcel and Kopecka (in press) to manifest a high degree of typological mixing between verb and satellite framing.

We discuss the relationship between the conflation patterns identified by Talmy and the **distributed spatial semantics** patterns identified by Sinha and Kuteva (1995), and critically evaluate the significance of the mapping patterns we identify in Amondawa for motion event typology. We propose that the categorical distinction of verb-framed (VF) vs. satellite-framed (SF) is most appropriately applied at the level of **construction** (Fillmore & Kay, 1987; Goldberg, 1995; Croft, 2001), and that languages as whole systems are better characterized in terms of mapping preferences or tendencies in usage.

PATH AND MANNER: GENERAL CONSIDERATIONS

The typology proposed by Talmy (1983, 1985, 1991), which motivates many recent studies of the linguistic organization and expression of **path** and **manner** of motion, is based on conflation patterns in mappings from conceptualization to expression. Specifically, Talmy's typology is based on the observation that in VF languages, **path** is typically conflated into the verb of motion, whereas in SF languages it is typically expressed by a satellite particle, while **manner** is typically conflated into the motion verb (see also Slobin, 2000, 2004, 2006).

Conflation is only one of the mapping phenomena characterizing the semantics and morphosyntax of space and motion. The complementary phenomenon of **distribution** (i.e., one conceptual element mapping to more than one morpheme in a single syntagmatic chain, sometimes through morphemic reduplication) is also ubiquitous in the language of space; its most general characteristic is **distributed spatial semantics,** or many to many mapping from conceptualization to expression (Sinha & Kuteva, 1995; see also Zlatev, 2003).

Before proceeding to a description and analysis of Amondawa, we review and critically discuss the principal issues arising from the motion typology literature.[3]

First, we note that the VF-SF distinction, if intended as a strict criterion of classification, applies only to simple Path of Motion constructions in which the Figure, but not the Ground, is expressed and which we call the **basic motion construction**. The distinction is typified by examples 1 (VF pattern) and 2 (SF pattern), all of which can be translated as 2a, uttered in the context of a boy leaving a house.

1a.	(BP)	*o rapaz*	**saiu**
1b.	(F)	*le garçon*	**est sorti**
2a.	(E)	*the boy*	**went out**
2b.	(NL)	*de jongen*	**ging weg**

In 1a and 1b, the respective verbs (boldface) are path-conflating, equivalent to English 'exit,' while in 2a and 2b, the verbs are simple 'go' motion verbs. What is criterial is the use, in the SF constructions, of the path-expressing morpheme as a verbal particle, which is obligatory for the specification of path in SF languages, but only very rarely permissible in the basic motion construction in VF languages. In BP, the basic SF construction does occur in restricted directional contexts, in which the crossing of the boundary of the Ground (Slobin and Hoiting, 1994) is unexpressed, but never in collocation with a path-conflating verb. Note that 3a is a translation equivalent of Dutch 2b, 'the boy went away,' not involving boundary crossing.

3a.	(BP)	*o rapaz*	*foi*	*embora*
		the boy	went	away
3b.	(BP)	°*o rapaz*	*foi*	*para fora*
		the boy	went	out
3c	(BP)	°*o rapaz*	*saiu*	*embora/[para fora]*
		the boy	exited	away/out

In both VF and SF languages, a motion verb can be combined with an adpositional complement specifying both Path and Ground, in what we call the **fully specified motion construction**:

---

[3] In the examples, we use the following conventions:
/ denotes alternative; [...] denotes optional addition; /[...] denotes scope of alternative if more than one morpheme or word; {ell. ...} denotes unexpressed elliptical content; [.] (in the second, italicized gloss line) denotes morphological conflation, or specifies the form class of a morpheme.
Morphological abbreviations. 3s: third singular person prefix; NOM: nominalizer; ADV: adverb; POSTP: postposition; GER: gerundive form.

4a. (BP)	*o rapaz*	*saiu*	*da*	*casa*
	the boy	exited	from.the	house
4b. (BP)	*o rapaz*	*entrou*	*na*	*casa*
	the boy	entered	into.the	house
4c. (E)	the boy	went	into	the house
4d. (NL)	*de jongen*	*ging*	*het huis*	*uit*
	the boy	went	the house	out

In fully specified VF motion constructions, when the boundary of the Ground is crossed, the motion verb is (almost) always path-conflating, and thus the Path may be specified in both the verb and the adposition in an overtly distributed fashion (Sinha & Kuteva, 1995). In fully specified SF motion constructions, boundary crossing is also commonly morpho-syntactically marked. In Dutch, boundary crossing is marked by postposition of the locative particle to specify Path (Sinha & Kuteva, 1995), while in English it is marked by modifying the particle with *of* or *to*. It is the boundary crossing constraint, of which more below, that may also explain the choice in Dutch of the particle *weg* 'away' in 2b above, since the postposing of the particle in constructions such as 4d, together with the deictic implicature of the 'go' verb, induces a preference against the use of *uit* 'out' in constructions such as 2b.

In VF languages, an alternative in some contexts to the fully specified motion construction is a construction in which the Ground is expressed as the direct object of a path-conflating verb. This construction is restricted to directional paths in which boundaries of the Ground are not, or at least not necessarily, crossed, such as 'descending the stairs' and 'crossing the road.' The admissibility of such adposition-free constructions in English is unusual in SF languages and is presumably a consequence of English lexical and constructional borrowing from French.

VF and SF languages differ in their mapping patterns for expressing manner of motion. SF languages favor the conflation of manner into the verb of motion, and thus typically have a larger class of manner verbs than VF languages. SF languages routinely employ manner-conflating verbs as main verbs in both basic and fully specified motion constructions, while VF languages cannot do so, except in highly restricted elliptical contexts. The BP examples below are translation equivalents of the preceding English sentences.

5a. (E)	the boy	ran	in[to	the house]
5b. (BP)	*°o rapaz*	*correu*	*em/*	*[na casa]*
5c. (E)	the boy	ran	out [of the house]	
5d. (BP)	*?o rapaz*	*correu*	*para fora {ell. da casa}*	
5e. (BP)	*°o rapaz*	*correu*	*de*	

Note that the expanded version of example 5b is acceptable as a construction involving motion-as-activity at a location, as opposed to motion resulting in change of location, but it is arguable that this sense does not count as a fully specified motion construction (see Pourcel & Kopecka, in press). Alternatively, and more conservatively, one could say that such usage is restricted in VF languages to non-boundary crossing cases (see below).[4]

Slobin (2004, 2006) observes that this typological distinction is correlated not only with a higher type frequency of manner verbs in SF languages, but also with a discursive and stylistic difference in **manner salience**, with texts written in SF languages displaying higher token frequencies of manner-conflating motion verbs.

However, VF languages can specify manner of movement adverbially, using gerundives, in both the basic and the fully specified motion constructions:

---

[4] We prefer the former formulation, while our reviewer favors the latter. Although we discuss the boundary crossing issue here, we do not attempt to do so exhaustively.

6a. (BP) *o rapaz   foi/ [saiu   da   casa]   devagar*
          the boy went / [exited from.the house] slowly
          'the boy came slowly out of the house'
6b. (BP) *o rapaz   foi/ [saiu   da   casa]   correndo*
          the boy went/ [exited from.the house] running
          'the boy ran out of the house'

The gerundive use of the manner verb is also possible in SF constructions with generic motion main verbs, but more frequent is the use of the manner-conflating verb as main verb with other modifiers:

6c. (NL) *Het meisje   kwam   lopend   het   huis   uit*
          the girl   came   running   the   house   out of
          'The girl came running out of the house'
6d. (NL) *Het meisje   liep   langzaam   het   huis   uit*
          the girl   walked slowly   the   house   out of
          'The girl walked slowly out of the house'

Slobin and Hoiting (1994; see also Slobin, 2006) have noted a boundary crossing constraint in VF languages, such that the use of manner-conflating motion verbs is permissible only in contexts where the boundary of the Ground is not crossed. This can be considered as a generalization or another instance of the same constraint applying to 3a to 3c above, limiting the use of the generic motion verb in basic motion constructions and is the converse of the obligatory use of a path-conflating verb in fully specified motion constructions in VF languages when the boundary of the Ground is crossed (see examples 2 to 4 above). The boundary crossing constraint, as noted above, also seems to be related to the contexts of permissibility, in VF languages, of path-conflating verb constructions in which the Ground is the direct object. We note, however, that the boundary crossing constraint on manner-conflating verbs in VF languages is not absolute; all the examples in 7 are acceptable in Brazilian Portuguese, including 7c, which involves boundary crossing.

7a. (BP) *A menina   correu   no   parque*
          The girl   ran   in.the   park
          'The girl ran in the park'
7b. (BP) *A menina   correu   para   o   parque*
          The girl   ran   to   the park
7c. (BP) *A menina   correu   para   dentro do   parque*
          The girl   ran   to   inside of.the park
          'The girl ran into the park'

The question of boundary crossing in motion events is clearly complex. It has been analyzed in terms of telicity (Aske, 1989) and of motion activities vs. motion events (Pourcel & Kopecka, in press), as well as of the spatial properties of the Ground, and we do not have space to try to resolve it here, although it will be relevant to the analysis of Amondawa. We can, however, note that in 7c above the Path is highly specified and distributed over different morphological elements, whereas the only acceptable reading of the morphologically simpler expression in 7a is of what Pourcel and Kopecka call a 'motion activity occurring in a location,' rather than a motion event.

The standard account of the VF-SF distinction focuses on the conflation of semantic material into the verb. As we have noted, conflation is only one aspect of the **distributed semantics** and morpho-syntax of space and motion (Sinha & Kuteva, 1995), in which distribution or reduplication also figures strongly. Sinha and Kuteva (1995) proposed that languages may vary along the dimension of *overt vs. covert* distributed semantics. In brief, overt distribution involves the multiple morphological realization of a semantic aspect (e.g., Path) in the same syntagmatic chain, as in 'the plane circled around'; whereas covert distribution involves its morphological reduction, as in 'the horse jumped the fence' (as opposed to 'the horse jumped over the fence').

There appears to be no clear correlation between overt/covert distributed semantics and satellite/verb framing of path of motion. The examples of languages favoring overtly distributed spatial semantics cited by Sinha and Kuteva included Bulgarian (a Slavic, SF language) and Japanese (a VF language obeying the boundary crossing constraint). Pourcel and Kopecka (in press), however, suggest that SF languages display a more overt distribution of manner information than VF languages. The former, for example, can and do use default manner verbs in motion constructions (e.g., 'walk up the stairs'), whereas the latter neither use such default main verbs nor employ them redundantly as gerundives. Rather, in VF languages, gerundive forms, as Pourcel and Kopecka (in press) point out, are used to foreground non-default information. In summary, although the distributed spatial semantics approach suggests that a typology based on conflation alone may not be sufficient to capture all the data reviewed, it does not necessarily contradict the SF-VF distinction.

Other data, however, have been claimed to directly challenge Talmy's typology, at least in term of its absoluteness and exhaustiveness. Ameka and Essegbey (2006), Slobin (2006), and Zlatev and Yangklang (2006) have suggested that serial verb languages exemplify a third type (termed by Slobin 'equipollently framed'). Serializing languages (such as Thai) typically have high type frequencies of both path- and manner-conflating verbs of motion, along with verbs that conflate both path and manner. These languages also do not obey the boundary crossing constraint and can treat all verbs as main verbs in serial verb constructions (SVCs), without employing a gerundive form for manner verbs, as would be typical for VF languages. In terms of the basic motion construction, Thai, at least, does not employ satellites to express path, always conflating path into a verb. Serial verb languages thus seem to display properties of both satellite and verb framing, even though, in terms of the basic motion construction, they are arguably closer to the VF paradigm. Doubt has also been cast on the classification of languages generally assumed to belong unambiguously to one or other category. Pourcel and Kopecka (in press), for example, characterize French (a Romance language usually classified as VF) as exhibiting a mixed or hybrid system, with verb framing dominating (see also Pourcel, 2004; Kopecka, 2006).

Our brief critical review has established a number of issues that will guide our description and analysis of the linguistic organization of motion events in Amondawa. First, there are a number of clustered phenomena, in different construction types, that point to the pervasiveness of the VF- SF distinction. Second, however, with the exception of the mapping patterns in the basic motion construction, none of these differences can be said to be strictly criterial. Differences appear as tendencies rather than absolutes, along with exceptions, the motivations of which are difficult to establish unambiguously. Third, conflation patterns alone are unlikely to provide the entire explanation for the patterns observed, which also depend on distributed mappings of space, motion, and manner elements to diverse, multiple form classes. Fourth, there is doubt about the exhaustiveness and absoluteness of the VF-SF typological distinction, and whether exceptions represent anomalies, further typological groups, or typologically mixed patterns.

MOTION, PATH, AND MANNER IN AMONDAWA

Path is expressed by three form classes in Amondawa.

  A. **Path-conflating motion verbs** include the following (NB the verb stem is obligatorily prefixed for person and number):

-ho	go
-hem	exit
-xi	enter
-jupin	ascend/climb
-jym	descend

This closed class, which (although we do not claim to have provided an exhaustive list) is small, is supplemented by verbs co-conflating manner, path, and/or causality similar to English 'pull' and 'jump.'

B. **Postpositions**, which are obligatory when specifying path of motion in relation to a Ground, include:

pe	at, to
pupe/pype	in, inside, into, to the inside
wi	from, out of
re	up, up in, up on, up into, up onto
katy	nearby (stative)
aramo	over, above
urumõ / urymõ	under, below, beneath
pywõ	by, past (path, dynamic)
rupi	along (a path)

The postpositions, when used dynamically, specify path of motion. They are all polysemous, and are also used to describe static scenes, except perhaps *wi*. Stative uses are those in which no verb of motion is employed. Since there is no copular verb in Amondawa, that means that stative uses are those in which either a stative dispositional or relational verb occurs, or in which Ground and Figure nominals are collocated. There are also grammatical (e.g., instrumental) uses that depend upon construction type.

There is no evident reason to suppose that stative meanings of the postpositions are more basic than dynamic meanings, or vice versa. Unlike the prepositions in Dutch, English, French, and Portuguese, there is no morpho-syntactic marking of dynamic meanings in Amondawa. Furthermore, unlike Japanese postpositions, Amondawa postpositions specify path, sometimes encoding multiple path components (i.e., source and goal). Consequently, and given their obligatory use in fully specified motion constructions, the motion verb and the postposition often encode the same information in an overt and redundantly distributed fashion, as in example 8 (NB Amondawa verbs are not inflected for tense; the default reading for Tupi verbs is perfective).

8. | kurumin | ga | **o-jupin** | ga | aiapykaw-a | **re** |
   |---|---|---|---|---|---|
   | boy | he | 3s-ascend | he | bench-NOM | up onto |
   | Fig | | Motion.**Path** | Fig | Goal | **Path** |

   'The boy climbed [up] onto the bench'

C. Optional **directional adverbs**, which can be considered as quasi-verbs, including:

ura	inside the Ground
hua	coming (toward speaker)
awowo	going (away from speaker)

The meanings of directional adverbs are highly context dependent, because of deixis and participants' construal of the referential situation. The glosses given above are approximate. These items differ from the other classes grammatically, although their precise grammatical status is difficult to establish. They cannot be used as main verbs; they receive no inflection and they are optional and rather free in their position in the construction. This is in contrast to the postpositions, which are obligatory and which always follow noun phrases. Nevertheless, these directional adverbs may encode the same directional and path information as the verbs and postpositions. The possibility of combining all three of these classes in construction frames, as in example 9, places Amondawa among the typological set of languages with an overtly and redundantly distributed spatial semantics. In example 9, the path information is distributed redundantly over no less than three items.

9. wiña **ura** **wi** jawara i-**hem** hua
   that ADV.**out of** POSTP.**out of** dog 3s-**exit** ADV.coming
   'The dog came out of that {ell. house}'

Based upon its basic motion construction, Amondawa should be classified as a VF language, on the basis of simple verb-noun constructions expressing the motion of a Figure along a Path, as in examples 10–13:

10. O-ho jawara
    3s-go dog
    'The dog went out'
11. O-ho kuñaguera hea
    3s-go woman she
    'The woman went out'
12. O-xi jawara
    3s-enter dog
    'The dog went in'
13. O-jupin kurumin ga
    3s-ascend boy he
    'The boy climbed'

Note that it is ungrammatical to add a postposition, without a noun, to such constructions, which is a strong diagnostic for a VF language. In other words, the Amondawa postpositions cannot be used as satellites.

In fully specified motion constructions, that is, when the path of motion is specified relative to a Ground, it is obligatory to express path information both in the motion verb and in the postposition, as in example 14. In contrast, the expression of path information in the adverb is optional, as in example 9.

14a. O-xi kuñanguera hea tapyia pe
     3s-enter woman she house POSTP.to
     'The woman went into the house'
14b. O-jupin kurumin ga ywa re
     3s-ascend boy he tree POSTP.up into
     'The boy climbed [up] the tree'

This type of construction is consistent with a VF pattern, but the fact that the postposition is obligatory is not, since, as we have noted, VF languages also typically have constructions in which the Ground is expressed as the direct object of a path-conflating verb (e.g., 'he crossed the road'). If the acceptability of constructions such as examples 15a and 15b is criterial for being a VF language, Amondawa cannot be considered a VF language.

15a. (F) Il monte l'escalier
         He ascends the stairs
         'He is going upstairs'
15b. (BP) Ele sobe a escada
          He ascends the stairs
          'He is going upstairs'

As noted in the previous section, VF languages (including Japanese), but not SF languages, typically obey the boundary crossing constraint (Slobin & Hoiting, 1994). That is, path-conflating verbs can, but manner-conflating verbs cannot, be used in situations in which a boundary is crossed. Amondawa does not obey this constraint, as demonstrated in examples 16 and 17:

16. *O-ñan kurumin ga awowo tapyia ura wi*
    3s-run boy he ADV.going house ADV.out of POSTP.out of
    'The boy ran out of the house'
17. *O-wewe wyrai'ia awowo ajayra pupe*
    3s-fly bird ADV.going nest POSTP.into
    'The bird flew into the nest'

Examples 16 and 17 express boundary crossing using manner-conflating verbs. If obeying the boundary crossing constraint serves as a criterion to be classified as a VF language, Amondawa is not verb framed. However, the constraint is not strictly criterial, since it can be violated in VF languages in contexts involving rapid or instantaneous motion (Özçalıskan, under review).

As Zlatev and Yangklang (2004) point out, serializing languages do not obey the boundary crossing constraint, since a manner verb, together with a path verb, can form part of an expression conceptualizing a boundary crossing event. The counter-example to the boundary constraint provided by Amondawa (if it is nonetheless considered as 'basically' verb framed) is even stronger than serializing languages, since Amondawa only employs single main verbs in examples 16 and 17, which frame the boundary crossing events in essentially the same way as their English translations.

Amondawa also employs serially collocated verb constructions, as well as dual-verb constructions in which both verbs constitute main verbs even if they are not adjacent, as in examples 18–21:

18. *Jawara o-hem o-ña hua tapyia wi*
    dog 3s-exit 3s-run ADV.coming house POSTP.out of
    'The dog ran out of the house'
19. *O-hem hea tapyia wi o-ñan hua*
    3s-exit she house POSTP.out of 3s-run ADV.coming
    'She ran out of the house'
20. *O-ñan kunanguera hea awowo o-xi awo tapyia pe*
    3s.run woman she ADV.going 3s.enter here house POSTP.into
    'The woman ran into the house here'
21. *O-mbaraka hea o-hem hua tapyia wi*
    3s-sing she 3s-exit ADV.coming house POSTP.out of
    'She went singing out of the house'

Note, however, that in the above examples, unlike in true serial verb constructions, path is expressed in a distributed fashion by both the postposition and the path-conflating motion verb.

In VF languages, an alternative but canonical construction for specifying both path and manner in a single construction, using more than one verb, is to employ the gerundive form of the manner-conflating motion verb, as in Brazilian Portuguese examples 6a and 6b above. Amondawa employs analogous constructions, in which the gerundivizing suffix *–wo* (or *–awo*) is attached to the manner verb, whether this is a verb of motion or another verb type.

22. *O-hem hea i-kunda-wo hua tapyia wi*
    3s-exit she 3s-limp-GER ADV.coming house POSTP.out of
    'She limped out of the house'
    Lit. 'She came limping out of the house'
23. *O-hem hea o-pyka-wo tapyia wi*
    3s-exit she 3s-smile-GER house POSTP.out.of
    'She went out of the house smiling'

However, Amondawa is not typical of VF languages in its employment of gerundive constructions, since it also permits constructions in which the gerund suffix is attached, not to the manner verb, but to a path-conflating verb of motion:

24. O-mbaraka hea o-xi-awo tapyia pe
    3s-sing she 3s-enter-GER house POSTP.to
    'She went into the house singing'
    Lit. 'She sang entering the house'

Constructions such as example 24 are not permissible in typical VF languages, although they can be in SF languages, such as English.

25a. (BP) °Ela cantó entrando na casa
     she sang entering into.the house
     'She sang going into the house'
25b. (BP) Ela entró cantando na casa
     she entered singing into.the house
     'She went into the house singing'

Pourcel (2004) has recorded instances in French spontaneous speech similar to the construction in example 24, where the main verb is a manner-conflating verb of motion. She calls this a 'verb framed reverse pattern' (see also Pourcel & Kopecka, in press, who call it a 'Path-adjunct framing pattern'):

26. (F) Il court en traversant la rue
    He runs in crossing the road
    'He is running across the road'
    Lit. 'He runs crossing the road'

Neither in English, nor in most verb framed languages, such as Brazilian Portuguese, are constructions such as example 26 permitted:

27. (BP) °Ele corre atrevasando a rua
    He runs crossing the road

We do not have an example of such a construction in Amondawa, but we have an example that uses a generic motion verb gerund in the same syntagmatic string as a path-conflating main verb.

28. Jawara i-hem u-a ko katy
    Jaguar 3s-exit go-GER here POSTP.towards
    Fig Motion.Path Motion Goal Path
    'The jaguar came out and went this way here'
    Lit. 'The jaguar exited going toward here' or 'The jaguar went out going toward here'

It is clear that the incidence of combining verbs of motion, including both generic, path-conflating, and manner-conflating verbs, in different constructions, such as serial, non-adjacent serial, and main verb plus verb gerund, is frequent in Amondawa; thus, Amondawa can be characterized as both flexible and overt in its distribution of manner and path information.

DISCUSSION AND CONCLUSIONS

Amondawa regularly employs path-conflating motion verbs in a wide variety of constructions, and on the basis of the Amondawa basic motion construction, it should be classified as a VF language. By the same criterion, it cannot be an SF language. However, other characteristics of the language are atypical of, and in some respects violate, the paradigm of a VF language. Path-specifying postpositions are obligatory in all but basic motion constructions in Amondawa, so that the fully specified motion construction, including the postposition, is the only way to express motion in relation to a Ground. We have noted in our fieldwork, also, that the basic motion construction is infrequent, and speakers have a strong preference for expressing Ground as well as Figure.

The employment of gerundives in Amondawa, which allows a high degree of flexibility in the selection of the main verb, is not a typical verb-framed pattern. Moreover, the boundary crossing constraint on the employment of manner-conflating motion verbs in fully specified motion constructions, typical of VF languages, does not apply to Amondawa. There are thus good reasons to resist categorizing Amondawa as a 'typical' VF language.

How then should Amondawa be classified? It displays some characteristics similar to the third, or equipollently framed, category of serial verb languages. It employs serial and multiple verb constructions, and, similarly to serial verb languages, it also violates the boundary crossing constraint. The flexibility displayed by Amondawa in its multiple verb constructions suggests that it is higher in manner salience than VF languages, but we have yet to establish this. It would, however, be incorrect to classify Amondawa as a serial verb language proper, because of the regularity of non-adjacent dual-verb constructions, relatively free word order, and the obligatory path-specifying postposition. However, if equipollent framing is considered as a general category comprising languages with high manner salience, frequent use of path-conflating verbs, and high frequency of path-specifying particles, then perhaps that is where Amondawa belongs. If so, it occupies a place on a continuum, together with other languages with a 'mixed' profile, such as French, as analyzed by Pourcel and Kopecka (in press).

This would be a solution preferable to proposing another discrete category, but carries with it the danger that the equipollent category becomes a kind of 'aporia' class, of diverse languages that fail to fit the original, and still fruitful, VF-SF distinction. There are other possible solutions that we can suggest, which may not be mutually exclusive. One would be to consider the typology as applying, not to languages, but to **construction types**, and to catalogue such types according to their specific patterns of mapping from linguistic conceptualization to linguistic expression. Languages could then be specified in terms of mapping preferences, tendencies, and relative frequencies, rather than strictly exclusive categories. Part of this solution would be to rethink the typology of motion and manner not only in terms of clines and/or adding additional types, but rather in terms of locating of languages in a multi-dimensional space of typological variation, including not just conflation but also distribution.

Another way forward is suggested by Pourcel and Kopecka (under review), who conclude that 'morphosyntactic criteria alone cannot account for [a language's] coding strategies … typological properties should be understood in a broader context of actual language usage rather than in terms of structural factors alone.' They also emphasize the need for analyzing the interaction between semantics and pragmatics in determining speakers' choices among constructional alternatives. We consider their approach to be consistent with the approach taken by Sinha and Kuteva (1995), who also highlight the importance of speaker situatedness and construal in analyzing the distribution of semantic information in spatial constructions.

Finally, although we recognize the importance of further research into the relations between contemporary Kawahib languages and historic, or Old Tupi, we would suggest that in attempting to typologically analyze languages such as Amondawa, socio-cultural and historical (not just genetic) factors should be taken into account. Amondawa was a purely oral language until the last decade, and it is possible that its apparent constructional freedom is related to the absence of a long history of the kind of standardization that has been undergone by languages more familiar to most linguists and psychologists, in the course of the process of their orthographization. Although this remains at this stage no more than a hypothesis, we hope to pursue in our future work the elucidation of the relations between text, context, structure, and usage that has been the hallmark of the research of our distinguished colleague and mentor, Professor Dan Isaac Slobin.

REFERENCES

Ameka, F., & Essegbey J. (2001). Serialising languages: Satellite-framed, verb-framed or neither? Paper presented at the *32nd Annual Conference on African Linguistics*, Berkeley, CA, March 22–25.

Aske, J. (1989). Path predicates in English and Spanish: A closer look. *Proceedings of the 15th annual meeting of the Berkeley Linguistics Society* (pp. 1–14).

Croft, W. (2001). *Radical construction grammar. Syntactic theory in typological perspective.* Oxford, UK: Oxford University Press.

Fillmore, C., & Kay, P. (1987). *The goals of construction grammar.* (Berkeley Cognitive Science Program Technical Report No. 50). University of California, Berkeley.

Goldberg, A. (1995). *Constructions: A construction grammar approach to argument structure.* Chicago: University of Chicago Press.

Kopecka, A. (2006). The semantic structure of motion verbs in French: typological perspectives. In M. Hickmann & S. Robert (Eds.), *Space in languages: Linguistic systems and cognitive categories* (pp. 83–101). Amsterdam: John Benjamins.

Özçalışkan, S. (under review). 'Doors, fences, and thresholds': The many ways of crossing a boundary in English and Turkish.

Pourcel, S. (2004). Rethinking 'thinking for speaking.' *Proceedings of the 29th annual meeting of the Berkeley Linguistics Society* (pp. 349–358).

Pourcel, S., & Kopecka, A. (under review). Motion events in French: Typological intricacies. *Linguistic Typology*.

Sampaio, W. (1999). A referência remissiva número-pessoal nos prefixos verbais da língua uru-eu-uau-uau. Unpublished manuscript, Federal University of Rondônia.

Sampaio, W., & da Silva, V. (1998). *Os povos indígenas de Rondônia: Contribuições para com a compreensão de sua cultura e de sua história* (2nd ed.), Porto Velho: UNIR.

Sinha, C., & Kuteva, T. (1995). Distributed spatial semantics. *Nordic Journal of Linguistics 18*, 167–199.

Slobin, D. I. (1997). The origins of grammaticizable notions: Beyond the individual mind. In D. I. Slobin (Ed.), *The crosslinguistic study of language acquisition: Vol. 5. Expanding the contexts* (pp. 265–323). Mahwah, NJ: Lawrence Erlbaum Associates.

Slobin, D. I. (2000). Verbalized events: A dynamic approach to linguistics relativity and determinism. In S. Niemeier & R. Dirven (Eds.), *Evidence for linguistic relativity* (pp. 107–138), Amsterdam: John Benjamins.

Slobin, D. I. (2004). The many ways to search for a frog: Linguistic typology and the expression of motion events. In S. Strömqvist & L. Verhoeven (Eds.), *Relating events in narrative: Typological and contextual perspectives* (pp. 219–257). Mahwah, NJ: Lawrence Erlbaum Associates.

Slobin, D. I. (2006). What makes manner of motion salient? In M. Hickmann, and S. Robert (Eds.), *Space in languages: linguistic systems and cognitive categories* (pp. 54–81). Amsterdam: John Benjamins.

Slobin, D. I., & Hoiting, N. (1994). Reference to movement in spoken and signed languages. *Proceedings of the 20th annual meeting of the Berkeley Linguistics Society* (pp. 487–505).

Talmy, L. (1983). How language structures space. In H. L. Pick, Jr. & L. P. Acredolo (Eds.), *Spatial orientation: Theory, research and application* (pp. 225–282). New York: Plenum Press.

Talmy, L. (1985). Lexicalization patterns: Semantic Structure In lexical forms. In T. Shopen (Ed.), *Language typology and syntactic description: Vol. 3. Grammatical categories and the lexicon* (pp. 57–149). Cambridge, UK: Cambridge University Press.

Talmy, L. (1991). Path to realization: A typology of event conflation. *Proceedings of the 17th annual meeting of the Berkeley Linguistics Society* (pp. 480–520).

Zlatev, J. (2003). Holistic spatial semantics of Thai. In E. Casad & G. Palmer (Eds.). *Cognitive linguistics and non-Indo-European languages* (pp. 305–336). Berlin: Mouton de Gruyter.

Zlatev, J., & Yangklang, P. (2004). A third way to travel: The place of Thai (and other serial verb Languages) in motion event typology. In S. Strömqvist and L. Verhoeven (Eds.), *Relating events in narrative: Typological and contextual perspectives* (pp. 159–190). Mahwah, NJ: Lawrence Erlbaum Associates.

Part IV

Language and Cognition
Universals and Typological Comparisons

Introduction

MELISSA BOWERMAN
Max Planck Institute for Psycholinguistics

The problem that troubles me is how to determine just what sorts of things should be considered as "preprogrammed." To what extent is a human child "wired up" with linguistic competence—and with specifically linguistic competence?...this is a knotty question indeed.

Dan I. Slobin (1966, p. 87)

LMC [the Language Making Capacity] constructs similar early grammars from all input languages. The surface forms...will, of course, vary...what is constant are the basic notions that first receive grammatical expression...

Dan I. Slobin (1985, p. 1161)

The activity of thinking takes on a particular quality when it is employed in the activity of speaking. In the evanescent time frame of constructing utterances in discourse one fits one's thoughts into available linguistic frames...I propose that, in acquiring a native language, the child learns particular ways of thinking for speaking.

Dan I. Slobin (1996, p. 76)

There is no problem to which Slobin has returned more persistently over many decades than the developmental relationship between language and cognition. The problem is stunningly complex, and in his attempts to find the right balance between two primary sources of structure—cognitive biases inherent to the child vs. semantic structuring principles provided by the input language—Slobin has traversed the whole landscape of the modern era of developmental and linguistic research.

Slobin's initial probes into the language and cognition puzzle took place during the late 1960s and 1970s, just as the domination of U.S. psychology by behaviorism was waning and it was no longer taboo to speculate about invisible mental representations. For American researchers working on child development, the work of Piaget—already famous in Europe but mostly unknown in the United States—burst on the scene, altering forever the way we looked at infants. Far from being a tabula rasa, Piaget showed, infants are active cognizers, and by the end of the first year and a half of life they have already built up representations of objects, events, locations, and causes.

Strange though it now seems, the idea that infants' conceptual understanding might play an important role in language acquisition was at first not at all obvious. Although it was increasingly acceptable to invoke mental representations, the kinds of representations that at first attracted child language scholars were not those of Piaget but those of Chomsky (1965)—innate notions of putative linguistic universals such as subjects, predicates, direct objects, nouns, and verbs (e.g., McNeill, 1966). Interest in the possible role of cognition in language acquisition came in large part as a reaction to Chomsky. A number of theorists accepted Chomsky's argument that language involved structures far more complex and abstract than had been envisioned, but they balked at his claim that these structures were innate, and specific to language. Cognitive development seemed to offer an alternative route into the kinds of representations needed.

In path-breaking theoretical and empirical work on this possibility, Slobin pointed out that "if you ignore word order, and read through transcriptions of two-word utterances in the various languages we have studied, the utterances read like direct translations of one another... There is a great similarity of basic vocabulary and basic meanings conveyed by the word combinations" (1970, p. 177). The basic meanings identified—to do with location, agency, naming, and the like—were exactly the kinds of meanings that Piaget had stressed in his work on sensorimotor development (Brown, 1973), which suggested that these meanings originate on the basis of universal cognitive processes and are only later mapped to language.

In his seminal 1973 paper "Cognitive prerequisites to the development of language," Slobin marshalled these findings in support of "a very strong developmental psycholinguistic universal": that "the rate and order of development of the semantic notions expressed by language are fairly constant across languages, regardless of the formal means of expression employed" (p. 187). This hypothesis provides a powerful research tool for crosslinguistic research, argued Slobin. If we hold a given meaning constant, we can compare across languages to determine how easily children master the forms with which their language conventionally expresses it, and this information will provide clues to children's predispositions for the construction of grammar. This proposal was the driving principle behind Slobin's immensely successful Operating Principles approach. Crucially, it gave strong developmental priority to cognition: The child's task was to identify the forms associated with already known meanings.

Although Slobin's emphasis was initially on Piaget-style concepts such as spatial location, he realized that these did not exhaust the possibilities. In particular, he noted in his "Cognitive prerequisites" paper that "we are just beginning to sense the intimate relations between linguistic universals and cognitive universals, and are far from an adequate developmental theory of either" (Slobin, 1973, p. 176). This remark foreshadowed a hypothesis that he would make explicit only later: That children's "semantic intentions stem not only from 'general cognitive development' but from particular ways of thinking and interacting which, in the human species, are most intimately related to our means of expression in structured language" (Slobin, 1985, pp. 1243–1244). Research soon began to flesh out this idea. For example, Clark (1976) found that children's early object word overextensions are guided by shape categories that also dominate the semantics of numeral classifier systems, while Andersen (1978) identified parallels between children's early acquisition of words for body parts and universals of body part terminology. Findings like these suggested that the organization of meaning in both languages and language learners is molded by fundamental propensities of human perception and cognition (see Clark, 2001, for further examples and discussion).

Slobin's own interest in this matter was directed primarily to the "grammaticized portion" of language. Talmy (1983, 1988, and Chapter 29 of this volume) had argued influentially that the meanings of grammatical morphemes (e.g., case endings, tense and aspect markers, and adpositions) are universally highly constrained, and likely to be innate. In his own work on the acquisition of markers of transitivity, Slobin was finding evidence that children indeed orient toward a core set of meanings for grammatical forms: Although the surface forms vary, "what is constant are the basic notions that first receive grammatical expression" (Slobin, 1985, p. 1161). The existence of these "basic notions," along with the regularities imposed on morphosyntax by the workings of the Operating Principles (Slobin, 1973, 1985), meant that children's first grammars were essentially alike—"a universally specifiable 'Basic Child Grammar' which reflects an underlying ideal form of human language" (Slobin, 1985, p. 1160).

This bold and interesting claim attracted considerable attention, but the tide in the linguistic and language-developmental literature had already begun to turn away from a monolithic view of the cognitive underpinnings of language, with its emphasis on universals of language, cognition, and language acquisition, toward a more nuanced view in which crosslinguistic variation came in for increasing attention. Always sensitive to both advances in linguistic theory and new empirical evidence, Slobin began to rethink his views. One influence was studies suggesting that even very young children are far more sensitive to the specific semantic categories of the input language than had previously been recognized: Meanings once assumed to be universal in young children were in hindsight now seen to be language specific (e.g., Choi & Bowerman, 1991; Bowerman & Choi, 2001). A second major influence was the growing understanding among linguists of the psycholinguistic processes of grammaticalization, whereby independent lexical items lose syntactic flexibility and become phonologically reduced and semantically bleached, until they end up over time as grammatical morphemes (see chapter 25, this volume [Bybee]). Steeping himself in this literature, Slobin (1997, 2001) came to the conclusion that he had been wrong to credit young children with a priori knowledge of "special meanings" for grammatical morphemes. Rather, he now believed, the universal "look" of the meanings of such morphemes could best be accounted for by reference to psycholinguistic processes that play out in the discourse of fluent speakers.

Slobin's change of mind about the existence of privileged semantic notions did not leave a void in his theorizing. He had already begun to think more seriously about systematic crosslinguistic differences in the expression of meaning. This process had been set in motion by the outcome of his major crosslinguistic project, together with Berman, on children's frog story narrations. In an eloquent summing up of the project, Berman and Slobin state that

> We began the study with an expectation that there was a basic set of semantic notions that all children would try to express by some means or other, whether or not grammatically-marked in their language...We were repeatedly surprised to discover how closely learners stick to the set of distinctions that they have been given by their language...We are left, then, with a new respect for the powerful role of each individual language in shaping its own world of expression, while at the same time representing but one variant of a familiar and universally human pattern. (1984, p. 641)

This remark seems to prefigure Slobin's disillusionment with the notion of cognitively and semantically privileged meanings, and it helps to explain his renewed interest in learning:

> ...now—partly to my surprise—I find myself thinking things that I said long ago...: [rather than invoking innate knowledge], I would rather think of the child as learning [semantic categories] through feedback... It seems to me more reasonable to suppose that it is language that plays a role in drawing the child's attention to the possibility of dividing nouns on the basis of animacy; or verbs on the basis of duration, or determinacy, or validity; or pronouns on the basis of social status, and the like. (Slobin, 2001, p. 443, reflecting on his views in Slobin, 1966)

During the long period during which Slobin emphasized the priority of cognition in language acquisition, including the idea of a privileged core set of grammaticizable notions, there had been little room for Whorfian thoughts: Semantics was seen to follow underlying cognitive dispositions, certainly not to guide them. But with his newfound recognition of the importance of learning and "the powerful role of each individual language in shaping its own world of expression," Slobin was ready to rethink the issue of language relativity. In doing so, he chose to focus not on the relationship between language and world view, or habitual thought, as Whorf and his predecessors had done, but on the more dynamic problem of what takes place online, as speakers try to convey their experiences through language. He took an agnostic view toward linguistic determinism:

> Whatever effects grammar may or may not have outside of the act of speaking, the sort of mental activity that goes on while formulating utterances is not trivial or obvious, and deserves our attention. We encounter the contents of the mind in a special way when they are being accessed for use. (Slobin, 1996, p. 76)

This agnosticism was critically important to the success of the Thinking for Speaking idea. For many who had gone through the cognitive revolution, the idea that language could have a fundamental influence on cognition was still unthinkable. By explicitly decoupling attention to crosslinguistic semantic variation from linguistic determinism—that is, by distinguishing "thinking online for language" from thinking in general—Slobin succeeded brilliantly in showing that one did not have to embrace Whorf to be fascinated by the challenges of explaining semantic diversity. Indeed, Slobin himself long resisted the idea that thinking for speaking filtered through to deeper levels of thought. But in opening the door to semantic diversity, and trying to find the right place for it in his theoretical thinking about language and cognition, his resistance diminished: Although still recognizing that nonlinguistic cognition is a powerful force in language acquisition, he found that its influence is less absolute than he had once supposed. Cognition lays the groundwork for language acquisition, but as language is acquired, mastering its requirements can, in turn, come to sway what speakers pay attention to when they are speaking, and even when they are not (Slobin, 2003).

The themes I have highlighted in Slobin's long career of work on language and cognition are picked up, reworked, and carried into new territory by the chapters in this section. Basic issues of cognitive prerequisites for language acquisition, and how these interact with other possible determinants of acquisition, are explored in Verhoeven and Vermeer's chapter. Cognitive abilities are found to be strong predictors of acquisition of both Turkish and Dutch as a native language and Dutch as the second language by ethnic Turkish children, although the cognitive skills tested feed differently into L1 and L2. Sociocultural factors such as ethnic group membership, home language, and parental education are also important predictors of language proficiency. The study makes clear that language acquisition has multiple interacting determinants, a finding that reminds us of Slobin's early emphasis on "communicative competence," according to which grammar learning does not take place in isolation but is fundamentally embedded within a cultural context (see Budwig & Ervin-Tripp, Introduction to Part I, this volume).

The developmental relationship between language and cognition is also explored in Aksu's chapter on the acquisition of evidentials in Turkish. Evidentials are obligatory grammaticalized devices with which speakers must express an "epistemic stance" concerning how they know something, e.g., by direct experience or by hearsay or inference. These forms are of great interest for the Thinking for Speaking hypothesis, because they require speakers to keep track of the source of their knowledge. Could this requirement, over time, come to influence cognition? Studying learners of Turkish over a broad age range, Aksu finds a complex succession of reciprocal interactions in which "the direction of influence between language and cognition changes depending on the level of knowledge representations available." Recall that in his early work, Slobin assumed a unidirectional influence from cognition to language. Here, however, we see precisely the sorts of complex interactions between these two factors to which the notion of Thinking for Speaking opens the door.

Two chapters are fundamentally concerned with the semantic "Ur-state" of the language learner: Brown & Levinson (whose handy term this is) and Gentner & Bowerman. Are all patterns of organizing a given semantic domain equally easy to learn, or do children have some inherent preferences for one organization of meaning over another? In his hypothesis for Basic Child Grammar, as we saw, Slobin argued in favor of privileged meanings, but he later rejected this proposal to suggest that children readily learn the categories displayed in the input. But in these two chapters we see evidence that some semantic systems are, just as he had thought, more in line with children's intrinsic biases than others.

Brown and Levinson concentrate on the finding that "in many societies people neither speak nor spatially reckon in terms of left and right, but rather in terms of fixed directions like north and south." (Slobin [2003, p. 176] has termed this finding "perhaps one of the most powerful thinking-for-speaking effects that has been demonstrated.") Our Kantian philosophical tradition suggests that relative (left–right) systems should be easier; children might work up to an absolute system only gradually, through an early reliance on landmarks (e.g., "X is looking toward the barn" would be earlier and easier than "X is looking northward"). But this turns out to be false: Tzeltal Maya children learn the absolute system of their language very early, and without reliance on landmarks. The authors evaluate this evidence together with new findings on how great apes solve spatial location tasks, and suggest that absolute spatial coding is in fact the hominid default. Children learning an absolute system can build directly on this cognitive bias, but children learning a relative system must override it with the help of language.

Gentner and Bowerman wonder whether Slobin did not go too far when he rejected his own hypothesis that some meanings are cognitively privileged for mapping to grammatical morphemes, and ask whether some ways of classifying topological spatial relations might after all be more "natural" for learners than others. To avoid circularity, "cognitively natural" cannot be simply equated with what children learn early. The authors propose instead to make predictions about naturalness based on the relative frequency of alternative categorization schemes in the world's languages, reasoning that naturalness for human cognizers should be reflected in both crosslinguistic prevalence and ease of acquisition. In a test of this hypothesis, the authors find that learners of English, which has a common categorization system for topological relations, indeed master their system earlier and with fewer errors than learners of Dutch, which has a rare system.

Taken together, the findings by Brown and Levinson and Gentner and Bowerman echo, in the sphere of semantics, what Slobin's (1973, 1985) Operating Principles approach long ago convincingly demonstrated for morphosyntax: that some patterns of linguistic organization match children's starting preferences better than others. Initial biases, whether in semantics or morphosyntax, can be overridden when it is necessary to do so to learn the input language, but it may take a little longer.

One of the most important themes in this "Language and Cognition" section of the volume is, not surprisingly, "Thinking for Speaking." Not surprising because this construct is the most recent of Slobin's many contributions to the language and thought debate, and it gives rise to many questions and directions that are still being creatively followed up. Several of the papers we have already considered touch on Thinking for Speaking, but it is the trio of papers by Pourcel; Strömqvist, Holmqvist, and Andersson; and McNeill that delve into this topic the most deeply, focusing on the domain to which Slobin himself returned over and over: the encoding of motion events.

In a series of innovative studies, Slobin (e.g., 2003, 2004) has shown differential effects of Thinking for Speaking on the salience of manner of motion for speakers of satellite-framed languages vs. speakers of verb-framed languages. But are these effects limited to the time of speaking or listening, or—as Slobin (2003) speculates—do they also affect speakers' memories of and overall conceptualization of motion events? To test this, Pourcel presented adult native speakers of English (satellite-framed) and French (verb-framed) with an engaging new elicitation stimulus, a 5-minute motion scenario from a Charlie Chaplin film. In line with predictions, the English speakers reported the manner in which motions took place more frequently than the French speakers. Crucially, they did so considerably more accurately, both in immediate recall and in a prompted recall task a day later. These effects on memory constitute a clear Whorfian effect, a strengthening, as Pourcel points out, of the Thinking for Speaking idea to encompass more general effects of language on mental representation.

Strömqvist et al. and McNeill also elicited narrations of motion events, not with the goal of exploring the direct effects of language on cognition but in order to assess Slobin's claim that Thinking for Speaking is a special form of thinking. These authors note that there is a risk of circularity in the Thinking for Speaking claim: We infer that speakers channel their attention differently on the basis of how they talk, but perhaps the structure of their language simply forces them to talk this way. Ideally, we need evidence about cognition that is independent of language. For Strömqvist et al., this comes from gaze behavior: They compare the eye movements and fixation patterns of two groups of participants, one who looked at the pictures of the frog story (Berman & Slobin, 1984) while narrating the tale, and another who saw the same the pictures but was not asked to tell the story. Systematically different patterns of gaze behavior were found in the two groups, according well with the claim that attention is distributed differently when speaking is required than when it is not.

For McNeill, the independent evidence about cognition comes from the spontaneous gestures that often accompany speech. McNeill argues that the imagery behind the gesture and the speech constitute "unlike modes of cognition…that are co-expressive of the same underlying thought unit," forming what he terms a "growth point" in which imagery and language interact. He shows that in Tweety and Sylvester cartoon narrations the co-speech gestures produced by speakers of different languages for the same cartoon events are systematically different, and are also timed differently with speech. McNeill argues that the impact of language on cognition is optimally revealed in the dynamic unfolding of language over time, just as the Thinking for Speaking hypothesis implies.

Stoll and Bickel take as their starting point Slobin's demonstration that differences in language structure and in discourse style can affect which aspects of events speakers of different languages habitually attend to. A potentially telling difference in discourse style, in their view, is the use of overt NPs. Even when languages in principle allow speakers to omit arguments, there is striking variation in how frequently this occurs. In comparing narrations of the short film known as the *Pear Story*, the authors find that speakers of Belhare, a language of Nepal, provide far fewer lexical NPs in argument positions than speakers of Russian. This difference goes hand in hand with different styles of information management in the two languages. In particular, the authors show that there are "thinking-for-speaking and thinking-for-listening effects on how much we orient our attention to the identities and characteristics of participants when we tell a story."

Slobin's work on the topic of language and cognition, as on every other topic, has continually uncovered connections between ideas from diverse sources, and woven them into a rich conceptual tapestry that inspires further questions. With Stoll and Bickel's paper, we can begin to appreciate how the diverse lines of inquiry Slobin has set in motion are branching out into new territory, and suggesting connections with themes developed in other lines of research. For example, how are the discourse differences that Stoll and Bickel observe in the treatment of story protagonists, as indexed by the density and function of lexical NPs in the narratives, related to issues of preferred argument structure in adult and child speech (Allen, 2007; Clancy, 2003; Du Bois, 2003)? And are these discourse differences related to the variation shown in recent work (e.g., Choi, 2000) in the extent to which caregivers in different language communities stress object names and properties when they are talking to children, vs. events and relationships?

Early on in his career, Slobin played a pivotal role in demonstrating how firmly language acquisition rests on a cognitive basis, and our field was immeasurably enriched by the crosslinguistic work that flowed from this insight. This would have been enough for one lifetime. But, having established the debt of language to cognition and introducing the role of language universals and typology into the heady mix, Slobin now turned his attention to how language might act back upon cognition. In working out his innovative ideas about Thinking for Speaking, Slobin has profoundly inspired a new generation of scholars and kicked off a whole new chapter of research on the language-and-cognition puzzle.

REFERENCES

Allen, S. E. M. (2007). Interacting pragmatic influences on children's argument realization. In M. Bowerman & P. Brown (Eds.), *Crosslinguistic perspectives on argument structure: Implications for learnability* (pp. 191–210). Mahwah, NJ: Lawrence Erlbaum Associates.

Andersen, E. (1978). Lexical universals of body-part terminology. In J. H. Greenberg (Ed.), *Universals of human language: Vol. 3. Word structure* (pp. 335–368). Stanford: Stanford University Press.

Berman, R.A., & Slobin, D. I. (Eds.) (1994). *Relating events in narrative: A crosslinguistic developmental study*. Hillsdale, NJ: Lawrence Erlbaum Associates.

Bowerman, M., & Choi, S. (2001). Shaping meanings for language: Universal and language-specific in the acquisition of spatial semantic categories. In M. Bowerman & S. C. Levinson (Eds.), *Language acquisition and conceptual development* (pp. 475–511). Cambridge, UK: Cambridge University Press.

Brown, R. (1973). *A first language: The early stages*. Cambridge, MA: Harvard University Press.

Choi, S. (2000). Caregiver input in English and Korean: Use of nouns and verbs in book-reading and toy-play contexts. *Journal of Child Language, 27*, 69–96

Choi, S., & Bowerman, M. (1991). Learning to express motion events in English and Korean: The influence of language-specific lexicalization patterns. *Cognition 41*, 83–121.

Chomsky, N. (1965). *Aspects of the theory of syntax*. Cambridge, MA: The MIT Press.

Clancy, P. (2003). The lexicon in interaction: Developmental origins of Preferred Argument Structure in Korean. In J. W. Du Bois, L. E. Kumpf, & W. J. Ashby (Eds.), *Preferred Argument Structure: Grammar as architecture for function* (pp. 81–108). Amsterdam: John Benjamins.

Clark, E. V. (1976). Universal categories: On the semantics of classifiers and children's early word meanings. In A. Juilland (Ed.), *Linguistic studies offered to Joseph Greenberg on the occasion of his sixtieth birthday (Syntax)* (Vol. 3, pp. 449–462). Saratoga, California: Anna Libri.

Clark, E.V. (2001). Emergent categories in first language acquisition. In M. Bowerman & S.C. Levinson (Eds.), *Language acquisition and conceptual development* (pp. 379–405). Cambridge, UK: Cambridge University Press.

Du Bois, J. (2003). Discourse and grammar. In M. Tomasello (Ed.), *The new psychology of language* (Vol. 2, pp. 47–87). Mahwah, NJ: Lawrence Erlbaum Associates.

McNeill, D. (1966). Developmental psycholinguistics. In F. Smith & G. A. Miller (Eds.), *The genesis of language: A psycholinguistic approach* (pp. 15–84). Cambridge, MA: The MIT Press.

Slobin, D. I. (1966). Comments on "Developmental psycholinguistics": A discussion of McNeill's presentation. In F. Smith & G. A. Miller (Eds.), *The genesis of language: A psycholinguistic approach* (pp. 85–91). Cambridge, MA: The MIT Press.

Slobin, D. I. (1970). Universals of grammatical development in children. In G. B. Flores D'Arcais & W. J. M. Levelt (Eds.), *Advances in psycholinguistics* (pp. 174–186). Amsterdam: North-Holland.

Slobin, D. I. (1973). Cognitive prerequisites for the development of grammar. In C. A. Ferguson & D. I. Slobin (Eds.), *Studies of child language development* (pp. 175–208). New York: Holt, Rinehart & Winston.

Slobin, D. I. (1985). Crosslinguistic evidence for the language-making capacity. In D. I. Slobin (Ed.), *The crosslinguistic study of language acquisition: Vol. 2. Theoretical issues* (pp. 1157–1256). Hillsdale, NJ: Lawrence Erlbaum Associates.

Slobin, D. I. (1996). From "thought and language" to "thinking for speaking." In J. J. Gumperz & S. C. Levinson (Eds.), *Rethinking linguistic relativity* (pp. 70–96). Cambridge, UK: Cambridge University Press.

Slobin, D. I. (1997). The origins of grammaticizable notions: Beyond the individual mind. In D. I. Slobin (Ed.), *The crosslinguistic study of language development: Vol. 5. Expanding the contexts* (pp. 265–323). Mahwah, NJ: Lawrence Erlbaum Associates.

Slobin, D. I. (2001). Form–function relations: How do children find out what they are? In M. Bowerman & S. C. Levinson (Eds.), *Language acquisition and conceptual development* (pp. 406–449). Cambridge, UK: Cambridge University Press.

Slobin, D. I. (2003). Language and thought online: Cognitive consequences of linguistic relativity. In D. Gentner & S. Goldin-Meadow (Eds.), *Language in mind: Advances in the study of language and thought* (pp. 157–191). Cambridge, MA: The MIT Press.

Slobin, D. I. (2004). The many ways to search for a frog: Linguistic typology and the expression of motion events. In S. Strömqvist & L. Verhoeven (Eds.), *Relating events in narrative: Vol. 2. Typological and contextual perspectives.* (pp. 219–257). Amsterdam: John Benjamins.

Talmy, L. (1983). How language structures space. In H. Pick & L. Acredolo (Eds.), *Spatial orientation: Theory, research, and application* (pp. 225–282). New York: Plenum.

Talmy, L. (1988). The relation of grammar to cognition. In B. Rudzka-Ostyn (Ed.), *Topics in cognitive linguistics* (pp. 165–205). Amsterdam: John Benjamins.

33

Language as Mind Tools
Learning How to Think Through Speaking[1]

PENELOPE BROWN and STEPHEN C. LEVINSON

Max Planck Institute for Psycholinguistics

> ... the expression of experience in linguistic terms constitutes *thinking for speaking*—a special form of thought that is mobilized for communication. ... We encounter the contents of the mind in a special way when they are being accessed for use. ... In the evanescent time frame of constructing utterances in discourse one fits one's thoughts into available linguistic frames. "Thinking for speaking" involves picking those characteristics of objects and events that (a) fit some conceptualization of the event and (b) are readily encodable in the language. *I propose that, in learning a native language, the child learns particular ways of thinking for speaking.* [our emphases]
>
> **Dan I. Slobin (1996, p. 76)**

Although relative newcomers to the field of child language, we have a long association with Dan Slobin stemming back to our graduate school days at Berkeley in the early 1970s. Dan was a frequent associate at the Language Behavior Research Lab, which housed linguistic anthropologists in those days. He had recently produced the ground-breaking *A field manual for cross-cultural study of the acquisition of communicative competence* (Slobin, 1967), which was the practical basis for a number of the first PhD dissertations examining child language development in non-Western societies (e.g., Stross, 1969; Mitchell-Kernan, 1972), was helpful in our own field research directed at adults in Mexico and in Tamilnadu, India, and has inspired a succession of such field manuals from the MPI, Nijmegen. Little did we realize then that, some 30 years later, Dan would still be a major intellectual stimulator of our research, including that reported here.

INTRODUCTION

In this chapter, we examine the implications of a major recent finding for Slobin's notion of 'thinking for speaking.' The finding is that in many societies people neither speak nor spatially reckon in terms of left and right, but rather in terms of fixed directions like north and south (see Majid, Bowerman, Kita, Haun, & Levinson, 2004, for a summary; Levinson, 2003, and Levinson & Wilkins, 2006 for the full facts). This implies a strong measure of cognitive diversity in one of the most crucial domains

---

[1] This chapter is based on 'Linguistic and cultural factors in learning an absolute spatial system,' a talk by P. Brown delivered at the Piaget Society meetings, Berkeley, California, in June 2001. A revised version was presented at the Workshop on Developmental Studies in Spatial Language and Cognition in Geneva in February 2005. We are grateful to participants at these two venues for helpful feedback.

of human cognition. This came as an unwelcome surprise to the psychological establishment, which has assumed strong universals in the spatial domain (see Li & Gleitman, 2002, and rejoinder in Levinson, Kita, Haun, & Rasch, 2002). Now, the interesting question is how this cognitive diversity comes about. Assuming we humans all start out the same, do infants start out as left-right conceptualizers (pretty much the psychological and philosophical orthodoxy), and then some of them learn another way to think, letting the left-right system atrophy? Or do they start out unbiased either way, perhaps pruning out one of the two pre-existing systems, or, on a blank slate view, building one or both from scratch? Or even, radical thought, do infants start out as north-southers, and then some of them (us Westerners) learn the left-right trick and let the north-south one atrophy?

One of the reasons that these questions are deeply interesting from a developmental perspective is that the north-south systems, and anything of the kind using fixed arbitrary directions, are highly abstract. For example, east is not a point but a direction which you can never reach. It's at precisely N090°, and whatever level of approximation is psychologically realistic, it involves angles and metric measurement. Unlike left and right, east has nothing to do with egocentric location—if X is east of Y, then Y is west of X, regardless of the viewpoint. But if I am travelling from Y to X via Z in a straight line, at one point I'll be west of Z, but later east of it. If Z is not on that line, then the direction of X from Z must be calculated from the distance and direction of Z from Y—this is the classical dead-reckoning of sailors. To run a north-south system consistently you need to be able to compute all this, and you need to know without a compass where north (or its local arbitrary equivalent) is. That is a lot of cognitive machinery to master. In societies which primarily use such a system, when do children start to manage this?

In the literature cited above we believe we have made a strong case for the covariation of language coding and conceptual coding for non-linguistic purposes like spatial memory or wayfinding. That is to say, if you speak in one of these two major ways, that's the way you think (and vice versa), as tested by a wide battery of tasks (see Levinson, 2003). One of our central cases was Tenejapa, where adults showed this strong linkage between language and cognitive style. The Tenejapans are a group of indigenous Mayans who live in Chiapas, Mexico, and speak a dialect of Tzeltal. In this chapter, we want to explore a little further the development of such a north–south system in Tenejapan children. Our earlier findings show that this abstract fixed-bearing system is learned remarkably early by children, with the semantic oppositions mastered by 3;6, practical comprehension demonstrable by 4, and systematic production in novel tasks between 5 and 7 years (Brown, 2001; Brown & Levinson, 2000). Here our focus is on *how* children learn this system, and in particular we want to explore whether this abstract system of fixed directions is gradually acquired, being scaffolded out of simpler, more concrete concepts like landmarks in the environment (so that, e.g., 'south' is learned as 'toward the school'). If such a gradual abstraction is discernible, 'thinking for speaking' could be the essential mechanism: one learns gradually to use the right words in the right situation, until the frame of mind that fits the native concepts becomes automatically on-line during language production. But if the child never passes through a series of approximations (e.g., using landmarks instead of abstract directions), some other account would seem to be necessary.

In assessing the role of 'thinking for speaking' it is important to bear the bigger picture, beyond the facts presented in this chapter, in mind. A striking part of the bigger picture is that, as mentioned, the patterns of conception evoked by 'thinking for speaking' have a persistence outside the "evanescent time frame of constructing utterances" (Slobin, 1996, p. 76). Adult spatial memory, when tested in non-linguistic tasks, matches the conception required by their language in a stable way (Levinson, 2003). In this particular domain, then, where we find cultural cognitive diversity and the cognition covarying with the language, 'thinking for speaking' may be too weak a mechanism to predict the cognitive effects outside a language task (in fact, Slobin has always been careful to distance himself from stronger Whorfian claims). If we put this together with the findings in this chapter, we may need a rather different kind of explanation, a matter we return to in the conclusions.

Before getting down to details, some preliminaries need to be explained. First, some terminology. We have argued elsewhere that there are distinct subdomains of spatial conception, notably deixis, topology, and frames of reference (Levinson, 2003). Deictic discriminations are basically about distance from ego (as in 'this' vs. 'that'), or direction to or from ego (as in 'coming' vs. 'going').[2] They give radial characterizations, not vector directions (you can 'come here' from any direction). Topological distinctions are essentially concerned with relations of contact, containment, or propinquity between a thematic object or 'figure' and a landmark object or 'ground.' Frame of reference distinctions involve the larger spatial framework which allows us to determine the direction of one object with respect to another one separated in space. Frames of reference are thus essentially coordinate systems, which in human cognition are nearly always polar coordinates. Investigation shows that languages use just three main frames of reference (Levinson, 2003): **intrinsic** relations which use the intrinsic facets of the landmark object to extract a direction (as in 'at the back of the post office'), **relative** relations which use our bodily coordinates and express directions in terms of left, right, front, and back, and finally **absolute** relations which use fixed, arbitrary bearings like north and south. Most languages use an intrinsic system for at least a few kinds of spatial relations, some use all three systems, but some use predominantly relative (left-right) systems (as in urban Western settings) or absolute (north-south-like) systems (as in Tenejapa). Some of the abstract properties of these different frame of reference systems will be crucial to what follows.

There is one aspect of this tripartite typology of frames of reference (intrinsic, relative, absolute) that has sometimes been misconstrued.[3] There is another bipartite typology into egocentric vs. allocentric frames. This roughly partitions relative (primarily egocentric) vs. intrinsic and absolute (primarily non-egocentric). (This is an approximation, good enough for current purposes, because the tripartite typology actually allows variable 'centers' or origins of the coordinates—see Levinson, 2003, chapter 2.) So non-egocentric thinking can be of two different types: one can either think that the obelisk stands at the front of the sphinx (intrinsic), or one can think that it stands to the north of it (absolute). When a gaming mogul has the array rebuilt in Las Vegas, he can get the one conception right and the other wrong, or vice versa. In the task to be described below, which is open to solution in any of the three frames of reference, Tenejapan children relied heavily on the two non-egocentric frames, intrinsic and absolute. So did adults, but they used a different proportion of the two, and moreover used a special form of intrinsic. For that reason we'll need to explain in a little more detail below the difference between landmark-based directions —which we hold to be a special kind of intrinsic—and directions based on abstract bearings (absolute).

LEARNING SPATIAL FRAMES OF REFERENCE IN TZELTAL

Tenejapan Tzeltal has no terms for 'left' and 'right' directions, i.e., no systematic relative system (though as we shall see, there are marginal relative uses of certain absolute and intrinsic terms). Instead, to express directions Tzeltal uses either an intrinsic system (especially if figure and ground are close), as in 'the bottle is at the face (front) of the chair,' or an absolute system which is based on, but abstracted from, the slope of the land in Tenejapa from a high south to a low north, as indicated in Figure 33.1. As the figure makes clear, the system offers four labeled quadrants of 90 degrees, oriented slightly rotated from grid north or magnetic north (the term for the east vs. west direction is actually the same, 'across'). So one would say of the bottle in Figure 33.1 that it is 'uphill (i.e., south) of the chair.' The system is fully abstract in the sense that it applies anywhere, even on the flat in quite different country miles away: 'uphill' is fixed once and for all as southerly. (See Brown & Levinson, 1993, for the details.)

Tzeltal was one of the first reported cases where speakers routinely use an absolute system of spatial reference, even in table-top space (Brown & Levinson, 1993; Levinson & Brown, 1994) and where this absolute usage was shown to correlate with nonlinguistic thinking (Levinson, 1996). It

---

[2] We are painting with a very broad brush—deictic discriminations in specific languages actually involve many other parameters.

[3] Misconstrued, for example, by Li and Gleitman (2002)—see the rejoinder in Levinson et al. (2002), and the full exposition in Levinson (2003).

Figure 33.1   The Tzeltal 'uphill'/'downhill' system.

is also one of the first where children's acquisition of such a system has been investigated. We know quite a lot about children learning a relative (left/right/front/back) system (work that goes back to Piaget and Inhelder, 1956). But we know relatively little about how children learn to use an absolute system at all scales, from the scene right in front of their eyes to distant spaces, as the default everyday way of talking about where things are. What evidence we have to date comes from a handful of widely dispersed speech communities: Bali (Wassman & Dasen, 1998), the Marquesas (Cablitz, 2001, 2002), India and Nepal (Mishra, Dasen, & Niraula, 2003; Niraula, Mishra, & Dasen, 2004; Mishra & Dasen, 2005; Dasen, Mishra, Niraula, & Wassman, 2006; Dasen & Mishra, 2008), and two Mexican Mayan communities, Tzotzil (de León, 1994) and Tzeltal (Brown, 2001). All concur that the absolute system emerges relatively early and is easily acquired compared with relative systems.

Focusing here on the Tzeltal case, we have explored children's acquisition of their spatial systems through the use of interactional 'space games,' where a 'Director' describes a spatial scene portrayed in a photograph and on the basis of this description a 'Matcher,' screened from view, reproduces the scene with toys. This task produces descriptions like the one shown in Figure 33.2.

These informal communicative tasks place a premium on the ability to calculate and describe small-scale spatial relations on the fly. Preliminary results from these tasks as well as from longitudinal language samples were reported in Brown and Levinson (2000) and Brown (2001). As already sketched, we found that Tzeltal children master the basic semantic oppositions of the absolute system by about age 3;6; they can understand instructions in novel spatial tasks like our Farm Animal games by about age 4, and they can produce instructions successfully in these games—demonstrating mastery of the abstract geographical axes—by age 5;8 to 7;8, well before Western children have fully mastered a left/right system.

In this chapter, using a larger set of space games, our focus is more specific. We want to track the emergence of the absolute system relative to other systems, and specifically we want to examine whether children start off relying on visible or local landmarks and then use this to bootstrap themselves into the much more abstract absolute system. But first we need to sketch the different

Tzeltal in English gloss:
Director:
"There's a tree standing there right <u>in the middle</u>. (topological)
There comes <u>to our fronts</u> a little drinking trough. (deictic, intrinsic)
A little bit far away, <u>coming</u>. (deictic motion)
<u>Comes</u> a cow, he licks. (deictic motion)
He's <u>bent over</u> there. (topological shape)
Thus his butt goes to <u>sunset</u>. <u>Uphill</u> of the tree. (absolute)
<u>Comes</u> another one, black-spotted. (deictic motion)
Thus he <u>comes</u> to <u>downhill</u> of the tree. A bit far ..."
(deictic motion + absolute)

Figure 33.2 The 'farm animals' task: Picture–object matching.

strategies children use, and explain why a landmark system, despite its allocentric nature, is fundamentally different from an absolute system.

ABSOLUTE COORDINATES VS. LANDMARKS

In the Farm Animal games, four kinds of information are (potentially) needed to accurately reproduce the spatial arrays depicted:

Placement information: e.g., cow uphill of horse
Facing information: e.g., horse facing tree
Distance information: e.g., how far apart
Position information: e.g., standing, sitting, leaning

It is placement and facing information which specify a direction of one object in relation to another, requiring a coordinate system to project the direction, so it is on these two that we concentrate here. In Tzeltal, deictics can supply a direction ('coming' or 'going,' i.e., toward or away from speaker), with the coordinate anchored by participants. The absolute and intrinsic systems are the primary resources for supplying nondeictic directional coordinates ('cow uphill of horse, pig at man's back'). But landmarks (concrete entities in the surrounding environment, either local or distant) can also be drawn upon ('cow toward the door,' 'facing Red Cliffs'), and it is necessary to clarify the distinction between absolute coordinates and landmark directions. These are both allocentric frames, so they may seem to be the same kind of thing—in fact in the developmental literature 'environmental' frames generally refer only to visible, locally available landmarks or cues around ego. But these local landmarks are best treated as a kind—albeit a special kind— of *intrinsic* frame of reference, not an absolute one, for reasons that have to do with their logic and geometry—you can walk around a tree, but you can't walk around east. Figure 33.3 makes the point that the landmark description

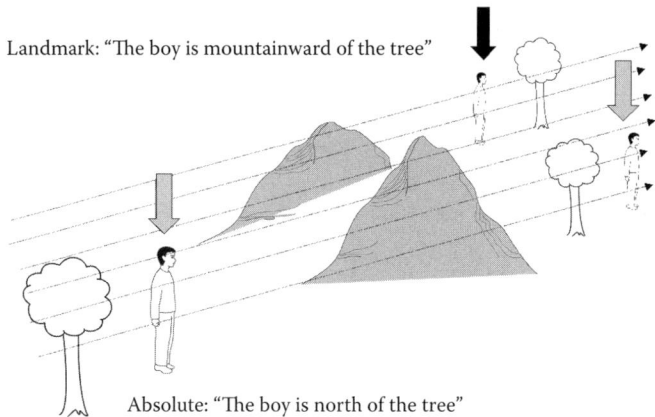

Figure 33.3 Landmark vs. true absolute systems.

"The boy is mountainward of the tree" specifies a different direction on the other side of the mountain, whereas the absolute description "The boy is east of the tree" does not. In this respect landmark descriptions are like arrays described in an intrinsic system: the internal organization of the array (here: boy, tree, mountain) has to be satisfied, but the description tells you nothing about the direction of the whole array, unlike an absolute description. Think about the array being in a large box: now ask yourself if the description tells you how the box is oriented. If it does, the description is in an orientation-bound frame, either relative or absolute; if it doesn't, it's in an intrinsic frame. Although by this test, landmark systems are best treated as a special kind of intrinsic system, the language Tzeltal does not treat them grammatically or semantically in the same way as other intrinsic expressions (like 'at the front of'). Therefore, in the treatments below we code and label landmark responses separately from other intrinsic responses.

It has to be conceded that as the virtual box (the size of the intrinsic array) gets larger and larger the distinction between absolute descriptions and intrinsic landmark use may effectively blur, but it is important to understand the conceptual distinction. For one thing, there's reason to think that landmark use of one kind or another is probably universal, but absolute systems are not—many languages have no way to indicate abstract fixed bearings, and speakers of most do not employ them colloquially and would certainly never use them to describe small-scale arrays.

Now, an abstract absolute system, requiring an internalized 'mental compass,' is presumably harder to learn to use than landmarks. If we assume (not unreasonably) that children everywhere can readily use local environmental cues in spatial tasks, we would predict that children start out with landmark terms, then slowly graduate to the more abstract absolute terms. Early on, children may even understand adults' absolute terms in landmark ways (see de León, 1994, on children's use of absolute terms in the related language Tzotzil). According to this commonsense view, landmark usage should precede absolute terms used absolutely. This we now set out to check.

FARM ANIMAL INTERACTIONAL GAMES

Method

The task focuses on production for children aged 5 and older. The data are primarily cross-sectional, supplemented by some longitudinal data. The elicitation stimuli consist of 12 Farm Animal photos, portraying toy farm animals, people, trees, fences, and drinking troughs in various arrays. Participants were 5 adult Director-Matcher pairs, 4 pairs of adult Directors to child Matchers, and 22 child Director-Matcher pairs in 4 age groups ranging from age 5 to 16. The participants were grouped as described in Table 33.1.

TABLE 33.1   Data Summary: Tzeltal Farm Animal Games

Group	Players (D=Director, M=Matcher)	Number of D-M Pairs Sampled	Age Range* of Ds	Age Range of Ms
I	D age 5–7	5	5;7–7;8	4;3–13+
II	D age 8–10	8	8;1–9;8	6;1–13+
III	D age 11–13	6	11–13+	6;0–9+
IV	D age 14–16	3	14+–16+	7+–14+
V	Adult D to Child M under age 7	4	adult	4;1–6;9
VI	Adult D to Adult M	5	adult	adult

* + in the age indicates that the child was unable to provide exact date of birth.

Visually screening off the Director from the Matcher proved impracticable with the children, so for all the child games the Directors were seated behind the Matcher so that they could see the Matcher's progress and respond to misconstruals, but the Matchers could not see the Director's stimulus photo and had to rely on the verbal descriptions. In the adult–adult games, Director and Matcher were side by side, visually screened from each other.

Analysis

The interactional games were videorecorded and transcribed in the field. Spatial descriptions produced by all Directors in the data establishing a direction, an angle on the horizontal, were identified and coded into the following categories:

deictic (DEIC):[4] 'coming,' 'going' [toward/away from speaker]
absolute (ABS): *ajk'ol* 'uphill,' *alan* 'downhill,' *k'atal* 'acrossways,' *moel* 'ascending,' *koel* 'descending' [when used with the absolute frame of reference, 'uphill' and 'ascending' meaning roughly south, 'downhill' and 'descending' roughly north]
intrinsic (minus landmark) (INTR):[5] 'back,' 'face,' 'foot,' 'butt,' etc. [bodypart terms used as Grounds within the scene being constructed]
relative (REL): *k'atal* 'across' [when used to mean across speaker's line of gaze']; also absolute or intrinsic terms used relatively (e.g., *moel* 'upward' used to mean 'farther away from us' or *pat* 'back' used projectively to mean 'behind']
landmark (LND): 'the bed,' 'the door,' 'the electricity post,' 'the path,' etc. [landmark terms used as Grounds outside of the scene being constructed]
sunset/sunrise (SS):[6] 'sun setting place,' 'sun rising place'

A total of 5332 spatial descriptors establishing a direction were coded (note that many utterances employ more than one descriptor—e.g., 'put the cow uphill coming (toward us)' is coded as ABS (for 'uphill') and DEIC for 'coming'). Examples of each category are given in Table 33.2.

---

[4] In coding the data we did not consider all types of 'deictic' usage, since virtually every utterance included morphemes meaning (roughly) 'this' or 'that.' We restricted ourselves to deictic uses of the directionals *tal* 'coming' and *bel* 'going,' which indicate directions (for placement or facing) toward or away from the speaker. Other categories of spatial language that we also coded for (distance, position, topological 'at') are not relevant to specifying direction and orientation of objects in the array and are therefore ignored in what follows. We also have omitted from the data reported here any forms ambiguous between absolute and relative or intrinsic interpretations, e.g., where *k'atal* can mean either 'across the north/south slope of the land' (ABS) or 'across the line of our sight (REL),' unless it was clear in the context which interpretation was intended.
[5] The intrinsic system of Tzeltal is not described here, but see Brown & Levinson (1993), Levinson (1994), Brown (2006). It involves a fixed set of body parts like 'face,' 'back,' 'side' with precise spatial meanings.
[6] As mentioned, these are intermediate between ABS and LND terms; they provide geocentric directions but these are tied to specific mountains and are subject to significant solstitial variation, unlike the true absolute terms.

TABLE 33.2 Examples of Spatial Descriptions (in Gloss) in Farm Animal Games

ABS	INTR	LND	SS	REL	DEIC
pig to downhill (5–7)	underneath the pig's nose (5–7)	(toward) edge of the bench (5–7)	to sunset (11–13)	at the back of (i.e., behind) the little tree (8–10)	uphillward coming here (5–7)
uphillward to above the tree (8–10)	pig in the middle (between trees) (8–10)	(toward) the lime tree (8–10)	to sunrise, to sunset (adults)	first, last (meaning left, right) (11–13)	put it coming here (8–10)
and the little tree just uphill here; put the cow below it! (11–13)	put the pig at the fence's back (i.e., outside it) (14–16)	toward where there's a nail (in the table) (8–10)		put the trough acrossways [relative to our line of sight] (adults)	and the pig here coming downhill-ward (11–13)
to downhill put its little nose; well sideways here to downhill (14–16)	make the horse look at the tree (11–13)	toward Turuwit (mountain) (11–13)			

Note: Absolute (ABS), Intrinsic (INTR), Landmark (LND), Sunset/Sunrise (SS), Relative (REL), deictic (DEIC); age group of speaker in parentheses.

Results

A summary of the results for each age group is provided in Table 33.3. For each of the six different age groups, we present the proportion of linguistic forms in the Directors' Farm Animal descriptions for each of the six spatial categories described above.

Most noteworthy in these results is the fact that the spatial descriptors for all of the groups look remarkably the same in several categories: deictic information was always the most frequently used, and, with the single exception of the adult-adult group, absolute and intrinsic descriptions were always second and third most frequent. The outstanding difference across groups is in the use of landmark terms: these were very rare (6% or less) in the child groups from age 5 to 13, and rather more frequent (12%) from age 14 to 16. Adults when speaking to child Matchers under the age of 7 used around 10% landmark terms, but when speaking to other adults, landmark usage jumped dramatically to 25%, with a corresponding drop in the proportion of absolute terms by the adults.

We can see that the children in Group I hardly used LND descriptions (just 3% of their 464 spatial descriptors). In fact these were all produced by children aged 7; the 5- to 6-year-olds used no landmark terms. Those used by the 7-year-olds are restricted to just three types: '(to) the edge of table/bench,' '(to) where mama is,' and 'beside Ermi's hand.' These children in Group I relied very heavily on the deictic adverbs 'coming/going' (42%). They also used intrinsic body parts freely: e.g., 'put its nose at the cow's chest.' Four of the five children used absolute terms as well, about as often as intrinsic; absolute was usually used correctly but was often not explicit with respect to the figure and

TABLE 33.3 Directional Language Usage in Tzeltal Farm Animal Games

	DEIC	ABS	INTR	LND	SS	REL	Total
I. CHILD 5–7	42%	27%	27%	3%	0	0	464
II. CHILD 8–10	38%	35%	23%	5%	0	0	968
III. CHILD 11–13	40%	28%	24%	6%	2%	1%	889
IV. CHILD 14–16	35%	29%	25%	12%	0	0	469
V. ADULT – CHILD	40%	27%	22%	10%	0	0	860
VI. ADULT – ADULT	30%	14%	22%	25%	8%	1%	1682
							5332

ground objects. For specifying precise angles the children used gesture, not landmark terms. The 3% exceptions indicated that lack of landmark usage was not always due to lack of competence—some of the 7-year-olds at least were capable of using landmarks, but on the whole used absolute instead. On the basis of their usage we may conclude that children aged 5–7 know where the absolute 'up'/'down' directions are, and know that they are the conventional way to express directional information.

The children in Group II, aged 8–10, showed a dramatic improvement in the explicitness of spatial descriptions. All of them used absolute terms accurately, and distinguished absolute placement ('cow downhillward of horse') vs. absolute facing ('cow facing downhillward') information. They still had very little landmark usage (5% of their total spatial descriptions), but showed some productivity: all but one of the 8 children used landmarks at least once and their 44 tokens were distributed across 24 different types (e.g., 'to Letti,' 'to the roof,' 'to the orange tree,' 'in line with Mario'). They very occasionally used absolute terms in a relative frame of reference (where 'up' = 'away from me'), a usage possibly derived from schooling in Spanish.

The children in Group III, aged 11–13, were confident in their use of absolute terms. Four of the six children in Group III also showed a range of uses of landmark terms, with 49 tokens and 15 types of a similar range to that of Group II; one child (age 11) also used the sunset/sunrise terms.

Landmark terms were much more in evidence in the data from the 14- to 16-year-olds in Group IV, comprising 12% of their spatial descriptors, with 25 distinct tokens. Predominantly, these references were 'to you/me,' 'to your/my bodypart,' or else to the edge of the table/bench on which the array was being constructed. The range of the rest was comparable to that of the children in Groups II and III.

Adults speaking to children under 7 also used relatively few landmark terms. Clearly the adults treated landmarks and sunset/sunrise terms as not suitable for directing children in this task. It was with the adult-adult pairs where the use of landmarks really came into its own; here the Directors produced 410 tokens. The adults exploited a feature of landmarks—an ad hoc landmark can be found in any conceivable direction—to provide precise characterizations of exact angles at which to place the referent.

All the data for children and adults are graphically represented in Figure 33.4.

To sum up, child Directors by age 5–7 already described the spatial relations depicted in this task naturally and frequently in absolute terms such as *ajk'ol* 'uphill' or *alan* 'downhill.' There was, incidentally, and contrary to the suggestions in Li & Gleitman (2002), no apparent facilitation of absolute usage when the players were outdoors as opposed to indoors. There was almost no landmark usage among the youngest, and landmark usage is the only category showing a developmental trend

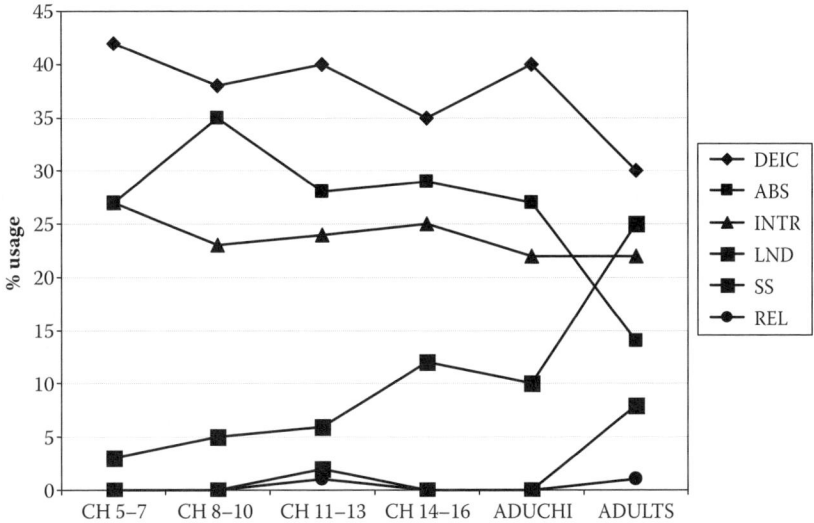

Figure 33.4 Proportions of types of directional usage in Tzeltal Farm Animal Games.

of gradual increase with age. There was only marginal sunset/sunrise usage by anyone except the adult pairs. Relative usage of intrinsic terms ('back' as 'behind') and of absolute terms ('acrossways' meaning 'at an angle orthogonal to viewer's line of gaze') occasionally appeared in the data of adults, but were extremely rare in the children's data.

We may conclude on the basis of the evidence from their performance on these space game tasks that Tzeltal children do *not* use landmarks at first, prior to absolute, at least not in this task. When they have difficulties communicating, they do not fall back on local ad hoc visible landmark cues. This is in contrast to the adults, who, when there are problems, switch strategies and use local ad hoc landmarks (the dog, the bed, the electricity post, etc.). In these data, landmark usage does not precede absolute, even if it is supposedly simpler, more concrete, and 'more natural.'

The children's failure to use landmarks is probably due to less flexibility and inventiveness than adults—they are less good at seeing what the Matcher doesn't understand and at thinking of a new way (e.g., a more fine-grained angle) to phrase the spatial relation at issue. And they are less concerned with precision, more willing to say 'yes, it's the same,' when the array produced by the Matcher is not exactly the same as that portrayed in the stimulus photo. Tzeltal adults, however, find precision important in this task and landmarks make greater precision of angle possible.

CONCLUSIONS

Our results from these space games show the following:

1. Children use the abstract absolute system confidently and frequently from the earliest age cohort we have sampled here (from age 5). There is in fact remarkably little development in the use of directional language from age 5 to age 16: children of all ages use pretty much the same proportions of absolute, intrinsic, and deictic specifications to make the spatial discriminations required by the task. Only in a few cases do any of them use a relative frame of reference, making front-back or acrossways discriminations relative to their own viewpoint.
2. We find no evidence of development from children's use of the more concrete landmark cues to the more abstract absolute system, as one might have a priori expected. It could be that this development has already occurred by age 5, the earliest age sampled (as suggested by the Tzotzil study of de León, 1994). However, that seems unlikely, as the only developmental trend in the data is in the reverse direction: the increase of landmark specifications over successive age groups.
3. The production data of adults vary depending on the addressee. When adults talk to child Matchers, their data show a similar pattern of distribution of the different categories as that produced by the older children. When they talk to adult Matchers, their use of absolute specifications is halved, and their use of landmark specifications increases by threefold.
4. The explanation for the increase of landmark specifications is clear enough. Adults are attempting a level of precision that cannot be communicated by the abstract absolute system alone, which only divides directions into four 90-degree quadrants. To give more precise angles, local landmarks can be brought into play, so one can say in effect 'heading southward, toward Red Cliffs,' now precise to, say, 20 degrees of arc. Caring about precision and having the inventive means to produce it are what mark fully adult speech.

We turn now to consider how consistent these results are with a 'thinking for speaking' perspective. Clearly, speaking in terms of absolute coordinates rather than left–right ones does require at the very least a different conceptualization of a scene at the time of speaking. But from a developmental perspective, we would expect a gradual increase of mastery of the absolute system over the age-range we are examining—after all, such a system presupposes a complex geometry of the kind sketched in Figure 33.3. And the only half-way house would seem to be a landmark system. But we find no such development. This suggests that the acquisition of an appropriate 'thinking for speaking' in early to middle childhood is not the only thing going on in this domain.

On the other hand, there are some telling details that fit a 'thinking for speaking' perspective. A typical finding in that perspective is a special progression toward a dominant pattern in a language, where minor alternatives exist. For example, although English allows locutions of the kind *He entered the room on all fours*, speakers are likely to prefer *He crawled into the room*, because that fits the predominant tendency in English to encode manner in the verb and path in the preposition. Further, a typical Slobin finding is that children gradually acquire this preference, and for a while (usually around age 8) 'hypercorrect,' banning the available alternatives, before developing in their teens a more adult flexibility that permits the minor alternative encodings for special effects (Berman & Slobin, 1994). A glance at Figure 33.4 shows that some such patterns can be detected: Children indeed use a quarter more absolute specifications at ages 8 to 10 than at the other ages. And adults freely use landmark specifications where helpful to the task, reducing their absolute usage concomitantly—a pattern of flexibility that teenagers can be seen gradually acquiring.

The study described above, then, suggests that the early development of the absolute system is a mystery, but otherwise the 'thinking for speaking' perspective fits the data.

We turn now to see how the 'thinking for speaking' perspective fits the wider picture derived from other studies of absolute thinking and speaking. A first point concerns the time stability of the cognitive style involved in speaking a specific language. In the 'thinking for speaking' perspective this cognitive style is "evanescent," it's a frame of mind invoked just for speaking: you have to think in the categories of the language in order to voice your thoughts, but when you've stopped speaking, all bets are off—the Tenejapans, for example, might then go back to *thinking* in terms of left and right. In short, 'thinking for speaking' makes of the speaker only a fleeting Whorfian. But we have a wide range of data from other studies that show that Tenejapans think just like they speak, in absolute and intrinsic terms, even when not involved in language production (see Levinson, 1996, 2003, pp. 146–169). We think this is best explained in what could be called "bottle-neck Whorfianism": if your language provides no output for left/right thoughts, you'll have to remember spatial arrays in (say) north/south terms which do permit linguistic expression. Otherwise, when it comes time to speak, the thoughts will be in the wrong format, and one which cannot be post hoc converted into the right one for speaking (Levinson, 2003, pp. 57–58). So the non-verbal cognition data require a stronger version of the Slobin paradigm, a 'thinking for later possible speaking.' A developmental version of this would hold that the child gradually learns to think the right way, so that plain thinking comes over time to match 'thinking for speaking.'

A different set of studies addresses the issue of why we see so little development in the child's mastery of the absolute frame of reference. These suggest that there is something special about the domain of spatial coordinate systems, which is not to be found in other domains explored in the 'thinking for speaking' paradigm. The distinctions between the coding of manner and path in language, a domain where the 'thinking for speaking' paradigm works so well, are distinctions which would hardly arise in a non-linguistic species. But spatial thinking obviously has a rich phylogenetic history before language, and indeed there is a huge literature on the spatial cognition of different species, where spatial coordinate systems have played a prominent role. Thus it makes sense to come back to the questions raised at the outset: what is the prelinguistic Ur-state of spatial cognition in the human infant? Is she a relative thinker, an absolute thinker, both, or none of the above, a blank slate perhaps?

Recently, work in our research group has thrown some light on these questions about underlying cognitive initial states, which are obviously difficult to answer directly. The approach has been to examine our nearest primate relatives, as well as human infants and children, using the very same non-linguistic cognitive tasks. A first study (Haun, Call, Janzen, & Levinson, 2006) examined a different but related aspect of spatial thinking: whether we identify locations by object properties of the landmark or by the place where the target is. The study looked at all the members of our family, the Hominidae, that is, all the great apes including humans. All the apes, including 1-year-old human infants, remembered locations primarily in terms of the place where the target is rather than its object properties. This amounts to using a coordinate system—either absolute or relative—in preference to a topological system, mere propinquity to a featured landmark. But 3-year-old (German) children reversed this preference. Since language is one of the major new conceptual tools mastered between 1 and 3, we interpret this as showing a likely effect of language on spatial thinking: 3-year-olds have learned through language to attend to object properties of the target (this is what learning concrete nouns is largely about). In other words, being a linguistic species may make a difference to the underlying, phylogenetically inherited spatial cognition: it introduces new possible strategies.

But now we want to know, of that initial preference for a coordinate system, which kind—absolute or relative—is the preferred kind for non-linguistic members of our Hominidae family. A second study (Haun, Rapold, Call, Janzen, & Levinson, 2006) examined the issue of relative vs. absolute frames of reference directly. Again all the great apes were examined together with 4-year-old German children, using a relational task in which bait was shown being hidden under one of three cups, and then the subject was rotated and had to choose between another set of three cups to find the object. The results show that across the great apes there's a preference for absolute (or at least allocentric) spatial coding in this task. And the German 4-year-olds do the same. Using a slightly more complex variant of the task for older humans (five cups rather than three), we compared adults and children of around 8 years old in two cultures, one (= Akhoe Hai//om speakers of Namibia) where the spatial language preference is absolute, and one (Netherlands Dutch) where the language preference is relative. The results on this non-linguistic task show that by age 8 or over, the preference goes along with the language —we find cognitive diversity matching the linguistic diversity.

We interpret these results as showing that a blank-slate approach to human spatial cognition is clearly wrong. All the evidence points to a phylogenetic bias throughout our family Hominidae in favor of a preference for absolute, or at least allocentric, spatial coding. This is in startling contradiction to the long tradition, most strongly voiced by Kant, that has viewed our own Western left–right systems as conceptually foundational (see Levinson, 2003, pp. 9–14).

So now we have perhaps some insight into the lack of observed developmental trends in the Tenejapan data: the children do not have to slowly abstract out an absolute system from a more concrete landmark system, for they are able to build directly on the underlying primate default in favor of, plausibly, absolute coding. They still have to learn, of course, to instantiate the special Tzeltal form of this system, with its specific named directions, 90-degree quadrants, and so forth, which is why we see the telling features of 'thinking for speaking' predicted by Slobin (hypercorrection at age 8, growing flexibility in the teens). In contrast, Western children, by implication, have to override this primate default in favor of a system that emphasizes an egocentric, relative conceptualization of space. This suggests that left–right systems should be slower to acquire, and so indeed they seem to be. The acquisition of language apparently makes possible this cognitive flexibility to override or modify a default—in this case, we have not only 'thinking for speaking,' but 'speaking for thinking.'

REFERENCES

Berman, R., & Slobin, D. I. (1994). *Relating events in narrative: A crosslinguistic developmental study*. Hillsdale, NJ: Lawrence Erlbaum Associates.

Brown, P. (2001). Learning to talk about motion UP and DOWN in Tzeltal: Is there a language-specific bias for verb learning? In M. Bowerman & S.C. Levinson (Eds.), *Language acquisition and conceptual development* (pp. 512–543). Cambridge, UK: Cambridge University Press.

Brown, P. (2006). A sketch of the grammar of space in Tzeltal. In S.C. Levinson & D. Wilkins (Eds.), *Grammars of space* (pp. 230–272). Cambridge, UK: Cambridge University Press.

Brown, P., & Levinson, S. C. (1993). 'Uphill' and 'downhill' in Tzeltal. *Journal of Linguistic Anthropology*, 3(1), 46–74.

Brown, P., & Levinson, S. C. (2000). Frames of spatial reference and their acquisition in Tenejapan Tzeltal. In L. Nucci, G. Saxe, & E. Turiel (Eds.), *Culture, thought, and development* (pp. 167–197). Mahwah, NJ: Lawrence Erlbaum Associates.

Cablitz, G. H. (2001). *Marquesan: A grammar of space*. PhD. dissertation. Kiel: Christian-Albrechts-Universität.

Cablitz, G. H. (2002). The acquisition of an absolute system: Learning to talk about space in Marquesan (Oceanic, French Polynesia). In E. V. Clark (Ed.), *Papers of the 2002 Stanford Child Language Research Forum* (pp. 40–49). Stanford: CLSI.

Dasen, P. R., & Mishra, R. C. (2008). Spatial language and concept development: The theoretical background and overview. In N. Srinivasan, A. K. Gupta, & J. Pandey (Eds.), *Advances in cognitive science* (pp. 242–254).New Delhi: Sage.

Dasen, P. R., Mishra, R., Niraula, S., & Wassman, J. (2006). Développement du langage et de la cognition spatiale géocentrique. *Enfance, 58,* 146–158.

De León, L. (1994). Exploration in the acquisition of geocentric location by Tzotzil children. In J. Haviland & S. C. Levinson (Eds.), *Spatial conceptualization in Mayan languages*, special issue, *Linguistics* 32(4/5), 857–884.

Haun, D., Call, J., Janzen, G., & Levinson, S. C. (2006). Evolutionary psychology of spatial representations in the Hominidae. *Current Biology, 16,* 1736–1740.

Haun, D., Rapold, C. J., Call, J., Janzen, G., & Levinson, S. C. (2006). Cognitive cladistics and cultural override in Hominid spatial cognition. *Proceedings of the National Academy of Sciences of the USA, 103*(46), 17568–17573.

Levinson, S. C. (1994). Vision, shape, and linguistic description: Tzeltal body-part terminology and object description. *Linguistics, 32*(4/5), 791–855.

Levinson, S. C. (1996). Frames of reference and Molyneaux's question: Cross-linguistic evidence. In P. Bloom, M. Peterson, L. Nadel, & M. Garrett (Eds.), *Language and space* (pp. 109–169). Cambridge, MA: The MIT Press.

Levinson, S. C. (2003). *Space in language and cognition: Explorations in cognitive diversity*. Cambridge, UK: Cambridge University Press.

Levinson, S. C., & Brown, P. (1994). Immanual Kant among the Tenejapans: Anthropology as empirical philosophy. *Ethos, 22*(1), 3–41.

Levinson, S. C., Kita, S., Haun, D., & Rasch, B. (2002). Returning the tables: Language affects spatial reasoning. *Cognition, 84,* 155–188.

Levinson, S. C., & Wilkins, D. (2006). *Grammars of space*. Cambridge, UK: Cambridge University Press.

Li, P., & Gleitman, L. (2002). Turning the tables: Language and spatial reasoning. *Cognition, 83*(3), 265–294.

Majid, A., Bowerman, M., Kita, S., Haun, D., & Levinson, S. C. (2004). Can language restructure cognition? The case for space. *Trends in Cognitive Sciences, 8*(3), 108–114.

Mishra, R., & Dasen, P. R. (2005). Spatial language and cognitive development in India: An urban/rural comparison. In W. Friedlmeier, P. Chakkarath, & B. Schwartz (Eds.), *Culture and human development: The importance of cross-cultural research to the social sciences (in honour of Gisela Trommsdorff's 60th birthday)* (pp. 153–179). Hove, UK: Psychology Press.

Mishra, R. C., Dasen, P. R., & Niraula, S. (2003). Ecology, language, and performance on spatial cognitive tasks. *International Journal of Psychology, 38*(6), 366–383.

Mitchell-Kernan, C. (1972). *Signifying, loud-talking and marking*. Champaign IL: University of Illinois Press.

Niraula, S., Mishra, R. C., & Dasen, P. R. (2004). Linguistic relativity and spatial concept development in Nepal. *Psychology and Developing Societies, 16,* 99–124.

Piaget, J., & Inhelder, B. (1956). *The child's conception of space*. London: Routledge and Kegan Paul.

Slobin, D. I. (Ed.). (1967). *A field manual for cross-cultural study of the acquisition of communicative competence*. Berkeley: Language Behavior Research Laboratory.

Slobin, D. I. (1996). From 'thought and language' to 'thinking for speaking.' In J. J. Gumperz & S. C. Levinson (Eds.), *Rethinking linguistic relativity* (pp. 70–96). Cambridge, UK: Cambridge University Press.

Stross, B. (1969). *Language acquisition by Tenejapan Tzeltal children*. Unpublished PhD dissertation, University of California, Berkeley.

Wassman, J., & Dasen, P. R. (1998). Balinese spatial orientation: Some empirical evidence for moderate linguistic relativity. *Journal of the Royal Anthropological Institute, 4*(4), 689–711.

34

Why Some Spatial Semantic Categories Are Harder to Learn than Others
The Typological Prevalence Hypothesis[1]

DEDRE GENTNER
Northwestern University

MELISSA BOWERMAN
Max Planck Institute for Psycholinguistics

…to some extent, the language structures itself as it is learned.

Dan I. Slobin (2001, p. 441)

RECOLLECTIONS

For me (Dedre) Dan has been a protean figure. I first met him when I was a graduate student at the University of California, San Diego and he was a young professor at Berkeley. He was brilliant, charismatic, and compelling, yet at times engagingly shy. We stayed connected through a circle of friends centered in Nijmegen and the Bay Area, a group united by a passion for psychologically juicy theories of language acquisition and for crosslinguistic approaches—both signature positions of Dan's throughout his career. This has led to a many shared quests, and, ultimately, to deep bonds of friendship and respect.

Dan and I (Melissa) fledged in the same academic nest at Harvard and were influenced by many of the same mentors, prime among them Roger Brown, but also Bruner, Miller, and Lenneberg. But Dan was there just before me, and had already finished and gone to Berkeley the year I arrived. Although I met him when he came back for a visit, I did not really get acquainted until I participated in his course at the famous 1968 U. C. Berkeley summer school, "Language, Society, and the Child." I remember worrying about how to address him—could I presume to call him "Dan"? Now after years of friendship this makes me laugh, because Dan was then only 29 years old! But such was already his influence and natural authority. Down the years, Dan and I saw each other often—in Berkeley (conveniently, my home town), at the Max Planck Institute, and at conferences around the world. Language acquisition, of course, was often the focus of our discussions and sometimes heated

---

[1] We gratefully acknowledge the support of the Max Planck Institute for Psycholinguistic Research at Nijmegen, and of NSF SLC Grant SBE-0541957, the Spatial Intelligence and Learning Center (SILC).

arguments, but our conversations roamed increasingly over a wide range of other topics—travel, anthropology, philosophy, politics, art, family, and always music. Many is the evening that ended with Dan at the piano and me at the flute, struggling our way through a Bach sonata. For me Dan has been a cherished comrade through life—a fellow explorer of ideas and places, an invaluable sounding board, and a constant inspiration.

INTRODUCTION

The most fundamental issue in the study of first language acquisition is to distinguish between two sources of structure and determine how they interact: the capacities and predispositions learners bring to the task themselves on the one hand, and the contribution of the language being learned on the other. For several decades, Dan Slobin's research has brought clarity and insight to the way we pose these questions and how we attempt to answer them. In this chapter we take up the problem in a domain that Dan has returned to again and again—the expression of spatial relations.

Space has been a major focus of work by Slobin and others for many reasons. First and most important, it provides an excellent arena for crosslinguistic comparison. Space is fundamental to human cognition, and all languages provide ways to talk about spatial relations, but they do so in different ways. For example, what one language does with prepositions, another does with case endings or in the verb (Johnston & Slobin, 1979; Slobin, 1973). How do these formal differences affect the language learner? Another advantage of the spatial domain is that developmentalists can increasingly draw on detailed studies of the meanings of spatial forms, both in English (e.g., Herskovits, 1986; Regier, 1996) and across languages (e.g., Levinson & Wilkins, 2006). Still another advantage is that words for spatial relations, such as *up, down, in,* and *on,* are acquired early relative to other relational terms (e.g., Bloom, 1973; R. Brown, 1973). This means that we can glimpse possible interactions between language and cognition at a very early stage of development. Finally, there is a practical consideration: It is relatively straightforward to test learners' grasp of the meaning of spatial terms, since the referent situations—e.g., an apple *in* a bowl, a cookie *on* a plate—are concrete and can easily be exemplified (e.g., Bowerman & Pederson, 1992, in preparation; Coventry & Garrod, 2005; Feist, in press; Johnston & Slobin, 1979).

In his pioneering early work on the development of spatial language, Slobin stressed the critical role played by the cognitive maturation of spatial concepts that are assumed to be universal, such as "containment" and "support" (Slobin, 1973; Johnston & Slobin, 1979). This research showed that spatial forms are acquired in a relatively consistent order across languages, and that this order conforms well with the order in which spatial concepts emerge in nonlinguistic cognition (Piaget & Inhelder, 1956). Inspired later by Talmy's (1975, 1985) typological work, Slobin (1985) proposed that the meanings children associate with spatial prepositions and other closed-class morphemes are shaped not only by nonlinguistic cognitive development but also by predispositions concerning the possible meanings of grammatical morphemes. Drawing on child language data from a large number of languages, Slobin suggested that children come to language acquisition equipped with a "privileged set of grammaticizable notions"—meanings onto which grammatical morphemes are preferentially mapped.

Still later, Slobin rethought this claim fundamentally (Slobin, 1997, 2001). One stimulus to his reconsideration was evidence from new studies showing that it is not only the morphosyntax of spatial forms that differs across languages, but also their *meanings*, and that children become sensitive to language-specific meanings well before the age of 2 (e.g., Bowerman, 1996a, 1996b; Bowerman & Pederson, 1992; Choi & Bowerman, 1991; Choi, McDonough, Bowerman, & Mandler, 1999; Levinson & Meira, 2003). These findings undermined the idea that there is a uniform set of core spatial concepts that are privileged in human cognition and in language acquisition. A second influence was Slobin's increasing interest in grammaticalization, the process by which grammatical morphemes arise gradually over time from open-class lexical items. Research on this phenomenon had shown that there is no clear dichotomy between grammatical morphemes and full lexical items, but rather a cline (Hopper & Traugott, 1993). This finding made it less plausible that children begin with a stock of universal "grammaticizable notions."

In the end, Slobin concluded that the meanings of grammatical morphemes do not reflect cognitive predispositions after all, but are shaped by psycholinguistic processes at play in rapid discourse among fluent speakers, such as the phonological reduction of high-frequency forms with accompanying semantic bleaching and schematization. Retracting his claims for cognitive prestructuring, Slobin returned to a position he had advanced much earlier: "It [now once again] seems to me more reasonable to suppose that it is *language* that plays a role in drawing the child's attention to the possibility of dividing nouns on the basis of animacy; or verbs on the basis of duration, or determinacy, or validity; or pronouns on the basis of social status, and the like" (Slobin, 1966, p. 89, as quoted in Slobin, 2001, p. 443, emphasis added).

THE TYPOLOGICAL PREVALENCE HYPOTHESIS

We strongly agree with Slobin's proposal to grant an important role to linguistic experience in the child's formation of semantic categories (e.g., Bowerman & Choi, 2003; Gentner, 1982, 2003). At the same time, we would like to come to the defense of an earlier Dan! Now that the shaping role of the input language has been established, it is time to revisit the role of nonlinguistic cognition in the formation of linguistic categories.

In particular, despite children's evident sensitivity to the contours of the spatial semantic categories of their local language, there is nonlinguistic evidence that not all ways of classifying a particular domain are equally easy for them. In the classification of topological spatial relationships, for example, Casasola and colleagues found that infants show sensitivity to containment relations across a wide range of different objects by as early as 6 months (Casasola, Cohen, & Chiarello, 2003); but even as much as a year later they still do not show nonlinguistic sensitivity to an abstract relation of support (relevant for the English word *on*) or tight fit (between complementary shapes across both containment and support—relevant for the early-learned Korean verb *kkita*) (Casasola & Cohen, 2002; Casasola, Wilbourn, & Yang, 2006).[2] Clearly, cognitive factors outside the linguistic input are at work here, just as Slobin originally assumed: Some ways of carving up a spatial domain are easier—hence perhaps cognitively more "natural"—than others.

Proposals about conceptual naturalness often have a circular logic: Children learn X before Y because X is more natural, and we know that X is more natural because children learn it more easily. In this chapter, we want to break through this circularity by linking conceptual naturalness in language acquisition to the relative prevalence of particular categorization patterns across languages. In particular, we adopt the following working hypothesis:

> *The Typological Prevalence Hypothesis*: All else being equal, within a given domain, the more frequently a given way of categorizing is found in the languages of the world, the more natural it is for human cognizers, hence the easier it will be for children to learn.

---

[2] Hespos and Spelke (2004) present evidence that infants as young as 5 months show sensitivity to the tight-fit/loose-fit distinction in a non-linguistic habituation task. But in these studies, the habituation and test trials utilized highly similar events, all involving very similar hollow and solid cylinders. Thus the intended relation was perfectly aligned across exemplars, with few distracting surface differences—an ideal situation in which to form a generalization, albeit one that does not go far beyond the materials given. In contrast, studies that have instantiated the tight-fit category with a wider range of objects and events, more representative of the full range of situations covered by the linguistic terms English *on* (support) and Korean *kkita* (tight fit) (e.g., Casasola & Cohen, 2002), have shown much later acquisition. As Gentner and Christie (in press) discuss, the question of "when do children acquire a given category" is bounded on the one side by an ideal learning sequence and on the other by realistically variable circumstances.

Typological frequency is, admittedly, an imperfect index to cognitive naturalness, because—as Dan has often reminded us—the distribution of particular classification patterns reflects socio-political as well as cognitive factors (some language families have undergone expansion, causing their semantic patterns to become more widespread, while others have dwindled, such that their perhaps equally "natural" patterns are more poorly represented). Nonetheless, just as linguistic typologists have long assumed (e.g., Croft, 1990), the difference between patterns that are extremely frequent vs. extremely rare may provide significant clues to the nature of language. All else being equal, crosslinguistic agreement in semantic categorization suggests relative uniformity in the way people readily conceptualize the domain, while disagreement suggests that the domain is more open to alternative conceptualizations, and so more in need of language-specific learning.

The idea that crosslinguistic frequency might predict ease of acquisition is of course not new. Jakobson (1971) argued that phonological distinctions that are universal across languages, such as the distinction between a maximally closed stop and a maximally open vowel, are the earliest to be acquired by children. Pinker (1984) suggested that in formulating implicit hypotheses about the meanings of inflections, children would sample crosslinguistically frequent distinctions before crosslinguistically rare ones. But the appeal to typological frequency has so far been little explored in the acquisition of semantic systems.

Gentner (1982) proposed a specific form of this hypothesis, applying it to the contrast between concrete nouns and relational terms such as verbs. Noting that verb meanings are more variable crosslinguistically than concrete noun meanings, she suggested that this difference reflects the greater naturalness (and therefore, by hypothesis, the greater ease of acquisition) of noun meanings over the linguistically more variable verb meanings: "... a language is freer in its choice of a system of relational meanings [than in its choice of concrete noun meanings], and this in turn means that a child learning the language is less able to guess those meanings purely by knowledge of the world" (p. 328). A more general form of the hypothesis was suggested by Bowerman (1985, p. 1306): "... the relative accessibility for children of alternative schemes for partitioning meaning in a given conceptual domain [may be] correlated with the frequency with which these schemes are instantiated in the languages of the world ... . It is plausible that relative frequency is correlated with 'ease' or 'naturalness' for the human mind..."

There is some evidence supporting the idea that semantic classifications that are crosslinguistically frequent tend also to be particularly accessible to children. For example, E. Clark (1976) showed that, across languages, the most common basis for children's overextensions of object words is object shape, and that the particular shape categories learners favor—round and long-and-thin—correspond precisely to the categories most frequently encoded by numeral classifiers in classifier languages (e.g., Mandarin, Japanese) around the world. (Numeral classifiers are morphemes obligatorily used in quantifying, e.g., "five *long-thin-class* pencil" or "how many *round-class* ball are there?") This correspondence, proposed Clark, suggests that both language acquisition and numeral classifier semantics are influenced and constrained by the same cognitive biases, which can ultimately be traced to fundamental properties of the human perceptual system.

Another suggestive parallel between early acquisition and crosslinguistic patterning concerns ways of expressing causation. Bowerman (1978) found that children learning English sometimes substitute *make* for *let* and vice versa (e.g., "Make (=let) me watch TV," "Don't let (=make) me go to bed"). This indicates that children implicitly recognize an abstract similarity between active (*make*) causation and permissive (*let*) causation, which parallels the crosslinguistic finding that it is common for languages to have a single causative marker that encompasses both meanings (Comrie, 1981).

In this chapter, we will put the Typological Prevalence hypothesis to the test in the domain of static topological relations—the kinds of relations denoted by prepositions in English sentences such as *The pencil is on the desk* and *There's a fish in the bowl*. This domain lends itself to the test both because children learn such forms early and because there is evidence about how different languages categorize such relations.

THE CATEGORIZATION OF STATIC TOPOLOGICAL SPATIAL SITUATIONS ACROSS LANGUAGES

Our evidence about what is typologically common or rare comes from a study by Bowerman and Pederson (1992, in preparation; reported briefly in Bowerman & Choi, 2001). These authors have surveyed how over 50 languages from over 30 different language families categorize static topological spatial situations. Native speakers were shown a large number of pictures of one highlighted object in a spatial relation with another, and asked to describe where the highlighted object was; additional data were collected by interviewing consultants about actual objects. The scenes described included topological situations of containment, surface contact, encirclement, and related functional and causal notions, including support from various directions, attachment, adhesion, and hanging, as well as other spatial relations not relevant to this discussion.

Figure 34.1 shows a sample of the pictures used. Each example represents a class of "situation types": (a) "support from below" (e.g., cup on table, man on roof), (b) "clingy attachment" (e.g., bandaid on leg, raindrops on window), (c) "hanging against" (e.g., picture on wall, coat on banister), (d) "point-to-point attachment" (e.g., apple on branch, string on balloon), (e) "encirclement with contact" (e.g., ribbon on candle, ring on finger), and (f) "full containment" (e.g., apple in bowl, rabbit in cage). These situation types were identified on the basis of the implicit classification of the scenes imposed by the spatial forms used in descriptions by speakers within and across languages. (The forms include prepositions, postpositions, case endings, spatial nominals, and so on.) Within any one language, instances of a situation type were encoded relatively uniformly. Across languages, two different situation types were sometimes associated with different forms, and sometimes mapped onto the same form (see Figure 34.1).

The situation types identified by examining shared and distinct encoding within and across languages were found to form a continuum, ordered as in Figure 34.1. (The actual scale includes additional situation types not shown here: for example, "marks on a surface" (e.g., freckles on face,

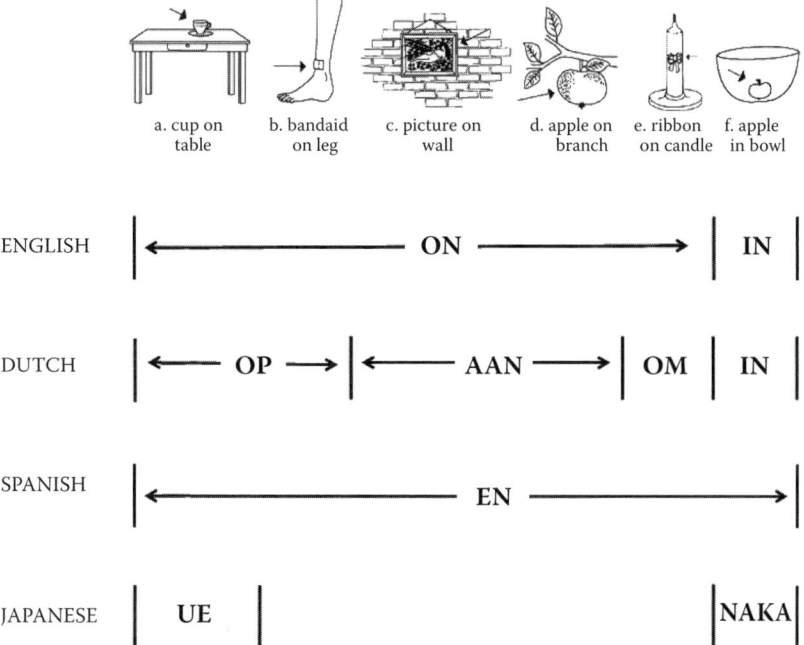

Figure 34.1 Samples from continuum of support and containment situations as lexicalized crosslinguistically (Bowerman & Pederson, 1992), with support from below on the left and containment or incorporation into another object on the right.

address on envelope), between (a) and (b); and "joined to a surface" (e.g., handle on pan or on cupboard door), between (c) and (d).) Languages vary in the number of distinctions they make along this continuum and in where one spatial word leaves off and the next begins, but if a word is used for more than one segment of the gradient, it covers *adjacent* segments, as illustrated in Figure 34.1. Thus, despite crosslinguistic variation in the semantic categorization of topological relations, there is strong crosslinguistic agreement on the extent to which different spatial scenes are underlyingly similar or different from each other.

Bowerman and Pederson found (1992; in preparation) that some ways of dividing up this continuum are very common crosslinguistically, while others are rare. In one widespread pattern, which occurs in languages genetically and geographically as diverse as English, Hungarian, Mandarin, and Mopan Mayan, the form used for support from below (far left) is extended far to the right along the gradient to a wide range of other situations involving contact and support. For example, the English preposition *on* is used for situations ranging from (a) to (e); only at (f) is another term, *in*, required. This categorization scheme makes a clear division between support and containment, with support construed very broadly.

Languages that lack an extended ON category[3] express clingy attachment, hanging, and other surface contact situations in the intermediate range of Figure 34.1 in various ways, some of which are shown in the figure: for example, they may provide a single form that covers the entire domain (e.g., the Spanish preposition, *en* 'in, on'); or—in a sort of mirror image of the English system—they may extend the form used most prototypically for containment relations leftward along the continuum to situations in which the figure, although not "contained" by the ground, is tightly attached to it or incorporated into its exterior (not shown; Tarafit Berber is such a language). Another fairly widespread pattern is to use special spatial terms only for prototypical 'on' and 'in-' relations, but not for adhesion, hanging, and other kinds of tenuous support. For example, Japanese uses an all-purpose locative marker *-ni* —which could be translated as 'at'—for many spatial situations, including (b)–(e); there are also two specific terms used together with *ni* that apply only to the canonical ON and IN situations— *ue* ('upper region, top, above') for the canonical support situation (a) and *naka* ('interior region') for the canonical containment situation (f).

Intriguingly, the most exotic pattern for the handling of ON relations (contact and support) was found in two languages closely related to English: Dutch and German. Like English, these languages use spatial prepositions for all the kinds of relations shown in Figure 34.1, but they make some unusual category splits. In the research reported in this chapter, we compare the acquisition of the typologically common English system with that of the typologically rare Dutch system.

THE DUTCH VS. ENGLISH SYSTEMS

Overall, the Dutch and English systems for expressing topological relationships are formally similar, and belong to the same typological pattern: both languages are "satellite-framed" (Talmy 1991), and have many forms that can function either as prepositions (*The papers are IN the drawer*) or as verb satellites (here, particles) (*Put the papers IN*). Yet the English strategy for partitioning the continuum shown in Figure 34.1 is common, whereas the Dutch strategy is rare, shared (although not exactly) in Bowerman and Pederson's sample only by the closely related language German.

Dutch and English agree in distinguishing IN relations (containment) from non-IN relations ((f) vs. (a)–(e) in Figure 34.1); in this they are in good company, since use of a special word for containment relations, as distinct from other kinds of relations, is crosslinguistically very common. But they

---

[3] We use capitals, as in "the ON category," to denote a range of scenes and situation types—in this case, the broadest extension of words for a contact and support situation in Bowerman and Pederson's sample (as suggested by examples (a) through (e) in Figure 34.1). In contrast, we use italics, as in "the *on* category," to denote the semantic category associated with a specific word in a specific language. This allows us to discuss differences in the way English and Dutch divide up the extensional range of the ON category.

differ in their partitioning of ON relations (the arena of contact and support), as shown in Figure 34.1. In Dutch, one preposition (*op*) is used for canonical support-from-below relationships like (a) and for adhesion relations like (b); another preposition (*aan*) is needed for situations of hanging and attachment (c)–(d), and still another preposition (*om*) for situations of encirclement with contact (e) (as well as encirclement more generally).

The *op-aan* distinction seems to reflect implicit force dynamics in how the figure (the located object) is related to the ground (the reference object) (Bowerman, 1996b; van Staden, Bowerman, & Verhelst, 2006). *Op* is used when the figure is viewed as stably in position—not in any salient way acted on by an underlying force that tends to separate it from the ground. Let us call this "solid support." *Aan*, in contrast, is used when the figure maintains its position (i.e., resists separation from the ground through forces like gravity or pulling in any direction) by virtue of being attached by one or more fixed points (typically hanging or projecting); this we will call "tenuous support." As for encirclement, the Dutch preposition *om* has a translation equivalent in English *around*; but when there is contact and support as well as encirclement, especially for smallish objects, contact typically overrides support for speakers of English, who routinely use *on*, e.g., for a ring on a finger, a stacking ring on a pole (child's toy), a diaper on a baby, and a ribbon on a candle. In Dutch, however, encirclement routinely takes precedence over contact: a ring is typically said to be *om* 'around' a finger or a pole, a diaper is *om* a baby, and a ribbon is *om* a candle.

PREDICTING THE ACQUISITION OF SPATIAL SEMANTIC CATEGORIES

We are now in a position to draw predictions for patterns of acquisition. Recall that, according to the Typological Prevalence hypothesis, semantic categories that are crosslinguistically common reflect a way of partitioning a domain that is conceptually relatively "natural" for human cognizers. These categories should be learned quickly and relatively error-free; i.e., a word for such a category should be extended rapidly and correctly across varied instances of the category. Semantic categories that are crosslinguistically rare, by hypothesis, reflect more marked, less accessible ways of classifying. They should be learned with more difficulty and give rise to more errors (substitutions of other forms for the conventional forms), and these errors may well reflect crosslinguistically more common ways of partitioning the domain (Bowerman, 1993).

We tested the Typological Prevalence hypothesis by investigating the development of topological spatial prepositions in first-language learners of Dutch and English (henceforth, for ease of reference, simply "Dutch [or English] children"). If there is no role for cognitive naturalness, and it is exposure to language alone that determines children's semantic categories, then both sets of children should learn their respective systems equally early. But if conceptual naturalness is related to crosslinguistic prevalence, as we propose, then Dutch children should take longer than English children to learn their ON system because the Dutch pattern is rare and the English pattern is common. More specific predictions are these:

1. English children should show proficiency with their term (*on*) for a range of situations of contact and support (ON situations) before Dutch children show proficiency with their three terms (*op*, *om*, and *aan*) that partition the ON category.
2. Dutch and English children should be equally early to show proficiency with *in* 'in' (Dutch) and *in* (English) for instances of containment (IN situations), since this category is similar in Dutch and English. Further, this category should be mastered relatively early, since it is crosslinguistically common.
3. Within Dutch, the *op* category should be acquired earlier than the *aan* and *om* categories. This is because the *op* category, by hypothesis, is relatively "natural," since it saliently includes "support from below," which is canonical for support, as well as certain other "solid support" situations that many languages encode with the same morpheme. In contrast, the *aan* category (tenuous support: figure tending to separate from ground unless held back)

is crosslinguistically extremely rare as a category distinct from other contact-and-support relations. As for *om*, although a term to describe encirclement situations (AROUND) is fairly common crosslinguistically, the Dutch pattern of routinely applying an AROUND term to situations involving contact and support as well as encirclement is rare in Bowerman and Pederson's sample.

4. The advantage of English over Dutch should be greatest for categories that are least common in the world's languages. Thus, learners of English and Dutch should perform equally well in correctly describing situations involving "solid support" (*op* in Dutch). The advantage predicted in (1) for English children will appear mainly among items involving "tenuous support" and encirclement with contact. This is because, as noted above, almost every language has a term prototypically applied to support from below and often other "solid support" scenes such as "clingy attachment," whereas very few languages have a special term for "tenuous support" (Dutch *aan*), and few languages routinely describe small-scale encirclement involving contact and support with an AROUND-type word (Dutch *om*).

5. Because the English-style ON category is, by hypothesis, a cognitively natural grouping, the errors made by Dutch children in encoding such relations should not be random, but should tend to involve substitutions within the larger ON category (e.g., *op* for situations where adults would say *aan* or *om*).

TESTING THE TYPOLOGICAL PREVALENCE HYPOTHESIS

To test these predictions, we carried out an elicited production task with native speakers of Dutch and English. In each language there were ten children in each of five age groups: 2-, 3-, 4-, 5-, and 6-year-olds, as well as a group of 10 adults. To ensure that the children understood the topological situations with which we presented them, we used objects rather than pictures. Most of the trials involved a large dollhouse with its furnishings and doll occupants, together with some larger toys and familiar household objects. Children were shown configurations of objects and asked to state the location of a specified object, e.g., *Where is the mirror?* We used a practice task to show children that we wanted them to respond with a specific location, such as *on the wall* (*aan de muur*), rather than by simply pointing and saying *There*.

There were 32 key stimulus configurations, shown in Table 34.1: eight exemplars for each of the four Dutch prepositions: *op, aan, om,* and *in*. The 24 items in the first three of these sets—let's call them OP, AAN, and OM items—can be routinely described by *on* in English (although English speakers can also choose to say *around* for the OM items). But we keep these sets distinct for analysis, since our predictions differentiate among them for both Dutch and English learners. We also included eight filler items requiring prepositions such as *behind* (*achter*) and *under* (*onder*), to provide variety and

TABLE 34.1 Stimulus Configurations, Arranged by Lexical Category in Dutch/English

op/on	aan/on	om/on	in/in
cookie on plate	mirror on wall	necklace on neck	cookie in bowl
toy dog on book	purse on hook	rubber band on can	candle in bottle
bandaid on leg	clothes on line	bandana on head	marble in water
raindrops on window	lamp on ceiling	hoop around doll	stick in straw
sticker on cupboard	handle on pan	ring on pencil	apple in ring
lid on jar	string on balloon	tube on stick	flower in book
top on tube	knob on door	wrapper on gum	toy cup in tube
freckles on face	button on jacket	ribbon on candle	hole in towel

discourage development of a particular response set. Thus, each child received 40 stimuli, as well as 4 practice items.[4]

After the warm-up and practice phase, the test items were presented. Children were encouraged to handle and describe the items. Then the experimenter named the figure and ground objects and asked the child to tell the location of the figure: e.g., *Look! See the mirror?*; *What's this? This is the wall*; *Now, where is the mirror?* If the child reacted by simply pointing or saying *Here/There* we repeated the question, and if the child still failed to produce a prepositional phrase, we offered a sentence frame for the child to complete: e.g., *The mirror is…* If the child still failed to provide a prepositional phrase, we recorded the response and introduced a filler item (with an irrelevant preposition) to recalibrate the child. Testing was identical for both Dutch and English children, and the instructions and questions were direct translations for the most part: e.g., *Where is the mirror?* (English) and *Waar is de spiegel?* (Dutch).[5] Children found the task very engaging.

The results are consistent with the Typological Prevalence hypothesis. Figure 34.2a shows the proportions of children and adults who used the target prepositions for each of the four sets of items tested for Dutch, and Figure 34.2b shows these proportions for English. Consistent with Prediction (1), Dutch children are slower to acquire their *op-aan-om* system of support relations than their English counterparts are to acquire their single term *on*. That is, Dutch children are less able than English children to encode these situations in the same way that adult speakers of their language do. An analysis of variance over both languages and all four sets of spatial relations (OP, AAN, OM, and IN) showed a significant effect of language $F(1, 90) = 15.24$, $p < .0001$, reflecting greater use of the target prepositions among English than Dutch children. (For this analysis we omitted the two *aan* items that showed inconsistent responding among adult Dutch speakers [see Footnote 4], leaving 30 items shown in Table 34.1.) For example, English-speaking 3- to 4-year-olds produced target prepositions 77% of the time overall, as compared to 43% among the Dutch-speaking children.

Prediction (2) was also borne out: the two language groups did not differ in their proficiency with the IN category, and the category was acquired early by both groups. Even 2-year-olds encoded the 8 IN items correctly 67% of the time in both languages (*in* for English and *in* 'in' for Dutch); among 4- to 6-year-olds, the rate was up to 98% for Dutch and 88% for English.

Prediction (3) is that within Dutch, *op* should be learned and applied correctly earlier than either *aan* or *om*. Consistent with this prediction, Dutch children were 73% on target for the OP items, as opposed to 44% for the AAN items and 55% for the OM items, as shown in Figure 34.2a. This difference appears even more strongly in the youngest group: Dutch 2- to 3-year-olds performed much better on the OP items ($M = .64$) than on either the AAN items ($M = .20$), $t(19) = 4.86$, $p < .001$ or the OM items ($M = .31$), $t(19) = 7.12$, $p < .001$. We did not find a significant difference between the AAN and OM items, although there is a nonsignificant advantage for OM at every age. As can be seen in Figure 34.2b, even in English, where the OP, AAN, and OM items all have the same label (*on*), there is a (nonsignificant) advantage for the OP items in the younger children—a hint that even in English there could be an advantage for the canonical "solid support" items.

Prediction (4) is that English- and Dutch-speaking children should perform similarly on the OP items, with the English advantage appearing mainly in the rare AAN and OM subclasses. This prediction was also borne out. The two groups do not differ on the OP items: both English and Dutch children produced the appropriate term (*on* or *op*, respectively) at a high rate ($M = .66$ for English

---

[4] Two of the eight supposed *aan* items (button on coat, knob on cupboard) were removed from the analysis after we discovered that some Dutch adults used *op* (as well as *aan*) for these items. Because our hypothesis predicts that Dutch children will be slower to learn how to encode AAN situations than OP situations, we had to be sure that the AAN situations we presented to children were consistently encoded with the word *aan* by Dutch adults.

[5] In colloquial Dutch, questions and statements about location are often formed with posture verbs like *staan* 'stand,' *zitten* 'sit,' *liggen* 'lie,' or *hangen* 'hang' (van Staden, Bowerman, & Verhelst, 2006). But because some of these verbs typically collocate with particular prepositions—e.g., *hangen* with *aan*, *staan* with *op*—we used the neutral copula form to avoid predisposing the choice of preposition. The fact that Dutch children were highly correct on both *in* and *op* (both of which would normally take posture verbs) suggests that these children understood the instructional format.

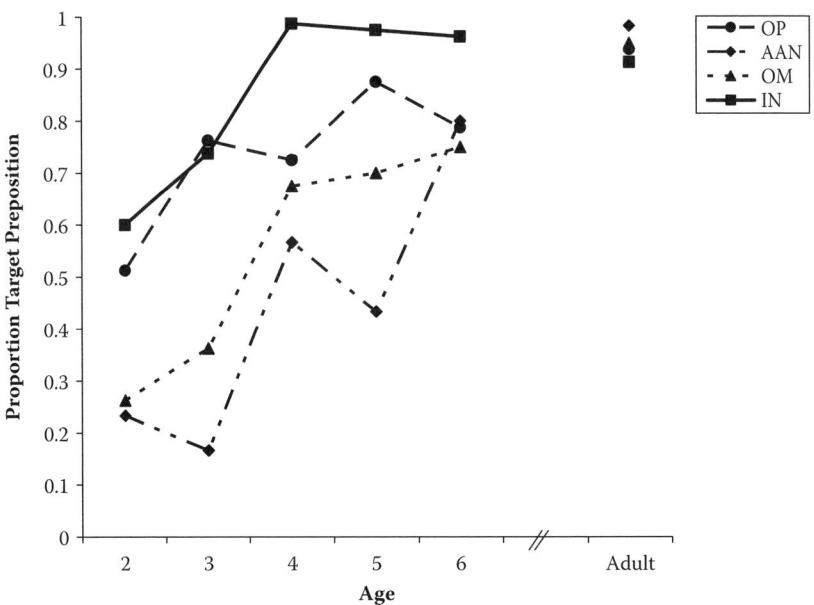
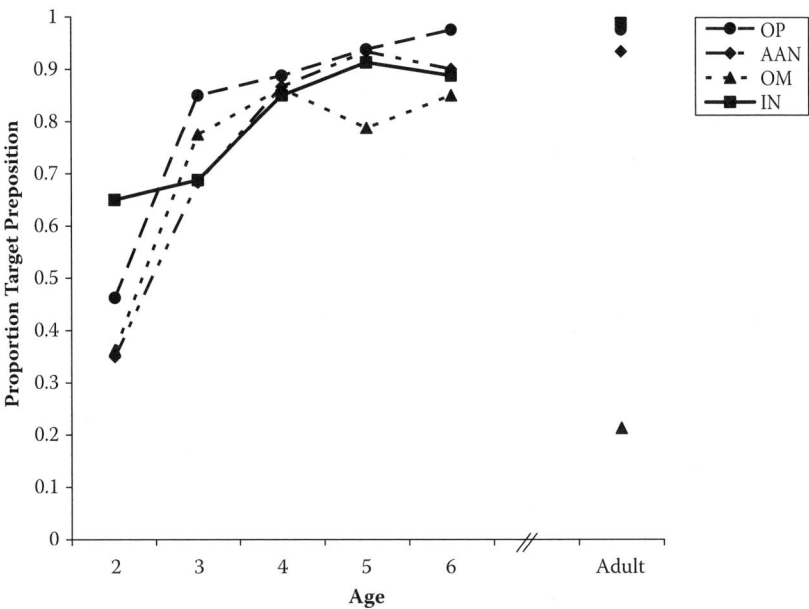

Figure 34.2 Proportion target prepositions (correct responses) across age for (a) Dutch and (b) English.

TABLE 34.2 Proportion of *op*, *om* and *aan* Responses (Including Errors) Among Dutch Children

Children's Response	Correct Response		
	Op	*Aan*	*Om*
No Preposition	.12	.23	.18
Op	**.73**	.23	.15
Aan	.04	**.42**	.07
Om	.02	.03	**.55**

Note: Bold type indicates correct use of target preposition.

and .64 for Dutch). In contrast, 2- to 3-year-old English children were more likely than their Dutch counterparts to produce their target preposition for both the AAN items ("tenuous attachment") and the OM items[6] (encirclement with contact). (For AAN items, $M = .52$ in English and .20 in Dutch; $t(38) = -3.31$, $p < .01$, two-tailed; for OM items, $M = .57$ in English and .31 in Dutch, $t(38) = -2.47$, $p < .05$, two-tailed.)

Prediction (5) is that when Dutch children make errors, they will often choose another preposition within the ON category (contact and support)—most probably *op*, the term for situations of "solid support." The detailed results, shown in Table 34.2, bear out this prediction. Although the target response dominates in each category, *op* responses (i.e., overextensions of *op*) occur for 23% of the AAN items and 15% of the OM items. *Aan* and *om* were rarely overextended to items in the other categories.

GENERAL DISCUSSION

Summary

Our aim in this study was to predict which semantic categories children find easy or hard to learn in the domain of spatial relations. It is clear that neither of the simple positions—cognition-first or language-first—will do. Past research has demonstrated that cognitive predispositions cannot be the whole story, since children learn language-specific spatial semantic categories even before age 2 (e.g., Bowerman & Choi, 2001; Casasola, 2005; Hespos & Spelke, 2004). Yet, just as Slobin's (1985) research suggested, children are indeed more predisposed toward some ways of categorizing space than others. As a way of gaining purchase on children's predispositions, we have proposed the Typological Prevalence hypothesis, according to which the frequency with which distinctions and categories are found across the world's languages provides a clue to conceptual "naturalness," with highly frequent category systems being cognitively more accessible, hence easier to learn, than rare ones.

Dutch and English spatial terms present an excellent testing ground for this hypothesis. The two languages share many typological and semantic properties, and their speakers are culturally similar as well, reducing the likelihood of variation due to nonlinguistic cultural differences. But the two languages differ markedly in an important respect. According to Bowerman and Pederson's (1992, in preparation) analysis (see also Feist, 2000) of how languages of the world partition the ON-IN continuum, it is very common for otherwise dissimilar languages to have a large ON category,

---

[6] One unexpected finding is that English adults produced very few *on* responses (21%) for the OM items; they frequently chose the term *around* instead (e.g., "The ribbon is around the candle"). English children did not manifest this tendency; for example, 5- and 6-year-old English children produced 79% and 85% *on* responses for the OM items. We suspect that the adults' *around* responding was inflated by a tendency (implicit or explicit) to seek contrast in their responses; that is, they preferred to say *around* for encirclement because *on* was the natural response for the other 16 ON items. Indeed, when we presented a new group of English-speaking adults with only one of our encirclement (*om*) situations, and asked "Where is the X?," the great majority used the term *on* rather than *around*.

comparable to the category associated with English *on*. Much rarer, in contrast, is the Dutch-style division of ON relations (contact and support) into three smaller categories—"solid support" (e.g., support from beneath: *op*), "tenuous support" (e.g., hanging, joining by screws: *aan*), and encirclement with contact (*om*). Thus, the Typological Prevalence hypothesis predicts that the English ON system will be easier for children to acquire than the Dutch ON system. Conveniently, both languages share a highly common IN category (containment: *in* in English and *in* 'in' in Dutch), and learners of both languages are predicted to show rapid and comparable learning of this category.

When we tested Dutch and English children in an elicited production task, we found strong support for the Typological Prevalence hypothesis:

1. English learners acquired their single term (*on*) for the ON category much earlier than Dutch learners acquired their three terms (*op, om,* and *aan*).
2. Both Dutch and English children acquired the IN category early and at about the same time, also consistent with the hypothesis. The lack of language differences in the IN category helps dispel the possible concern that the differences seen in the two ON systems might reflect a mismatch between the two populations in their overall level of language development.
3. Within Dutch, the crosslinguistically rare categories associated with the prepositions *aan* ("tenuous support") and *om* (encirclement with contact) are acquired much later than the crosslinguistically more common category associated with *op* ("solid support").
4. The advantage of English over Dutch was greatest for items in semantic subclasses that are rarely singled out for distinctive labeling in the world's languages—the categories associated with *aan* and *om* in Dutch.
5. When Dutch children made errors in encoding ON relations, they limited their choices to other prepositions of contact and support, especially tending to overextend *op* to situations that adults would describe with *aan* or *om*. This is a rather strong indication of the naturalness of the extended ON category, because if the Dutch children were simply using high-frequency spatial prepositions when they were uncertain, they would have shown a broader set of substitution errors, including use of the early-learned and highly frequent preposition *in*.

In sum, the Typological Prevalence hypothesis successfully predicted the performance of the two language groups, not only globally but also in fine detail. These results suggest that some ways of classifying a particular domain are indeed more natural for children than others, and specifically, that the inherent difficulty of a category can be predicted on the basis of typological data.

Alternative Explanations

Before embracing the Typological Prevalence hypothesis, however, let us consider some possible alternative explanations for our findings.

Category size. First, could the English advantage result from differences in the size of the categories to be learned, rather than their semantic makeup? Perhaps it is easier to learn a single highly general category like that of English *on* rather than several more specific subcategories like those of Dutch *op, aan,* and *om*. But there is abundant evidence that in semantic learning, the path of development by no means always goes from general to specific; in fact, it often goes from specific (more bound to particular contexts and referents) to general.

For example, children initially often underextend words, e.g., using *up* only when asking to be picked up in someone's arms rather than for a full range of "motion upward" (Gentner, 1982). Further, learning several small categories can be no more difficult than learning a single more encompassing category. For example, during the same time frame that English-speaking children learn a single verb for putting on clothing (*put on*), Korean-speaking children learn three different verbs that obligatorily distinguish putting clothing onto the head vs. trunk/legs vs. feet (Choi & Bowerman, 1991). Similarly, while learners of English are acquiring the verb *eat*, learners of Tzeltal Maya are learning and using appropriately a small set of verbs that obligatorily distinguish eating events according to what is consumed, e.g., tortillas or other grain-based items vs. bananas and other soft things vs. meat (P. Brown, 2001). (See Bowerman, 2005, for a recent overview of the role of category size in crosslinguistic perspective; and see also Fulkerson & Haaf, 2006, for experimental evidence that, in the domain of novel objects, 12-month-old children can learn narrow categories with the help of linguistic labeling more easily than broader categories that subsume them.) There is no reason, then, to assume that learning a single large ON category is necessarily easier than learning three smaller categories.

Word frequency is another factor that could affect acquisition rate. Perhaps the overall English advantage stems simply from the fact that *on* is more frequent in adult English than is any of the three prepositions applied to the more finely broken-down ON relations in Dutch. Similarly, perhaps the advantage within Dutch for *op* over *aan* and *om* results from its (possibly) greater frequency. We think this explanation is unlikely, in light of R. Brown's (1973) landmark study of the acquisition of the 14 grammatical morphemes acquired earliest in English (among them, the prepositions *in* and *on*). His analysis of the recorded utterances of three children (Adam, Eve, and Sarah) showed a highly stable order of acquisition, which was not correlated with the frequency of these morphemes in parental speech to the children. Brown concluded that at the extremely high levels of frequency associated with grammatical morphemes, frequency is not a determining factor in the order of acquisition.

Finally, perhaps differences in the ease of acquiring English *on* vs. the Dutch *op-aan-om* system could be due to differential polysemy: i.e., perhaps the Dutch prepositions have more different senses than *on* does. Although it seems plausible that words with multiple senses are more difficult to learn (because the word-to-world mapping is more variable), the English word *on* seems to be at least as polysemous as Dutch *aan* and *om*. For example, *on* is used not only for spatial relations but also in phrases like *turn on the light* and *turn on the water*—uses acquired very early by English-speaking children. And within Dutch, there are at least as many high-frequency alternative senses for *op* as for *aan* and *om* (e.g., *eet X op* 'eat X up,' *(X is) op* '(X is) all gone,' *let op* 'watch out'), yet spatial *op* is acquired earlier than spatial *aan* and *om*. So it seems unlikely that polysemy explains the lag in Dutch acquisition relative to English.

These alternative explanations, then, fail to convincingly explain the pattern of results in our study as well as the Typological Prevalence hypothesis does. Of course, the crosslinguistic prevalence of certain category systems will not always be a good guide to ease of learning, since as Slobin (1997, 2001) has pointed out there can be other reasons for prevalence besides cognitive naturalness, such as political hegemony and communicative utility.

Conclusions

The Typological Prevalence hypothesis aims to link crosslinguistic patterns with developmental patterns in acquisition, as Slobin has done so fruitfully throughout his career. It generates several detailed predictions, all of which appear to hold for the acquisition of the Dutch and English prepositions that encode ON and IN types of relationships. In a sense, this hypothesis occupies a kind of middle ground between two positions Slobin has delineated in his path-breaking career. At one extreme is the view that children come pre-equipped with linguistically relevant categories, which they then map onto their specific language (Slobin, 1973, 1985). At the other extreme is the view that children learn the semantic categories associated with spatial and other grammatical morphemes strictly from the input language itself (Slobin, 1997, 2001). Neither of these positions can explain the evidence.

Spatial categories are clearly not all equipotent in acquisition. For example, when infants are given an equally intensive learning experience, they acquire the concept of containment more readily than the concept of support (e.g., Casasola & Cohen, 2002), and young children find it easier to learn an allocentric frame of reference than an egocentric frame (Haun, Rapold, Call, Janzen, & Levinson, 2006). But learners of English vs. Korean acquire strikingly different, and at a number of points crosscutting, systems of spatial semantics in a comparable time frame (Bowerman & Choi, 2001; Choi & Bowerman, 1991), and this argues against the strong view that there is a prelinguistic set of spatial categories that are simply mapped directly onto language.

Both the "concepts first" and the "language first" positions ignore the learning process. We suggest recasting the question, asking not "which (if any) spatial categories exist pre-linguistically?" but "which semantic categories of space does a child most readily learn with the help of her language?". Suppose that hearing a common label for two situations prompts children to compare them (Bowerman & Choi, 2003; Gentner & Namy, 1999, 2006). When the experiential commonalities are obvious to the child, this alignment process will lead rapidly to the relevant abstraction. But when the shared structure is not obvious, as may be the case for typologically rare categories, then learning the category will take longer; the child will have to hear more situations labeled by the joint term before she discovers it.

In sum, these findings offer support for the Typological Prevalence hypothesis. Semantic categories whose members share cognitive and perceptual commonalities that are salient for humans—as signaled by their crosslinguistic frequency—can be acquired with little or no prompting from the input language, while those that are less natural—as indexed by their crosslinguistic rarity—will require more language experience to be learned. Clearly, then, learners come equipped with *both* pre-existing cognitive biases for semantic organization *and* a phenomenal ability to learn semantic categories from the linguistic input. It has been one of Dan Slobin's signal contributions that he has constantly kept his eye on the crucial importance of *both* of these two often seemingly conflicting determinants of language acquisition, thereby forcing attention to the knotty problem of how to reconcile them.

REFERENCES

Bloom, L. (1973). *One word at a time*. The Hague: Mouton.
Bowerman, M. (1978). Systematizing semantic knowledge: Changes over time in the child's organization of word meaning. *Child Development, 49*, 977–987.
Bowerman, M. (1985). What shapes children's grammars? In D. I. Slobin (Ed.), *The crosslinguistic study of language acquisition: Vol. 2. Theoretical issues* (pp. 1257–1319). Hillsdale, NJ: Lawrence Erlbaum Associates.
Bowerman, M. (1993). Typological perspectives on language acquisition: Do crosslinguistic patterns predict development? In E. V. Clark (Ed.), *The proceedings of the twenty-fifth annual Child Language Research Forum* (pp. 7–15). Stanford: Center for the Study of Language and Information.
Bowerman, M. (1996a). Learning how to structure space for language: A crosslinguistic perspective. In Bloom, P., Peterson, M. A., Nadel, L., & Garrett, M. F. (Eds.), *Language and space* (pp. 385–436). Cambridge, MA: The MIT Press.
Bowerman, M. (1996b). The origins of children's spatial semantic categories: Cognitive versus linguistic determinants. In J. Gumperz & S. C. Levinson (Eds.), *Rethinking linguistic relativity* (pp. 144–176). Cambridge, UK: Cambridge University Press.
Bowerman, M. (2005). Why can't you "open" a nut or "break" a cooked noodle? Learning covert object categories in action word meanings. In L. Gershkoff-Stowe & D. H. Rakison (Eds.), *Building object categories in developmental time* (pp. 209–243). Mahwah, NJ: Lawrence Erlbaum Associates.
Bowerman, M., & Choi, S. (2001). Shaping meanings for language: Universal and language-specific in the acquisition of spatial semantic categories. In M. Bowerman & S. C. Levinson (Eds.), *Language acquisition and conceptual development* (pp. 475–511). Cambridge, UK: Cambridge University Press.
Bowerman, M., & Choi, S. (2003). Space under construction: Language-specific spatial categorization in first language acquisition. In D. Gentner & S. Goldin-Meadow (Eds.), *Language in mind: Advances in the study of language and cognition* (pp. 387–428). Cambridge, MA: The MIT Press.
Bowerman, M., & Pederson, E. (1992, November). Crosslinguistic perspectives on topological spatial relationships. Paper presented at the 87th annual meeting of the American Anthropological Association, San Francisco, CA.
Bowerman, M., & Pederson, E. (in preparation). INwards from ON and ONwards from IN: The crosslinguistic categorization of topological spatial relationships.

Brown, R. (1973). *A first language: The early stages.* Cambridge, MA: Harvard University Press.
Brown, P. (2001). Learning to talk about motion UP and DOWN in Tzeltal: Is there a language-specific bias for verb learning? In M. Bowerman & S. C. Levinson (Eds.), *Language acquisition and conceptual development* (pp. 512–543). Cambridge, UK: Cambridge University Press.
Casasola, M. (2005). Can language do the driving? The effect of linguistic input on infants' categorization of support spatial relations. *Developmental Psychology, 41,* 183–192.
Casasola, M., & Cohen, L. B. (2002). Infant categorization of containment, support and tight-fit spatial relationships. *Developmental Science, 5,* 247–264.
Casasola, M., Cohen, L. B., & Chiarello, E. (2003). Six-month-old infants' categorization of containment spatial relations. *Child Development, 74,* 679–693.
Casasola, M., Wilbourn, M., & Yang, Y. (2006). Can English-learning toddlers acquire and generalize a novel spatial word? *First Language, 26,* 186–205.
Choi, S., & Bowerman, M. (1991). Learning to express motion events in English and Korean: The influence of language-specific lexicalization patterns. *Cognition, 41,* 83–121.
Choi, S., McDonough, L., Bowerman, M., & Mandler, J. (1999). Early sensitivity to language-specific spatial categories in English and Korean. *Cognitive Development, 14,* 241–268.
Clark, E. V. (1976). Universal categories: On the semantics of classifiers and children's early word meanings. In A. Juilland (Ed.), *Linguistic studies offered to Joseph Greenberg on the occasion of his sixtieth birthday* (Vol. 3, pp. 449–462) *Syntax.* Saratoga, CA: Anna Libri.
Comrie, B. (1981). *Language universals and linguistic typology: Syntax and morphology.* Oxford, UK: Basil Blackwell.
Coventry, K. R., & Garrod, S. C. (2005). Spatial prepositions and the functional geometric framework. Towards a classification of extra-geometric influences. In L. A. Carlson & E. van der Zee (Eds.), *Functional features in language and space: Insights from perception, categorization and development* (pp. 149–162). Oxford, UK: Oxford University Press.
Croft, W. A. (1990). *Typology and universals.* Cambridge, UK: Cambridge University Press.
Feist, M. I. (in press). Space between languages. *Cognitive Science.*
Fulkerson, A. L., & Haaf, R. A. (2006). Does object naming aid 12-month-olds' formation of novel object categories? *First Language, 26,* 347–361.
Gentner, D. (1982). Why nouns are learned before verbs: Linguistic relativity versus natural partitioning. In S. Kuczaj (Ed.), *Language development: Vol. 2. Language, thought and culture* (pp. 301–334). Hillsdale, NJ: Lawrence Erlbaum Associates.
Gentner, D. (2003). Why we're so smart. In D. Gentner & S. Goldin-Meadow (Eds.), *Language in mind: Advances in the study of language and thought* (pp. 195–235). Cambridge, MA: The MIT Press.
Gentner, D., & Christie, S. (in press). Language and cognition in development. To appear in M. M. Spivey, K. McRae, & M. Joanisse (Eds.), *The Cambridge handbook of psycholinguistics.* New York: Cambridge University Press.
Gentner, D., & Namy, L. L. (1999). Comparison in the development of categories. *Cognitive Development, 14,* 487–513.
Gentner, D., & Namy, L. L. (2006). Analogical processes in language learning. *Current Directions in Psychological Science, 15,* 297–301.
Haun, D. B. M., Rapold, C., Call, J., Janzen, G., & Levinson, S. C. (2006). Cognitive cladistics and cultural override in Hominid spatial cognition. *Proceedings of the National Academy of Sciences, 130,* 17568–17573.
Herskovits, A. (1986). *Language and spatial cognition: An interdisciplinary study of the prepositions in English.* Cambridge, UK: Cambridge University Press.
Hespos, S., & Spelke, E. (2004). Conceptual precursors to language. *Nature, 430,* 453–455.
Hopper, P. J., & Traugott, E. C. (1993). *Grammaticalization.* Cambridge, UK: Cambridge University Press.
Jakobson, R. (1971). *Studies on child language and aphasia.* The Hague: Mouton.
Johnston, J. R., & Slobin, D. I. (1979). The development of locative expressions in English, Italian, Serbo-Croatian and Turkish. *Journal of Child Language 6,* 529–545.
Levinson, S., & Meira, S. (2003). 'Natural concepts' in the spatial topological domain — Adpositional meanings in crosslinguistic perspective: An exercise in semantic typology. *Language, 79,* 485–516.
Levinson, S. C., & Wilkins, D. (Eds.). (2006). *Grammars of space: Explorations in cognitive diversity.* Cambridge, UK: Cambridge University Press.
Piaget, J., & Inhelder, B. (1956). *The child's conception of space.* London: Routledge & Kegan Paul.
Pinker, S. (1984). *Language learnability and language development.* Cambridge, MA: Harvard University Press.

Regier, T. (1996). *The human semantic potential: Spatial language and constrained connectionism*. Cambridge, MA: The MIT Press.

Slobin, D. I. (1966). Comments on "developmental psycholinguistics": A discussion of McNeill's presentation. In F. Smith & G. A. Miller (Eds.), *The genesis of language: A psycholinguistic approach* (pp. 85–91). Cambridge, MA: The MIT Press.

Slobin, D. I. (1973). Cognitive prerequisites for the development of grammar. In C. A. Ferguson & D. I. Slobin (Eds.), *Studies of child language development* (pp. 175–208). New York: Holt, Rinehart & Winston.

Slobin, D. I. (1985). Crosslinguistic evidence for the language-making capacity. In D. I. Slobin (Ed.), *The crosslinguistic study of language acquisition: Vol. 2. Theoretical issues* (pp. 1157–1256). Hillsdale, NJ: Lawrence Erlbaum Associates.

Slobin, D. I. (1997). The origins of grammaticizable notions: Beyond the individual mind. In D. I. Slobin (Ed.), *The crosslinguistic study of language acquisition: Vol. 5. Expanding the contexts* (pp. 265–323). Mahwah, NJ: Lawrence Erlbaum Associates.

Slobin, D. I. (2001). Form-function relations: How do children find out what they are? In M. Bowerman & S. C. Levinson (Eds.), *Language acquisition and conceptual development* (pp. 406–449). Cambridge, UK: Cambridge University Press.

Talmy, L. (1975). Semantics and syntax of motion. In J. Kimball (Ed.), *Syntax and semantics* (Vol. 4, pp. 181–238). New York: Academic Press.

Talmy, L. (1985). Lexicalization patterns: Semantic structure in lexical forms. In T. Shopen (Ed.), *Language, typology and syntactic description: Vol. III. Grammatical categories and the lexicon* (pp. 57–149). Cambridge, UK: Cambridge University Press.

Talmy, L. (1991). Path to realization: A typology of event conflation. *Proceedings of the Berkeley Linguistics Society, 17*, 480–519.

van Staden, M., Bowerman, M., & Verhelst, M. (2006). Some properties of spatial description in Dutch. In S. C. Levinson & D. Wilkins (Eds.), *Grammars of space: Explorations in cognitive diversity* (pp. 475–511). Cambridge, UK: Cambridge University Press.

35

Cognitive Predictors of Children's First and Second Language Proficiency

LUDO VERHOEVEN
Behavioral Science Institute, Radboud University

ANNE VERMEER
Tilburg University

Language is constructed anew by each child, making use of innate capacities of some sort, in interaction with experiences of the physical and social worlds.

Dan I. Slobin (1985, p. 1158)

As the first author of this chapter, I met Dan Slobin for the first time in 1987 during my stay in Berkeley as a postdoc just after I finished my dissertation work on the language and literacy development of Turkish children in the Netherlands. I became heavily influenced by his theoretical framework on the language-making capacity of the child. Among the varieties of languages Slobin has taken into account in his work, Turkish has been a topic of special interest and I shared his passion for the study of Turkish language and culture (for a synopsis, see Verhoeven, 1991a). I was also highly impressed by Berman and Slobin's (1994) work on relating events in narratives which neatly showed how the construct of language achievement by the child can be seen as the result of a complex interaction between morpho-syntax, lexicon, and discourse functions. It resulted in a collaborative attempt at a follow-up volume in which typological and contextual perspectives on narrative development were further explored (Strömqvist & Verhoeven, 2005).

INTRODUCTION

The purpose of this study was to shed light on cognitive predictors of monolingual and bilingual children's early first and second language proficiency in relation to their sociocultural background. The scope of the present study is highly motivated by Dan Slobin (1973), who taught us how cognitive prerequisites may have an impact on language acquisition. As outlined in Slobin (1985), it can be seen as particularly relevant to study the notion of cognitive determinism from a crosslinguistic and a crosscultural point of view by comparing children learning different languages in different cultural settings. To honor the contributions of Dan Slobin to the field of child language, we are pleased to report on a study in which we examined cognitive predictors of the language achievement of 4-year-old children from two different sociocultural backgrounds in the Netherlands: children acquiring

Dutch as a native language, and minority children, many of whom were Turkish children, acquiring Dutch as a second language.

Language development goes hand in hand with children's cognitive and sociocultural functioning. In a broad range of theoretical paradigms, the interaction between language and cognitive development has been stressed—the perceptual and psycho-motor dependency in language acquisition (e.g., Piaget, 1955), the necessary interface between vocabulary growth and concept formation (Cromer, 1991), the premise of an innate universal rule-governed grammar (e.g., Chomsky, 1965, 1986), the continuity assumption referring to the symbolic nature of language development (e.g., Pinker, 1991), or the evidence of operating principles underlying children's language-making capacity (Slobin, 1985). From a sociocultural point of view, it has been stressed that children pick up language in social contexts with the help of caregivers and peers. In theoretical models such as that proposed by Bronfenbrenner and Ceci (1994), the development of psychological functions associated with language and communication goes beyond the well-established behavioral genetics paradigm by allowing for direct environmental measures and mechanisms of child–environment interaction.

The discussion on the relation between language and cognition and the influence of the environment on both has a long tradition. Language and thinking are so closely connected that speaking about the latter is not possible without mentioning the former. Central questions in these are whether linguistic knowledge is separate from knowledge of the world, and whether language development can be seen as 'rote-learning' rather than 'rule-learning.' The generative linguists have a clear point of view: the language ability of human beings is a specialized, autonomous module with innate information about (the possible rules of a) language (Chomsky, 1965, 1995). A cognitive view on rule discovery comes from Slobin (1973, 1982, 1985), who introduced the notion of the child's 'language making capacity' as a set of operating principles which were defined as strategies for the perception, production, and analysis of speech. These principles were supposed to be part of the initial equipment of language acquisition being phrased as 'self-instructions' which lead to the construction of a 'basic child grammar' that guides the perception and production.

Opposite to the rule-governed representations of language stands the view of the connectionists, in which linguistic and non-linguistic knowledge are not differentiated as such, and in which rules do not play such an important role (cf. Elman, Bates, Johnson, Karmiloff-Smith, Parisi, & Plunkett, 1996). For instance, the distribution of 'regular' and 'irregular' rules is taken to be a reflection of frequency of occurrence of a particular form. In other words, a form that is more frequent is acquired earlier, and retrieved faster from memory, irrespective of the question whether it is a 'base' form or not. It is the frequency of various regular and irregular morphological rules in daily speech that can account for the acquisition of these forms in German (Bybee, 1995), English (Marchman, Plunkett, & Goodman, 1997), or Dutch (Vermeer, 1997; Lowie, 1998). Thus, in a connectionist approach, associative memory plays a major role: namely, linking aspects of words or sentences with a more or less arbitrary label or manifestation.

The 'symbolic' approach (Pinker, 1991) takes in a certain way a middle course between the two aforementioned positions: on the one hand, language is regarded as a system of symbols and rules; on the other hand, 'irregular' forms are represented lexically, and thus they are not derived from a rule. According to Karmiloff-Smith (1997), cognitive development and language development are intimately related within the broader context of symbolic development. In this neo-Piagetian view, starting from the end of the sensorimotor development, the child starts to show the ability to deal with objects in a symbolic way. In the beginning, the child uses symbols that bear some physical similarity to their referents. In the course of language development, the child's symbolic processing is extended to arbitrary signs with socially shared meanings.

Although a broad range of empirical studies has given insight into the factors involved in first language development, the study of second language development and its relationships to cognitive functioning is relatively young. In research on the determinants of success in proficiency in the first or second language, sociolinguistic studies rarely incorporate cognition as a variable (see Genesee, 1976; Cummins, 1991). The focus is oriented toward group characterizing variables such as sex, ethnicity, schooling, and home language (cf. Verhoeven, 1991b; Verhoeven & Vermeer, 2006). However, the question about the relative influence of the various factors underlying success in language acquisition in relation to cognitive factors remains unsolved. That is also the case with the role of the first language in relation to cognition and second language acquisition. For instance, in Cummins' interdependency hypothesis (Cummins, 1991; Verhoeven, 1994), the language-component 'Cognitive Academic Language Proficiency' (CALP) leans heavily on cognition. This hypothesis claims that if the CALP in the first language of ethnic minority children is not well developed, then CALP will also not develop in their second language. Given the (otherwise not very precisely defined) character of CALP, that causal relationship has probably more to do with cognition than with proficiency in the first or second language. However, this claim has not been validated in empirical research so far.

The present study deals with the relationship between sociocultural factors, cognitive factors, and the early first and second language proficiency of children starting kindergarten in the Netherlands. Recently, the influx of ethnic minority children in Dutch schools increased to over 15 percent of the school population, with great regional differences. Institutional and attitudinal support, parental education, gender, and socioeconomic stratum (SES) have earlier been referred to as important determinants of second language development and community language maintenance (see Extra & Verhoeven, 1993, 1998; Verhoeven, 1991b). However, it is by no means clear what the linguistic situation of the minority children is like at the beginning of kindergarten, nor what role various cognitive and sociocultural factors play in the process of first and second language acquisition, such as the question of 'rule learning' versus 'rote learning.' In order to shed more light on this, in the present study an attempt will be made to find answers to the following research questions:

1. How do the Dutch language proficiency levels in L1 vs. L2 in 4-year-old native Dutch children and ethnic minority children compare?
2. How do measures of rule discovery, symbolic processing, conservation, and verbal naming relate to monolingual children's Dutch or Turkish children's Turkish as L1 and Dutch as L2?
3. To what extent can the children's Dutch and Turkish language proficiency be explained by their cognitive abilities, sex, home language use, parental education, and the socioeconomic index of the school?

METHOD

Participants

From 80 schools all over the Netherlands, a sample of 910 children was randomly selected, just as they started primary school. Among them, 462 were native Dutch children from lower-middle-class families, and 448 had an ethnic minority background. The minority children originated from Mediterranean countries, such as Turkey and Morocco, or ex-colonies, such as Surinam and the Dutch Antilles. Of the minority children 178 were Turkish, of which over 80% spoke only or almost only their mother tongue at home. A total of 147 children originated from Morocco, 71 from Surinam, and 52 from the Dutch Antilles. The mean age of all groups was 4:7 years, with a standard deviation of 5 months. Sex was equally divided in both groups. All children were born and raised in the Netherlands.

The ethnic minority children belonged to the second and third generation of immigrants who came to the Netherlands during the past few decades. Turks form the largest minority group in the Netherlands. In 2003, they numbered 341,000 and there were about 55,000 Turkish children in Dutch primary schools. Moroccans constitute the third largest minority group, numbering 295,000 and with approximately 49,000 Moroccan children enrolled in Dutch primary schools (SCP, 2003). The language patterns of these children can be characterized as follows. They live in primarily ethnic language speaking homes with parents who are almost always monolingual speakers of the ethnic language. The early language input of the children is restricted to this language, and the Dutch language enters into their lives only gradually, through Dutch playmates and school. The language situation of ex-colonial minority groups in the Netherlands, on the other hand, is totally different in that in their country of origin they have at least some exposure to Dutch. In the last two decades of the millennium, large cohorts of about 321,000 immigrants from Surinam (the second largest minority group), and 129,000 from the Dutch Antilles came to the Netherlands, of which about 40,000 and 13,000 children, respectively, were enrolled in Dutch primary schools. Extra and Verhoeven (1998) provides a more extensive overview of the sociolinguistic background of these ethnic groups.

INSTRUMENTS

Language Proficiency Tests

The children's Dutch language proficiency was evaluated by ten tasks of the Revised Dutch Language Proficiency Test (TAK), a standardized discrete-point test for the assessment of oral proficiency in Dutch as L1 and L2 for 4- to 10-year-olds (cf. Verhoeven & Vermeer, 2001). The following tasks were administered (the maximum score is indicated in the parentheses):

- Auditory Discrimination task (50), in which 50 pairs of Dutch phonemes had to be distinguished.
- Articulation task (45), in which a sample of 45 words had to be imitated.
- Receptive Vocabulary task (96), in which the child had to point to a picture (out of four) of the right referent for an orally presented word.
- Word Definition task (45), in which the child was asked to explain or describe the meaning of a given word.
- Function Words task (42) and Syntactic Patterns task (42). In both tasks, three pictures were shown together with an oral sentence and the child was asked to point to the corresponding picture.
- Sentence Reproduction task (40), in which 20 sentences had to be imitated.
- Morphology task (24), in which the plural of nouns and the past tense of orally given words had to be formed by the child, with picture support ('This is one key, these are two ...').
- Text Comprehension task (24), in which six short stories were read, each text being followed by four questions to be answered by the child.
- Story Telling task (32), consisting of two series of eight pictures about which the child had to tell a story. Each of the two stories was evaluated regarding 16 aspects of cohesion and coherence.

All tasks were sufficiently reliable, with Cronbach's alpha between .90 and .97.

The mother tongue proficiency of the Turkish children was evaluated by means of three tasks of the Diagnostic Test on Bilingualism (see also Narain & Verhoeven, 1994). The following tasks were administered (the maximum score is in parentheses):

- Receptive Vocabulary task (60), in which, as in the Dutch language test, the child had to point to a picture (out of four) of the right referent for an orally presented word.
- Function Words task (65), in which three pictures were shown, together with an orally presented sentence, of function words with respect to form, color, quantity, space, and relation between events. The child was asked to point to the picture corresponding to the right function word. An example: *In which picture the cat is sitting under the chair?*
- Sentence Reproduction task (40), in which sentences with a broad variety of morpho-syntactical constructions had to be reproduced.

All tasks were sufficiently reliable, with Cronbach's alpha between .90 and .95 (Narain & Verhoeven, 1994.

Cognitive Tests

The cognitive development of the children was assessed by four tasks of the Revised RAKIT, a Dutch standardized cognition test for children (Bleichrodt, Drenth, Zaal, & Resing, 1984), which has been proven to be reliable and valid with ethnic minority children (Resing, Bleichrodt, & Drenth, 1986). The tasks were chosen with respect to the four aspects in relation to language acquisition and cognition mentioned in the introduction: 'rule-discovery' as in the view of generativist linguistics, 'symbolic processing' as in Pinker's conception, the notion of 'conservation' as in the views of Piaget, and 'verbal naming' as in the view of connectionism. The following tasks were administered with the instruction for the minority children being given in both L1 and L2 (the number of test items appears in parentheses):

- Rule Discovery (30). This task is related to logical, inductive reasoning on principles of classification. The child has to choose one abstract figure (out of four) that does not fit the rule that applies to the other three figures.
- Symbolic Processing (2 × 18). This task measures the memory span for 18 concrete and 18 abstract figure sequences. The child has to reproduce with toy blocks the order of the figures shown on a card for five seconds.
- Conservation (40). This task investigates the ability to cope with number, volume, length, distance, weight, surface, and calculation of probabilities. It is based on conservation tasks developed by Piaget (1955). The child has to compare multiple-choice items with four figures on these aspects.
- Verbal Naming (2 × 10). Verbal naming is a task for memory of 'paired associates.' A series of 10 pictures of animals is shown, and with each picture a certain name is given. The child has to reproduce that name in the second and third turns of the series.

The reliability of the tasks was good, as in previous studies, with Cronbach's alpha being between .83 and .91 for the populations in the research reported here (Bleichrodt, Drenth, Zaal, & Resing, 1987).

Sociocultural Data

By means of teacher questionnaires, the following background data were gathered: age, sex, ethnic group (Dutch vs. minority), home language use, socioeconomic status (SES), parental educational level, and the socioeconomic index of the school. The degree of using the first or second language at home for ethnic minorities was measured on a five-point scale: exclusively Dutch, above all Dutch, both languages equally often, above all the mother tongue, and exclusively the mother tongue. The children's socioeconomic background was defined in two ways. As a global measure of socioeconomic status (SES), we used the two-category classification system (Dutch schools use it for funding consideration): high SES (children from middle-class families) vs. low SES (children from working-class families). We used a more refined system to categorize parental education. Four categories of parental education were established: basic education, lower vocational training, middle vocational education, and higher education. The Socioeconomic School Index (SSI) consists of three categories: high, intermediate, and low, depending on the proportion of children from high versus low SES.

Procedure The Dutch language tasks of the TAK and the cognitive development tasks of the RAKIT were individually administered to all children by trained experimenters from the Center of Test Development (CITO, Arnhem) in a separate room in the school, across three or four sessions.

113 Turkish children also performed a Turkish language task which was administered by native language-speaking teachers or research assistants. Teacher questionnaires for collecting the sociocultural data were administered by psychology graduate students.

In order to explore the group differences in cognitive and first and second language abilities of the children, t-tests were carried out. Pearson correlations and multiple regression analyses were conducted to explore the relationships between language abilities on the one hand, and sociocultural and cognitive factors, on the other.

RESULTS

Variation in Language Proficiency

In Table 35.1, the means and standard deviations of the Dutch language and cognitive tasks are presented for the Dutch children and the minority children.

It can be seen that the Dutch native children performed better than the ethnic minority children on all linguistic and cognitive tasks. The differences in vocabulary were particularly large. The t-tests on each task showed that all differences were significant ($p < .001$).

The Turkish children attained substantial scores on the Turkish language proficiency tasks. The means are 40.4 (S.D. = 10.1) for Receptive Vocabulary (maximum = 60), 46.6 (S.D. = 9.1) for Function Words (maximum = 65), and 25.1 (S.D. = 6.9) for Sentence Reproduction (maximum = 40).

Relations Between Language Proficiency and Cognitive Abilities

The mean of the z scores of the ten language proficiency tasks (TAK) was calculated as an index for Dutch language proficiency for Dutch children and the minority children, respectively. In addition, the mean of the z scores of the three Turkish proficiency tasks was calculated to index the native Turkish language proficiency for the Turkish children. Table 35.2 shows the correlations between the above three language proficiencies, on the one hand, and the four cognitive tasks, on the other.

TABLE 35.1 Means and Standard Deviations of Native Dutch and Ethnic Minority Children on Cognitive Tasks and Dutch Language Proficiency Tasks (Maximum Scores in Parentheses)

	Dutch Natives		Ethnic Minorities	
	Mean	SD	Mean	SD
Cognitive Tasks				
Rule discovery (30)	17.6	5.4	14.5	6.2
Symbolic Processing (36)	8.0	3.1	6.8	3.1
Conservation (40)	22.6	7.4	18.1	8.4
Verbal Naming (20)	8.0	3.4	5.6	3.0
Dutch Language Tasks				
Auditory Discrimination (50)	34.4	12.7	27.9	15.4
Articulation (45)	40.8	5.3	38.0	7.3
Receptive Vocabulary (96)	41.3	14.7	21.4	14.1
Word Definition (45)	9.7	6.2	3.9	4.4
Function Words (42)	26.3	6.4	18.5	8.0
Syntactic Patterns (42)	24.6	7.1	17.5	7.9
Sentence Reproduction (40)	18.8	11.4	9.2	9.9
Morphology (24)	11.0	4.5	4.0	4.8
Text Comprehension (24)	11.8	5.8	5.8	5.6
Story Telling (32)	10.1	6.7	5.8	5.8

TABLE 35.2 Correlations Between Dutch Language Proficiency and the Cognitive Measures of Rule Discovery, Symbolic Processing, Conservation, and Verbal Naming ($* = p < .05$; $** = p < .01$)

	Rule Discovery	Symbolic Processing	Conservation	Verbal Naming
L1 Dutch	.48**	.21*	.38**	.49**
L2 Dutch	.30**	.20*	.37**	.57**
L1 Turkish	.34**	.07	.31**	.10

With respect to learners of Dutch as a mother tongue (L1 Dutch), we found relatively high correlations between language proficiency, and rule discovery and verbal naming, and a moderate correlation between language proficiency and conservation. For the native Turkish language proficiency of the Turkish children (L1 Turkish), we found significant correlations with rule discovery and conservation. There was no significant correlation between verbal naming and Turkish language proficiency.

With respect to ethnic minority learners of Dutch (L2 Dutch), we saw a high correlation between Dutch language proficiency and verbal naming and a moderate correlation between Dutch language proficiency and conservation, but a much lower correlation between language proficiency, on the one hand, and rule discovery and symbolic processing, on the other.

Predictors of Dutch Language Proficiency Table 35.3 presents the correlations between the criterion variable of Dutch Language Proficiency and the predictor variables of ethnic group, sex, cognition (mean of the z-scores of the four cognitive tasks), parental education, home language use, and socioeconomic index of the school. It can be seen that all variables except sex yielded significant correlations.

Table 35.4 presents the results of a stepwise multiple-regression analysis with Dutch Language Proficiency as the dependent variable and ethnic group, sex, cognition, parental education, home language use, and socioeconomic index of the school as predictor variables. In order to control for the influence of ethnic group (native Dutch vs. ethnic minority children), this factor was entered as the first step in the analysis, all other variables as the next step.

TABLE 35.3 Correlations Between Dutch Language Proficiency, Cognition, Ethnic Group, Parental Education, Home Language Use, Sex, and Socioeconomic School Index (SSI) of All Children ($** = p < .01$)

	Cognition	Ethnic Group	Parent Educ.	Home Lang.	Sex	School Index
Dutch L Prof.	.63**	.59**	−.49**	−.55**	.07	−.32**

TABLE 35.4 Multiple Regression Analysis (After Four Steps) for All Children with Dutch Language Proficiency as Criterion Variable and Cognition, Ethnic Group, Parental Education, Home Language Use, Sex and Socioeconomic School Index as Predictor Variables ($*** = p < .001$)

Variable	Beta	R
Cognition	.42	
Ethnic Group	.25	
Parental Education	.20	
Home Language Use	−.13	.76***

TABLE 35.5 Correlations Between Proficiency in Turkish, and Dutch Language Proficiency, Ethnic Group, Cognition, Parental Education, Home Language Use, Sex, and Socioeconomic School Index (SSI) (* = $p < .05$)

	Dutch LP	Cognition	Parent Educ.	Sex	Home Lang.	School Index
Turkish	.24*	.26*	–.01	.01	–.03	–.04

TABLE 35.6 Multiple Regression Analysis (After Four Steps) for Turkish Children with Dutch Language Proficiency as Criterion Variable, and Turkish Language Proficiency, Ethnic Group, Cognition, Parental Education, Home Language Use, Sex, and Socioeconomic School Index as Predictor Variables (*** = $p < .001$)

Variable	Beta	R
Cognition	.33	
Parental Education	.29	
Home Language Use	–.28	.57***

The multiple regression analysis showed cognition, ethnic group, parental education, and home language to be significant predictors of children's Dutch proficiency. These variables explained 76% of the variance in Dutch proficiency scores. Neither sex nor the socioeconomic school index played a significant role. As can be seen from Table 35.4, the predictive power of cognition as compared to the other predictors was relatively high.

Predictors of Turkish Children's First and Second Language Proficiency

Table 35.5 shows the correlations between the native Turkish proficiency of the 179 Turkish children and the various other variables.

The Turkish children showed low but significant correlations between proficiency in Dutch and Turkish, and between Turkish proficiency and cognition. A stepwise multiple regression analysis was carried out with these Turkish children's Dutch language proficiency as the dependent variable, and native Turkish proficiency, cognition, parental education, home language use, sex, and socioeconomic school index as predictors. Table 35.6 shows that only cognition, parental education, and home language use turned out to be significant predictors, while native Turkish language proficiency was not.

DISCUSSION

The main aim of this study was to gain insight into the sociocultural and cognitive predictors of early first and second language proficiency. With the use of multiple regression analysis, the extent to which different cognitive factors are related to children's proficiency of Dutch as a first and second language, and to minority children's native Turkish language proficiency was also examined. In this closing section, the results will be summarized and discussed.

Variation in Language Proficiency

Our first research question was concerned with possible differences in language proficiency and cognitive skills among first and second language learners. With respect to this question, the study showed that 4-year-old minority children lag significantly behind in the acquisition of Dutch as compared to their Dutch peers. These results were in line with other studies on Dutch proficiency of native and ethnic minority children in Dutch elementary education (cf. Mulder, 1996). The differences in mean scores turned out to be quite substantial for all tasks except the articulation task. The largest differences were found for the vocabulary measures. Such differences can be explained by ethnic minority children's later and less frequent contact with Dutch than their monolingual Dutch native peers. The language differences can at least partly be perceived as a consequence of restricted input of Dutch in addition to issues related to affect, peer relationships, and social identity (cf. Leseman, 1994; Leseman & Sijsling, 1996).

Relations Between Language Proficiency and Cognitive Abilities for L1 and L2

With respect to the question how language proficiency relates to rule discovery, symbolic processing, conservation, and verbal naming, the different correlation patterns of first and second language-learning children are interesting. Rule discovery appears to be a crucial predictor variable of language proficiency but more for L1 than for L2. Furthermore, the data make clear that symbolic processing abilities play a less substantial role in both first and second language learning. Conservation showed a moderate but significant correlation with both L1 and L2 proficiency. Verbal naming as a rote learning task appears to be more critical in second-language learning than in first-language learning. A possible explanation for the lack of correlation between verbal naming and Turkish language proficiency is that the limited and restrictive language input in kindergarten provided fewer opportunities for associative learning.

On the basis of these findings, one may conclude that L1 processes in young children can be characterized as both connectionist and generative in nature, whereas the nature of L2 processes can above all be defined as connectionist.

Predictors of Language Proficiency With respect to the determinants of Dutch language proficiency, cognitive abilities turn out to be the strongest predictor, followed by ethnic group membership, parental education, and home language use. These factors explain more than half of the variance in the Dutch language proficiency scores. For Turkish language proficiency, we found a similar pattern: cognitive abilities show up as the strongest predictor variable, followed by parental education and home language use. The strong prediction of cognitive abilities is in line with the outcome of earlier studies on the relationship between language and cognitive development. Slobin (1985) showed that rule-based strategies seem to be a prerequisite for the emergence of linguistic achievement. Furthermore, Adams and Gathercole (1996) demonstrated that children's working memory and naming skills make a significant contribution to the variance in speech development independently of age. In a similar vein, Ellis and Sinclair (1996) showed that the short-term maintenance of sequence information and the short-term rehearsal of sequences promote the consolidation of long-term storage of language sequences. They concluded that cognitive abilities related to the labelling, sequencing, and rehearsal of information are heavily involved in the acquisition of vocabulary and syntax in both first and second language.

Furthermore, we may conclude that apart from cognitive factors, sociocultural factors do play a role in predicting children's language proficiency. Ethnic group membership which marks the acquisition of Dutch as L1 vs. L2 turns out to be a significant determinant of children's proficiency in Dutch. Due to restricted input, the minority children lag behind their monolingual peers in all aspects of Dutch proficiency under consideration. Moreover, we found parental education and home language to be significant predictors of children's proficiency in Dutch. This was also the case for the prediction of first language proficiency in the group of Turkish children. This result is consistent with the outcome of earlier studies examining the relationship between language proficiency and sociocultural factors (Verhoeven, 1991b; Snow, Barnes, Chandler, Goodman, & Hemphill, 1991; Snow, 1995).

An important question is to what extent the minority children's first language proficiency predicts their level of second language proficiency. Although for Turkish children a positive correlation between language proficiency in the home language and the second language was evidenced ($r = .24$), the multiple regression analysis showed that the predictive power of home language proficiency disappeared after cognitive and sociocultural factors were taken into account. Cummins' (1991) hypothesis of interdependencies taking place in first and second language learning largely neglects the role of these factors in explaining differential language learning success. Thus, it can be argued that a strictly linguistic explanation of individual differences in bilingual development is not feasible. In order to arrive at a better understanding of the notion of interdependence, it is important to relate sociocultural and cognitive factors to the outcome of processes of L1 and L2 acquisition.

Some Limitations Regarding the Present Study There are, of course, a number of limitations to the present study. First of all, it should be mentioned that in the present study children's language proficiency has been assessed strictly by their linguistic competence. To arrive at a better understanding of children's communicative competence we also need insight into children's pragmatic knowledge and performance (see Verhoeven, 1992; Verhoeven & Vermeer, 1992). Second, the present study lacks a longitudinal design. Quasi-experimental studies, such as the present one, can only be seen as a starting point in research on cognitive factors in first and second language proficiency. In order to arrive at a better understanding of the relationship between language and cognition, we are in need of longitudinal studies in which the impact of cognitive abilities and sociocultural factors on language development is examined over time, and in which the predictive validity of these cognitive measures is investigated. Finally, the present study gives no account of the consequences of bilingual development. In several earlier studies, it was shown that children who acquire a high proficiency in two or more languages at an early stage enjoy an advantage in a number of cognitive domains (for an overview see Bialystok & Ryan, 1985; Cummins, 1991). We will investigate this aspect more in detail in the near future, when we have data on these children in subsequent years.

Educational Implications The results of the present study show cognitive skills to be of critical importance for the development of language skills in monolingual and bilingual children. Teachers must recognize that cognitive skills may facilitate or impede the course of language development. Insight into rule-based language mechanisms and conservation principles as well as memory of symbolic items can be seen as generally important for children's language learning.

For bilingual learners, vocabulary knowledge appears to be an extremely important factor. Intensive vocabulary acquisition should be emphasized. Children should build a large vocabulary in combination with frequent and repeated use in order to automatically access word meanings in communication. It is by fostering vocabulary learning in a variety of natural contexts that the process of bilingual language acquisition can be optimally supported (cf. Vermeer, 2001; Nation, 2001).

REFERENCES

Adams, A., & Gathercole, S. E. (1996). Phonological working memory and spoken language development in young children. *The Quarterly Journal of Experimental Psychology, 49(1),* 216–233.

Berman, R. A., & Slobin, D. I. (1994). *Relating events in narrative: A crosslinguistic developmental study.* Hillsdale, NJ: Lawrence Erlbaum Associates.

Bialystok, E., & Ryan, E. B. (1985). A metacognitive framework for the development of first and second language skills. In D. L. Forrest-Pressley, G. E. Mackinnon, & T. G. Walter (Eds.), *Metacognition, cognition, and human performance* (pp. 207–252). New York: Academic Press.

Bleichrodt, N., Drenth, P., Zaal, J., & Resing, W. (1984). *Revisie Amsterdamse Kinder Intelligentie Test.* Lisse: Swets & Zeitlinger.

Bleichrodt, N., Drenth, P., Zaal, J., & Resing, W. (1987). *Revisie Amsterdamse Kinder Intelligentie Test: Handleiding.* Lisse: Swets & Zeitlinger.

Bronfenbrenner, U., & Ceci, S. J. (1994). Nature-nurture reconceptualized in developmental perspective: A bio-ecological model. *Psychological Review, 101(4),* 568–586.

Bybee, J. (1995). Regular morphology and the lexicon. *Language and Cognitive Processes, 10*(5), 425–456.
Chomsky, N. (1965). *Aspects of the theory of syntax.* Cambridge, MA: The MIT Press.
Chomsky, N. (1986). *Knowledge of language: Its nature, origin, and use.* London: Praeger.
Chomsky, N. (1995). *The minimalist program.* Cambridge, MA: The MIT Press.
Cromer, R (1991). *Language and thought in normal and handicapped children.* Oxford, UK: Blackwell.
Cummins, J. (1991). Interdependence of first and second language proficiency in bilingual children. In E. Bialystok (Ed.), *Language processing in bilingual children* (pp. 70–89). Cambridge, UK: Cambridge University Press.
Ellis, N. C., & Sinclair, S. G. (1996). Working memory in the acquisition of vocabulary and syntax: Putting language in good order. *The Quarterly Journal of Experimental Psychology, 49*(2), 234–250.
Elman, J. L., Bates, E., Johnson, M., Karmiloff-Smith, A., Parisi, D., & Plunkett, K. (1996). *Rethinking innateness: A connectionist perspective on development.* Cambridge, MA: The MIT Press.
Extra, G., & Verhoeven, L. (1993). *Community languages in the Netherlands.* Lisse: Swets & Zeitlinger.
Extra, G., & Verhoeven, L. (1998). *Bilingualism and immigration.* Berlin: Mouton/deGruyter.
Genesee, F. (1976). The role of intelligence in second language learning. *Language Learning, 26*(2), 267–280.
Jackendoff, R. (1992). *Languages of the mind: Essays on mental representation.* Cambridge, MA: The MIT Press.
Karmiloff-Smith, A. (1997). *Beyond modality: A developmental perspective on cognitive science.* Cambridge, MA: The MIT Press.
Leseman, P. (1994). Socio-cultural determinants of literacy development. In L. Verhoeven (Ed.), *Functional literacy: Theoretical issues and educational implications* (pp. 163–184). Amsterdam: John Benjamins.
Leseman, P., & Sijsling, F. F. (1996). Cooperation and instruction in practical problem solving. Differences in interaction styles of mother-child dyads as related to socioeconomic background and cognitive development. *Learning and Instruction, 26*(2), 307–323.
Lowie, W. (1998). *The acquisition of interlanguage morphology: A study into the role of morphology in the L2 learner's mental lexicon.* Unpublished doctoral dissertation, University of Groningen.
Marchman, V., Plunkett, K., & Goodman, J. (1997). Overregularization in English plural and past tense inflectional morphology: A response to Marcus (1995). *Journal of Child Language, 24*(3), 767–779.
Mulder, L. (1996). *Meer voorrang, minder achterstand? Het onderwijsvoorrangsbeleid getoetst.* Nijmegen, the Netherlands: Instituut Toegepaste Sociologie.
Narain, G., & Verhoeven, L. (1994). *Ontwikkeling van tweetaligheid bij allochtone kleuters.* Tilburg, the Netherlands: Tilburg University Press.
Nation, I. S. P. (2001). *Learning vocabulary in another language.* Cambridge, UK: Cambridge University Press.
Piaget, J. (1955). *The child's construction of reality.* London: Routledge & Kegan Paul.
Pinker, S. (1991). Rules of language. *Science, 253,* 530–535.
Pustejovsky, J. (1995). *The generative lexicon.* Cambridge, MA: The MIT Press.
Resing, W., Bleichrodt, N., & Drenth, P. (1986). Het gebruik van de RAKIT bij allochtoon etnische groepen. *Nederlands Tijdschrift voor de Psychologie, 41*(2), 179–188.
SCP. (2003). *Rapportage Minderheden 2003.* Den Haag: Sociaal en Cultureeel Planbureau.
Slobin, D. I. (1973). Cognitive prerequisites of for the development of grammar. In C. A. Ferguson & D. I. Slobin (Eds.), *Studies of child development* (pp. 175–208). New York: Holt, Rinehart & Winston.
Slobin, D. I. (1982). Universal and particular in the acquisition of language. In E. Wanner & L. R. Gleitman (Eds.), *Language acquisition: The state of the art* (pp. 128–170). Cambridge, UK: Cambridge University Press.
Slobin, D. I. (1985). Crosslinguistic evidence for the language-making capacity. In D. I. Slobin (Ed.), *The crosslinguistic study of language acquisition* (pp. 1157–1256). Hillsdale, NJ: Lawrence Erlbaum Associates.
Snow, C. E. (1995). Issues in the study of input: Finetuning, universality, individual and developmental differences, and necessary causes. In P. Fletcher & B. MacWhinney (Eds.), *The handbook of child language* (pp. 180–193). Oxford, UK: Basil Blackwell.
Snow, C., Barnes, W., Chandler, J., Goodman, I., & Hemphill, L. (1991). *Unfulfilled expectations: Home and school influences on literacy.* Boston: Harvard University Press.
Strömqvist, S., & Verhoeven, L. (Eds.). (2005). *Relating events in narrative: Typological and contextual perspectives.* Mahwah, NJ: Lawrence Erlbaum Associates.
Verhoeven, L. (1991a). Acquisition of Turkish in a monolingual and bilingual setting. In H. E. Boeschoten & L. Verhoeven (Eds.), *Turkish linguistics today* (pp. 113–149). Leiden, the Netherlands: Brill.
Verhoeven, L. (1991b). Predicting minority children's bilingual proficiency: Child, family and institutional factors. *Language Learning, 41*(2), 205–233.

Verhoeven, L. (1992). Assessment of bilingual proficiency. In J. H. A. L. de Jong & L. Verhoeven (Eds.), *The construct of language proficiency* (pp. 125–136). Amsterdam: John Benjamins.

Verhoeven, L. (1994). Transfer in bilingual development: The linguistic interdependency hypothesis revisited. *Language Learning, 44*(3), 381–415.

Verhoeven, L., & Vermeer, A. (1992). Modeling communicative second language competence. In L. Verhoeven & J. H. A. L. de Jong (Eds.), *The construct of language proficiency* (pp. 163–173). London: John Benjamins.

Verhoeven, L., & Vermeer, A. (2006). Sociocultural variation in literacy achievement. *British Journal of Educational Studies, 54*, 189–211.

Verhoeven, L., & Vermeer, A. (2001). *Taaltoets Alle Kinderen*. Arhnem, the Netherlands: Cito.

Vermeer, A. (1997). Breedte en diepte van woordenschat in relatie tot toenemende taalverwerving en frequentie van aanbod. *Gramma, 6*(3), 169–187.

Vermeer, A. (2001). Breadth and depth of vocabulary in relation to acquisition and frequency of input. *Applied Psycholinguistics, 22*(2), 217–234.

36

Relativistic Application of Thinking for Speaking

STÉPHANIE POURCEL

Bangor University

> The language or languages that we learn in childhood are not neutral coding systems of an objective reality. Rather, each one is a subjective orientation to the world of human experience.
>
> **Dan I. Slobin (1996, p. 91)**

I first encountered Dan Slobin's ideas on motion and linguistic relativity in 2000, while struggling to define my doctoral focus of investigation. His ideas proved so enlightening that they inspired my entire research paradigm, and they continue to do so today. It was in February 2003 that I eventually met Dan for the first time, in Berkeley, at the occasion of the 29th Annual Meeting of the Berkeley Linguistics Society. I offered a critical talk entitled 'Rethinking Thinking for Speaking' after which Dan kindly invited me for sushi. This was the start of a continuous relationship and correspondence on our shared interests in language and cognition, and the domains of motion and vision. Dan proved to be an invaluably supportive mentor while I completed my doctoral research, and to this day Dan contributes his time and insights generously to the development of my work. Needless to say, his generosity and devotion to the field and its researchers is yet another powerful source of inspiration.

INTRODUCTION

It is the aim of this chapter to explore Slobin's interest in the relationship between language and cognition in the domain of motion, in accordance with his preference for empirical approaches to theoretical questions. To this end, I propose to complement Slobin's neo-Whorfian notion of Thinking for Speaking with experimental data pertaining to "cognitive processes" (Slobin, 2003, p. 158) to support his "impressions" that motion events are "more active, dynamic, or violent" (Slobin, 2003, p. 172) to English speakers than to French speakers, and that there are indeed "cognitive consequences of differential encoding of manner of motion" reaching into "memory for events" and "speakers' conceptualizations of motion events" overall (Slobin, 2003, pp. 263–264).

For this purpose, the chapter begins with an outline of Thinking for Speaking (e.g., Slobin, 1996) followed by an overview of Slobin's empirical and theoretical insights into motion typology (e.g., Slobin, 2004). Finally, the chapter presents a crosslinguistic study—largely inspired by Slobin's research—which adapts the Frog Story methodology to elicit spontaneous narratives from native speakers of English and French. The present study, however, is an innovative contribution to Slobin's work in two respects: (i) it uses a dynamic motion scenario in the form of a film extract from Charlie Chaplin, and (ii) it analyzes the elicited narratives for accuracy of recall, hence testing the Whorfian question in memory.

THINKING FOR SPEAKING

Slobin (e.g., 1996, 2000, 2003) has put forward a neo-Whorfian proposal, known as Thinking for Speaking, which suggests that language influences event conceptualization *in the act* of speaking. The argument constitutes a mild neo-Whorfian position, as it constrains the scope of language influences on cognition to the here-and-now of language processing—what Slobin (e.g., 2003, p. 158) has also referred to as "the online effects of language on thought processes." Indeed, Slobin (1996, p. 76) does not propose to examine "whatever effects grammar may or may not have outside of the act of speaking," that is, Whorfian linguistic relativity per se. Rather, he (1996, p. 76) offers to explore "a special form of thought that is mobilized for communication," namely, Thinking for Speaking. This 'form of thought' concerns the processing of specific information relating to the reality to be communicated. The selection of these specific aspects of reality is determined by the aspects that must be expressed in language for communication to be successful in a given language. It is thus insofar as speakers must attend to certain semantic parameters in their language that attention and other cognitive functions are influenced in the process of linguistic production and comprehension. Overall then, the idea behind Thinking for Speaking is that cognitive functions, such as attention and memory, are 'mobilized' and channelled according to native linguistic categories, semantic codability, lexicalization patterns, and discourse preferences, while processing language for production and comprehension purposes. One may infer, then, that the profiling preferences found in specific languages cause speakers' attention to be allocated to the profiled selection of information found in the scene or entity being communicated, *during* language planning and decoding.

Thinking for Speaking has attracted great attention in recent cognitive science. Indeed, the idea represents a truly neo-Whorfian proposal insofar as Whorf's principle of linguistic relativity offered an examination of the effects of language on linguistic *and* non-linguistic cognition as well. That is, Whorfian relativity entails *pervasive* effects of language on cognition. This position represents a rather extreme stand with far-reaching and controversial consequences. As a result, Whorf's relativity has not always been popular in modern science. Slobin's reformulation, on the other hand, offers somewhat of a mid-way position, which appears to reconcile relativistic notions with contemporary requirements for scientific plausibility and demonstrability in cognitive studies. As such, Thinking for Speaking is an attractive proposal to consider.

However, I wish to retain an open mind in this chapter and argue that it is difficult to conceive of 'online' only effects of language on cognition, and that Thinking for Speaking is quite compatible with a degree of 'true' Whorfian relativism. This suggestion has been voiced by Slobin in more recent proposals (e.g., Slobin, 2003). The question this chapter addresses thus goes beyond the 'whether' of language effects, and asks about the extent of these effects. In so doing, the present study not only seeks to offer support to Slobin's notion of Thinking for Speaking, but also aims to establish whether Slobin's proposal may be taken further and closer to Whorf's original ideas. To do so, an additional objective of this chapter is to show how Thinking for Speaking may be approached empirically via domain investigations at the linguistic and at the cognitive levels. Slobin has offered numerous linguistic empirical studies but the cognitive level yet remains to be fully investigated. This chapter therefore offers an exploration of the cognitive basis for Thinking for Speaking, and it presents crosslinguistic data in support of Slobin's Thinking for Speaking and of Whorfian relativity as well.

THE DOMAIN OF MOTION

A second set of aims in this chapter is to reflect Slobin's interests in the domain of motion, which he identified as

> an ideal arena for the Whorf hypothesis—in ways in which the color domain was not—because there are no biologically determined concepts here waiting to be labelled. (Slobin, 2000, p. 122)

Indeed, this domain is highly interesting because it corresponds to a natural domain which is experienced, conceptualized, and expressed by all members of the species. At the same time, this domain is sufficiently complex not to be subject to biological physio-motor determinism. This complexity ensues (a) from the several components animating its dynamics, e.g., figure, ground, path, and manner, and (b) from the contextualization of motion within larger events involving objective as well as subjective states, e.g., goals, causes, motion sequences, consequences, and symbolisms. In other words, motion conceptualization is not a simple matter of visuo-motor processing, arguably the same for all members of the species. As Talmy (1988, p. 171) explains, motion events do not correspond to

> Euclidean-geometric concepts—e.g., fixed distance, size, contour, and angle—as well as quantified measure, and various particularities of a quantity: in sum, characteristics that are absolute or fixed.

In short, unlike more basic natural domains such as color, rate, shape, material, and so on (Talmy, 1988), motion is typically not conceptualized as a—possibly arbitrary—agent or event property, but as an integral event itself with meaningful purport. Given the quantitative and qualitative complexity of even the simplest of motion events, their processing is of an order complex enough to cause selective attention to some of its components rather than others. Furthermore, due to their typical contextualization within larger life situations, the cognitive conceptualization of motion events may also depend on that situational context, such as agent goals, and emotions.

MANNER SALIENCE IN THE LINGUISTIC FRAMING OF MOTION EVENTS

The schematic complexity of motion events is reflected in the language resources and patterns used in natural languages to communicate motion events. Indeed, this domain is not restricted to isolated lexical items in its expression, but instead reaches to the sentence level, involving grammatical relations with dynamic semantic import, and to the discursive level, incurring set fashions of framing motion scenes with selective foregrounding of its various conceptual components (Slobin, 1997, 2004). The motion component most notable for selective foregrounding in crosslinguistic expression has been identified as the manner of motion (Slobin, 2004). Based on this understanding, Slobin (2004) has elaborated a typological 'cline of Manner salience' along which the world's languages are ranked relative to their preferential fashions of speaking about motion. On the one hand, 'high-manner-salient' languages provide "an accessible slot for manner" (Slobin, 2004, p. 250) in elements such as main verbs (e.g., English, Russian), serial-verb constructions (e.g., Mandarin, Thai), morphemes in bipartite verbs (e.g., Algonquian, Athabaskan), preverbs (e.g., Jaminjungan languages), or ideophones (e.g., Basque, Japanese). On the other hand, 'low-manner-salient languages' (e.g., Romance, Semitic, Turkic languages) "require additional morphology" (Slobin, 2004, p. 253) to encode manner information, such as gerunds, adverbs, prepositional phrases, so that "manner is subordinated to path" and is altogether optional in expression (Slobin, 2004, p. 250).

Given this understanding, Slobin (2003, pp. 163–164) has hypothesized "a set of cognitive consequences of differential encoding of manner of motion," so that "if a language provides fine-grained, habitual, and economical expression of manner of motion…manner of motion will be salient in memory for events and in verbal accounts of events." His study presents an extensive analytical review of crosslinguistic data, including elicitations, conversations, oral and verbal narratives, news report analyses, and more. This substantial body of linguistic data is useful in documenting crosslinguistic resources for motion expression, together with usage patterns and codability with respect to the manner dimension of motion.

To then tackle the Whorfian question concerning the cognitive consequences of crosslinguistic variability, Slobin innovated an approach whereby subjects were asked to recollect and re-tell a written narrative translated literally from Spanish. Importantly, the text contained no manner verbs. Instead, it expressed ground and agent details, thus making manner inferences possible. Specifically, Slobin asked English and Spanish subjects to recall the manners of motion in the story. His findings report accounts of vivid and elaborate mental images for manner by English speakers, as opposed to poor imagery recall by Spanish speakers. Interestingly, the study also used bilinguals, who responded either in terms of vivid or of poor imagery for manner depending on whether they were tested in English or Spanish, respectively. These findings are strongly suggestive of language effects on cognition in terms of the nature of the evidence brought to address speakers' conceptualization of motion events. However, these findings rely on linguistic data elicited in response to a linguistic stimulus, and may thus be perceived as circular (Pourcel, 2004). I suggest that these findings require further testing for full validation, and this testing crucially needs to involve non-linguistic stimuli, so as not to probe responses via semantic interference. Slobin himself admits that most of his data:

> rely on an inferential argument: speakers of typologically different languages vary in their linguistic construals of events, across a wide range of situations of language use. There seem to be quite clear differences in habitual ways of talking about the sorts of events that all human beings experience and care about. *More elusive have been clear demonstrations that these sorts of online attention may also have long-term and pervasive effects on mental representation and conceptual processes.* (Slobin, 2003, p. 179, emphasis added)

MANNER SALIENCE IN THE COGNITIVE REPRESENTATION OF MOTION EVENTS

As stated previously, it is the main aim of this chapter to answer Slobin's call for such demonstrations by showing that systematic linguistic differences in the expression of motion engender "long-term and pervasive effects on mental representation and conceptual processes" (Slobin, 2003, p. 179). To fulfil this aim, the present research has adapted Slobin's methodology for collecting crosslinguistic narrative data (e.g., Slobin, 1996, 2000). Instead of using a book of static pictures, such as *Frog, where are you?* (Mayer, 1969), the present research has chosen a film extract from Charlie Chaplin's *City Lights* to render the dynamicity inherent in motion more realistically via moving pictures. The present stimulus thus differs in format from the Frog Story cartoons; however, in accordance with Slobin's stimulus, it presents a story-based approach to motion to contextualize isolated events within a complex interactive framework. We may call this type of stimulus a *motion scenario*, defined as

> a real-life framework in which motion events are embedded and take on significance. A motion scenario comprises internal schematic diversity, e.g., diversity of paths, fine-graining of manners, and also dimensions external to the motion itself, e.g., agent goals, states, emotions, non-motion events, physiological senses, and cultural dynamics. (Pourcel, in press)

This contextualization seems important in experimental settings in order to re-create a conceptual experience resembling that habitually known to subjects, and therefore more likely to yield naturalistic reactions to the stimulus. Indeed, motion typically occurs within a situational context, involving basic motion components, such as figures, grounds, paths, and manners, but also more complex motion components, such as motivations, causes, sequences, implications, as well as events and entities not pertaining to motion, such as emotions, appearances, non-motion events, and the like. In the present study, the motion scenario—lasting 4.5 minutes—relates a suicide attempt, which takes place at night and on a river quay. The plot involves two main characters: a drunken gentleman who is the suicidee, and Charlie Chaplin, who ends up being his life saver. Given this basic plot, the motion scenario involves the following components:

> three characters, or figures, i.e., Charlie, the suicidee, and a police officer;
> one main location, i.e., a river quay;
> several grounds, e.g., river, staircase, platform, bench;
> several objects, e.g., suitcase, rope, stone, handkerchief, flower, hats, canes, jacket, shoes;
> several manners of motion, e.g., strolling, shuffling, hopping, running, pushing, swaying, jumping, climbing, stumbling, shaking, swimming, tittering, bumping, flying, spinning, kicking, crouching;
> several path types, e.g., up, down, across, in, out, over, around, along;
> several motion types, e.g., spontaneous, caused, human, object;
> several non-motion events, e.g., smelling, looking, crying, talking;
> several psychological and emotional states, e.g., despair, surprise, anger, panic, gratitude, relief, suspicion, annoyance, joy, fear;
> several agentive intentions, e.g., death, safety, rescue, rest;
> a cultural context comprising, e.g., symbols, ideologies, morals, ethics.

This film extract was taken from a silent movie. Although six text boards[1] were shown during this 4.5-minute extract, most meanings, entailments, intentions, and critical aspects of the plot were therefore not signalled by language acts, but by motion and other events instead. This motion scenario was therefore filled with motion events and, as such, constituted an ideal type of stimulus for the examination of motion conceptualization. Note, as well, that the presence of non-motion events provided natural distractors from the focus of the stimulus. Finally, both language groups under observation—French and English—were equally acquainted with the Charlie Chaplin film tradition and, therefore, minimal cultural interference was expected.[2]

This motion scenario was shown to over 20 native speakers of English and French. Recall that in Slobin's (2004) cline of manner salience, English represents a high-manner-salient language, and French a low-manner-salient language. The overall aim was to assess whether memory for manner details present in the stimulus would differ across these two native populations. The full procedure consisted of two tasks, and subjects were tested individually. Stimulus visualization proceeded in silence. The first task was an immediate recall task implemented straight after visualization. Each subject was asked to provide a narrative account, from memory, of the scenario in as much detail as deemed pertinent. These post-visualization narratives therefore enabled the monitoring of accurate memory for the scenario, involving both its non-motion and its motion events. The second task was a late prompted recall task administered 24 hours later, on the following day. Each subject met the experimenter again and answered 31 questions pertaining to the scenario. This test enabled the monitoring of accurate memory for specific aspects of the scenes, which might have been left unreported in the narrative accounts.

The specific hypothesis addressed by these two tasks sought to resolve whether the semantic salience of manner in high-manner-salient languages entails the cognitive salience of manner in the

---

[1] The text boards displayed during the extract read (1) "Night," (2) "Tomorrow, the birds will sing," (3) "No, I am going to end it all," (4) "Be brave! Face life!," (5) "I'm cured, you're my friend for life," and (6) "Let's go home and get warmed up!"
[2] Note that the present film extract was chosen from one of the less famous films in this tradition—*City Lights*—and none of the subjects but one had seen this particular extract before.

minds of speakers of high-manner-salient languages. In other words, in both immediate and late recall, it was predicted that manner details would be better memorized by English speakers than by French speakers. Therefore, we should expect (1) greater mention of manners of motion in English narratives as a result of manner cognitive salience in conceptualizing the stimulus in recall conditions, and (2) greater recall accuracy for manner specifics by English subjects. In sum, the memory performance of the two language groups, in reaction to the same stimulus, should present both quantitative and qualitative divergences with particular respect to manners of motion.

Narrative Performance

The first task elicited 47 narratives in total (N_E = 22, N_F = 25). Narrative length averaged 3 minutes in speaking time across subjects in both language groups, corresponding to an average mean of 42 utterances per speaker.

Narratives were first analyzed as per type of lexical unit. This analysis thus concentrated on the word level, and particularly on monolexemic units for encoding path and manner information. That is, the analysis provides a count of all single path and manner words found in the narratives (e.g., *cross, into, walk, limp*). In other words, the analysis monitors the quantitative distribution of motion lexical units used in the subjects' narratives. The analysis indicates that the path-encoding lexical units are the ones most widely found in motion discourse in both French and English—in comparison to semantic information on manner, cause, result, grounds, or other—as shown in Figure 36.1. This finding is indicative of the core schematicity of path in motion events, as suggested by Talmy (1991), for instance. In addition, according to the narrative data, mean frequencies for path items are equivalent across both language groups, as shown in Figure 36.1. On the other hand, the analysis reveals a significant crosslinguistic difference in the quantitative encoding of manner in lexical units.

As predicted by Slobin (2004), manner information is consistently and significantly more frequent at the lexical level in English than in French. Figure 36.1 shows that, on average, 22 manner lexical units were found in each English narrative, as opposed to 14.7 in each French narrative.

Given this interesting discrepancy, a type analysis was performed for manner items. The token analysis offers a count of the *different* lexical units used for encoding manner, as opposed to all the lexical units for manner. For instance, the item 'stroll' counts as one token, though a dozen occurrences may be found across the English narratives. This analysis has the advantage of showing the qualitative use of manner items at the semantic level of word production. According to Slobin, we should expect English speakers to display a more varied range of manner words. This expectation is supported by the present study, as shown in Figure 36.2.

Figure 36.2 illustrates an important difference between French and English narratives in terms of the semantics of manner items. Only 54 distinct manner tokens are employed in the French texts,

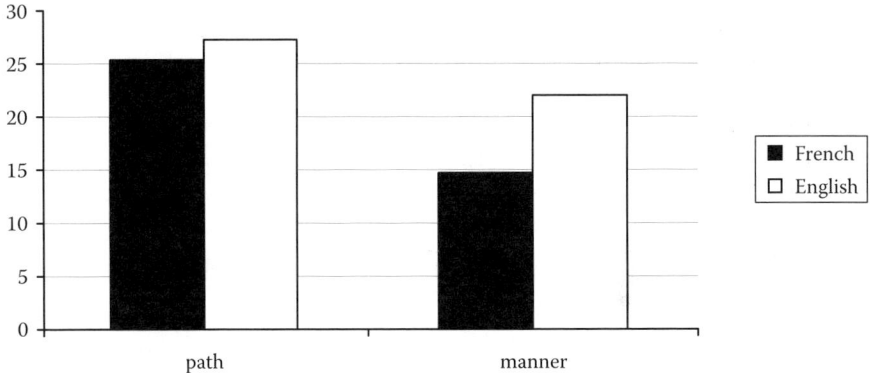

Figure 36.1 Mean frequencies of lexical unit type per speaker.

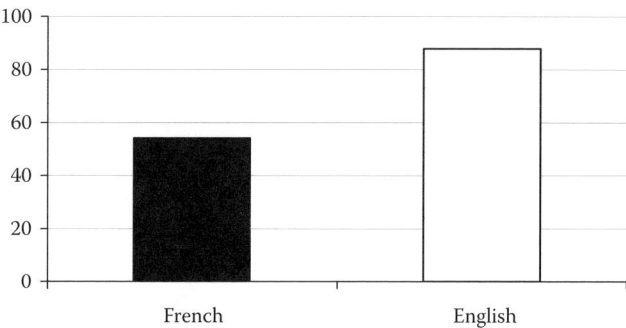

Figure 36.2 Frequency of manner tokens across narratives.

as opposed to 88 distinct tokens in the English data. In other words, English speakers make greater use of manner lexical units at both the quantitative and qualitative levels of expression.

Finally, narratives were also analyzed at the discourse level by examining information statements. A statement constitutes one type of conceptual information about the scene on, for example, path, manner, vision, emotion, and so forth. Consider, for instance, the following narrative sequence:

1. a man comes down some stairs
2. he's sort of drunkenly stumbling
3. down the steps
4. in his evening dress pin suit tuxedo

This excerpt from the English sample data was broken down, as shown in (1)–(4), into three types of information statements, namely, path-and-ground (1 and 3), manner (2), and figure (4). The present analysis focuses specifically on statements relating manner and path information. The crosslinguistic distribution of these types of statements resembles that reported in the lexical type analysis (compare Figure 36.1 and Figure 36.3). Indeed, path statements figured equally in each group's narratives, whereas manner statements were found with consistently greater frequency in the English data set.

The narrative data presented in this study offer ample demonstration of the differential use of and reference to manners of motion across the French and English languages. This study therefore supports Slobin's research and further predictions regarding languages such as French in their comparatively poorer attention to manner details—at least in language.

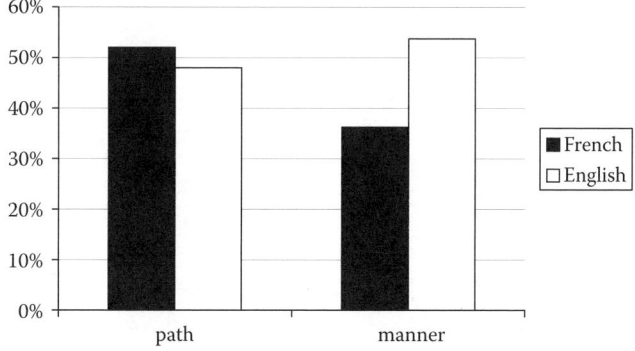

Figure 36.3 Proportions of motion statement type per language group.

Immediate Recall

The previous section confirmed Slobin's predictions regarding the differential semantic salience of manner-of-motion in English and French. Along a cline of relative manner salience, English proves consistently more prone to pay attention to manner details and to express such details in language than French. Based on this template, the relativist hypothesis—as mentioned above—predicts that the greater semantic salience of manner in English should incur greater cognitive salience of manner in the minds of English speakers. In other words, rhetorical facts should induce specific conceptual realities.

In this section, the narratives were analyzed for the accuracy of the information they offered. The analysis was at the statement level, as defined previously. Given that the narratives were elicited after stimulus visualization, they correspond to what the subjects recalled from memory regarding the motion scenario. Erroneously recalled statements were taken as indicative of memory failure and, therefore, of low levels of cognitive salience relative to the specific type of information they expressed. Note that only objective statements were subjected to recall analysis. Objective statements are descriptive and relate information whose truth value may be verified upon viewing the stimulus. In other words, any statement relating inferential information, subjective impressions, and the like, was not analyzed for accuracy of recall. Objective statements constituted over 80% of statements in both groups' narratives.

Erroneous statements were analyzed relative to the type of information they encoded. An erroneous statement, or recall error, consists of a piece of information which is either (i) not present in the stimulus (i.e., over-commission), or (ii) present in the stimulus but incorrectly recalled. An error instance of type (i) might be a statement about Charlie Chaplin's friend falling in the water a third time in the film extract, when he only fell in twice; and an error instance of type (ii) might be a statement about Charlie's friend jumping in the water, when he only ever fell in. Note that information present in the stimulus but omitted in the narrative did not count as a recall error.

The manner salience hypothesis predicted that manner information should be better recalled by English speakers than by French speakers, hence suggesting that manner of motion is more cognitively salient to English speakers.

Figure 36.4 displays error rates for path and manner information. The manner and path error data display important crosslinguistic discrepancies which, I therefore suggest, may be attributed to the distinct rhetorical styles in French and English for conveying these types of information.

The error rates reported in Figure 36.4 confirm the relativistic prediction that manners of motion are better recalled in memory than path information by English subjects and, vice versa, that path information is better recalled in memory than manner information by French subjects. These differences are strongly suggestive of greater attention to manner details by English speakers and to path properties by French speakers. In other words, manner was more cognitively salient to English speakers than path information during motion visualization and recall. Likewise, path was

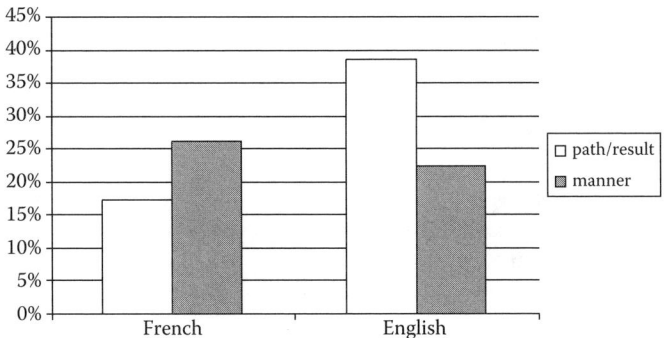

Figure 36.4   Immediate recall error rates.

more cognitively salient to French speakers than manner information during motion visualization and recall.

Figure 36.4 reports a much greater difference in error rates for paths and manners in the English data than it does in the French data. In addition, French speakers made significantly fewer errors on path information than the English subjects. It has been noted earlier that the French and English samples in this study made equivalent mention of path information. This finding was therefore not predicted by the working hypothesis. This discrepancy needs not be antithetical to relativistic arguments, however. A possibility may explain this difference, in agreement with Whorfian tenets, as linked to the distribution of attention to motion details. Indeed, if the manner salience–based hypothesis is correct (which it appears to be), then manner receives greater cognitive salience to English speakers. This greater salience may be to the detriment of other elements in motion, such as path. The present data seems to suggest that this is so, to the extent that manner errors are found in 22% of manner statements whereas path errors are found in 38% of path statements in the English data sample. No such contrast is found in the French data, where manner errors appear in 26% of manner statements and path errors in 17% of path statements. In other words, it is possible that English habitual levels of attention tend to be more 'single-focused' onto manners. In contrast, French habitual levels of attention appear to be more evenly distributed over paths and manners. It should therefore not be surprising that a single attentional focus may yield fewer errors on that given focus than a dual attentional set of foci. The results reported so far thus correlate with the differences found across the two languages for conveying manner information, so that it may be concluded that greater attention to manner in language leads to greater attention to manner in non-linguistic cognitive tasks—a truly Whorfian conclusion.

This immediate recall task therefore offers support to the Whorfian postulate according to which specific fashions of speaking entail specific fashions of thinking—here about motion events and outside the act of speaking. These findings also constitute a preliminary demonstration that 'online attention' to manner details in motion scenarios has "pervasive effects in mental representation and conceptual processes" (Slobin, 2003, p. 179)—here, in immediate recall memory.

Late Recall

Twenty-four hours after the film viewing and the narrative elicitations, 29 English-speaking and 33 French-speaking subjects[3] took part in a prompted recall session. The late recall task was implemented by using a questionnaire consisting of 31 questions. The aim of the questionnaire was to assess accuracy of memory for specific conceptual aspects of the stimulus, as opposed to relying on what subjects may have found relevant to narrate in free prose. With a targeted questionnaire, elements either forgotten or erroneously recalled are clearly identified, whereas in spontaneous narratives, the unsaid does not clearly equate with the forgotten, and the pressure of oral expression may induce unintended inaccuracies.

Questions included references to various conceptual elements of the motion scenario, including grounds ($N_Q = 1$), temporality ($N_Q = 2$), figures ($N_Q = 6$), manners ($N_Q = 14$), paths ($N_Q = 8$), objects ($N_Q = 2$), and causality ($N_Q = 2$), e.g.,

i. Ground question: Could you describe what is on the scene grounds at the very start? There's a river, for instance, where is it?
ii. Time question: Does the millionaire give his friendship to Charlie after the first or after the second fall in the water?
iii. Figure question: Do both men have a hat?
iv. Manner question: Does Charlie walk down the stairs one step at a time?
v. Path question : A policeman arrives. Where does he come from? And where is he going?
vi. Cause question: Is it the millionaire who causes Charlie to fall in the water the first time?

---

[3] Note that a greater number of subjects took part in the late recall task.

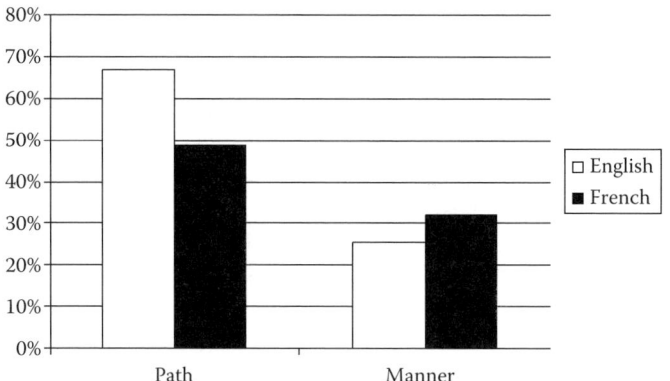

Figure 36.5 Late recall error rates.

The motion-related answers about path and manner were analyzed to test Hypothesis 2, according to which manner details should be better memorized by English than by French native speakers. The late recall also sought to test whether English speakers focus less on path information, as found in the immediate recall task. The other questions were used as distractors.

Figure 36.5 displays the proportions of error rates for manner and path questions, respectively. These error rates show that the French subjects made more errors in answering manner questions than the English subjects. The graph also confirms earlier findings (see Figure 36.4), whereby English speakers produce significantly more errors on path details than French speakers. These findings agree with the relativistic prediction expressed in hypothesis (2) and voiced by Slobin, according to whom "if a language provides fine-grained, habitual, and economical expression of manner of motion... manner of motion will be salient in memory for events" (Slobin, 2003, pp. 163–164). The late recall findings, together with the immediate recall findings, therefore offer evidence for "pervasive effects on mental representation and conceptual processes" of habitual patterns of linguistic expression (Slobin, 2003, p. 179).

CONCLUSION

The study reported in this chapter is inspired by Dan Slobin's research. This inspiration ranges across a number of considerations central to Slobin's work, including a focus on the domain of motion, the aim of understanding the influential relation of language to cognition, and especially memory, and an overall epistemological stance favoring data-driven explorations of linguistic and cognitive phenomena. Regarding this latter point, the present study has sought to offer innovative methodological contributions by contextualizing motion events within a real-life scenario, and by offering linguistic analyses of meaning representation beyond the lexical level of expression. The examination of informational distribution in narrative is a step toward understanding the dynamics of discursive patterns in crosslinguistic research. Such an aim echoes Slobin's approach to typological descriptions in language (e.g., Slobin, 2004) on the basis that "language use is determined by more than lexicalization patterns" (Slobin, 2004, p. 220) and that rhetorical, or narrative, styles found in language use converge in elaborating the framing of events in linguistic semantics. Overall then, the findings of this study offer an appreciation of both narrative and cognitive styles across French and English native populations, as relating to the domain of motion.

Linguistically, two different styles emerged for reporting the stimulus events in each language. Discrepancies were found between the two language groups at the lexical and discursive levels. Token, type, and statement analyses demonstrated that path of motion is equally mentioned in both languages, but that manner of motion is expressed with greater frequency and finer nuancing in English narratives. Slobin's narrative findings were therefore confirmed by the present data, which lend further support for conceiving of English as a high-manner-salient language, and of French as a low-manner-salient language. On this basis, the study explored Slobin's prediction that manner of motion should be more salient in cognition to English speakers than to French speakers.

Cognitively, error analyses of the immediate and late recall tasks revealed greater memory accuracy for manner details by the English speakers than the French speakers, and better memory accuracy for path by French speakers than English speakers. These results are perfectly congruent with relativistic hypotheses according to which semantic salience incurs cognitive salience, as voiced by Slobin (e.g., 2003) and also by Whorf (1956). Besides, this is the case whether one attends to specific information for purposes of communication or not. These memory findings on contextualized motion scenes from Charlie Chaplin are thus indicative of differing narrative *and* conceptual styles across the French and the English population samples, and they offer preliminary evidence for both Thinking for Speaking and linguistic relativity in the domain of motion, as well as a clear demonstration that online attention to manner "may have long-term and pervasive effects on mental representation and conceptual processes" (Slobin, 2003, p. 179). In doing so, this study encourages the continued pursuit of relativistic explorations in the domain of motion in other languages.

REFERENCES

Mayer, M. (1969). *Frog, where are you?* New York: Dial Press.
Pourcel, S. (2004). Rethinking thinking for speaking. *Proceedings of the twenty-ninth annual meeting of the Berkeley Linguistics Society* (pp. 349–358).
Pourcel, S. (in press). Motion scenarios in cognitive processes. In V. Evans & S. Pourcel (Eds.), *New directions in cognitive linguistics*. Amsterdam: John Benjamins.
Slobin, D. I. (1996). From 'thought and language' to 'thinking for speaking.' In J. J. Gumperz & S. C. Levinson (Eds.), *Rethinking linguistic relativity* (pp. 70–96). Cambridge, UK: Cambridge University Press.
Slobin, D. I. (1997). Mind, code, and text. In J. Bybee, J. Haiman, & S. A. Thompson (Eds.), *Essays on language function and language type* (pp. 437–467). Amsterdam: John Benjamins.
Slobin, D. I. (2000). Verbalized events: A dynamic approach to linguistic relativity and determinism. In S. Niemeier & R. Dirven (Eds.), *Evidence for linguistic relativity* (pp. 107–138). Amsterdam: John Benjamins.
Slobin, D. I. (2003). Language and thought online: Cognitive consequences of linguistic relativity. In D. Gentner & S. Goldin-Meadow (Eds.), *Language in mind: Advances in the investigation of language and thought* (pp. 157–191). Cambridge, MA: The MIT Press.
Slobin, D. I. (2004). The many ways to search for a frog: Linguistic typology and the expression of motion events. In S. Strömqvist & L. Verhoeven (Eds.), *Relating events in narrative: Vol. 2. Typological and contextual perspectives* (pp. 219–257). Mahwah, NJ: Lawrence Erlbaum Associates.
Talmy, L. (1988). The relation of grammar to cognition. In B. Rudzka-Ostyn (Ed.), *Topics in cognitive linguistics* (pp. 165–205). Amsterdam: John Benjamins.
Talmy, L. (1991). Path to realization: A typology of event conflation. *Proceedings of the seventeenth annual meeting of the Berkeley Linguistics Society* (pp. 480–520).
Whorf, B. L. (1956). *Language, thought, and reality*. Cambridge, MA: The MIT Press.

37

Thinking for Speaking and Channeling of Attention
A Case for Eye-Tracking Research

SVEN STRÖMQVIST, KENNETH HOLMQVIST,
and RICHARD ANDERSSON[1]

*Humanities and Linnaeus Centre for Cognition, Communication and Learning,
Lund University*

INTRODUCTION

The stunningly productive new wave of research on language, cognition, and linguistic relativity guided by works such as Berman and Slobin (1994) and Gumperz and Levinson (1996) is emerging in a time when a deeper understanding of "the cognitive and communicative consequences of linguistic diversity" (Slobin, 2002, pp. 7–23) has a pivotal role to play both for research strategies in the scientific community and for the everyday life of citizens in a world of many languages and crosscultural communication. Thus, *thinking for speaking* (Slobin, 1996) is an important corrective to the view that we would be better off on this planet if we were all speaking but one language. To amplify this point, consider Cassin (2004, personal communication), who presents an analysis of the vocabulary of European philosophies with a special focus on "untranslatable" terms, such as, for example, "philosophy of *mind*" "philosophie de l'*ésprit*"—"*Geist*eswissenschaft." Cassin argues that the diversity of languages represents a plurality of viewpoints. Applied to differences in terminological traditions between academic disciplines, this plurality presents a problem for translation, but it also presents a resource of perspectives for conceptualizing a problem or phenomenon. In the domain of neuroscience there is a growing interest in the cognitive control of neural activity (e.g., Badre, Poldrack, Paré-Blagoev, Insler, & Wagner, 2005; Miller, D'Esposito, & Wills, 2005) and language plays a powerful role in cognitive control and regulation of brain activity. Here, the notion of *thinking for speaking* can help promote cooperation between scholars in the linguistic and cognitive sciences on the one hand and brain scientists on the other. Another research challenge concerns a partly new and extended model of the linguistic production process. According to the standard view (e.g., Hayes & Flower, 1980; Levelt, 1989), building a linguistic utterance or a text fragment is much like a logistic process where pre-specified conceptual good gets packaged, transported, and repackaged. The notion of *thinking for speaking* is suggestive of a more dynamic interplay between

---

[1] We would like to thank Joost van de Weijer for methodological discussions and advice on statistical analysis.

language and thought, such that the conceptual content to be dressed up in words may be influenced by grammatical demands and rhetorical habits.

One important claim Slobin has made about the cognitive consequences of thinking for speaking is the channeling of speakers' attention influenced by the typological characteristics of language, as shown in the following quote:

> If particular aspects of the pictured situation are regularly encoded in a language, we can conclude that those aspects attract the attention of speakers in the course of constructing a verbalized expression of their perceptions. Our data present a number of instances in which there seem to be clear differences between languages with regard to the event components which are encoded by their speakers. We propose that such differences are due to the channeling of attention in the course of thinking for speaking. (Berman & Slobin, 1994, p. 613)

Berman and Slobin's ground-breaking volume from 1994 was based on crosslinguistic developmental analyses across five languages and three phyla. The claims and conclusions in the above quote were further amplified and richly exemplified in a follow-up volume 10 years later edited by Strömqvist and Verhoeven (2004) where analyses of picture-story retellings across fourteen languages and six phyla were included. Consider, as an illustration, Example 1, where a speaker of Tzeltal, a Mayan language, describes a particular scene of the frog story, based on a 24-page wordless picture book *Frog, where are you?* (Mayer, 1969), where the main character, a boy, has fallen down from a tree (example taken from Brown, 2004).

(1) *jipot **jawal** ta lum*
'He [the boy] has been thrown **lying_face-upwards_spread-eagled** to the ground.'

Mayan languages are very rich in positionals, a class of verbal roots, detailing information about spatial position and body posture. The attempt at a literal translation into English of the positional *jawal* in Example 1 suggests that a narrator who wishes to encode the detailed body-posture information in question into a linguistic form will have a much easier time as a speaker of Tzeltal than as a speaker of English. Consequently, a Tzeltal speaker has acquired the habit of detailing information about body posture to an extent to which an English speaker has not. In effect, this kind of difference in linguistic habits can result in a different channeling of attention in speakers of different languages when they are faced with the same event-description task. Speakers of Tzeltal can be expected to channel their attention toward the body posture of the boy to a larger extent than can speakers of English.

Research based on the frog-story task evidences many other systematic differences in thinking for speaking between speakers of languages that are less far apart in terms of typological traits than English and Tzeltal. Talmy's well-known typology of verb-framed versus satellite-framed languages (Talmy, 1991, 2000) has paved the way for several of these observations. Thus, speakers of Germanic languages detail distinctions of manner of motion to a far greater extent than do speakers of Romance languages (Slobin, 2004). Further, speakers of Germanic languages also tend to detail information about direction of motion and complex paths to a greater extent than speakers of Romance languages (ibid). However, past research on attention channeling has its methodological limitations. Although speakers' linguistic behavior can be used as evidence to hypothesize the channeling of attention, it is not conclusive if the speakers are simply forced by the language structure to produce such behavior, or they are actually channeling their attention to the specified stimuli. In other words, evidence other than linguistic behavior is needed to support the hypothesis in a non-circular way. One such possible evidence may come from the study of speaker's eye movement while speaking. In the present chapter, we have taken the picture story method used by Berman and Slobin (1994) to our eye-tracking lab, in order to find out whether the eye movements and fixation patterns of the story-telling subjects are indicative of channeling of attention during thinking for speaking.

Mayer's wordless picture book *Frog, where are you?*, which was used by Berman and Slobin (1994) and Strömqvist and Verhoeven (2004), consists of a set of 24 pictures, each depicting a scene in the story. The participants are asked to tell the story in their own words as they browse through the booklet at their own pace, picture by picture. In this narrative task, therefore, a considerable amount of the information to be encoded into a linguistic form is selected from a visual array of objects. In effect, the frog-story task allows us to explore eye-fixation patterns as an indicator of channeling of attention. Using a similar rationale, Holsánová (2001) employed eye-tracking technology to study the interplay between speech and visual attention during a picture description task. A pilot study where a frog-story narration was recorded by a combination of audio and eye-tracking equipment is described in Holmqvist, Holsánová, Johansson, and Strömqvist (2005).

The systematic time-locked interrelationship between visual search and concurrent articulated speech has brought forth a rapidly growing paradigm called the "Visual-world" to the study of cognition and psycholinguistics, and it is increasingly used to investigate models of speech production and comprehension (for instance, Trueswell & Tanenhaus, 2005; Griffin & Spieler, 2006; Henderson & Ferreira, 2004). This paradigm is an important point of departure for the present study. Furthermore, we will explore the combined speech and eye-tracking data in terms of a partly new model of the language production process—whether in speech or writing (Strömqvist, 2006). The model rests on the assumption that the information to be structured by means of language is richer than that of the resultant linguistic product and that central aspects of the planning phase, therefore, concern orienting in a rich information array and, eventually, selecting certain aspects while leaving others out. This process may lead to a product which the producer (speaker or writer) experiences as satisfactory, and in many situations the producer is happy with his first attempt at building an utterance or a discourse fragment. In other situations, the producer is discontented with his first attempt and can spend a lot of effort on reflecting, reorienting, and revising. According to this view, building a linguistic utterance or a text fragment is less like a logistic process where well-specified semantic goods get packaged, transported, and repackaged, but more like building a working model of your thoughts—much like the working models or sketches an architect produces in order to structure, refine, and elaborate his ideas. The working model is necessarily selective and perspectival ('perspectival' in the sense that it imposes a certain perspective on the information array). You build the working model of your thoughts on the conditions of the particular language you speak (*thinking for speaking*) and on the conditions (communicative conditions and processing constraints) associated with spoken, signed, or written language. The model is summarized in Figure 37.1 (from Strömqvist, 2006).

Slobin's claim that thinking for speaking has cognitive consequences and that one of them is channeling of attention can be further broken down into at least two main claims. The first one is that thinking for speaking is different from non-linguistic modes of thinking for expressing, such as, for example, thinking for painting, sculpturing, or composing music. The second one is that linguistic diversity results in a diversity of thinking for speaking. Research so far has focused on exploring and giving empirical substance to the second claim. In this study, we focus on the first claim.

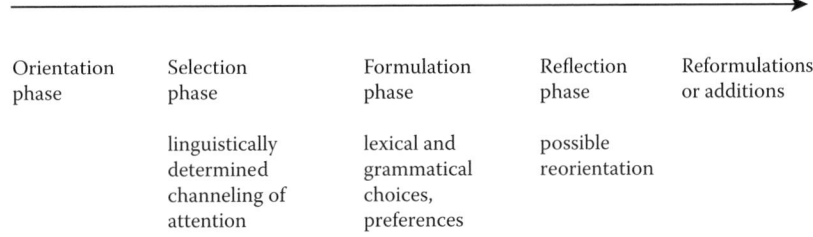

Figure 37.1 Toward a model of the dynamic process from first thoughts to an elaborated text fragment. (From Strömqvist, in press. With permission.)

METHOD

Twenty-two adult speakers of Germanic languages—12 Swedish speakers and 10 English speakers—were recruited to perform the frog-story task in our eye-tracking lab at Lund University.[2] The subjects were available from a translation experiment totally unrelated to the present investigation and they were collapsed into one subject group on the assumption that the difference between the two closely related Germanic languages, English and Swedish, would make no significant difference whatsoever for the purposes of the present investigation (and, as we shall see, there was no significant effect of language on the results). The subjects were instructed to tell a story based on the 24 pictures of the frog story, which were displayed to each subject on a computer screen, one picture at a time, for 15 seconds each. The pictures were 800 × 600 pixels in resolution and were scaled to fill the full screen of the 19-inch monitor. The subjects were distanced on average 650 millimeters from the screen.

In a control condition, a group of 12 independent subjects, all Swedish speakers, were presented with the same set of pictures, in the same order and with the same time constraints. These subjects were instructed to look at the pictures as if they were at an exhibition, and they were not asked to tell a story based on the pictures. However, we expected that it would not take the control subjects long to figure out that they were looking at a picture story. In effect, if a narrative interpretation of the picture series would be an overruling determinant to the attentional pattern measured by the eye tracker, we would expect a very similar pattern in both the spoken narrative condition and in the silent picture (control) condition. Conversely, if thinking for speaking is a determinant to the attentional pattern under investigation—powerful enough to influence the way visual attention is organized over and above the narrative interpretation—the pattern in the two conditions could be expected to be different.

The task was administered by means of the stimulus presentation software E-prime[3] and each stimulus picture was active for 15 seconds, whereupon E-prime immediately shifted to the next picture. The eye movements of the subject were recorded by means of a headmounted eye tracker with head tracking.[4] An eye camera and a scene camera were placed on a bicycle helmet worn by the speaker. On top of the bicycle helmet, there was a magnetic sensor made by Polemus (the Fastrak) that kept track of the head in the six dimensions (6D[5]) of position and direction. The eye tracker calculated a vector for the gaze direction that eminated from the eye of the subject. The head position and direction together with the eye direction allowed for a real-time calculation of the position where the combined eye-head vector hit the stimulus picture plane. This setup allowed the subject freely to move his/her head during the course of the recording for a more natural narrative setting, but still provided us with absolute coordinates of where the subjects were looking on the screen.

For each participant, the eye tracking part of our setup produced two output formats. First, one format was a MPEG-2 video of the visual field with an overlaid gaze cursor showing where the subject was looking. This video also contained the spoken narratives of the subjects. The other format was a data file which contained the absolute coordinates of where the subjects looked every 20 milliseconds. The video and the data file were synchronized with each other to allow for analyses with high temporal resolution.

Figure 37.2 shows a screenshot from one of the video recordings. The subject is in the process of describing the scene where the dog—the faithful companion of the boy during his search for the frog—is falling out of a window. The white circle points at the position in the picture where the subject's dominant eye gaze was directed to 4.13 seconds after the activation of the picture. The picture is slightly tilted because the subject is tilting his head.

---

[2] Visit the home page of the lab for more information: http://www.sol.lu.se/humlab/eyetracking/
[3] http://www.pstnet.com/products/e-prime/
[4] Maker: SensoMotoric Instruments Gmbh. Model: iView X HED. Software: iView X 1.6. Sampling frequency was 50 Hz.
[5] The three regular position dimensions: x (width), y (height), z (depth), and also the three direction dimensions: azimuth, elevation, and roll. Website: http://www.polhemus.com/fastrak.htm

Figure 37.2 Screenshot from a picture-story retelling task using eye-tracking.

In this way, we obtained 22 frog-story narrations with complete eye-tracking data. For the present study, we focus on only 1 of the 24 pictures of the frog story, namely, the one that depicts the dog's fall out of the window. Again, it should be noted that the present study is not aimed at revealing crosslinguistic differences in attentional preferences. The purpose of this study is to provide evidence that there is a systematic interaction between the information selected for linguistic encoding by the subjects on the one hand and their selective visual channeling of attention on the other.

For the purpose of quantitative analysis, four mutually exclusive areas of interest (AOIs) were defined for the picture in question: one AOI for the boy, one for the dog, one for the lower part of the window representing the source of the locomotion path, and one for the ground representing the goal of the locomotion path. The four AOIs are shown in Figure 37.3.

The eye-tracking data was analyzed using iView Analysis by SMI, and a fixation was defined as a sum of gaze hits, each lasting 20 milliseconds, equal to or longer than 80 milliseconds, and located in an area with the radius of 10 pixels. By means of our analysis software, we could then derive the distribution of visual attention—in terms of total gaze times for all fixations—across the four AOIs over a given period of time. Figure 37.4 shows this type of distribution for one subject during the 15 seconds when the picture in question was displayed on the computer screen. Each AOI received a lane across the window of the protocol shown in Figure 37.4, where bars in the lane marked B indicated the time duration when the subject was looking at the boy, W the window, D the dog, and G the ground. The protocol in Figure 37.4 shows that, during the first 2 seconds, the subject was first looking at the dog, then shifted to the window, then to the boy, then back to the window, and then back to the dog again.

In order to grasp the phonetic and temporal properties of the speech wave, we used the phonetic analysis package PRAAT (Boersma, 2001; Boersma & Weenink, 2006). Transcripts of the phrases spoken by the subject are entered in the lower part of Figure 37.4 together with information about the length of the phrases and the length of silent pauses. The space in Figure 37.4 does not allow for a strict temporal alignment of the transcripts to the AOI protocol, but the onsets of the phrases are indicated by means of thin solid lines from a point in the AOI protocol to the beginning of the phrase as it is rendered in the transcript below the protocol. In this way, we produced a complex protocol inspired by the multimodal time-coded score sheets developed by Holsánová (2001) (see also Andersson, Dahl, Holmqvist, Holsánová, Johansson, Karlsson, Strömqvist, Tufvesson, & Wengelin, 2006).

For ease of reading, the complete set of transcribed phrases together with an English translation is rendered in Table 37.1. For example, around the 6th second, the subject started saying "rakt NER på marken" 'straight DOWN to the ground' just after his visual attention had been directed exactly

Figure 37.3 Four areas of interest for eye-tracking analysis.

at the AOI Ground (see Figure 37.4). Still a little later, around the middle of the 15-second period, there was a silent pause which was 1.239 seconds long. The onset of that pause in relation to the AOI protocol is indicated by a dashed line. The dashed line indicates that the long pause occurred while the subject was looking at one AOI only (Dog), thus keeping his visual exploration of the picture to a minimum. Figure 37.4 illustrates the types of complex time-coded data which form the empirical basis for our investigation.

RESULTS

From the point of view of content structure, the example in Table 37.1 and Figure 37.4 is representative of the majority of the 22 elicited retellings of the dog's fall from the window. Twenty-one of them contain a description of the physical motion event. The subjects produced these descriptions after having made an initial pause of around 2 to 3 seconds right after the picture appeared on the computer screen. These event descriptions are rich in verb particles and prepositional phrases (PP), where the noun of the PP refers to the source of the locomotion. Nineteen subjects produced an utterance containing the construction [Verb+particle+PP], for example, "fell out of the window."

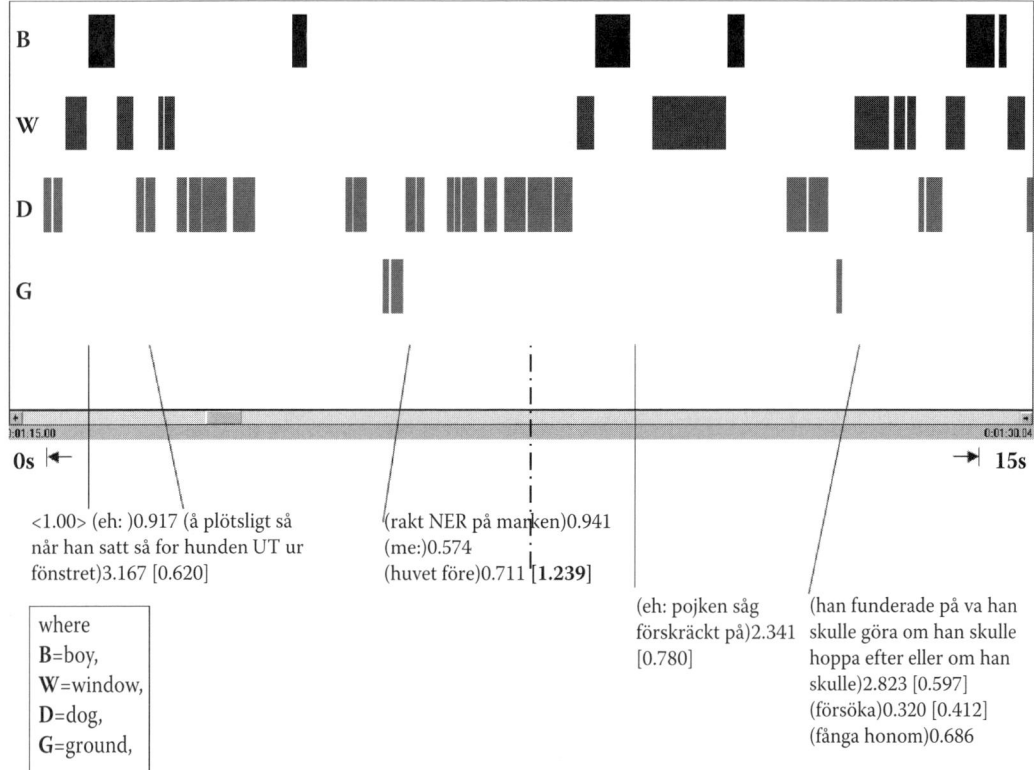

Figure 37.4 A multimodal protocol with time-coded eye and speech data. (For an English translation of the Swedish narrative, see Table 37.1.)

Three of the 21 subjects spent the rest of their 15 seconds in silence, whereas 18 subjects moved on to say something more. Five of them extended their first descriptions using the construction [particle+PP] to refer to the goal of the locomotion, for example, "down to the ground." The majority (13) of them, however, moved on to say something of a very different semantic character. They made statements about the boy's state of mind (see Table 37.1 for an illustration) or they made emotive or evaluative comments, for example, "ouch, he's gonna get hurt." These additional comments invariably occurred after the description of the physical event, during the second half of the 15 seconds. Just as in Table 37.1, there was a tangible silent pause in connection with the transition from the earlier

TABLE 37.1   Relating an Event in Narrative: Transcripts and Translation of the Stream of Speech

Swedish Original	English Translation
<1.00> (eh:) 0,917 (å plötsligt så när han satt så for hunden ut ur fönstret) 3,167 [0,620]	<1.00> (ah:) 0,917 (and suddenly as he was sitting the dog went out of the window) 3,167 [0,620]
(rakt ner på marken) 0,941 (me:) 0,574 (huvet före) 0,711 **[1,239]**	(straight down to the ground) 0,941 (with:) 0,574 (head first) 0,711 **[1,239]**
(eh: pojken såg förskräckt på) 2,341 [0,780]	(ah: the boy was watching anxiously) 2,341 [0,780]
(han funderade på va han skulle göra om han skulle hoppa efter eller om han kulle) 2,823 [0,597] (försöka) 0,320 [0,412] (fånga honom) 0,686	(he was wondering what he should do if he should jump after or if he should) 2,823 [0,597] (try) 0,320 [0,412] (to catch him) 0,686

Note: <n> | n marks the time in seconds after the activation of the picture when the subject starts speaking
(xxx)n | n marks the duration in seconds of the phrase enclosed by the preceding brackets
[n] | n marks the length in seconds of a silent pause
x: | : marks phonetic lengthening

phase with the description of the physical event to the later phase with the cognitive/emotive/evaluative comment (the pause in question in Table 37.1 is in boldface **[1.239]** for ease of reference).

From the point of view of distribution of visual attention, the example in Figure 37.4, again, serves as an illustration which is representative of the majority of the subjects. During the first couple of seconds, the subject in Figure 37.4 was looking at several of the AOIs—first the dog, then the window, and then the boy. Then, just in advance of starting to speak, the subject narrowed down the range of AOIs to just the window and the dog. In the subsequent utterance, he encoded into a linguistic form exactly the two objects corrersponding to these two AOIs: the dog as grammatical subject and the window as landmark. After this first utterance, the subject made a pause ("[0.620]"—see Table 37.1) and during that pause, he focused his attention on the AOI "ground" (see Figure 37.4), whereupon he said "rakt ner på marken" 'straight down to the ground,' thus encoding into a linguistic form exactly the AOI he just looked at. For 18 of the 19 (out of a total of 22) subjects who used the construction [verb+particle+PP] to refer to the window (source of the locomotion) in their first utterance describing the physical motion event, it holds that they focused their visual attention at the window AOI within 1 second before the onset of the utterance. For the 5 subjects who extended their first descriptions using the construction [particle+PP] to refer to the ground (goal of the locomotion), the same time-locking relationship holds true. Around the middle of the 15 seconds, just around the long pause between the subject's description of the physical motion event and his description of the boy's state of mind, the subject was looking steadily at just one AOI (the dog). Here, again, the subject serving as an illustration in Table 37.1 is typical of a majority of all subjects.

All these kinds of changes are summarized on a group level by the black bars in Figure 37.5 in terms of average number of shifts of AOIs per second. (The gray bars summarize the corresponding distribution in the control condition.) For example, the value 2 on the vertical axis thus indicates two shifts, that is, a change of visual attention across three AOIs.

The black bars in Figure 37.5 show that the number of shifts peaked during the first 2 seconds of the picture-story retelling task, then there was a drop from second 2 to 3, whereupon the number of shifts stayed relatively stable for another 4 seconds and then dropped further from the 6th to the 7th second. After the 7th second the amount of shifts rose a little, but it never approached the peak as observed during the first two seconds. Among the changes in amount of attentional shifts, second by second, in Figure 37.5, the changes from the 2nd to the 3rd, from the 6th to the 7th, and from the 7th to the 8th second were statistically significant (repeated measures ANOVA, $p < .05$), yielding

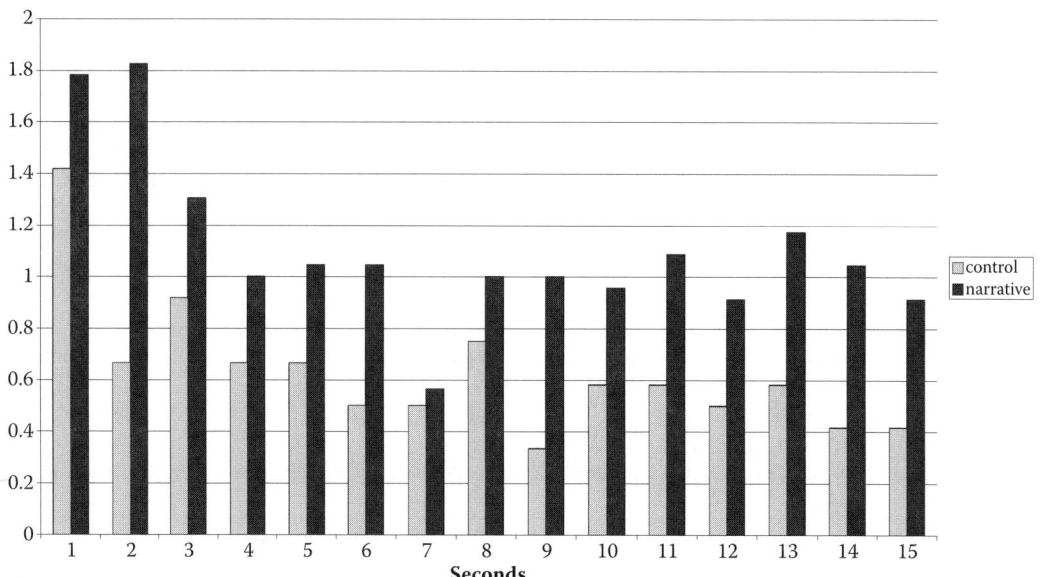

Figure 37.5 Changes in amount of visual attention during 15 seconds of a picture-story retelling task.

four distinct phases. In accordance with our assumptions, there was no significant effect of language between the English and Swedish speakers among our subjects ($F[1,21] = 0.122$, $p > .05$).

The corresponding pattern in the control condition was clearly different. The pattern resulting from the control condition is summarized by the gray bars in Figure 37.5 together with the pattern from the spoken narrative condition (black bars), for ease of comparison.

Figure 37.5 shows that, in the control condition, there was a peak in number of shifts during the 1st second only, and then there was a drop from second 1 to 2. Then the number of shifts stayed low. The change from second 1 to 2 was the only significant change (repeated measures ANOVA, $p < .05$) throughout the 15 seconds in the control condition. Also, the average number of shifts of AOIs is somewhat lower in the control condition than in the spoken narrative condition. We do not have a satisfactory explanation for this observation, but it may be the case that the arousal level in the subjects is greater in the spoken narrative condition (because of the higher demands on performing) and that an increased arousal level covariates with more saccades. This is a hypothesis for further experimental testing.

In short, then, the linguistic narrative condition imposed a lot of structure on the distribution of visual attention. The distribution, however, relates to spontaneous, task-driven data and lends itself to several interpretations. Here, we will try to interpret the data in terms of a tentative model of the linguistic production process from first thoughts to a ready-made text or text fragment. Consider, again, the model sketched in Figure 37.1 (Strömqvist, 2006). It consists of five phases: (1) an orientation phase, where the subject overviews the information domain to be talked or written about; (2) a selection phase, where a subset of the information overviewed is selected; (3) a formulation phase, where the information is encoded into a linguistic form; (4) a reflection phase, where the linguistic construction accomplished is pondered upon; and, (5) a final phase, where reformulations or additions are made. The orientation phase and the selection phase are intimately interrelated in that the selection presupposes the orientation and in that the selection implies that certain information overviewed in the orientation phase is left out. Also, the formulation phase and the selection phase are intimately interrelated, since the selection is partly driven by linguistic demands and rhetorical habits (thinking for speaking).

As for the distribution of visual attention, we interpret the prolonged phase (as compared to the control condition) of peaking number of shifts of AOIs at the very beginning of the 15 seconds when the picture is displayed to the subject as indicative of the orientation phase. The finding that it is prolonged as compared to the non-linguistic control condition testifies to the additional effort the subject has to expend on exploring the picture and choosing which information to exclude and which to include for subsequent linguistic encoding. The following drop in shifts of AOIs indicates the transition from the orientation phase to the selection phase, and the systematic time-locking relationship between AOIs focused upon during this phase and AOIs subsequently encoded into a linguistic form testify to the interrelationship between the selection phase and the formulation phase.

A semantic dimension which is already well attested in crosslinguistic studies and which is also present in the study reported here is the degree to which narrators of a motion event encode or detail information about direction and landmarks. Just as expected from speakers of Germanic languages, almost all (21 out of 22) subjects of the present study produced a lot of detail about direction and landmarks. Nineteen of them used the construction [verb particle PP] to describe the motion event, for example, "fell out of the window." And 18 of these 19 subjects focused their visual attention at the AOI corresponding to the window within 1 second before the onset of the utterance.

The selection phase produces a "filtering effect" (Berman & Slobin, 1994, p. 9), that is, some information filters through to the subsequent linguistic utterance, whereas other information is filtered out. When the utterance is produced, the narrator finds himself in a new situation. He has just said what first came to his mind or, at least, what his semantic preferences were in terms of describing the motion event. He can now spend some time reflecting on what he just said and/or whether there is something more he wants to say. If he choses to say something more, it will not have the status of his first preference, but rather the status of an elaboration, addition, comment, or the like.

The further drop in amount of shifts of AOIs from the 6th to the 7th second occurs in the region where many subjects make a transition from the linguistic construction of the physical motion event to the linguistic construction of a state-of-mind or an emotive or evaluative stance. We interpret this drop as indicative of a pause during which the subject reflects upon his linguistic construction of the motion event so far and decides to extend the linguistic construction of the physical motion event with more information of the same kind (5 subjects) or reorient toward a different kind of semantic content, namely, state-of-mind or emotive or evaluative stance (13 subjects). The reflection phase is followed by a phase of reformulations or additions when the visual attention is back at a similar level of shifts of AOIs as just before the reflection phase.

The minimal level of shifts of AOIs in the reflection phase—as contrasted with the maximal level of shifts in the orientation phase—lends itself to a supplementary interpretation, which, admittedly, is more speculative. During the initial orientation phase, you assess the landscape (in a broad sense) which you are going to describe by means of a language. If this is an outer landscape—as it is in the picture story—you look extensively in order to search for relevant information. This is what all 21 of the 22 subjects in the current study did. In contrast, in the phase of additions or reformulations, the majority of the subjects in our study chose to talk about an inner landscape (again, in a broad sense). That landscape did not have any clearly perceivable correlates in the picture and required more imagination on the part of the narrator. Thus, there was no reason for the subjects to conduct a visual search of the picture in order to plan these descriptions, something which would help explain the dip in shifts of AOIs during the subjects' phase of reorientation.

FURTHER RESEARCH

We hope that this first study has served its purpose of demonstrating that thinking for speaking and channeling of attention is indeed a case for eye-tracking research. Needless to say, a lot of work remains to be done to tease out the precise relations between thought, speech, and visual attention and to integrate the notions of thinking for speaking and channeling of attention with a model of the linguistic production process. Among many ways to proceed, which we are considering in our lab, combining eye-tracking with electrophysiological measures might help validate assumptions about the cognitive differences between the different phases from first thoughts to a ready-made text fragment outlined in the tentative model in Figure 37.1.

An obvious step to take in further research is to investigate the impact of linguistic diversity on channeling of attention. We do not yet have corresponding eye-tracking data for speakers of a language group which is known to be characterized by little or no encoding of landmarks. But there exist comparable data for linguistic forms used by Spanish speakers to describe the scene with the dog's fall out of the window. Thus, a quick look at frog stories in the CHILDES archive[6] produced by 22 Spanish speakers (Sébastian corpus: 12 adult subjects; Aguilar corpus: 10 12-year-olds) revealed that only 4 of the 22 subjects used PP (e.g., "se cae de la ventana" '(he) falls from the window'). Eight of them used V only (e.g., "se cae" '(he) falls') and nine did not explicitly encode information about the fall at all and said, for example "tiene un accidente" '(he) had an accident.' Our expectation is that speakers of a linguistic community, such as the Spanish one, where there is no preference for encoding information about landmarks, will not channnel their attention toward landmarks during the selection phase.

Another line for further research is comparing speaking to writing. The communicative conditions and processing constraints of writing are typically very different from those of speaking, and so, *thinking for writing* can be expected to be different from *thinking for speaking* (Strömqvist et al., 2004). For example, in terms of our model in Figure 37.1, thinking for writing can be expected typically to contain more reflexion and contingent reformulation/revision than thinking for speaking.

These hypotheses now await testing in our lab.

---

[6] See http://childes.psy.cmu.edu/data/Frogs

REFERENCES

Andersson, B., Dahl, J., Holmqvist, K., Holsánová, J., Johansson, V., Karlsson, H., et al. (2006). Combining keystroke logging with eye tracking. In L. van Waes, M. Leijten, & C. Neuwirth (Eds.), *Writing and digital media* (pp. 166–172). Amsterdam: Kluwer.

Badre, D., Poldrack, R. A., Paré-Blagoev, E. J., Insler, R. Z., & Wagner, A. D. (2005). Dissociable controlled retrieval and generalized selection mechanisms in ventrolateral prefrontal cortex. *Neuron, 47,* 907–918.

Berman, R. A., & Slobin, D. I. (Eds.). (1994). *Relating events in narrative: A crosslinguistic developmental study.* Hillsdale, NJ: Lawrence Erlbaum Associates.

Boersma, P. (2001). Praat, a system for doing phonetics by computer. *Glot International, 5*(9/10), 341–345.

Boersma, P., & Weenink, D. (2006). Praat: Doing phonetics by computer (Version 4.4.13) [Computer program]. Retrieved March 8, 2006, from http://www.praat.org/

Brown, P. (2004). Position and motion in Tzeltal frog stories. In S. Strömqvist & L. Verhoeven (Eds.), *Relating events in narrative—typological and contextual perspectives* (pp. 36–57). Mahwah, NJ: Lawrence Erlbaum Associates.

Cassin, B. (2004). *Vocabulaire Européen des philosophies, Dictionnaire des intraduisibles.* Paris: Les éditions du Seuil.

Griffin, Z. M., & Spieler, D. S. (2006). Observing the what and when of language production by monitoring speakers' eye movements. *Brain and Language, 9*(3), 272–288.

Gumperz, J., & Levinson, S. (Eds.). (1996). *Rethinking linguistic relativity.* Cambridge, UK: Cambridge University Press.

Hayes, J. R., & Flower, L. S. (1980) Identifying the organisation of the writing process. In L.W. Gregg & E. R. Steinberg (Eds.), *Cognitive processes in writing* (pp. 3–30). Hillsdale, NJ: Lawrence Erlbaum Associates.

Henderson, J. M., & Ferreira, F. (Eds.). (2004). *The interface of language, vision, and action: Eye movements and the visual world.* New York: Psychology Press.

Holmqvist, K., Holsánová, J., Johansson, V., & Strömqvist, S. (2005). Perceiving and producing the frog story. In D. Ravid, & H. Bat-Zeev Shyldkrot (Eds.), *Perspectives on language and language development* (pp. 289–302). Dordrecht, the Netherlands: Kluwer.

Holsánová, J. (2001). *Picture viewing and picture descriptions—Two windows to the mind.* Unpublished doctoral dissertation. Lund, Sweden: Department of Cognitive Science, Lund University.

Levelt, W. (1989). *Speaking.* Cambridge, MA: The M.I.T. Press.

Mayer, M. (1969). *Frog, where are you?* New York: Dial Press.

Miller, B. T., D'Esposito, M., & Wills, H. (2005). Searching for "the top" in top-down control. *Neuron, 48,* 535–538.

Slobin, D. I. (1996). From "thought and language" to "thinking for speaking." In J. Gumperz & S. Levinson (Eds.), *Rethinking linguistic relativity* (pp. 70–96). Cambridge, UK: Cambridge University Press.

Slobin, D. I. (2002). Cognitive and communicative consequences of linguistic diversity. In S. Strömqvist (Ed.), *The diversity of languages and language learning* (pp. 7–23). Lund, Sweden: Lund University Centre for Languages and Literature.

Slobin, D. I. (2004). The many ways to search for a frog: Linguistic typology and the expression of motion events. In S. Strömqvist & L. Verhoeven (Eds.), *Relating events in narrative—typological and contextual perspectives* (pp. 219–257). Mahwah, NJ: Lawrence Erlbaum Associates.

Strömqvist, S. (2006) Learning to write: A window on language, communication and cognition. In J. Bérnicot (Ed.), Pragmatique développementale: Perspectives Européennes, special edition of *Le langage et l'Homme, 41*(2), 157–180.

Strömqvist, S., Nordqvist, Å., & Wengelin, Å. (2004). Writing the frog story —developmental and cross-modal perspectives. In S. Strömqvist & L. Verhoeven (Eds.), *Relating events in narrative—typological and contextual perspective* (pp. 359–394). Mahwah, NJ: Lawrence Erlbaum Associates.

Strömqvist, S., & Verhoeven, L. (Eds.). (2004). *Relating events in narrative—typological and contextual perspectives.* Mahwah, NJ: Lawrence Erlbaum Associates.

Talmy, L. (1991). Path to realization: A typology of event conflation. *Proceedings of the seventeenth annual meeting of the Berkeley Linguistics Society, 17,* 480–519.

Talmy, L. (2000). *Toward a cognitive semantics: Vol. II. Typology and process in concept structuring.* Cambridge, MA: The MIT Press.

Trueswell, J. C., & Tanenhaus, M. K. (Eds.). (2005). *Approaches to studying world-situated language use: Bridging the language-as-product and language-as-action traditions.* Cambridge, MA: The MIT Press.

38

Imagery for Speaking

DAVID MCNEILL
University of Chicago

INTRODUCTION

The Whorfian hypothesis has alternately attracted and annoyed linguists and psycholinguists for generations. The polar reactions tend to come in waves. We currently seem to be entering a phase of attraction, due in no small part to Dan Slobin's innovative extension of the Whorfian hypothesis to encompass thinking for speaking. The classic Whorfian hypothesis is fundamentally static. It presumes the synchronic view of language that has dominated linguistics ever since Saussure's famous Course (Saussure, 1966, original compiled posthumously by his students from lectures and published around 1915). As usually understood, the Whorfian hypothesis (Whorf, 1956) is the doctrine that holds that language influences 'habitual thought'—the very term a synchronic reference: thought abstracted from realtime dynamics to form a system of relationships viewed in toto, visible at a single theoretical instant. Lucy's (1992a, 1992b) elucidation of the Whorfian hypothesis confirms this crystalline structure, in the form of projected analogies between language and thought that by their nature are grasped synchronically. It is to Dan Slobin in his Berkeley Linguistics Society paper, "Thinking for Speaking" (Slobin, 1987), that we turn to get the first sight of a truly dynamic version of the Whorfian hypothesis—thinking generated, as Slobin says, because of the requirements of a linguistic code: "'Thinking for speaking' involves picking those characteristics that (a) fit some conceptualization of the event, and (b) are readily encodable in the language"[1] (p. 435). That languages differ in their thinking for speaking affordances is a version of the relativity hypothesis, now realized on the realtime dimension of speech and its unfolding.

My contribution to this approach is to bring in gestures. The imagery embodied in gestures also differs across languages. Duncan and I wrote on this theme in relation to thinking for speaking in McNeill and Duncan (2000). The current contribution is an updating of our joint paper, drawing on the growth point hypothesis we presented there and the considerable further development of the hypothesis in McNeill (2005). I will demonstrate gestures at work in thinking for speaking in four languages. To provide a theoretical framework, I will first define "gesture," and then present a theoretical dynamic model—the growth point or GP—to explicate the role performed by gestures in thinking for speaking. The overall approach is presented at length in McNeill (2005).

Duncan and I observed in our paper that a skeptical view of thinking for speaking could maintain that it operates only at the level of linguistic expression; there are indeed differences across

---

[1] The expression, 'thinking for speaking' suggests to some readers a temporal sequence: thinking first, speaking second. We posit instead an extended process of thinking while speaking, but keep the thinking for speaking formulation to maintain continuity with Slobin and his writings, and to capture the sense of an adaptive function also conveyed by for, with the caveat that we do not mean by this a thinking → speaking temporal sequence.

languages in how data and experience are expressed, but to infer also from these differences in thinking risks circularity. To counter such a view, some way is needed to externalize cognition in addition to language. We thus considered speech and gesture jointly as an enhanced 'window' onto thinking and showed how the co-occurrences of speech and gesture in different languages enabled us to infer thinking for speaking in Slobin's sense (McNeill and Duncan, 2000).

WHAT IS 'GESTURE'?

Kendon (1980) distinguished five kinds of 'gestures.' I subsequently arranged the distinctions along a continuum that I named the Gesture Continuum (McNeill, 1992; later elaborated into the Gesture Continua, McNeill, 2000). Here is the original Continuum:

Gesticulation → Speech-Linked → Pantomime → Emblems → Signs

The gestures with which we are concerned are the gesticulations. As one moves along the Continuum, two kinds of reciprocal changes occur. First, the degree to which speech is an obligatory accompaniment of gesture decreases from gesticulation to signs. Second, the degree to which gesture shows the properties of a language increases over the same span. Gesticulations are obligatorily accompanied by speech but have properties unlike language. Speech-linked gestures are also obligatorily performed with speech, but time with speech in a different manner—sequentially rather than concurrently, and in a specific linguistic slot (filling in for a missing complement of the verb, for example). Pantomime or dumb show by definition is not accompanied by speech. Emblems such as the "OK" sign have independent status as symbolic forms. Signs in American Sign Language (ASL) and other sign languages are obligatorily not accompanied by speech, and the languages themselves have the essential properties of all languages. Clearly, therefore, speech and gesticulation (but not the other points along Gesture's Continuum) combine properties that are unalike, and this combination occupies the same performance instant. A combination of unalikes at the same time is a framework for an imagery-language dialectic.

A DYNAMIC APPROACH

McNeill (2005) presents a dynamic conception of language as an imagery-language dialectic, in which gestures provide imagery. Thinking for speaking appears at several places in this dialectic, with imagery for speaking the first of these. Gesture is an integral component of language in this conception, not merely an accompaniment or ornament. Such gestures are synchronous and co-expressive with speech, not redundant, and are not signs, salutes, or emblems. They are frequent—about 90% of spoken utterances in narrative discourse are accompanied by them (Nobe, 2000). The synchrony of speech forms and gestures creates the conditions for an imagery-language dialectic. A dialectic implies:

- a conflict or opposition of some kind, and
- resolution of the conflict through further change or development.

The synchronous presence of unlike modes of cognition, imagery, and language, that are co-expressive of the same underlying thought unit, sets up an unstable confrontation of opposites. Even when the information content in speech and gesture is similar it is present in contrasting semiotic modes, and a dialectic occurs. This very instability fuels thinking for speaking as it seeks resolution. Instability is an essential feature of the dialectic, and is a key to the dynamic dimension. The concept of an imagery-language dialectic extends a concept initiated (without reference to gesture) by Vygotsky, in the 1930s (cf. Vygotsky, 1987):

> The relation of thought to word is not a thing but a process, a continual movement back and forth from thought to word and from word to thought. In that process, the relation of thought to word undergoes changes that themselves may be regarded as development in the functional sense. Thought is not merely expressed in words; it comes into existence through them. (1987, p. 218)

This conception also recaptures an insight lost for almost a century, that language requires two simultaneous modes of thought—what Saussure, in recently discovered notes composed around 1910, termed the 'double essence' of language (although he too expressed this without reference to gestures; cf. Harris, 2002; Saussure, 2002).

Gesture is naturally opposed to linguistic form; they present the same underlying idea unit in two forms. At the point where speech and gesture are synchronous they are co-expressive. The idea unit ties them together and explains the synchrony. The opposition between them is semiotic, different ways of packaging information, and exists even when the referential content of speech and gesture is the same. In gesture, information is embodied globally, as a whole, instantaneously, and concentrates in one symbol what may be distributed across several surface elements of speech. Simultaneously, in speech, the same idea unit is represented analytically, combinatorically, and linearly. In this semiotic opposition the idea unit exists at the same moment in two semiotically opposite forms, a contrast that fuels thought and speech, animating it in a dialectic.

The smallest unit of the imagery-language dialectic is posited to be a 'growth point' (hereafter GP), so named because it is theoretically the initial unit of thinking for speaking out of which a dynamic process of organization emerges. A GP combines imagery with linguistic categorial content, and the theory is that such a combination is unstable and thus initiates cognitive events. In the GP interactions between language and imagery occur in both directions, it is not that imagery is input to language or language to imagery; the effects are mutual, but in this chapter the emphasis is on imagery and how it is affected by language, in keeping with the thinking for speaking focus.

A GP is an empirically recoverable idea unit, inferred from speech-gesture synchrony and co-expressiveness. An example recorded in an experiment (offered in part because of its ordinariness) is a description by a speaker of a classic Tweety and Sylvester escapade, which went in part as follows: "and Tweety Bird runs and gets a bowling ba[ll and drop**s it down** the drainpipe]."[2] Speech was accompanied by a gesture in which the two hands thrust downward at chest level, the palms curved and angled inward and downward, as if curved over the top of a large spherical object (see Figure 38.1).[3] At the left bracket, the hands started to move up from the speaker's lap to prepare for the downward thrust.

Then her hands, at the very end of "drops," paused briefly in the curved palm-down position, frozen in midair (the first underlining). Next was the gesture stroke—the downward thrust itself—timed exactly with "it down" (boldface). Movement proper ceased in the middle of "down," the hands again freezing in midair until the word was finished (the second underlining). Finally, the hands returned to rest (up to the right bracket). The two pauses or holds and the continuing preparation phase itself reveal that the downward thrust was targeted precisely at the "it down" fragment: the downward thrust was withheld until the speech fragment could begin and was maintained,

---

[2] Notation for indicating gesture phase timing in relation to speech: [is the onset of the gesture phrase, when the hands move from rest or a previous gesture into position to perform the stroke;] is the end of the gesture phrase; boldface is the gesture stroke itself, the meaning-bearing phase of the gesture, performed with effort, and the only phase that is obligatory; underlining is a pre- or poststroke hold, a brief cessation of motion that tends to ensure the synchrony of stroke and targeted speech. Gesture phrases can occur inside other gesture phrases and this is marked by a double '[[' and ']]' (cf. line 2 of Ex. 1). The preparation phase is the interval between the onset of motion '[' and the beginning of the stroke or prestroke hold; the retraction phase is that between the end of the stroke or poststroke hold and the end of motion ']'. In the speech transcript, a '/' is a silent pause and a '°' is a self-interruption. The onset of preparation is the first indication the idea unit in the stroke has come to life—in this example, with the word "ball" in the preceding clause. A prestroke hold suggests the linguistic material co-occurring with the stroke was targeted. A poststroke hold suggests the stroke and its speech are not merely co-occurring but are a single production. Finally, the end of retraction can be seen as the switching off of the idea unit.

[3] Computer art in this and all following figures by Fey Parrill.

Figure 38.1 Gesture stroke accompanying "it down" in the sentence "and drops it down the drainpipe." (From McNeill (2005). Used with permission.)

despite a lack of movement, until the fragment was completed. Significantly, even though the gesture depicted downward thrusting, the stroke bypassed the very verb that describes this motion, "drops," the preparation continuing right through it and holding at the end.

The fragment, "it down," plus the image of a downward thrust, was the GP. It is impossible to fully understand the source of any GP without elaboration of its relationship to context. This relationship is mutually constitutive. A GP cannot exist without a context, because it is a point of differentiation within it; and the context is created, in part, to make the differentiation possible. While context reflects the physical, social, and linguistic environment, it is also a mental phenomenon, a representation; the speaker constructs it in order to make the intended contrast, the GP, meaningful within it. Theoretically, a growth point is a psychological predicate in Vygotsky's (1987) sense, a significant contrast within a context (also Firbas, 1971).

A further concept, the catchment, provides an empirical route for finding this context. A catchment comprises gestures in a discourse stretch with recurring form features and reveals the theme or field of oppositions from which the GP is differentiated. To identify the catchment in the "it down" case, we look for other gestures during the narration in which the hands are shaped and/or move similarly to the target gesture and ask if these gestures comprise a family with thematic continuity. We find such a family; in the speaker's rendition, all such two-handed gestures had to do with the bowling ball conceptualized as an antagonistic force, directed contra-Sylvester. The whole episode, of which the case study is a part, was construed by this speaker not merely as a cinematic episode but as a confrontation of antagonistic forces—Sylvester vs. Bowling Ball. We can thereby further specify the "it down" GP: it was a psychological predicate specifying how the bowling ball was this antagonistic force:

Ways of Thwarting Sylvester: Bowling Ball Down

So the field of oppositions (Ways of Thwarting Sylvester) was differentiated as an image of a downward path, and categorized as "it" and "down."

This analysis explains why the verb "drops" was excluded from the GP. The verb describes what Tweety did, not what the bowling ball did (it went down as the antagonistic force), and thus "drops" was not a significant contrast in the field of oppositions involving the bowling ball. The core idea of "it down" was the bowling ball and its action, not Tweety and his. The origin of the verb in this case is explained by separate unpacking (see McNeill, 2005).

GPS IN FOUR LANGUAGES

This dynamic approach can also be applied crosslinguistically. We observe that idea units are not independent of the language spoken, even when referential content is the same; given the same objective reality idea units can differ across languages. The languages to be described cover a range of types—English, Mandarin, Spanish, and the Deaf Sign Language of Taiwan (TSL).

METHODOLOGICAL PRELIMINARIES

Sources of Data

We have collected narrations of a Tweety & Sylvester cartoon stimulus in some 20 languages, with substantial collections in English, Spanish, and Mandarin. The English speakers were students at the University of Chicago. The Mandarin narrators were mostly students or spouses of students at the University of Chicago, many recent arrivals. The Spanish speakers were monolinguals recorded in Guadalajara, Mexico.[4] The TSL narrations were recorded in Taipei by Susan Duncan. Both male and female speakers participated in all languages. The narrators viewed a 6-minute film ("Canary Row") and retold it immediately from memory to a listener who had not seen it; narrator and listener were told that the listener would be asked to retell the story, a provision to encourage a full and clear description from the primary speaker. There was no mention of gesture, the emphasis was on storytelling. The resulting stories have coherence, including those by non-English speaking subjects. (The cartoon was selected in part because it makes limited use of speech and has a highly repetitive storyline with amusing surface variations.) Because we use a standard stimulus we are able to compare retellings across languages of the same episodes, thus holding referential content constant.

Coding

All narrations were transcribed, translated where necessary into morpheme-by-morpheme glosses by bilingual transcribers, plus idiomatic English, and coded for gestures, with the emphasis on the exact temporal location in relation to speech of the preparation, stroke, and retraction phases, plus any pre- and poststroke holds. Motion event content (both speech and gesture) was coded using Talmy's (2000) motion event semantic components—figure, path, manner, and/or ground (gestures frequently combine several components).

COMPARISON ACROSS LANGUAGES

In the following analyses, languages are compared for a specific cartoon episode that involves the following drama: Sylvester the cat, pacing on a sidewalk, is attempting to reach Tweety, a canary, perched tantalizingly in a window high above. He decides to use a drainpipe running up the side of the building. The pipe conveniently ends just at Tweety's window. Sylvester tries this twice, each time with catastrophic results. His first effort is on the outside of the pipe, climbing it like a rope.

---

[4] The recordings in Guadalajara were conducted by Lisa Miotto and Karl-Erik McCullough. The gesture motion events project was carried out with Susan Duncan.

He reaches Tweety but is battered off the windowsill by Tweety's fierce protector, Granny. On his second try (the case study episode), Sylvester climbs the pipe on the inside, hoping for concealment. Tweety nevertheless sees him, rushes off screen, and returns with an enormous bowling ball, which he releases into the pipe. The ball and Sylvester meet explosively mid-pipe. He is next seen shooting out the bottom of the pipe, the bowling ball now inside him. A living bowling ball, he rolls (or is rolled) down a sloping street, legs spinning helplessly at his side, and disappears into a bowling alley. After an ominous pause, we hear tenpins being knocked over. This collection of motion events and how they are packaged comprises points of comparison across languages.

Crucial for comparing English and Spanish is Talmy's (2000) motion events typology, according to which these two languages (and many others) differ in how they package motion event semantic components. In satellite-framed (or 'S-type') languages (including English, German, Scandinavian languages, Chinese), path is encoded outside the verb, in a so-called satellite or preposition—cf. the different directions of walking in "walk in/out/across/through, etc." Manner in contrast is encoded within the verb—cf. the different ways of getting across in "walk/run/stride/stagger/sidle, etc., across." In contrast, in verb-framed (or 'V-type') languages (such as Spanish, French, Italian, Turkish, Japanese, ASL), path is encoded inside the verb and manner is outside either in a new verb or gerund (cf. Sp. "sale volando" 'exits flying'), or is omitted altogether. In what follows, we see how gestures differ in these two kinds of languages.

Gestural Paths Tend to Be Straight-Line Segments in English and Unbroken Wholes in Spanish

S-type and V-type languages typically induce different imagery modes (cf. Özyürek et al., 2005). Given the GP theory, this implies distinct thinking for speaking approaches. In S-type English, imagery of path or direction is broken into straight-line segments. In Spanish, the V-type, path is more often a single unbroken whole. The cross-language difference becomes clear when complex, curvilinear paths such as the bowling ball episode are compared—in the S-type, the path devolves into a series of short segments. The same path in the V-type is preserved in its full curvilinear complexity. GPs in English thus tend to focus on segments and how they relate, while those in Spanish focus on wholes. Different contexts would tend to be constructed by speakers of the two languages to make these GPs possible—in English, where the segments of the path may have communicative dynamism, what Slobin (1996) has described as "elaborated trajectories of motion," versus, in Spanish, contexts in which the path as a whole stands out, perhaps what he described as "elaborated descriptions of the static locations of objects" (p. 78).

In English The general rule seems to be that the gestures of English speakers convey path information synchronized with path satellites. The exceptions are that some path gestures align with ground/landmark elements. But overall, complex curvilinear paths break down into a series of more or less straight path segments (paths 1, 2, 3, and 5 in the following align with satellites, 4 and 6 with ground/landmark elements):

> Example 1
> (1) [/ and it **goes** <u>down</u>]
> (2) but [[it **roll**][s **him out°**]]
> (3) [[down **the** / <u>/</u>]
> (4) [/ **rain**<u>spo</u>]]
> (5) [ut/ **out** i][nto
> (6) **the** **sid**<u>ew</u>]alk/ <u>into</u> a] [bowling a**lley**

The statements and their linked gestures are shown in Figure 38.2, and the match-up is perfect. Visuospatial cognition consisted of six straight-line segments. Such a division is expected from the kind of analytic path-satellite treatment directionality receives in S-type languages.

 PATH 1 [/ and it **goes** down]

 PATH 4 [/ **rain**spo]]

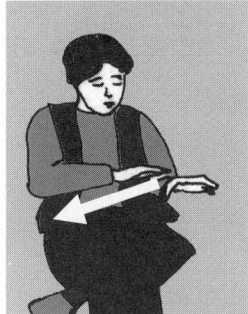 PATH 2 but [[it **roll**][s **him out***]]

 PATH 5 [ut/ **out** i][nto

 PATH 3 [[down **the** //]

 PATH 6 **the** sid<u>ew</u>]alk/ <u>into</u> a] [bowling **alley**

Figure 38.2   English speaker's six path segments for Sylvester's trip down the pipe, accompanied by "and it goes down but it rolls him out down the rain spout out into the sidewalk into a bowling alley and he knocks over all the pins." Compare to Figure 38.3. The hand performed two similar strokes in Path 6. (From McNeill (2005). With permission.)

In Spanish   Spanish speakers, in contrast, often seem to represent the same scene without significant segmentation. Example 2 is a description by a monolingual Spanish speaker. In speech there was onomatopoeia, a frequent verb substitute in our Spanish-language productions:

Example 2
[enton**ces SSS**]
then he-falls ONOM
then SSSS he falls

The accompanying gesture traced a single, unbroken path down and to the right (Figure 38.3—there are no pauses or interruptions). For the very same event, what had been segmented in English was a single curvaceous trajectory in Spanish.

To quantify this crosslinguistic difference, Table 38.1 shows the number of path segments contained in gestures depicting path from Sylvester's encounter with the bowling ball to the denouement in the bowling alley, for both Spanish and English descriptions. All speakers, regardless of language,

Figure 38.3 Spanish speaker's single continuous arc for Sylvester's trip down the pipe, accompanied by "entonces SSS" ('then SSS he falls'). Compare to Figure 38.2. (From McNeill (2005). With permission.)

segment, but English speakers break the trajectory into 43 percent more segments than do Spanish speakers. On average, each English speaker produced 3.3 segments, while each Spanish speaker produced 2.3 segments. Extremes of segmentation, moreover, strongly favor English. Five English speakers divided the trajectory into six or more segments, compared to only one Spanish speaker going so far. Thus Spanish speakers, even when they divide paths into segments, have fewer of them. And since they do not introduce lapses of gesture the segments are also broader, covering more speech (however, when speech describes a boundary or change of state—conditions that necessitate a new clause in Spanish—any accompanying path gesture stops and a new gesture or a gesture cessation

TABLE 38.1 Segmentation of Paths by English- and Spanish-Speaking Adults

Number of Gesture Segments	Number of Speakers	
	English (N=21)	Spanish (N=18)
0	0	1
1	3	5
2	7	6
3	3	4
4	2	1
5	1	0
≥ 6	5	1

TABLE 38.2 Gestures With Spoken References to Rolling

	Manner in Gesture	Non-Manner in Gesture
Spanish Adults (18)	80%	20%
English Adults (21)	43%	57%

ensues; English speakers, in contrast, at these same points, simply continue the path gesture, since in this language no new verb or clause accrues; McNeill & Duncan, 2000).

Gestures Expand Manner in Spanish, Modulate Manner in English

Manner is the other diagnostic motion event component, along with path, separating the S-type and V-type languages. Manner imagery is accessible to speakers of both types of language, but enters into GP formation in different ways. Table 38.2 provides an overview of gestural manner with a specific verb, "rolls" in English, "rodar" in Spanish. Perhaps surprisingly, Spanish has a higher incidence of gestural manner with this verb.

In Spanish   In Spanish speech, manner requires a second verb or gerund and is often omitted altogether (Slobin, 1996, 2004). Nonetheless, a manner gesture can combine imagery with other motion components in speech, typically the ground/landmark. The result is an expansion of the Spanish sentence to include manner without actually lexicalizing it. The effect seems to be that different kinds of surfaces, situations, etc., imply their own manners of action; we shall see an example of this constraint below.

One result of the expansion is a 'manner fog'—a blanketing of manner via gesture when there is no manner in speech. An example is shown in Example 3, a description of Sylvester climbing the inside of the pipe:

Example 3
  (1) e entonces busca la ma[ner**a (silent pause)**]
      and so he looks for the way
      Gesture depicts the shape of the pipe: **ground**.
  (2) [de **entra**][r // **se met**][**e por e**l]
      to enter REFL goes-into through the
      Both hands rock and rise simultaneously: **manner** + **path** *combined (left hand only through "mete")*
  (3) [de**sague** //] [// si?]
      drainpipe...yes?
      Right hand circles in arc: **manner** + **ground** *(shape of pipe).*
  (4) [de**sague entra** /]
      drainpipe, enters
      Both hands briefly in palm-down position (clambering paws) and then rise with chop-like motion: **manner** + **path** *combined.*

Manner gestures appeared in the second, third, and fourth lines, despite a total absence from speech. Thus, while manner may seem to be absent when speech alone is considered, it may be present, even abundant, in visuospatial thinking. In this example manner is categorized as motion along a path and/or as a ground element (the pipe). In the ground (pipe) GPs, the speaker seems to have conceived of the pipe and its shape as constraining a certain kind of manner. The swirling gesture with "desague" in (3) is an illustration—circling around, a constraint on manner arising from the interior contour of the pipe[5] (English speakers sometimes convey this as well, but use a verb for it, e.g., "barreling").

In English In English, imagery modulates lexical manner, either emphasizing it or downplaying it. Such a role is correlated with the obligatory presence of manner in S-type verbs. A verb like "rolls" contains manner regardless of communicative dynamism. If manner is part of the GP manner is likely to appear in a gesture synchronized with the verb; but if manner is not the point of differentiation the gesture can lack manner, emphasize path or some other motion event component, and may not synchronize with the verb at all (or there can be no gesture, of course). Thus gesture modulates manner. Whereas a manner fog adds manner when it is lacking from speech, modulation adjusts the manner that is present in speech. The direction in which the modulation goes—enhancement or minimization—can be traced to the communicative weight given to manner in the context of speaking. The following examples, from different speakers, show enhancement and minimization, respectively, and how they correspond to different contextual weightings of manner.

The enhancement example was at the end of a series of references to the bowling ball, where its manner of motion would plausibly have been highlighted (cf. Parrill, 2008). The gesture contains manner and synchronizes with the manner verb, "rolls." This content and co-occurrence with the gesture highlight manner and suggest that it was part of the psychological predicate, as shown in Example 4.

> Example 4 (enhancement)
> and he drops a [bowl]ing ball [in**to** the rain spout]
> [and it **goes do**wn]
> and it° [/] ah°
> you [**can't tell if the bow**ling ball /]
> [is un° /] [is **und**er Sylvester
> **or ins**ide of him]
> [but it **rolls him out**]°
> (= *gesture with manner: Both hands sweep to right and rotate as they go, conveying both path and manner*)

In the minimization example, despite the same verb, "rolls," the gesture skips the verb and has no manner content of its own. It shows path, and co-occurs with the path satellite, "down." Both the timing and the shape of the gesture thus suggest that manner was not a major element of the speaker's intent, and that "rolls," while referentially appropriate, was de-emphasized and functioned as a verb referring to the fact of motion with manner content downplayed (the speaker could just as well have said "goes down," avoiding lexical manner, but this would have meant editing out what the speaker also knew—Sylvester was rolling; the manner component in "rolls" referred without adding to communicative dynamism). This situation is shown in Example 5:

> Example 5 (minimization)
> [the canary] # [th**rows**°] #
> [puts a # [bowling] [ball] #
> into] # [the **drain** spout as the]
> [**cat** is climbing up /and]
> [it **goes** into his] [mouth] / *(topic switch to Sylvester)*
> [and **of course**] #
> [**into** his stomach] #
> [and he rolls # **down** the drain spout] (= *gesture with path but no manner: Left hand plunges straight down, in synchrony with the satellite*)
> [and [**across**] [the **street**] into [the bowling] alley #]

---

[5] Observation due to Sue Duncan.

English, Compared to Mandarin, Is Enslaved to Predication

Mandarin and English are each languages of the S-type but differ in many other ways. A less-than-obvious difference emerges from the gesture data. English, more than Mandarin, seems committed to predicates as the loci of gestures.

Example 6 (English—committed)
[so it **hits** him on **the hea**][d and he winds up **rolling down the stre**]et

The speaker performed a rolling down gesture as she was saying "hits him on the head." Gesture and speech comprised a sensible combination, the gesture showing the consequence of the action that speech described. However, the hand did not return to rest but held in place waiting (in fact, twice) for the predicate; then the gesture repeated on a larger scale. The larger gesture had the character of a repair, was exaggerated, as if to correct the 'misplaced' previous version.

Mandarin, perhaps because it has alternate construction strategies such as topic and comment, seems less wedded to predication (also, on the English side, word order inflexibility could promote tighter linkages of gestures to predicates). We find Mandarin examples in which a gesture depicting an action co-occurs with a noun phrase referring to the instrument of that action, not the verb phrase identifying the action itself. An action-instrument combination also makes sense; in fact, much the same kind of sense as the English speaker's cause-effect combination. The predicate, however, when it comes, is free of gesture. It is as though the predicate—far from a repair—is felt to be redundant, a repetition of something already conveyed, and is included only to meet standards of well-formedness. An example is the following:[6]

Example 7 (Mandarin—free)
lao tai-tai [na   -ge   da **bang hao**]-xiang gei   ta   da-xia
old lady hold CLASSIFIER big stick seem CAUSE him hit down$_{\text{verb-satellite}}$
'The old lady seemed to have knocked him down with a big stick'
Left hand in grip moves downward sharply from head to waist.

Despite the spacing, there were no pauses or hesitations. The speaker, as she said "da bang" (a big stick), performed a gesture that seemingly held the stick while executing a downward blow. Her hand then went to rest and remained there as she continued on to the predicate, the meaning of which was close to that of the gesture. There were no further gestures. Thus, unlike English, a gesture depicting an action with speech not part of the predicate was not repaired; to the contrary, the predicate was treated like a repetition.

Thus the languages show opposite inclinations toward predicates, revealed in the treatment of gestures. In terms of GPs, the English speaker's initial gesture-speech combination, although sensible, was not a successful growth point, because it attempted to swallow what for her belonged to the predicate.[7] Such was not a barrier for the Mandarin speaker, who in fact released the predicate from service once the instrument-action combination had been created with the gesture. Imagery is categorized differently—in English it is tied to predication; in Mandarin it may seek other partners.

GPs with Manner in Sign Languages

What of sign languages? It goes without saying that a sign language uses imagery for speaking in one sense of image; however, this is a regularized kind of imagery. Sign languages conventionalize

---

[6] Example, transcription, and translation due to Sue Duncan. Although we don't have numerical data, Duncan has often noticed such combinations in daily Mandarin speech.

[7] Gestures in English do occur outside predicates, but as Exs. 6 and 7 suggest, the gravitational pull of the predicate is greater in English.

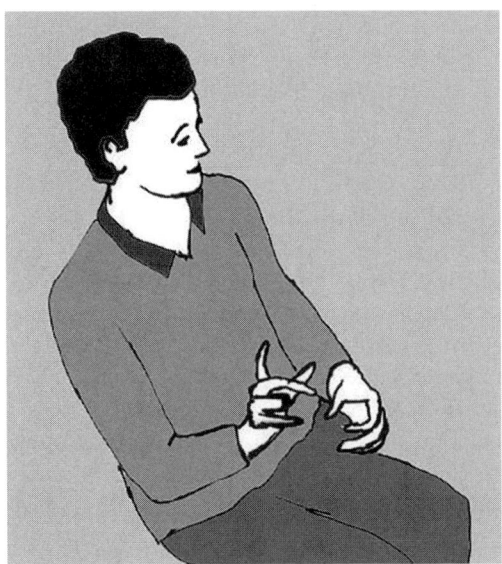 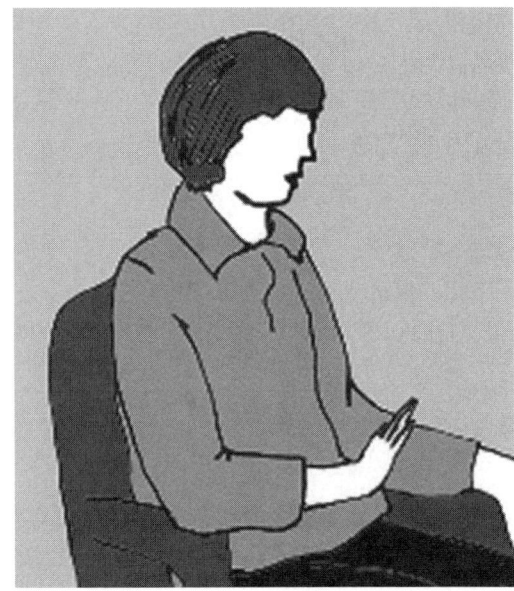

Figure 38.4 Possible gesture (left panel) with the TSL sign for 'animate being with more than two legs,' deformed for iconicity at the same discourse junctures where gestures also occur by hearing speakers (recorded by S. Duncan). Compare to English speaker's gesture for the same event (right panel). Both illustrations from McNeill (2005) are used with permission.

space and motion (utilizing space and motion as the linguistic medium). Conventionalization alters the semiotic quality of signs. A sign is analytic, segmented, and combinatoric—the semiotic of the language side. But it would be odd if sign languages did not have GPs. So what would the gestural side of a signed GP look like? Duncan (2005) proposes that sign deformation signals a gesture occurrence. She has recorded this phenomenon in Taiwan sign language (TSL) at points of newsworthy content, the same points where speaking narrators also perform gestures. The deformations modify the sign to highlight what is significant in the immediate discourse context. Thus we can examine TSL gestures in signing to see if, here too, manner imagery is adapted to linguistic form in the environment of a sign. Figure 38.4 (left panel) illustrates a sign using a classifier in TSL for animate beings with more than two legs (animals, crawling babies). The standard form of the classifier is the thumb, the index finger, and the middle finger extended and spread apart, the other fingers curled in, with the palm down. However, when describing Sylvester going up the pipe on the outside, the signer modified the classifier by having the first and second fingers, instead of extending outward motionlessly, alternatingly 'walk up' in space (also the left hand, at leg level, was curved, apparently to show the pipe, but this location was not a locus for the 'walking'). The thumb was extended, which indicates that we see here the sign modified. What is key is that also the fourth finger was extended, an extension that is not part of the canonical form but was perhaps added to be the third leg as specified in the canonical sign (unmoving but extended).[8] If so, imagery for speaking (signing) was modified to meet the sign's conventional form. The GP was something like the image of climbing, linguistically categorized as having been done by a creature with more than two legs. The right panel of Figure 38.4 shows a hearing English speaker's version of the same cartoon event. Here, the gesture emphasizes interiority and ascent, just as did the TSL gesture/sign, but lacks protuberances for legs (the squeezed upright fingers showing direction and compression) and in fact does not depict clambering at all. So perhaps the emphasis in TSL, but not in English, on climbing was another case of thinking for speaking adapting to the affordances of the language, due to linguistic features of the

---

[8] This interpretation supercedes the one offered, with puzzlement, in McNeill (2005).

sign finding special significance in images of clambering feet (presumed feet, since they were not in fact visible in the stimulus).

GENERAL SUMMARY

The different uses of gesture in these four languages provide evidence that visuospatial cognition during thinking for speaking differs systematically across languages. Four major ways in which gestures co-occur with speech have been observed:

(a) Gestural paths tend to be broken into straight-line segments in English and remain unbroken curvilinear wholes in Spanish.
(b) Gestural manner tends to expand the encoding resources of Spanish and to modulate them in English, following the packaging of manner information in these languages—unavoidable manner in English, all-too-avoidable in Spanish.
(c) Gestures reveal a 'tyranny of predication' in English GPs that is lacking or minimal in Mandarin.
(d) Gestures combine with signs through distortions to provide imagery, and create signed GPs.

CONCLUSION: A STRONG/WEAK PARADOX

We began this chapter with the Whorfian hypothesis. Now it is time to expose a paradox in the 'strong' and 'weak' versions of this hypothesis. Depending on what we mean by 'strength,' the weak version is stronger. I would prefer not to use the muscular analogy at all: it misses the real distinction, which is that the 'strong' version is static, the 'weak' version, in its thinking for speaking form, is dynamic. The strong version, so-called, refers to habitual thought, and proposes that the effects of language on cognitive dispositions do not require the production of speech to activate them—'strong' in this sense means that the influence of language does not depend on the unfolding of a process, namely, speech. Thinking for (and while) speaking, on the other hand, occurs during acts of speech only, hence is 'weaker.'

Apart from the time-honored but dubious distinction between 'language' and 'speech,' there is another way to think about this comparison, and in this alternative the weak outpowers the strong. The question is, on which dimension of language is the influence on thought stronger? And here the dynamic dimension is clearly the place: the impact of language on thought is readily demonstrated in the dynamic unfolding of language where thinking for speaking takes place. To judge from the years of controversy and waves of endorsement followed by rejection, the impact of language on thought on the static dimension is hard to discern: this is the paradox, but also the remedy. Slobin's thinking for speaking hypothesis is the breakthrough that reveals the dynamic dimension of the Whorfian hypothesis, where an impact of language on thought is readily observed.

REFERENCES

Carroll, J. B. (Ed.). (1956). *Language, thought, and reality: Selected writings of Benjamin Lee Whorf.* Cambridge, MA: The MIT Press.
Duncan, S. (2005). Gesture in signing: A case study from Taiwan Sign Language. *Language and Linguistics,* 6, 279–318.
Firbas, J. (1971). On the concept of communicative dynamism in the theory of functional sentence perspective. *Philologica Pragensia,* 8, 135–144.
Harris, R. (2002). Why words really do not stay still. *Times Literary Supplement,* July 26 issue, p. 30.

Kendon, A. (1980). Gesticulation and speech: Two aspects of the process of utterance. In M. R. Key (Ed.), *The relationship of verbal and nonverbal communication* (pp. 207–227). The Hague: Mouton.

Lucy, J. A. (1992a). *Language diversity and thought: A reformulation of the Linguistic Relativity Hypothesis.* Cambridge, UK: Cambridge University Press.

Lucy, J. A. (1992b). *Grammatical categories and cognition: A case study of the Linguistic Relativity Hypothesis.* Cambridge, UK: Cambridge University Press.

McNeill, D. (1992). *Hand and mind.* Chicago: University of Chicago Press.

McNeill, D. (2000). Catchments and contexts: Non-modular factors in speech and gesture production. In D. McNeill (Ed.), *Language and gesture* (pp. 312–328). Cambridge, UK: Cambridge University Press.

McNeill, D. (2005). *Gesture and thought.* Chicago: University of Chicago Press.

McNeill, D., & Duncan, S. D. (2000). Growth points in thinking-for-speaking. In D. McNeill (Ed.), *Language and gesture* (pp. 141–161). Cambridge, UK: Cambridge University Press.

Nobe, S. (2000). Where do most spontaneous representational gestures actually occur with respect to speech? In D. McNeill (Ed.), *Language and gesture* (pp. 186–198). Cambridge, UK: Cambridge University Press.

Özyürek, A., Kita, S., Allen, S., Shanley, E. M., Furman, R., & Brown, A. (2005). How does linguistic framing of events influence co-speech gestures?: Insights from crosslinguistic variations and similarities. *Gesture, 5,* 219–240.

Parrill, F. (2008). Subjects in the hands of speakers: An experimental study of syntactic subject and speech–gesture integration. *Cognitive Linguistics, 19,* 283–299.

Saussure, F. de (1966). *Course in general linguistics* [C. Bally & A. Sechehaye, Eds., in collaboration with A. Riedlinger; W. Baskin, trans.]. New York: McGraw-Hill.

Saussure, F. de (2002). *Écrits de linguistique général* [compiled and edited by S. Bouquet & R. Engler]. Paris: Gallimard.

Slobin, D. I. (1987). Thinking for speaking. In J. Aske, N. Beery, L. Michaelis, & H. Filip (Eds.), *Proceedings of the thirteenth annual meeting of the Berkeley Linguistics Society* (pp. 435–445). Berkeley: Berkeley Linguistics Society.

Slobin, D. I. (1996). From "thought and language" to "thinking for speaking." In J. J. Gumperz & S. C. Levinson (Eds.), *Rethinking linguistic relativity* (pp. 70–96). Cambridge, UK: Cambridge University Press.

Slobin, D. I. (2004). The many ways to search for a frog: Linguistic typology and the expression of motion events. In S. Strömqvist & L. Verhoeven (Eds.), *Relating events in narrative: Vol. 2. Typological and contextual perspectives* (pp. 219–257). Mahwah, NJ: Lawrence Erlbaum Associates.

Talmy, L. (2000). *Toward a cognitive semantics.* Cambridge, MA: The MIT Press.

Vygotsky, L. S. (1987). *Thought and language.* [Edited and translated by E. Hanfmann & G. Vakar; revised and edited by A. Kozulin]. Cambridge, MA: The MIT Press.

39

Evidentials:
An Interface Between Linguistic and Conceptual Development[1]

AYHAN AKSU-KOÇ
Yeditepe University and Boğaziçi University, Istanbul

> [T]here is a process of thinking for speaking in which cognition plays a dynamic role within the framework of linguistic expression[.]
>
> **Dan I. Slobin (2003, p. 158)**

As a young graduate student at Berkeley, in the summer of 1972, I was invited to join a wonderful group of people in Dubrovnik where they were preparing to launch the first comprehensive crosslinguistic study of language acquisition. This first encounter with Dan Slobin was the beginning of my inquiry into language and my first insights and enthusiasm went into the exploration of evidentials. The same excitement prevailed during the years when I looked on and off into the question of what the cognitive underpinnings for their acquisition might be. Given the 'meta' nature of this semantic/pragmatic domain, the results of this search have not crystallized easily. In this chapter I tried to systematize what I have learned, using again some of Dan's guiding principles as the key, and our shared curiosity for what the linguistic mind can achieve as the motivating force. But of course, what I have learned from him—about language, about development, and about how to look at both—has just remained in the background, together with all I learned about how to give and how to guide, that is, about friendship and mentorship.

The past three decades have witnessed a move away from the unidirectional Piagetian assumption that language maps onto an independently built cognitive domain to investigations showing the formative role of language in conceptual growth along the lines suggested by Vygotsky (1978). This neo-Whorfian perspective gained momentum with Slobin's crosslinguistic work (Slobin, 1985, 1987, 2003), Bowerman's arguments for the role of language in shaping cognition (Bowerman, 1985; Bowerman & Levinson, 2001), and studies in linguistic anthropology (Gumperz & Levinson, 1996). This view is best expressed in Slobin's (1987) notion of 'thinking for speaking' which states that no utterance is a direct representation of perceived reality because mental representations submit to, and are shaped by, the categories of the language spoken. In this process where "cognition plays a dynamic role within the framework of linguistic expression," language has online effects on thought (Slobin,

---

[1] I would like to express my sincere thanks to my editors Jiansheng Guo and Kei Nakamura for their critical suggestions on an early draft of the chapter, and to my colleague Ageliki Nicolopoulou for her fine-tuned comments on the last draft.

2003, p. 158). These online effects are particularly revealing in children's acquisition of grammaticized distinctions that some languages observe. A case in point is evidential languages where every utterance is a function of both a representation corresponding to its informational content and a pragmatic tag corresponding to the particular mode of access to or source of that information.

In this chapter, I explore the developmental relations between language and cognition by bringing together findings from my earlier work on the acquisition of this grammatical category (Aksu-Koç, 1988) and my recent studies exploring its conceptual correlates in social cognition (Aksu-Koç & Alıcı, 2000; Aksu-Koç, Aydın, Avcı, Sefer, & Yaşa, 2005). I examine the nature of this competence tapped through spontaneous speech and experimental data, arguing that these data reveal different types of knowledge corresponding to different levels of accessibility—namely, procedural, computational, and explicit (Karmiloff-Smith, 1992). My claim is that in the process of acquisition, the direction of influence between language and cognition shifts with the level of knowledge representation achieved in each domain. To this effect, I present data which indicate that developments in the two domains first proceed simultaneously when knowledge is procedural, then become successively reciprocal as knowledge becomes progressively more explicit—initially in the cognitive and later in the linguistic domain. During this process the nature of their interface changes from 'online' to 'theoretical.'

FUNCTIONS OF EVIDENTIAL MARKERS

Evidentials, defined as the grammaticized means for expressing epistemic stance through the specification of knowledge source, constitute a sophisticated interface between language and cognition.[2] Evidential markers indicate whether information has been acquired through direct experience or indirectly through hearsay, inference, or deduction (Aikhenvald, 2003; Chafe & Nichols, 1986).

Recent treatments of evidentiality view it as a category on a par with epistemic modality (Aikhenvald, 2003; Mushin, 2001; Palmer, 2001). Palmer (2001), for example, proposes that both are types of propositional modality, with epistemic modality expressing the speakers' judgments about the factual status of the proposition and evidential modality indicating the evidence speakers have for its factual status. Thus, both modalities indicate a certain epistemic stance or discourse perspective by expressing speaker attitudes toward knowledge.

My initial analysis together with Dan Slobin on the semantics and pragmatics of Turkish evidentials capitalized on this function. Slobin and Aksu (1982, pp. 196–198; Aksu-Koç, 1988) proposed that the epistemic stance expressed by the inferential/reportative particle -(I)mIş is "information new for unprepared minds," and later I proposed (Aksu-Koç, 1995, p. 281) that the epistemic stance expressed by the deductive/belief particle -DIr is "information assimilated in knowing minds." My contention is that the underlying function unifying the different forms is to express the speakers' psychological stance toward experience.

Recently, Johanson (2000, p. 61) has proposed that evidentials anchor the speech act to a reference point on a continuum of "indirectivity" and present the information "by reference to its reception by a conscious subject." This is not far from our characterization since both views take as pivotal the subjective positioning of speakers with respect to the asserted content. Similarly, Mushin (2001, pp. 29–30) shares our view that evidential use is determined by the "degree to which the speaker has assimilated the information and integrated different kinds of evidence." In sum, various authors converge on the fact that evidentials specify the source of information, and more recently they emphasize their function for situating speakers in terms of their subjective relation to the information rather than for qualifying its truth or factuality (Bacanlı, 2005; Johanson, 2000; Mushin, 2001; Palmer, 2001).

---

[2] Evidentiality is grammaticalized in some language families such as American Indian, Turkic, Iranian, and South-East Asian but not in most Indo-European languages which, however, have lexical means to express similar distinctions (Aikhenvald & Dixon, 2003; Chafe & Nichols, 1986; Johanson & Utas, 2000).

Let me now briefly turn to evidential marking in Turkish to show how it maps onto particular discourse perspectives and knowledge representations. Turkish uses tense-aspect-mood inflections to make a four-way distinction regarding mode of access to information (Aksu-Koç, 1988). The direct experience marker -*DI* encodes a neutral perspective and presents the event as a *representation of reality* (e.g., *Pencere kırıl-DI* '[I know that][3] the window got broken'). *–MIş* encodes indirect experience inferred from physical evidence and marks 'new information,' underscoring a *representational change* in the speaker's mind (e.g., *Pencere kırıl-mIş* '[I infer that] the window got broken'). The reportative *-(I)mIş* encodes the perspective of a speaker who has accessed information through language (*Pencere kırıl-mIş* '[I am told that] the window was broken') and indicates the availability of a *linguistic representation*. Finally, the belief marker -*DIr*[4] expresses *generalized representations* deduced from the speaker's well-assimilated knowledge about habitualities (*Pencere kırıl-mış-TIr* '[I think/deduce that] the window got broken'). Given that a choice of one of these inflections as pragmatic operators is obligatory, speakers end up conveying a particular epistemological perspective by reference to a particular source in every utterance.

COGNITIVE CORRELATES OF EVIDENTIALITY

In view of the above functions, the use of evidential markers should rest on, or alternatively, help develop an understanding of the representational status of the mind given the conditions of knowledge acquisition or source. This understanding is achieved as children engage in different levels of perspective taking.

In their three-step ontogenetic sequence for the concept of person and associated social-cognitive abilities, Tomasello, Kruger, and Ratner (1993) offer perspective taking as a general mechanism that lays the foundations for further conceptual and linguistic developments. They propose that before the end of the first year, children engage in *simple perspective taking* by internalizing the behavior of the other through imitation and thus develop a concept of *intentional agent*. Language emerges on this foundational level of social-cognitive competence, and the use of evidential markers in discourse starting around 18–24 months is presumed to rest on this capacity.

By age 4, children start *coordinating different perspectives* and develop a concept of *mental agent*. While 3-year-olds fail to hold in mind two different perspectives and understand that others' beliefs may differ from their own, 4-year-olds can grasp the causal link between reality, mental states, and action. They can track changes in their own and others mental states, and thus differentiate true and false beliefs (Flavell, 1999; Nelson, 1996; Perner, 1991), which provides evidence for metarepresentational capacity. This theory of mind (ToM) development is relevant to evidentiality since understanding *the conditions of representational change*, hence understanding the different types of relation between information and its source, calls upon metarepresentation. Gaining skill in coordinating perspectives should support the construction of a 'theory of knowledge' that represents the understanding that knowledge may arise from different types of sources.

Finally, Tomasello et al. (1993) observe that school-age children engage in *integrated perspective taking* which results in the development of the concept of person as a *reflective agent* and the understanding of second-order mental states. These social-cognitive capacities entail both metapragmatic processes for tracking respective mental states in terms of their relation to reality, and metarepresentational processes for tracking the contents of those mental states. They thus provide the cognitive basis for a 'theory of evidentiality' which refers to the additional understanding that different sources get encoded in language through different forms.

---

[3] Materials in square brackets represent the meaning of the evidential inflections which function like speech-act verbs or pragmatic operators.

[4] *–DI* and *–mIş* are multifunctional tense-aspect-mood inflections whereas the post clitics *–ImIş* and *–DIr* are indicators of mood. The particular function of the forms depend on context.

A key cognitive process that evidential languages call upon is, then, source monitoring which involves tracking the source of knowledge by remembering the circumstances under which it is gained (Johnson, Hashtroudi, & Lindsay, 1993). Source monitoring or source memory, as it is often called, poses extra cognitive demands since, in addition to the information itself, the source has to be encoded, stored, and retrieved (Gopnik & Graf, 1988; O'Neill & Gopnik, 1991; Wimmer, Hofrege, & Perner, 1988; Woolley & Bruell, 1996). In evidential languages, where source is marked for purposes of "epistemological stance selection" (Mushin, 2001, p. 151), source memory should gain further importance. In discussing the online effects of language on cognition, Slobin (2003, p. 178) refers to 'thinking for potential speaking' by noting that "those event components that must be attended to in thinking for speaking must also be mentally stored for future speaking." This means that speakers of evidential languages must systematically attend to, encode, and store in a retrievable form, two types of information for future speaking: information relevant to event components at the semantic level, and information relevant to source at the pragmatic level.

The question is how these cognitive competencies and evidential functions align during the course of development. Let me first turn to empirical evidence for some answers.

CONSTRUCTING THE DOMAIN OF EVIDENTIALITY

Early Use of Evidentials in Spontaneous Speech

Contrary to what might be expected, children are quite precocious in acquiring evidential markers. Data from Turkish (Aksu-Koç, 1988) and Korean (Choi, 1995), where evidential use is obligatory, show that this development is underway before age 2, and from Cantonese (Lee & Law, 2000), where their use is optional, before age 3.

In Turkish, children first mark a contrast when referring to direct experience between old/assimilated (-DI) vs. new information (-mIş) around age 2. And just before age 3, children also make a distinction when referring to indirect experience between inferences from results (-mIş) vs. deductions based on well-assimilated knowledge (–DIr). Use of -ImIş to mark reported speech is also observed at this time (Aksu-Koç, 1988; Aksu-Koç, 1998). Choi (1995) reports a very similar sequence for Korean. Children first mark a three-way opposition when referring to direct experience among new information, information already assimilated into an existing knowledge system, and information that is certain and shared. The particles for reported speech and inferred information emerge somewhat later, just before age 3. In Cantonese (Lee & Law, 2000), children also first talk about direct experience, using the surprise/new information marker contrastively with the form for old/shared information. The reported speech and elaboration markers are acquired around 3 years.

The context appropriate use of evidentials in all three languages reveals that children display early sensitivity to distinctions between old vs. new information,[5] and that by age 3 they are differentially marking types of knowledge source. To the extent that "new information is an unshared perspective on an event" (O'Neill, 2005, p. 93), marking new vs. old information entails shifting perspectives and is therefore related to developments in ToM that have consequences for understanding evidentiality. In the following section I present relevant findings from my research exploring their interface.

Evidentiality and Representational Capacities

In thinking for speaking in an evidential language, speakers are unconsciously monitoring the status of the information to be conveyed and express their discourse stance with the choice of a particular inflection. In listening for understanding, on the other hand, they are decoding these epistemic tags to evaluate the informational perspective of their interlocutor. Hence, children acquiring an

---

[5] Salience of the contrast between new vs. old information for children younger than 2 has been much discussed in the literature and is related by O'Neill (2005) to levels of ToM development.

evidential language can be expected to be sensitized to their own and others' mental representations in their constantly changing roles of speaker and listener in discourse. More specifically, practice in evidential marking may be expected to facilitate children's grasp of the *causal link* between different types of evidence and corresponding mental states. We investigated this hypothesis in a number of studies.

Aksu-Koç et al. (2005) examined whether evidentials, together with other linguistic variables, were predictors of children's ToM performance, using the false-belief verb *san* in task administration with 3- and 4-year-olds. To assess ToM skills we used the unexpected contents task,[6] and to assess evidential comprehension, a task that required matching a given utterance to the correct one among three pictures representing relevant semantic content. More than 80% of 3½- to 4-year-olds succeeded on both the representational change (RC) and the false belief (FB) questions. However, children's performance on the evidentials task was poor and did not differentiate between age groups. This may be because of the high task demands, as will be discussed in the next section.

Comparison of our results with those reported for English-speaking children (de Villiers & Pyers, 2001) tested on the same ToM task revealed that 60% of the Turkish-speaking 3- and 4-year-olds passed both the RC and FB questions whereas only 30% of the English-speaking children did so. The precocity of Turkish-speaking children on ToM compared to English-speaking peers, which strongly suggests the effects of language on cognition, may be due either to the grammaticized marking of evidentiality in Turkish or to the effects of the false belief verb used in task administration. To differentiate between these two explanations, in another study we included a control condition using the neutral verb *düşün* 'think' in task administration. The results indicated that Turkish-speaking children had the same high level of performance on RC (75% passing) regardless of age and verb type (Aksu-Koç et al., 2005). We can therefore safely assume that the determining factor for the high performance on the RC task is not the false belief verb used during task administration, but rather early competence in using the inferential *–mIş*, the form that punctuates changes experienced in representational states. On FB questions, on the other hand, 4-year-olds displayed a significantly higher performance than 3-year-olds, and a trend for higher performance when the false belief verb *san* was used. Furthermore, 4% of the variance was explained by evidential comprehension. These results strongly suggest the influence of specific linguistic forms on specific cognitive changes along the same lines suggested by Gopnik and Meltzoff's (1986) specificity hypothesis: that is, the evidential marker *-mIş* seems to foster the ability to track personal representational change, while both evidentials and the false belief verb *san* foster the ability to understand false beliefs of others.

Aksu-Koç and Alıcı (2000) investigated the relation between children's comprehension of information source indicated by direct experience *(-DI)* vs. belief *(-DIr)* statements, and their representational change and false belief understanding. Three- to six-year olds tested on the unexpected contents ToM task again displayed early competence in tracking personal mental representations (75% success at 3 years and a non-significant increase with age). On FB questions, a comparable level of performance (85%) was reached at 4 years although 50% of the 3-year-olds also provided evidence for the ability to read other minds in view of their perspectives on reality. On the language comprehension task, children at all ages were significantly more successful in identifying the information source for *-DI* than *-DIr* utterances but this performance did not predict ToM performance. Instead, the number of mental state/belief terminology (*-DIr*, verbs and adverbs such as *think, know, perhaps, may be*) spontaneously used by the children in explaining the information source for each utterance was significantly affected by FB understanding as well as by age. Children who were successful on the FB task used more belief terms ($M = 12.47$) than those who were not ($M = 4.06$), and

---

[6] In this task the child is shown a familiar candy box (Smarties) and asked what he thinks is in it. After his answer (typically correct: candy) the box is opened to reveal 'pebbles' instead, and then it is closed. To assess representational change understanding the child is asked what he thought was in the box before it was opened; if he answers "pebbles" he fails, if he answers "candy" he passes. To assess false belief understanding the child is asked what a friend who did not see the contents of the box would think is in it; if he answers "pebbles" he fails, if he answers "candy" he passes.

5- and 6-year-olds used more of such terminology ($M = 15.25$) than 4-year-olds ($M = 5.87$). These results indicate that changes in ToM representational capacities around 4 years of age promote the understanding of other minds and subsequently enhance the use of epistemically modalized language (lexical and grammaticized) to talk about mental states. In short, they point to the effects of cognitive development on language.

Put together with the spontaneous speech data, these findings relating the representational capacities of the mind and linguistic marking of evidentiality show that there are successive reciprocal relations between the two domains. Early procedural use of evidential markers in discourse expressing different perspectives on events leads to advances in cognition, which foster developments for metarepresentational capacity. This capacity in turn, by enhancing mind reading abilities, leads to increases in the use of mental language, including more sophisticated use of evidential markers.

These findings obtained with spontaneous and experimental methodologies help articulate the relations between language and cognition at different points in development. However, as the children's low level of performance on the language tasks reveals, there is a developmental lag between knowledge children display in contexts of natural interaction versus in experimental tasks. This brings me to a consideration of the issue of levels of knowledge representation before discussing my findings on evidentials as source markers.

LEVELS OF KNOWLEDGE REPRESENTATION

As will be discussed in detail later, I have explored the acquisition of evidentials in Turkish using different types of data and have found that: (1) in experimental tasks children display knowledge of the functions of the different forms about a year later than that observed in spontaneous speech; and (2) children show higher levels of performance on production than on comprehension tasks. These findings require some explanation because later performance in experimental contexts gives rise to questions about what it is that children know when they use these forms spontaneously at a younger age, and what makes comprehension, which typically precedes production, lag behind. Some methodological explanations can be offered: most experimental tasks invite children to take part in an artificial situation and to share the experimenter's assumptions regarding the meaning of the contrived event; in turn, they pose demands on children that tax their memory capacities as well as their role-taking abilities.

Even if we grant these methodological explanations, my contention is that the discrepancy observed here is more foundational. Specifically, I believe it is a function of different levels of knowledge tapped by different methodologies that can be explained along the lines proposed by Karmiloff-Smith (1992). In her model, the basic level of representation is implicit and constituted of nonsymbolic, nonpropositional procedures that are goal-directed. It represents "direct knowledge constructed through interactions with the environment" (Nelson, 1996, p. 14). The next level is explicit but only to the extent that knowledge is computationally accessible and procedures can be decomposed and recombined internally. Level 3 is achieved when representations become consciously accessible, can be reflected upon, manipulated, and verbally expressed. Cognitive progress is a result of movement from one level to the next, when representations at one level become automatic and mastered enough to be analyzed and reintegrated at the higher level. This process involves what Karmiloff-Smith (1992, pp. 17–18) calls "representational redescription," which refers to "a cyclical process by which information already present in the organism's independently functioning, special purpose representations, is made progressively available, …, to other parts of the cognitive system." It operates within each domain of knowledge and results in increasing degrees of explicitness. Language, itself subject to redescription and explicitation, assumes a dual role and becomes the instrument of redescription for other domains as well as itself, and transforms their representations to a linguistic code, making new representational relationships possible.

This model of levels of knowledge provides an appropriate framework for explaining the discrepancy between results obtained using different methodologies, as well as illuminating aspects of my research on source monitoring, which, as I argued above, is another component of evidentiality.

EVIDENTIALITY AND SOURCE KNOWLEDGE

I explored children's knowledge of evidentials as indicators of informational perspective or source experimentally with 3- to 6-year-olds using both production and comprehension tasks (Aksu-Koç, 1988, 1998). To spontaneously elicit the direct experience *(-DI)* and the inferential *(-mIş)* markers that are obligatory in Turkish, children were asked to describe events acted out with toys that displayed either all phases of an event (direct experience) or just the beginning and the end (requiring inference). The results indicated that the semantic/pragmatic conditions for the use of *-DI* was consolidated by 3½ years ($M = 87\%$ correct) whereas the same level of competence was achieved for *-mIş* around 4 years (Aksu-Koç, 1988). When children were asked to produce utterances on behalf of a character who could talk about a situation only on the basis of well-assimilated general information, 4-year-olds preferred *-DI* as if the character had direct experience, whereas 5- to 6-year-olds correctly expressed the belief status of their utterance using *-DIr* (Aksu-Koç, 1998).

For the comprehension tasks, I used short picture-stories that depicted characters who had different informational perspectives on events and children were presented an utterance and asked to point to its speaker. The results confirmed the pattern obtained for production, indicating that children were more successful in identifying the speakers of direct experience than indirect experience utterances: 70% correct use was reached for *-DI* items at 4½ years, and 50% for the inferential *-mIş* by 5 years. As for the contrast between *-DI* vs. *-DIr*, at all ages children preferred a direct experiencer (80% correct for *-DI*, 40% correct for *-DIr* items) regardless of whether the character had perceptual evidence for the event or just general knowledge (Aksu-Koç, 1998).

These results show that the perspective of a direct experiencer has developmental primacy over that of the indirect experiencer and confirm the findings from spontaneous speech. They also indicate that children's performance on experimental tasks is later than that observed in their spontaneous speech, and overall children show lower levels of success on experiments that require their comprehension as opposed to their production. These are counterintuitive results but can be explained by appealing to levels of knowledge representation.

The production tasks required children to describe events from given information perspectives which needed to be marked by appropriate evidential forms. In this sense, these tasks tapped procedural knowledge—that is, the set of independently functioning, special-purpose, linguistic representations displayed in spontaneous speech. Comprehension tasks, on the other hand, in asking for speaker-utterance matching, required computing and keeping in mind the speaker perspective signaled by an evidential form, the metarepresentational capacity to identify the speaker with that knowledge perspective, as well as the metapragmatic capacity required to coordinate the two. These tasks, therefore, required computational knowledge available as Level 2 representations accessible upon experimental probing, or explicit knowledge available as Level 3 representations accessible for both problem solution and verbalization.

The type of knowledge children were accessing in responding to these task demands was inferred from an analysis of their justifications as to why they chose a specific character or information perspective to match a given utterance (Aksu-Koç, 1988; Aksu-Koç & Alıcı, 2000). Three-year-olds provided no evidence for computational or explicit knowledge: the mode of access to knowledge was not even a parameter, the choice of character was random, and the only identifiable perspective was that of the child's. The justifications of 4-year-olds, in line with Tomasello et al.'s (1993) proposal for understanding the person as a mental agent, offer evidence for coordination of perspectives and meta representational capacity. They explicitly identified who witnessed the event and had knowledge about it, thus causally linking modes of information access to knowledge states. However, these perspectives did not integrate different types of evidence since children claimed that only direct experiencers could know and talk about the event, ignoring other types of source as evidence. Their responses reflected partial, nonsystematic (Level 2) representations of the knowledge source that yields certain types of computations but not others, and no awareness of linguistic marking of different sources. Five-year-olds could identify the speakers of utterances marked for direct or indirect experience, and understood that each refers to a different type of evidence as a basis for talk. However, they could not link these epistemic perspectives with the appropriate linguistic forms systematically. Thus, although they displayed an explicit 'theory of knowledge' that rests on Level 3 representations of 'information source–knowledge state' configurations, their understanding of how these are expressed by grammaticized forms appeared to remain implicit (Level 2). Only older 5- and 6-year-olds could reflect on the different linguistic forms as indicators of different informational perspectives, providing evidence for Level 3 representations of knowledge *about* language *in* language with an integrated 'theory of evidentiality.'

In summary, children's initial 'theory of knowledge' emerges around age 4 and assumes direct perception as the only valid information source. Awareness of knowledge states accessed through inference, hearsay, and deduction is achieved by age 5. Nonevidential languages such as English indicate a similar progression regarding children's basis for a theory of knowledge: Children regard perception as a source around 4 years, language as a source between 4 to 5 years, and inference from linguistic premises after 5 years of age (Montgomery, 1992; O'Neill & Gopnik, 1991; Perner, 1991; Pillow, 1989; Wimmer, Hofrege, & Perner, 1988; Woolley & Bruell, 1996). Children's 'theory of evidentiality,' on the other hand, is mapped onto their theory of knowledge as the Turkish data have shown: children achieve explicit awareness of evidential marking after they understand different modes of knowledge acquisition.

A possible conclusion suggested by these data is that children's understanding of the link between knowledge states and knowledge source is not initially affected by the linguistic encoding of source in language. Although Turkish children use evidentials at the procedural level before age 3, their understanding appears to be determined by a 'theory of knowledge' held independently of language, and very similar to that of children acquiring nonevidential languages. This might suggest that there is no influence of language on cognition in this domain. However, I have also presented data that provide evidence for the effect of language on cognition by showing that: (1) the use of evidentials before age 3, when representations are as yet procedural in each domain, fosters coordination of perspectives and metarepresentational capacity; and (2) the development of a 'theory of evidentiality' follows the increase in the variety and frequency of use of epistemically modalized terminology subsequent to developments in ToM between 3 and 5 years. The present analysis has shown that language is at work at the procedural level whereas cognition takes precedence in the explicitation of knowledge and the building of theories.

CONCLUDING REMARKS

In this chapter, I undertook the evaluation of the acquisition of evidentials to articulate the developmental relations during the interface of language and cognition. I also considered findings from my work on early acquisition, on the relations between language and ToM, and on the understanding of different modes of knowledge acquisition that get specified in language with different forms. As I argued, the direction of influence between language and cognition changes depending on the level of knowledge representations available.

The procedural use of evidentials guided by Level 1 representations is early and constitutes online evidence that children attend to source information as well as event characteristics both at the time of nonlinguistic coding and at the time of speaking. In line with Slobin's (2003) suggestion that effects at speaking time present the critical interface between language and cognition, I take this early spontaneous use as the first or unarticulated dialogue between language and cognition.

As children participate in discourse, presenting and interpreting information from different epistemic perspectives, the procedures they use become automatic enough to be redescribed. Our data suggest that abstracted representations become available as Level 2 representations first in the cognitive then in the linguistic domains sometime between 3 and 5 years. Obligatory use of evidentials for epistemic stance selection contributes to cognition by enhancing skills for coordination of perspectives, which in turn, are manifested in the capacity for metarepresentation displayed in mindreading abilities. At this point in development the interface of language and cognition is dominated by cognitions about knowledge acquisition that are partial and unidirectional since they privilege direct perception as the only valid information source. These advances in ToM lead to increased use of lexical and grammatical constructions that refer to mental states and other epistemic notions. Increase in the type and frequency of use of mental state vocabulary can be said to support the internal reorganization and redescription of the linguistic elements into Level 2 representations, making them accessible for purposes of computation and judgment required in experimental contexts.

By age 5 children come to regard different types of evidence as a legitimate source for knowledge acquisition and display an integrated 'theory of knowledge.' Only subsequently do they articulate 'linguistic [evidential] marker—information source—knowledge state' corespondences. Thus the flexibility of thought brought about by metarepresentational capacity in general, and Level 2 developments in language in particular, make reflection of language upon itself possible, yielding verbally explicit Level 3 representations and a linguistically informed 'theory of evidentiality.'

Thus, relations between language and cognition proceed both at a general level, where language functions as the instrument of redescription, and at a specific level, through the use of different semantic, syntactic, and morphological structures. The specific interactions between language and ToM have been subject to much research focusing on mental verbs, false belief verbs, complement clauses, as well as evidentials (e.g., Astington & Jenkins, 1999; Astington & Pelletier, 2000; de Villiers & de Villiers, 2000; Lee, Olson, & Torrance, 1999; Shatz, Diesendruck, Martinez-Beck, & Akar, 2003; Vinden, 1996) and a comprehensive overview by Astington and Baird (2005) explores these multifaceted relations. These relations, outlined only for evidentials here, should be conceived within the more general context of changes that pertain to the whole system of language. Most crucial is the shift around 3 to 5 years from Level 1 procedural nondifferentiated representations to Level 2 domain-specific representations which result in the abstraction of language from its procedural context of use to make it available as a general representational tool. Proponents of similar models of levels of consciousness such as Jacques and Zelazo (2005) also stress the significance of language for ToM at the general level. They propose that language, as the driving force for self-reflection, brings about flexible thought and action at a higher level of consciousness by virtue of its pervasive features such as labeling or arbitrariness. The increases in the level of consciousness, in turn, they offer, allow for flexible selection of perspectives from which to reason. Viewing it from this perspective, evidential marking in language contributes to developments in cognition also at the general level; cognitive flexibility is promoted by the continued obligatory selection of different epistemic perspectives in discourse.

Finally, let me point to several lines of research that should yield further knowledge about this interface of language and cognition. First, crosslinguistic replications with nonevidential and other evidential languages are necessary for confirming the present claims. Studies exploring the role of evidential marking on developments in source memory, an issue we are currently researching, will also be particularly informative. Another question concerns how children progress in instantiating different epistemic stances in conversational and narrative discourse in evidential vs. nonevidential languages. The most challenging question is the nature of the cognitive underpinnings around 2–3 years, when knowledge is still procedural. As we know more about these questions, I think we will have further insight into the language–cognition interface. We have seen that competence in source marking in language does not immediately translate into an explicit understanding of knowledge acquisition but requires a gradual development. We have also seen, however, that the implicit guidance this affords is by no means negligible, lending support to the neo-Whorfian interpretations of this relationship.

REFERENCES

Aikhenvald, A. Y. (2003). Evidentiality in typological perspective. In A. Y. Aikhenvald & R. M. W. Dixon (Eds.), *Studies in evidentiality* (pp. 1–31). Amsterdam: John Benjamins.

Aikhenvald, A. Y., & Dixon, R. M. W. (Eds.). (2003). *Studies in evidentiality*. Amsterdam: John Benjamins.

Aksu-Koç, A. (1988). *The acquisition of aspect and modality: The case of past reference in Turkish*. Cambridge, UK: Cambridge University Press.

Aksu-Koç, A. (1995). Some connections between aspect and modality in Turkish. In P. M. Bertinetto, V. Bianchi, Ö. Dahl, & M. Squartini (Eds.), *Temporal reference aspect and actionality: Vol. 2. Typological perspectives* (pp. 271–287). Torino: Rosenberg & Sellier.

Aksu-Koç, A. (1998, August). Changes in the basis for children's assertions: The acquisition of *–DIr*. Paper presented at the Ninth International Conference on Turkish Linguistics, Oxford University, Oxford.

Aksu-Koç, A., & Alıcı, D. M. (2000). Understanding sources of beliefs and marking of uncertainty: The child's theory of evidentiality. In E. V. Clark (Ed.), *The proceedings of the 30th annual Child Language Conference* (pp. 123–130). Stanford: Center for the Study of Language and Information.

Aksu-Koç, A., Aydın, Ç., Avcı, G., Sefer, N., & Yasa, Y. (2005, July). The relation between mental verbs and theory of mind performance: Evidence from Turkish children. Paper presented at the 10th International Congress for the Study of Child Language, Berlin.

Astington, J. W., & Baird, J. A. (2005). Introduction: Why language matters? In J. W. Astington & J. A. Baird (Eds.), *Why language matters for theory of mind* (pp. 3–25). Mahwah, NJ: Lawrence Erlbaum Associates.

Astington, J. W., & Jenkins, J. M. (1999). A longitudinal study of the relation between language and theory of mind development. *Developmental Psychology, 35*, 1311–1320.

Astington, J. W., & Pelletier, J. (2000). Theory of mind and metacognitive vocabulary development in first and second languages. Unpublished manuscript, Institute of Child Study, University of Toronto.

Bacanlı, E. (2005). Türkçedeki dolaylılık işaretleyicilerinin pragmatik anlamları. [The pragmatics of indirectivity markers in Turkish]. *Modern Türklük Araştırmaları Dergisi, 3*, 35–47.

Bowerman, M. (1985). What shapes children's grammars? In D. I. Slobin (Ed.), *The study of language acquisition: Vol. 2. Theoretical issues* (pp. 1257–1319). Hillsdale, NJ: Lawrence Erlbaum Associates.

Bowerman, M., & Levinson, S. C. (Eds.). (2001). *Language acquisition and conceptual development*. Cambridge, UK: Cambridge University Press.

Chafe, W., & Nichols, J. (Eds.). (1986). *Evidentiality: The linguistic coding of epistemology* (pp. 261–272). Norwood, NJ: Ablex.

Choi, S. (1995). The development of epistemic sentence-ending modal forms and functions in Korean children. In J. Bybee & S. Fleischman (Eds.), *Modality in grammar and discourse* (pp. 165–204). Amsterdam: John Benjamins.

de Villiers, J. G., & de Villiers, P. A. (2000). Linguistic determinism and the understanding of false beliefs. In P. Mitchell & K. J. Riggs (Eds.), *Children's reasoning and the mind* (pp. 191–228). East Sussex, UK: Psychology Press.

de Villiers, J. G., & Pyers, J. E. (2001). Complementation and false belief representation. In M. Almgren, A. Barrena, M. J. Ezeizabarenna, I. Idiazabal, & B. A. MacWhinney (Eds.), *Research on child language acquisition. Proceedings of the 8th conference of the International Association for the Study of Child Language* (pp. 984–1005). Somerville, MA: Cascadilla Press.

Flavell, J. (1999). Cognitive development: Children's knowledge about the mind. *Annual Review of Psychology, 50*(2), 1–45.

Gopnik, A., & Graf, P. (1988). Knowing how you know: Young children's ability to identify and remember the sources of their beliefs. *Child Development, 59*, 1366–1371.

Gopnik, A., & Meltzoff, A. (1986) Relations between semantic and cognitive development in the one word stage: The specificity hypothesis. *Child Development, 57*, 1040–1053.

Gumperz, J. J., & Levinson, S. C. (Eds.). (1996). *Rethinking linguistic relativity*. Cambridge, UK: Cambridge University Press.

Jacques, S., & Zelazo, P. D. (2005) Cognitive flexibility: Implications for theory of mind. In J. W. Astington & J. A. Baird (Eds.), *Why language matters for theory of mind* (pp. 144–162). Mahwah, NJ: Lawrence Erlbaum Associates.

Johanson, L. (2000). Turkic indirectives. In L. Johanson & B. Utas (Eds.), *Evidentials: Turkic, Iranian and neighbouring languages* (pp. 61–87). Berlin: Mouton de Gruyter.

Johanson, L., & Utas, B. (Eds.). (2000) *Evidentials: Turkic, Iranian and neighboring languages*. Berlin: de Gruyter.

Johnson, M. K., Hashtroudi, S., & Lindsay, D. S. (1993). Source monitoring. *Psychological Bulletin, 114,* 3–28.

Karmiloff-Smith, A. (1992). *Beyond modularity: A developmental perspective on cognitive science.* Cambridge, MA: The MIT Press.

Lee, H. T., & Law, A. (2000). Evidential final particles in child Cantonese. In E. V. Clark (Ed.), *The proceedings of the 30th annual Child Language Conference* (pp. 131–138). Stanford: Center for the Study of Language and Information.

Lee, K., Olson, D. R., & Torrance, N. (1999). Chinese children's understanding of false beliefs: The role of language. *Journal of Child Language, 20,* 1–21.

Montgomery, D. E. (1992). Young children's theory of knowing: The development of a folk epistemology. *Developmental Review, 12,* 410–430.

Mushin, I. (2001). *Evidentiality and epistemological stance.* Amsterdam: John Benjamins.

Nelson, K. (1996). *Language in cognitive development: The emergence of the mediated mind.* Cambridge, UK: Cambridge University Press.

O'Neill, D. K. (2005). Talking about "new" information: The given/new distinction and children's developing theory of mind. In J. W. Astington & J. A. Baird (Eds.), *Why language matters for theory of mind* (pp. 84–105). Mahwah, NJ: Lawrence Erlbaum Associates.

O'Neill, D. K., & Gopnik, A. (1991). Young children's ability to identify the sources of their beliefs. *Developmental Psychology, 27,* 390–397.

Palmer, F. R. (2001). *Mood and modality.* Cambridge, UK: Cambridge University Press.

Perner, J. (1991). *Understanding the representational mind.* Cambridge, MA: The MIT Press.

Pillow, B. H. (1989). Early understanding of perception as a source of knowledge. *Journal of Experimental Child Psychology, 47,* 116–129.

Shatz, M., Diesendruck, G., Martinez-Beck, I., & Akar, D. (2003). The influence of language and socioeconomic status on children's understanding on false belief. *Developmental Psychology, 39,* 717–729.

Slobin, D. I. (Ed.). (1985). *The crosslinguistic study of language acquisition: Vol. 1. The data* (pp. 839–878). Hillsdale, NJ: Lawrence Erlbaum Associates.

Slobin, D. I. (1987). Thinking for speaking. *Proceedings of the Berkeley Linguistic Society, 13,* 435–444.

Slobin, D. I. (2003). Language and thought on-line: Cognitive consequences of linguistic relativity. In D. Gentner & S. Goldin-Meadow (Eds.), *Language in mind* (pp. 157–192). Cambridge, MA: The MIT Press.

Slobin, D. I., & Aksu, A. A. (1982). Tense, aspect and modality in the use of the Turkish evidential. In P. Hopper (Ed.), *Tense-aspect: Between semantics and pragmatics* (pp. 185–200). Amsterdam: John Benjamins.

Tomasello, M., Kruger, A. C., & Ratner, H. H. (1993). Cultural learning. *Behavioral and Brain Sciences, 16,* 495–511.

Vinden, P. G. (1996). Junin Quechua children's understanding of mind. *Child Development, 67,* 1707–1716.

Vygotsky, L. S. (1978). *Mind in society.* Cambridge, MA: Harvard University Press.

Wimmer, H., Hogrefe, J., & Perner, J. (1988). Children's understanding of informational access as source of knowledge. *Child Development, 59,* 386–396.

Woolley, J. D., & Bruell, M. J. (1996). Young children's awareness of the origins of their mental representations. *Developmental Psychology, 32,* 335–346.

40

How Deep Are Differences in Referential Density?[1]

SABINE STOLL
Max Planck Institute for Evolutionary Anthropology, Leipzig

BALTHASAR BICKEL
University of Leipzig

> The language or languages that we learn in childhood are not neutral coding systems of an objective reality. Rather, each one is a subjective orientation to the world of experience, and this orientation affects the ways in which we think while we are speaking.
>
> **Dan I. Slobin (1996, p. 91)**

INTRODUCTION

*I*n his work on rhetorical typology, Dan Slobin (1996, 1997a, 1997b, 2000) demonstrated that differences in discourse style and linguistic structure can have an impact on how speakers of different languages habitually attend to different aspects of situations—at least during speaking. His case is typological differences in the coding and structuring of motion events.

Another area that reveals important differences in discourse style is the use of overt NPs. In an experimentally controlled comparison of various languages in which argumental NPs are optional from a strictly syntactic point of view ('pro-drop'), Bickel (2003, 2005) found significant differences among different speech communities in the use of overt NPs in discourse. NP use was assessed in this research by the Referential Density (henceforth RD) measurement, defined as the ratio of overt NPs to all possible argument slots (also cf. Noonan, 2003). In one of the languages studied, Belhare (Sino-Tibetan, Nepal), on average, only approximately 40% of all available argument positions are overtly realized. This contrasts with discourse habits in high-RD languages, such as Maithili (Indo-European, Nepal and India), in which approximately 60% of argument positions are filled, creating a style that seems overly explicit to speakers of low-RD languages.

So far, research on referential density has primarily concentrated on the presence vs. absence of NPs. The questions we investigate in this chapter concern the kind of NPs that are used,

---

[1] We are grateful to Lekh Bahadur Rai for his help with data collection on Belhare and to Michail Lurie, Tatjana Krugljakova, Madelaine Taoubi for their help with data collection and analysis in Russia. We thank Jiansheng Guo and Kei Nakamura for helpful comments on an earlier draft. Research on Belhare discourse was supported by the Swiss National Science Foundation, Grant 610-062717.00 (2001–2002, Bickel, PI).

concentrating, as in previous research, on narratives produced under experimental control. Specifically, we ask the questions: (1) Do the differences in RD result from the use of lexical NPs or from the use of pronouns? (2) To the degree that they result from the use of lexical NPs, do these differences reflect different strategies of how speakers and listeners manage referential information in discourse?

In general, the degree of referential information of NPs (their *informativeness*, for short) defines a continuum ranging from very explicit lexical NPs ('the old farmer over there') to generic NPs ('people') and pronouns ('they') to zero anaphora ('and ø went home'). Whether a given pronoun is closer to lexical NPs or zeros on this continuum depends on its semantic structure. It is close to zero when the pronoun encodes nothing beyond the existence and number of referents, as in the case of English plural pronouns (*they*) or generally in pronouns of many other languages (e.g., Turkish or Belhare). Pronouns are closer to generic NPs when they encode such features as gender (English *she* vs. *he*) or honorific degree and distance (Maithili *u* 'third person nonhonorific,' *o* 'third person honorific,' *i* 'third person proximate'). However, in actual discourse such differences frequently do not matter much because referents often happen to have the same gender, honorific degree, or spatial distance, and this minimizes the overall contribution that pronouns can make to what listeners learn about referents (informativeness), and how easy it is to track their identity in discourse (reference tracking).

If the typological difference in RD results from the presence or absence of pronouns, then the difference in RD typology might have little impact on the amount of referential information that is processed by speakers and hearers during narrative exchange, and consequently might have little impact on what Slobin calls 'thinking for speaking' and 'thinking for listening' (Slobin, 2000).

By contrast, if the difference in RD values results from the different degrees to which lexical NPs are used, the typological differences in RD would suggest a much deeper issue. If speakers of high RD languages use more lexical NPs, their narrative discourse is bound to convey more descriptive information about referents. This, then, might well create an entirely different way of thinking about referents—specifically, about the information made explicit about referents—when telling a story or listening to one.

However, in order to understand the role that lexical NPs play in the processing and management of information in narrative discourse, it is not enough to simply count NPs. It is essential to also analyze the distribution of these NPs over time in a narrative and to determine the discourse function that they assume at different points in time. The discourse functions of lexical NPs vary widely within narratives: NPs can be used to introduce a referent, so that the listener learns something about this referent. NPs can also be used to re-identify referents after a certain amount of discourse time. A third important function is to disambiguate referents, i.e., if several referents are interacting, NPs are used to specify the referents for the listener.

In this chapter, we use a narrative production experiment contrasting a low-RD language and a language that we expect to have a high degree of RD to discuss these issues. In order to isolate discourse factors in NP use from syntactic issues, we limit ourselves to languages where the presence of NPs is never (or almost never) enforced by purely syntactic principles, and where we can therefore safely assume that NP use reflects pragmatics alone. For the low-RD language we chose Belhare because discourse in this language has the lowest RD values known to us (Bickel, 2003). For what we expect to be a high-RD language, we chose colloquial spoken Russian, a language that allows dropping of argumental NPs in almost all syntactic contexts, but where NPs still often appear to be used under many pragmatic conditions.

In sum, the three focal issues of this chapter are: first we test whether our expectation of the RD distributions in Belhare and Russian bear out. Second, we analyze whether there is a difference in the types of NPs used in the two languages, i.e., whether one of the two languages uses significantly more lexical NPs than the other language. Then, third, we analyze the discourse functions of the NPs and compare their role for information management.

METHODS

Subjects

In each language we tested 10 speakers. In Belhare the speakers were mostly illiterate, and the Russian speakers only had minimal education and not much day-to-day exposure to written forms of communication. Both participant groups live in close-knit rural societies, which minimizes a possible effect on RD conventions from the degree of mutual familiarity among participants (see Bickel, 2003, 2005 for discussion).

Material and Procedure

We compared narratives produced in response to the same stimulus so as to avoid an impact on NP use stemming simply from differences in content. The stimulus we used was a short (6 minutes) video clip called the Pear Story. The film was developed in the late 1970s by Wallace Chafe and colleagues with the specific goal in mind to collect data from very different cultures (Chafe, 1980). The story is about a man collecting pears and someone taking away these pears. The story opens with a man picking pears and collecting them in several baskets. Then a young man (who has no further bearing on the story) walks by with a goat. After this, a young man approaches with a bicycle, sees the baskets with the pears, takes one of the baskets and bikes off with it. He sees a girl, and while looking at her, he stumbles over a stone and all the pears fall out of the basket. A group of young men approach and help him collect the pears. They help him get back on the bike and walk away. Then one of them comes back and hands back a hat to the young man, which he had dropped earlier. The young man hands each of them a pear to thank them. They walk further—chewing on their pears—to the tree where the farmer had just realized that one basket is missing. In the story, five human referents can be introduced and re-identified.

The film was shown on a color laptop computer with a 14-inch screen. The subjects watched the movie individually in a separate room. The instructions were given by a native speaker research assistant just before the film was shown. Each subject received the same set of instructions (in colloquial speech).

The film was shown twice, because some Belhare participants had little experience with movies and the participants from both groups were not used to experimental situations.

The participants watched the film and then were led to another room where they told the story to a listener who was unfamiliar with the film. The time gap between watching the video and telling the story was about 2–3 minutes. The stories were tape-recorded and then transcribed and coded. We only included those subjects who actually told the story depicted in the film. This resulted in 10 speakers per language. Three Russian subjects and six Belhare subjects were excluded because they merely described the pictures in isolation.

Coding

Each narrative was broken down into one-predicate units ('clauses'), in which complex predicates (of the kind 'do whistling' instead of 'whistle'), or compound verb constructions (like 'pick-take,' common in Belhare) counted as one predicate. To facilitate analyses, we excluded all metapragmatic units (e.g., 'listen!,' 'did you get it?,' etc.). We also excluded all embedded clauses, because in many cases, their NP positions are referentially dependent on the main clause arguments and do not allow, therefore, a straightforward assessment of the pragmatic factors on NP realization.

For each clause, we then determined the number of syntactically possible overt arguments. In some cases, notably with some nonfinite forms (of the kind 'while collecting the pears'), the number of possible overt arguments is less than the lexical valence of the verb because subjects cannot be overt in these contexts in Belhare or Russian (or English, for that matter). It was not always straightforward to differentiate arguments from adjuncts in the specific case of locative expressions. As a basic principle, we counted as a possible argument any possible expression whose case assignment or case interpretation was governed by the lexical predicate. As a result of this, and in line with Bickel (2003), we included goal expression of motion verbs as arguments: in both Russian and Belhare, locative case interpretation is governed by whether or not the verb entails directed motion (i.e., 'to go' vs. 'to walk' type verbs, where 'go'-type verbs impose a directional interpretation onto a locative case, while 'walk'-type verbs do not). True adjuncts do not enter such dependencies with predicates.

Then, we counted the number of actual overt arguments in each clause, differentiating between lexical nouns and pronouns, the latter including spatial pronouns like 'there' or 'this,' or numerals like 'one' (both when intended as a numeral and when intended as an indefinite or generic pronoun). Appositional structures ('he, the young man') were counted as single lexical NPs.

We summed the number of overt arguments in each narrative and divided this by the number of possible arguments in the same narrative. The resulting number is the general Referential Density (RD) of this narrative. The highest possible RD is 1.00, indicating that all possible arguments are expressed overtly in the surface structure. Then, we calculated the Lexical RD (RD_{lex}) by including only the lexical NPs and excluding all pronouns (as defined above plus numerals like 'one'). We divided the sum of the overt lexical NPs by the number of total possible arguments in a narrative, and we obtained RD_{lex} for that narrative. RD_{lex} was calculated to test whether there is a qualitative difference between the RDs of the two languages.

For an analysis of the discourse function of the NPs, we analyzed when and how in the story the referents were introduced. Specifically, we analyzed whether they were mentioned immediately at their first occurrence in the story to specify the kind of referent, or whether they were only explicitly introduced later on for disambiguation when other referents ask for disambiguation.

RESULTS

Referential Density

As expected, Belhare speakers produced narratives with much lower referential density than Russian speakers. The Belhare narratives in our sample had a mean RD of .40 (SD = .06) and Russian had a mean RD of .67 (SD = .07). The difference between the two languages was statistically significant, $t(18) = -8.50, p < .001$.[2] The plots in Figure 40.1 show the distribution of RD values among Russian and Belhare speakers.

Lexical NPs vs. Pronouns

In a second step, we tested whether this difference in RD was due to the use of nouns or pronouns. We calculated the lexical RD (RD_{lex}), excluding all pronouns. The Belhare sample had a mean RD_{lex} of .32 (SD = .08); Russian had a mean RD_{lex} of .47 (SD = .07). Again, the difference between the two languages was significant, $t(18) = -4.49, p < .001$. The distributions of RD values in each language are shown in Figure 40.2.

This suggests that the difference in the overall RD cannot be reduced to a difference in pronoun use, since the difference was still significant in RD_{lex}, where pronouns were removed.

---

[2] Figure 40.1 suggests an outlier in the Russian sample, with RD = .49. Removing this outlier does not affect these results, $t(17) = -11.46, p < .001$.

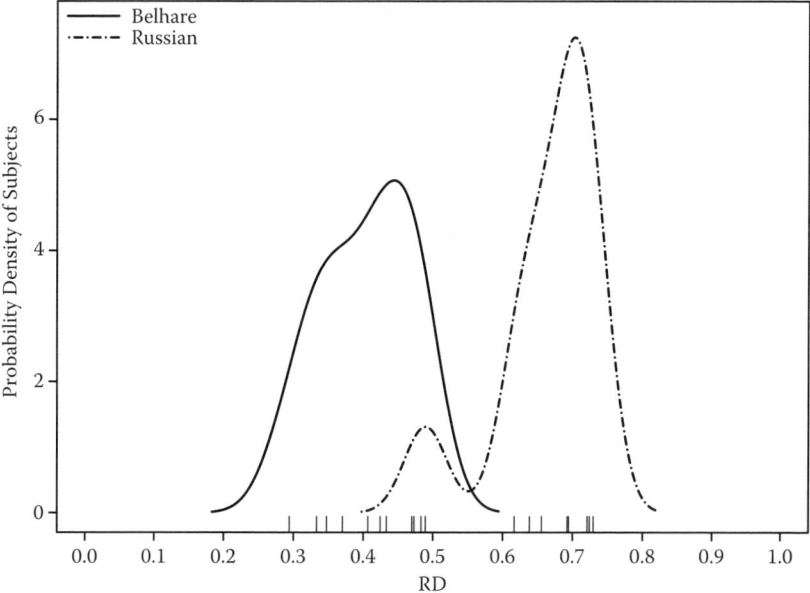

Figure 40.1   Referential Density (RD) in Belhare vs. Russian.

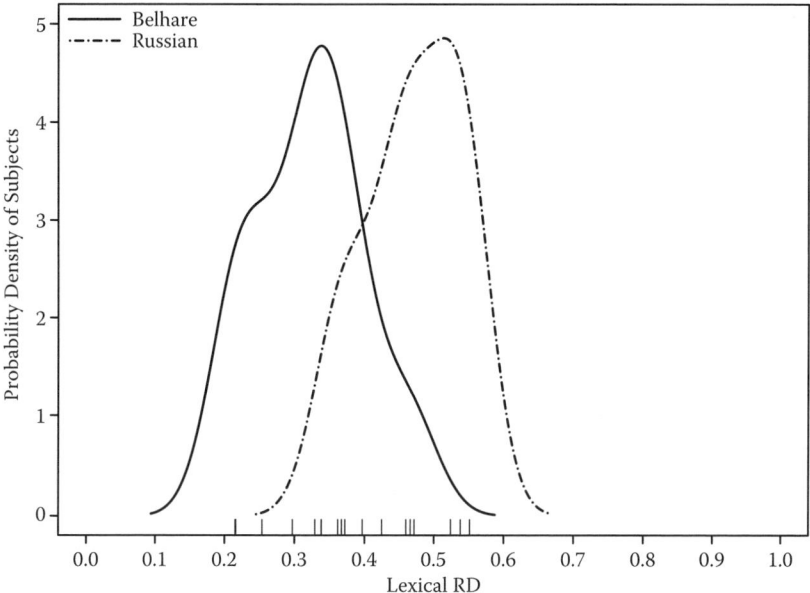

Figure 40.2   Lexical Referential Density (RD_{lex}) in Belhare vs. Russian.

Discourse Functions of Overt NPs and Information Management

In Russian, all human referents in the Pear Story were introduced by a lexical NP when they first appeared, regardless of the location in the text. A typical beginning of a Pear Story in Russian looks like the following (protagonists are underlined, and false starts are marked by '}'):[3]

(1) Sad. Na reke, vidno, derevnja.
Garden.sNOM on river.sLOC visible village.sNOM
<u>Xozjain</u> sobiraet, ja} grushi v sadu.
owner.sNOM collect.3sNPST.IPFV pear.pACC in garden.sLOC
Sobral odnu korzinu. Pojavljaetsja.
collect.smPST.PFV one.sfACC basket.sACC appear.3sNPST.IPFV.REFL
<u>drugoj muzhchina s kozoj</u>.
another.smNOM man.sNOM with goat.sINSTR
Koza bleet. Oni proshli.
goat.sNOM baa.3sNPST.IPFV they go.by.pPST.PFV
Muzhchina s kozoj proshli mimo.
man.sNOM with goat.sINSTR go.by.pPST.PFV close
A xozjain sada poshel nabirat'
and owner.sNOM garden.sGEN go.3sPST.PFV collect.INF
vtoruju korzinu. Tut im priexal <u>mal'chik</u>,
second.sfACC basket.sACC here 3pDAT come.smPST.PFV boy.sNOM
<u>naverno, ego syn</u>, na velosipede.
probably 3smGEN son.sNOM on bicycle-sLOC
(Female, 66 years)

'A garden. Near the river a village is visible. The <u>owner</u> is collecting appl} pears in the garden. (He) collected one basket. <u>Another man with a goat</u> appears. The goat is baa-ing. They went by. The man with the goat went by. And the owner of the garden went to collect the second basket. Here, <u>a boy</u> came towards them on a bicycle, <u>probably his son</u>.'

First the speaker sets the scene by means of nominal sentences. Then, the protagonists are introduced either by their role in the story or by a core characteristic: 'the owner,' 'another man with a goat,' and 'a boy, probably his son.'

Occasionally, the Belhare Pear Stories were similar in these respects. But a much more common strategy was to introduce human referents by a numeral like 'one' or indeed nothing at all. A typical Belhare Pear Story begins like the following:

(2) ʌbo pʌila syau phighe. syau phighe kina dhakie
now first apple pick.3sPST apple pick.3sPST and basket.LOC
andhe. ʌni ... ʌni meri sassa tahe, <u>ibaŋ</u>.
fill.in.3s>3sPST then then goat pull.CVB come.3sPST one.HUMAN
meri sassa tahe kina yolleŋ phetkhatthe,
goat pull.CVB come.3sPST and over.there move.on.level.3s> 3sPST
khe phetkhatthe. ina meri khatlotthe. kina
like.this move.on.level.3s>3sPST that goat take.away.3s>3sPST and
saikil}... saikille tahe, <u>ibaŋ</u>. (B99.10)
bicycle bicycle.LOC come.3sPST one.HUMAN

---

[3] Interlinear glossing follows the Leipzig Glossing Rules (http://www.eva.mpg.de/lingua/files/morpheme.html), except that we use lower case 'f,' 'm,' 'n' for feminine, masculine, and neuter gender, respectively. 'MED' stands for 'mediative case,' which expresses 'from' and 'via' relations.

'Now, first, (someone) picked apples. (S/he) picked apples and filled (them) into a basket. Then… then, <u>one</u> came along pulling a goat. (S/he) came pulling a goat and took (it) over there across; (s/he) took (it) over there across like that ((gesturing)). (S/he) took away that goat. And then, a bicycle} … <u>one</u> came on a bicycle.'

The first human referent is not introduced at all, not even with a pronoun. All that we know is contained by the event in which the referent participates, i.e., that he or she picked apples (the local substitute for pears, because pears were unknown to the local people). The following two referents, the person coming with a goat and the one coming with the bicycle, are each introduced by the numeral *i* 'one' with the human classifier *-baŋ*, but no lexical noun is used. Interestingly, each time, the numeral appears in an afterthought position, after the main verb (Belhare is a verb-final language).

The example in (2) was fairly representative of Belhare narratives. A quantitative analysis of all subjects showed that of the three human referents at the beginning of the story (the farmer picking pears, the man with the goat, and the boy taking away one basket with pears), speakers used lexical nouns in only 21% of the cases (pooling all speakers together), and where speakers used a lexical noun, they used it only for one of the three referents. In 61% of all Belhare cases, speakers used the numeral *ibaŋ*, occasionally expanded into *ibaŋ maʔi*, where *maʔi* is a generic noun meaning 'person, human being' that does not contain any information beyond what is already conveyed by the human classifier *-baŋ* (and that is also used as indefinite pronoun). The remaining 18% of the cases were introduced by zero anaphora, in the way we observed at the beginning of example (2).

While referential information is relatively thin, Belhare narratives place great emphasis on the nature and sequencing of events: hardly any event is mentioned just once; most are taken up in what is known as tail-head linkage (where the preceding predicate is repeated at the beginning of the next sentence, as in 'Picked apples. Picked apples and filled them into a basket'), leading to emphasis by repetition. This is a general strategy of Belhare discourse, shared with many other languages of the world (cf., e.g., Foley, 1986).

In Russian, the lexical NP used for introducing a referent serves as the identifier of the same referent later in the text, after another referent is introduced. In example (1) above, the referent introduced as 'Another <u>man with a goat</u>' (*muzhchina s kozoj*) is taken up again exactly by this label two clauses later in the story: 'Another <u>man with a goat</u> appears. The goat is baa-ing. They went by. The <u>man with the goat</u> went by.' Similarly, the main protagonist of the story is introduced in (1) as a boy (*mal'chik*), and it is by this term that the protagonist is referred back to later in the story. The story begun in (1) continues as follows:

(3) *Vsjal   korzinu   odnu,   postavil*
    take.sm.PST.PFV basket.sACC one.sfACC   put.smPST.PVF
    na velosipede, povez   ee.   Povez
    on bicycle.sLOC carry.smPST.PFV   3sfACC carry.smPST.PFV
    ee.   Potom   <u>devochka</u>   priexala,   tozhe na   velosipede.
    3sfACC then   girl.sNOM   come.sfPST.PFV also   on   bicycle -sLOC
    Vzjala   vtoruju   korzinu.   i   èto.
    take.sfPST.PFV   second.sfACC   basket.sACC   and   that
    Spotknulis'   na   velosipedax.   <u>Mal'chik</u>
    stumble.pPST.PFV.REFL   on   bicycle.pLOC   boy.sNOM
    s   korzinoj,   s   korzinami,   s   sumkami   upal.
    with   basket.sINST   with   basket.pINSTR,   with   bag.pINST
    fall.smPST.PFV
    Pojavilis'   <u>rebjata</u>,   kotorye   pomogli
    appear.pPST.PFV.REFL   guy.pNOM   which.pNOM   help.pPST.PFV
    <u>mal'chiku</u>   sobrat'   frukty   v   korzinu.
    boy.sDAT   collect.INF.PFV   fruit.pACC   in   basket.sACC

Postavili		*ee,*	*i*	*on*	*povez.*		*Tak.*
put.pPST.PFV		3sACC	and	3smNOM	carry-sPST.PFV		so
Vo	*vremja*	*stolknovenija.*		*Vo*	*vremja,*	*kak*	*upal*
in	time.sACC	collision.sGEN		in	time	how	fall.smPST.PFV
<u>*mal'chik,*</u>	*ego*	*upala*			*shljapa.*	<u>*Rebjata*</u>	*poshli*
boy.sNOM	3smGEN	fall.sfPST.PFV			hat.sNOM	guy.pNOM	go.pPST.PFV
dal'she,	*kotorye*	*pomogali*			*emu,*	*ètomu*	
further	which	help.pPST.IPFV			3smDAT	this.smDAT	
sobrat'		*frukty.* (Female, 66 years)					
collect.INF		fruit.pACC					

'Here came a <u>boy</u> towards them on a bike, <u>probably his son</u>. (He) took a basket, put it on the bicycle and carried it away. (He) carried it away. Then, a girl arrived, also on a bicycle. (She) took the second basket. And so. They stumbled on the bicycles. The <u>boy with the basket, with the baskets, with the bags</u>, fell. (Some) <u>guys</u> showed up, who helped the <u>boy</u> to collect the fruits into the basket. (They) lifted it up. And he carried (it) away. So. During the time of collision, when the <u>boy</u> fell, his hat fell off. The <u>guys</u> who had helped him, this one to collect the fruits went further.'

The first few clauses describe what the boy did, and because there is continuity of referents, all subject NPs are dropped here. But when new human referents appear—the girl (*devochka*), and later, the other boys (*rebjata*)—the speaker refers back to the protagonist with the same lexical labels as before, 'boy' (*mal'chik*). Thus, by introducing labels early on, the speakers later has a straightforward means to uniquely identify referents and to disambiguate them when necessary. The paragraph shows that a lexical NP is used whenever there is an introduction of a new referent or a switch to another referent independent of the location in the narrative.

The rhetorical style of Belhare is fundamentally different. In Belhare, lexical labels are introduced only when two protagonists are interacting with each other and it is necessary to identify them. The identity of referents is not given away in advance, so to speak, but only when it becomes absolutely necessary to avoid confusion. The continuation of the story reproduced in (4) illustrates this:

(4)
saikille	*tahe*	*kina*	*saikille*		*syau*	*annhatthe.*	
bicycle.LOC	come.3sPST	and	bicycle.LOC		apple	fill.in.3s>3s PST	
syau	*annhatthe*		*kina khatcahe.*	*khatcahe*	*kina*	*pheri*	*tahe.*
apple	fill.in.3s>3sPST		and go.3sPST	go.3sPST	and	again	come.3sPST
ʌni	*ʌrko*	*keti*	*tahe,..*	*saikillamma.*	*ʌni*		*saikil*
then	other	girl	come.3sPST	bicycle.MED	then		bicycle
ntuhechi	*kina*	*kohareʔ*	*ŋkoharechi.*	*ŋkoharechi*	*ʌni ..*		*keti*
crash.3dPST	and	fall.3sPST	fall.3dPST	fall.3dPST	then		girl
yulleŋ	*khatcahe.*	<u>*keta*</u>	*caĩ*	*inetto*	*utumbhut*		*sopyakthe.*
over.there	go3sPST	boy	TOP	there.FOC	3sPOSS.knee		pat.IPFV.3sPST
sopyakthe	*ʌni car-janaʔ*		*car-janaa*		*ek*		*chin*
pat.IPFV.3sPST	then four-HUMAN		four-HUMAN.ERG		one		moment
syau	*ŋkobhe*		*kina ibaŋŋa*		*saikil*		*phoghe*
apple	pick.up.3ns>3s.PST		and one.HUMAN.ERG		bicycle		lift. 3s>3sPST
kina	*khatcahe*						
and	go.away.3sPST						

'(S/he) came on a bicycle and then (s/he) filled the apples (into the basket) on the bicycle. (S/he) filled in the apples and then went away. (S/he) went away and then again came. Then, <u>another girl</u> came, … on a bicycle. Then, (they) crashed (their) bicycles (into each other) and (he) fell} (they) fell. (They) fell and … the <u>girl</u> went over there. As for the <u>boy</u>, (he) patted his

TABLE 40.1 Strategy Used for the First-Time Introduction of Human Referents in the Belhare Pear Story Corpus

	Not Interacting with Established Referents (Farmer, Man with Goat, Boy)		Interacting with Established Referents (Girl, Boys)	
Lexical	6	21%	14	88%
Numeral	17	61%	2	12%
Zero	5	18%	0	0%
Total	28		16	

knee right there (where he was). (He) patted his knee and then four} <u>four</u> (guys) picked up apples for a while, and then one lifted up the bicycle and then (s/he) went away.'

To continue with the story started in (2), the narrative in (4) first uses zero consistently for six verbs to refer to the protagonist who was introduced in (2) by an indefinite NP (*saikille tahe, ibaŋ* 'one came on a bicycle'). However, when another referent is introduced who will interact with (i.e., to crash with) the on-going referent, the speaker uses a lexical NP for the first time in the narrative to refer to the new referent: *ʌrko keti* 'another girl.' This choice seems to be motivated by the need to differentiate the second character from the protagonist, as they interact with each other (i.e., they crash into each other). In line with this, a few clauses later, the protagonist, too, is—for the first time in the entire story—identified by a lexical NP (*keta* 'boy'), marked by the contrastive topic particle *caĩ*. Note that, before this point in the narrative, neither gender nor age of the protagonist was ever mentioned.

The usage pattern in this example is typical. Table 40.1 contrasts the way in which human referents are introduced in contexts where they do not interact with previously established referents (i.e., the farmer picking pears, the man with goat, and the boy taking away one basket with pears) as opposed to contexts (necessarily later in the story) where the new referents interact with previously entailed (though not overtly mentioned) referents (i.e., the girl and people coming to help the protagonist after the crash).

The choice among the three types of introduction (lexical, numeral, zero) differs significantly between the two contexts (without vs. with interacting referents) in the entire Belhare text sample (Fisher Exact Test pooling all subjects, $p = .00007$). Comparing subjects individually, we found that the mean ratio of lexical vs. non-lexical introductions was significantly smaller in the non-interaction contexts than in the interaction-contexts (.17 vs. .91, Wilcoxon signed-ranks test, $p = .004$). In fact, as noted earlier, no subject ever introduced more than one of the three referents in the non-interaction context by lexical means. By contrast, in interaction contexts, when disambiguation becomes relevant, only two subjects used a non-lexical strategy (numerals) for one of the two referents. Thus, there is a general and statistically significant trend across subjects and the entire sample to use lexical NPs much more frequently for introducing referents when they interact with each other.

DISCUSSION

The results of our study suggest (i) that Russian speakers tend to produce narratives with higher RD than Belhare speakers, (ii) that Russian speakers specifically produce narratives with a higher *lexical* RD, and (iii) that Russian speakers use lexical NPs in an argument position for different narrative discourse functions from Belhare speakers—at least in the context provided by our experiment. In the following, we discuss our finding first (i) and then findings (ii) and (iii).

Referential Density in General

Why do Russian and Belhare narratives differ in RD? Here we consider two possible causal factors. One possible explanation could be found in the differences in grammatical structures of the two languages. Although both Belhare and Russian grammars allow dropping pronouns in most syntactic contexts, they differ in a number of ways, and some of these typological differences in grammar can be expected to cause differences in their RDs. Bickel (2003) proposes that the major typological factor regulating RD is the role that NP properties, most prominently case, play in the way grammatical relations are defined. In this regard, Russian and Belhare differ strongly from each other: in Russian, but not in Belhare, case features of argument NPs influence person agreement on verbs, even if the NP is not overtly realized, while in Belhare no NP property influences the choice of verbal agreement forms.

For example, in Russian, verb person agreement is strictly tied to nominative case features. Only if the highest-ranking argument of a predicate is in the nominative case can it trigger person agreement in the verb; if it is in any other case, it will trigger a neutral third-person singular form. Compare the examples in (5):

(5) a. *(ja)*   *xoch-u*   *idti*   *domoj.*
     1sNOM   want-1sNPST.IPFV   go.INF.IPFV   home
     'I want to go home.'
   b. *(mne)*   *xoch-et-sja*   *idti*   *domoj.*
     1sDAT   want-3sNPST.IPFV.REFL   go.INF.IPFV   home
     'I want to go home.'

In (5a), the highest argument of 'want' ('I') is in the nominative, and therefore triggers first-person singular agreement in the verb (*xochu*). By contrast, in (5b) the highest argument is in the dative case, and this triggers a neutral third-person singular form in the verb (*xochetsja*).

This is very different in Belhare, where the verb agrees with the person of the subject and object regardless of the other grammatical properties of these arguments (Bickel, 2004a, 2004b, 2006):

(6) a. *(han)*   *khar-e-ga*   *i?*
     2sNOM   go-PST-2   Q
     'Did you go?'
   b. *(han-na)*   *kii?-t-u-ga*   *i?*
     2s-ERG   fear-NPST-3P-2   Q
     'Do you fear him/her/it?'
   c. *(han-naha)*   *ŋ-kipma*   *kai?-t-u-ga*   *i?*
     2s-GEN   2sPOSS-fear   come.up-NPST-3P-2   Q
     'Are you afraid of him/her/it?' (etymologically: 'Did your fear arise?')

The second-person arguments in (6) trigger the same second-person agreement (-*ga*) forms regardless of their case (nominative in 6a, ergative in 6b, genitive in 6c—which exhausts the range of argumental cases in Belhare).

Thus, although NPs are not required to be overt in either language, they play a considerably more important role in the mechanics of grammar in Russian than in Belhare. The constant need to monitor the grammatical properties of NPs in Russian may lead to NPs being overtly realized more often in discourse, and this would predict the observed increase in RD.

There are several other typological differences that one might expect to affect the RD of a language, but based on the findings in Bickel (2003), they seem less likely to play a role in RD regulation. One set of differences is morphological. Belhare is a polysynthetic (but non-incorporating) language. The Russian morphological system is somewhat less elaborate, and certainly much less complex in terms of the number of categories marked and the intricacies of allomorphy and affixal positions.

A related difference is that Belhare transitive verbs agree with both subject and object for number and person, while in Russian the verb agrees with one argument only (the one in the nominative, cf. above) in number and person, and, for the past tense singular, in gender. While these differences may be thought to be a likely factor in causing RD differences because rich agreement would seem to favor more NP dropping, the findings in Bickel (2003) falsify this as a general hypothesis: the Maithili agreement system is as rich as the Belhare one (both having double agreement in transitive verbs), yet the two languages have radically different RD conventions (with Maithili showing a significantly higher RD than Belhare). And Bickel (2005) finds that speakers of Kyirong, a Tibetan variety, use overt NPs as little as Belhare speakers (i.e., both languages have a low RD), even though Kyirong has no agreement morphology at all.

Lexical Referential Density and Information Management

A main issue for the status of referential density in the two languages was the type of NP speakers used. Thus, the question we were interested in is whether this difference in RD is merely due to a variation in the use of pronouns or rather due to a cognitively deeper difference in the use of lexical NPs.

Our experiment suggests that Russian speakers not only mention significantly more NPs but they also specifically use significantly more lexical NPs. A closer inspection of the Pear narratives suggests that the difference is to a large degree due to the way human referents, the protagonists of the story, are introduced as soon as they occur in the story. The crucial contrast between Russian and Belhare speakers in our experiment consists of two different principles of information management: in Russian, protagonists are each labeled and described by a lexical NP at the outset, and then, during the narrative, they are referred to by the same labels for the purpose of tracking switches in reference. It appears that Russian speakers find it important to specify referents even before this becomes absolutely necessary for the purpose of reference tracking. In Belhare, by contrast, lexical labeling of referents tends not to be given away 'for free' at the outset but occurs only when the speaker is forced to do so by the communicative demands of reference tracking, i.e., when communication would break down unless referential identities are explicated.

The difference between these two types of information management is one of cultural tradition, and as such invites relativistic 'irritation' when speakers in one tradition look at the products of other traditions.

From a Russian or, for that matter, English perspective, Belhare narratives seem to leave out much essential information, and examples like (2) seem to go against all we expect from a 'good' narrative. But note that Belhare Pear Stories are by no means inadequate for understanding the narrative and tracking referents across events. The opening paragraph in (2) makes clear that there are three different referents: although referents were not lexically labeled, the use of 'one' indicates that there are distinct, new referents. The subsequent paragraph in (4) continued with one of these referents by zero anaphora (cf., the first few lines), but then the speaker introduced the contrasting lexical labels *keti* 'girl' vs. *keta* 'boy' just in time when the two interacted and needed to be distinguished.

Reading Russian Pear Stories with Belhare in mind suggests information overflow that is communicatively inappropriate: Why would one want to specify the identity of referents if there is no need to distinguish referents since they are not directly interacting with each other? In some cases, even a non-Belhare speaker would deem the referential information provided by Russian speakers as communicatively excessive: we noted in Pear Stories that Russian speakers often invent lexical attributes for referents that have no basis in the visual stimulus: e.g., in (1) the Russian speaker says that the one who is picking pears is the owner of a garden. It seems that the cultural need of providing explicit lexical labels is so strong that speakers would rather invent properties of referents than not be explicit.

Of course, within each cultural tradition, the information flow in narratives is naturally perceived as just right—Belhare listeners do not find Belhare narratives under-explicit and do not request more information; and Russian listeners do not find Russian narratives over-explicit or too liberal in inventing properties of referents.

CONCLUSIONS

It is commonly assumed that behind all apparent differences in the use of overt NPs and other referential coding devices, speakers of all languages comply with universal principles on how much referential information can be reasonably conveyed by a given stretch of discourse. Rich supporting evidence for this assumption comes from Du Bois and colleagues' findings on preferred argument structure, which suggests a universal upper limit of one lexical NP per clause on average (DuBois, 1987, 2003; DuBois, Kumpf, & Ashby, 2003). Our present findings suggest that below this threshold, there are significant differences between speech communities in information management, specifically in the amount of lexical information that speakers are expected to give away when telling a story beyond what is strictly needed for tracking the identities of referents across events. Thus, while there is a universal upper limit on informativeness, our study suggests that human minds are more flexible and diverse when it comes to the lower limits on informativeness.

This, then, suggests thinking for speaking and thinking for listening affects how much we orient our attention to the identities and characteristics of participants when we tell a story. What must be left for future research is the question of whether these effects have a larger impact on cognition, beyond the information processing that happens during a conversation: could it be that the typological differences in information management we found relate to larger differences in the cultural valuation of identities and referents as opposed to events, or in general cultural strategies of information dissemination? In an ethnographic study, Besnier (1989) suggests that Tuvaluan (a Polynesian language) speakers often withold essential information to the effect that the information can only be established through collaborative conversational exchange, not by the speaker alone. As Duranti (1997) suggests, this ties into a general view of sharing responsibility on information.

It remains to be seen whether the difference we found between Russian and Belhare rhetorical style correlates with such differences in the ideology of information dissemination, or with general differences in the attentional balance between referents and events, or with both. At any rate, progress regarding this issue is inspired by and represents a further expansion of the kind of controlled comparative research across different languages and cultures that Slobin launched with the Frog Story project over a decade ago (cf. Berman & Slobin, 1994).

REFERENCES

Berman, R. A., & Slobin, D. I. (Eds.). (1994). *Relating events in narrative*. Hillsdale, NJ: Lawrence Erlbaum Associates.

Besnier, N. (1989). Information withholding as a manipulative and collusive strategy in Nukulaelae gossip. *Language in Society, 18*, 315–341.

Bickel, B. (2003). Referential density in discourse and syntactic typology. *Language, 79*, 708–736.

Bickel, B. (2004a). Hidden syntax in Belhare. In A. Saxena (Ed.), *Himalayan languages: Past and present* (pp. 141–190). Berlin: Mouton de Gruyter.

Bickel, B. (2004b). The syntax of experiencers in the himalayas. In P. Bhaskararao & K. V. Subbarao (Eds.), *Non-nominative subjects* (pp. 77–112). Amsterdam: John Benjamins.

Bickel, B. (2005, February). Referential density in discourse: Typological and sociological factors. Paper presented at the ZAS, Berlin.

Bickel, B. (2006). Clause-level vs. predicate-level linking. In I. Bornkessel, M. Schlesewsky, B. Comrie, & A. D. Friederici (Eds.), *Semantic role universals and argument linking: Theoretical, typological and psycholinguistic perspectives* (pp. 155–190). Berlin: Mouton de Gruyter.

Chafe, W. (1980). *The pear stories: Cognitive, cultural, and linguistic aspects of narrative production*. Norwood, NJ: Ablex.

DuBois, J. W. (1987). The discourse basis of ergativity. *Language, 63*, 805–855.
DuBois, J. W. (2003). Discourse and grammar. In M. Tomasello (Ed.), *The new psychology of language* (Vol. 2). Mahwah, NJ: Lawrence Erlbaum Associates.
DuBois, J. W., Kumpf, L. E., & Ashby, W. J. (Eds.). (2003). *Preferred argument structure: Grammar as architecture for function*. Amsterdam: John Benjamins.
Duranti, A. (1997). *Linguistic anthropology*. Cambridge, UK: Cambridge University Press.
Foley, W. A. (1986). *The Papuan languages of New Guinea*. Cambridge, UK: Cambridge University Press.
Noonan, M. (2003, September). Crosslinguistic investigation of referential density. Paper presented at the 5th Biannual Conference of the Association for Linguistic Typology, Cagliari.
Slobin, D. I. (1996). From "thought and language" to "Thinking for speaking." In J. J. Gumperz & S. C. Levinson (Eds.), *Rethinking linguistic relativity* (pp. 70–96). Cambridge, UK: Cambridge University Press.
Slobin, D. I. (1997a). Mind, code, and text. In J. Bybee, J. Haiman, & S. A. Thompson (Eds.), *Essays on language function and language type dedicated to Talmy Givón* (pp. 437–467). Amsterdam: John Benjamins.
Slobin, D. I. (1997b). Typology and rhetoric: Verbs of motion in English and Spanish. In M. Shibatani & S. A. Thompson (Eds.), *Grammatical constructions* (pp. 195–219). Oxford, UK: Oxford University Press.
Slobin, D. I. (2000). Verbalized events: A dynamic approach to linguistic relativity and determinism. In R. Dirven & S. Niemeier (Eds.), *Evidence for linguistic relativity* (pp. 107–138). Amsterdam: John Benjamins.

Appendix A

Dan Slobin's Mentors, Models, Influences, and Connections
A Self-Portrait

(PowerPoint Slides Presented by Dan Slobin at the Special Symposium in His Honor at the 10th International Congress for the Study of Child Language, Berlin, July 2005)

Dan I. Slobin

Harvard Center for Cognitive Studies (founded 1960)

Advisory Committee:
  Roger W. Brown, Jerome S. Bruner,
  John B. Carroll, H. Stuart Hughes,
  Roman Jakobson, George A. Miller,
  C. Frederick Mosteller, Willard V. Quine

"Cognitive studies are concerned with what people know, and there is no simple relation between what they know and what they do. The real problem is to see beyond their behavior to the underlying rules and concepts that characterize this knowledge."

(*Second Annual Report*, 1962)

Jerry Bruner

"The categories in terms of which we group the events of the world around us are constructions or inventions. They do not 'exist' in the environment. We select and utilize certain cues rather than others...

Since different cultures have different languages, and since these languages code or categorize the world into different classes, might it not be reasonable to expect some conformance between the categories normally employed by speakers and those contained in the language they use?"

(Jerome S. Bruner, Jacqueline J. Goodnow, & George A. Austin, *A study of thinking*, 1956)

Jerry Bruner

"The very use of language presupposes certain underlying cognitive processes required for its use."

(*Studies in cognitive growth*, 1966)

Vygotsky

Piaget

Roger Brown

"Because linguistic invariance is much simpler than invariance of reference, language guides the child in his cognitive socialization."

(*Words and things*, 1966)

"We suspect that the changes sentences undergo as they shuttle between persons in conversation are the data that most clearly expose the underlying structure of language."

(Roger Brown, Courtney Cazden, Ursula Bellugi, *The child's grammer from I to III*, 1967)

Noam Chomsky

"The central fact to which any significant linguistic theory must address itself is this: a mature speaker can produce a new sentence of his language on the appropriate occasion, and other speakers can understand it immediately, though it is equally new to them...

On the basis of a limited experience with the data of speech, each normal human has developed for himself a thorough competence in his native language."

(*The logical basis of linguistic theory*, 1962)

Eric Lenneberg

"The central and most interesting problem is whether the emergence of language is due to very general capabilities that mature to a critical minimum at about eighteen months to make language and many other skills possible, or whether there might be some factors specific to speech and language that come to maturation and are somewhat independent from other, more general processes."

(*The natural history of language*, 1966)

George Miller

"Just as we induce a three-dimensional space underlying the two dimensional pattern on the retina, so we must *induce a syntactic structure underlying the linguistic string of sounds in a sentence.* And just as the student of space perception must have a good understanding of projective geometry, so a student of psycholinguistics must have a good understanding of grammar."

(*Some psychological studies of grammar*, 1962)

Roman Jakobson

"Psychologists must bear in mind the equal importance of studying the signification of context and that of their components by themselves: for instance, syntactic structures and words. The wholes and parts are mutually determined."

(*Linguistics in relation to other sciences*, 1967)

Sue Ervin-Tripp   Erving Goffman   John Gumperz

Dell Hymes   John Searle   Julian Boyd

More teachers: Doctoral students

1960s
David Argoff
Jan Brukman
Douglass Carmichael
Robin Chapman
Lorraine Fitzgerald
Pulin Garg
Susanna Hoffman
Richard Howell
Keith Kernan
Claudia Mitchell-Kernan
David Nichols
Jacqueline Sachs
Brian Stross
Janet Tallman
Leonard Talmy
Nicholas Thompson
Peyton Todd

1970s – 1980s
Ayhan Aksu-Koç
Mary Sue Ammon
Fatima Badry
Michael Bamberg
Bartholomew Body
Penny Boyes-Braem
Nancy Budwig
Anne Carter
Elizabeth Charlson
Patricia Clancy
Katherine Demuth
Janet Dougherty
Eva Eckert
Anne Eisenberg
Mary Erbaugh
Dennis Galvan
Julie Gerhardt
Teresa Jacobsen
Judith Johnston
Brian MacWhinney
Virginia Marchman
Daniel Morrow
Ageliki Nicolopoulou
Ljubica Radulovic
Susan Rattray
Gisela Redeker
Tanya Renner
Iskender Savaşir
Geoffrey Saxe
Eugenia Sebastián
Marilyn Silva
Amy Strage
Diane Sunar
Darlene Turner-Charles

1990s – 2000s

Michelle Anthony	Robert Mannheimer
Jon Aske	Laura Michaelis
David Bailey	Kevin Moore
Therese Baumberger	Keiko Nakamura
Yael Biederman	Kyung-ju Oh
Joyce Tang Boyland	Şeyda Özçalişkan
Nancy Chang	Maria Pak
Lisa Dasinger	Lillian Park
Rebecca Des Roches	Eric Pederson
Seiko Fujii	Jennie Pyers
Adele Goldberg	Paula Rogers Radetzky
Joseph Grady	Iliana Reyes
Jiansheng Guo	Susan Rivera
Phillip Hull	Sarah Shull
Christopher Johnson	Lauren Silver
Aylin Küntay	Richard Sprott
Marlon Kuntze	Sabine Stoll
Amy Weinberg Lieberman	Sarah Taub
Reyna Lindert	Helen Thumann
Molly Losh	Ceil Toupin
Wolfgang Mann	Inge Zwitserlood

Post-docs, Visiting Scholars, Research Collaborators

Ayhan Aksu-Koç	Susan Duncan
Mary Sue Ammon	Natalys Durova (Russia)
Michelle Anthony	Jane Edwards
Francesco Antinucci (Italy)	Sonja Eisenbeiss (Germany)
David Argoff	Elizabeth Engber-Pedersen (Denmark)
Michael Bamberg	Susan Ervin-Tripp
Elizabeth Bates	Charles Ferguson
Edith Bavin (Australia)	Dennis Galvan
Heike Behrens (Germany)	Xosé Ramón García Soto (Spain)
Ruth Berman (Israel)	John Gumperz
Raphael Berthele (Switzerland)	Jiansheng Guo
Thomas Bever	Roni Henkin (Israel)
Balthasar Bickel (Germany)	Annette Herskovits
Yael Biederman	Nini Hoiting (Netherlands)
Aura Bocaz (Chile)	Iraide Ibarretxe-Antuñano (Spain)
Melissa Bowerman (Netherlands)	Takehiko Ito (Japan)
Penelope Brown (Netherlands)	Harriet Jisa (France)
Joan Bybee	Judith Johnston
Soonja Choi	Jelena Jovanovic
Patricia Clancy	Annette Karmiloff-Smith (UK)
Eve Clark	Anetta Kopecka (Poland, France)
Doğan Cüceloğlu (Turkey)	Aylin Küntay (Turkey)
Katherine Demuth	Marlon Kuntze

Maarten Lemmens (Belgium)	Tanya Renner
Stephen Levinson (Netherlands)	Matthew Rispoli
Yonata Levy (Israel)	Jacqueline Sachs
Amy Weinberg Lieberman	Chikako Sakura
Elena Lieven (UK)	Iskender Savaşir (Turkey)
Reyna Lindert	Svenka Savić (Serbia)
Brian MacWhinney	Bambi Schieffelin
Virginia Marchman	Eugenia Sebastián (Spain)
Aida Martinović-Zić	Gunter Senft (Germany)
Yo Matsumoto (Japan)	Marilyn Silva
David McNeill	Magdalena Smoczyńska (Poland)
Xiaochun Miao (China)	Gloria Soto
Ruth Miller	Sven Strömqvist (Sweden)
Juan Pablo Mora Gutiérrez (Spain)	Ayshe Talay-Ongan (Turkey)
Gary Morgan (UK)	Yukiko Sugiyama (Japan)
Keiko Nakamura (Japan)	Leonard Talmy
Bhuvana Narasimhan (Netherlands, India)	Sarah Taub
Kyung-ju Oh (Korea)	Helen Thumann
Kyoko Ohara (Japan)	Ceil Toupin
Öget Oktem-Tanör (Turkey)	Ludo Verhoeven (Netherlands)
Şeyda Özçalişkan (Turkey)	Christiane von Stutterheim (Germany)
Enrique Palancar (Spain)	Stefan von Tetzchner (Norway)
Miguel Pérez Pereira (Spain)	Richard Weist
Miguel Pérez Pereira (Spain)	Gordon Wells (Canada)
Stephanie Pourcel (UK)	Charles Welsh
Jennie Pyers	David Wilkins
Ljubica Radulović (Croatia)	Cynthia Hsin-feng We (Taiwan)
Hrafnhildur Ragnarsdóttir (Iceland)	Karl Zimmer
Judy Reilly	Jordan Zlatev

THE WORLD

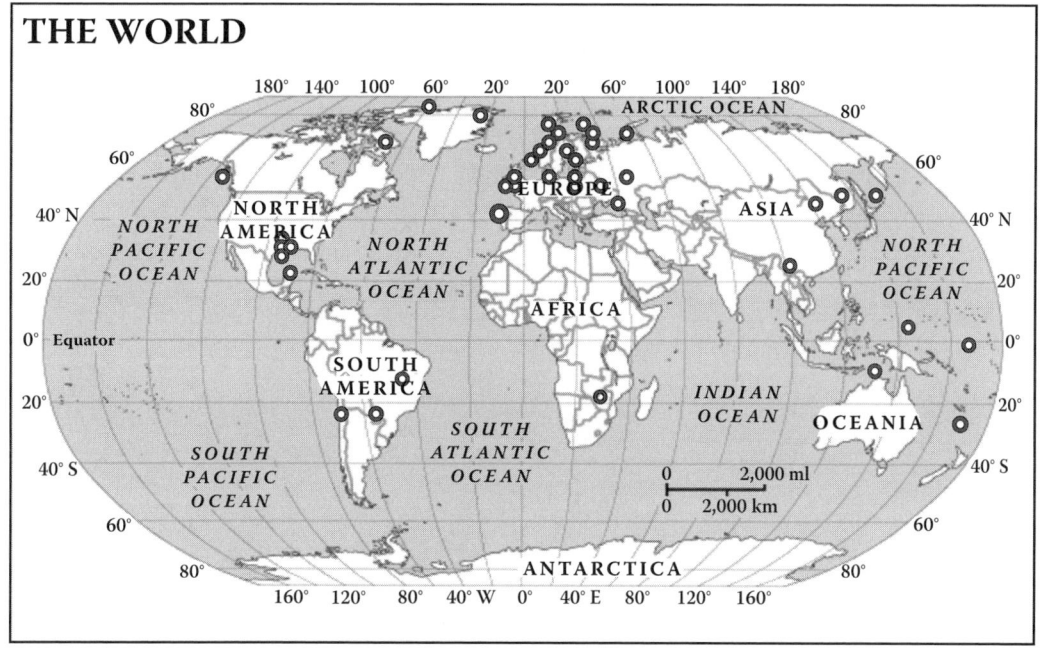

Wisława Szymborska

My apologies
to great questions
for small answers.

Appendix B

Bibliography of Dan Isaac Slobin's Publications, 1960–

Poems

Slobin, D. I. (1994). "Sensing Sense" "From My Son's Bed" In B. R. Strahan, D. J. Napoli, & E. N. Rando (Eds.), *Speaking in tongues: Poems by linguists*. Falls Church, VA: Black Buzzard Press.

Slobin, D. I. (2005). "To right the writing," "Fiat Lux," "Verbs of Motion," "Written Lines." In A. Sunshine (Ed.), *Poetry by linguists*. Chicago: Atlantis-Centaur.

Dissertations

Slobin, D. I. (1960). *Antonymic phonetic symbolism in three natural languages*. Unpublished senior honors dissertation, Department of Psychology, University of Michigan.

Slobin, D. I. (1963). *Grammatical transformations in childhood and adulthood*. Unpublished doctoral dissertation, Harvard University.

Academic

1961

Slobin, D. I. (1961). *New design in elementary second language teaching: Field demonstration in the State of Israel and evaluation*. Technical Report, Language Research, Inc., Cambridge, MA.

1962

Miller, G. A., Ojemann, K. E., & Slobin, D. (1962). *A psychological method for investigating grammatical transformations*. Technical Report, Center for Cognitive Studies, Harvard University.

1963

Slobin, D. I. (1963). Some aspects of the use of pronouns of address in Yiddish. *Word, 19,* 193–202.

1964

Slobin, D. I. (1964). The fruits of the first season: A discussion of the role of play in childhood. *Journal of Humanistic Psychology, 4,* 59–79.

1965

Slobin, D. I. (1965). To open the mouths of babes: Review of R. Ray Battin and Olaf Haug, Speech and language delay: A home training program. *Contemporary Psychology, 10,* 74–76.

1966

Ervin-Tripp, S. M., & Slobin, D. I. (1966). Psycholinguistics. *Annual Review of Psychology, 17,* 435–474. [Translations: Argentina, France, Italy, Russia]

Slobin, D. I. (Ed.). (1966). *Handbook of Soviet psychology*. Special double issue of *Soviet Psychology & Psychiatry, 4*(3–4).

Slobin, D. I. (1966). Grammatical transformations and sentence comprehension in childhood and adulthood. *Journal of Verbal Learning and Verbal Behavior, 5,* 219–227.

Slobin, D. I. (1966). The acquisition of Russian as a native language. In F. Smith & G. A. Miller (Eds.), *The genesis of language: A psycholinguistic approach* (pp. 129–148). Cambridge, MA: The MIT Press.

Slobin, D. I. (1966). Comments on "Developmental psycholinguistics": A discussion of McNeill's presentation. In F. Smith & G. A. Miller (Eds.), *The genesis of language: A psycholinguistic approach* (pp. 85–91). Cambridge, MA: The MIT Press.

Slobin, D. I. (1966). Soviet psycholinguistics. In N. O'Connor (Ed.), *Present-day Russian psychology: A symposium by seven authors* (pp. 109–151). Oxford, UK: Pergamon.

Slobin, D. I. (1966). Review of *Psycholinguistics: A survey of theory and research problems* (C. E. Osgood & T. A. Sebeok, Eds.). *American Scientist, 54,* 111A–112A.

1967

Slobin, D. I. (Ed.). (1967). *A field manual for cross-cultural study of the acquisition of communicative competence.* Berkeley, CA: Language-Behavior Research Laboratory.

Slobin, D. I. (Ed.). (1967). *Vygotsky memorial issue: In honor of the seventieth birthday of Lev Semyonovich Vygotsky.* Special issue of *Soviet Psychology,* 7(3).

1968

Slobin, D. I. (1968). Antonymic phonetic symbolism in three natural languages. *Journal of Personality and Social Psychology, 10,* 301–305.

Slobin, D. I. (1968). Recall of full and truncated passive sentences in connected discourse. *Journal of Verbal Learning and Verbal Behavior, 7,* 876–881.

Slobin, D. I. (1968). Imitation and grammatical development in children. In N. S. Endler, L. R. Boulter, & H. Osser (Eds.), *Contemporary issues in developmental psychology* (pp. 437–443). New York: Holt, Rinehart & Winston. [Translation: France]

Slobin, D. I. (1968). *Early grammatical development in several languages, with special attention to Soviet research.* Technical Report No. 11, Language-Behavior Research Laboratory, University of California, Berkeley.

Slobin, D. I. (1968). Review of *Directions in psycholinguistics* (S. Rosenberg, Ed.) *International Journal of American Linguistics, 34,* 161–163.

Slobin, D. I., Miller, S. H., & Porter, L. W. (1968). Forms of address and social relations in a business organization. *Journal of Personality and Social Psychology, 8,* 289–293.

1969

Slobin, D. I. (Ed.). (1969). *Soviet psycholinguistics.* Special issue of *Soviet Psychology,* 9(3).

1970

Slobin, D. I. (1970). Universals of grammatical development in children. In G. B. Flores d'Arcais & W. J. M. Levelt (Eds.), *Advances in psycholinguistics* (pp. 174–186). Amsterdam: North-Holland. [Translation: Germany]

1971

Slobin, D. I. (1971). *Psycholinguistics.* Glenview, IL: Scott Foresman. [Translations: Argentina, Germany, Iceland, Italy, Japan, Malaysia, Russia]

Slobin, D. I. (Ed.). (1971). *The ontogenesis of grammar: A theoretical symposium.* New York: Academic Press.

Slobin, D. I. (1971). Developmental psycholinguistics. In W. O. Dingwall (Ed.), *A survey of linguistic science* (pp. 298–411). College Park, MD: University of Maryland Linguistics Program.

Slobin, D. I. (1971). Grammatical development in Russian-speaking children. In A. Bar-Adon & W. F. Leopold (Eds.), *Child language: A book of readings* (pp. 343–348). Englewood Cliffs, NJ: Prentice-Hall.

Slobin, D. I. (1971). On the learning of morphological rules: A reply to Palermo and Eberhart. In D. I. Slobin (Ed.), *The ontogenesis of grammar: A theoretical symposium* (pp. 204–223). New York: Academic Press.

Slobin, D. I., & Welsh, C. A. (1971). Elicited imitation as a research tool in developmental psycholinguistics. In C. B. Lavatelli (Ed.), *Language training in early childhood education* (pp. 170–185). Urbana: University of Illinois Press.

1972

Brožek, J., & Slobin, D. I. (Eds.). (1972). *Fifty years of Soviet psychology: An historical perspective.* White Plains, NY: International Arts & Sciences Press.

Slobin, D. I. (1972). Seven questions about language development. In P. C. Dodwell (Ed.), *New horizons in psychology 2* (pp. 179–215). Harmondsworth, UK: Penguin. [Translation: Spain]

Slobin, D. I. (1972). *Leopold's bibliography of child language: Revised and augmented edition.* Bloomington: University of Indiana Press.

Slobin, D. I. (1972). Children and language: They learn the same way all around the world. *Psychology Today, 6*(2), 71–74, 82.

1973

Ferguson, C. A., & Slobin, D. I. (Eds.). (1973). *Studies of child language development.* New York: Holt, Rinehart & Winston.

Slobin, D. I. (1973). Cognitive prerequisites for the development of grammar. In C. A. Ferguson & D. I. Slobin, (Eds.), *Studies of child language development* (pp. 175–208). New York: Holt, Rinehart & Winston. [Translations: Germany, Iceland, Poland, Russia]

1974

Slobin, D. I. (1974). Berklijski projekat o razvoju jezika u raznim jezičkim sredinama [The Berkeley project on language development in different linguistic environments]. In M. Jočić & S. Savić (Eds.), *Modeli u sintaksi dečjeg govora [Models of child language syntax].* Novi Sad, Yugoslavia: Institute za Lingvistiku.

1975

Slobin, D. I. (1975). On the nature of talk to children. In E. H. Lenneberg & E. Lenneberg (Eds.), *Foundations of language: Vol. 1. A multidisciplinary approach* (pp. 283–297). New York: Academic Press. [Translation: Spain]

Slobin, D. I. (1975). Beginnings of language, Language development. In R. E. Schell (Ed.), *Developmental psychology today* (2nd ed.) (pp. 143–161, 223–241). New York: CRM/Random House.

1977

Slobin, D. I. (1977). Language change in childhood and in history. In J. Macnamara (Ed.), *Language learning and thought* (pp. 185–214). New York: Academic Press.

1978

Slobin, D. I. (1978). A case study of early language awareness. In A. Sinclair, R. Jarvella, & W. J. M. Levelt (Eds.), *The child's conception of language* (pp. 45–54). Heidelberg, Germany: Springer-Verlag.

Slobin, D. I. (1978). Suggested universals in the ontogenesis of grammar. In V. Honsa & M. J. Hardman-de-Bautista (Eds.), *Papers on linguistics and child language: Ruth Hirsch Weir Memorial Volume* (pp. 249–264). The Hague: Mouton.

1979

Ammon, M. S., & Slobin, D. I. (1979). A cross-linguistic study of the processing of causative sentences. *Cognition, 7,* 3–17.

Johnston, J. R., & Slobin, D. I. (1979). The development of locative expressions in English, Italian, Serbo-Croatian and Turkish. *Journal of Child Language, 6*, 531–547.

Slobin, D. I. (1979). *Psycholinguistics* (2nd ed.). Glenview, IL: Scott Foresman. [Translation: Brazil]

1980

Cüceloğlu, D., & Slobin, D. I. (1980). Dil reformu ve kişi algılaması [Language reform and person perception]. *Psikoloji dergesi (Ankara)*, No. 9, 4–9.

Cüceloğlu, D., & Slobin, D. I. (1980). Effects of Turkish language reform on person perception. *Journal of Cross-Cultural Psychology, 11*, 297–326.

Slobin, D. I. (1980). The repeated path between transparency and opacity in language. In U. Bellugi, & Studdert-Kennedy, M. (Eds.), *Signed and spoken language: Biological constraints on linguistic form* (pp. 229–243). Weinheim, Germany: Verlag Chemie.

1981

Slobin, D. I. (1981). Psychology without linguistics = language without grammar. *Cognition, 10*, 275–280.

Slobin, D. I. (1981). The origins of grammatical encoding of events. In W. Deutsch (Ed.), *The child's construction of language* (pp. 185–199). London: Academic Press.

Slobin, D. I. (1981). L'apprentissage de la langue maternelle. *La Recherche, 12*, 572–578. [Translation: Spain]

1982

Bybee, J. L., & Slobin, D. I. (1982). Rules and schemas in the development and use of the English past tense. *Language, 58*, 265–289.

Bybee, J. L., & Slobin, D. I. (1982). Why small children cannot change language on their own: Suggestions from the English past tense. In A. Ahlqvist (Ed.), *Papers from the 5th International Conference on Historical Linguistics* (pp. 29–37). Amsterdam/Philadelphia: John Benjamins.

Slobin, D. I. (1982). Universal and particular in the acquisition of language. In E. Wanner & L. R. Gleitman (Eds.), *Language acquisition: The state of the art* (pp. 128–172). Cambridge, UK: Cambridge University Press.

Slobin, D. I. (1982). Preface. In M. Beverdige (Ed.), *Children thinking through language* (pp. ix–x). London: Edward Arnold.

Slobin, D. I., & Aksu, A. A. (1982). Tense, aspect and modality in the use of the Turkish evidential. In P. J. Hopper (Ed.), *Tense and aspect: Between semantics and pragmatics* (pp. 185–200). Amsterdam/Philadelphia: John Benjamins.

Slobin, D. I., & Bever, T. G. (1982). Children use canonical sentence schemas: A crosslinguistic study of word order and inflections. *Cognition, 12*, 229–265.

1983

Slobin, D. I. (1983). What the natives have in mind. In R. W. Andersen (Ed.), *Pidginization and creolization as language acquisition* (pp. 236–253). Rowely, MA: Newbury House.

1984

Slobin, D. I. (1984). Child language and the bioprogram. *Behavioral and Brain Sciences, 7*, 209–210.

Slobin, D. I. (1984). La construcción de la gramática por el niño. In M. Monfort (Ed.), *La intervención logopédica: II. Symposio de Logopedia* (pp. 45–57). Madrid, Spain: Ciencias de la Educación Preescolar y Especial (CEPE).

1985

Aksu-Koç, A. A., & Slobin, D. I. (1985). Acquisition of Turkish. In D. I. Slobin (Ed.), *The crosslinguistic study of language acquisition: Vol. 1. The data* (pp. 839–878). Hillsdale, NJ: Lawrence Erlbaum Associates.

Slobin, D. I. (Ed.). (1985). *The crosslinguistic study of language acquisition: Vol. 1. The data* Hillsdale, NJ: Lawrence Erlbaum Associates.
Slobin, D. I. (Ed.). (1985). *The crosslinguistic study of language acquisition: Vol. 2. Theoretical issues*. Hillsdale, NJ: Lawrence Erlbaum Associates.
Slobin, D. I. (1985). The child as linguistic icon-maker. In J. Haiman (Ed.), *Iconicity in grammar* (pp. 221–248). Amsterdam/Philadelphia: John Benjamins.
Slobin, D. I. (1985). Crosslinguistic evidence for the Language-Making Capacity. In D. I. Slobin (Ed.), *The crosslinguistic study of language acquisition: Vol. 2. Theoretical issues* (pp. 1157–1256). Hillsdale, NJ: Lawrence Erlbaum Associates.
Slobin, D. I. (1985). Why study language crosslinguistically? In D. I. Slobin (Ed.), *The crosslinguistic study of language acquisition: Vol. 1. The data* (pp. 3–24). Hillsdale, NJ: Lawrence Erlbaum Associates.

1986

Aksu-Koç, A. A., & Slobin, D. I. (1986). A psychological account of the development and use of evidentials in Turkish. In W. Chafe & J. Nichols (Eds.), *Evidentiality: The linguistic coding of epistemology* (pp. 159–167). Norwood, NJ: Ablex.
Slobin, D. I. (1986). The acquisition and use of relative clauses in Turkic and Indo-European languages. In D. I. Slobin & K. Zimmer (Eds.), *Studies in Turkish linguistics* (pp. 277–298). Amsterdam/Philadelphia: John Benjamins.
Slobin, D. I., & Talay, A. (1986). Development of pragmatic uses of subject pronouns in Turkish child language. In A. A. Aksu-Koç & E. Erguvanlı Taylan (Eds.), *Proceedings of the Turkish Linguistics Conference: August 9–10, 1984* (pp. 207–228). Istanbul, Turkey: Boğaziçi University Press.
Slobin, D. I., & Zimmer, K. (Eds.). (1986). *Studies in Turkish linguistics*. Amsterdam/Philadelphia: John Benjamins.

1987

Berman, R. A., & Slobin, D. I. (1987). *Five ways of learning how to talk about events: A crosslinguistic study of children's narratives* (Technical Report No. 46). Institute of Cognitive Studies, University of California, Berkeley.
Slobin, D. I. (1987). From the Garden of Eden to the Tower of Babel. In F. Kessel (Ed.), *The development of language and language researchers: Essays in honor of Roger Brown* (pp. 9–22). Hillsdale, NJ: Lawrence Erlbaum Associates.
Slobin, D. I. (1987). Thinking for speaking. *Proceedings of the Annual Meeting of the Berkeley Linguistics Society, 13*, 435–444. [Translation: Russia]
Slobin, D. I. (1987). Preface. In E. Dromi, *Early lexical development* (pp. ix–x). Cambridge, UK: Cambridge University Press.

1988

Slobin, D. I. (1988). Confessions of a wayward Chomskyan. *Papers and Reports on Child Language Development, 27*, 131–136.
Slobin, D. I. (1988). The development of clause chaining in Turkish child language. In S. Koç (Ed.), *Studies on Turkish linguistics* (pp. 27–54). Ankara, Turkey: Middle East Technical University.
Slobin, D. I., & Bocaz, A. (1988). Learning to talk about movement through time and space: The development of narrative abilities in Spanish and English. *Lenguas Moderna (Santiago de Chile), 15*, 5–24.

1989

Slobin, D. I. (1989). Foreword. In E. Bates & B. MacWhinney (Eds.), *Crosslinguistic studies of sentence processing* (pp. vii–ix). Cambridge, UK: Cambridge University Press.

1990

Slobin, D. I. (1990). The development from child speaker to native speaker. In J. W. Stigler, R. A. Shweder, & G. Herdt (Eds.), *Cultural psychology: Essays on comparative human development* (pp. 233–256). Cambridge, UK: Cambridge University Press.

1991

MacWhinney, B., Osmán-Sági, J., & Slobin, D. I. (1991). Sentence comprehension in aphasia in two clear case-marking languages. *Brain and Language, 41,* 234–249.

Slobin, D. I. (1991). Aphasia in Turkish: Speech production in Broca's and Wernicke's patients. *Brain and Language, 41,* 149–164.

Slobin, D. I. (1991). Can Crain constrain the constraints? *Behavioral and Brain Sciences, 14,* 633–634.

Slobin, D. I. (1991). Learning to think for speaking: Native language, cognition, and rhetorical style. *Pragmatics, 1,* 7–26.

1992

Slobin, D. I. (Ed.). (1992). *The crosslinguistic study of language acquisition* (Vol. 3). Hillsdale, NJ: Lawrence Erlbaum Associates. [Introduction: pp. 1–13]

1993

Slobin, D. I. (1993). Is spatial language a special case? *Behavioral and Brain Sciences, 16,* 249–251.

Slobin, D. I. (1993). Adult language acquisition: A view from child language study. In C. Perdue (Ed.), *Adult language acquisition: Cross-linguistic perspectives* (pp. 239–252). Cambridge, UK: Cambridge University Press.

Slobin, D. I. (1993). Coding child language data for crosslinguistic analysis. In J. A. Edwards & M. D. Lampert (Eds.), *Talking data: Transcription and coding in discourse research* (pp. 207–219). Hillsdale, NJ: Lawrence Erlbaum Associates.

Slobin, D. I., Dasinger, L., Küntay, A., & Toupin, C. (1993). Native language reacquisition in early childhood. *The Proceedings of the Annual Child Language Research Forum, 24,* 179–196.

1994

Berman, R. A., & Slobin, D. I. (1994). *Relating events in narrative: A crosslinguistic developmental study.* Hillsdale, NJ: Lawrence Erlbaum Associates.

Sebastián, E., & Slobin, D. I. (1994). Development of linguistic forms: Spanish. In R. A. Berman & D. I. Slobin (Eds.), *Relating events in narrative: A crosslinguistic developmental study* (pp. 239–284). Hillsdale, NJ: Lawrence Erlbaum Associates.

Slobin, D. I. (1994). *Crosslinguistic aspects of child language acquisition* (Sophia Linguistica Working Papers in Linguistics No. 35). Tokyo: Sophia University.

Slobin, D. I. (1994). Passives and alternatives in children's narratives in English, Spanish, German, and Turkish. In B. Fox & P. Hopper (Eds.), *Voice: Form and function* (pp. 341–364). Amsterdam/Philadelphia: John Benjamins.

Slobin, D. I. (1994). Talking perfectly: Discourse origins of the present perfect. In W. Pagliuca (Ed.), *Perspectives on grammaticalization* (pp. 119–133). Amsterdam/Philadelphia: John Benjamins.

Slobin, D. I., & Hoiting, N. (1994). Reference to movement in spoken and signed languages: Typological considerations. *Proceedings of the Annual Meeting of the Berkeley Linguistics Society, 20,* 487–505.

1995

Slobin, D. I. (1995). Converbs in Turkish child language: The grammaticalization of event coherence. In M. Haspelmath & E. König (Eds.), *Converbs in cross-linguistic perspective: Structure and meaning of adverbial verb forms—adverbial participles, gerunds* (pp. 349–371). Berlin/New York: Mouton de Gruyter.

Slobin, D. I., & Küntay, A. (1995). Nouns and verbs in Turkish child-directed speech. *Proceedings of the Annual Boston University Conference on Language Development, 14*, 323–334.

1996

Küntay, A., & Slobin, D. I. (1996). Listening to a Turkish mother: Some puzzles for acquisition. In D. I. Slobin, J. Gerhardt, A. Kyratzis, & J. Guo (Eds.), *Social interaction, social context, and language: Essays in honor of Susan Ervin-Tripp* (pp.. 265–286). Hillsdale, NJ: Lawrence Erlbaum Associates.

Slobin, D. I. (1996). Aspectos especiales en la adquisición del español. In M. Pérez Pereira (Ed.), *Estudios sobre la acquisición del castellano, catalán, eusquera y gallego* (pp. 27–59). Santiago de Compostela, Spain: Universidade de Santiago de Compostela.

Slobin, D. I. (1996). Beyond universals of grammatical development in children. In W. J. M. Levelt (Ed.), *Advanced psycholinguistics: A Bressanone retrospective for Giovanni B. Flores d'Arcais* (pp. 82–88). Nijmegen, The Netherlands: Max Planck Institute for Psycholinguistics.

Slobin, D. I. (1996). From "thought and language" to "thinking for speaking." In J. J. Gumperz & S. C. Levinson (Eds.), *Rethinking linguistic relativity* (pp. 70–96). Cambridge, UK: Cambridge University Press. [Translation: Poland]

Slobin, D. I. (1996). Two ways to travel: Verbs of motion in English and Spanish. In M. S. Shibatani & S. A. Thompson (Eds.), *Grammatical constructions: Their form and meaning* (pp. 195–220). Oxford, UK: Clarendon Press.

Slobin, D. I. (1996). Introduction. In X. R. García Soto (Ed.), *Era unha vez un neno... Estudio da evolución da linguaxe en nenos galego-falantes* (pp. 11–17). Santiago de Compostela, Spain: Sotelo Blanco.

Slobin, D. I., Gerhardt, J., Kyratzis, A., & Guo, J. (Eds.). (1996). *Social interaction, social context, and language: Essays in honor of Susan Ervin-Tripp*. Hillsdale, NJ: Lawrence Erlbaum Associates.

1997

Slobin, D. I. (Ed.). (1997). *The crosslinguistic study of language acquisition* (Vol. 4). Mahwah, NJ: Lawrence Erlbaum Associates. [Introduction: pp. xi–xiii]

Slobin, D. I. (Ed.). (1997). *The crosslinguistic study of language acquisition: Vol. 5. Expanding the contexts*. Mahwah, NJ: Lawrence Erlbaum Associates. [Introduction: pp. xi–xiii]

Slobin, D. I. (1997). Mind, code, and text. In J. Bybee, J. Haiman, & S. A. Thompson (Eds.), *Essays on language function and language type: Dedicated to T. Givón* (pp. 437–467). Amsterdam/Philadelphia: John Benjamins.

Slobin, D. I. (1997). The origins of grammaticizable notions: Beyond the individual mind. In D. I. Slobin (Ed.), *The crosslinguistic study of language acquisition: Vol. 5. Expanding the contexts* (pp. 265–323). Mahwah, NJ: Lawrence Erlbaum Associates.

Slobin, D. I. (1997). The universal, the typological, and the particular in acquisition. In D. I. Slobin (Ed.), *The crosslinguistic study of language acquisition: Vol. 5. Expanding the contexts* (pp. 1–39). Mahwah, NJ: Lawrence Erlbaum Associates.

1998

Shirai, Y., Slobin, D. I., & Weist, R. (Eds.). (1998). The acquisition of tense/aspect morphology. *Special issue of First Language, 18*. [Introduction, pp. 245–253]

Slobin, D. I. (1998). A typological perspective on learning to talk about space. In H. Ragnarsdóttir & S. Strömqvist (Eds.), *Learning to talk about time and space: Proceedings from the 3rd NELAS Conference, Reykjavík, 1994* (Gothenburg Papers in Theoretical Linguistics 80) (pp. 1–29). Göteborg, Sweden: Kompendiet.

Slobin, D. I. (1998). How language can direct thought: Linguistic relativity and linguistic determinism. In R. L. Atkinson, R. C. Atkinson, E. F. Smith, D. J. Bem, & S. Nolen-Hoeksma (Eds.), *Hilgard's introduction to psychology* (13th ed.) (p. 342). Fort Worth, TX: Harcourt Brace.

Slobin, D. I. (1998). Language and thought. LSA Fields of Linguistics. Linguistic Society of America website: http://lsadc.org/web/thought.html.

1999

Küntay, A., & Slobin, D. I. (1999). The acquisition of Turkish as a native language. A research review. *Turkic Languages, 3*, 151–188.

Özçalışkan, Ş., & Slobin, D. I. (1999). Learning how to search for the frog: Expressions of manner of motion in English, Spanish, and Turkish. *Proceedings of the Annual Boston University Conference on Language Development, 23*(2), 541–552.

Slobin, D. I. (1999). Review of K. Hirsh-Pasek & R. M. Golinkoff, The origins of grammar: Evidence from early language comprehension. *Journal of Child Language, 26*, 208–215.

2000

Hoiting, N., & Slobin, D. I. (2000). Foreward. In C. Chamberlain, J. P. Morford, & R. I. Mayberry (Eds.), *Language acquisition by eye* (pp. xv–xvii). Mahwah, NJ: Lawrence Erlbaum Associates.

Özçalışkan, Ş., & Slobin, D. I. (2000). Climb up vs. ascend climbing: Lexicalization choices in expressing motion events with manner and path components. *Proceedings of the Annual Boston University Conference on Language Development, 24*(2), 558–570.

Özçalışkan, Ş., & Slobin, D. I. (2000). Expression of manner of movement in monolingual and bilingual adult narratives: Turkish vs. English. In A. Göksel & C. Kerslake (Eds.), *Studies on Turkish and Turkic languages* (pp. 253–262). Wiesbaden, Germany: Harrasowitz Verlag.

Slobin, D. I. (2000). Verbalized events: A dynamic approach to linguistic relativity and determinism. In S. Niemeier & R. Dirven (Eds.), *Evidence for linguistic relativity* (pp. 107–138). Amsterdam/Philadelphia: John Benjamins.

2001

Hoiting, N., & Slobin, D. I. (2001). Typological and modality constraints on borrowing: Examples from the Sign Language of the Netherlands. In D. Brentari (Ed.), *Foreign vocabulary in sign languages* (pp. 121–137). Mahwah, NJ: Lawrence Erlbaum Associates.

Küntay, A., & Slobin, D. I. (2001). Discourse behavior of lexical categories in Turkish child-directed speech: Nouns vs. verbs. In M. Almgren, A. Barreña, M.-J. Ezeizabarrena, I. Idiazabal, & B. MacWhinney (Eds.), *Research on child language acquisition: Proceedings of the 8th Congress of the International Association for the Study of Child Language* (pp. 928–946). Somerville, MA: Cascadilla Press.

Slobin, D. I. (2001). Form function relations: How do children find out what they are? In M. Bowerman & S. C. Levinson (Eds.), *Language acquisition and conceptual development* (pp. 406–449). Cambridge, UK: Cambridge University Press.

Slobin, D. I., Hoiting, N., Anthony, M., Biederman, Y., Kuntze, M., Lindert, R., et al. (2001). Sign language transcription at the level of meaning components: The Berkeley Transcription System (BTS). *Sign Language & Linguistics, 4*, 63–96. [BTS coding manual available online at http://www.Colorado.EDU/slhs/btsweb/]

2002

Bowerman, M., Brown, P., Eisenbeiss, S., Narasimhan, B., Slobin, D. I. (2002). The crosslinguistic encoding of goal-directed motion in child-caregiver discourse. *Proceedings of the Stanford Child Language Research Forum, 31*, 1–122. http://csli-publications.stanford.edu/CLRF/2002/CLRF-2002-toc.html.

Hoiting, N., & Slobin, D. I. (2002). What a deaf child needs to see: Advantages of a natural sign language over a sign system. In R. Schulmeister & H. Reinitzer (Eds.), *Progress in sign language research. In honor of Siegmund Prillwitz / Fortschritte in der Gebärdensprachforschung. Festschrift für Siegmund Prillwitz* (pp. 267–278). Hamburg, Germany: Signum.

Hoiting, N., & Slobin, D. I. (2002). Transcription as a tool for understanding: The Berkeley Transcription System for sign language research (BTS). In G. Morgan & B. Woll (Eds.), *Directions in sign language acquisition* (pp. 55–75). Amsterdam/Philadelphia: John Benjamins.

Küntay, A., & Slobin, D. I. (2002). Putting interaction back into child language: Examples from Turkish. *Psychology of Language and Communication, 6*, 5–14.

Matsumoto, Y., & Slobin, D. I. (2002). A bibliography of linguistic expressions for motion events. *Meiji Gakuin Review*, No. 684, 83–158. [Version of 2005 available at http://www.lit.kobe-u.ac.jp/~yomatsum/motionbiblio.html]

Slobin, D. I. (2002). What language is "mentalese"? *Behavioral and Brain Sciences, 75*, 700–701.

Slobin, D. I. (2002). Cognitive and communicative consequences of linguistic diversity. In S. Strömqvist (Ed.), *The diversity of languages and language learning* (pp. 7–23). Lund, Sweden: Lund University, Centre for Languages and Literature.

Slobin, D. I. (2002). Language evolution, acquisition, diachrony: Probing the parallels. In T. Givón & B. Malle (Eds.), *The evolution of language out of pre-language* (pp. 375–392). Amsterdam/Philadelphia: John Benjamins.

2003

Özçalışkan, Ş., & Slobin, D. I. (2003). Codability effects on the expression of manner of motion in Turkish and English. In A. S. Özsoy, D. Akar, M. Nakipoğlu-Demiralp, E. Erguvanlı-Taylan, & A. Aksu-Koç (Eds.), *Studies in Turkish linguistics* (pp. 259–270). Istanbul, Turkey: Boğaziçi University Press.

Slobin, D. I. (2003). Language and thought online: Cognitive consequences of linguistic relativity. In D. Gentner & S. Goldin-Meadow (Eds.), *Language in mind: Advances in the investigation of language and thought* (pp. 157–191). Cambridge, MA: The MIT Press.

Slobin, D. I., Hoiting, N., Kuntze, K., Lindert, R., Weinberg, A., Pyers, J., Anthony, M., Biederman, Y., & Thumann, H. (2003). A cognitive/functional perspective on the acquisition of "classifiers." In K. Emmorey (Ed.), *Perspectives on classifier constructions in sign languages* (pp. 271–296). Mahwah, NJ: Lawrence Erlbaum Associates.

2004

Narasimhan, B., Bowerman, M., Brown, P., Eisenbeiss, S., & Slobin, D. I. (2004). "Putting things in places": Effekte linguisticher Typologie auf die Sprachentwicklung. In G. Plehn (Ed.), *Max-Planck Gesellschaft Jahrbuch 2004*. Göttingen, Germany: Verlag Vandenhoeck & Ruprecht.

Slobin, D. I. (2004). How people move: Discourse effects of linguistic typology. In C. L. Moder & A. Martinovic-Zic (Eds.), *Discourse across languages and cultures* (pp. 195–210). Amsterdam/Philadelphia: John Benjamins.

Slobin, D. I. (2004). The many ways to search for a frog: Linguistic typology and the expression of motion events. In S. Strömqvist & L. Verhoeven (Eds.), *Relating events in narrative: Vol. 2. Typological and contextual perspectives* (pp. 219–257). Mahwah, NJ: Lawrence Erlbaum Associates.

Slobin, D. I. (2004). From ontogenesis to phylogenesis: What can child language tell us about language evolution? In J. Langer, S. T. Parker, & C. Milbrath (Eds.), *Biology and knowledge revisited: From neurogenesis to psychogenesis* (pp. 255–285). Mahwah, NJ: Lawrence Erlbaum Associates.

2005

Slobin, D. I. (2005). Relating events in translation. In D. Ravid & H. B. Shyldkrot (Eds.). *Perspectives on language and language development: Essays in honor of Ruth A. Berman* (pp. 115–129). Dordrecht, The Netherlands: Kluwer.

Slobin, D. I. (2005). Linguistic representations of motion events: What is signifier and what is signified? In C. Maeder, O. Fischer, & W. Herlofsky (Eds.), *Iconicity inside out: Iconicity in language and literature 4* (pp. 307–322). Amsterdam/Philadelphia: John Benjamins.

Slobin, D. I. (2005). Issues of linguistic typology in the study of sign language development of deaf children. In B. Schick, M. Marschark, & E. Spencer (Eds.), *Sign language development by deaf children: Where have we been, and where are we going?* (pp. 20–45). Oxford, UK: Oxford University Press.

Slobin, D. I. (2005). Cross-linguistic comparative approaches to language acquisition. *The Encyclopedia of Language and Linguistics* (2nd ed.). Oxford, UK: Elsevier.

Slobin, D. I., & Tomasello, M. (2005). Thirty years of research on language, cognition, and development: The legacy of Elizabeth Bates. *Language Learning & Development, 1*(2), 139–149.

Tomasello, M., & Slobin, D. I. (Eds.) (2005). *Beyond nature-nature: Essays in honor of Elizabeth Bates*. Mahwah, NJ: Lawrence Erlbaum Associates. [Introduction: pp. xv–xxiv]

2006

Slobin, D. I. (2006). What makes manner of motion salient? Explorations in linguistic typology, discourse, and cognition. In M. Hickmann & S. Robert (Eds.), *Space in languages: Linguistic systems and cognitive categories* (pp. 59–81). Amsterdam/Philadelphia: John Benjamins.

Slobin, D. I. (2006). Review of S. Liddell, Grammar, gestures, and meaning in American Sign Language. *Language, 82,* 176–179.

2007

Hoiting, N., & Slobin, D. I. (2007). From gestures to signs in the acquisition of sign language. In S. D. Duncan, J. Cassell, & E. T. Levy (Eds.), *Gesture and the dynamic dimension of language: Essays in honor of David McNeill* (pp. 51–65). Amsterdam/Philadelphia: John Benjamins.

Slobin, D. I., & Bowerman, M. (2007). Interfaces between linguistic typology and child language research. *Linguistic Typology 11,* 213–226.

2008

Slobin, D. I. (2008). Breaking the molds: Signed languages and the nature of human language. *Sign Language Studies, 8,* 114–130.

Slobin, D. I. (2008). The child learns to think for speaking: Puzzles of crosslinguistic diversity in form-meaning mappings. *Studies in Language Sciences 7,* 3–22.

Slobin, D. I. (2008). Putting the pieces together: Commentary on "The Onset and Mastery of Spatial Language in Children Acquiring British Sign Language" by G. Morgan, R. Herman, I. Barriere, & B. Woll. *Cognitive Development, 20,* 20–23.

Current

Frishberg, N., Hoiting, N., & Slobin, D. I. (in press). Transcription. In R. Pfau, M. Steinbach, & B. Woll (Eds.), *Handbook of sign language linguistics* (Series: Handbooks of Language and Communication). Berlin: Mouton de Gruyter.

Lemmens, M., & Slobin, D. I. (in press). Positie- en bewegingswerkwoorden in het Nederlands en in het Frans [Positional and motion verbs in Dutch and French]. *Mededelingen van de Koninklijke Academie voor Nederlandse Taal en Letterkunde.*

Slobin, D. I. (in press). Relations between paths of motion and paths of vision: A crosslinguistic and developmental exploration. In V. M. Gathercole (Ed.), Routes to language: *Studies in honor of Melissa Bowerman.* Mahwah, NJ: Lawrence Erlbaum Associates.

Slobin, D. I. (in press). Review of M. Bowerman & P. Brown (Eds.), Crosslinguistic perspectives on argument structure: Implications for learnability. *Journal of Child Language.*

Slobin, D. I., Bowerman, M., Brown, P., Eisenbeiss, S., & Narasimhan, B. (in press). Putting things in places: Developmental consequences of linguistic typology. In J. Bohnemeyer & E. Pederson (Eds.), *Event representation.* Cambridge, U.K.: Cambridge University Press.

Author Index

A

Abbot-Smith, K., 101
Adam, S., 76
Adger, C.T., 176n2
Ahlsén, E., 382
Aikhenvald, A.Y., 532, 532n2
Aksu-Koc, A., 532, 535, 536
Aksu-Koç, A., 83, 139, 277, 284, 408, 531–542
Albert, L., 277–292
Albro, E.R., 243
Alici, D.M., 535, 536
Allen, S., 29, 176, 522
Ameka, F., 432
Ameka, R., 404
Ammon, M.S., 2
Andersen, H., 347
Andersson, B., 509
Andersson, R., 505–516
Antinucci, F., 42, 44
Aparici, Melina, 151n6
Ashby, W.J., 549
Aske, J., 431
Aslin, R.N., 327
Astington, J.W., 539
Atanassova, M., 69n1, 70, 73, 75, 77
Avci, G., 532, 535
Aydin, C., 532, 535

B

Bacanli, 532
Baddeley, A.D., 384
Badre, D., 505
Baird, J.A., 539
Bamberg, M., 3, 60, 82, 89, 127–139, 177, 189, 197, 226, 230, 234, 243, 249, 277
Bandi Rao, S., 327
Bard, E.G., 107
Baressi, 381n3
Barker, M., 300
Barlow, M., 346
Barnes, W., 489
Bar-Shalom, E., 18
Bates, E., 84, 322, 327, 379, 380, 482
Bauer, P.J., 70, 76
Baughn, C.R., 243
Bauman, 138
Bavelas, J., 364
Bavin, E.L., 137–148, 139n2, 411
Beardsall, L., 226, 237
Behrens, H., 55–68, 57, 70
Bencini, G.M.L., 378
Bennett-Kastor, T., 82
Benson, M.S., 243
Bentivegna, C., 226
Berko, J., 95

Berman, R., 2, 43–44, 55, 75, 82–84, 121–126, 128n1, 129–130, 137–139, 149–162, 150n3, 176, 176n3, 177, 177n5, 179, 189, 194, 197, 211–212, 222, 227, 241, 243, 254, 265n1, 277, 284, 389, 404, 408, 415, 481, 505–506, 513, 554
Berndt, R., 377
Berthele, R., 163–174, 169, 171n4, 172, 408, 411, 412
Besnier, N., 554
Bever, T., 321–332, 324, 325, 326
Bialystok, E., 490
Bickel, B., 543–556
Bickerton, D., 299
Bleichrodt, N., 485
Bloom, L., 300, 466
Blum-Kulka, S., 176n3, 179, 188
Bock, J.K., 107, 109n3, 114, 115, 378, 384
Boersma, P., 509
Bokus, B., 277
Boles, L., 381, 384
Bonamo, K., 328
Bowerman, M., 3, 42, 55, 70, 71n2, 76, 195, 196, 211, 222, 264, 443–450, 451, 465–480
Boyce, S., 380
Braine, M.D.S., 312–313, 318, 350
Brand, R., 327–328
Branigan, H., 107
Brecher, B., 379
Brent, M.R., 327
Bresnan, J., 97
Bretherton, I., 237
Breull, M.J., 534, 538
Bright, W., 336, 350, 375n1
Bronfenbrenner, U., 482
Browman, C.P., 380
Brown, A., 29, 70, 522
Brown, J., 226, 237
Brown, P., 76, 165, 176, 177n6, 179, 180, 180n10, 194, 451–464, 477
Brown, R., 18, 19, 82, 196, 376, 466, 477
Bruner, J., 246, 247, 312–313
Buczowska, E., 71n2
Budwig, N., 3, 11–16, 42, 43, 51, 101, 189, 368
Budwig & Ervin-Tripp, 2
Burger, L.K., 379
Buscha, J., 57
Butcher, C., 33n2, 300
Butterworth, B., 378
Bybee, J., 299, 345, 345–356, 361, 482

C

Cablitz, G.H., 454
Cahana-Amitay, D., 155
Calbris, G., 359
Call, J., 308, 461, 462, 477
Cameron, R., 107
Campbell, C., 353

Caplan, C., 377
Caramazza, A., 376
Carapella, J., 72
Caroll, J.B., 1
Carpendale, J., 286
Carstens, V., 97
Cartwright, T.A., 327
Casasola, M., 467, 475, 477
Casoula, WIlbourn & Yang, 467
Cassidy, K., 327
Cassin, B., 505
Cazden, C,, 188
Ceci, S.J., 482
Chafe, W., 300, 532, 532n2
Champaud, Christian (AU), 209–224
Chandler, J., 489
Chandler, M., 277, 286
Chao, Y., 195
Charest, M., 369
Chater, N., 327
Chen, C., 28
Chen, L., 193–208, 194, 195
Chiarello, E., 467
Chipere, N., 59
Choi, S., 35, 70, 76, 109, 196, 211, 222, 264, 466–467, 469, 475–476, 478, 534
Choinoid & Clark, 328
Chomsky, N., 4, 127, 194, 311–312, 314, 315n1, 318–319, 323, 342, 349, 482
Chovil, B., 364
Christiansen, M.H., 328
Christie, S., 467n2
Cienki, A., 362
Clahsen, H., 95, 107
Clancy, P.M., 35, 51, 105–118, 109, 189
Clark, B., 349
Clark, E., 18, 25, 195, 211, 301, 468
Claudi, U., 301, 346, 347
Cleland, A., 107
Code, C., 377, 379
Coerts, J.A., 31
Cohen, L,, 379
Cohen, L.B., 467, 477
Collis, G.N., 278
Comrie, B., 70, 71, 382
Connelly, M., 95
Conrad, R., 29
Conti-Ramsden, G., 369
Cook-Gumperz, J., 48
Coventry, K.R., 466
Crago, M.B., 176
Croft, W., 349, 428, 468
Cromer, R., 195, 482
Crystal, D., 336, 341
Culler, J., 245
Cummins, 483, 490
Curtin, S., 327

Dale, P.S., 17
Dale, R., 328
Damrad-Frye, R., 138, 139, 226, 234, 243, 277
Dasen, P.R., 454
Dasher, R.B., 350
Dasinger, L., 87
de León, L., 175–192, 454, 456, 460
de Villiers, J.G., 534n5, 539
de Villiers, P.A., 539
Dehaene, S., 379
Delancey, S., 390
Dell, G.S., 379
Demuth, K., 93–104, 95, 96, 98
D'Esposito, M., 505
Dimroth, C., 336
Dixon, R.M.W., 31, 532n2
Dodge, M., 33n2
Doke, C.M., 95
Dravins, C., 382
Drenth, P., 485
Dressler, W., 382, 383
Drew, P., 133
Du Bois, J.W., 82, 106, 114, 115, 189, 549
Dudis, P.G., 358
Duncan, S., 29, 361, 517, 521, 521n4, 522, 526n5, 527n6, 528
Dunn, J., 226, 237
Duran, P., 59
Duranti, A., 42, 43, 49, 51, 52, 554
Durkheim, E., 173

E

Eaton, J.H., 278
Eichinger, L.M., 56, 59
Eisenbeiss, S., 95, 107
Eisenberg, A., 196, 203, 205, 254, 264
Eisenberg, P., 57
Ellis, D., 93–104
Elman, J.L., 482
Ely, R., 17–27
Engberg-Pederson, D., 176, 179
Engberg-Pederson, E., 411
Engelen, B., 57
Engle, R.A., 364
Engstrand, O., 410
Epstein, S., 328
Ervin, S.M., 43
Ervin-Tripp, N., 11–16, 42, 43, 51
Ervin-Tripp, S., 43, 51, 52, 176n2
Essegbey, J., 404, 432
Euskaltzaindia, 412
Extra, G., 483
Eyer, D.W., 49–50

F

Fauconnier, G., 357
Feist, M.I., 466, 475
Feldman, H., 30
Fenson, L., 17

D

da Silva, V., 412, 427–442
Dahaene, S., 304
Dahl, J., 509

Ferguson, C., 166n2
Ferreira, F., 507
Filipovic, L., 212
Fillmore, C., 428
Finch, S., 327
Firbas, J., 520
Fitch, T., 264
Fitch, W.T., 312, 314
Fivush, R., 76
Flavell, J., 533
Fleischman, S., 419
Flores-Ferrán, N., 107
Flower, L.S., 505
Fodor, J.D., 327
Foley, W, 152n9, 549
Fournier, 422n3
Francis, W.N., 17
Franklin, M., 28, 33
Frawley, W., 377
Freeman, M., 134
Fu, V.R., 28
Fujita, I, 381, 384
Fulkerson & Haaf, 477
Fung, H., 242
Furman, R., 29, 522
Furuyama, N., 364

G

Garai, K.J., 408
Garrod, S.C., 466
Garton, A., 301
Gebelt, J., 226
Gee, J., 3, 43, 51
Gelman, S., 28
Genesee, F., 482
Gennari, S.P., 264
Gentner, D., 196, 465–480, 467, 467n2, 476, 478
Georgakopoulou, A., 134
Gerber, M., 50
Gerhardt, J., 1, 3
Gerken, L.A., 98, 327
Gillette, J., 327
Givón, T., 82, 299–310, 345, 347
Gleason, J. Berko, 17–27, 376
Gleitmann, H., 327
Gleitmann, L., 29, 30, 203, 264, 327, 452, 453n3, 459
Godden, D.R., 384
Goffman, 165
Goikoetxea Arrieta, J.L., 412
Goldberg, A., 378, 428
Goldin-Meadow, S., 27–40, 33n2, 33n3, 35n4, 36n5, 264, 264n1, 300, 361
Goldstein, L., 380
Golinkoff, R., 327, 327–328
Gomez, R.L., 327
Gonzalez-Mena, J., 49–50
Goodglass, H., 381n3
Goodman, I., 489
Goodman, J., 482
Goodwin, M., 106, 114, 176n2
Gopnik, A., 534, 535, 538
Gopnik, M., 91

Gordon, D.P., 43, 51, 52
Gordon, J.K., 379
Gossen, G., 178, 180
Gottfried, M., 382–383
Gotts, S.J., 379
Gould, S.J., 299
Graf, P., 534
Greenberg, J., 345
Greimas, A.J., 245, 248
Gries, S., 107
Griffin, Z.M., 114, 507
Gruber, J., 368
Gumperz, J.J., 52, 164, 176n2, 210, 211, 505, 531
Guo, J., 1, 1–10, 193–208
Gurjanov, M., 107
Guthrie, M., 93
Gvozdev, A. N., 42

H

Haden, C., 76
Hadler, M., 107
Haiman, J., 150, 353
Hale, K., 137, 146
Halle, M., 323
Halliwell, J., 378
Hamano, S., 404
Hanks, W., 132, 360
Harnisch, R., 56
Harris, R., 519
Hashtroudi, S., 534
Haskill, A., 372
Haspelmath, M., 349
Haun, D., 451, 453n3, 461, 462, 477
Hauser, M.D., 312, 314
Haviland, J., 176, 177, 178, 180n9, 226, 360
Hayashi, M., 381, 384
Hayes, J.R., 505
Hazen, N.L., 76
Heath, S.B., 237, 242
Heinämäki, O., 73
Heine, B., 301, 346, 347, 349, 353
Helbig, G., 57
Hemphill, L., 489
Henderson, J.M., 507
Hendriks, H., 82, 213
Hendriks, S., 90
Henriks, H., 82, 209–224
Henzen, W., 56
Herskovits, A., 466
Hespos, S., 467n2, 475
Hickmann, M., 82, 90, 176n3, 179, 209–224, 213
Highter, M., 203, 254, 264
Hirsh-Pasek, K., 327–328
Hoff-Ginsburg, E., 327
Hoffmann, L., 57
Hoffmeister, R., 29, 31
Hofrege, J., 534, 538
Hohenstein, J., 196, 205
Hoiting, N., 4, 364, 390, 429, 431
Holland, J.H., 350
Holmqvist, K., 505–516, 507, 509
Holsánová, H., 507, 509

Hoogstra, L., 242
Hopper, P.J., 42–47, 49, 51, 350, 353, 467
Hoyle, S., 176n2
Hsueh, F., 195
Huang, J., 195
Huang, S., 411
Hudelot, C., 277, 284, 286
Hudson, J.A., 226, 243
Huennemeyer, F., 301
Hünnemeyer, F., 346, 347
Hunt, K.W., 150
Huttenlocher, J., 76, 379
Huxley, R., 368
Hyams, N., 35

I

Ibarretxe-Antuñano, I., 8, 275, 403–414
Idiata, D.F., 95
Ilgaz, H., 249
Inhelder, B., 327, 454, 466
Insler, R.Z., 505
Internicola, R., 73
Ishii, S., 234n9
Ishizuka, T., 29

J

Jackendoff, R., 317
Jacques, S., 539
Jakobson, R., 181, 468
Janda, R.D., 348, 353
Janzen, G., 461, 462, 477
Jarema, G., 378
Jenkins, J.M., 539
Johanson, L., 532, 532n2
Johansson, V., 158, 507, 509
Johnson, A., 50
Johnson, J.R., 72
Johnson, M., 42, 361, 482
Johnson, M.K., 534
Johnston, J.R., 466
Jonsdottir, M., 410
Joseph, K., 369

K

Kadzielawa, D., 378
Kahn, P.H., 18
Kail, M., 82, 90
Kakehi, H., 404
Kako, E., 203, 254, 264
Kamio, A., 381, 384
Kant, Immanuel, 333, 462
Kaplin, E., 381n3
Karasik, C., 177, 178, 180
Karlsson, H., 509
Karmiloff-Smith, A., 82, 249, 312, 327, 482, 532, 536
Katzenberger, I., 82, 150n3, 158

Kay, P., 428
Kellert, S.R., 18
Kemmer, S., 346
Kendon, A., 359, 360, 362, 364, 518
Kent, R., 377
Keyser, A., 381, 382, 383
King, R., 226
Kita, S., 29, 360, 451, 453n3, 522
Klein, W., 210, 333–344, 342n7
Kleinman, S., 379
Kobayashi, H., 236
Koçbas, Dilara (AU), 81–92
Koch, P., 171, 410, 412
Kolk, H., 381, 382, 383
Konieczna, E., 71n2
Kopecka, A., 210n2, 212, 415–426, 428, 430–432, 436
Krause, M., 65
Kruger, A.C., 533
Kucera, H., 17
Kumpf, L.E., 549
Kunene, 95
Kunene, E.C.L., 95
Küntay, A., 43, 81–92, 134–135, 138–139, 189, 225–226, 227n2, 229n6, 234, 238, 243, 277
Kuteva, T., 428, 429, 430, 431, 437
Kyratzis, A., 1, 41–54, 48, 176n2

L

Labov, W., 129, 133, 138, 164, 166, 176n2, 179, 226
Lakoff, G., 42, 361
Lalonde, C.E., 277, 286
Lambrecht, K., 83, 87
Lamendella, J., 299
Landau, B., 211
Langacker, R.W., 47, 48, 52, 346
Lanza, E., 410
LaPolla, R., 314, 316, 317
Lappin, S., 411n5
Lasnik, H., 328
Lasser, I., 336
Laughlin, R., 176, 177, 177n4, 178, 180
Law, A., 534
Leary, A.P., 350
LeBaron, C., 360, 361
Leclanche, J.-L., 418, 420–424
Lecours, A.R., 377, 379
Leden, A., 56
Lederer, A., 327
Lee, C., 111
Lee, H.T., 534
Lee, K., 539
Leheckova, H., 375
Lehmann, C., 346, 347
Leiwo, M., 410
Lemmens, M., 212
Leonard, L., 368, 369, 372
Leondar, B., 243
Leseman, P., 489
Levelt, W., 378, 505
Levinson, S., 52, 76, 165, 180, 180n10, 210, 211, 360, 451–464, 453n3, 457n5, 466, 478, 505, 531
Lewin, R., 300

Lewis, C., 278, 286
Li, C., 195
Li, P., 452, 453n3, 459
Liang, J., 82, 90
Liddell, S., 358, 359, 360, 364
Lieven, E., 1–10, 3, 51, 91, 95, 101, 293–298, 328, 368, 379, 415n1
Lightfoot, D., 327, 347, 351, 352, 353
Lin, C.-Y.C., 28
Lindsay, D.S., 534
Lleó, C., 98
Lobeck, A., 411n5
Lockman, J.J., 76
Loeb, D., 368, 369, 372
Loebell, H., 107
López Calixto Méndez, M., 177, 178, 188
Lowery, J., 379
Lowie, W., 482
Lowrie, D.A., 364
Lucy, J., 210, 517
Lukatela, G., 107
Lukatela, K., 107
Lust, B., 35
Lyytinen, P., 70

M

Machobane, M., 96, 97
MacWhinney, B.J., 18, 42, 44, 57, 84, 308, 322, 327, 379, 380
Magnúsdóttir, S., 382
Mair, W.N., 169
Majid, A., 451
Malt, B., 264
Malvern, D.D., 59
Mandler, J., 466
Maratsos, M.P., 82, 91
Marchman, V., 60, 482
Marcus, G.F., 327
Martin, N., 379
Martin, S., 228, 277–292
Marty, L., 101
Massey, J., 29, 203, 264
Masur, E., 18
Matisoff, J.A., 396–397
Matthiessen, 150
Mayberry, R.I., 29
Mayer, M., 2, 129, 137, 176, 194, 197, 227, 404, 506
Maynard, S., 227, 235
McCabe, A., 138, 179, 226, 235, 237
McDonough, L., 466
McElree, B., 325
McGann, W., 90, 249
McGraw, N., 203, 254, 264
Mchombo, S., 97
McNeill, D., 28, 29, 357, 358, 359, 361, 362, 517–530
McVeigh, B., 228
Meadow, K., 29
Meeussen, A.E., 93
Mehler, J., 321
Meier R.P., 29
Meira, S., 466
Melson, G.F., 18

Meltzoff, A., 535
Menn, L., 375–388
Michaels, S., 188
Miller, B.T., 505
Miller, G., 322
Miller, M., 57
Miller, P., 28, 37, 226, 242
Miller, R., 42, 44
Miller, W., 43
Mills, A.E., 95
Milroy, L., 164, 165
Mimouni, Z., 378
Minami, M., 138, 235, 237
Mintz, J., 242, 327
Mishra, R.C., 454
Mitchell-Kernan, C., 176n2, 451
Moerk, E.L., 327, 328
Mofokeng, S.M., 95
Moloi, F., 96
Montgomery, D.E., 538
Moore, M., 368
Morgan, J.L., 328
Morris, D., 362
Mulder, L., 489
Munger, M.P., 243
Munn, P., 237
Munnich, E., 211
Mushin, I., 532, 534
Mylander, C., 27–40, 28, 30, 33, 33n2, 33n3, 35
Myres, S., 97

N

Naigles, L., 196, 203, 205, 254, 264, 327
Nakamura, K., 138, 139, 225–240, 227n2, 229n6, 243, 277, 531n1
Namy, L.L., 478
Narain, G., 484, 485
Narasimhan, B., 101
Nash, D., 137
Nation, I.S.P., 490
Neeman, Y., 158, 408
Nelson, K., 242, 533, 536
Nespoulous, J.-L., 377, 379
Newcombe, N.S., 70, 76
Newmeyer, F.J., 353
Newport, E.L., 29, 327
Nichols, J., 532, 532n2
Nicolopoulou, A., 241–252, 277, 531n1
Nippold, M.A., 188
Niraula, Mishra & Dasen, 454
Niraula, S., 454
Nir-Sagiv, B., 149–162, 150n3, 157
Nobe, S., 518
Noonan, M., 410, 543
Norde, M., 348
Núñez, R., 76, 361
Nuyts, J., 210

O

Obler, L.K., 376, 380
O'Brien, C., 42, 43, 51
Ochs, E., 42, 43, 49, 51, 52, 176n2, 225, 226
Oehlrich, J.S., 73
Oesterreicher, W., 171, 412
Ogiela, D., 372
Ogino, M., 236
Ogura, M., 352
Oh, K., 253–262
Oh K., 253–262, 264
Ohara, K.H., 404
Olsen, S., 61
Olson, D.R., 539
O'Neill, D.K., 534, 534n5, 538
Osgood, C.E., 1
Özçaliskan, S., 203, 254, 263–276, 264, 300, 408, 415n1, 435
Özyürek, A., 27–40, 29, 522

P

Pagliuca, W., 346, 347, 350
Paley, V., 242, 246
Palmer, F.R., 532
Papafragou, A., 29, 203, 264, 327
Paré-Blagoev, E.J., 505
Parill, F., 358
Parisi, D., 482
Pawlak, A., 69n1, 70, 72, 73, 75, 77
Pederson, E., 210, 466, 469, 470, 472
Pelham, S., 368
Pelletier, J., 539
Pence, K., 327–328
Perdue, C., 342n7
Pérez López, E., 177
Perkins, R., 346, 347, 350
Perner, J., 278, 534, 538
Pesco, D., 176
Peters, A., 105, 106
Peterson, C., 179, 226, 237
Phillips, B., 17–27
Phillips, S.B.V.D., 28, 37
Piaget, J., 454, 466, 482
Pick, H.L., 76
Pickering, M., 107
Piérart, B., 212
Pillow, B.H., 538
Pine, J.M., 51, 91, 101, 368, 369
Pinker, S., 327, 468, 482
Plank, F., 352
Plaut, D.C., 379
Plemmenou, E., 107
Plunkett, K., 482
Poldrack, R.A., 505
Poplack, S., 107
Port, R.F., 350
Potter, J., 133
Pourcel, S., 428, 430–432, 436, 493–504
Propp, V., 245
Pyers, J.E., 534n5
Pyraube, 212

R

Radke-Yarrow, M., 226
Ragnarsdóttir, H., 405n2, 410
Rapold, C.J., 462, 477
Rasch, B., 453n3
Ratner, H.H., 533
Ravid, D., 150, 155
Redington, M., 327
Regier, T., 466
Reh, M., 346, 347
Reilly, J., 138, 139, 151n6, 230, 237
Reilly, K.F., 381, 384
Renner, T., 83
Resing, W., 485
Rice, M., 368, 369
Richards, B.J., 59
Richards, N., 328
Richner, E., 242–243, 245–249, 277
Rimmon-Kenan, S., 245
Rispoli, M., 109, 367–374, 368, 369, 370, 371, 372
Roach, A., 379
Roberts, I., 346, 347, 348, 350, 351, 352, 353
Rodkin, P.C., 243
Roland, F., 82, 90
Rorty, A., 246, 247
Rosado, E., 157
Roussou, A., 346, 347, 348, 350, 351, 352, 353
Rowe, D.W., 242
Rowland, C.F., 51, 101, 368
Rumbaugh, Sue Savage (AU), 299–310
Ryan, E., 490

S

Saffran, J.R., 327
Sakas, W.G., 327
Saltzman, J., 28, 33
Sampaio, W., 412, 427–442
Sancar, B., 27–40
Sanchez-Lopez, I., 82
Sankoff & Brown, 301
Sansa-Tura, S., 83
Sanz, T.M., 325
Sasanuma, S, 381, 384
Saussure, F. de, 517, 519
Savage, C., 379
Savage-Rumbaugh, S., 300
Savarnejad, A., 44
Savasir, I., 3, 42, 43, 51
Savic, M., 107
Saxton, M., 328
Scales, B., 242, 248
Schieffelin, B.B., 42, 44, 109, 176n2, 225, 226
Schiffrin, D., 82, 226
Schlesigner, 312
Schuele, C., 372
Schultze-Bernt, E., 390, 400
Schütze, C., 368, 369, 370, 372
Schwartz, A., 90, 249
Schwarze, C., 169
Scollon, R., 300
Sebeok, T.A., 1

Seely, D., 328
Sefer, N., 532, 535
Sengul, C.J., 301
Shanley, E.M., 522
Shapiro, L.R., 243
Sijsling, F.F., 489
Sikic, N., 383
Silverstein, M., 31
Simpson, J., 137
Sinha, C., 412, 427–442, 428, 429, 430, 431, 437
Sizemore, M., 358, 362, 364
Skinner, 312
Slobin, D., 1–8, 17, 27, 29, 35–37, 41–44, 50–51, 55, 64–65, 69–71, 71n2, 72–73, 75, 77, 81–82, 90, 93, 95, 102, 105–106, 115, 127–128, 128n1, 129–130, 134–135, 137–138, 146, 149–150, 153, 160, 163, 169, 175–177, 177n5, 179, 188–189, 193–197, 203, 205–206, 209, 211–212, 221–222, 225, 227, 241, 243, 253–255, 263–264, 265n1, 275, 277, 285, 299, 311–313, 318n5, 319, 321–322, 326, 328, 333, 345–346, 349–351, 357, 361, 364, 367, 370, 372, 375–376, 380, 389–390, 400, 403–405, 405n2, 408–409, 409n4, 410, 415–416, 425, 427, 429, 431–432, 437, 451, 461–462, 465–467, 477–478, 481–483, 493, 495–497, 502–503, 505, 513, 517, 531–532, 534, 538, 543–544, 557
Slobin, D. & Bever, 327
Sloman, S.A., 264
Smith, C., 72
Smith, M.C., 114
Smith, N., 364
Snow, C., 489
Snyder, W., 18
Sonnenstuhl, I., 107
Spelke, E., 467n2, 475
Sperry, L., 226
Spieler, D.S., 507
Srivastava, S., 101
Stahl, D., 59
Stark, J.A., 382, 383
Stein, N.L., 243
Stein, S., 42, 43, 51, 172, 243
Stern, C., 1
Stern, W., 1
Stevens, K.N., 323
Stoll, S., 543–556
Strecker, B., 57
Streeck, J., 360, 361
Strömqvist, S., 2, 82, 137, 176, 189, 227, 229, 277, 405n2, 410, 481, 505–516
Stross, B., 451
Sugiyama, Y., 404
Sutton, P., 141
Suzman, S.M., 95
Svek, W.R., 379
Sweetser, E., 76, 357–366, 358, 361, 362, 364
Swift, M., 70, 76

T

Talmy, L., 29, 55, 70, 169–170, 194–195, 210, 212, 221, 253, 263, 349, 389–404, 415–416, 418, 428, 432, 466, 494, 506, 521, 522
Tanangkingsing, M., 411
Tannen, D., 19, 114, 226
Taub, S.F., 358, 363
Tekdemir, G., 139, 277, 284
Theakston, A., 51, 95, 368, 379
Thompson, S., 42, 43, 44, 45, 46, 47, 49, 51, 150, 195
Thornton, R., 368
Thráinsson, H., 382
Tolchinsky, L., 151n6, 157, 158
Tomasello, M., 59, 95, 101, 308, 312, 314, 379, 533
Toolan, M.J., 242, 245
Torrance, N., 539
Toupin, C., 87
Townsend, D. & Bever, 323
Trabasso, T., 243
Traugott, E.C., 346, 350, 353, 467
Travis, L., 107, 328
Trondhjem, F.B., 176, 179, 411
Tsonope, J., 95
Turner, M., 357
Turvey, M.T., 107

U

Umiker-Sebeok, J., 226
Utas, B., 532n2
Uttal, D.H., 28

V

Vainikka, A., 95
Valian, V., 321, 328
van Gelderen, E., 346, 351, 353
van Grunsven, M., 381, 382, 383
van Hell, J.G., 150, 150n4
van Staden, M., 471
Van Valin, R., 72, 152n9, 311–320, 317n4, 318n5
Veneziano, E., 277–292
Vennemann, T., 352
Verhelst, M., 471
Verhoeven, L., 2, 82, 137, 150, 150n3, 150n4, 151, 176, 176n3, 189, 227, 229, 277, 481–492
Verjat, I, 212
Vermeer, A., 481–492, 482
Vijayan, S., 327
Vinden, P.G., 539
Virbil, J., 377, 379
Vishton, P.M., 327
Visser, M., 97
Vygotsky, L.S., 518, 520, 531

W

Wade, A., 364
Wagner, A.D., 505
Waletzky, J., 129, 133, 138, 176n2, 179, 226
Warden, D., 82, 91
Warren, R.K., 19, 384
Warren-Leubecker, A., 18
Wassman, J., 454
Watters, J., 93
Weenink, D., 509
Weintraub, J., 242, 248
Weist, R.M., 69–80, 70, 71n2, 72, 73, 75, 77
Welmers, W.E., 93
Wexler, K., 368, 369, 370, 372
Wheeldon, L.R., 114
Whorf, B.L., 211, 503, 517
Wigglesworth, G., 82, 83, 90
Wilbur, R., 29
Wilkins, D., 176, 210, 410, 411, 451, 466
Williams, K., 242
Wills, H., 505
Wilson, P., 411n5
Wimmer, H., 278, 534, 538
Witkowska-Stadnik, K.., 71n2
Wolf, S.A., 188, 242
Woolley, J.D., 534, 538
Wortham, 189
Wray, A., 114
Wright, S., 301
Wu, D.Y.H., 28
Wulfeck, B., 379, 380
Wulff, S., 107
Wysocka, H., 69n1, 70, 71n2, 73, 75, 77
Wysocka, J., 70

Y

Yang, C., 327
Yangklang, P., 194–195, 390, 404, 411, 432, 435
Yasa, Y., 535

Z

Zaal, J., 485
Zahn-Wexler, C., 226
Zamora, A., 158
Zaretsky, E., 17–27
Zei, B., 383
Zelazo, P.D., 539
Zheng, M., 28, 33, 35–37, 264, 264n1
Ziesler, Y., 95–96
Zifonum, G., 57
Zlatev, J., 194–195, 390, 404, 411, 429, 432, 435
Zuazo, K., 412
Zurif, E., 376

Subject Index

A

A Cross-Linguistic Study of the Processing of Causative Sentences, 2
A Field Manual for Cross-Cultural Study of the Acquisition of Communicative Competence (Slobin), 2, 451
Accusing statements, 45–48, 50, 52
Adverbials encoding manner, use of in English and Turkish, **268**
Affective behaviors, used by Japanese children in narratives, 230
Agrammatic aphasia (Broca's aphasia), 380
Agreement contexts, 96
Algonquian language, 495
Alternative manner expressions, mean number of, **258**
American children, 237
 transitive actors, intransitive actors, and patients in two-gesture sentences, 31
American Indian language, 532n2
American Sign Language (ASL), 29, 31, 357–361, 363–364, 518, 522
Amondawa language (Tupi Guariní language), 412, 427–440
 directional adverbs, 433
 motion, path, and manner in, 427–440
 path-conflating motion verbs, 432
 postpositions, 432–433
Animal terms, acquisition of, 17–27
 Brown corpus: Adam and Sarah, 20
 coding categories by corpus, **21**
 data, 18
 data analysis, 19
 decontextualized talk, 22
 discussion of study, 24
 in English, 17–27
 future directions of study, 25–26
 Gleason corpus: families at dinner, 21
 introduction to study, 17
 method of study, 18
 results of study, 20
 in Russian, 17–27
 Russian Corpus: Tanja and Varya (Protassova Corpus), 22
 types and tokens by speakers for the longitudinal data, **20**
 Warren corpus: children at play, 21–22
Anomic aphasia, 377
Apes, teaching grammar to, 299–310
Aphasia, 375–388
 agrammatic Broca's aphasia, 377, 380
 anomic, 377
 child language and, 375–388
 competing word orders, 381
 competition in aphasic speech production, 379–380
 Dan Slobin's contribution to aphasia research, 376
 defining simplicity, 376–378
 discussion, 384–385
 German language and, 377–378
 introduction: defining "simplicity," 375–376
 predictability and its effects on production, 380–381
 psycholinguistic definition of simplicity, 385
 psycholinguistics and, 375–388
 psycholinguistics of production, 378–379
 semantically related words and phrases in competition, 382–384
 speech errors, 375–388
 varieties of, 377
 Wernicks's aphasia, 377
Arabic language, 154
Arrente language, 411
ASN, 364
Athabaskan language, 495
Atsugewi language (Hokan language of Northern California), 393
Attention, channeling of, 505–516
 eye-tracking research, 505–516
Austronesian language family, 195
Authors
 English/American, 254
 Korean, 254

B

Bambi, 19
Bantu Acquisition Workshop at Smith College, 93n1
Bantu languages, 93–104, 97
 Bantu noun class systems, sample of, **94**
 children's acquisition of, 102
 noun class prefix system, 93
"Basic Child Grammars," 42, 128
Basque language, 403–405, 408–412
Belhare language (Sino-Tibetan language), 544–553
Bend It Like Beckham, 364
Berkeley Linguistics Society, 493, 517
Berkeley Transcription System (BTS), 4
Berkeley's Crosslinguistic Acquisition Project, 376
Berman, R., 75, 129
Bern Swiss dialect, German language and, 164
Black-winged monkey stories, 178
 Tzotzil (Mayan) language, 186–187
Boston Diagnostic Aphasia Examination, 381n3
Boston VA Medical Center, 377
Boundary-crossing events, distribution of by verb type, **273**
Bowerman, M., 3
Boyd, J., *561*
Brazilian Portuguese language. *See* Portuguese language, Brazilian
Breakdown of M+(D) constructions by deictic verb presence by age, *202*
Breakdown of M+P+(D) constructions by deictic verb presence by age, *202*
Breakdown of P+(D) constructions by deictic verb presence by age, *203*
Bristol Language Development Project, 427

Broca's aphasia, 377, 383
Brock-Levelt model of speech production, 383
Brown, R., 1, 3, 127, *559*
Brown data, 25
Bruner, J., 3, 127, *558*
Budwig, N., 3
Bybee, J., 137

C

Caddo language, 398
Camaroonian languages, 93
Canary Row (Tweety and Sylvester), 521–522
Canonical forms, 327
Cantonese language, 533
Causal connectors, used by Japanese children in narratives, 233–234
Causative event, structure of, *317*
Cebuano language, 406
Center of Test Development (CITO, Arnheim), 485
Chantyal language, 405, 406, 408, 410, 411
Chaplin, Charlie, 496, 497
Character representation, 242, 244–245, 247–248
  actors, 247–248
  agents, 247–248
  central and secondary characters, 249–250
  characters as mental agents, 247–248
  children's narratives and, 241–252
  complexity, 245
  comprehensive and socioculturally informed approach to, 248
  from conceptions of the mind to conceptions of the person, 248
  development, 245
  future research in, 246–249
  inner life and, 245
  reconsidering "main character," 249–250
Characters
  Bruner: the "Dual Landscape" of narrative and the "Morphology" of persons, 246
  early precursors to mentalistic portrayals, 243–244
  as intentional agents, 243
  narratology and, 245–246
  orienting framework for, 245–246
  speech of used by Japanese children in narratives, 232
Characters, attribution of internal states to, 280–281
  emotional states, 280
  epistemic states, 280
  intentional states, 280
  physical sensations, 280
Chief, Lian-Cheng, 399
Child language, 375–388, 451–464
  aphasia and, 375–388
  English, 209–224
  French, 209–224
  typological constraints on motion in, 209–224
CHILDES database, 4, 18, 57, 83, 215n4, 514
Children, 453–454
  first and second language proficiency, 481–492
  language acquisition, 367–372
  percentage correct interpretations of simple sentences by, **322**
  verb constructions used in peer disputes, 41–54

Children, deaf
  in China, 28–40
  in Turkey, 28–40
  in U.S., 28–40
Children's first and second language proficiency, cognitive predictors of, 481–492
  cognitive tests, 485
  discussion of study, 488–490
  educational implications, 490
  first and second languages, 489–490
  instruments, 484–486
  introduction to study, 481–483
  language proficiency and cognitive abilities, 486–487, 489–490
  language proficiency tests, 484–485
  limitations regarding the present study, 490
  method of study, 483–484
  participants in study, 483–484
  predictors of Dutch language proficiency, 487–488
  predictors of language proficiency, 489–490
  predictors of Turkish children's first and second language proficiency, 488
  results, 486–488
  sociocultural data, 485–486
  variation in language proficiency, 486, 488–489
Children's language learning, homesign and, 37
Children's narrative development
  cognitive vs. typological issues, 179–181
  evidentials, 180–181
  Tzotzil (Mayan) children, 179–181
Children's narratives, 241–252
  from actors to agents to persons in, 247–248
  character representation in, 241–252
  evaluative devices in, 226
  evaluative expressions in, 225–239
  Japanese, 225–239
  Tzotzil (Mayan), 175–192
  Tzotzil (Mayan) children, 175–183
China, homesign in, 27–40
Chinese children
  transitive actors, intransitive actors, and patients in two-gesture sentences, *31*
Chinese language, 212, 334, 407, 409
Chomsky, N., 3, 312, 314, 318, *560*
City Lights (movie with Charlie Chaplin), 496, 497
CLAN, 19
CLAS data, 382
  German language and, 382
CLASNET working paper series, 376
Clause packaging in narratives, 149–162
  age-related comparisons, 157–160
  clause packaging, 150–151
  crosslinguistic and developmental trends, 153–160
  crosslinguistic comparisons, 154–157
  data sources and analysis, 151–153
  discussion of study, 160
  introduction to study, 149–150
Clauses
  layered structure of, *316*
  mean number of per clause package, by age and language, *154*
  number of in adult Frog Stories, *182*
  number of in Tzotzil Frog Stories, *182*
  syntactic units of layered structure, **316**
Cognition (Journal), 2

Cognitive Academic Language Proficiency (CALP), 483
Cognitive hypothesis, 196
"Cognitive Prerequisites for the Development of Grammar" (Dan Slobin), 70, 105
Cohesion and the use of the evidential *la* (hearsay), *184*
Color adjectives, apes ability to modify
    results of testing for color adjectives after prior demonstration, **305**
    results of testing for color adjectives without prior demonstration, **305**
Color adjectives, modifying
    general design for study with apes, 304
    instruction and testing for study with apes, 304–306
    instructional sessions with study of apes, 304
    interpretation of study with apes, 305–306
    testing after prior demonstration in study of apes, 304
    testing without prior demonstration in study of apes, 304–305
Commands/prohibitions, 45–48, 50
"Communicative Action in the Social Lives of Very Young Children," 44
Competition Model, 380, 385
Complements, path of motion and, 406–408
Conceptions of mind and person, a more comprehensive and socioculturally informed approach, 248
Construction frames for indefinite and definite first mentions for the boy by different age groups in English and Turkish, **88**
Continuum of support and containment situations as lexicalized crosslinguistically, samples from, *469*
Corpora, description of, **18**
Creole languages, 3
Cross Language Aphasia Study (CLAS), 376
Crosslinguistic Study of Language Acquisition (Dan Slobin), 69, 116
Cue validity, 380
Cummins' interdependency hypothesis, 483

D

Danish language, 405, 411
Deaf children
    American, 28
    Chinese, 28
    Turkish, 28
Deaf Sign Language of Taiwan (TSL), 521
Deafness
    homesign, 29–30
    language learning and, 29–30
Defining simplicity, aphasia and, 376–378
Demonstrative modifiers
    instructional trials in study with apes, 302
    interpretation of study with apes, 303
    results of study with apes (with physical pointing), **302**
    results of study with apes (without physical pointing), **303**
    study of apes learning grammar and, 302–303
    testing trials I in study with apes (with physical pointing cues), 302
    testing trials in study with apes (without physical pointing), 302
Demuth Sesotho corpus, 95, 97
Developmental primitives, 313

Diagnostic Test on Bilingualism, 484
Diahoi language, Kawahib languages (of Amazonia), 427
Dialects
    German language and, 171
Dialogic priming and acquisition of argument marking in Korean, 105–118
    conclusions of study, 114–116
Dialogic priming and argument marking in Korean
    data coding, 108–109
    discussion of study, 114–115
    introduction to study, 105–108
    methodology of study, 108–109
    participants and data, **108**, 108
    results of study, 109–114
Direction and perspective in German child language, qualitative analyses, 61–64
    complex paths, 64
    error analysis, 62–63
    pleonastic constructions, 63–64
Direction and perspective in German child language, quantitative analyses, 58–61
    emergence of perspectival particle verbs, 60–61
    proportion of particle verbs with hin- and her-, 58–60
Directional adverbs
    in Amondawa language (Tupi Guariní language), 433
Directional and perspectival particle verbs
    German language and, 56–57
Directional language usage in Tzeltal farm animal games, **458**
Directional particles, token frequency of, **58**
Directional usage in Tzeltal farm animal games, types of, *459*
Discourse functions of overt NPs and information management, 548–551
Discourse units expressing motion events containing manner and path gestures (American, Chinese, and Turkish children), *34*
Donald Duck, 19
Double participles, German language and, 57
Duden German Dictionary, 56
Dumbo, 19
Duncan, S., 521
Dutch language, 428–431, 469–477, 482
    aphasia in, 381
    CLAS data and, 382
    compared to English language, 470
    as first language, 482
    "Little Red Riding Hood," 383
    means and standard deviations of native Dutch and ethnic minority children on cognitive task and proficiency in, **486**
    proficiency in, 487–488
    as second language, 482
Dutch language proficiency
    correlation with Turkish language proficiency and other factors, **488**
    correlations with cognition, ethnic group, and other factors, **487**
    correlations with rule discovery, symbolic processing, conservation, and verbal naming, **487**
    multiple regression analysis for children with predictor factors, **487**
    multiple regression analysis for Turkish children, **488**
Dutch-speaking children, 470–477, 483, 486
Dyirbal language, 315, 317

Dynamic process from first thoughts to an elaborated text fragment, 507

E

Elicitation failures, simple taxonomy of
    type 1, informants protect their negative face, 165–166
    type 2, protect positive face and try to convince fieldworker to ask someone else, 166–167
    type 3, refusal to cooperate due to pragmatically odd task, 167–168
    type 4, cooperate willingly but without getting the nature of the task, 168–169
Elicited narrative, 81–92
    developmental and crosslinguistic analysis of first mentions, 83–90
    elicitation procedures, 177–179
    English character introductions in, 81–92
    Frog Story databases, 83
    lexical items and construction types in, 81–92
    methodological and ethnographic considerations, 177
    in an oral culture, 176–179
    relevant linguistic features, 83
    Turkish character introductions in, 81–92
Emotion verbs
    used by Japanese children in narratives, 231
English language, 1–2, 35, 70, 76, 81–93, 149, 153–154, 156, 160, 175, 209–224, 253–254, 315–316, 320–324, 342, 349, 361, 367, 377, 397, 405, 416, 428, 430, 435, 469–477, 482, 493, 495, 503, 506, 518, 521–522, 529, 553
    acquisition of animal terms, 17–27
    adverbials encoding manner in, **268**
    American, 226
    aphasia in, 381
    Californian, 151
    character introductions in elicited narratives, 81–92
    compared to Dutch language, 470
    fiction writing in, 260
    Frog Stories in, 138
    gestures in, 360, 363, 525–527
    main verb status and, 392
    motion events in, 253–263
    narratives in, 179, 243, 497–499
    path, expression of by children, 269–272
    predication in, 527
    proportions of motion statement type per language group, *499*
    space and time in, 73–74
    spatial motion in, 263–277
English speakers, 496
English speaker's six path segments for Sylvester's trip down the pipe, *523*
English-speaking adults, 87, 234, 475n6, 506, 513
    segmentation of paths by, **524**
English-speaking children, 158, 196, 205, 209–224, 234, 320, 470–477, 533
    expressing path in the verb, 269–270
    expressing path outside the verb, 270–272
    narratives of, 246–249
    spatial motion and, 263–277
Enrichment expressions
    used by Japanese children in narratives, 236

Episodic structure analysts, 243
Equipollent framing, 427
    main verb status and, 389–402
Ervin-Tripp, S., 3, *561*
Euskara Batua dialect, 412
Evaluative expressions in narratives
    affective behaviors, 228, 230
    causal connectors, 228, 233–234
    character speech, 228, 232
    coding for, 228
    emotion terms, 228
    emotion verbs, 231
    enrichment expressions, 228, 236
    frames of mind, 228, 230
    hedges, 228, 234–235
    Japanese children and, 229–237
    mental state verbs, 228, 231–232
    negative qualifiers, 228, 233
    onomatopoeia, 228, 235–236
    percentage of clauses containing in Japanese, **229**
    relative frequencies of evaluative expressions, 236–237
    Warlpiri children's Frog Stories, 137–148
    in Warlpiri children's Frog Stories, 139–140, **141**, 144–145
Event segmentation in the deer scene, **409**
Evidentiality
    constructing the domain of, 534–536
    representational capacities and, 534–536
    source knowledge and, 537–538
Evidentials, 531–542
    cognitive correlates of evidentiality, 533–534
    early use of in spontaneous speech, 534
    functions of evidential markers, 532–533
    levels of knowledge representation, 536–537
    linguistic and conceptual development, 531–542
    in spontaneous narratives, *186*
    in Tzotzil (Mayan) children's narratives, 175–192
Eye-tracking, 515
    analysis of, 505–516
    channeling of attention, 505–516
    four areas of interest for, *510*
    research in, 505–516
    results, 510–514
    thinking for speaking, 505–516
Eye-tracking research
    screenshot from a picture-story retelling task using eye-tracking, *509*

F

Fabliaux, 418
Farm animal interactional games (Tzeltal), 456–460
    analysis of study, 457–458
    conclusions of study, 460–462
    distance information in, 455
    facing information in, 455
    kinds of information in, 455
    method of study, 456–457
    placement information in, 455
    position information in, 455
    results of study, 458–460
    spatial description in, **458**
'Farm animals' task

picture-object matching, *455*
Finiteness, 333–344
 finite utterance organization, 341
 German language and, 336–337
 as an inflectional category, 336
 Kantian questions, 333–336
 language faculty and, 333–344
 prosodic properties of, 340
 semantic properties of, 338–341
 specific and non-specific interpretation of noun phrases, 338–339
 syntactic properties of, 337
 tense, 339–340
 the topic situation, 340–341
 universal grammar and, 333–344
Finnish language, 70, 75
 aphasia in, 380
 space and time in, 71–72
Finnish-speaking children, 77
Finno-Ugric language, 69, 71
First mentions, developmental and crosslinguistic analysis of
 adult patterns, 86–88
 developmental patterns, 88–90
 introductory constructions, 86
Frames of mind
 used by Japanese children in narratives, 230
French language, 90, 164, 169, 209–224, 253, 432, 435, 493, 503, 522
 aphasia in, 377
 children telling stories of false belief in, 277–292
 Middle French, 418
 Modern French (MF), 415, 417, 418, 419, 420–425
 motion events in, 415–426
 narratives in, 497–499
 Old French (OF), 416–425
 proportions of motion statement type per language group, *499*
 representation of motion events in, 415–426
 shift from satellite- to verb-framed pattern, 416
French-speaking children, 209–224, 265
 narratives of false belief, 277–292
Frog, where are you? (Mayer), 2, 83, 128n2, 129, 137, 139, 175–177, 194, 197, 227, 265, 404, 496, 506
 cover page and picture 1, *131*
 pictures 11 and 12, *129*
Frog book project, 128, 134, 137
Frog stories, 149, 168, 177–178, 493, 496
 data collection, 197
 databases, 83, 403
 elicited narrative and, 196
 studies, 160, 277
 Tzotzil (Mayan) language, 180–186, 188
Frog Stories (Berman & Slobin, 1994), 55
Frog Story (picturebook used by researchers), 82

G

Generative grammar, 323
Genetics psycholinguistics group, 277
Gerhardt, J., 3
German child language
 the data, 57–58, **58**
 direction and perspective in, 55–68
 directional and perspectival particle verbs, 56–57
 discussion, 64–65
 German directional and perspectival particle verbs, 56–57
 introduction, 55–56
German language, 2, 55–68, 90, 107, 131, 164, 194, 212, 253, 320, 470, 482
 aphasia in, 377–378
 Bern Swiss dialect, 164
 CLAS data and, 382
 dialects, 171
 directional and perspectival particle verbs, 56–57
 double participles in, 57
 early new high, 56
 finiteness in, 336–337
 "Little Red Riding Hood," 383
 Muotathal dialect, 165
 Muotathal Swiss dialect, 169, 170–172
 narratives in, 179
 old high German, 56
 pleonastic constructions, 63
 simple participles in, 56
 standard high German, 164, 169
 Swiss German dialect, 164
German Swiss dialects, 412
Germanic languages, 164, 210, 416, 506
 aphasia in, 380
Germanic languages, adult speakers of, 506
German-speaking children, 55–68
 Frog Story narrative and, 60
Gestural paths, 522–525
 as straight-line segments in English, 522
 as unbroken wholes in Spanish, 523–525
Gesture continuum, 518
Gestures
 analyticity and compositionality, 358–359
 in Anglo-American speakers, 362
 concreteness, 359–360
 conventionality, 360–362
 of deaf children, 34–37
 in English, 362, 525–527
 expand manner in Spanish, 525–527
 the heterogeneity of gesture, 364–365
 iconicity, analyticity, and convention, 362–363
 imagery for speaking, 518
 language and, 357–366, 357–367
 modulate manner in English, 525–527
 paths of in English and Spanish, 522–525
 in Spanish, 362, 525–527
 with spoken references to rolling, **525**
 stroke accompanying "it down" in the sentence "and drops it down the drainpipe," *520*
 with TSL sign for 'animate being with more than two legs,' *528*
Gleason dinner corpus, 21, 22, 25
Goffman, E., *561*
Goodglass, H., 377
Google, 2
GPS in four languages
 Deaf sign language of Taiwan (TSL), 521
 English, 521
 Mandarin, 521
 Spanish, 521
Grammar, study of apes and, 299–310, 307–308

instruction and testing sessions for the four systems, 302–307
instructional and testing methodology, 301–302
language evolution, 299–310
pre-grammar systems, 301
Grammaticalization Symposium (Eugene, Oregon), 346
Grammaticization, 345–346
gradualness, 346–367
grammaticizable categories, 349–351
implications for a theory of language, 345–356
research, 346
as a theory of language, 353
triggering experiences and economy principles, 351–353
unidirectionality, 347–349
Greek language, 107
Ground, 393–396
coding categories, 198–200
Gumperz, J., 3, *561*

H

Harvard University, 1, 4, 19
Center for Cognitive Studies, 127, 557
Hebrew language, 2, 149, 153–155, 160, 212, 408–409
aphasia in, 380
biblical, 154
Israeli, 151
narratives in, 179
Hebrew-speaking children, 158
Hedges
used by Japanese children in narratives, 234–235
Hindi language
aphasia in, 380
Hlobohang's production of coronal and non-coronal noun class prefixes, *99*
Hmong-Mien language family, 195
Homesign, 27–40
children's language learning and, 37
in China, 27–40
crosslinguistic study of, 27–40
deafness and language learning, 29–30
development of homesign systems, 28–29
expressing path and manner in motion events, 33
language-making skills that do not require a language model, 33–35
privileged forms and meanings, 35–36
sentence-level structure in, 30–33
in Turkey, 27–40
in the United States, 27–40
Hong Kong Sign Language (HKSL), 357–358, 361
Hungarian language, 71, 320, 470
children's acquisition of, 42
Hungarian-bilingual children, 69
Hyde, Mary, 377
Hyenswu's marked vs. unmarked arguments with marked vs. unmarked primes, *110*
Hymes, Dell, *561*

I

Icelandic language, 405, 410
CLAS data and, 382
Ideophones identified in Korean texts, **261**
Imagery for speaking, 517–530
coding, 521
comparisons across languages, 521–529
conclusion, a strong/weak paradox, 529
a dynamic approach, 518–521
gestural paths as straight-line segments in English and unbroken wholes in Spanish, 522–525
gesture and, 518
gestures expand manner in Spanish, modulate manner in English, 525–527
GPS in four languages, 521
GPS with manner in sign languages, 527–529
methodological preliminaries, 521
predication in English vs. Mandarin, 527
sources of data, 521
ways of thwarting Sylvester, bowling ball down, 520–521
Immediate recall error rates (French and English), *500*
Indefinite, definite, and possessive NPs used for the dog and the frog by different age groups in English and Turkish, **89**
Indo-European languages, 532n2
International Association for the Study of Child language (IASCL), 2
International Congress for the Study of Child Language, 5
International Symposium on First Language Acquisition, 2
Interpretations of simple sentences by children, percentage correct, **322**
Introduction of human referents in the Belhare Pear Story corpus, strategy used for, **551**
Inuit language, 76
Inuktitut language, 70, 76
Iranian language, 532n2
IsiSwati language, 102
IsiXhosa language, 102
IsuZulu language, 102
Italian language, 2, 35, 321–323, 522

J

Jakobson, R., 3, *560*
Jaminjong language, 400, 401, 495
Japanese acquisition data, 105
Japanese language, 225–239, 253, 401, 404, 411, 434, 458, 469, 522
acquisition of, 105
aphasia, 380
Frog Stories in, 138
narratives in, 243
Japanese-speaking adults, 227, 237
Japanese-speaking children, 225–239
affective behaviors in narratives of, 230
causal connectors used in narratives of, 233–234
characters speech in narratives of, 232
frames of mind used in narratives of, 230
use of evaluative expressions in narratives, 225–240
Japanese-speaking children, use of evaluative expressions in narratives, 227–238

coding of study, 227–229
language and affect, 225–240
method of study, 227–229
participants in study, 227
procedure of study, 227
results of study, 229–237

K

Kaluli language
    children's acquisition of, 42
Kant, Immanuel, 333, 462
Karipuna language, Kawahib languages (of Amazonia), 427
Karok language (a Native American language of California), 350
Kawahib languages (of Amazonia), 427, 437
Kendon's Continuum, 518
Klamath language (Penutian language), 393, 396
Korean language, 35, 76, 253, 254, 401
    acquisition of, 105
    argument-marking morphology, 107
    dialogic priming and acquisition of argument marking in, 105–118
    dialogic priming and argument marking in, 105–118
    fiction writing in, 260
    ideophones identified in Korean texts, **261**
    motion events in, 253–263
Korean-speaking children, 105–119, 476, 477
Kyirong language (Tibetan language), 553

L

Lahu language (Tibeto-Burman language), 396
Lakhota language (Siouan language of North America), 315, 317
Landmark vs. true absolute systems, *456*
Language
    cognition and, 443–556
    gesture and, 357–367
    universals and typological comparisons, 443–556
Language acquisition, 134, 214
    adults and derivational and recursive grammar, 323–326
    analysis by synthesis in language acquisition, 326–330
    background, 321–323
    children and, 41–54
    cognitive view of, 311
    crosslinguistic perspective, 11–120
    diachronic change and, 299
    general theory of learning and, 321–332
    introduction, 11–16
    Tzeltal language and, 453–454
Language acquisition device (LAD), 311, 312, 313, 314
Language acquisition, early phases:
    longitudinal naturalistic data, 214–220
    semantic content and utterance density, 217–219
    summary, 219–220
    verbs and other devices encoding motion, 215–217
Language as mind tools, learning how to think through speaking, 451–464
    absolute coordinates vs. landmarks, 455–456

farm animal interactional games, 456–460
introduction, 451–453
learning spatial frames of reference in Tzeltal, 453–455
Language Behavior Research Lab
    University of California, Berkeley, 451
Language Change in Childhood and History (Slobin), 2
Language comprehension strategies, 321
Language evolution (teaching grammar to apes), 299–310
Language faculty, 333–344
Language families, 195
Language proficiency in children
    cognitive predictors of, 481–492
    Dutch language, 483
    Turkish language, 483
Language varieties
    summary table (for frog stories), **164**
Language-Making Capacity (LMC), 105, 107, 114, 116
Language-making skills that do not require a language model, homesign and, 33–35
Languages
    Australian Aboriginal, 314
    satellite-framed, 427
    verb-framed, 427
Languages and their sources, **405**
Language-specific hypothesis, 196, 206
Late recall error rates (French & English), *502*
Latin language, 417
Layered structure of a simple English sentence, *316*
Lenneberg, Eric, 3, 127, *560*
lexical NPs vs. pronouns, 546–547
Lexical patterns in intra-linguistic translation, typological patterns in Old French and Modern French texts, **418**
Lexical referential density and information management, 553–554
Lexical referential density (RD_{lex}) in Belhare vs. Russian, *547*
Lexical unit type
    mean frequencies per speaker (French and English), *498*
Litlhare's production of coronal and non-coronal noun class prefixes, *99*
"Little Red Riding Hood," 383
    German language and, 383

M

MacArthur-Bates Communicative Development Inventory, 17
Main verb properties and equipollent framing, 389–402
    conclusion, 401
    expanded criteria for judging main verb status, 391–393
    introduction, 389–391
    main verb criteria applied to coverb constructions, 400–401
    main verb criteria applied to polysynthetic constructions, 393–396
    main verb criteria applied to serial verb constructions, 396–400
Main verb status, 390, 397
Maithili language (Indo-European), 543–544, 553

SUBJECT INDEX

Mandarin Chinese language, 35, 90, 193–208, 253, 315, 349, 398, 399–400, 406, 458, 470, 495, 518, 521
    expressing motion in, 193–208
    main verb status, 397
    motion event typology of, 203–205
    motion events and, 397
    motion expression typology of, 194–195
    motion expressions and, 195–196
    narratives in, 193–208
    predication in, 527
Mandarin-speaking adults, 194, 196, 198, 399
Mandarin-speaking children, 203–206
    child language development and, 195–196
    development of motion expressions, 205–206
    developmental trends across age groups, 201–203
    learning to express motion by, 193–208
    learning to express motion in narratives, 193–208
    motion expressions and, 195–196
    motion in narratives, 193–208
    results, language type as shown in adult speech, 200–201
Manipulative Activity Scene (MAS), 41–44, 50–52
Manner, 400, 427
    verbs and, 392
Manner, expression of by children in English and Turkish, 266–268
    expressing manner in the verb, 266–268
    expressing manner outside the verb, 268
Manner expressions
    expressions in motion events (English and Korean), 255–256
    translation in motion events (English and Korean), 256
Manner expressions, alternative
    in motion events (English and Korean), 258
Manner expressions (manner verbs and alternative expressions), mean number of, **258**
Manner information
    descriptions containing in motion events (English and Korean), 258–260
    distribution of across different linguistic means, **259**
    information in motion events (English and Korean), 256
Manner salience in cognitive representation of motion events, 496–502
    late recall, 501–502
    narrative performance, 498–501
Manner tokens, frequency across narratives (French and English), *499*
Manner verbs
    mean number of produced by English and Turkish speakers, *266*
    mean number per motion-event description by condition, **257**
    proportional use of in the language varieties in the sample [frog stories], *171*
    translations of, **259**
    types of used by English and Turkish speakers, **267**
    use in motion events (English and Korean), 255, 257
Marked and unmarked arguments, distribution by priming context, *110*
Massachusetts Institute of Technology (MIT), 1, 127
Max Planck Institute for Psycholinguistic Research, 5, 465
Mayan language, 180. *See also* Tzotl and Tzetl languages
Mental state verbs

Japanese children's use of evaluative expressions in narratives, 231–232
Michelangelo, 'David,' 343
Middle East morphology, 81
Miller, G., 3, 127, *560*
Minimalist Program (Chomsky), 323
Mopan Mayan language, 470
Morpheme–concept mapping within the dimensions of direction and perspective, prototypical patterns for Finnish and Polish, 72
Morphology
    acquisition of, 105–119
Motion, 390, 398–399
Motion, expression of in narratives by Mandarin-speaking children, 193–208
    child language development and Mandarin Chinese motion expressions, 195–196
    coding, 197
    conclusion and future research, 206
    data collection and coding categories, 197–200
    development of motion expressions, 205–206
    focus of the study, 196–197
    motion event typology of Mandarin, 203–205
    motion expression typology and Mandarin Chinese, 194–195
    results
        developmental trends across age groups, 201–203
        general, 200–203
        language type as shown in adult speech, 200–201
        of study, 200–203
    subjects and data, 197
    theoretical background and focus of the study, 194–197
    theoretical significance of the study, 201–202, 203–206
    thinking for speaking, 194
Motion, path, and manner, 432–436
    acknowledgments, 437–438
    in Amondawa language (Tupi Guariní language), 427–442, 432–436
    directional adverbs, 433
    discussion and conclusions, 436–437
    introduction, 427
    motion, path, and manner in Amondawa, 432–436
    path and manner: general considerations, 428–432
    path-conflating motion verbs, 432
    postpositions, 432
Motion, typical constraints on
    in French and English child language, 209
    motion across languages, 210–212
Motion, typological constraints on in French and English child language, 209–224
    concluding remarks, 220–222
    early acquisition phases, longitudinal naturalistic data, 214–220
    motion in French and English after three years: experimental data, 212–214
Motion across languages, 210–212
    Dan Slobin's contribution, 211–212
    developmental and cognitive implications, 211–212
    space across child languages, 211
    verb-framing and satellite framing, 210–211
Motion construction, 429
Motion events, 55, 393–396
    descriptions of, 254
    in English fictional writings and translations, 253–263
    expressing path and manner in, 33

in French and English, *220*
French language and, 415–426
in homesign, 33
in Korean fictional writings and translations, 253–263
mean number of described by children and adults, *271*
representation of, 415–426
types denoted, *220*
typology of, 427–440
utterance density for, *219*
Motion events in English and Korean fictional writings and translations, 253–262
conclusions of study, 261
discussion, 260–261
introduction, 253–254
manner verbs in sample texts, **257**
mean number of manner verbs per motion-event description by condition, **257**
method, 255
alternative manner expressions, 255–256
descriptions containing manner information, 256
manner verb use, 255
translation of manner expressions, 256
results, 257–260
alternative manner expressions, 258
descriptions containing manner information, 258–260
manner verb use, 257
translation of manner expressions, 259–260
sources of the sample, **255**
Motion events, representation in French, 415–426
conclusion, 424–425
introduction, 415–416
lexical patterns in translation, from old into modern French, 418–419
from a satellite- to a verb-framed pattern, a typological shift in French, 416–418
typological contrast in rhetorical style, from old into modern French, 419–424
Motion expressions
by age groups, **200**
coding categories, 197–198
in Mandarin language, 197–198
Motion expressions with ground information, *204*
Motion in French and English after three years, experimental data, 212–214
caused motion, 213–214
summary, 214
summary of data base for all children, **215**
voluntary motion, 212–213
Motion information expressed in verb roots, *217*
Motion information expressed outside of verb roots, *218*
Motion statement
proportions of type per language group (in French and English), *499*
Motion verb construction types of age, *201*
Motion verb types
coding categories, 198
in Mandarin language, 198
Motion verbs
categories of, *204*
mean adult verb types and type/token ratios for different categories of, **201**
verb types in, *203*
MPI for evolutionary anthropology in Leipzig, 57

Multimodal protocol with time-coded eye and speech data, *511*
Muotathal dialect
German language and, 165
Muotathal Swiss dialect, 408, 411, 412
German language and, 169, 170–172

N

Narrative Inquiry, 2006 (special issue), 134
Narrative representation
from actors to agents to persons in young children's narratives, 247–248
of characters as mental agents, 247–248
Narrative research and character
character representation and its development in narrative research, 244–245
episodic structure analysts and characters as intentional agents, 243
seeking earlier precursors to mentalistic character portrayals, 243–244
taking character more seriously, some steps toward an orienting framework, 245–246
Narratives
development of, 121–292
elicited, 81–93
evaluative expressions used by Japanese children in, 225–240
expressing motion in, 193–208
German language and, 179
linguistic, cognitive, and pragmatic perspectives, 121–292
relating an event in, transcripts and translation of the stream of speech, **511**
Warlpiri children's frog stories, 140–141
Narratives, elicited, 81–92
in an oral culture (Tzotzil-Mayan), 176–179
Tzotzil (Mayan) children's narratives, 176–179
Narratives, first and second
children's performance on Theory of Mind (ToM) tasks in, **284**
percentages of children producing internal states, epistemic states, false belief, and rectification of false belief in, **282**
Narratives, Japanese children's use of evaluative expressions in
causal connectors, 233–234
enrichment expressions, 236
hedges, 234–235
negative qualifiers, 233
onomatopoeia, 235–236
relative frequencies of evaluative expressions, 236–237
Narratives, second and third
percentages of children producing internal states, epistemic states, false belief, and rectification of false belief, **283**
Narratives of false belief, a study of French-speaking children, 277–292
analysis of the data, 280–281
attribution of internal states to the characters, 280–281
discussion, 284–286
false belief (FB), 280
first and second narratives, 281–283

introduction to study, 277–278
linguistic expression of second-order belief, 284
materials, 278–279
method of study, 278–281
procedure of study, 279–280
results of study, 281–284
subjects of study, 278
theory of mind in the narrative, 283–284
theory of mind tasks, 281
third narrative, 283
National Institute of Child Development, 300n2
Negative qualifiers
 results for language and Japanese children's use of in narratives, 233
Nguni languages, 102
Niger-Congo language family, 195
Nominal forms
 distribution of with indefiniteness and definiteness marking in all age groups for both language samples, **88**
Nominal marking
 for the boy in adult narratives in English and Turkish, **86**
 for the frog and the dog across ages in English and Turkish, **90**
 for the frog and the dog in adult narratives in English and Turkish, **86**
Noun class prefix system
 in Bantu languages, 93
Noun class prefixes
 acquisition of in Sesotho language, 98
 lexical effects in Sesotho language, 101
 percent production of under different phonological and syntactic conditions, 100
 in Sesotho language, 96
Noun class prefixes in Sesotho language, acquisition of, 93–104
 conclusion of study, 102
 discussion of study, 101–102
 distribution of null noun class prefixes in Sesotho, 96–98
 introduction to study, 93–96
 lexical effects, 101
 phonological licensing of null noun class prefixes, 98–99
 syntactic licensing of null noun class prefixes, 100–101
Noun class prefixes, null
 distribution of in Sesotho language, 96–98
 phonological licensing of in Sesotho language, 98–99
 syntactic licensing of in Sesotho language, 100–101
Nouns
 singular/plural nouns and prefixes in Sesotho language, 94
Numerals and quantifiers [instruction and testing for can apes learn grammar]
 results of numeral/quantifier test, **304**
Numerals and quantifiers, 303–304
 instruction sessions for study with apes, 303
 interpretation of study with apes, 304
 testing sessions for study with apes, 303–304

O

Old High German, German language and, 56
Old Tupi language, 437
Onomatopoeia, Japanese children's use of in narratives, 235–236
Operating Principles (OP), 2, 69–70, 93, 102, 105–106, 115, 128, 206
Orality
 in Tzotzil (Mayan) children's narratives, 175–192

P

Paradigms, principles and predictions of, 367–374
Parintintin language, Kawahib languages (of Amazonia), 427
Path, 390, 393–396, 398–399, 400, 427
 expressing in the verb, 269–270
 expressing outside the verb, 270–272
 expression of by children in English and Turkish, 269–272
 verbs and, 392
 verbs and complements, 406
Path elements per verb, **407**
Path of motion, 403–410
 intra- and inter-typological variation in, 403–410
 path and event granularity, 409
 paths, verbs, and complements, 406–408
 paths and verbs, 405–406
Path salience cline: verb-frames, satellite-framed, equipollently framed, *410*
Path salience in motion events, 403–414
 intra- and inter-typological variation in path of motion, 403–410
 path salience cline and possible explanations, 410–412
 problems in lexicalization patterns, 403–405
Path satellites, mean number of, **271**
Path verbs
 mean number of produced by English and Turkish speakers, 269
 proportional use of in different language varieties [frog stories], *170*
 types used by English and Turkish speakers, **270**
Path-conflating motion verbs
 in Amondawa language (Tupi Guariní language), 432
Paths, segmentation of
 by English-speaking adults, **524**
 by Spanish-speaking adults, **524**
Pear Story, 544–548
Perspective statements, 45–48, 50, 52
Phonetic analysis package PRAAT, 506
Piaget, 558
Piaget Society, 451n1, 485
Picture description vs. narrative cohesion, *183*
Pidgen languages, 3
Pleonastic constructions
 German language and, 63
Plot
 Warlpiri children's frog stories, 138–140
Poems by linguists (by Dan Slobin), 4
Polish language, 70, 75, 415
 space and time in, 71–72, 73–74
Polish-speaking children, 77

Portuguese language, 427
Portuguese language, Brazilian, 428, 429, 431, 435–436
Position of patients and transitive actors in two-gesture sentences containing acts (American and Chinese children), 32
Postpositions, in Amondawa language (Tupi Guaraní language), 432–433
Pourquoi l'aphasique peut-il dire "Je ne peux pas le dire" et pas "Elle ne peut pas la chanter?," 376
Predication in English and Mandarin, 527
Priming contexts for children's production of argument markers, **109**
Priscianus, *Institutiones grammaticae*, 334
Production probability of transitive actors, intransitive actors, and patients in two-gesture sentences (American and Chinese children), *31*
Pronoun productions of a 27-month-old
 with an extended paradigm, **370**
 with a limited paradigm, **369**
Proportion of *op, om* and *aan* responses (including errors) among Dutch children, **475**
Proto-Bantu, 93
Psycholinguistics, 375–388
 aphasia and, 375–388
 child language vs. aphasia, 375–388

R

Peferential density (RD), 543–544, 552–553
 in Belhare vs. Russian languages, *547*
 coding, 545–546
 differences in, 543–556
 discourse functions of overt NPs and information management, 548–551
 lexical NPs vs. pronouns, 546–547
 lexical referential density and information management, 553–554
 material and procedure of study, 545
 methods of study, 545–546
 results of study, 546–551
 subjects of study, 545
Resources for Infant Educators (RIE), 49–50
Revised Dutch Language Proficiency Test (TAK), 484
Revised RAKIT, 485
Role and Reference Grammar (RRG), 316
Romance languages, 163, 210, 495, 506
 aphasia in, 380
Romance–Germanic border (in Swiss Alpine area), 164
Romansh German, 164, 169
Rubert-Pugh, E., 301–308
Russian language, 175, 194, 495, 544–552, 553
 acquisition of animal terms, 17–27
 children's acquisition of, 42

S

Saisiyat language, 406, 411
SDpro and stereotypic error rates at 27, 30, and 33 months, **371**
Searle, John, *561*
Second language, acquisition of, 42–54

Semetic languages, 495
Sentence-level structure
 gesture order regularities, 31–33
 gesture production and deletion regularities, 30–31
 in homesign systems, 30–33
Sepedi language, 101
Serbo-Croatian children, 69
Serbo-Croatian language, 2, 71, 107, 321–323
 "Little Red Riding Hood," 383
Sesotho language, 93, 95, 101
 noun class prefixes, 96
 singular/plural nouns and prefixes in, 94
Sesotho-speaking adults, 95
Sesotho-speaking children, 97, 101
Setswana language, 93, 95, 101
Sign Language of the Netherlands, 31
Sign languages
 acquisition of, 3
 GPS with manner, 527–529
Signed English, 29
Simone and Kerstin data, 57
Simple participles, German language and, 56
Simple sentences, correct interpretations of by children, **322**
Sinclair, M., 277
Sino-Tibetan language family, 195
Siswati language, 95
Slavic languages, 69–70, 71
 aphasia in, 380
Slobin, D., 56, 71, 127–129, 189, 195, 206, 261, 311
 accomplishment and recognition, 5
 aphasia research, 376
 beginning of crosslinguistic studies, 1–2
 bibliography of publications, 565–574
 contribution of, 1–8, 211, 277, 345, 357, 367–368, 376, 385, 517, 543
 crosslinguistic studies, 1–2
 dynamic thinker, 2–4
 mentors and influences, 557–564
 mind of humanity, 4
 Operating Principles (OP), 102
 poetic portrait, xxi
 post-docs, visiting scholars, research collaborators, 562
 recollections of, 81, 93, 105, 137, 149, 163, 175, 193, 225, 241, 263, 299, 389, 403, 415, 427, 451, 465–466, 481, 493, 531
 'Renaissance Man,' 4–5
 teachers and doctoral students, 561–562
Snow White experiment, 361
Social Science Research Council, Korea Program, 105n1
Societé Linguistique de Paris, 333
Society for Research in Child Development, 5
Sotho group of languages, 101
South-East Asian languages, 532n2
Southwest Project in Comparative Psycholinguistics, 1
Spacial Intelligence and Learning Center (SILC), 465n1
spacial relations, 465–480
Spanish, 521
Spanish language, 2, 149, 153–154, 156–157, 160, 175, 177, 188, 194, 212, 361, 381, 404, 408–409, 416, 469, 514, 518, 521–522, 529
 Colombian, 107
 gestures in, 522–527
 Iberian, 151
 main verb status and, 392–393

narratives in, 179
Spanish speakers, 496
Spanish speaker's single continuous arc for Sylvester's trip down the pipe, 524
Spanish-speaking adults, segmentation of paths by, **524**
Spanish-speaking children, 159, 196, 205
Spatial and temporal systems, two core dimensions of, **71**
Spatial descriptions, 457
    absolute, 457
    categories of, 457
    deictic, 457
    examples of in farm animal games, **458**
    intrinsic, 457
    landmark, 457
    relative frequencies of evaluative expressions, 457
    sunrise/sunset, 457
Spatial language data, collecting, 163–174
    introduction, 163–164
    a simple taxonomy of elicitation failures, 165–169
    speech communities, 164–165
    successful elicitation, 169–172
    summary and discussion, 172–173
Spatial motion, 263–277
    how children express boundary-crossing events in English and Turkish, 272–274
    how children express manner in English and Turkish, 266–268
    how children express path in English and Turkish, 269–272
    how children learn to talk about motion in typologically distinct ways, 264–266
    learning to express motion events in English and Turkish: concluding remarks, 274–275
    learning to talk about in language-specific ways, 263–276
    tightening the constraints on lexicalization, 272–274
    typology of motion events, 263–264
Spatial prepositions, apes ability to learn, 306–307
    general design of study, 306
    instructional sessions, 306
    interpretation of results, 307
    results of tests
        for prepositions following demonstration, **306**
        for prepositions without prior demonstration, **307**
    testing
        following demonstration, 306–307
        without prior demonstration, 307
Spatial semantic categories, typological prevalence hypothesis, 465–480
    categorization of static topological spatial situations across languages, 469–470
    Dutch vs. English systems, 470–471
    general discussion, 475–478
alternative explanations, 476–477
    conclusions, 477–478
    summary, 475–476
    introduction, 466–467
    predicting the acquisition of spatial semantic categories, 471–472
    recollections, 465–466
    testing the typological prevalence hypothesis, 472–475
    typological prevalence hypothesis, 467–468
Speech errors, aphasia and, 375–388
Speech production
    competing word orders in aphasia, 381

    competition in aphasia, 379–380
    semantically related words and phrases, 382–384
Spiderman, 19
Squliq language, 406, 411
Standard High German, 412
    German language and, 164, 169
Stimulus configurations arranged by lexical category in Dutch/English, **472**
"Stone Story," 278
Storytelling, 127–137. *See also* Narratives
    coding for story length, 228
    evaluative elements, 138
    frog-book projects, from 'relating events in Time' to 'Relating Events in Narrative,' 127–133
    informative elements, 138
    narrative clauses, 138
    relating events in time or in narrative, from cognition to discourse, 134–135
    so what is so special about 'Narrative'?, 133–134
Swedish language, 405, 410, 506
    CLAS data and, 382
Swedish-speaking adults, 506, 513
Swiss German dialect, 164, 166, 169
    German language and, 164
Swiss National Science Foundation, 543n1
Sylvester the cat, 521–522
Syntactic architecture, 152
    asymmetric parataxis, 152
    endotaxis, 152
    of high-school narrative openings in three languages, 153
    hypotaxis, 152
    isotaxis, 152
    symmetric parataxis, 152
Syntactic structures (Chomsky), 323

T

Tagalog language, 406, 409, 411
Tai-Kadai language family, 195
Taiwan sign language (TSL), 528
Talk, decontextualized, 22
Talmy, Leonard, 3
Tarafit Berber language, 470
Target prepositions (correct responses)
    proportion across age for Dutch and English, *474*
Temporal and spatial relations
    cognitive pre-requisites and linguistic creativity, 75–77
    introduction to operating principles, 69–70
    mono-/bi-referential location in space/time, 72–73
    one-to-one mapping of, 69–80
    research motivation, 70–71
    space and time systems for Polish and Finnish, 71–72
    space/time research
        design, 73–74
        hypothesis, 73
        results, 74–75
Tenharim language, Kawahib languages (of Amazonia), 427
Thai language, 315, 406, 407, 411, 432, 495
"The Cookie Theft," 381, 382
    Boston Diagnostic Aphasia Examination, 381n3
"The Frog Story," 75
The world (Wilawa Szymborska), 563

SUBJECT INDEX

Theoretical perspectives on language development, language change, and typology, 293–442
    introduction, 293–298
Theory of mind (ToM)
    development, 533
    tasks, 283
"Thinking for Speaking," 3
Thinking for speaking, 451–464, 505–516, 517n1, 531
    conclusion, 502–503
    domain of motion, 495
    eye-tracking research, 505–516
    gestures and, 517–530
    manner salience
        in the cognitive representation of motion events, 496–502
        in the linguistic framing of motion events, 495–496
    method of study, 508–510
    relativistic application of, 493–504
Thinking for writing, 514
Three Blind Mice, 19
Transformational grammar, 1
Transition from analysis in terms of ontological categories to syntactic categories, *314*
Transitivity, 42–54
Transitivity and the grammar in toddlers' peer disputes
    accusing, commanding, and perspective-sharing, 41–54
    discussion, 50–52
    introduction, 42–43
    study of verb constructions, 44–50
    transitivity in toddler's verb constructions in different speech acts within disputes, 46–50
Translations
    English to Korean, 259–260
    Korean to English, 259–260
    of manner + satellite constructions from old into modern French, **423**
Tsou language, 406, 411
Turkey, homesign in, 27–40
Turkic languages, 495, 532n2
Turkish language, 2, 81–93, 175, 226, 253, 321–323, 367, 408, 411, 481, 522, 533
    adverbials encoding manner in, **268**
    character introductions in elicited narratives, 81–92
    evidentials in, 532
    frog stories in, 138
    narratives in, 179, 243
    path, expression of by children, 269–272
    proficiency in, 487–488
    spatial motion in, 263–277
Turkish language proficiency
    correlation with Dutch language proficiency, ethnic group, and other factors, **488**
Turkish-speaking adults, 87
Turkish-speaking children, 481, 483, 486, 533, 538
    expressing path
        in the verb, 269–270
        outside the verb, 270–272
    spatial motion and, 263–277
Tweety Bird, 521–522
Typological contrast in rhetorical style, from old into modern French
    manner of motion in intra-linguistic translation, 422–424
    path of motion in intra-linguistic translation, 419–422
Typological prevalence hypothesis, 465–480
Tzeltal farm animal games, data summary, **457**
Tzeltal Frog Stories, 177n6
Tzeltal language (Mayan), 70, 76, 180, 194, 334, 476, 506
    farm animal interactional games, 456–460
    learning spatial frames of reference in, 453–454
    in Tenejapa, Mexico, 452
    Tzeltal 'uphill'/'downhill' system, *454*
Tzotzil (Mayan) children's narratives, study of, 175–192
    children's narrative development, cognitive vs. typological issues, 179–181
    comparison of elicitation from printed stimuli vs. spontaneous narratives, 180–187
    conclusions, 187–189
    elicitation from printed stimuli vs. spontaneous narratives, 180–187
    frogs and black-winged monkeys, 175–192
    introduction, 176
    orality, evidentials and authorship in, 175–192
    schooling in adult participants, *182*
    studying elicited narratives in an oral culture, 176–179
Tzotzil (Mayan) language, 175–176, 177, 180–181, 189
    orality in, 188
Tzotzil (Mayan)-speaking children, 176

U

United States, homesign in, 27–40
Universal grammar (UG), 311–321, 333–344
    allure and illusion of, 318–319
    human language faculty and, 342–343
    language acquisition without a LAD (language acquisition device), 311–314
    nature of universals, 314–318
University of California, Berkeley, 1, 81, 93, 105, 116, 163, 241, 263, 403, 427, 451, 465, 531
    Humanities Graduate Research Grant, 225n1
    Psychology Department, 41
University of Chicago, 521
University of Montreal, 376
University of Oregon, 137
Uru-eu-uau-uau, Kawahib languages (of Amazonia), 427
Utterance density, semantic content and, 217–219

V

Verb constructions
    coding categories, 198–200
    in Mandarin language, 198
    proportion of with low transitivity parameters in different speech acts, **46**
    used by toddlers in peer disputes, 41–54
Verb stems (types) with particles, number of, **59**
Verbs
    minus-ground and plus-ground, **406**
    and other devices encoding motion, 215–217, *216*
    path of motion, 406–408
    path of motion and, 405–406
    polysynthetic, 393
    types of used by English and Turkish speakers in boundary-crossing descriptions, **274**
Verbs, directional and perspectival particle verbs

German child language, 56–57
Verbs with hin- and her-
   rank order and age of first occurrence of, *61*
Visual attention, changes in during a picture-story retelling task, *512*
Vygotsky, Lev, 3, *558*

W

Warlpiri children's frog stories
   age, story items, plot components and search statement by group, **140**
   conclusions, 146
   evaluation, 138–140
   evaluative elements, 139–140, 144–145
   main events/items coded, *141*
   number of children using types of evaluative elements, **141**
   plot, 138–140
   plot and evaluation, 137–148
   study of, 137–138
   Warlpiri narratives, 140–141
Warlpiri language (Australian indigenous language), 137, 411
Warlpiri narratives, 140–141
   data, 140–141
   story events, 141–144
Warlpiri-speaking
   adults, 137
   children, 137
Warren corpus, 25
Welsh language, aphasia in, 380
Wenceng's marked vs. unmarked arguments with marked vs. unprimed marks, *111*
Wernicks's aphasia, 377
West Greenlandic language, 406, 407, 411
Western Ejagam language, 93
Whorf hypothesis, 1, 495, 517, 529
Winnie-the-Pooh, 113
Workshop on Developmental Studies in Spatial Language and Cognition, 451n1

Y

Yiddish language, 4

Z

Zulu language, 95, 102